CRITICAL SURVEY
OF
DRAMA

CRITICAL SURVEY

OF

DRAMA
Second Revised Edition

Volume 5
Jane Martin - Lennox Robinson

Editor, Second Revised Edition
Carl Rollyson
Baruch College, City University of New York

Editor, First Editions, English and Foreign Language Series
Frank N. Magill

SALEM PRESS, INC.
Pasadena, California   Hackensack, New Jersey

Editor in Chief: Dawn P. Dawson
Managing Editor: Christina J. Moose
Developmental Editor: R. Kent Rasmussen
Project Editor: Rowena Wildin
Research Supervisor: Jeffry Jensen
Research Assistant: Michelle Murphy

Acquisitions Editor: Mark Rehn
Photograph Editor: Philip Bader
Manuscript Editor: Sarah Hilbert
Assistant Editor: Andrea E. Miller
Production Editor: Cynthia Beres
Layout: Eddie Murillo and William Zimmerman

Library of Congress Cataloging-in-Publication Data

Critical survey of drama / edited by Carl Rollyson.-- 2nd rev. ed.
    p. cm.
Previous edition edited by Frank Northen Magill in 1994.
"Combines, updates, and expands two earlier Salem Press reference sets: Critical survey of drama, revised edition, English language series, published in 1994, and Critical survey of drama, foreign language series, published in 1986"--Pref.
Includes bibliographical references and index.
ISBN 1-58765-102-5 (set : alk. paper) -- ISBN 1-58765-107-6 (vol. 5 : alk. paper) --
1. Drama--Dictionaries. 2. Drama--History and criticism--Dictionaries. 3. Drama--Bio-bibliography. 4. English drama--Dictionaries. 5. American drama--Dictionaries. 6. Commonwealth drama (English)--Dictionaries. 7. English drama--Bio-bibliography. 8. American drama--Bio-bibliography. 9. Commonwealth drama (English)--Bio-bibliography. I. Rollyson, Carl E. (Carl Edmund) II. Magill, Frank Northen, 1907-1997.
PN1625 .C68 2003
809.2'003—dc21
    2003002190

Fourth Printing

PRINTED IN THE UNITED STATES OF AMERICA

CONTENTS

VOLUME 5

COMPLETE LIST OF CONTENTS

VOLUME 1

VOLUME 2

VOLUME 3

VOLUME 4

VOLUME 5

VOLUME 6

VOLUME 7

AMERICAN DRAMA

VOLUME 8

CRITICAL SURVEY
OF
DRAMA

JANE MARTIN

Born: Kentucky; date unknown

PRINCIPAL DRAMA

The Boy Who Ate the Moon, pr. 1981, pb. 1988
Cul de Sac, pr. 1981, pb. 1988
Talking With, pr. 1982, pb. 1983
Coup/Clucks, pr. 1982, pb. 1984
Shasta Rue, pr. 1983, pb. 1988
Summer, pr. 1984, pb. 1995
Travelin' Show, pr. 1987, pb. 1988
What Mama Don't Know: Five Plays, pb. 1988
Vital Signs, pr., pb. 1990
Cementville, pr., pb. 1991
Criminal Hearts, pr., pb. 1992
Keely and Du, pr., pb. 1993
Middle-Aged White Guys, pr., pb. 1995
Pomp and Circumstance, pb. 1995, pr. 2000
Jack and Jill, pb. 1995, pr. 1996
Jane Martin: Collected Plays, 1980-1995, pb. 1995
Tumblin' After, pr. 1996
Mr. Bundy, pr. 1998, pb. 1999
Anton in Show Business, pr., pb. 2000
Flaming Guns of the Purple Sage, pr., pb. 2001
Jane Martin: Collected Plays, 1996-2001, pb. 2001
White Elephant, pr. 2001
Good Boys, pr. 2002

OTHER LITERARY FORMS

The pseudonym "Jane Martin" has been used exclusively for the purpose of writing for the stage. Though it is feasible that the same individual has been responsible for writing other forms of literature, there is no known connection between the "Jane Martin" name and any writing other than dramatic works.

ACHIEVEMENTS

First produced in at the Actors Theatre of Louisville's Humana Festival in 1981, Jane Martin would eventually become the theater's most often produced playwright. Acclaimed by critics, audiences, and fellow playwrights alike, Martin has become known for her biting wit, her contemporary onstage explorations of social issues, and her playful sense of the stereotypical absurd.

Though Martin has never had a single play produced on Broadway, her name has become well known in the theater community, and she is frequently produced—especially in smaller theaters that thrive on her small casts and monologue-form drama. Her mysterious identity has been a favorite subject of critics over the years, though the quality of her plays has retained a surprising ability to overshadow the secondary "identity controversy" that surrounds them.

Martin is a three-time recipient of the American Theater Critics New Play Award—for *Talking With*, *Keely and Du*, and *Jack and Jill*. This speaks both to Martin's ability to write timely plays and to the centrality in modern theater criticism of the Actors Theatre of Louisville's Humana Festival—where the majority of Martin works have premiered. The Humana Festival and Martin have been central to the growth of small regional theaters working outside the New York theater scene.

BIOGRAPHY

The Actors Theatre of Louisville's program biography for Jane Martin states that she was born in Kentucky and lists her works. This is, in fact, the entirety of hard facts that the general public has about the mysterious Martin. Remarkably for a world as gossipy as that of the theater, Martin has managed to keep her actual identity a much-discussed secret since she entered the theater scene in 1981. Her first work, *The Boy Who Ate the Moon*, was produced at the Actors Theatre of Louisville in 1981 and received a fair amount of critical notice. Her second work, *Talking With*, was also successful, winning her an American Theater Critics New Play award and a nationally recognized name.

Originally, it was rumored that Martin had secretively slipped a manuscript under the door of Actors Theatre of Louisville artistic director Jon Jory, an act that resulted in Martin's first professional production.

This theory did not last long among the gossip-mongering of the Humana Festival, however. Eventually, all the rumors surrounding Martin's identity would center on Jory himself. In recent years, almost every theory of Martin's identity has revolved around Jory, and reporters have gone to great lengths to prove the Jory-Martin connection. Jory has even received a call from a Louisville reporter who had examined his tax returns, pre- and post-Jane Martin. Jory, as well as his supposed collaborators, has continually denied responsibility for the "Jane Martin" body of works and consistently encourages reporters to focus on the plays themselves, rather than the identity of their playwright.

The Jory-Martin theories have probably sprouted more from convenience than anything else, as Jory is the only obvious choice to assume Martin's identity. The speculation around Jory has stemmed from the fact that he has directed every premiere of a Martin play and is in fact the only individual who will "admit" to having met Martin in person. Atypical of the modern-day production process, Martin has apparently never appeared in person to the actors in her plays (at least not to their knowledge).

Either way, the anonymity and ambiguous gender of Martin has had the interesting effect of focusing critics' appraisals on the works themselves, rather than on the character of the playwright or her background. Reluctant to pointedly criticize Martin as a playwright because they know nothing about her, reviewers tend to focus on the merit of the plays alone—perhaps the effect that Martin desired in hiding her identity.

Jory has in fact produced plays under his own name. Those that believe him to be Martin see it as a separate persona contrived to allow him to write outside his own gender. Alternative theories have had him collaborating with his wife, Marcia, the theater's literary manager Alexander Speer, or a reclusive Louisville socialite. Many critics take the assumption that Jory is Martin to be fact. There is, in fact, no concrete evidence to this effect, only circumstantial. Many assumed that Martin's last hurrah would come with *Anton in Show Business* in 2000—the same year Jory resigned as artistic director of the Actors Theatre of Louisville. This turned out not to be true, as evidenced by Martin's *White Elephant* and her *Good Boys*, which premiered at the Guthrie Theater Lab—directed, of course, by Jory.

ANALYSIS

The mystery of Jane Martin's identity makes it difficult to solve the other mystery, which is the conundrum of her work. With *Talking With*, Martin seemed to establish herself as a feminist dramatist intent on examining women and gender and the role women play in society. By her later works—especially works such as *Anton in Show Business* in which gender is tertiary—this view of Martin had nearly deteriorated. A comparison of her earlier monologue-style shorts to mid-career full-length works such as *Mr. Bundy* to her most famous *Keely and Du* reveals a playwright with a wide range of social issues at hand and with specific aims in tackling them.

Eventually, the "social issue" play—in which Martin takes on a pressing social issue with her trademark dark wit—would define the course of Martin's career. This type of work was a favorite of the Humana Festival and thus a favorite of Martin's, and it would become the core of the Martin œuvre. Subjects addressed by Martin have included gender studies, the state of the American theater, abortion, and Republican politics.

There are two basic forms that Martin has used in her work as a writer. The first is the style seen in works such as *Talking With*—a string of unrelated monologues on similar subjects. Martin's forte has been in writing character monologues, in which a lone actor addresses the audience directly. She is well known for her short plays and her comic monologues—she in fact has helped make the ten-minute play a valid form of theatrical expression. She has also written traditionally staged dramas, with the fourth wall intact. These are plays such as *Mr. Bundy* and *Keely and Du*. Although her earlier work leaned toward the shorter monologue style, her later work has tended to be in a more conventional dramatic style.

Infused into every social or political study of Martin's drama is a keen eye for southern gothic—her characterizations favor the down-and-out, the stereotypical backwoods hick, the ill-informed religious fanatic. Her comedy is dark, though her style is not pessimistic—she simply has a fascination with the darker, absurd side of humanity. Realistic character development is not usually Martin's goal in writing—she tends to work in stereotypes, and her characters are often mouthpieces of sorts. One favorite tactic of Martin's is to make her own points clear by presenting a character whose point of view is diametrically opposite to her own and then exposing the individual's folly.

Especially notable in Martin's style is the pointed wit with which she deals with her subjects. Although it cannot be said that all of her plays are comedies—*Keely and Du* borders on tragedy—it can be said that all of her plays are comic, no matter how dark the subject matter. She is known for her playful irreverence for the conventional and her quick sense of retort.

It is a useful exercise when dealing with the work of Martin to examine how a work might be viewed differently if Martin were not female, but a male writing under a female moniker. In *Keely and Du*, for instance, the play revolves around women who are upset with the confines of a patriarchal system. When viewed as a female-written work, it is clearly written as feminist drama. When viewed as male-written, however, the focus of both of the women on how their lives revolve around men becomes suspect.

TALKING WITH

With this play, Martin emerged on the national theater scene, winning her first of three American Theatre Critics New Play awards and creating rumors regarding her identity. Premiered, like most of her works, at the Humana Festival, and directed, like all her works, by Jory, *Talking With* soon received productions all over the country. The play is a collection of eleven short monologue scenes, in which different incarnations of women express a variety of insecurities and revelations in ten-minute segments.

The scenes are ostensibly unrelated, though each monologue is written with a keen eye toward gender politics and male-female relationships. The opening monologue, for instance, features an actress backstage, fifteen minutes before curtain. She speaks to the audience directly about the one-sided relationship

of theater, the nakedness of being alone on a stage in front of strangers, and her desire to know intimate details about the audience members just as they know intimate details about her. In this, the title words are brought to light—Martin desires that her works be less of a "talking-to," as theater tends to be, and more of an open conversation. It also speaks to the fact that she, herself, has chosen not to reveal her identity to her audience of strangers.

The style of *Talking With*—monologues by women, directly addressing the audience—has become the style that audiences associate most commonly with Martin. In her earlier work, she almost exclusively wrote either in monologue or in ten-minute shorts, and *Talking With* seems to be her most successful effort with the format. Her sense of playfulness comes out often in these scenes—the characters of *Talking With* are generally painted with broad absurdist strokes—an actress who threatens to kill a cat at an audition, a southern woman taken in by religious snake handling, a woman who thinks she is giving birth to a dragon. Martin also, in this play and others, favors writing about the less educated, the down-and-out—most of her characters speak in vernacular southern dialects and sometimes crude poetry.

KEELY AND DU

After the success of *Talking With* and other short offerings by Martin, many critics doubted her ability to write a traditionally structured drama. *Keely and Du* was a definitive answer to these critics—it is a dark dramatic exploration into the politics of abortion and features multiple characters onstage in conventional dramatic conflict. The most earnestly serious of Martin's plays, *Keely and Du* is surprising in that its controversial topic—abortion—generated a surprisingly minimal amount of backlash. This is perhaps because theatergoers, especially those at one of Martin's plays, tend to be liberal; therefore, Martin may have been preaching to the choir. It also may be because of the empathetic way in which *Keely and Du* accommodates both sides of the issue. Though Martin's standpoint is clear, both sides of the argument are given a fair hearing.

The play is mostly a dialogue between two women—Keely and Du. Keely is a young rape victim who has been kidnapped from an abortion clinic by a religious faction, of which Du is an integral member. Matronly Du is responsible for taking care of captive Keely until her child is born—her militant faction is attempting to use Keely to make a political statement about the evil of abortion, and Keely was chosen to represent rape victims in the plan.

As is typical of Martin's style, the play relies heavily on dialogue rather than action—necessarily, as Keely spends most of the action chained to a bed. The scenes are short and mark the change in Keely's relationship with Du. Eventually, a kind of "Stockholm Syndrome" sets in, and both women bond over their frustration with men who make decisions for them. For a time, the play moves away from the abortion topic altogether and becomes a simple feminist dialogue about the submissive tendencies of women.

The other characters of the play pop in and out of the holding room. Of these, Walter is the most notable—he is a stereotype of both militant religious fervor and of oppressive alpha male-ism. In Keely and Du, outside her broad satire of Walter, Martin avoids the cleverness of her other works, relying mostly on dark parody for the humor of the piece.

ANTON IN SHOW BUSINESS

Many critics expected this 2000 Humana Festival work to be a last hurrah for Martin, as it marked the end of Jory's reign as artistic director at the Louisville theater. It ended up not to be, though its subject matter—the dire straits of American theater—certainly reads like one.

Anton in Show Business was written to be a heavy satirical blow to the sacred cows of theater, among them ego-driven actors, clueless board members, and corporate ownership of artistic ventures. The play-within-a-play features a small theater attempting to put on Anton Chekhov's *Tri sestry* (pr., pb. 1901, revised pb. 1904; *The Three Sisters*, 1920). Martin promptly uses this framework to send up the state of theater—mostly by using a character who sits in the audience, heckling the very play that she is writing.

The overall message behind *Anton in Show Business* is that theater, the strong point of which should be narrative, has gotten too far from its roots in storytelling, influenced too heavily by the media, especially television. Many people see this viewpoint—which Jory has also expressed in public—as a definitive connection between Jory and Martin. In reality, it is probably only proof that Martin is indeed someone well inside theater—someone knowledgeable about the financial functioning of contemporary theater as well as its deepest inadequacies.

Another notable quality of *Anton in Show Business* is its dramatic distance from the feminist playwright evident in *Talking With*—gender is a kind of nonissue here, and this demonstrates how Martin has somewhat divorced herself from the lone-woman-on-stage format of her earlier life.

BIBLIOGRAPHY

Healy, Samantha Rachel. "Love and Pain." *American Theatre* 17 (July, 2000): 26. Healy gives a short history of the Humana Festival and explains Martin's role in its growth. She also reviews Martin's play *Anton in Show Business*.

Rich, Frank. "Stage: *Talking With*, A Find from Louisville." Review of *Talking With*, by Jane Martin. *The New York Times*, October 4, 1982. Rich reviews the Manhattan Theater Club production of *Talking With*, examines the writing of Martin, and speculates on her identity.

Leah Green

FRANCISCO MARTÍNEZ DE LA ROSA

Born: Granada, Spain; March 10, 1787
Died: Madrid, Spain; February 7, 1862

PRINCIPAL DRAMA
Lo que puede un empleo, pr. 1810, pb. 1812
La viuda de Padilla, pr. 1812, pb. 1814

Morayma, wr. 1818, pb. 1827

La niña en casa y la madre en la máscara, pr. 1821, pb. 1830

La boda y el duelo, wr. c. 1828, pr., pb. 1839

Edipo, pb. 1829, pr. 1832

Aben Humeya: Ou, La révolte des naures sous Philippe II, pr., pb. 1830

Aben Humeya: O, La rebelión de los moriscos, pb. 1830, pr. 1836

La conjuración de Venecia año de 1310, pb. 1830, pr. 1834

Los celos infundados: O, El marido en la chimenea, pr. 1833, pb. 1845

El español en Venecia: O, La cabera encantada, pb. 1843

Amor de padre, wr. 1849, pb. 1861

El parricida, pb. 1856

Obras dramáticas, pb. 1933

OTHER LITERARY FORMS

Francisco Martínez de la Rosa initiated his fruitful literary career with several poetic odes that quickly attracted his contemporaries' attention. Furthermore, his participation in the Cádiz resistance against the French invasion during the War of 1808-1814 brought this young liberal into the political arena. Throughout his life, he contributed to Spanish affairs with several treatises and fundamental political statutes and documents. This political involvement naturally inclined him toward historical research, which inspired his historical novel, *Doña Isabel de Solís, Reyna de Granada* (1837-1846), and several historical treatises, among them the monumental *El espíritu del siglo* (1835-1851). His diverse literary interests also led him in 1829 to publish a translation of Horace's *Ars poetica* (c. 17 B.C.E.; *The Art of Poetry*, 1567) called *Traducción de la Epístola de Horacio a los Pisones sobre arte poética* and to write his *Poética* (1831).

ACHIEVEMENTS

Although Francisco Martínez de la Rosa cultivated all literary genres, he regarded his writing merely as a substitute for political action during idle periods in prison or in exile. Nevertheless, he occu-

pies a primary place in the Spanish Romantic drama because his *La conjuración de Venecia año de 1310* was the first play with Romantic characteristics to be represented on a Spanish stage. Mariano José de Larra, the period's sharpest and severest critic of the time, hailed the play as the best seen in Madrid, pointing out both the dramatic and the political achievements of Martínez de la Rosa. Indeed, in April, 1834, this successful first performance was contemporaneous with the publication of the *Estatuto Real*, the new constitution of the nation written by him, and by his signing of the Quadruple Alliance. Despite these successes, Martínez de la Rosa is remembered today by modern critics only for the historical significance of *La conjuración de Venecia año de 1310*.

Ironically, Martínez de la Rosa cannot be classified as a convinced Romantic, because in politics and literature alike, he was a moderate. This is a reflection of his transitional position between neoclassical and Romantic poetics. Russell P. Sebold considers Romantic poetics to be a consequence of the transformation of the poetic rules in the eighteenth century from mechanical and closed to organic and open. In those terms, Martínez de la Rosa stands as an evolutionary rather than a revolutionary figure, although he was the first Spanish dramatist to write a play that upheld the new spirit of liberty surrounding the Cádiz resistance against Napoleon. *La viuda de Padilla*, staged in the besieged city, contrasts with the neoclassical tragedies that exploited past national heroes for despotic objectives. Martínez de la Rosa's tragedy incorporates the Romantic emphasis on freedom and antiabsolutism while nevertheless retaining many Enlightenment values.

BIOGRAPHY

Francisco de Paula Martínez de la Rosa Berdejo Gómez y Arroyo was born in Granada to a bourgeois family on March 10, 1787. He was soon admired for his prodigious intellectual abilities, and by age twelve, he had already entered his hometown's university. In 1804, he received a Ph.D. in civil law, and in April, 1805, he was awarded the chair of philosophy at the University of Granada. That same year marked his beginnings in the poetic genre with some religious odes that he composed for the festival of Corpus Christi. Among his literary contacts, José Joaquín de Mora, noted later for his Romantic polemic with Juan Nicolás Böhl de Faber, contributed to his acceptance in the Cádiz literary circle of Antonio María Alcalá Galiano, who would become another important Romantic spokesman.

During the war against Napoleon, in 1810, Martínez de la Rosa sailed from Cádiz to London. There he met José María Blanco White, who introduced him to English parliamentary government, which Martínez de la Rosa defended in "La revolución actual de España." Upon his return to the besieged city of Cádiz, he was elected to the first Spanish Parliament, the Cortes, and premiered his two first plays. Later he stood out as a leader of the liberal group that unsuccessfully tried to persuade Ferdinand VII to accept the new constitution. Jailed in 1814, Martínez de la Rosa wrote poems and a tragedy, *Morayma*.

With Rafael del Riego's liberal uprising of 1820, Martínez de la Rosa returned to the political arena. As a Cortes deputy for Granada, he contributed to several key legislative projects. Later he was named head of the government. Because he opposed the dominant revolutionary tendencies of the period from 1820 to 1823, he left Spain in 1823 and lived mainly in Paris until his return in 1831. During this period of exile, he produced the majority of his literary accomplishments; he enjoyed the acclaim of the Paris public for his play *Aben Humeya: Ou, La révolte des naures sous Philippe II*. While in Paris, he also wrote his principal play, *La conjuración de Venecia año de 1310*.

After the death of Ferdinand VII, the regent called upon Martínez de la Rosa to head the new government. Nevertheless, the moderate views expressed in his *Estatuto Real*, which displeased both ends of the political spectrum, and his failure with the Carlist uprising forced him out. Despite this political disappointment, he had been able to witness the Madrid success of the premiere of *La conjuración de Venecia año de 1310*. In the following years, Martínez de la Rosa actively opposed the reforms of the Count of

Toreno and Francisco Mendizábal. In 1839, he was nominated to the presidency of the Spanish Language Royal Academy. His political opposition to the new liberal regent, General Espartero, forced him into a second exile in Paris in 1840, where he continued to work on his *El espíritu del siglo*.

When Elisabeth II was crowned in 1844 and called for a moderate government, Martínez de la Rosa again played a key political role, as ambassador, cabinet minister, member and president of the Cortes, and president of the council of state. A year before his death in Madrid on February 7, 1862, he published his complete dramatic works in three volumes. His plays certainly won for him more popular acclaim than did his conservative politics.

ANALYSIS

Francisco Martínez de la Rosa's venture into the theater in 1812 was accompanied by the battle echoes of the French siege of Cádiz. Both the comedy *Lo que puede un empleo* and his patriotic tragedy *La viuda de Padilla*, reminiscent of the nationalistic works of the Italian playwright Vittorio Alfieri, were immediately acclaimed. Although it seems that the comedy was written as a complement to the tragedy, it was premiered earlier than *La viuda de Padilla*.

LA VIUDA DE PADILLA

In *La viuda de Padilla*, a historical drama, Martínez de la Rosa sought to encourage the patriotic spirit of the people of Cádiz by presenting a story of personal courage in another siege, that of sixteenth century Toledo. The protagonist, María Pacheco, was the widow of Francisco Padilla, one of the Castilian leaders during the War of the Communities against the absolutism of Charles I. With historical perspective, as Rafael Seco points out, the play not only reflects the resistance against the French invaders but also foreshadows the troubles that lay ahead for the Liberals with the return of Ferdinand VII's absolute rule in 1814.

La viuda de Padilla differs from neoclassical tragedy in its treatment of Spain's past. Instead of presenting a national hero whose behavior ought to reinforce the enlightened despotism of absolute rule, Martínez de la Rosa's tragedy is a declaration of the rights of humanity against tyranny and oppression. Historically, the play is inaccurate; the real claims of the Castilian followers of Padilla are not advanced, and in fact his widow, María Pacheco, did not remain in Toledo but actually fled to Portugal. Nevertheless, the play projects the moderate views of Martínez de la Rosa that characterize his later works and political beliefs: Violent revolutions are not the answer to the needs of the new system, and the people, the masses, are not to be entrusted with historical decisions. In the last scene, as Charles's troops override the Toledo defenders, María Pacheco commits suicide. As she is dying, she disdains her people's pleas for clemency from the victors. Her point of view reflects the maxim "Everything for the people, but without the people." Martínez de la Rosa was sending the clear message that the heroes of the new bourgeois order could come only from the top of the social hierarchy.

LO QUE PUEDE UN EMPLEO

Lo que puede un empleo is the first of Martínez de la Rosa's neoclassical comedies. Although, at the end of his life, he ventured into the cape and sword (*capa y espada*) genre with *El español en Venecia: O, La cabera encantada*, his other comedic attempts closely follow the structural and thematic patterns that Leandro Fernández de Moratín established at the turn of the century. In *Lo que puede un empleo*, a typical comedy of manners, the anagnorisis, or comic discovery, is centered on a political conflict. The expulsion of the conservative usurper Melitón is linked to the intervention of the liberal Don Luis, who, as the *honnête homme*, is the agent of the happy ending and new social order. The deceived and corrected father, Don Fabián, recognizes the virtues of his future son-in-law, Don Luis's son, Teodoro, despite his liberal tendencies.

LA NIÑA EN CASA Y LA MADRE EN LA MÁSCARA

In *La niña en casa y la madre en la máscara*, the social order is restored when the usurper, Don Teodoro, who courts both an irresponsible mother, Doña Leoncia, and her innocent daughter, Doña Inés, is unmasked. As Mariano José de Larra claimed in an 1835 critique, however, Martínez de la Rosa appears trapped within the structural patterns of the comedy; consequently, the moral discourse of Don Pedro, and

thus the marriage of the pale Don Luis to Doña Inés, seems false. When Larra claimed that spectators should be able to infer the moral of the play from the action itself and not have to rely on a spokesperson, he was pointing out the historical deficiencies of the genre, too close to Moratín's comic practice. That is the case of *La boda y el duelo*, a work that thematically and structurally recalls Moratín's *El sí de las niñas* (wr. 1801, pr., pb. 1806; *When a Girl Says Yes*, 1929).

LOS CELOS INFUNDADOS

Probably the most refreshing of Martínez de la Rosa's comedies is *Los celos infundados: O, El marido en la chimenea*, an intrigue comedy. A jealous older husband, Don Anselmo, is corrected through the scheming seduction of his wife's brother, Don Eugenio, who has just arrived in Cádiz from La Habana with his cousin. The cousin assumes the identity of Don Eugenio and because Don Anselmo has never met either of them, Don Eugenio now impersonates a friend of his cousin so that he can thereby pretend to court Don Anselmo's wife, Doña Francisca. Although the play is very amusing, Larra again found that verisimilitude was lacking. He conceded that a jealous husband whose wife remained loyal when courted by a stranger might then feel secure about his wife's faithfulness, but he argued that, contrary to the resolution of the play, the jealous husband would not retain his equanimity after discovering that the so-called stranger was really his brother-in-law.

From the point of view of comedy, Martínez de la Rosa could hardly be called an innovator, except for his insertion of a political message in *Lo que puede un empleo*. Nevertheless, his plays were successfully staged throughout his career, and he showed his skill as a playwright with his incursion into the cape and sword mode and by the use of verse and prose in these plays.

MORAYMA

While in prison, Martínez de la Rosa attempted his second tragedy with a national theme, *Morayma*. In contrast to the Castilian background of *La viuda de Padilla*, the setting of *Morayma* is King Boabdil's Alhambra palace after the rebellion of the Abencerrajes in the fifteenth century. During the uprising, the Abencerrajes's chief, Albinhamad, Morayma's husband, has been killed. Because Boabdil may not harm his stepsister, he decides to ban the rest of the Abencerrajes, and thereby separate Morayma from her son. Alí, the chief of the Zegríes and victor over the Abencerrajes, falls in love with Morayma and tries to save her son. After being betrayed, Alí is killed while escaping with Morayma's son. Morayma dies as a result of her painful loss, and at the end of the play, Boabdil shamelessly flees from the scene of the crime. Boabdil's depiction in the tragedy recalls the ruthless return to power of Ferdinand VII. *Morayma* already uses character, thematic, and spatial motifs that would be encountered later in *Aben Humeya: O, La rebelión de los moriscos* and in the more romantic *La conjuración de Venecia año de 1310*.

For example, Alí's efforts to reconcile Boabdil and the Abencerrajes, in act 2, scene 4, are similar to Rugiero's promises, in *La conjuración de Venecia año de 1310*, to safeguard the lives of his wife's family. Furthermore, Rugiero's death is accompanied by the death of his wife, who cannot overcome the pain of seeing her lover condemned, in the same way in which Morayma dies after Alí's and her son's death. Moreover, not only is the thematic motif of the maternal responsibility expressed by Morayma, a topic which appears in later plays (as Robert Geraldi has noted), but also both Muley Carime in *Aben Humeya: O, La rebelión de los moriscos* and Juan Morosini in *La conjuración de Venecia año de 1310* admit an inability to understand their paternal role.

These three all involve a *coup d'état*, as well as nighttime scenes and lugubrious spaces—underground paths in a castle in the first two, and the Morosini pantheon in the cemetery in *La conjuración de Venecia año de 1310*. Despite these similarities and the distinctively Romantic historical setting, *Morayma* can hardly be called a Romantic play, because in *Morayma* all three stage unities are enforced, although different spaces within the palace are used. This neoclassical flexibility in the unity of space can be found in Ignacio de Luzán's *Poética* (1737) as well as in Pierre Corneille's theater. These similarities found in Martínez de la Rosa's later historical dramas reinforced the evolution of the neoclassical theatrical patterns into Romantic ones through the more adaptable poetic rules.

ABEN HUMEYA: O, LA REBELIÓN DE LOS MORISCOS

Aben Humeya: O, La rebelión de los moriscos recounts the Moriscos' rebellion against Philip II within a somewhat weak time unity, condensing the historical events of five months into a twenty-four-hour period. On its Spanish premiere in 1836, the play failed to appeal to the public, particularly to Larra, who disliked Martínez de la Rosa's politically conservative positions of that period. Nevertheless, the play resembles *La conjuración de Venecia año de 1310*, which two years earlier had been very well received. Both plays use religious holidays and festive moods in contrast with the preparation and staging of a rebellion; in both, the collaboration of outsiders helps the conspirators prepare a plan, while spies intervene to unveil the future plans of both Muley Carime and Rugiero. In both plays, the sound of wind predicts evil and catastrophe.

Both plays also show structural similarities to sentimental comedy. In Martínez de la Rosa's plays, one finds the conflict of the family feelings of two men overridden by their duties as executors of justice. In *Aben Humeya: O, La rebelión de los moriscos*, the protagonist is forced to give his father-in-law the poison that punishes him for treason because he has attempted to save Abén Humeya's wife and family through a pact with the Christians. After the failure of the conspiracy in *La conjuración de Venecia año de 1310*, Pedro Morosini judges and condemns his son Rugiero during a tragic anagnorisis. If the lachrymose scenes of Don Justo condemning his son Don Torcuato in *el delincuente honrado* (tragicomedies) have the *rex ex machina* denouement of the royal pardon, in Martínez de la Rosa's dramas, the spectator is dismayed by the condemnation and death of the heroes. Formally, both dramas use prose instead of verse, another feature of *el delincuente honrado*.

If both plays witness the failure of rebellions, it is not simply because Martínez de la Rosa held deep reservations concerning popular movements but also because dramatists of this period were increasingly conscious of the claims of historical accuracy. In any case, *Aben Humeya: O, La rebelión de los moriscos*, like *Morayma*, warns against tyranny based on bloody oppression and injustice, as well as insisting that the attempt to replace tyranny through violent means evolves into internal strife and a repetition of the original tyrannical pattern it strived to suppress. *La conjuración de Venecia año de 1310*, through Marcos Querini's discourse in act 1, scene 3, recalls the ideological purpose of the neoclassical tragedies and *La viuda de Padilla:* The people should be directed through changes and not allowed political choice. This ideological declaration certainly reflects Martínez de la Rosa's moderate views. As Francisco Ruiz Ramón claims, both plays treat the theme of freedom as an elegy rather than from the Romantic point of view of a hymn.

INFLUENCE OF NEOCLASSICISM

If, ideologically, Martínez de la Rosa's theater may be described as a reflection of his moderate views, the formal aspects of his plays also support this stance. Because the poetic rules had evolved from authority to reason, nature and art did not exclude but rather complemented each other. Therefore, as early as 1773, this new poetic appeared with its Romantic touches in the work of an apparent neoclassicist, José Cadalso, as Sebold notes.

In his "Apuntes sobre el drama histórico," which appeared in volume 5 of his *Obras literarias* (1827-1830), Martínez de la Rosa justifies this neoclassical flexibility, adding to his dramas the *dulce et utile* precept found in Luzán and Moratín. In *La conjuración de Venecia año de 1310*, he would therefore present himself as an eclectic descendant of the spectacular Romanticism of the end of the eighteenth century, while in his "Anotaciones sobre el drama histórico" (1830), he clarifies the theory for these changes.

As a neoclassicist interested in didacticism, he defends the action rule so that the spectators may clearly understand the play, while he offers concessions to the spatial rule, an "innovation" already found in Luzán and *Morayma*. Regarding the time unity, his flexibility overcomes the suffocating twenty-four-hour limit. With respect to language, he recom-

mends the verisimilitude of tone defended by Luzán and Denis Diderot.

LA CONJURACIÓN DE VENECIA AÑO DE 1310

La conjuración de Venecia año de 1310 takes place in 1310, during the dreadful time of the feared Venetian Tribunal and the failure of the famous conspiracy against the political control of a few families. One of the conspirators is Rugiero, an adopted Venetian of obscure origins, secretly married to Laura Morosini, the daughter of Juan Morosini and the niece of Pedro Morosini, the president of the hated Venetian Tribunal. In act 1, at the palace of the Ambassador of Genoa, Rugiero plots with the other conspirators to overthrow the Venetian oligarchy. In act 2, at night, in the Morosini pantheon, Pedro Morosini receives the account of his spies. Interrupted by Laura's and Rugiero's entry, he reveals the conspirators' plans to her as well as to the hidden enemies. Captured by the spies, Rugiero is taken away, and Laura faints. The lack of verisimilitude of this act is compensated for by the very romantic setting of the pantheon. In act 3, inside the Morosini palace, Laura confesses her secret marriage to her father. In this moving scene of paternal understanding, she convinces him to try to save Rugiero. When Juan confronts his brother, in a typical sentimental comedy dilemma, Pedro pledges his allegiance to the judicial prerogatives he serves. Act 4 recounts the failure of the conspiracy in several animated popular scenes. Martínez de la Rosa changed the date to Mardi Gras and therefore renders the act into a very appropriate Romantic tableau later used in José Zorrilla y Moral's *Don Juan Tenorio* (pr., pb. 1844; English translation, 1944). The last act takes place in the lugubrious Hall of the Tribunal, which leads to the jails and torture rooms. As in a sentimental comedy, friendship turns into heroism when Julián Rossi refuses to declare against his former *condottiero*, Rugiero. Then Juan Mafei, another conspirator, is condemned in a hearing that recalls Christ's sentencing. When the tribunal is unable to make the now insane Laura testify, Rugiero is brought in, and Pedro Morosini discovers that he is in fact judging his own son. The former had been captured at sea and separated from his parents when he was a baby. This dramatic anagnorisis causes Pedro Morosini to faint, while the judges condemn Rugiero to death. In the lachrymose finale, Laura dies when she sees the scaffold, and Rugiero is taken away.

The play contains many manneristic Romantic motifs found in later Spanish dramas: torture, a carnival, a conspiracy, disguised suggestions of incest, onstage violence, mention of pirates, and so on. Besides these obvious motifs, marriage, as in Ángel de Saavedra's *Don Álvaro: O, La fuerza del sino* (pr., pb. 1835; *Don Álvaro: Or, The Force of Destiny*, 1964) is a source for parental opposition. Passionate love is abruptly ended by death, as in Antonio García Gutiérrez's *El trovador* (pr. 1836), Juan Eugenio de Hartzenbusch's *Los amantes de Teruel* (pr. 1836; *The Lovers of Teruel*, 1938), and *Don Álvaro*. The three protagonists in Martínez de la Rosa's, Saavedra's, and Gutiérrez's plays have obscure origins and therefore conform to Jean-Jacques Rousseau's notion of the noble savage who is destroyed by society; all three find their destinies determined by fate.

La conjuración de Venecia año de 1310 thus exemplifies the evolution of eighteenth century poetics into Romanticism. It combines the sentimental comedy structure and spectacular elements of the early Romantic examples à la Cadalso with the more nineteenth century manneristic Romantic elements that one finds in plays written after 1834. Although it remains Martínez de la Rosa's best-known work, his other historical plays are also of interest for the light they shed on the transformation of Spanish drama in the early nineteenth century.

OTHER MAJOR WORKS

LONG FICTION: *Doña Isabel de Solís, Reyna de Granada*, 1837-1846.

POETRY: *Zaragoza*, 1811; *Poemas*, 1831; *Poesías*, 1833.

NONFICTION: "La revolución actual de España," 1810; "Manifiesto a la Nación," 1814; "Anotaciones sobre el drama histórico," 1830; *Poética*, 1831; *Hernán Pérez del Pulgar el de las Hazañas: Bosquejo histórico*, 1834; *El espíritu del siglo*, 1835-1851; *Libro de los niños*, 1839; *Discours: Quelle est l'influence de l'esprit du siècle actuel sur la littérature?*, 1842; *Bosquejo histórico de la política de España desde los tiempos de los Reyes Católicos hasta nuestros días*, 1857.

TRANSLATION: *Traducción de la Epístola de Horacio a los Pisones sobre arte poética*, 1829 (of Horace's *Ars poetica*).

MISCELLANEOUS: *Obras literarias*, 1827-1830 (5 volumes).

BIBLIOGRAPHY

Cook, John A. *Neoclassic Drama in Spain: Theory and Practice*. 1959. Reprint. Westport, Conn.: Greenwood, 1974. An analysis of neoclassical drama in Spain. Bibliography.

Geraldi, Robert. "Francisco Martínez de la Rosa: Literary Atrophy or Creative Sagacity?" *Hispanófila* 77 (1983): 11-19. Geraldi examines Martínez de la Rosa's works in regard to their progressiveness.

Kosove, Joan Lynne Pataky. *The "Comedia Lacrimosa" and Spanish Romantic Drama 1773-1865*. London: Tamesis, 1977. A look at the relationship between sentimental comedy and Spanish Romantic drama.

Mayberry, Robert, and Nancy Mayberry. *Francisco Martínez de la Rosa*. Boston: Twayne, 1988. A general study of the life and work of Martínez de la Rosa. Bibliography and index.

Ojeda Escudero, Pedro. *El justo medio: Neoclasicismo y romanticismo en la obra dramática de Martínez de la Rosa*. Burgos, Spain: Universidad de Burgos, 1997. An examination of the neoclassicism and Romanticism found in the dramatic works of Martínez de la Rosa. Bibliography. In Spanish.

Pérez Magallón, Jesús. *El teatro neoclásico*. Madrid: Ediciones del Laberinto, 2001. Covers the neoclassical movement in Spanish theater. Bibliography. In Spanish.

José María Naharro-Calderón

GREGORIO MARTÍNEZ SIERRA *and* MARÍA MARTÍNEZ SIERRA

Gregorio Martínez Sierra
Born: Madrid, Spain; May 6, 1881
Died: Madrid, Spain; October 1, 1947

María Martínez Sierra
Born: San Millán de la Cogolla, Spain;
    December 28, 1874
Died: Buenos Aires, Argentina; June 28, 1974

PRINCIPAL DRAMA

Teatro de ensueño, pb. 1905

Vida y dulzura, pr. 1907 (with Santiago Rusiñol)

Hechizo de amor, wr. 1908, pb. 1917 (*Love Magic*, 1917)

Juventud, divino tesoro, pr. 1908

La sombra del padre, pr. 1909

El ama de la casa, pr. 1910

Primavera en otoño, pr. 1911 (*Autumn Spring*, 1927)

Canción de cuna, pr. 1911, pb. 1917 (*The Cradle Song*, 1917)

El palacio triste, pr. 1911, pb. 1913

Lirio entre espinas, pr. 1911, pb. c. 1930 (*A Lily Among Thorns*, 1923)

El enamorado, wr. 1912, pb. 1917 (*The Lover*, 1919)

Madame Pepita, wr. 1912, pb. 1917 (English translation, 1923)

El pobrecito Juan, wr. 1912, pb. 1917 (*Poor John*, 1920)

Mamá, pr. 1913 (based on Henrik Ibsen's *Et dukkehjem*; *Mama*, 1923)

Madrigal, pr. 1913 (English translation, 1931)

Los pastores, pr. 1913, pb. 1922 (*The Two Shepherds*, 1923)

Margot, pb. 1914

Las golondrinas, pr. 1914 (with José Maria de Usandizaga)

La mujer del héroe, pr. 1914, pb. 1922 (*Wife to a Famous Man*, 1923)

La pasión, pr. 1914, pb. 1915

El amor brujo, pr. 1915 (music by Manuel de Falla)

Amanecer, pr. 1915

El reino de Dios, pr. 1915, pb. 1922 (*The Kingdom of God*, 1923)

El sombrero de tres picos, pr. 1916 (music by de Falla)

Navidad, pr. 1916 (*Holy Night*, 1928)

Sueño de una noche de agosto, pr. 1918, pb. 1922 (*The Romantic Young Lady*, 1923)

Rosina es frágil, pb. 1918

Cada uno y su vida, pb. 1919

El corazón ciego, pr. 1919, pb. 1922

Don Juan de España, pr. 1921

Mujer, pb. 1925

Seamos felices, pr. 1929

Triángulo, pr. 1930 (*Take Two from One: A Farce in Three Acts*, 1931)

La hora del diablo, pr. 1930

Sortilegio, pr. 1930

OTHER LITERARY FORMS

Gregorio Martínez Sierra has been credited with more than two hundred titles in addition to the numerous articles that appeared in literary periodicals. Recent scholarship has unearthed the fact that his wife, María Martínez Sierra, collaborated in most works credited to Gregorio, and she was also the principal author of many of these works. Because it is not possible to ascertain with certainty which works were done by each, the couple will be treated as an artistic unit for the purposes of this article. *Diálogos fantásticos* (1899; fantastic dialogues) is a lyric work consisting of philosophical remarks made by Life, Death, Heart, Head, Soul, Truth, and other personified elements. *Flores de escarcha* (1900; frost flowers), a collection of stories written in the somewhat artificial style of the modernists, expresses a deep faith in nature's inherent wholesomeness.

Martínez Sierra wrote several novels and novellas, among them *Tú eres la paz* (1906; *Ana María*, 1921), a romantic novel that not only foreshadowed the author's involvement with his leading actress, Catalina

Bárcena, but also introduced the strong, intelligent, and long-suffering female character that later appeared in many of his dramas.

ACHIEVEMENTS

Gregorio Martínez Sierra was one of Spain's most prolific writers. He is primarily known for his theatrical works, which captivated the Spanish public during the first half of the twentieth century, but his artistic genius encompassed many literary genres and activities. Besides the numerous plays credited to his name, Martínez Sierra wrote poetry, short stories, novels, operettas, and essays. As if this were not enough to satisfy his enormous creative instincts, he founded several prestigious literary journals, *Vida moderna* (modern life), *Helios* (the sun), and *Renacimiento* (renaissance); established two highly respected publishing houses, *Renacimiento* and *Estrella* (star); managed his own theater company; directed many innovative dramas; supervised the filming of some of his more popular plays; and wrote original film scripts for Metro-Goldwyn-Mayer, Paramount, and Fox Studios.

The breadth and depth of his activities startle the imagination and cause one to question whether such uncommon literary talent could possibly belong to but one individual. In fact, Martínez Sierra's genius lay in his uncanny ability to collaborate with fellow artists. Though it was suspected for many years, it was not until the publication of Patricia W. O'Connor's incisive study, *Gregorio and María Martínez Sierra* (1977), that concrete evidence was presented revealing to what extent Martínez Sierra's talent consisted in serving as a catalyst to other artists. Specifically, his wife, María, is now known to have collaborated with him on virtually all the plays attributed to him, and she was the principal author of many of these works. Although María Martínez Sierra has been granted her rightful place in literary history as Spain's first great woman dramatist, Gregorio's importance should not diminish in the least. On the contrary, his role as muse and catalyst was essential in the literary partnership that he shared with his wife. Together, this couple produced some of the most popular drama of twentieth century Spain.

BIOGRAPHY

Because the literary Gregorio Martínez Sierra is actually two people, Gregorio and his wife, María (née de la O Lejárraga García), a focus on both individuals is essential to illuminate the circumstances surrounding the artistic development of one of Spain's most popular dramatists. Both Gregorio and María were born to middle-class Castilian families, Gregorio in 1881 and María in 1874. Whereas Gregorio was reared in a staunch Catholic setting, María was taught from her earliest years to question traditional beliefs. As a young boy, Gregorio manifested a general attraction to literature and a specific love for the theater. It was in 1897 that Gregorio and María met for the first time. Gregorio was a rather shy individual but found himself deeply attracted to María, who was seven years his senior. Their mutual love of literature seemed to fuse their lives inexorably together. Years later, as their marriage began to deteriorate, the literary union that initially had brought them together seemed to intensify.

After their marriage in 1900, María supported the two of them by teaching, allowing Gregorio free rein to pursue his literary interests. In 1901, he founded the first of three periodicals, *Vida moderna*, which only survived for four issues. Undaunted by this failure and encouraged by the support of such established writers as Juan Ramón Jiménez, Ramón Pérez de Ayala, and Pedro González Blanco, he cofounded the respected but ephemeral periodical *Helios*. In 1904, his novel *La humilde verdad* (the humble truth) won third prize in a literary contest. This success led to a commission to write another novel. María took the opportunity to suggest that Gregorio and she take a short vacation from Spain. Gregorio's health had been weakening, and she was afraid that if they remained in Madrid, he might fall prey to tuberculosis. In 1905, they left for Paris, where in the succeeding weeks they had the good fortune to meet several influential artists who, in later years, would collaborate with Gregorio. While María worked on the novel *Ana Mariá*, Gregorio returned with the well-known Catalonian dramatist Santiago Rusiñol to Madrid, where they worked on a Castilian version of Rusiñol's play, *Buena gente* (1906; good people). When Gregorio returned to Paris, María and he decided to tour Europe together. Once Gregorio's health seemed substantially restored, they returned to Madrid, where, in 1907, two fateful events awaited them: the performance of their first play, *Vida y dulzura* (life and sweetness), which was written in collaboration with their good friend Rusiñol, and Gregorio's initial encounter with Catalina Bárcena. Catalina was to become Gregorio's mistress, and together they would dominate the Spanish theater, he as Spain's leading director and she as his leading actress. María would be the invisible force behind her husband's rising fame, writing many of the plays that would be credited to Gregorio.

With the successful performance of *La sombra del padre* (the father's shadow) in 1909, Gregorio found himself in the envious position of being courted by the theater establishment. By now, Gregorio was amorously involved with the young actress Catalina. He suggested that María and he take a vacation in Italy, but that she should go on ahead of him while he completed business in Madrid. It was during this critical time in their marital relationship that the inspiration for their most renowned play was born. While in Nice and Florence, María visited many churches, where she was attracted to the beautiful portrayals of the Virgin holding her child. The idea of a virgin mother prompted María to focus on the concept of maternity. She discussed this idea with Gregorio, and two years later, *The Cradle Song* was to captivate the imagination of the entire Spanish people, winning the Royal Academy's prize for best work of 1911.

Except for a sudden bout with typhoid fever, in 1911, the remainder of Gregorio's life was filled with innumerable successes. While Gregorio enjoyed the public's adulation, María remained quietly in the background, writing the plays that would bear Gregorio's name. In 1915 and 1916, Gregorio collaborated with Spain's most prominent composer, Manuel de Falla, to produce two very successful musicals, *El amor brujo* (love's sorcery) and *El sombrero de tres picos* (the three-cornered hat). After a year of touring the provinces with Catalina, Gregorio decided to found his own theater company with Catalina as his leading actress. For eight years, from 1916 to 1924, the

Eslava Theater in Madrid would present some of the most avant-garde dramas in Spain.

Gregorio, because of the highly successful writing of his wife, is best known today as one of Spain's finest dramatists. It should be recalled, however, that Gregorio's personal strength lay in directing. Considered by his contemporaries to be Spain's premier director, he introduced many innovative techniques to the art of directing. For example, he is credited with separating the art of directing from that of staging and set design. While Gregorio was running his theater, María found herself attracted to the international feminist movement. During these years, she wrote several volumes of essays on the modern woman's role in society. In 1922, Catalina gave birth to a girl, precipitating Gregorio's formal separation from María. From 1924 until 1930, Gregorio and Catalina toured with their theater group throughout Europe and the Americas, returning to Madrid in 1929 to open two new plays, *La hora del diablo* (the devil's hour) and *Take Two from One*. María, in the meantime, divided her time between Madrid and Nice. Besides continuing to work on new plays, she involved herself quite seriously in the Socialist and feminist movements. The physical separation between María and Gregorio caused economic complications for María. Because all the royalties went to Gregorio, he decided, in 1930, that María should receive the royalties of all their works produced outside Spain.

In 1931, Gregorio and Catalina went to Hollywood, where, for four years, Gregorio involved himself with the film industry. María, back in Spain, became more and more politically committed. She successfully ran as a Socialist candidate for a seat in the Republic's Cortes (legislative body), which she held until the outbreak of the Civil War in 1936. Following the outbreak of war, María went to Switzerland, and then on to Nice, where she settled. Gregorio and Catalina fled to Argentina, where they continued their theatrical and filming activities. Gregorio's health began to deteriorate. Suffering from a severe abdominal illness, Gregorio returned to Spain in 1947, where he died of cancer on October 1, two weeks after his arrival home. María resided in Nice until 1950, when she left for the United States in the hope of selling some of her stories to the Walt Disney Studios. Unsuccessful in this attempt, María left, in 1953, for Mexico, where she published her autobiographical account entitled *Gregorio y yo* (Gregorio and I).

From 1953 to 1974, María lived in Buenos Aires, where she remained active, writing articles for various periodicals until her death on June 28, 1974. Gregorio and María Martínez Sierra, together, dominated the Spanish stage for the greater part of the first half of the twentieth century. Their unique literary partnership gave to the world some of the most tender and loving scenes the Spanish theater has ever produced.

ANALYSIS

Gregorio Martínez Sierra's prolific output transcends any brief attempt at analysis. One can, however, analyze the various styles, techniques, and dramatic themes that make his drama unique. Concerning his style, there is a definite movement away from the abstract and poetic language of the modernist mode to a more concrete and realistic portrayal of life. Although his style acquired an ever greater simplicity, his themes remained relatively constant. For example, there is a profound faith in nature's healing qualities, as well as a strong moralistic overtone in almost all of his plays. It was not until 1910, however, that Martínez Sierra developed the dramatic formula that would become synonymous with his name. With the premiere of *El ama de la casa*, Martínez Sierra combined a simple and direct style with the recurring theme of maternal love. Given the substantial contributions of María Martínez Sierra, it is not surprising that the women in Martínez Sierra's plays are more believable than the men. In Spanish society, which frequently stereotyped its women as either pure and innocent maidens to be cared for by their husbands, or dangerous and alluring temptresses to be encountered as prostitutes or mistresses, the plays of the Martínez Sierras reminded audiences that women transcend any stereotype and are more than capable of contributing equally with men to society's well-being.

Martínez Sierra's theatrical career as dramatist and director spanned almost the entire first half of the twentieth century. Beginning in 1907, with his first dramatic production, *Vida y dulzura*, his presence on the Spanish stage continued to grow in stature. For example, four years later, in 1911, with the performance of *The Cradle Song*, he was given one of the Spanish Royal Academy's highest recognitions when his play was chosen as that year's outstanding drama. The three decades that were to follow saw the production of more than forty original plays, as well as the direction of many other Spanish and foreign dramas. During the years 1916 through 1924, he managed his own drama company, producing highly acclaimed plays from Madrid's Eslava Theater and introducing many innovative techniques in the art of directing. Although the last decade of his life was lived mostly outside Spain, first in the United States and later in Argentina, his influence both within and without his mother country continued unabated until his death in 1947. Because of the large number of plays credited to Martínez Sierra, the analysis of individual dramas will focus on those plays that are considered most representative.

Martínez Sierra's early drama reflected a modernist heritage characterized by a rather languid style, melancholy in tone and moralistic in content. Nevertheless, there is a definite progression away from the ethereal and toward the concrete. Through the influence of Santiago Rusiñol, the renowned Catalonian dramatist, Martínez Sierra began to cultivate a simple and more direct style that focused on the everyday domestic occurrences that would be more likely to please the Spanish public.

TEATRO DE ENSUEÑO

Martínez Sierra's initial attempt at theater, *Teatro de ensueño* (dream theater), consisted of a collection of modernist pieces that, for the most part, lacked the necessary dramatic tension to be produced onstage. Nevertheless, it included a work entitled *Saltimbanquis* (the tumblers), which was later set to music. *Teatro de ensueño*'s first dramatic sketch, "Por el sendero florido" (along the flowery path), tells of the grief experienced by a young man whose wife literally works herself to death for love of her husband. A source of joy to her husband when alive, she becomes an even greater blessing to him when he associates his wife's love with the life-giving warmth of the sun.

The second piece, "Pastoral," depicts, in allegorical terms, humankind's often misguided quest for happiness. The protagonist, Alcino, represents Everyman, as he searches for his idyllic Sun Queen. Unable to recognize the pure and innocent love of his companion Rosa María, who represents opportunity, Alcino loses his chance for true love. Nevertheless, he has learned the important lesson that happiness often is very close at hand if one but opens one's eyes.

Teatro de ensueño's third sketch is entitled "Cuento de labios en flor" (story of lips in flower). Of the three sketches, this is the most poetic. Two sisters, Blanca and Rosalina, fall in love with a young artist. Their love for each other, however, moves each one to sacrifice her own happiness for that of the other. Each sister throws herself into a stream so that the other might experience the artist's love. All ends well when they are reunited through nature as two water lilies.

Although these poetic sketches, with their clear moral teachings, resemble stylized parables rather than complex human dramas, they do possess, in embryonic form, the seeds of dramatic conflict that would come to full fruition by 1911. For example, from the protagonist of "Pastoral" would develop the more believable yet equally weak-willed and dependent male characters of Martínez Sierra's later plays. Similarly, the self-sacrificing wife of "Por el sendero florido" and the sisters of "Cuento de labios en flor" foreshadow the strong-willed, self-sacrificing, and intelligent female characters that have come to be associated with his better-known dramas.

VIDA Y DULZURA

Martínez Sierra's first play performed for a Madrid audience, *Vida y dulzura*, was written in collaboration with Santiago Rusiñol. The dramatic action revolves around a young woman's quest to choose her own destiny. Reared in a highly intellectual atmosphere, Marcela has acquired a true love of learning and scientific investigation. Nevertheless, she sees in her parents' fondness for intellectual pursuits a certain lack of openness and spontaneity. Although her parents hope that she will marry the learned but dull Dr. Dalmau, she finds herself attracted to Enrique, a

pleasant young man whose simple manner fails to impress Marcela's parents. By her shrewdness, Marcela eventually convinces both the doctor and her parents that she must follow the dictates of her heart and not the well-meaning but sterile wishes of others. *Vida y dulzura* is an uncomplicated play with a simple message: Life, if it is to have meaning, must be experienced fully. One must follow one's heart as well as one's head.

JUVENTUD, DIVINO TESORO

In *Juventud, divino tesoro* (youth, that divine treasure), an aging Don Juan named Emilio finds himself deeply attracted to his innocent and beautiful niece, Clara. The young girl easily deceives herself into thinking that her uncle's love is all she would ever want in life until she encounters Pedro, a handsome cousin, who convinces her that she is meant to love someone her own age. The uncle, who at first refuses to accept the loss of Clara, is urged to forget his own hurt by devoting himself to the needs of others. Although this play met with only modest success, it is worthy of comment for several reasons: First, it was Martínez Sierra's first performed play that was credited to his name alone. Second, the play's very simple plot reappeared ten years later, but more developed this time, in the very popular drama *Rosina es frágil* (Rosina is fragile). Last, this play introduced the theme of loving service to others as an efficacious way of overcoming one's loneliness. This motif would reappear many times in subsequent plays, especially in his religious dramas, which focus on convent life.

LA SOMBRA DEL PADRE

La sombra del padre is of special interest in that its central figure, unlike the majority of Martínez Sierra's protagonists, is a male character. Don José is a successful man who has come home to his family after seventeen years in Argentina, where he has worked diligently in order to provide a secure and comfortable life for his wife and seven children. The father's disillusionment over his children's lack of respect for work is heightened by his belief that his wife has not sacrificed herself enough for her children, as a loving mother should. Don José decides to return to Argentina with their youngest son so that at least one child might learn the proper value of work. Although she is a weak and submissive wife, Feliciana demonstrates more insight than her husband when she begs him to stay with the family because the children need both a father's authoritative voice and a mother's loving support. In the end, Don José accedes to the wishes of his wife, and the play ends on an optimistic note that together they might provide both a spiritually and materially secure home for their children. In many of Martínez Sierra's plays, the female protagonist is the dominant figure, while her male counterpart lacks strength of character and is unable to confront the ordinary responsibilities associated with adulthood.

EL AMA DE LA CASA

El ama de la casa (mistress of the house) was pivotal in Martínez Sierra's artistic development, for it marked the moment when he as a dramatist found the dramatic formula that he would employ repeatedly during the next two decades with unparalleled success. (It should be recalled here that when using the name Martínez Sierra or the pronouns "he" and "his," one is referring either to the collaborative work of María and Gregorio Martínez Sierra or to María's work alone.) Beginning with this play, his style would be simple and direct, and his female protagonist would be an intelligent, self-sacrificing, and capable woman, sometimes a loving wife, other times a virgin, but always a woman filled with the desire to lose herself in the service of others. His recurring theme would be the idea of maternal love, a love characterized by a willingness to renounce one's own desires in order to serve the needs of those under one's charge.

In *El ama de la casa*, the protagonist is Carlota, a childless widow who marries a widower who has three nearly grown children. The play focuses on Carlota's ability to bring order, peace, and prosperity to a household that has sorely missed the loving but strong hand of a dedicated mother. Carlota not only fulfills her wifely and motherly responsibilities with a fervor that is truly admirable but also takes over her husband's failing business affairs and manages to rescue him from financial disaster. In a sense, Carlota mothers both her husband and his children. In an important scene, in which Carlota defends her motherly

concern for and active involvement in the affairs of her husband and children, she defines the essence of woman as being nothing more and nothing less than that of being a mother.

THE CRADLE SONG

In *The Cradle Song*, his best-known play, Martínez Sierra breaks with traditional dramatic structure, wherein human conflict is developed to its eventual climax and subsequent cathartic effects. Instead, he chooses to focus on two significant moments within the lives of a group of cloistered nuns. In act 1 of *The Cradle Song*, an abandoned baby is discovered by one of the sisters. This providential event causes myriad reactions on the part of the nuns, awakening in them their dormant urge to nurture new life. When the town doctor offers to adopt the child, the sisters agree to rear it within the loving atmosphere of their community. When the second act begins, eighteen years have passed. It is the day that the grown child, Teresa, is to be married and, therefore, leave her convent family behind. As in the first act, the audience witnesses the profound effects such a momentous event produces in the lives of these virgin mothers. The innovative structure of *The Cradle Song* allows Martínez Sierra to explore in depth the maternal instinct present within the feminine psyche. It should be recalled that for Martínez Sierra, women were meant, above all, to be mothers. If their maternal instinct were to be smothered or interfered with in any way, a noticeable change either in their personality or in their health most assuredly would occur.

Act 1 focuses on the sisters' way of sublimating their maternal inclinations. One sister suffers from imaginary illnesses, while another regularly dreams of escape. One young nun has no appetite and cries repeatedly for seemingly no reason. With the arrival of Teresa, the nuns are given the opportunity to express their motherly instincts in a normal, healthy manner. One nun, in particular, is given the responsibility of caring for the child. In her assigned role as principal mother, Sister Juana blossoms into a tender and loving woman. In contrast, the community's vicaress refuses to allow herself to express her maternal feelings toward Teresa and is portrayed as a cold and bitter woman whose feminine interior remains hidden behind a hardened and cold exterior. In order to underline the drama's principal message, Martínez Sierra presents a lyric interlude extolling woman's intrinsic need to express her motherly feelings. Because of its idyllic setting, *The Cradle Song* is frequently viewed as a sentimental portrayal of idealized maternal love. When one reflects, however, on the sisters' natural inclination to love selflessly the innocent child given to their charge, and their profound frustration on being forced to renounce this love, there is an implied criticism of woman's lot in society.

SEAMOS FELICES

In general, as noted previously, the female protagonist in Martínez Sierra's plays far outshines the lead male character. Whereas she is usually intelligent, sensitive, and strong-willed, he is narrow-minded, impetuous, and insecure. Nevertheless, in *Seamos felices* (let's be happy), the male protagonist, although ultimately the one who is brought to a new awareness through the wise counsel of his wife, is not so much her inferior as her partner and friend. Moreover, the focus in this play changes from that of a woman's struggle to achieve happiness in a male-dominated society to that of a husband's and wife's quest to experience the joy that springs from a mutual willingness to share each other's talents.

Fernanda and Emilio are a happily married couple. When financial problems arise, Fernanda, who is an excellent pianist, tells her husband that she has been asked to make a concert tour that will contribute greatly to their financial situation. At first, Emilio refuses to allow his wife to share in accepting the family's economic responsibilities, for to allow Fernanda to help support the two of them would imply that he has failed in one of his basic manly duties. Fernanda's commonsensical approach to her husband's refusal, however, convinces Emilio that his wife's sincere offer to share responsibly, as an equal, is the best way to ensure true conjugal bliss. When one recalls the titles of such earlier dramas as *Cada uno y su vida* (to each his own) and *Mujer* (woman), which seem to pit female against male in an ageless struggle of the sexes, the "us" of *Seamos felices* indicates a certain maturity and depth of understanding on the part of Martínez Sierra concerning the male-female relationship. Indeed, *Seamos felices*'s fundamental message that true equality between the sexes will exist when each person is open to the other's talents and potential make this play a timeless representation of the human condition.

OTHER MAJOR WORKS

LONG FICTION: *Almas ausentes*, 1900; *Horas de sol*, 1901 (novella); *Pascua florida*, 1903; *La humilde verdad*, 1904; *Tú eres la paz*, 1906 (*Ana Mariá*, 1921); *Aventura*, 1907; *El agua dormida*, 1907 (novella); *Beata primavera*, 1907 (novella); *El peregrino ilusionado*, 1908; *Torre de Marfil*, 1908; *El amor catedrático*, 1910; *Todo es uno y lo mismo*, 1910.

SHORT FICTION: *Cuentos breves*, 1899; *Flores de escarcha*, 1900; *Sol de la tarde*, 1904.

POETRY: *El poema del trabajo*, 1898; *La casa de la primavera*, 1907.

NONFICTION: *Cartas a las mujeres de España*, 1916; *Feminismo, feminidad, españolismo*, 1917; *Nuevas cartas a las mujeres*, 1932; *Gregorio y yo*, 1953.

EDITED TEXT: *Un teatro de arte en España*, 1926.

MISCELLANEOUS: *Diálogos fantásticos*, 1899; *La selva muda*, 1909; *Obras completas*, 1920-1930 (14 volumes).

BIBLIOGRAPHY

Douglas, Frances. "Gregorio Martínez Sierra." *Hispania* 5 (November, 1922): 257-369. A look at Martínez Sierra and his work, from about the time of the couple's separation.

_____. "Gregorio Martínez Sierra." *Hispania* 6 (February, 1923): 1-13. A further examination of the dramatist and his works.

O'Connor, Patricia W. *Gregorio and María Martínez Sierra*. Boston: Twayne, 1977. A basic study of the life and works of Gregorio and María Martínez Sierra. O'Connor provides evidence for María's participation in the writing of their works.

_____. *Women in the Theater of Gregorio Martínez Sierra*. New York: America Press, 1967. A study of the central, strong woman character in Martínez Sierra's plays.

Richard Keenan

EDWARD MARTYN

Born: Masonbrook, Ireland; January 31, 1859
Died: Dublin, Ireland; December 5, 1923

PRINCIPAL DRAMA

The Heather Field, wr. c. 1893, pr., pb. 1899
Maeve, pb. 1899, pr. 1900
An Enchanted Sea, pb. 1902, pr. 1904
The Place-Hunters, pb. 1902
The Tale of a Town, pb. 1902, pr. 1905
Romulus and Remus, pb. 1907
Grangecolman, pr., pb. 1912
The Dream Physician, pr., pb. 1914

OTHER LITERARY FORMS

Edward Martyn is known exclusively as a playwright, although he also published a novel, *Morgante the Lesser* (1890), under the pseudonym Sirius. The novel's combination of wit and scatology makes Martyn a remote relation of Jonathan Swift and François Rabelais, and as a shaggy-dog story, it owes a debt to Laurence Sterne. In addition, the novel belongs to a rich Gaelic and Anglo-Irish tradition of satires on learning. Its interest is confined exclusively to literary history, however, thanks to its turgid style and flaccid pace. Perhaps its most surprising aspect is its authorship. Nothing in the rigorous Ibsenite realism of his major plays or in the ascetic idealism of his private life would lead one to suspect that Martyn ever perpetrated a work that might well be ascribed to Alfred Jarry.

ACHIEVEMENTS

Edward Martyn has a permanent, if minor, place in the history of the Irish Literary Renaissance. Because this cultural phenomenon undertook no less than to change, or indeed to review, the mind of a nation, a minor contribution to it should not necessarily be considered negligible. William Butler Yeats, in one of his summaries of Martyn's achievements, dismissively mentions Martyn merely as one of Lady Augusta Gregory's neighbors who "paid for our first performances" (those, that is, of the Irish Literary Theatre, the company that in 1904 became the Abbey Theatre). In fact, Martyn was a founding member of the Irish Literary Theatre, and his play *The Heather Field* was the company's second production. Moreover, Martyn brought to the company a set of theatrical ideals, heavily influenced by the drama of Henrik Ibsen, which offered an alternative to Yeats's concept of "peasant drama." This alternative remained underdeveloped, and partly as a result, Martyn's playwriting career stagnated. In *The Heather Field*, however, Martyn demonstrated, intriguingly but embryonically, how his approach could have spoken in realistic terms about contemporary Irish idealism.

Far from being merely the nascent Irish theater's well-disposed financier, Martyn was as committed to the renaissance as was any of its other initiators. Despite more lasting contributions to other spheres of Irish culture and the fact that he was, by temperament, better equipped to be a critic than an artist, Martyn's position in the anterooms of fame is assured. He gave significant impetus to one of the twentieth century's most distinctive theatrical undertakings.

BIOGRAPHY

Edward Martyn was born to an illustrious family of Irish Catholic aristocrats at Masonbrook, near Loughrea, County Galway, on January 31, 1859. His father died the following year, and Edward and his brother were reared in the Martyn family home, Tulira Castle (which he subsequently inherited).

When Martyn was eight years old, the family moved to Dublin, where Martyn briefly attended Belvedere College. A further move, to London, led to his enrollment, in 1870, at Beaumont College, Windsor (like Belvedere, a prominent Jesuit school). Completing his secondary education in 1876, Martyn—in an unusual move for a Catholic—entered Christ Church College, Oxford, in 1877. There he had an undistinguished career and left, without taking his degree, in 1879, though not before falling under the influence of the aesthetic philosophy of Walter Pater.

The following year found Martyn in Paris, in the company of his cousin and subsequent nemesis, the Irish novelist George Moore. Paris gave him access to such contemporary artistic movements as Symbolism and Impressionism (Martyn had an important collection of Impressionist paintings, notably of works by Edgar Degas). Extensive travel in Europe put him in touch with other important cultural developments, such as Wagnerism and Hellenism. The latter proved an important enthusiasm on Martyn's return to Tulira Castle, and he divided his time between Tulira and London artistic circles, in which he cultivated the acquaintance of, among others, Arthur Symons and Aubrey Beardsley.

In 1885, however, Martyn underwent a spiritual crisis of some severity, resulting in the replacement of virtually all the modern tastes that he had formed with a more pious and ascetic regimen. The most important survivors of this reevaluation were the drama of Ibsen and the music of Giovanni Palestrina. It is tempting, with this crisis in mind, to view Martyn's contribution to the Irish Literary Theatre as, in part, rehabilitative. The crisis certainly contributed to the scathing attitude, and essentially inchoate argument, of his pseudonymous novel, *Morgante the Lesser.*

The Irish Literary Theatre was founded by Yeats, Martyn, and Lady Gregory in 1899, and in its early days, Martyn, as well as Yeats, was its principal playwright. By 1902, however, Martyn had resigned from the venture, partly because of artistic differences with Yeats but partly also because of the arrival of George Moore. (Moore was later to subject Martyn to merciless satire in his three-volume memoir of those years, *Hail and Farewell,* 1911-1914—treatment to which Martyn eventually responded in kind in *The Dream Physician.*)

The matter at issue between Moore and Martyn was the latter's play *The Tale of a Town.* In response to Yeats's criticism of it, Moore revised the piece, which was then staged under the title *The Bending of the Bough* (pr. 1900). After resigning from the Irish Literary Theatre, Martyn continued his playwriting career. He directed a large share of his energies to other areas of Irish culture, however, particularly to music.

In 1902, after protracted negotiations, the Palestrina Choir was established at the Pro-Cathedral, Dublin. The choir was exclusively Martyn's idea, and at the time of its inauguration he referred to it as "the chief interest of my life." This interest reflected an unorthodox approach to bringing art to the people. A unique expression of the Irish Literary Renaissance's ethos, the choir was financed almost exclusively by Martyn. As a result of this venture's success, Martyn devoted further time and money to beautifying provincial churches with tapestries, stained glass, and similar ornamentation.

After his break with Yeats and Moore, Martyn also developed a strong interest in, and commitment to, the Gaelic League, an organization devoted to the restoration of the Irish language. Martyn believed Irish to be second only to Greek among the world's languages. As a practical expression of his commitment, he set about rehabilitating traditional Irish music. He was instrumental in organizing an annual outlet for amateur performers called Feis Ceoil (music festival). At one of these, a tenor named James Joyce performed. Perhaps the most substantial expression of Martyn's involvement with the non-Yeatsian renaissance was his presidency of Sinn Féin (the renaissance's political manifestation) from 1904 to 1908.

In 1906, Martyn helped establish the Theatre of Ireland. Its principles were identical to those of the more successful Irish Theatre, which Martyn founded in 1914, assisted by Thomas MacDonagh and Joseph Plunkett, both of whom were executed for their parts in the Easter Rising of 1916. These principles echo Martyn's lifelong admiration of drama, which was intellectual in theme and which availed itself of contemporary European dramaturgical models. Despite numerous vicissitudes, the Irish Theatre managed to remain open until 1920.

Martyn's activities on behalf of the Irish Theatre marked the end of his public life. He died in Dublin on December 5, 1923, a lonely and neglected figure. He was unmarried.

ANALYSIS

Inspired by the most impressive contemporary models and fortified by the principles derived from them, Edward Martyn had perhaps too clear an intellectual formula for his work and an insufficiently coherent aesthetic approach. Adherence to his formula made the work repetitive, two-dimensional, and lacking in vitality. Like so many of his protagonists, Martyn failed to live up to the promise of his ideals. Yet those ideals, particularly in their eschewal of sentimentality, and the works that attempt to articulate them provide an important perspective from which to view the theatrical accomplishments of his contemporaries.

THE HEATHER FIELD

Martyn made his name as a dramatist with *The Heather Field*, and his subsequent works consist of a series of not very startling variations on that play. Without being autobiographical, *The Heather Field* draws on important features of Martyn's life.

The play is set in the wild country of the author's native western Ireland. The action takes place in the context of the Land War, as the struggle between peasants and landlords over conditions of tenure was called. The play is not absolutely contemporaneous with the events it relates; the Land War was at its height from the late 1870's to the mid-1880's and had simmered down considerably by the turn of the century. Nevertheless, the play's references to events still fresh in the minds of an Irish audience emphasize Martyn's rejection of prehistoric material as the vehicle of his vision and have something in common with the belief of James Joyce (another Ibsenite) that art may be won from the life of one's own unpromising times. This belief is implicit in all of Martyn's plays. Regardless of whether one accepts that the handling of the belief conforms to the tenets of realism, the plays' intellectual bases are firmly grounded in realism.

In addition, the protagonist of *The Heather Field*, Carden Tyrrell, is a landlord, as Martyn himself was. He is given a surname whose Irish associations are as notable in their own right as is the name Martyn. Tyrrell is provided with one of Martyn's own formative experiences, that of hearing exalted song from the choir of Cologne Cathedral. Tyrrell is also an "improving" landlord—that is, one who takes an interest in his property (which a great number of Irish landlords did not). In fact, the play contains an unexamined paradox concerning Tyrrell's social commitments: He makes every effort to reclaim land and enlarge his holdings, yet he is notably unsympathetic to the causes of the Land War. This paradox is subsumed under the more divisive and irreconcilable aspects of Tyrrell's case. Martyn is less interested in his protagonist's social situation than in his psychological condition. It should be noted, however, that *The Heather Field* is an important step forward in the representation of typical Irish types not as figures of fun but as serious embodiments of predicaments experienced by the majority of conscious humanity. By remaining faithful to conditions with which he was intimately familiar, Martyn helped to enlarge the stock of Irish dramatic characters. By dignifying stereotypes, he offered the basis for a new dramatic perspective on Irish life.

The plot of *The Heather Field* is somewhat spare. Tyrrell conceives an overweening ambition to reclaim the wild, infertile areas of his demesne. To this end, he has risked his fortune draining the heather field of the title. This project is, ostensibly, a success: Productive grass has evidently supplanted pretty, barren heathland. As a result, Tyrrell is determined to go forward and put the whole of his property in financial jeopardy in order to expand his reclamation scheme. Barry Ussher, a friend and neighbor, attempts to dissuade Tyrrell from his rash ambition but to no avail. Moreover, Tyrrell's wife, Grace (like most of Martyn's protagonists, Tyrrell is unsuitably married, a fate which the author himself assiduously avoided), is aggressively opposed to the scheme, so much so that she attempts to have her husband certified as insane. Only the timely intervention of Barry Ussher thwarts such a development, Tyrrell being so engrossed in his dream of fertility that he cannot perceive Grace's tactics or defend himself against the two doctors summoned to the house to carry out Grace's design. As events reveal, however, official certification of insanity becomes a formality. In the third act, spring has come round again and with it the triumph of heather over grass. The result is that Tyrrell, refusing to accept that nature has declined to answer his needs, loses his mind. He cannot tell past from present, or anything else about himself and the real world that has frustrated his dreams.

Establishing a theme that was to recur in Martyn's work, *The Heather Field* is a critique of idealism—or perhaps of idealism in a solipsistic formulation. Tyrrell does not recognize that his ambition is flawed on practical grounds. He cannot accept the fact that the world will not necessarily accommodate the needs he foists on it. His indifference to society, both in the polite sense of the word and in the historical sense, throws him back on his own psychic resources, which wilt under the pressure. Tyrrell's isolation is subjectively crucial and objectively crippling. The belief that the reclamation scheme is the signature of his integrity leads inevitably to his disintegration. As practical dramatic evidence of his situation, Tyrrell seems to exist in the play in order to contest what everyone else says to him rather than adjust to it. The only relaxation of this intransigent manner occurs in exchanges with his young son, Kit, who is being reared as a child of nature. These exchanges ironically portray the child as father to the man: the child's genuine, naïve wonder of the same state of mind—a pursuit of the natural that requires the face of nature to be redrawn.

One of the rewards of *The Heather Field*, therefore, is in identifying the protagonist's problems from an intellectual standpoint. In terms of its theatrical dynamics, however, the play is less satisfactory. The dialogue is written in prose of a rather leaden variety, and the scenes are conceived as set pieces in an argument rather than as occasions in a man's life. These drawbacks are nevertheless redeemed by the strength of Tyrrell's commitment to his ideal: It does, after all, cost him everything. The audience's involvement with his fate is sustained by the persuasiveness with which the ideal is conveyed. It is clear that for Tyrrell, the heather field and the dream of rehabilitation that it duplicitously facilitates offer the possibility of beauty, renewal, and completeness. It is an alternative to history, both personal (his marriage) and social (the Land War). Tyrrell claims to hear voices when he is out in the field, the voices of a German choir, the definitive experience of beauty that he received in his formative years, and it is these voices

he welcomes when nature fails and madness overwhelms him.

The author's unsparing revelation of his protagonist's irreconcilable tensions gives the play its dramatic strength and also lends to it a cultural significance of which Martyn may have been only incidentally aware. The play is a fascinating and idiosyncratic example of a distinctively Irish genre, consisting of works, in a variety of literary forms, which deal with the decline of the Big House, the generic term for the homes of the landed gentry.

As noted, Martyn's other plays repeat the themes of *The Heather Field*, but whereas *The Heather Field* contains a degree of tacit sympathy for Tyrrell (if only because all the other characters are narrower in spirit than he is), the critique of idealism in later plays is rather more bitter. In fact, what causes subsequent works to have destructive endings is not idealism of the characters as such, but its frustration.

GRANGECOLMAN

Grangecolman is a case in point. The action is set in the Colman family home, a large old house outside Dublin, and the plot is concerned with the hauntings of an irrecoverable past. This theme is conveyed with a symbolic explicitness that borders on the obtuse and that, at the same time, leaves the intellectual burden of the play vague and generalized.

The household consists of old Michael Colman, the last of his line, his daughter Catherine, and her ne'er-do-well husband, Lucius Devlin. Michael is an antiquarian, a pursuit which in the Irish literature of the generation before Martyn's epitomized impotent reclusiveness. Catherine, who, with her husband, espouses the contemporary feminism, is a doctor, but her career has been blighted because of Lucius's irresponsible financial speculations. To assist him with his research, Michael hires young Clare Farquhar. Her grace and energy have a restorative effect on the old man's morale. This development, in turn, arouses Catherine's hostility.

Early in the play, the notion of the house's decline is introduced. Incursions, by thieves from the outside and ghosts from within, are feared. Miss Farquhar, handling a revolver, promises to deal with intruders of whatever kind. The audience soon learns, however, of the depth of Catherine's jealousy of Clare, whose vitality and resolve are at odds with Catherine's self-abnegating temperament. Catherine's hostility erupts in her peremptory dismissal of Clare from her duties.

Ignorant of this development, Michael proposes marriage to Clare, a step that Catherine naturally opposes, using the occasion to voice the ideals of feminism and independence, which, for all of her enthusiasm for them, have evidently driven her into a dead end. Leaving the scene in an agitated state, she later returns, impersonating the family ghost. Clare takes the revolver and kills her.

Undoubtedly the plot's gothic machinery gets in the way of the play's intellectual brooding. Nevertheless, there is no escaping the ideological impasse to which Catherine's idealism has led. Once again, the world resists the pressure placed by the mind on it, with catastrophic results for the mind's proprietor. The contrived nature of the scenario diminishes the play's surface plausibility, while at the same time drawing attention to the situation's latent incoherence. In the dialogue, Martyn shows himself to be as tone-deaf as ever to the rhythms of human speech, but the consistency of the play's gloom and pessimism in a sense works to sanction its shortcomings. It seems remarkable that a committed Catholic such as Martyn continued to write plays that implicitly deny the possibility of faith. The depiction of conditions that are apparently beyond redemption—a prominent feature throughout Martyn's work—is given its most funereal presentation in *Grangecolman*, a play that, in the hands of a more adept playwright, would have fully realized itself as a plainsong dirge for the past, present, and future and for cultural recuperation, social commitment, and personal vanity.

THE DREAM PHYSICIAN

In his last play, *The Dream Physician*, Martyn resorted to an uncharacteristic mode that perhaps he should have cultivated—namely, satire. (*The Tale of a Town* is the other major dramatic example of Martyn's satiric powers.) The basic framework of the plot is no more than a pretext for the author to have the last word about the role of Yeats and George Moore (particularly the latter) in the Irish Literary Renaissance. The surgery that exposes these luminaries' pretensions in act 4 is wholly out of keeping with the play's stilted pace, but the results are hilarious. Moore is presented as the fraudulent, malicious, self-seeking George Augustus Moon, and Yeats is caricatured as Beau Brummell, whose self-appointed destiny is to save the soul of his people with the aid of a banjo.

The plot concerns Shane Lester, who has betrayed his Anglo-Irish origins by becoming president of, and later member of Parliament for, an Irish nationalist group. His wife, Audrey, a social butterfly, cannot forgive Shane for this shift in allegiance, and she and her husband have a violent fight, during the course of which Audrey believes that she has killed him. Nothing will expunge this fantasy—the dream of the title. Audrey is confined to bed in a semicatatonic state, despite Shane's numerous entreating visits. A nurse, Sister Farnan, is engaged to care for Audrey, and it is she who suggests that the patient will snap out of her dream if confronted with a reality to which she cannot possibly assent. This reality is provided by the antics of Moon and company, and exposure to it has the desired therapeutic effect: The play ends with Audrey and Shane reconciled. Moon's posturing makes him the dream physician; the imbalance resulting from his pretensions makes it impossible to take seriously what he represents. By virtue of experiencing that impossibility, Audrey is restored to a reality that she can take seriously, her husband's.

Clearly, however, *The Dream Physician* is itself imbalanced, formally and thematically. Martyn was unable to work out a unified relationship between the more general theme of Shane's idealism, embodied in his nationalist leanings, and the more local and personal bouts of character assassination, which have little or nothing to do directly with Shane. This failure places the play in danger of being a unique example of a hopelessly implausible genre, the revenge farce. After the sobriety of most of its predecessors, however, it is pleasant to encounter a spirited Martyn. The caricatures of Moore and Yeats show all the signs of being an insider's work. Less successful are the cartoons of Lady Gregory (Sister Farnan) and James Joyce. Joyce was allegedly the model for Otho, Audrey's insufferable brother, who finally comes to life when he denounces Moon because his beloved, Moon's grandniece, "a woman of genius" who signs her poetic effusions "La Mayonaise" (Mayo was George Moore's native county), proves to be nonexistent.

OTHER MAJOR WORK

LONG FICTION: *Morgante the Lesser*, 1890 (as Sirius).

BIBLIOGRAPHY

Courtney, Marie Therese. *Edward Martyn and the Irish Theatre*. New York: Vantage Press, 1956. A detailed portrait of Martyn in the context of Irish theatrical history. Courtney examines his involvement in the establishment of a national theater movement from both a biographical and an artistic point of view and assesses the eventual effect of that involvement on Martyn. All Martyn's dramatic works are thoroughly evaluated.

Feeney, William J., ed. *Edward Martyn's Irish Theatre*. Vol. 2 in George Spelvin's *Theatre Book*. Newark, Del.: Proscenium Press, 1980. These essays examine the Irish Theatre established by Martyn and discuss plays of its writers, including Martyn's *Romulus and Remus* and Thomas MacDonagh's *Pagans*.

Gwynn, Denis. *Edward Martyn and the Irish Revival*. 1930. Reprint. New York: Lemma, 1974. An early attempt to describe Martyn's role in the Irish Literary Renaissance. Much of the focus is on Martyn's contributions to the development of Irish drama. The study, however, also contains information on his other cultural commitments, with the result that an overall sense of Martyn's cultural context emerges.

Hogan, Robert, and James Kilroy. *The Irish Literary Theatre, 1899-1901*. Atlantic Highlands, N.J.: Humanities Press, 1975. Contains a considerable amount of detailed information regarding Martyn's involvement in the events that led to the eventual formation of Ireland's national theater. Includes accounts of the production and reception of Martyn's plays. The volume also provides extensive scholarly support for the study of the formative period of modern Irish theater.

Setterquist, Jan. *Edward Martyn*. Vol. 2 in *Ibsen and the Beginnings of Anglo-Irish Drama*. 1951-1960. Reprint. New York: Gordian Press, 1974. The impact of Henrik Ibsen's revolution in the social and critical role of the drama on the fledgling Irish theater is examined. Martyn's complicated attitude toward Ibsen's example is central to this study's argument, and Martyn's plays are also seen in the context of the Ibsenite dimension of the contemporary Irish drama.

George O'Brien

JOHN MASEFIELD

Born: Ledbury, Herefordshire, England; June 1, 1878
Died: Near Abingdon, England; May 12, 1967

PRINCIPAL DRAMA

The Campden Wonder, pr. 1907, pb. 1909 (one act)
The Tragedy of Nan, pr. 1908, pb. 1909
Mrs. Harrison, pb. 1909 (one act)
The Tragedy of Pompey the Great, pr., pb. 1910
The Witch, pr. 1911 (adaptation of a Norwegian play)
Philip the King, pr. 1914 (one act)
The Faithful, pr., pb. 1915
The Sweeps of Ninety-Eight, pr., pb. 1916
Good Friday: A Dramatic Poem, pb. 1916, pr. 1917
The Locked Chest, pb. 1916, pr. 1920 (one act)
Esther, pr. 1921 (adaptation of Jean Racine's play)

Melloney Holtspur: Or, The Pangs of Love, pb. 1922, pr. 1923

A King's Daughter: A Tragedy in Verse, pr. 1923

Tristan and Isolt: A Play in Verse, pr. 1923, pb. 1927

The Trial of Jesus, pb. 1925, pr. 1927

The Coming of Christ, pb. 1928

Easter: A Play for Singers, pr. 1929

End and Beginnings, pb. 1933

A Play of St. George, pb. 1948

OTHER LITERARY FORMS

John Masefield is noted for his lyric and narrative poetry, and because of poems such as "Sea Fever" and "Cargoes," he will continue to be read. For more than sixty years, however, he was prolific in many other genres as well. Between 1902 and 1966, Masefield wrote more than forty volumes of poetry or verse plays and more than twenty novels, in addition to short stories, essays, reviews, biographies, historical works, addresses, and prefaces, totaling about fifty books in all. Masefield's first book of verse was *Salt-Water Ballads* (1902), and his narrative poem *The Everlasting Mercy* (1911) caused a sensation with its realistic diction. Masefield wrote eight other book-length narrative poems, the most important being *The Window in the Bye Street* (1912), *The Daffodil Fields* (1913), *Reynard the Fox: Or, The Ghost Heath Run* (1919), *Right Royal* (1920), and *King Cole* (1921). His sea poems and ballads are about the life of the common sailor, and his narrative verse describes the lot of the rural folk of the Malvern Hills in his native Herefordshire.

Masefield's fiction is varied and uneven; his most popular and successful novels were his books about the sea and strange lands, written in the vein of Joseph Conrad and Robert Louis Stevenson—tales such as *Captain Margaret* (1908), *The Bird of Dawning* (1933), and *Victorious Troy* (1935). Although not a great critic, Masefield was a thoroughly professional man of letters who turned out well-focused articles and reviews by the hundreds, as well as book-length studies. In the field of history, Masefield gave accounts of World War I debacles in *Gallipoli* (1916) and *The Battle of the Somme* (1919). He told the story

of the evacuation of Dunkirk in *The Nine Days' Wonder* (1941). In addition, Masefield wrote about maritime history in *Sea Life in Nelson's Time* (1905), *On the Spanish Main* (1906), and *The Conway from Her Foundation to the Present Day* (1933). Masefield's autobiographical works include *In the Mill* (1941), *New Chum* (1944), *So Long to Learn* (1952), and *Grace Before Ploughing* (1966).

ACHIEVEMENTS

John Masefield's plays have lost much of their appeal for stage audiences, but some of his dramatic work, such as that written about the common people, has a vitality to recommend it, particularly his most successful play, *The Tragedy of Nan*, which reveals Masefield's ability to tell a vivid story in dramatic terms. It is not likely that any of his plays will become standard reading in drama courses, nor are any

John Masefield in 1935. (Library of Congress)

likely to be revived for production, yet Masefield should be commended for trying to infuse the English commercial theater in the early twentieth century with dramatic works of serious artistic intent. In the years after World War I, Masefield largely abandoned this ambition. The postwar plays were the products of an avocation rather than a true vocation. Though some of these plays were staged by local amateur dramatic clubs, Masefield wrote them primarily for his own edification and for the entertainment of his family and friends.

Although Masefield was writing plays after George Bernard Shaw, Henrik Ibsen, August Strindberg, and Anton Chekhov had established the dimensions of early modern drama, his dramatic values have the conventionalities of Victorian theater. Despite their conventional manner, his plays never appealed to a wide popular audience, nor, for the most part, did they satisfy the critics. Masefield's endeavors as a playwright did, however, enhance his reputation in Georgian literary circles, and his mastering of the dramatic conventions enabled him to write novels with well-constructed plots and carefully focused characterizations.

Whatever the merits of his drama, it is for his achievements as a poet that Masefield will be remembered. His tenure as England's poet laureate, from 1930 until his death in 1967, was one of the longer ones.

BIOGRAPHY

John Edward Masefield was born on June 1, 1878, in the small town of Ledbury in rural Herefordshire, England; he was the son of George Edward and Carol Parker Masefield. Masefield's father, a fairly successful solicitor, died at the age of forty-nine following a period of mental disorder that may have been caused by the death of Masefield's mother, who died from complications following childbirth in 1885. Left an orphan when he was only six years old, Masefield was taken in by his aunt and uncle, who reared him in pleasant circumstances in a Victorian country house called The Priory. There, young Masefield learned to love the waters, woods, and flowers of Herefordshire, and from his aunt's teaching he acquired a love for

literature, particularly the narrative poems of Henry Wadsworth Longfellow. In 1888, Masefield was sent to the King's School in Warwick as a boarding student. Homesick and unhappy at Warwick, Masefield ran away from school, and though he was to return, it was obvious that this experience with formal education was not to produce the desired results.

Masefield was allowed to join the merchant navy, leaving home at thirteen and enlisting as a midshipman; he was posted to the HMS *Conway*, a famous training ship. During his days as apprentice seaman, he took long voyages to South America and around Cape Horn, but the arduous life of a sailor was not to his liking, and he jumped ship in New York, giving up his berth as sixth officer on the White Star liner *Adriatic*. The young Masefield's disgraceful behavior caused his uncle to disinherit him, and Masefield was forced to take whatever work he could find. For some time, he lived a nearly vagrant life in Greenwich Village, where he started to write poetry seriously. Masefield remained in New York for two years before returning to London in 1897, where he took a post as a bank clerk, a position he held for three years, during which time he started to publish some of his own verse and to meet some of the London literati, becoming acquainted with William Butler Yeats, Lady Augusta Gregory, and John Millington Synge, along with others whom he came to know during regular gatherings in Bloomsbury. Masefield's first book of poems, *Salt-Water Ballads*, was published in 1902 and enjoyed immediate success, becoming popular with the public and critics alike.

Masefield met Constance Crommelin in 1903, and they were married the same year, when he was twenty-five years old and his bride was thirty-five. Despite the difference in their ages, the marriage seems to have been as happy as most. Masefield acquired a job as an editor and settled in Greenwich with his wife and baby daughter. In 1904, Masefield received an offer to write for the *Manchester Guardian*, but newspaper writing deflected him from his main interest at this period—writing plays. He managed to turn out a series of dramas, despite the demands of producing reviews and articles for the *Manchester Guardian* seven days a week. Although most of Masefield's early dramatic writings were unfinished or destroyed, he completed and produced his first play, *The Campden Wonder*, in 1907. In addition to writing six more plays in the years before World War I, he produced novels, stories, sketches, his first long verse narratives, and more ballads and poems, although he considered himself to be primarily a playwright. In 1910, about the time of the birth of his son Lewis, he become involved with Elizabeth Robins, an American actress and leader of the suffragettes. Although she was nearly fifty and he was only thirty-one, he became totally enamored of her. For her part, she accepted Masefield's attentions with reservation, and their affair was conducted under the guise of an imaginary mother-son relationship, he calling her "mother" and she addressing him as her "little son." Most of Masefield's ardor went into his letters; he often wrote her as many as two a day. Their actual meetings were confined primarily to rendezvous at the British Museum, where "mother" and "son" would tour the galleries. Finally, Robins, having tired of Masefield's filial pose and the maternal role imposed on her, called off the relationship.

After a period of desolation caused by Robins's withdrawal, Masefield moved his family to an old manor house in the Berkshire hills. It was at this time that he wrote the long narrative poem *The Everlasting Mercy*, which established his fame as the premier poet of the Georgian period.

Masefield's life as a literary country squire was disrupted by the start of World War I. Although he tried to enlist in the army, Masefield was not able to join a combat branch because of his poor medical record but was accepted for service in the British Red Cross, going to France in 1914 with the British Expeditionary Force. Later, in 1915, he was posted to the Dardanelles, where he participated in the debacle at Gallipoli. Because of his literary reputation, he was relieved of his duties as a field officer and sent by the Red Cross to promote the war effort with two lecture tours of the United States.

As the war ended, Masefield moved his residence again, settling at Boar's Hill, near Oxford. His neighbors there included Gilbert Murray, Sir Arthur Evans, and Robert Bridges. Masefield became the landlord

for a young war-poet, Robert Graves, to whom he leased a cottage on his property. Masefield also became a friend to Edmund Blunden, another war-scarred writer who was returning to Oxford to be a professor of poetry. The two young veterans saw Masefield as a mentor who, like them, was opposed to modernists such as Ezra Pound, T. S. Eliot, and Edith Sitwell, and stood, like them, rooted in the native English tradition.

The postwar years were good ones for Masefield. He was the originator of annual verse recitals called the Oxford Recitations and devoted himself to writing plays again as well as history books about the war. He founded a local amateur theatrical company in 1919 that put on the plays of Euripides, William Shakespeare, and John Galsworthy. The Hill Players, as they were called, performed in a theater called the Music Room from 1922 until 1932, staging several experimental plays by young, unknown playwrights as well as some of Yeats's later plays and Masefield's own *Tristan and Isolt* and *The Trial of Jesus*. In effect, Masefield had created his own private theater, where he could try out his plays without worrying about commercial success. He could give young dramatists a vehicle for their plays and could cast his friends and family in the parts.

At the end of the decade, Masefield was named poet laureate, and in 1930, he moved from Boar's Hill to Pinbury Park, near Cirencester in Gloucestershire. There, Masefield lived in a grand house with great rows of oak trees, playing his part as a public figure with quiet dignity, but, as before, another world war disturbed his serene life.

Masefield once again offered his services to the nation and, during the dark days of the early war years, produced an inspiring story of the escape of the British Army from the beaches of Dunkirk. Personal grief came to him in this war: His son Lewis was killed in action in the African desert while serving with the Royal Ambulance Corps. The aging Masefield never fully recovered from the heartbreak caused by his son's death. In the years after the war, his life was given over to letter writing, by which he kept up a wide range of friendships, and to completing his sequence of autobiographical works. His official duties as poet laureate kept him occupied in cultural affairs, promoting the Royal Academy of Dramatic Art and serving as president of the National Book League. In the autumn of 1959, his wife became ill, and she died in 1960 at the age of ninety-three. Masefield's life became increasingly reclusive, but he continued to write. Among the works required by his office were poems on the deaths of T. S. Eliot and President John F. Kennedy, Jr. Indeed, Masefield's energy as a writer seemed inexhaustible, and he produced his last book, *In Glad Thanksgiving* (1967), when he was eighty-eight years old. On May 12, 1967, he died and was cremated. His ashes were placed in the Poets' Corner of Westminster Abbey, though he had requested that they should be scattered in the winds and waters of his native downs.

ANALYSIS

John Masefield was always more the poet than the dramatist. His plays nevertheless retain historical interest, both as expressions of his many-sided talent and as reflections of diverse trends in British drama of the late nineteenth and the early twentieth century.

Very early in his career as a writer, Masefield developed an interest in playwriting. His deep study of Shakespeare and his personal association with Yeats, Lady Gregory, and Synge instilled in Masefield a desire to revive the English drama as his friends were attempting to rekindle the drama of Ireland by infusing it with the vitality of mythic and folk elements. Masefield saw what could be done with folk materials in plays such as Synge's *Riders to the Sea* (pb. 1903) and *In the Shadow of the Glen* (pr. 1903). His own first play, *The Campden Wonder*, is a one-act drama in the expressionistic-symbolic mode of Yeats, to whom it was dedicated. Using the colloquial idiom, it deals with a brutal story that Masefield had heard about a hanging in Chipping Campden of three innocent people. This first effort was followed by several more one-act plays: *Mrs. Harrison*, a sequel to *The Campden Wonder* and also an exercise in sustained naturalism; *The Sweeps of Ninety-Eight*, an amusing comedy with a historical background concerning the outwitting of the British Navy by an Irish rebel in 1798; and another short play, *The Locked Chest*, which is a suspenseful drama about a clever wife who tricks her confused husband.

GOOD FRIDAY

Good Friday, also written during this period, is a morality play in rhymed verse. Its subject is the Passion of Christ, and Masefield employs an austere style in imitation of the cycle plays of medieval drama, but his modern idiomatic phrases are somewhat out of keeping with the spirit of the original. Nevertheless, the play contains a moving account of the Crucifixion, simple and vivid in its effects:

> We were alone on the accursed hill
> And we were still, not even the dice clicked
> On to the stone . . .
> And now and then the hangers gave a groan,
> Up in the dark, three shapes with arms outspread.

Overall, in the period between 1907 and 1916, Masefield finished ten plays. During this decade, he produced some of his most important dramatic works, including longer, full-length plays such as *The Tragedy of Nan*, *The Tragedy of Pompey the Great*, *Philip the King*, and *The Faithful*.

THE TRAGEDY OF NAN

The first of these, *The Tragedy of Nan*, was produced at the New Royalty Theatre under the direction of Harley Granville-Barker. It had a long and successful stage run in repertory theaters in England and abroad. Based on a true "country tragedy" of the early nineteenth century, it is a play with the capacity to move audiences. The poignant plot details the plight of Nan Hardwick, an orphaned charity girl whose father is hanged for stealing sheep. She is taken in by a stingy uncle whose family is unkind to her, but her life is made bearable by the attention paid her by Dick Gurvil, a local youth of uncertain moral fiber who has plans to marry Nan. Her chances for happiness are destroyed when her mean-spirited aunt, who wants him for a husband to one of her own daughters, reveals to Dick that Nan is a murderer's daughter. Fearful that he cannot expect a dowry from Nan and that he will be disinherited by his own father, he breaks off their engagement and marries one of Nan's cousins. Nan realizes the defective character of her lover, but her pain and humiliation at losing him are nevertheless acute. In an ironic turn of events, it is discovered that her father was the victim of a miscarriage of justice: He was innocent of the charges, and she is paid a large sum of money in compensation for his death. Her former fiancé realizes that she is a richer prize than the cousin, so he turns to her again with a proposal of marriage. In a fury at his duplicity and temerity, Nan stabs him in the heart with a bread knife, saying that he must be killed to keep him from preying on any more innocent women. She then throws herself in the Severn River, closing the play on a note of unrelieved tragedy.

Although a summary of the play makes it appear like a study in naturalism, it is, in fact, less so than Masefield's early plays; nevertheless, some contemporary drama critics indicted the drama for its use of dialect, vicious characters, and commonplace scenes to tell an ugly story. In general, *The Tragedy of Nan* seems most to echo Thomas Hardy's novel *Tess of the D'Urbervilles* (1891): Both are rustic melodramas that feature pure, beautiful country girls who are the playthings of cruel fate. Like Hardy's Tess, Nan is truly a tragic protagonist, and her death induces the proper feeling of catharsis in the audience.

THE TRAGEDY OF POMPEY THE GREAT

Masefield followed *The Tragedy of Nan* with *The Tragedy of Pompey the Great*, which was written during the winter of 1908-1909 and produced for the stage in 1910, opening at the Aldwych Theatre in London under the direction of Harcourt Williams. Masefield began this history play as a one-act drama in which he tried to dramatize the life of the ill-fated Roman general as it was depicted in Sir Thomas North's translation (1579) of Plutarch's *Bioi paralleloi* (c. 105-115 C.E.; *Parallel Lives*, 1579). The events of the story required a fuller treatment, however, and Masefield expanded his play into a complete three-act drama. The tragic career of Pompey, who goes down to defeat with brave dignity in his struggle with Caesar, embodies a theme often found in Masefield's work: the idea that the greatest victories are those of the spirit. Masefield draws Pompey's character in more complimentary terms than history does, making him into a magnanimous, peace-loving general.

As a play, *The Tragedy of Pompey the Great* has some arresting scenes, with battles on land and sea

that provide an opportunity for striking stage effects, but as Aristotle states in *De poetica* (c. 334-323 B.C.E.; *Poetics*, 1705), spectacle is the lowest artistic ingredient of the drama. The main weakness of this play, though, is its lack of dramatic tension. Masefield idealizes Pompey as a highly principled aristocratic leader who opposes Caesar's mob appeal and egalitarian policies. Masefield's Pompey, much like Shakespeare's Brutus, is motivated by a patriotic desire to preserve the ideals of Republican Rome. Unfortunately, Caesar is not among the *dramatis personae* of Masefield's play; as a result, there is no dramatic tension between Pompey and a worthy antagonist. Instead, there is only an extended exposition of Pompey's character. Pompey's tentative idealism is no match for the single-minded Caesar's ambition; his efforts at compromise and his rational appeals to avert civil war are not successful, and strife breaks out with seeming inevitability. In this respect, some reviewers saw the play as an effort by Masefield to warn audiences of the threat to peace that international tensions posed in the period just before the outbreak of World War I.

THE FAITHFUL

One of Masefield's next plays, *The Faithful*, a total departure from any of his previous dramatic works, reflects the vogue for Oriental culture that swept England and France during the early years of the twentieth century. Using Japanese rather than Roman history as his subject, Masefield—inspired perhaps by Yeats's adaptations of Nō plays—tried a more experimental form of drama in *The Faithful*. The play opened at the Birmingham Repertory Theatre in 1915 and ran until 1918. After the end of the war, it had a run of more than forty performances on Broadway, where it enjoyed a critical rather than a commercial success. The play is about the forty-seven *rōnin* (masterless samurui), whose tragic story Masefield at first planned to tell in a verse narrative because he could not envision a dramatic structure for the story. Inspired in part by Granville-Barker's productions of Shakespeare's *Twelfth Night: Or, What You Will* (pr. c. 1600-1602) and *The Winter's Tale* (pr. c. 1610-1611), which, Masefield said, "showed me more clearly than any stage productions known to me the power and sweep of Shakespeare's constructions," he created a play of considerable lyric eloquence—a play that has all the blood and gore of a Jacobean tragedy, presented with a ritualistic air that mutes the violence and invests the action with a timeless quality.

The action, set in medieval Japan, revolves around a revenge plot. The play's villain is an upstart tyrant named Kira, a newly rich daimyo, or feudal lord, who causes the death of a young rival, Asano. In the conflict that results, Asano's followers try to avenge their leader, but the rebels are routed and their families are scourged by the ruthless Kira. Finally, however, the tide turns, and Kira is executed by one of Asano's followers, the heroic Kurano. The curtain comes down with all the survivors preparing to commit seppuku, or ritual suicide. The pseudo-Japanese quality of the drama annoyed some of the play's critics, who questioned its historical and cultural credibility, but Masefield should be given credit for his attempted synthesis of Western and Oriental dramatic modes. All in all, *The Faithful* is an interesting example of the impact of Japanese theater on the dramatic arts in England.

MELLONEY HOLTSPUR

Only a few of Masefield's post-World War I plays attracted any serious critical attention. One that did was a fantasy melodrama entitled *Melloney Holtspur*, a seriocomic ghost story about the way in which the peccadilloes of a past generation are passed on to the present. Written in the spirit of the supernaturalism of Sir James Barrie, the play was praised for its upbeat treatment of such solemn themes as ancestral sins and atonement. In addition, Masefield translated Jean Racine's play *Bérénice* (pr. 1670; English translation, 1676); he also adapted Racine's *Esther* (pr., pb. 1689; English translation, 1715). Masefield's last effort at playwriting was *A Play of St. George*. This drama in verse and prose, which was never staged, treats the famous legend of England's patron saint.

OTHER MAJOR WORKS

LONG FICTION: *Captain Margaret*, 1908; *Multitude and Solitude*, 1909; *Lost Endeavour*, 1910; *The Taking of Helen*, 1923; *Sard Harker*, 1924; *Odtaa*, 1926; *The Hawbucks*, 1929; *The Bird of Dawning*,

1933; *Victorious Troy: Or, The Hurrying Angel*,1935; *Basilissa*, 1940.

SHORT FICTION: *A Mainsail Haul*, 1905; *A Tarpaulin Muster*, 1907.

POETRY: *Salt-Water Ballads*, 1902; *Ballads*, 1903; *The Everlasting Mercy*, 1911; *The Widow in the Bye Street*, 1912; *The Story of a Round-House and Other Poems*, 1912; *Dauber: A Poem*, 1913; *The Daffodil Fields*, 1913; *Philip the King and Other Poems*, 1914; *Good Friday and Other Poems*, 1916; *Sonnets and Poems*, 1916; *Lollington Downs and Other Poems*, 1917; *The Cold Cotswolds*, 1917; *Rosas*, 1918; *A Poem and Two Plays*, 1919; *Reynard the Fox: Or, The Ghost Heath Run*, 1919; *Enslaved and Other Poems*, 1920; *Right Royal*, 1920; *King Cole*, 1921; *The Dream*, 1922; *Sonnets of Good Cheer to the Lena Ashwell Players*, 1926; *Midsummer Night and Other Tales in Verse*, 1928; *South and East*, 1929; *The Wanderer of Liverpool*, 1930 (poems and essay); *Minnie Maylow's Story and Other Tales and Scenes*, 1931; *A Tale of Troy*, 1932; *A Letter from Pontus and Other Verse*, 1936; *Ode to Harvard*, 1937; *Some Verses to Some Germans*, 1939; *Guatama the Enlightened and Other Verse*, 1941; *Natalie Masie and Pavilastukay: Two Tales in Verse*, 1942; *Wonderings (Between One and Six Years)*, 1943; *I Want! I Want!*, 1944; *On the Hill*, 1949; *Poems*, 1953; *The Bluebells and Other Verse*, 1961; *Old Raiger and Other Verse*, 1961; *In Glad Thanksgiving*, 1967.

NONFICTION: *Sea Life in Nelson's Time*, 1905; *On the Spanish Main*, 1906; *Shakespeare*, 1911; *Gallipoli*, 1916; *The Battle of the Somme*, 1919; *Chaucer*, 1931; *The Conway from Her Foundation to the Present Day*, 1933; *The Nine Days' Wonder*, 1941; *In the Mill*, 1941; *New Chum*, 1944; *So Long to Learn*, 1952; *Grace Before Ploughing*, 1966.

CHILDREN'S LITERATURE: *Martin Hyde*, 1910; *Jim Davis*, 1911; *The Midnight Folk*, 1927; *The Box of Delights*, 1935.

MISCELLANEOUS: *A Book of Both Sorts: Selections from the Verse and Prose*, 1947.

BIBLIOGRAPHY

Babington-Smith, Constance. *John Masefield: A Life.* Oxford, England: Oxford University Press, 1978.

This full biography was prepared with the active cooperation of Masefield's family and friends. The circumstances of individual plays are discussed but little critical evaluation is attempted. Complemented by a select list of books by Masefield and an index.

Binding, Paul. *An Endless Quiet Valley: A Reappraisal of John Masefield*. Woonton, Almeley, Herefordshire, England: Logaston,1998. Binding provides a critical analysis of Masefield's works, examining them within their historical framework. Index.

Drew, Fraser. *John Masefield's England: A Study of the National Themes in His Work*. Rutherford, N.J.: Fairleigh Dickinson University Press, 1973. As the title suggests, this work looks at the specific qualities of Masefield's "Englishness" through the corpus of his work. Bibliography and index.

Dwyer, June. *John Masefield*. New York: Frederick Ungar, 1987. This volume appears in the useful Literature and Life series and covers the whole corpus of Masefield's work. Includes a bibliography and an index.

McDonald, Jan. *The New Drama, 1900-1914*. Basingstoke, England: Macmillan, 1986. A chapter on Masefield's *The Campden Wonder* and *The Tragedy of Nan* sets Masefield within the context of the Court Theatre and Harley Granville-Barker but sees him as somewhat atypical of the other "new dramatists." The chapter argues that these two early plays show evidence of a power and originality of style that could have befitted English drama had Masefield developed them. Bibliography and index.

Sternlicht, Sanford. *John Masefield*. Boston: Twayne, 1977. This volume, one of Twayne's English Authors series, covers both life and works in a clear, well-focused way. It contains a bibliography and an index.

Hallman B. Bryant,
updated by David Barratt

PHILIP MASSINGER

Born: Salisbury, England; November 24, 1583 (baptized)

Died: London, England; March 18, 1640 (buried)

PRINCIPAL DRAMA

The Fatal Dowry, pr. c. 1616-1619, pb. 1632 (with Nathaniel Field)

Sir John van Olden Barnavelt, pr. 1619, pb. 1883 (with John Fletcher)

The Custom of the Country, pr. c. 1619-1620, pb. 1647 (with Fletcher)

The Little French Lawyer, pr. c. 1619-1623, pb. 1647 (with Fletcher)

The Virgin Martyr, pr. c. 1620, pb. 1622 (with Thomas Dekker)

The False One, pr. c. 1620, pb. 1647 (with Fletcher)

The Double Marriage, pr. c. 1621, pb. 1647 (with Fletcher)

The Maid of Honour, pr. c. 1621, pb. 1632

The Unnatural Combat, pr. c. 1621, pb. 1639

The Duke of Milan, pr. c. 1621-1622, pb. 1623

A New Way to Pay Old Debts, pr. 1621-1622(?), pb. 1633

The Beggar's Bush, pr. before 1622, pb. 1647 (with Fletcher)

The Prophetess, pr. 1622, pb. 1647 (with Fletcher)

The Bondman, pr. 1623, pb. 1624

The Renegado: Or, The Gentleman of Venice, pr. 1624, pb. 1630

The Parliament of Love, pr. 1624, pb. 1805

The Elder Brother, pr. 1625(?), pb. 1637 (with Fletcher)

The Roman Actor, pr. 1626, pb. 1629

The Great Duke of France, pr. 1627(?), pb. 1636

The Picture, pr. 1629, pb. 1630

Believe as You List, pr. 1631, pb. 1849

The Emperor of the East, pr. 1631, pb. 1632

The City Madam, pr. 1632(?), pb. 1658

The Guardian, pr. 1633, pb. 1655

A Very Woman: Or, The Prince of Tarent, pr. 1634, pb. 1655

The Bashful Lover, pr. 1636, pb. 1655

The Dramatic Works of Thomas Dekker, pb. 1953-1961 (4 volumes; Fredson Bowers, editor; includes collaborations with Dekker)

The Dramatic Works in the Beaumont and Fletcher Canon, pb. 1966-1976 (4 volumes; Bowers, editor; includes collaborations with Fletcher)

Selected Plays of Philip Massinger, pb. 1978 (Colin Gibson, editor)

Philip Massinger (Library of Congress)

OTHER LITERARY FORMS

Philip Massinger wrote a few commemorative poems, commendations of other playwrights, and dedicatory epistles in verse and prose. These have been collected by Donald Lawless in a 1968 monograph, *The Poems of Philip Massinger with Critical Notes.* Massinger's reputation, however, rests firmly on his plays.

ACHIEVEMENTS

Philip Massinger's missing plays are the stuff of legend: An eighteenth century book dealer, Joseph Warburton, bought and stacked away in a closet an undetermined number of Massinger manuscripts, which his cook mistook for scrap and used, sheet by sheet, to line pie plates and start fires. What outlived the cook is a body of competently, sometimes brilliantly, plotted plays, which are variations on three or four themes and character types.

In the past, critics such as Arthur Symons and Ronald Bayne have complained that Massinger's works offer no new insights into the relationship between human beings and society, no existential questions about the right and wrong of a character's course. They found his thinking conventional and his heroines smug. Later critics, such as Mark Mugglio and A. P. Hogan, attempted to rescue Massinger from

such charges by arguing that he was subtly challenging the very assumptions his plays seem to support.

In fact, Massinger's plays do make conventional assumptions about art, society, and human motives. Art teaches pleasantly; society naturally forms a hierarchy in which those of good blood, well educated, rule over those of less exalted natures. Humans act from love, greed, ambition, or simple fellowship. Working from these assumptions, Massinger dramatizes the unsuccessful attempts of citizens who wish to rise above their natural stations. He twits the younger generation for its impatience, he upholds loyalty as an almost ultimate value, and he polishes with loving care his portraits of the loyal and the innocent, the gruff and the greedy.

Though he does not challenge his culture's values, Massinger can still fascinate and delight a modern audience for three reasons. First, he fills his scenes with accurate observations of daily details. He savors the dodges by which a shrewd merchant secures a mortgage, the puff pastries and sherry sauces that a good chef can concoct, the pearl necklaces and tavern reckonings on which social status so often depends. Even in his most serious plays, one finds him lavishing stage time on the petty rituals and daily clutter that make people feel comfortably at home in the middle class. Through Massinger, one becomes intimate with the Renaissance Everyman, a hearty and surprisingly broad-minded figure.

Second, Massinger composes good, though not memorable, poetry and satisfying plots. His characters can dependably explain themselves and can use the common stock of images. Having apprenticed himself to such masters of double and triple plots as Thomas Dekker and John Fletcher, Massinger could weave most pleasing tapestries of contrasting threads. The saint's sweetness shows grandly against a background of sinners; the jealous man's frenzy, against the loyal anger of his wife.

Third, Massinger had an apparently lifelong fascination with the way that passion attacks reason. He continually examines the "something snapped" movement of a character's mind. In a Massinger character, passion's attack can numb the will as suddenly as the wasp's sting paralyzes the spider. Like Robert Burton in his *The Anatomy of Melancholy* (1621), Massinger concentrates sometimes on symptoms, sometimes on causes, sometimes on cures for the victims of jealousy or of "heroical love." His impassioned characters may be enrapt by Providence (as in *The Virgin Martyr*) or entrapped by their own possessive natures (as in *A New Way to Pay Old Debts*) or by the lure of other characters (as in *The Maid of Honour*). Whatever the causes, they act with a compulsiveness and are cured, if they are cured at all, by mechanisms that call into question the notion of free will perhaps more strongly than their creator intended.

BIOGRAPHY

Philip Massinger was baptized on November 24, 1583, at Salisbury, England, the son of Arthur and Anne Crompton Massinger. His father, "an honest gentleman and a loving man," served as trusted retainer to the powerful Henry Herbert, earl of Pembroke. As Pembroke's retainer, Arthur Massinger held various minor political offices, sat three times in Parliament, and handled many of the earl's financial affairs. Massinger's mother came from a similarly

professional family, but one whose political connections were smudged by more or less open Roman Catholicism. (Young Massinger may well have grown up Catholic; he treats Papists sympathetically, and their doctrines underlie at least three of his plays.) Early editors speculated that Massinger was reared as a page in a Pembroke household, where he could become familiar with the routines of gentry life. At the age of eighteen, he entered Oxford University, his father's alma mater. Though he may have stayed there until Arthur's death around 1606, he left without a degree.

Massinger's whereabouts after leaving Oxford are conjectural; probably he worked as an actor. By 1613 he was certainly scriptwriting in London, collaborating with other scriptwriters for hungry London audiences. Because playwriting paid very little, Massinger lived for some time on the fringes of poverty. In two letters, he seeks cash advances "without which we cannot be bailed" from prison for debt. Like a modern young screenwriter, he joined forces with one or another of the more established writers—Thomas Dekker, Nathaniel Field, Robert Dabourne—and worked for several of London's major production companies. Though Massinger wrote tragedies, tragicomedies, and comedies throughout his career, there was a general drift toward lighter plays as his career advanced.

By 1617, Massinger had begun what became his most fruitful writing partnership—with John Fletcher, who had succeeded William Shakespeare as chief writer for the King's Men, a highly acclaimed acting company. Massinger and Fletcher worked together on at least a dozen (and perhaps as many as nineteen) plays, mostly tragicomedies. In 1625, when Fletcher died in the great London plague, Massinger succeeded him as the company's chief writer. From then until his own sudden death in March, 1640, Massinger wrote almost exclusively for the King's Men.

ANALYSIS

The shaping and testing of will is certainly not Philip Massinger's only theme, but its development in several of his major plays amply illustrates both his talents and his limitations. Whether the will is tested by the demands of religion, the lure of lucre, the icy grip of jealousy, or the sweetness of an infatuation, Massinger manages to stir the theme deep into a play, to arrange characters and events to illustrate it. If he did not challenge the social or psychological conventions of his day as John Webster or John Ford did, he did make dramatically vivid and sometimes convincing cases for the wisdom of those conventional attitudes.

It is in Massinger's studies of passion, whether the conclusion is tragic or comic, that one sees most clearly both his strengths and his limitations—both his famous seriousness as a dramatist and teacher, and the problems critics find with his use of conventions. Four plays particularly illustrate Massinger's "anatomy" of passion and will: *The Virgin Martyr*, *The Maid of Honour*, *The Picture*, and *A New Way to Pay Old Debts*.

THE VIRGIN MARTYR

In *The Virgin Martyr*, Massinger collaborated with Dekker to produce a hagiography with a decidedly Romish coloring. Massinger believed in ritual, ceremony, and order, as well as in the power of prayer to change determinations. With a certainty bordering on superstition, he believed that those who adhere to a set body of moral codes will have an almost magical effect on their world.

Dorothea, the virgin martyr, has such an effect. She adheres to Christian dogma and practices the virtues of generosity, compassion, self-control, and rational argument. She gladly accepts martyrdom as payment for three benefits: heaven for herself; conversion of Antoninus, the young Roman who loves her; and a gift of fruit and flowers for Theophilus, her prosecutor. At her dying request, "A holy fire/ yields a comfortable heat" in Antoninus; soon thereafter, Theophilus, receiving his miraculous bouquet, sets about becoming Rome's next Christian martyr. Thus, prayer's power triumphs—perhaps over the free will of the converts.

Yet *The Virgin Martyr*, contrary to what the title leads us to expect, is not entirely Dorothea's story; her self-control in the face of physical torment is merely the simplest of several versions of self-control tested. Massinger gives as much attention to Anto-

ninus, the governor's son, and Artemia, the emperor's daughter. Antoninus passionately loves Dorothea, yet when Artemia chooses him for her consort, he cannot safely refuse. He temporizes, then rushes off to pursue Dorothea again. The Christian virgin, completely occupied with prayer and good works, shows no interest in a pagan lover. She would rather feed the poor and instruct the ignorant.

Antoninus does not love Dorothea for her virtue—he simply loves her, irrationally. Of Artemia's proposal, he complains, "When I am scorched/ With fire, can flames in any other quench me?/ What is her love to me, greatness, or empire,/ That am slave to another?" That Dorothea's love brings him "assured destruction" bothers him not a whit, and when he attempts to color his passion with reason, the attempt largely fails.

Artemia, like Antoninus, covers passion with reasonable answers, yet ultimately, the pagan princess exercises a self-control that makes her admirable. Given her choice of husband, she bypasses kings and follows her affection for Antoninus; when she finds that he loves Dorothea, she impulsively wants him dead. She orders his execution but soon relents. Regaining control, she gives up her interest in him, "That all may know, when the cause wills, I can/ Command my own desires." At the play's end, she chooses a more appropriate husband, the emperor Maximinus, grounding love and affection to him on a clearly rational basis.

The question of will is examined from two other perspectives as well—those of Theophilus's daughters and of Dorothea's servants. The daughters, at the play's start, have newly renounced their Christianity and returned to their father's pagan gods. Tortures and reasoning had not worked, but the knowledge that their father chose his cultural convictions over even paternal feelings brought the girls back to Jove's altar. Massinger casts their conversion from Christianity in convincing psychological terms; their father's will has overwhelmed them. (Later, Dorothea uses reason to bring them back to Christ.)

The other perspective is that of Dorothea's two reprobate servants, Hircius and Spungius, who provide a not very comic commentary on their mistress's intellectualism. Drunkard and whoremaster respectively, they squander, with mechanical predictability, money entrusted to them for the poor. They embrace Christianity or paganism, depending on which sect puts the readiest cash into their hands. They claim no will at all. As Spungius says, "The thread of my life is drawn through the needle of necessity, whose eye, looking upon my lousy breeches, cries out it cannot mend them." Derogatory comparisons and flat punch lines give these characters some cleverness but no will. Their conversations counterpoint Dorothea's rational control.

THE UNNATURAL COMBAT

Several of the themes and characters of *The Virgin Martyr* turn up in later Massinger works. *The Unnatural Combat*, for example, is the study of a father's incestuous passion for his daughter. Malefort, the father, habitually does as he pleases; he has dispatched prisoners of war, disregarded friendship, and done away with one wife to make room for a second. Massinger has his audience learn these things gradually as he builds a picture of an effective military leader, but one whose power comes from utterly undisciplined appetites. Malefort gradually loses the sympathy of the audience until, halfway through the play, he kills his own son in a duel. His saving grace has been his care for his daughter. Now he suddenly realizes that he wants the girl incestuously, and the habit of taking what he wants—of unbridled, undisciplined will—is so strong in him that his real and painful struggle to give her up is doomed to fail.

The Malefort character resembles that of Theophilus in *The Virgin Martyr* and has even stronger resemblance to the Duke of Milan in the play of that title. There, the possessive will of Duke Sforza demands that, should he die, his chaste and innocent wife be killed, lest she someday enjoy a second love. Sforza's possessive will, like Malefort's, derives from his habitual and public indulgence of his appetite for Marcelia, and, like Malefort's, it is fatal. Domitian and his wife in *The Roman Actor* share the same lack of disciplined will.

THE RENEGADO

The willful will-lessness Massinger portrays in these characters is opposed in the likes of Dorothea

and Artemia. Massinger is particularly interested in the influence of such characters on others. In *The Renegado*, for example, the stalwart Christian hero converts the equally stalwart pagan heroine by having a Jesuit sprinkle her with holy water as she passes by, a rapid-transit baptism. In this case, the ritual itself effects the change in will. (Such a belief in ritual's power to summon up prevenient grace served as a kind of watershed in the early seventeenth century, separating Papists from Anglicans. Thus, critics tend to think Massinger was a Catholic.) In a humanized, toned-down form, Massinger's interest in the way wills fixate, interact, and change informs three of his mature works, *A New Way to Pay Old Debts*, *The Picture*, and *The Maid of Honour*. These three plays are vintage Massinger; all three deserve close study.

A NEW WAY TO PAY OLD DEBTS

In *A New Way to Pay Old Debts*, Massinger packs the *deus ex machina* in mothballs and stores it backstage along with the thunderbolts and heavenly flowers. The play, often considered his masterpiece, depends on human goodwill and gets most of its energy from one man's bad will. *A New Way to Pay Old Debts* transfers the single-minded bad man of *The Unnatural Combat* to the world of London city comedy, reshaping him into a Sir Giles Overreach, a character based on the real-life monopolist Sir Giles Mompesson. Sir Giles moves so firmly over Massinger's stage that, despite a highly conventional comic plot, the play almost loses its status as comedy.

A New Way to Pay Old Debts contains all the conventions of Jacobean double-plot comedy. In one of its plots, Frank Wellborn, Overreach's nephew, schemes to regain the land his uncle has deceitfully appropriated. In the other plot, Wellborn's younger friend, Tom Allworth, schemes to win Overreach's daughter Margaret. Each plotter uses a similar device. Wellborn asks Widow Allworth, Tom's mother, to pretend that she is infatuated with him; Overreach jumps to furnish Wellborn with riches as bait to catch the wealthy lady. Allworth asks Lord Lovell, his employer, to pretend that he is infatuated with Margaret Overreach. Her father jumps to furnish Margaret with riches, a marriage contract, and all things necessary for eloping with a lord. Thus, Wellborn regains his wealth and Tom Allworth gets Margaret. To complete the symmetry of the plots, Widow Allworth and Lord Lovell become a loving couple.

The play is rich in imagery. A gang of butlers and chefs at the Allworth house, with names such as Furnace and Order, keep up a running account of the way various schemers use food and fancy dress as weapons in their battle of wits. Among Overreach's retainers is a crooked, pathetically thin judge whose perpetual hunger mirrors the insatiable appetites of his master. The vignettes of taverners and tailors clamoring for payment and the scenes of banqueting and muted bits of courtship would make the play a good one even without its gargantuan villain. Yet for most audiences, the play belongs to Sir Giles—and he goes mad.

The role, like that of Shylock in Shakespeare's *The Merchant of Venice* (pr. c. 1596-1597), is a rich one. Sir Giles has more land, more money, more luxuries, and more dreams than any other two characters combined. A commoner by birth, he has parlayed small sums into huge fortunes. Early in the play, he gives detailed instructions for ruining a neighbor and appropriating his land—beginning with cutting his fences, firing his barns, and trampling his grain; moving on through protracted lawsuits and phony writs; and concluding with the forced sale of the land for a fraction of its worth. Bitter against those who claim aristocratic status from birth, Overreach relishes the knowledge that his servants are the widows of gentlemen he has ruined, that his daughter wears elaborately jeweled dresses, that his home far outshines those of the gentry.

Yet despite this bitterness, Sir Giles wants more than anything else to see his daughter married to a nobleman, to call her "right honorable" and bounce young lordlings on his knee. To achieve that aim, he virtually orders the girl to prostitute herself to Lord Lovell so that a marriage between them will be necessary. He oversees preparations for her courtship with a vigor and a compulsiveness that almost win the sympathy of modern democratic audiences, whatever their original effect may have been. When he finds that his plans have failed—that she has eloped not with a lord but with a dependent page—he goes mad.

Critics disagree on whether Massinger intended Sir Giles's ambition to gain the sympathy it does. Certainly, Massinger did not believe that usurers should cheat the poor or that citizens and lords should intermarry. He does, however, structure the play's last scene so that Sir Giles, at last sure of his goal, receives one irreversible blow after another. When Wellborn counsels the "true valor" of repentance after the penultimate revelation, Sir Giles replies, "Patience, the beggar's virtue/ Shall find no harbour here." Though he has competently manipulated people throughout his career and has adopted patience when it suited his purpose, the anger he had hidden earlier has cut a deep underground channel in him, and now it floods out in murderous fury. When others prevent his carrying out his threats, his mind snaps. In his frenzy, he cries out one last lucid line before drowning in hallucinations: "Why, is not the whole world/ Included in myself?" It is a question Massinger's tragic protagonists—Malefort or Sforza—might have asked, and one that Sigmund Freud would have found revealing.

THE PICTURE

In *A New Way to Pay Old Debts*, Massinger examined human will in the context of greed and social ambition. In *The Picture*, the context is jealousy and trust. The play teaches that loyalty begets loyalty, while mistrust begets mistrust. When soldier Mathias goes to Hungary to seek fortune as a mercenary, he leaves behind his lovely wife, Sophia. He secretly takes with him, however, a magic picture of her, a likeness that will turn yellow if she is sexually tempted and black if she is unfaithful to him. Mathias soldiers so well that meek King Ladislaus and his gorgeous wife Honoria stand indebted to him. His boasts about his wife, however, arouse Honoria's envy. Like the spoiled and willful villains of Massinger's early tragedies, she decides to destroy what stands in her light, namely the constant love of Mathias and his wife. She sends goatish courtiers off to seduce Sophia and offers herself to Mathias. In a series of parallel scenes, Mathias, strengthened by the Picture, resists Honoria while his wife resists Ubaldo and Ricardo. The courtiers (and her husband's long delay in returning home) eventually convince Sophia that her husband is unfaithful; in jealous anger, she decides that she, too, will embrace wantonness. As the lines of the Picture turn yellow and begin to blacken, Mathias, in anger, gives in to the queen's kisses. Conscience, religion, and "love to goodness for itself," however, soon recall Sophia from her wayward schemes. As the Picture correspondingly regains its natural colors, Mathias finds it easy to lecture the queen on the value of married love.

The Picture trumpets Massinger's theme of will. Honoria has been badly spoiled. Her husband proclaims himself her slave, gives her charge of the treasury, and knocks timidly at her bedroom door at night, unsure of admission, while dependable observers voice authorial comments on such submissiveness. Willfulness reigns so supremely in Honoria that she sees Mathias and Sophia's loyalty as something else for her to overcome. "I thought one amorous glance of mine could bring all hearts to my subjection," she complains. "I cannot sit down so with mine honour." Accustomed to having her way, she no longer questions whether her way is just.

It takes the Picture, indirectly, to save her. A day's journey from the palace waits a good woman, one capable of doubt and anger but essentially honorable. While Honoria and Mathias circle each other like amateur wrestlers looking for a headlock, Sophia manages her household in Bohemia. As the match in Hungary gets tougher, she loses her sense of humor, punishing servants for pranks. When she succeeds in bringing her suspicions and fears under control and chooses "goodness for itself," the long-distance reformations begin. First Mathias chooses chastity, then Honoria learns humility, and Ladislaus gains in fortitude.

This growth in the characters' virtue comes through a magic totem, just as Theophilus's conversion had come from flowers and the pagan princess's Christianity had come through a sprinkle of water. The problem of *deus ex machina* has thus surfaced again, yet in *The Picture*, Massinger backs away from superstition. Sophia is outraged to learn that her husband relies on a picture instead of doing, as she has, the very hard work of trusting one's spouse. Her sense of humor becomes astringent: She will teach the courtiers a lesson, so she pretends to make assig-

nations, robs them of their clothes, dresses them in women's garb, and sets them to work spinning wool. She will teach Mathias, too, so she disorders the house for his homecoming, ignores his royal guests, and pretends to have become promiscuous. In the play's final scene, it takes the entire cast's pleading to keep Sophia from entering a convent.

Sophia's lessons work. The lecherous courtiers renounce womanizing. Her pretense rouses an almost murderous wrath in her husband. When he is made aware how unjust and unstable his jealousy makes him, he learns to value trust. The royal Hungarians also find a better marital balance. Sophia's actions produce these effects directly, not through flowers or thunderbolts. Her will is strong enough to affect the other characters' wills, in a purely human way.

THE MAID OF HONOUR

The anatomy of will shapes *The Maid of Honour* as fully as it does *The Picture*, yet the test cases differ. Sophia and Mathias, and Honoria and Ladislaus, have to learn to control but not ignore their jealousies. In *The Maid of Honour*, the test case is the oath. Almost every character in the play makes and wants to break an oath, yet for Massinger oath-breaking inevitably signals a disordered will. (Massinger rarely questions whether a conventionally condemned action is right or wrong but rather whether the character has will enough to choose the course assumed right. In his better plays, such as this one, even the very good characters are capable of moral failure.)

The title character, Camiola, is a lovely, charmingly honest young maid. She cherishes oaths; being naturally inclined to "deal in certainties," she likes having things spelled out, contracted. She believes in the social order that has produced her. When the king's brother, Bertaldo, sends eye beams toward her, she tells him she loves him but denies his passionate suit. "Reason, like a tyrant," forbids a match between his royal blood and even the richest and fairest of citizens, which she grants herself to be. Besides, she is convinced that "when what is vow'd to heaven is dispens'd with/ To serve out ends on earth, a curse must follow," and Bertaldo, as a Knight of Malta, has vowed lifelong celibacy. Thus, at the play's start, she sacrifices her love.

Such a sacrifice, however, is not easily made. Like any self-confident, honest, and infatuated young woman, Camiola sees in his "sweet presence/ Courtship and loving language" evidence that Bertaldo possesses "so clear a mind, . . . furnished with Harmonious faculties moulded from Heaven." She proclaims that her passion for Bertaldo rests on his solid virtues, on "the judgment of my soul." (In fact, her catalog of his virtues relies heavily on the superficial.) Because she is rich and charming, she has had little need for or practice in renunciations. When he leaves, she is sure her sun has set forever. Her passions fight so fiercely against reason that she first takes to her bed, then tries to recover by amusing herself with the vain suit of a fop, Signior Sylli, himself a prodigious breaker of oaths.

Bertaldo, frustrated, embarks on a time-honored cure for the constellation of feelings that Robert Burton called "heroical love": He goes to war. An ally of Sicily has invaded the kingdom of Duchess Aurelia and is in need of assistance. The war is patently unjust, as even the ally's ambassador admits, but Bertaldo needs a fight, and his brother, King Roberto, allows him to go. In fighting against the duchess, Bertaldo is breaking yet another of his knightly oaths, to protect the innocent. Back in Sicily, his brother the king sends an ambassador of his own to Duchess Aurelia. His mission: to swear falsely that Bertaldo is fighting without the king's consent. Most of the play's characters see promises as convenient ways to get what they want. They use oaths willfully. Fulgentio, the king's favorite, for example, uses them to turn the king against his brother, and, when Camiola scorns him, he swears to tell "every man in every place" that she is a strumpet.

Because Camiola is strong-willed rather than willful, she keeps her resolutions even when they are inconvenient. Yet once, temporarily, she falters. She has refused Bertaldo on two counts—the difference in their social classes and his vow. When, in the course of battle, he is captured and refused ransom by his brother, she gladly sends fifty thousand gold crowns to redeem him. Buying him from slavery, she believes, makes her his social equal and thus frees her to marry him. In her exuberance at finding a way

around the problem of class, she apparently forgets his vow. She sends off a betrothal contract with the ransom money. She employs as messenger a man who, she knows, loves her loyally from a distance. Anticipating Bertaldo's gratitude, she lives a dance of glee, daydreaming their future together.

In a play about the importance of vows, Massinger, moralist, will not let a heroine, no matter how charming, build a happy future on broken promises. Bertaldo does sign the betrothal agreement but almost immediately finds himself the object of another infatuation. The normally level-headed Duchess Aurelia, like Camiola, sees his courtly bearing as proof of a wise and noble nature. Forgetting past offenses, she offers him marriage, a dukedom, and a papal dispensation from his vow of celibacy. Bertaldo, like the spoiled Honoria, has few scruples. He accepts and returns home in triumph, doubly promised.

Massinger's conclusion owes much to Shakespeare's *All's Well That Ends Well* (pr. c. 1602-1603). Bertaldo, like Bertram, is publicly exposed. The duchess shakes off her infatuation and Camiola wins fair title to the now repentant man. Then, in a plot twist destined to perplex readers for centuries, Camiola abandons the court, abandons Bertaldo—whom she now pities as a weakling—and marries herself to the Church as a nun.

Massinger may have intended Camiola's decision as a comic resolution, but several things qualify the reaction audiences have to it. Though she has proved strong-willed and loyal, Camiola is very young. She has misjudged Bertaldo's character through her own inexperience. She has a flair for drama that needs careful control. She choreographs the entire last scene of the play, from exposing Bertaldo to taking the veil, deliberately arranging events to "deserve men's praise, and wonder too," and she does so immediately on learning of his betrayal. Thus, the will, which has guided her throughout the play in delightfully good-hearted ways, shows itself even in the act of renouncing itself.

OTHER MAJOR WORKS

POETRY: *The Poems of Philip Massinger with Critical Notes*, 1968 (Donald Lawless, editor).

MISCELLANEOUS: *The Plays and Poems of Philip Massinger*, 1976 (5 volumes; Philip Edwards and Colin Gibson, editors).

BIBLIOGRAPHY

Adler, Doris. *Philip Massinger*. Boston: Twayne, 1987. Adler briefly comments on the life, then analyzes the plays in historical and dramatic contexts. Promotes Massinger as a political analyst concerned with the dangers to England represented by corrupt Stuart courts, especially by such men as Robert Carr and George Villiers—and also Sir William Davenant, who was promulgating values at court that the poet could not accept.

Clark, Ira. *The Moral Art of Philip Massinger*. Lewisburg, Pa.: Bucknell University Press, 1993. Clark examines morality and ethics in the dramatic works of Massinger. Includes bibliography and index.

_____. *Professional Playwrights: Massinger, Ford, Shirley, and Brome*. Lexington: University Press of Kentucky, 1992. Clark analyzes and criticizes the plays of Massinger, John Ford, James Shirley, and Richard Brome, known as the Carolines. Includes bibliography and index.

Garrett, Martin, ed. *Massinger: The Critical Heritage*. New York: Routledge, 1991. This volume provides a critical look at the dramatic works of Massinger. Bibliography and index.

Howard, Douglas, ed. *Philip Massinger: A Critical Reassessment*. Cambridge, England: Cambridge University Press, 1985. Contains valuable essays by eight scholars, with an appendix by Anne Barton on "Massinger's distinctive voice." Topics include the collaboration with John Fletcher, charity and social order, and Massinger's theatrical language. Plays treated in depth include *The Maid of Honour, The City Madam*, and *A New Way to Pay Old Debts*.

Sanders, Julie. *Caroline Drama: The Plays of Massinger, Ford, Shirley, and Brome*. Plymouth, England: Northcote House in association with the British Council, 1999. Sanders examines the works of the Carolines: Massinger, John Ford, James Shirley, and Richard Brome. Includes bibliographical references and index.

Elizabeth Spalding Otten,
updated by Howard L. Ford

W. SOMERSET MAUGHAM

Born: Paris, France; January 25, 1874
Died: Saint-Jean-Cap-Ferrat, France; December 16, 1965

PRINCIPAL DRAMA

A Man of Honor, wr. 1898-1899, pr., pb. 1903
Loaves and Fishes, wr. 1903, pr. 1911, pb. 1924
Lady Frederick, pr. 1907, pb. 1912
Jack Straw, pr. 1908, pb. 1911
Mrs. Dot, pr. 1908, pb. 1912
The Explorer, pr. 1908, pb. 1912
The Noble Spaniard, pr. 1909, pb. 1953
Penelope, pr. 1909, pb. 1912
Smith, pr. 1909, pb. 1913

Landed Gentry, pr. 1910 (as *Grace*), pb. 1913
The Tenth Man, pr. 1910, pb. 1913
The Land of Promise, pr. 1913, pb. 1913, 1922
Caroline, pr. 1916, pb. 1923 (as *The Unattainable*)
Our Betters, pr. 1917, pb. 1923
Caesar's Wife, pr. 1919, pb. 1922
Home and Beauty, pr. 1919, pb. 1923 (also as *Too Many Husbands*)
The Unknown, pr., pb. 1920
The Circle, pr., pb. 1921
East of Suez, pr., pb. 1922
The Constant Wife, pr., pb. 1926
The Letter, pr., pb. 1927
The Sacred Flame, pr., pb. 1928

The Breadwinner, pr., pb. 1930
The Collected Plays of W. Somerset Maugham, pb.
   1931, 1952 (3 volumes, including 18 plays)
For Services Rendered, pr., pb. 1932
Sheppey, pr., pb. 1933

OTHER LITERARY FORMS

W. Somerset Maugham was a celebrated writer of novels and short stories. In addition, he published ten important books of travel, autobiography, criticism, and miscellaneous essays. He was a constant contributor to periodicals, and he furnished prefaces, stories, and chapters to more than two dozen anthologies and books by other writers. Many of his works have been translated into foreign languages.

Maugham's novels began with a story of London slum life, *Liza of Lambeth* (1897), and closed with *Catalina: A Romance* (1948), a love story of no great importance. Of the eighteen novels published between these two, at least five are of major importance: *Mrs. Craddock* (1902), *Of Human Bondage* (1915), *The Moon and Sixpence* (1919), *Cakes and Ale* (1930), and *The Razor's Edge* (1944).

Of the collections of short stories, only the three volumes of *The Complete Short Stories* (1951) need be mentioned here. The publishing history of the individual stories is extremely intricate. An excellent detailing is provided in Raymond Toole Stott's *Maughamiana: The Writings of W. Somerset Maugham* (1950). Stott traces the publishing history of Maugham's short stories from "Don Sebastian," which appeared in *Cosmopolis* magazine in October, 1898, through the publication of "Mr. Know-All" in the April 16, 1949, issue of *Everybody's Weekly*. Of special value is Stott's tracing of the stories that appeared in *Nash's Magazine*, *Cosmopolitan*, *Hearst's International Magazine*, and *Good Housekeeping* from November, 1920, to March, 1947. Maugham's stories that were written in French and published in three French periodicals receive separate treatment.

Maugham's travel books include *The Land of the Blessed Virgin: Sketches and Impressions in Andalusia* (1905), *On a Chinese Screen* (1922), *The Gentleman in the Parlour: A Record of a Journey from Rangoon to Haiphong* (1930), and *Don Fernando* (1935). Literary criticism and autobiography are curiously mixed in *The Summing Up* (1938) and *A Writer's Notebook* (1949), later printed together as *The Partial View* (1954). The autobiographical *Strictly Personal* (1941) details Maugham's flight from France in World War II. *The Writer's Point of View* (1951) is a lecture to aspiring writers delivered to the National Book League in London. Other essays and criticism are to be found in *The Vagrant Mood: Six Essays* (1952), *Ten Novels and Their Authors* (1954), and *Points of View* (1958). All these books may be said to be both frank and secretive. In his works, Maugham expresses himself freely on many public and some private subjects, but he guards his innermost privacy carefully.

ACHIEVEMENTS

That W. Somerset Maugham was one of the more successful English writers of the first half of the

W. Somerset Maugham (Library of Congress)

twentieth century is clear enough, even though the fact is sometimes obscured by that preliminary rising and falling of popular and academic estimation that accompanies the settling of a writer into his place in history. Early criticism tended to portray Maugham's plays as cynical, shallow, and witty, after the manner of Restoration comedy and of Oscar Wilde. Appreciation of Maugham's broader and more serious themes—poverty, social injustice, the possibilities inherent in the relationships between the sexes, privilege versus responsibility, and the ultimate nature of human good and evil—has emerged gradually over three-quarters of a century and has established that Maugham the playwright was a thoughtful observer and critic of life.

Maugham's reputation as a serious dramatist seems likely to continue growing as scholars and critics reconsider his plays, and the success of revivals indicates that at least some of the plays will be part of the living repertoire of English drama for some time to come.

BIOGRAPHY

William Somerset Maugham was born in the British Embassy in Paris, which ensured his British citizenship. He passed his early life in France and, although he was staunchly English, he never lost his attachment to France, living and vacationing there whenever he could and, in the end, dying in his longtime home, the Villa Mauresque on Saint-Jean-Cap-Ferrat.

Maugham was born into a "legal" family: His father, Robert Ormond Maugham, was a solicitor for the British Embassy in Paris; his grandfather was reputedly one of the founders of the Law Society in England; and Maugham's brother Frederick Herbert Maugham, first viscount Maugham of Hartfield, was an outstanding lawyer, politician, and writer. His mother, Edith Mary Snell Maugham, a woman of great beauty and sensitivity, was socialite of some note in Paris. Her death at forty-one (January 13, 1882) was a shock from which Maugham never fully recovered. Her portrait stood at his bedside for the rest of his life. Edith Maugham bore six sons in all. Among those who survived to adulthood, Henry

Neville Maugham was an unsuccessful writer who committed suicide in 1904, while Charles Ormond Maugham went into the law and eventually headed the family law firm in Paris.

In 1884, Maugham was uprooted from his Parisian home and was sent to live with his uncle, the Reverend Henry MacDonald Maugham, vicar of Whitstable, Kent, and his aristocratic German wife. While his older brothers were romping their way through Dover College, young Maugham was enrolled in the famous King's School in Canterbury. There, the stuttering youngster had a very hard time of it until he left behind what was, in his opinion, the brutal staff of the lower forms. In later life, he became one of the school's chief benefactors and established a library there, which bears his name.

In 1890, Maugham was sent to the Riviera to recover from lung disease, a complaint that plagued him in one form or another periodically throughout his life. There he discovered French literature, an influence that was to be lasting. In *The Summing Up*, Maugham declared that it was the fiction of Guy de Maupassant that most influenced him when he set about becoming a writer.

In 1891, Maugham left the king's school and persuaded his uncle to send him to Heidelberg, where he acquired a lasting taste for philosophy from Kuno Fischer, attended his first play, and became much involved with the students' informal discussions of drama.

From 1892 to 1895, Maugham studied medicine at St. Thomas's Hospital in London, gaining much experience of life in the wards, in the clinic, and as an obstetrical clerk in the Lambeth district of London, then a slum of incredible squalor. The first fruit of his medical experience was the novel *Liza of Lambeth*, the success of which so encouraged Maugham that he turned down the offer of an assistantship at St. Thomas's. He decided later that this had been a great mistake, since it robbed him of a further chance to study human nature under stress and at its most primitive. Abandoning medicine, except for his wartime tour in the ambulance corps, Maugham began his writing career in earnest. He also began his lifelong habit of travel.

In the next several years, Maugham traveled in Spain and Italy, saw his first full-length play, *A Man of Honor*, performed by the Imperial Theatre Stage Society in 1903 (an error, he ultimately concluded, because it labeled his work as "intellectual" and frightened off the commercial managers), and even tried his hand at editing. After finding editing uncongenial, he established residency in Paris.

The year 1907 was a gala one for Maugham. After years of struggle, he had determined in 1903 to write plays with the deliberate goal of producing "surefire" commercial successes. *Lady Frederick*, his first attempt under the program, languished for several years before being produced at the Court Theatre; however, within the year, four of Maugham's plays were running simultaneously in London: *Lady Frederick*, *Jack Straw*, *Mrs. Dot*, and *The Explorer*. All but the last were resounding commercial successes. This triumph freed Maugham from nagging money worries, and he would never again be forced to resume them.

A series of commercially successful but artistically mediocre plays followed, with only *Smith*, *Loaves and Fishes*, and *The Land of Promise* having some pretense to addressing serious themes, namely social caste and religious hypocrisy.

In 1913, Maugham began having an affair with Syrie Wellcome, a married woman. The alliance was quite open and was accepted by Maugham's set. The outbreak of World War I found Maugham signing up for ambulance service, an occupation he found to be physically rigorous but oddly free from responsibility in that he was under orders and thus free from personal decision making. In 1915, through Syrie, with whom he was sharing an apartment in Rome and whom he was to marry that same year, he transferred to the intelligence branch of the British forces and was sent as a spy to Lucerne and Geneva, Switzerland. The Swiss police were at once suspicious, and he found that writing was necessary for a cover. In August, he published his great novel, *Of Human Bondage*, which he had begun in 1911 and in which autobiography and imaginative invention were so intertwined that he observed in his later life that he could not distinguish one from the other.

In 1916, Maugham went to the South Seas for his health, his always weak lungs having given way to bronchitis during the rugged Swiss winter. It is an open question whether he was also traveling on an intelligence assignment. His companion was Gerald Haxton, a dashing American whom Maugham had met in the ambulance service and who was to be his special friend for years to come. The trip gave Maugham the material for his short story "Miss Sadie Thompson" (better known under the later title "Rain") as well as for his novel *The Moon and Sixpence*, about the art and career of Paul Gauguin.

The Russian Revolution was well under way when Maugham, in 1917, was posted to St. Petersburg to keep the Kerensky government in the war. Maugham seems not to have fully realized the preposterousness of the mission and later suggested that, had he been sent earlier, he might have had a chance of success. Once again, his lungs gave way, this time with tuberculosis, and he entered Banchory Sanitorium in Scotland. He found the hospital a perfect place in which to relax and write, in spite of the bitter cold, which, according to the medical theories of the time, had to be freely admitted into the sickroom along with the fresh air.

During 1919, Maugham determined to enter on unlimited travels. *The Moon and Sixpence* having been seen through the press, he visited the South Seas again and toured the Far East, the United States, Europe, and North Africa. Meanwhile, he kept up a regular flood of publication of all kinds.

In 1927, Syrie and Maugham were divorced. The parting was not friendly, and Maugham observed at her death in 1955 only that he was at last free of alimony payments. In 1928, Maugham bought the charming Villa Mauresque on Saint-Jean-Cap-Ferrat, west of Nice, France, which remained his home for the rest of his life except for the period of World War II. In the same year, *Ashenden: Or, The British Agent* was published, and in 1930, *Cakes and Ale*, one of Maugham's best works, appeared.

In 1933, Maugham announced his retirement from playwriting, stating quite simply that he had lost touch with the public and had no desire to resume the contact, since it would require him to master the tastes of a new generation of theatergoers, which was a drudgery he was not willing to undertake.

After a visit to the West Indies in 1936 and another to India in 1938, Maugham was dislocated by World War II. No friend of the Germans, he found it prudent to put his treasured art in the care of French friends and flee Nice to escape probable arrest. London proved incompatible, and he weathered the war in South Carolina and Massachusetts.

In 1944, *The Razor's Edge*, Maugham's mystic novel, which expresses his deep belief that human kindness is the central fact of life, was published. To Maugham's grief, Haxton died the same year.

From the war years onward, Maugham's interest in film deepened, climaxing, a few years after his return to Villa Mauresque, with the filming of *Quartet* (1949). *Trio* (1950) and *Encore* (1951) followed, along with a new interest in television as a medium.

Honors came to the aging author: In 1952, Oxford University awarded Maugham a doctorate, and two years later, the Garrick Club made him a Companion of Honor. In 1959, Maugham made his final visit to the Far East. In 1962, he published *Looking Back*. From that point on, he lived a rather solitary and antisocial life until he died on December 16, 1965, at Saint-Jean-Cap-Ferrat.

ANALYSIS

An examination of the body of W. Somerset Maugham's plays must begin with a paradox: Maugham, who claimed that he could write nothing that was not based on his personal experience or on his observation of the experience and personality of others, came, as a playwright, as close as it is possible to come to the impersonality of T. S. Eliot's objective correlative, the evoking of emotion by dispassionately presenting objects or situations without comment. Maugham achieved that aesthetic distance that makes his plays independent of whatever personal experience triggered them. It is hardly surprising, in an age devoted to the public confession and to the propagandizing of whole programs of social theory, that Maugham's aloofness was mistaken for cruelty, cynicism, failure of nerve and of sensitivity, vacuousness, and simple avarice and mendacity. Indeed,

Maugham's assiduous cultivation of several public identities to mask his basic kindliness, his bisexuality, and his serious concern for the human condition, with its struggle for freedom in the face of the deterministic pressures that beset it from all directions (not the least of which were the conventions that condemned women to a demeaning social role), has hindered a full appreciation of his artistic achievement in drama.

Maugham's statements about his own plays have tended to blur his intentions further rather than clarifying them. In *The Summing Up*, in one of his clearer statements about his comedies, Maugham wrote that they followed the Restoration tradition in being dramas of conversation, not of action. Unfortunately, he added that the comedies treat the follies and vices of the fashionable with "indulgent cynicism." In the preface to the first volume of *The Collected Plays of W. Somerset Maugham*, which includes eighteen plays by which Maugham wished to be known, he further muddied the waters by declaring that the purpose of drama is solely to please and delight, that playwriting is merely "a graceful accomplishment" and "the most ephemeral of all the arts." He followed this by denying that plays are, in fact, art at all because they must appeal to the common denominator of the audience's passion and not to the intellect of its individual members. Thus, he argued, the theater of ideas is possible only on the most elementary level, a notion he also discussed in *The Summing Up*. Yet, in *The Summing Up*, he also argued that an art that exists only to give pleasure is no art at all, or at least is of little consequence. Art, he asserted, if it is to be considered one of the most important aspects of life, must teach "humility, tolerance, wisdom, and magnanimity." Proper art, he added, leads not to beauty but to right action. Perhaps it is irony, perhaps it is only the mask of humility slipping a bit, but Maugham concluded the discussion by remarking that the most effective sermon the artist preaches is the one he has no notion that he is preaching. One suspects that he knew well enough the sermons in his plays. In the best of them, the audience never suspects the presence of the playwright in the pulpit and takes Maugham's ideas for their own.

Maugham's comedies follow the classical tactic of ridiculing humankind's vices and follies and, in doing so, combine obvious pleasure with more or less subtle teaching. The plays, insofar as they treat universal subjects, will remain viable, in spite of Maugham's own predictions, because his theatrical techniques are solid as well as unusually skillful. That they still play well in the twenty-first century makes the case.

LADY FREDERICK

Lady Frederick, by far Maugham's best play before *Our Betters*, was one of the famous "four at one time" plays of his early triumph. Maugham had decided that the way to a playhouse manager's heart was through interesting an actress in her part, and he wrote *Lady Frederick* with this scheme in mind. His formula was to present the average woman's ideal, a heroine who is a good-hearted, titled adventuress, a "wanton of impeccable virtue" who gets her way in everything. The managers saw his point, but neither an American nor a British actress would touch a part that called for her to appear onstage neither dressed for the day nor with her hair arranged nor with her makeup on. Not until 1907, when Otho Stuart, manager of the Royal Court Theatre, unexpectedly needed a stopgap play, did *Lady Frederick* get produced. It was a smash hit; just how Stuart persuaded an actress to take the part is not clear. The previously rejected *Jack Straw* (written in 1905), *Mrs. Dot* (written in 1904), and *The Explorer* (written in 1899) joined *Lady Frederick* on the stage in 1908; all but *The Explorer* enjoyed good runs.

Lady Frederick, potboiler or no, is good theater, a combination of bedroom and drawing-room comedy shot through with the witty repartee that makes comparison with Wilde as inevitable as it is misleading. The essentially trifling game of sorting out partners is played against a background of the romantic and decadent habits of the upper classes. Two scenes in particular fit Maugham's theory of "big scenes" comedy. In one, Lady Frederick, whose great talent is to charm whomever she pleases, turns away the wrath of an unpaid dressmaker by treating her as a social equal. In the second, Lady Frederick invites her stripling suitor, "Charlie," the marquess of Mereston, to her dressing room, where she treats him to the dubious spectacle of a middle-aged woman transforming herself from a morning fright into the artificially youthful charmer who had infatuated him. The scene was an impressive, if shocking, success.

OUR BETTERS

Our Betters, produced nearly a decade later, is much superior to *Lady Frederick* in technique and impact. Although it deals with an infinitely small segment of humanity—wealthy, title-hunting American women and their foreign husbands and gigolos—it offers universal insights concerning sexuality, idleness, ignorance, and egocentric indifference.

Pearl, Lady Grayston, heads a set of self-exiled American women. Her lover, who financially backs her social climbing, is a gross, not quite brutal, extremely wealthy American businessman. Into this environment of false values and sensual abandon wanders Bessie Saunders, Pearl's younger sister. She and her rejected suitor, Fleming Harvey, act as commentators on the action, as she gradually comes to see the corruption of this imitation European society that at first attracts her. Pearl, who is caught *flagrante delicto* with an English adventurer, brazenly brings her set to heel again through a series of shabby tricks. Only Bessie and Fleming escape, after Bessie makes a scathing denunciation of the uselessness of the women who are now neither Americans nor the aristocrats they pathetically ape. Interspersed with this intrigue are scenes in which the misery of people who marry for false reasons and the hopelessness of women who have been brought up to no purpose is examined. On the whole, the play denounces the human waste produced by a frivolous, even a vicious, civilization that puts wealth and leisure into the hands of people who have neither the responsibility, the education, nor the instincts to employ it creatively.

HOME AND BEAUTY

Home and Beauty, which was produced in the United States as *Too Many Husbands*, is an example of Maugham's romping farce. The play revolves around a selfish young woman whose first husband was reported killed in World War I and who married his best friend shortly thereafter; she has had a child by each. When the first husband shows up from the dead, there is surprisingly little conflict. Stage irony develops as it becomes clear that neither man is keen to become the official husband, and a *ménage à trois* creaks along until the wife, to their untold relief, decides to divorce them both. If there is social commentary at all, it is aimed at the antiquated English divorce laws, which are ruthlessly parodied in the last act.

THE CONSTANT WIFE

The Constant Wife is a nearly perfect example of drawing-room comedy, but it is also clearly a play of ideas. It reverses the plot of William Shakespeare's *The Taming of the Shrew* (pr. c. 1593) in that the wife tames the philandering husband and makes him agree to her "sauce for the gander" fling with her lover before settling down to a marriage of equals. It also works with the theme of the "new woman," a staple from Henrik Ibsen and George Bernard Shaw. The point is that a wife is in honor bound to be faithful to her husband so long as she is financially dependent on him, the more so because wealth, servants, and modern conveniences have robbed her of all meaningful domestic functions. Financially independent, however, she is free to love where she chooses. Although the play inevitably suggests Ibsen's *Et dukkehjem* (pr., pb. 1879; *A Doll's House*, 1880), it is notably different in that Constance achieves her independence before making her gesture of defiance. The gesture may seem somewhat tawdry, but it is more satisfying than kissing and making up would be.

THE BREADWINNER

The Breadwinner is another study of marriage conventions. A husband-father revolts from his conventional role of the taken-for-granted provider and from the meaningless life thrust on him as a stockbroker. His children grown and his wife provided for, he simply leaves to lead his own life in America without a twinge of conscience. The picture of the parasitic wife and the egocentric, unloving children is a devastating commentary on the "lives of quiet desperation" led by most men. The husband points up his plight as a taken-for-granted provider when he observes that people are quite able to accept other people's sacrifices without feeling much pain, in spite of their protestations to the contrary.

FOR SERVICES RENDERED

For Services Rendered, one of Maugham's last four plays—plays written, he said, to "suit himself"—is perhaps his bitterest. In it, he examines the plight of one war veteran who is blind and another who will be financially ruined by the indifference of people who profited from his sacrifices and who could help him if they would. The play closes on a mad scene in which a daughter dances and sings patriotic songs while her father mouths the most blithering platitudes about home and family.

St. John Ervine disliked the play, arguing that the Ardsleys were made unnecessarily spineless simply to serve the needs of the satire. Even so, he declared it to be "a moving and sincere tragedy, with moments of great beauty." John Fielden was yet more perceptive: He saw that, through the focus of a nation's self-serving disregard for the welfare of its returned soldiers, Maugham was making a point against a larger attitude that allows people to "bravely make light of the suffering of others."

SHEPPEY

Sheppey, Maugham's last play, is a sort of morality play, fantasy, and allegory combined; it turns on the question of what would happen to an ordinary person who accidentally became enormously wealthy and decided to dispose of that wealth on strictly Christian principles. The answer is that the world would follow his family in declaring him mad. John Fielden rejected the play as weak, while Desmond MacCarthy found Sheppey a highly sympathetic character in whom theatergoers could take refuge from the otherwise too bitter satire. He saw it as a mark of Maugham's skill that he could make Sheppey sympathetic without sentimentalizing him. Richard Ward paid a high compliment indeed in declaring that, while *Sheppey* was far from Maugham's best play, none better achieved the purpose of art, the expression of spiritual reality in material terms.

THE CIRCLE

The Circle is generally considered to be Maugham's masterpiece. It combines the often brutal wit of drawing-room comedy with drama of ideas. Once more, the upper classes and their marriage habits are the target of satire. The aftermath of the elopement of a married woman, who is willing to give up child, reputation, position, and security for the companionship of the man she loves, is placed under microscopic observation. Some thirty years after the elopement, she returns to her son's country house with her lover and encounters, unexpectedly, the man who is still legally her husband. Age has not been kind to the wife, a former beauty, or to her lover, a politician of great promise gone to seed, and worse, in self-imposed exile. In contrast, the husband has aged well, though beneath his facade of cleverness and self-satisfaction lurks a selfish bitterness. The abandoned son is himself a rising politician; his wife is bored with him and is planning an elopement in her turn. Attempts are made to dissuade her. First her father-in-law and then the mother-in-law and her lover cut to ribbons the notion of romantic love, painting a picture of the slow horror of a life in adulterous exile. The knowledge that their class code ties them together more inescapably than marriage laws rankles both of the aging lovers. Yet, even after seeing what silly, shallow, unhappy people their lives have made them—the mother-in-law, a painted harridan, and her lover, a testy, bridge-playing drunk—the daughter-in-law decides to elope and does so with the aid of the older couple. The play closes with their knowing laughter coupled with the blind laughter of the now twice-duped father-in-law.

The Circle, then, examines English marriage laws, the codes of love in upper-level social circles, and, very quietly, the notion that women will achieve equality with men only when they can earn their living exactly as men do. Meanwhile, they are condemned to a degrading marriage or to a romantic flight to a situation that is at least equally degrading. The circle is fortune's wheel—there is no getting off it, and eventually it smashes its riders.

OTHER MAJOR WORKS

LONG FICTION: *Liza of Lambeth*, 1897; *The Making of a Saint*, 1898; *The Hero*, 1901; *Mrs. Craddock*, 1902; *The Merry-Go-Round*, 1904; *The Bishop's Apron*, 1906; *The Explorer*, 1907; *The Magician*, 1908; *Of Human Bondage*, 1915; *The Moon and Sixpence*, 1919; *The Painted Veil*, 1925; *Cakes and Ale*, 1930; *The Narrow Corner*, 1932; *Theatre*, 1937; *Christmas Holiday*, 1939; *Up at the Villa*, 1941; *The Hour Before Dawn*, 1942; *The Razor's Edge*, 1944; *Then and Now*, 1946; *Catalina*, 1948; *Selected Novels*, 1953.

SHORT FICTION: *Orientations*, 1899; *The Trembling of a Leaf: Little Stories of the South Sea Islands*, 1921; *The Casuarina Tree: Six Stories*, 1926; *Ashenden: Or, The British Agent*, 1928; *Six Stories Written in the First Person Singular*, 1931; *Ah King: Six Stories*, 1933; *East and West: The Collected Short Stories*, 1934; *Cosmopolitans*, 1936; *The Favorite Short Stories of W. Somerset Maugham*, 1937; *The Round Dozen*, 1939; *The Mixture as Before: Short Stories*, 1940; *Creatures of Circumstances: Short Stories*, 1947; *East of Suez: Great Stories of the Tropics*, 1948; *Here and There: Selected Short Stories*, 1948; *The Complete Short Stories*, 1951; *The World Over*, 1952; *Seventeen Lost Stories*, 1969.

SCREENPLAY: *Trio*, 1950 (with R. C. Sherriff and Noel Langley).

NONFICTION: *The Land of the Blessed Virgin: Sketches and Impressions in Andalusia*, 1905 (also known as *Andalusia*, 1920); *On a Chinese Screen*, 1922; *The Gentleman in the Parlour: A Record of a Journey from Rangoon to Haiphong*, 1930; *Don Fernando*, 1935; *The Summing Up*, 1938; *Books and You*, 1940; *France at War*, 1940; *Strictly Personal*, 1941; *Great Novelists and Their Novels*, 1948; *A Writer's Notebook*, 1949; *The Writer's Point of View*, 1951; *The Vagrant Mood: Six Essays*, 1952; *The Partial View*, 1954 (includes *The Summing Up* and *A Writer's Notebook*); *Ten Novels and Their Authors*, 1954 (revision of *Great Novelists and Their Novels*); *The Travel Books*, 1955; *Points of View*, 1958; *Looking Back*, 1962; *Purely for My Pleasure*, 1962; *Selected Prefaces and Introductions*, 1963.

MISCELLANEOUS: *The Great Exotic Novels and Short Stories of Somerset Maugham*, 2001.

BIBLIOGRAPHY

Calder, Robert. *Willie*. London: Heinemann, 1989. Through interviews with friends of Maugham and through letters made available for the first time (and published here), Calder offers a most informed account of the playwright and novelist. Contains an excellent discussion of Maugham's early life in Paris and the strong influence of French literature on his writing style. Also contains a detailed study of his experiences as a doctor, which contributed to his development. Photographs, bibliography, index.

Connon, Bryan. *Somerset Maugham and the Maugham Dynasty*. London: Sinclair-Stevenson, 1997. Connon examines the influence that the Maugham family had on the life and works of W. Somerset Maugham. Includes Bibliography and index.

Curtis, Anthony, and John Whitehead, eds. *W. Somerset Maugham*. London: Routledge and Kegan Paul, 1987. This book offers reprints of reviews of Maugham's plays, novels, short stories, and essays from 1897 to 1965. Many distinguished names appear as critics of his work; among them are Virginia Woolf, Max Beerbohm, Theodore Dreiser, Katherine Mansfield, Rebecca West, D. H. Lawrence, and Evelyn Waugh. A treasure trove of critical information. Bibliography and index.

O'Connor, Sean. *Straight Acting: Popular Gay Drama from Wilde to Rattigan*. Washington, D.C.: Cassell, 1998. O'Connor explains the influence that Oscar Wilde had on three gay or bisexual playwrights who wrote from the 1920's to the 1950's: Maugham, Noël Coward, and Terence Rattigan. Bibliography and index.

Rogal, Samuel J. *A Companion to the Characters in the Fiction and Drama of W. Somerset Maugham*. Westport, Conn.: Greenwood Press, 1996. An alphabetical listing of the characters—animal, human, unnamed, named—in Maugham's drama and fiction. Each entry identifies the work in which a character appears and the character's role in the overall work.

_____. *A William Somerset Maugham Encyclopedia*. Westport, Conn.: Greenwood Press, 1997. This encyclopedia covers the works of Maugham, from his plays and fiction to his travel narratives as well as important events and people in his life. A short bibliography appears after each entry. Also includes a bibliography of selected criticism and an index.

Whitehead, John. *Maugham: A Reappraisal*. London: Vision Press, 1987. Whitehead studies Maugham from his beginnings as a late Victorian writer to the close of his literary career, showing how he retained his public for almost sixty years. Whitehead gives Maugham high marks for three novels, four plays, and a number of short stories, and he pays tribute to his underestimated skill as an essayist, concluding that the "baggage with which Maugham set out for the future was not, after all, as slender as he feared."

B. G. Knepper,
updated by Mildred C. Kuner

FRANÇOIS MAURIAC

Born: Bordeaux, France; October 11, 1885
Died: Paris, France; September 1, 1970

PRINCIPAL DRAMA

Asmodée, pr. 1937, pb. 1938 (*Asmodée: Or, The Intruder*, 1939)

Les mal Aimés, pr., pb. 1945

Le Passage du malin, pr. 1947, pb. 1948

Le Feu sur la terre: Ou, Le Pays sans chemin, pr. 1950, pb. 1951

OTHER LITERARY FORMS

Although François Mauriac began his career as a poet, he worked in almost every literary genre. He wrote literary criticism, journalism, religious works, biographies, and several volumes of memoirs. However, he is known primarily as a novelist. His career as a dramatist extended only from 1937 to 1951 and resulted in four plays. His career as a novelist began in 1913 and lasted even beyond his death. The publication of *Un Adolescent d'autrefoix* (1969;

François Mauriac (© The Nobel Foundation)

Maltaverne, 1970) marked the appearance of his twenty-ninth book of fiction.

ACHIEVEMENTS

François Mauriac was elected to the prestigious French Academy in 1933 and won the Nobel Prize in Literature in 1952. He was also remarkable for his patriotism and courage. Although he was denied entrance to the army at the outset of World War I, he served in the ambulance corps from 1914 to 1917. He contributed to the literary arm of the French Resistance during World War II, protested in print against the use of torture by the French during the Algerian War, and was a founding member of the still-prospering magazine, *L'Express*.

BIOGRAPHY

François Mauriac was born in Bordeaux, France, on October 11, 1885, the son of a well-to-do family.

He grew up in Bordeaux and Les Landes, a sparsely populated pine-forested region south of the city, which would later become the settings of most of his fiction and drama.

As a young man, he abandoned his university studies in Paris to become a poet, but he soon turned to writing fiction. In the late 1920's, Mauriac experienced a religious crisis that eventually resulted in his renewed Roman Catholic convictions, which generally inform the body of his work but are especially crucial after 1930. Indeed, Mauriac is often referred to as a Catholic writer of Catholic literature, although he did not always welcome that categorization, preferring, like Georges Bernanos and the American Flannery O'Connor, to be known as a writer who was also Catholic. In the 1920's and 1930's, Mauriac published his best novels, although some critics have argued that his later novels do not receive the popular respect and admiration due them.

In the 1930's, Georges Bourdet, administrator of the state-subsidized Comédie Française, persuaded Mauriac to write for the theater. Having a play performed at the Comédie Française constitutes a peak in a playwright's career, just as it is a great honor for an actor to perform there. Mauriac eventually wrote four plays, all of which were produced in prominent Paris theaters. *Asmodée* was his most successful play, but after *Le Feu sur la terre*, he lost interest in the theater. Indeed, by 1960, he had written to a friend that he no longer felt any affinity with the theater and even avoided attending theatrical productions. However, he continued to write other works, primarily memoirs, until his death in 1970.

ANALYSIS

Like his novels, François Mauriac's plays indicate his preoccupation with cruelty and hypocrisy in the stifling atmosphere of the bourgeois family. Perhaps even more than his novels, Mauriac's plays expertly exploit the confinement and terrible constraints of homes and families in which power, meanness, and evil threaten any presence of goodness, love, and faith in God. Psychological and spiritual tension are magnified in spatial situations in which family members cannot escape each other, try to hide and fail, meet in secret, conspire, and scheme in rooms of remote houses, resorts, and estates.

This spatial and physical tension, as well as other qualities of Mauriac's plays, indicate his admiration for the plays of seventeenth century French classicism, particularly those of Jean Racine (whose biography Mauriac wrote in 1928). However, although Racine's plays are tragedies in the Greek tradition (most often culminating in a death or deaths and ending in some kind of explanatory denouement), Mauriac's plays are open-ended to some degree. A character may be trapped in his or her life and perhaps held prisoner in some way by others, but other characters escape to some kind of freedom. In this somewhat limited sense, the endings of Mauriac's plays are happy, at least for some characters.

Although Mauriac is known to many as a Catholic writer, it is not easy to determine in his plays—or in many of his novels—what if any Catholic or even Christian perspective is present. Clerics—former, present, and future priests—appear in some of the plays, but they are not major characters (except perhaps for Blaise Coûture of *Asmodée*). None of Mauriac's characters seems to speak consistently or insistently in favor of God, religion, or Catholicism, and good does not resoundingly triumph over evil in the plays. The Roman Catholic presence in Mauriac's drama resides in more subtle phenomena. For example, the sudden, unexpected realization that one ought to sacrifice one's own happiness for that of another may show how grace works in people's lives. Or one character may realize that he must cut his ties with the past, as tempting as they are, to honor commitments to the present and future, commitments made as signs of love.

These realizations contain the ultimate Christian message in Mauriac's plays: that those who love may suffer, but they do what they know is right. They accept their losses and give what they can to others.

ASMODÉE

The play's title aptly indicates the conflict between its characters. Asmodée is a biblical demon, known in the French literary tradition for lifting the roofs of houses to discover what was really going on inside, behind the facade that people ordinarily presented to the world. The Asmodée in the play is Englishman Harry Fanning, who comes to France as an exchange student. It turns out that Harry is twenty years old, not fifteen, as the family had expected. As a result of Harry's surprising sophistication, his presence in the de Barthas home, headed by the beautiful widowed mother, Marcelle, exposes the passions and frustrations of the members of the household. Harry toys with the affections of Marcelle, seventeen years older than he, but he truly falls in love with her daughter, seventeen-year-old Emmanuelle, who had been planning on life in a convent. Harry disrupts the relationship between Marcelle and Blaise Coûture, the children's tutor (and Marcelle's secret admirer). While Blaise pursues Marcelle, over whom he has exercised a sinister control, he breaks the spirit of Mademoiselle, the family governess, who loves him. Blaise is a former seminarian, dismissed from his school for unspecified bad attitude. His frustration with his failed career finds some release in the spiritual control he has over Marcelle.

Ultimately, the play focuses on Marcelle's epiphany: Although she had foolishly cultivated an attraction to Harry, she sacrifices her own happiness, recognizing that even though Emmanuelle will not be taking holy vows, the daughter's happiness with Harry is God sent. As the play ends, Marcelle faces life in her own home under Blaise's spell—as the despondent Mademoiselle looks on. Several years later, Mauriac wrote that he saw Blaise as a victim of his own pride, driven to use others for his own ends instead of trying to win their souls for God.

LES MAL AIMÉS

Les mal Aimés deals with the Virelade family, a father and his daughters, Marianne and Elisabeth. The girls' mother abandoned the family to live with another man when the children were very young, leaving the father bitter and viciously manipulative. A young neighbor, Alain, sustains a long flirtation with Elisabeth but betrays her in favor of her much younger sister. When the father threatens to kill Alain and when Elisabeth fears that Marianne loves Alain so much that she could not live without him, she gives him up. Indeed, Monsieur Virelade persuades Elisabeth to give Alain up so that Marianne will not kill herself. Elisabeth does as her father wishes; she has made similar sacrifices, for the good of others, before.

Alain and Marianne marry, but the union is not a happy one. Alain misses Elisabeth's intellectual stimulation. Near the end of the play, Elisabeth is tempted into running off with Alain, who in reality still loves her. Alain and Elisabeth leave the Virelade estate together, but Elisabeth cannot bring herself to carry out such treachery. She and Alain return home. The play ends with tensions unresolved: Marianne and Alain are still together, even though both know that Alain really loves Elisabeth. The future looks bleak in a family locked in a love-hate embrace. As is the case in *Asmodée*, Mauriac suggests that sexual love is a destructive force, tearing families apart and distracting people from their true moral obligations.

LE PASSAGE DU MALIN

In this play, Mauriac again examines the maneuvering for power within a family. In this case, Emilie Tavernas is the head of a family that she supports by means of a school she founded. She is a strong woman with a history of dominating young female protégées, frequently expressing her belief in the value of the soul over the life of the body. Ironically however, the play's opening scenes establish the distinct notion that Emilie is homosexual. She and her husband apparently have no sexual life, and Emilie has been spending most of her time with her latest discovery, Agnès.

However, into Emilie's life comes Bernard, a fascinating character, a classic seducer in the French tradition, who possesses women then casts them aside. He eloquently persuades Emilie to spend a night with him, and she sees herself afterward as a changed person—and free of her family. It turns out that Bernard truly wants Emilie's love. However, the liaison between Bernard and Emilie collapses when he sees that Emilie cannot overcome her shame and sense of sin at what she has done. Although Bernard succeeded in conquering her physically, she does not—and will not—love him. Although Bernard has liberated her sexually, Emile refuses to give in to physical passion. Bernard is stung, having fallen in love with

one of his victims for the first time. Emilie is left a sad figure: She regretfully—but by active choice—reassumes her family roles.

LE FEU SUR LA TERRE

Mauriac sets his drama in Les Landes, the country of sand and pines where out-of-control fires sweep the acreages, both in reality and in Mauriac's novels. The title, *Le Feu sur la terre* (the earth on fire), reflects the play's atmosphere: one of impending disaster, tension, the need for decisions, and the heat of passion.

Osmin du Prat de La Sesque is a classic Mauriac bourgeois villain: egotistical, money-hungry, closed-minded, and hypocritical. His adversary is his son, Maurice, who has deceived his father by studying art instead of law while in Paris. The father and son represent a classic cultural conflict, that of materialism and art or the life of the spirit. Maurice returns home to repay his father's financial investment in his education and to introduce his wife, Andrée, and their son, Eric. However, Maurice is torn between his quest for personal freedom as well as his love for his wife and son and his strong, unusual bond with his older sister, Laure. Readers of *Asmodée* will see a similarity between Laure and Blaise Coûture: They are both characters who fulfill themselves by absorbing another's personal autonomy.

The essential struggle in the play is between Andrée and Laure for love of and control of Maurice, whose allegiances are certainly ambivalent. Andrée eventually wins out, but the play's last scene is perhaps the most touching in Mauriac's theater. Although the character of Laure is essentially hateful, one can feel compassion for her as she tenderly expresses her nostalgia for her former relationship with Maurice, knowing all the while that things can never be the same again—that things are as they ought to be but are nevertheless difficult to bear.

OTHER MAJOR WORKS

LONG FICTION: *Le Baiser au lépreux*, 1922 (*The Kiss for the Leper*, 1923, 1950); *Genetrix*, 1923 (English translation, 1950); *Le Fleuve du feu*, 1923 (*The River of Fire*, 1954); *Le Désert de l'amour*, 1925 (*The Desert of Love*, 1929); *Thérèse Desqueyroux*, 1927

(*Thérèse*, 1928); *Destins*, 1928 (*Destinies*, 1929); *Le Noeud de vipères*, 1932 (*Vipers' Tangle*, 1933); *Le Mystère Frontenac*, 1933 (*The Frontenac Mystery*, 1952); *La Fin de la nuit*, 1935 (*The End of the Night*, 1947); *Les Anges noirs*, 1936 (*The Dark Angels*, 1950); *Les Chemins de la mer*, 1939 (*The Unknown Sea*, 1948); *La Pharisienne*, 1941 (*Woman of the Pharisees*, 1946); *Galigaï*, 1952 (*The Loved and the Unloved*, 1952); *L'Agneau*, 1954 (*The Lamb*, 1955); *Un Adolescent d'autrefoix*, 1969 (*Maltaverne*, 1970).

POETRY: *Les Mains jointes*, 1909; *L'Adieu à l'adolescence*, 1911; *Orages*, 1925; *Le Sang d'Atys*, 1940.

NONFICTION: *La Vie de Jean Racine*, 1928; *Souffrances du chrétien*, 1928 (translated in *Anguish and Joy of the Christian Life*, 1964); *Dieu et Mammon*, 1929 (*God and Mammon*, 1936); *Bonheur du chrétien*, 1929 (translated in *Anguish and Joy of the Christian Life*); *Blaise Pascal et sa sœur Jacqueline*, 1931; *Le Romancier et ses personnages*, 1933; *Journal*, 1934-1953 (memoir); *Vie de Jésus*, 1936 (*Life of Jesus*, 1937); *Le Cahier noir*, 1943 (*The Black Notebook*, 1944); *Mes Grands Hommes*, 1949 (memoir; *Great Men*, 1952); *Écrits intimes*, 1953 (memoir); *Bloc-notes, 1952-1957*, 1958 (memoir); *Mémoires intérieurs*, 1959 (memoir; English translation, 1960); *Le Nouveau Bloc-notes*, 1961-1970 (memoir); *Ce que je crois*, 1962 (memoir; *What I Believe*, 1963); *De Gaulle*, 1964 (English translation, 1966); *Nouveaux Mémoires intérieurs*, 1965 (memoir; *The In-*ner Presence, 1968); *Mémoires politiques*, 1967 (memoir); *Le Dernier Bloc-notes, 1968-1970*, 1971 (memoir).

BIBLIOGRAPHY

Flower, John. *Intention and Achievement: A Study of the Novels of François Mauriac*. Oxford, England: Clarendon, 1969. Focuses on the earlier novels (pre-1930), but Flower is a respected Mauriac scholar.

Flower, John, and Bernard Swift, eds. *François Mauriac: Visions and Reappraisals*. New York: Berg, 1991. Looks at new ways of interpreting Mauriac's work and career. Presents what is perhaps a more nuanced picture of the author and his work than that typical of pre-1960's criticism.

Jarrett-Kerr, Martin. *François Mauriac*. London: Bowes and Bowes, 1954. A short but classic introduction to Mauriac, with greatest attention to the pre-1930 novels.

Maloney, Michael F. *François Mauriac: A Critical Study*. Denver: Swallow, 1958. A brief but nevertheless substantial introduction to Mauriac.

O'Connell, David. *François Mauriac Revisited*. New York: Twayne, 1995. The best introduction to Mauriac and his entire career, including his theater, for English-speaking readers. Penetrating, original, well-written analysis throughout, up-to-date scholarship, very helpful bibliography.

Gordon Walters

VLADIMIR MAYAKOVSKY

Born: Bagdadi, Georgia, Russian Empire (now
  Mayakovsky, Georgia); July 19, 1893
Died: Moscow, U.S.S.R.; April 14, 1930

PRINCIPAL DRAMA
  Vladimir Mayakovsky: Tragediya, pr. 1913, pb.
    1914 (*Vladimir Mayakovsky: A Tragedy*, 1968)
  Misteriya-buff, pr., pb. 1918, revised pr., pb. 1921
    (*Mystery-bouffe*, 1933)

  Chempionat vsemirnoy klassovoy borby, pr. 1920,
    pb. 1935 (*The Championship of the Universal
    Class*, 1973)
  *A chto y esli? Pervomayskiye grezy v burzhuaznom
    kresle*, pr. 1920, pb. 1934
  *Pyeska pro popov, koi ne pobnimayut, prazdnik
    chto takoye*, pr. 1921, pb. 1934
  Kak kto provodit vremya, prazdniki prazdnuya, pr.
    1922, pb. 1934

Radio-Oktyabr, pr. 1926, pb. 1927 (with Osip Brik)
Klop, pr., pb. 1929 (*The Bedbug*, 1931)
Banya, pr., pb. 1930 (*The Bathhouse*, 1963)
Moskva gorit, pr. 1930, pb. 1936 (*Moscow Is Burning*, 1973)
The Complete Plays, pb. 1968

OTHER LITERARY FORMS

Vladimir Mayakovsky, a versatile artist, is best known for his poetry, which ranges from the epic to the satiric and from the grandiose to the mundane. His poem *Chelovek* (1916; man) explores cosmic themes in the form of a parody. Parodying the stages in the life of an Orthodox saint, Mayakovsky moves from his own nativity to his resurrection and finally to his reappearance on earth. Mayakovsky, the martyr-saint, does battle with divine forces, undergoes the terrors of "the bullet and the razor," ascends into a lifeless heaven, and returns a lonely man alienated from the universe. In *150,000,000* (1920; English translation, 1949), Mayakovsky pits the giant Ivan, a symbol for 150 million cold, hungry, desperate Russians, against the grotesque capitalist warrior Woodrow Wilson, who sinks to the bottom of the sea. In *Pro eto* (1923; *About That*, 1965), Mayakovsky transforms a story of rejected love into an agon on his own martyrdom and his resurrection into a futuristic world. Finally, in his magnum opus, *Vladimir Ilich Lenin* (1924; English translation, 1939), he mixes comic and epic styles to re-create the glories of the Russian Revolution. The use of cosmic imagery, the parody of Christian themes, the creation of futuristic worlds, and the techniques of propaganda seen in these poems are also found in Mayakovsky's dramas.

Mayakovsky also wrote screenplays, most of which were unsuccessful. In *Ne dlya deneg rodivshiisya* (1918; not born for money), he adapted Jack London's novel *Martin Eden* (1909), rewriting the ending to have Eden feign suicide, renounce the bourgeois world, and become a worker; Mayakovsky himself dismissed this script and many of his earlier ones as too bourgeois. He felt more comfortable, however, with his later film scenarios. His most innovative work, *Serdtse kino* (1926; heart of cinema), recounts the love story of a painter and film star who leads one life on film and then steps off the screen to lead another. Mayakovsky's experimentation with montage, accelerated motion, and angled views carried over into his dramas, which are cinematic in style.

Mayakovsky not only wrote manifestos and started literary journals but also designed posters, composed advertising jingles, and produced children's literature, much on the level of sheer propaganda.

ACHIEVEMENTS

Vladimir Mayakovsky has been deemed the poet laureate of the Russian Revolution. As a member of the Futurist movement, he broke with the heroic literature of the past and the sentimentality of bourgeois realism to fight for a democratic art that would allow the free word of the creative personality to be "written on the walls, fences, and streets of our cities." He wanted literature to cry out to the people, abandon traditional imagery, praise the urban landscape, and hail the coming of the utopian commune. To accomplish this artistic revolution, Mayakovsky created a literature that eschewed the notions of absolute value and eternal beauty and struck out at the heart of the masses—a literature in which poetic devices were valued more for their effectiveness as propaganda than for their aesthetic qualities. As a poet, art critic, literary editor, and film auteur, Mayakovsky battled against the Symbolists, who wanted to reduce art to mysticism, and the Formalists, who emphasized artistic technique over message.

As a dramatist, Mayakovsky formed an association with director Vsevolod Meyerhold, and together they revolutionized modern theater. In plays ranging from cosmic parody in *Mystery-bouffe* to topical satire in *The Bathhouse*, Mayakovsky assisted Meyerhold in creating a utopian art "which would not only pose problems of today but would project decades into the future." Mayakovsky also tried to move theater away from dreary, slice-of-life realism. In his prologue to *Mystery-bouffe*, he set forth his dramatic credo. Realizing that the stage was "only one third of the hall," Mayakovsky brought the action of the drama into the audience, breaking the bonds of "key-

Vladimir Mayakovsky

cialist poets, and at the tenth anniversary of his death, Bagdadi (Mayakovsky's birthplace) was renamed Mayakovsky, and Sadova-triumfalnaya Square was converted into Mayakovsky Square. (Much later, in 1958, a memorial statue of Mayakovsky was erected in this square.) Increasingly, however, Mayakovsky fell out of favor, and production of his plays was suppressed until the mid-1950's, when the liberalization that followed Stalin's death brought the rehabilitation of many writers. Mayakovsky enjoyed a significant revival in the late 1950's and 1960's, and his plays have become a standard part of the repertoire in many Eastern Bloc countries.

BIOGRAPHY

Vladimir Vladimirovich Mayakovsky, born in Bagdadi, Georgia, Russian Empire, was an unpromising student who early in his life became involved in revolutionary activities. In 1905, a year of upheaval in Russian politics, Mayakovsky joined a Marxist society at his school and later became a propaganda worker for the Bolsheviks. Even after being expelled from school and arrested, Mayakovsky, a fervent revolutionary, persisted in underground activities and was imprisoned three times before he was fifteen years old.

By 1910, however, Mayakovsky had rechanneled his revolutionary zeal in the direction of creating socialist art. He soon enrolled in the Moscow College of Painting, Sculpture, and Architecture, where he was introduced to modern art by David Burlyuk, an expressionist turned cubist. Turning to poetry, Mayakovsky joined the Russian Futurists, who wanted to revolutionize poetry by advocating a total disregard for the poetic and linguistic conventions of the past. In 1913, Mayakovsky wrote, directed, and acted in his first drama, *Vladimir Mayakovsky*, performed at the Luna-Park Theatre in St. Petersburg on December 2. Despite exorbitant ticket prices, the show played to packed houses, and onstage, Mayakovsky outshouted the boos from the audience. Having launched his career as a dramatist, Mayakovsky toured Russia as a poet-performer and lecturer.

Then came the turning point in Mayakovsky's life—the Russian Revolution. The Russian literary

hole" realism. Instead of creating believable characters hidden behind the proscenium arch and seen against the background of decorative scenery, he created grotesque figures—slapstick clowns bouncing across constructivist, three-dimensional sets composed of ropes, grids, and platforms—in other words, a theater of spectacle.

Mayakovsky turned the stage into a soapbox and spared no one from the barbs of his satire. He not only portrayed capitalists as brutal and vicious exploiters but also attacked his enemies within the Soviet regime. In his dramas, odious, boot-licking artists, gaudy philistines, and pompous bureaucrats are magnified into grotesque caricatures.

Even though his constant criticism of the artistic establishment did not endear him to many of his contemporaries, he was accorded a state funeral with 150,000 participants. In 1938, Joseph Stalin proclaimed Mayakovsky one of the most important so-

critic Viktor Shklovsky said, "Mayakovsky entered the Revolution as he would enter his own home." Filled with pride when he heard Red soldiers singing his song on their way to storm the Winter Palace, Mayakovsky celebrated the Revolution in epic poems, posters, propaganda slogans, and mass lectures. On November 7, 1918, in collaboration with avantgarde director Meyerhold, Mayakovsky commemorated the first anniversary of the Revolution with his second play, *Mystery-bouffe*. In this theatrical spectacle, Mayakovsky mixed circus antics with poetic monologues and combined allegory with satire. The first version of *Mystery-bouffe* was unsuccessful, so in May, 1921, Mayakovsky staged a revised version, which was later performed in German before the Third Comintern Congress.

After *Mystery-bouffe*, Mayakovsky continued to write epic verse and to travel Europe as a cultural ambassador and a Soviet propagandist. In 1923, Mayakovsky cofounded the journal *Lef*, and his line "time forward March!" was the battle cry for a new art that would lead humanity into the age of technology. He also took his revolutionary message to America in 1925, touring the United States from Coney Island to the Chicago stockyards and winning the praises of *The Daily Worker*, which acclaimed him as "the famous proletarian poet." By 1926, Mayakovsky was at the height of his career.

By 1927, however, the tide of Soviet politics was changing. The Soviet society was searching for stability, and revolutionary art was giving way to socialist realism. Critics attacked Mayakovsky's art as bombastic and bohemian and accused him of lacking sincerity and concern for individual human problems. In a spirit of rebellion, Mayakovsky met his critics head-on with *The Bedbug*, a scathing attack on Soviet philistines who were returning to the capitalist practices of prerevolutionary Russia. Although the drama was successful in its 1929 staging, the critics accused Mayakovsky of creating poster art. In 1930, in his final effort to establish his theater of spectacle, Mayakovsky produced *The Bathhouse*, which not only satirized the Soviet bureaucracy but also lampooned the Soviet literary establishment. The play closed after three performances. Having been refused an exit visa,

despondent over the boycott of his exhibition "Twenty Years of Work," and disillusioned over the failure of *The Bathhouse*, Mayakovsky shot himself on April 14, 1930. A revolutionary to the last, Mayakovsky left a suicide note to one of his literary adversaries whom he had placated, stating that he (Mayakovsky) "ought to have fought it out."

ANALYSIS

Vladimir Mayakovsky stretched the limits of theater. He was a witty satirist and a clever creator of performance art. Today, Western audiences might find his plays dated and preachy. Many of them are filled with topical allusions and puns that are not easily translatable. Also, his dramas depend heavily on complicated theatrical devices and performance routines that work better on the stage than on the page. Yet there is an element in his work that transcends topicality and ideological biases. Anyone who has dealt with the shabby art of social climbing or felt stranded in the myriad complexities of massive modern bureaucracies can appreciate the pointed satire of Mayakovsky's plays.

VLADIMIR MAYAKOVSKY

Early in his career, Mayakovsky wrote three articles calling for the rejection of realistic theater in favor of a theater that would combine the elements of dance and rhythmic speech to "give expression to powerful emotions." Such an expression is found in Mayakovsky's first drama, *Vladimir Mayakovsky*. In the summer of 1913, on cigarette boxes and scraps of paper, Mayakovsky feverishly scribbled verses, which later developed into a drama with the working title "The Railroad," perhaps inspired by the suicide of one of Mayakovsky's fellow boarders who threw himself under a train. Though this suicide motif is introduced into the drama, the play focuses on many personal reflections of the author.

In fact, *Vladimir Mayakovsky* is a monodrama in which there is only one character—Mayakovsky, the suffering poet. The other "characters" are all dreamlike reflections of various elements of his ego. The play, which has no clear plot, is a series of long interior monologues written in fractured verse. With a painted city in the background, Mayakovsky takes center stage, while various cardboard, masklike characters surround him with pleas, observations, and exhortations.

Although the play is not a tragedy per se, it has many elements of a traditional tragedy. First, the drama is structured like a classical tragedy with a prologue, an epilogue, various choral speeches, and long monologues describing offstage violence. More important, the play follows the ritual structure of tragedy. Mayakovsky, the scapegoat hero, offers his "soul on a platter to be dined on by future years" and bares his neck to the "wheel of a locomotive." Surrounded by a chorus of maimed characters suffering from an emotional blight, Oedipus-like Mayakovsky with his "foot swollen" addresses his supplicants as "my children" and, arrayed in his toga, sacrifices their tears "to the dark god of storms." Finally, the drama exposes the fatalistic philosophy of tragedy as the protagonist refers to the people as "bells on the dunce cap of God" and, in an ironic twist, announces that "somewhere in Brazil, most probably there is one really happy man."

This early drama picks up some of the themes and techniques that Mayakovsky developed in his later plays. First, in typical Futuristic style, the play calls for the destruction of past cultures. Second, Mayakovsky presents a future-oriented visionary who invents slicing machines while his friend develops traps for bedbugs. Third, the play abounds in images of urban technology. By stroking cats, one character produces electricity to make the streetcars rush and the lights glow. Finally, the play addresses a revolution, in which people are chopped up on plates from "fancy salons," and a postrevolutionary period, in which a poet-prince declines the laurel wreath and takes up the woes of his people. In later plays, Mayakovsky explored the triumphs of revolution and the dangers of postrevolutionary backsliding.

In *Vladimir Mayakovsky*, Mayakovsky showed his flair for theatricality. In the play's production, actors carrying cardboard masks popped out to say their lines, while Mayakovsky, dressed in a yellow tunic, intoned his lines from a rostrum. According to one critic, the play contained shouts, howls, and the simulation of a trance. Also, the set consisted of a futuris-

tic view of an urban landscape that had no connection with the play's content. Mayakovsky was on his way to building a theater of spectacle.

Produced, directed, and acted by Mayakovsky, *Vladimir Mayakovsky* opened in 1913 to mixed reactions. Mayakovsky outshouted catcalls; reviewers found the performance mediocre, and one fellow Futurist found the show flat. Yet one audience member issued a reaction that could sum up the effect of all of Mayakovsky's dramas: "I had come to make fun of a clown and when the clown suddenly started talking about me the laugh froze on my lips."

MYSTERY-BOUFFE

During the Revolution, Mayakovsky created propaganda posters and "living newspapers" and, according to one of his comrades, dreamed of "a revolutionary mass theatre of the future where thousands of people as well as hundreds of cars and airplanes would fill a gigantic arena creating for millions the vision of say, the heroic epic of the October Revolution." *Mystery-bouffe* is a scaled-down attempt to recreate exactly such an event. The world has sprung a leak, causing a worldwide flood. Rushing to the North Pole are the two classes: the Clean, represented by various world rulers ranging from the Negus of Abyssinia to the English prime minister, Lloyd George, and the Unclean, represented by the workers of the world. When the Pole floods, the Unclean build an ark for both groups. Yet, plagued by food shortages, the wily capitalists try to trick the workers into subservience by creating a monarchy. When this ploy fails, the capitalists establish a "republic," but the workers, realizing that they will be ruled by "A czar with a hundred mouths," throw most of the Clean overboard. Inspired by the Man of the Future, who promises them that they will inherit the earth, the Unclean overthrow Hell and Heaven—Hell is not as horrible as the atrocities of imperialist wars, and Heaven is filled with ineffective visionaries. Having stolen the thunderbolt of the Lord of Hosts, they return to an earth plagued by Chaos, whom the workers destroy in order to open the way for the earthly paradise.

In *Mystery-bouffe*, Mayakovsky continues to explore the cosmic vision he set forth in *Vladimir Mayakovsky*. This time, instead of creating mock tragedy, he parodies the structure of the medieval mystery cycle, which includes the Flood (worldwide revolution), the storming of Hell (the refuge of the bourgeois), the conquest of Heaven (the haven of idle speculators), the final victory over Chaos (stagnation), and the coming of the New City (the earthly paradise). As well as parodying the mystery cycle, Mayakovsky, in true primitivist fashion, condenses the history of class warfare from autocracy to socialism into a few comic scenes. Thus, by going beyond the narrow confines of realism, Mayakovsky created a comedy with historical vision.

Just as he did in *Vladimir Mayakovsky*, Mayakovsky introduces a visionary. The Man of the Future, a secular messiah, hands down a new Sermon on the Mount, promising an earthly paradise full of technological wonders. Thus, in *Mystery-bouffe*, as in his other major dramas, Mayakovsky views the world of the present from the eyes of a future generation. He also praises the marvels of a mechanized world. Chaos, the enemy of humanity, devours machines and gobbles up railroads, whereas the workers, the real saviors of the new world, keep the locomotives running and the steamships whistling. Nowhere is Mayakovsky's utopian vision more clearly defined than in his picture of the earthly paradise, a world of skyscrapers with trains, streetcars, and automobiles "wrapped in rainbows."

In true propagandist style, Mayakovsky caricatures the enemies of Communism: the greedy capitalists, who are useless baggage in the world of the future; the compromising Mensheviks, who would sell out world revolution; the inactive intellectuals, who fawn over the passive ideals of Leo Tolstoy and Jean-Jacques Rousseau; and the Soviet merchants, who are throwbacks to the old order of bourgeois capitalism. Mayakovsky even instructed his actors to exaggerate the actions of the Clean and to play the Unclean workers in a heroic fashion.

Perhaps the greatest significance of *Mystery-bouffe* lies in the collaboration of Mayakovsky and Meyerhold. Together they transformed the stage from a two-dimensional, photographic representation of reality into a constructivist circus with ropes, platforms, cylinders, and a host of tumbling performers who brought the world of the stage into the audience. Nevertheless, *Mystery-bouffe* was a failure. The play was criticized for being abstract and unintelligible. Certainly, from the perspective of the late twentieth century, the drama is heavy-handed and dated, but Mayakovsky himself recognized this fact when he instructed future generations to alter the play's content to fit their needs.

THE BEDBUG

In the early 1920's, Mayakovsky completed some agitprop skits (satiric playlets that combined topical events with jingles, cartoon-tableaux, and circus antics). Not until late in the decade did he complete another major play. When the revolutionary fervor died down, Mayakovsky turned his satire inward on the Soviet regime of the New Economic Policy. In *The Bedbug*, he satirizes those Soviet backsliders who had reverted to the crude and vulgar lifestyles of the bourgeois. Prisypkin, a worker with calluses on his hands and a union card in his pocket, is seduced into guzzling vodka, playing sentimental songs, dancing the foxtrot, and following other reactionary bourgeois pursuits. Changing his name to Pierre Skripkin and jilting his proletariat girlfriend, Zoya Berezkina, Prisypkin marries Elzevira Renaissance, a grotesque sex symbol ("Each breast weighs eighty pounds, I'll bet!") with affected French mannerisms. Their wedding at the Renaissance beauty salon is a mixture of maudlin sentimentality, conspicuous consumption, and all-out drunken debauchery, ending up in a brawl and a fire that reduces the beauty salon and everyone in it to ashes.

Prisypkin's unscathed body, buried under the ice, is discovered in the futuristic world of 1979. The power structure in this highly organized, completely sanitized society resurrects Prisypkin only to find out that he infects their society with such bad habits as drinking vodka, engaging in modern dances, and falling in love. Finally, the people capture Prisypkin, along with the bedbug he has brought with him, and put him in the zoo, where he is displayed as *Philistinius vulgaris*. In desperation, Prisypkin urges the audience to join him, but his plea is dismissed as a fit of lunacy.

In *The Bedbug*, Mayakovsky again attacks the enemies of socialism by creating grotesque caricatures.

In Oleg Bayan, the effete, self-indulgent poet who teaches Prisypkin how to wiggle his behind correctly and scratch his back discretely, Mayakovsky lampoons Vladimir Sidorov and other such reactionary poets of his time, who not only recognized their doubles onstage but also demanded an apology. The Renaissance beauty parlor revealing its tawdry decor of hair tonics, curling tongs, and perfumes; the hawking merchants peddling everything from lamp shades to sausage balloons; and the odious gang of parasites indulging in debauchery and creating havoc—all create a dismal picture of life under the Soviet regime of the New Economic Policy.

This dismal picture does not end with the present society, however, for in *The Bedbug*, even Mayakovsky's utopian future comes across more like an Orwellian dystopia than an earthly paradise. It is a sterile, automated world with mechanical voting arms, mass meetings, and elaborate cleansing and purifying paraphernalia. Even worse, it is an emotionless world where love is defined as a pathological condition. According to one account, Mayakovsky had to testify that his play was not a satire on the socialist future, but a fantasy world that was purified but not purified enough to withstand the infectious habits of Prisypkin.

This play also illustrates Mayakovsky's use of theatricality. In Meyerhold's production, actors marched through the audience hawking bras, and the performer playing Prisypkin created a thick-lipped, slit-eyed, fat-bellied, pigeon-toed grunter. The set consisted of everything from the kitsch art of the period to the futuristic scenery of metal, plastics, and glass, accented by flashing lights, blaring microphones, and flickering film projectors. Mayakovsky's theater of spectacle contained everything from temperance propaganda to clown acts. The production of *The Bedbug* attained moderate success although it played to mixed reviews. Though heavy-handed at times, *The Bedbug* is a clever satire in the tradition of Molière, and it is still Mayakovsky's most popular play.

THE BATHHOUSE

The Bathhouse, Mayakovsky's last play produced in his lifetime, is his most vicious attack on his own contemporaries. This time, Mayakovsky targets the Soviet bureaucrat. Pobedonosikov, a paper-shuffling, cliché-mouthing, indifferent bureaucrat surrounded by boot-lickers and incompetents, is too busy to deal with the problems of ordinary people, so when Chudakov, an inventor, gets caught in red tape and bureaucratic shuffles in his effort to obtain a patent for his time machine, he sneaks the machine into Pobedonosikov's apartment. The machine is accidentally triggered into action, producing the Phosphorescent Woman, a Communist prototype from the year 2030, who paints a picture of a glorious Communist future and promises to take all qualified Communists there. Only Pobedonosikov and his cohorts are left behind as Pobedonosikov discovers that he and his kind are "not needed for communism."

Vladimir Lenin, father of the Bolshevik Revolution, wrote "Our worst internal enemy is the bureaucracy," and Communist Party decrees in Mayakovsky's time had already criticized the cumbersome Soviet bureaucracy. Mayakovsky's attack, however, was deadly and personal. When asked why he titled the play *The Bathhouse*, he flippantly remarked, "Because it is the one thing the play doesn't have." Yet later he wrote, "*The Bathhouse* washes bureaucrats." It does, indeed. Pobedonosikov lets needy people wait in endless lines outside his door while he shuffles papers and dictates wordy, nonsensical memorandums. Instead of conducting important business, he uses his contacts for personal advantage, spouts meaningless clichés in bureaucratese, and chastises his wife for not keeping up appearances. He is depicted as "scum" that must be washed out of the system.

Pobedonosikov, however, is only one part of a complex system. Accompanying him are a host of unconcerned clerks who spend their days screening him from the people, and boot-licking artists who try to paint heroic portraits of him. Everywhere in the play there are official bureaus with lengthy acronyms, but nothing ever gets done. People with genuine demands are informed that they should not be "pestering a big government agency" with their "petty problems." Projects are left unfinished, plans unformulated, and people frustrated, while socialism becomes a "matter of bookkeeping."

As in other Mayakovsky satires, the present is evaluated through the eyes of the future. The Phosphorescent Woman praises the true Communists who have struggled against a world of "parasites and enslavers." She promises a new age of technological transformations in which labor will move "from the assembly line to the control panel—from the file to the comptometer." Yet, before such utopian transformations can be accomplished, Pobedonosikov and his crew must be purged from the system.

In *The Bathhouse*, Mayakovsky again attacks the theater of his day. In a Pirandello-like third act, Pobedonosikov becomes a character watching the play about himself. Pobedonosikov complains to the director that he has been presented in a "bad light," that the caricature of him is "unnatural" and "not lifelike." He and his cohorts demand a drama of "poeticized reality." In this clever piece of metatheater, Mayakovsky attacks the realistic school of the Moscow Art Theatre as well as the Russian ballet theater, which tried to "poeticize" life. He reduces the objects of his satire to grotesque types, breaks with fourth-wall realism, and tries to jar his audience into action. Again he tries to create a theater of spectacle that will magnify, not mirror, reality so as to "transform the boards of the stage into a rostrum."

Yet *The Bathhouse* was Mayakovsky's theatrical downfall. It not only flopped, closing after three performances, but it also outraged Mayakovsky's enemies, who accused him of writing abstract dramas for coterie audiences and of failing to create heroic workers who would overcome the bureaucracy. Even Mayakovsky himself was not satisfied with his comedy and was willing to accept criticism, yet he defended his plays as "dramatic material of real value." Soon after the closing of *The Bathhouse*, Mayakovsky killed himself.

MOSCOW IS BURNING

Shortly after his death, *Moscow Is Burning*, Mayakovsky's last dramatic work, was produced on April 21, 1930. The drama, having been written to commemorate the Revolution of 1905, is a propaganda spectacle filled with slogans, fireworks, circus acts, and grand marches. In *Moscow Is Burning*, with its cast of five hundred, Mayakovsky went beyond theatrical satire and finally created a circus spectacle. This comedy has little literary merit and depends more on performance antics and improvisation than on genuine satire.

OTHER MAJOR WORKS

POETRY: *Ya*, 1913; *Oblako v shtanakh*, 1915 (*A Cloud in Pants*, 1945); *Chelovek*, 1916; *Fleita-pozvonochnik*, 1916 (*The Backbone Flute*, 1960); *150,000,000*, 1920 (English translation, 1949); *Pro eto*, 1923 (*About That*, 1965); *Vladimir Ilich Lenin*, 1924 (English translation, 1939); *Khorosho!*, 1927 (*Fine!*, 1939); *Vo ves' golos*, 1930 (*At the Top of My Voice*, 1940); *Polnoe sobranie sochinenii*, 1955-1961 (13 volumes); *Mayakovsky: Poems*, 1965; *Poems*, 1972.

SCREENPLAYS: *Ne dlya deneg rodivshiisya*, 1918 (adaptation of Jack London's novel *Martin Eden*); *Baryyshnya i khuligan*, 1918; *Serdtse kino*, 1926; *Dekadyuvkov i Oktyabryukhov*, 1928.

NONFICTION: "Kak rabotaet respublika demokraticheskaya," 1922; "Kak delat' stikhi?," 1926 (*How Are Verses Made?*, 1970).

BIBLIOGRAPHY

Briggs, A. D. F. *Vladimir Mayakovsky: A Tragedy.* Oxford, England: W. A. Meeuws, 1979. This biography of Mayakovsky covers his life until his suicide as well as examines his works. Bibliography and index.

Payne, Robert. Introduction to *Mayakovsky: Plays.* Reprint. Translated by Guy Daniels. Evanston, Ill.: Northwestern University Press, 1995. The introduction to this translation of the major plays of Mayakovsky provides some critical analysis and a description of his life. Bibliography.

Stapanian, Juliette R. *Mayakovsky's Cubo-futurist Vision.* Houston, Texas: Rice University Press, 1986. Stapanian discusses the Futurism presented in Mayakovsky's work. Bibliography and index.

Terras, Victor. *Vladimir Mayakovsky.* Boston: Twayne, 1983. Terras presents a biography of Mayakovsky, along with analyses of selected works. Bibliography and index.

Paul Rosefeldt

MARK MEDOFF

Born: Mount Carmel, Illinois; March 18, 1940

PRINCIPAL DRAMA

The Wager, pr. 1967, pb. 1975

Doing a Good One for the Red Man, pr. 1969, pb. 1974

The Froegle Dictum, pr. 1971, pb. 1974

The War on Tatem, pr. 1972, pb. 1974

The Kramer, pr. 1972, pb. 1976

When You Comin' Back, Red Ryder?, pr. 1973, pb. 1974

The Odyssey of Jeremy Jack, pr., pb. 1974 (with Carleene Johnson)

The Ultimate Grammar of Life, pr., pb. 1974

The Halloween Bandit, pr. 1976

Children of a Lesser God, pr. 1979, pb. 1980

The Hands of Its Enemy, pr. 1984, pb. 1987

The Majestic Kid, pr. 1985, pb. 1989

The Heart Outright, pr. 1986, pb. 1989

Big Mary, pb. 1989

The Hero Trilogy, pb. 1989

Stumps, pr. 1989, pb. 1995

Stefanie Hero, pr. 1990, pb. 1994

Kringle's Window, pb. 1994

The Homage That Follows, pb. 1995

Showdown on Rio Road, pr. 1996, pb. 1998 (with Ross Marks)

Crunch Time, pr. 1997, pb. 1998 (with Phil Treon)

Road to a Revolution, pr. 2001

Tommy J and Sally, pr. 2002

OTHER LITERARY FORMS

In addition to his plays, Mark Medoff wrote the screenplays for the films *Children of a Lesser God* (1986, with Hesper Anderson), *Clara's Heart* (1988), *The Majestic Kid* (1988), and *City of Joy* (1992). A story he wrote is anthologized in *Prize College Stories* (1963), and his first novel, *Dreams of Long Lasting*, appeared in 1992.

ACHIEVEMENTS

Although some of his early works found their way to the Off-Broadway circuit, Mark Medoff's real achievement rests with his Tony Award-winning *Children of a Lesser God*, the first major play since *The Miracle Worker* to depict deafness onstage, but unique in that the play was written to be played by a deaf actress, Phyllis Frelich. Written in a stunning dramaturgical style, in which the speeches are signed in American Sign Language, Medoff explores not only the love story of the two protagonists but also the hidden assumptions about "being different" that can result in prejudices in the "normal" person.

The 1980 Tony Award was added to the Drama Desk Award and the Outer Critics Circle Award the same year; it was Medoff's second Outer Critics Circle Award, the first coming from *When You Comin' Back, Red Ryder?*, which also won an Obie Award and the Jefferson Award. A Guggenheim Fellowship in 1974-1975 allowed Medoff to pursue his writing while holding a faculty position at New Mexico State University. The film version of his play has also garnered many awards, including the Academy Award for Best Actress.

However, Medoff should not be categorized as simply the author of a moving, popular play. Throughout his career, he has examined masculinity and the victimization of women, the contemporary state of the American West, and the way people are tempted by ambition and competitiveness even though these drives can more often than not be bad for their character. Medoff pioneered the dramatic exploration of a sort of Western identity that became very much in the air in the 1970's. This is a vision of the American West inflected by defeat and disillusionment in Vietnam and the contemporaneous social changes taking place on the home front, but that still retains a sense of the old mythic themes of the West, such as the vastness of the landscape, an epic stoicism, and a cleansing violence.

BIOGRAPHY

Mark Howard Medoff was born to educated parents (his father a physician and his mother a psychologist) and was educated at the University of Miami and at Stanford University. Intending to undertake a writing career, he gradually moved toward teaching and found unexpected rewards. While pursuing his professional playwriting career, he advanced in academia, chairing the Department of Drama at New Mexico State University, a position that would allow him to mount college productions of his work before attempting professional productions in the regional or New York market.

Medoff is an adoptive Westerner, which brings his work about the West both advantages and disadvantages. He moved to New Mexico in 1966 after life spent in far more metropolitan areas. Rather than seeing this position as a grim exile to be hurriedly escaped from by obtaining a permanent position at a more conveniently located college, Medoff took New Mexico as an opportunity. He saw that here he had a taproot into the American spirit at its most stark and elemental. Medoff would have been a brilliant play-

Mark Medoff in 1974. (AP/Wide World Photos)

wright in any event, but his living in New Mexico gave him his subject.

Medoff's relationship with Phyllis Frelich and her husband, Robert Steinberg, began in 1977, when Medoff promised Frelich, an accomplished deaf actress, to write a play for her. The resulting three-year collaboration moved to Broadway after Steinberg and Frelich helped Medoff refine the play's ideas into a finished script. John Rubenstein replaced Steinberg for the Broadway run, winning a Tony for his work, as did Frelich. After a long hiatus, during which Medoff wrote and rewrote his next two works, *The Hands of Its Enemy* was performed Off-Broadway to mixed reviews, with Frelich again cast as a deaf person and with Steinberg as her interpreter. *The Heart Outright* received a workshop production at the American Southwest Theatre Company, where Medoff served as artistic director from 1984 to 1987. Medoff also worked with Frelich in *Road to a Revolution*.

The Hero Trilogy, consisting of *When You Comin' Back, Red Ryder?*, *The Heart Outright*, and *The Majestic Kid*, was published in 1989, with an introduction by the author. His film work includes *Clara's Heart* (1988) and *City of Joy* (1992), as well as the screen version of his own play, *The Majestic Kid* (1988). He has received many awards, including the Media Award of the President's Committee on Employment of the Handicapped and an Oscar Award nomination for Best Screenplay for *Children of a Lesser God* in 1987.

In 2000, Medoff became professor emeritus of theater at New Mexico State and took up a position as adjunct professor of theater at the University of Oklahoma as well as serving as a consultant in theater to the English department of the University of Mew Mexico.

ANALYSIS

Because of his practice of carefully rewriting every detail of his work and testing it in readings and workshops and because his academic duties limit his writing time to the mornings, Mark Medoff has only a modest number of plays to his credit. Although some theatrical stylization is also present (as in his early *The War on Tatem*, in which a narrator helps the audience through several years of a young man's experiences, or in *Children of a Lesser God*, in which time is condensed by eliminating blackouts and other theatrical devices, allowing characters to move in and out of the stage frame at will), Medoff stays with realistic plots and psychologically believable characters. Although on the surface Medoff deals with a variety of topics, placing his plays in quite different locales and social settings (a college dormitory room, a restaurant, a home for the deaf, a rehearsal stage, and the like), certain themes gradually emerge in Medoff's work as concerns that are central to the playwright's artistic vision and as recurring motifs important to understanding the larger ideas of his plays. Three major concerns can be discerned: the journey to self-realization, violence as an event that precipitates that journey, and the relation of language to meaning, in its ability to obfuscate as well as its limitations for full communication.

Deafness is a built-in metaphor for all Medoff's themes, in that the deaf person must suffer not only the handicap but also the prejudices of the hearing public, who perceive deaf persons as somehow less than whole, as if the inability to speak the oral language somehow precludes their experiencing the same emotions and having the same thoughts as the hearing. This violence done to the deaf makes them highly sensitive to the limitations of all communication.

In Medoff's plays, he often expresses a concern with the manipulation of language to achieve his characters' ends. In every play, the dialogue hinges on wordplay: vague references, subtle and obscure distinctions in the language, and a preciseness on the part of one character in order to intimidate another, less verbally accomplished person. Some of the battles are entirely verbal for a large part of the play. In *The War on Tatem*, for example, Louis does everything that he can, verbally, to avoid and then to ameliorate the actual fight, and he succeeds until his brother, less verbal and less cowardly, gets Louis to act on his principles with something besides words. The entire conflict of *The Wager* centers on Ward's ignorance of the subtleties of the (often unspoken) dialogue between Leeds and Honor. A typical line,

showing how Leeds can manage the language to suit his ends, is: "You think I'm cleverer than you think I am, when in fact you think I'm cleverer than I am. And that's one of the reasons why I'm king and you clean the stables." Leeds, too, is possibly hiding something from himself. Hints of homosexuality or impotence are sprinkled through the play, and his ultimate discovery may be that his attraction to Honor may finally bring his sexual preferences to the surface. In *Children of a Lesser God*, the entire action revolves around the question of whether Sarah is somehow obligated to learn to read lips or whether she has a right to stay within her own range of expression and expect others to enter into it. The mode of communication becomes the arena of conflict not only for Sarah and James but also for Sarah and the "real" world of the hearing.

The single most important aspect of Medoff's plays is the discovery by the protagonist of his or her own identity, a discovery often precipitated by the introduction of the possibility of violence. All of his plays are really moments when the search for self is intensified by circumstances. *Children of a Lesser God* is not merely James's play, in which he discovers that deaf people are whole people; it is, most important, a journey taken by Sarah into articulating a truth for herself, one that has lain embedded in her anger and defensive attitudes. When she tells James about the "joining" that they can never have, she is telling herself for the first time as well. The whole "speech" to the panel is in fact her manifesto for her future, and she comes to it only after her relationship with deafness is replaced by her relationship with James. It is no coincidence that James's last name is Leeds, the name of the character in *The Wager*, because in both cases a man hurries to assumptions about a woman, who must during the course of the action set him straight about those assumptions. Honor and Sarah are alike, too, in that they both are clearheaded about their defense systems against humanity but must discover who they are during the play itself. They both become more satisfied with themselves after the male (in both cases Leeds, a name that takes on significance in the abstract) helps them through the complexities of self-argument.

THE WAR ON TATEM

Thematically, there seems to be an underlying sense of incipient violence in many of Medoff's plays. The early one-act play titled *The War on Tatem*, far from a fully mature work, begins the exploration of a theme that seems to follow Medoff from play to play in steadily more sophisticated form. The "war" is a gang war in Miami Beach, between adolescents who do not even know the function of a gang but know only that they must "fight it out" for some sort of vague control over an even vaguer territory. Here is the primeval impulse toward winning and keeping a territory; the young boys make a comedy of an inclination that becomes deadly serious a few years later in urban areas and that carries with it the seeds of nationalism and war. Tough-guy King Myron sends his challenge to Louis Dunbar via messenger. Louis, the leader of a sorry group of youngsters known as the Tatem Perch, knows that a showdown is inevitable, but he avoids it as long as he can, with glibness and clever talk. When, however, Myron picks on Louis's little brother, Louis sees that it is time for action. He gets a bloody nose for his trouble, but the lesson is learned and a reputation is saved. Most important, Louis comes to know things about himself that he carries with him into adult life and, as twenty-year-old narrator, explains in retrospect to the audience.

THE WAGER

From this modest beginning, Medoff continued to explore the basic human trait of avoidance of violence. His notion is clearest in the two early full-length works that made their way to New York: *The Wager* and *When You Comin' Back, Red Ryder?* In *The Wager*, for example, two college men, Ward and Leeds, lounge in their dormitory room discussing the possibility of seducing Honor, the wife of a neighbor, Ron. Very early, and for no immediately explainable purpose, Leeds carries a revolver, an image that shadows the play as it moves toward its climax, exaggerated in a second-act scene in which Honor's husband brandishes a machine gun. The play moves within the possibilities of violence; Leeds is described in a stage direction: "A dangerous explosiveness rages beneath his very cool exterior." The sense is that un-derneath the complex patina of social conventions lies the ever-present possibility of physical violence, which exposes all the hypocrisy behind which normal personalities hide from raw forces. The "dance" of word games, double entendres, subtle reverse psychological ploys, and the like is interrupted by the unequivocal burst of energy implied in the violent act.

THE KRAMER

The Kramer is an allegory of power relationships reminiscent of the work of Harold Pinter. It reveals Medoff as not simply a social realist but also someone concerned with the clash of principles on a suprapersonal level. Art Malin, a hapless, ordinary man, is manipulated by the brilliant but demonic Bart Kramer into acting amorally. Kramer urges Malin to be unfaithful to his wife and to generally exploit people. Unlike in most of Pinter's plays, the intended victim of the ontological scam fights back. Malin stands up to Kramer and tells him that he will not have his values distorted or preyed on. Yet his escape has been a narrow shave, as Kramer's promise of an alleviation of his mediocre condition was surely a temptation for Malin.

WHEN YOU COMIN' BACK, RED RYDER?

Violence bursts to the surface in *When You Comin' Back, Red Ryder?*, a play that explores more directly and visually the question of bravery and cowardice in the face of danger. Teddy, a dangerous man who is making his way across the country by his wits, confronts the self-protective and falsely safe inhabitants of a run-down wayside restaurant. At stake—besides the very expensive violin held "hostage" by Teddy throughout the play—is the presence or absence of bravery in the face of violence: Stephen, a frightened young man, is forced into humiliating acts before his girlfriend, Angel, and in the process discovers his own manliness. Teddy is not so much a real threat as he is the embodiment of all the threats to one's comfortable mental existence, a challenger not simply to the body but also to protective attitudes and self-deceit. Nor is Teddy a simpleminded brute; his cruelty is calculated and clever, and it stems from a rudimentary but accurate understanding of how humans act toward one another. He instinctively senses the affection of Angel for Stephen and forces Stephen to "look bad" in front of her.

The violence he does to the married couple Richard and Clarisse, who have stopped for breakfast, is parallel to the Stephen-Angel plot: Richard is forced by Teddy to choose his wife's humiliation over the dollar value of the violin; when he turns his back on Clarisse, the false values of their marriage are exposed. It should be remembered, however, that Richard has been shot (a flesh wound) by this time and that Teddy still holds the gun, so the choice is not as simple as the wife chooses to interpret it. The dilemma, however, does seem to expose the duplicity and thinness of the marriage. Thus, Teddy, without destroying the violin, destroys the marriage. Ironically, after Teddy's departure, Richard himself destroys the violin in anger and as a gesture of what he has lost. Like Stephen, however, Clarisse is freed by the violence of the events to identify herself, finally, as a whole person no longer burdened with the falseness that the marriage forced on her. Thus, Medoff's plays explore how honest the characters are with themselves, given a situation that forces them to back away from all the facades and face who they really are behind the masks of social acceptability. Although on the surface the plays are about violence, they are in fact about the realizations that come from the introduction of violence to an otherwise false and superficial life. Acting as a catalyst for the reaction that lies dormant within the human personality, violence, like agitation in a test tube, begins the chain reaction that results in a satisfaction, a neutralizing, of the disparate "chemicals" of the human personality.

CHILDREN OF A LESSER GOD

Children of a Lesser God is about minorities faced with the choice of whether or not to join the mainstream. As such, it is relevant not only to deaf people but also to women, African Americans, Latinos, Asians, gays and lesbians, and other American minorities. *Children of a Lesser God* is particularly salient in a feminist perspective. As a person with a disability, Sarah is assigned, because of her disability, a vulnerable and dependent position parallel to the one traditionally assigned to women, a category to which she also belongs. Sarah has to face the decision of whether to "join" James and therefore the mainstream or remain true to her previous identity. However, she also has to come to terms with the way in which she is genuinely disadvantaged and disempowered. This realization must be made before Sarah can come to terms with her own predicament. Long before the academic alignment of disability and gender studies, Medoff had arrived at an intuitive apprehension of their congruence.

THE HANDS OF ITS ENEMY

The themes of self-awareness and the difficulties of verbal communication are continued in Medoff's next play, *The Hands of Its Enemy*, in which a stage director guides a woman on her journey to self-realization. The title refers to the existential saying "Life is in the hands of its enemies." Here, the play-within-a-play form is employed as a device for exploring the ways in which a novice playwright (a deaf woman, played by Frelich in New York) hides the truth from herself about a violent incident in her past. As the rehearsals progress on her autobiographical play, the director admonishes her for writing a "little revenge play" instead of a "large play about domestic violence." The playwright has written a play about a wife's revenge on her husband, instead of about the pain and violence of her own experience. This self-disguise of one's real anguish is central to all Medoff's plays. He sees his characters as exposing themselves to themselves in the course of the play.

CRUNCH TIME

Toward the end of the 1990's, Medoff cowrote two plays, *Crunch Time* with Phil Treon and *Showdown on Rio Road* with Ross Marks. Though there is no way of knowing for what portion of the plays Medoff was responsible, the two works do have similar themes. One of them is the metaphor of team sports as a way to discuss competitiveness and community in contemporary America. The other is how children growing up are often repressed or constrained by socially normative identities.

In *Crunch Time*, after Coach Larson, the beloved coach of the local high school women's basketball team, dies, he is replaced by Fluffy Murdock, who claims to have formerly been an assistant coach with perennial college basketball powerhouse Duke University. Murdock stuns the star of the team, Robyn Wingstrom, by jettisoning Coach Larson's ethic of interdependency and team play. He urges instead a more ruthlessly competitive approach. Murdock is revealed to be a satanic figure who threatens harm to Robyn's beloved grandfather if she does not adhere to his philosophy. Robyn, though, manages to con Murdock into thinking she has adopted his point of view when she really has not. In this way, she wins the game and (for the moment) vanquishes Murdock. At the end of the play, she is reunited with her grandfather (who had been hospitalized, then disappeared) and her boyfriend Brendon. As her grandfather helps Brendon with his paper on the Vietnam War, a sense of generational continuity and social fellow-feeling is reconstituted, dispelling Murdock's devilish individualism. Medoff and Treon capture the grain of what it feels like to be an American teenager—the clothes they wear, the food they eat, and the way they talk. *Crunch Time* was a very relevant play to the time in which it was produced, a time that Medoff and Treon imply was plagued by vindictive self-aggrandizement. *Crunch Time* served to enlighten audiences in a time in which the prominence of women's sports was growing along with worries about competitiveness among child and teenage athletes and their parents.

SHOWDOWN ON RIO ROAD

Showdown on Rio Road concerns Victor, a teenage gang member from Brooklyn who moves to New Mexico. There, he finds socially conformist teenage identities of machismo and assertiveness that conflict with his interest in playing the piano, which he worries people will see as effeminate. Mirroring this conflict, Big Meat Boyle, the feared gang leader whose reputation percolates throughout the earlier portion of the play, is in fact revealed to be a girl named Marilisa. At the end of the play, teenage stereotypes are dispelled and everyone gets to be the constructive, healthy citizens they really wish to be. This conclusion is a a rare victory for incipient civilization over looming barbarism in Medoff's and much other contemporary American drama. Although the sociological portraits seem to come from an earlier era, perhaps the 1950's, the slang and reference used by the teenagers are completely of the 1990's. Both

Crunch Time and *Showdown on Rio Road* are presumably intended for performance by high school theater students, yet they raise issues relevant for a more general audience.

ROAD TO A REVOLUTION

Shortly thereafter, Medoff returned to the theme of deafness and to working with Phyllis Frelich. *Road to a Revolution* concerns the controversy in 1988 at Gallaudet University, the renowned university for deaf students in Washington, D.C., when the students demanded a deaf president. Premiering at Deaf West Theater in Hollywood, *The Road to Revolution* expands Medoff's exploration of disability as a marker in the way people construct power relationships. As the deaf students fight for their rights, they learn that disability does not mean disenfranchisement. A rare example of student revolution in the 1980's, the Gallaudet students' struggle is an inspiration for marginalized people everywhere. More straightforwardly political than *Children of a Lesser God*, Medoff's play lacks some of the earlier work's dramatic power—perhaps because *Road to a Revolution* was originally conceived as a film script. *Road to a Revolution* went on a national tour in spring, 2002.

TOMMY J AND SALLY

In 2002, Medoff had a new play premiered by the Woolly Mammoth Theater Company in Washington, D.C., under the direction of Paul Devin Baker. In *Tommy J and Sally*, Medoff explores the tangled racial legacy of American history and memory. The title alludes to president Thomas Jefferson's rumored sexual liaison with his African American slave, Sally Hemings, which became prominent in late 1990's headlines as historians unearthed new evidence and reanimated debate ensued from all quarters. Here, the races are reversed: Tommy J (played in the premiere by Craig Wallace) is a black man obsessed by the celebrity allure of Sally Hemmings (Medoff changed the spelling from the historical person), a white, bubbly blonde star pop singer played in the Woolly Mammoth production by Sue Anne Morrow. Tommy breaks into Sally's room, thinking that he knows her under another name. The play is quite remarkable; it is a phantasmagoric reverie that uses historical themes as an abstract template to underline a thoroughly contemporary and independent drama. It can be compared to another play on similar issues, Suzan-Lori Parks's *Topdog/Underdog*, which won the 2002 Pulitzer Prize in Drama. Medoff might have been expected to simply replay themes from the 1970's, the era when his drama received the most public acclaim. Instead, *Tommy J and Sally* shows he has remained, albeit very neglected, at the cutting edge.

Medoff is most linked to the cultural climate of the 1970's. Had American literature and culture continued on the path they seemed to be on in 1980, Medoff might well be a seminal American playwright. His last four plays, including *Tommy J and Sally*, show him regaining the element of relevant social commentary that so intrigued his earlier audiences. This may animate a comeback. As it is, his work, though obscure other than for *Children of a Lesser God*, offers a vivid and various portrait of the late twentieth century United States.

OTHER MAJOR WORKS

LONG FICTION: *Dreams of Long Lasting*, 1992.

SCREENPLAYS: *Children of a Lesser God*, 1986 (with Hesper Anderson); *Clara's Heart*, 1988; *The Majestic Kid*, 1988; *City of Joy*, 1992; *Homage*, 1996 (adaptation of his play *The Homage That Follows*); *Santa Fe*, 1997.

RADIO PLAY: *The Disintegration of Aaron Weiss*, 1977.

BIBLIOGRAPHY

Barnes, Clive. "*Children of a Lesser God* Flows Like a Symphony." Review of *Children of a Lesser God*, by Mark Medoff. *Post* (New York), March 31, 1980. Barnes states that in any season this play would be "a major event, a play of great importance, absorbing and interesting, full of love, understanding and passion." Finds it to be "a play that opens new concepts of the way of a man with a woman, and even new thoughts on the means and matter of human communication."

Erben, Rudolf. *Mark Medoff.* Boise, Idaho: Boise State University, 1995. This fifty-five-page pamphlet by a German scholar is the most comprehensive and authoritative work available so far on Medoff. Though *Children of a Lesser God* is highlighted, coverage is given of Medoff's entire career. Erben, a seminal figure in Medoff studies, provides not only plot summaries but also interpretive discussions. Published in a series on Western writers, Erben's work places Medoff in the context of the reconsideration of Western myths and images that took place in the 1970's and afterward. Also contains an extensive bibliography listing academic pieces, not just newspaper articles.

_____. "The Western Holdup Play: The Pilgrimage Continues." *Western American Literature* 23 (February, 1989): 311-322. A study of "hold-up" plays, among them *The Petrified Forest*, the 1935 Robert E. Sherwood play, which introduced the genre. *When You Comin' Back, Red Ryder?* is almost a sequel to the Sherwood play; like Mantee, "Teddy is a mixture between cowboy and gangster." Stephen's and Angel's sexual reunion, ten years later, is the subject of *The Heart Outright*. The genre is an offshoot of the "Lifeboat or Snowbound" dramatic convention.

Holden, Stephen. "Mark Medoff Tells of Softness in a Macho World." *The New York Times*, May 21, 1989, p. A68. A penetrating analysis of *The Heart Outright*, "a psychological melodrama in which Stephen's fighting spirit is severely tested and found wanting." Holden believes that the "themes of machismo and cowardice in American life" are not fully explored, and the central character is "a gentle soul in a barbaric Cowboys and Indians environment [who] merely wants to do the decent thing."

Kerr, Walter. "The Stage: *Children of a Lesser God.*" Review of *Children of a Lesser God*, by Mark Medoff. *The New York Times*, March 31, 1980, p. C11. A favorable but reserved review of the Longacre Theater opening on Broadway. Cites the provocative opening of the play, a misdirection by the character, around whom the play is built. "We remain eager to know what last barriers can be broken down," Kerr states, but "as the committed couple begins to run into difficulties, so does the dramatist."

Medoff, Mark. *The Hero Trilogy*. Salt Lake City: Gibbs Smith, 1989. A collection of *When You Comin' Back, Red Ryder?*, *The Heart Outright*, and *The Majestic Kid*, with individual introductions to each play, plus an introductory autobiographical essay, "Adios, Old West," in which

Medoff remarks on his relationship to Western heroes, his views of women, film directors, and other matters.

Thomas J. Taylor,
updated by Nicholas Birns

HENRY MEDWALL

Born: England; fl. 1486-1500
Died: Place unknown; after 1501

PRINCIPAL DRAMA
Fulgens and Lucres, pr. c. 1497, pb. c. 1513-1519
Nature, pr. c. 1500, pb. c. 1530
The Plays of Henry Medwall, pb. 1980

OTHER LITERARY FORMS
Henry Medwall is known only for his two plays.

ACHIEVEMENTS
Henry Medwall was the first vernacular dramatist in English, and he wrote two of the most significant plays in the history of English drama. *Fulgens and Lucres*, the first vernacular play to be printed in England, is also the first to show the influence of classical antiquity, the first on an entirely secular theme, the first in which a woman is the central character, the first—aside from the Wakefield Master's *Secunda Pastorum* (fifteenth century; commonly known as *The Second Shepherds' Play*)—to incorporate an extensive secondary plot, and the first English romantic comedy. *Nature*, a Humanist morality play, is notable for its lively characterizations of the Vices, its allusions to contemporary London, and the excellence of its verse.

BIOGRAPHY
Henry Medwall's London origins are reflected in his works' occasional references to the unsavory haunts of his native Southwark. He probably came

from a family involved in the cloth trade. From 1475 to 1480, he attended Eton as a king's scholar and proceeded to King's College, Cambridge, where he studied for three years. His precipitate departure, without his taking a fellowship, may have been a result of the shift in political power on the accession of Richard III. He continued to dine occasionally at King's and more than once was present at theatrical performances there on feast days. In London, he entered legal service, either with John Morton, bishop of Ely, later archbishop of Canterbury and chancellor of England, or with Oliver Kyng, both of whom were prominent in government after Henry VII's accession in 1485. He was definitely in Morton's employ by 1490, when he was ordained to minor orders of acolyte and dean. In 1491, Cambridge granted him the degree of master of civil law. In 1492, he received a benefice, the living of Balinghem near Calais, which he held in absentia. A grant of another living, in Norfolk, was never ratified.

Morton, who became a cardinal in 1493, died in 1500, after which Medwall's career seems to have ended. After he resigned his living in 1501, nothing further is known of him. There is no indication on the title page of *Fulgens and Lucres* as to whether he was still alive; the description of him as "late chaplayne to. . .John Morton" may merely refer to the ending of his appointment.

Because he never took full orders, the extent of Medwall's ecclesiastical employment is uncertain. His chief legal occupation was as notary public, and he seems to have reached a position with Morton of considerable power and trust, for he was the keeper of important records after Morton's death. His attachment to Morton's household, where Thomas More was in youthful service, and the printing of his two plays by John and William Rastell, suggest that he was associated with the circle of John Rastell and John Heywood.

ANALYSIS

Henry Medwall's plays reflect the aristocratic, humanistic, social, and political preoccupations of their audience, as well as the physical conditions under which they were performed. Drawing on diverse dramatic and intellectual influences, they achieve remarkable unity and focus and succeed in their purpose of combining entertainment and instruction. Although the dearth of extant plays from this period makes it difficult to judge the extent of Medwall's innovativeness, it is possible to appreciate his dramatic genius in its own right and at the same time to use his plays as an index to the progress of dramatic form and to theatrical conditions in the court drama of his time.

Both plays were probably written for performance in the Great Hall at Lambeth Palace, the residence of Medwall's patron, Cardinal Morton, at banquets during winter festivals. The audience (aside from the servants) was aristocratic and intellectual and included, if passing references in both plays are to be credited, women as well as men. The situation was an intimate one, with the dining audience seated at tables on three sides of the hall and the play taking place in the center of the floor, down the length of the hall, with entrances through the two doors in the screen at the end opposite the high table (possibly raised) where sat the host with his chief guests. The play took place, therefore, in the midst of the audience, and Medwall shows his genius in adapting and exploiting this close relationship to manipulate the relationship between reality and illusion and to provide humor.

FULGENS AND LUCRES

In *Fulgens and Lucres*, Medwall makes a virtue of the physical closeness that renders illusion impossible. The play begins as two characters, differentiated only by the speech prefixes "A" and "B," step forward, apparently from the audience, to anticipate the coming performance and summarize the plot. When the rival suitors of the main plot enter, A and B take service with them and proceed thereafter to shift in and out of the play, discussing its moral and intellectual argument and mediating between it and the audience. Medwall uses A and B to guide his audience's response to the play's moral theme.

The main plot is based on Buonaccorso da Montemagno's treatise *De Vera Nobilitate* (c. 1428), translated into English by John Tiptoft, earl of Worcester, about 1460 and printed by Caxton in 1481. Lucres, daughter of the Roman senator Fulgens, is sought in marriage by Cornelius Flavius, a dissolute aristocrat, and Gayus Flaminius, a virtuous commoner. Her father leaves the choice to her, and she urges the suitors to plead their respective cases in a debate, intending to choose the suitor who proves himself more noble. In the source, this debate takes place before the senate, and no decision is rendered, though the outcome points to Gayus. Limitations of cast size and considerations of dramatic interest and focus led Medwall to have Lucres herself be the audience and judge of the debaters, thus providing English drama with its first heroine. Her decision in favor of Gayus is announced in the play.

The play considers a moral question: the source of true nobility. This was a particularly topical matter because Henry VII's government restrained the power of the old nobility and promoted accomplished commoners, such as Morton, to high office. The emergence of this new class encouraged a strong interest in Humanism, which emphasized innate virtue. Because Medwall's audience must have included both old and new nobility, he took pains to avoid offending either. He distanced the argument by setting it in ancient Rome, and the brunt of his criticism is directed not at Cornelius's inherited nobility but at his abuse of it by indulgence in ostentation and pride, theft, murder, riot, and sloth. Lucres makes it clear that honor with inherited nobility is preferable to honor without it, but when the ideal is unavailable, as in this case, honorable poverty is preferable to dishonorable nobility. Her insistence that her decision applies to her case alone and is not to be taken as a general rule provides a critically neutral setting for exploring the question. Finally, that A and B disagree with her conclusion admits the possibility of disagreement, although Medwall has steered the audience toward agreeing with Lucres by characterizing her as intelligent and virtuous and placing the opposite opinion in the mouths of A and B, who are scurrilous rogues without honor or nobility.

It may be no coincidence that virtually the first subplot in an English play originated in a household in which young Thomas More, as a page of fourteen, used to get up and improvise merry parts for himself during the Christmas plays, as his son-in-law and biographer William Roper tells us. Whether More's antics inspired in Medwall the idea for A and B or whether More may even have played one of them is unknown. In any event, their shifting character and status allow Medwall to control the audience. The illusion of their improvisation makes A and B seem more "real," and their comic confusions therefore achieve a sense of spontaneity, while being carefully controlled by the author.

A and B provide a comic parallel to the main plot and prepare for the coming debate by prefiguring it. As servants of Gayus and Cornelius, they become rivals for the affections of Lucres' serving maid Joan, who puts them to a test as Lucres has done with her suitors: They must show their relative merits. This they proceed to do in a song contest, a wrestling match, and a mock tournament, which seems to involve beating buttocks with blunt spears (perhaps mops or brooms), with the competitors' hands tied. Joan, comically apostrophized as "flower of the frying pan," is the "lady" honored by the joust. Like Lucres, she exercises control over the two suitors, eventually rejecting both. Although the elevated tone of the main plot allows no outlet for expression of the physical side of love, A and B's scatological jokes in their wooing of Joan fill this need and express the license appropriate to Christmas revelry.

In structure, the play falls into two parts. The division was probably occasioned by the exigencies of the dining situation. As A points out at the end of the first part, the members of the audience "have not fully dyned." The first part of the play has been presented between courses of the midday dinner, and at the end of it, A directs the usher to fill the diners' glasses with the best wine, at the request of the "master of the fest" (probably Morton). When the play resumes, it is evidently still the same day, for A refers to the earlier part as taking place "today." Medwall builds this social requirement into the structure of the play by applying the break to the suitors' needs as well: They need time to prepare their speeches. The play is given a natural time scheme: Lucres has appointed the suitors "to be here/ Sone, in the evynyng aboute suppere" to receive her decision.

As the first part presented diversions in song, wrestling, mock tournament, and bawdy jest, the second—the text of which, because of this diversion, is shorter—includes a mummers' dance. As the comic wooing and mock tournament farcically prefigure the suitors' debate, the dance prefigures it romantically (Cornelius offers it as a wooing device). These actions recall the wooing contest of courtly love poetry. By these means, and by the suspense created with the interval, attention is directed to the debate as the climactic event of the play. The intelligentsia, many trained in law, were accustomed to regarding public disputation as entertaining and diverting. The debate itself seems to draw on two earlier traditions: the medieval *demande d'amour* and the classical *controversia*. Medieval love literature often poses a question about love—for example, whether a rich or a wise suitor is preferable—and the question is followed by a debate. The *controversia* was an exercise in pleading by students of oratory and came to be a rhetorical showpiece for the entertainment of lawyers, in which two disputants argued each side of a philosophical question, with the choice (as in *Fulgens and Lucres'* source) left to the audience. In the play, Lucres rounds off the argument by revealing her choice to B, while conflict is avoided by her not being seen to reveal it to the suitors: She intends to write to them. This avoidance of conflict should not be regarded as a dramatic flaw because conflict would distract the audience from the play's main purpose of reaching a resolution to the problem of choice in an exemplum framed to illustrate a moral question.

The conclusion, the choice of Gayus, has been well prepared for in advance by the characterizations and relations of the characters to one another. Cornelius's excess in sartorial ostentation, which exemplifies pride, is revealed in the first part by B. In the second part, B has to rebuke Cornelius for not behaving according to his rank in waiting on the mummers instead of letting them wait on him; this characterizes him as somewhat foolish. Cornelius is undercut in that his message to Lucres is given bawdy signification by B's mistaking of words. Gayus, on the other hand, is portrayed as modest and direct, kind and considerate. In the debate, Cornelius offers Lucres a life of idleness. Gayus's speech expresses his piety and his military and political activity, and he promises Lucres moderate but sufficient wealth and harmony of disposition. The characters' relationships are subtly demonstrated: Cornelius appeals to Lucres' father, and he later approaches her indirectly again in the courtly form of wooing with mummers. Gayus, on the other hand, has a sensitive scene with Lucres herself early in the play and expresses his love to her directly.

Medwall takes and incorporates into the structure of his play traditional Christmas games and entertainments: mummings and disguisings, song and dance, wrestling, jousting, and debate. The parody and the sense of topsy-turveydom characteristic of Christmas revelry in the tournament is apparent in the use of a kitchen wench as its lady, in Cornelius's subservience to the mummers, and in A and B's occasional cheekiness to their noble audience. A and B draw on the seasonal tradition of the Lord of Misrule as leaders of the Christmas games. The inclusion of these elements illustrates A's elucidation of dramatic theory at the beginning of the second part, when he mentions that "Dyvers toyes" are mingled with the substance of the play "To styre folke to myrthe and game/ And to do them solace," so that all the spectators will be pleased, both those that like serious and those that like comic matter. B expresses at the end of the play its other purpose:

> Not onely to make folke myrth and game,
> But that suche as be gentilmen of name
> May be somwhat movyd

> By this example for to eschew
> The wey of vyce and favour vertue;
> For syn is to be reprovyd
> More in them, for the degre,
> Than in other parsons such as be
> Of pour kyn and birth.
> This was the cause principall,
> And also for to do with all
> This company some myrth.

He then brings the audience into the play by inviting them to rewrite it if they wish.

The play's purpose, then, is to entertain the audience and to teach them, by leading them to participate in exploring the moral question so that the ideal of virtue mingled with nobility—hinted at but not realized in the play itself—may reach fruition in them. The shifting relationship of reality and illusion attains this conclusion: The lesson of the play may be taken into the real life of the spectators.

Fulgens and Lucres was probably performed by a small, professional company of four men, with two boys to play Lucres and Joan, unless one boy played both female roles (they do not appear together). That Fulgens appears only at the beginning suggests that the actor playing him had to double as Gayus. It is not known whether this troupe of actors, or the dancers, were permanently attached to Morton's household. The musicians probably were members of the household. Costume, judging from the description of Cornelius's elaborate clothing and the engraving of a well-dressed medieval man and woman that Rastell selected for the title page, was contemporary and, along with the jokes, the place references, and the characters of A and B, would have added topicality to the moral. The dominant verse form is rhyme royal, but there is a colloquial fluency in the comic sections achieved through the rhythm, the division of stanzas between speakers, and the use of slang and colloquial expressions. It has been suggested that because there is a Spanish dance and a line of Flemish in the mumming section, the play was written in 1497 to honor a visit of the Spanish and Flemish ambassadors, but this is very tenuous, and the tone is better suited to a less formal occasion. There is no evidence permitting closer dating.

NATURE

Though there is no evidence of *Nature*'s having been composed later than *Fulgens and Lucres*, it was published later. *Fulgens and Lucres* was published by John Rastell, who, in printing what appears to be the first vernacular play in English, embarked on a daring venture. *Nature* was published some twenty years later by his son, William Rastell. It is in line with the native English morality play, which patterns the journey human beings make through life, from their birth into the world as its ruler, through their succumbing to sin, to their salvation through contrition, confession, and adoption of virtue. A conflict for the mastery of humankind's soul is carried on between personified virtues and vices. Humankind, whose personal attributes the Virtues and Vices represent, is passive between them, though in *Nature* it is not lacking in characterization. In *Nature*, the Virtues and Vices prepare an offstage battle, but the audience does not see them in conflict with each other. There is a dramatic cause for this in that humankind's backsliding after virtue has won it over gives the play its structure, and a theatrical cause in that the actors probably doubled as Vices and Virtues. Medwall innovatively conceives of the relationship of Man to his attendant virtues and vices as that of a ruler in relation to his courtiers. He uses a political metaphor to symbolize the human state as the Virtues and Vices offer themselves as attendants to Man sitting on his throne.

There are two concurrent structural patterns in *Nature*, as in other moralities of the period, a construction that foreshadows that of William Shakespeare's *Henry IV* (pr. c. 1597-1598). Over the course of the play, there is a progression through the ages of humankind, from birth through maturity to old age. The cycle of temptation, fall, and redemption, however, is repeated, as it may be in the life of a person. It appears once in the first half, at the end of which Man suddenly repents, without apparent motivation, and again in the second, when age has made sin impossible.

The opening of the play, in which Nature, a medieval deity, after a long speech on natural order, sends Man to the World with Reason on one side and Sen-

suality on the other, advising him to take Reason as his chief guide, is based on John Lydgate's poem *Reson and Sensualyte* (c. 1430). Medwall takes this as his starting point, his vantage point from which to explore dramatically the age-old conflict of the Vices and Virtues. In so doing, he makes sin the result of unreason: Man banishes Reason and thus becomes prey to the Vices. The play proceeds from this point more compactly and clearly in its allegory and its line of action than the poem does.

The play was apparently performed in the same setting as *Fulgens and Lucres*, the Great Hall, with its entrance doors through which the actors come and go, and the winter fire. Unlike *Fulgens and Lucres*, however, the first half occurs at night, with the second apparently taking place on another day. The time scheme, which encompasses the whole life of Man, is telescoped. The opening is more ceremonial than that of *Fulgens and Lucres*: The World enters with Worldly Affection, who carries the garments Man is to don, and sits down silent. Then Nature, accompanied by Man, Reason, Sensuality, and Innocencye, enters, sits, and begins to speak. Nature advises Man and sends him on his journey to the World (actually from one end of the hall to the other), where he is dressed and ascends the World's throne. He begins as a pious ruler, submissive and grateful to God. In selecting his court, however, he dismisses Reason and Innocencye, retaining as advisers Worldly Affection and Sensuality. The Deadly Sins, beginning with Pride and Bodily Lust in the first half and all the others in the second half, find easy access. They are disguised, in traditional fashion, as Virtues: Pride as Worship, Lechery as Love, Wrath as Manhood, Gluttony as Good Fellowship, Sloth as Ease, Envy as Disdain, and Covetousness as Worldly Policy.

Vice is most clearly exemplified in the character of Pride, who is dominant among the Vices. The chief manifestation of sin, as in *Fulgens and Lucres*, is sumptuous dress. Man's first assumption of apparel is not essentially sinful; it signifies the conferring of rulership and majesty. At the same time, however, it signals temptation. Pride, who is dressed in garments exactly echoing those of Cornelius, will purvey to Man far better garments. During the play's first half, these are in the making, and in the second half, Man's wearing of them signals a descent into deeper sin. Sumptuous dress is culpable not only because it indicates personal vanity and addiction to changing foreign fashion but also because it supports the exploitation of the poor. As with Cornelius, it signifies poor stewardship of worldly goods. Medwall thus expresses support for Henry VII's policies against livery and maintenance and in favor of fiscal moderation.

Like *Fulgens and Lucres*, *Nature* is a didactic play, giving advice not only to people generally but specifically to the ruling class. Like Medwall's other play, it is varied with mirthful elements, though it does not contain extensive subsidiary entertainments. Particularly diverting are the vividly salacious descriptions of Man as a haunter of the stews, where, as a tavern customer, he consorts with the whore Margery in the first part, and in the second, jests with Sensuality and Bodily Lust about Margery, who has missed him so much during his temporary sojourn with Reason that she has joined a "convent," the Green Friars, where entrance is free to all men. The characterization of the Vices, especially in the second half, provides diversion as well as the chief dramatic interest. They muster troops for a battle against Reason. Medwall has made their defeat and desertion of Man dramatically powerful in showing that it has an internal cause, springing from their own characteristic weaknesses. After mastering Man, they defeat themselves and each other and desert the field. Bodily Lust is disinclined to go anywhere near blows and bloodshed. Gluttony comes in, like Falstaff in Shakespeare's *Henry IV*, with a bottle and a cheese as his sword and buckler and expresses his intention of keeping out of the way of gunshot. Sloth is afraid and feigns sickness. Wrath storms off in a rage, though he does not actually desert. Envy, resenting Pride's ostentatious appearance, sends him off in a dudgeon with a false report that Man has taken away his office.

With the disappearance of the Vices, the dramatic aspect of the play ends. Man, by reason of age, can no longer sin actively; the Vices have gone to seek a new master. He can approach only Covetousness to wait on him, but Covetousness is busy with church-men. Reason leads Man to be addressed by the Virtues in turn and encourages him to continue in the path of virtue, and the play ends as "they syng some goodly ballet," this harmony contrasting with the discord of the Vices.

Again, the basic verse form is rhyme royal, but the play is remarkable in containing the first example of prose speech in English drama, an aside by Pride to Sensuality. The language of the Vices is dynamic and colloquial, that of the Virtues formal and measured. In several places, notably Nature's opening speech, the verse rises to heights of quite notable poetry. Metrical ease and rhythmic unobtrusiveness are among Medwall's virtues. A rather interesting feature of the original printed text is the marking of caesuras, which seem to designate pauses for the actor, so it is possible to gain some idea of the pacing and rhythm of speech. The more colloquial speeches have fewer of these and seem therefore to have been spoken rapidly.

The setting is contemporary London, with its peculiarly urban haunts of vice, and again the costume, judging from Pride's apparel, is contemporary. The Vices talk familiarly to the audience, as do A and B (who exhibit some characteristics of the morality Vices), insulting them and asking them for favors, and there are references to the hall setting and furniture. The cast is larger than that of *Fulgens and Lucres*, requiring at least eight or nine players. That Innocencye is addressed as both a boy and a woman may suggest that he was played by a boy dressed as a woman. He could have doubled as Pride's son Garcius.

Until the twentieth century, Medwall's reputation was low, and it was believed to have been poor in his own day, because of a fabricated account by John Payne Collier of Henry VIII's walking out in boredom during a performance of *The Finding of Truth*, a supposed play by Medwall. The discovery in 1919 of the sole surviving copy of *Fulgens and Lucres* and the exposure of the fabrication led to recognition of his significance. *Nature*, which has been known to specialists since the beginning of the seventeenth century, has been, until recently, somewhat in the shade critically because of the bias against morality plays. The success of performed moralities, however, and an increasing tolerance of religion and ribaldry on the stage have allowed it, too, to be given its critical due. Medwall is now appreciated for his dramatic flair, his linguistic vitality and rhythmic ease, structural tightness, vivid characterization, good jokes, and especially for the way in which he controls his material, shaping traditional elements to his central purpose while giving them fresh life and guiding the responses of his audience to his moral themes and to his humor.

BIBLIOGRAPHY

Medwall, Henry, and M. E. Moeslein. *The Plays of Henry Medwall: A Critical Edition.* New York: Garland, 1981. The section on Medwall's life is dotted with general information about Tudor England that is not immediately or definitely applicable to the dramatist. Contains a consideration of the language, style, and versification in the plays, a discussion of Medwall's literary reputation, and a separate introductory section for each play with extensive commentary. Lengthy and in the main valuable, but with extraneous comments. Includes an appendix for life records and illustrations. Unattractive format.

Nelson, Alan H., ed. *The Plays of Henry Medwall.* Totowa, N.J.: Rowman and Littlefield, 1980. Contains a substantial amount of material on Medwall's life, including connections with the powerful cardinal John Morton and the young Thomas More. Offers interesting comments on the morality play technique and the language of Medwall's two surviving plays. Includes a listing of documents pertaining to Medwall's life, texts of both plays with notes and a glossary, and illustrations.

Reed, A. W. *Early Tudor Drama: Medwall, the Rastells, Heywood, and the More Circle.* 1926. Reprint. New York: Octagon Books, 1969. Establishes Medwall's place at the very beginning of the new drama developing just before 1500. Discusses Medwall's relationship with Cardinal John Morton and possible connections with Thomas More. Presents information on Medwall's association with John Rastell, himself a playwright, who printed *Fulgens and Lucres*, and whose son William printed *Nature*.

Whall, Helen M. *To Instruct and Delight: Didactic Method in Five Tudor Dramas.* New York: Garland, 1988. Sees *Nature* as a failure (too instructive and insufficiently delightful) and *Fulgens and Lucres* as a success (highly didactic; marvelously entertaining, and almost perfect). Medwall's source for his best play is viewed as a product of Renaissance rhetoric, oratory and debate, and Medwall's best play is found to be gently persuasive, with its concepts of true nobility presented with diplomacy and good humor.

Arthur Kincaid,
updated by Howard L. Ford

MENANDER

Born: Athens, Greece; c. 342 B.C.E.
Died: Piraeus, Greece; c. 291 B.C.E.

PRINCIPAL DRAMA

Orge, 321 B.C.E. (*Anger*, 1921)
Samia, 321-316 B.C.E. (*The Girl from Samos*, 1909)
Dyskolos, 317 B.C.E. (*The Bad-Tempered Man*, 1921; also known as *The Grouch*)

Perikeiromenē, 314-310 B.C.E. (*The Girl Who Was Shorn*, 1909)
Aspis, c. 314 B.C.E. (*The Shield*, 1921)
Epitrepontes, after 304 B.C.E. (*The Arbitration*, 1909)
Comedies, pb. 1921
The Plays of Menander, pb. 1971

OTHER LITERARY FORMS

Menander is not known to have written anything but comedies.

ACHIEVEMENTS

Though not extremely popular in his own lifetime—winning only eight victories in the dramatic festivals at Athens—Menander was lionized in the generations following his death as the greatest of some seventy authors of New Comedy. He was the acknowledged leader in the canonical triad of New Comedy writers recognized by Hellenistic critics: Philemon, Diphilus, and Menander. The fact that of the comic writers only Menander's work survives in any quantity among the papyrus rolls of Egypt attests his overwhelming supremacy among readers in the Hellenistic and Roman periods. Further evidence of his influence is his survival in the Latin adaptations of Plautus and Terence, for whose plays he was not the only but a favorite source. As the first grand master of domestic, romantic comedy, Menander can claim through his Roman imitators a vast literary progeny that includes William Shakespeare, Ben Jonson, Molière, Restoration comedy, P. G. Wodehouse, and even the flood of situation comedy that gluts the modern television screen.

Perhaps because his plays were not included in the traditional school curriculum of late antiquity, Menander did not survive the decline of learning in the Middle Ages. Where texts of more edifying authors such as Homer and Sophocles found their way into the monastic libraries of Western Europe before the great libraries of Byzantium were burned, Menander's work was completely lost, and until the twentieth century nothing was known of him directly save for a few quotations. Only his reputation survived, so that such Romantic philhellenes as Johann Wolfgang von Goethe were tempted to extravagant—but highly speculative—estimations of his literary worth. Following Napoleon's entry into Egypt in 1798, the infant science of papyrology began investigating hordes of papyrus texts—used for mummy wrappings, stuffed in the hides of alligators, and stored in long-buried libraries—and in 1898, the first lines of Menander appeared in the form of eighty nearly complete lines of the *Georgos* (fourth century B.C.E.; the farmer). It was not until the twentieth century, with the discovery in 1905 of the Aphroditopolis papyrus and its publication two years later, that Menander reentered literary history with considerable parts of *The Arbitration*, *The Girl Who Was Shorn*, and *The Girl from Samos*, and smaller fragments of two other plays. The subsequent trickle of fragments was punctuated dramatically in 1959 when a papyrus acquired by a Swiss collector, M. Bodmer, added *The Bad-Tempered Man*, the most complete text so far, to the corpus. Smaller important accretions came in 1965 and 1969, bringing the usable total of Menander up to a plump three-hundred-plus pages (F. H. Sandbach's 1972 Oxford Classical Text), but even this collection became technically obsolete in 1977 with the publication of some hundred lines from the beginning of the *Misoumenos* (fourth century B.C.E.; the man who was hated). By this process, Menander has become antiquity's "new" author, virtually unknown until the twentieth century and still coming out in newly discovered bits as if he were a contemporary playwright. The rediscovery of Menander is a continuing process, and few are willing to predict that it will end soon.

Critical appraisal of Menander has been shaped by the slow recovery of his plays, the piecing together of his fragments into plausible reconstructions, and the comparison of Roman adaptations with Menandrian originals (or scraps thereof). Conclusions likely to stand the test of still further discoveries can now be studied against the background of adequate textual evidence. Judgments characterizing Menander as "the last great poet of Athens" or "the final flower of Athenian genius" (T. J. P. Williams) are safe enough: Alexandria replaced Athens as the center of literary activity in the Hellenistic era (323-332 B.C.E.), and the sheer craftsmanship of Menander's language, characterization, and scene building are now beyond serious doubt. Some may prefer to reserve words such as "great poet" and "poetic genius" for poets of a weightier genre than New Comedy, and most readers will agree that Menander pales beside the great master of Old Comedy, Aristophanes, who died some sixty years before Menander began writing. On present evidence it seems unlikely that Menander will regain the eminence he enjoyed in late antiquity. Rather than attempt to find in his works the qualities of a world-class author, it is more profitable to consider the character of his achievement in its historical context.

Old Comedy reached its peak at the end of the fifth century B.C.E. with Aristophanes, who brought the talents of a uniquely gifted poet to an irreverent, obscene, and politically satirical dramatic ritual. As the Athenian love affair with public life soured in the fourth century, Aristophanes' last plays lost some of their topicality and licentious pugnacity. All but a few scraps of a transitional Middle Comedy have been lost, but it appears that mythological travesty, romance, melodrama, and domestic comedy became the popular stage material. Euripides had already broached the clear distinction between tragedy and comedy in *Alkēstis* (438 B.C.E.; *Alcestis*, 1781), *Helenē* (412 B.C.E.; Helen, 1782), *Iōn* (c. 411 B.C.E.; Ion, 1781), *Iphigeneia ē en Taurois* (c. 414 B.C.E.; *Iphigenia in Tauris*, 1782), and *Iphigeneia ē en Aulidi* (405 B.C.E.; *Iphigenia in Aulis*, 1782). Consequently, Euripidean echoes in Menander are probably nothing new, as Euripides was the most popular of the great Attic tragedians in the century following his death. Type characters such as the cunning slave, the braggart warrior, the gold-digging *hetaera*, and the loquacious cook were a common stock-in-trade of the dramatic tradition inherited by Menander. Given the absence of actual plays from those sixty years between Aristophanes and Menander, however, it is impossible to tell exactly when and how "New" comedy appeared and how it affected the development of Menander's art. Beyond any doubt, Menander's plays are mainstream New Comedy, and for later writers he was the definitive master of the form, but the process of give-and-take that constitutes every artist's relation to his form is now lost.

One aspect of Menander's contribution to his age that deserves special mention is the rational and humane values that underlie all his extant writing. For those who view him from a modern perspective, this quality is best described in terms of the classical humanism that flourished in late antiquity. For Me-

nander's contemporaries, the word was *philanthropia*; it included the virtues of altruism, compassion for folly as well as suffering, an attachment to family values, and a determination to defend the rights of humanity that cut across barriers of wealth, age, and class. The weak side of such a philosophy is a sentimental unwillingness to accept the human capacity for evil. Its obvious strong side made Menander the most popular spokesperson of civilized values in the ancient world: "I am a human being; I consider nothing human to be alien to me."

BIOGRAPHY

Little of the information or gossip that has survived has a direct bearing on Menander's work. The *Suda* (a literary and historical encyclopedia compiled around the end of the tenth century C.E. and preserving, albeit in corrupt form, much ancient scholarship) describes him as an Athenian of good family, son of Diopeithes and Hegestrate. The comedian Alexis (by some accounts his maternal uncle) is said to have taught him his craft, and Diogenes Laertius says that he studied philosophy under Theophrastus, Aristotle's successor as head of the Peripatetic school. Although politically inactive himself, his political associations with the oligarchic faction in Athens brought his career and even his person into danger on at least one occasion. A scholiast to Ovid's *Ibis* (after 8 C.E.; English translation, 1859) preserves the story that he died by drowning while swimming at the Piraeus. Plutarch reports that he was at the height of his powers when he died. A well-to-do family background fits the subjects of Menander's plays, who are generally prosperous citizens and their associates, slaves, concubines, and parasites. The connection with Theophrastus is also plausible: Theophrastus's sketches of eccentric types in *Charaktēres* (fourth century B.C.E.; *The Characters*, 1699) are sometimes very close to Menandrian personalities, and there is a general assumption of Peripatetic beliefs about motivation and conduct in the plays.

ANALYSIS

Among the stage conventions that Menander inherited is the five-act structure, which derived from the usual form of classical tragedy as described in Aristotle's *De poetica* (c. 334-323 B.C.E.; *Poetics*, 1705) minus the choral portions: What was formerly prologue, three episodes, and the exodos became the five acts. All that remains of the chorus in New Comedy is unscripted song and dance, a kind of *entr' acte* typically motivated by an actor's exit line referring to the arrival of "a band of drunken revellers." Menander seems also to have accepted Aristotle's dictum that plot is the soul of a drama. Like many truisms about ancient men of letters, this comes in the form of an anecdote. Plutarch records that when asked about his current work in progress, Menander replied, "I've composed my comedy. The plot's worked out—I have only to fit lines to it." It may well be that after designing the action, Menander wrote comedy as rapidly as Shakespeare. He demonstrates a similar fluency of diction, instinct for economy, and rapid, logical movement from act to act. Character is molded to action so that developments in plot are well motivated, and Menander has a special talent for making a single speech or vivid detail serve multiple purposes, such as plot development, revelation of character, and scene painting. This observation has deservedly become a cliché of modern criticism. A deeply classical author in spite of his Hellenistic date, Menander observes the unities of time and place as well as the old three-actor rule, which required that no more than three speaking actors be on the stage at any time. This allowed productions to go ahead with a minimum of trained actors supported by a complement of walk-ons who had no lines to speak.

Menander's plays are realistic in the portrayal of character and behavior, but the slice of fourth century B.C.E. Athenian life that New Comedy represents is paper-thin, exclusively domestic in scope, and hemmed in by convention. The Greek passion for recognition scenes, which can be traced as far back as Homer's *Odyssey* (c. 750 B.C.E.; English translation, 1614), had come to dictate an excessive reliance on coincidence (for example, a citizen's long-lost daughter turns out to be the unfortunate girl whom the boy next door has just saved from the grasp of a repulsive pimp), and Menander's audiences demanded their fair share of unfair stereotypes. Rape plays a surprisingly prominent role in this gentle form of comedy: A young man rapes an unknown girl at a nocturnal festival, or he rapes the girl he loves in order to avoid having to submit to an arranged marriage. All these patterns of character and plot revolve around a single basic situation, repeated with variations ad infinitum in New Comedy. Every Menandrian plot that has come to light has to do with sex, love, and the family. A play may represent the process by which a boy wins a girl in marriage, or that by which married lovers who have been estranged are reunited.

This erotic preoccupation is always within the limits of decency, if one is willing to allow for the curious employment of rape (sometime in the past) as an expedient of plot. Furthermore, sexual love (*eros*) is brought to some kind of resolution with family love (*philia*). Menander in particular is reluctant to let a play end on a note of family disharmony. It is especially important that father be reconciled with son, given the patriarchal bias of Athenian audiences and their dependence on reliable family ties. Beneath the constant fuss over love, sex, and the family, it is not difficult to perceive a social concern that must have been close to Menander's Hellenistic audiences. Throughout most of their history, the Greeks have preferred marriages arranged by heads of households to those love matches that depend entirely on the initiative and inclinations of the couple who marry. Yet, for a period of time beginning in the fourth century B.C.E., cosmopolitan Greeks who could afford the luxury entertained the notion that an ideal marriage was erotically charged; sexual, emotional passion was added to friendly cooperation as a component of such unions. Romantic love emerged as the mythos of such thinking, and New Comedy became its medium. Some of Menander's plays are concerned with the conflict between the morality of arranged marriages and that of love matches. Fathers must be reconciled to their sons' wayward inclinations; plots must be manipulated so that the girl whom the young man marries turns out to be socially acceptable. By whatever means, love must prevail. New Comedy does not herald any sweeping or permanent cultural change among the Greeks. What it does signify is a belief that the union of man and woman should be more than an expedient for pleasure or profit. This idea was to have further development in Western Europe in a later era.

Menander's plays are chiefly about people. Although Menander is an acute observer, his analysis does not go deep: just far enough to suggest depth. As is perhaps appropriate to the medium in which he wrote, he presents credible, lifelike, and seemingly individual characters, sketched in by a series of suggestive details rather than exhaustively presented. The tradition that grew up around him might be called a theater of humanism because of its willingness to look behind the traditional comic masks and find in real people a more satisfying object of entertainment.

THE GIRL FROM SAMOS

None of this means that Menander put ethics before entertainment. Although his comedies reflect the concerns of a thoughtful audience in the midst of cultural change, they served primarily as light entertainment for playgoers who appreciated a well-made play. The stage was set to represent two houses, with sometimes a third house, an inn, or a shrine between them. With this conventional setting, writers often wove their plots around the goings-on in two households; typically a well-to-do young man falls in love with the girl next door. This is what happens in *The Girl from Samos*. The house on the left belongs to Demeas, a rich old Athenian, and his adopted son Moschion. Also in residence is the title character, Chrysis, who is the old man's concubine; a clever slave; and a cook. The house on the right belongs to Niceratus, a poor old Athenian, and his daughter Plangon.

In the first act, young Moschion explains that his foster father, Demeas, has left town on a business trip with his friend and neighbor Niceratus, leaving Chrysis pregnant but with orders to get rid of the child, who would be illegitimate. During the old man's absence, Chrysis has had the baby (because of a break in the text, one does not know whether it was stillborn or abandoned), and Moschion has raped Plangon, the girl next door, during a nocturnal cele-

bration of Adonis Day. As always in comedy, Plangon has had a baby as a result, and the good-natured Chrysis has agreed to nurse this infant as her own in order to conceal Plangon's shame from her straitlaced father and make it possible for Moschion, who is eager to do the right thing, to marry Plangon. Chrysis assures Moschion that Demeas is so much in love with her that she will easily persuade him to let her keep the baby. Moschion's job will be to persuade Demeas to accept Plangon as a daughter-in-law even though she is too poor to have a dowry. As news of the old men's arrival is announced, Moschion shows considerable nervousness. The fathers' conversation as they come in from the harbor reveals that they have independently agreed that Moschion and Plangon should marry, thus by coincidence confirming what the young couple have already decided. As the first act ends, it looks as if nothing stands in the way of a happy ending.

The second act introduces the first complication, in which Demeas is enraged to find out (he thinks) that Chrysis has not disposed of her baby by him, but Chrysis, as promised, persuades him to let her keep it. In the third act, there is a new complication as Demeas learns that the baby is not in fact the one that he sired, but that Moschion is the father. This suggests a love triangle pitting father against son, a common specter in New Comedy that normally turns out to be illusory. Demeas is unwilling to believe that his son would plot against him, and in a rage he expels a bewildered Chrysis for seducing his innocent boy. Chrysis takes refuge next door with Niceratus.

Reversals come thick and fast in act 4. Niceratus and Moschion both remonstrate with Demeas for his harshness with Chrysis, but when Demeas reveals his knowledge that Moschion is the child's father, Niceratus turns on Moschion and goes to his house to expel Chrysis. As Moschion tells his father the truth about Chrysis, Niceratus sees his own daughter suckling the child that was supposed to be Chrysis's baby: Now he is in a rage to find out who dishonored his daughter, and he threatens to kill the baby. Chrysis, carrying the baby, rushes in terror from the house where she has just taken refuge; Demeas astonishes her by offering his house as sanctuary. Now it is Demeas's turn to placate his neighbor: Some god must be the father, and Moschion will make an honest girl of her. In act 5, Moschion, miffed at his father's earlier suspicion that he would intrigue with Chrysis, plans to punish his father by pretending that he will enlist as a mercenary and leave home. Demeas precludes this gesture by apologizing for his suspicions, but he reproves his foster son for forgetting his years of good treatment and being ready to expose Demeas's error to the world. Niceratus ends these reproaches by summoning Moschion to the wedding, which can now be celebrated.

The Girl from Samos is a good example of what Menander and his audiences loved: a complicated plot involving a small number of characters in domestic entanglements over love, moving from one error to another, with each complication bringing some new recognition or reversal and some new good or bad will between the persons involved. It is no coincidence that a description of comic plots elicits phrases that Aristotle used in describing tragedy. Peripatetic theory appears to have had a formative influence on Menander, and his plays sometimes border on tragic situations: The love triangle that seems to Demeas to pit him against his son is reminiscent of Euripides' *Hippolytus* (428 B.C.E.; English translation, 1781), in which Theseus dooms his son in the belief that he tried to rape Phaedra. The art of plot design calls for an exciting series of potentially unhappy developments. Each character perceives some new disaster as the plot goes through its changes, and only the audience knows the whole truth. There are fewer evil people in this world than victims of misunderstanding. Their passions usually rise from a love for father, son, daughter, or lover, and all such passions are lovingly resolved in the end. Menander's care in the representation of character is motivated by a benign perspective of human nature which assumes that to understand is to forgive and that there is always a certain logic in the most bizarre behavior. This view of life's tumult was later to find expression in Vergil's phrase *forsan et haec olim meminisse iuvabit*: "Perhaps sometime it will be a pleasure to remember even these things."

THE BAD-TEMPERED MAN

By virtue of its relatively recent discovery in nearly complete form—it is the only Menandrian play so far to have been recovered intact—*The Bad-Tempered Man* is often the only work of Menander that students of drama read. This is unfortunate, because it is an early effort (317 B.C.E.). Rustic Knemon is a Scrooge type. He lives in a shack near Athens with an ancient slave woman, Simiche, and his innocent daughter Myrrhine, who piously tends the shrine of Pan next door. Myrrhine's mother has long since moved out; she lives on the other side of the stage with her son by an earlier marriage, a worthy young man named Gorgias. This imperfect idyll is disturbed when Sostratus, a wealthy young Athenian out hunting with a companion, sees and falls in love with Myrrhine. All these circumstances are explained by Pan in the prologue.

Act 1 begins as Sostratus tells his friend, the parasite Chaireas, how he sent his slave Pyrrhias to break the ice with the girl's father before making a formal offer of marriage. Pyrrhias runs on in terror: Knemon has flown into a rage at his approach and has chased him off the farm. Pyrrhias exits in a panic as Knemon stamps on and into his house, not as dangerous though every bit as choleric as reported. Myrrhine now comes out carrying a water jug, and a nearly swooning Sostratus is able to fetch water for her. Daos, the slave of Myrrhine's half-brother Gorgias, views this overture with suspicion and vows to see that she is protected.

In act 2, Gorgias warns Sostratus that he will tolerate no improprieties, but Sostratus convinces him of his honorable intentions. He enlists the aid of Gorgias, whose slave Daos (in the hope that this city-slicker will sprain his back and be off) suggests a plan by which Sostratus will impress Knemon by working in the fields like a common farmer. Knemon is prevented in act 3 from seeing this demonstration of worthiness because Sostratus's superstitious mother and his sister Plangon arrive to sacrifice to Pan at the little shrine next door: Their insolent slave Geta and the self-important cook Sikon harass Knemon with requests for various pots that they neglected to bring and are viciously reviled in return. A weary and disheveled Sostratus, who has labored in vain, returns to the scene just in time to hear that Knemon's slave Simiche has dropped a mattock down the well; Knemon flies into another rage—now he must go down the well after the mattock, and his planned day's work is ruined.

As act 4 opens, Simiche hobbles on with the news that Knemon has fallen into the well (much to the cook's delight). Sostratus soon returns with an account of Knemon's rescue, which features his own moonish attentions to the beauteous Myrrhine. Knemon returns and makes a speech in which he acknowledges the error of his misanthropic self-sufficiency; he puts Myrrhine in Gorgias's care and grants half his estate as dowry for her, clearing the way for her betrothal to Sostratus. At the same time, however, he asks to be allowed to live in his old solitary way. Menander thus limits the conversion of the title character, implicitly confirming the Greek belief that basic character does not change. A real transformation in the manner of Charles Dickens' Scrooge is not conceivable in Menander's intellectual framework. The fifth act begins with Sostratus's father Kallipides agreeing to bestow his daughter on the worthy Gorgias with a lordly dowry of three talents, thus making the plot symmetrical: City boy weds country girl, country boy weds city girl. In a strange coda, the city slave Geta and the cook Sikon take their revenge on Knemon for his earlier hostility by harassing him mercilessly for various wedding provisions and forcing him—now a pathetic figure—to go dancing into the shrine of Pan where festivities are under way.

By any reckoning, *The Bad-Tempered Man* must be considered a minor achievement. There is little depth in the presentation of the title character, and the plot shows few of the ironic reversals that enliven *The Girl from Samos*. At best, some of Menander's characteristic preoccupations reveal themselves at an early stage of their development: a love of symmetry, a talent for dovetailing motivations that lock the plot into an organic whole, and an interest in the inner dynamics of personality—in this case, the misanthrope's.

BIBLIOGRAPHY

Frost, K. B. *Exits and Entrances in Menander.* New York: Clarendon Press, 1988. An examination of the dramatic techniques involving entrances and exits used by Menander. Bibliography and index.

Henry, Madeleine Mary. *Menander's Courtesans and the Greek Comic Tradition.* New York: Peter Lang, 1985. A study examining the role of courtesans in Menander's comedies.

Katsouris, Andreas G. *Menander Bibliography.* Thessalonike, Greece: University Studio Press, 1995. A bibliography listing the works on and by Menander. Indexes.

Sutton, Dana Ferrin. *Ancient Comedy: The War of the Generations.* New York: Twayne, 1993. A look at the comedies of Menader, Aristophanes, Plautus, and Terence. Bibliography and index.

Walton, J. Michael, and Peter D. Arnott. *Menander and the Making of Comedy.* Westport, Conn:" Greenwood, 1996. A critical analysis of Menander's work and an analysis of his contribution to comedy. Bibliography and index.

Wiles, David. *The Masks of Menander: Sign and Meaning in Greek and Roman Performance.* New York: Cambridge University Press, 1991. Wiles compares the comedies of Menander with those of Plautus and Terence and looks at the stage histories of Greek and Roman theater. Bibliography and index.

Zagagi, Netta. *The Comedy of Menander: Convention, Variation, and Originality.* Bloomington: Indiana University Press, 1995. A critical analysis of the comedic dramas of Menander. Bibliography and index.

Daniel H. Garrison

LOUIS-SÉBASTIEN MERCIER

Born: Paris, France; June 6, 1740
Died: Paris, France; April 25, 1814

PRINCIPAL DRAMA

Jenneval: Ou, Le Barnevelt français, pb. 1769, pr.
  1781 (based on George Lillo's play *The History
  of George Barnwell*)
Le Déserteur, pb. 1770, pr. 1771 (*The Point of
  Honor*, 1800)
Olinde et Sophronie, pr., pb. 1771
Le Faux Ami, pr., pb. 1772
L'Indigent, pb. 1772, pr. 1782 (*The Distressed
  Family*, 1787)
Jean Hennuyer, évêque de Lisieux, pr., pb. 1772
  (*Jean Hennuyer, Bishop of Lisieux*, 1773)
Le Juge, pr., pb. 1774
Childéric I, roi de France, pb. 1774
La Brouette du vinaigrier, pb. 1775, pr. 1784
Théâtre complet, 1778-1784 (4 volumes)
Le Campagnard: Ou, Le Riche Désabusé, pb. 1779,
  pr. 1790
Le Charlatan: Ou, Le Docteur Sacroton, pb. 1780,
  pr. 1787
La Demande imprévue, pr., pb. 1780 (adaptation of
  David Garrick's play *The Lying Valet*)
L'Habitant de la Guadeloupe, pb. 1782, pr. 1786
  (*The Merchant of Guadeloupe*, 1802)
La Destruction de la Ligue, pb. 1782
La Mort de Louis XI, roi de France, pb. 1783
Charles II, roi d'Angleterre, pb. 1784
Montesquieu à Marseilles, pb. 1784
Portrait de Philippe II, roi d'Espagne, pb. 1785
La Maison de Molière, pr. 1787, pb. 1788 (based
  on Carlo Goldoni's play *Il Molière*)
Le Nouveau Doyen de Killerine, pr. 1788, pb. 1790
Le Ci-devant Noble, pr. 1791, pb. 1792

OTHER LITERARY FORMS

Louis-Sébastien Mercier was an incredibly prolific writer, if somewhat repetitive. He published a
wealth of material in almost every genre that was
used in the eighteenth century and classified his
works according to the following scheme: novels, political treatises, moral or philosophical works, historical plays, dramas, comedies, fantasies, polemics,
newspaper articles, academic discourses, dialogues,
poetry, and translations.

ACHIEVEMENTS

In contrast to his own predictions, Louis-
Sébastien Mercier has been remembered neither as
the prophet of the French Revolution nor as the greatest French author of his time. Nevertheless, the versatile writer did promote ideas that led to the formation
of the new republic, and he is still remembered as the
most outspoken advocate of the eighteenth century's
major theatrical innovation, *le drame*.

Mercier earned this reputation in 1773, when he
defined the new genre in his controversial treatise *Du
théâtre: Ou, Nouvel essai sur l'art dramatique*.
Though he borrowed many ideas for this study, he expressed them with a precision and vigor that set this
study apart from similar eighteenth century works,
including those by the more original dramatic theore-
ticians Denis Diderot and Pierre-Augustin Caron de
Beaumarchais. Mercier's essay was also more provocative than the works that had come before it. Calling for a complete break with the strict neoclassical
tradition, he surprised even his fellow reformers with
the scorn he displayed for such established reputations as those of Jean Racine and Nicolas Boileau.
The document immediately created a scandal, and the
extravagance in Mercier's attacks eventually brought
him ridicule. Nevertheless, in the stifling atmosphere
projected by eighteenth century French theatrical institutions, the young reformer's fervor and audacity
served to encourage his contemporaries in their drive
to reinvigorate stage performance.

A number of the principal elements of *le drame*
have survived to become incorporated into its parent
forms, *la tragédie* and *la comédie*. Since the eighteenth century, for example, the majority of playwrights in all genres have preferred prose to verse
and have felt free to chose protagonists from all

walks of life. Though in his own plays Mercier did not initiate many changes, he did set new standards in the presentation of visual detail, demonstrating exceptional precision both in the marking of stage directions and in the description of scenic decor. Mercier must also be commended for the courage he displayed in his choice of subject matter, for he never feared presenting beliefs that were politically dangerous. Because of their anticlerical and antimonarchist nature, many of his plays were never allowed to reach the stage, but through their publication, he managed to influence both public opinion and the styles of his fellow playwrights.

In spite of the durability of many of their theatrical reforms, however, the specific genre that Mercier and his contemporaries termed *le drame* has survived only in name. The plays that resulted from their theoretical excursions were immensely popular when first performed, but later generations have almost invariably considered them inferior to seventeenth century tragedies. Mercier's own dramas have fared worse than many. In fact, even before his death his reputation was suffering. The playwright's incredible vanity caused him a number of difficulties during his early years, but in consideration of his youth, it was generally forgiven him. Unfortunately, his ego only became more pronounced as he grew older, and he was labeled an eccentric. In his later years, he published a series of invectives against the most established reputations in letters, unwisely predicting that his own name would outlive them all. In addition, he published wild theories on the subject of physics, claiming that his ideas would supplant those of Sir Isaac Newton and Nicolaus Copernicus. A number of critics have argued that, in addition to spoiling his reputation among his contemporaries, this incredible conceit may have contributed to the neglect that his name and works suffered throughout the nineteenth and most of the twentieth centuries. In any case, there has never been a sustained revival of interest in his drama. Conversely, attention has been paid to his prose fiction. Critical reexaminations of this work have shown a Romantic thrust in his writing, and he has been labeled as a native precursor of French Romanticism.

BIOGRAPHY

Louis-Sébastien Mercier was born into and reared in the bourgeois class that, during his lifetime, would bring about the French Revolution. Social and political reforms were dominant themes in all his writing. He demonstrated his literary inclinations early, writing in a popular poetic genre before his twentieth year. Like many of his contemporaries, however, Mercier turned to prose, arguing that it was a more natural means of expression. He would be one of the first dramatists to write in prose.

Before he was twenty-five, Mercier proved his scholarly abilities and was named professor of rhetoric at the College of Bordeaux, but he missed being at the center of activity and soon returned to Paris. He had not been back long before he won a prize for eloquence, given by the French Academy. In the years that followed, he made money doing translations, and he completed his first novel, *L'An 2440* (1770; *Memoirs of the Year Two Thousand Five Hundred*, 1772). In this genre, he gained both his first recognition and his first notoriety as an author: The book was very popular, but it was banned by the authorities.

Mercier did not begin to work for the theater until he was twenty-nine years old, but he became immediately impassioned in his new occupation. His first dramas were taken directly from German and English plays, including those of William Shakespeare. Mercier had always preferred these works to the neoclassical tragedies of his immediate predecessors, and in his first original dramas he incorporated many foreign elements. A number of his contemporary French critics considered these plays too experimental, however, and they did not meet with the success that he would have liked. His treatise *Du théâtre: Ou, Nouvel essai sur l'art dramatique* was in large measure an expression of this dissatisfaction.

The essay created such a scandal that the Comédie-Française halted preparations for his play *Natalie*. When the playwright countered with fierce attacks in pamphlets, the institution took away his membership. Infuriated, he took the directors of the institution to court and lost, but he refused to be beaten. He began to publish his dramas, and they met with much success. Filled with optimism, he took them to be produced outside Paris, and in the years that followed, he enjoyed the greatest triumphs of his career as a playwright. His plays were so popular in other cities in France that he was invited to return to the capital and produce his dramas at one of the Comédie-Française's rival institutions, the Comédie-Italienne. Produced for the first time in Paris, his dramas *The Merchant of Guadeloupe* and *La Brouette du vinaigrier* were major successes, and by popular demand *The Distressed Family* was returned to the stage.

While writing plays, Mercier began the first two volumes of what would be his major prose work, *Le Tableau de Paris* (1782-1788; *Paris*, 1802). Resembling a guided tour through the city, the work contained a number of pointed social criticisms. Like *Memoirs of the Year Two Thousand Five Hundred*, it was very popular with the public but banned by the authorities. Anticipating further censure, Mercier wisely moved to Switzerland, where he finished ten more volumes. *Paris* brought Mercier international recognition and was particularly well received in Germany. During these same years, he published another successful novel, entitled *Mon Bonnet de nuit* (1784). In it he repeated many of his earlier contentions and criticisms.

Anticipating the coming revolution, Mercier returned to Paris in 1788 and began propagating his ideas more directly in two journals, *Annales patriotiques* and *Chronique du mois*. He was named a deputy at the Convention from Seine-et-Oise and sided with the moderates. When extreme factions took hold of the revolutionary government, Mercier fell out of favor and even went to jail, but he escaped death during the Terror and eventually returned to government. In 1795, he was elected to the Council of Five Hundred.

Mercier's eccentricities became increasingly pronounced in his later years. In his legislative position, he inveighed sharply against tributes to both René Descartes and Voltaire, and wrote diatribes against various circles and academics. When he opposed legislation aimed at providing mass instruction, he was nicknamed "Jean-Jacques Monkey," a reference to his admiration for the philosopher Jean-Jacques Rous-

seau. In spite of this derision, however, he was still influential, and in 1803 he was named as a member of the Institute of History and Ancient Literature.

Upon leaving the government, Mercier was named professor of history in the Écoles Centrales in Paris. With more spare time on his hands, he devoted himself to the studies of science and literature, reproducing many of his former criticisms in scholarly articles. Few names were spared his critical treatment: In addition to writers and physicists, Mercier attacked such philosophers as John Locke and Étienne Condillac, as well as the artists Raffaello Raphael and Tiziano Titian. He continued studies he had begun in physiognomy, an eighteenth century pseudoscience, but at the same time he began a study on the nature of language, which, as H. Temple Patterson has pointed out, had an important influence on Victor Hugo. This work Mercier entitled *Néologie: Ou, Vocabulaire des mots nouveaux* (1801).

In 1814 Mercier died in Paris, the capital whose beauty and contradictions he had poignantly captured in his prose fiction. In spite of his eccentricities, he had a few close friendships, and in a state funeral, he was eulogized as an active thinker and a devoted public servant.

ANALYSIS

In his study *Du théâtre: Ou, Nouvel essai sur l'art dramatique*, Louis-Sébastien Mercier put forward the high expectations he had for the stage. Like almost every viewpoint he put forward, his theories on drama must be considered in relation to his political, moral, and social ideas. Associating classical tragedy with the nobility and the monarchy, Mercier stated that the genre's characters, settings, feelings, and modes were alien to the lives of average Frenchmen. In its place, he argued for a theatrical form that would reflect values common to all economic classes. Echoing his fellow reformers, he argued that protagonists in drama should be modeled after honest people from all walks of life, and he asserted that, for the sake of realism, they should speak in prose rather than in verse. In addition, he believed that the theater should open people's lives to new experiences. With particular eloquence, he urged his fellow dramatists to celebrate those moments of greatness and nobility that any person might experience, and he argued with vehemence that theater should serve society's common interests by promoting high moral values.

In practice, the dramatist met a number of these theoretical objectives. For example, he succeeded in staging provocative situations, investing the lives of what would otherwise be termed ordinary characters with dramatic interest. At the same time, however, his plays were by no means provincial. He brought the experience of his wide travels to the Parisian stage, utilizing diverse settings and cosmopolitan casts of characters. Above all, he ensured that his plays promoted moral values, and often his spectators or readers are moved to empathize with the victims of unjust social institutions. At his best, Mercier dramatizes a social problem through the use of well-conceived plots, as in one of his earliest efforts, *The Point of Honor*. Though the play's effect is often diminished by an exaggerated sentimentality, the young deserter's plight exemplifies the inadequacy of an arbitrary military code. In plays such as *The Merchant of Guadeloupe*, Mercier achieves a powerful effect through the opposition of contrasts. In *The Distressed Family*, in which one act is played in the poor family's quarters and another in the rich man's abode, the contrast is sharply portrayed through the visual medium.

To the detriment of his work, however, Mercier was often tempted to subordinate dramatic considerations, using the stage as a platform to air his social and political convictions. This fault is displayed in all his dramas, and sometimes asserts itself as their dominant mode. In the last half of *Jean Hennuyer, Bishop of Lisieux*, for example, the lead character speaks as if he is reading one of Mercier's philosophical papers. Although these plays were very popular when first published and produced, the public's interest in them did not last. Ironically, it is most likely because of the success of the eighteenth century's social and political reforms that these plays can no longer find an audience: There is no longer any novelty in what were, at one time, revolutionary ideas. In many of Mercier's dramas, the playwright's desire to depict life accurately conflicts with a stronger impulse to present moral exemplars. Although it can be argued

that characters such as the selfless notary in *The Distressed Family* are sometimes found in everyday life, the veracity of such thoroughly morally perfect characters as the vinegar merchant in *La Brouette du vinaigrier* is sometimes called into question.

THE POINT OF HONOR

The second original play that Mercier wrote, *The Point of Honor*, was his first to be performed, and it was a huge popular success. It was eventually given a private audience before the royal family. When Mercier offered the play for performance, the question of how to treat deserters was being widely debated; the military's solution was an automatic death penalty. In *The Point of Honor*, Mercier successfully dramatized his reasons for opposing this severe punishment. The action is situated in a small town on the border between France and Germany, where a young deserter, Durimel, has been staying as a boarder in the home of a German woman, Madam Luzère. In the opening scene, an older man, Mr. Hoctau, is asking Madam Luzère for the hand of her daughter, Clary. Though the woman insists that her daughter has already been promised to Durimel, Mr. Hoctau persists because the younger man is French and has no prospects. Insisting that money and nationalism are more important than love is, Mr. Hoctau immediately takes on the role of villain, and his intolerant behavior sets a tone against which the young deserter will appear favorable. In the scenes that follow, Durimel is shown to be a brave and sensitive young man. To Madam Luzère, he explains the reasons for his desertion: When an authoritarian captain for no reason humiliated him, he lashed back in uncontrollable rage; subsequently fearing for his life, he ran.

The play's central conflict begins when the French army comes to occupy the German town, and it becomes necessary to hide Durimel. In the role of villain, Mr. Hoctau turns Durimel over to the French authorities. The action is complicated by the appearance of two officers in the French army, St. Franc and Valcour. Madam Luzère learns that the captain, St. Franc, lost his son when the boy was very young, but she does not suspect that the son could be Durimel. So much of the play is devoted to this revelation, however, that the audience can have no doubt. St.

Franc eventually finds his son, only to learn of the impending execution, but in spite of the young soldier's understandable reasons for deserting, there is nothing the captain can do. In this way, Mercier successfully demonstrates a potential problem inherent in the inflexible law. In addition, the playwright forces his audience to empathize with the situation from two highly emotional viewpoints, that of the father and that of the potential wife.

In the scenes that follow, the other French officer, Valcour, devises a means for Durimel's escape. For a few long scenes, Durimel and his father agonize over the decision of whether to take the opportunity, eventually deciding that their honor is more important than Durimel's life. Durimel forgoes the escape. Mercier certainly introduced these scenes to dramatize the young deserter's nobility and innocence. The device fails, however, for it is unimaginable that the father and son would allow the son's death, especially when the escape has been sanctioned by the other French officer. In Mercier's original ending, Durimel is killed, and the play ends with his father imploring Heaven, but the playwright was persuaded to substitute this ending with a happy one. According to tradition, the suggestion was made by Marie Antoinette.

THE DISTRESSED FAMILY

In much the same manner as *The Point of Honor*, *The Distressed Family* dramatizes an unjust social condition, but the more mature play, Mercier's fifth, was acclaimed for its especially effective use of scenic decor. The drama opens in the wretched living quarters of an impoverished brother and sister, Joseph and Charlotte. Both characters work night and day at the spinning wheel, earning just enough money to survive and to take a little food to their father, who has been unjustly imprisoned. The second act of the play is set in the lush home of their loud, reveling neighbor, De Lys. Utilizing a technique that others would copy, Mercier elaborately described both the incredible wealth of De Lys and the intense squalor of the poor family. More important, the playwright ensured that the conditions were re-created with painstaking detail onstage. The startling contrast between the two settings accurately depicts the disparity of wealth in eighteenth century France.

The settings were meant to strike the audience in the way that paintings do, and with Joseph and Charlotte spinning and complaining about their misfortunes, the play's first act is conspicuously, perhaps intentionally, undramatic. In the second act, however, De Lys reveals that he has had his eye on Charlotte, and the confrontation between these two characters shows Mercier at his best. De Lys is portrayed as a tough, often heartless nobleman, who refuses to consider that he will not have his way with Charlotte. Yet Charlotte is endowed with so much natural beauty and such a similarly unbending will that she successfully resists. Simultaneously attracted to and exasperated by her, De Lys offers her marriage, a proposal she also resists. Unfortunately, however, the quality of the drama deteriorates after this meeting, and eventually Charlotte learns that she is the sister of De Lys, rather than of Joseph. Though the similarity between the fiery Charlotte and the uncompromising De Lys has prepared the audience for this revelation, the plot mechanism that brings it about is too obviously contrived: Abandoned as a child and reared in a poor country family, the young woman only happens to be neighbors with De Lys by chance. The play ends with Charlotte taking half of her real brother's fortune, freeing her father, and marrying Joseph.

LA BROUETTE DU VINAIGRIER

The differences between the living conditions of the rich and the poor are presented with such exaggeration that *The Distressed Family* alternates between highly emotional melodrama and satire. A similar effect is created in Mercier's seventh play, *La Brouette du vinaigrier*. Class distinction is the subject of this drama, in which the young, humbly born Dominique aspires to marry the beautiful and rich Miss Delomer. Miss Delomer shares his tender feelings but knows that her father cannot consent to the union; Dominique belongs to a lower social order. As in *The Point of Honor*, *La Brouette du vinaigrier* opens with the villain, Mr. Jullefort, who wishes to marry Miss Delomer to enhance his already great fortune. By contrast, Dominique's simple but noble love is calculated to make him the favorite.

When Mr. Delomer goes bankrupt, Mr. Jullefort abandons Miss Delomer, and the outcome of the play seems obvious. Interestingly, however, both Dominique and Miss Delomer are still afraid to ask permission to be married, and Mr. Delomer prepares his daughter to be sent to a convent. In this way, Mercier effectively illustrates the residual power of class distinction and the helplessness of his characters before it. At the same time, however, his resolution to the conflict demonstrates one of his recurring weaknesses as a playwright: his willingness to present moral exemplars at the expense of verisimilitude. In *La Brouette du vinaigrier*, the exemplar is Dominique's father, who is the vinegar merchant. At the moment when all seems lost, the father reveals to his son and Mr. Delomer a barrel full of gold. The noble man has been saving all his life for just such an occasion, he has lived simply in spite of his secret wealth, and he is happy to turn it over to the couple so that they can get married.

In addition to complaining that the father's character is unbelievable, critics have argued that this outcome poses no tenable solution to the problems of class distinction. Undoubtedly, Mercier intended that all men should act as the humble vinegar merchant. Yet by providing the other characters with gold, the father does not really force them to alter their rigid views; on the contrary, he provides means by which those attitudes may continue.

JEAN HENNUYER, BISHOP OF LISIEUX

In addition to these often satiric melodramas, Mercier is known for a series of history plays similar to Shakespeare's. A number of Mercier's most important works belong to this category—including *Childéric I, roi de France*; *La Destruction de la Ligue*; and *Charles II, roi d'Angleterre*—but these plays in particular were never allowed to be performed. In fact, only one such play ever slipped past the censors. In *Jean Hennuyer, Bishop of Lisieux*, Mercier builds a drama surrounding the historical events of the massacre of Saint Bartholomew's Day. On this day in 1572, the Catholic king Charles IX signed a peace treaty with the French Protestants, but when their defenses where down, he ordered his troops to slaughter them. In Mercier's historical reenactment, the playwright makes the most of this opportunity to strike at the monarchy, cleverly placing his largely Catholic audience in a Protestant home and focusing on the similarities between French families of either religion. The play opens with a newlywed, Laure, who awaits the return of her husband, Arsenne. Arsenne has gone to Paris with his fellow Protestants to sign the treaty and is late in returning. Like any young newlywed, Laure is concerned over her husband's tardiness, but the other characters, Laure's brother and Arsenne's father and sister, tell her that she must have patience. In this ingeniously constructed situation, Mercier uses his audience's knowledge of the events surrounding the massacre to create the play's tension.

Eventually Arsenne does return, and he relates the events of the massacre to his family and fellow Protestants. From various sources, the assembled characters learn that no Protestants are to be spared, and they prepare to defend themselves. Arsenne's father does not believe, however, that the noble Catholic bishop of Lisieux, Jean Hennuyer, could possibly sanction such an event in his diocese, and he convinces his fellow Protestants to seek refuge in the church. Arsenne's father has guessed right, and the Protestants are spared.

The last half of *Jean Hennuyer, Bishop of Lisieux* illustrates Mercier at his worst. Armed with a historical figure who truly demonstrated exemplary moral courage, Mercier cannot resist the opportunity to turn the play into a polemic. The king's lieutenant tries to force Hennuyer to commit himself to the slaughter, and in keeping with historical facts, the bishop refuses. Rather than dramatizing any doubts or fears that Hennuyer might have had, however, Mercier forces his character to make speech after speech about honor and duty. The bishop is eloquent, as Mercier himself so often was, but there is virtually no dramatic interest in the entire second act of the play. The fault in *Jean Hennuyer, Bishop of Lisieux* illustrates the difference between Mercier and a greater dramatist, such as Shakespeare, who might well have portrayed Hennuyer as a little less certain about going against his king. Indeed, the transitory popularity of eighteenth century drama in general might be explained by the playwrights' own reluctance to treat themes of personal conflict, preferring to restrict their attention to the promotion of moral values.

OTHER MAJOR WORKS

LONG FICTION: *L'An 2440*, 1770 (*Memoirs of the Year Two Thousand Five Hundred*, 1772); *Mon Bonnet de nuit*, 1784.

SHORT FICTION: *Satire contre Racine et Boileau*, 1808.

NONFICTION: *Songes et visions philosophiques*, 1768; *Du théâtre: Ou, Nouvel essai sur l'art dramatique*, 1773; *Éloges et discours philosophiques*, 1776; *Le Tableau de Paris*, 1782-1788 (12 volumes; *Paris*, 1802); *Portraits des rois de France*, 1785; *Le Nouveau Paris*, 1799 (6 volumes; *New Picture of Paris*, 1800); *Néologie: Ou, Vocabulaire des mots nouveaux*, 1801.

BIBLIOGRAPHY

Majewski, Henry F. *The Preromantic Imagination of L.-S. Mercier*. New York: Humanities Press, 1971. Majewski provides criticism and interpretation of Mercier's works, while focusing on his pre-Romantic qualities. Bibliography.

Pusey, W. W. *Louis-Sébastien Mercier in Germany: His Vogue and Influence in the Eighteenth Century*. 1939. Reprint. New York: AMS Press, 1966. Pusey examines Mercier's influence on German literature in the eighteenth century. Bibliography.

Wilkie, Everett C. *Mercier's "L'An 2440": Its Publishing History During the Author's Lifetime*. Cambridge, Mass.: Harvard University Library, 1986. This short work, in detailing the publishing history of *Memoirs of the Year Two Thousand Five Hundred*, a banned book, sheds light on the political aspects of Mercier's work.

Keith Bowen

PIETRO METASTASIO
Pietro Antonio Domenico Trapassi

Born: Rome; January 3, 1698
Died: Vienna, Austria; April 12, 1782

PRINCIPAL DRAMA

Gli orti esperidi, pr., pb. 1721
Didone abbandonata, pr. 1724, pb. 1733 (libretto; *Dido Forsaken*, 1952)
Siroe, re di Persia, pr. 1726, pb. 1734 (libretto)
Catone in Utica, pr. 1728, pb. 1734 (libretto)
Ezio, pr. 1728, pb. 1733 (libretto)
Artaserse, pr. 1730, pb. 1733 (libretto; *Artaxerxes*, 1761)
Adriano in Siria, pr. 1731, pb. 1733 (libretto; *Adrian in Syria*, 1767)
Demetrio, pr. 1731, pb. 1733 (libretto; *Demetrius*, pb. 1767)
Sant'Elena al Calvario, pr. 1731
Issipile, pr. 1732, pb. 1733 (libretto; *Hypsipyle*, 1767)
La morte d'Abele, pr. 1732, pb. 1734 (libretto; *The Death of Abel*, 1768)
L'Olimpiade, pr., pb. 1733 (libretto; *The Olympiad*, 1767)
La clemenza di Tito, pr. 1734, pb. 1737 (libretto; *The Mercy of Titus*, pb. 1767)
Temistocle, pr. 1736, pb. 1737 (*Themistocles*, 1767)
Attilio Regolo, wr. 1740, pr., pb. 1750 (libretto; *Atilius Regulus*, pb. 1767)
Zenobia, pr. 1740 (libretto; English translation, 1767)
Isacco, figura del Redentore, pr. 1740
Il re pastore, pr. 1751 (libretto)
L'eroe cinese, pr. 1752
The Works of Metastasio, pb. 1767 (2 volumes)

OTHER LITERARY FORMS

In addition to his plays, Pietro Metastasio wrote a number of oratorios, some stylized love songs of lyric charm called *canzonetta*, and several volumes of criticism and letters.

ACHIEVEMENTS

Pietro Metastasio created the first great libretti in opera. Though they were written primarily as dramatic vehicles for music, his melodramas, as they were called, were so poetic and so dramatically effective that they were often performed as independent plays.

In the century or more before Metastasio, the libretto had sunk from its primacy in the works of the early operatic composers, such as Claudio Monteverdi, to mere episodic threads between scenes of spectacle and exaggerated action, even low comedy. The music, particularly as it allowed for feats of virtuosity and vocal fireworks, made the libretto an almost vestigial part of the performance; indeed, the poetry of most of the libretti during the hundred years before Metastasio was negligible.

Following the pioneering reform of his predecessor, Apostolo Zeno, Metastasio brought an impressive artistic integrity to the form. Subordinating the merely spectacular, he simplified plot structure, creating scenes that both enhanced the music and delineated character and idea. His melodramas were thematically controlled: logical, dignified, and poetic.

His lyric gift was the key to his art. The poetic language had a conciseness, a precision, a fluency that meshed the action perfectly with the music. In effect, he was not only the first great librettist but also the first modern one. In his hands, the opera became genuinely dramatic as well as musical. His influence was such that almost all of his major works were set to music by many major composers: Giovanni Battista Pergolesi, Antonio Vivaldi, Alessandro Scarlatti, Johann Sebastian Bach, George Frederick Handel, Wolfgang Amadeus Mozart, and Ludwig van Beethoven.

BIOGRAPHY

Pietro Metastasio was born Pietro Antonio Domenico Trapassi, the fourth child of a poor family living in Rome. Though little is known of his early years, he seems to have been a precocious child, gifted with the ability to create lyrics spontaneously. The first important event of his childhood years occurred in 1708, when, at the age of ten, he was reciting and singing extemporaneous verse to a group of playmates and he was noticed by the influential lawyer and literary man Gianvincenzo Gravina. So impressed was he with the boy's ability that Gravina secured permission from the parents to adopt him and carried the boy into a world of classical and legal studies.

Though the story sounds improbable, the practice of extemporary declamation was not an unusual one in Italy at that time. As a form of public entertainment, it often dazzled and frequently awed the audience, who watched as poets vied with one another to expatiate in eight-line rhyming stanzas on any subject offered. Metastasio himself relates in his letters how, one evening at Gravina's, he improvised eighty stanzas at a single sitting. Such a feat exhausted the youth, however, and Gravina, fearful for the boy's health, soon put a stop to such improvisations.

Gravina himself was a member of an important literary club. A coterie of artists and poets who had originally come together in a Roman garden in 1690, the group formalized its association, founding an academy called Arcadia. Its members were devoted to the writing of simple, classically inspired verse, poetry of pastoral clarity and elegance free from the artificial mannerism of the seventeenth century baroque poet Giambattista Marino and his followers.

Arcadia was an important early influence on the work of the young Pietro Trapassi. Indicative of his respect for the classics, Gravina had already changed the boy's family name to "Metastasio," a Greek translation of Trapassi, meaning "crossing" and symbolizing, appropriately, the crossing from a humble, untutored station to a position of cultivated study and discipline. Metastasio's admission to the Academy in 1718, at the age of twenty, provided him with examples of Italian neoclassical poetry that he would bring to theatrical brilliance in his melodramas. The Academy taught him the importance of verse that was musical, precise, clear—verse in which importance was given to the sound of the word, the rhythm of the phrase.

Ironically, Gravina died shortly before Metastasio's formal admission to the Academy, but he left his protégé a large inheritance so that, for the first time in his life, Metastasio was independent. Both the law and literature now consumed his interest, and he continued to write lyric and conventional love poetry that began to attract notice. By 1719, he had moved to Naples, taking a position as law clerk in the office of one of that city's most respected jurists. Meanwhile, his fame as a poet was spreading.

Though he had produced only one minor dramatic work, *Justin* (1717), published in the same volume as his short poems (*Poesie*), Metastasio received a commission from the viceroy in Naples to write a dramatic serenade in honor of the birthday of Elizabeth, the wife of Charles VI, emperor of Austria and ruler of Italy. He responded with *Gli orti esperidi*, a short play that was to be a critical turning point in his life and career. The female lead of Venus was sung by Marianna Bulgarelli, one of the most famous actresses and singers of the era. Known as La Romanina, she was impressed by the lyric beauty of the piece and was further taken by the handsome young poet, whose courtliness and quiet elegance so naturally complemented his genius. She fell in love with Metastasio and took him as her protégé.

His relationship with La Romanina was the most significant in his career. Though married, she encouraged Metastasio to live in her household in Rome, where he would have more opportunity to pursue his art. That the two became lovers is probable but not certain. Metastasio's letters to her are complimentary, tactful, discreet; hers to him have not survived. What is certain is that Romanina convinced him to give up the law and to turn his attention full-time to poetry. She provided him with an intellectually stimulating environment, introduced him to theatrical friends, writers, and artists, and, according to some biographers, served as a critical sounding board for the development of his craft. In her salon, he immersed himself in the study of music. Their relationship was to last until her death in 1734.

For her Metastasio wrote his first melodrama—a play meant to be performed with music. *Dido Forsaken* was a sensational success. Nothing like it had appeared in the Italian theater before. The melodrama was compact and logical, and the poetry was of a high order, serving not as an excuse for the music but

as an integral part of it. *Dido Forsaken* is one of the first truly modern operatic scripts.

Some half-dozen melodramas followed, and by 1730, Metastasio was one of the best-known dramatists in Italy. On the retirement of Apostolo Zeno as official poet to the Viennese court, Metastasio was offered the post. He arrived there in April, 1730, and from that date until his death more than half a century later, he wrote the works that were to establish him as the greatest of Italian librettists.

His life at court took on the regularity and the ease that made it possible for him to produce with great facility, though his life became, from a biographer's point of view, one of routine uneventfulness. The first decade of his stay in Vienna, the capital of the Holy Roman Empire, was the most productive of his career. From 1730 to 1740, he wrote the greatest melodramas—libretti—of the age. They appeared quickly, dazzlingly, in succession: *Demetrius*, *The Olympiad*, *The Mercy of Titus*, *Themistocles*, and *Atilius Regulus*.

The Countess D'Althan, who had first known Metastasio when he was in Naples, became his patron and his confidante during these Viennese years; she filled the intellectual and emotional void left by Romanina's death at the height of his achievements. Although he refused to learn German, he was always courtly and diplomatic. Some contemporary accounts scorn his servility, his readiness to bow and to kiss the hand that fed him. He lived relatively isolated from the events at court, seemingly unconcerned with the momentous historical events of the era.

After 1740, Metastasio's powers began to wane. He had been engaged in almost ceaseless writing, often by command, always for an occasion; by 1750, his melodramas had become competent and crafty but little else.

His final years were not happy. Afflicted with a nervous disorder sometimes identified as hypochondria, Metastasio found writing increasingly difficult. He was aware, too, that the operatic world was beginning to turn away from his style of heroic tragedy— the *opera seria*—in preference for a more bourgeois, less aristocratic tradition exemplified by Christoph Willibald Gluck and Mozart. In addition, the lighter comic drama—the *opera buffa*—made the Metastasian conflicts of love and duty seem stodgy and old-fashioned, reliquaries of a pre-Enlightenment age.

By the time of his death in 1782, Metastasio's vogue had passed. Yet his influence was such that a medal was struck, bearing the phrase "The Italian Sophocles," in honor of Europe's most outstanding musical dramatist. His reputation is secure as a great librettist who was also a first-rate poet.

ANALYSIS

The Metastasian themes that seemed so old-fashioned in the late eighteenth century were the very epitome of an artistic reflection of order, of monarchy, of a world controlled by reason and distrustful of the passions. The heroes and heroines of Pietro Metastasio's dramas are highborn princes, kings and queens who ultimately subdue their baser drives and who adhere to an ideal—patriotism, duty, honor. Conflicts in a Metastasian drama are therefore not physical but psychological. Characters often philosophize and rarely bleed. The action of the drama—static by standards of a later theatrical tradition—revolves about the protagonist's resolution of the conflict, a resolution sometimes closed by death but more often also by happiness and salvation. In the end, dignity triumphs; order is restored.

DIDO FORSAKEN

Dido Forsaken, Metastasio's first melodrama and his earliest success, is an excellent introduction to his work because it illustrates some of the major characteristics of his later Viennese period. In his introduction to the drama, Metastasio notes that his source was Vergil's *Aeneid* (c. 29-19 B.C.E.; English translation, 1553), in deference to the classics, which typified the eighteenth century's idea of imitation and adaptation of Greek and Roman literary models. His plot is straightforward and uncomplicated. Dido, widowed queen of Carthage, has fallen in love with Aeneas, the Trojan warrior who has escaped from the fall of Troy and who has been shipwrecked on her North African shores. Aeneas loves Dido, as well, but his mission—he has been ordained by the gods to found Rome—must take precedence over his feelings. After declaring his love, he sets sail for Italy

and his destiny. Angry, then forlorn, Dido hurls herself on her own funeral pyre, and in the concluding scene, Neptune rises from the sea and quenches the flames.

To this basic plot, Metastasio fuses an element from Ovid, who, he declares in the same introduction, portrays Iarbas, King of the Moors, as one of Dido's suitors who destroys Carthage after Dido's death. In the interest of "good theater," however, Metastasio introduces Iarbas in disguise and pits him as a rival of Aeneas. Interestingly, the Elizabethan playwright Christopher Marlowe had earlier written with Thomas Nashe *Dido, Queen of Carthage* (pr. c. 1586-1587), in which Iarbas is portrayed as Aeneas's chief rival. If Metastasio knew of Marlowe's play, however (which seemed unlikely), he took little from it.

Metastasio's piece on Dido, unlike that of Marlowe, is a tight, three-act tragedy that opens with Aeneas having already announced his intention of leaving Dido. Metastasio thereby limited the action to the conflict of emotions and places dramatic emphasis on the psychological forces rather than on the physical. The epic sweep of Aeneas's story is distilled into a lyric cameo.

Moreover, Metastasio limited the number of characters. To the three major ones forming the basis of the action, he introduced only three others: Selene, Dido's sister ("Anna" in the *Aeneid*), who is secretly in love with Aeneas; Araspe, Iarbas's confidant, who is secretly in love with Selene; and Osmida, Dido's confidante, who is secretly plotting with Iarbas for the queen's overthrow. This use of confidants is a marked characteristic of Metastasian drama. The confidant is an effectively economical device for externalizing the conflict by providing alternative courses of action for the main character. The confidant is, in effect, a dramatization of the protagonist's inner voice, thus eliminating the need for the dramatic monologue or the soliloquy. This second group of characters also provides the grounds for a subplot of intrigue—as opposed to the honesty of Aeneas's and Dido's motives—and keeps the play from becoming static by maintaining a tension of opposing forces that alternates with each scene or clusters of scenes.

With almost mathematical precision, the scenes of swordplay between Aeneas and Iarbas—no one dies and there is no bloodshed or violence depicted—occur near the end of act 1 and again near the beginning of act 3, perfectly balancing the main, largely declamatory scenes portraying the emotions of love and hate and the sentiments of duty, honor, loyalty, and even repentance.

Declamation, in fact, is a strategic principle in the structure of *Dido Forsaken*. The characters declare their love, proclaim their intentions, and assert their feelings in neat, compact recitative—a middle way between speech and song, between spoken dialogue and sung verse. Significantly, major scene clusters conclude with a character's singing in arietta, or small aria, placed not only for virtuoso effect but also for dramatic emphasis and tension.

Despite the declamation, Dido herself is portrayed as a woman of genuine passion. Though she is willing to die for Aeneas, she is not an infatuated ingenue, but rather a queen who knows how to rule. Angry at Aeneas for denying her love, she reminds him shrewdly that she has presided over Carthage all these years without him, and without him has seen it prosper. She bitterly mocks him at his delay, sarcastically asking him why he was not already in Italy, subduing kings and winning other kingdoms. She is a woman of spirit: When she kills herself at the end, it is as much an act of strength as a gesture of despair.

DEMETRIUS

Dido Forsaken is one of Metastasio's few melodramas in which the protagonist dies. Those representative of his best work end in reconciliation. These works of his Viennese period established the classic format and structure of the Metastasian drama. The first work of this period, one of his best, is *Demetrius*, a heroic melodrama suffused with idyllic sentiment. Its author claimed in his letters that the play brought tears to the eyes of even the most bearlike members of the audience when it was performed in 1731.

The plot, like that of *Dido Forsaken*, is clear and uncomplicated. There is the same limitation on the number of characters, the same logical distribution of arietta among the principals, and the same technique of using the confidant to externalize the conflict,

which is resolved by the triumph of Reason and Order over emotional turmoil. Unlike *Dido Forsaken*, *Demetrius* ends happily; no one dies, no one is sacrificed.

Cleonice, Queen of Syria, is loved by Alcestes, a shepherd risen to the rank of soldier and reared by a nobleman, Phenicius, who is also the father of Olinthus. Alcestes is in reality Demetrius, son of King Demetrius, who died in exile and who gave his son to Phenicius to rear incognito until such time as he could assume his rightful throne.

Cleonice, meanwhile, must choose a husband to share her throne and is pressured by Olinthus to decide in his favor. The queen, however, loves Alcestes, though she is ignorant of his royal lineage. Urged by the people to choose a consort, she is torn between her love for Alcestes and her duty as queen to choose among the nobled blood and to respect "decorum." She is encouraged in her choice of a prince by her confidante, Barsene, who is secretly in love with Alcestes and wants him for herself.

The major scenes of the melodrama center on Cleonice's confrontations with Alcestes, during which she explains her dilemma and her reasons for choosing honor over love, loyalty to the idea of sovereignty over personal feelings. In the end, however, Phenicius arranges for Alcestes' true identity to be revealed, the lovers are united, and the play concludes with a grand chorus of reconciliation.

The theme of *Demetrius* is the triumph of harmony over the chaos consequent to the submission to personal desires. Writing for an absolute monarchy, Metastasio is stating in dramatic form the philosophical and political idea that reason, represented by the monarchy, brings order to a disordered world. Cleonice understands, as she tells Alcestes, that the crown is often a burdensome jewel, that the price of sovereignty is selflessness: "Tyrannical Honor! Because of you I must forever be deprived of what I hold dear."

That she is united with Alcestes in the finale is typical of the idyllic sentiment popular in the eighteenth century, and to later tastes, such an ending appears trite, even comic. In the world order that Metastasio was upholding, her union with the real Demetrius is the logical reward for her loyalty, the natural result of putting honor above personal happiness.

The plot of *Demetrius* is the reverse of that of *Dido Forsaken*. Where Aeneas spurned Dido's love in pursuit of a higher destiny, so Cleonice refuses Alcestes' love in deference to her high responsibility. Both Aeneas and Cleonice illustrate a glorious self-abnegation in the interest of what should be.

Demetrius is superior to *Dido Forsaken* in the greater depth of characterization. Olinthus, for example, who is reconciled at the end, is a Hotspur, a fiery, hot-tempered youth who has no false modesty about his preeminence as a match for Cleonice or his desire for the throne. He provides the main physical conflict in the melodrama, which succeeds in holding an audience's interest even though there are no spectacular effects. Only the verbal sparring keeps the play on the move.

THE OLYMPIAD

The Olympiad is the most perfectly structured of Metastasio's melodramas and, like *Demetrius*, the product of his "golden age" of accomplishment. The play reveals both the strengths and the weaknesses of the poet's work. It illustrates Metastasio's mastery of the melodramatic formula already worked out in the previous plays, but it is a mastery that relies on repetition of and variation on established themes rather than on artistic experimentation, innovation, or growth. Metastasio simply reworked previous material and ideas, polishing, trimming, redressing.

The plot is drawn from classical sources, Herodotus and Pausanias, and the general story outline was probably already known to the courtly audience for whom the work—like all eleven of the melodramas of this period—was first performed. Such foreknowledge on the part of the audience allows the poet to begin, much in the manner of the classical Greek epics, late in the sequence of events. By means of this technique, called *in medias res*, the characters allude to previous actions, bringing the audience up to date naturally. Such a method provides for a remarkable compactness and for a direct, unflagging progress toward the denouement.

The source is a complicated, involved story that seems a cognate version of the Oedipus legend and

that, curiously, anticipates the proxy idea contained in Edmond Rostand's late Romantic drama *Cyrano de Bergerac* (1897; English translation, 1898). Clistenes, king of Sicyon, is warned by an oracle that his infant son, twin to his sister Aristea, will one day kill his father. The king thus orders the boy to be thrown into the sea, but the baby is saved by Amyntus, who takes him to Crete, giving him to a childless royal couple to rear as their own. Years later, the young man, called Lycidas, falls in love with Argene, but the king forbids the relationship and Argene thus flees to Elis, where she lives as a shepherdess.

Meanwhile, Lycidas saves the life of Megacles, a young man famous for his athletic prowess. The two men become fast friends. When it comes to pass that the Olympic Games are to be held in Elis, Lycidas decides to participate, sees Aristea, and falls in love with her. She has arrived in Elis with her father, Clistenes, who was to preside over the Games. To win the love of Aristea—Lycidas is unaware that she is really his twin—he determines to win glory in the Games and sends for his friend, Megacles, persuading him to participate in the Games in his name. Disguised as Lucidas, Megacles wins the Games and gains the love of Aristea.

The major conflict is Megacles' loyalty to Lycidas, a loyalty that prevents him from returning Aristea's love. At the climax, Megacles is discovered as the false Lycidas, Lycidas almost strikes Clistenes in anger but relents, and by the final scene, all is made straight and reconciliation ensues. Happiness reigns for all. That Metastasio could create an effective vehicle from such a clumsy welter of detail is a tribute to his ability as a craftsman. He opens the play only a short time before the Games are to begin, and in the five short scenes of act 1, he has all the relationships drawn and the background clarified. Furthermore, *The Olympiad* relies less on the confidants and more on love scenes among the four principals. In addition, effective dramatic use is made of the chorus, especially in the climactic scenes in which the choral ariettas provide suspense and excitement. The action is thus condensed and the theme of loyalty is intensified.

The Olympiad remains one of Metastasio's finest achievements, not because of its subject matter but because of the way such potentially spectacular yet dangerously confusing material is handled. The play shows the reasons for Metastasio's reputation as one of the century's greatest musical dramatists—logical intensity, clarity of outline, quickness of movement, and, above all, structure remarkably adaptable to the musical score.

OTHER MAJOR WORKS

POETRY: *Poesie*, 1717.

NONFICTION: *Estratto della Poetica d'Aristotele*, 1782.

BIBLIOGRAPHY

Charlemont, James Caulfield. *Lord Charlemont's History of Italian Poetry from Dante to Metastasio: A Critical Edition from the Autograph Manuscript.* Lewiston, N.Y.: Edwin Mellen Press, 2000. This volume, edited by George Talbot, presents Lord Charlemont's critical review of Italian poetry, including the dramas of Metastasio.

Fucilla, Joseph. Introduction to *Three Melodramas*, by Pietro Metastasio. Lexington: University of Kentucky Press, 1981. Fucilla presents a brief discussion of the life of Metastasio and his works, focusing on the three melodramas that are translated in this volume, *Dido Forsaken*, *Demetrius*, and *The Olympiad*.

Lee, Vernon (Violet Paget). "Metastasio and the Opera." *Studies of Eighteenth Century Italy.* 1907. Reprint. New York, Da Capo Press, 1978. Lee examines Metastasio's relationship with the opera, for which he wrote the first great libretti.

Neville, Don. *Metastasio at Home and Abroad: Papers from the International Symposium Faculty of Music, the University of Western Ontario.* London, Ont.: University of Western Canada, 1996. This collection of papers examines Metastasio largely from the musical perspective. Bibliographical references.

Stendahl. *Haydn, Mozart, and Metastasio.* New York: Grossman, 1972. This classic study by the nineteenth century author Stendahl examines the life of Metastasio along with those of composers Joseph Haydn and Wolfgang Amadeus Mozart.

Edward Fiorelli

THOMAS MIDDLETON

Born: London, England; April 18, 1580 (baptized)
Died: Newington Butts, Surrey, England; July 4, 1627

PRINCIPAL DRAMA

The Honest Whore, Part I, pr., pb. 1604 (with Thomas Dekker)

The Family of Love, pr. c. 1604-1607, pb. 1608

The Phoenix, pr. 1604, pb. 1607

Your Five Gallants, pr. 1604-1607, pb. 1608

A Trick to Catch the Old One, pr. c. 1605-1606, pb. 1608

A Mad World, My Masters, pr. c. 1606, pb. 1608

Michaelmas Term, pr. c. 1606, pb. 1607

The Roaring Girl: Or, Moll Cutpurse, pr. c. 1610, pb. 1611 (with Dekker)

The Witch, pr. c. 1610, pb. 1778

A Chaste Maid in Cheapside, pr. 1611, pb. 1630

No Wit, No Help Like a Woman's, pr. c. 1613-1627, pb. 1657

More Dissemblers Besides Women, pr. c. 1615, pb. 1657

A Fair Quarrel, pr. c. 1615-1617, pb. 1617 (with William Rowley)

The Widow, pr. c. 1616, pb. 1652 (with Ben Jonson and John Fletcher?)

The Major of Queenborough, pr. c. 1616-1620, pb. 1661 (with Rowley)

The Old Law: Or, A New Way to Please You, pr.
c. 1618, pb. 1656 (with Rowley and Philip
Massinger)
Anything for a Quiet Life, pr. c. 1621, pb. 1662
(with John Webster?)
Women Beware Women, pr. c. 1621-1627, pb. 1657
The Changeling, pr. 1622, pb. 1653 (with Rowley)
A Game at Chess, pr. 1624, pb. 1625
The Selected Plays of Thomas Middleton, pb. 1978

OTHER LITERARY FORMS

Thomas Middleton's nondramatic work includes a
number of youthful, less accomplished works. He
produced *The Wisdom of Solomon, Paraphrased*
(1597), a poem based on the Book of Solomon;
Micro-cynicon (1599), a volume of satiric poems;
The Ghost of Lucrece (1600), a narrative poem; and
The Black Book (1604) and *Father Hubburd's Tales*
(1604), two satiric pamphlets, the latter of which includes poetry. Through the rest of his career, the main
body of Middleton's writing that was not for the theater consisted of the lavish public or court entertainments known as masques, pageants, or shows. Middleton was the author of at least seven Lord Mayors's
shows—huge allegorical spectacles honoring the city,
performed outdoors using expensive sets and costumes. In 1603, he collaborated with Thomas Dekker
and Ben Jonson on a coronation pageant, *The Magnificent Entertainment Given to King James*, and in
1625, he was in charge of a pageant to welcome
Charles I to London after King James's death. Between 1604 and 1625, he wrote at least six other
masques and entertainments for the court and for important occasions.

ACHIEVEMENTS

Like most of the dramatists of his day, Thomas
Middleton lived as a practicing man of the theater
without apparent concern for claiming literary stature. As with William Shakespeare (but in contrast to
Jonson), the evidence suggests that he cared little
about having his works published. Apparently the
success he sought was that of the playwright whose
works were performed, not read. Yet his works do
have stature, both in reading and in performance. He

created a number of interesting and insightful comedies, several substantial tragicomedies, and the most
fascinating political satire of the age. Four of his
comedies are frequently described as masterpieces,
and two of his tragedies are considered great works.
The four comedies, all dating from the first half of his
career (1604-1613), are *A Chaste Maid in Cheapside*;
A Mad World, My Masters; *The Roaring Girl*; and *A
Trick to Catch the Old One*. The two tragedies, both
written later (1620-1627), are *The Changeling* and
Women Beware Women. (To these might be added
The Revenger's Tragedy of 1606-1607, generally attributed to Cyril Tourneur but believed by some critics to be Middleton's work.) Middleton is judged by
some to be the third great playwright, after Shakespeare and Jonson, in a period notable for its abundance of gifted dramatists.

BIOGRAPHY

Very little is known about Thomas Middleton's
life except what can be determined from legal and

Thomas Middleton (Hulton Archive by Getty Images)

theater records. Middleton's father was a bricklayer but also a gentleman who acquired a sizable estate by buying London property. Middleton was born in 1580, and when he was five, his father died, leaving an estate of more than three hundred pounds to his wife. She then wisely placed the estate in trust to three advisers to protect herself and her children from fortune hunters. Soon, she married Thomas Harvey, an adventurer who had just returned from Sir Walter Raleigh's expedition to colonize Roanoke Island. Apparently, marrying Middleton's mother was also a business venture and apparently Harvey did not know about the trust; as a result, between 1587 and 1599 there was constant litigation as Harvey attempted to gain control of his wife's fortune. From the age of seven on, young Middleton was in the midst of an ugly family situation that undoubtedly encouraged his later bent for satire.

At eighteen, Middleton entered Oxford, where he studied for at least two years but left without taking a degree. By 1601, he had left Oxford for his new love, the theater, and in the following year was receiving payment from Philip Henslowe, the theater owner, for collaborations with Dekker and John Webster. About this time, Middleton married Mary Marbeck, the sister of an actor.

At first, Middleton was writing for the Lord Admiral's Men, but beginning in 1603, he began writing primarily for Paul's Boys and the Children of the Chapel Royal, two companies of professional "child" actors (actors in their early and middle teens). For the private indoor theater called the Blackfriars, which served a well-to-do, sophisticated audience, Middleton wrote a number of his most satiric and successful city comedies. During the years when Jonson wrote *Volpone* (pr. 1605) and when Shakespeare was approaching the end of his career, Middleton became established as one of the leading English playwrights.

Soon, Middleton was working more for the adult companies, especially the Prince's Men and the Lady Elizabeth's Men. He came to associate more with Dekker and Webster and with William Rowley and to write a broader type of comedy. Middleton suffered from indebtedness and had to struggle through lawsuits. By 1609, he was living at Newington Butts be-

cause it was close to the theater district, and he apparently lived there until his death. Beginning about 1613, Middleton turned increasingly to writing and producing Lord Mayors's shows, and this led in 1620 to his appointment as city chronologer, by which time he was probably fairly well-to-do. During this period, he tried his hand at several tragicomedies, a genre made popular by Francis Beaumont and John Fletcher. Finally, in the 1620's came his two great tragedies, *The Changeling* and *Women Beware Women*.

In 1624, *A Game at Chess*, probably Middleton's last play, created a huge scandal. At the time, anger toward Catholic Spain was especially high in England, and Middleton provided a focus for this sentiment. His play is an elaborate allegory in which a game of chess reflects the contemporary international situation. The play was a phenomenal success, drawing capacity crowds for nine days in succession, an unusually long run for the theater in that era. Finally, because of protests by the Spanish ambassador over the play's seditious nature, the Privy Council ordered the play closed down and, according to one report, had Middleton imprisoned. In any case, he was soon involved with overseeing the printing of the play, which was also very successful. Although *A Game at Chess* was probably very lucrative for Middleton, he left very little behind for his widow when he died three years later, at the age of forty-seven. Her death followed two weeks after his own.

Analysis

As is the case with many writers of the Elizabethan and Jacobean stage, Thomas Middleton's canon has never been definitively established. For several reasons, it is extremely difficult to determine what is his work: The concrete evidence is scanty. Many plays were published in pirated editions, and Middleton frequently collaborated in writing his plays. Many critics do not believe that Middleton has a distinct style. Indeed, T. S. Eliot, in an essay highly praising Middleton as an artist, went so far as to say that he felt no sense of a distinct personality unifying the plays: To Eliot, Middleton was simply a name connecting a number of works.

Although the controversy surrounding Middleton's authorship has not been resolved, the critical consensus is that there are stylistic and thematic patterns connecting those plays that are definitely by Middleton. In fact, the Victorians had already perceived a pattern in Middleton's plays: To them, Middleton's viewpoint was immoral. Modern criticism consistently rejects this reading but acknowledges that Middleton's subject matter was frequently low and often shocking and was presented with little apparent value judgment by the author. Middleton's comedies, usually set in the city and usually antiromantic, are pictures of lust, greed, and ambition. They are frequently called "realistic," and the term applies well in one sense. The modern reader must not expect consistent realism or naturalism in the modern sense, for, like all plays of the period, Middleton's plays employ many nonrealistic conventions. Still, they are realistic in that they are filled with the language and behavior of the least elegant characters of London—with the bravado of grocers and the gabble of grocers' wives, with the slang of whores and the cant of thieves, and with the equally unrefined attitudes and language of various gentlemen and gentlewomen, who are also hungry for gold and glamour. In all of this uproar, Middleton is remarkably detached. Authorial judgments are made, but they are implied through subtle ironies rather than directly stated.

Middleton worked at first with a comedy of humors in the tradition of Roman comedy and under the immediate influence of Jonson. In these early comedies, he developed an increasing interest in character, in the psychology of human behavior and particularly the psyche's response to sin. Often, Middleton's characters undergo startling but carefully prepared-for conversions as their sins overwhelm them. Also, he became fascinated with presenting contemporary London life from a woman's point of view: Middleton often placed female characters at the center of his plays. Consistent with his psychological interest, Middleton from the beginning stood apart from his characters, allowing them to speak and act with little authorial intrusion. Irony is an increasingly persistent effect in these plays, and it is often gained through the aside and the soliloquy. With these conventions, Middleton reveals inner fears and desires, often in conflict with a character's public pose. Middleton's detached, ironic stance and his intense psychological interest are even more apparent in the tragedies later in his career. In these plays in the tradition of Shakespeare, Webster, and John Ford, he continued to use sin and retribution, particularly sexual degradation, as major themes. As in his earlier plays, he typically blended prose with blank verse, a verse that is never ornate but that rises to eloquence when the scene demands it.

There is something particularly modern about Middleton's attitude toward his material; perhaps it is a moral relativism. This modernity shows up in his persistent exploration of the psyche's complexity and in the ironies through which this complexity is expressed. His characters cannot be dismissed or summarized easily—a disturbing fact to previous ages looking for more decisive, discriminating judgments. Yet to the modern age, this is the highest kind of morality, and for that reason, Middleton's reputation will probably endure.

THE ROARING GIRL

Written in collaboration by Middleton and Dekker, *The Roaring Girl* centers on a real-life London woman named Moll Frith. Moll was reputed to be a prostitute, bawd, and thief, but the playwrights present her as a woman of great spirit and virtue whose reputation is maligned by a petty, convention-bound society. In the play, as in real life, Moll dresses in men's clothes, smokes a pipe, and wears a sword. This unconventionality, the play suggests, leads to her spotted reputation. She is a roaring girl—a brash woman-about-town—but beneath this lack of femininity is a courageous, high-principled woman. Moll intervenes in the main plots and is involved in skirmishes with many of the characters, consistently displaying her ability to stand up for the oppressed and mistreated, most eloquently when they are women.

The main plot of *The Roaring Girl* involves a young man, Sebastian Wengrave, and a young woman, Mary Fitzallard, in love with each other but prevented from marrying because Sebastian's father, Sir Alexander Wengrave, wants a well-to-do daughter-in-law.

Sebastian plots to outwit his father: He will pretend to be in love with the infamous Moll, and when his small-minded father learns this, he will agree to the union with Mary simply to get rid of Moll. The plan temporarily backfires, however, because Sir Alexander at first reacts by employing a false-witted humor character named Ralph Trapdoor, "honest Ralph," to tempt Moll to theft and have her executed. Moll resists his temptations and instead exposes Trapdoor as a coward, ultimately eliciting a confession and an apology from him. She is also instrumental in helping Sebastian win Mary and even in bringing on a complete conversion of his father, who eventually sees Moll with the eyes of true judgment rather than through his willful prejudices.

Accompanying the main plot are two parallel stories of couples whose marriages are tested by callous gallants. One of these men, Laxton, leads on Mrs. Gallipot until she tricks her supremely gullible husband into giving thirty pounds to him. Ultimately, however, she becomes disgusted with her would-be seducer and denounces him to her husband, whose eyes are finally opened. Similarly, a "gentleman" named Goshawk tries to seduce Mrs. Openwork; her husband, however, is far shrewder than Gallipot. He outmaneuvers Goshawk, and together husband and wife expose Goshawk's lechery. In both of these plots, marriage survives its attackers, but the differences between the marriages are equally important. Given Gallipot's blindness and Mrs. Gallipot's lechery, their marriage survives largely because Laxton prefers money to sex. The Openworks' marriage, on the other hand, survives because of the intelligence and integrity of the marriage partners.

A major motif in *The Roaring Girl* is the reversal of gender stereotyping. Moll wears masculine clothes; Mary disguises herself in men's clothes; Mrs. Gallipot speaks scornfully of her "apron" husband; and Moll several times overcomes male antagonists by means of her sword and the manly art of bullying. These reversals of sex roles are one of the means of uniting the many elements of the play: They reveal that appearances count for little, that the reality of a person's character shows up only through certain kinds of trials. Such trials or tests are quite frequent in the play. For example, Openwork tests Goshawk's integrity, Goshawk tests Mrs. Openwork's virtue, and Laxton tests Mrs. Gallipot's. Moll's honesty is tried by Sir Alexander through Trapdoor, and Moll herself tests the courage and integrity of many characters. The play overturns conventional assumptions that men have a monopoly on courage and that all women are the daughters of Eve. Instead, the play implies that men and women must be judged carefully and on their individual merits. Throughout the play, Moll stands as a lively, unconventional, attractive woman—an ancestor of the Shavian heroine. She is the one shining example of integrity in the play and one of the great creations of the period.

A CHASTE MAID IN CHEAPSIDE

In contrast to *The Roaring Girl*, which was coauthored by Middleton and Dekker, *A Chaste Maid in Cheapside* was written by Middleton alone. Also, in contrast to the eponymous protagonist of *The Roaring Girl*, the "chaste maid" of the title is a minor character. The play focuses instead on several men—Allwit, Sir Walter Whorehound, and Yellowhammer—who embody the values of London's Cheapside district (an area notorious for its unchaste women—and men). The play is admirable for its complex interweaving of many plots and for Middleton's detached stance, which creates such effective satire.

Yellowhammer, a goldsmith, and his wife, Maudlin, have two children: One is sweet, silent Moll, the chaste maid of the title, and the other is Tim, a foolish young man who is overly impressed with himself for having done well in Latin at Cambridge. The parents' overriding concern is to "sell" their children to prosperous spouses. They plan to have Moll marry Sir Walter Whorehound (in spite of his last name), and they hope to marry Tim to Sir Walter's "niece" (even though, as they eventually learn, she is actually his cast-off whore). In the meantime, Allwit (a play on the term "wittol," a willing cuckold) has been living comfortably without working because he and his wife have been quite willing for wealthy Sir Walter to "keep" Mistress Allwit as his mistress. In fact, Allwit is quite content that Sir Walter has fathered all of Mistress Allwit's children. The central conflict in the play develops when Allwit learns that Sir Walter might marry Moll: Allwit must prevent this if he and his wife are to remain in Sir Walter's keep.

A romantic plot runs through the play: Moll and a penniless young gentleman, Touchwood Junior, want to marry, but her greedy father opposes the plan. Another plot involves Touchwood Senior, who is so sexually potent that his wife (and many other women as well) are continually bearing his children. As a result, he and his wife have agreed that they must separate for a time because of the expense of increasing the size of their family. Finally, a related plot involves Sir Oliver Kix and his lady, relatives of Sir Walter, who are miserable because they are childless.

The ways the plots develop and are resolved reveal their related purposes. Touchwood Senior generously fathers a child for Sir Oliver. This of course resembles the Allwit/Sir Walter arrangement but with the important exception that Sir Oliver has no idea that he is a cuckold. Because Sir Oliver and Lady Kix now have an heir, they take the place of their relative, Sir Walter, in line for the family fortune and thus ruin his chances to win Moll. Meanwhile, however, Sir Walter and Touchwood Junior have a sword fight because of Moll, in which Sir Walter is seriously wounded. Thinking that he is dying, Sir Walter undergoes a kind of deathbed conversion and delivers an angry sermon to Allwit, who callously throws his former benefactor out. Then, in a burlesque of a tragicomic ending, the characters assemble for what they believe is the funeral of Touchwood Junior (dead from the sword fight) and of Moll (dead of grief), but in the middle of the ceremony both characters arise from their coffins and reveal that they are married.

In the outcome of the play, a rough poetic justice operates. Touchwood Junior wins Moll, and Tim Yellowhammer finds himself married to Sir Walter's "niece," who is almost what he deserves. Although Sir Walter has repented and become a sort of moral spokesman, his rejection by Moll and his loss of fortune are a suitable penance for his earlier lechery. On the other hand, the treatment of Allwit violates the pattern. Throughout the play, he has served as a remarkably detached commentator on morals and manners. For example, in one sharply satiric scene, he delivers the author's cutting observations about the hypocrisy of the Puritan women when they come to the christening of the Allwit's child. This uncomfortable intimacy between the audience and such a character complicates the audience's judgment of him and at least disconcerts the audience as they condemn him. Ultimately, Allwit is left with a comfortable home and has begun to play the role he will adopt thereafter—that of the hypocritically "moral" citizen. At this point, Middleton chooses realism over a toosimplistic moralism: Although comedy demands a degree of poetic justice, life reminds one that degenerate behavior often goes unpunished.

THE CHANGELING

Middleton's greatest and most frequently read play is *The Changeling*. Coming near the end of an extraordinary period in England drama, it is often described as the last great English tragedy. The play's psychological realism makes it particularly appealing to the modern temperament. *The Changeling* was written in collaboration with William Rowley, and scholars generally agreed that Rowley wrote almost all of the subplot, while Middleton wrote almost all of the main plot and was responsible for the unity of the whole.

Set in Spain, *The Changeling* centers on a young woman, Beatrice, who falls in love with one young man, Alsemero, whom she first meets five days after she has become betrothed to another man, Alonzo. Beatrice believes that fate has been unfair to her in causing her to find true love five days too late. She is desperate to break off the engagement to Alonzo but feels bound to its because of her father's insistence and because she would be dishonoring her vow. To resolve this dilemma, she exploits DeFlores, a poor gentleman employed as a servant to her father. Beatrice finds DeFlores physically repulsive, but DeFlores is passionately attracted to her. Noticing this, Beatrice flatters him into thinking that she finds him handsome and then easily persuades him to kill Alonzo. All along, she blindly assumes that payment in gold will satisfy him; she fails to see that DeFlores (whose name suggests "deflower") expects to have her as his reward.

For his own part, DeFlores, having seen that Beatrice can cold-bloodedly arrange her fiancé's murder, understandably assumes that she will no longer have scruples about yielding her virginity to him. This radical, but psychologically plausible, misunderstanding creates considerable tension until DeFlores must finally state the payment that will satisfy him. Beatrice is shocked that he would "murder her honor," at which DeFlores points to her moral blindness: "Push, you forget yourself!/ A woman dipped in blood, and talk of modesty?" DeFlores reminds her that she is now "the deed's creature," that her moral innocence is gone now that she has commissioned a murder. Beatrice first becomes furious and then kneels and implores him to spare her, but he stands triumphant over her, grandly declaring, "Can you weep fate from its determined purpose?/ So soon may you weep me."

Alsemero and Beatrice are soon married, but Alsemero, largely because he is obsessed with being sure of his wife's purity, proposes to administer a virginity test. Because she has been seduced by DeFlores, Beatrice is able to pass the test only by deception. She realizes that she will fail the next test, her wedding night, and she plots to have her maid Diaphanta take her place in the wedding bed for a few hours. Diaphanta stays too long; she is awakened by a fire in the house, started by DeFlores, who kills her in the ensuing confusion. At this point, Beatrice recognizes that she has come to love DeFlores, revealing, in the psychological terms of the play, that she has been reduced to his level. Finally, Alsemero discovers Beatrice and DeFlores together and confronts her as a whore. As the confessions at last come out, DeFlores kills Beatrice and then himself, and her husband and father are left with the horror of what has happened.

The subplot of *The Changeling* takes place in an insane asylum, where Alibius, who runs the madhouse, jealously keeps his wife, Isabella, closely guarded. Two inmates who are merely feigning madness, Antonio and Franciscus, and Lollio, Alibius's subordinate, all try to seduce Isabella. Although she has more of a motive for unfaithfulness than does Beatrice, she remains loyal to her vows and eventually shames her husband into treating her better. This subplot works as a comic contrast to the main action of the tragedy. Lollio unsuccessfully tries to use Isabella's apparent unfaithfulness to blackmail her into yielding to his lust, and the scene in which this occurs is pointedly placed between the two private meetings between Beatrice and DeFlores. On several occasions, the madmen in the asylum run across the stage shouting out their dangerously uncontrolled desires, provoking their keepers to use the whip on them. This image of uncontrolled human appetite held in check reflects on the main plot: Beatrice and DeFlores—and, arguably, Alsemero, because of his failure to honor Beatrice's betrothal—fail to check their own libidinous desires.

The main plot of *The Changeling* was based on a moralistic narrative by John Reynolds called *The Triumphs of God's Revenge Against the Crying and Execrable Sin of Willful and Premeditated Murder* (1621); Middleton's version makes changes that soften the harsh judgment of the original. In the source story, Beatrice is continuously self-possessed, but in the play she is pictured as distracted, out of control, moved by an overwhelming fate. She frequently allows this fate, operating through her willful temperament, to distort her sense of morality. Through a heavy use of the soliloquy and the aside, Middleton reveals the intense inner struggles and desires of his characters, particularly Beatrice and DeFlores. Ultimately, Beatrice is disgusted with her sinful behavior, even though, in contrast to many of the great figures of Shakespearean tragedy, she is not fully enlightened about her errors at the end; a part of her tragedy lies in her moral blindness. DeFlores, by contrast, gains less sympathy but, like Shakespeare's Macbeth, more stature by always behaving with his eyes open.

WOMEN BEWARE WOMEN

As in *The Changeling*, the characters in *Women Beware Women* are obsessed with lust; like Beatrice, they become totally degraded because of it. Also as in *The Changeling*, two plots borrowed from two distinct sources are woven together ingeniously, each one commenting on the other. The main plot deals with a marriage that at first seems wholesome, perhaps even romantic. Leantio, a Florentine businessman, has married a Venetian woman, Bianca, who appears not to regret having given up family riches for love. When he leaves her with his mother as her chaperone, the Duke of Florence sees the beautiful, foreign Bianca and desires her. In order to pander to their sovereign, a brother and sister, Hippolito and Livia, plot to bring the two women to their house so that the duke can seduce Bianca. While Livia distracts Leantio's mother with a game of chess, Hippolito conducts Bianca on a tour of the house. Hippolito suddenly presents the duke to Bianca and leaves her alone with him. Bianca halfheartedly resists the duke but soon yields to his passionate wooing and his promises of wealth. While this is occurring, the chess game below provides brilliant ironic commentary on the seduction above. When Leantio returns, Bianca treats him scornfully and openly flaunts her new lover. Leantio strikes back by becoming the lover of Livia, who has developed a sudden passion for him.

The subplot presents the relationship between Hippolito and his niece Isabella, who at first seem to have a pure, loving friendship. When Hippolito tries to seduce his niece, however, Isabella rejects him in horror. As in the main plot, Livia intercedes to help her brother by telling Isabella a lie—that she is not really a blood relative of Hippolito. Relieved of the threat of incest, Isabella can now express her love for Hippolito. Thus far, Isabella is essentially an innocent victim, but she is not so innocent when she agrees to go ahead with an arranged marriage in order to cover her love affair. She is betrothed to a coarse, stupid man, the ward of a character named Guardiano.

Both plots revolve around women who appear to be virtuous but who quickly reveal their frailty. Isabella at first appears to be a foil to Bianca, but she is scarcely her moral superior. In both plots, Livia schemes to destroy a woman in order to please her brother. Eventually, Hippolito learns about Livia's relationship with Leantio and, strangely, defends her honor by fighting and killing him. In anguish, Livia retaliates by revealing Hippolito's relationship with his niece, and this brings on the series of revenges in the denouement. During a masque to celebrate the wedding of the duke to Bianca, fictitious violence turns out to be real revenge and suicide. At the end,

death comes to Isabella, Guardiano, Livia, Hippolito, the duke, and Bianca.

As a summary of its plot suggests, *Women Beware Women* is a play of almost unrelieved horror and baseness. The play's only decent character, the cardinal, appears late in the action as a commentator on this baseness. Several of the main characters highlight their moral confusion by adopting moral poses in the midst of their depravity; Isabella's marriage with Guardiano's ward is an example of this defense mechanism, as is Hippolito's concern for his sister's honor even though at the time he is knowingly committing incest. Similarly, the lecherous duke deludes himself that he will become a virtuous person simply by marrying Bianca. At the center of the intrigue stands Livia, outwardly a good-humored, sociable woman but underneath a vastly dangerous person because of her extraordinary indifference to moral standards. Hippolito, as he dies, has some sense of what the tragedy has been about: "Lust and forgetfulness has [*sic*] been amongst us,/ And we are brought to nothing." Through this and other reminders near the end, and above all through the many ironies of the play, audiences are able to see the tremendous waste of healthy instincts destroyed by lust and ambition.

OTHER MAJOR WORKS

POETRY: *The Wisdom of Solomon, Paraphrased*, 1597; *Micro-cynicon*, 1599; *The Ghost of Lucrece*, 1600.

MISCELLANEOUS: *The Magnificent Entertainment Given to King James*, 1603 (with Thomas Dekker and Ben Jonson); *The Black Book*, 1604; *Father Hubburd's Tales*, 1604 (includes poetry); *Sir Robert Sherley*, 1609; *The Works of Thomas Middleton*, 1885-1886 (8 volumes; A. H. Bullen, editor).

BIBLIOGRAPHY

Brittin, Norman A. *Thomas Middleton*. New York: Twayne, 1972. Presents in a chronology and an introduction what little is known of Middleton's life, then marches through the generally accepted canon. The final chapter outlines the critical response to Middleton, and the annotated secondary bibliography is a good guide.

Chakravorty, Swapan. *Society and Politics in the Plays of Thomas Middleton*. New York: Oxford University Press, 1996. A look at the political and social world that surrounded Middleton and found its way into his plays. Bibliography and index.

Daileader, Celia R. *Eroticism on the Renaissance Stage: Transcendence, Desire, and the Limits of the Visible*. New York: Cambridge University Press, 1998. Daileader looks at the depiction of women and eroticism in the works of Middleton and Shakespeare. Bibliography and index.

Heinemann, Margot. *Puritanism and Theatre: Thomas Middleton and Opposition Drama Under the Early Stuarts*. New York: Cambridge University Press, 1980. Heinemann considers a series of problems: Why do Middleton's tragedies differ in tone from others of the period? Why did his work change so much over his career? How could *A Game at Chess* have been staged in the midst of a political crisis? Heinemann finds the answers in the plays' political settings.

Heller, Herbert Jack. *Penitent Brothellers: Grace, Sexuality, and Genre in Thomas Middleton's City Comedies*. Newark: University of Delaware Press, 2000. Heller looks at Calvinism, sex, and city and town life in Middleton's comedies. Bibliography and index.

Martin, Mathew R. *Between Theater and Philosophy: Skepticism in the Major City Comedies of Ben Jonson and Thomas Middleton*. Newark: University of Delaware Press, 2001. A scholarly study that looks at skepticism as it appeared in the comedic dramas of Middleton and Jonson. Bibliography and index.

Elliott A. Denniston,
updated by Frank Day

EDNA ST. VINCENT MILLAY

Born: Rockland, Maine; February 22, 1892
Died: Austerlitz, New York; October 19, 1950

PRINCIPAL DRAMA

The Princess Marries the Page, pr. 1917, pb. 1932
Two Slatterns and a King, pr. 1917, pb. 1921
Aria da Capo, pr. 1919, pb. 1920
The Wall of Dominoes, pb. 1921
The Lamp and the Bell, pr., pb. 1921
Three Plays, pb. 1926
The King's Henchman, pr., pb. 1927 (libretto; music by Deems Taylor)
Conversation at Midnight, pb. 1937, pr. 1961

OTHER LITERARY FORMS

Edna St. Vincent Millay is known primarily for her poetry rather than for her plays. In 1912 at the age of twenty, she entered a poetry contest with "Renascence." Although her poem only finished fourth, it was included in *The Lyric Year*, which consisted of the top one hundred poems out of approximately ten thousand submitted. The critical reaction was overwhelming positive, and she came to the attention of the American literary community. She continued to write poetry for the rest of her life, selling her work to magazines and collecting it into books periodically. To earn a living after graduating from college, she wrote short stories and satirical sketches under the pseudonym Nancy Boyd. They were collected into *Distressing Dialogues* (1924).

ACHIEVEMENTS

Edna St. Vincent Millay is generally considered the leading poet of the Jazz Age, the 1920's, as F. Scott Fitzgerald is considered that decade's leading novelist. Her second volume of poems, *A Few Figs from Thistles* (1920), made her one of the leading spokespersons for her generation. Millay also became recognized as a major feminist for smoking cigarettes in

Edna St. Vincent Millay (Library of Congress)

public when this was illegal for women and for advocating sexual freedom.

Millay was the second recipient of the then-new Pulitzer Prize in Poetry in 1923 for *The Ballad of the Harp Weaver*, and eight sonnets that appeared in *American Poetry 1922: A Miscellany*. These poems were reprinted that year in *The Harp-Weaver and Other Poems*.

Like those of her contemporaries Edgar Lee Masters and Dorothy Parker, Millay's volumes of poetry were best sellers. She toured the country several times to read her poems to the public. In 1927, *The King's Henchman* was the first opera broadcast on nationwide radio, and she herself read her poems eight times on nationwide radio in 1932. In 1938, a poll named her as one of the ten most famous women in the United States.

BIOGRAPHY

Edna St. Vincent Millay was the daughter of Cora Buzzell and Henry Millay. Cora divorced Henry for physical abuse and compulsive gambling when Millay was eight years old. Vincent, as she was called, grew up in Camden, Maine, with her mother and two younger sisters. Because Henry rarely sent them money, Cora had to support them by her meager earnings as a practical nurse and as a maker of women's hairpieces. After graduating from high school, Millay stayed home and worked in Camden to take care of her sisters. The publication of "Renascence" brought her to the attention of Caroline Dow, dean of the YWCA Training School of New York City, who enabled her to attend Vassar. There she acted in several theatrical productions and wrote three plays. Her schoolwork was exemplary, but her disregard for the rules of conduct almost prevented her from graduating in 1917.

After one last summer in Camden, Vincent moved to the Greenwich Village neighborhood of New York City, wrote short stories and more poetry, and became associated with the Provincetown Players, the Washington Square Players, and the Theatre Guild. She acted in several plays and both wrote and directed *Aria da Capo* in a Provincetown Player production. It received a rave review from Alexander Wollcott. In addition, she came into contact with other writers such as John Reed, Louise Bryant, Susan Glaspell, E. E. Cummings, Wallace Stevens, Theodore Dreiser, and Sherwood Anderson. In 1923, she married Dutch businessman Eugen Boissevain, descended from French Huguenots and twelve years her senior. They lived on a farm, named Steepletop after a wildflower that grew in the area, in Austerlitz, New York, for the rest of their lives, only leaving for trips and summer vacations to Maine. Although she had an intense love affair with fellow Pulitzer Prize-winning poet George Dillon, she remained married to Boissevain until his death in 1949. She herself passed away one year later after years of addiction to alcohol and morphine.

Once Vincent achieved popular success, she supported her mother until Cora's death in 1931 and arranged for her youngest sister Kathleen to attend Vassar. Kathleen also became a writer and poet, but Vincent always overshadowed her. Kathleen eventually became an alcoholic and died in 1943. The middle sister Norma became an actress, appearing in the original production of *Aria da Capo*, before marrying a painter. She survived both her siblings and inherited Steepletop, where she lived until her death in 1986, and became Millay's literary executor.

Except for feminism, Vincent was apolitical in college. However, she became associated with leftist causes first by attending the 1918 trial of Max Eastman, editor of *The Masses*, and others charged with violating the Sedition Act and then by protesting the 1927 executions of Italian immigrant anarchists Nicola Sacco and Bartolomeo Vanzetti, who had been convicted for murder. Vincent was arrested following a demonstration in Boston and personally pleaded with the governor of Massachusetts for clemency.

ANALYSIS

Edna St. Vincent Millay's plays can be divided into romances and political plays. It is ironic that her best-known play, *Aria da Capo*, is a political allegory, while her reputation as a poet suffered for writing anti-fascist poetry in the late 1930's and for participating in the American propaganda effort during World War II. She wrote three one-act plays, *The Princess Marries the Page*, *Two Slatterns and a King*, and *The Wall of Dominoes*, as a student at Vassar. Except for the third Vassar play, which has never been performed, Millay wrote all her plays in verse. The romantic plays emphasize the concepts of honor and integrity and the ideals of love and friendship. *Aria da Capo* is the one most frequently revived, with 471 licensed productions alone in the decade following her death. *Conversation at Midnight*, on the other hand, was not performed until after her death and is rarely revived.

ARIA DA CAPO

In music, an aria da capo is a three-part song in which the third part repeats the first. Millay's *Aria da Capo* is a one-act expressionist morality play divided into three parts. The characters are Thyrsis and Corydon, young shepherds; Pierrot, an artist; Columbine, a young woman; and Cothurnus, stage manager and the Masque of Tragedy. Dressed as harlequins and sitting at a table, Pierrot and Columbine begin by caricaturing the bohemian types Millay knew in Greenwich Village and commenting on the radical

movements of the era. Then Cothurnus interrupts them so that the shepherds can come onstage and perform their pastoral scene. After the harlequins leave, Cothurnus prompts the shepherds to build a wall that divides the stage into two territories. They discover that Thyrsis has all the water, and he refuses to allow Corydon's sheep to drink. Then Corydon discovers diamonds in his territory. Finally, Thyrsis finds a black root. They agree to trade a bowl of water for a bowl of diamonds. Thyrsis poisons the water with the root, and Corydon strangles Thyrsis with a necklace of diamonds. They die simultaneously. After Cothurnus pushes the table over the bodies and leaves, Pierrot and Columbine return and make disparaging remarks about the corpses. The harlequins take Cothurnus's offstage advice to use the tablecloth to hide the bodies and then resume their dialogue.

The harlequinade is an eighteenth century theater form, and the pastoral dates back to the ancient Greeks; the juxtaposition of both genres is a form of expressionism. The story, a play within a play, is an old one, similar to that of Cain and Abel. Because Corydon and Thyrsis separate and develop the concept of private property rather than engage in the pursuit of music and other constructive occupations, the naturally innocent shepherds develop distrust, egotism, and violence. The dialogue is mostly in blank verse in iambic meter, especially between the shepherds. The harlequins speak in shorter units with a smaller number of run-on lines and with a more colloquial vocabulary. Cothurnus's dialogue, on the other hand, is quite dignified.

THE LAMP AND THE BELL

The Lamp and the Bell is a spectacle Millay wrote for the fiftieth anniversary of the founding of Vassar College, an all-woman institution. There are forty-eight speaking roles and many nonspeaking roles for musicians and children, and Millay intended it to be performed outdoors in five acts. The medieval setting requires extensive costuming, and the action is spread over several years. Based on the fairy tale *Rose White and Rose Red*, it centered on the love between two women who are stepsisters.

A widower king with a daughter (Beatrice) marries a woman (Octavia), also with a daughter (Bianca).

Four years later, the two girls have become fast friends. However, Octavia sends Bianca away because she feels the girls are too close. Four months later, Beatrice falls in love with Mario, a neighboring king who is visiting. Guido, the court jester and illegitimate nephew of the king who lusts after Beatrice, and Octavia scheme to prevent their marriage by summoning Bianca home. Bianca also falls in love with Mario, who chooses Bianca. Beatrice never tells Bianca of her feelings for Mario. The king dies during the wedding, and Beatrice becomes queen. Five years later, Beatrice sustains an injury while fighting off bandits but accidentally kills Mario. Two years later, Bianca dies but not before forgiving Beatrice and entrusting her with the custody of her two children. Guido leads a revolt against Beatrice, but the people rise up to prevent it.

THE KING'S HENCHMAN

Millay's libretto for Deems Taylor's opera, *The King's Henchman*, was based on a story from the *Anglo-Saxon Chronicles* (tenth century). King Eadgar of the West Saxons sends his best friend Aethelwold to evaluate Aelfrida, daughter of the Thane of Devon, as a possible queen and to arrange their marriage should he find her suitable, which Eadgar defines as beautiful. Aethelwold, however, falls in love with Aelfrida and she with him. He betrays his king and friend by sending word that she is unsuitable as a queen, meaning too ugly, when she is the very opposite. Their marriage is an unhappy one because of Aethelwold's guilt and Aelfrida's boredom. She desires to visit Eadgar's court and to see the world. Eventually, Eadgar visits them and realizes that Aethelwold had lied to him when he meets the beautiful Aelfrida. Aethelwold kills himself out of shame.

It is interesting to contrast this story with *The Lamp and the Bell*, in which the two women friends remain faithful to each other, although they love the same man. In the case of *The King's Henchman*, a man betrays his best friend for a pretty face.

Millay uses a banquet in the opening act to convey background information and to send Aethelwold on his mission. Her words consisted only of those in the English vocabulary in some form prior to the Norman Conquest. The verse includes alliterative measures common in Old English poetry, the choruses have strong rhythms, and images are plentiful.

CONVERSATION AT MIDNIGHT

Some critics debate whether *Conversation at Midnight* should even be considered a play. Certainly Millay intended it to be read rather than performed, but George Bernard Shaw and Johann Wolfgang von Goethe also felt similarly regarding some of their plays on occasion. *Conversation at Midnight* is a Platonic dialogue among seven men who have different occupations, ages, and ideological beliefs. Although it is not explicitly stated in the character descriptions, it is implied that they are all Anglo-American, so there are no perspectives from other ethnic groups. They include Merton, a sixty-eight-year-old Republican Protestant stockbroker; Lucas, a twenty-five-year-old advertising writer; Father Anselmo, a forty-five-year-old Catholic priest; John, a forty-five-year-old painter who votes Democrat when he votes at all; Pygmalion, a forty-year-old short story writer who never votes; Ricardo, a forty-three-year-old agnostic liberal; and Carl, a forty-three-year-old communist poet. They meet for drinks at Ricardo's home to discuss a wide variety of subjects. Millay uses several different poetic styles, including rhyming couplets, lyrics, free verse, and sonnets.

The conversation begins with the subject of hunting and dogs. Carl objects to Merton paying five dollars weekly to care for his dog when other people live in poverty. Then the conversation moves in turn to religious faith, modern developments such as airplane flight and the vacuum cleaner, and the abuse of language. When Father Anselmo laments the degradation of Latin, especially Church Latin, the conversation returns to religious faith. From there, they discuss the question of war and violence. John argues that nations fight for living space, Ricardo says that humans have an instinct for violence, Carl blames capitalism, and Pygmalion cites boredom as the cause of wars. After this debate, Lucas brings up the subject of love, and all the men find agreement in their critique of women. The conversation then breaks into two groups to discuss economic motives, proletarian poetry, communism, and tradition. Toward the end, they discuss the world situation at hand, especially the rise of Hitler, Stalin, and Mussolini, but the conversation degenerates to trading insults before the gathering breaks up.

Millay intended the conversation to contrast and compare the opposing ideologies current in 1937 (with the exception of Nazism and fascism) and this fact makes the play seem dated at times. Unlike Plato, Millay's dialogue has neither a winner nor a loser, although Father Anselmo leaves the gathering early. Although Ricardo's point of view is closest to that of Millay, each participant is an eloquent, decent, and witty spokesman for his point of view.

OTHER MAJOR WORKS

POETRY: *Renascence and Other Poems*, 1917; *A Few Figs from Thistles*, 1920; *Second April*, 1921; *The Ballad of the Harp-Weaver*, 1922; *The Harp-Weaver and Other Poems*, 1923; *The Buck in the Snow and Other Poems*, 1928; *Edna St. Vincent Millay's Poems Selected for Young People*, 1929; *Fatal Interview*, 1931; *Wine from These Grapes*, 1934; *Huntsman, What Quarry?*, 1939; *Make Bright the Arrows*, 1940; *There Are No Islands Any More*, 1940; *Invocation to the Muses*, 1941; *Collected Sonnets*, 1941; *The Murder of Lidice*, 1942; *Collected Lyrics*, 1943; *Poem and Prayer for an Invading Army*, 1944; *Mine the Harvest*, 1954; *Collected Poems*, 1956.

NONFICTION: *Distressing Dialogues*, 1924 (as Nancy Boyd); *Letters*, 1952.

TRANSLATIONS: *The Flowers of Evil*, 1936 (of Charles Baudelaire; with George Dillon)

BIBLIOGRAPHY

Brittin, Norman A. *Edna St. Vincent Millay*. New York: Twayne, 1967. This critical analysis devotes one chapter to Millay's dramas and one subsection to each play.

Epstein, Daniel Mark. *What Lips My Lips Have Kissed: The Loves and Love Poems of Edna St. Vincent Millay*. New York: Henry Holt and Company, 2001. Although the author's emphasis is on Millay's love affairs and their connection to specific love poems, he discusses *Aria da Capo* and Millay's career as an actress in part two.

Milford, Nancy. *Savage Beauty: The Life of Edna St. Vincent Millay*. New York: Random House, 2001. The author was the first biographer to have access to Millay's private papers, and she also discussed them extensively with Norma Millay.

Thesing, William B. *Critical Essays on Edna St. Vincent Millay*. New York: G. K. Hall, 1993. A comprehensive collection of essays that includes early reviews and more modern scholarship. Harriet Monroe, Louis Untermeyer, Mark Van Doren, Allen Tate, Louise Bogan, and Edmund Wilson are among the authors that provide their interpretations and analysis.

Thomas R. Feller

ARTHUR MILLER

Born: New York, New York; October 17, 1915

PRINCIPAL DRAMA

The Man Who Had All the Luck, pr. 1944, pb. 1989
All My Sons, pr., pb. 1947
Death of a Salesman, pr., pb. 1949
An Enemy of the People, pr. 1950, pb. 1951 (adaptation of Henrik Ibsen's play)
The Crucible, pr., pb. 1953

A Memory of Two Mondays, pr., pb. 1955
A View from the Bridge, pr., pb. 1955 (one-act version)
A View from the Bridge, pr. 1956, pb. 1957 (two-act version)
Collected Plays, pb. 1957 (includes *All My Sons*, *Death of a Salesman*, *The Crucible*, *A Memory of Two Mondays*, *A View from the Bridge*)
After the Fall, pr., pb. 1964

Incident at Vichy, pr. 1964, pb. 1965

The Price, pr., pb. 1968

The Creation of the World and Other Business,
    pr. 1972, pb. 1973

The American Clock, pr. 1980, pb. 1982

Arthur Miller's Collected Plays, Volume II, pb.
    1981 (includes *The Misfits, After the Fall,
    Incident at Vichy, The Price, The Creation of
    the World and Other Business, Playing for
    Time*)

The Archbishop's Ceiling, pr., pb. 1984

Two-Way Mirror, pb. 1984

Danger: Memory!, pb. 1986, pr. 1988

Plays: One, pb. 1988

Plays: Two, pb. 1988

Plays: Three, pb. 1990

The Ride Down Mt. Morgan, pr. pb. 1991

The Last Yankee, pb. 1991, pr. 1993

Broken Glass, pr., pb. 1994

Plays: Four, pb. 1994

Plays: Five, pb. 1995

Mr. Peter's Connections, pr. 1998, pb. 1999

Arthur Miller (Inge Morath/Magnum)

OTHER LITERARY FORMS

Although Arthur Miller's major reputation is as a playwright, he has published reportage, *Situation Normal* (1944); a novel, *Focus* (1945); a novelized revision of his screenplay *The Misfits* (both 1961); a screenplay entitled *Everybody Wins* (1990); a collection of short stories, *I Don't Need You Any More* (1967); three book-length photo essays in collaboration with his wife, Ingeborg Morath, *In Russia* (1969), *In the Country* (1977), and *Chinese Encounters* (1979); and one television drama, aired in 1980, *Playing for Time*. Most studies of Miller's career neglect his nondramatic writing, even though he has demonstrated an impressive command of the short-story form and has proved himself remarkably adept at blending reportage, autobiography, and dramatic reflection in his later essay-length books, such as *"Salesman" in Beijing* (1984) and *Spain* (1987). All the important themes of his plays are explored in his nondramatic work, which also contains considerable comment on the nature of drama. *The Theater Essays of Arthur Miller* (1978), edited by Robert A. Martin,

and *Conversations with Arthur Miller* (1987), edited by Matthew C. Roudané, are essential to an understanding of Miller's theory of drama, his career in the theater, his political views, and his work as a whole; as is his autobiography, *Timebends* (1987).

ACHIEVEMENTS

Arthur Miller has been acclaimed as one of the most distinguished American dramatists since Eugene O'Neill, the father of modern American drama. Because of his direct engagement with political issues and with the theoretical concerns of contemporary drama, he has frequently been a significant spokesperson for his generation of writers. His reputation seems secure both nationally and internationally, and his plays continue to be performed live or through screenplay adaptations all over the world.

Miller successfully synthesized diverse dramatic styles and movements in the belief that a play should embody a delicate balance between the individual and society, between the singular personality and the polity, and between the separate and collective elements of life. Miller is a writer of social plays whose concern with the moral problems in American society led him to probe the psychological causes of behavior. He builds on the realist tradition of Henrik Ibsen in his exploration of the individual's conflict with society but also borrows Symbolist and expressionist techniques from Bertolt Brecht and others. He bases his plays on the assumption of an objective reality that is comprehensible as well as a subjective reality that makes life problematic and ambiguous. Therefore, all attempts to interpret his work from either an exclusively political or an exclusively psychological standpoint fail, for Miller regards his plays as indissoluble amalgamations of inner and outer realities.

Miller's achievement as a dramatist has been recognized with numerous awards. These include the Pulitzer Prize in 1944 for *Death of a Salesman*; the New York Drama Critics Circle Award for *All My Sons* in 1947 and for *Death of a Salesman* in 1949; the Antoinette Perry Award in 1949 for *Death of a Salesman* and for *The Crucible*. In 1956, Miller received an honorary Doctor of Humane Letters degree from the University of Michigan, and he was elected to the National Institute of Arts and Letters in 1958. During the 1990's, he received the William Ingle Festival Award for distinguished achievement in American theater and the Edward Albee Last Frontier Playwright Award. In 1998, Miller was named Distinguished Inaugural Senior Fellow of the American Academy in Berlin. In 1999, he received the Tony Award for Best Revival of a Play (*Death of a Salesman*) and in 2001 a National Endowment for the Humanities fellowship and the John H. Finley Award for Exemplary Service to New York City.

BIOGRAPHY

Arthur Miller grew up in New York City with an older brother and a younger sister. His father was a prosperous businessperson until the Crash of 1929, after which the family suffered through the Depression, a period that had a major impact on Miller's sense of himself, his family, and his society, and one

that figures prominently in many of his dramas, essays, and stories. During the Depression, Miller drove trucks, unloaded cargoes, waited on tables, and worked as a clerk in a warehouse. These jobs brought him close to the kind of working-class characters who appear in his plays. His observation of his father's fall from financial security and of the way the people immediately around him had to struggle for even a modicum of dignity placed Miller in a position to probe individuals' tenuous hold on their place in society.

Although Miller had been a poor student in school, he was inspired by Fyodor Dostoevski's implacable questioning of individual impulses and societal rules in *The Brothers Karamazov* (1879-1880), and eventually he was able to persuade the University of Michigan to admit him. Almost immediately he began to write plays that were to receive several Hopwood awards. If Miller was not exactly a Marxist during his college years (1934-1938), he was certainly a radical insofar as he believed that American society had to be made over, to be made fair to the masses of people who had been ruined by the Depression.

His early student plays contain sympathetic portrayals of student militants and union organizers as well as compassionate characterizations of small business owners and professional people caught in the economic and political tyranny of capitalism. In the fall of 1938, after his graduation from the University of Michigan with a bachelor of arts degree in English language and literature, Miller joined the Federal Theatre Project in New York City, for which he wrote numerous radio plays and scripts until 1943. Some of these works express his irrepressible interest in social and political issues. In 1940, Miller married Mary Grace Slattery, and a daughter, Jane, was born in 1944. They divorced in 1956.

From Miller's earliest student plays to *Death of a Salesman*, there is an evolution in his treatment of individuals in conflict with their society, a gradual realization of conflicts within individuals that both mirror the larger conflicts in society and define a core of singularity in the characters themselves. Undoubtedly, Miller's intense involvement in public affairs in the 1940's and 1950's—his support of various liberal and radical causes and his subsequent testimony about his political commitments before the House Committee on Un-American Activities in 1956 are two examples—reflected and reinforced his need to write social plays.

Miller's marriage to Marilyn Monroe in 1956, far from being the perplexing and amusing sideshow the press made of it, had a significant impact on his writing, not only by encouraging him to focus on female characters in ways he previously had not but also by stimulating him to enlarge on and reconsider the theme of innocence that he had adumbrated in earlier plays. After his divorce from Monroe in 1961, he wrote some of his finest plays and continued to participate in local, national, and international affairs—including two terms as international president of PEN, the worldwide writers' organization. He was a delegate to the Democratic conventions of 1968 and 1972. Miller married Ingeborg Morath, a Austrian-born photojournalist, in 1962, and the couple collaborated on several travel books. After serving as a lecturer at the University of Michigan in the mid-1970's, Miller retired to a large Connecticut estate, where he continued to write and where he indulged in such hobbies as carpentry and gardening. In 1997, he petitioned the Czech government to halt arrests of dissident writers. His international reputation expanded during the 1980's, when he directed *Death of a Salesman* in Beijing, China. Throughout the 1990's, Miller continued to receive numerous awards for distinguished achievement. In early 2002, his wife died.

ANALYSIS

A back injury prevented Arthur Miller from serving in the armed forces during World War II, but in characteristic fashion, he became involved in the war effort by gathering material for a screenplay, "The Story of GI Joe," which was never filmed but instead became the basis of his book *Situation Normal*, in which he reported on army camps in the United States and on soldiers' attitudes toward the war in which they were preparing to fight. For the most part, the soldiers had no great interest in the democratic principles for which Miller believed the war was fought, but he elevated one war hero, Watson, to a representative position as a figure whose intensely

avowed loyalty to his company represents the democratic solidarity many others cannot articulate. Miller admitted candidly the skepticism of Watson's company commander, who doubted Watson's whole-hearted commitment to rejoin his fellow soldiers in one of the most dangerous theaters of the war: "The company pride that made him do the great things he did do is gone now and he is left unattached, an individual," who yearns for—yet probably fears—returning to men he knows he will never see again. Thus, *Situation Normal* was transformed into the drama of how Miller's innocent convictions about the war were challenged by psychological and social complexities; indeed, the book is informed by a crisis of conviction that Miller did not fully recognize until the writing of *After the Fall* and *Incident at Vichy*.

THE MAN WHO HAD ALL THE LUCK

Even in an early play, *The Man Who Had All the Luck*—Miller's first Broadway production—there is some awareness of the dangers inherent in the innocent attitude of characters such as David Frieber, who insists that the world conform to what his employer, Shory, calls "the awards of some cloudy court of justice." At twenty, Frieber is still a child, Shory suggests, and Frieber admits that he does not know what he is supposed to be. He believes that he must somehow earn everything that comes to him. That good fortune and the complex interplay of societal forces he cannot control also contribute significantly to his success is an idea that disturbs him. In his quest to become self-made, he withdraws from society, from his family, and ultimately from himself. In the midst of his guilty obsession with the fact that others have aided him, he is unable to see that he has already demonstrated his resourcefulness. In his delusion that he can measure himself, he gives up everything he owns and starts a new business. Frieber's lunacy seems somewhat forced—much too strident, making it all too obvious that Miller has a point to prove. Moreover, Frieber's quasi-philosophical declamations disturb what is otherwise rather well-executed midwestern dialogue.

ALL MY SONS

Miller comes even closer to fluent dialogue and carefully crafted dramatic structure in *All My Sons*, his first Broadway success and the first play he deemed mature enough to include in his *Collected Plays* of 1957. Critics have long admired the playwright's suspenseful handling of the Keller family's burden: the father's permitting defective parts to remain in warplanes that subsequently crash. Not only does Joe Keller fail to recognize his social responsibility, but also he allows his business partner to take the blame and serve the prison term for the crime. Gradually, events combine to strip Keller of his rationalizations. He argues that he never believed that the cracked engine heads would be installed and that he never admitted his mistake because it would have driven him out of business at the age of sixty-one, when he would not have another chance to "make something" for his family, his highest priority. "If there's something bigger than that I'll put a bullet in my head!" he exclaims. He also claims that other businessmen behaved no differently during the war and that Larry, his son who died flying a warplane, would have approved of his actions: "He understood the way the world is made. He listened to me," Keller contends. He maintains these arguments, however, as a man who has clearly been challenged by his surviving son, Chris, who questions his father's very humanity when the full truth of Joe's irresponsibility is exposed: "What the hell are you? You're not even an animal, no animal kills his own, what are you?" Joe Keller's tough, resilient character crumbles quickly after Larry's former fiancée, Ann, discloses Larry's last letter, in which he expresses his intention to crash his plane in shame over his father's culpability. The play turns somewhat melodramatic with Joe's reversal of viewpoint, his discovery of his social responsibility, and his human loss in the deaths of the young fliers. His statement, "They were all my sons," depends heavily on Larry's self-abnegating idealism and on other contrived plot devices, as Leonard Moss instructively points out. Miller resorts to the theatrical trick of the last-minute revelation rather than relying on character development. Nevertheless, the logic of destroying Joe's innocent disregard of the world at large—he is not so much deeply cynical as he is profoundly unaware of the ties that must hold society together—is compelling, especially because he cries

for moral direction. "What do I do? he asks his wife, Kate, thus strengthening Chris's imperative that his father reckon the consequences of his terrible moral oversight. If audiences are still gripped by the final events of *All My Sons*, it is because the play's early scenes convincingly dramatize familiar aspects of family and community, with characters who know one another very well, who are quick to respond to the nuances of conversation and to what is unspoken but clearly implied.

What disables Miller's plays before *Death of a Salesman* is not so much an inadequate understanding of dramatic form; rather, both his dramatic and nondramatic prose lack artistic tact. He tends to overstate social problems, to give otherwise inarticulate characters such as Lawrence Newman in the novel *Focus* an inappropriately self-conscious language that is meant to identify their cumulative awareness of societal sickness—in Newman's case, of anti-Semitism. Like so much of Miller's writing, however, *Focus* transcends its faults because of its author's incisive portrayal of events that relentlessly push Newman to the brink of self-knowledge.

DEATH OF A SALESMAN

In *Death of a Salesman*—originally entitled "The Inside of His Head"—Miller brilliantly solves the problem of revealing his main character's inner discord, rendering Willy Loman as solid as the society in which he tries to sell himself. Indeed, many critics believe that Miller has never surpassed his achievement in this play, which stands as his breakthrough work, distinguished by an extremely long Broadway run, by many revivals, and by many theater awards, including the Pulitzer Prize in 1949. *Death of a Salesman* seems destined to remain an American classic and a standard text in American classrooms.

Willy Loman desperately wants to believe that he has succeeded, that he is "well liked" as a great salesman, a fine father, and a devoted husband. That he has not really attracted the admiration and popularity at which he has aimed is evident, however, in the weariness that belabors him from the beginning of the play. At the age of sixty-three, nearing retirement, Willy dreads confronting the conclusion that his life has gone offtrack, just like the automobile he cannot keep from driving off the road. His mind wanders because he has lost control: He has trouble keeping up with the bills; he feels hemmed in at home by huge, towering apartment buildings; his sales are slipping drastically; and his sons have thwarted his hope for their success.

Earlier in his career, Miller might have made a good but unremarkable play out of Willy's dilemma, a drama about how American society has misled him and stuffed him with unrealizable dreams until a conflict between social structures and individual desires becomes inevitable. Instead, Miller learned from the mistakes in his earlier plays not to divide individual and social realities too neatly or too simply, so that in *Death of a Salesman*, he created a great play that is not merely about a victim of society.

Willy is not easily categorized; he is both simple and complex. On the one hand, he has all the modern conveniences that stamp him as a product of society; on the other hand, he is not content to be simply another social component. As he tells Linda, his wife, who tries to soothe his sense of failure, "some people accomplish something." "A man has got to add up to something," he assures his brother, Uncle Ben. Willy resists the idea that his life has been processed for him—like the processed American cheese he angrily rejects for Swiss, his favorite. Still, he wonders, "How can they whip cheese?" and thus he can be diverted from self-scrutiny to the trivialities of postwar consumer society.

Willy worries that he talks too much, that he is fat and unattractive, but he also brags about his persuasive abilities, his knack for knowing how to please people. Similarly, he alternately regards his son Biff as a bum and as having "greatness"; Willy's automobile is alternately the finest of its kind and a piece of junk. Willy is a mass of contradictions who asks why he is "always being contradicted." He has never been able to sort himself out, to be certain of his course in life. He is insulted when his friend Charley offers him a job, because the job offer and Charley's self-assured demeanor—he keeps asking Willy when will he grow up—remind Willy of Uncle Ben, a man who is "utterly certain of his destiny," who once extended to Willy a tremendous opportunity in Alaska, an oppor-

tunity Willy rejected with regret in favor of a salesperson's career. He lives with the might-have-been of the past as though it were his present and even confuses Charley with Ben. As a result, scenes from Willy's past and present follow—and indeed pursue—one another successively in a fuguelike fashion that shows his awareness of his failure to progress.

There is a grandeur in Willy's dreams of success; his self-deceptions are derived from his genuine perceptions of life's great possibilities, which are like the big sales he has always hoped to make. This is why Linda abets his penchant for self-aggrandizement. She knows that he has not been a successful salesperson, but she tempers his faults: "You don't talk too much, you're just lively." At the same time, she is utterly believable as a housewife who has to know how much money her husband has brought home from work. After Willy exaggerates his sales from one trip, Linda quietly but firmly brings him back to reality by simply asking, "How much did you do?"—a question that becomes more pointed if the actress playing the role delicately emphasizes the word "did."

When the play is read aloud, there is an uncanny power in some of its simplest and seemingly pedestrian lines, lines that capture the nuances and innuendos of colloquial language. This subtly effective dialogue is enhanced by a powerful use of human gesture that distinguishes *Death of a Salesman* as a completely realizable stage drama. Toward the end of the play, for example, after Biff, "at the peak of his fury," bluntly tells Willy, "Pop, I'm nothing!" Biff relents, breaks down, sobs, and holds on to Willy, "who dumbly fumbles for Biff's face." This brief intimate encounter encapsulates everything that can be learned about Willy and Biff and about the play's import, for the son renounces the father's ridiculous belief in the son's superiority even as the son clings to the father for support. While Biff rejects Willy, he embraces him and has to explain himself to Willy, who is "astonished" and at first does not know how to interpret his son's holding on to him. Willy does not understand why Biff is crying. Willy has always been blind to Biff's needs, has always "fumbled" their relationship, yet—as so often—Willy transforms Biff's words of rejection into an affirmation. The Biff who leans on him is the son who "likes me!" Willy exclaims, after their close but momentary contact. This fleeting instance of family solidarity, however, cannot overcome the abiding family conflicts and misunderstandings, epitomized by Willy's delusion that the insurance money accrued from his suicide will finally make him the good provider, the person who furthers his son's magnificent future.

AN ENEMY OF THE PEOPLE

Miller followed *Death of a Salesman* with his 1951 adaptation of Henrik Ibsen's *En folkefiende* (pb. 1882; *An Enemy of the People*, 1890). Miller transforms Ibsen's language into American idioms and shortens the play to emphasize the impact of Dr. Stockmann's confrontation with his community, which will not acknowledge its polluted water, its own moral and political corruption. Stockmann's battle against public opinion clearly foreshadows John Proctor's struggle with his society's self-inflicted evil in *The Crucible*. *The Crucible* is far more complex than Miller's adaptation of Ibsen's play, however, because Proctor is much more complicated than Stockmann, and the motivations of the Puritans are not as easily fathomed as those of Stockmann's townspeople, who are primarily worried about their economic welfare. Even so, *An Enemy of the People* prefigures the fundamental questions raised in *The Crucible* about the value of human dignity and individuality and the kind of justice one can expect from a majority culture, especially when that culture begins to doubt its own coherence.

THE CRUCIBLE

With incisive historical summaries, Miller, in *The Crucible*, characterizes the community of Salem, Massachusetts, in 1692, which has been beset by property disputes, by a slackening in religious fervor, and by an increasing lack of trust among its citizens. Rather than face their inner turmoil, some of Salem's citizens search for scapegoats, for people who can take on the society's sense of defeat and frustration, who can be punished, and who can carry away by means of their execution the society's burden of guilt. In short, the Puritans seek signs of the devil and devil-worship in their midst in order to dissolve their

own dissension. Although John Proctor, like Stockmann, speaks against his community's blindness to the true causes of its corruption, he does not share to the same degree Stockmann's naïveté, youthful outrage at injustice, and virtually pure innocence as a dissident. On the contrary, Proctor eventually opposes the witch-hunt, because he accepts his own part in having made that hysterical clamor for scapegoats possible. He knows that he has not acted quickly enough to expose Abigail, the chief instigator of the witch-hunt, because he has feared his own exposure as an adulterer. What finally exercises his conscience is not simply that he had previously given way to his lust for Abigail but that he had deluded himself into thinking he no longer cared for her and had even reprimanded his wife, Elizabeth, for failing to forgive him. Elizabeth is unbending but not without cause, for she intuits her husband's tender feelings toward Abigail and suspects that he refuses to know his own mind. Proctor almost relinquishes his good name by confessing to witchery, until he realizes that however deep his guilt and responsibility may be for the community's corruption, he cannot surrender his integrity, his cherished individuality. Like Willy Loman, Proctor reaffirms his own name—"I am John Proctor!"—and prefers his own crucible to his society's severe test of him for its redemption.

The Crucible is not only Proctor's play, however, and as important as its moral and political implications are—it was first received as a parable on McCarthyism and the 1950's hysteria over communism in the United States—it deserves analysis as a dramatic whole in the same way that *Death of a Salesman* does. In Miller's superb creation of scenes that require a company of carefully choreographed actors and actresses, he is able to dramatize an entire society and to show the interplay of individual and group psychology. Proctor would not be regarded as such a powerful personality were it not for the full panoply of personalities out of which he emerges. In this respect, *The Crucible* has a finer equilibrium as a social play than does *Death of a Salesman*, which is inescapably dominated by Willy Loman's consciousness. Miller's accomplished use of the Puritans' formal idioms suggests their rigid judgments of one another.

Perhaps he even exaggerates the archaisms of their language in order to stress the gravity of their world-view, although at the same time, he dramatizes a childishness in their readiness to credit the workings of witchcraft. There is a great deal of humor, for example, in one of the play's early scenes, in which Mrs. Putnam's energetic entrance explodes the seriousness of reports that the Reverend Parris's child, Betty, has been bewitched. Mrs. Putnam, every bit as excited as a child, immediately glances at Betty and wonders, "How high did she fly, how high?" The simple, naïve directness of these words catches the audience up in a kind of enthusiasm for the marvelous that will soon infect Abigail and her female followers as well as the whole society of Salem. By varying his speakers' styles to conform to the precise demands of each dramatic situation, Miller wins the audience's absolute confidence in the psychological reality of his characters.

A MEMORY OF TWO MONDAYS

Miller's excursion into the Puritan past was followed by the writing of two one-act plays, *A Memory of Two Mondays* and *A View from the Bridge* (later revised as a two-act play), both of which he regarded as having arisen from his personal experience, although it took him some time to discover the autobiographical elements of the latter play. *A Memory of Two Mondays* covers the Depression period before Miller's admission to the University of Michigan, and the play centers on the discrepancy between human needs and work requirements. Kenneth, the most melancholy character in the play, also has the greatest feeling for life and for its poetry. In the end, however, he has forgotten the poems he recites to Bert, the only character who escapes the tedium of the automobile parts warehouse, who will read the great books and save enough money to go to college. The other characters remain very much imprisoned in their everyday lives. Bert's leavetaking is hardly noticed, even though he lingers in obvious need of making more out of his friendships at the warehouse than others are willing to acknowledge. Earlier, he and Kenneth had washed the windows of the warehouse to get a clear look at the world in which they were situated; now Kenneth is a drunk and Bert must stand apart, like

his author, remembering the meaning of what others have already forgotten because of the demands of their jobs. Although *A Memory of Two Mondays* is one of Miller's minor achievements, it is also one of his most perfectly executed dramas in that the impulse to rescue significance from Bert's departure is sensitively qualified by the consciousness of human loss.

A VIEW FROM THE BRIDGE

Miller's one-act version of *A View from the Bridge* is also a memory play—in this case based on a story he had heard and pondered for several years. Eddie Carbone, a longshoreman, is driven to violate the most sacred ties of trust that bind his community by his compulsion to possess his niece, Catherine—a compulsion that he denies and displaces by conceiving an unreasoning dislike for his wife's young relative, Rodolpho, an illegal immigrant whom Eddie has agreed to harbor. Eddie implies that Rodolpho is a homosexual, an unnatural man who will marry Catherine merely to make his stay in the country legal. Eddie's desperate need to have Catherine becomes so uncontrollable that, when she and Rodolpho make plans to marry, he informs on Rodolpho and his brother, Marco, who are apprehended in circumstances that expose Eddie to his neighborhood as an informer. In Marco's view, Eddie must be confronted with his subhuman behavior. In words reminiscent of Chris's charge in *All My Sons* that his father is not human, Marco calls Eddie an animal who must abase himself. "You go on your knees to me!" Marco commands Eddie, while Eddie expects Marco to give him back his "good name." They fight, and Eddie dies, stabbed by Marco with the former's own knife. In a sense, Eddie has stabbed himself; the play has shown all along that Eddie's mortal wound has been self-inflicted.

Eddie's cry for self-respect recalls similar pleas by Willy Loman and John Proctor, and the concern in *A View from the Bridge* with informing and betrayal of friendships and blood ties echoes themes from Miller's student plays through *The Crucible*, foreshadowing not only his own refusal to "name names" in his testimony before the House Committee on Un-American Activities but also Quentin's fundamental exploration of many different kinds of betrayal in *After the Fall*. Yet Miller first wrote *A View from the Bridge* as if he were aloof from its central story, as if it were a parable that he did not understand. He even provides a narrator, Alfieri, an attorney who ruminates over the significance of the story as Miller admits he had done in writing the play.

The one-act version of *A View from the Bridge* seems aloof from the audience as well. There is very little attempt to probe the characters' psychology, so that what Miller gains in dramatic force by presenting events swiftly and starkly, he loses in the audience's inability to empathize with circumscribed characters. Miller acknowledges these faults and notes that the two-act version more fully develops his characters' psychology, particularly that of Eddie's wife, Beatrice. Catherine, too, is a much-improved character in the two-act version. She tentatively expresses her divided feelings about Eddie, whereas in the one-act version, she is far less self-searching, almost woodenly immune to his passion. In the two-act, she desires to appease Eddie's growing fears of her approaching adulthood. She loves him for his devotion to her, but her childlike behavior, as Beatrice points out to her, only encourages his possessiveness. Thus, Catherine tries gradually to separate herself from Eddie so that she can attain full maturity. As a result, Eddie's rigid refusal to admit his perverse passion for Catherine, even when Beatrice confronts him with it, makes him singularly willful and more particularly responsible for his tragedy than is the case in the one-act version, in which all the characters, except Alfieri, are rather helplessly impelled by events. In this respect, Rodolpho is a more credible suitor for Catherine in the two-act version because he is somewhat more commanding (she pleads with him, "I don't know anything, teach me, Rodolpho, hold me") in capturing her love and therefore a stronger counterweight to Eddie's authority.

A View from the Bridge in two acts still does not overcome all the play's weaknesses. For example, Alfieri, like many narrators in drama, seems somewhat intrusive in his use of elevated language to wrest an overarching meaning from characters and events, even though he is an active participant in some fine scenes. Nevertheless, the play is as beautifully written and moving as any of Miller's major works, and its main character is almost as powerfully drawn as Willy Loman and John Proctor, who, like Eddie Carbone, will not "settle for half"—will not be content with less than their lives' joy. Because of an ample sense of self, they allow themselves, in Alfieri's words, "to be wholly known."

AN INTERLUDE

Miller arrived at an impasse upon his completion of the two-act version of *A View from the Bridge*, which was successfully produced in England in 1956, and he did not have another new work staged until 1964. Various explanations have been offered for this long gap in his dramatic production—including his marriage to Marilyn Monroe, the attendant publicity that interfered with his working life, and the trying and time-consuming process of defending his political activities. Of crucial importance, however, seems to have been his feeling that what he had been working for in his plays had not been sufficiently understood by his public. At any rate, he wrote several plays that did not satisfy him, a number of short stories, and a screenplay, *The Misfits*, that was subsequently revised as a novel. He may have turned to other literary forms from a belief that he had temporarily exhausted what had been an evolving sense of dramatic structure. Nondramatic prose seems to have permitted him to explore certain themes and narrative viewpoints that he had not been able to incorporate fully in *A View from the Bridge*, for his next produced play, *After the Fall*, successfully fuses narrative and dramatic discourse in the figure of its central character, Quentin, who constantly forces the audience into the explicit position of auditors rather than into the intermittent role of eavesdroppers addressed by a narrator as in *A View from the Bridge*.

AFTER THE FALL

How does one live in a world beset by death? This question is relentlessly probed in *After the Fall*, with its concentration-camp tower serving as one of the central metaphors for the human betrayal of life. As was so often true in the camps, the characters in *After the Fall* are divided against themselves. Not only can kind men kill, but also intelligent men can act like idiots, and Maggie—innocent in so many ways—is horribly transformed into a hater of life. Quentin, who is Maggie's momentary stay against confusion, witnesses "things falling apart" and wonders, "Were they ever whole?" He proves to be incapable of protecting Maggie, so concerned is he with his own survival. In the very act of saving her from her pills—from her death—he defends himself by strangling her, suffocating her just as surely as the pills would have done. He discovers the limits of his own love for her, and Maggie sees his human incapacity for unconditional love as a betrayal, just as Quentin interprets the limitations of his mother's love as a betrayal of him. Thus, for Maggie, Quentin comes at "the end of a long, long line" of men who have degraded her, betrayed her, killed her. He is, in other words, an accomplice in the general evil of the world, and therefore his presence as an "accomplice" in the ultimate evil that is the concentration camp is not altogether unfitting. He has been his mother's accomplice in the degradation of his father and an accomplice in the death of his friend, Lou, who sensed that Quentin could not wholeheartedly defend his reputation and that he was not, in fact, a true friend. Quentin craves his own safety, and he feels the guilt of the survivor as the concentration-camp tower "blazes into life."

Maggie has no identity to hold back, no reserves of self to compensate for her disappointment in Quentin. She thinks of herself as "nothing" and hopes to please everyone by becoming "all love." (The metaphor's abstractness virtually ensures her inability to develop a defined self.) Ironically, her generosity eats her up—people eat her up—because she does not possess the normal defenses of a separate ego. Maggie requires from Quentin the same selflessness she represents. She wants him to look at her "out of [his] *self.*" Quentin has abetted her by acting more like a child than an adult. Like William Faulkner's Quentin Compson in *The Sound and the Fury* (1929), Miller's Quentin is an idealist and something of a Puritan; he romanticizes Maggie's innocence and believes that she must be saved from herself and from a corrupt world. In some ways, he seems as thoroughly innocent as Quentin Compson's brother Benjy, an idiot—

the word itself is applied to Miller's protagonist more than once, and it recurs obsessively as he recalls how others have employed the term to deny and attack one another. No more than Benjy or Maggie can Quentin accept the separateness of the adult world of his mother, his friends, and his wives.

These failures of love, of human connection, force Quentin to reexamine the moments of hopefulness that recur, one might say, idiotically—for no apparently sensible reason—throughout the play. From the concentration-camp tower and on "the mountain of skulls" where no one can be "innocent again," Quentin observes the "fallen Maggie," who once seemed like a proof of victory, and he realizes that his brothers both died in and built the camp, that Maggie's fall is his fall, and that without that fall he would have no hope, for hope in the real world is "not in some garden of wax fruit and painted trees, that lie of Eden," but in the knowledge of human destructiveness, of human idiocy, which will not go away and so must be taken to heart. In the full knowledge of his failures, Quentin embraces his life at the end of the play, whereas Maggie is seen rising from the floor "webbed in with her demons, trying to awake." Her partial consciousness reflects her inability to take full responsibility for her life, to see that she was not simply a victim but in charge of her emotions. The hardest thing Quentin must do is reverse the force of the play's dominant metaphor, making the idiot serve not as a rejection of the broken, fragmented facts of life but as an acceptance of the flawed face of all people. That reversal of rejection is accomplished by saying hello to Holga, his third partner in life, who has provided the dream—the metaphor, in truth—of how lives such as Quentin's ("Why do I make such stupid statements!") and Maggie's ("I'm a joke that brings in money") can tentatively approach redemption.

After the Fall sometimes suffers from a vagueness of rhetoric and from overstatement, so that Quentin's confessions overwhelm the dramatic action and diminish the substantiality of other characters. Miller restrains Quentin's verbosity in the revised stage version quoted here (printed in 1964, the same year as the production of the original stage version, available in *Collected Plays, Volume II*). A television adaptation (1974) removes nearly all of Quentin's verbiage, but in none of these versions is Miller entirely successful in balancing Quentin's subjective and objective realities. Edward Murray argues, for example, that not all scenes are consistently staged "in the mind, thought, and memory of Quentin," as the play would have it. Hence it is difficult to find a "warrant," a certifiable viewpoint, for some of the play's action. In *Death of a Salesman*, on the contrary, the audience is compelled to move in and out of Willy's mind and is thereby able to comprehend his reality both subjectively and objectively. In part, Murray's objection may be met by carefully following Quentin's struggle to *know* his past, not simply to repossess it as Willy does. How does one achieve a viewpoint, Quentin asks, when there is no objective basis on which to recreate one's past? In the disagreements over Quentin's motives (some critics emphasize his self-criticism, others his self-exculpation), Miller adumbrates an ambiguity of viewpoint explored more successfully in *The Price*.

INCIDENT AT VICHY

Some reviewers of the first production of *Incident at Vichy* mistook it as a message play and faulted Miller not only for his didacticism but also for teaching a lesson already learned about Nazism and people's inhumanity toward others. It is a very talky drama, and given the various arguments advanced, it is easy to regard the characters as representative figures rather than as whole personalities. That this is not the case, however, is evident in the play's refusal to locate a winning argument, a resolution of the crisis of conviction besetting each character as his most cherished opinions are found wanting, are exposed as contradictory and self-serving. Even Leduc, who does a large amount of the debunking, discovers that he is not free of self-aggrandizing illusions. The Major reveals Leduc's privileged sense of himself, and Von Berg forces on him a pass to freedom, which he must take at the cost of another's imprisonment. Von Berg's self-abnegating act of love for another man—although a moving statement of his belief that there are people in the world who would sacrifice themselves rather than permit evil to be done to others—is

not dramatized as a final answer to the self-interested pleas of the other characters, however, and it does not cause the reversal of belief Miller coerced from Joe Keller after his son Larry's suicide in *All My Sons*. On the contrary, Von Berg is faced at the end of the play with an uncomprehending Major, a man who scorns gestures of self-sacrifice, except insofar as he is "an idealist" who ironically sacrifices himself for the perpetuation of the totalitarian system he serves.

For all the characters, then, Vichy France during World War II is a place of detention where their self-justifications are demolished as they await their turns in the examination room, in which their release or their final fate in the concentration camps will be determined. Like Quentin, they are all vulnerable to the suspicion that they have not lived in "good faith." In other words, it is their questionable integrity, not their shaky ideas, that is ultimately at stake. *Incident at Vichy* is Miller's most existential play, in the sense that there is no exit from the dilemmas it portrays, no consoling truths to which characters can cling permanently; instead, there are only approximations of the truth, certain accurate perceptions, but there is nothing like the requiem, the coda, the summing up to be found in *Death of a Salesman*, *The Crucible*, and *A View from the Bridge*.

THE PRICE

In *The Price*, Miller combines the best features of *After the Fall* and *Incident at Vichy*. Once again, the issue of coming to others in "good faith" is paramount, as Esther realizes in characterizing the surprise appearance of her husband Victor's brother, Walter. Walter returns to their boyhood apartment, where Victor is selling the family possessions because the building has been condemned. Walter has not seen his brother in sixteen years and wants to explain to him why he chose such an independent course, why he failed to support their father as Victor had done, to the detriment of his career. The immensely successful Walter feels stymied by the past and suggests that he and Victor took "seemingly different roads out of the same trap" created by their father's pose of helplessness after the failure of his business in the Crash of 1929. While Victor chose to "invent" a life of self-sacrifice, Walter chose to adopt a career of self-advancement. "We're like two halves of the same guy," Walter insists. His point is well taken in terms of Miller's dramatic development, for Victor and Walter are also opposite sides of Quentin, whose family background is somewhat similar to theirs and who engages in similar debates with himself concerning the calls of self-denial and self-preferment; indeed, like Quentin, Victor and Walter are having what is essentially an argument with themselves in front of auditors (Esther and the furniture dealer, Gregory Solomon). Because Walter and Victor can go over the same ground of the past, their recollections are both arguable and utterly convincing as parallel but divergent interpretations. Thus, the audience responds to one character's point of view in the context of the other's and follows precisely the process by which these characters form their histories. Walter excuses himself by showing that in objective terms his father was not helpless; he had four thousand dollars he asked Walter to invest for him. Walter rejects the vision of family harmony that Victor worked so steadily to maintain; there was no love between their mother and father, only a business arrangement, as Walter brutally reveals with vivid memories of how their mother failed to support their father in his terrible need. Victor dismisses Walter's narrowly conceived interpretation of his father and their family. "A system broke down," he reminds Walter, referring to the Crash, "did I invent that?" Victor fights against Walter's simplification of their father's psychology. Embedded in Victor's words is an echo of Miller's original title for *Death of a Salesman*: "What about the inside of his head? The man was ashamed to go into the street!"

In the dialogue between these "archetypal brothers," as Neil Carson calls them, the nature of individual psychology and social reality, which Miller explores in all of his plays, is debated, and nowhere is that exploration more finely balanced, more convincingly conceived, than in *The Price*, where the two brothers—for all of their representativeness—steadfastly remain individual and irreconcilable. Moreover, the other two characters, Esther and Solomon (a kibitzer who is Miller's funniest and wisest creation), are just as credibly presented, as they mediate between the hard positions held by Victor and Walter.

Esther is one of Miller's most complex female characters, as her lyric memory at the end of the play demonstrates, for her wistful words richly embody all the wonderful promise of a life gone sour, just as Solomon's last actions—he is listening to a "laughing record" from the 1920's, "sprawling in the chair, laughing with tears in his eyes, howling helplessly to the air"—recall all the characters' hilarious and painful memories, leaving the audience perfectly poised in this drama of life's alternative expressions.

THE CREATION OF THE WORLD AND OTHER BUSINESS

The Creation of the World and Other Business—with its archetypal brothers (Cain and Abel), its battle between God and Lucifer (who stand as the alternatives between which Adam and Eve must choose), its feel for human beings in a state of natural but problematic innocence, and its grappling with injustice—is an inevitable outgrowth of themes Miller has pursued throughout his career. When the play first appeared, however, it startled reviewers with its departure from Miller's realistic, domestic settings. They did not receive it favorably, and the play failed in its initial Broadway production, which is unfortunate, because it contains some of Miller's shrewdest writing and a surprisingly innovative rendition of the Edenic myth. The play's humor saves it from becoming a ponderous retelling of the familiar biblical account. The wide-ranging use of idiomatic expressions in English, Yiddish, and French mixed with the English of the Authorized Version of the Bible sets up a fascinating juxtaposition between the traditional story and the contemporary language that gives the whole play an uncanny freshness and irreverence. God calls Adam and Eve "my two idiotic darlings," and the profoundly comic nature of their moral and sexual education gradually acquires credibility. Would not the experience of being the first man and woman constitute the first comedy as well as the first tragedy? This is the question Miller appears to have posed for himself in this play, for Adam and Eve do not know what to do. Not having a history of feelings about God, about humanity, and about their sexuality, they must discover their sentiments about all of these things, and Lucifer would like to show them the shortcuts, to rationalize life, to avoid conflict before it begins. In order to follow him, however, Adam and Eve must accept the primacy of intellect over love.

LATER PLAYS

Several of Miller's later plays, including *The American Clock*, *The Archbishop's Ceiling*, and *Danger: Memory!*, proved far more successful in London than in New York, a fact the playwright attributed at one point to the discomfort his American producers felt in dealing with "psychopolitical themes." Deeply cognizant of the dangers of social coercion and excessive conformity, Miller continued to hunger for the sense of community he described in one of his books of photo essays, *In Russia*:

> No one who goes to the theater in Russia can fail to be struck by the audience. . . . It is as though there were still a sort of community in this country, for the feeling transcends mere admiration for professionals doing their work well. It is as though art were a communal utterance, a kind of speech which everyone present is delivering together.

OTHER MAJOR WORKS

LONG FICTION: *Focus*, 1945; *The Misfits*, 1961.

SHORT FICTION: *I Don't Need You Any More*, 1967; *Homely Girl, A Life, and Other Stories*, 1995.

SCREENPLAYS: *The Misfits*, 1961; *Everybody Wins*, 1990; *The Crucible*, 1996.

TELEPLAY: *Playing for Time*, 1980.

NONFICTION: *Situation Normal*, 1944; *In Russia*, 1969 (photo essay; with Inge Morath); *In the Country*, 1977 (photo essay; with Morath); *The Theater Essays of Arthur Miller*, 1978, revised and expanded 1996 (Robert A. Martin, editor); *Chinese Encounters*, 1979 (photo essay; with Morath); *"Salesman" in Beijing*, 1984; *Conversations with Arthur Miller*, 1987 (Matthew C. Roudané, editor); *Spain*, 1987; *Timebends: A Life*, 1987; *Arthur Miller and Company*, 1990 (Christopher Bigsby, editor); *The Crucible in History and Other Essays*, 2000; *Echoes Down the Corridor: Collected Essays, 1947-2000*, 2000; *On Politics and the Art of Acting*, 2001.

CHILDREN'S LITERATURE: *Jane's Blanket*, 1963.

MISCELLANEOUS: *The Portable Arthur Miller*, 1995 (Christopher Bigsby, editor).

BIBLIOGRAPHY

Bigsby, C. W. E. *File on Miller*. New York: Methuen, 1987. Contains a detailed, up-to-date chronology, synopses of the major and minor plays and of the drama on television and radio, and excerpts from nonfiction writing, with each section accompanied by critical commentary. Also includes a comprehensive bibliography of Miller's essays, interviews, and secondary sources (collections of essays, articles, chapters in books, and book-length studies).

Bigsby, Christopher, ed. *The Cambridge Companion to Arthur Miller*. Cambridge, England: Cambridge University Press, 1997. Contains a detailed chronology, an essay on the tradition of social drama, and chapters on the early plays, the major plays, and Arthur Miller in each of the decades from the 1960's through the 1990's. There follow chapters on Miller's involvement with cinema, his fiction, and his relationship with criticism and critics. Includes a bibliographic essay and an index.

Bloom, Harold, ed. *Arthur Miller*. New York: Chelsea House, 1987. This volume consists of essays on Miller's major drama from *All My Sons* to *The American Clock*, a brief introduction discussing Miller's significance, a chronology, a bibliography, and an index. Includes important early essays (Raymond Williams and Tom F. Driver on the playwright's strengths and weaknesses) and later criticism by Neil Carson, C. W. E. Bigsby, and E. Miller Buddick.

_____, ed. *Arthur Miller's "Death of a Salesman."* New York: Chelsea House, 1988. Contains critical discussions published between 1963 and 1987, a chronology of Miller's life, a comprehensive bibliography of books and articles, and an index. In spite of reservations about Miller's importance as a writer, Bloom explains in his introduction how the play "achieves true aesthetic dignity" and discusses the particular merits of the essays in this collection.

Murphy, Brenda. *Miller: Death of a Salesman*. Cambridge, England: Cambridge University Press, 1995. This comprehensive treatment of Miller's play *Death of a Salesman* discusses its Broadway production, productions in English and in other languages, and media productions. Also provides a production chronology, a discography, a videography, and an extensive bibliography and index.

Schleuter, June, and James K. Flanagan. *Arthur Miller*. New York: Frederick Ungar, 1987. Contains a comprehensive narrative chronology, a thorough first chapter on Miller's literature and life to 1985, chapter-length discussions of his major plays (including *The Archbishop's Ceiling*), and a concluding chapter on his later one-act plays. Extensive notes, bibliography of Miller's work in all genres, select secondary bibliography of books and articles, and index.

Carl Rollyson,
updated by Victoria Price

YUKIO MISHIMA
Kimitake Hiraoka

Born: Tokyo, Japan; January 14, 1925
Died: Tokyo, Japan; November 25, 1970

PRINCIPAL DRAMA

Kantan, wr. 1950, pb. 1956 (English translation, 1957)

Yoro no himawari, pr., pb. 1953 (*Twilight Sunflower*, 1958)

Dōjōji, pb. 1953 (English translation, 1966)

Aya no tsuzumi, pr. 1955, pb. 1956 (*The Damask Drum*, 1957)

Aoi no ue, pr., pb. 1956 (*The Lady Aoi*, 1957)

Hanjo, pb. 1956 (English translation, 1957)

Sotoba Komachi, pb. 1956 (English translation, 1957)

Kindai nōgakushū, pb. 1956 (includes *Kantan, The Damask Drum, The Lady Aoi, Hanjo,* and *Sotoba Komachi; Five Modern Nō Plays*, 1957)

Tōka no kiku, pr., pb. 1961

Sado kōshaku fujin, pr., pb. 1965 (*Madame de Sade*, 1967)

Suzakuke no metsubō, pr., pb. 1967

Waga tomo Hittorā, pb. 1968, pr. 1969 (*My Friend Hitler*, 1977)

Chinsetsu yumiharizuki, pr., pb. 1969

OTHER LITERARY FORMS

Yukio Mishima was a critic, an essayist, and a poet (though largely unpublished in the latter genre) as well as a dramatist. His aesthetic is carefully set forth in *Taiyō to tetsu* (1968; *Sun and Steel*, 1970) and *Hagakure nyumon* (1967; *On Hagakure*, 1977). No doubt, however, he is best known as one of Japan's most accomplished and prolific novelists of the immediate post-World War II period, and it is as a novelist that he will be known to future generations. His major novels include *Kamen no kokuhaku* (1949; *Confessions of a Mask*, 1958), *Kinkakuji* (1956; *The Temple of the Golden Pavilion*, 1959), *Gogo no eikō* (1963; *The Sailor Who Fell from Grace with the Sea*, 1965), and his tetralogy, *Hōjō no umi*, published between 1969 and 1971, and translated into English between 1972 and 1974 as *The Sea of Fertility: A Cycle of Four Novels*, comprising *Haru no yuki* (1969; *Spring Snow*, 1972), *Homba* (1969; *Runaway Horses*, 1973), *Akatsuki no tera* (1970; *The Temple of Dawn*, 1973), and *Tennin gosui* (1971; *The Decay of the Angel*, 1974). In addition to the above-named works and several other significant novels, Mishima published some fine short fiction and a large quantity of other writings, ranging from literary criticism to slick formula fiction produced strictly to maintain his expensive lifestyle.

ACHIEVEMENTS

The paradoxical Yukio Mishima brought to the West an awareness of modern Japan both as a unique culture and as a lively leader in the world, as a nation with much in common between its individuals and those of other cultures and an appreciation of the complexities of contemporary life. Most important, perhaps, he drew attention to human problems and human verities that stretch across the entirety of history. It was appropriate that he chose for much of his drama the ancient and classical Nō form as base, as its ultimate concerns are based in timelessness.

The young Mishima early gained the attention of the established novelist Yasunari Kawabata. Kawabata, winner of the Nobel Prize in Literature in 1968, was to be an advocate of Mishima's work throughout his career. He participated in Mishima's wedding to Yoko Sugiyama on June 1, 1958, and himself committed suicide seventeen months after Mishima. It

was Kawabata who said of Mishima's work, "Such a writer appears once in three hundred years."

BIOGRAPHY

Yukio Mishima was born Kimitake Hiraoka, the son of a government bureaucrat. Mishima's life was unusual from the outset. His physically ill grandmother, Natsuko, virtually kidnapped the firstborn of her son Azusa and his wife, Shizue, sequestering the child in her quarters. The young Mishima lived with her, enduring that strained situation. When he was ready for the seventh grade, however, she allowed him to move back to his parents' section of the house. Mishima said that as early as the age of five, he learned to prefer an imaginary world, often of violence, to the real world. As early as the age of four he was to begin a pattern of falling in love with pictures in books. A favorite picture was of Joan of Arc, whom he assumed to be a male. Mishima candidly reported that his first erotic arousal occurred when he was looking at a photograph of Guido Reni's portrait of Saint Sebastian pierced by arrows.

Mishima attended the exclusive Peer's School in Tokyo. He was too young for the draft in early World War II but was called up later, only to fail the physical, and so returned to work in the aircraft factory where he had been employed. Fame was to come to him following the publication of the novel *Confessions of a Mask*. He complemented his writing of plays and novels by creating his own persona, pursuing bodybuilding and mastering English. Mishima visited the United States on a world tour, which included Latin America and Greece, in 1951 and 1952. This trip was to be the first of several journeys to the United States, including one in 1957 and another, with his wife, Yoko, in 1960.

Mishima and his wife had two children by the early 1960's. By the middle of the decade, he was probably the best-known living Japanese with the exception of the emperor. Mishima was frequently a nominee for the Nobel Prize; one of his champions is said to have been the then-United Nations Secretary General, Dag Hammarskjöld.

Yukio Mishima in 1970, shortly before his death.
(Hulton Archive by Getty Images)

Nevertheless, in 1968, it was his mentor Kawabata who was named Nobel laureate for literature. Mishima was disappointed but nevertheless often appeared in public with his very shy teacher to help Kawabata cope with his unwanted fame. Among Mishima's other close friends were novelist Kōbō Abe, Kabuki actor Utaemon Nakamura, critic-historian Donald Keene, writer-film-producer Donald Richie, and popular female impersonator Akihiro Maruyama.

On November 25, 1970, after delivering the last book of his tetralogy, *The Decay of the Angel*, to his publisher, Mishima, accompanied by a select squad of his Shield Society (a handpicked private legion of just under one hundred university men), seized the Eastern Military Headquarters in downtown Tokyo, spoke to the troops, urging an overthrow of the current government and a return of absolute power to the emperor, and then committed ritual suicide (seppuku). He was in his forty-fifth year.

ANALYSIS

Yukio Mishima's dramatic works share with his others a concern with action in the face of the void. His conviction that every act is necessarily a political act is a significant one, and it provides a unifying force in the plays, as does his conviction that, in things great or small, any action, ultimately, is better than no action. This constant often leads to tortured situations reminiscent of Jean-Paul Sartre. Indeed, it is easy to see why Mishima preferred Sartre to Albert Camus, philosophically, despite Mishima's dislike of the political Left and his outright contempt for bureaucracy.

Mishima favored modern adaptation to extend great art through all time. Donald Keene, one of his foremost translators, has noted that Mishima believed that his modern Nō plays should be as effective in a performance in Central Park as on a traditional Nō stage. This belief reminds one of William Butler Yeats's conviction that set properties and cast were too complex if all could not be fitted into a taxi, brought to a destination, and performed in a private home.

Mishima's negative critics point to the stiff nature of characters, as well as the restricted action in his conventional plays, claiming that he was overly influenced by the French period drama of Jean Racine. These so-called drawbacks, however, served a larger purpose in *Madame de Sade* and *My Friend Hitler*, which may be compared to the dramas of Aeschylus and Sophocles, in which unspeakable, bloody, or violent acts are described rather than acted onstage.

Flawlessly educated, Mishima had perfect command of the classical as well as the modern Japanese language. His grasp of Eastern and Western literature was equaled by few, if any, of his peers. The same was true of his understanding of history and politics, as well as philosophy. Jean Cocteau, whom he met in Paris, and Oscar Wilde were two writers who exercised great influence on him. Both, like Mishima, were flamboyant public figures. One is reminded that Mishima's experiment with becoming a boxer parallels Cocteau's becoming the manager of a professional prizefighter. Mishima also was interested in the multifaceted Italian writer Gabriele D'Annunzio, who not only wrote in a number of forms but also shared an interest in the martyrdom of Saint Sebastian and who became a military activist and daring airplane pilot. Mishima himself was eventually to help train Japanese self-defense force troops in parachute jumping (a skill that he taught himself), in addition to forming and financing his own small, private army, dedicated to the protection of the emperor.

The plays published in *Five Modern Nō Plays*, written between 1950 and 1955, have been performed, in various groupings, by a number of small theater groups throughout the United States. *Sotoba Komachi*, *The Lady Aoi*, and *Hanjo* have probably been acted more frequently than *The Damask Drum* and *Kantan*. Similarities discovered in opposites and the dictatorship of desire—even beyond the grave—and the agonies attendant thereto are the motivating force behind them all.

SOTOBA KOMACHI

In *Sotoba Komachi*, the primary characters are an arrogant Poet (who remains nameless) and an ugly Old Woman, who is soon to be discovered by the audience as Komachi, the formerly devastating beauty, reincarnated. Beauty and torment are welded in all the works of Mishima. Komachi historically tormented her suitor, refusing to give herself unless courted for one hundred nights. The suitor died on the ninety-ninth night.

Both of the primary characters are developed sympathetically. The Poet, who at first harshly tells the Old Woman, whom he stumbles on in the park late at night, that someone as old and vile as she should leave that spot for young lovers, is destined to change his insult that she is "a profanation." When Komachi tells him that she is ninety-nine years old, he recoils yet again, though he is drawn to look at her more closely. During the course of their exchange, the park empties, and Komachi reminisces about her love for Captain Fukakusa eighty years previously. Here Mishima is freer still with his modernization of the classic Komachi and introduces an onstage flashback to a ball at which Fukakusa was courting Komachi— but Viennese waltzes, not Japanese music, provide background as various couples appear and discuss the romance of Komachi and her captain. The audience suddenly realizes that fate is destined to repeat itself as the Poet begins to see the Old Woman as absolutely beautiful and begins to pay court to her. Komachi's hundredth night has again come around. To her credit, she tries to warn the young man, but he is totally enthralled by his new vision of her. The play, carried by Mishima's powerful dialogue, at once masterful in its timing and economical but eloquent in its progress, concludes with his dying and Komachi's acceptance of "a hundred more years to wait," as she returns to counting cigarette butts garnered that day. She is seen at the final curtain as she was when the curtain rose. The play is classic Mishima—including his obsessive interest in cycles, despite his personal disclaimer of belief in reincarnation. His claimed belief in active nihilism is seldom more accurately manifested than in this koanlike play.

Bondage to an emotional state and/or obsession is a frequent theme for Mishima and probably goes back even to his preadolescent intoxication with Reni's portrait of Saint Sebastian, ultimately leading to a commissioned series of portraits of himself in various dying situations—including one of himself as Saint Sebastian, arms bound above his head and ar-

rows appearing to protrude from his torso. In *The Damask Drum* and *Hanjo* such pain and torture are enacted at an essentially intellectual-emotional level. *The Lady Aoi* also works at that level but features spirit possession, torture of a physical sort, and murder, too.

THE DAMASK DRUM

The Damask Drum centers on an old janitor, Iwakichi, who falls madly and impossibly in love with a woman whom he has never met but has observed across the alley from the office building where he cleans. He has spied her repeatedly in a fashionable dress shop just across the way. Iwakichi confesses to the clerk Kayoko that he must have sent the mystery lady thirty unanswered love letters, in addition to seventy more that he has burned after writing. (The mystery of the hundredth occasion reminds one of *Sotoba Komachi*.) After their exchange, Iwakichi and Kayoko continue to spy on the adjacent office and observe the activity there during their night shift. Eventually tiring, Kayoko takes her leave of the old man, carrying with her yet another love letter for the mystery lady from him. Across the way, three sophisticated male customers and the proprietress of the shop discuss the old man's obsessive passion. The proprietress confesses that she has used the old man's letters as wipers for her dog's combs, never showing them to Mrs. Hanako Tsukioka, who is the object of the old man's passion. The girl Kayoko arrives with the thirtieth letter, which they read aloud.

The discourse that follows concerns questions of romance, the erotic, and fashion—then returns to the old man, whom they decide to discipline for his cheeky courtship. They contrive to give Iwakichi a stage prop, a drum that is made of damask and therefore soundless. The drum is accompanied by a note that hints that Mrs. Tsukioka will grant the old man her favors when she hears the drum beating. On his failure to be heard, as they laugh at him from across the alley, Iwakichi commits suicide by jumping from his window ledge. Stage lighting soon indicates that night has come, and Mrs. Tsukioka is "back" at the scene to meet the ghost of Iwakichi. Now it is their turn to speak of love and its flaws. Responding to her challenge, yet again, to make the drum sound, the ghost pounds away, only to fall into despair on the hundredth beat and disappear. "I would have heard if he had only struck it once more," avers the lady—less kind and less intelligent than the earlier Komachi but less cruel than Rokujō in *The Lady Aoi.*

THE LADY AOI

In *The Lady Aoi* there are but four characters, the three major ones being Aoi, her husband, Hiraku, and Lady Rokujō. The action opens in a hospital, which, it seems, may use sexual therapy. This element is intended by Mishima to shock. Though Mishima was hostile to the theories of Sigmund Freud and his disciples, he was keenly, if unhappily, aware of their influence on the twentieth century; hence, that influence appears in this modern version of a tale from the Genji cycle. Spirit possession is the mainspring of this intense play's action, which presents an effective story of love and of hate growing from betrayed love. Not the Genji figure, Hiraku, but his chosen, Aoi, is killed by the spirit of Rokujō, whose ability to manifest in both spirit and person is stunningly effective in this jarring masterwork.

KANTAN

Kantan, the earliest of the five plays in the collection, is perhaps the least effective of Mishima's Nō plays. Although it may remind one of Eugène Ionesco's *L'Avenir est dans les œufs: Ou, Il Faut de tout pour faire un monde* (pr. 1953; *The Future Is in Eggs: Or, It Takes All Sorts to Make a World,* 1960), or perhaps of the works of Harold Pinter or Samuel Beckett, the dialogue does not always cohere, and one is not quite sure if this incoherence is the playwright's intention. *Kantan* does contain some delightful whimsy, and dreams and near-romps abound as eighteen-year-old Jirō imagines that he becomes a dictator and power broker. He awakens to a new love for real life and his doting nurse, Kiku, as magical flowers burst into bloom everywhere. *Kantan* is the stuff of opera or ballet and should be splendidly adaptable to such works.

HANJO

The homoerotic theme is dominant in *Hanjo,* one of the most powerful and economical of Mishima's works. True to Mishima's desire, it could well be played in any theater in the world—or even in Central Park. *Hanjo* is a drama of love and alienation, in which the loyal, long-suffering lesbian wins. Hanako, a beautiful girl, has gone mad after being deserted by her handsome lover, Yoshio. She is taken off the streets, loved (and painted) and nurtured by a middle-aged artist, Jitsuko Honda. Jitsuko's idyll is jeopardized by a newspaper story, telling of her rescue of the girl and even providing her name and address. Her worst fears are soon realized, for Yoshio sees the story and subsequently finds them. His identification of Hanako is confirmed by matching a pair of fans that they had exchanged as symbols of undying loyalty. A brutal psychological battle between Yoshio and Jitsuko ensues, and which Jitsuko presumes that she has lost. Yet the tables turn when Hanako insists to the young man, "You are not Yoshio. Your face is dead." She maintains this claim and eventually dismisses him. Jitsuko is gentle in dealing with Yoshio in his defeat but cannot resist exultantly exclaiming "Oh, wonderful life!" when he finally has gone.

DŌJŌJI

It is in the Nō play *Dōjōji,* which first found print amid nine short stories of the volume *Manatsu no shi* (1953; *Death in Midsummer and Other Stories,* 1966), that Mishima perhaps stands more revealed than in any of his other plays, in the person of a young lady named Kiyoko. (It may be worth noting that Mishima's female characters tend to have more dimensions than his men—unlike those of Ernest Hemingway, with whom he is often paralleled.) *Dōjōji*'s other characters are the Antique Dealer and the Apartment House Superintendent (both unnamed), and five nondescript men and women patrons of the antique shop. The setting is "a room in what is in fact a secondhand furniture shop, though it is so filled with antiques— both Oriental and Occidental—that it might properly be called a museum." Like the classical version of this Nō play, Mishima's version involves unabated passion. In the traditional play, *Kanegamisaki* (the cape of the temple bell), a hermit is loved by a stunning beauty. Rejecting her, he takes refuge by hiding under the huge Dōjōji temple bell. Crazed by her desire for him, she transforms herself into a great and outraged serpent whose fire burns the ungrateful hermit as it coils around the bell.

Mishima's Kiyoko, a dancer, keeps to the passion with something of a plot reversal suitable to modern times. She desires a huge wardrobe (with, appropriately, the form of a bell carved into its doors) from the antique shop. The cabinet is about to be sold to the highest bidder among a number of interested, affluent parties, but the sale is spoiled by Kiyoko telling of the murder of a young lover who hid inside—obviously unsuccessfully—from a jealous husband. After the potential buyers have been driven away, Kiyoko reveals to the Dealer that indeed a man had died inside the wardrobe, but that it was her lover, Yasushi, who jilted her for an older woman because she (Kiyoko) was too beautiful. Yasushi chose to hide in the wardrobe to avoid the world, to live and, in fact, to die there (suicide is suggested). Kiyoko browbeats the Dealer but still cannot afford the wardrobe. She leaps inside and locks herself in, crying out that she will disfigure her features with acid. Panic ensues, but when she finally emerges, her face is unchanged. It is at the very end of the play that Mishima and his character seem to merge. Kiyoko says, "Nothing can bother me, no matter what happens. Who do you suppose can wound me now?" Soon the Dealer replies, "You'll be ruined, your heart will be torn to shreds. You'll end up no longer able to feel anything." To this Kiyoko replies, "Still, nothing that happens can ever change my face."

LONGER PLAYS

The longer and more conventional plays, *Madame de Sade* and *My Friend Hitler*, have much in common. Like many plays, for all but an unusually specialized or attentive audience, they may be deemed to read better than they play. Ironically, this gives them a point in common with traditional Nō, which some prefer to have explicated rather than to attend. More traditional critics claim that the plays are sometimes overwhelmed by dialogue at the expense of action.

In these two plays, the most horrible acts of violence and violation are described in frequently long, descriptive speeches, in which the actors simply face off and deliver—hence it is easy to lose a sense of outrage. Yet, as noted above, one may compare this type of play with the classical Greek drama, in which the violence was described instead of witnessed.

MADAME DE SADE

Madame de Sade, the first of these two plays of the theater of tirade, was finished in 1965 and played successfully in Tokyo, opening in November of that year. Its five characters are all female. They are Renée, Sade's wife; Mme de Montreuil, her mother; Anne, her younger sister; Baronesse de Simiane; the cruel Comtesse de Saint-Fonde; and Charlotte, who is housekeeper to the Montreuils. Much of the main debate of the play swings between the decadent Saint-Fonde, who states that God is both lazy and decrepit after proclaiming herself "utterly bored with the artifices of love and the nasty machinations . . . even my own bad reputation." She describes love as a mixture of honey and ashes, announcing that she has concluded that the highly religious Montreuil was correct earlier when describing the truth as "whips and sweets, that's all." The fascinating exchanges and revelations proceed, often staggering in their implications. The third and final act, following a major soliloquy of Renée, ends after embracing the notion that Sade embodies the cruel essence of reality; the arrival of the Marquis de Sade, himself, is heralded by a knock at the door. The maid describes the bloated, down-at-heels, albeit dignified appearance of the man, who has been long in prison. Renée, Madame de Sade, seeming to have arrived at a sudden decision, stuns the audience by announcing her decision to "never see him again." As the maid leaves to communicate this to the Marquis de Sade, the curtain falls. Remarkable as it is, there is a classic Zen koanlike quality to this play; a rap on the head by the playwright in the role as Zen master—and the audience is left to find the truth on its own.

MY FRIEND HITLER

My Friend Hitler, also in three acts, has as its characters Adolf Hitler, the arms magnate Alfried Krupp, the SA Captain Ernst Roehm, and left-wing Nazi Gregor Strasser. The play is set on the infamous "night of long knives," when, in late June and early July of 1934, Hitler gave his blessing to the SS, led by Hermann Göring, Heinrich Himmler, Rudolf Hess, Joseph Goebbels, and others, to liquidate all leadership of the rival SA paramilitary organization. The SA, a less elite, though larger, group of Hitler's back-ers, was headed by Captain Roehm, who believed himself to be Hitler's best friend. The leftist Strasser, who also helped in Hitler's rise to power, has become unable to tolerate Hitler's leadership, while Roehm, like many of his men a motorcycle-riding, hard-drinking bully, believes that Nazi leadership will soften unless it rests on a continual revolution. The dialogue between them is spirited and fascinating, as is that between Hitler and Krupp, the only man before whom Hitler trembles.

Donald Richie calls the work an "allegory in iron," and that it is. It ran successfully in Tokyo in January, 1969, but has not been presented in English except as laboratory theater at St. Andrews College in 1982, in the Hiroaki Sato translation. Again, Mishima—who said that he could never identify with Hitler, though he had some sympathy for Benito Mussolini—leaves the spectator with tense irresolution at the play's end. As gunfire continues in the background, signaling the continuing execution of SA leaders, Hitler, now recovered from his terror of the intimidating Krupp, accepts the latter's congratulations for cutting down both the Left and the Right, walking to center stage to state, "Yes, government must take the middle road."

OTHER MAJOR WORKS

LONG FICTION: *Kamen no kokuhaku*, 1949 (*Confessions of a Mask*, 1958); *Kinjiki*, 1951, and *Higyo*, 1953 (combined as *Forbidden Colors*, 1968); *Shiosai*, 1954 (*The Sound of Waves*, 1956); *Kinkakuji*, 1956 (*The Temple of the Golden Pavilion*, 1959); *Kyōko no ie*, 1959; *Utage no ato*, 1960 (*After the Banquet*, 1963); *Gogo no eikō*, 1963 (*The Sailor Who Fell from Grace with the Sea*, 1965); *Haru no yuki*, 1969 (*Spring Snow*, 1972); *Homba*, 1969 (*Runaway Horses*, 1973); *Akatsuki no tera*, 1970 (*The Temple of Dawn*, 1973); *Tennin gosui*, 1971 (*The Decay of the Angel*, 1974); *Hōjō no umi*, 1969-1971 (collective title for previous four novels; *The Sea of Fertility: A Cycle of Four Novels*, 1972-1974).

SHORT FICTION: *Kaibutsu*, 1950; *Tōnorikai*, 1951; *Manatsu no shi*, 1953 (*Death in Midsummer and Other Stories*, 1966).

NONFICTION: *Hagakure nyumōn*, 1967 (*The Way of the Samurai*, 1977); *Taiyō to tetsu*, 1968 (*Sun and Steel*, 1970); *Yukio Mishima on "Hagakure": The Samurai Ethic and Modern Japan*, 1978.

EDITED TEXT: *New Writing in Japan*, 1972 (with Geoffrey Bownas).

MISCELLANEOUS: *Hanazakari no mori*, 1944 (short fiction and plays); *Eirei no koe*, 1966 (short fiction and essays).

BIBLIOGRAPHY

Miller, Henry. *Reflections on the Death of Mishima*. Santa Barbara, Calif.: Capra, 1972. A noted author's comments on the death of Mishima.

Napier, Susan Jolliffe. *Escape from the Wasteland: Romanticism and Realism in the Fiction of Mishima Yukio and Oe Kenzaburo*. Cambridge, Mass.: Harvard University Press, 1991. A look at romanticism and realism in the works of Mishima and Kenzaburo Oe. Bibliography and index.

Nathan, John. *Mishima: A Biography*. 1974. Reprint. Cambridge, Mass.: Da Capo Press, 2000. The classic biography of Mishima, with a new preface by Nathan. Index.

Scott-Stokes, Henry. *The Life and Death of Yukio Mishima*. Rev ed. New York: Noonday Press, 1995. The revised edition of Scott-Stokes' 1974 biography of Mishima, covering his life and works. Bibliography and index..

Starrs, Roy. *Deadly Dialectics: Sex, Violence, and Nihilism in the World of Yukio Mishima*. Honolulu: University of Hawaii Press, 1994. A study of Mishima's literary works, with emphasis on his philosophy.

Wolfe, Peter. *Yukio Mishima*. New York: Continuum, 1989. A basic biography of Mishima that covers his life and works. Index.

Yourcenar, Marguerite. *Mishima: A Vision of the Void*. Chicago: University of Chicago Press, 2001. This edition of a biography of Mishima published in 1986 contains a foreword by Donald Richie, a well-known critic and Japan expert.

Ronald H. Bayes

MOLIÈRE
Jean-Baptiste Poquelin

Born: Paris, France; January 15, 1622 (baptized)
Died: Paris, France; February 17, 1673

PRINCIPAL DRAMA

L'Étourdi: Ou, Les Contre-temps, pr. 1653, pb. 1663 (verse play; *The Blunderer*, 1678)

Le Dépit amoureux, pr. 1656, pb. 1663 (adaptation of Niccolò Secchi's *L'Interessé*; *The Love-Tiff*, 1930)

Les Précieuses ridicules, pr. 1659, pb. 1660 (*The Affected Young Ladies*, 1732)

L'École des maris, pr., pb. 1661 (verse play; *The School for Husbands*, 1732)

L'École des femmes, pr. 1662, pb. 1663 (verse play; *The School for Wives*, 1732)

La Critique de "L'École des femmes," pr., pb. 1663 (*The Critique of "The School for Wives,"* 1957)

L'Impromptu de Versailles, pr. 1663, pb. 1682 (*The Versailles Impromptu*, 1714)

Tartuffe: Ou, L'Imposteur, pr. 1664, revised pr. 1667, pb. 1669 (verse play; English translation, 1732)

Dom Juan: Ou, Le Festin de Pierre, pr. 1665, pb. 1682 (*Don Juan*, 1755)

L'Amour médecin, pr. 1665, pb. 1666 (*Love's the Best Doctor*, 1755)

Le Misanthrope, pr. 1666, pb. 1667 (verse play; *The Misanthrope*, 1709)

Le Médecin malgré lui, pr., pb. 1666 (*The Doctor in Spite of Himself*, 1672)

Amphitryon, pr., pb. 1668 (verse play; English translation, 1755)

L'Avare, pr. 1668, pb. 1669 (*The Miser*, 1672)

Le Bourgeois Gentilhomme, pr. 1670, pb. 1671 (*The Would-Be Gentleman*, 1675)

Les Fourberies de Scapin, pr., pb. 1671 (*The Cheats of Scapin*, 1701)

Les Femmes savantes, pr., pb. 1672 (verse play; *The Learned Ladies*, pr., pb. 1693)

Le Malade imaginaire, pr. 1673, pb. 1674 (*The Imaginary Invalid*, 1732; also known as *The Hypochondriac*)

Dramatic Works, pb. 1875-1876 (3 volumes)
The Plays of Molière, pb. 1926 (8 volumes)

OTHER LITERARY FORMS

Molière is known only for his plays.

ACHIEVEMENTS

Molière possessed a brilliant imagination, constantly creating new characters and easily moving from one type of comedy to another. His imagination was, however, carefully controlled through reason, by which he avoided excess. Reality is the point of departure for his wildest creations, and his comedies owe their depth to his keen observation of humanity. When Molière began writing for the theater there was little comedy, except for Pierre Corneille's first works, and what there was leaned heavily toward the extravagant. Molière soon realized that, more than any other genre, comedy required a basis in truth. Consequently, he was not particularly concerned with original subjects or careful plots, but rather with the portrayal of manners and the study of character.

Therefore, Molière made free use of any subject or plot that came his way, borrowing in whole or in part from earlier French works of any genre, or from Latin, Italian, and Spanish sources. Although he was capable of devising clever plots, he believed that simple ones were better if the audience was to concentrate on the substance of the play. As for denouements, any or none would do, once he had said what he intended.

Molière was thoroughly familiar with the milieus of his day and represented them all faithfully as settings for his characters and their foibles. What interested Molière more than sociological truth, however, was universal truth. His precious ladies, pedants, and nouveaux riches could be of any era. More important than a wealth of exterior detail was this portrayal of universal types. These were to replace the conventional figures—boastful captains, scheming parasites, sweet ingenues, young lovers, and the like—of traditional comedy. Despite their universality, however, Molière's characters were not created according to simple formulas. On the contrary, they are complex to an extreme, each possessing the general traits of the type observed and abstracted by Molière from reality, yet endowed with enough of the particulars to make each a real human being. There is no one stock servant in Molière's work, but a series of individualized servants. His Miser is a lover as well. The Hypocrite is also a lecher. Molière's dramatic universe is a very real one.

Molière made special use of those of his observations that could make the spectator laugh at humanity. Although the comedy almost always contains a serious meaning, its forms are extremely varied, and its tones range from the most farcical to the most subtle, all arranged with the utmost skill during the course of a single play. Thus, the spectator may remain unaware of how disagreeable a subject is until, the performance over, he reflects on it further. Especially telling is Molière's device of making certain characters repeat words and gestures that reveal the vice or passion that controls each. By this technique, the characters are reduced almost to the status of machines and thus inspire, not sympathy or pity, but ridicule.

Molière believed that human nature was basically good and sensible, and he opposed any artificial constraints placed on it. Such constraints came not from society, which is a collection of human natures whose discipline reasonable people accept; rather, they had their source in perverse individuals who conformed neither to human nature nor to society. Molière has been criticized for excessive optimism and conformism, but however conservative his solutions to the problems that he posed, there can be no doubt that he was forthright and courageous in posing them.

BIOGRAPHY

Very little is known of the personal life of Molière, born Jean-Baptiste Poquelin.

He left no diary, no memoirs, no correspondence, no autobiography. The first biography, J.-L. Le Gallois Grimarest's *Vie de Monsieur de Molière* (1705), is interesting, but it was not published until thirty-two years after Molière's death, and is therefore considered questionable by most modern scholars. Anything written by his contemporaries was polemical in nature.

Molière was baptized January 15, 1622, on the rue Saint-Honoré. He was of a good bourgeois family that had recently come to Paris from Beauvais. His father was a merchant and "upholsterer by appointment of the King," having received the title from his brother. Molière's mother died in 1632, and his father soon remarried, only to become a widower again in 1636.

Between 1632 and 1639, Molière attended the Collège de Clermont, studied law in Orléans, and be-

Molière (Library of Congress)

came a lawyer. In addition, in 1637, his father arranged for his son to succeed him in his official charge. Molière was not much interested in the law, however, and his practice was not brisk, nor was he inclined to follow in his father's footsteps.

It is said that Molière's grandfather often took him to the Hôtel de Bourgogne to see French tragedy and Italian comedy. Around 1640, Molière probably met Tiberio Fiurelli, known as Scaramouche in the Italian theater, and became closely associated with the Béjart family. Its members were involved in the arts, particularly theater, and were somewhat eccentric, but they lived in the fashionable Marais section of Paris and had some good connections. Their oldest daughter, Madeleine, known as an actress, was the sometime mistress of the Baron de Modène and mother of a child recognized by him. At a time when "actor" and "outlaw" were considered synonymous by many, Molière chose the life of the theater. He was giving up the security and respectability offered him, not only by the right to succeed his father, but also by the legal profession. At first, he chose not to write for the theater, instead pursuing a career as an actor.

The Illustre Théâtre was founded in 1643 by the Béjarts and other actors, including Molière, not for profit at first but simply for their entertainment and that of the bourgeoisie of Paris. The troupe was under the protection of Gaston, the duke of Orléans, brother of Louis XIII, who did not always remember to pay his actors. They rented and appointed a former tennis court as a theater, opened their doors in 1644, and were soon in serious financial difficulty. Marie Hervé, mother of the Béjart girls, helped her children and Molière, who had by then taken this name and was head of the troupe. Despite all measures, matters grew worse. In 1645, Molière was sued by numerous creditors and experienced a brief sojourn in debtors' prison. He had made many friends among Parisian men of letters and their noble patrons, however, and formulated his philosophy of the theater. He had not wasted his time.

On his release from prison, Molière decided to leave Paris to try his luck in another troupe. Madeleine soon joined him. At the behest of a number of dramatic authors, the duke of Épernon received

Molière, Madeleine, and her brother and sister into his troupe. They toured the provinces under the direction of Charles Dufresne until 1650, when the duke withdrew his support and Dufresne left the troupe. Molière assumed leadership during this awkward time, but in 1652 the troupe found a new patron in the prince of Conti. Again, the intercession of men of letters in Paris had been instrumental. The prince was an enlightened man who enjoyed such company, and he came to prize Molière's intelligence and culture highly. Unfortunately, the prince's spiritual advisers persuaded him to lead a more austere life, and in 1657 he withdrew his patronage.

By this time, the troupe was doing well artistically and financially. It contained a number of artists who were or would become celebrated. A fine actor, Molière was an equally fine director. He was a hard taskmaster but earned his actors' respect and affection, and the turnover in his troupe was always remarkably low.

The players decided that, after a lengthy sojourn in Rouen, they would spend the winter of 1658 in Paris, which they had revisited sporadically, maintaining numerous contacts. In Paris, they rented the Marais Theatre for eighteen months and were granted the protection of Philippe, duke of Orléans, who paid them no more faithfully than had Gaston. On October 24, 1658, they played Corneille's *Nicomède* (pr., pb. 1651; English translation, 1671) and then Molière's *The Love-Tiff* before Louis XIV. The king was so pleased with Molière's work that he accorded the troupe the use of the Petit-Bourbon on the days that the Italians did not play there. They performed in the fine hall there until 1660, when, for unknown reason, they moved to a smaller theater that was badly in need of repairs. Despite all efforts, the theater remained a makeshift affair. The troupe remained there, more or less permanently, until 1671, when it relocated to the Palais-Royal, which was properly remodeled and appointed.

The old Corneillean repertoire was no longer successful. Moreover, there was considerable bias on the part of good dramatic authors against offering their works to any troupe until 1667, when Corneille allowed *Attila* (English translation, 1960) to be mounted at the Petit-Bourbon, and 1670, when he gave Molière *Tite et Bérénice* to perform. Molière had found it necessary to create his own repertoire, a task that he had already begun in a modest way in the provinces. His comedies were well received, and the troupe seemed firmly established. The players at the Hôtel de Bourgogne and the Marais became increasingly more disgruntled. The triumph of *The Affected Young Ladies* in 1659 brought its author the active enmity of his rivals as well as the admiration of his public. Molière would never leave Paris again. His most important plays remained to be written. They were to win for him the highest praise, his contemporaries' and posterity's, and engage him in the fiercest of polemics with certain factions.

Molière was a short, rather ugly man with severe curvature of the spine, and he was by nature serious and somewhat taciturn. Nevertheless, his great art and talent brought him many friends, admirers, and patrons, and he enjoyed their company. He especially enjoyed being received by the notables of his day, whose invitations he insisted on reciprocating rather elegantly. During his life he had several mistresses, usually actresses, beginning with Madeleine Béjart, with whom he had a lifelong association, although he was not the most attentive of lovers.

At about the age of forty, Molière married pretty Armande Béjart, then about seventeen years of age and said variously to be Madeleine's sister or daughter (perhaps by Molière). As was to be expected, their life was not a happy one. He was jealous of her as he had been of no other, and she seems to have given him considerable cause. Three children were born during their marriage, but Esprit-Madeleine was the only one to whom he was greatly attached and perhaps the only one that he fathered. Despite all vicissitudes, he continued to love Armande, and she was with him when he died in 1673.

Molière's had always been a generous nature, emotionally as well as financially. Temperamental, not easy to live with, and always willing to engage in fierce polemic, he was nevertheless very forgiving. He was known not only to reconcile with but also to lend substantial sums of money to former enemies.

Louis XIV was Molière's greatest patron, showering him with money and favors and protecting him from powerful enemies. After 1665, Molière's group was known as "the King's troupe," a name preferred to that of the Hôtel de Bourgogne, and was requested to perform at Versailles, Saint-Germain, and Chambord. For inexplicable reasons, Jean-Baptiste Lully, the Florentine composer and sometime collaborator with Molière, became Louis's favorite with respect to theatrical entertainment in 1672, only one year before Molière's death. Although he had protected Molière in some extremely delicate situations, the king now preferred Lully's frivolous productions to Molière's masterpieces, and he granted the Italian exclusive rights over all works in which he had had a part. In vain, Molière tried legal means to oppose Louis's will. Fortunately, he had long had important protectors at court, such as the king's sister-in-law, Henriette d'Angleterre, and the prince of Conti, as well as numerous influential friends in various Parisian circles, including men of letters such as Nicholas Boileau.

After some initial difficulties concerning Lully's rights and the search for another composer, *The Imaginary Invalid*, originally created for the court, was a success at the Palais-Royal. Despite his ill health, Molière played the title role. It was during the fourth performance that he fell seriously and visibly ill; however, the show continued because the prince of Conti and other notables were in the audience and the actors needed to work. After the performance, Molière was taken home, where his hemorrhaging grew worse. His wife was called, and his servants tried to find a priest who would come to an actor's deathbed. When one finally arrived an hour later, Molière was dead.

ANALYSIS

Molière's first comedies were composed of elements borrowed from a variety of comic genres, high and low, ancient and modern, foreign and domestic. In each, he revealed considerable skill in development of character, observation of manners, construction of plot, or a combination of all these laced with much amusing physical activity. There was little original invention until *The Affected Young Ladies*, which was a *petite comédie*, a short farce designed to be performed after a longer serious work, but a farce containing satire of the excesses of certain manners of the day. Still specializing in the farce, of which he would remain a master, Molière continued his search for originality. *The School for Husbands*, in three acts, is the first of his plays to add a social thesis, however disguised by humorous treatment, to the observation of manners and character.

THE SCHOOL FOR WIVES

The School for Wives, Molière's first major play, centers on the vain Arnolphe, who has taken the aristocratic name of M. de la Souche. Hoping to acquire the peace and happiness of a conjugal life in his old age, he wishes to marry his young ward, Agnès, who is being reared in solitude and ignorance. He praises the virtues of this unnatural form of education to his friend, Chrysalde, who protests against his plan in the name of common sense. Meanwhile, Horace, the son of Oronte, a great friend of Arnolphe, has fallen in love with Agnès and has even been successful in communicating with her. He confides in Arnolphe himself, whom he does not know by the name of de la Souche, and of whose role as guardian and jailer he is unaware.

In act 2, Arnolphe, after scolding his servants, Alain and Georgette, for having allowed Horace to enter the house, questions Agnès. She is innocent and docile and willingly gives him the details of her meeting with Horace, who has moved her, she admits ingenuously. Arnolphe decides to marry Agnès without delay and orders her to throw stones at the suitor if he dares to declare himself. In act 3, Arnolphe lectures Agnès further and makes her read the disagreeable "Maxims on Marriage"; later, Horace reports to Arnolphe the vain precautions taken by the jealous old man: Agnès had thrown Horace a stone, but only after attaching a love note to it.

As act 4 reveals, Arnolphe is prepared to fight for Agnès and issues orders to his servants accordingly. Nevertheless, Horace informs him that he has been able to visit Agnès and that he intends to elope with her during the night. Arnolphe calls for the notary to draw up a marriage contract and plans an ambush for Horace. In the fifth and final act, Horace is surprised

by Alain and Georgette and severely beaten. Feigning death, he succeeds in abducting Agnès but foolishly entrusts her to Arnolphe, whom he still does not connect with the jealous old man. Arnolphe's declarations of love do not touch Agnès, however, who now knows what true love is. Agnès's father, who opportunely returns from America, allows her to marry Horace.

In five acts, this *grande comédie* exemplifies the formula that Molière had developed for his theater through a series of shorter pieces. As in *The School for Husbands*, the theme is the proper education of young women. The setting is a real one drawn from contemporary society. Arnolphe and Chrysalde are French bourgeois; Alain and Georgette are French peasants. At the same time, all the characters are highly personalized. Agnès is a remarkable portrait of a young woman who, acting on her instincts, becomes aware of her love for Horace and becomes aware of herself as a person. Arnolphe, the principal character, is both ridiculous, because of his obsession to keep Agnès in ignorance and be master of the house, and tragic, because of his unrequited love for Agnès and his despair at losing her, which ennobles him. In part through Chrysalde, one of his numerous mouthpieces, and in part through a conventional denouement, Molière reveals an important tenet of his philosophy: It is stupid and dangerous to try to suppress natural emotion, for it always wins out in the end.

THE CRITIQUE OF "THE SCHOOL FOR WIVES"

The School for Wives was so successful as to earn for its author additional favors from the king and more polemics from diverse factions. Supported by Louis and the *honnêtes gens*, Molière responded to his enemies' attacks in *The Critique of "The School for Wives,"* a one-act play in prose, by means of a series of caricatures and his definition of art as the portrayal of truth. The setting is Uranie's salon, where a discussion of Molière's play is taking place. Célimène, a *précieuse*, attacks Molière's immorality and vulgarity, and is in turn attacked by Uranie for her affected prudery. The marquis criticizes the play for having made the common people laugh, whereupon Dorante defends their common sense and good judgment. The pedant Lysidas considers the play an insignificant piece that cannot be compared with serious plays. He casts doubt on the judgment of the court in applauding Molière's work, for it breaks all the rules of art. Once again, it is Dorante who acts as the author's spokesman by stating that comedy is as difficult as tragedy to create and more true to life. For him the greatest rule is to please, and he sides with the court in its approbation of *The School for Wives*. Molière's enemies were not stilled; they counterattacked with other short plays, accusing him of being too personal, impious, and immoral in his private life.

THE VERSAILLES IMPROMPTU

At the insistence of the king this time, Molière wrote another one-act piece in prose, *The Versailles Impromptu*, performed for Louis in October of 1663. Molière represents himself as director and actor in the midst of a rehearsal for a play to be given before the king. Having mocked the actors of the Hôtel de Bourgogne, Molière proceeds to give each of his players advice appropriate to his role and defends his theater, whose goal is to depict manners, not personalities. Whatever his enemies may say of his work does not disturb him, but he forbids them to intrude on his privacy. The piece concludes with an announcement from the king postponing the performance of the play under rehearsal.

TARTUFFE

Tartuffe, perhaps the most controversial of Molière's comedies, was first given in its original version, now lost, as a part of *Les Plaisirs de l'île enchantée*, a week of the most extravagant entertainment offered by Louis XIV at Versailles in 1664 in honor of Louise de la Vallière. *Tartuffe* (then titled *Tartuffe: Ou, L'Hypocrite*) not only gave rise to another fierce polemic, but also was finally banned by the king at the insistence of the Company of the Blessed Sacrament, a secret society dedicated to reforming manners, who were concerned that Molière had them in mind when he presented his hypocrite as a cleric. Molière modified and expanded the play from three to five acts, and Louis authorized its performance (entitled *L'Imposteur*) at the Palais-Royal in 1667. Although Molière had made the hypocrite a layperson and softened his satire, the police and the

Archbishop of Paris took advantage of the king's trip to Flanders to shut down the successful play. After more efforts by Molière and Louis, the comedy was again authorized in 1669 and performed triumphantly as *Tartuffe: Ou, L'Imposteur*.

As the play begins, Mme Pernelle, pleased that her son, Orgon, has welcomed such a pious man into his household, roundly criticizes each member of the family who accuses Tartuffe of hypocrisy, including the outspoken servant Dorine. Returning from the country, Orgon inquires most solicitously about Tartuffe's health (not his wife's) and gives his brother-in-law, Cléante, an evasive answer regarding the proposed marriage of his daughter to Valère.

Complications develop in act 2: Despite Mariane's dislike for Tartuffe, Orgon wants his daughter to marry him rather than the man whom she loves and who loves her. Dorine's remonstrances are of no avail with Orgon, and she comforts the timid Mariane and settles the lovers' quarrel that Orgon's wishes have incited. In act 3, Orgon's son Damis tries to intervene also, but Dorine makes him promise to leave matters to his stepmother, Elmire. The latter sends for Tartuffe, who finally appears. The young woman begs him to give up Mariane. The hypocrite takes advantage of the situation to try to seduce Elmire, who agrees not to reveal his scandalous behavior if he will favor the marriage of Mariane and Valère, but Damis, who overhears everything from a nearby closet, informs his father. Tartuffe feigns humility and deceives Orgon, who turns against his son and makes Tartuffe his heir.

Tartuffe is evasive when, in act 4, Cléante begs him to reconcile Orgon and Damis. Orgon wishes to hasten his daughter's wedding to Tartuffe despite the protests of Cléante and Mariane. In order to disabuse her husband, Elmire has him hide under a table, summons Tartuffe, and pretends to respond to his passion. Finally understanding that he has been tricked by an impostor, Orgon comes out of his hiding place and orders Tartuffe to leave the house. The hypocrite abandons his mask and threatens Orgon, for the house belongs to him now.

The concluding act brings about the anticipated reversal. Orgon regrets having turned all his worldly possessions over to Tartuffe, including a strongbox containing the papers entrusted to him by a friend who is in political trouble. Mme Pernelle continues to have faith in Tartuffe when M. Loyal arrives with a court order to evict Orgon. Valère offers to help Orgon escape, for the incriminating strongbox has been turned over to the king's officers. Tartuffe appears in person with an officer to have Orgon arrested, but it is Tartuffe who is arrested instead; the king had been alerted to the impostor's fraudulent activities and knew of Orgon's services to the royal cause during the rebellion of the Fronde. The *deus ex machina* ending finds the king praised and Valère and Mariane about to be married.

In *Tartuffe*, Molière claimed to attack hypocrisy only and took pains to have Cléante, his spokesman, distinguish carefully between true and false piety. Despite praise of the former, the only avowed Christians in the work, Orgon and his mother, are depicted as ridiculous, whereas the principal characters shown in a good light, Elmire and Cléante, are not religious persons. The emphasis in *Tartuffe* is clearly on human rather than divine wisdom, very much in the spirit of the eighteenth century philosophes.

Tartuffe's is a skillful plot that maintains interest in its theme, the rise and fall of a religious hypocrite, from the lively, realistic exposition to the unlikely denouement. It is the perfect model of a comedy of character as well. Although all the characters are complex, drawn from life, it is Tartuffe who stands out, not only for his hypocrisy, but his keen intelligence, strong will, and great powers of dissimulation. For all his cleverness, however, he has a weakness, his sensuality coupled with greed, and this brutal passion causes his downfall.

DON JUAN

Between 1664 and 1669, Molière produced ten comedies in addition to reworking *Tartuffe*. Among them was *Don Juan*, whose Spanish subject had become popular in Italy and France. Molière's version, a five-act play in prose, was very successful, but again, he was opposed by the religious faction. No doubt the libertine's cynicism, his perverse seduction, his impious "articles of faith," and his unrepentant sins were shocking to audiences of the time. Still more shocking was his novel recourse to hypocrisy in the last act, although in the end Don Juan remains an unregenerate sinner and is led off to Hell.

As the play begins, Don Juan informs his valet, Sganarelle, that his happiness consists in seducing all women without becoming attached to any. Elvire, whom he has abandoned, attempts in vain to win him back. Shipwrecked on the coast during a storm, Don Juan and Sganarelle are taken in by some peasants. There, Don Juan seduces two young women, whom he deceives with promises of marriage. Pursued by Elvire's brothers, he hides in the forest with Sganarelle.

In act 3, to the horror of his valet, Don Juan explains his "articles of faith," which may be summarized as "two and two are four." He meets a poor man and tries to bribe him with alms to blaspheme. Then he saves the life of one of Elvire's brothers. In an act of bravado, he invites the statue of a Commander whom he killed in the past to dine; the statue accepts with a gesture.

In the fourth act, Don Juan is insolent to his father, Don Louis, who rebukes him for his scandalous life, and he remains insensitive to the prayers of Elvire, who, before retiring to a convent, would like to bring him to repentance. He sits down to dine, and the statue appears to remind him of his invitation. Sganarelle is terrified, but Don Juan retains his composure.

In the final act, Don Juan, having pretended to repent before his father, explains to Sganarelle that henceforth he intends to wear the mask of a hypocrite; it is in this manner also that he responds to the challenge of Elvire's brothers. At this point, a ghost appears to tell Don Juan that he has only a moment in which to repent if he wishes divine mercy. Hardhearted, he mocks this warning. The Commander's statue arrives, takes him by the hand, and Don Juan is engulfed in the invisible flames of Hell.

At first glance, *Don Juan* does not seem to be related to its author's earlier works. Molière did wish to try something new. The play requires several changes of scene and machinery to achieve stage effects. It includes the supernatural along with the realistic, phantoms and an animated statue along with peasants drawn from real life. Similarly, the comedy of the almost burlesque scene with M. Dimanche alternates with the tragic qualities of Don Louis's vehement speech to his son.

Yet this work is related to Molière's serious concerns. For the first time in the succession of versions of the Don Juan story, the principal character is not only debauched but also a hypocrite. As long as he is a seducer and blasphemer, divine mercy will spare him; when in the last act he pretends to be converted, he goes too far, and divine patience is exhausted. While in *Tartuffe* it is the king who intervenes to punish the hypocrite, in *Don Juan* it is Heaven. Molière thus uses another occasion to attack his enemies' false piety, but again religion, false or sincere, finds itself in a weak position. Atheism is defended by a vicious but intelligent and charming aristocrat, whereas the defender of religion is a sensible yet somewhat obtuse valet.

THE MISANTHROPE

A five-act comedy in verse, *The Misanthrope*, on which Molière had been working since 1664, finally appeared in 1666. Although well received by the intellectual elite, the work did not enjoy great favor with the general public, who preferred Molière's farces, comedies with music and ballet, and satire.

In the salon of a young widow, Célimène, whom he awaits, the misanthropic Alceste rails to his friend, the indulgent Philinte, against the worldly hypocrisy that makes him detest humankind. Nevertheless, he loves the coquettish Célimène. Oronte asks Alceste for his opinion of a love sonnet that he has composed. Reticent at first, Alceste finally blurts out his opinion of the piece, which he finds detestable. Furious, Oronte withdraws, followed by Alceste and Philinte, who leave together.

As act 2 begins, Alceste has brought Célimène home, where he reproaches her for her fickleness and tries to make her declare her love. The arrival of two dandies, Acaste and Clitandre, suitors of Célimène, interrupts the scene between the lovers. Philinte and Eliante, Célimène's cousin, arrive, and a conversation takes place in which the young widow draws satiric portraits of friends in their absence. Célimène's clever but biting tongue makes Alceste indignant, and

he is not spared her witty attacks. Alceste must leave, for he is being sued by Oronte because of his critical judgment of the sonnet.

In act 3, Acaste and Clitandre make a pact: The one who can first give clear proof of Célimène's love for him shall be declared the winner. During a visit with Arsinoë, Célimène is provoked by her guest's innuendos regarding her flirtations into giving the prude her comeuppance. Her vanity wounded, Arsinoë tries in vain to charm Alceste, but she succeeds in troubling him with regard to Célimène's love, offering to furnish him evidence that she is betraying him.

The fourth act adds further complications. When Philinte tells Eliante how Alceste and Oronte have patched up their differences, she reveals her admiration for the misanthrope's heroic sincerity; in turn, Philinte declares his love to her. Alceste, however, arrives in a rage, for Arsinoë has produced a note written by Célimène to Oronte. Alceste offers his heart to Eliante, and, when Célimène appears, he heaps reproach on her. Lying artfully, she justifies herself and triumphs over Alceste, who loves her more than ever despite shame for his weakness. Her explanation is interrupted by the arrival of the burlesque valet, Dubois, with the news that Alceste has lost an important lawsuit and risks arrest.

The conclusion plays against comic conventions. Alceste decides to leave society, against Philinte's advice, and he wants to know if Célimène is ready to accompany him. She arrives with Oronte, and when the two suitors demand that she choose between them, she is embarrassed and asks Eliante, who refuses, to judge. When Acaste and Clitandre appear and read notes that make it clear to all how false Célimène has been with her several suitors, her salon is deserted. Only Alceste remains to offer himself if she will follow him. She accepts him as a husband but refuses to leave Paris. Alceste will not marry her under these conditions, and, as Eliante agrees to marry Philinte, he prepares to go to his retreat alone.

Unlike most of Molière's plays, which take place in a bourgeois setting, *The Misanthrope* depicts the aristocracy of the period. The often crude humor of an earlier time has been replaced by refined manners.

An elegant elite frequents Célimène's salon where visiting, conversation, and gallantry are the preferred diversions. The charming young widow's guests reveal their wit by improvising verbal portraits, engaging in subtle analyses of amorous themes, and judging one another's latest verses. Molière reveals, however, that beneath this society's brilliant exterior there lies mediocrity and profound hypocrisy: Polite manners thinly veil coldness; the art of conversation consists of clever but malicious gossip or sarcastic repartee between supposed friends; gallantry is coupled with contempt for women and love.

The Misanthrope is a love story, too, told as it is ending. From the first scene between Alceste and Célimène one knows that they are incompatible, for they disagree on everything, especially love, which for her is only flirtation, for him total commitment. Love has blinded Alceste, and he indulges himself in the hope of reforming Célimène, until he begins to suspect that he has been betrayed. He then scorns Célimène, and he scorns himself for being unable to stifle his passion. When he is certain that Célimène does not love him, he rejects her as being unworthy of him and takes refuge in voluntary exile. Contrary to the traditions of comedy, the lovers separate at the end.

Finally, *The Misanthrope* is a perfect comedy of character. The characters' features are less striking than those found in *Tartuffe*, but they are more delicately modeled. Alceste, whose soul is noble, has a disagreeable temperament. He is the opposite of Philinte, who is a man of the world, outwardly indulgent to his fellows, although he really despises them. In contrast to Célimène, the eternal coquette, young, beautiful, and witty, but heartless, stand the wise Eliante and the prudish Arsinoë. Among the secondary figures at whom Molière points the finger of ridicule, Oronte, the would-be poet whose vanity leads him to commit nasty, cowardly acts, is outstanding.

Each age sees *The Misanthrope* differently, according to its own preoccupations, and discovers a new wealth of emotions and ideas. Whereas the seventeenth century found Alceste odd and ridiculous, later periods have appreciated his heroic and pathetic side.

LATER WORKS

Molière's career changed direction when, in 1669, the ban on *Tartuffe* was finally lifted. He felt vindicated, and he took care thereafter not to write highly controversial works. Charged with the organization of royal entertainments, he produced the farces and comedies with music and dance that had always won for him general acclaim, as well as a number of novel pieces, often in collaboration with Lully and on one occasion with Corneille. There was, as always, much satire, but of politically powerless types. For example, because of his ill health, Molière found doctors an increasingly favorite object of his attacks.

THE ACTOR AND DIRECTOR

Molière's worst enemies admitted that he was an extraordinary comedic actor. Despite the efforts of traditionalists to make him fit a classical mold, it is more accurate to say that he followed Gallic and Italian traditions. Not only did Molière know Scaramouche but also he was on familiar terms with the whole Italian troupe and their work; he imitated the costumes and traits of both Scaramouche and Sganarelle. Above all, he learned the art of caricature and mime, long popular in France and so necessary for the Italians in a foreign country, and applied their synthetic approach to re-create life in his theaters. Molière developed a stylized walk, posture, and facial expression by which he became known to his public for many years in whatever role he played. There were important modifications from time to time, depending on the roles and changes in Molière's physical condition, but his basic philosophy remained the same.

Molière governed his troupe with cordial familiarity and firm authority. He was a most exacting director at a time when directing had not advanced far, and he made fine actors and actresses of mediocre talents. As has been noted, Molière's first efforts to recruit a repertoire met with small success; he was obliged to create his own, one that served as a model closely followed by his successors for many years. Among Molière's many duties was that of keeping order among the spectators in his theater, not always an easy task at the time. It seems that Molière was as successful on this count as on the many others required to create the national theater in France that is his glory.

BIBLIOGRAPHY

Calder, Andrew. *Molière: The Theory and Practice of Comedy.* Atlantic Highlands, N.J.: Athlone Press, 1993. An analysis of the comedic dramas of Molière. Bibliography and index.

Carmody, James Patrick. *Rereading Molière: Mise en scène from Antoine to Vitez.* Ann Arbor: University of Michigan Press, 1993. An examination of the production of Molière's plays and their stage history. Bibliography and index.

Finn, Thomas P. *Molière's Spanish Connection: Seventeenth Century Spanish Theatrical Influence on Imaginary Identity in Molière.* New York: Peter Lang, 2001. A look at the influence of Spanish drama on identity in the works of Molière. Bibliography and index.

Kroen, Sheryl. *Politics and Theater: The Crisis of Legitimacy in Restoration France, 1815-1830.* Berkeley: University of California Press, 2000. This look at Restoration France examines Molière's *Tartuffe* and its influence. Bibliography and index.

Lalande, Roxanne Decker. *Intruders in the Play World: The Dynamics of Gender in Molière's Comedies.* Madison, N.J.: Fairleigh Dickinson University Press, 1996. A critical analysis of Molière's plays from the perspective of gender. Bibliography and index.

Norman, Larry F. *The Public Mirror: Molière and the Social Commerce of Depiction.* Chicago: University of Chicago Press, 1999. Norman examines depiction in the plays of Molière. Bibliography and index.

Scott, Virginia. *Molière: A Theatrical Life.* New York: Cambridge University Press, 2000. A biography of the dramatist that examines his life as a member of the theater rather than as man of letters. Bibliography and index.

Richard A. Mazzara

FERENC MOLNÁR

Born: Budapest, Hungary; January 12, 1878
Died: New York, New York; April 1, 1952

PRINCIPAL DRAMA

A doktor úr, pr., pb. 1902
Józsi, pb. 1904
Az ördög, pr., pb. 1907 (*The Devil*, 1908)
Liliom, pr., pb. 1909 (English translation, 1921)
A testőr, pr., pb. 1910 (*The Guardsman*, 1910)
A farkas, pr., pb. 1912 (*The Wolf*, 1914)
A fehér felhő, pr. 1916 (*The White Cloud*, 1929)
Farsang, pr., pb. 1917 (*Carnival*, 1924)
Úri divat, pr., pb. 1917 (*Fashions for Men*, 1922)
A hattyú, pr. 1920, pb. 1921 (*The Swan*, 1922)
A vörös malom, pr. 1922, pb. 1923 (*The Red Mill*, 1928)
Égi és földi szerelem, pr., pb. 1922 (*Heavenly and Earthly Love*, 1923)
Az üvegcipő, pr., pb. 1924 (*The Glass Slipper*, 1925)
Játék a kastélyban, pr., pb. 1926 (*The Play's the Thing*, 1926)
Olimpia, pr., pb. 1928 (*Olympia*, 1928)
The Plays of Ferenc Molnár, pb. 1929
Egy-kettő-három, pb. 1929 (*One, Two, Three*, 1930)
A jó tündér, pb. 1930 (*The Good Fairy*, 1932)
Valaki, pr., pb. 1932 (*Arthur*, 1946)
Delila, pr., pb. 1937 (*Delilah*, 1947)
Romantic Comedies: Eight Plays by Ferenc Molnár, pb. 1952

OTHER LITERARY FORMS

After Ferenc Molnár achieved recognition as a playwright, only half-hearted attention was given to his accomplishments in other genres; nevertheless, he produced a respectable body of work in areas outside drama. Molnár always considered himself a journalist, and he achieved distinction in both the Hungarian and the international press. With his many volumes of collected editorials, sketches, *feuilletons*, and satires, he emerged as a faithful chronicler of life in Budapest and left an indelible mark on Hungarian short prose. As a journalist, he valued keen observation, precise description, and wit. His urbane, vibrant, meticulously constructed short stories reveal a remarkable narrative ability in his realistic characterization, his control of plot and technique, and his consummate skill with dialogue. Molnár also wrote a number of novels that were widely popular at the time of their publication. Although they are characterized by brilliant style, cleverly calculated plots, and sensitively drawn characters, their range is rather narrow. While most of these autobiographical novels are perhaps merely interesting period pieces, *A Pál-utcai fiúk* (1907; *The Paul Street Boys*, 1927), a moving tale about youth, is regarded as a masterpiece. Molnár completed his nostalgic autobiography, *Utitárs a száműzetésben* (1958; *Companion in Exile: Notes for an Autobiography*, 1950), in the United States. This loosely constructed work provides rare glimpses into his rich, colorful life.

Ferenc Molnár in 1952. (AP/Wide World Photos)

ACHIEVEMENTS

Ferenc Molnár's most significant achievement was, without doubt, in drama. The first Hungarian playwright to become internationally famous, he achieved critical, popular, and financial success both at home and abroad, writing forty-two plays, most of which were performed all over the world. Some twenty-six films and three musical comedies produced in the United States were based on his plays. Although his can be considered a remote language and a scarcely known culture, Molnár overcame the literary isolation of his native land, entertaining audiences of many countries, calling their attention to Hungary, and creating a demand for export dramas. His plays made Budapest one of the theater centers of the world.

At the age of eighteen, Molnár became famous as a journalistic prodigy, two years later as a promising novelist, and, in 1902, as an accomplished playwright. He sustained this popularity all through his life. Rewards were heaped on him. For his distinguished service as a reporter at the front during World War I, he was recognized by the emperor, who conferred the Franz Joseph Order on him in 1916. The same year, his new play, *The White Cloud*, written in the army headquarters, won for him the Academy's prestigious Voinits Award and membership in the Kisfaludy Society, an exclusive literary association. In 1927, after the Paris premiere of *The Swan*, Molnár was decorated with the Cross of the Legion of Honor by the president of France. He then received a hero's welcome in the United States: Theater directors and publishers besieged him with offers, President Calvin Coolidge received him at the White House, and, before his departure, the author was made a staff member of the magazine *Vanity Fair*.

Molnár fused Hungarian stage tradition and Western influences into a cosmopolitan amalgam, yet his unerring dramatic instinct, dazzling technique, vivid style, and accurate timing were uniquely his own. He wrote only what was natural to him, and he avoided obscure language, pseudo-Symbolism, forced social commentary, and intellectual aloofness. His talent not only entertained but also enlightened. The relativity of truth and the almost indiscernible difference between illusion and reality became Molnár's major dramatic themes, areas in which he preceded and to a certain extent even inspired Luigi Pirandello.

BIOGRAPHY

A true cosmopolitan, Ferenc Molnár was born to a wealthy family and lived in luxury most of his life. The son of Dr. Mór Neumann, a prosperous Jewish physician, and Jozefa Wallfisch, a frail, sickly woman, Molnár and his only sister, Erzsébet, were reared by nannies and taught by tutors as young children. In 1887, Molnár entered the Református Gimnázium, a Calvinist high school, where, at the age of fourteen, he began to write, launching a student newspaper and undertaking his first dramatic venture. After he was graduated in 1895, Molnár enrolled at the University of Budapest to study law, where he formed the habit of sitting in the Central Café to study and entertain friends with his *bons mots* and puns. His father quickly sent him to Geneva to continue his legal training there but to no avail. While abroad, Molnár began to write in earnest, sending home vivid reports to be published in the Budapest papers. He also finished a novel, *Magdolna és egyéb elbeszélések* (1898), while traveling in France. After returning home, he abandoned law and became a full-time journalist, working for József Vészi's *Budapesti napló*. Soon he published a new novel, *Az éhes város* (1901; the hun-

gry city), and saw the opening of his first play, *A doktor úr* (the lawyer).

In the ensuing years, Molnár published at least one book a year, and his fame grew rapidly. His charm, wit, and banter made him the favorite author of the bourgeoisie and the idol of the literary set. In 1906, he married his editor's daughter, Margit Vészi, a gifted artist. Their daughter Márta was born the following year, when Molnár became internationally renowned for the production of *The Devil*. The next year, his father died, and his marriage disintegrated. After the failure of *Liliom*, Molnár became ill but was soon involved with Hungary's leading actress, Irén Varsányi, for whom he wrote several plays. He then divorced his wife and basked in the phenomenal success of *The Guardsman*. During the next four years, he published several volumes of essays and stories and translated more than thirty French plays. During World War I, he worked as a correspondent, sending vibrant accounts from the front, which were printed both at home and in the *London Morning Post* and *The New York Times*. Between 1920 and 1924, Molnár wrote seven plays in rapid succession. His personal life was similarly hectic: His ten-year affair with Hungary's prima donna Sári Fedák culminated in their marriage in 1922, and, after much scandal, in their divorce two years later. In 1926, he married Lili Darvas, an accomplished actress, and presented her in *The Play's the Thing*. They traveled extensively, and in the 1930's, sensing the approach of war, Molnár allowed his absences from Hungary to grow longer; he moved from country to country with his new secretary-companion, Wanda Bartha, who remained with him until her death.

Seeking refuge from the Nazis, Molnár emigrated to the United States. He arrived in New York in January, 1940, and moved into the Hotel Plaza, where he stayed until his death. In his new home, he again wrote constantly, learning English, working assiduously on plays, novels, and his autobiography. After he became an American citizen, he suffered his greatest tragedy when Mrs. Bartha committed suicide in 1947. His health failing, he sought solace in hard work until his final collapse on March 22, 1952. On April 1, 1952, the celebrated Hungarian hedonist died in exile as a forlorn American recluse.

ANALYSIS

Ferenc Molnár's literary career bloomed at a time when Hungary was experiencing a social and cultural renascence after having achieved a relative independence within the Dual Monarchy. As Budapest became a lively, industrialized metropolis where the arts began to flourish, Molnár emerged both as a lionized dramatic spokesperson of the new class and a leading figure in the international theater world.

Molnár had no significant links with any fashionable literary movements of his time, but he used the tenets of particular trends when and if they suited his purpose. In his graceful, whimsical, sophisticated drawing-room comedies, he provided a felicitous synthesis of naturalism and fantasy, realism and romanticism, cynicism and sentimentality, the profane and the sublime. He delivered his plots with accurate dramatic timing, using witty, sparkling, spicy dialogues. He wrote elegant satiric dramas on manners, human frailties, and illusions; he portrayed suave, lovelorn gentlemen and perfumed, cunning women, or thugs and servants, even princes and princesses, all engaged in the battle of the sexes. Molnár was an undisputed expert of stagecraft. The inextricable fusion of his life with the theater gave him a theatrical versatility along with a vast knowledge of the tricks of the stage. The ease and vigor of his innovative talent, the ability to construct plays faultlessly, the discipline and sense of dramatic proportion, make Molnár one of the finest theatrical craftsmen of his era. He has, however, been criticized as being too superficial and glib in his treatments, tending to rely on wit and charm rather than attempting to delve into the substance of the themes he addressed.

Molnár's turbulent life was one of hard and incessant work. He wanted primarily to be an entertainer, not a preacher or propagandist, and he succeeded. By his special skill, he provided the public with escape, festivity, and an illusory world in which conflicts were fun and amenable to solution. A true artist, he contributed prodigiously to the literary heritage of the world by spreading truth and joy among his public.

THE DEVIL

The first comedy to attract notice to him was *The Devil*, which after its production in Hungary was translated into all major languages. It had a long, spectacular run in the United States. At one time in New York, four companies were playing it simultaneously. The story concerns the pretty young wife of an elderly, jealous banker and an artist, her old beau, whom the husband hires to paint her portrait. After their initial innocent encounter the devil appears, eager to make the two young people happy by rekindling their old flame. They virtuously resist the temptation, but in the end, because of the Devil's clever tricks and manipulations, the wife leaves her husband to join the painter while the Devil smiles diabolically. The importance of this play is in its theme, rather than its plot. In *The Devil*, Molnár launched his theories about women and jealousy, topics he would expand in later works. His female characters seem to be distorted versions of George Bernard Shaw's Life Force—cunning, unfathomable, fickle, and illogical. Men, forever intrigued, baffled, and ultimately defeated, are at their mercy. Introduction of a negative supernatural element is also related to Molnár's theme of the relativity of truth as applied to women, but it goes beyond that. As a protagonist of duplicity, temptation, and malignancy, the Devil becomes a symbolic Jungian shadow, or Freudian Id. The play can thus be interpreted as an allegorical study of the evil instincts inherent in humankind. The characterization is subtle and colorful, the dialogue inventive and sparkling—showing some influence from Oscar Wilde, especially in the Devil's monologues, which are rich with epigrams and paradoxes.

LILIOM

From powdered dandies and scheming ladies, Molnár turned to thugs and simple servants in his next play, *Liliom*, doubtless his most famous drama. Staged and filmed worldwide, both the play and its musical version, *Carousel* (1945), are classics. Liliom, a tough barker at an amusement park, marries Julie, a naïve servant. Failing in his efforts to steal and kill for money to provide for his pregnant wife, he commits suicide. At a celestial court, he learns that after purging himself for sixteen years, he could gain salvation by one good deed. Having served his probation, Liliom returns to earth, but his daughter refuses his gift: a star he stole on the way. In exasperation, he strikes the young girl. As a result, the incorrigible sinner is escorted back to Hell as unredeemable.

This touching allegory examines the questions of redemption while portraying human suffering in Budapest's contemporary underworld. It also provides a thorough analysis of the relation of the hero to his family, to society, and to his playwright; the last, by extension, may also reflect the relationship of human beings to God. Most people view *Liliom* as a tender, romantic love story, others as a fable of humankind's dual nature. Some emphasize the sociological message: the destruction of a downtrodden, deprived couple by the evils of society; others see the play as an acerbic satire on the justice of both heavenly and earthly courts, which brazenly discriminate against the poor.

The character portraits are remarkable. The dualistic hero, a twenty-eight-year-old loud, passionate man, is not a villain, only a maladjusted creature who ends up doing the wrong things in spite of all his good intentions. Liliom, who lives with disarming simplicity all the little pleasures of life, is Molnár's paradoxical Everyman. Julie, the fragile, shy, uneducated peasant girl, is the author's most unforgettable heroine: Through her unswerving love and blind loyalty to Liliom, the ignorant Julie becomes the epitome of saintly womanhood.

Liliom's loose structure is crafted with boundless originality. By changing acts into seven flexible scenes, Molnár maintains a fluency of action. This format suits the rapid yet subtle shifts from reality to fantasy. Most scenes begin with a casual realism and colloquial dialogue, then grow into imaginary realms of romance or fancy.

Oscillating between tragedy and comedy, the play borders on melodrama. The style is similarly eclectic: highly poetic, symbolic, colloquial, grotesque, and sentimental, alternating from scene to scene. The dialogue is pungent with idioms and reflects a racy folksiness. The emotional tone is a combination of pathos, irony, and rhapsodic passion. Like the myth and the fairy tale, *Liliom* is unusually rich in allusions and symbolism built on contrast. The title, *Liliom*, both identifies and characterizes the hero in the vernacular. In the city's slums, it was common to apply the name "lily," the white flower of innocence, to roughnecks. Thus, Liliom's name symbolizes both fundamental goodness and brutality. The clever and playful synthesis of realism and fantasy makes the play titillating; its human topic, universal themes, and profound beauty make it an exhilarating, deeply moving drama.

THE GUARDSMAN

Molnár contrasts relative and absolute truth, creating a play-within-a-play in his next comedy, *The Guardsman*, written for and about his lover, Irén Varsányi, Hungary's leading actress. A perfect example of the wages of jealousy, *The Guardsman* portrays a famous actor who believes that he is not loved for himself and so needs to masquerade as what he believes his wife desires. Using his histrionic powers to impersonate the Guardsman, his alleged rival, he sets out to seduce his own wife, an equally talented Actress. The action of the play turns on the business of this enterprise. The Actor pursues the tactics of a lover hoping to be rebuffed; instead, she encourages his attention. The husband thus must choose between wounding his professional pride and losing his faith in his spouse. The play ends with the Actress claiming that she knew that the guardsman was her husband in disguise all along. Consequently, the self-revelation of the Actor is devoid of meaning because of his wife's pretense of pretense. Here, Molnár creates a supreme form of the art of make-believe by venturing the most improbable encounter between a couple.

Ultimately, the author does not deal simply in lies; he deals in illusions of the truth that are made true only because people believe in them. The opposing characters are both "right" because there is no way to establish where the forever elusive line between reality and pretense may lie hidden. In this play, no truth can be known, only verisimilitude. The style is gracious and poetic, the dialogue is swift and full of sanguine exuberance even when illustrating Molnár's underlying philosophy. By leaving the couple nameless, Molnár underlines the satiric intent and projects a universal image. This entertaining play is still popular in theaters around the world.

THE PLAY'S THE THING

The Play's the Thing is further evidence that in Molnár's mind the dividing line between theater and life was beginning to disappear; what one experiences in real life reappears in theatrical scenes; truth as illusion, pretense as reality. Moreover, the play instructs the audience in how to cope with an embarrassing situation and offers a living manual for playwriting. Like other Molnár plays, its merit lies in its superb craftsmanship and theme rather than in its plot. A dreamy young composer, Adam, and his older colleagues, Turai and Mansky, arrive unheralded at a castle, where they accidentally overhear a passionate conversation between Adam's fiancée and her former lover, both noted Thespians. The heartbroken composer threatens suicide. Seeking a solution to this unfortunate situation, Turai concocts a play that incorporates the incriminating verbal exchange as part of the dialogue. At night, the makeshift farce, "a French comedy," is enacted, with Turai as stage manager. Adam is relieved to discover that his beloved was only rehearsing earlier. Slight as the story is, it is developed with a masterful technique. Turai is Molnár himself, controlling and enjoying the action as he leisurely spins out its gossamer thread. The improvised scene works enchantingly as a triple travesty: of pretentious actors, French farce, and "the play's the thing" itself. Through Turai's reflections, Molnár takes the audience into his confidence and teaches them the secrets of writing a play.

The comedy, however, is not as glib as it might at first appear. Entertainingly Molnár criticizes the art of pretense and, in the process, laughs at himself. He careens on the borderline between stage and reality, demonstrating that what goes on beyond the walls of the theater is not life but histrionics, simply another play. Like Pirandello, Molnár provides no less than a chunk of life, featuring not fictitious characters but "real" people. Conversely, all real people are actors and all real lives consist of mere role-playing; after all, "the play's the thing." This play is an engrossing, mercilessly cynical farce with complete characterizations and sparkling dialogue, adorned with quips and blatant gags, and P. G. Wodehouse's English rendition is as brilliant as the original.

THE SWAN

Similarly enchanting are Molnár's light farces that present romance among the aristocracy. *The Swan* is a beguiling comedy about a princess who is compelled to forsake genuine love for family interest. Because her marriage to the heir apparent to the throne will reinstate the family hegemony, the princess obediently but reluctantly abandons her sweetheart, a "common" tutor. The author effectively criticizes royal disregard for the sacredness of the individual, yet, despite the frequent satiric thrusts at the foibles of princely households, the play is not "a relentless satire of royalty," as contemporary critics have claimed. The general tone is playfully ironic and mocking; equally sardonic is the rendition of the royal suitor's smug superiority, pompous mannerisms and ponderous phraseology. The effective characterization makes the imperial cast identifiably human. The action, spectacularly set in high-class splendor, is swift and absorbing. The dialogue is graceful, rapidly moving with an admirable economy of words. There is a pleasing mixture of the romantic and the satiric, touching pathos and sophisticated raillery. The dramatic structure, classically designed with a meticulous rise and fall of the action, is faultless. *The Swan* is still widely played, and its three American motion-picture versions also attract large audiences.

OLYMPIA

Elaborating on the same theme, in *Olympia*, Molnár presents a love affair between a Magyar hussar and an Austrian princess, while assailing the cruelty of aristocratic exclusivity at the expense of the commoner. In both comedies, the victim is an honest, passionate Hungarian who retaliates for having been used as a clown, rebelling against the smug hauteur and sophisticated viciousness of the Austrian royalty. *Olympia*'s political allusions and social message made the play quite popular in Europe; in the United Stages, its numerous film versions fared much better than its stage production.

OTHER MAJOR WORKS

LONG FICTION: *Magdolna és egyéb elbeszélések*, 1898; *Az éhes város*, 1901; *Égy gazdátlan csónak története*, 1901 (*The Derelict Boat*, 1926); *Éva*, 1903

(English translation, 1926); *Rabok*, 1907 (*Prisoners*, 1925); *A Pál-utcai fiúk*, 1907 (*The Paul Street Boys*, 1927); *A zenélő angyal*, 1933 (*Angel Making Music*, 1935); *Kekszemű*, 1942 (*The Blue-Eyed Lady*, 1942); *The Captain of St. Margaret's: Twenty-five Chapters of Memoires*, 1945; *Isten veled szivem*, 1947 (*Farewell My Heart*, 1945).

SHORT FICTION: *Muzsika*, 1908; *Ketten beszélnek*, 1909 (*Stories for Two*, 1950); *Széntolvajok*, 1918.

NONFICTION: *Pesti erkölcsök*, 1909; *Hétágú síp*, 1911; *Ma, tegnap, tegnapelőtt*, 1912; *Az aruvimi erdő titka és egyéb szatirák*, 1916; *Égy haditudósitó emlékei*, 1916; *Ismerősök*, 1917; *Husbands and Lovers*, 1924; *Toll*, 1928; *Utitárs a száműzetésben*, 1958 (*Companion in Exile: Notes for an Autobiography*, 1950).

BIBLIOGRAPHY

Györgyey, Clara. *Ferenc Molnár*. Boston: Twayne, 1980. This basic biography examines the life and works of Molnár. Includes index and bibliography.

Rajec, Elizabeth M. *Ferenc Molnár: Bibliography.* 2 vols. Wien: H. Böhlaus, 1986. Rajec provides a bibliography of primary and secondary sources in English, German, and Hungarian on Molnár. Indexes.

Várkonyi, István. *Ferenc Molnár and the Austro-Hungarian "Fin de Siecle."* New York: Peter Lang, 1992. Várkonyi examines the life and works of Molnár as well as intellectual life in Austro-Hungary during the twentieth century. Bibliographical references.

Clara Györgyey

HENRY DE MONTHERLANT

Born: Paris, France; April 21, 1896
Died: Paris, France; September 21, 1972

PRINCIPAL DRAMA

Fils des autres, pr. 1941, pb. 1944

La Reine morte, pr., pb. 1942 (*Queen After Death*, 1951)

Fils de personne, pr. 1943, pb. 1944 (*No Man's Son*, 1951)

Un Incompris, pr. 1943, pb. 1944

Malatesta, pb. 1946, pr. 1950 (English translation, 1951)

Le Maître de Santiago, pb. 1947, pr. 1948 (*The Master of Santiago*, 1951)

Demain il fera jour, pr., pb. 1949 (*Tomorrow the Dawn*, 1951)

Celles qu'on prend dans ses bras, pr., pb. 1950

La Vile dont le prince est un enfant, pb. 1951, pr. 1967

Port-Royal, pr., pb. 1954 (English translation, 1962)

Brocéliande, pr., pb. 1956

Don Juan, pr., pb. 1958

Le Cardinal d'Espagne, pr., pb. 1960 (*The Cardinal of Spain*, 1969)

La Guerre civile, pr., pb. 1965 (*Civil War*, 1967)

OTHER LITERARY FORMS

Although he is best known as a playwright, Henry de Montherlant also had an extensive career as a novelist and essayist. He excelled more in the genre of the former than in that of the latter, for his essays, though often brilliant, never arrive at objective conclusions.

ACHIEVEMENTS

Robert B. Johnson, the American scholar who knew Henry de Montherlant best, remarked that the author's plays are poetic statements on the human condition, transcending time, and therefore likely to endure. This view is shared by the French critic Michel Mohrt, who also pointed out the quality of Montherlant's pessimism that led him to the notion of people's total freedom: from God, from their fellow human beings, even from their own makeup. Hope, the invention of the coward, makes one walk on crutches and live in the future, instead of stepping serenely on one's own feet and existing in the present. If God is posited as absent; if dependence on others is viewed as useless; and if one refuses to excuse anything by invoking one's physical and intellectual limitations, freedom is immediate and complete. Montherlant's plays, then, focus on his characters' struggle to come to terms with the awesome liberty of humankind.

The dramatist was not popular at first because the majority of his spectators questioned the value of freedom at the cost of retreat from God, from others, and from oneself. Montherlant's answer, that the ensuing lucidity was worth any price, no matter how high, pleased the elite theatergoers, but not the rest. His plays were and are considered too cerebral. In the post-World War II era, however, when existentialism burst on the literary scene and attracted a popular following, Montherlant's plays benefited from the similarity between his ideas and those of Jean-Paul Sartre, Simone de Beauvoir, and other exponents of the new school. A wave of intellectualism swept across the French stage, and Montherlant's dramas began to be produced frequently and successfully. Readers and spectators were then faced with the reality of a war just ended and with the specter of another looming on the horizon. Scarred by the concentration camps and already threatened by the restrictions and constrictions of new ghettos and gulags, they found it easy to conceive of the absence of God and the basic loneliness of humanity. The lucidity announced by Montherlant seemed, then, a plausible alternative.

Since the 1970's, however, as the vogue for existentialism has steadily declined, Montherlant's theater has been less well received. To be sure, his plays are still presented and are well attended, but one can no longer speak of mass receptivity. The anti-theater of Samuel Beckett, Eugène Ionesco, and others has replaced the logically composed and intellectual dramas of Montherlant. That is not to say that he does not have a chance to survive in the twenty-first century. Once the anti-theater gives way to a new dramatic school, the well-written plays penned by Montherlant may well become popular again on French and other stages.

BIOGRAPHY

Henry-Marie-Joseph-Millon de Montherlant did not hide the details of his life. He spoke to interviewers, wrote numerous self-revealing articles, and published a diary entitled *Carnets* (1957) covering the years 1930-1944, as well as a second volume entitled *Va jouer avec cette poussière* (1966), detailing his life through 1964. From various essays published subsequently in magazines and newspapers, much is known about the years between this cutoff date and his death by suicide in 1972.

Montherlant's upbringing was decidedly Catholic, first at the École Saint-Pierre and, as a teenager, at the École Sainte-Croix, from which he managed to get himself expelled because of a variety of small infractions. By the time he reached the age of twenty, both of his parents had died. It was then, in 1916, that he volunteered for front-line combat in World War I and was gravely wounded. Although he recovered, the experience left an indelible mark on him and pushed him toward cynicism. He began to practice all sorts of sports, as if to prove to himself that his physical abilities were still intact, and he enjoyed especially bullfighting, which he went on to pursue on numerous occasions, even though he was injured more than once. He wrote intermittently all this time, novels and essays, but it was at the request of a friend, Jean-Louis Vaudoyer, director of the Comédie-Française, that he embarked seriously on a dramatic career. Between 1942 and 1965, he was to write a dozen plays, three of which, *Port-Royal*, *The Cardinal of Spain*, and *Brocéliande*, were staged directly at the French national theater, a feat of considerable rarity.

In the late 1960's, Montherlant began to watch his body decay more and more, a calamity which, as he stated often, he was neither able nor willing to endure. The proud physical being he had been all along refused to put up with slow movement, with blindness, with the humility of dependence on a part-time, and then full-time nurse. In the course of the morning of September 21, 1972, though he could no longer see at all, he put the finishing touches to his will and wrote a letter to the chief of his police precinct in order that his action not be doubted in any way; whereupon, he put a bullet in his head, opting to remain the master of his destiny, in full compliance with the tenets that he had always held.

ANALYSIS

Reflecting their creator's belief in the self-sufficiency and freedom of the individual, most of the characters of Henry de Montherlant fight to maintain or to acquire liberty. Given this premise, threats to freedom come mostly from the outside, although sometimes from within an individual who is attracted by an easy way out. Such challenges must be met head on, according to Montherlant, for there is no compromise possible. The opposition between the spiritual race of the pure and the intransigent, which he claims as his own, and the ersatz race of compromisers is at the core of his best plays. Those characters with whom he sympathizes are clearly the ones who say no to modest, moderate, middle-of-the-road positions. If, in the process of saying no, they lose a privileged status, or even their life, they will have had a chance to breathe the rarefied, precious air of the Parnassian heights where heroes and heroines dwell in singular splendor.

QUEEN AFTER DEATH

It is in *Queen After Death* that these ideas first crystalize. Montherlant transforms the legend of Inés de Castro into a play of grandeur. Passion and duty clash in strong and weak characters, and one or the other wins according to the virility or femininity of the persons involved. If events have an almost hormonal explanation, it is because once all sentimentality has been purged, the physical reigns paramount. Ferrante, the King of Portugal, according to custom but also in the interest of political expediency, has arranged for his son, Pedro, to marry the Infanta of Navarre. Pedro, however, has already been married in secret to Inés de Castro, who is now pregnant. Faced with his father's authority, Pedro hesitates enough to give the king the courage to order the death of Inés. The son's feminine makeup, even more accentuated than that of the two rival women, suggests neither flight, nor any other solution. Ferrante, on the other

hand, is not being a bad father. He is fully aware of duty to family and to state, but between the two there is no compromise, and he is willing to sacrifice the first to the second even at the expense of changing from a moral being into a hateful, amoral subperson. Like Ferrante, the infanta accepts her defeat and returns to Navarre in dignity, if in sadness. Inés, on the other hand, like Pedro feminine and sentimental, appears to be a likely victim of Ferrante's decisiveness, for, after all, in the real world only the fit have the upper hand and deserve to survive.

MALATESTA

Even more than Ferrante, Sigismond Malatesta of Rimini, the hero of *Malatesta*, displays the qualities of the pure and the intransigent. Not merely taking on a son and his wife, as did Ferrante, Malatesta is pitted against Pope Paul II himself, who wishes to remove the hero from his post. None of Malatesta's friends, least of all Porcellio, his best friend, is willing to help, and so Malatesta, unperturbed, arranges the pope's assassination without assistance. A poetic duel of words takes place between hero and pope in act 2, and Montherlant is to be given credit for putting valid, human, and humane arguments in the mouths of both, even though the author clearly sympathizes with Malatesta. In the following act, Porcellio betrays his master and poisons him. In the final act, one learns the reason for Porcellio's betrayal: Once Malatesta had saved his life, and Porcellio, for as long as Malatesta is alive, will owe his life to him. Yet, a free individual cannot owe anything to anyone, for dependence, no matter what its origin, belittles, humiliates, and erases the humanity of people. Porcellio has no choice but to kill his benefactor in order to regain his freedom. The giver must never be forgiven the sin of giving.

Notwithstanding the events, all the main characters admire one another: Malatesta reveres the pope and understands very clearly his political motivation; the pope appreciates Malatesta's qualities of leadership, which, in fact, are so good that in the long run they might prove dangerous; Malatesta loves Porcellio's mind, and in his company reveals in discussions of philosophy and metaphysics; and Porcellio, grateful to Malatesta, shares the latter's delight in the virtuosity of their debates. Were it not that the self-sufficiency of each is endangered by the others, there would be no tragedy. Yet tragedy there must be, for without it there is no purity. It is interesting to note that the minor characters in the play (as in many other plays of Montherlant) are not driven to a tragic ending, for theirs is a stability that does not reach beyond, a complacence based on mediocrity. Isotta, Malatesta's wife; Vannella, Malatesta's mistress; and the other minor figures were born to serve, are content in so doing, and wish no more, for anything else would detract from their comatose existence. Malatesta may be temporarily lured, especially by the thirteen-year-old beauty Vannella, but having used his mistress, as is his right, he reasserts his independence.

THE MASTER OF SANTIAGO

In *The Master of Santiago*, Montherlant's most Christian and most Jansenist play, the dichotomy between contemplation and action is fully explored. All religions, but especially Christianity, must somehow reach a compromise between their sociopolitical functions and the duty of each individual to save his own soul. Don Alvaro, Knight of the Order of Santiago, whose mission is to convert the Indians of the New World, scorns the efforts he directs. He is aware of the compromises involved, of their ultimate futility, and he chooses to isolate himself from the concerns inherent in his post. On a domestic level, he would like to see his daughter, Mariana, give up her love for, and impending marriage with, Jacinto, so that she, too, may be freed from the degradation of living with another human being. In the beginning, she resists, but in the end she is persuaded that the institution of the family is an obstacle to grandeur and to salvation: Is this not the very reason why Catholic priests are not permitted to marry and why members of contemplative orders are closest to God?

Mariana's conversion to Montherlantean ideals recalls the final attitude of the infanta in *Queen After Death*, just as the makeup of Don Alvaro presents similarities with that of Ferrante. To be sure, such extreme asocial attitudes as depicted constantly by the playwright may, for many, damage the verisimilitude of the characters; yet, these remain believable within the context of the severity of their psychology, which transcends the customary norms of society. Life is a social contract by which much is gained and something is lost. For those who refuse compromise, however, no loss, no matter how small, is worth any gain, no matter how large. Montherlant and his protagonists, it seems, look back nostalgically at the asceticism of the primitive Church. They see it threatened by modern Christian morality, which glorifies marriage, family, children, and other societal concerns that blur and blunt the primacy of the individual.

CELLES QU'ON PREND DANS SES BRAS

The dramatist's scorn for women has already been noted. His almost legendary misogyny comes through in no uncertain terms in *Celles qu'on prend dans ses bras*. The title of the play is in fact the playwright's definition of women: They are the ones destined to fall, and in so doing to cause the fall of man. Man's arms must not surrender and catch those luring creatures whom Saint Francis himself feared. Montherlant is known to have often recalled the saint's conviction that nuns were the invention of the devil, for they are a constant source of temptation. Lay women are even more so—witness Ravier's reaction when faced with Christine. He is fifty-eight, rich, powerful, and independent. She is barely twenty, poor, beautiful, and she needs Ravier's help on behalf of her father. In a moment of weakness, he provides the help requested. She is grateful, and a liaison ensues. Ravier knows, then, that he has lost, that he is lost, that nothing good can come out of a situation in which a woman is linked to a man through gratitude, and a man is linked to her through biological attraction. Ravier aspires to purity and intransigence but is unable to pay the price for their attainment.

PORT-ROYAL

If in *Celles qu'on prend dans ses bras* both man and woman are weak, *Port-Royal* presents a group of women whose determination to say no is as unswerving as that of Montherlant's most aggressive male characters. It should be noted at the outset, however, that these are no ordinary women: They are Jansenist nuns, belonging to a sect known for its austerity and for which Montherlant had a special penchant. The sisters of Port-Royal were indeed of a singular breed.

For the playwright, they exemplified the highest level of asceticism, a level at which only exiles exist. They exhibited the frustration, the desperation, and the isolation of the potent and the principled, of the genuinely devout who rejected the mixture of politics and religion of the Vatican, of the Jesuits, in a word, of the compromisers. Not even the threat of excommunication, not even the menace of physical extinction, could make them retreat, let alone capitulate. Theirs was thirst for freedom, like Antigone's, quenchable only in death.

Montherlant was attracted by their story when he read Blaise Pascal's *Les Lettres provinciales* (1656-1657; *The Provincial Letters*, 1657) and Charles-Augustin Sainte-Beuve's *Port-Royal* (1840-1859). The Archbishop de Péréfixe, representing the Vatican, is the advocate of law and order, the enemy of any kind of particularism. The Church of Rome has ordered him to have the Jansenist sisters sign a document recanting their heresy. He is very persuasive in his speeches to the straying nuns. He pleads from the heart and from the mind. He enumerates the privileges that would be restored to them; he exalts the value of regimen over rebellion; he cautions that the admission of one divisive belief would inevitably bring forth others, endangering the very singularity of the Jansenist credo as well as that of the Church. It is so easy to say yes, he points out, using all the familiar arguments that Creon had uttered to the anarchic Antigone. Temporarily, some of the sisters hesitate. They fear, not so much the loss of their lives, but their doubts. In all human thinking there is a chance of error, and, besides, their resistance might irreparably harm all of Christendom.

Sister Angélique de Saint-Jean gives courage to the other sisters. She possesses a nobility and a dignity reminiscent of those of Ferrante, of Alvaro, and a strong constitution not unlike that of the archbishop. The debates between the two well-matched antagonists are devoid of maudlin sentimentality, each being unwilling and unable to capitulate. They both understand that the power to refuse to sign is greater than the power asking for signature. The ensuing destruction of Port-Royal by the Jesuits in 1710 is viewed by Montherlant as a gesture of frustration on the part of an immense authority that lost a struggle against a handful of women. What emerges also from the play is the dramatist's belief that often people are punished not because they are heretics, but because any departure from the fold is considered dangerous to the majority. The sisters of Port-Royal are clearly Christian and clearly Catholic. The rigidity of their practice, however—their orthodoxy—may make new conversions difficult, may inspire others to stray; from the perspective of the pragmatic Church hierarchy, such threats cannot be tolerated. Quantity must win over quality, Montherlant concedes, but the victory can only be temporary. *Port-Royal* aroused a strong response in its first audiences and was immediately acclaimed as a masterpiece; it remains perhaps Montherlant's finest work.

THE CARDINAL OF SPAIN

Almost equally successful was the author's next great play, *The Cardinal of Spain*. The work of a playwright whose mastery of dramatic technique was at its height, *The Cardinal of Spain* concerns two figures of sixteenth century Spain, Cardinal Francisco Ximenez de Cisneros and Juana la Loca. Cisneros's predecessors on the Montherlantean stage are Ferrante, Don Alvaro, and Malatesta. Like them, the cardinal walks a tightrope, attempting to strike a balance between spiritual duty to others and duty to himself. As a cardinal, he is aware that he cannot scorn others, that he must love them and administer to their needs; as an intelligent individual, he is equally aware of the humiliation of serving others, of the others' frequent unworthiness, of the fact that nothing really changes no matter how valiant the effort because of people's stubbornness and imbecility and natural petrification. Cardona, the cardinal's nephew (whose predecessor is Pedro of *Queen After Death*), weak, jealous of his uncle's power, will betray him and cause his death. Instead of being freed from his uncle's authority, as he had hoped, he is imprisoned by guilt. It is the cardinal who, through death, is provided with an escape from the irreconcilable conflict between fulfilling his office and retaining his dignity.

The heroine, Juana la Loca, has the physical and mental stamina of the Infanta of Navarre, with whom she shares a masculinized temperament. There is no madness about her; there is only the stark reality of her sanity. The dialogues between her and the cardinal are models of the dramatist's elegant and noble language. The two understand each other perfectly, and their enmity is only one of circumstance. They both find commerce with men demeaning, and they both long for the repose of indifference, of renunciation. That these can only be reached through feigned madness and real death is no fault of their own. From the gravitational pull of social existence there are no other means of escape—a recurring Montherlantean view, which helps to explain his own loneliness and ultimate suicide.

CIVIL WAR

Men who view death as being more meaningful than life appear in the dramatist's last great play, *Civil War*. This time it is in the pagan ambience of the Rome of Cesar and Pompei that the action takes place. Having now reached old age, and having to bear all the frailties involved, Montherlant's cynicism goes a step further: Not only is one's own death often desirable, but also the annihilation of many is frequently needed for the purification of a race or of a society. Civil wars are especially helpful and necessary in this respect. He points out, for example, that when the Greeks had stopped killing one another, they became the slaves of foreigners. Besides, the horror of war disappears when fighting is viewed as a sacrificial rite.

The ambition of the leaders, Cesar and Pompei, of the traitor, Laetorius, of Cato, Pompei's general, is used by the protagonists less for the attainment of an immediate and temporal victory than for the purpose of courting danger so that death might ultimately result. There is an ecstasy in war that allows people to escape the drabness and dreariness of routine existence, as revealed in the play by the voice of the chorus. Much as Jean Giraudoux does in *La Guerre de Troie n'aura pas lieu* (pr., pb. 1935; *Tiger at the Gates*, 1955), Montherlant suggests that national and international strife belongs to the natural state of things, and leads to the realization of the self, as does procreation for primitive societies, and as cloning might for more advanced ones. A state of peace, devoid of violent action and brutality, would soften people's minds and bodies, would atrophy whatever meager capacities they possess. Amoral or offensive as such a thought may be, it is expected of the pure and the intransigent as fashioned by Montherlant's personal view and dramatic conception.

OTHER MAJOR WORKS

LONG FICTION: *Le Songe*, 1922 (*The Dream*, 1962); *Les Bestiares*, 1926 (*The Bullfighters*, 1927; also known as *The Matador*, 1957); *Les Jeunes Filles*, 1936-1939, 1943 (*The Girls: A Tetralogy of Novels*, 1968; includes *Les Jeunes Filles*, 1936 [*Young Girls*, 1937; also known as *The Girls*, 1968]; *Pitié pour les femmes*, 1936 [*Pity for Women*, 1937, 1968]; *Le Démon du bien*, 1937 [*The Demon of Good*, 1940; also known as *The Hippogriff*, 1968]; and *Les Lépreuses*, 1939 [*The Lepers*, 1940, 1968]).

NONFICTION: *Carnets*, 1957; *Va jouer avec cette poussière*, 1966.

BIBLIOGRAPHY

Becker, Lucille Frackman. *Henry de Monttherlant: A Critical Biography*. Carbondale: Southern Illinois University Press, 1970. A biography of Montherlant that covers his life and works. Bibliography.

Gerrard, Charlotte Frankel. *Montherlant and Suicide*. Madrid, Spain: J. Porúa Turanzas, 1977. A critical analysis of the works of Montherlant, with emphasis on his attitude toward suicide. Bibliography and index.

Golsan, Richard Joseph. *Service Inutile: A Study of the Tragic in the Theatre of Henry de Montherlant*. University, Miss.: Romance Monographs, 1988. This study examines the tragic elements in the dramatic works of Montherlant. Bibliography.

Johnson, Robert Borwn. *Henry de Montherlant*. New York: Twayne, 1968. A basic biography of Montherlant that covers both his life and works. Bibliography.

Alfred Cismaru

LEANDRO FERNÁNDEZ DE MORATÍN

Born: Madrid, Spain; March 10, 1760
Died: Paris, France; June 21, 1828

PRINCIPAL DRAMA

El barón, wr. 1787, pr. 1803, pb. 1825 (verse play; *The Baron*, 1805)

El viejo y la niña, pr. 1790, pb. 1825 (verse play)

La mojigata, wr. 1791, pr. 1804, pb. 1825 (verse play)

La comedia nueva: O, El café, pr. 1792, pb. 1825

El sí de las niñas, wr. 1801, pr., pb. 1806 (*When a Girl Says Yes*, 1929)

La escuela de maridos, pr. 1812, pb. 1825 (adaptation of Molière's play *L'École des maris*)

El médico a palos, pr. 1814, pb. 1825 (adaptation of Moliére's play *Le Médecin malgré lui*)

OTHER LITERARY FORMS

Leandro Fernández de Moratín is chiefly recognized for his plays although he did contribute to the Spanish literary world a rather large and varied corpus of writings. He wrote much verse, most of which is undistinguished, although he did win honorable mention in a 1779 poetry contest held by the Spanish Royal Academy for a narrative poem *La toma de Granada*. Three years later, the Spanish Royal Academy again awarded him honorable mention for *Lección poética: Sátira Contra los vicios introducidos en la poesía castellana*, a satire on the literary vices of the day.

In 1798, he undertook a translation of *Hamlet, Prince of Denmark* (pr. c. 1600-1601). Although his command of English was not perfect, his prose translation was probably the best in a Romance language up to that time. Moratín also translated two comedies by Molière: in 1812, *L'École des maris* (pr., pb. 1661; *The School for Husbands*, 1732) and in 1814, *Le Médecin malgré lui* (pr., pb. 1666; *The Doctor in Spite of Himself*, 1672). Unlike his translation of *Hamlet, Prince of Denmark*, these are free adaptations that stray considerably from the original but refrain from deforming them. Moratín was a great admirer of the French dramatist, from whom he learned to avoid the unbelievable series of mistaken identities and circumstances found in earlier comedies and to focus on the true nature and emotions of his fellow human beings. He may well have had another motive for translating French plays, however, since they were both staged after the French invasion, when Spain was ruled by King Joseph Bonaparte. Late in life, perhaps when he had lost the illusions and optimism of his youth, he finished a translation of Voltaire's *Candide: Ou, L'Optimisme* (1759; *Candide: Or, All for the Best*, 1759). Moratín's translation of the famous satiric tale appeared posthumously in 1838.

In 1789, he published a prose satire, *La derrota de los pedantes*, which achieved considerable renown. In 1812, he edited a seventeenth century account of an *auto-da-fé* that had taken place in the year 1610. Moratín's contribution consists primarily of notes that ridicule, in a Voltairean fashion, the absurdities of the investigation and condemnation of witches.

After leaving Madrid in 1812, he resumed the task of writing a history of the Spanish theater. Moratín worked on this study periodically throughout his life and left in manuscript form the *Orígenes del teatro español* (1830), which was published by the Academy of History. This history was the first significant study of the theater before Lope de Vega Carpio. In addition to the valuable essay, it contains a catalogue of plays and an anthology. Elsewhere, he treated other periods so that his total work on this subject forms a survey of the Spanish theater to his own time. Two intriguing works by Moratín are his *Diario* (1968) and his *Epistolario* (1973). Moratín was a rather shy bachelor, but his *Diario* and correspondence reveal a merry, lively facet of his personality.

ACHIEVEMENTS

It is remarkable that Leandro Fernández de Moratín, despite writing only five original comedies, is a major figure of the Spanish theater. His scant production appears insignificant, for example, when compared to the 80 and 113 plays written, respectively, by his contemporaries Antonio Valladares y Sotomayor and Luciano Comella y Villamitjana. Moratín, however, had a lasting impact on generations of Spanish dramatists, who admired his command of language, his carefully structured plots, and his good taste. The result was that his plays served as models for several generations of playwrights. In fact, he has been called the most influential dramatist in Spanish literature next to Lope de Vega.

Moratín merits being placed in the same category with the greatest genius of the Spanish stage because of his signal contributions to the reform of the Spanish theater. The great aesthetic concern of the eighteenth century was the reformation of the theater, and Moratín, primarily through *La comedia nueva* and *When a Girl Says Yes*, gave a new direction to the theater just as Lope de Vega had done in the previous century with his *comedia*. With *La comedia nueva*, which mocked a popular but decadent genre, Moratín played a crucial role in convincing playwrights to turn from an inferior form of the heroic comedy. *When a Girl Says Yes* was a resounding success and provided playwrights with a model for a type of play that achieved great popularity in the decades that followed. So great was the success of this type of play that historians of literature speak of the School of Moratín to describe the dramatists who followed Moratín's path in creating plays dealing with simple problems about ordinary people. They learned from Moratín that such a play could maintain the interest of a large public while moving them to both laughter and tears. From this point onward, the Spanish theater took a direction that the intense but brief reign of Romanticism did not fundamentally alter. Since Moratín, the realistic, middle-class drama has dominated the Spanish stage.

Moratín was an innovative dramatist because he gave his comedies a sentimental and tearful tone. He presented the ridiculous or laughable side of life while also creating lovers who touched the hearts of the spectators. Moratín was an acute observer of his contemporaries, observing with humor or irony the foibles of human nature. He held up a mirror to the middle class while teaching a moral lesson. His portrayal of ordinary people and simple events is characterized by a concern for detail, usually associated with the realists of the nineteenth century.

Moratín's themes reflect the spirit of the time. For example, they appear in the paintings and etchings of his friend Francisco de Goya. Their contrasting personalities, however, caused a marked difference in treatment. Goya's pessimism produced grotesque caricatures whereas Moratín's plays have a strong note of sentimentality and optimism. Moratín avoids Goya's bitter irony and treats his characters with a softer touch. Another important contribution of Moratín to the Spanish stage was his establishment of higher technical standards. He participated actively in the rehearsals of his plays to correct the unprofessional attitude of some actors and directors. In 1799, when *La comedia nueva* was in production, he made seven demands concerning the actors and actresses, the rehearsals, sets, and costumes, which were granted him by the Judge Protector of the Theaters of Madrid. His desire for high quality productions was an important part of the theater reform of the period.

BIOGRAPHY

Leandro Fernández de Moratín was born in Madrid on March 10, 1760, into a prominent literary family. Though Nicolás, his father, never achieved the distinction of his son, he enjoyed considerable stature in the literary circles of his time. The lives of the Moratíns, father and son, span the period of neoclassicism in Spain. Nicolás was born in 1737, the year that marked the beginning of the neoclassical period in Spain with the publication of Ignacio de Luzán y Claramunt's *Poética*. By 1760, when the father was beginning his career in Madrid, the neoclassical movement was receiving official support, and when Nicolás died in 1780, the son, Leandro, was ready to continue the family tradition, which he did until his death in 1828.

Living during the height of neoclassicism in Spain, Moratín gave this movement some of its greatest successes. His theater represents a continuation and improvement of the efforts of his father. Like his father, Moratín had an extremely facile wit His distrust of this gift, however, explains why he wrote only five original comedies. He had deep reservations concerning prolific authors, for he believed that "to write a lot is to write badly." Moratín was probably influenced by Luzán's belief that good dramatists limit their production to a few carefully written plays. The classical dictum to polish a work through much study and effort was not lost on Moratín.

Moratín's father was a jeweler for the royal family, and he encouraged his son to take up that profession, knowing how difficult it was to earn a living as a writer. Moratín followed his father's advice and worked as a jeweler from 1780, the year of his father's death, until about 1786. In that year, Moratín's commitment to the theater became obvious, for he read his first play, *El viejo y la niña*, to a Madrid theatrical company. Despite his obvious predilection, he was named secretary to a prominent Spanish banker, whom he accompanied to France. While there, he wrote a verse play entitled *The Baron*. In 1789, he took minor religious orders, becoming an abbé.

Between 1792 and 1796, Moratín lived in various European countries, first traveling to France under the auspices of the government. Because of the chaos and violence in France, he fled to England, where he stayed for almost two years. After studying English and the English drama, particularly the works of William Shakespeare, he traveled through Flanders, Germany, and Switzerland en route to Italy, where he lived from 1793 to 1796. He returned to Spain in 1796 and became active in the theater. From 1797 until 1811, Moratín was a government official in charge of an office providing the public with certified translations of a commercial and legal nature. In 1808, he fled the oncoming French troops of Napoleon Bonaparte, but later he returned and was named Royal Librarian by Joseph Bonaparte. In 1812, he fled Madrid with the retreating French troops, never to return. He spent the following years in both Spain and France, where he died in 1828.

Analysis

The foundation of Leandro Fernández de Moratín's theory of comedy was neoclassical; therefore, he wrote his comedies following Aristotelian and Horatian tenets, with modifications based on the innovations of some of his contemporaries, such as Denis Diderot. Moratín defined comedy as an imitation in dialogue of an action occurring in one place and within a few hours, among people of the middle class. He also believed that comedy should have a moral aim; it should ridicule the vices and errors of society and recommend truth and virtue. To understand Moratín's theater fully, it is necessary to recognize his desire to achieve verisimilitude. He was able to attain naturalness in language, the characters, exits and entrances, and other details of the structure because he had a profound understanding of the customs and psychology of his countrymen. While admiring the universal values of neoclassicism, he firmly believed that a Spanish play had to be "clothed in a mantilla and a basquine skirt"; that is, it had to adapt cosmopolitan theories and traditions to contemporary Spanish society.

El viejo y la niña

Moratín's first produced play, *El viejo y la niña*, contains ideas that concerned him throughout his career: the education and general upbringing of women. Moratín, a lifelong bachelor, defended the right of women to be free of domineering relatives and to seek a satisfying emotional life. *El viejo y la niña* presents the unfortunate situation of a girl of nineteen married to a seventy-year-old widower. Isabel, an orphan, marries after believing that the young man whom she loved was obliged to marry another woman. Later, the young people learn that they had been duped. Realizing the hopelessness of their situation, the young man prepares to leave for America. Meanwhile, the jealous husband plots to spy on his wife, a decision that brings about his ruin, for Isabel discovers his plan and decides to enter a convent.

This seemingly innocent play caused Moratín considerable problems. The censors apparently could not condone Moratín's treatment of marriage, for they mutilated the play by cutting lines so that the dialogue became meaningless. Finally, in 1790, a license to perform the play was granted, probably through the influence of Manuel Godoy, who was later to be a favorite of the king and queen and a minister of the government.

El viejo y la niña is a well-constructed play that follows the unities of time, place, and action. The exposition of the conflict is rapid and amusing. The scene in which Don Roque forces his servant to hide under the sofa in order to spy on the young couple is excellent farce. The sad denouement carries the message by demonstrating both the lamentable results of an unequal marriage based on a deception and the fate of those who allow themselves to marry someone other than the one they love.

LA COMEDIA NUEVA

After the great achievements of Lope de Vega, Pedro Calderón de la Barca, and other dramatists of the seventeenth century, the Spanish theater lost momentum. In the eighteenth century, dramatists continued the patterns of the previous epoch or imitated neoclassical dramatists of other nations. In this period of limited experimentation, Spanish theatergoers were enthralled with plays that emphasized elaborate stage machinery. The heroic *comedia* became increasingly popular, and the parodic play within *La comedia nueva* gives one an idea of the overblown language and unrealistic action typical of that genre.

La comedia nueva, first performed in February, 1792, is a satire on dramatic criticism. It is a play about the foibles of an aspiring playwright, his family, and his friends, who are taught a lesson in accordance with the tradition of the neoclassical comedy. Encouraged by his wife and a pedantic friend, who presumes to be a literary critic, the young protagonist of *La comedia nueva*, Eleuterio, writes a drama in the popular style of the day. This play, *El gran cerco de Viena*, opens with the grandiose entrance of the Emperor of Poland, other notables, ladies, and horsemen. The Emperor describes the siege of Vienna by the Turks and how his people have been reduced to eating rats, toads, and filthy insects. The remainder of the play is a series of melodramatic scenes: a lady dying of hunger after refusing to be the Vizier's concubine, a storm, a prayer by the Vizier to his idols, a dance, a funeral, and so on. Finally, on the entrance of a hungry mother and crying child, the public refuses to tolerate any more and creates such a turmoil that the curtain is lowered permanently on *El gran cerco de Viena*.

In contrast to Eleuterio's play, the action of *La comedia nueva* is extremely simple. The aspiring playwright, his family, and friends have lunch shortly before the performance of *El gran cerco de Viena*. They arrive only in time to observe the disastrous ending of the play because the watch of the playwright's pedantic friend had stopped. The audience's reaction to his play, as well as the advice of the elderly Don Pedro, convince the aspiring dramatist that talent, dedication, and knowledge are necessary in order to write for the theater.

Moratín denied having any specific models for his satire. Nevertheless, some believe a priest, Cristóbal Cladera, to be the model for the pedantic critic, who is one of Moratín's outstanding creations, and Luciano Comella y Villamitjana to be the inspiration for the aspiring playwright. Comella y Villamitjana, a prolific dramatist of the time, believed that he was the object of the satire and appealed unsuccessfully to the authorities to suppress the play.

THE BARON

The Baron is set in a bourgeois household of a widow who is being duped by an impostor who is seeking her money and her daughter. The foolish mother is determined that her daughter will marry the baron rather than the handsome, wealthy young villager whom she loves. Because this is a comedy, the fraudulent baron is finally unmasked and the two young lovers marry. The baron's machinations are so ridiculous that even the widow eventually sees through them and learns that her pride and envy almost made her fall into the impostor's trap. Clearly, the play conveys the conservative message that one should not strive to escape from one's social class, particularly through marriage. Moratín also returned in this play to his attacks against the venality and the abuse of marriage. The reviews of *The Baron* were mixed, but the opening run of the play was quite a box-office success. An interesting sidelight to *The Baron* is the fact that, sixteen years before its premiere, Moratín had written a very similar musical play with the same title to please the count of Cabarrus, a banker for whom he worked.

LA MOJIGATA

Moratín's fourth play, *La mojigata*, had its premiere in May, 1804, fifteen months after *The Baron*, even though he had written a first version as early as 1791. The title signifies an individual who feigns humility in order to achieve her end. The author included in the first edition of the play a Latin maxim: "When a bad man pretends to be good, he is then worse." This saying applies to Clara, whose father has reared her in a very strict fashion. He believes Clara to be a devout and obedient daughter who wishes to renounce her inheritance and enter the convent. In contrast to Clara is her cousin Inés, reared by a permissive father who concludes that his method is superior when he observes Clara's deceitfulness. The action of the play explains how the clever Clara gets her comeuppance when a rich relative, hearing that she intends to enter the convent, gives his money to her cousin. Inés, however, decides to share her fortune with Clara, and conditions are established so that Clara will have to reform her character, as will her future husband, Claudio, a dissipated and dishonest young man. Contemporary critics disagreed on certain aspects of the play. One believed that Clara's vice was not sufficiently perverse and that the dissipated young gallant and his servant were morally worse than Clara. In response, another critic wrote that Moratín's intention was not to attack hypocrisy but to make his audience aware of the effects of the improper training of children.

WHEN A GIRL SAYS YES

Moratín's fifth original play, *When a Girl Says Yes*, is generally considered his masterpiece. In the early 1790's, Moratín had destroyed a play entitled "El tutor," which may have been the embryo for *When a Girl Says Yes*. At any rate, by 1801, he had completed a version of *When a Girl Says Yes* that he read on several occasions to friends. In October, 1804, he read one act per day for three consecutive days in the home of the prime minister Manuel Godoy. In November of 1805, he read it to the company of actors of the Cruz theater in Madrid. The company later performed it on January 24, 1806.

When a Girl Says Yes is an extremely well-constructed play that served playwrights as a model of dramatic craftsmanship for many years. Like other Moratín plays, it provided instruction on being a parent or guardian. Moratín shows his concern over the deleterious results of the improper rearing of children.

The plot is simple. A widow, Doña Irene, wishes to marry her sixteen-year-old daughter to Don Diego, a wealthy gentleman of fifty-nine. Francisca, the young daughter, has led a sheltered life in a convent school, where she has been trained not to question authority. She is far from enthusiastic about her mother's plan, because she has fallen in love with an army officer. She is not aware that the handsome young man is Diego's nephew, Carlos. The intrigue is developed skillfully through misunderstanding and dramatic irony. The tension builds to a climax in the final act when the three principals despair of their situation. Don Diego has told his nephew to leave the city; Francisca is heartbroken over his departure; and the elderly suitor is hurt and jealous because another man loves his fiancée. Don Diego is a reasonable man, however, and the conflict is resolved happily for the young couple. As the spokesman of the play's moral, he berates a society that encourages girls to hide innocent feelings and considers them "proper if they are expert in the art of silence and lying." The action of the play conveys the message of the inappropriateness of a marriage between an elderly gentleman and a young girl and the failure of an education that makes young women hide their true emotions. The play's appeal resides in part in the universality of the conflict between the values of parents and children and the idea of love conquering all. The mother, Doña Irene, is Moratín's finest comic character, surpassing Don Hermógenes, the pedantic critic of *La comedia nueva*. She is a self-centered chatterbox who gives little thought to what she herself says, and less to others. She cannot pass up the opportunity to marry her only surviving daughter to the wealthy Don Diego. Doña Irene never changes; when she realizes that the nephew will receive his uncle's money, her single-mindedness comes through as she quickly turns her attention to the young man and praises her daughter for her excellent choice of a husband.

When a Girl Says Yes was an extraordinary box-office success. At a time when an exceptional run of a new play was eight or ten nights, *When a Girl Says Yes* played for twenty-six successive nights, concluding its run on Ash Wednesday, when the theaters had to be closed for Lent. Its popularity was so great that the competing Caños del Peral Theater changed its bill ten times, finally presenting a spectacular show whose major attraction was a short play with four bulls. The play passed through a lengthy legal process before the authorities in both Madrid and Barcelona. In November, 1819, it was prohibited because of its disrespect for ecclesiastical matters and the education provided by religious schools. The play was Moratín's fifth and final original play. He once wrote a friend that he would have written at least five or six more if he had not been subjected to such harassment. Indeed, it is known that after the attacks on *When a Girl Says Yes*, he destroyed some five or six uncompleted plays.

OTHER MAJOR WORKS

LONG FICTION: *La derrota de los pedantes*, 1789.

POETRY: *La toma de Granada*, 1779; *Lección poetica: Sátira contra los vicios introducidos en la poesía castellana*, 1782; *Poesías completas*, 1995.

NONFICTION: *Orígenes del teatro español*, 1830; *Diario*, 1968; *Epistolario*, 1973.

TRANSLATIONS: *Hamlet*, 1798 (of William Shakespeare's play); *Candide*, 1838 (of Voltaire's tale).

MISCELLANEOUS: *Obras dramáticas y líricas*, 1825 (3 volumes); *Obras póstumas*, 1867-1868 (3 volumes).

BIBLIOGRAPHY

Deacon, Philip. Introduction to *El sí de las niñas*, by Leandro Fernández de Moratín. Newburyport, Mass.: Focus Information Group, 1995. In his introduction to Moratín's *When a Girl Says Yes*, Deacon provides information on Moratín's life and on the play. Bibliography.

Dowling, John. *Leandro Fernández de Moratín*. New York: Twayne, 1971. A biography of Moratín covering his works and life. Bibliography.

_____. "Moratín's *La comedia nueva* and the Reform of the Spanish Theater." *Hispania*. 53 (1970): 397-402. An analysis of the influence of Moratín's play *La comedia nueva* on Spanish theater.

Edward V. Coughlin

ALBERTO MORAVIA

Born: Rome, Italy; November 28, 1907
Died: Rome, Italy; September 26, 1990

PRINCIPAL DRAMA

Gli indifferenti, pr., pb.1948

La mascherata, pr. 1954, pb. 1958

Beatrice Cenci, pr. 1955, pb. 1958 (English translation, 1965)

Teatro, pb. 1958, 1976

Il mondo è quello che è, pr., pb. 1966 (*The World's the World*, 1970)

L'intervista, pr., pb. 1966

Il dio Kurt, pr., pb. 1968

La vita è gioco, pb. 1969, pr. 1970

L'angelo dell'informazione e altri testi teatrali, pb. 1986

La cintura, pb. 1986

OTHER LITERARY FORMS

Alberto Moravia's role as a leading figure in twentieth century Italian literature resulted from his lifelong commitment to writing prose fiction in what he described as theatrical form. A prolific author of novels, short stories, essays, film scripts, travel books, and movie reviews, Moravia achieved international respect. He collaborated with other authors and noted directors on screenplays for the more than twenty of his novels that were adapted for film. For a time he coedited the magazine *Nuovi argomenti* and regularly contributed articles to the Milan newspaper *Corriere della sera*. He also wrote a weekly movie column for *L'esspresso*. Moravia traveled a great deal, often meeting with significant political figures and regularly interacting with other artists. As a young author, he served as a special correspondent to the periodicals

Libera Stampa and later to *La gazzetta del popolo*. His travel writings include volumes of exceptional quality on India, China, and Africa.

ACHIEVEMENTS

The immediate success of Alberto Moravia's first work, *Gli Indifferenti* (1929; *The Indifferent Ones*, 1932), signaled the beginning of a new era for Italian literature. Published when he was only twenty-two years old, the novel is considered by many to have been his greatest. Moravia's replacement of the traditionally ornamental Italian prose with unrelenting realism and his themes of ennui and despair paved the way for the development of existential literature. In the postwar years, he became the first Italian writer of the twentieth century to achieve international recognition. The consistent popularity and sale of his works contributed to his later prominence and wealth. In 1952 he received the prestigious Strega prize for a collection of short stories, *I racconti, 1927-1951* (1952), selections from which have been translated and published as *Bitter Honeymoon and Other Stories* (1954) and as *The Wayward Wife and Other Stories* (1960). He received the Viareggio Prize in 1961 for *La noia* (1960; *The Empty Canvas*, 1961). Throughout the 1970's Moravia occupied a prominent role in Italy. Political parties vied for his support and the press routinely reported his views on a variety of events and people, including his own literary achievements and personal life. In 1984 he became a Communist member of the European Parliament, planning to devote his entire tenure solely to promoting nuclear disarmament.

BIOGRAPHY

Alberto Pincherle Moravia was born the son of an architect in Rome, Italy, on November 28, 1907. Moravia's father, of Jewish descent, came to Rome from Venice and his mother, née De Marsanich, was Catholic, a countess of Dalmatian origin. At the age of nine, Moravia contracted tuberculosis of the leg bone. He remained ill, except for periods of brief improvement, for the next nine years. As a result he did not receive a formal education and never graduated from high school. His long confinement also exacerbated the normal tensions of family life for the Pincherles,

Alberto Moravia (Library of Congress)

causing Moravia to develop negative views of the role of family relationships. He felt little rapport with either his mother, who was primarily concerned with acceptance in the bourgeois society of Rome, or his father, an atheist who lived a solitary existence and seldom spoke to his children. He was unhappy and bored living at home and rejected the family values that he later described as being dominated by prudence, self-interest, ignorance, and hedonism.

However, Moravia took full advantage of the two opportunities available to him. As a child, he developed impressive skill in languages. His mother planned a future career in diplomatic service for him and so engaged a succession of foreign governesses. He learned to speak French fluently before learning Italian, later adding English and German. Moravia also had access to his father's library, from which he read a rich selection of drama, especially works by Carlo Goldoni, Molière, Jean Racine, and William Shakespeare. Later he systematically read a succession of great authors, discovering two lifelong favorites in Fyodor Dostoyevsky and James Joyce.

Moravia began writing very early in life, an activity that helped him cope with the enforced isolation resulting from his illness. Failing to recover from the disease at home, Moravia was eventually sent to a sanatorium for a period of two years. During this time, his activity was restricted to reading. On being discharged from the sanatorium at eighteen, he resumed writing and in the next five years wrote three short stories and a novel. Although agonizingly difficult in the beginning, writing later proved to be the means by which Moravia endured what he believed to be the decadence and hypocrisy of bourgeois existence.

Moravia's first novel, *Gli Indifferenti*, was published at his father's expense in 1929. Soon afterward Moravia began a series of travels through Europe, unaware of the great popularity his first novel was enjoying. Recognizing the book's success, Moravia's father agreed to support his son's writing efforts. For the next decade, Moravia spent his time writing and traveling, activities financed in part by his father and in part by his work as a newspaper correspondent. In 1935 he published a second novel, *Le ambizioni sbagliate* (*Wheel of Fortune*, 1937; also known as *Mistaken Ambitions*), and traveled to New York and Mexico.

In 1936 Moravia met a fellow writer, Elsa Morante, who became his companion and later his wife. In 1936 and 1937 he traveled to China and Greece and published two more books. In 1941 Moravia and Elsa Morante were married. By this time Fascist authorities in Italy had begun censoring all publication, and although Mussolini at first approved the text of Moravia's *La Mascherata* (1941; *The Fancy Dress Party*, 1947), all copies were confiscated soon after publication because of its satiric indictment of dictatorship. Moravia and Morante were forced to flee Rome in 1943 and spent the winter in the Ciociaria area south of Rome. In 1944, near war's end, the two returned to Rome and Moravia's writing career continued thereafter without further interruption. In 1952,

the Roman Catholic Church listed his complete works on the Index of Prohibited Books because of their sexual forthrightness, an act that encouraged Moravia's further use of sexuality as a literary device. Although the 1950's were highly productive for Moravia's career, his marriage to Morante disintegrated. He later became involved first with author Dacia Maraini and subsequently with Carmen Llera, whom he married in 1986. Moravia died of a cerebral hemorrhage in his Rome apartment in September of 1990.

ANALYSIS

Alberto Moravia led Italian literature away from the romanticism of the past and championed the realism he believed suited the twentieth century. As a realist, he intended his writing to bear witness to reality in a manner that affirmed the objective existence of both people and things. Moravia explored the world and the psychological state of his characters in relation to each other. He shunned "artistic" prose as mere verbal exercises and mythologizing as falseness. He concentrated exclusively on character and situation. His fiction proved to be so dramatic in quality that more than twenty of his novels were adapted into films.

Moravia's plays provided a direct platform for the expression of ideas he found stylistically difficult to include in his novels, yet they seldom captivated audiences with the same power that his fiction achieved. In Moravia's drama, characters often make long speeches embodying their author's views of reality and the human condition. Productions of his plays were short-lived and received little critical acclaim. Many have yet to be translated into English. Over time, Moravia came to believe that theater in Italy had been surpassed in quality by film and that the country's bourgeois audiences lacked vitality and diversity and so were only interested in drama as a social event. In the public view, Moravia's collection of essays *L'uomo come fine e altri saggi*, 1964 (*Man as an End: A Defense of Humanism: Literary, Social and Political Essays*, 1965) more attractively expressed many of his principal ideas and beliefs, ones that were difficult to communicate in his chosen novel form and that were not well received as plays.

GLI INDIFFERENTI

The drama version of *Gli Indifferenti* (the indifferent ones), produced in 1948, recasts the story of the meaningless life of a young Italian male, a plot clearly drawn from Moravia's own youth and his disenchantment with Italian society. In the play, the young man's sister is seduced by his mother's lover, but despite the dishonor to himself and his family, the young man remains powerless to react effectively.

LA MASCHERATA

La mascherata (the masquerade) is a dramatic version of the novel banned by Mussolini for its satiric indictment of his regime. Set in a Latin American country replete with the oppression, spying, and self-centeredness of the ruling classes that parallels Italy in the 1930's, the story revolves around a dictator who is modest, shy, and clumsy around women. The dictator intends to further his goal of enacting a benign government by ridding his regime of the true villain, the repressive chief of police.

BEATRICE CENCI

Produced in 1955, *Beatrice Cenci* is based on a historical event—the famous Cenci case, the story that had fascinated both English poet Percy Bysshe Shelley and French novelist Stendhal. An aging aristocrat known for his wanton behavior and violent temper, Count Francesco Cenci sexually abuses his daughter Beatrice. A conspiracy unfolds in which Beatrice, her stepmother Lucrezia, and the Governor of the Castle of La Petrella, Olimpio, plot to rid themselves of their monstrous oppressor. The Count, who has experienced "goodness" as stultifying, finds excitement and identity in terrifying and mistreating others. His abuse of Beatrice initiates her desperate attempt to regain her innocence by the murder of her abuser. She allows the already married Olimpio to become her lover to recruit him. After the death of Francesco, Beatrice is repulsed by Olimpio's plan that the two of them live a normal life as if they were man and wife and decides to enter a nunnery as a last hope of regaining her innocence. She plans to mortify herself in obedience and humble herself in prayer, to give up her selfhood in sacrifice and in doing so to defeat hypocrisy in its most odious and virulent form. In spite of Beatrice's good intentions, all of the con-

spirators are arrested, and at the end of the play, the audience is left to contemplate the emptiness of life itself.

THE WORLD'S THE WORLD

Moravia wrote for the theater again in 1966 in the tautologically titled *The World's the World*. In this two-act play, a group of people retire to a villa to undergo experimental language therapy in hopes of improving their lives by reducing their use of emotion-laden words. The therapist contends that a cleansed rhetoric rich in euphemisms, common sayings, and clichés will heal the sickness brought on by such contaminated terms as "soul," "love," "marvelous" and "God."

IL DIO KURT

This 1968 play exploring the evils of governmental oppression recapitulates Moravia's protests against fascism. In *Il dio Kurt* (the god Kurt) an SS commander forces Jews in a concentration camp to enact the story of Oedipus. The Oedipal theme of incest is used metaphorically (if perhaps not convincingly) to reveal the fallacy of racial superiority.

LA VITA È GIOCO

The following year's production, *La vita è gioco* (life is a game), recalls the social satire of *The World's the World*. Moravia evokes gamesmanship as a deceitful occupation used to manipulate society into sidestepping important issues such as inequality, poverty, war, and other societal ills created by excessive consumerism. In all, the play is a comedic treatment of kidnapping, dishonor, and death.

OTHER MAJOR WORKS

LONG FICTION: *Gli indifferenti*, 1929 (*The Indifferent Ones*, 1932; also known as *The Time of Indifference*, 1953); *Le ambizioni sbagliate*, 1935 (*Wheel of Fortune*, 1937; also known as *Mistaken Ambitions*); *La mascherata*, 1941 (*The Fancy Dress Party*, 1947); *Agostino*, 1944 (English translation, 1947); *La Romana*, 1947 (*The Woman of Rome*, 1949); *La disubbidienza*, 1948 (*Disobedience*, 1950); *L'amore coniugale*, 1949 (*Conjugal Love*, 1951); *Il conformista*, 1951 (*The Conformist*, 1951); *Il disprezzo*, 1954 (*A Ghost at Noon*, 1955); *La ciociara*, 1957 (*Two Women*, 1958); *La noia*, 1960 (*The Empty*

Canvas, 1961); *L'attenzione*, 1965 (*The Lie*, 1966); *Io e lui*, 1971 (*Two: A Phallic Novel*, 1972); *La Vita interiore*, 1978 (*Time of Desecration*, 1980); *1934*, 1982 (English translation, 1983); *L'uomo che guarda*, 1985 (*The Voyeur*, 1986); *Il viaggio a Roma*, 1988 (*Journey to Rome*, 1990).

SHORT FICTION: *La bella vita*, 1935; *L'imbroglio*, 1937; *I sogni del pigro*, 1940; *L'amante infelice*, 1943; *L'epidemia: Racconti surrealistici e satirici*, 1944; *Due cortigiane*, 1945; *L'amore coniugale e altri racconti*, 1949; *I racconti, 1927-1951*, 1952; *Bitter Honeymoon and Other Stories*, 1954 (selections from *I racconti*); *Racconti romani*, 1954 (*Roman Tales*, 1956); *Nuovi racconti romani*, 1959 (*More Roman Tales*, 1963); *The Wayward Wife and Other Stories*, 1960 (selections from *I racconti*); *L'automa*, 1963 (*The Fetish*, 1964); *Una cosa è una cosa*, 1967 (*Command and I Will Obey You*, 1969); *I racconti di Alberto Moravia*, 1968; *Il paradiso*, 1970 (*Paradise and Other Stories*, 1971; also as *Bought and Sold*, 1973); *Un'altra vita*, 1973 (*Lady Godiva and Other Stories*, 1975; also as *Mother Love*, 1976); *Boh*, 1976 (*The Voice of the Sea and Other Stories*, 1978); *La cosa e altri racconti*, 1983 (*Erotic Tales*, 1985).

NONFICTION: *Un mese in U.R.S.S.*, 1958 (travel sketch); *Saggi italiani del 1959*, 1960; *Un'idea dell'India*, 1962 (travel sketch); *L'uomo come fine e altri saggi*, 1964 (*Man as an End: A Defense of Humanism, Literary, Social and Political Essays*, 1965); *La rivoluzione culturale in Cina*, 1967 (travel sketch; *The Red Book and the Great Wall*, 1968); *A quale tribù appartieni?*, 1972 (travel sketch; *Which Tribe Do You Belong To?*, 1974); *Impegno controvoglia: Saggi, articoli, interviste*, 1980; *Lettere dal Sahara*, 1981; *L'inverno nucleare*, 1986; *Passeggiate africane*, 1987; *Vita de Moravia*, 1990 (with Alain Elkann; *Life of Moravia*, 2000).

CHILDREN'S LITERATURE: *Tre storie della preistoria*, 1977; *Quando Ba Lena era tanto piccola*, 1978; *Un miliardo di anni fa*, 1979; *Cosma e i briganti*, 1980; *Cama Leonte diventò verde lilla blu*, 1981; *Storie della preistoria*, 1982.

BIBLIOGRAPHY

Freed, Donald, and Joan Ross. *The Existentialism of Alberto Moravia*. Carbondale: Southern Illinois University Press, 1972. Delineates the elements of existentialism as found in Moravia's philosophy and art.

Peterson, Thomas Erling. *Alberto Moravia*. New York: Twayne, 1996. Comprehensive coverage of the life and works of Moravia. Includes critical analysis of major works, as well as information on personal and public activities. Describes the political climate in Italy and its relevance to Moravia's life.

Rebay, Luciano. *Alberto Moravia*. New York: Columbia University Press, 1970. Concise critical biography in the Columbia Essays on Modern Writers series. Covers Moravia's life and literary accomplishments through *L'attenzione*, 1965 (*The Lie*, 1966).

Margaret A. Dodson

AGUSTÍN MORETO Y CABAÑA

Born: Madrid, Spain; 1618
Died: Toledo, Spain; October 28, 1669

PRINCIPAL DRAMA

El lincenciado Vidriera, wr. before 1648, pb. 1653 (based loosely on Miguel de Cervantes' novella)

La cena del rey Baltasar, wr. before 1649, pb. 1796

El Eneas de Dios: O, El caballero del sacramento, wr. before 1651, pb. 1661 (based on Lope de Vega Carpio's *El caballero del sacramento*)

San Franco de Sena, pb. 1652

Hasta el fin nadie es dichoso, pb. 1654 (based on
　　Guillén de Castro y Bellvís's *Los enemigos
　　hermanos*)

Trampa adelante, pb. 1654

Antioco y Seleuco, pb. 1654

De fuera vendrá quien de casa nos echará, pb.
　　1654 (based on Lope de Vega's *De cuando acá
　　nos vino*)

El desdén con el desdén, pb. 1654 (*Love's Victory:
　　Or, The School for Pride*, 1825)

La fuerza de la ley, pb. 1654

Lo que puede la aprehensión, pb. 1654 (based on
　　Lope de Vega's *Mirad a quien alabáis* and on
　　Tirso de Molina's *La celosa de sí misma*)

El mejor amigo, del rey, pb. 1654 (based on the
　　anonymous *Cautela contra cautela*)

*La misma conciencia acusa: O, Despertar a quien
　　duerme*, pb. 1654 (based on Lope de Vega's *El
　　despertar a quien duerme*)

El poder de la amistad, pb. 1654

El valiente justiciero, pb. 1657 (based on Lope de
　　Vega's *El infanzón de Illescas*)

La vida de San Alejo, pr. 1657, pb. 1658

Amor u obligación, pb. 1658

El más ilustre francés, San Bernardo,
　　pb. 1659

No puede ser guardar una mujer, pb. 1661
　　(based on Lope de Vega's *El mayor imposible*;
　　Sir Courtly Nice: Or, It Cannot Be, 1685)

Fingir y amar, pb. 1661

Los más dichosos hermanos, pb. 1662

Las travesuras de Pantoja, pb. 1662

El caballero, pb. 1662

El lindo don Diego, pb. 1662 (based on Castro y
　　Bellvís's *El narciso en su opinión*)

Primero es la honra, pb. 1662

Cómo se vengan los nobles, pb. 1668 (based on
　　Lope de Vega's *El testimonio vengado*)

El defensor de su agravio, pb. 1671

Industrias contra finezas, pb. 1676

Yo por vos y vos por otro, pb. 1676

OTHER LITERARY FORMS

Agustín Moreto y Cabaña is known almost exclusively for his full-length plays. In addition to those plays listed above, which are generally accepted as written solely by Moreto, there are several more on which he collaborated and a few whose authorship is in question. He also wrote some thirty-eight one-act plays, or *teatro menor*, as well as at least fourteen poems and a few *villancicos*.

ACHIEVEMENTS

Because very little is known about Agustín Moreto y Cabaña's life and nonliterary activities, his reputation rests almost exclusively on his abilities as a dramatist. Interestingly, even those abilities have been long in question, this in spite of his prolific and popular dramatic production. The critical tendency to downplay Moreto's achievements can be traced to a comment by a contemporary, Jerónimo de Cáncer y Velasco, who, as incoming secretary of the Academia Castellana, presented a composition to the members of the academy in which he criticized Moreto of plagiarism, of going through copies of old plays and selecting those which would be of use to him in his own writings.

Although on the same occasion, Cáncer y Velasco also made critical remarks about other illustrious contemporaries, all of which were without doubt taken as lighthearted jabs, as the spirit of the occasion would have dictated, and in spite of the fact that the plagiarism with which Moreto was charged was an accepted practice of the time and was engaged in by such famous Spanish dramatists as Lope de Vega Carpio, Pedro Calderón de la Barca, and Tirso de Molina, the charges seem to have stuck and to have done Moreto's reputation considerable damage during the centuries that followed. It has only been in modern times that the criticism has been challenged by such authors as Ruth Lee Kennedy, Frank P. Casa, and James A. Castañeda. As Kennedy points out, Moreto did, in fact, use works by other authors as the basis for about half his major plays, a fact that she attributes to the "customs of the time." Whatever one's view regarding the originality of some of his works, Moreto was and continues to be one of the leading dramatists of Spain during the Golden Age, a time when Spain's drama was a shining light among the literatures of the Western world.

BIOGRAPHY

Agustín Moreto y Cabaña was born to Agustín Moreto and Violante Cabaña, both of whom had come from Italy and settled in Madrid. The exact date of his birth is unknown, although he was baptized on April 9, 1618. The family was apparently affluent, as a result of the elder Moreto's success as a merchant. Moreto attended the University of Alcalá, from which he was graduated in December of 1639. His earliest known literary effort, a poem eulogizing the poet Juan Perez Montalbán on the occasion of the latter's funeral, predates his graduation by a few months.

By 1642, he was a cleric of minor orders in the Church of Santa María Magdalena, in Toledo. By the time his father died, in January of 1643, Moreto was a member of the Academia Castellana. Moreto died on October 28, 1669.

ANALYSIS

The numerous plays written by Agustín Moreto y Cabaña alone or in collaboration with other writers cover a wide variety of subjects, both religious and secular. He wrote many different types of plays, some totally original and some clearly taken from identifiable sources. Among his works are found some of the best plays of his time, some of the best, in fact, in all of Spanish drama. Although long having been praised for his skill in developing and presenting his themes and characters, Moreto has also been condemned for his lack of originality.

Although Moreto wrote five religious plays by himself and collaborated in the writing of nine more, none of his really outstanding works is among them. Although not all modern critics share her views, Kennedy is quite negative in her appraisal of this category of his drama: "In his secular theatre Moreto was, as we shall see, ahead of his time. In the religious *comedia* he is entirely of his own day. Moreover, if put in comparison with other dramatists of his time, he cannot, in this genre, be said to rise above the level of mediocrity."

SAN FRANCO DE SENA

An example of Moreto's religious drama, *San Franco de Sena*, was first published in 1652. Casa notes that its publication took place one year after the establishment of the cult of that saint in Madrid and was probably written as part of the celebration in honor of San Franco. The critics' comments on its artistic value range from very negative to extremely laudatory. Kennedy says, for example, in reference to Moreto's writing of religious drama in general: "His works show clearly that he had not that appreciation of the mystical, that understanding of the sublime, nor that comprehension of the tragic depths of life which enabled his great contemporary [Calderón] to transform pictures of the commonplace into scenes of moving beauty and grandeur." Angel Valbuena Prat, on the other hand, considers *San Franco de Sena* to represent the most profound aspect of Moreto's dramatic genius. Perhaps Casa represents a more measured and realistic judgment in his assessment of this particular work: "While [Moreto] does not deal with a complex theological problem, as does Tirso in *El condenado por desconfiado*, he treats with artistry and profound feeling the theme of contrition and forgiveness."

San Franco de Sena deals with Franco's sinful life and his later repentance and conversion to a life as a pilgrim and ascetic. The play illustrates the concept that "the greatest sinners make the greatest saints." In the first act, he is a shameless criminal and sinner. Among other things, he duels with and kills Aurelio, Lucrecia's suitor. The latter, mistaking him for Aurelio, leaves with Franco and is dishonored by him. She, in fact, becomes as much a sinner and outlaw as he, for a time leading her own band of bandits.

Having introduced his main characters in the first act, the author continues to demonstrate their evil nature in the second, which deals in large part with Franco's attempts to rescue his sick father from the local police. On his way to the city to do so, he is confronted by an example of divine intervention, not at all unusual in Golden Age theater. As he passes the home of the slain Aurelio, Franco sees a cross marking the spot where Aurelio died. As he stops to extinguish the light on the cross, because the memorial bothers him, he hears a voice warning him to desist. He persists anyway and an arm miraculously appears and stops him. He is startled by the occurrence but in no way dissuaded from his sinful life. As he passes the same spot with his father, having killed his father's guards, he again hears a voice. This time the voice tells him to go and gamble, that in losing he will win.

He does in fact soon engage in a card game with other criminals. After he loses all of his possessions, he offers to bet his sight, a sacrilege that astonishes even his fellow gamblers. He is stricken blind and at once realizes the enormity of his sins and begins to repent. The balance of the play deals with Franco's contrition and penitence, as well as with Lucrecia's repentance. She, having been constrained by a Guardian Angel, also eventually sees the error of her ways and turns to a life of righteousness.

The source of Moreto's play was a work written by Father Gregorio Lombardello, in which was detailed the life, sins, and conversion of the saint. While following the historical account in the broadest of terms, the author employed considerable originality in developing his play, including the addition of numerous characters and events.

The popularity that Moreto has enjoyed through the centuries is attributable far more to his secular than to his religious plays. Kennedy divides the former into two main groups: plays of plot (which she further divides into plays of novelistic interest and plays of intrigue) and plays of character and idea. It is from the latter group that his fame principally derives. Of these, eighteen of which Kennedy attributes to his authorship alone, the two most popular are *Love's Victory* and *El lindo don Diego*.

LOVE'S VICTORY

Love's Victory was first published with a collection of Moreto's plays in 1654 and has been published many times since, including translations into several languages. It has been variously described as "the best *comedia* which our language possesses" and "among the four best plays of the Castilian repertoire." Not only has it been translated into several languages, but it also has served as the basis of a number of adaptations.

The play begins with the arrival of Carlos, count of Urgel, and his servant Polilla in Barcelona. The count is expressing to his servant his love for Diana, the daughter of the Count of Barcelona. Diana is an unusual beauty, of whom all the available young noblemen present are enamored. Diana is completely uninterested in any of them and disdainful of their advances. Her disdain only intensifies Carlos's interest, and, under the instigation and coaching of Polilla, he decides to fight fire with fire, or disdain with disdain, from whence the original title. The ploy works. The more uninterested he appears, the more determined she becomes to make him fall in love with her, with the intention of maintaining control over her own feelings.

The second act is devoted to the development of the theme and to the conflict between the two protagonists, he struggling with himself to appear aloof and uninterested and not to give away his true feelings, and she ever more determined to accomplish her own ends. She says in an aside: "I've got to make this man love me if it costs me my very soul." Polilla, meanwhile, enters into Diana's service under the name Caniquí. He acts as a go-between and constantly urges his master not to weaken in his resolve.

The climax comes in the third act, with both Carlos and Diana going so far as to tell each other that they are in love with someone else. In the final scene, they both proclaim their love for each other and receive her father's blessing. Carlos has conquered disdain with disdain. Of this play Castañeda states, "The psychological dimensions of love, vanity, disdain and ambition are carefully woven into a plot which, although it highlights the momentary weaknesses in resolve of the protagonist, also illustrates step by logical step his inexorable progress toward victory, if he will only follow the sage counsel of Polilla. This servant, one of Moreto's greatest comic creations, plays a truly dominant role."

EL LINDO DON DIEGO

El lindo don Diego is the second of Moreto's two masterpieces, which are in large part responsible for his continued popularity. It was first published in 1662 and is based on an earlier play by Guillén de Castro y Bellvís titled *El narciso en su opinión* (1618). As has been pointed out by a number of critics, Moreto's rendition of the story of the insufferable dandy, Don Diego, is a vast improvement over the original. In the words of Castañeda,

> Moreto's adaptation . . . represents gigantic improvement over its humorous but loosely structured source. Frank Casa ably studies the systematic transformation wrought by Moreto to give dramatic cohesiveness to this play which, close behind *El desdén con el desdén* enjoys an undisputed place of honor very near the pinnacle occupied by the greatest plays of the Spanish Golden Age.

The play begins with a dialogue between Don Tello and Don Juan. The former announces to the latter that he has arranged for his two daughters, Doña Inés and Doña Leonor, to marry, respectively, their cousins, Don Diego and Don Mendo. Unknown to Don Tello, Doña Inés and Don Juan are lovers. Don Juan is shocked by the news and accuses Doña Inés of treachery, although he soon learns that she knows nothing of her father's plans. Although she is as dismayed as he at the prospect of being obliged to marry Don Diego, whom she has as yet not met, she says that she can plead with her father but cannot go against his wishes.

The servant, Mosquito, enters and describes the two cousins. Don Mendo is in every way an admirable young gentleman. Don Diego, on the other hand, is a complete dandy and a fool. Don Diego is certain that he is the greatest thing that ever walked. Every time he looks at himself, Mosquito reports, he admires himself and praises God. He is astonished that anyone could be as perfect as he and is sure that any woman would swoon at the sight of him. He is so preoccupied with his looks that, after having spent nine hours primping in front of his mirrors, he complains about being rushed.

His only concern regarding Doña Inés is whether she is worthy of him. She at first tries to make a bad impression, but he misinterprets everything and is convinced that she and her sister are madly in love with him and jealous of each other.

The conflict is finally resolved when, through an intrigue arranged by Mosquito, the maid Beatriz impersonates a countess and convinces Don Diego that he should marry her. Because marriage with a countess would be more advantageous to him, Don Diego declines to accept Doña Inés, with the result that she and Don Juan are reunited, with her father's blessing. The "countess" suddenly becomes a maid and, at the conclusion of a very well done and comic work, everyone is happy except Don Diego, who has been shown for the fool that he is.

BIBLIOGRAPHY

Casa, Frank P. *The Dramatic Craftsmanship of Moreto*. Cambridge, Mass.: Harvard University Press, 1966. A significant study of Moreto and his plays. Casa defends Moreto's practice of borrowing themes from other writers.

Castañeda, James A. *Agustín Moreto*. New York: Twayne, 1974. A concise but thorough treatment of Moreto's life and works.

Exum, Frances, ed. *Essays on Comedy and the Gracioso in Plays by Agustín Moreto*. York, S.C.: Spanish Literature Publishing, 1986. These essays examine the role of the gracioso, or fool, in the comedies of Moreto, particularly Polilla in *Love's Victory*. Includes bibliographies.

Kennedy, Ruth Lee. *The Dramatic Art of Moreto*. Northampton, Mass.: Smith College, 1932. An early, classic work on Moreto and his works. Bibliography.

Rissel, Hilda. *Three Plays by Moreto and Their Adaptation in France*. New York: P. Lang, 1995. Rissel examines three plays by Moreto that were performed in France in the seventeenth century. Bibliography and index.

Rosco N. Tolman

JOHN MORTIMER

Born: London, England; April 21, 1923

PRINCIPAL DRAMA

The Dock Brief, pr. 1957 (radio play and televised),
    pr. 1958 (staged), pb. 1958 (one act)
I Spy, pr. 1957 (radio play), pr. 1958 (televised),
    pb. 1958, pr. 1959 (staged)
Call Me a Liar, pr. 1958 (radio play and televised),
    pb. 1960, pr. 1968 (staged)
What Shall We Tell Caroline?, pr., pb. 1958 (one
    act)
Lunch Hour, pr., pb. 1960 (one act)
The Wrong Side of the Park, pr., pb. 1960
Lunch Hour and Other Plays, pb. 1960 (includes
    Collect Your Hand Baggage, *David and
    Broccoli*, and *Call Me a Liar*)
Collect Your Hand Baggage, pb. 1960, pr. 1963
    (one act)
Two Stars for Comfort, pr., pb. 1962
A Voyage Round My Father, pr. 1963 (radio play),
    pr. 1970 (staged), pb. 1971
A Flea in Her Ear, pr. 1966, pb. 1967 (adaptation
    of Georges Feydeau's play)
The Judge, pr., pb. 1967
Cat Among the Pigeons, pr. 1969, pb. 1970
    (adaptation of Feydeau's play)
Come as You Are: Four Short Plays, pr. 1970, pb.
    1971 (includes *Mill Hill*, *Bermondsey*,
    Gloucester Road, and *Marble Arch*)
Five Plays, pb. 1970 (includes *The Dock Brief*,
    What Shall We Tell Caroline?, *I Spy*, *Lunch
    Hour*, and *Collect Your Hand Baggage*)
The Captain of Köpenick, pr., pb. 1971 (adaptation
    of Carl Zuckmayer's play)
I, Claudius, pr. 1972 (adaptation of Robert Graves's
    novels *I, Claudius* and *Claudius the God*)
Collaborators, pr., pb. 1973
Heaven and Hell, pr. 1976, pb. 1978 (2 one-acts:
    The Fear of Heaven and *The Prince of
    Darkness*)
The Bells of Hell, pr. 1977, pb. 1978 (revision of
    The Prince of Darkness)

The Lady from Maxim's, pr., pb. 1977 (adaptation
    of Feydeau's play)
John Mortimer's Casebook, pr. 1982 (includes *The
    Dock Brief*, *The Prince of Darkness*, and
    Interlude)
Edwin, pr. 1982 (radio play), pr. 1984 (televised),
    pb. 1984 (stage version)
When That I Was, pr. 1982
Edwin and Other Plays, pb. 1984
A Little Hotel on the Side, pr. 1984, pb. 1985
    (adaptation of Feydeau and Maurice
    Desvalliers's play)
Three Boulevard Farces, pb. 1985
Charles Dickens' A Christmas Carol, pr. 1994, pb.
    1995 (adaptation of Charles Dickens' novel)
Naked Justice, pr., pb. 2001

OTHER LITERARY FORMS

In addition to his stage plays, John Mortimer has
written in a variety of other genres. His earliest work
was as a novelist (*Charade*, 1947; *Rumming Park*,
1948; *Answer Yes or No*, 1950; *Like Men Betrayed*,
1953; *The Narrowing Stream*, 1954; and *Three Winters*, 1956); in the late 1950's, he wrote the first of
many screenplays on which he has worked; he began
writing specifically for television in 1960 and has
since then written such popular successes as the
Rumpole of the Bailey series (1975, 1978, 1979) and
Brideshead Revisited (1981; adaptation of Evelyn
Waugh's novel). He also continued to be a regular
newspaper critic and interviewer. Mortimer has published an autobiography, *Clinging to the Wreckage: A
Part of Life* (1982). His later works include the novels
Titmuss Regained (1990) and *Dunster* (1992) and in
the 1990's and into the twenty-first century, a series
of short-story collections based on his Rumpole character.

ACHIEVEMENTS

John Mortimer won the Italia Prize in 1958 for
The Dock Brief, which the British Broadcasting Corporation's Third Programme produced in 1957. He

received a Writers Guild of Great Britain award for best original teleplay in 1969 for *A Voyage Round My Father*, a Golden Globe award nomination in 1970 for his screenplay *John and Mary*, and was the British Film and Television Academy's writer of the year in 1980. He was named a Commander of the British Empire in 1986 and received an honorary degree from Exeter University in the same year. He has served as the dramatic critic for London's *New Statesman, Evening Standard*, and *The Observer*.

BIOGRAPHY

John Clifford Mortimer was born on April 21, 1923, in Hampstead, London, to Clifford and Kathleen May Smith Mortimer. His father was a barrister who went blind when Mortimer was still young but continued to practice law. Mortimer studied at Harrow School in Middlesex from 1937 to 1940, and at Brasenose College, Oxford, from 1940 to 1942. Because of his poor eyesight, he was exempted from military service during World War II and worked as an assistant director and scriptwriter with the Crown Film Units. He was called to the bar in 1948, and in the years since has practiced law in London while writing for radio, television, the theater, film, and newspapers. He became Queen's Counsel in 1966 and Master of the Bench, Inner Temple, London, in 1975. As a barrister, he has been a leading figure in freedom of speech and press cases; in part as a result of his efforts, the Lord Chamberlain's censorship authority was abolished with the passage of the Theatre Act of 1968, which—according to Mortimer—raised the status of playwrights "to the most carefully protected of all public performers." Mortimer married Penelope Fletcher (a novelist, known first as Penelope Dimont and then as Penelope Mortimer) in 1949. They were divorced in 1972, and Mortimer remarried in the same year, to Penelope Gollop.

A regular contributor to *The Times* of London, Mortimer enters the intellectual world from four directions at once: As a barrister, he holds forth in essays and letters to the editor on events that have an impact on the world of law; as a television writer, his name is ubiquitous among the credits of dramatic and comic specials; as a stage writer, his plays continue to find audiences in London and the provinces; and as a detective novel writer and inventor of the famous Rumpole character, he has produced a best-selling novel every few years. He was awarded the Cross of the British Empire in 1986 and was named chairman of the Council of the Royal Society of Literature in 1989. In 1991, in a typical gesture of responsible citizenship, Mortimer appeared at one of his old schools in a charity appearance to raise money for school equipment.

Mortimer settled in Chiltern Hills, north of London, with his second wife, Penelope, and the younger of their two daughters, Rosamond, spending considerable time campaigning against overdevelopment near his rural home, Turville Heath, which he immortalized in *A Voyage Round My Father*.

ANALYSIS

In his autobiography, John Mortimer says that a novice writer is obsessed by "the panic-stricken search for a voice of his own. His ears are full of noises, a cacaphony of sweet airs from the past and the even more delightful sounds of the present." Early in his career as a dramatist, Mortimer found a proper voice, as a writer of comedies of manners, sex farces, and Chekhovian one-act plays in which he attempted "to chart the tottering course of British middle-class attitudes in decline." He has said that comedy "is the only thing worth writing about in this despairing world," which "is far too serious to be described in terms that give us no opportunity to laugh." His choice of subject matter, he has written, "was dictated by myself, my childhood, and such education as I was able to gather . . . ," for he believes that a writer "can only work within that narrow seam which penetrates to the depths of [his] past." Within such a "narrow seam" he has created memorable moments in the theater. Though his farces, such as *Marble Arch* and *Mill Hill*, are little more than whimsies, other plays have enduring merit, particularly *The Dock Brief, The Judge*, and *Collaborators*, and the autobiographical *A Voyage Round My Father* is a major achievement. Mortimer has been a diligent practitioner of the brief play ("In a one-act play the enthusiasm has no time to die") and must be credited with demonstrating not only the commercial but also the artistic viability of the form on the modern stage; concerning the latter, he has written:

> A play, even if it lasts not more than five minutes, should be able to contain at least one life, with a character that can be conceived as stretching backwards and forwards in time, with an existence longer than those moments which actually take place on the stage. A play is a demonstration, in which an audience can recognize something about themselves. As with a picture, this can be achieved by a few lines in the right position.

Mortimer's experience with writing radio plays and his mastery of the dramatic form, as well as his work in the cinema, prepared him for television scriptwriting. He clearly prefers radio plays, which he has described as having many advantages: "They are not subject to the technical mischances and distractions of the theatre and television. They call on the audience to make a great effort of imagination and in them words must be used, as they were in the Elizabethan theatre, to paint scenery or suggest changes of light." On the other hand, "If you're in a theatre where you know everything is unreal and you know it's all an act of the imagination—and you know that all you have are actors standing on a platform—then you can do anything, just because it's entirely imaginary. But if you're in the cinema where you have to try to be literal, then I think it's much harder." His television scripts have developed his largest audiences and gained for him his most widespread critical acclaim, particularly the *Rumpole of the Bailey* series, which began in 1975, and the 1981 adaptation of Evelyn Waugh's novel *Brideshead Revisited*. During the decades in which he has been writing plays—for radio, stage, and television—Mortimer has demonstrated his ability to conceive of clever situations and manage them deftly, to create believable characters even when they are stereotypes, to write dialogue that abounds with witticisms, and to endow even his whimsies with the insight of a perceptive social conscience. He has led theatergoers to a better understanding of themselves while making them laugh.

THE DOCK BRIEF

The Dock Brief features an old barrister whom success has eluded for a half century (and who may be, Mortimer has speculated, "a distant cousin of a far more extrovert creation, 'Rumpole of the Bailey,' whom I wouldn't begin to think about for another fifteen years"). The barrister is randomly selected to defend "an equally unsuccessful criminal" who is accused of murdering his wife. In the man's cell, the two rehearse their courtroom scenario, assuming the roles of judge, witnesses, and jurors. At the actual trial, the barrister becomes befuddled and loses the case, but the judge frees the defendant because the barrister's incompetence has rendered the legal process "ever so null and void." The pair rationalize that the counsel's "dumb tactics" won the day, and they depart whistling and dancing. Funny though it is, *The Dock Brief* also has a message: "I wanted to say something about the lawyer's almost pathetic dependence on the criminal classes, without whom he would be unemployed, and I wanted to find a criminal who would be sorrier for his luckless advocate than he was for himself." The play also exemplifies Mortimer's belief that comedy should be "truly on the side of the lonely, the neglected, the unsuccessful" and "against established rules and . . . the imposing of an arbitrary code of behaviour upon individual and unpredictable human beings." When *The Dock Brief* was revived in London in 1982, it was as part of *John Mortimer's Casebook*, which also includes *The Prince of Darkness* and *Interlude* and is a trilogy that criticizes three pillars of society: the law, the Church, and medicine.

WHAT SHALL WE TELL CAROLINE?

What Shall We Tell Caroline?—Mortimer's first play written expressly for the theater—is a sensitive character study in which a curmudgeonly headmaster who is constantly at odds with his wife convinces an assistant to continue a pretended affair with her, for "If we stopped quarreling over her now . . . think how empty her poor life would be." Caroline, their overprotected eighteen-year-old daughter, silently observes the sparring, but at the close of the one-act play she announces her intention to go to London to live and work. Her escape from the stifling home environment anticipates Mrs. Morgan's desertion of her husband in *I Spy* and Paddy's flight to Paris in *Collect Your Hand Baggage*. The play also foreshadows later works in which variants of the *ménage à trois* motif are present, such as *The Wrong Side of the Park*, *Bermondsey*, *Gloucester Road*, and *Collaborators*. The characters in all of these plays—including *The Dock Brief* and *What Shall We Tell Caroline?*—have a comic vitality touched with pathos. They have trouble communicating with others and coping with life, and they make accommodations that only superficially resolve their problems. Except for *The Dock Brief*, all of these plays are about unhappy marriages.

THE WRONG SIDE OF THE PARK AND TWO STARS FOR COMFORT

In 1959, "with a good deal of trepidation," Mortimer wrote his first full-length play, *The Wrong Side of the Park*, which opened in London the following year with Peter Hall directing and starring Margaret Leighton. The central character, according to Mortimer, was his house in the Swiss Cottage section of London, but this *ménage à trois* play also features "an anglicized Blanche Dubois" who is wed to a "dull boy" and lives in squalor with her in-laws. When she is attracted to a lusty boarder who reminds her of her first husband, she fantasizes about her first marriage, but in a somewhat contrived happy ending, she is reconciled with her present husband, who is made to seem better than he actually is. Although reviewers praised Mortimer's original treatment of old-hat subject matter, some said that the play was too long, with neither characters nor plot adequately sustained. It enjoyed a modest popular success, with a run of 173 performances. In 1962, *Two Stars for Comfort*, Mortimer's next full-length play, had an even longer run of 189 performances, with Trevor Howard as a solicitor-turned-publican "who," Mortimer has said, "always told people what he thought they wanted to hear, an extension of the pleasure principle which only works in the extremely short term." A reworking of an early, unpublished novel, the play is the first in which Mortimer presents the law as a repressive force.

THE JUDGE

The law as repressor is also a theme of *The Judge*, which was criticized for diffuseness when it opened

in London in 1967 (it ran for only sixty-seven performances). According to one reviewer: "Conditioned by his naturalistic habits, [Mortimer's] plotting is ill served by his non-naturalistic structure." Writing about the play years later, Mortimer saw as a primary weakness the fact that its "central character remained entirely in the resonant and archetypal stage; it was a play that appeared, I noticed to my embarrassment when I saw it, with its symbols showing." These fundamental flaws notwithstanding, *The Judge* is an intriguing study of obsession and a disturbing look at how the law sometimes functions. In it, Mortimer's nameless high court judge (who has a reputation for severity) returns to his hometown for his last assize before he retires; obsessed with guilt for having abandoned in his youth a local girl he thought he made pregnant, he comes home to be judged instead of to judge. The girl, Serena, who is now middle-aged, is content with her life, running an antique shop that also provides a variety of sexual services. Mortimer skillfully develops a number of character-revealing and tension-building episodes that give a context to the judge's attempts to force a confrontation with Serena, which he manages to achieve in the penultimate scene: refusing to accept her forgiveness, demanding in vain that she "proceed to judgment," and finally trying unsuccessfully to carry out his own sentence on himself as his last judicial act.

A VOYAGE ROUND MY FATHER

The law also is central in the autobiographical *A Voyage Round My Father*, Mortimer's best and most popular stage play. It was performed at the Haymarket Theatre, London, in 1971 and ran for 501 performances, with Alec Guinness as the father, Leueen MacGrath as the mother, and Jeremy Brett as the son. (Sir Laurence Olivier starred in the 1982 television adaptation.) Spanning more than twenty years, it dramatizes the symbiotic relationship between the playwright and his blind father. According to Ronald Bryden, in a review of a 1970 production at the Greenwich Theatre of the first version of the play, its "style is an expression of the father's. . . . His jokes and stories are the public face of a very private man, whose privacy Mortimer respects, and it is that chosen persona, clownish, dignified, amusing and amused, which Mortimer celebrates lovingly." In his autobiography, Mortimer tells of anxieties he had about the work:

> I had written a play which was about to open; into it I had collected my memories of my father, and written lines for him, so that a man who had filled so much of my life seemed to have left me and become someone for other people to read about and perform. In one way I felt detached from it; but a play is a public exhibition with its own peculiar dangers, another sort of trial. Not for the only time in my life I felt that the theatrical drama in which I was involved was more real than the Old Bailey and the due process of law. Also I was about to tell a wider public a fact which, in our small family, had been the subject of a discreet conspiracy of silence, something, which in our English determination to avoid the slightest embarrassment, we never mentioned. My father had been blind.

Shaping forces other than the father also are in the play—teachers, girls, wartime experiences, friends—and all closely parallel real people and events. Despite the far-reaching concerns of this drama of two lives, however, the play is not at all diffuse. Instead of being divided into separate scenes, the episodes flow into one another, united by the son as the reflective narrator, bridging past and present and providing a clearly defined point of view.

The action begins with the old father recalling wistfully with his son his regular ritual of drowning earwigs that attacked the dahlias in his garden ("a cross between Trooping the Colour and a public execution"), moves to the boy being taught to whistle by a girl who reappears in a later adolescent initiation scene, and then proceeds to the boy's school experiences with a simpleminded headmaster and masters who still suffered the aftereffects of World War I shell shock and battle fatigue. Years later, through the intercession of two lesbians who run a bookshop, the son gets a wartime job as an assistant director with a propaganda film unit. Then, soon after meeting a film writer (whom he marries when she is divorced), he decides to study law. Pervading the play is a series of episodes involving the iconoclastic blind father, whose world is bound by his garden and the courtroom, each of which he strives to dominate: the ear-

wigs that prey on his flowers and the barristers for the opposition. Though the father pretends not to take much of life very seriously, he has a sense of dignity that proscribes mention of his blindness, and he engages in selfless acts of kindness toward children and animals. Neither a demonstratively affectionate husband nor an openly loving parent, he does occasionally express his feelings, about marriage, for example: "You know, the law of husband and wife might seem idiotic at first sight. But when you get to know it, you'll find it can exercise a vague medieval charm." In the same speech, to his son, he adds: "Learn a little law, won't you? Just to please me. . . ." The son's reaction (as narrator, to the audience) reveals the first of several conjunctions of the views of father and son: "It was my father's way to offer the law to me—the great stone column of authority which has been dragged by an adulterous, careless, negligent and half criminal humanity down the ages—as if it were a small mechanical toy which might occupy half an hour on a rainy afternoon." Despite this statement, the episodes that show the father at work in the courtroom and the son's faltering attempts to emulate him present the law as something more than a mere mechanical toy.

A Voyage Round My Father is a memory play with a son as narrator and raisonneur; Tennessee Williams's *The Glass Menagerie* (pr. 1944) inevitably comes to mind. Mortimer's narrator, however, is not haunted by the past as Williams's Tom Wingfield is; he merely retells it. At the end of the play, after his father dies, the son says: "I'd been told of all the things you're meant to feel. Sudden freedom, growing up, the end of dependence, the step into the sunlight when no one is taller than you and you're no one else's shadow. I know what I felt. Lonely."

COLLABORATORS

Collaborators, which had a 1973 London run of 167 performances, similarly has autobiographical connections. In *Clinging to the Wreckage*, Mortimer writes about Henry Winter, a pacifist and conscientious objector who was his closest Oxford friend, through whom Mortimer met his first wife, and who became a physician. Years later, Winter killed a patient's wife, with whom he was having an affair, and then committed suicide. In the *Collaborators*, the main character is also named Henry Winter. Winter is a struggling barrister who also writes radio plays and enjoys cooking (one of Mortimer's own recreations); his wife, Katherine, has been wed once before (which was the case with Penelope Fletcher); and he is on the verge of having an affair with his secretary as a means of escape from the teetering marriage. He meets Sam Brown, an American for whom he starts writing a screenplay about marriage (Mortimer worked as a screenwriter for a time in California), a project that becomes a three-way collaboration, with the American becoming part of the Winter household and alternately wooing husband and wife. Soon, Mortimer's play for his West End audience becomes indistinguishable from the script that the Winters are doing for Brown, just as the reality of their lives becomes intertwined with the fiction of the screenplay they are writing. Midway into *Collaborators*, Katherine suggests to Henry: "I'm not asking you for gimmicks, Henry. . . . Forget the action sequences. Forget the box office even. Suppose we start to examine two people mistaken about each other from the start." By the final curtain, the foreign intruder is gone, the husband's nubile secretary has been scared off, and the married couple is alone—scarred by their domestic sparring and wearied by children grown tall enough "to eat the pornography" (which is moved to a higher shelf). Having collaborated on their screenplay, Katherine and Henry are ready now to collaborate anew on another project, their marriage. It is inevitable that one will want to compare *Collaborators* with Edward Albee's *Who's Afraid of Virginia Woolf?* (pr. 1962)—the situation and pacing are to a degree similar—but Mortimer is wittier than Albee.

EDWIN

In 1982, Mortimer continued to work familiar territory and at the same time to expand his horizons with the productions of *When That I Was* and *Edwin*. *When That I Was* is a one-character play featuring Jack Rice, an old actor at Shakespeare's Globe. *Edwin* began as a radio play for the British Broadcasting Corporation (starring Emlyn Williams, it was broadcast as one of the British Broadcasting Corporation's Sixtieth Anniversary Plays), then was made

into a television play with Alec Guinness, and has since been published in a stage version. It is a one-act play featuring a retired judge, Sir Fennimore Truscott; his wife, Margaret; and a neighbor, Tom Marjoriebanks, a potter. Truscott fantasizes that Tom was Margaret's lover in years past and fathered Edwin, the Truscotts' son, but the more the old men talk about Edwin, the less interested each is in claiming the young man as his son, for Edwin's lifestyle is repellent to both of them. They finally decide to confront Margaret with the matter and ask her to settle the dispute. She responds: "I mean, you may love someone . . . you may love the way they spin a potter's wheel with such outrageous confidence, or go to work at the Law Courts each morning trembling with fear and trying to put a ridiculously brave face on it. And you may love the way someone prunes roses, stooping so easily, or weeds the strawberry bed all day in the hot sunshine . . . with the dark stain of sweat growing on the back of his shirt." Oblique though her answer may be, its import is clear: Neither the senile judge nor the foppish potter sired Edwin. Cattermole, the longtime gardener, is the one. The play concludes with the old men as friends, no longer rivals, and thankful, at least, that the wine being stored as a legacy for Edwin they now can drink because the young man is not their concern any more. Says Truscott: "Not ours, Tom. Let's thank God for it. Not ours!" Whimsy tempered with a semitragic note is the prevalent tone of this play, as it is of so many of its predecessors. Though the characters may find it hard to cope with their lot—Truscott, for example, once retired and dozing in his basket chair, forever pretends that he still is on the bench—they eventually make accommodations with reality, reconciled to their lot in life.

THE FEAR OF HEAVEN

The Fear of Heaven, a 1976 one-act play, concerns two Englishmen who think they are in heaven because the ceiling of their Italian hospital room has a celestial fresco. One of the men dies, while the other lives; at the play's end, the survivor celebrates his good fortune ("Fletcher dead! And I'm alive. Harmlessly alive") at the same time that he laments his fate ("You know what I have discovered? Everything *in-*

teresting happens to Fletcher!"). This ambivalence, which typifies the lives of so many of Mortimer's characters, mirrors life as he sees it. Near the end of *Clinging to the Wreckage*, he tells this anecdote:

> In the years that were to come, I was to invent a down-at-heel old barrister with a certain low courtroom cunning who was to become the hero of a television series. I sat in the usual embarrassed silence with an East End totter whom I had been defending on a charge of attempted murder. He had been accused of stabbing the man next door with the knife he used to cut up carrots for the pony that drew his cart. The motive suggested was that the son of the next-door neighbour had stolen my client's Victory Medal. As we sat together, the totter and I, in the cells beneath the Old Bailey, waiting for a word from the Jury, and as I thought, as usual, of all the things I might have said, art took its revenge on life. "Your Mr. Rumpole could've got me out of this," the totter said, "so why the hell can't you?"

OTHER MAJOR WORKS

LONG FICTION: *Charade*, 1947; *Rumming Park*, 1948; *Answer Yes or No*, 1950; *Like Men Betrayed*, 1953; *The Narrowing Stream*, 1954; *Three Winters*, 1956; *Paradise Postponed*, 1985; *Summer's Lease*, 1988; *Titmuss Regained*, 1990; *Dunster*, 1992; *Under the Hammer*, 1994; *Felix in the Underworld*, 1997; *The Sound of Trumpets*, 1998.

SHORT FICTION: *Rumpole of the Bailey*, 1978; *The Trials of Rumpole*, 1979; *Regina Rumpole*, 1981; *Rumpole's Return*, 1981; *Rumpole and the Golden Thread*, 1983; *The First Rumpole Omnibus*, 1983; *The Second Rumpole Omnibus*, 1987; *Rumpole à la Carte*, 1990; *Rumpole on Trial*, 1992; *The Best of Rumpole*, 1993; *Rumpole and the Angel of Death*, 1995; *The Third Rumpole Omnibus*, 1997; *Rumpole Rests His Case*, 2001.

SCREENPLAYS: *Ferry to Hong Kong*, 1959 (with Lewis Gilbert and Vernon Harris); *The Innocents*, 1961 (with Truman Capote and William Archibald); *Guns of Darkness*, 1962; *I Thank a Fool*, 1962 (with others); *Lunch Hour*, 1962 (adaptation of his play); *The Running Man*, 1963; *Bunny Lake Is Missing*, 1964 (with Penelope Mortimer); *A Flea in Her Ear*, 1967 (adaptation of his play); *John and Mary*, 1969.

TELEPLAYS: *David and Broccoli*, 1960; *Desmond*, 1968; *Rumpole of the Bailey*, 1975, 1978, 1979; *Rumpole's Return*, 1980; *Brideshead Revisited*, 1981 (adaptation of Evelyn Waugh's novel); *A Voyage Round My Father*, 1982; *Paradise Postponed*, 1986; *Titmuss Regained*, 1991.

NONFICTION: *No Moaning at the Bar*, 1957 (as Geoffrey Lincoln); *With Love and Lizards*, 1957 (with Penelope Mortimer); *Clinging to the Wreckage: A Part of Life*, 1982; *In Character*, 1983; *Character Parts*, 1986; *Murderers and Other Friends: Another Part of Life*, 1994; *The Summer of a Dormouse*, 2000.

BIBLIOGRAPHY

Barnes, Clive. "'Little Hotel' on Slight." Review of *A Little Hotel on the Side. Post* (New York), January 27, 1992. A review of the "racily idiomatic adaptation" of a French farce, here in Mortimer's version called *A Little Hotel on the Side*. The Belasco Theater was the site for this second offering of the first season for Tony Randall's National Actors Theater. As in all farce, "the story doesn't matter."

Hayman, Ronald. *British Theatre Since 1955: A Reassessment*. Oxford, England: Oxford University Press, 1979. Mortimer is grouped with Robert Bolt and Peter Shaffer, and all are seen as playwrights who "have repeatedly tried to move away from naturalism, [oscillating] between writing safe plays, catering for the West End audience, and dangerously serious plays, which might have alienated the public they had won." Contains an overview of *The Dock Brief, Two Stars for Comfort*, and *The Judge*.

Honan, William H. "The Funny Side of Social Issues." *The New York Times*, May 12, 1990, p. A13. Honan profiles Mortimer in midtown Manhattan, promoting *Titmuss Regained*. He finds that Mortimer admires Anthony Trollope and Charles Dickens and shares their intent "not only to expose human foible but to elucidate the social issues raised by his story." Provides a good conversational biography, starting with the 1958 radio play *The Dock Brief*.

Rusinko, Susan. *British Drama, 1950 to the Present: A Critical History.* Boston: Twayne, 1989. Chronicles the major movements and important dramatists emerging from Britain in the mid- to late twentieth century, providing a context for the life and works of Mortimer.

Stevens, Andrea. "The Smile Button for Tragedy." *The New York Times*, January 26, 1992, p. B47. A brief but informative look at *A Little Hotel on the Side.* Mortimer says, and Stevens quotes, that "[f]arce is tragedy played at about 120 revolutions a minute." Interviewed by telephone, Mortimer remarks that "all these pompous middle-class men and well-upholstered women [in his work]—

underneath they are selfish little children."

Taylor, John Russell. *The Angry Theatre: New British Drama.* Rev. ed. New York: Hill and Wang, 1969. A separate chapter provides a good long discussion of Mortimer's traditional influences and place among more experimental peers, but with the same subject, "more often than not the failure of communication, the confinement to and sometimes the liberation from private dream-worlds." Treats *The Dock Brief, The Wrong Side of the Park, Two Stars for Comfort,* and about a dozen shorter plays.

Gerald H. Strauss,
updated by Thomas J. Taylor

TAD MOSEL

Born: Steubenville, Ohio; May 1, 1922

PRINCIPAL DRAMA

The Happiest Years, pr. 1942

Jinxed, pb. 1947, pr. 1949 (televised)

The Lion Hunter, pr. 1952

Madame Aphrodite, pr. 1953 (televised), revised pr. 1961 (staged)

The Five Dollar Bill, pr. 1957 (televised), pb. 1958

All the Way Home, pr. 1960, pb. 1961 (adaptation of James Agee's novel *A Death in the Family*)

Impromptu, pr., pb. 1961

That's Where the Town's Going, pr. 1962 (televised), pb. 1962

OTHER LITERARY FORMS

Although Tad Mosel is best known for his Pulitzer Prize-winning stage play *All the Way Home*, much of his best work was written for the hour-long or ninety-minute drama venues in early television. Between 1953 and 1962, more than twenty original Mosel scripts appeared on television. By the mid-1960's, virtually all television drama was in series with recurring characters, though Mosel had one last teleplay

broadcast in 1968, and a television version of his stage hit *All the Way Home* in 1971. For the American Bicentennial in 1976, he wrote two episodes of the Public Broadcasting Service (PBS) series *The Adams Chronicles.* He also wrote two screenplays, *Dear Heart* (1964, a revision of his 1956 teleplay *The Out-of-Towners*) and *Up the Down Staircase* (1967). His books include an anthology of his teleplays, *Other People's Houses: Six Television Plays* (1956), and a biography of actress Katherine Cornell (1978).

ACHIEVEMENTS

There is no doubt that Mosel's greatest accolades came from his 1961 Broadway hit *All the Way Home*, which ran for 333 performances, was nominated for a Tony Award, and won the New York Drama Critics Circle Award and the Pulitzer Prize in Drama. But even before that success, he had established himself as one of the top names in television drama in the 1950's. In 1967 his screenplay for *Up the Down Staircase* was nominated for a Writer's Guild of America award. For decades a member of the editorial board of *TV Quarterly*, the journal of the Academy of Television Arts and Sciences, Mosel was also an influential member of the Writer's Guild of America and was a delegate to the meetings that created the International Writer's Guild. Mosel received honorary doctorates from two Ohio colleges: the College of Wooster in 1963 and his hometown college, the College of Steubenville, in 1969.

BIOGRAPHY

Tad Mosel was born George Ault Mosel, Jr., in 1922 in Steubenville, Ohio, a small industrial city on the Ohio River. Though his family moved to New York only eight years later, his teleplays, notably *Ernie Barger Is Fifty*, *The Lawn Party*, *Presence of the Enemy*, and *That's Where the Town's Going*, are often set in small Ohio River towns and consciously crafted from his memories of Midwestern life. His father, George Ault Mosel, Sr., an advertising executive, and his wife, Margaret, shared their love for the theater with their son, taking him as a child to serious dramas instead of typical children's fare. He particularly recalled being star-struck by Katharine Cornell in George Bernard Shaw's *Saint Joan* (pr. 1923, pb. 1924) in 1936, at the age of fourteen. More than forty years later, he wrote a biography of the stage legend.

Entering Amherst College in 1940, Mosel immediately found a home in the college theater department, which produced his play *The Happiest Years* early in his junior year. World War II interrupted his undergraduate work, however, and he served in the U.S. Air Force Weather Service, also editing his squadron's newspaper. After the war, Mosel completed his degree requirements at Amherst, receiving a B.A. in 1947, and did graduate work at the Yale School of Drama. At Yale he studied more experimental modern playwrights and wrote a Luigi Pirindello-inspired one-act that became one of his most-acted pieces, *Impromptu*.

During his Yale years, the new medium of television was in need of original scripts, and Mosel was contracted to expand a treatment into a script for *Chevrolet Tele-Theater* in 1949. Unsure of the new medium's potential, he landed a steady job as a clerk for Northwest Airlines while he continued to write scripts for the weekly drama series *Omnibus* and to pursue graduate study at Columbia. Then in 1953,

only months after completing his master's degree, he sold his first original teleplay, *Ernie Barger Is Fifty*, to the Columbia Broadcasting System (CBS), and he was established full time as a television writer.

All the Way Home, a stage success in 1961, was one of three Mosel plays in New York that year: The one-act experimental drama *Impromptu* and his musical *Madam Aphrodite* (music and lyrics by Jerry Herman) both appeared Off-Broadway. A successful film adaptation of *All the Way Home* in 1963 gave him the Hollywood contacts to adapt one of his teleplays into the 1964 film *Dear Heart*, and three years later, he wrote the screen adaptation of *Up the Down Staircase*.

In 1975, when WNED-TV in New York prepared for the U.S. bicentennial by creating a miniseries on one of the founding families of the United States, *The Adams Chronicles*, Mosel was chosen to write two of the episodes, including one about the *Amistad* case, which Mosel explored in film drama two decades before Stephen Spielberg's film *Amistad* (1997). In his later years, Mosel devoted himself to teaching rather than writing, though as late as 1984, a new Mosel original drama was produced at Kenyon College in Ohio.

ANALYSIS

Equally versatile in three dramatic media—live stage, television, and film—Tad Mosel has a knack for adapting material from one medium to another. His stage hit *All the Way Home* was adapted from James Agee's posthumous novel *A Death in the Family*; his film *Dear Heart* was expanded and revised from his own teleplay; he adapted the stage play and film classic *The Petrified Forest* for television; his last film *Up the Down Staircase* adapted a popular novelized autobiography of a young teacher's experience at a tough city school; and he rewrote his teleplays *The Five Dollar Bill* and *That's Where the Town's Going* as stage versions for a dramatic publisher. In going from novel to stage, he skillfully compressed the action, eliminated minor characters, and transmuted some of the narrator's words into dialogue. In going from television to film, he took advantage of the possibilities of exterior shots and expanded action in many locations.

Stylistically, Mosel's plays tend to be dramatic realism—with the notable exception of *Impromptu*. They tend to be about ordinary people at peak moments in their lives and to move toward bittersweet or unresolved endings. As such, they are typical of most plays of the mid-twentieth century, but what is extraordinary is that Mosel wrote this way for early television, when audiences, and sometimes network executives, were said to demand neat resolutions and happy endings. Thematically, Mosel's drama, both on stage and on television, tends to explore societal conventions, with at least one character, not always the protagonist, consciously running counter to those conventions. The unconventional character is frequently an alcoholic, an artist, or simply an average American opposed to changes in American society.

ALL THE WAY HOME

Readers of the James Agee novel *A Death in the Family*, on which Mosel's play is based, are confronted with profound structural differences between the two works. The narrative style of the novel is stream of consciousness, in which past and present flow back and forth between the current experience of the characters and their memories. Time is very fluid in Agee's novel. In the play, on the other hand, Mosel has ordered the action so that it progresses chronologically. Critics praised a Public Broadcasting Service (PBS) *Masterpiece Theatre* dramatization of the novel in 2002 for adapting the stream-of-consciousness style for television, comparing Mosel's adaptation unfavorably. Yet Mosel's decision to edit the action in a linear fashion was probably the right one for 1961, and its rightness is confirmed by the play's receiving the Pulitzer Prize in Drama that year.

In this play, the unconventional character, a common Mosel type, is the title character of the novel, Jay Follet, whose death provides the tragic climax to the play. He is light and easy-going in general, though a point of tension in his marriage is his chafing at the religious strictures, not so much of his society, but of his devoutly Catholic wife, Mary, and her family. In the opening scene, Mary hesitates even to tell her six-year-old son Rufus about her pregnancy until she checks with a priest. This religious tension is confined to the narration in the novel, though

Mosel brilliantly inserts just enough consciousness of it into the play's dialogue for the audience to feel the tension.

Another tension that Mosel is able to keep visible between the lines is Mary's concerns over the alcoholism of Jay's brother Ralph. Mosel's dialogue makes it clear, without explicitly stating it, that Mary at one time had similar concerns for Jay, but that he had given up drink for his family, and she perceives Ralph's visit in the opening scene to be a potentially bad influence on her husband and the family. The family tensions over alcohol are part of the received matter of the novel Mosel is dramatizing, but the situation parallels his 1958 CBS teleplay *Presence of the Enemy*. In both plays, the alcoholic brother is presented with some sympathy for the judgmental way in which his frailty is stigmatized, though in neither play is he the moral center. The way that these concerns are made visible in a very indirect way is typical of Mosel's dramatic technique.

IMPROMPTU

This play, which Mosel calls a product of his "Pirandello period" during graduate school at Yale, is not at all typical of his style, yet is one of his best and most-performed works. Mosel mentions the Italian playwright Luigi Pirandello because the plot and structure of *Impromptu* are very much like those of Pirandello's *Sei personaggi in cerca d'autore* (pr., pb. 1921; *Six Characters in Search of an Author*, 1922), in which a group of actors are given the task of producing a play without scripts or directors, ordered to do so by a tyrannical and unseen stage manager.

As innovative as that plot may sound, it was already old hat in theatrical circles when the play was first performed in 1961—or even when it was first written in the late 1940's. Yet, there is more to the play than a self-consciousness in which actors toy with the conventions of characterization. First, Mosel deliberately simplifies the cast for this short, one-act play. There are only four characters, two male (Ernest and Tony) and two female (Winifred and Lora). Ernest and Winifred are the seasoned theatrical professionals; Tony and Lora are the younger and less experienced ones. Yet there is a difference between Ernest's experience and Winifred's: for Ernest, the aging leading man, his experience gives him a false sense of self-importance as he gives orders to the others, especially Tony. For Winifred, experience has only made her cynical. She provides a great deal of the play's humor, but it is usually at the expense of another character.

In addition to exploring the conventions of dramatic characterization, however, *Impromptu* also probes into the twentieth century actor's presuppositions about acting, a fact that doubtless accounts for its popularity among community and professional companies. Ernest's self-importance and Winifred's cynicism will not allow either of them to go beyond the level of playing stereotypes. Tony, on the other hand, wants to be more emotionally realistic, but the only way he can do so is to be himself rather than a character. Lora finds a middle ground in her desire to play against her type casting. She is always cast as the ingénue, and she wants to play the matron. With Winifred it is the other way around. When arguing over such casting difficulties leads to Tony's leaving, Winifred finally breaks through her cruel pose and defends him, though the play ends with Tony gone and others unsure if their play was successful.

THAT'S WHERE THE TOWN'S GOING

This stage adaptation of Mosel's television play illustrates his gift for dramatic compression. In *That's Where the Town's Going*, he illustrates the tensions between the past and future of a small Midwestern town with just four characters, only three of whom are central to the plot. The difference between the past and present of the town is expressed partly through characterization, for Hobart Cramm was a poor boy from the "wrong" side of town (River Street), and Wilma and Ruby Sills were the rich girls from the "posh" side (Ohio Street). However, now that all three are middle aged, the town has changed, Cramm is a successful New York businessperson, and the sisters, reluctant to admit that the glory of their family name has faded, blame one another for the fact that neither one ever married. The play is a realistic portrait of the fate of small Midwestern towns in the 1960's: The population was shifting from downtown areas to planned housing developments such as the Shadyside of the play—optimistically named, as one

character observes, for there is not a single tree in the area. The Sills' property, conversely, has retained its trees, but only by filling them with concrete. The abandonment of the downtown reflects the abandonment of Wilma Sills, who had once turned down Cramm's proposal of marriage because his prospects seemed so poor. When Wilma turns down his second proposal, her sister Ruby, who had always criticized Cramm, marries him instead, leaving Wilma with her regrets.

OTHER MAJOR WORKS

SCREENPLAYS: *Dear Heart*, 1964; *Up the Down Staircase*, 1967.

TELEPLAYS: *Ernie Barger Is Fifty*, 1953; *Other People's Houses*, 1953; *The Haven*, 1953; *The Figgerin' of Aunt Wilma*, 1953; *This Little Kitty Stayed Cool*, 1953; *The Remarkable Case of Mr. Bruhl*, 1953; *Guilty is the Stranger*, 1955; *My Lost Saints*, 1955; *The Lawn Party*, 1955; *Star in the Summer Night*, 1955; *The Waiting Place*, 1955; *The Petrified Forest*, 1955 (adaptation of Robert E. Sherwood's play); *The Out-of-Towners*, 1956; *Other People's Houses: Six Television Plays*, 1956; *The Morning Place*, 1957; *Presence of the Enemy*, 1957; *The Five Dollar Bill*, 1957; *The Innocent Sleep*, 1958; *A Corner of the Garden*, 1959; *Sarah's Laughter*, 1959; *The Invincible Teddy*, 1960; *Three Roads to Rome*, 1960; *That's Where the Town's Going*, 1962; *Secrets*, 1968; *All the Way Home*, 1971.

NONFICTION: *Leading Lady: The World and Theatre of Katherine Cornell*, 1978 (with Gertrude Macy).

BIBLIOGRAPHY

Burack, A. S. *Television Plays for Writers*. Boston: The Writer, 1957. This anthology of teleplays from the golden age of live television in the 1950's opens with a helpful introduction addressed to would-be writers and includes an afterword by each writer. Mosel's comments describe how the supposed limits of the medium of television are not as confining as they seem and actually lead to a creative discipline.

Mosel, Tad. *Other People's Houses: Six Television Plays*. New York: Simon and Schuster, 1956.

Mosel's generous introductions to each of the six plays in this anthology give us the most complete picture available of his ideas on the craft of drama.

Tessier, Brian. "There Was Gold Dust in the Air." http://emmys.com/foundation/archive/vault/fal 1998/page3.html. Text of Mosel's comments used as fillers for the 1998 Emmy Awards Show, available on the Emmy website. Presents Mosel's recollections of the early days of television.

John R. Holmes

SŁAWOMIR MROŻEK

Born: Borzęcin, Poland; June 26, 1930

PRINCIPAL DRAMA

Profesor, pr. 1956, pb. 1968 (*The Professor*, 1977)

Policja, pr., pb. 1958 (*The Police*, 1959)

Męczeństwo Piotra Oheya, pr., pb. 1959 (*The Martyrdom of Peter Ohey*, 1967)

Indyk, pb. 1960, pr. 1961

Na pełnym mrozu, pr., pb. 1961 (*Out at Sea*, 1961)

Karol, pr., pb. 1961 (*Charlie*, 1967)

Strip-Tease, pr., pb. 1961 (*Striptease*, 1963)

Zabawa, pb. 1962, pr. 1963 (*The Party*, 1967)

Kynolog w rozterce, pb. 1962, pr. 1963

Czarowna noc, pr., pb. 1963 (*Enchanted Night*, 1967)

Śmierć porucznika, pb. 1963, pr. 1964

Utwory sceniczne, pb. 1963

Wybór dramatów, pb. 1963, 1987, revised and enlarged pb. 2000 (2 volumes)

Krawiec, wr. 1964, pb. 1977, pr. 1978

Tango, pb. 1964, pr. 1965 (English translation, 1966)

Poczwórka, pb. 1967, pr. 1968

Testarium, pb. 1967, pr. 1968 (*The Prophets*, 1972)

Six Plays, pb. 1967

Woda, pb. 1967 (radio monologue)

Drugie danie, pb. 1968, pr. 1977 (*Repeat Performance*, 1967)

Vatzlav, pr., pb. 1970 (English translation, 1970)

Three Plays, pb. 1972

Rzeźnia, pr. 1973 (radio play), pr. 1975 (staged), pb. 1997

Szczęśliwe wydarzenie, pr., pb. 1973

Emigranci, pr. 1974, pb. 1975 (*The Emigrés*, 1976)

Garbus, pr., pb. 1975

Serenada, Polowanie na lisa, Lis filozof, pr., pb. 1977

Lis aspirint, pb. 1978, pr. 1979

Pieszo, pb. 1980, pr. 1981

Ambasador, pr. 1981, pb. 1987

"Striptease," "Tango," "Vatzlav": Three Plays, pb. 1981

Alfa, pr., pb. 1984 (*Alpha*, 1984)

Kontrakt, pr. 1986, pb. 1995

Portret, pr. 1987, pb. 1995

Milosc na Krymie: Komedia tragiczna w trzech aktach, pb. 1994

OTHER LITERARY FORMS

Sławomir Mrożek began his career as a writer of sketches and short stories, some of which are collected in *Słoń* (1957; *The Elephant*, 1962). More stories by Mrożek have been collected and translated into English as *The Ugupu Bird* (1968). His published fiction in Polish includes *Półpancerze praktyczne* (1953), *Wesele in Atomice* (1959), *Postępowiec* (1960), *Deszcz* (1962), and *Opowiadania* (1964). He also has published a book of satiric drawings, *Polska w obrazach* (1957). Although Mrożek writes drama primarily for the stage, he has adapted for television *Dom na granicy* (1967; *The Home on the Border*, 1967), from his short story of the same title, and he has written a monologue for radio titled *Woda* (1967). His radio play *Rzeźnia* was produced onstage in Warsaw in 1975. Adaptations of Mrożek's work include "Siesta," adapted by Martin Esslin, from the short story of the same name for the British Broadcasting Corporation in 1963; a comic opera adapted by Henryk Czyz from Mrożek's play *Kynolog w rozterce*; and Tom Stoppard's adaptation of Nicholas Bethell's translation of *Tango* for the Royal Shakespeare Company production in 1966. Mrożek also contributed regularly to the Polish avant-garde magazine *Dialog* from 1959 to 1967.

ACHIEVEMENTS

While Sławomir Mrożek was awarded both the literary prize in 1957 by the Warsaw magazine *Przegląd Kulturalny* and the Millennium Award of the Jurzykowski Foundation in New York in 1964, his achievements are perhaps greater in the contributions he has afforded Polish theater. Mrożek is generally regarded as the first Polish dramatist in the Theater of the Absurd, although as his work becomes more accessible to audiences outside Poland, he is emerging as one of the leaders of international postabsurdist drama. Mrożek's career can be divided into two phases. The first phase, which culminated with his important work *Tango*, is characterized by what the dramatist himself describes as a concern with exploring metaphors and ideas. His plays since *Tango* are marked by a less experimental and more direct political and social style.

Another of Mrożek's great achievements is his use of allusions recognizable in both East and West. His early stories parody works by Samuel Beckett, Henrik Ibsen, George Bernard Shaw, and Oscar Wilde. *Tango* has been described as a *Hamlet* play, and *Vatzlav* encompasses both the structure of Everyman and the techniques of Bertolt Brecht. Mrożek's plays are also characterized by an audacious theatricality. In *Striptease*, a huge hand enters through a door to make demands of the two men imprisoned there, whereas in *Rzeźnia* (the slaughterhouse) a horde of barnyard animals invades a music-hall concert.

Mrożek has benefited from Western interest in Eastern European literature brought about, in part, by the Soviet invasion of Czechoslovakia in 1968 and the Solidarity movement in Poland during the early 1980's. The political content of his early plays, cleverly conveyed through irony and metaphor, proved attractive to audiences on both sides of the Iron Curtain. His later works, such as *The Emigrés* and *Alpha*, tend to be didactic and realistic, rather than suggestive and fantastic. Nevertheless, he retains his sense of absurdity, his satiric bite, and his concern with form.

BIOGRAPHY

The son of a village postmaster, Sławomir Mrożek was born on June 26, 1930, in Borzęcin, near Krakow, Poland. In 1939, the Soviet army moved into

Sławomir Mrożek in 1990. (Hulton Archive by Getty Images)

Poland to meet the Nazis, and independent Poland's twenty-one-year life came to an end. Mrożek spent the remainder of his boyhood near Krakow in a country under foreign domination. Although he never completed a university degree, the playwright studied architecture and painting at the Academy of Fine Arts in Krakow; he also studied oriental art and philosophy for a time. His interest in structure and artifice, as evidenced in the areas he chose to study, seems to have carried over into his fiction and his dramatic works.

In the postwar years, the normally active Polish theater suffered from a strict adherence to its Soviet satellite government's policy of socialist realism; Mrożek saw his first play after the war, but he was not initially attracted to the stage. Rather, he began by drawing cartoons and writing humorous sketches for the Krakow newspapers in 1955. The so-called thaw of 1956 removed some restrictions on the creative expression of Polish artists. One year later, the appearance of Mrożek's illustrated collection of stories and sketches called *The Elephant* helped establish him as a satirist and a writer of fantasies, which were very often thinly disguised, humorous attacks on the bumbling Polish bureaucracy. By 1958, Mrożek was editing a weekly, *Postępowiec*, to which he contributed more satiric pieces. Meanwhile, he became involved with an improvisational theater group called Bim-Bom, for which he wrote a short play called *The Professor* as part of a presentation called "Joy in Earnest" in 1956.

Mrożek, as evidenced by his story "Escape Southward," in *The Elephant*, rejected the avant-garde as a supportive environment for creative effort relatively early in his career. In the story, an apeman and three village boys happen on a competition at the headquarters of the Association for Polish Writers in which the participants spit, belch, and recite original works on dandruff and sweat glands. The apeman manages to win first prize with a series of inarticulate grunts leading to the word "cauliflower," and at the climax of his delivery he throws a dead rat at the audience. Mrożek remained independent of mob art—avant-garde or otherwise—and began to contribute plays to *Dialog*, which was edited by Adam Tarn.

Most of his plays, beginning with *The Police* in 1958, were first published there. He supplemented his income as a playwright through journalism, illustrations, theater criticism, and through translations of English poetry into Polish.

Produced at Warsaw's Teatr Dramatyczny in June of 1958, *The Police* examines in cartoon style what happens when the only remaining revolutionary in a totalitarian state swears allegiance to the government. As represented in this play, Mrożek's vision, both frightening and hilarious, became increasingly popular on Polish stages; eight more of his plays were produced in the next six years. He soon became Poland's best-known playwright outside Poland as well; in 1961, Mrożek had his American premiere in New York City, where the Phoenix Theater presented *The Police*.

Having been awarded both the literary prize in 1957 by the Warsaw magazine *Przegląd Kulturalny* and the Millennium Award of the Jurzykowski Foundation in New York in 1964, Mrożek left his native country for Genoa, Italy, in 1964. His intensely Polish play, *Tango*, in which, as Adam Tarn has noted, he both satirizes the Polish character and falls under its spell, premiered in Belgrade, Yugoslavia, on April 21, 1965, and some six weeks later was produced in Poland.

The success of *Tango*, coupled with Mrożek's outspoken criticism of the Soviets, contributed to a growing international reputation. In 1968, while living in Paris, he publicly denounced the Soviet invasion of Czechoslovakia; consequently, his passport was revoked, and he was declared *persona non grata* by the Polish government. His work was banned in Poland from 1968 until 1974, and, although he continued to write during that time, his plays became more overtly political. Freed from the constraints imposed by the Communist government, but also cut off from the theatrical traditions that he had reshaped in his plays, Mrożek lost some of the ingenuity and evasiveness that contributed to the power of his earlier work. *The Emigrés*, which has had many successful productions around the world since its premier in Paris in 1974, treats the cyclic movement of history that has created in Poland under totalitarian rule a contemporary phenomenon of émigré literature, of which Mrożek is a part, to rival the tradition of Polish émigré art—the work of Adam Mickiewicz and of Juliusz Słowacki, for example—which was vital to the cultural life of Poland in the years of foreign domination in the nineteenth century. Mrożek's response to Solidarity can be found in *Alpha*, which concerns a charismatic revolutionary, modeled on Polish labor leader Lech Walesa, kept under house arrest in an unnamed European country. During *Alpha*'s English-language premiere in New York City in 1984, Mrożek himself was exploring yet another facet of the theater by directing a production of his play *Ambasador* in West Germany.

ANALYSIS

Through the plays of Sławomir Mrożek, observed Kott, the Poland that meant nowhere to Alfred Jarry in *Ubu roi* (wr. 1888, pr., pb. 1896; English translation, 1951) is now everywhere indeed. Both Mrożek's short fiction and his plays, although influenced by an Absurdist tradition of which Jarry is a part, translate the experience of modern Poland into a striking vision that depends on the tension between the surreal and the real. Whereas Jarry used a fantastical Poland as a metaphor for a destructive banality that allows human cruelty to thrive, Mrożek renders his actual experience in Poland as an ironic nightmare in which the reality of daily life is shaped by a regimen of absurdity and bureaucratic banality. The world he captures has survived the grotesque experience of World War II only to be forced to accept the inevitable prospect of endless Soviet domination. Mrożek captures the absurd workings of this society in a concise, usually unelaborate style marked by an ironic sensibility cultivated as a response to illogical happenings and to absurdity as inextricable parts of existence.

Theater critics outside Poland have often found themselves at a loss in discussing the peculiarities of Mrożek's work as well as the traditions of the Polish theater to which his plays are indebted. Martin Esslin has called him an absurdist who creates political theater; Daniel Gerould has dubbed Mrożek, along with his countryman Tadeusz Różewicz, heir to a legacy of Polish avant-garde drama; and *Tango* has been de-

scribed as both an Aesopian satire and a Shavian play of ideas. Mrożek's plays, however, exceed the limits of any one school or movement. His development as a dramatist is a chronicle of formal innovation and experimentation in response to theater history and to the culture and history of Poland. Yet, as Jan Kott, the Polish critic, has noted, in Mrożek's plays the references go beyond Poland to encompass all Europe.

Nowhere is this clearer than in Mrożek's attempts to redefine the theater in the wake of the triumph of the absurdists, an endeavor analogous to the work of such dramatists as Edward Bond, Václav Havel, Arthur Kopit, and Stoppard. As one of his Polish precursors, Stanisław Ignacy Witkiewicz (Witkacy), intended to do, Mrożek redefines the drama through a revolution in form, and his plays spring from a dramatic consciousness that shares Witkacy's belief that the playwright must shake off old habits and stop repeating the past. All of Mrożek's work during the first part of his career generically addresses itself to the problem of form in postabsurdist art, and *Tango* deals specifically with the questions of form as a necessary component of social, political, and cultural history. The opening of *Tango* in Poland in 1965 is considered the most explosive night in Polish theater since the premiere of Stanisław Wyspiański's *Wesele* (pr., pb. 1901; *The Wedding*, 1933), and the numerous productions of *Tango* throughout the world have focused attention on both Mrożek and Polish drama. His plays have been produced in Canada, France, Great Britain, Norway, the Soviet Union, the United States, and West Germany.

Czesław Miłosz has observed that Mrożek often employs a sly parody of styles in his work, and both his fiction and his plays have been described as parables. The absurd, grotesque, totalitarian environment that had conditioned Mrożek's thinking deprives him of bestowing on his works the customary happy ending or simple moral associated with such tales. His short fiction is populated with children, talking animals, elves, and snowmen who migrate to the mountains when spring threatens to melt them into puddles. Yet, side by side with the fantastical are everyday quarreling comrades, petty bureaucrats, unsuccessful suitors, aging relatives, foolish soldiers, and dishonest zookeepers. The result is a highly stylized universe that allows Mrożek, like Franz Kafka before him, to balance the grotesque with the whimsical imagination.

Thus, Mrożek blends the fantastical and the real, and the result, like the superimposition of one drawing on another, is striking in its visual effect. In "On a Journey," a traveler in a horse-drawn chaise riding through an utterly believable country landscape notices that men in postal uniforms are standing at measured intervals along the road. The coachman informs the traveler that the men constitute the region's wireless telegraph: One yells to the next, and he yells to the next, and so on. During *The Martyrdom of Peter Ohey*, in which a tiger is supposedly discovered in a middle-class family's bathroom, an entire circus is set up in the family's apartment without moving a single piece of furniture.

In response to totalitarian doublespeak, Mrożek often subverts language through substituting an unlikely vocabulary for an expected one. Mrożek describes an idyllic, rural wedding celebration in "A Wedding in Atom-town" but imposes on this conventional setting the trappings of nuclear jargon in place of colloquial speech. In preparation for the wedding, the bride is given electrolysis and put in a compression chamber, and, when a fight erupts during the wedding celebration, the guests deploy short-range rockets and cuff one another with atomic knuckledusters. Arguments for cannibalism in *Out at Sea* are presented by each character in speeches that use the rhetorical devices of political oratory, and two of the speakers stage a brief rally, where they wave a banner that reads, "We Want Food." The two men forced into a room by a huge hand in *Striptease* attempt to deal with the inexplicable appendage in logical, philosophical language that scarcely masks their fear and helplessness. Implausible, but appropriate, such language choices function in Mrożek's work beyond mere satire to substantiate the intrinsic imaginative validity of each particular story and play.

Mrożek's targets are by no means limited to the manifestations of the repressive political and social climate in Poland. Pressure to conform, and thus surrender the imagination, comes not only from the

state, but also from the established artistic community. His portraits of the artist can be scathing; he attacks both aesthete and social realist in his short stories. Mrożek, however, was never strongly aligned with an active, subversive avant-garde in his country, as his satire of the Polish avant-garde in "Escape Southward" demonstrates. Moreover, the same story presents Mrożek at his most amusing and his most forceful in that it makes a travesty of the international avant-garde masterpiece, Beckett's *En attendant Godot* (pb. 1952, pr. 1953 *Waiting for Godot*, 1954). His portraits of the foolish Eleanor and the ineffectual Stomil in *Tango* provide further evidence of his disparagement of the avant-garde, yet, paradoxically, his own drama is indebted to two of his Polish avant-garde precursors, Witold Gombrowicz and Witkacy. For Mrożek, the imagination, which cannot be subjected to state law or the pressure of artistic peers, seems even more alluring, more triumphant, when cast against a background of ideological indoctrination and rigid artistic conventions.

His conception of the artist and of art itself lies squarely in the Romantic tradition that has evolved from Johann Wolfgang von Goethe and Percy Bysshe Shelley down through the existentialists. In *Tango*, artists are construed as historically gifted people who, unlike other men, are united with the spirit of women and children, and Mrożek's experiences under tyranny have led him to see that Shelley's proud boast that poets are indeed the unacknowledged legislators of the world is taken seriously by men in power. They fear that the poet's effect might loosen their hold, and consequently they suppress a force they understand too well as a threat to their own security. As the brutish Eddie tells Stomil near the end of act 3 of *Tango*, "Nothing to worry about so long as you keep quiet and do what I say." The artist in Mrożek's work embodies many Romantic qualities: He is a solitary figure, he rebels against artistic convention, he struggles for the triumph of the imagination, and he is a political progressive.

This artistic stance is particularly apt in the Polish theater, which is often used as a forum for the presentation of ideas for cultural and political debate. Despite the particular dramatic technique at work in sophisticated Polish theater, the major Polish plays of the past one hundred years inevitably involve the clash of ideas. Wyspiański's plays, for example, decidedly romantic and full of spectacle, ultimately deal with political and social issues. The same audience that applauded Wyspiański also cultivated a taste for the unelaborate intellectual play of ideas. In addition, the oddity of Polish nationalism, grounded in cultural heritage and Roman Catholicism rather than in geographical reality, has resulted in a number of paradoxes that have helped shape the themes and techniques of modern Polish theater; Mrożek's work continues this tradition.

Soviet repression did not alter this, although it forced Mrożek, while living in Poland, to develop an oblique dramaturgy that, while receiving government approval, served to reinforce, in its allusions and idioms, Polish national feeling. Mrożek's introduction to *The Police*, in which he carefully explains that "this play does not contain anything except what it contains," is an example of ingenious equivocation that invites the audience to look for everything he says is not there. Most of Mrożek's early plays contain direct, if often subtle, allusions to the political situation of contemporary Poland; this state of affairs, which helped shape the vision of Mrożek's fiction, is concisely rendered in one exchange in the third act of *Tango*. Stomil asks if he can still have his own opinion. "Of course," replies Eugene. "As long as it agrees with ours."

THE POLICE

The Police, Mrożek's first play to receive considerable attention, puts onstage a world in which this kind of totalitarian attitude has triumphed. The last remaining prisoner in a police state disavows all of his former revolutionary beliefs and swears allegiance to the heads of state, the Infant King, and his Uncle the Regent, thus effectively rendering the police obsolete. The Chief of Police, disturbed by the prospect of an entire bureaucratic system deprived of purpose, persuades the loyal Sergeant, in the name of saving the police, to shout out a window that the Regent, uncle to the Infant King, is a "dirty swine." This accomplished, the Chief arrests the Sergeant, and the police again have a *raison d'être*. The play's action degener-

ates into an absurd series of arrests and counterarrests by characters with cartoonlike aspects that help push their world closer to fantasy. The connection between the fantasy of the play and the absurd reality of life in a police state, apparent to Mrożek's audience from the onset, is clearly stated in the Sergeant's final, futile yell in act 3: "Long live freedom!"

THE MARTYRDOM OF PETER OHEY

The initial premise of *The Martyrdom of Peter Ohey* is more absurd than that which sets the plot of *The Police* in action. The structure of the play, hinted at by the pseudo-epic subtitles that Mrożek gives to each scene, is episodic, piling one absurdity on another and leading to Ohey's death by gunshot. Of all Mrożek's plays, *The Martyrdom of Peter Ohey* is closest to the Theater of the Absurd, especially to the work of Eugène Ionesco. Like Ionesco's Berenger in *Rhinocéros* (pr., pb. 1959; *Rhinoceros*, 1959), Mrożek's Ohey confronts the impossible and is left to find the refuge of self insufficient. Ohey's son insists that he has been bitten by the tiger, but he shows no markings; his daughter is carrying on with the Scientist in her bedroom, which is ostensibly a temporary tiger-observation center; and his wife, an Ionesco-like creation who admonishes the children to brush their teeth before meals or risk poisoning the soup, confesses to her husband in a satire of Jungian jargon how the tiger has stolen her heart away. Deserted by his family and tyrannized by the forces of society gathered in his house, Ohey agrees to sacrifice himself to the unseen and unreal tiger by playing decoy for a Maharaja's hunt. In the final moments of the play, Mrożek makes the allegorical functions of his characters explicit, and like Ionesco and Edward Albee, uses the form of the absurd as a vehicle for social comment. Confronted by a Foreign Office Man, a Circus Manager, and a Scientist, Ohey declares in act 3, "My house is a milling ground for politics, science, art, and authority." Ohey goes to his death in the third act to escape these contemporary furies with words that foreshadow Arthur's sentiments in *Tango*: "This age does not please me and I have no wish to seek slavishly for its approval."

Everything is possible in the play—a circus, a jungle safari through Ohey's dining room, two murders offstage while characters comment like newscasters—because Mrożek's absurdist technique depends on implausibility. As a result of the focus that Peter Ohey procures through the overwhelming and absurd events thrust on him in the play, he emerges from this fantastic world as more than a mere two-dimensional figure. Peter Ohey is one of Mrożek's few characters to have an actual name. He suffers, has fears, changes in the course of the action, and serves as Mrożek's spokesman by the play's end.

OUT AT SEA AND CHARLIE

This emphasis on character is not developed in either *Out at Sea* or *Charlie*, one-act plays that were published and produced in 1961. Murder figures prominently in both plays, as it does in *The Martyrdom of Peter Ohey*, but the action of these plays, abrupt and effective, stresses situation over character. In *Out at Sea*, Fat, Medium, and Thin, three survivors of a shipwreck, dressed in tuxedos, sit on chairs on a raft and debate, because they are hungry, which of their party they will eat to survive. The political metaphor of cannibalism is presented in a stylized way through such details as a tablecloth, china, cutlery, silverware, and a vase of flowers. The grotesque flourishes of *Out at Sea* seem to evolve logically from the preposterous premise of the play. For this technique, Mrożek is indebted to the plays of Gombrowicz, whose theater relies primarily on developing terrifying situations. This influence is also apparent in *Charlie*, in which an Oculist saves his own life by convincing a murderous Grandpa in need of glasses that one of his regular eye patients is the Grandpa's traditional—and, like the tiger in *The Martyrdom of Peter Ohey*, imaginary—enemy.

STRIPTEASE

Striptease, originally produced in Sopot on the same program with *Charlie*, is a much richer, more complex piece that demonstrates Mrożek's mastery of theater idiom as well as political metaphor. Two identically dressed bureaucrats carrying briefcases, Mr. I and Mr. II, are forced into a room. A huge hand appears and demands that the men take off their clothing. They comply, but not without bickering between themselves, until a second hand wearing a red glove appears and beckons them to follow. The first hand puts dunce caps over their heads while they, clad in their underwear and clinging to their briefcases, stumble out after the second hand. Certainly, *Striptease* can be read as a political allegory in which two men, representing opposite concepts of freedom, are subjected to a tyrant who treats them both in the same way.

Striptease bears some resemblance to Harold Pinter's *The Dumb Waiter* (pr. 1959 in German, pr. 1960 in English) and to Stoppard's *Rosencrantz and Guildenstern Are Dead* (pr. 1966) in its delineation of a force that controls the existence of two men and capriciously makes them victims, and it is no less overtly theatrical than either play. The doors that open and close by themselves and the huge hand entering and exiting call attention to the artifice of the stage. The play makes no pretense at being anything but pure theater, and the logical answer to the men's queries about how they arrived in the room is, for the audience, from the wings. Mr. I and Mr. II are a variation of the music-hall duo, and Mrożek utilizes, as did Beckett in *Fin de partie: Suivi de Acte sans paroles* (pr., pb. 1957; *Endgame: A Play in One Act, Followed by Act Without Words: A Mime for One Player*, 1958), the rubric of vaudeville sketches in which performers are controlled and defeated by objects and props.

THE PARTY

Whereas *Striptease* relies on an essential theatricality for its effect, *The Party* investigates the ritualistic aspects of theater. Three farmers in search of a party they cannot find create one of their own; they engage in praying, singing, dancing, playacting, fighting, and hanging. They seek meaning in an empty room through trying to shape a party out of the fragments of rituals that they recall. Finally, they open up an old cupboard that contains masks, costumes, shoes, and props. One of them, designated as B, exclaims, "There's a whole theater here!" They proceed to try on the dresses, slip on high-heeled shoes, and wear the larger-than-life masks that represent the King, the Virgin, and Death. Mrożek's farmers momentarily reenact the primitive essentials of the drama—the formless energy of Dionysus ritualized into the Apollonian formality of drama. The actors pretend to be farmers who pretend to be actors, and the cycle of the theater ritual is complete.

ENCHANTED NIGHT

Enchanted Night explores not so much ritual as the dimensions of reality discerned by the mind. Through a progression from the reality of a hotel room that two traveling officials share into a dream that they experience simultaneously, Mrożek offers a sophisticated parody of the mechanics of expressionism. The beginning of the play carefully establishes the objects in the hotel room and the feelings of the two men that will be integral to the dream that evolves from them—their discussion about women, the noise of the railroad nearby, the painting of the Venus de Milo, the smell of lilac soap. The play's movement from reality to dream and back again, a structuring device often used in the poetry of the Romantics, criticizes human inability to reach the ideal. Despite the insight that Old Man and Old Boy gain about themselves in their dream of the ideal, when they awake they do not remember a thing. The use of dreams in *Enchanted Night* also demonstrates Mrożek's relationship to the twentieth century Polish theater techniques of Julius Osterwa, who attempted through psychological chamber theater to explore the entire interior aspect of character and concentrate on mood and atmosphere.

TANGO

No play by Mrożek, however, makes use of dramatic modes, both Polish and non-Polish, in the way *Tango* does. It is an outgrowth of and advance over all of his earlier work, and, as noted above, it signals the conclusion of the first phase of his playwriting career. *Tango* is the artistic expression of a reality more dramatic than drama, a world whose power, as Stomil says in act 2, "erodes all forms and that goes for tragedy too." *Tango* stands as Mrożek's answer to Stomil's question in the play's second act: "What can we do? Tragedy impossible, farce a bore—what's left but experiments?"

Tango, set in the mid-1960's, takes place in the cluttered, disorganized home of a family that encompasses three and one-half generations. Eugenia and her brother, Uncle Eugene, remnants of the late nineteenth century, live with Eugenia's daughter Eleanor and her avant-garde artist husband, Stomil, both of whom belong to the generation of André Breton and Tristan Tzara. On hand is a fat and boorish butler, Eddie (or Edek), who plays cards with the family, sleeps with Eleanor, and attempts to exploit the decadence of the household for his own advantage. This morass of confusion proves intolerable for Arthur, the twenty-five-year-old son of Eleanor and Stomil, who attempts to force the household to reorganize itself through the imposition of old rituals and customs on its members, an endeavor to which the play's ironic subtitle "The Need for Order and Harmony," alludes. Part of Arthur's scheme involves marriage to his eighteen-year-old cousin, Ala, a half-generation younger than he is chronologically but years ahead of him emotionally. With the help of Uncle Eugene, Arthur stages a *coup d'état* and forces the family, at gunpoint, to revert to the old ways that embodied meaning before the major upheavals of the twentieth century.

Just before his marriage to Ala, however, Arthur gets drunk and despairs of his method of returning to old customs. He decides instead to exercise absolute power over life and death to create meaning. In a moment of weakness brought on by Ala's disclosure that she has been unfaithful to him with Eddie, a lie she invents to distract Arthur from ordering Uncle Eugene's death, Arthur humanizes himself in a fit of jealous rage. Eddie, who has Arthur's gun, stages a brief counterrevolution; attracted by the idea of pure force, he uses his physical prowess to end Arthur's brief exercise with power by killing him with two swift blows to the back of the neck. Eddie assumes control over the household, and, as the play ends, dances a tango with Uncle Eugene over the corpse of the misguided, although idealistic and romantic, Arthur.

The world to which *Tango* alludes is real, but it is at the same time deliberately nonrealistic, a poetic construct of reality. Mrożek intends to portray in the guise of a three-act chronicle of one household a parable of life in the twentieth century. Eugenia represents the old generation, once shocked by people such as Eleanor and Stomil, but now bored and cynical, frittering away existence in useless poker games. Uncle Eugene, with his memoirs and his nostalgia for the order of the past, stands for the aristocracy displaced by the cultural and political events of the twentieth century. Eleanor and Stomil, married in 1928, are the aging, now ineffectual artists who once achieved their goal of destroying all artistic tradition and, consequently, all form. They also represent an entire generation that could not wrestle with the necessity of form as a political reality and thus sacrificed Poland's brief independence as a nation to Germany and the Soviet Union. Whereas Arthur embodies the spirit of the romantic visionary desperate to have the world conform to an impossible ideal, Ala functions as a representative of the apolitical, personal liberation movement that began to spread through most social strata in the 1960's. Eddie, with his gross habits and small, square moustache, represents the ignorant but powerful mob that resorts to Hitlers and Stalins to assert itself. Mrożek, a socialist-humanist, cannot reconcile himself to tyranny in any form. The triumph of Eddie in *Tango*, on a political level, alludes to the subjugation of humanistic social ideals by inhuman force—the revisionist Marxism of the Soviet Union—which is a way of life for the victimized Poles.

Like Shaw's *Heartbreak House* (wr. 1913-1919, pb. 1919) and its Chekhovian antecedents, *Tango* uses an extended family to chart the passing of a way of life. It once took courage for Stomil and Eleanor to dance the tango in public; when Eddie and Uncle Eugene dance the tango at the play's end, it becomes a *pas de deux* of force and submission. Art and politics are partners in history, and *Tango* is addressed to an era of the triumphal dance of tyranny on the corpse of visions and ideals.

THE PROPHETS AND REPEAT PERFORMANCE

The Prophets and *Repeat Performance*, which was not produced in Poland until eleven years after its publication, explore in different ways some of Mrożek's concerns in *Tango*. *The Prophets* mixes historical figures such as the Magi with caricatures of political types in a grotesque, futuristic fantasy about two identical men who both claim to be the one, true prophet for mankind. Whereas this play ends with a cataclysmic spectacle of revolution that asserts, through a series of absurd and Surrealistic de-

vices, a Marxist view of the inevitable dialectic of history, *Repeat Performance* insists on an inescapable need for rebellion in each generation. The Ghost, an allegorical figure who represents the spirit of rebellion, once courted Daddy through fascism but now woos Daddy's son, Little Fellow, simply by being anti-Daddy.

VATZLAV

Vatzlav, which had its English-language premiere at Canada's Stratford Festival in 1971, follows the adventures of a shipwreck survivor through a world that is composed of Mrożek's arbitrary reconstruction of history. Comprising seventy-seven scenes, *Vatzlav* is nearly cinematic in its movement, a development that can be linked to Mrożek's debt to silent-film comedy in some of the pre-*Tango* plays. *Vatzlav* contrasts the destruction represented by the bloodsucking capitalist Mr. Bat with Vatzlav's various rebirths and transformations. The play ends with a hopeful image. Cradling in his arms a baby who is the child of Justice, Vatzlav prepares to cross the border of the play into the world. "You wait here," he says to the audience in scene 77. "If I don't come back, you'll know I've made it. Then you can follow."

THE EMIGRÉS

This guarded optimism is not reflected in *The Emigrés*, a gritty, naturalistic play in which two Eastern European men square off against one another in a basement apartment that they share in a Western European city. Mrożek seems to have inverted the theatrical techniques of *Striptease* and *The Party* in *The Emigrés* to examine the relationship between two expatriates of opposing views who, trapped together, try without success to celebrate New Year's Eve. They are singularly obsessed with the country they have left, however, and their freedom, ironically, forces them to confront their own inadequacies in the new life they lead.

LATER WORKS

Certain other works that Mrożek has written since *Tango* explore relatively new territory for the playwright, although most retain his sense of irony and his ability to convey the grotesque. *The Home on the Border*, adapted for television from his short story of the same name, concerns the inhabitants of a cabin who have an international border running directly through their home. *Rzeźnia*, originally written for radio, demonstrates the inability of art to withstand intrusions by life. His one-act plays *Serenada, Polowanie na lisa, Lis filozof,* and *Lis aspirint* employ the methods of beast fables to comment on decaying civilization, and *Alpha*, which premiered at New York City's La Mama ETC in October, 1984, uses direct contemporary allusion to the celebrity status of Lech Walesa to examine ironically the nature of revolutionary leadership in a media-saturated world.

OTHER MAJOR WORKS

SHORT FICTION: *Półpancerze praktyczne*, 1953; *Słoń*, 1957 (*The Elephant*, 1962); *Wesele in Atomice*, 1959; *Postępowiec*, 1960; *Deszcz*, 1962; *Opowiadania*, 1964 (2 volumes); *The Ugupu Bird*, 1968.

TELEPLAYS: *Dom na granicy*, 1967 (adaptation of his short story; *The Home on the Border*, 1967).

MISCELLANEOUS: *Polska w obrazach*, 1957; *Dziela zebrane*, 1994-1998 (collected works; 12 volumes).

BIBLIOGRAPHY

Czerwinski, E. J. *Contemporary Polish Theater and Drama, 1965-1984*. New York: Greenwood Press, 1988. Provides history and criticism of Polish theater in the mid- to late twentieth century. Bibliography and index.

Gerould, Daniel, ed. *Twentieth Century Polish Avant-Garde Drama: Plays, Scenarios, Critical Documents*. Ithaca, N.Y.: Cornell University Press, 1977. Explores Poland's experimental theater and provides translations of major plays and documents.

Kott, Jan. *Theatre Notebook, 1947-1967*. Translated by B. Taborski. Garden City, N.Y.: Doubleday, 1968. Provides translated analysis of Polish theater.

Miłosz, Czesław. *The History of Polish Literature*. 1969. 2d ed. Berkeley: University of California Press, 1983. Provides history and criticism of Polish literature. Bibliography and index.

O'Neill, Michael C. "A Collage of History in the Form of Mrożek's *Tango*." *The Polish Review* 28, no. 2 (1983). Explores historical references in *Tango*.

Stephan, Halina. *Transcending the Absurd: Drama and Prose of Sławomir Mrożek*. Atlanta, Ga.: Rodopi, 1997. The first monographic study devoted to Mrożek, this work centers on his development as a playwright and provides criticism and interpretation of Mrożek's life and works. Bibliography and index.

Michael C. O'Neill

HEINER MÜLLER

Born: Eppendorf, East Germany; January 9, 1929
Died: Berlin, Germany; December 30, 1995

PRINCIPAL DRAMA

Das Laken: Oder, Die unbefleckte Empfängnis, wr. 1951, pb. 1966, pr. 1974

Die Reise, wr. 1951-1952, pb. 1977 (based on a Nō play by Zeami Motokiyo)

Die Schlact: Szenen aus Deutschland, wr. 1951-1974, pr., pb. 1975 (*The Slaughter*, 1977; also pb. as *The Battle*, 1989)

Traktor, wr. 1955-1961, pb. 1974, pr. 1975 (*Tractor*, 1989)

Germania Tod in Berlin, wr. 1956-1971, pb. 1977, pr. 1978

Der Lohndrücker, pb. 1957, pr. 1958 (with Inge Müller; *The Scab*, 1989)

Zehn Tage, die die Welt erschütterten, pr., pb. 1957 (with Hagen Stahl; based on John Reed's *Ten Days That Shook the World*)

Die Korrektur: Ein Bericht vom Aufbau des Kombinats "Schwarze Pumpe," first version

pb. 1958, second version pr. 1958, pb. 1959
(with Inge Müller; *The Correction*, 1958)

Klettwitzer Bericht, pb. 1958

Glücksgott, wr. 1958, pb. 1975 (adaptation of
Bertolt Brecht's fragment "Die Reisen des
Glücksgotts")

Die Bauern, wr. 1964, pr., pb. 1975 (revision of the
comedy *Die Umsiedlerin: Oder, Das Leben auf
dem Lande*, 1961)

Philoktet, pb. 1965, pr. 1968 (based on Sophocles'
play; *Philoctetes*, 1981)

Der Bau, pb. 1965, pr. 1980

Herakles 5, pb. 1966, pr. 1974 (*Heracles 5*, 1989)

Ödipus Tyrann, pr., pb. 1967 (based on Friedrich
Hölderlin's translation of Sophocles' play)

Prometheus, pb. 1968, pr. 1969 (based on
Aeschylus's play)

Drachenoper, pr. 1969, pb. 1970 (libretto in
collaboration with Ginka Tscholakowa for Paul
Dessau's opera *Lanzelot*)

Horizonte, pr. 1969, pb. 1975 (first scene of an
adaptation of Gerhard Winterlich's play
Horizonte)

Waldstück, pr. 1969, pb. 1985 (compilation of
different versions of Winterlich's *Horizonte*)

Weiberkomödie, pr. 1970, pb. 1971 (based on Inge
Müller's radio play *Die Weiberbrigade*)

Macbeth, pr., pb. 1972 (based on William
Shakespeare's play)

Der Horatier, pr., pb. 1973 (based on Bertolt
Brecht's play; *The Horatian*, 1976)

Zement, pr. 1973, pb. 1974 (based on a novel by
Fyodor Vasilyevich Gladkov; *Cement*, 1979)

Mauser, pr. 1975, pb. 1976 (based on Bertolt
Brecht's play *Die Massnahme*; English
translation, 1975)

Medeaspiel, pb. 1975 (scenario; *Medeaplay*,
1984)

*Leben Gundlings Friedrich von Pruessen Lessings
Schlaf Traum Schrei: Ein Greuelmärchen*, pb.
1977, pr. 1979 (*Gundling's Life Frederick of
Prussia Lessing's Sleep Dream Scream*, 1984)

Hamletmaschine, pb. 1977, pr. 1978
(*Hamletmachine*, 1980)

Quadriga, pb. 1978 (scenario)

Fatzer, pr. 1978, pb. 1994 as *Der Untergang des
Egoisten Johann Fatzer* (adaptation of Bertolt
Brecht's fragment "Fatzer")

Der Auftrag: Erinnerung an eine Revolution, pb.
1979, pr. 1980 (*The Task*, 1984)

Philoktet 1979, pb. 1979 (outline for a drama with
ballet)

Herzstück, pb. 1981, pb. 1982 (*Heartpiece*, 1984)

Quartett, pb. 1981 (based on Pierre Choderlos de
Laclos's novel *Les Liaisons dangereuses*;
Quartet, 1984)

*Verkommenes Ufer Medeamaterial Landschaft mit
Argonauten*, pb. 1983 (*Despoiled Shore:
Medeamaterial: Landscape with Argonauts*,
1984)

Wolokolamsker Chaussee I, pr., pb. 1985

Bildbeschreibung, pr., pb. 1985 (*Description of a
Picture/Explosion of a Memory*, 1987)

Shakespeare Factory 1, pb. 1985

Shakespeare Factory 2, pb. 1989

Germania 3 Gespenster am Toten Mann, pb. 1996
(*Germania Three Ghosts at Dead Man*, 2001)

OTHER LITERARY FORMS

Since 1959, Heiner Müller, who began his career
as a journalist and editor of a monthly journal on
modern art, has devoted himself to the writing of
plays, for which he is best known. He has, however,
published lyric poetry, prose, and a great number of
articles, interviews, and commentaries on the theory
of drama. In 1994, Müller published his autobiography under the title *Krieg ohne Schlacht: Leben in
zwei Diktaturen* (war without battle: life under two
dictatorships) in which he examined his life under the
Nazi dictatorship from 1933 to 1945 and under the
dictatorship of the Socialist Unity Party in East Germany between 1949 and 1989.

ACHIEVEMENTS

Although in 1970, in his critical introduction to
postwar German literature, Peter Demetz named Peter Hacks as Bertolt Brecht's most sophisticated disciple, the American critic changed his mind when he
assessed the problems of German theater in 1986, rat-
ing Heiner Müller's achievements as among the most

important on the German stage. Müller is the only German playwright who has been able to combine his commitment to socialism with an avant-garde, if not postmodernist, consciousness. In the West German press of the early 1980's, he was named as the most famous East German dramatist since Brecht, who was, although successful abroad, most controversial at home. In terms of the theory and practice of drama, Arlene Akiko Teraoka, in her 1985 study of Müller's postmodernist poetics, regarded him as "the most significant playwright since Brecht to emerge out of East Germany, if not out of *any* of the German-speaking countries of postwar Europe."

By deconstructing both bourgeois and orthodox socialist models of drama, history, and revolution, Müller has gone beyond the conventions of dramatic action of individual characters in conflict with history or fate and has created a new form of dramatic discourse that includes the anonymous voices of the oppressed, the nonrational, the nonmale, and the nonwhite of the Third World. In his ideology and dramatic idiom, Müller has traveled a long distance from Brecht, toward Jean Genet and Antonin Artaud, and has intersected with the postmodernist forms of Samuel Beckett, Edward Bond, Richard Foreman, and Robert Wilson. He has created a theater composed of the anarchic forms of montage, ritual, pantomime, comic-strip scenes, and street-theater demonstrations of terror, cruelty, and obscenity.

In 1979, Müller received the Drama Prize of the Mülheim Theater in West Germany. In 1985, he was awarded the West German Büchner Prize and in 1986 the East German National Prize. In 1990, he received the Kleist Prize.

BIOGRAPHY

Born in Eppendorf, Saxony, in 1929, Heiner Müller was one of two sons of a working-class family. His father was a member of the Social Democratic Party and subject to the persecutions of the Nazi regime. Müller's childhood trauma began with the arrest of his father, who was put in a concentration camp in 1933, released, and reimprisoned when he refused to accommodate to the Nazi regime. After 1949, Müller's father was expelled from the Socialist Unity Party because of his "Titoism" (his opposition to the personality cult that had formed around Joseph Stalin) and left the German Democratic Republic (GDR) for West Germany in the early 1950's in order to avoid the threat of government persecution.

During the last year of World War II, Müller was drafted and experienced the total defeat of the German army in 1945. After the liberation of Germany,

Heiner Müller in 1995. (AP/Wide World Photos)

he was employed as an administrator for various cultural organizations in the GDR, and then worked as journalist and editor of the journal *Junge Kunst* (young art), until he was hired by the Maxim Gorky Theater in East Berlin (1958-1960), where he learned his stagecraft. In the late 1950's, Müller wrote a number of plays in collaboration with his wife, Inge Müller (1925-1966), for which they were awarded the Heinrich Mann Prize in 1959. After 1959, Müller continued to devote himself to the writing of plays. From 1970 to 1976 he served as dramaturge of the former Brecht company, the Berliner Ensemble, and later of the East Berlin Volksbühne.

Like many of his colleagues, Müller has had his share of conflicts with the Socialist Unity Party, the ruling party in the GDR, and with government officials responsible for the direction of cultural developments in the GDR. During the early 1960's, many of his plays were publicly criticized by party functionaries and were canceled after only a few performances or were never produced. At the same time, Müller was expelled from the East German Writers' Union. Therefore, from the mid-1960's to the early 1970's, Müller concentrated on adapting Greek, Shakespearean, and Brechtian plays. This was the period of a socialist classicism, to which both Hacks and Müller contributed important plays.

After 1971, when Erich Honecker came into office as first secretary of the Socialist Unity Party, a number of changes in official cultural politics took place that allowed for a greater divergence of literary productions. The premiere of *Cement* by the Berliner Ensemble in 1973 was the first production of a major play by Müller since 1958. At the same time, many of his plays were made available in print in the GDR, while a West Berlin publishing house began with the publication of Müller's collected works. The production of *Mauser* by the Austin Theater Group at the University of Texas in 1975 brought international recognition to Müller.

In the mid-1970's, Müller had his breakthrough as a postmodernist playwright. Although the East German theater reacted with some reservation to his development as a postmodernist, theaters in the West have welcomed the products of this phase. With the exception of *The Task*, most of his postmodernist plays were premiered in West Germany or Belgium. *Hamletmachine* was premiered by the Théâtre Mobile in Brussels in 1978.

Müller, a resident of East Berlin, traveled widely to participate in the production not only of his own plays but also of other playwrights' works. For example, he collaborated with Robert Wilson on *the CIVIL warS* (partial pr. 1983 and 1984; includes *Knee Plays*) in 1984. After German reunification, he became a member of the management team of the Berliner Ensemble, the former Bertolt Brecht theater in East Berlin. In 1993, there were reports about Müller's collaboration with the Stasi, the East German secret police, dating back to 1978. Subsequent investigation, however, showed that Müller did not betray any of his friends and managed to help several of his colleagues. In 1994, Müller was operated on for cancer of the throat. He went to Los Angeles to recover from his operation. When he returned to Berlin, he was appointed the artistic director of the Berliner Ensemble. He died in December, 1995, and was buried next to Brecht in a Berlin cemetery.

ANALYSIS

Heiner Müller's development as a dramatist must be seen in the context of the international debate concerning a poetics for postmodernist drama. After 1971, Müller presented his work as a contemporary dramatist in terms of the poetic productions of a postmodernist artist in a postcapitalistic world system, as Teraoka has shown. In the works of this phase, beginning in 1971 with the completion of *Germania Tod in Berlin*, he engaged in the deconstruction of certain models of enlightenment or socialist drama in favor of alternative models of Third World drama. Investigating the issues of cultural colonialism and the exportation of revolution, the role of the intellectual in the revolutionary process, and, especially, the role of the European socialist intellectual in the conflicts of the Third World, Müller was current in terms not only of his topics but also of his dramatic techniques. In his revolutionary postmodernist aesthetics, Müller associated himself with the antiliterary traditions of contemporary literature, which work toward the elimination of the aesthetic autonomy of the work of art and the disappearance of the author behind the text as part of a universal discourse.

In an essay, "Der Schrecken, die erste Erscheinung des Neuen: Zu einer Diskussion über Postmodernismus in New York" (1979; "Reflections on Post-Modernism," 1979), Müller defined his place and role within modernist and contemporary European literature. For Müller, quoting Franz Kafka, "literature is an affair of the people." The revolutionary artist must write from the standpoint of the oppressed people within the dominant structures of imperialism, capitalism, and colonialism. For Müller, the "oppressed people" are the masses of the Third World in Africa, Asia, and Latin America, living in a world that is divided between the two power blocs of capitalism and socialism. The author in the socialist world, who is still privileged by virtue of his talent, has the goal of working toward his self-abolition. This goal is closely connected to the revolution of the Third World, which will establish, according to Müller, Marx's "realm of freedom," in which the author as privileged creator and art as private property no longer exist. In this situation, there are only two alternatives for the language of the contemporary author: either the self-abolition of the privileged voice or participation in a collective discourse—in Müller's words, "the silence of entropy, or the universal discourse which omits nothing and excludes no one."

Only gradually did Müller come to this perspective. His dramatic œuvre can be divided into three major periods: from the early 1950's to the early 1960's, when Müller dealt with contemporary problems in industry and land reform in the GDR; from the mid-1960's to the early 1970's, when the playwright followed the trends of a socialist classicism, employing mythology and the models of classical drama; and from the mid-1970's to 1995, when Müller explored the causes and consequences of failed revolutions in Germany and the demise of the German working-class movement. In this last period he focused on the issues of cultural colonialism, the exportation of revolutions, and, especially, the struggles of the Third World.

In his first phase, Müller explored the contradictions, evolving from the collaboration of communists and former Nazis, within the new collective work system under socialism. Plays such as *The Scab*, *The Correction*, *Die Umsiedlerin* (the homeless one), which was to be revised as *Die Bauern* (the peasant), and *Der Bau* (the wall) belong to this period.

THE SCAB

The play most typical for this period is *The Scab*, dealing with the need for increased production under poor working and living conditions in the GDR in 1949. Following the Soviet model of rewarding exemplary workers, the GDR had singled out workers surpassing production norms for extra pay and special privileges. The protagonist of the play is such an "activist," hated and distrusted not only by his coworkers but also by management and the party. Their distrust is not without reason: The protagonist had denounced workers for sabotage during the Nazi regime in order to save his own life. The fulfillment of socialist production plans, however, requires the collective labor of all workers. There is no room for private revenge. The protagonist, who is beaten by his coworkers after work, and his adversaries on different levels have to work together to complete an important project. The dialectics of the play show that collective labor under socialism is a matter not of individual choice but of historical necessity.

THE ADAPTATIONS

During the second phase of his work, in the late 1960's and early 1970's, Müller did adaptations of Greek, Shakespearean, and Brechtian plays: *Ödipus Tyrann* (based on Friedrich Hölderlin's translation of Sophocles' play), *Macbeth* (based on Shakespeare's play), *Philoctetes* (based on Sophocles' play), *Prometheus* (based on Aeschylus's play), *The Horatian* (based on Brecht's play), *Mauser* (based on Brecht's play *Die Massnahme*), and *Cement* (1972, based on Gladkov's novel) make up the corpus of his middle period.

PHILOCTETES

The work most typical of this period is *Philoctetes*. The original play by Sophocles has a rare happy ending, returning the protagonist and his invincible bow from his isolation on the island of Lemnos to the

Greek army before Troy, where his festering wounds are healed. In Müller's version, the return of Philoctetes is engineered by Ulysses for the sole purpose of rallying the troops for battle. Ulysses uses Achilles' son to carry out his plan, deceiving Philoctetes into believing that he is rescued to be taken home to Greece. When Achilles' son finally tells Philoctetes about the lie, a battle ensues, during which Philoctetes is killed. Now Ulysses exploits the death of Philoctetes, concocting a new lie in the service of the war against Troy. The Trojans are said to have invaded Lemnos and killed Philoctetes because he refused to join their side. With this propaganda story, Ulysses hopes to inspire the Greek army to fight the Trojans with increased fury and desire for revenge. On its most obvious level of interpretation, the drama has been understood as an anti-imperialist play, showing the cynical exploitation of human values for the sake of aggressive wars, but the pervasive pessimism of the play that also informs the character of Achilles' young son has rendered the obvious interpretation questionable. The dialectics of Müller's *Philoctetes* are enigmatic, but not without direction.

MAUSER

That the dialectics of Müller's plays are not always in line with party-approved directions shows in *Mauser*, a "learning play" based on a theme from Mikhail Sholokhov's novel *Tikhii Don* (1928-1940; *And Quiet Flows the Don*, 1934). In this play, an old comrade who has administered revolutionary justice in the city of Vitebsk, to defend the Soviet system during the civil war, is put to death by his own comrades because he continued killing people without party mandate. The revolution no longer needs him; it needs his death. As in Brecht's *Die Massnahme* of 1930, the death sentence is not executed before the accused has confirmed his own sentence.

CEMENT

Although written in 1972 and instrumental in his rehabilitation in the GDR with its production by the Berliner Ensemble in 1973, Müller's *Cement*, based on Gladkov's novel of 1925, portraying the national effort of reconstruction in the Soviet Union after the October Revolution of 1917 and the subsequent civil war, points in the same direction as *Mauser* and per-haps even Müller's earlier *The Scab*. As during the socialist reconstruction in the GDR, counter-revolutionaries were also needed for the reindustrialization in the Soviet Union after 1917. *Cement* is not, however, a historical drama, but rather a dramatic analysis of revolution in general and a thoroughgoing critique of the Soviet Revolution during the bureaucratic rationalization under the New Economic Policy after 1921. In this regard, *Cement* belongs to Müller's third phase. Of special interest is the concept of the role of women in the revolution, which is far more radical than the traditional Soviet interpretation. The female protagonist sacrifices her child for the revolution. Her daughter starves to death in a children's home. Her mother wants to construct a new world and is prepared to pay the price: her old love and her child. In reference to mythology, the true revolutionary woman is revealed as a second Medea.

GERMANIA TOD IN BERLIN

During his third phase, Müller produced the most challenging and most avant-garde work of his career as a playwright. Plays such as *Germania Tod in Berlin*, *The Slaughter*, *Gundling's Life Frederick of Prussia Lessing's Sleep Dream Scream*, *Hamletmachine*, and *The Task* constitute Müller's breakthrough of the 1970's.

Germania Tod in Berlin (Germania dead in Berlin) is a dramatic collage of German history from the first century to 1953. According to Müller, Germany manifests itself through the fraternal strife of two brothers, from the Roman time of Arminius and Flavius to the divided Germany of the twentieth century. While one of the brothers loves freedom and fatherland and wants to liberate his people from servitude, the other brother is concerned only with his individual wealth, glory, and honor and thinks only about his personal freedom. This constellation repeats itself throughout German history, with the defeat and death of the altruistic brother at the hands of the egocentric brother. Still, the unselfish brother never gives up hope, in spite of defeat and death. In this play, Müller appears to be clinging to the last vestiges of hope in German history. In the play's final scene, the bricklayer Hilse, a counter-figure to Gerhart Hauptmann's quietist weaver Hilse in his drama *Die Weber* (pb.

1892; *The Weavers*, 1899), is almost stoned to death by members of a juvenile gang who ridicule his socialist work ethic. When he finally dies of cancer, Müller's Hilse sees in his hallucinations Rosa Luxemburg returning from her grave and red flags flying over a united Germany. In contrast to his namesake's meaningless death in Hauptmann's day—in which the old weaver is killed by a stray bullet after refusing to take part in the revolt against the ruling class—Müller's Hilse knows what he fought and died for, even though his final goal remains visionary.

GUNDLING'S LIFE FREDERICK OF PRUSSIA LESSING'S SLEEP DREAM SCREAM

Gundling's Life Frederick of Prussia Lessing's Sleep Dream Scream is a dramatized critique of the German Enlightenment in nine scenes. The synthetic title of the play lists the major figures of the comic-strip plot: Jacob Paul von Gundling (1673-1731), a professor of history and law and president of the Prussian Academy of Sciences; Frederick II, king of Prussia (1712-1786); and Gotthold Ephraim Lessing (1729-1781), the major dramatist of the German Enlightenment. The first scene portrays the degradation of Gundling as intellectual at the court of Frederick William I, king of Prussia. Scenes 2-7 present the transformation of Frederick II from poet-king and Enlightenment intellectual into a military tyrant, and scenes 8-9 show the resignation of Lessing and the self-destruction of the younger dramatist Heinrich von Kleist (1777-1811). In the concluding scene, Lessing meets with the last president of the United States in an American junkyard, while figures from his dramas embrace and kill one another. Enlightenment is exposed as treason of the intellectual, his adaptation to the authoritarian state and service to universal oppression. The reason of language is reduced to absurdity, resulting in the systematic deconstruction of the model of Enlightenment drama.

HAMLETMACHINE

Hamletmachine, of 1977, is Müller's most enigmatic play, presenting the total deconstruction of European drama by means of a collage of fragments from that tradition. Consisting of five scenes, the play shows the Hamlet figure at the funeral of his father and raping his mother, while the Ophelia figure de-

stroys the home where she has been imprisoned, and takes to the street as a prostitute. While the Hamlet player represents the intellectual betraying the revolution, the Ophelia player embodies the voice of the oppressed. In the end, Hamlet withdraws into a suit of armor, before murdering Karl Marx, Vladimir Ilich Lenin, and Mao Zedong, who appear totally defenseless as naked women. Ophelia is left behind on the stage in a wheelchair among the corpses. Her last words are a call to revolution in the Third World against European colonialism. Form and logic of classical bourgeois drama are abandoned in favor of an anarchic vision.

THE TASK

The Task is based on the model of the Brechtian learning play, specifically, Brecht's *Die Massnahme* (pr. 1930; *The Measures Taken*, 1960). While Brecht's play deals with the mission of four agitators sent from Moscow to export the revolution to China, Müller's play reconstructs the failure of three revolutionaries, sent from France to accomplish a revolution in eighteenth century Jamaica. The three figures of Müller's play represent the various types of revolution in history: The bourgeois intellectual Debuisson stands for the French Revolution, the peasant Galloudec for the communist revolution, and the former slave Sasportas for revolution in the Third World. At the center of the play is a reenactment of Georg Büchner's drama *Danton's Tod* (pb. 1835; *Danton's Death*, 1927) as "theater of the revolution," with Sasportas playing Robespierre and Galloudec playing Danton. Sasportas declares the "theater of the white revolution" historically finished.

As a black revolutionary, Sasportas adds a new voice to the revolutionary discourse, expressing its superiority over the dominant European models of the French Revolution as well as Marxist communism. While Debuisson betrays the revolution by returning to his former life as a slave owner and Galloudec is not able to provide any leadership, Sasportas introduces an authentic alternative to the European models, continuing the revolutionary movement in Jamaica. As Antoine, the adjudicating voice in *The Task*, representing the "control chorus" of the Brechtian model, becomes directly involved in the betrayal of the revolution, Müller's play emerges as a deconstruction of the Brechtian learning play. By abandoning the indispensable control function of reason, *The Task* shows a shift from Brecht to the theater of Jean Genet and Antonin Artaud.

GERMANIA THREE GHOSTS AT DEAD MAN

Müller's last play, *Germania Three Ghosts at Dead Man*, is a loose sequence of scenes showing his total disillusionment with German socialism and its history during the last seventy years from Ernst Thälmann, the leader of the German Communist Party during the 1930's, to Walter Ulbricht, the East German Communist Party leader of the 1960's. The Dead Man's Ridge is a contested battleground in France during World War I where a great number of German soldiers lost their lives. The "ghosts" of socialism appear at their symbolic Dead Man's Ridge. At the center of the play is a scene showing Joseph Stalin signing the nonaggression pact with Adolf Hitler in 1939 and exploiting Hitler's attack on the Soviet Union for his own power politics. These scenes with historical characters are interspersed with scenes displaying the nameless perpetrators and victims of aggression, rape, and genocide during World War II. Bertolt Brecht's widow, Helene Weigel, and the assistant directors at the East Berlin theater appear in a brief scene rehearsing Brecht's *Coriolan* (wr. 1952-1953, pb. 1959, adaptation of William Shakespeare's play *Coriolanus*; *Coriolanus*, 1972) without paying attention to the uprising of the East German workers in 1956. The moral of Müller's play is that Brecht's revolutionary legacy is ignored for the sake of artistic production. Müller's last play ends with the pessimistic conclusion that Brecht's name is as good as forgotten.

OTHER MAJOR WORKS

NONFICTION: *Krieg ohne Schlacht: Leben in zwei Diktaturen*, 1994 (autobiography).

MISCELLANEOUS: *Explosion of a Memory: Writings by Heiner Müller*, 1989; *Theatremachine*, 1995 (plays, poems, essays); *Werke*, 1998-2001 (4 volumes); *A Heiner Müller Reader: Plays, Poetry, Prose*, 2001.

BIBLIOGRAPHY

Barnett, David. *Literature Versus Theater: Textual Problems and Theatrical Realization in the Later Plays of Heiner Müller*. New York: Peter Lang, 1998. Monograph dealing with the texts of Müller's later plays with regard to their literary merits and their production on the stage.

Demetz, Peter. *After the Fires: Recent Writing in the Germanies, Austria, and Switzerland*. San Diego, Calif.: Harcourt Brace Jovanovich, 1986. Survey of German literature after 1970 with chapters on individual authors, including Müller.

_____. *Postwar German Literature: A Critical Introduction*. New York: Pegasus, 1970. Survey of German literature between 1945 and 1970 with chapter on Müller.

Huettich, H. G. *Theater in a Planned Society: Contemporary Drama in the German Democratic Republic in Its Historical, Political, and Cultural Context*. Chapel Hill: University of North Carolina, 1978. Study of theater in the GDR through the 1970's, including the role of Müller as dramatist.

Kalb, Jonathan. *The Theater of Heiner Müller*. New York: Cambridge University Press, 1998. Magisterial study of Müller's plays and their productions, including his plays after 1990.

Silberman, Marc. *Heiner Müller*. Amsterdam: Rodopi, 1980. Report on the state of research on Müller.

Teraoka, Arlene Akiko. *The Silence of Entropy or Universal Discourse: The Postmodernist Poetics of Heiner Müller*. New York: Peter Lang, 1985. Highly acclaimed assessment of Müller's plays in terms of postmodernist aesthetics.

Ehrhard Bahr

KAJ MUNK
Kaj Harald Leininger Petersen

Born: Maribo, Denmark; January 13, 1898
Died: Silkeborg, Denmark; January 4, 1944

PRINCIPAL DRAMA

Pilatus, wr. 1917, pb. 1937, pr. 1941

Sampson, wr. 1917, pb. 1949

Operationen, wr. 1920, pb. 1942

En Idealist, wr. 1923, pr., pb. 1928 (*Herod the King*, 1953)

Ordet, wr. 1925, pr., pb. 1932 (*The Word*, 1953)

Fugl Fønix, wr. 1926, pr. 1938, pb. 1939

Kærlighed, wr. 1926, pr. 1935, pb. 1948

Fra Tidehvervet, wr. 1928, pb. 1948

Havet og Menneskene, wr. 1929, pb. 1948

Kardinalen og Kongen, wr. 1929, pb. 1948

I Brændingen, pb. 1929, pr. 1937

Cant, pr., pb. 1931 (English translation, 1953)

De Udvalgte, pr., pb. 1933

Hamlet, pr. 1935, pb. 1938

Sejren, pr., pb. 1936

Døden, pb. 1936, pr. 1942

Diktatorinden, pr. 1938, pb. 1948

Han sidder ved smeltediglen, pr., pb. 1938 (*He Sits at the Melting Pot*, 1944)

Puslespil, pr. 1939, pb. 1949

Egelykke, pr., pb. 1940 (English translation, 1954)

Kongen, pb. 1941, pr. 1948 (radio play)

Niels Ebbesen, pb. 1942, pr. 1943 (English translation, 1944)

De Herrer dommere, pb. 1942, pr. 1947 (radio play)

Før Cannae, pb. 1943, pr. 1945 (*Before Cannae*, 1953)

Ewalds Død, pr., pb. 1943 (*The Death of Ewald*, 1949)

Alverdens urostiftere, wr. 1943, pb. 1947

Atterdag, pb. 1949

Five Plays by Kaj Munk, pb. 1953

OTHER LITERARY FORMS

Kaj Munk was a prolific dramatist, and he was no less active as an essayist, poet, and preacher. Many of his sermons have been published, as well as much of his poetry and his essays, which dealt with a wide variety of topics, especially with the Danish theater and politics.

ACHIEVEMENTS

A Danish writer once stated that if one were to ask throughout Denmark which two people had meant the most to the country under the German Occupation, the answer would no doubt be the king and Kaj Munk. If one were to ask which single person's death had made the greatest impression, the answer would surely be Kaj Munk's.

That Munk became such an important influence in Denmark during the twenty years that he served as village priest in Vedersø, and particularly during the nearly four years that he lived under the Occupation, was the result not only of his literary abilities but also, to an even greater extent, of his strength of character, his extraordinary ability to rally the people of his country to resist the oppressor and to stand up for what was right. That Munk was a small-town preacher provided him with a pulpit from which to expound his ideas to his people, but his audience quickly became much broader. Even before the war, he was well known throughout Scandinavia for his ability as a writer of drama. Many of his plays were presented in Norway and Sweden as well as in Denmark. Later he became well known in Germany, England, and elsewhere. Munk is remembered today at least as much for his political stance—as a rallying point for those opposed to the Occupation—as for his literary achievements. Of the latter, his drama is of great importance.

BIOGRAPHY

Kaj Munk was born Kaj Harald Leininger Petersen on January 13, 1898, at Maribo on the South Danish island of Lolland. He was the only child of Carl and Anna Mathilde Petersen. His father died when he was only eighteen months old and his mother when he was five and a half years old. He was adopted and reared by his mother's cousin, Marie Munk, and her husband, Peter. The Munks had no children of their own, and Marie had promised Anna Mathilde, as the latter lay on her deathbed, that she would rear the child and would love him and care for him as her own. The Munks were yeoman farmers, and Kaj was brought up in a wholesome, healthy environment, full of love and close to the land, and was instilled with a love for learning and a deep and lasting faith.

Munk, though rather frail, was an inquisitive and talented student who demonstrated unusual literary abilities at a very early age. When he was eight years old, he was visited during an illness by his schoolmaster, who wrote: "What a surprise when I turned the paper over and found it covered from top to bottom with poems. I nearly fell over backwards at the sight of what had been written there by a boy of eight years. The contents were naturally immature, but the rhyme, as well as the arrangement of the words, was witness to a very real sense of language."

Munk was educated first at the country school at Vejleby, then at Maribo Realskole, and later at the neighboring Nykøbing Latin School. While he was enrolled at the Realskole, under the remarkable tutelage of an unusually capable headmaster and a young, talented staff, Munk first became truly excited about learning. Munk was especially impressed by the poetry of Adam Gottlob Oehlenschläger. While in his last year at the Nykøbing Latin School, Munk wrote his first play, *Pilatus*, which is of particular interest not only because it is the first example of his dramatic talent but also because it contains the seeds of the later important work *He Sits at the Melting Pot*.

At the age of nineteen, Munk enrolled at the University of Copenhagen. During his years at the university, he experienced some of his most carefree, happiest times, although he never lost sight of his educational goals and was a very serious student. He lived at the prestigious student residence Regensen,

Kaj Munk (Kongelige Bibliotek)

where he became "Klokker," or head student. He continued to be active as a writer and, though enrolled as a student of theology, underwent considerable inner turmoil regarding his own faith and whether his life should be spent as a priest or a writer. He ultimately became both.

At the University of Copenhagen, Munk began to write his first publicly produced play, *Herod the King*. He was preparing for his finals in theology when a professor happened to remark, in a lecture on Herod the Great, that it was too bad that William Shakespeare had never tried his hand at this material. The chance comment was taken as a challenge by the receptive student, and before finishing his finals,

Munk had written four-fifths of the play, which he finished soon after assuming his duties as village priest at Vedersø.

Munk became pastor at Vedersø, a small village on the west coast of the Danish mainland, in 1924. His friends could not believe that, having been so happy in the city, he could tolerate for long the life of the small town. In fact, life was somewhat difficult for a time, but he became very fond of the area and beloved by its people. He was married to a young woman who was a native of the area, Lise Jørgensen, on January 13, 1929. During the years that followed, Munk's fame—as a playwright, public speaker, and journalist—increased. Nevertheless, he was always a pastor first. He never neglected his duties toward his flock and, in spite of his increasing fame and wealth, remained humble and dutiful in visiting his parishioners and in carrying out his duties where they were concerned. He even took a certain satisfaction in the knowledge that his words and thoughts, which originated in such an unimportant place, could have a significant impact on the outside world.

During these early years at Vedersø, Munk began to achieve success as a playwright, beginning with the presentation by the Copenhagen Royal Theater of *Herod the King* in 1928. He went on to write more than thirty plays, and by the late 1930's, Munk productions were being simultaneously presented in as many as nine principal cities in Denmark and Sweden. As Munk was both a preacher and a playwright, he often mixed the two. He considered drama to be, among other things, one way of preaching the word of God. Some of his plays are thus quite didactic, although he always sought first to entertain.

As the world, and particularly Europe, became ever more involved in conflict, Munk's plays began to take on decidedly political overtones. *He Sits at the Melting Pot*, written in 1938, is very critical of the Germans, especially of their attitude toward Jews. After the Occupation, which took place on April 9, 1940, Munk continued to write critical political drama, such as *Niels Ebbesen*, written in 1940, and *Before Cannae*, of 1943. Much of his writing in the last few years of his life was suppressed by the Occupation forces. It nevertheless was widely dispersed and had a great impact, both at home and abroad. Munk felt himself especially akin to Niels Ebbesen, the Jutland patriot who had successfully defied the Germans six hundred years earlier.

When Adolf Hitler and Benito Mussolini first took power, Munk had actually admired them and had considered a strongman type of government desirable. He became increasingly disenchanted with the developments in Europe, however, and became both a dedicated and an effective critic of Nazism. Munk refused to still his criticism even when ordered to do so by the Danish Ministry of Ecclesiastical Affairs, which in March, 1943, in a circular addressed to members of the clergy, instructed them to abstain from all public comment on the struggle of the Norwegian Church. In an open letter to the minister, Munk wrote, "I hereby take the liberty to inform the honored Church Ministry that I intend not only to disobey its orders, but to act directly against them. . . . It is better that Denmark be endangered in her relations to Germany than in her relations to our Lord Jesus Christ." In a similar vein, in a sermon entitled "Render Therefor unto Caesar the Things That Are Caesar's and unto God the Things That Are God's," Munk said:

> Much might be demanded of us: our money, our labor, the best years of our youth, our health, our very lives. But if Caesar demands that we call black white, tyranny freedom, violence justice, and falsehood truth, we shall answer him: "It is written, thou shall have no other gods but me. . . . By our death we shall conquer. We must obey God before man.

Little of what Munk wrote or preached during the Occupation was not directed in some way or another at the Germans. Although other notables fled to Sweden or elsewhere, he refused to do so, preferring instead to remain, to do what he could and to face the consequences. He concluded his final sermon, on New Year's Day, 1944, with these words: "Therefore he who knows what is right and does not do it, for him it is a sin." He then encouraged his parishioners to continue the struggle against the Nazis. On January 4, at about eight o'clock in the evening, a car arrived, filled with five agents of the Gestapo. Under orders from Berlin, Munk was taken from his wife and five children and was shot in the head and left in a roadside ditch. Munk had become too much of a thorn in the side of the Germans. Ironically, by murdering him, they made of him a martyr and an even more potent adversary.

ANALYSIS

In *Himmel og Jord* (1938) and in the preface to *I Brændingen*, Kaj Munk sets forth his theories of drama. He states a desire to see the Danish theater return to the "grand drama" of earlier years. He proposes a bold approach to drama, in which the true world is depicted. He says that the public is better off watching motion pictures, in which dramatic things happen, than watching an insipid stage production.

HEROD THE KING

Herod the King was Munk's first play to be presented at the Royal Theatre in Copenhagen but certainly not his greatest success. It was, in fact, met with a decided lack of enthusiasm on the part of the critics. It was later drastically revised, and the result was much more successful than the original had been. The play is fundamentally about the struggle between the king and God. It presents Herod as a person who will stop at nothing to remain in power. No sacrifice is too great if it will accomplish that end—even the murder of his own beloved wife.

This is only one of a number of Munk's plays portraying larger-than-life characters, such as kings, emperors, and dictators. Act 1 begins with Herod's sister, Salome, trying to influence him in the selection of a high priest. Salome is involved in plots and intrigues throughout the play, and she ultimately succeeds in turning the king against his lovely wife Miriamne, by wrongly accusing her of unfaithfulness, upon which Herod has Miriamne put to death.

In the first act, Herod clearly outlines his goal: "At last, at last—Edom's foot on Jacob's neck! Now my aim is to wield a ruthless scepter with a hated hand over this people, until I did. . . . No, I do not declare war on God. For what do I know of God? No, but—if He declares war on me, if He still sides with Jacob, well, then, I am a son of Edom and I shall not abandon my goal." Later, he says: "I have

but one goal: to wear my crown so that none can wrest it from me. For this I must sacrifice everything on earth."

Herod's love of power and his defiance of God can lead only to his ultimate failure and damnation. In act 8, Herod says: "My life has been one long fear—fear that He up there might at last rob me of my crown." Then, hearing that the son of David has been born in Bethlehem, he orders that every male child less than two years of age be put to the sword. He finally realizes that he has failed, that the Messiah, the King of the Jews, has escaped his sword. He ends the play with these words: "I am alone with God. . . . Then wilt Thou hear me. . . . See, I kneel to Thee— forgive me my sins, my struggle, my defiance. But let the child die. . . . Give me back the crown for which I have sacrificed the blood of my beloved—my body and soul—all that I had. Take pity on me, my Emperor, my Master, Thou God of Jacob—take pity on They servant, Thy slave, Thy fool." With those words, Herod dies, realizing finally the futility of his defiance of God and that his sacrifice has been for nought.

THE WORD

The Word was received with enthusiasm but was not without its critics. It presents the common, country folk and deals almost exclusively with religion. The theme is clearly laid out in the first act. The action takes place in the home of a seventy-five-year-old farmer, the father of three sons. The eldest son, Mikkel, is married and has two daughters. The second, Johannes, was studying for the priesthood but has apparently gone mad and imagines himself to be Jesus Christ. The youngest, Anders, hopes to marry a neighbor girl, Esther.

The subject of miracles continually arises. Interestingly, it is the local pastor who is most certain that miracles cannot happen in the modern world. On his first visit to the farmer's home, the new pastor meets Johannes, who introduces himself as Jesus of Nazareth, and says: "You believe in miracles of two thousand years ago, but not in one now. Why do you believe in the dead Christ, but not in the living?" The priest later says, as they discuss a play by Bjørnstjerne Bjørnson called *Over ævne, annet stykk*

(1805; *Beyond Our Power*, 1913): "An incurable is supposed to be cured by a miracle—I remember. It simply couldn't happen nowadays." The old farmer also repeatedly says that he does not believe in miracles.

The second act takes place in the home of Rueben, Esther's father, and represents a conflict between two groups within the state church. The group represented by Reuben is extremely conservative, believes in miracles, and is quite hostile toward those who do not share their beliefs. Because of these differences, Reuben will not let his daughter marry Anders, although they are all Lutheran.

The climax of the play occurs in the third and fourth acts, with the death of Inger, Mikkel's wife, in childbirth. Johannes disappears for three days, reappearing just as the casket is about to be closed. He appears now to be in his right mind, although not very happy to return to a reality filled with fear. He insists that Inger is not dead and calls on her to awaken, which she does. The pastor still cannot believe what he has witnessed, saying that it is a physical impossibility. The doctor attributes Inger's "revival" to the issuing of death certificates by amateurs—he is convinced that she was not really dead. The rest accept the miracle.

In *The Word*, Munk presents the religious beliefs of the people whom he knew so well and loved so deeply. In addition, he was able to accomplish in fiction what he had failed to do in real life, when as a youngster he had tried so hard to restore his grandmother to life.

CANT

Cant focuses once again on a larger-than-life character, in this case King Henry VIII of England. Here Munk is particularly critical of the hypocrisy that passed for religion at the time. The play deals principally with the question of divorce, or rather annulment, as the Catholic Church did not allow divorce. The king wished to have his marriage to the queen annulled, ostensibly because she was unable to present him with a living son but in truth because he had been seduced by the beauty of the young Anne Boleyn. When the pope himself refuses to grant the annulment, the local churchmen prefer to follow the

wishes of the king and bend the precepts of the Church to appease him. Anne herself is later beheaded when falsely accused of adultery, and the king is never presented with a male heir to the throne.

HE SITS AT THE MELTING POT

In *He Sits at the Melting Pot*, his play about pre-World War II Germany, Munk first incurred the wrath of the Nazis, who had him murdered six years later. The title comes from the opening verse of a Danish hymn by B. S. Ingemann: "The great Artificer comes; all-loving is his purpose./ He sits at the melting-pot and diligently purifies the silver." Munk wrote the play during a visit to Berlin, where he was able to see the Third Reich in action. *He Sits at the Melting Pot* is an almost purely political play and is extremely critical of the Germans, particularly of their anti-Semitism and their attempts to restructure the world and its history in order to make it fit their view of reality. In his introduction to the play, Munk says:

> The earth is on fire. There have been times in the history of humankind when it was possible to forget this; but our own time is not one of these. . . . Are these flames that beset us the flames of destruction? We do not know. . . . The earth is in the meltingpot. . . . It is the god in hell who shovels in the coal under God's melting-pot. That is why the heat is so terrific. And it has to be, in order that the dross may be cleansed away.

The play takes place in the study of Professor Mensch, a noted and somewhat elderly professor of archaeology. The universality of the name is no accident: Mensch is a good, learned man who has little time for the realities of the mundane world around him. His only interest is in his work. Little else concerns him. As the play begins, he and his assistant, Fräulein Schmidt, are studying some shards that he has brought back from a collecting expedition he has made to the Holy Land. They are excited beyond their wildest dreams when they realize that a sketch that they had been able to reassemble from the fragments is actually a likeness of Jesus Christ, done by a contemporary.

Professor Mensch and Fräulein Schmidt are interrupted by a visit from Professor Dorn, who is very concerned about three things: rising in the ranks of

National Socialism (he hopes to become the Minister of Culture); a treatise he has written in an attempt to prove that Christ was really of Aryan, rather than Jewish, stock (the thesis has been contested in print by the local bishop); and one Dr. Helm, a university librarian, who, it has been discovered, is probably a Jew and has apparently falsified his Aryan certificate. Professor Mensch expresses his own distaste for the Jews, but he does not want to get involved. He simply wants to be left alone to do his research.

In the third act there is a confrontation between Professor Dorn and Bishop von Beugel. The latter says: "The core of our controversy as to whether Christ was Aryan or no is really this: shall Germany worship truth or—itself?" Later the bishop says to Dorn, "So you mean to go on? Profaning the name of Germany with your methods from the Inquisition— with every kind of devilry from the Middle Ages!" When Fräulein Fürst, Dr. Helm's fiancé, finds out that he is a Jew, she is scandalized. She cannot believe that she could have allowed herself to be touched by him and feels that she should have somehow been able to tell.

Professor Mensch has decided to present the Führer with his picture of Christ and is to be awarded the National Prize. When Professor Dorn insists that he must not tell the Führer that the obviously Jewish face is that of Christ, Mensch smashes the picture. He does not care about the National Prize; he cares only about the truth. He learns also that his assistant, Fräulein Schmidt, is really Sarah Levi and is Dr. Helm's sister. She and the professor decide to leave Germany together.

Although *He Sits at the Melting Pot* is about German society under the Third Reich and is particularly critical of the persecution of the Jews, it is also about all humankind, personified by Mensch. God sits at the melting pot and purifies His creation. Professor Mensch begins as a capable but weak individual and ends as a strong person who is able to overcome his weaknesses.

NIELS EBBESEN AND BEFORE CANNAE

Two plays written by Munk during the Occupation, *Niels Ebbesen* and *Before Cannae*, deal with the moral issues of the war by means of a historical analogue. In the former, Munk clearly identifies himself with the real person after whom the play is named. Niels Ebbesen had defied the Germans and was instrumental in the struggle against them in the fourteenth century. *Before Cannae* is a one-act play that principally consists of a dialogue between Hannibal and Fabius Cunctator. It does not require much imagination to see the parallels between the two generals of the play and their real-life counterparts, Hitler and Winston Churchill, and Rome is easily recognizable as London. In this play, one notes Munk's final rejection of dictatorship and his embracing of democratic principles.

OTHER MAJOR WORKS

LONG FICTION: *Dette dødsens legeme*, 1938.

POETRY: *Os baerer den himmelske glaede*, 1934; *Knaldperler*, 1936; *Elleve Kaj Munk digte*, 1937; *Navigare necesse*, 1941; *Svaerg det, drenge*, 1941; *Det unge nord*, 1942; *Danmark: Lidt om folk og faedreland fortalt de kaereste af mine landsmaend børnene*, 1943; *Den skaebne ej til os*, 1943.

NONFICTION: *Rub og Stub*, 1922; *Vedersø— Jerusalem retur*, 1934; *Liv og glade dage*, 1936; *Himmel og Jord*, 1938; *Ved Babylons Floder*, 1941 (*By the Rivers of Babylon*, 1945); *Foraaret saa sagte kommer*, 1942; *Med sol og megen glaede*, 1942; *Jesus' historier genfortalt for de smaa*, 1943; *Tre praedikener*, 1943; *Sømandsvise*, 1943; *Lukas— Evangeliet*, 1944.

BIBLIOGRAPHY

Harcourt, Melville. *Portraits of Destiny*. New York: Sheed and Ward, 1966. In one of the essays in this volume, Harcourt examines the life and works of Munk, the Danish writer and activist.

Rosco N. Tolman

ALFRED DE MUSSET

Born: Paris, France; December 11, 1810
Died: Paris, France; May 2, 1857

PRINCIPAL DRAMA

La Nuit vénitienne: Ou, Les Noces de Laurette, pr.
    1830, pb. 1834 (*The Venetian Night: Or,*
    Laurette's Wedding, 1905)

La Coupe et les lèvres, pb. 1833 (*The Cup and the*
    Lips, 1905)

À quoi rêvent les jeunes filles, pb. 1833, pr. 1880
    (*Of What Young Maidens Dream*, 1905)

André del Sarto, pb. 1833, pr. 1848 (English
    translation, 1905)

Les Caprices de Marianne, pb. 1833, pr. 1851 (*The*
    Follies of Marianne, 1905)

Fantasio, pb. 1834, pr. 1866 (English translation,
    1853)

On ne badine pas avec l'amour, pb. 1834, pr. 1861
    (*No Trifling with Love*, 1890)

Lorenzaccio, pb. 1834, pr. 1896 (English
    translation, 1905)

Un Spectacle dans un fauteuil, pb. 1834 (second
    series, 2 volumes)

La Quenouille de Barbarine, pb. 1835, revised wr.
    1851, pr. 1882 (*Barbarine*, 1890)

Le Chandelier, pb. 1835, pr. 1848 (*The Chandelier*,
    1903)

Il ne faut jurer de rien, pb. 1836, pr. 1848

Un Caprice, pb. 1837, pr. 1847 (*A Caprice*, 1847)

Il faut qu'une porte soit ouverte ou fermée, pb.
    1845, pr. 1848 (*A Door Must Be Either Open or*
    Shut, 1890)

L'Habit vert, pr., pb. 1849 (with Émile Augier; *The*
    Green Coat, 1915)

Louison, pr., pb. 1849 (English translation, 1905)

On ne saurait penser à tout, pr. 1849, pb. 1853
    (*One Can Not Think of Everything*, 1905)

Carmosine, pb. 1850, pr. 1865 (English translation,
    1865)

Bettine, pr., pb. 1851 (English translation, 1905)

L'Âne et le ruisseau, wr. 1855, pb. 1860, pr. 1876
    (*Donkey and the Stream*, 1905)

Comedies, pb. 1890
A Comedy and Two Proverbs, pb. 1955
Seven Plays, pb. 1962

OTHER LITERARY FORMS

Alfred de Musset established his reputation as a poet and was, in fact, best known as a poet throughout the greater part of an artistic career of almost thirty years. It was not until 1847, with the successful productions of *A Caprice* (a comedy published ten years earlier) in St. Petersburg and at the Comédie-Française, that Musset began to enjoy comparable distinction as a dramatist. Additionally, Musset published an extensive amount of fiction, most of it in the form of *contes*, or tales, which are often full of wit and spirit but have fallen, perhaps undeservedly, into almost total neglect. In 1836, Musset's one major novel was published, the semiautobiographical *La Confession d'un enfant du siècle* (*The Confession of a Child of the Century*, 1892). This work is most notable for its vivid evocation of an era and its philosophical climate; the novel is a striking, extended depiction of nineteenth century *mal de siècle*. Musset's nondramatic canon is rounded out by a number of often perceptive and forward-thinking critical reviews in the fields of literature, music, and the visual arts.

ACHIEVEMENTS

The early nineteenth century in France was an age of tremendous theatrical activity. Indeed, the theater was regarded by all literary factions—romantics, neoclassicists, *philosophes*—as the proving ground for the determination of true literary worth. The era was, nevertheless, more notable for its pronouncements about the nature of drama than for the viability of the theater that it produced. In this light, it is remarkable that Alfred de Musset's "armchair theater" (as he referred to his style of dramatic writing), a theater designed to be read, not produced, should have not only survived its time but also increased in stature, while the works of most of his contemporaries have faltered. Musset's *comédies* and *proverbes*, moreover, seem to be anachronisms in a period remarkable for its general lack of literary and dramatic humor. Their deft touch and light, ironic style, which owe much to the critical spirit of the eighteenth century, must have struck his fellow romantics as an outright challenge. This aspect of Musset's drama was nurtured not only by his early exposure to Enlightenment literature and philosophy but also by his wide reading in several languages and his familiarity and respect for the ironic comic tradition of such earlier masters as Molière and Marivaux. Even in the arena of that pet genre of the romantics, the historical drama, it was Musset, not Victor Hugo, Alexandre Dumas, *père*, or Alfred de Vigny, who, in *Lorenzaccio*, created the finest example of the genre in French theatrical literature.

Despite their being intended for a reading public, Musset's best plays have been discovered as emi-

nently suited for the stage, thanks to their author's seemingly innate sense of the dramatic situation. During Musset's lifetime, no one, least of all Musset, could have foretold that several of the plays would become staples of the classic repertory, nor could anyone possibly appreciate the foreshadowing of cinematic technique in the fluid, dramatic movement of Musset's theater. Filmmaker Jean Renoir, for example, in *La Règle du jeu* (1939; *The Rules of the Game*, 1950) owes much to this latter aspect of Musset's art (Renoir's original concept of the film was, in fact, a retelling of *The Follies of Marianne*). In the twentieth century, Eric Rohmer embarked on a series of films whose collective generic heading, "Comédies et proverbes," refers directly to Musset's dramatic conception and subject matter.

It is clear, in France at any rate, that Musset's stature as a dramatist is well established. It can only be hoped that the neglect of his theater in the English-speaking world will be rectified by increased critical attention and greater visibility on the stage.

BIOGRAPHY

Louis Charles Alfred de Musset was born in Paris on December 11, 1810, the second child of Victor-Donatien de Musset and Edmée-Claudine Guyot Desherbiers. The genealogy of the Musset family was aristocratic and could be traced back as far as the twelfth century. Alfred's father had survived the French Revolution in spite of his noble descent, partially as a result of his liberal sympathies, and he had served as a soldier and civil servant under the Republic and Napoleon Bonaparte's First Empire. Victor-Donatien was a man of literary tastes and scholarly temperament. An ardent admirer of Jean-Jacques Rousseau, he not only wrote a biography of the great eighteenth century philosopher and writer but also published an edition of Rousseau's works. There had been a similar literary background in Alfred's mother's family, and consequently, the young boy was reared in an atmosphere of books and periodicals. The young Musset's readings of *The Thousand and One Nights*, Miguel de Cer-

Alfred de Musset (Hulton Archive by Getty Images)

vantes's *El ingenioso hidalgo don Quixote de la Mancha* (1605, 1615; *The History of the Valorous and Wittie Knight-Errant, Don Quixote of the Mancha*, 1612-1620, better known as *Don Quixote de la Mancha*), and Ludovico Ariosto's Renaissance epic, *Orlando furioso* (1516, 1521, 1532; English translation, 1591), established a precocious taste for the exotic, the fantastic, and the ironic, a taste that nourished his poetic and dramatic composition throughout his artistic career.

From the ages of nine to seventeen, Musset studied at the Collège Henri IV in Paris, where he quickly established and maintained a reputation as a student of great talent and application, typically winning a number of prizes at the conclusion of each school year. On leaving this school, Musset, at his father's suggestion, made some trifling efforts to study first law and then medicine but was quickly bored and disgusted by both professions. His studies at home and school had established in him a strong preference for the arts, and he took up further studies in foreign languages, music, and drawing. Musset displayed some talent in the latter and contemplated a future as a painter. With the composition of his first poems (written under the influence of his readings of the eighteenth century poet André Chenier), however, Musset set his sights unalterably on a literary career.

While still at school, Musset was introduced to two figures of considerable importance in the Parisian literary scene, two of the artists who helped inaugurate the new romantic movement in early nineteenth century France: Charles Nodier and Victor Hugo. Both were poets and novelists and were the hosts of literary clubs that attracted the participation of most of the literary hopefuls of the day. Hugo hosted a club called the Cénacle, and it was there that Musset, at the urging of the literary critic Charles Augustin Sainte-Beuve, first read his poems, which were received enthusiastically. At the same time, Musset's noble descent, youthful charm, affability, and good looks guaranteed him an effortless entrée into Parisian high society. He was soon drawn into the circle of wealthy young dandies, among whom he developed what became a lifelong predilection for wine, gambling, and women.

In 1828, Musset's translation of Thomas De Quincey's 1821 novel, *Confessions of an English Opium Eater* (to which he had interpolated some original, personal material), was published anonymously. This literary exercise, together with the success of his poetry readings at the Cénacle, convinced him to find a publisher for his own original work, and, in 1829, *Contes d'Espagne et d'Italie* (1829; *Tales of Spain and Italy*, 1905) appeared. This brief collection, containing several tales in verse, a short drama, and some fantasy poems, jolted romantic circles with its indirect jibes at the exotic brand of poetry exemplified by Hugo's recent collection, *Les Orientales* (1829; English translation, 1879). That same year, at the request of the manager of the Odéon Theater, Musset composed a play entitled *The Venetian Night*. It was hissed down at its first performance, and its failure proved a deep psychological blow for the twenty-year-old playwright, who resolved never again to write specifically for the stage. Significantly, the greater portion of his subsequent drama was of the closet variety, pieces created for reading only, not production.

Musset immediately returned to the hedonistic life that he had somewhat modified by this burst of literary activity, but, with the death of his father in 1832, he was impelled to provide for himself and his mother (with whom he continued to live for the greater part of his life) by further writing. He soon published the first volume of *Un Spectacle dans un fauteuil* (1833, first series, two volumes; *A Performance in an Armchair*, 1905), a collection of poems and two verse plays. The volume was not a great success, but it did attract the attention of Musset's friend from Cénacle days, Sainte-Beuve. The critic's favorable review resulted in an invitation from François Buloz, editor of the fortnightly literary magazine *Revue des Deux Mondes*, to become a regular contributor of poetry, drama, and fiction. It was in this review that the first of Musset's plays to reveal truly his particular dramatic genius, *The Follies of Marianne*, made its appearance; it was also at a dinner party given by Buloz in June, 1833, that Musset made the acquaintance of the talented writer of notorious reputation, George Sand. A mutual fascination was immediately aroused in the two authors, and approximately two months later they inaugurated their brief but tempestuous affair.

What began idyllically and peacefully was destined in a very short time to turn acrimonious and bitter. A trip with Sand to Italy, ending in Venice during the winter of 1833-1834, was marked not only by mutual financial embarrassments but also by sometimes violent and abusive quarrels. Sand became ill soon after their arrival in Venice, and Musset took the opportunity to drink heavily and sample the charms of Venetian women. Just as Sand began to recover, Musset became severely ill, suffering from fever and delirium for almost two weeks. While devotedly nursing her lover, Sand was drawn to the attractive, sensitive attending physician, Pietro Pagello, and became his lover within the month. When Musset finally recovered, he recognized the nature of the relationship that had developed between the two people who had practically saved his life. After a brief period of jealous recrimination and display, Musset left Sand and Pagello together with his blessing and returned alone to Paris. The characteristics Musset displayed in this "Venetian drama" would recur in his subsequent relationships. His temperament was a curious combination of the libertine, the ardent idealistic lover, and the paranoid.

The entire episode was, by his own admission, the most crucial and devastating of his life. When Sand left Pagello and Italy to return to France the following autumn, there was a short-lived reconciliation, but the intensity and devotion of their brief time together could not be rekindled. In spite of the personal pain suffered, the relationship proved to be a source of artistic nourishment for both writers. Musset's play *Fantasio* was published at the height of the affair, and shortly after the rupture, the comedy *No Trifling with Love* and the historical drama *Lorenzaccio* were published. In addition, the break with Sand served directly as inspiration for some of Musset's finest poetic achievements, notably the four *nuit* poems, works concerning the acceptance of lost love and the transformation of experience into art.

The final break with Sand in early 1835 had cured Musset, at least temporarily, of his self-destructive, hedonistic proclivities and provoked a four-year period of considerable literary activity. Four plays came out of this period as well as a number of poems, tales, and a semiautobiographical novel, *The Confession of a Child of the Century*. In 1839, however, at the age of twenty-eight, Musset returned to his former habits of heavy drinking, gambling, and womanizing. In the succeeding years, he was to have a number of amorous relationships of varying seriousness and success. Perhaps the most enduring of these was his affair with a Madame Jaubert, a relationship that evolved into a devoted friendship. Like Sand before her, Madame Jaubert recognized the young man's need for a mother figure of similar intellectual tastes and sympathies to whom he could turn for conversation and compassion.

Since his father's death, Musset had always suffered from financial anxieties, but these largely disappeared in 1838 with his appointment as librarian for the Ministry of the Interior. He retained this post until the 1848 revolution, when he was dismissed for suspected Royalist sympathies. By the time of his dismissal, however, Musset had begun to enjoy a revival of interest in his dramatic œuvre, and the performance of his plays now assured him a fairly reliable income. With the success of *A Caprice* in Russia and at home at the Comédie-Française in 1847, Musset's reputation as a playwright began to create a mounting demand for his work. He revised and expanded several earlier works and received commissions from leading actors and theater managers for new ones.

In 1852, after two attempts, Musset made a third and successful bid for election to the Académie Française. After many years of remaining in the family home with his mother, he now lived there alone under the care of a housekeeper. He continued to write but composed no new poetic or dramatic works of particular importance. Since 1842 at the latest, he had been suffering from heart trouble, and, in the winter of 1856, his health began to deteriorate rapidly. He died at home on May 2, 1857.

ANALYSIS

Alfred de Musset himself divided his theater into three distinct categories: *comédies, proverbes,* and historical drama. The bulk of the plays fall under the rubric of "comedies," with *The Follies of Marianne, Fantasio, No Trifling with Love*, and *Il ne faut jurer de rien* heading the list in terms of critical and popular esteem. The so-called *proverbe dramatique* was a one-act form inherited from the eighteenth century (originating in family and salon theatricals) in which the action was devised to illustrate a well-known aphorism. Musset, typical of his refusal to dismiss summarily the literary and dramatic inheritance of the seventeenth and eighteenth centuries (a repudiation common among romantic writers and propagandists), adapted and enlarged the scope of the form, perfecting it in such plays as *A Caprice, A Door Must Be Either Open or Shut*, and *One Can Not Think of Everything*. Of the final category, historical drama, there are only two examples, both of whose subjects are drawn from the late Italian Renaissance: *André del Sarto* and *Lorenzaccio*. Of his dramatic oeuvre, the four plays written in the span of two years, 1833 and 1834, *The Follies of Marianne, Fantasio, No Trifling with Love*, and *Lorenzaccio*, are now generally acknowledged as Musset's finest and most enduring contributions to dramatic literature.

Theoretical pronouncements regarding the nature of drama abounded in early nineteenth century France, but the age, active as it was in actual composition of new plays, left relatively little in the way of a viable repertory. Musset, however, was no theorist. He did not leave behind any manifestos à la Hugo, nor did he intend to bequeath a body of dramatic literature conceived for stage production. The disastrous premiere of *The Venetian Night* had turned his attention to the composition of plays meant to be enjoyed exclusively as literature. In part because he created those plays in a condition of freedom from the demands and limitations of produced drama, as his age conceived it, Musset generally avoided the pitfalls and shortcomings which, in retrospect at least, damaged the viability of the theater of his contemporaries. Moreover, it was Musset's closet drama that most successfully realized romantic conceptions of and aspirations for drama, particularly the desire to revive a Shakespearean theater that comingled tragic, comic, and fantastic elements. Without necessarily

intending it, Musset was in the avant-garde in the most significant sense: He was a visionary capable of realizing theory in actual artistic practices.

Whatever freedom Musset displayed in matters of theory and dramatic construction, in terms of thematic concern his theater remained loyal to the great concerns of the romantic stage. Particularly characteristic is Musset's examination of the place and the role of the man of imagination (the artist) in society and of the disparity between the ideal and the real, between what is aspired to and what is achieved. Even more idiosyncratic is the "youth-oriented" perspective of much of Musset's theater. It has often been remarked apropos of Musset's verse that his great overriding theme is the perpetually reiterated drama of youth: the fears of approaching adulthood and responsibility and a sense of the impending betrayal of youth's idealism and energy. Where in the poetry, however, there is a tendency toward the puerile and the mawkishly sentimental, in the plays, Musset seems to have discovered the most effective medium for the exploration of his views on this theme. The very dialectical impulse inherent in the nature of dramatic dialogue (one character speaks, another reacts) perhaps accounts for Musset's ability to avoid overly simplistic thematic statements while providing a sense of irony that, at least to modern readers, seems a breath of fresh air for the romantic theater.

Critical investigation has been slow to appreciate and evaluate Musset's achievement. Scholars and theater literary managers alike hardly knew what to make of this "stage of dreams." What they sensed as inattention to the demands of actual production could be excused only because of the literary aspirations of the plays; stageworthy they could not be. In modern times, however, critical estimation and an ever-increasing number of appearances on the boards (in France) made amends for tentative beginnings, and Musset has come to be generally considered the most significant and innovative playwright of French Romanticism. In the best of his theater, Musset realized many of the theoretical aspirations of dramaturgy in his day. Perhaps the most significant of his achievements, however, was his sensitivity in depicting the darker recesses of the human heart and mind, and his comprehension of and sympathy for the human condition.

Fantasio

Fantasio, first published in *Revue des Deux Mondes* in January of 1834, is the least performed of the major comedies, and its production history is typical of the early fate of most of Musset's plays. The play first appeared at the Comédie-Française nine years after Musset's death, revised by the playwright's brother, Paul, who tampered with the order of several scenes, expanded the original two acts into three, and altered the nature of the relationship between Fantasio and Elsbeth into something approaching a more conventional love interest. Both theatrical producers and literary critics throughout the rest of the nineteenth and early twentieth centuries mistook this inept, structurally and spiritually unfaithful version for the original, and the play received little serious consideration. It was not until later productions that the piece was performed using the original text. Critics have additionally, and perhaps misguidedly, expended immense energy in the examination of the play as a depiction of the author's emotional and psychological state, a habit characteristic of Musset criticism (admittedly amply generated by the author's frequent informal pronouncements on the relationship of his life and work).

The action is divided into two acts and occurs in Munich; the time is unspecified. In the first act, the King of Bavaria has arranged a marriage of political convenience between his daughter, Elsbeth, and the Prince of Mantua, a man personally unknown either to the king or to the princess. An abrupt change of scene finds three young men carousing in the street, drinking and discussing the forthcoming royal wedding. The youths are joined by a handsome young companion, Fantasio, who immediately confesses to a state of spiritual and intellectual ennui. He is not only pursued by his creditors but is also prey to a decidedly cynical perspective of the world, in which both God and love are dead, and a life of true adventure is no longer possible. Presently, a funeral procession passes by: It is for the king's jester, Saint-Jean. A taunting remark by one of the pallbearers provokes

Fantasio to masquerade as a new jester for the court. In the meantime, on his arrival at an inn outside the city, the Prince of Mantua confides to Marinoni, his aide-de-camp, a scheme to switch roles and costumes in order to observe incognito his future wife and father-in-law.

The second act opens with Elsbeth's avowal of dismay at the arranged marriage and her sorrow at the death of the beloved Saint-Jean. Fantasio appears in the palace gardens in the disguise of the hunchbacked jester himself and engages the princess in a witty conversation, using the traditional liberties of the jester's role to comment disparagingly on arranged marriages. Later, when Fantasio catches sight of her weeping, he decides to help Elsbeth out of her unfortunate personal situation. Several scenes follow in which the prince and Marinoni so fumble their assumed roles that they deeply offend the king and the princess. Fantasio stations himself in a window, seizing the opportunity to snatch off the prince's wig as he passes on the street below. The enraged prince demands the jester's imprisonment and declares war on Bavaria. When Elsbeth visits Fantasio in prison, she discovers his true identity. In return for releasing her from an unbearable personal situation, she frees the young man, promising to allow him to return as jester whenever he tires of the everyday world of creditors and responsibility.

Fantasio has all the appearance of a whimsical potpourri of political satire, social commentary, philosophy, sentiment, fantasy, and farce. There is an almost improvisational air created by the rapid shifts of scene and the general absence of dramatic action. The very "weight" of the two acts seems capricious: The first act is divided into three scenes, the second act into seven. Moreover, the first act is almost entirely expository (the lengthy second scene functions somewhat in the manner of a philosophical dialogue), and there is no real action until the second act. In spite of its chameleonlike surface, the play is bound together by several features, notably its delight in linguistic play and its obvious thematic emphasis on the concept of the self (signaled by the costume switches and role reversals among the characters).

In the long scene of act 1, even before Fantasio has the inspiration for his change of roles, his mind is clearly occupied by the philosophical implications of human role-playing and the conflict between external appearances and internal reality:

> That gentleman passing by is charming. Look at him: What lovely silk breeches! What delightful red flowers on his waistcoat. . . . I am positive that that very man has a million ideas in his head which are absolutely foreign to me: his essence is peculiar to him alone. Alas! everything men say to one another amounts to the same thing; the ideas they propose are almost invariably identical from conversation to conversation; but somewhere deep inside these individual machines, what creases, what hidden crannies! Each man carries an entire world inside him. An unremarked world which is born and dies in silence! What solitudes all these human bodies!

Fantasio has described the egocentric problem of the artist (and, by extension, of all humankind): the desire to escape the confines of one's own flesh. Despite Fantasio's sense of ennui and his frustration with the ways of the world, one strength remains: his imagination. A jester's funeral procession is enough to spark his mind. Fantasio instinctively understands that the feeling, imaginative person can always step into another individual's shoes. His exchange of roles is more than a simple exchange of outward appearance; Fantasio is successful at his masquerade because he has a powerful sense of empathy with others.

The prince and Marinoni stand in marked contrast to Fantasio's resilient adaptability. They fumble their exchanged roles so pitifully that they annoy the entire court. They are mere puppets, incapable of adapting themselves to the unfamiliar task of projecting themselves into another man's skin. The prince's great sense of outrage at Fantasio's prank reveals his limitations in the perception of his role; he allows his clothing and the superficial appurtenances of his rank to define his identity. Unlike Fantasio, the prince has no inner resources on which to rely; he has, in fact, no "self," and he patently lacks the key to freedom—imagination.

In the world of *Fantasio*, the self is caught in a conflict between personal will and the larger forces of human destiny. All the major characters walk this tightrope: Elsbeth must marry a man whom she does not know and does not love; the welfare of a nation depends on a politically expedient marriage; Fantasio is faced with the possibility of surrender to his creditors and, worse, to his world-weary frame of mind. Fantasio's ability to see life from different perspectives, however, is his trump card, the measure of his ability to survive. The literal prison from which Elsbeth frees him at the end of the play corresponds to the mental-spiritual prisons he describes in act 1 and from which he is liberated by an act of imagination. Fantasio's fate is, to some extent, then, of his own making; he earns his freedom as a reward for teaching the meaning of freedom to another human being. By issuing Fantasio an open-ended invitation to return to Elsbeth's garden and to his role as jester, Musset places his hero in a never-never land that he was not to grant to the protagonists of any of his subsequent plays.

NO TRIFLING WITH LOVE

Musset's next play, *No Trifling with Love*, published in *Revue des Deux Mondes* in July of 1834, has often struck critics as even more stylistically and structurally whimsical than *Fantasio*. Perdican, the son of a provincial baron, and Camille, his cousin, return separately to the château where they were reared together, he from the university, she from a convent school. Their arrival is preceded by that of Perdican's tutor, the bibulous Master Blazius, and by that of Camille's spindly, sour-tempered governess, Dame Pluche; these two stock characters are greeted with ironic formality by a chorus of local peasants. Also drawn with the broad strokes of caricature are the pompous, dull-witted baron and the village curate, Master Bridaine. The baron, who has assumed that his niece will marry his son when they reach the appropriate age, is piqued and confused by Camille's prudish reserve in greeting her cousin, a reaction that is soon discovered to arise from her decision to enter the convent. Her cool attitude is in striking contrast with Perdican's warm and nostalgic rediscovery of the pleasures and acquaintances of childhood.

The young girl's decision to take the veil does not seem fixed, however, and she is aroused half-consciously by her cousin's attentions. She begins to play a double game, maintaining a show of icy reserve yet somehow leading the young man on. Perdican, frustrated by Camille's ostensible rejection of their past lives and of his present attentions, pays court to an attractive village girl, Rosette, Camille's foster sister. Camille requests a rendezvous with Perdican before her return to the convent. In an impassioned scene, the cousins exchange their antithetical views of life and love. Camille reveals that her experience at the convent as the confidante of one of the nuns, Sister Louise, has altered her views of worldly pleasure and human commitment. Before entering the convent, Sister Louise had suffered a failed love affair and has bitterly confided her disappointment and frustration to the young schoolgirl. Perdican accuses Camille of arriving at her present state of heart and mind vicariously. In his view, Camille has rejected life without experiencing it herself.

This emotionally charged interview wounds the vanity of both parties and provokes a contest of mutual deceit. The contest revolves around the pawn Rosette, who is herself torn between her sincere attraction for Perdican and her suspicion concerning the sincerity of his declarations. In the final scene, Perdican encounters Camille at prayer and, overhearing her declaration of love for him, rushes to take her in his arms. The two immediately hear a terrifying cry from behind the altar. Rosette has overheard them and has fallen dead from grief and shock. There is no longer any question of a relationship between the cousins, and Camille bids Perdican a brief and austere farewell.

For more than a century, critics have tried to assign a generic tag to this peculiar play. Musset termed it a *proverbe* (it certainly adheres to the concept of the form, with its dramatic illustration of the aphoristic title), yet critics have often categorized it with the "comedies" in view of its complexities: its expanded length (three acts), its highly stylized techniques (the extensive use of the chorus, something in the manner of Greek drama, and the narration of much of the plot by the stock characters), its sometimes startling shifts of style and mood, and its melodramatic conclusion. The play, in fact, spans generic differences, creating

its own structure. The binding force of what appears superficially as a hodgepodge must be discovered not so much in form, but in language and theme.

Critic David Sices proposed that the underlying theme that permeates the stylistic, structural mosaic of *No Trifling with Love* is the concept of the multiple, unintegrated personality. Musset is not merely trying to dramatize the conflicts of personality between the two protagonists, or those between the protagonists and the stock characters. He has set himself the additional and more intricate task of dramatizing the multiple aspects of the individual personality itself. It is Camille's and Perdican's internal psychological complexity and the unintegrated segments of their own individual personalities—the unstable states of belief, opinion, and emotion—that constitute the obstacle to their ultimate union and guide their conduct throughout. The comic impulse traditionally tends toward union and resolution, and, significantly, that is precisely the state which this peculiar comedy cannot attain.

Somewhere within Camille, in spite of her cold exterior, is a warm, passionate young woman who longs for love almost as much as she fears it. Because of her experiences at the convent school, she eschews the actual commitment of a relationship with its human instability and unreliability. She has gained a false experience of human love (because it is not her own), yet she cannot quite control her desire to experience love for herself. Her stiffness contrasts sharply with her only half-conscious attempts to draw her cousin on to further declarations of affection. Perdican is an intelligent, articulate, and sensual young man who also happens to be stubborn and sensitive. His warm affection and desire for the anchoring values of his childhood contrast with his only half-conscious callowness in using Rosette as a pawn. The two cousins are unable to stabilize the various and contending fragments of thought and emotion that motivate their behavior. Musset's sensitivity in portraying this instability moves the play in the direction of psychoanalysis.

Interwoven with this serious central plot is the two-dimensional framework of the comic characters. Everything about Blazius, Bridaine, Pluche, and the baron is conventional and lacking in depth. Like the prince in *Fantasio*, they function mechanically and are, consequently, baffled by the vital, three-dimensional contest between the two young cousins. Only in the battle between Blazius and Bridaine for the place of honor at the baron's table is there a comic echo of the more serious battle between the protagonists, and this subplot serves to underscore the banality of the world they represent. Indeed, the stock characters are, in a sense, depictions of the human personality devoid of youthful hopes and ideals.

The "message" of the play is hard; Musset offers no escape into the magical garden of possibility, as in *Fantasio*, for Camille and Perdican, no second chance for the hapless Rosette. All that is offered is one small light against the encroaching darkness: To have loved is to have lived.

LORENZACCIO

The plot of Musset's superb historical drama *Lorenzaccio*, based on the murder of the sixteenth century Florentine tyrant Alessandro de Medici by his cousin Lorenzo (popularly known by a pejorative form of his name, Lorenzaccio), is grandiose in scope (a full five-act tragedy) and highly involved, with intertwining plots and a large cast of characters. Three parallel conspiracies aimed at the destruction of Alexandre (as he is called in French) combine in this vast canvas depicting the moral life of a modern political city. The central action involves the conduct and the philosophical struggles of the young Lorenzo.

Alexandre, the illegitimate son of Lorenzo II de Medici, has ruled Florence for six years as duke with the combined support of Pope Clement VI and the Holy Roman Emperor Charles V. His corrupt and decadent conduct threatens the welfare of the entire city, from aristocracy to thriving merchant class. No effective attempt at revolt has been successfully organized, however, and only the ever-increasing number of exiles from the city, both forced and voluntary, signals popular discontent.

Lorenzo, noted in earlier days for his studious and idealistic nature, has returned to his native Florence from Rome with the intention of assassinating his tyrannical cousin and helping to restore the Florentine Republic. To accomplish this end, he assumes a mask of corruption and cowardice in order to remain unsuspected by both the duke, with whom he becomes a companion in debauchery, and the citizenry in general. His only confidant is the elderly patriarch of one of Florence's leading patrician families, Philippe Strozzi. To him alone, Lorenzo reveals not only the nature of the insidious role he has assumed but also the terrible consequences of his action. He has become the role that he plays and is incapable of regaining his lost sense of innocence and integrity. Moreover, although resolved to carry out his original plans, he has come to recognize the futility of his act in a city in which the citizens are too spineless to validate the murder by the reestablishment of the Republic. Using his young aunt as a decoy, Lorenzo sets an ambush for the lustful duke and stabs him to death in bed. His moment of exaltation is brief, and he flees for safety to Venice, where he is murdered, his body ignominiously tossed into a canal. The play concludes with the installation of Cosimo de Medici on the ducal throne, thus squelching once again any hope for the reinstitution of the Republic; Lorenzo's predictions have been borne out.

One of the extraordinary aspects of Musset's play is that it is largely accurate historically. At the beginning of their affair in the summer of 1833, George Sand turned over to Musset the manuscript of a *scène historique* concerning Lorenzo's plot. The *scène historique* was a popular form, derived from the more full-blown historical drama, which aimed at the straightforward dramatization of historical events as they happened, without artistic elaboration. Musset used this work as the foundation for a much larger concept, considerably expanding the number of characters and scenes, thoroughly researching the events and correcting Sand's inaccuracies, giving a sense of private lives and psychological depth to his characters, and, finally, centering the action on Lorenzo.

Most impressive is the play's pervasive Shakespearean scope and spirit. There are many echoes of the great tragedies (such as *Macbeth*, pr. 1606, pb. 1623, and *Othello, the Moor of Venice*, pr. 1604, revised 1623) in the language, themes, and dramatic situations of *Lorenzaccio*. The most obvious is the theme of action (and its antithesis, inaction), clearly derived from *Hamlet, Prince of Denmark* (pr. c. 1600-1601), which runs throughout the play, from Lorenzo's philosophical and practical hesitations to the cowardly compliance of the Florentine citizens. Intimately bound up in this theme are the themes of the significance of action and the illusion of human ideals. Lorenzo is the quintessentially disillusioned man, and the collective disillusionment of the Florentines is brilliantly sketched in the numerous street exchanges among members of the city's aristocracy and business community. The ultimate disillusionment of the almost allegorically positivistic Philippe Strozzi, occurring at the murder of his daughter, is conveyed with a telling sense of poignant dramatic effect. The pattern of failed ideals filters down even to characters who appear only once or twice.

One example of the way in which Musset utilizes a minor character and scene to add thematic resonance occurs in the second scene of act 2, in which Lorenzo, in the company of Cardinal Valori, encounters a young painter, Tebaldeo Freccia. Tebaldeo admits that in the presence of such masters as Raphael and Michelangelo his own stature is small indeed. Lorenzo is moved by Tebaldeo's humility and instantly recognizes a fraternity between himself and the painter who can only partially realize his vision. The theme of the artist who attempts to reorder the world in the act of creation is a mirroring of Lorenzo's attempt to reorder the political world of Florence. Like Tebaldeo, Lorenzo will immediately sense the limitations of his creative act after completing Alexandre's murder. The failure of art is inherent in the larger theme of disillusionment in human action.

In the end, corruption, not virtue, appears to be humankind's natural state; Musset's vision of human progress and perfectability is unmitigatedly dark. Lorenzo does "define" himself by his one fatal act, but, paradoxically, the definition gives no meaning to anyone or anything outside himself. The reinstatement of Medici control over the city argues the essential meaninglessness of history and of the sum of individual and collective experience. The definition endowed by action is the most for which the individual can hope. It is not difficult, in this regard, to understand the interest stirred by the play among the existentialist writers of the years surrounding World War II. The play is not without its faults: In structure, dialogue, and thematic statement, it has been accused of long-windedness and repetition. Nevertheless, its largely successful attempts to contain the vastness of life within the scope of its broad canvas as well as the brilliant characterization of the title role make *Lorenzaccio* the preeminent example of romantic historical drama.

OTHER MAJOR WORKS

LONG FICTION: *La Confession d'un enfant du siècle*, 1836 (*The Confession of a Child of the Century*, 1892).

SHORT FICTION: *Les Deux Maîtresses*, 1837 (*Two Mistresses*, 1905); *Emmeline*, 1837 (English translation, 1905); *Le Fils du Titien*, 1838 (*Titian's Son*, 1892); *Frédéric et Bernerette*, 1838 (*Frederic and Bernerette*, 1892); *Margot*, 1838 (English translation, 1905); *Histoire d'un merle blanc*, 1842 (*Adventures of a White Blackbird*, 1892); *Pierre et Camille*, 1843 (*Pierre and Camille*, 1905); *Le Secret de Javotte*, 1844 (*Secret of Javotte*, 1905); *Les Frères Van Buck*, 1844; *Mimi Pinson*, 1845; *La Mouche*, 1854 (*The Beauty Spot*, 1892).

POETRY: *Contes d'Espagne et d'Italie*, 1829 (*Tales of Spain and Italy*, 1905); *Un Spectacle dans un fauteuil*, 1833 (first series, 2 volumes; *A Performance in an Armchair*, 1905); *Rolla*, 1833 (English translation, 1905); *Poésies complètes*, 1840 (*Complete Poetry*, 1905); *Poésies nouvelles*, 1852 (*New Poetic Works*; definitive edition in *The Complete Writings*); *Premières poésies*, 1852 (*First Poetic Works*; definitive edition in *The Complete Writings*).

TRANSLATION: *L'Anglais mangeur d'opium*, 1828 (of Thomas de Quincey's *Confessions of an English Opium Eater*, 1821).

MISCELLANEOUS: *The Complete Writings*, 1905 (10 volumes).

BIBLIOGRAPHY

Bishop, Lloyd. *The Poetry of Alfred de Musset: Styles and Genres*. New York: Peter Lang, 1987. Although this work focuses on Musset's poetry, it provides valuable information on his life and literary output. Bibliography and index.

Kelly, Linda. *The Young Romantics: Victor Hugo, Sainte-Beuve, Vigny, Dumas, Musset, and George Sand and Their Friendships, Feuds, and Loves in the French Romantic Revolution.* New York: Random House, 1976. Kelly examines the French Romanticists, including Musset, Victor Hugo, Charles Augustin Sainte-Beuve, Alfred de Vigny, and George Sand, and their intellectual world. Bibliography and index.

Levin, Susan M. *The Romantic Art of Confession: De Quincey, Musset, Sand, Lamb, Hogg, Frémy, Soulié.* Columbia, S.C.: Camden House, 1998. Levin's work on the confession literature of Romanticists such as Musset, Thomas De Quincey, James Hogg, George Sand, and Charles Lamb sheds light on the life of Musset, as revealed in his semiautobiographical novel. Bibliography and index.

Rees, Margaret A. *Alfred de Musset.* New York: Twayne, 1971. A basic biography of Musset, covering his life and works. Bibliography.

Sices, David. *Theatre of Solitude: The Drama of Musset.* Hanover, N.H.: University Press of New England, 1974. Musset translator and scholar Sices provides a close look at the dramatic works of the French writer. Contains a bibliography and index.

Theodore Baroody

N

GNAEUS NAEVIUS

Born: Ancient Capua (now in Italy); c. 270 B.C.E.
Died: Utica, North Africa (now in Tunisia);
  c. 201 B.C.E.

PRINCIPAL DRAMA

COMEDIES

Acontizomenos, c. 250-205 B.C.E. (*Speared*)

Agitatoria, c. 250-205 B.C.E. (*The Driver's Play*)

Ariolus, c. 250-205 B.C.E. (*The Soothsayer*)

Agrypnuntes, c. 250-205 B.C.E. (*Wide-awakes*)

Appella, c. 250-205 B.C.E. (*The Circumcised*)

Carbonaria, c. 250-205 B.C.E. (*The Collier Maid*)

Clamidaria, c. 250-205 B.C.E. (*The Cloak*)

Colax, c. 250-205 B.C.E. (*The Flatterer*)

Corollaria, c. 250-205 B.C.E. (*The Garland Seller*)

Dementes, c. 250-205 B.C.E. (*The Madmen*)

Demetrius, c. 250-205 B.C.E.

Dolus, c. 250-205 B.C.E. (*The Fraud*)

Figulus, c. 250-205 B.C.E. (*The Potter*)

Glaucoma, c. 250-205 B.C.E. (*Cataract*)

Gymnasticus, c. 250-205 B.C.E. (*The Gym-Teacher*)

Lampadio, c. 250-205 B.C.E.

Leon, c. 250-205 B.C.E.

Nautae, c. 250-205 B.C.E. (*The Sailors*)

Personata, c. 250-205 B.C.E. (*A Masked Play*)

Proiectus, c. 250-205 B.C.E. (*The Outcast*)

Quadrigemini, c. 250-205 B.C.E. (*The Quadruplets*)

Stalagmus, c. 250-205 B.C.E.

Stigmatias, c. 250-205 B.C.E. (*The Branded Slave*)

Tarentilla, c. 250-205 B.C.E. (*The Girl from Tarentus*)

Technicus, c. 250-205 B.C.E. (*The Charlatan*)

Testicularia, c. 250-205 B.C.E. (*A Play About Testicles*)

Triphallus, c. 250-205 B.C.E.

Tunicularia, c. 250-205 B.C.E. (*The Little Tunic*)

TRAGEDIES

Andromacha, c. 250-205 B.C.E. (*Andromache*)

Danae, c. 250-205 B.C.E.

Equos Troianus, c. 250-205 B.C.E. (*The Trojan Horse*)

Hector proficiscens, c. 250-205 B.C.E. (*Hector's Departure*)

Hesiona, c. 250-205 B.C.E. (*Hesione*)

Iphigenia, c. 250-205 B.C.E.

Lycurgus, c. 250-205 B.C.E.

HISTORICAL

Clastidium, c. 250-205 B.C.E.

Romulus: Sive, Lupus, c. 250-205 B.C.E. (*Romulus: Or, The Wolf*)

Remains of Old Latin, pb. 1935-1940 (E. H. Warmington, editor; contains English translations of proceeding plays)

OTHER LITERARY FORMS

Gnaeus Naevius created a Roman national epic with his poem in Saturnian verse, the *Bellum Punicum* (c. 250-205 B.C.E.; *The Punic War*, 1935-1940). He also authored the historical epic *Annales* (c. 250-205 B.C.E.; *Annals*, 1935-1940).

ACHIEVEMENTS

In the *Bellum Punicum*, Gnaeus Naevius claimed to have fought with distinction in the First Punic War. Testimony that he made this statement comes through Varro, who quoted Naevius, and Gellius, who quoted Varro. Even so, a greater achievement was the new life Naevius brought to the Roman stage. Naevius followed Livius Andronicus, enlivening Roman drama considerably, in part through what Terence called his *neglegentia*. Terence's use of the word "carelessness" probably refers to Naevius's willingness to modify the Greek originals from which he worked.

It is also likely that Naevius invented the poetic form known as the *fabula praetexta* or *praetextata*. The *toga praetexta* was the purple-bordered toga worn by Roman magistrates as a mark of their office, and correspondingly the *fabulae praetextae* were plays with characters drawn from Roman history or myth who might have worn such a toga. The effect gave antiquity to such Roman customs, for Romulus would wear the gown of a Roman senator.

Similarly, such dress allowed references to other customs. In a fragment from the *Clastidium* (which probably dealt with the Roman victory there in 222 B.C.E.), there is a reference to the triumph that the hero can expect when he returns to his native land. Though some critics maintain that Naevius also invented the form known as the *fabula Atellana* (a series of verse jokes exchanged as banter between two actors) and the *fabulae togatae* (comedy on Italian themes), there is no evidence that he did so. Reliable arguments trace the *Atellanae* to Oscan sources.

Naevius was the pioneer of the Roman national epic, a form that Vergil would use in writing the *Aeneid* (29-19 B.C.E.; English translation, 1553). Like the *Aeneid*, Naevius's *Bellum Punicum* established the antiquity of Roman origins, tracing the city's legendary connections to Aeneas's flight from Troy and his establishment of a Trojan settlement in Italy; unlike Vergil's elegant poem, however, the *Bellum Punicum*, to judge from the fragments that remain, was close stylistically to the prose chronicles of the Roman analyst historians. The poem originally formed a continuous whole, but Suetonius reports that it was subsequently divided into seven books by the scholar Octavius Lampadio. The main body of the poem, telling of the First Punic War, was preceded by a lengthy recounting of legendary history starting with Aeneas.

Though Naevius wrote imitations of Greek tragedies, as did the other Roman dramatists, his play *Romulus* treated the youth of Romulus and Remus, and his *Clastidium* a contemporary historical event. He was, then, the first Roman dramatist to adapt native materials to a literary form specifically Greek.

BIOGRAPHY

Because Gnaeus Naevius fought in the First Punic War (264-241 B.C.E.), he could not have been born much later than 260 B.C.E. The second century C.E. commentator Aulus Gellius, in *Noctes Atticae* (c. 180 C.E.; *Attic Nights*, 1927), records Naevius's prideful and possibly self-composed epitaph, in which he declares that the Muses themselves weep for him, if deities ever mourn for human beings, for his death signals the end of the true Latin language in Rome. Gellius remarks that the epitaph is filled with Campanian pride, and this remark has been used to support the traditionally held view that Naevius's birthplace was in Campania. It consequently seems reasonable to assume that Naevius came from that region's principal town, Capua, which prided itself on its ancient origins. There is no firm evidence that the epitaph was self-composed, however, and Gellius's comment simply follows the tradition, firmly established even in his own time, that Campania was Naevius's birthplace.

It is clear, however, that Naevius became proficient in the Latin language relatively early in his life and that he came to see himself as an urbane man whose personal interests were identifiable with those of Rome itself. His literary output indicates his special interest in Roman historical and political affairs, and from his own testimony in his *Bellum Punicum* it is clear that he fought in the First Punic War.

The Punic War took Naevius to Sicily, called Magna Graecia by the Romans because of its extensive Greek settlements, and it was there that he was able to see Greek life at first hand, as well as the permanent stone theaters built in Greek style where the plays of Greek dramatists were given. This is not to imply that his experiences in Sicily were pleasure-filled. High-level incompetence and poor treatment of the common soldiers by their commanders were rife, and it may be that Naevius developed even this early in his life the sharp wit that appeared in his plays.

Two important events occurred in 235 B.C.E.: Spurius Carvilius Ruga became the first Roman to divorce his wife, and Naevius presented his first play at the public games. There is a stronger connection between these two events than there would at first appear to be, for Romans traditionally maintained the sanctity and permanence of the marriage vow just as they frowned on publicly sponsored drama. That both things happened in the same year indicates an increasing willingness to accept Greek institutions and practices. By the time of Plautus, marriage itself would become acceptable matter for ridicule in Roman comedy.

Naevius, however, pursued his career in the theater by continuing to adapt Greek originals. Indeed, he was to do so for the next thirty years, though he managed, as his predecessor Livius Andronicus never had, to infuse a distinctly Roman tone into his works. In addition to beginning the practice of staging historical dramas in Roman dress (*fabulae praetextae*), he began to lampoon the aristocracy. His attacks on a wealthy and powerful consular family, the Metelli, were so sharp that he was brought up on charges under the provision of the ancient code of the Twelve Tables, which required capital punishment for those found guilty of slander.

Even politics was a forbidden subject. Public allusions to contemporary political matters were punishable by flogging, and Naevius might have suffered this punishment. Plautus reports the flogging of "a foreign poet" in lines 210-211 of *Miles Gloriosus* (*The Braggart Warrior*, 1767); and Festus, a grammarian of the third century C.E., maintains that this man was Gnaeus Naevius. Gellius notes that Naevius was imprisoned for his stage attacks and wrote recantations into two plays, *Ariolus* and *Leon*, which brought his release. Saint Jerome claims that the Metelli and others he had attacked exiled Naevius to Utica in North Africa and that he died there in 201. Cicero, in *Brutus* (46 B.C.E.; English translation, 1776), though he says nothing about either the imprisonment or exile, gives 204 as the date of Naevius's death. To accept 204 as the date of death, however, makes it impossible to maintain that Naevius died at Utica, for Scipio's siege of that city ended only in the year 202. Although some modern scholarship sets forth the year 199, the commonly accepted year of death is 201.

ANALYSIS

Although little of his work actually survives, it is clear that Gnaeus Naevius was a prolific dramatist.

Nearly forty titles have been attributed to him, and assuming that they were all his, this would mean that he wrote more than one play each year during his theatrical career. If one can judge reliably based on the meager fragments, independence and free speech were his recurring themes. Several of his comedies, given their outrageous titles (*Cataract, A Play About Testicles, Triphallus*) no doubt brought unconventional subject matter to the stage, and the very number of his comedies, when considered against a mere seven tragedies, implies that he found in comedy a greater opportunity for innovation. The tragedies, no matter what innovations Naevius might have introduced in meter or detail, were essentially adaptations, translations based on Greek originals. It is logical that his ingenuity and patriotism would lead him to create his historical dramas in Roman dress, and though only two of these titles remain, they likely constituted the most significant dramatic contribution he made to Roman drama.

Stylistically, his plays had the strong bias toward rhetorical effects which Romans would continue to admire in the works of Quintus Ennius. Both Cicero and Seneca quote a heavily alliterated line from *Hector's Departure* drawn from Hector's farewell to his father Priam. Although it is difficult to be certain on the basis of one line, Naevius's Hector appears to have an almost consular nobility in this scene, fighting for his city rather than for personal glory. Cicero also quotes Lycurgus's ornate words to his bodyguard. His guard is called "custodian of the royal person" (*regalis corporis custodias*), the forest "branch-bearing groves" (*frundiferos locos*) where trees unsown grow "by skill" (*ingenio*). Such rhetoric, while somewhat precious and perhaps overdone by classical standards, shows that Naevius was experimenting, even in his tragedies, to create a literary Latin language.

Comedy provided an even greater opportunity for innovation. Although the characters of the fragments are derived from the stock plots of Greek New Comedy, Naevius clearly chose plots into which he could infuse distinctly Italian references and points of view. He depended on topical puns and political allusions to make the plays his own. Titles such as *The Soothsayer, The Collier Maid,* and *The Garland Seller* imply that the characters of these plays were colorful commoners. The discussion of the cuisine of Praeneste and Lanuvium (boiled pig's stomach and nuts) which survives from the *Ariolus* (Loeb fragments 22-26) illustrates the broad localized tone which Naevius brought to his Greek plots. In *The Little Tunic*, the largest fragment (Loeb 97-100) mentions the Compitalia (the crossroads festival) and the Lares (Roman household gods).

Though Tarentum was a Greek colony and though Naevius's *The Girl from Tarentus* probably derives from a lost Greek original by Alexis, Naevius could have assumed that many former soldiers in his audience knew the place and what many Romans viewed as its degeneracy. Indeed, his tale of two young men "on the town" in Tarnetum probably had a familiar ring. Terence, the Roman playwright, reports that *The Flatterer*, a play from Menander's original, was translated by Plautus and Naevius. This could imply two plays, or it might mean a Plautine reworking of the original play. In either case, it indicates the affinity between the two Roman comedians.

The fragments allow only brief remarks about plot lines and characterizations. Does the *Appella* concern a circumcised man (*a pellis*), a Jew, or possibly a woman from Apulia? Evidently, *Wide-awakes* concerned a gang of street thieves, while *Speared* was a murder play, presenting a hero who was wrongly accused of fratricide. Courtesans and pimps, wise slaves and foolish masters, young lovers and hopeless love ultimately realized—this is the stuff of Naevius's comedies. It would find its fullest development in Plautus and Terence.

OTHER MAJOR WORKS
POETRY: *Bellum Punicum*, c. 250-205 B.C.E. (*The Punic War*, 1935-1940).
HISTORICAL EPIC: *Annales*, c. 250-205 B.C.E. (*Annals*, 1935-1940).

BIBLIOGRAPHY
Goldberg, Sander M. *Epic in Republican Rome*. New York: Oxford University Press, 1995. Goldberg's study of the epic in Republican Rome touches on Naevius.
Gruen, Erich S. *Studies in Greek Culture and Roman Policy*. Berkeley: University of California Press, 1996. This study on the ancient Greeks and Romans provides insight into Naevius's life and works.
Rowell, H. T. "The Original Form of Naevius's *Bellum Punicum*." *American Journal of Philology* 68 (1947): 21-46. Although this article focuses on Naevius's *The Punic War*, it provides some insight into this dramatist's life and other works.

Robert J. Forman

THOMAS NASHE

Born: Lowestoft, Surrey, England; November, 1567
Died: Yarmouth(?), England; 1601

PRINCIPAL DRAMA
Dido, Queen of Carthage, pr. c. 1586-1587, pb. 1594 (with Christopher Marlowe)
Summer's Last Will and Testament, pr. 1592, pb. 1600
The Isle of Dogs, pr. 1597 (with Ben Jonson; no longer extant)

OTHER LITERARY FORMS
Thomas Nashe was primarily a pamphlet writer, although he wrote a work of long fiction (*The Unfortunate Traveller: Or, The Life of Jack Wilton*, 1594), a long poem (*The Choise of Valentines*, 1899), and several songs and sonnets in addition to the plays listed above.

ACHIEVEMENTS
Thomas Nashe was best known during his own day as the writer of pamphlets, who used lively rhe-

Thomas Nashe (Hulton Archive by Getty Images)

the story of a young page who, after serving in the army of King Henry VIII, travels to Europe to find a means of earning a living. The underworld realism that Nashe presents in his descriptions of Jack Wilton's escapades has earned him a reputation for being more than a mere pamphleteer, a hurler of invective. The book is not a unified work of art; its characters, other than Jack himself, are not particularly memorable. Its descriptions of the harshest elements of human life, such as disease, hunger, torture, rape, and murder, place it in stark contrast to the sweet absurdities of romance; it thus shows the way to the modern novel.

BIOGRAPHY

Thomas Nashe was born in November, 1567, the second son of William Nashe, a minister in Lowestoft, moving in 1573 to West Harling in Norfolk, where his father took up the duties of rector. There Nashe likely remained until he left for Cambridge in 1581 or 1582.

R. B. McKerrow and others have suggested that young Nashe's early education was probably accomplished at home with his father as tutor, a likely suggestion because no suitable school existed in West Harling. Wherever he acquired his schooling, it was of such quality as to allow young Nashe to enter St. John's College, Cambridge, where, as Nashe himself later wrote in *Nashe's Lenten Stuffe* (1599), *Have with You to Saffron-Walden* (1596), and the preface to Robert Greene's *Menaphon* (1589), he did well in his studies and enjoyed the academic life. Although he complained that the curriculum at Cambridge was weighted too heavily toward vague theology and too little toward the ancient philosophers, he nevertheless praised St. John's and was proud of his college's reputation for sound scholarship. The Puritan influence at Cambridge, with its emphasis on utilitarian training rather than on Humanistic inquiry, did not please the inquisitive Nashe.

Nashe received his bachelor's degree from Cambridge in 1586 and left school in 1588 without taking his master's degree. Whether he ended his education because he lacked funds to continue (his father had

torical devices, a ready wit, and outrageous personal attacks to get the better of the pompous scholar Gabriel Harvey. Harvey, who took himself and his ideas seriously, was no match for Nashe, the young University Wit who used words as a soldier did a rapier. The attacks that Nashe leveled at the Puritans have none of the romantic niceties of Thomas Lodge, the euphuistic panegyrics of John Lyly, or the literary balance of Thomas Deloney: His language is direct, stark, without pedantry. Nashe offers no pleasant dialogues or polite deviations. When Harvey suggested a truce in the war of words between Nashe and him, Nashe responded that he would make "Uncessant warres with waspes and droons," and he dismissed Harvey simply as a dunce. The magnificent invective found in the speeches of William Shakespeare's Falstaff, Prince Hal, and (especially) Kent was almost certainly derived from the monstrous hyperbole and the extravagant vituperation Nashe hurled at his adversaries.

Among modern students of literature, Nashe is remembered for his most unusual work, the picaresque novel of adventure *The Unfortunate Traveller*. It tells

died in 1587) or because he did not fit well into the Puritan narrowness at the school is not clear, but it is clear from his comments in *The Anatomie of Absurditie* (1589) that he thought Cambridge had failed him.

Leaving Cambridge with no resources but a ready wit, Nashe followed the lead of fellow University Wits Robert Greene and Christopher Marlowe by moving to London to attempt to support himself as a professional writer. Nashe may have been acquainted with both Greene and Marlowe at Cambridge; it is certain that he knew both in London. Like Nashe, both loved poetry and detested Puritans. In the same year that he left Cambridge, Nashe published *The Anatomie of Absurditie*, a dull, preachy work reflecting his inexperience and brashness. Nashe's intent was to use the satiric pamphlet form against the satiric pamphlets of the Puritans, chiefly against Philip Stubbs's *The Anatomie of Abuses* (1583), but his fervor to condemn the lack of learning and discrimination shown in the narrow Puritan tracts blossomed into a general diatribe against bad books, bad science, bad poetry (generally that produced by the ballad-mongers), bad actions, bad thinking—bad everything. The result was that in trying to accomplish too much, he succeeded in accomplishing nothing much.

Many of Nashe's early works were dedicated to various personages of noble birth, the hope clearly being that the noble person might like the quality of the work, be flattered, and be moved to reward the young writer. *The Anatomie of Absurditie* was dedicated to Sir Charles Blount, who, perhaps seeing that the work had little intrinsic value, offered Nashe no support. As a young writer struggling to sustain life while he earned his reputation, Nashe needed patrons. He dedicated several of his pamphlets to a variety of people in a position to offer him assistance, but he never found much support for his work from among nobility. Finally, after the dedication of *The Unfortunate Traveller* to Henry Wriothesley, earl of Southampton, Nashe decided that patrons were more trouble than they were worth. Hating hypocrisy in others and finding himself forced into hypocrisy in order to be paid for his work, Nashe turned to writing only for his middle-class readers and depending on them to reward his efforts.

What gave Nashe's literary career its largest boost was neither patrons nor the excellence of his ideas. What gave him the chance to display his vigorous style of writing and gained for him public attention was the famous Martin Marprelate controversy. The controversy, which was begun by a Puritan attack against the Anglican Church, centered on whether the Church should be ruled by a hierarchy of bishops or by the preachers. From the beginning, with the publication in 1572 of the Puritan pamphlet *Admonition to Parliament*, the Puritans had had the better of the argument, especially after an unusually gifted writer entered the lists on the side of the Puritans. This author, unfortunately but necessarily anonymous, called himself Martin Marprelate and wrote some eight pamphlets that effectively routed the less lively, less witty apologists for the Anglicans.

Nashe entered the lists against Martin on behalf of (and probably hired by) the prelates, writing *An Almond for a Parrat* (1590). Using the same type of invective, parody, hyperbole, and specious logic used by Martin, Nashe portrayed his adversary as a hypocrite, a heretic, and a traitor, an attack that drew a response from Gabriel Harvey, a friend of Edmund Spenser who, unlike Martin, was not anonymous, not without influence, and not as capable a writer as Nashe. It was in this battle of wits that Nashe found his place as a writer, low though the place was. Here the verbal street-fighter had the great good fortune to be attacked by a man of reputation who was his inferior both in wit and in writing ability. Beginning with a slap at Harvey in his preface to Greene's *A Quip for an Upstart Courtier* (1592) and ending with *Have with You to Saffron-Walden*, Nashe earned a reputation and a fair living from his anti-Harvey prose. Finally, in 1599, Archbishop of Canterbury John Whitgift ordered a halt to future writings by both men and confiscated their existing works.

Nashe's most important work is a picaresque novel published in 1594, *The Unfortunate Traveller*. A kind of pamphlet itself, but longer and more complex, the work was not particularly popular during his lifetime, but today it is his best-known work.

Nashe left London in 1597 when the authorities decided that *The Isle of Dogs*, a play he had begun and which Ben Jonson had finished, was "seditious." Jonson was jailed and Nashe sought, but the famous pamphleteer had fled to Yarmouth, in Norfolk. By 1598 or early 1599, he had returned to London, where *Nashe's Lenten Stuffe* was entered in the Stationers' Register. After *Nashe's Lenten Stuffe*, Nashe wrote no more, and in 1601 history records a reference to his death.

ANALYSIS

As a young man who chose to make his living as a writer, Thomas Nashe would almost certainly have tried his hand at drama. With the strong traditions of native English drama at his back, classical drama in his brain, and Renaissance hybrid drama daily before his eyes, Nashe could hardly have escaped the temptation to enter the field. His contributions to dramatic literature are not as plentiful as those to prose, nor perhaps as plentiful as he might have wished. Evidence indicates that Nashe participated to a greater or lesser extent in the writing of five plays.

Nashe's first experience with drama probably occurred while he was at Cambridge. A contemporary of his wrote that Nashe "had a hand in a show called *Terminus et non terminus*," but neither the play nor the extent of Nashe's participation in it is known. The next reference connecting Nashe to drama was made by Nashe's friend Robert Greene. In *Greene's Groatsworth of Wit Bought with a Million of Repentance* (1592), Greene draws a comparison between Christopher Marlowe and "yong *Iuvenall*, that byting satyrist, that lastly with mee together writ a comedie." Because Nashe had been closely associated with Greene and because he best fits the description that Greene gives, most scholars believe that Nashe is "yong *Iuvenall*." Which of Greene's plays received Nashe's contribution is not clear, although some scholars offer *A Knack to Know a Knave* (pr. 1592) as a possibility. There is no evidence, however, to lead to any definite conclusion. The third play with which Nashe is connected is *Dido, Queen of Carthage*. Although the title page lists "Christopher Marlowe, and Thomas Nash, Gent." as authors, most scholars believe from internal evidence that Nashe had little if any part in the authorship. A final play, also co-authored, this time with Ben Jonson, was presented in 1597. *The Isle of Dogs*, no text of which is extant, was reported to the Privy Council as being "a lewd plaie . . . contanyng very seditious and sclanderous matter." An order was issued to prohibit the play's being acted, and warrants were issued for the arrests of both Nashe and Jonson. Nashe, who later wrote that he had "begun but the induction and first act of it" and was unaware of what was added without his consent later, fled London and escaped prosecution. Jonson, on the other hand, was jailed.

SUMMER'S LAST WILL AND TESTAMENT

It is Nashe's fourth try at drama that survives in full and from Nashe alone. *Summer's Last Will and Testament* was published in 1600, but it was almost certainly written and presented in 1592 at the home of Archbishop Whitgift in Croydon. Written not for the public but for a private audience and a special occasion, *Summer's Last Will and Testament* shows little of what Nashe might have accomplished had he attempted a complete drama in the tradition of Thomas Kyd, Marlowe, Shakespeare, Jonson, and others. Nashe himself distinguishes between regular English drama and his work by including in his prologue the assertion "nay, 'tis no play neither, but a show," and truly the work is more in the form of a seasonal pageant than a play. Nashe's pageant is in the form of a debate, or a series of debates, and therefore *Summer's Last Will and Testament* is not far removed from the style of his pamphlets.

Written almost certainly to be performed by amateur players as informal entertainment at the home of Archbishop Whitgift, *Summer's Last Will and Testament* treats two themes (with the usual digressions that help identify Nashe's style): the hot summer just drawing to a close and the plague then devastating London. Will Summers, the famous jester of Henry VIII, is cast as narrator, chorus, and general analyst of the proceedings, serving as Nashe's apologist for the light content of the pageant. In a self-deprecating vein, Nashe has Will reflect on the suitability of having a famous jester as commentator for this particular drama: "One fool presents another; and I, a fool by nature and by art, do speak to you in the person of the idiot our playmaker." In answer to his own question about the significance of the ideas in the work, Will remarks, "Deep-reaching wits, here is no deep stream for you to angle in." After he delivers the "scurvey Prologue" Nashe wrote for him, a speech Will criticizes regularly while delivering it, he decides to stick around to "flout the actors and him [Nashe] at the end of every scene." Almost true to his word (he rarely waits until the end of scene to comment), Will Summers condemns the ideas, language, and acting throughout the work.

Will Summers's denigrating comments are the best part, except for an occasional excellent lyric poem, of an otherwise dull drama. After an overly long speech early in the first scene on the subject of begging, Will swears that it was as boring as a sermon: "So we come here to laugh and be merry, and we hear a filthy beggarly oration in the praise of beggary. It is a beggarly poet that writ it." "This play," he says, "is a gullimaufry," an absurd mixture—and indeed it is.

As the action continues, Will Summers becomes less intrusive, probably because he is bored to sleep, but he still interrupts every scene with his witty comments. The work consists, after the introductory comments and prologue, of ten scenes and an epilogue. The central character, Lord Summer (a personification of the season, not to be confused with Will Summers) appears in each scene, his purpose to interview his "officers" to determine what is left of the wealth he gave to them. With the help of Vertumnus (god of the changing seasons), Summer questions and argues with Autumn, Winter, Ver (spring), Solstitium (solstice), Sol (sun), Orion, Harvest, Bacchus and his companions, and Christmas and Backwinter (sons of Winter). Various Morris dancers, clowns, and maids round out the *dramatis personae*.

Lord Summer enters, supported by Winter and Autumn. In attendance are satyrs and wood nymphs, who sing the song "Fayre Summer Droops," a conventional lament on the passing of summer, which helps to set the elegiac theme of the entire work. Summer reinforces the theme by pronouncing his own impending death and seeking to settle his affairs by calling his "officers" to account for how they have used what Summer gave them.

Ver enters, accompanied by singers and dancers, and announces to old Summer, "What I had I have spent on good fellows, in these sports you have seen, which are proper to the spring, and others of like sort—as giving wenches green gowns, making garlands for fencers, and tricking up children gay." Summer condemns Ver as a "monstrous unthrift," but Ver fortunately has Nashe to help him defend himself and therefore builds a magnificent argument using appeals to authority and to nature in praise of begging. Considering his servant prodigal, dying Summer announces that Ver shall hereafter always be accompanied by Lent, whose "scarcity may countervail thy waste."

Solstitium enters next, an old hermit carrying a set of balance scales. Representing the summer solstice, the one day when the sun appears balanced before it starts its southward journey, Solstitium is the golden mean, and he gains moralizing Summer's unqualified approval: "I like thy moderation wonderous well," says Summer. "A pattern is to princes and great men." Both Summer and Solstitium give sage advice, but neither is as witty as Ver—or, for that matter, as witty as Sol, Orion, Harvest, or Bacchus, who follow.

Sol is accused by Autumn of wronging Daphne by descending "to Thetis' lap," but Sol defends himself admirably in lyric blank verse. Orion and his huntsmen are called next to be condemned by Autumn for causing unhealthy days: The hunting dogs that Orion leads cause the season's dog days. Orion, Nashe-like, accepts the challenge to debate and presents an excellent defense of dogs, "proving" quite beyond doubt that dogs are the rarest of creatures. Harvest, who enters next, is accused by Summer of hoarding and selfishness. After merely singing several merry songs as a response, Harvest effectively defends his selflessness, his liberality. Bacchus enters extolling the virtues of drink, asking Winter and Summer to drink with him. When they refuse, Bacchus turns to Will Summers, who accepts and is dubbed Sir Robert Toss-pot. Bacchus happily uses Plato and Aristotle to support his praise of wine. Disgusted, Lord Summer says, "no more of this. I hate it to the death," and has Bacchus removed.

Announcing that "worse servants no man hath,"

Summer is ready to resign his crown in favor of Autumn. Winter complains in the classical Nashe fashion of misapplied learning that autumn is the favorite time of useless scholars, poets, and philosophers. Winter/Nashe's use of learning to condemn learning is, as G. R. Hibbard points out, reminiscent of the king in Shakespeare's *Love's Labour's Lost* (pr. c. 1594-1595), who comments on Berowne's similar argument by saying, "How well he's read to reason against reasoning." Summer, to quiet Winter, makes him Autumn's guardian, but now Autumn complains that Winter's two sons, Christmas and Backwinter, are so horrible that Winter deserves no consideration. Called to appear before Summer, Christmas and Backwinter prove to be at least as bad as Autumn had suggested. Christmas enters with no music, declaring that he believes hospitality to be out of date and downright sinful. Backwinter rudely threatens to be worse than Winter. They are both ordered out by Summer.

Left then to the business of his last will and testament, Summer itemizes his effects: his crown, flowers, long days, short nights, and the like. Announcing "here Summer ends," old Summer is carried out by the singing satyrs and woodnymphs who brought him in.

The plot of *Summer's Last Will and Testament* is, as has been shown, slight. Will Summers puts it quite completely in one sentence of the prologue: "Summer must come in sick; he must call his officers to account, yield his throne to Autumn, make Winter his executor, with tittle tattle Tom boy." The characters, whom Hibbard sees as individualized rather than "mere allegorical ghosts," are still little more than figures for the witty arguments of Nashe. Summer is facing death, but he has not the stature to be an emblem for humanity. When Nashe brings his audience to face death, it is by means of his excellent lyric poem "Song: Adieu, farewell earths blisse," not by means of old Summer. Summer is himself moved to awareness by the song.

The pageant presented by Nashe as entertainment at Croydon is witty enough, moral enough, and properly debunked by Will Summers. The arguments offered in their own defense by the various servants of Summer, because they include topical subjects, personal references to members of the audience, and displays of learning and rhetorical devices, would surely have pleased the audience for whom they were presented. Such characters as Ver, Orion, and Bacchus provide the same kind of diversion as did the holiday Lord of Misrule in their unpragmatic actions and sophistic defenses of those actions. Summer offers the proper social balance with his moral objections to misrule, but, in the hands of the anti-Puritan Nashe, Summer never becomes so dull a moralizer as to become a churl. The play is unified, consistent, and complete—an evening's pleasant entertainment. It would not have been a success on the London stage, but Nashe did not have that audience in mind when he wrote the play.

Some elements of general social interest to a modern audience are included in *Summer's Last Will and Testament*. The representation of Christmas, for example, as an inhospitable churl points to a significant problem in sixteenth century England—the decline of the community-based system with the introduction of free enterprise. A subject addressed most clearly during Nashe's time by Thomas Deloney, the lack of charity shown by people for their neighbors, was a problem addressed by many writers of the day, including Shakespeare and Nashe's friend Greene. Nashe has Christmas enter his pageant unaccompanied by festive music (or music of any kind). Christmas is against tradition, against authority, against enjoyment—in short, he is a Puritan. Like Shakespeare's Malvolio, Christmas, because he is virtuous, expects there to be no cakes and ale. Autumn calls him "a pinchbeck, cutthroat churl,/ That keepes no open house, as he should do,/ Delighteth in no game or fellowship,/ Loves no good deeds, and hateth talk." Harvest, the direct opposite of Christmas in the pageant, represents the discharge of social obligations. Harvest has distributed his crops equitably and with goodwill. He declares that he "keeps good hospitality" and presents good evidence of his claim. Persuaded, Summer praises Harvest above all of his servants.

Analysis of social problems, however, is not a major part of Nashe's pageant. If the social implications are slight, the personal reference narrow, and the arguments usually merely rhetorical, what is there to the pageant to interest someone other than an antiquarian? What pervades the work from beginning to end—sometimes relegated to the background, sometimes brought to the front—is the theme of impending death. The days are hot, the plague threatens each life, and summer is dying. The song that ushers old Summer onstage, "Fayre Summer Droops," raises the specters of tears, sorrow, and the grave. The song that leads Summer out announces the sad news that "short days, sharp days, long nights come on apace." Each of the two stanzas of that song, "Autumn hath all the summer's fruitful treasure," ends with the refrain, "From winter, plague, and pestilence, good Lord deliver us." As Summer dies, so must we all. Human weakness in the face of natural elements, a truth exhibited daily to Nashe and his audience at Croydon, is the theme of *Summer's Last Will and Testament.*

This theme is nowhere more apparent or more poignantly expressed than in what is generally considered to be the best of Nashe's lyrics, "Song: Adieu, farewell earths blisse," sung to the dying Summer by Will Summers. Nashe recognizes in the refrain that follows each of the six stanzas that he is sick, that he must die, and he prays: "Lord have mercy on us." In a logical development, Nashe first introduces the theme of the medieval morality play *Everyman*: "Fond are lifes lustful ioyes." In succeeding stanzas, he develops each of the "lustful ioyes" in turn. "Rich men" are warned not to trust in their wealth, "beauty" is revealed as transitory, "strength" is pictured surrendering to the grave, and "lust" is useless to dissuade Hell's executioner. In a very specific, orderly manner and in spare lines of iambic trimeter, Nashe presents the theme of the pageant: Man's death-lament and prayer for mercy. One stanza will show the strength of the whole poem:

> Beauty is but a flowre,
> Which wrinkles will deuoure,
> Brightnesse falls from the ayre,
> Queenes have died yong and faire,
> Dust hath closed Helen's eye.
> I am sick, I must dye:
> Lord, have mercy on vs.

OTHER MAJOR WORKS

LONG FICTION: *The Unfortunate Traveller: Or, The Life of Jack Wilton*, 1594 (includes poetry).

POETRY: *The Choise of Valentines*, 1899.

NONFICTION: Preface to Robert Greene's *Menaphon*, 1589; *The Anatomie of Absurditie*, 1589; *An Almond for a Parrat*, 1590; Preface to Sir Philip Sidney's *Astrophel and Stella*, 1591; *Pierce Penilesse, His Supplication to the Divell*, 1592 (includes poetry); Preface to Robert Greene's *A Quip for an Upstart Courtier*, 1592; *Strange News of the Intercepting of Certain Letters*, 1592 (includes poetry; also known as *The Four Letters Confuted*); *Christ's Tears over Jerusalem*, 1593; *The Terrors of the Night*, 1594; *Have with You to Saffron-Walden*, 1596; *Nashe's Lenten Stuffe*, 1599.

BIBLIOGRAPHY

Crewe, Jonathan V. *Unredeemed Rhetoric: Thomas Nashe and the Scandal of Authorship.* Baltimore, Md.: The Johns Hopkins University Press, 1982. A study of the conflict between orthodox values and a cynical perception of society's injustice and exploitation that cuts across Nashe's career, complicating and adding tension to his work. At all levels of discourse there is a split between the manifest rhetorical purpose and the latent anarchy of the language.

Hilliard, Stephen S. *The Singularity of Thomas Nashe.* Lincoln: University of Nebraska Press, 1986. Hilliard discusses the concept of "singularity," or individuality, in Nashe's life and work. In sixteenth century terms, Nashe's controversial standing as an author reflects, according to Hilliard, Elizabethan ambivalence about singularity, a quality both prized and condemned—a difference from, yet also a threat to, the social order. Nashe's singularity was both a literary goal and a condition forced on him by his estranged status.

Holbrook, Peter. *Literature and Degree in Renaissance England: Nashe, Bourgeois Tragedy, Shakespeare.* Newark: University of Delaware Press, 1994. Holbrook's study of Renaissance literature in England examines the works of Shakespeare and Nashe. Bibliography and index.

McGinn, Donald J. *Thomas Nashe*. Boston: Twayne, 1981. Contains insightful commentary on Nashe's life and works. Focuses on Nashe's works as portrayals of the various types of middle-class Londoners—their appearance, their manners, and their customs. Contains a bibliography, chronology, and appendix.

Nicholl, Charles. *A Cup of News: The Life of Thomas Nashe*. Boston: Routledge and Kegan Paul, 1984. Nashe's writings, according to Nicholl, offer a vividness of presentation that makes them perhaps more representative of Elizabethan England than

the works of almost any other writer. He goes on to say that this aspect of his work is partly why Nashe is described as a "pamphleteer" rather than an "author." Bibliography, illustrations, documents.

Nielson, James. *Unread Herrings: Thomas Nashe and the Prosaics of the Real*. New York: Peter Lang, 1993. This study examines Nashe's use of realism in his works. Bibliography.

Eugene P. Wright,
updated by Genevieve Slomski

JOHANN NESTROY

Born: Vienna, Austria; December 7, 1801
Died: Graz, Austria; May 25, 1862

Principal drama

Der Zelträger Papp, pr. 1827, pb. 1910 (adaptation of Hermann Herzenskron's *Die Heirat durch die Pferdekomödie*)

Der Tod am Hochzeitstage: Oder, Mann, Frau, Kind, pr. 1829

Nagerl und Handschuh: Oder, Die Schicksale der Familie Maxenfutsch, pr. 1832 (adaptation of Charles-Guillaume Étienne's *Cendrillon*)

Der böse Geist Lumpazivagabundus: Oder, Das liederliche Kleeblatt, pr., pb. 1833 (adaptation of Carl Weisflog's *Das grosse Los*)

Robert der Teuxel, pr. 1833 (adaptation of Giacomo Meyerbeer's *Robert le Diable*)

Die Familien Zwirn, Knieriem und Leim: Oder, Der Welt-Untergangs-Tag, pr. 1834

Weder Lorbeerbaum noch Bettelstab, pr. 1835 (adaptation of Karl von Holteis's *Lorbeerbaum und Bettelstab*)

Zu ebener Erde und im ersten Stock: Oder, Die Launen des Glücks, pr. 1835, pb. 1838

Eine Wohnung ist zu vermieten in der Stadt, Eine Wohnung ist zu verlassen in der Vorstadt, Eine

Wohnung samt Garten ist zu haben in Hietzing, pr. 1837

Das Haus der Temperamente, pr. 1837, pb. 1891

Der Färber und sein Zwillingsbruder, pr. 1840 (adaptation of Adolphe de Leuven and Leon Lherie's *Le Brasseur de Preston*)

Der Talisman: Oder, Die Schicksalsperücken, pr. 1840, pb. 1841 (adaptation of Charles Desiré Dupeuty and F. de Courcy's *Bonaventure; The Talisman: Or, The Wigs of Fate*, 1967)

Das Mädl aus der Vorstadt: Oder, Ehrlich währt am langsten, pr. 1840, pb. 1845 (adaptation of Paul de Kock and Charles-Victor Varin's *La Jolie Fille du faubourg*)

Einen Jux will er sich machen, pr. 1842, pb. 1844 (adaptation of John Oxenford's *A Day Well Spent: The Matchmaker*, 1957)

Liebesgeschichten und Heiratssachen, pr. 1843 (adaptation of John Poole's *Patrician and Parvenu: Or, Confusion Worse Confounded; Affairs and Wedding Bells*, 1967)

Der Zerrissene, pr. 1844, pb. 1845 (adaptation of Frédéric Auguste Duvert and Auguste Théodore Vaux-Roussel de Lauzanne's *L'homme blasé; A Man Full of Nothing*, 1967)

*Das Gewürzkrämerkleeblatt: Oder, Die
    unschuldigen Schuldigen*, pr. 1845 (adaptation
    of Joseph-Philippe Lockroy and Auguste
    Anicet-Bourgeois's *Les Ers*)
Unverhofft, pr. 1845, pb. 1848 (adaptation of Jean
    Bayard and Philippe Dumanoir's *Boquillon à la
    recherche d'un père*)
Der Unbedeutende, pr. 1846, pb. 1849
Die schlimmen Buben in der Schule, pr. 1847
    (adaptation of Lockroy and Anicet-Bourgeois's
    Le Maître d'école)
Freiheit in Krähwinkel, pr. 1848, pb. 1849
    (*Freedom Comes to Krähwinkel*, 1961)
Judith und Holofernes, pr. 1849, pb. 1891
    (adaptation of Friedrich Hebbel's *Judith*)
*Kampl: Oder, Das Mädchen mit Millionen und die
    Näherin*, pr., pb. 1852 (adaptation of Ferdinand
    Raimund's *Der Alpenkönig und der
    Menschenfeind*)
*Theaterg'schichten durch Liebe, Intrige, Geld und
    Dummheit*, pr. 1854
Frühere Verhältnisse, pr. 1862
*Häuptling Abendwind: Oder, Das greuliche
    Festmahl*, pr. 1862, pb. 1912 (adaptation of
    Jacques Offenbach's *Vent du soir: Ou,
    L'Horrible Festin*)

OTHER LITERARY FORMS

Johann Nestroy is chiefly known for his comedies,
although his most famous "couplets" (brief operatic
songs) and epigrammatic sayings from within these
plays have been compiled into separate collections.

ACHIEVEMENTS

Johann Nestroy was praised as the "Aristophanes
of Vienna" by his contemporaries, and the more than
eighty comedies and farces that he wrote during his
lifetime support that praise. As dramatist and actor,
he marks the culmination and finale of the long tradition of the Viennese folk theater, which had its roots
in the baroque age and its first significant representative in the famous Josef Anton Stranitzky, who took
over the directorship of the newly constructed comedy house near the Kärntnertor in 1712. Within fourteen years Stranitzky had created that unique Vien-

nese folk theater that achieved its highest expression
at the beginning of the nineteenth century in the
hands of Nestroy and Ferdinand Raimund.

While Raimund seemed to cling to the idealism of
a past age in his fairy-laden dream plays, Nestroy was
a realist who excelled in the parody of this fairy
world as well as in social criticism of the new middle
class in the growing metropolis of Vienna and has
been called "the first realistic writer of German comedy" as well as "the greatest German comedy writer"
altogether.

"Opposition to the spirit of his time, and not only
his time, dominated his work," remarks Franz H.
Mautner in his introduction to Nestroy's plays. One
of the great dramatists of the twentieth century, the
Swiss writer Friedrich Dürrenmatt, remarks in the
notes to *Der Besuch der alten Dame* (1956; *The Visit*,
1958), "One should treat me as a sort of deliberate
Nestroy, and one will get far." In his essay *Problems
of the Theatre* (1955), there is no other author whom
Dürrenmatt mentions nearly as often as Nestroy.
Modern comedy and especially Dürrenmatt's tragicomedies have prompted a reevaluation of Nestroy's
plays. What had been regarded as his failure by earlier critics has proved to be Nestroy's strength after
all. He is, observes Mautner, a modern writer in his
passion for a theater that shuns the illusion of reality.

Nestroy himself regarded his playwriting as only a
vehicle for his acting, writing role after role for himself, preferring to leave literary fame to others: "I
don't aspire to poetic laurels. My things should please,
entertain, people should laugh, and it also should
make me some money, so that I can laugh, that's the
whole purpose." Nestroy cared little about his written
texts, constantly improvising onstage and filling the
scripts with their best lines only then. (Even a so-
called complete critical edition that appeared between 1924 and 1930 does not include all his plays
because some remain known of by title solely and
others were discovered only relatively recently.)

Because of his busy schedule, which did not permit him time to revise manuscripts, his farces, which
were primarily intended for the stage and not as
works of literature, lacked some of the polish provided by other dramatists of the time. Critics have

commented that these witty parodies and farces were not comedies in the true sense of the word and charged that these dramatic works lack a deeper humor that springs from personal experience. In addition to this problem, Nestroy frequently failed to create an internally coherent and convincing plot. His characterization is also weak. Minor roles often remain stereotypes, and his women lack individuality altogether, with the notable exception of Salome Pockerl in *The Talisman*.

Nestroy's ample use of Viennese dialect and the fact that he was his own best interpreter onstage limited his popularity primarily to Vienna during his lifetime. Northern Germany, especially, remained closed to him, since the standard of High German spoken in that region was usually the language reserved for Nestroy's more despicable characters. Only a few of his comedies now belong to the standard repertoires of the German-speaking stage outside Vienna. During the 1950's and 1960's, five of his plays were translated into English, but even with these translations, Nestroy remains virtually unknown on the American stage, with the exception of *The Matchmaker*, which Thornton Wilder adapted as *The Merchant of Yonkers* in 1938, the revised version of which became a Broadway success as *The Matchmaker* in 1954.

BIOGRAPHY

Johann Nepomuk Eduard Ambrosius Nestroy was born on December 7, 1801, in Vienna. His father immigrated to Vienna from Silesia and became a successful trial lawyer who intended the same career for his son. Nestroy's mother, the daughter of a well-to-do Viennese commercial inspector, died of consumption at a relatively young age. During Nestroy's adolescence, the family's prosperity vanished quickly, and the wheel of fortune that sends Nestroy's characters up and down with such unpredictable regularity tumbled Nestroy himself from a secure childhood into growing poverty hidden under the pretense of a life unchanged. Instead of the law, Nestroy pursued a career in the opera, making a successful debut in Vienna as Sarastro in Wolfgang Amadeus Mozart's *Die Zauberflöte* (1791; *The Magic Flute*). After a year, he went as an opera singer to Amsterdam, Brünn, and fi-

nally to Graz for a more permanent engagement. He married, but his wife, Maria Philippine, with whom he had a son, left him after a short time. In Graz, he then met the actress Marie Weiler, whom he could not marry, because Austrian law prohibited a second marriage. They lived together, and he had two children by her.

In Graz, Nestroy switched over to the comic theater and endeared himself to audiences in 1831, in the role of Sansquartier in Louis Angely's popular farce *Sieben Mädchen in Uniform* (seven girls in uniform; for his performance, the farce was temporarily retitled *Zwölf Mädchen in Uniform*, meaning twelve girls in uniform). In this role he seems to have developed the farcical gestures and comic devices that would later become his mark as playwright and actor. This farce also launched his career as a playwright because it did not fill the evening and thus prompted him to write a farcical prologue to round out the bill. In 1831, Karl Carl, the director of the Viennese theater, engaged Nestroy as actor and playwright first for the Theater an der Wien and later for the Theater in der Leopoldstadt. The immediate printing of Nestroy's works was prevented by the harsh contract that Nestroy signed with Carl. This exploitative contract provided that everything that Nestroy wrote, including individual scenes, had to be submitted to the Carl-Theater first for consideration, and that Carl retained the exclusive option on the text for eighteen months after its first performance. By that time, a text was well worn and apparently of no further interest to the playwright. The contract lasted until Carl's death in 1854, when Nestroy, in addition to his acting and writing careers, also assumed the directorship of the Theater in der Leopoldstadt.

Nestroy ended his career as director of that theater in 1860, when he retired to Graz. After 1860, Nestroy only appeared in some guest performances in Vienna and was seen onstage for the last time in 1862, in his *Häuptling Abendwind*. Not quite four months later, he died in Graz.

ANALYSIS

Johann Nestroy's works stand at the end of the Viennese folk-theater tradition, and at the beginning of the modern theater of tragicomedy. Appreciation for the striking modernity of Nestroy's vision has continued to grow, as is evidenced by Tom Stoppard's adaptation *On the Razzle* (1981), and Nestroy's work is seen in the context of the profound influence of Austrian culture on the modern mind.

Nestroy shares with modern playwrights their predominantly intellectual-ironic-objective stance, their skepticism, and especially their aversion to false pathos. In particular, he shares with Bertolt Brecht the effect of deliberate alienation. Nestroy even anticipated Brecht's technique of alienation through song in his couplets. Parody in Nestroy's work and in modern plays serves the identical purpose of alienating the audience from ideas and values long held sacred and opening the spectator's eye to a new perspective. Indeed, Nestroy's affinity with modern playwrights such as Dürrenmatt and Eugène Ionesco runs deeper still, for he often went beyond the parodistic reinterpretation of a given situation to a parody of language itself, a parody of overused and meaningless phrases and metaphors, of virtuous banalities and proverbs, even to a parody of the pompous theatrical language of his time, which he effectively contrasted with the Viennese folk dialect. Franz Mautner postulates that Peter Handke's 1966 *Pubikumsbeschimpfung und andere Sprechstücke* (plays about language), which closely investigate each word as to its possible range of meanings, are unthinkable without Nestroy's example. Present-day theatrical devices such as the division of the stage into two or more independent spheres of action are also common occurrences in Nestroy.

Nestroy's shunning of the illusion of theatrical reality can be traced to the influence of the *commedia dell'arte* on his writing. This influence can be seen best in his characters and plots. Originality is not important to him, and he usually borrows the plot from other works, including the comedies of antiquity. His farces consist of an artful mechanism held in motion by stock characters, burlesque situations, and theatrical coups. There are jealous lovers, fathers who want to prevent their children's marriages, cunning servants, and crafty craftsmen. His plays are filled with the Viennese lower and middle classes:

the shoemakers and tailors, the rich merchants and parvenus, the servants and masters. In some ways, these farces must have been regarded by their audiences in the same manner in which the more intelligent television situation comedies are received today.

DER TOD AM HOCHZEITSTAGE

Reflecting the heritage of the Viennese folk theater, magic plays a significant role in Nestroy's work. Its representatives have become all too human, however, their virtuous or evil qualities reduced in scale. Clearly, the effects of romanticism are noticeable in Nestroy, even though he was anything but a romantic writer. One of his earliest plays, *Der Tod am Hochzeitstage* (death on the wedding day), is not far removed from romantic Symbolism. Its protagonist Dappschädl, "the fool of melancholy," dreams of what could have happened if his wife had not died twenty-five years earlier. In his despair, he throws himself on his servant girl Seppi, and as his mournful feelings well up, he tries to seduce her. This early comedy is a mixture of magic and disillusionment, a parody of romantic witchcraft that expresses the absurd in life.

NAGERL UND HANDSCHUH

Nestroy employed a specifically Viennese locale for the first time in his play *Nagerl und Handschuh* (Nagerl and the glove). This "parody of an often satirized theme" (Cinderella) replaces the shoe with a glove and the gruesome ending for the older sisters with a happy one.

DER BÖSE GEIST LUMPAZIVAGABUNDUS

It was a play in the following year, however, *Der böse Geist Lumpazivagabundus* (the evil spirit Lumpazivagabundus), that signified Nestroy's breakthrough as the most prominent Viennese actor and playwright of his time. As with most of his plays, Nestroy here drew on an earlier source, Carl Weisflog's *Das grosse Los* (1827; the winning ticket). In good baroque fashion, and again like most of his plays, it has a double title, the second half of which lifts the veil on that which is about to happen just enough to whet the audience's appetite (in this case the subtitle, "Das liederliche Kleeblatt" means "the roguish trio"). The real world of nineteenth century

Vienna and the fairy kingdom encounter each other in this story of three dissolute journeymen: a shoemaker, a tailor, and a carpenter. The old magicians of the realm, led by Mystifax, complain to the Fairy King Stellaris about Lumpazivagabundus, who has seduced their sons and daughters into a dissolute life. The king commands Fortuna to return their squandered possessions to them, but Lumpazivagabundus mocks that wealth will never better the young. As if to prove his point, Hilaris, the son of Mystifax, exclaims that only love can conquer the dissolute, and he demands the hand of Brillantine, Fortuna's daughter. Fortuna refuses, even though Amorosa takes the side of the lovers. Finally, Fortuna offers the following condition: Three dissolute humans shall receive wealth from her horn of plenty. If two of them make wise use of their gifts, Brillantine and Hilaris shall not marry; if two squander their wealth obstinately, Amorosa will be victorious.

The action then shifts to the city of Ulm, where the audience is introduced to the shoemaker Knieriem, a student of beer and astrology, the squanderous tailor Zwirn, and the carpenter Leim, who has become melancholic after the loss of his beloved Pepi. At the inn, they discover that the main drawing in the city's lottery will be held on the following day. During the night, Fortuna allows each of them to dream about the same number, 7359, and the next morning they buy this ticket with their last pennies. They win a considerable amount of money, which they divide evenly, and then they go their separate ways. Leim will try to regain his lost Pepi, Zwirn wants to lead the life of a Don Juan, and Knieriem will give himself entirely to the study of wine and beer, since his astrological observations have foretold the impending doom of the world. In one year, they plan to meet again at the house of Pepi's father, Master Hobelmann, in Vienna. Because Leim is now equipped with money, Hobelmann is happy to consent to Pepi's marriage. Zwirn, meanwhile, has become a parvenu in Prague and entertains worthless friends and passions with his quickly diminishing fortune. When the year has passed, Zwirn and Knieriem appear penniless at Master Hobelmann's door. In the famous letter scene, Hobelmann pretends that Leim is lying on his deathbed in Nuremberg, but he has left some money behind for his friends. They resolve immediately to rush to Nuremberg in order to help him. In spite of their dissolute lives, they have demonstrated their good hearts. Leim appears, and the three are reunited. The two squanderers do not want to settle down, however, and they march on to the next inn. There, Stellaris, horrified by so much slovenliness and angered by the success of Lumpazivagabundus, catches up with them and banishes the two into the underworld. Fortuna declares herself the loser of the bet, and Hilaris and Brillantine are allowed to marry. Amorosa does not give up her hope, though, that Zwirn and Knieriem can become decent human beings through the power of love. In the end, she succeeds, and in a peaceful apotheosis, the three craftsmen appear, seated on different floors of the same house, working diligently, surrounded by wives and children, until the evening bell calls them all to dancing and merriment.

The play became an unsurpassed success at the Theater an der Wien. With it, Nestroy modified the traditional form of the magical farce into his own vehicle of expression. The contemporary critic Karl Meisl observed that Nestroy still employed the magic convention to motivate the dramatic action, but it was no longer intrinsically necessary and might even be eliminated altogether. The traditional bet waged between the forces of good and evil, which has notable forerunners in Raimund's *Das Mädchen aus der Feenwelt: Oder, Der Bauer als Millionär*, (pr. 1826, pb. 1837; *The Maid from Fairyland: Or, The Peasant as Millionaire*, 1962), and particularly in Johann Wolfgang von Goethe's *Faust: Eine Tragödie* (pb. 1808, pb. 1833; *The Tragedy of Faust*, 1823, 1828) served to illustrate Nestroy's ironic and paradoxical view of the world, since Lumpazivagabundus, the representative of slovenliness, remains victorious. His counterpart is Fortuna, a force who is similarly negative in a classical system of values. The old juxtaposition of virtue and vice has thus been abolished a priori, and the "Everyman in reverse," as the play has been called, proved to its amused audience that it was much more enjoyable and took much less pain to go to Hell than to walk the path of virtue.

Some critics stress that Nestroy also sounded, for the first time, a political note in *Der böse Geist Lumpazivagabundus* and especially in the refrain to the famous couplet "Die Welt steht auf keinen Fall mehr lang" (This world will not exist much longer in any case). To this line Nestroy apparently added still greater relevance by delivering it with strong emphasis on the definite article, thus making the allusion to the shaky condition of the social order of his time. In the character of Knieriem, who sings this couplet, the author and actor Nestroy, for the first time, had made the coarsest of the poor his central comic figure and spokesperson. Knieriem was drawn and acted with a realistic quality that led another contemporary critic to observe, "Mr. Nestroy is a genre painter who conceives the most common scenes from life with such a sure and efficient hand and puts them on the stage so drastically that the viewer seems to shy away stunned as from a portrait so life-like that one expects it to speak any second."

DIE FAMILIEN ZWIRN, KNIERIEM UND LEIM

Die Familien Zwirn, Knieriem und Leim (the families of Zwirn, Knieriem and Leim) takes place twenty years after *Der böse Geist Lumpazivagabundus*. Leim and Knieriem are now married, but Zwirn has remained an itinerant skirt-chaser and tailor and at the same time has become an apprentice to a quack named Paracelsus. The play was a parody of the then popular "improvement-plays" but lacked the originality and drive of its predecessor. Nestroy hinted at the reason for its mediocrity in a line from one of his later plays: "That's how it goes with continuations, there simply no longer is the same interest."

WEDER LORBEERBAUM NOCH BETTELSTAB

In *Weder Lorbeerbaum noch Bettelstab* (neither laurel tree nor beggar's staff), Nestroy deals with his own profession of comedy writing. The poet Leicht is chided because his comedy contains witty ideas. Blasius, the son of a rich manufacturer, tells him that comedy should never be witty but rather sentimental and good-hearted so that one can laugh with one eye and weep with the other. The conventions of Nestroy's period are satirized when Blasius continues: "We are upright and good people, and we want our hearts touched in everything we see."

ZU EBENER ERDE UND IM ERSTEN STOCK

The second play of 1835, *Zu ebener Erde und im ersten Stock* (downstairs-upstairs), almost appears to be the model for the similarly titled British television series. The stage is divided throughout all three acts. The poor family of Schlucker, his wife, children, and brother-in-law Damian live downstairs; the millionaire, Goldfuchs, and his daughter Emilie lead an opulent life upstairs. The wheel of fortune turns constantly, however, and during the course of the play, downstairs becomes upstairs and upstairs, downstairs. The Schluckers win a large amount of money in the lottery, while Goldfuchs loses his fortune through bad speculations. Nestroy played the central character, Johann, the butler upstairs. The play has been called magical, but no fairies or magicians appear. Life itself performs the magical acts. This masterpiece, in which Nestroy comes closest to the spirit of his rival Raimund, has been rated higher than *Der böse Geist Lumpazivagabundus* by several critics.

DAS HAUS DER TEMPERAMENTE

Das Haus der Temperamente (the house of temperaments) sections the stage into four separate spheres, representing the four human tempers as character-types. As in *Zu ebener Erde und im ersten Stock*, the lives of the families living in one house are interwoven. Nestroy's stylistic principle of presenting the same action from varied viewpoints is particularly evident in this play.

THE TALISMAN

During the decade from 1840 to 1850, Nestroy wrote three of his most important plays. The first among these was *The Talisman*. Red hair makes life miserable for Titus Feuerfuchs, the barber's apprentice, and for Salome Pockerl, the goose-girl. A black wig with which he is rewarded for saving the master-barber's life inadvertently wins for him the favor of Flora Baumscher, the widow of a gardener. She puts him into her husband's clothing and makes him an overseer. In this job, he is espied by the chambermaid Constantia, similarly suffering from the tribulations of widowhood. She launches him on a new career as hunter for the court. Complications arise when the master-barber suspects in the black-wigged Titus a rival for the hand of Constantia. After the loss of the black wig during a brawl with the master-barber, Titus flees to become the secretary of a countess, now hiding himself under a blond wig. During an evening gathering, Titus is unmasked, however, by the vengeful widows and the master-barber as a wig thief and is thrown out of the house. Fortunately, Titus has a rich uncle who appears at this moment to save his disgraced nephew from destitution. New complications arise that finally compel Titus to forgo the inheritance and favors attained by the use of his wigs and to marry Salome Pockerl, who never objected to the color of his hair in the first place.

The Talisman is one of the high points of Nestroy's work, featuring his most fully realized female character (Salome Pockerl), exceptionally well-written dialogue, and the witty exposition of one of his recurring themes: the discrepancy between *Schein und Sein* (appearance and essence). By the beginning of the 1840's, Nestroy had perfected his particular variety of farce, but at the same time had not yet slipped into the glib routine that, according to several critics, characterizes his later plays. Yet even then he continued his practice of adapting the scripts of others. The source of *The Talisman* was the farce *Bonaventure* (1840), by the French authors Charles Desiré Dupeuty and F. de Courcy, which had premiered in Paris a few months earlier. Critic Helmut Herles has investigated Nestroy's gradual adaptation of the original into *The Talisman*, providing some valuable insights into Nestroy's method of adaptation.

The social criticism first noted in *Der böse Geist Lumpazivagabundus* seems to have gained ground. Nestroy's proximity to his contemporary Georg Büchner should not be overlooked here. A couplet in the third act shows Nestroy as a direct ancestor of Bertolt Brecht: "*Mit ein' orndlichen Mag'n/ Kann man alles ertrag'n*" (With a decent stomach one can endure everything) seems to reflect the same attitude as Brecht's famous "*Erst kommt das Fressen, dann kommt die Moral*" (First comes eating, then morality). W. E. Yates emphasizes that Titus recalls Brecht's Shui Ta in *Der gute Mensch von Sezuan* (wr. 1938-1940, pr. 1943; *The Good Woman of Setzuan*, 1948) when he states in an aside: "*Meine Stellung hier im Hause gleicht dem Brett des Schiffbrüchigen;*

ich muss die andern hinunterstossen, oder selbst untergehn" (My position here in the house equals the board of the ship-wrecked: I must push the others off or drown myself). Yates considers *The Talisman* a social allegory in which Nestroy uses the story of the wig—that is, the "talisman"—as a

presentation of a society in which prejudice is all-powerful, appearance all important, and merit unrewarded. Titus is excluded for reasons of birth (symbolized in the red hair he was born with from a world to which he aspires until he finally sees through the worthlessness of its standards.

The Talisman can also be seen as one of Nestroy's best portrayals of the Austrian capital during his lifetime: a Viennese Biedermeier idyll with its widows, gardeners, brewers, bakers, chambermaids, and poets, and with the satiric tableau of the literary salon of Frau von Cypressenburg.

In the character of Titus Feuerfuchs, Nestroy created the first and perhaps the best of a new breed which he was to repeat with Herr von Lips in *A Man Full of Nothing*: the articulate *raisonneur* and philosopher who stands above his time and dominates it with virtuosity.

THE MATCHMAKER

The second great play of this period, *The Matchmaker*, features a dazzling plot full of delightfully preposterous confusions. An exact English translation of *Ein Jux will er sich machen* (he wants to have some fun) would seem a more fitting title for Nestroy's work than *The Matchmaker*. This farce has been appropriately labeled the "first tragicomedy of an apprentice whose wildly flailing attempt to break out of the boredom of his existence into the adventure of the unknown is doomed to fail." Curiously enough, the play was based on a British farce, *A Day Well Spent*, by John Oxenford. As in most other instances, however, Nestroy considerably modified and expanded the original.

Nestroy returned in *The Matchmaker* to his earlier device of separating the stage into two contrasting spheres; acts 1 and 4 are situated in Zangler's small-town shop, while acts 2 and 3 take place in the big city. Nestroy also returned to an earlier age of innocence, as compared to the mood of *The Talisman* or even *Der böse Geist Lumpazivagabundus*; *The Matchmaker* came closer again to the pure farces of his early years. The action is highly improbable, as is the case in most of Nestroy's farces, while the lively tempo and the many comical quid pro quos lend a poetic aura to the interspersed realistic-satiric scenes, as, for example, those depicting the dull lives of Zangler's two employees Weinberl and Christopherl. One critic has observed that the masquerades—as for example that of Weinberl, who would like to be a swashbuckler just once in his life—are symbolic depictions of the general madness of the world. The wise simpleton of the play, the servant Melchior, responds to every incomprehensible event that he witnesses with the stock phrase "*Das is klassisch*" (that's classic). Humankind's foolishness, Nestroy seems to say to his audience in *The Matchmaker*, is its most characteristic feature.

Weinberl, on the other hand, is also a calmer reincarnation of the *raisonneur* and philosopher Titus Feuerfuchs, more resigned to the ways of the world than Titus was and, after his edifying adventures in the big city, perhaps more moderate in the demands which he will put on it.

A MAN FULL OF NOTHING

The third notable play in this fruitful decade was *A Man Full of Nothing*. Herr von Lips is disgusted with the world and bored with his friends in spite of all the wealth he has been able to amass. The locksmith Gluthammer, who has been called to Lips' mansion to install a new banister, is also at odds with the world because a certain Mathilde, for whom he had sacrificed all his possessions, has left him. In a conversation with Kathi, the young niece of Lips, Gluthammer laments his sad fate and confesses that he is still in love with Mathilde. Kathi has arrived to return a sum of money that her mother had borrowed from Lips many years earlier. Within the circle of his friends, Lips, who has never married, vows that he will marry the first woman whom he meets that day in order to break his boredom and disgust with the world. At this moment, a widow, Madame Schleier, appears to offer Lips tickets to a ball that she will hold at her country home in order to improve her

modest finances. Lips is bound by his vow and offers to marry her, which at first surprises and then delights the widow. Kathi is less enthusiastic, since she is secretly in love with Lips. After Kathi has heard that Madame Schleier's first name is Mathilde, she confides this to Gluthammer, who recognizes his long-lost love. Lips insists on his wedding plans and a fight ensues between him and Gluthammer, in the course of which they tumble over the yet unfinished banister down into a brook that runs in front of the house.

Lips, who believes that he has killed Gluthammer, disguises himself and hides from the police at the farm of his tenant farmer, Krautkopf, where Kathi is the housekeeper. She coaxes the farmer into hiring Lips as the new handyman. While Lips is at work, Gluthammer, who has also survived but believes himself to be the murderer of Lips, appears at the farm and implores his friend Krautkopf to hide him from the police. The farmer hides him in the grain silo. In the meantime, Lips's will has been probated, and his three best friends arrive at the farm in order to look at their newly inherited property. Lips can overhear his friends unnoticed and finds out their sentiments toward him. He is very disappointed, and when the will is left unguarded, he manages to affix an addendum to it which declares Kathi to be the sole heir. The probate judge discovers the addendum and declares it valid. Kathi, the rich heiress, is now wooed by the three friends. Lips grows increasingly jealous, but Kathi assures him that she will sell the whole estate and send the money to Lips, who now plans to flee abroad. The friends dislike the confidences between Kathi and the hired hand, and when one of them seizes him by the collar, he recognizes Lips. The probate judge proclaims that he must arrest Lips for murder, and that he will be locked up in the grain silo until the police can be summoned. There, Gluthammer and Lips encounter each other during the night, and each imagines that the ghost of the other has come to haunt him. From this climax, it is only a brief step to the end, when Lips and Kathi and Gluthammer and Mathilde are united in marriage.

In Lips, Nestroy created one of his most interesting and rewarding stage characters. *A Man Full of*

Nothing depicts most clearly a humanity victimized by its own masquerades and tricked by itself. In contrast to *The Talisman* and *The Matchmaker*, the responsibility for the protagonist's situation has been shifted from the outside to the inside. Oskar Maurus Fontana suggests that Lips is the incarnation of modern humanity with his self-inflicted disintegration and inner void. Once life is without meaning and all activity has become senseless, profound boredom is the unavoidable result. Such existential ennui on the stage of nineteenth century Vienna resurfaced in the twentieth century philosophies of such luminaries as Jean-Paul Sartre and Martin Heidegger.

Nestroy's contemporaries would not have missed his parody of the Byronic *Weltschmerz*, which afflicted the Romantic age and which had been similarly satirized in Georg Büchner's *Leonce und Lena* (1838; *Leonce and Lena*, 1927). Indeed, *A Man Full of Nothing* was Nestroy's ultimate satiric statement, in which satire of the world around him had turned into satire on itself, a parody of the sort of *Zerrissenheit* (torn state) that Nestroy's skepticism has produced.

In *A Man Full of Nothing*, Nestroy drew on French *comédie-vaudeville*, *L'Homme blasé* (1843) by Frédéric Auguste Duvert and Auguste Théodore Vaux-Roussel de Lauzanne. The two writers were regarded as among the leading *vaudevillistes* of the time, and W. E. Yates suggests that their play stood out from the common fare, being based on a relatively new comic situation. He further suggests that Nestroy did not really improve the original significantly, having reached a creative plateau in the mid-1840's after the peaks of the previous year: "Nestroy *develops* the characters of Kathi Krautkopf and Lips, but without having to alter the fundamentals of the characterization . . . and he takes over some of the limitations of the original, to the detriment of the finished work."

FREEDOM COMES TO KRÄHWINKEL

Freedom Comes to Krähwinkel deserves to be mentioned at least as the one play of Nestroy written most clearly under the influence of the revolution of 1848. Here Nestroy vents his disappointment that the revolution for freedom had quickly changed into a petty rebellion of the middle class.

KAMPL

During the following decade, Nestroy produced one more outstanding play, *Kampl*. The theme is again that of *Schein und Sein*. The protagonist, Kampl, has a double identity: as a doctor of the poor on the one hand, and as a fashionable health spa doctor on the other. He disguises himself only in order to do good more effectively. The fairies and evil spirits from the past have clearly become the opposing powers of love and money, and Kampl is a more modern version of Raimund's famous *Der Alpenkönig und der Menschenfeind* (pr. 1828, pb. 1837; *Mountain King and Misanthrope*, 1962).

BIBLIOGRAPHY

Harding, Laurence V. *The Dramatic Art of Ferdinand Raimund and Johann Nestroy: A Critical Study*. The Hague: Mouton, 1974. An examination of the plays of Nestroy and Ferdinand Raimund. Bibliography.

Yates, W. E. *Nestroy and the Critics*. Columbia, S.C.: Camden House, 1994. An analysis of the critical reaction to Nestroy's works. Bibliography and index.

_____. *Nestroy: Satire and Parody in Viennese Popular Comedy*. Cambridge, England: Cambridge University Press, 1972. A study of satire and parody as they appear in the works of Nestroy. Bibliography.

Klaus D. Hanson

NGUGI WA THIONG'O

Born: Kamiriithu village, near Limuru, Kenya;
January 5, 1938

PRINCIPAL DRAMA

The Black Hermit, pr. 1962, pb. 1968
This Time Tomorrow: Three Plays, pb. 1970
(includes *The Rebels*, *The Wound in My Heart*,
and *This Time Tomorrow*)
The Trial of Dedan Kimathi, pr. 1974, pb. 1976
(with Micere Githae-Mugo)
Ngaahika Ndeenda, pr. 1977, pb. 1980 (with Ngugi
wa Mirii; *I Will Marry When I Want*, 1982)
Maitu Njugira, pb. 1982 (with Ngugi wa Mirii;
Mother, Sing for Me, 1986)

OTHER LITERARY FORMS

Ngugi wa Thiong'o is primarily known as a novelist, having published one of the first English-language novels by an East African, *Weep Not, Child* (1964). This novel, *The River Between* (1965), *A Grain of Wheat* (1967), and *Petals of Blood* (1977) re-create the cultural history of the Gikuyu people and the emergence of modern Kenya. His fifth novel, *Caitaani Mutharaba-Ini* (1980; *Devil on the Cross*, 1982), combines elements of Gikuyu oral tradition with satire on neocolonial exploitation and realism portraying the victims of that exploitation. Writing fiction for the first time in his native Gikuyu, Ngugi completed his own translations into Kiswahili and English. In addition to his novels, Ngugi has also published a collection of early short stories, *Secret Lives and Other Stories* (1975), which gathers his work in this genre from the early 1960's to the mid-1970's.

Ngugi has also written extensively as a social and literary critic. His collection of literary criticism, *Homecoming: Essays on African and Caribbean Literature, Culture, and Politics* (1972), testifies to the maturation of his social vision, including speculations on Mau Mau, nationalism, socialism, and capitalism. A second collection of essays, *Writers in Politics* (1981; revised 1997), asserts that the function of

the writer in society is essentially a political one, however explicitly mute or vocal the writer may choose to be on social issues. In *Detained: A Writer's Prison Diary* (1981), Ngugi records his experience during his politically motivated incarceration, openly indicting the corruption of neocolonial Kenya and offering insights into his development as a writer and an activist. In a subsequent collection of essays, *Barrel of a Pen: Resistance to Repression in Neo-Colonial Kenya* (1983), Ngugi employs the ideals of the Mau Mau movement to analyze the role of writing and education in contemporary Kenya. His fourth collection of essays, *Decolonising the Mind: The Politics of Language in African Literature* (1986), addresses the need for awareness of the dominating colonial legacies of British culture and the obligations of a neocolonial writer in Africa to address his compatriots, his cultural and historical milieu, and his global readership. Ngugi gathered twenty-one short essays and speeches into his next collection, *Moving the Centre: The Struggle for Cultural Freedoms* (1993). In three sections, he addresses the challenges of freeing culture from Eurocentrism, from colonial legacy, and from racism, proposing that although its influence cannot be erased, the Western world should not be the primary shaper of culture in Africa and throughout the world. Ngugi's focus on language and form in African literature and art is revisited in his sixth critical work, *Penpoints, Gunpoints, and Dreams: Toward a Critical Theory of the Arts and the State of Africa* (1998). In this book, he traces the connections between art and politics, drawing on the example of Africa, where art has been widely used to expose the political sins of those in power.

Ngugi has also granted a number of interviews that have been published. In the 1960's, he contributed forty-four columns to the *Daily Nation*, a newspaper in Nairobi, useful for their witness to his humanistic and political growth as a writer and thinker. In 1990, Ngugi expanded his literary canvas still further by publishing two children's books, *Njamba Nene's Pistol* and *Njamba Nene and the Flying Bus*.

Because Ngugi's themes and concerns are often interwoven among his various modes of discourse, virtually all of his writings help provide an informative context for the reading of his drama.

ACHIEVEMENTS

Ngugi wa Thiong'o is the foremost writer of modern East Africa. Through his novels, essays, and plays, he has garnered the respect of both Africans and others. His fiction offers the single most impressive record of an African country's precolonial history, its exploitation under colonial rule, its turmoil in gaining independence, and its subsequent struggles to maintain a democratic government in the midst of neocolonial corruption. His essays, often forthrightly polemical, have resulted in the emergence of East African literature as a serious topic of criticism among scholars of world literature; he has also made a significant contribution to curriculum reform in African universities, emphasizing the study of African literature.

Ngugi's plays, like his early fiction, reveal a well-schooled and well-read background in British and European literature, but they evolve, as do his novels, from a humanistic, ethical focus to one of a leftist, radical program for social reform. By adapting *The Trial of Dedan Kimathi* and *I Will Marry When I Want* to experimental forms that include aspects of the Gikuyu oral tradition and by producing and writing the latter play in Gikuyu, Ngugi succeeded in reaching the masses with his drama and his concerns. His explicit commitment to democratic socialist reform and the strong popular support of Ngugi's *I Will Marry When I Want* resulted in Ngugi's detention.

While Ngugi, then known as James Ngugi, was recognized early as a promising young writer, his later work—perhaps because of political circumstances and his refusal to desist from polemics and activism—has not been accorded the same official status. His first play, *The Black Hermit*, was selected for performance at the 1962 Ugandan independence celebration, and *Weep Not, Child*, his first published novel, received an award from the East African Literature Bureau in 1965 and first prize in the 1966 Dakar Festival of Negro Arts. In that same year,

Ngugi traveled to the United States as an honored guest of the 1966 International PEN Conference.

Ngugi earned the Lotus Prize for Afro-Asian literature in 1973 and began a twenty-year period during which he produced works of high quality that earned him worldwide respect but little formal recognition in the form of awards. In the 1990's, however, he was acclaimed for a lifetime of important fiction, drama, and criticism. He received the Zora Neale Hurston-Paul Robeson Award in 1993 and in 1996 was given the Fonlon-Nichols Prize and the New York African Studies Association's Distinguished Africanist Award.

BIOGRAPHY

Ngugi wa Thiong'o was born James Ngugi in Kamiriithu village, twelve miles northeast of Nairobi, on January 5, 1938. His father, Thiong'o wa Nducu, was a farmer who had been dispossessed of his land in the White Highlands of the Kiambu District and forced to squat as a laborer on what had been his homeland. As a result of the British Imperial Land Act of 1915, many Gikuyu farmers—deprived of legal rights—had been reduced to farming the land of well-to-do British settlers or influential Africans who had been granted parcels in the confiscation of the fertile area by the British governor. Ngugi's father farmed for one of the few Africans who had retained property. His mother was one of four wives, and he was one of twenty-eight children in the extended family.

Until about the age of nine, Ngugi was reared according to a mixture of traditional Gikuyu customs and Christian principles. Beginning in 1947, he attended the mission school of Kamaandura in nearby Limuru for two years; subsequently, he completed his primary education in the village of Maanguu at a school established by the Karing'a, the Independence Schools Movement, a cooperative undertaking by Kenya's Africans who viewed education as a vital component in their struggle for freedom from British rule. From his earliest years in school, Ngugi experienced both the colonial and the nationalistic perspectives inherent in the respective curricula.

Ngugi received his secondary education at Alliance High School in Kikuyu. There Ngugi encountered principal Carey Francis, a man with rigid missionary views and a strict bias for the values of European civilization, who would become the prototype of the missionary headmaster in Ngugi's fiction. There, too, Ngugi acquired a complex religious sensibility, integrating biblical study and Christian mythology with his Gikuyu background. His experiences at Alliance High School constitute one of the shaping influences of his adolescent life.

During this period, Ngugi's family was deeply involved in the Mau Mau resistance. His brother, Wallace Mwangi, fought with the clandestine Mau Mau forces in the forests from 1954 to 1956. His parents, as well as other relatives, were detained for the subversion of colonial rule. A stepbrother was killed by government troops, and his home village was relocated. Ngugi himself did not engage in combat, and although his youth provided him with a measure of justification, he suffered considerable guilt. Reflection on the Mau Mau as an ideal model for the fight against social injustices would be a central theme in his work.

After Ngugi's graduation from high school, he entered Makerere University College in Kampala, Uganda, the only school then conferring degrees in English literature in East Africa. An outstanding student, he completed work in the Honors English program in 1963. During this period, Ngugi began his creative writing, editing the student journal *Penpoint*, writing several short stories, drafting his first two novels, and writing his first play, *The Black Hermit*, as well as two one-act plays, *The Rebels* and *The Wound in My Heart*. He also began writing columns for the Nairobi newspaper *Daily Nation*, a task that was to lead to a stint as a junior reporter in Nairobi in the year following his graduation. Also during this period, Ngugi married Nyambura in 1961 and had the first two of his five children.

In 1964, Ngugi continued his education, pursuing a degree in English studies at Leeds University in England. Exposed to the radical views of fellow students and finding himself in a community that encouraged open inquiry into social and political issues, Ngugi began work on Caribbean literature as well as the extensive drafting of *A Grain of Wheat*, projects

that helped him delineate his views into the most systematic line of thought that he had yet achieved. He also traveled to literary conferences in Damascus, New York, and Moscow, meeting a number of writers and widening his access to diverse social and literary perspectives. Although his teachers at Leeds encouraged him to complete his M.A. thesis, Ngugi chose to pursue his writing and returned to Kenya in 1967.

At Nairobi University, Ngugi worked to reform the curriculum, encouraging an emphasis on African studies, but he resigned in protest in March, 1969, siding with students who confronted the government for their lack of academic freedom. The next year found Ngugi in Makerere again, as a fellow in creative writing, where he helped conclude curriculum revisions and organized a writers' workshop. In March, 1970, while addressing a church conference in Nairobi, at which he renounced Christianity, James Ngugi was challenged by an old man who pointed out that his name was contrary to his denial; thereafter, the writer used the traditional Gikuyu name. By then, however, he was well-known as simply Ngugi. Later that same year, he went to Northwestern University, where he taught African literature. While in Chicago, Ngugi witnessed the degraded conditions of African American ghetto life, becoming convinced that American racism was the result of systematic economic and political exploitation. Returning in August, 1971, to head, eventually, the Nairobi University English Department, Ngugi completed the curriculum changes that he had helped initiate two years earlier. While his teaching was to continue until his detention, Ngugi had, by 1977, become the leading proponent of radical East African literature with the publication of *Petals of Blood*, his fourth novel.

After the successful and popular reception of *The Trial of Dedan Kimathi* and the release of *Petals of Blood*, Ngugi's activism provoked the anger of authorities during his staging of *I Will Marry When I Want* at the Kamiriithu Community Educational and Cultural Center in Limuru. Although the play had been granted a license for production, a district official revoked permission after only a few performances, fearing that peasants would be moved to challenge the power of the upper class. The government, perhaps fearing Ngugi's outspoken convictions, arrested him on December 31, 1977. Despite international protests, appeals, and special delegations to Nairobi, Ngugi was detained without charges or trial in Kamiti Maximum Security Prison until December 12, 1978. Although the conciliatory climate in the early months of President Arap Moi's government probably facilitated Ngugi's release, he was not reinstated at Nairobi University, which terminated his appointment shortly after his detention, despite Ngugi's repeated attempts to regain his position. Ngugi continued to write, working on three collections of essays, his prison diary, his novel in Gikuyu and his own translation of it, *Devil on the Cross*, and a new play, a musical in Gikuyu written in collaboration with Ngugi wa Mirii. In March, 1982, the authorities dismantled the Kamiriithu center just when the new musical, *Mother, Sing for Me*, was in its final rehearsal.

For a decade, Ngugi made his primary residence in London, occasionally serving as a visiting lecturer at various universities, and returning to Kenya whenever the government allowed. He remained a powerful freelance voice, speaking and writing on behalf of the landless, ordinary people and calling for social justice. In 1992 he joined the faculty of New York University, where he became the Erich Maria Remarque professor of languages and comparative literature, and a professor of performance studies. Identifying strongly with his fictional creation, Matigari, from the novel *Matigari ma Njiruungi* (1986; *Matigari*, 1989), written in the Gikuyu language and banned in Kenya, Ngugi is a committed writer who attacks neocolonialism and advocates reformist possibilities. Although optimistic about the future, Ngugi remains militant in his stance against oppression.

ANALYSIS

Ngugi wa Thiong'o's drama explores the issues germane to the transition within Kenya from a colony to an independent nation. Often unabashedly didactic in his plays, Ngugi probes the challenges that young black intellectuals must overcome if they are to alleviate conflicts of tribe, race, and religion that threaten the unity of nationalism. Although his early plays of the 1960's usually revolve around the qualities of

leadership, they also initiate themes concerning the tension between traditional, rural life and modern, urban life; the role of African women in developing a strong nationalism; and resistance to the continuation of colonial practices that perpetuate exploitation in the new country. As these themes evolve in the plays of the next decade, Ngugi's drama becomes even more decidedly didactic, using an idealized history of Mau Mau, straightforward calls to action, and realistic portrayals of the exploited that are interspersed with pageantry to evoke the grandeur of African culture and the tragedy of colonial history. From his earliest play *The Black Hermit* to his volatile *I Will Marry When I Want*, Ngugi gradually shifts his attention from the confusion of a central character beset by conflicts among his loyalties, to the community's determination to achieve a democratic voice in the political and economic development of the nation.

THE BLACK HERMIT

In *The Black Hermit*, the protagonist, Remi, the only university-educated member of a small tribe, wavers between loyalty to his customs and desires for his own happiness. As the play opens, the villagers await Remi's return from the city. He is, however, returning to a bewildering array of anxious expectations in the village. Before he left for the city, Remi had fallen in love with Thoni, but, by the time he had mustered courage enough to propose, he learned of his brother's marriage to her. Six months later, his brother was killed in a car accident; custom required that Remi marry his dead brother's wife, which he did, hesitantly, believing that Thoni did not love him. Just after the ceremony, he fled to the city. Thoni, however, does love him, and, having remained faithful, she is hopeful of their reconciliation on his return. His mother, Nyobi, expects him to comfort the abandoned Thoni and to start a family; the village priest wants Remi to reaffirm Christianity in the tribe; and the elders, having been convinced by Remi before his departure to support an African party in elections, hope that his return signals his willingness to lead them to power in the government.

Act 2 finds Remi still in the city and entangled in an affair with a white woman, Jane. While he must end the affair before returning, Remi realizes that

Jane does not have similar experiences under colonialism and cannot ever understand him, despite her sincere affection. Remi's belated admission that he has been married to Thoni while carrying on the affair provokes Jane's anger, and she leaves him, calling into question Remi's own sense of ethical standards. Meanwhile, Remi and his friend Omange debate the powers of the new black government. Both oppose tribalism and support the new nation, but Remi refuses to sanction the right of workers to strike, while Omange envisions a state based on black workers rather than foreign aid. Despite Remi's support for the government, he refuses to enter politics when the elders visit the city to plead for his return. When the priest visits him, he sends word of his return, but his motives are confused.

Upon his return to the anxious village, Remi rants against tribalism. Yet he reveals himself as an obsessed, arrogant intellectual whose egotism renders him incapable of recognizing the strengths and appreciating the values in his own people. He renounces Christianity, but he has sacrificed his own spiritual awareness and interpersonal sensitivity to his rigid, nearly desperate, adherence to unquestioned principles of nationalism. When Remi renounces his marriage to Thoni, she flees and kills herself. Having asserted his individuality as more important than the complexities of traditional, communal society, Remi realizes, too late, that he has not thwarted tribalism and custom but profaned the mutual love and respect on which the traditions are founded. He recognizes, in short, that African traditions must inform the evolution of African nationalism. Although Omange, the priest, Jane, and Remi himself are type characters in *The Black Hermit*, the elders suggest a ceremonial dignity and ritual wisdom, represented by "Africa's anthem" and sung in Kiswahili. The women Nyobi and Thoni provide models of genuine sensitivity in their mutual support to overcome the literal and figurative departure of Remi: Leaders, they assert, cannot take leave of compassion.

THIS TIME TOMORROW

The critique of leadership extends from *The Black Hermit* to the three one-act dramas in *This Time Tomorrow*. In *The Rebels*, a young man returns home with a Ugandan fiancé, Mary, only to find that his father has chosen a local girl to be his bride. When he hesitates to accept the arrangement dictated by custom, the humiliated prospective bride kills herself, and he loses Mary as well. Implicitly, the play attacks the lack of black unity among the emerging nations of East Africa. By his use of a Ugandan for the character of Mary, Ngugi focuses on tribal prejudice rather than racial or colonial repression as the source of conflict. *The Wound in My Heart* portrays Ruhiu, a Mau Mau detainee, who eagerly returns to his village after his release only to find his wife with a child from an adulterous affair with a white man. Before she can hear Ruhiu's reaction, his wife kills herself. The fatalism inherent in *The Black Hermit* and these two one-acts, despite their sympathy with the role of African women in the emerging nation, yields to the undeveloped social protest of *This Time Tomorrow*, a one-act attack on the affluent classes for their demolition of a slum in the interests of foreign investment and tourism. This play prefigures the social commitment of Ngugi's next two plays.

THE TRIAL OF DEDAN KIMATHI

In *The Trial of Dedan Kimathi*, Ngugi shifts his concern from confused though well-intentioned leading characters to the strength of group commitment in reforming colonial practices that continue in independent Kenya. The play shapes the historical Dedan Kimathi into a heroic figure who embodies the idealistic principles of Mau Mau resistance. By idealizing a myth of Mau Mau, Ngugi and Micere Githae-Mugo, his collaborator, hoped to create a call to action, extolling Mau Mau glory and criticizing the neocolonial betrayal of the Mau Mau goals for social justice. An appeal to popular audiences, the play eulogizes Kimathi while celebrating his resistance to colonial enemies and staging re-creations of his tribulations, both in the courtroom and in private confrontations in his cell. Using an extremely loose structure—by Western standards—of three "Movements" rather than formally designed acts, each of which includes "Trials" and randomly juxtaposed rather than tightly meshed scenes, Ngugi creates an atmosphere of sad, undefined urgency in which characters, events, time, place, and conflict "flow into one another" until the play feels like and appears to be "a single movement."

As the play opens, the audience views a crowded courtroom and hears the charges against Kimathi for possessing a revolver. Although the date of this trial is 1956, Kimathi's refusal to plead guilty or not guilty gives way to a mimed pageant of "the Black Man's History," showing Kimathi's silence to be a gesture of disdain for repressive colonial law. As "phases" of the pageant progress, gunshots, voices, whiplashes, and drumbeats fade to a mime of mourning that evokes slavery, orphaned children, forced labor on Kenyan plantations, and black betrayals of the Mau Mau resistance, concluding with defiant shouts of "anti-imperialist slogans."

With the unfolding of the First Movement, the audience is witness to a number of rapidly shifting scenes; they see the inhabitants of a village harassed and arrested for supporting Mau Mau fighters, intimidating interrogation of peasants that is abetted by a black informer, and an important discussion between a Woman and a Boy (a Girl later appears) who are symbolic of the birth of freedom and its hope for the future. Implicit in this First Movement is the African urban, colonial city as an archetype of corruption; the Boy is an orphan, who, with the Girl, hustles tourists in Nairobi and who himself eventually seeks to exploit the Girl for small sums of money. Confronting the Boy's sexist behavior toward the Girl, the Woman redefines manhood as possessing a socialist, ethical awareness of the country's needs and conflicts. When the Boy agrees to deliver a loaf of bread containing a gun to the scene of Kimathi's trial, he does so out of a vivid clarity about his choice of political ideals. The threat to the Woman and the Boy in this Movement is not only from the colonial soldiers but also from the black soldiers, informers, and collaborators, the "black masters" who hope to profit by preserving colonial rule. While Ngugi keeps the play set safely in the 1950's, the premise is obvious to the audience: Present neocolonial corruption in land reform and court decisions began in the Mau Mau period and has continued to thrive in postcolonial Kenya. To attack that corruption will require the courage and dedication of the Mau Mau.

In the Second Movement, scenes move rapidly between the street outside the jail where Kimathi is imprisoned, the courtroom, and Kimathi's cell, in which his four Trials take place. (The cell becomes, in a sense the courtroom, and the courtroom, in turn becomes a cell.) Meanwhile, the historical pageant continues to be mimed in the dimly lit background onstage. In costuming, demeanor, and dialogue, the contrast between the peasants and the elite is pronounced. Kimathi, in his trial, repudiates the double standard of colonial law, favoring, in the Judge's words, "Civilization . . . Investment . . . Christianity . . . [and] Order," and condemns colonially inspired individual betrayals and tribalism. He rejects an offer to spare his life in return for naming fellow Mau Mau, and he refuses a banker's offer to make him wealthy. In rejecting colonial claims of progress and paternalistic benevolence, Kimathi, clearly a spokesman for Ngugi, espouses an anticapitalistic, classless society of laborers who draw on their own customs for values rather than those of Christianity. In the Movement's closing, Kimathi, suffering from torture and beatings, refuses to surrender or to betray his compatriots.

The Third Movement begins with the Woman clarifying the plan to rescue Kimathi with the Boy and the Girl. She tells them stories that contribute to Kimathi's legendary status, honoring the qualities of his leadership. Thus, the Woman links respect for the oral tradition to qualities necessary for the people's support of a revolutionary leader. The major portion of the Movement consists of a flashback to Kimathi's command in a guerrilla camp in the Nyandarua forest. In long, didactic monologues, Kimathi, in the midst of directing the executions of British and African soldiers, justifies the Mau Mau war with mini-lectures on the pan-African arms supply to revolutionary movements, preaching self-sufficiency in weaponry, production, and education; the study of the lives of heroes as necessary training to comprehend history; and black pride as the basis for African self-determination. Calling for "unity and discipline in struggle," Kimathi touches on a number of issues, calling for the subordination of the individual's desires to the community's needs and calling explicitly for the implementation of an African socialist philosophy. As the flashback closes, Kimathi, in a demonstrative act of compassion, spares the lives of several collaborators, among them his younger brother. They escape, however, and flee to the British, to betray the Mau Mau again with their testimony against Kimathi in the closing courtroom scene. When the Woman, having failed in the rescue attempt, is detained, Kimathi is sentenced to hang, and the Boy and the Girl fire their gun as darkness falls on the stage. A moment later, the stage erupts with the Boy and the Girl—the potential of the uneducated masses now having attained a vision of their own wisdom and power from the Woman—leading a crowd of workers and peasants in a freedom song in which the audience is encouraged to participate. The ambiguous end of Kimathi's life is thus downplayed, despite the construction of his legend throughout the play. Instead of merely celebrating a heroic revolutionary leader, the play's conclusion emphasizes a revolutionary spirit that remains potent long after Dedan Kimathi and the Mau Mau resistance have passed away.

I WILL MARRY WHEN I WANT

Like *The Trial of Dedan Kimathi*, Ngugi's Gikuyu *I Will Marry When I Want* rejected the proscriptions for well-made drama in favor of an indigenous combination of mimed dance, historical realism, social vision, and heroic symbolism. Although the former play is passionate in rhetoric and plain in diction, it was accessible only to those who comprehend English, and it was written by playwrights for an audience. *I Will Marry When I Want*, on the contrary, grew not only from Ngugi's collaboration with Ngugi wa Mirii but also from the collective contributions of the Kamiriithu community center. Changes by actors and crew were incorporated into the play in both its script and its performance, as there was much opportunity for improvisation. Consequently, the play includes a greater number of Mau Mau songs and Christian hymns, a much more extensive use of ritual and dance, and many more proverbs and striking images than the earlier play of the same period. Unlike *The Trial of Dedan Kimathi*, *I Will Marry When I Want* is set in contemporary neocolonial Kenya. Further, to a greater extent than does the earlier play, it

embraces the entire history of the country—from before the coming of white settlers to a vision of a just, compassionate society of the future—centering on the village marriage ceremony as the symbol of a united, classless society. Ironically, Ngugi's dramas in the 1960's often presented marriage as an emblem of conflict and constraint. In *I Will Marry When I Want*, marriage is transformed from a deceptive scheme to swindle a poor family out of its land into an ideal that has the capacity to renew the strength of traditional family life in contemporary times.

The plot of *I Will Marry When I Want* pits the hypocritical piety of a Christian elite against the dignity and desperation of traditional Gikuyu, who are forced to work factory shifts or as farm laborers. The elite Ahab Kioi wa Kanoru and his wife Jezebel wa Kanoru conspire with foreign investors and Kenyan middlemen to swindle the poor Kiguunda and his wife, Wangeci, out of their last acre of land by coercing him to use his property as collateral for a loan to cover the costs of a Christian wedding between Kiguunda's daughter Gathoni and Kioi's son John Muhuuni. Kiguunda's land, on which stands his one-room house, has been selected for the site of an insecticide factory, thus keeping it at an agreeable distance from the homes of the wealthy and near the exploited laborers who will work there. Believing that Kioi plans a union of the two households, Wangeci condones the wedding, only to learn that John has abandoned the pregnant Gathoni. When Kiguunda insists on the marriage, Kioi dismisses them with contempt. When Kiguunda cannot meet the payments on the loan, he loses his furniture and, presumably, will eventually lose his house and his land as well. The play closes with Kiguunda drunk, Gathoni working as a prostitute in a local bar, and Wangeci crushed by hopelessness.

Both of Ngugi's plays of the 1970's call for adherence to traditional values in an egalitarian society. Those values, however anchored in the past, must be adaptable to changing conditions and responsive to the needs of the exploited, or they become only faint memories. Kiguunda's mimicry of Kioi's hollow Christian piety and his aspirations to the elite's ruthless materialism are as much responsible for his downfall as is Kioi's merciless conspiracy. Wangeci, for example, blinded by her own materialism, believes against all reason that Kioi actually wants to unite their two households. Kiguunda believes in neither a coherent social vision of freedom and justice nor a committed lifestyle of traditional values. Like the earlier betrayal of the Mau Mau, Kiguunda's betrayal of his own origins and values is a failure of leadership; Gicaamba, a factory worker and neighbor, provides the contrasting model. He opposes Kiguunda's flirtation with the elite Kioi and, throughout the play, portrays a leader who converts struggle and despair into pride in human dignity and protest against the elite. Echoed in the communal pageantry of song and dance, these attributes of leadership reverberate in speech rhythms of free verse, permitting easy identification and empathy by the audience. The audience, then, views a play wherein they themselves are the heroic force of social change, a dynamic relationship between stage and audience that evokes the drama of communal commitment overcoming the greedy whims of egocentric power brokers.

Entirely African in its design, *I Will Marry When I Want* represents the enactment of Dedan Kimathi's teaching: "unite, drive out the enemy and control your own riches, enjoy the fruit of your sweat." Ngugi's success as a dramatist is exemplified by the enthusiastic but violent reactions of audiences attending the first few performances before the government banned the play and detained Ngugi. *Mother, Sing for Me*, a musical that explores Kenya's past, was also suppressed. Few playwrights in the history of drama have suffered so for their power to move an audience to action.

OTHER MAJOR WORKS

LONG FICTION: *Weep Not, Child*, 1964; *The River Between*, 1965; *A Grain of Wheat*, 1967; *Secret Lives*, 1974; *Petals of Blood*, 1977; *Caitaani Mutharaba-Ini*, 1980 (*Devil on the Cross*, 1982); *Matigari ma Njiruungi*, 1986 (*Matigari*, 1989).

SHORT FICTION: *Secret Lives and Other Stories*, 1975.

NONFICTION: *Homecoming: Essays on African and Caribbean Literature, Culture, and Politics*, 1972; *Writers in Politics*, 1981, revision, 1997; *Detained: A Writer's Prison Diary*, 1981; *Barrel of a Pen: Resistance to Repression in Neo-Colonial Kenya*, 1983; *Decolonising the Mind: The Politics of Language in African Literature*, 1986; *Writing Against Neocolonialism*, 1986; *Moving the Centre: The Struggle for Cultural Freedoms*, 1993; *Penpoints, Gunpoints, and Dreams: Toward a Critical Theory of the Arts and the State of Africa*, 1998.

MISCELLANEOUS: *The World of Ngugi wa Thiong'o*, 1995 (Charles Cantalupo, editor; essays, poems, and interviews).

BIBLIOGRAPHY

Cantalupo, Charles, ed. *Ngugi wa Thiong'o: Texts and Contexts*. Edinburgh: Edinburgh University Press, 1997. A selection of contributions from a major conference held in 1994 to honor and examine Ngugi's work. Although the emphasis is on the prose works, the criticism touches on issues, including Ngugi's status as an exile and his use of the Gikuyu language, that also inform the drama.

Gikandi, Simon. *Ngugi Wa Thiong'o*. Cambridge Studies in African and Caribbean Literature series. Cambridge, England: Cambridge University Press, 2001. Examines each of Ngugi's works in the context of its historical background and in light of Ngugi's life. Gikandi asserts that Ngugi's novels are of primary importance to Ngugi himself, and that the drama and criticism are meant to supplement the novels.

Gugelberger, Georg M. "'When Evil-Doing Comes Like Falling Rain': Brecht, Alioum Fantoure, Ngugi wa Thiong'o." *Comparative Literature Studies* 24, no. 4 (1987): 370-386. Presenting a valuable tie-in with Brechtian ideas, Gugelberger cites Ngugi's use of a Bertolt Brecht poem in his prison diary and mentions Brecht's *Leben des Galilei* (1943; *Galileo*, 1947) in Ngugi's essay, "Freedom of the Artist." He points out that "both Brecht and Ngugi are facilitators of social change."

Lovesey, Oliver. *Ngugi Wa Thiong'o*. New York: Twayne, 2000. The best introduction to Ngugi's life and work for the general reader. Among its five chapters of criticism and analysis is one on "Performing Revolution: Plays and Film." Also includes a chronology and annotated bibliography.

Nazareth, Peter, ed. *Critical Essays on Ngugi Wa Thiong'o*. New York: Twayne, 2000. A collection of essays, most of them previously published, that examine themes, language use, and use of the oral tradition in Ngugi's novels.

Ndigirigi, Gicingiri. *Ngugi Wa Thiong'o's Drama and the Kamiriithu Popular Theater Experiment*. Lawrenceville: Africa World Press, 2000. The only book-length critical study devoted entirely to Ngugi's drama, this book treats the plays individually and as a continuum revealing the author's search for social relevance.

Ross, Robert L., ed. *International Literature in English: Essays on the Major Writers*. New York: Garland, 1991. G. D. Killam presents information on Ngugi, pointing out his progress from *The River Between*, Ngugi's second novel, to *Matigari*. Provides some direct discussion of his plays, especially the portrait of Dedan Kimathi and the "simple folk" of *I Will Marry When I Want*. Contains a strong bibliography of articles in African literature sources.

Sharma, Govind Narain. "Socialism and Civilization: The Revolutionary Traditionalism of Ngugi wa Thiong'o." *Ariel* 19 (April, 1988): 21-30. Offers comments on Ngugi's commitment to Marxism, his contempt for the middle class, and his observations on the Mau Mau Uprising, "the epitome of a revolutionary movement by the peasantry." Deals extensively with *I Will Marry When I Want* and *Devil on the Cross*, dividing African history into pre- and postimperialist eras.

Williams, Patrick. *Ngugi Wa Thiong'o*. Contemporary World Writers series. Manchester, England: Manchester University Press, 2000. Examines all Ngugi's writing through *Penpoints, Gunpoints, and Dreams*. Includes detailed analysis of all the major plays, in accessible and stimulating language.

Michael Loudon, updated by Thomas J. Taylor and Cynthia A. Bily

---

GIOVANNI BATTISTA NICCOLINI

Born: Bagni di San Giuliano, province of Pisa (now in Italy); October 29, 1782
Died: Florence, Italy; September 20, 1861

PRINCIPAL DRAMA

Polissena, pb. 1811, pr. 1813
Ino e Temisto, wr. 1814, pr. 1824, pb. 1825
Matilde, wr. 1815, pr., pb. 1825 (adaptation of John Home's play *Douglas*)
Nabucco, pr. 1816, pb. 1819
Medea, pr. 1816, pb. 1858 (based on Euripides' play)
Giovanni da Procida, wr. 1817, pr. 1830, pb. 1831
Edipo nel bosco delle Eumenidi, pr. 1823, pb. 1825 (based on Sophocles' play *Oedipus Tyrannus*)
Antonio Foscarini, pr., pb. 1827
Lodovico Sforza, pb. 1833, pr. 1847
Beatrice Cenci, wr. 1838, pb. 1844 (adaptation of Percy Bysshe Shelley's dramatic poem *The Cenci*)
Rosmonda d'Inghilterra, pr. 1838, pb. 1844
Arnaldo da Brescia, wr. 1838, pb. 1843 (*Arnold of Brescia: A Tragedy*, 1846)
Filippo Strozzi, pb. 1847
Mario e i Cimbri, pb. 1858

OTHER LITERARY FORMS

In addition to his plays, Giovanni Battista Niccolini wrote poetry, literary and historical essays, and articles that he contributed to the journal *Antologia*. Particularly influenced by classical Greek drama, Niccolini undertook, in addition to his own adaptations of Euripides and Sophocles, translations of several of Aeschylus's plays.

ACHIEVEMENTS

During his times, Giovanni Battista Niccolini was acclaimed in Italy as a great tragedian, particularly for *Arnold of Brescia*. His most popular work, *Giovanni da Procida*, produced in Florence in January of 1830, was received with great enthusiasm but, as a result of its political content, was banned until 1847. The play encapsulates the theme of Niccolini's lifework: patriotism and liberty in opposition to tyranny—both the neo-Guelfic tendencies of the period and the imperial ones. As Mario Sansone noted, however, Niccolini's plays, lacking realism and psychological insight, have not withstood the "corrosive work of time." A work such as *Arnold of Brescia* was very popular during Niccolini's day because the title character represented the ideal libertarian—an enemy of papal and imperial tyranny and an advocate of the popular republic, a system also favored by Niccolini. These time-bound concerns are expressed in several of Niccolini's other plays as well.

Stylistically, Niccolini is a transitional figure, representing the shift from classicism to Romanticism, as can be seen in *Matilde* (adapted from John Home's *Douglas* of 1757), whose plot, set in medieval times, is typically Romantic, and in *Nabucco*. The historical and nationalistic themes of both plays reverberate with passionate political eloquence.

Niccolini is thus important more as a representative of the ideals and trends of his age than for his individual plays. He used the theater as a social and political weapon to awaken the conscience of the Italian people against foreign invasion and tyranny.

BIOGRAPHY

Giovanni Battista Niccolini was born in Bagni di San Giuliano, in the province of Pisa (some reference works give Lucca as the province, but this is a mistake), on October 29, 1782, to a noble and prosperous Florentine family. Both his father, Ippolito, and his mother, Vincenza da Filicia, were descendants of noble families. Ippolito worked for the grand duke of Tuscany as superintendent of the baths. The young

Niccolini attended the Scolopi School in Florence and subsequently enrolled in the School of Jurisprudence of the University of Pisa. He received his doctorate in 1802.

As early as 1799, when Niccolini was still in his teens, he was an ardent republican, an outspoken liberal, and an anticlerical. It is said that he was influenced by his maternal uncle, Alemanno da Filicia. More notable, however, was the influence of the poets Ugo Foscolo and Giovanni Fantoni. In 1803, Foscolo dedicated to Niccolini some odes and sonnets, as well as *La chioma di Berenice*. Foscolo also seems to have cast Niccolini in the character of Lorenzo Alderani in *Le ultime lettere de Jacopo Ortis* (1802; *Last Letters of Jacopo Ortis*, 1970).

In 1804, Niccolini returned to Florence, where his family was experiencing financial difficulties because of his father's death. From 1804 to 1807, Niccolini worked in the Riformagioni Archive, earning a modest income. In 1807, he succeeded in obtaining a teaching position in history and mythology at the Academy of Fine Arts, where he worked also as librarian and secretary. He was also a member of the Accademia della Crusca (the most important linguistic academy in Italy, founded in Florence toward the end of the sixteenth century, whose purpose was to maintain the purity of the language), which presented him with the Premio della Crusca award for his first dramatic work, *Polissena*; the play was later staged in the Teatro Nuovo (previously called the Teatro della Pallacorda) in Florence on January 15, 1813. For a short period, Niccolini acted as tutor for the court pages of Elisa Baciocchi Bonaparte and as private librarian to the grand duke of Tuscany. *Polissena* pleased both public and critics, including critic Jean Sismondi, who generally did not have great sympathy for the classicists.

Starting in 1814, Niccolini became prolific in theatrical works: He wrote *Ino e Temisto* in 1814, a minor, less successful drama; *Matilde* in 1815, a Romantic drama adapted from John Home's *Douglas*, whose Scottish events are transplanted to medieval Sicily; and *Nabucco* in 1815, which was published in London in 1819 with the help of Gino Capponi, who believed that government censors would suppress it in Italy. *Nabucco* portrays, under the guise of a Babylonian milieu, the last years of Napoleon's deeds and events. *Matilde* and *Nabucco*, admired mostly for their style and eloquence rather than their dramatic power, represent the beginning of Niccolini's new way and his acceptance of Romanticism. Subsequent dramas, such as *Antonio Foscarini, Giovanni da Procida, Lodovico Sforza, Beatrice Cenci, Rosmonda d'Inghilterra, Arnold of Brescia*, and *Filippo Strozzi*, his major production, are imbued with patriotism, in accordance with his views as a political agitator. His tragedies were admired more for their poetic form and their political allusions than for their dramatic power. His models became William Shakespeare, George Gordon, Lord Byron, and Friedrich Schiller, and he took more liberties in his works, breaking away from the classical mold. When *Arnold of Brescia*, which had been printed in Marseilles, was smuggled into Italy in 1843, it provoked admiration on the part of the patriots and ire on the part of the provincial governments. Niccolini himself said, "I may not have written a good tragedy, but I did take a courageous action." *Arnold of Brescia* represented the neo-Ghibelline ideals of the time, in total opposition to the neo-Guelfic party, whose manifesto was Vincenzo Gioberti's *Primato morale e civile degli Italiani* (1843). *Arnold of Brescia*, therefore, became the "antidote" to Gioberti's work.

Niccolini had been leading a rather private life in his Florence home or in a villa at Popolesco (between Pistoia and Prato) inherited from his uncle Alemanno. After *Arnold of Brescia*, he slowed down and isolated himself even more. In 1848, when Pope Pius IX created great hopes with his short-lived liberalism, Niccolini was elected to the Tuscan Senate, but he never took part in any session. In 1860, he greeted as a liberator Victor Emmanuel II, with the verses of *Giovanni da Procida*. The same king recognized Niccolini as a prophet of the Risorgimento. Niccolini had remained a liberal and republican but had come to realize that only the House of Savoy could unify Italy.

On February 3, 1860, the citizens of Florence dedicated the Teatro del Cocomero to Niccolini with a bust and the recital of part of *Arnold of Brescia*. Niccolini died in Florence on September 20, 1861,

and was buried in the Church of Santa Croce. His dream of a united and free Italy would become reality only nine years later in that same Rome that is the setting for his famous tragedy.

ANALYSIS

Giovanni Battista Niccolini began his career as a dramatist under the influence of Greek tragedy and using its subjects and themes. Niccolini admired Aeschylus, whose *Hepta epi Thēbas* (467 B.C.E.; *Seven Against Thebes*, 1777), *Agamemnōn* (458 B.C.E.; *Agamemnon*, 1777), and *Choēphoroi* (458 B.C.E.; *Libation Bearers*, 1777) he translated into Italian; Sophocles, whose *Oidipous Tyrannos* (c. 429 B.C.E.; *Oedipus Tyrannus*, 1715) he adapted as *Edipo nel bosco delle Eumenidi*; and finally Euripides, whose *Mēdeia* (431 B.C.E.; *Medea*, 1781) he also adapted for the Italian stage. The influence of Seneca can also be seen in Niccolini's works.

Although Niccolini will not be remembered as a great dramatist, his contribution to the Italian theater holds dual significance: First, he was, during his lifetime, the dramatic voice for the unification of Italy; perhaps more important to the modern student of drama history, he stood at the crossroads of the classical and Romantic traditions, and both benefited from and advanced the latter by using its techniques to further his cause.

POLISSENA

Polissena, Niccolini's first tragedy, deals with the main character's torn soul and mind. She was given to Pyrrhus, Achilles' son, as war booty. She loves him, but with remorse, because he killed her father. The Greeks, who have defeated Troy, are led to believe that the gods will not allow them to leave Troy unless Achilles' ghost is placated by the sacrifice of one of Priam's daughters at the hand of someone dear to them. Polissena, caught between filial piety and love for her man, throws herself on Pyrrhus's sword. This tragedy, though eloquent and elegant in its verses, lacks dramatic power and the force of psychological anguish. It is far superior, however, to the subsequent *Edipo nel bosco delle Eumenidi* and *Ino e Temisto*, whose only distinction lies in their refined style and eloquence, a trademark of Niccolini.

MATILDE AND NABUCCO

In 1815, Niccolini wrote *Matilde*, based on John Home's *Douglas*, and succeeded in transposing the events surrounding a Scottish woman to the setting of feudal Sicily. This play is important, not so much for its artistic content, but because it represents Niccolini's abandonment of classical and mythological themes and the acceptance of a new, Romantic subject matter. Niccolini had come to believe (as evidenced in a letter he wrote to Cesare Lucchesini in 1824) that mythology was no longer viable in an antipoetic era. During the same year, 1815, he wrote *Nabucco*, which, although set in Babylon and Assyria, is a thinly disguised political allegory for events that were taking place in Paris. Nabucco (Napoleon) refuses to grant freedom or peace to his subjects, and as his enemies overcome him, he throws himself into the Euphrates, uttering the words, "May the waves submerge my lifeless body and every king await me tremblingly." (This is the same Nabucco who, earlier, says, "I on earth and God in Heaven!") Both *Matilde* and *Nabucco*, despite their weakness of plot and characterization, therefore can be seen as inaugurating a new, more Romantic, and more political trend in Niccolini's theater, the basis of which is a patriotic and civil commitment to freedom and rebellion against tyranny.

GIOVANNI DA PROCIDA

Giovanni da Procida was written in 1817 but staged only in 1830, after several modifications. Again, the theme is political liberty. The plot revolves around Giovanni's daughter Imelda, who, during the time of the Sicilian Vespers, secretly marries one Tancredi. Tancredi, reared in Italy, has not told her that he is really French by birth, revealing this fact only after the marriage. Giovanni enters, announcing his wish that Imelda marry his friend and fellow patriot Gualtiero, with whom he is plotting to expel the French occupiers. The plot is complicated by the revelation that Tancredi is the son of Eriberto, an enemy of Giovanni and one of the most ferocious of the oppressors.

As the revolt is about to explode, Giovanni finds himself caught in a dilemma, for Imelda is also carrying a child. Moreover, the audience learns, Tancredi and Imelda are actually brother and sister: Giovanni's wife was raped by Eriberto and, after giving birth to Tancredi, died of sorrow. In the meantime, the people revolt, and there is much bloodshed. Tancredi dies of heartbreak and shame on learning of the incestuous relationship. Giovanni incites the people to rebellion. Although private and family passions are better and more vividly presented in this tragedy, the main thrust is a political cry for freedom and rebellion. The Italian patriots did not hesitate to substitute the word Austrian for French in this cry: "Let the French cross the Alps and he'll be our brother again."

ANTONIO FOSCARINI

Antonio Foscarini, which was written in 1823 and staged in 1827, became a battleground for classicists and Romantics as well as for supporters and enemies of the Venetian government. Alvise Foscarini, the doge of Venice, has a son, Antonio, who has returned from an ambassadorial mission to Switzerland. Venice is in a state of tension. The council of state, fearing a plot, passes a law establishing death as the punishment for anyone who attempts to enter at night a foreign embassy and speak to the ambassador. Antonio loves one Teresa Navagero, who has been forced to marry the state inquisitor, Contarini. Antonio has been accused of advocating political reform and is therefore suspected of sedition.

In the third act, as the two lovers meet secretly and talk of their tragic love, Contarini's men arrive. Antonio has no choice but to attempt to hide in the palace of the Spanish ambassador. He is caught, arrested, and interrogated, but the inquisitors are unable to obtain any statement from him: To save Teresa, he obstinately refuses to reveal anything about her. The two inquisitors, Contarini and Loredano, know quite well that he is innocent. Teresa, meanwhile, seeing her lover lost, confesses her love for Antonio to the doge, but it is too late: Antonio has already been put to death. She kills herself with a stiletto. This passionate Romantic drama maintains in its forms and language the classical tradition, but its success in Italy was attributable primarily to its political overtones and ideas. The plot is smoother and less cumbersome than that of *Giovanni da Procida*. One senses that here Niccolini's move away from classicism is largely because of his politics as opposed to the ideology of Romanticism. Paradoxically, it was the tenets of Romanticism that allowed Niccolini the freedom to use the stage as a political weapon.

LODOVICO SFORZA

Niccolini's dramatic production continued with *Lodovico Sforza*, published in 1833. This tragedy, set in the late fifteenth century, centers on Italy's political subservience to France caused by the deeds and machinations of Lodovico il Moro. Niccolini believed that it was during this time that Italy's miserable condition of servitude began.

ARNOLD OF BRESCIA

Arnold of Brescia is considered Niccolini's most important work, and the underground nature of its publication—it was first printed in Marseilles, France, and smuggled into Italy in 1843—stirred enthusiasm and admiration among the patriots. There were several editions of this tragedy, but the first official one approved by the authorities was in 1848, by Le Monnier, in Florence.

Many critics admire the play's contents, philosophy, and poetic power. They do not, however, see it as work for the stage; rather, it is a long poem in hendecasyllables, composed to be heard and read. Stageability did not interest Niccolini as much as ideology: He said that even if he had not written a good tragedy, he was sure that he had performed a courageous deed. The political ferment and revolutions of 1848 throughout Italy sustained this argument.

In *Arnold of Brescia*, the title character, a friar, becomes the hero and prophet of a free and republican Italy as he is being burned and his ashes scattered in the Tiber. The plot is set in the twelfth century, during the descent of Barbarossa (Frederick I) into Italy to subjugate the rebellious communes. The action takes place in Rome, where the citizens have set up a free commune supported by Arnold of Brescia, who advocates independence from both the pope and the emperor. Arnold expounds his ideology from a piazza near the Campidoglio: The freedom he seeks must encompass all of Italy, so that there will be one people, one country. The cardinals warn the people that Barbarossa's armies will descend on Italy and subjugate everyone. They have elected pontiff Adrian IV,

an Englishman, who attempts conciliation with Arnold, but this is totally useless. The murder of Cardinal Guido, a fierce enemy of the republic, provokes the ire and the anathema of the new pope.

In the meantime, although Arnold and the republic have the support of Swiss soldiers from Zurich, Arnold's excommunication and the pope's reaction have forced Arnold to move to the countryside, where his friend Giordano urges him to side with the emperor so as to defeat the pope. Arnold refuses, saying that he does not wish the German tyrant to have the land that the Church usurps from the people of Italy. Arnold also refuses to save himself by joining the Swiss troops who have now been ordered to return to their land. He is unafraid of death and will face his destiny unbending in his firm republican conviction.

As the emperor descends into Italy, Arnold is in hiding, protected by Count Ostasio, whose wife betrays his secret in the hope of saving her husband. Arnold is captured by the imperial troops and put to death. The fire that consumes his body and the ashes that are scattered across the Tiber are meant to extinguish the people's ardor for liberty and Arnold's prophetic vision. The pope says: "Nothing remains in Rome of God's enemy but an infamous memory." One can understand how these words would inflame the souls of Italian patriots and incite them to rebellion. The wickedness of the pope and the emperor are portrayed vividly, and although the main characters are not well developed as dramatic figures, they are meaningful as symbols. Again, what predominates is the eloquent and lyric expression of ideals.

OTHER MAJOR WORKS

POETRY: *La pietà*, 1823; *Canzoniere nazionale*, 1863.

NONFICTION: *Dell'imitazione dell'arte drammatica*, 1825; *Discorso sulla tragedia greca*, 1844; *Lezioni di mitologia e di storia*, 1855; *Storia della casa Svevia in Italia*, 1873.

TRANSLATIONS: *I sette a Tebe*, 1816 (of Aeschylus's *Seven Against Thebes*); *Agamennone*, 1844 (of Aeschylus's *Agamemnon*); *Le coefore*, date unknown (published posthumously; of Aeschylus's *Libation Bearers*).

BIBLIOGRAPHY

Bondanella, Peter, and Julia Conaway Bondanella, eds. *Dictionary of Italian Literature*. Rev. ed. Westport, Conn: Greenwood, 1996. An entry describes the life and works of Niccolini.

Carlson, Marvin. *The Italian Stage from Goldoni to D'Annunzio*. Jefferson, N.C. : McFarland, 1981. A look at the state of Italian drama during Niccolini's time. Bibliography and index.

Kennard, Joseph Spencer. *The Italian Theater from the Close of the Seventeenth Century*. New York: Rudge, 1932. An examination of Italian theater, including Niccolini.

Giuseppe C. DiScipio

PETER NICHOLS

Born: Bristol, England; July 31, 1927

PRINCIPAL DRAMA

The Hooded Terror, pr. 1963 (televised), pr. 1964 (staged)

A Day in the Death of Joe Egg, pr., pb. 1967

The National Health: Or, Nurse Norton's Affair, pr. 1969, pb. 1970

Forget-Me-Not Lane, pr., pb. 1971

Neither Up nor Down, pr. 1972, pb. 1987

Chez Nous, pr., pb. 1974

The Freeway, pr. 1974, pb. 1975

Harding's Luck, pr. 1974 (adaptation of E. Nesbitt's novel)

Privates on Parade, pr., pb. 1977

Born in the Gardens, pr. 1979, pb. 1980

Passion Play, pr., pb. 1981

Poppy, pr., pb. 1982

A Piece of My Mind, pr., pb. 1987

Plays: One, pb. 1987, revised pb. 1991

Plays: Two, pb. 1991

Blue Murder pr., pb. 1996

So Long Life, pr., pb. 2000

OTHER LITERARY FORMS

Peter Nichols is a prolific writer who is the author of dramatic works for motion pictures and television as well as for the stage. Among his many teleplays are *A Walk on the Grass* (1959), *The Continuity Man* (1963), and *Daddy Kiss It Better* (1969); he has adapted for the small screen works by F. Scott Fitzgerald and Evelyn Waugh. His film scripts include *Georgy Girl* (1966; with Margaret Foster; adaptation of her novel) and adaptations of his stage plays, *The National Health* (1973), *Joe Egg* (1971), *Privates on Parade* (1983). Nichols also published his autobiography, *Feeling You're Behind* (1984), and three diaries: *Diaries, 1969-1977* (2000).

ACHIEVEMENTS

Peter Nichols has risen rather slowly through the ranks of his profession, with even *A Day in the Death of Joe Egg* undergoing limited runs in the initial London and New York productions. Nevertheless, he has become internationally recognized as one of Great Britain's leading playwrights, and his work has entered the standard repertory of professional, university, and community playhouses. His first official support came with an Arts Council Bursary, a small stipend, in 1961. With the first stage productions of his work, the awards began to accrue, including the John Whiting Award in 1969, four *Evening Standard* Best Play awards (1967, 1969, 1981, 1978), two Society of West End Theatres Best Musical awards (1978, 1983), the Ivor Novello Award for Best Musical Comedy (1977), the Tony Award for Best Revival (1985), and the New York Drama Critics Circle Award (1989). Though he has received limited critical attention, Nichols provides a rare blend of popular entertainment and intellectual challenge. Drawing on materials as diverse as English pantomime, military vaudeville, and intimate autobiography, Nichols has created plays with unique theatrical structures and intense, unusually extreme emotional effects. His work from the 1970's has been anthologized as representative of the best in contemporary British drama. Because he has so well captured the spirit of the times and done so in such wide-ranging topics and genres, his place in the history of dramatic literature has been secured.

BIOGRAPHY

Peter Richard Nichols was born and grew up in Bristol, in the generation that went through grammar school in the wake of local hero Cary Grant's rise to fame. Nichols has documented his early years in Bristol in two of his stage plays and, most extensively, in his autobiography, *Feeling You're Behind*. Nichols's family home, Palatine Lodge, was a rambling sort of unfashionable house located across the street from a large boys' orphanage that would serve during the war as an American military barracks. The presence of the orphanage, the example of Cary Grant, and the excitement of the American influx combined in Nichols's upbringing to create an environment that was alternatively daunting or rife with the potential for upward mobility.

Both of Nichols's parents were performers of a sort. His mother, Violet Poole, had certificates in both piano and voice from the London Academy of Music and tutored students at home during the week. After the war broke out, she began to perform occasionally in service reviews but always when husband Richard, a traveling salesperson, was away. The interest her performances aroused in the audience almost led to a split in the family during the war, but Nichols's parents eventually reunited. Richard Nichols was a self-styled musical-hall clown and classical music collector. The monologue passages in *Forget-Me-Not Lane* and the autobiography appear to have been lifted almost verbatim from the bitterly comic routines the elder Nichols rehearsed at home and then used in local club performances. When Peter Nichols first tried his hand at performance, as "the Miserable Mirth Maker" in wartime service reviews, his act owed something to his father's precedent. The strong, eccentric style developed by his father later constituted an important obstacle for the younger Nichols (who also had to overcome his father's admonition that motivation for

success should come from making a habit of "feeling you're behind"), until Peter managed to master and use the style for his own effects.

While attending Bristol Grammar School, Nichols cultivated a comic self-image, and his exploits with his best friend, Cliff Browne, a gifted cartoonist, centered on the kind of irreverent ironic invention that would later pepper the sentiment of plays such as *A Day in the Death of Joe Egg*. When Nichols joined the military after the war, however, his attitude shifted; he became a dedicated diarist, trying hard to impress the other servicemen with his sophistication. Stationed in a dismal camp near Calcutta during the Indian independence movement, a melancholy Nichols observed with some detachment the effects of political conflict and maintained the discipline of keeping a journal, as he would for the rest of his life. Transferred to the Royal Air Force (RAF) entertainment unit in Singapore, he worked with mostly male performers, among whom were many homosexuals and transvestites, and he colorfully documented the experience in his musical comedy *Privates on Parade*. The flamboyance of the entertainment unit and its productions left an impression on Nichols that encouraged bold choices in his later use of theatrical technique.

Nichols was eventually "invalided out" of the service because of repeated bouts with dysentery. On his return to Bristol, he enrolled in the Old Vic theater school and attempted a career in acting. Though he was able to gain occasional roles in local repertory companies, Nichols gradually became disillusioned with acting. First leaving on impulse to teach English for the Berlitz school in Florence, Nichols soon returned to England and entered teacher training at the Trent Park Training College. There, he met Bernie Cooper, the model for Ben Spray, and began the routine of classes and writing that would continue through his teaching years in the late 1950's and early 1960's. His academic years supplied Nichols with material for a number of television plays as well as parts of later stage works such as *Chez Nous*.

The first break came for Nichols through the British Broadcasting Corporation, and he began writing regularly for television. While his second teleplay was in production, Nichols suffered a collapsed lung and was hospitalized. Through his parents, he became reacquainted with Thelma Reed, a childhood friend of his brother whom he had used as a model for a television character. Her hospital visits led to their marriage in 1960. For the next few years, Nichols settled into a routine of television work and family life, though the latter was increasingly clouded by the realization of his eldest daughter's severe mental disability. When some screenplay work provided Nichols with the money to write daughter Abigail's story, she served as the model for Josephine—Joe Egg—in the play that would launch Nichols's career as a professional theater writer.

In 1967, the year *A Day in the Death of Joe Egg* premiered in Glasgow, Nichols began working steadily, producing a number of important plays, as well as some less successful thesis and autobiographical plays. The major plays have been regularly adapted by Nichols for the screen, and he has also continued to write occasional adaptations and scripts for television. His work for the stage has been generally acclaimed since 1967, when he began working with director Michael Blakemore. Later, Nichols would direct some of his own work, such as the Bristol Old Vic production of *Born in the Gardens* and the Guthrie production of *The National Health*. The intensity and theatrical inventiveness of *A Day in the Death of Joe Egg* continued through a series of plays on social issues and family life that peaked with *Passion Play* and his most accomplished musical, *Poppy*.

Nichols announced his retirement from the stage in 1983, at a relatively early point in his career as a playwright. The decision was regrettable—and apparently not final. His plans to work on a trilogy of novels resulted in an adaptation for the stage in 1987 entitled *A Piece of My Mind*, which chronicles a writer's failure to write in narrative form. Two more plays followed: *Blue Murder* and *So Long Life*. Nichols "preretirement" plays were collected in two volumes for the Methuen World Dramatists series, and the occasion of their republication offered Nichols an opportunity to comment on the biographical circumstances of their composition and to summarize his work. His own conclusion was that he valued the role of the audience in the theater. One example of this is an incident, Nichols recounts, that occurred during the "performance of *The National Health* when someone in the stalls had a cardiac arrest and, from a stage full of actors robed and masked for a surgical operation, one had to ask, 'Is there a doctor in the house?'" This demonstrates Nichols's unique intuition for opportunities to "cast the audience."

ANALYSIS

Critical analyses of Peter Nichols's major works have emphasized correspondences between events and characters in the plays and the playwright's personal experiences. For the most part, Nichols does not, in fact, write unadorned autobiography. When dealing with autobiographical material, Nichols has been able to bring much passion and insight to his work, but this material has been transformed in every instance by the bold use of theatrical devices. The difference in quality between Nichols's television work and his stage plays comes fundamentally from his skill in manipulating the communicative potential of the theatrical medium and not necessarily from his use of highly personal source material. His ability to sustain complex theatrical structures and to use them to exploit his subject matter makes Nichols unique in a generation of British playwrights who have typically written with great personal reflection and political commitment. Nichols might be considered somewhat conservative in comparison with his more radical peers, yet his use of theatrical resources allows the less controversial subject matter of his plays to have a strong emotional impact on his audiences.

The final impression of Nichols's work must include not only a high estimation of his technical abilities as a theatrical writer but also an appreciation of his traditional humanism. Nichols consistently argues for mercy in a secular world and does so in a way that typically avoids naïveté and maudlin sentiment. The laughter in his plays is not usually silly but based on a kind of intellectual recognition that there is some overlooked truth behind the way people ordinarily behave. In his domestic plays as well as his more political musical comedies, Nichols appeals for understanding rather than violence, for comprehension rather than conformity. He notes

> the danger of getting seduced by laughter for its own sake. But if understanding is the end of it all, or you manage to make the audience share your world view for a moment, or give them a glimpse of things they wouldn't have seen if they hadn't gone to the theater, then you've achieved something through laughter.

With such a point of view, Nichols cannot be dismissed as a merely "commercial" writer. He has created plays that entertain, but they often draw the spectators in only to challenge them, to encourage them to face themselves and their institutions from a new, more skeptically honest and intelligent vantage point.

A DAY IN THE DEATH OF JOE EGG

The pattern of biographical reception for Nichols began with the international success of *A Day in the Death of Joe Egg*. Many details from the play were drawn from Nichols's personal experience as the father of a spastic child; his decision to represent such a character onstage had such a strong aesthetic impact at the time that biographical revelations only increased the play's potential for sensationalist responses. The central character within the play, however, is not Joe Egg but Bri, the father, a young schoolteacher, and it is the father's thoughts—in opposition to those of his wife—that direct the course of the play's events. The argument between the married couple over their responsibility to the daughter provides a classically simple dramatic plot that has no biographical parallel; other particular events, such as the attempt to kill the child through exposure, are also inventions.

The play's sense of intimacy in performance comes not so much from the audience's knowledge of the writer's biography as from the use of direct address. Nichols has acknowledged that the demands of expressing the couple's thoughts about their child seemed to defy the kinds of representational strategies he had employed as a writer of realistic television plays. The child herself could not realistically speak, and the characters were dealing with such a taboo subject in such a pressurized personal situation that it seemed implausible that they would express their thoughts openly to one another. Thus, Nichols chose to have the stage figures acknowledge the audience as listeners. This decision motivated a kind of ironic semantic split that has since proved to be the most enduring, characteristic aspect of Nichols's style.

A Day in the Death of Joe Egg begins with a "teacher skit" that Nichols wrote for an impromptu salon audience during his own teaching years. In the skit, the teacher speaks directly to the members of the audience, treating them as his class. This device served as a kind of bridge that allowed the audience gradually to be acknowledged at a time when modern realistic plays seldom did so. The teacher skit dissolves fairly quickly, but the apparent realism into which it dissolves remains pervaded with the trappings of theater: gag spiders, mad doctor bits, intentional comic misinterpretations. When Bri finally returns to soliloquy, the theatrical gesture seems more honest, more stable, than the troubled domestic scene.

The device of splitting the situations and characters into multiple semantic perspectives continues through both acts of the play and represents a kind of structural logic in the play's development. Soon after Bri's first monologue, describing the monotony of his daily life and the revulsion he feels, Sheila gets a chance to tell her side of the story in a pair of extended speeches. The final moment of the act is a *coup de théâtre* of the same order, in which the actress playing Joe Egg skips onstage jumping rope, apparently healthy and normal. The audience realizes that she is merely a projection of Sheila's maternal fantasy when the actress calmly undercuts the childish image with an announcement of the intermission. In the first act, Nichols progressively applies the semantic split between confessional monologue and dishonest realistic behavior, between the character's thoughts and actions, to both Bri and Sheila. Then, when the same device is applied to Joe Egg, there is no inner life to reveal, no consciousness, only an actress embodying a role. In act 2 the realistic action of the play gets split twice again. Because of the intimacy the audience acquired with the leading characters in the first act, it is able to see through the lies and delusions that occur in the parts that follow. The principal events in the second part are two visits, the first by married friends Freddy and Pam, the second by Bri's mother, Grace. These visits gradually intensify both the pressures on the couple to justify their decisions and the audience's sympathy for the couple, who must deal with the heartless, trivial behavior of the other adults. The ironic effect of the realistic dialogue continues through to the play's conclusion, when Sheila has returned with Joe Egg from the hospital after Bri's attempts to allow the child to die. Bri has finally abandoned his wife and child when Sheila has a last witless word with Joe about how devoted her Daddy is. The play ends enigmatically, with the handicapped child alone onstage. The multiple meanings encouraged by the other theatrical devices are finally distilled into the emblematic figure of Joe Egg, hopelessly alive.

THE NATIONAL HEALTH

The splitting of characters and situations in *A Day in the Death of Joe Egg* causes not only pathos but comedy as well. The same strategy of creating bitter comedy through ironic juxtapositon characterizes the form of Nichols's second major play, *The National Health*. The play draws on Nichols's repeated hospital stays during his military service and when suffering a collapsed lung. Nichols has removed this play more completely from autobiography, however, by adding an independent interior play, a send-up of hospital soap opera. This decision to split the play into two parts is again based on the need to manipulate audience response. The first version of *The National Health* was a realistic television play called *The End Beds*. This play, of which Nichols was particularly proud, was roundly rejected by television producers; they preferred conventional, romantic hospital drama to Nichols's grim, mordant chronicle play. Nichols responded by incorporating both attitudes toward hospital experience into the same play and changing to a theatrical venue where television norms could be viewed with more detachment. With the exception of the title character, the interior play has little contact with the unfolding of the more realistic hospital scenes, yet the principle of comparison deepens and informs the whole work.

A progressive principle applies again as well. When the play begins, there are six beds in the hospital ward; when it ends, there is only one. This image of gradual decay finds reinforcement in many other details, such as the gradual amputation of a cheerful, singing patient's limbs or the discharge of a vigorous young motorcyclist who returns from another accident brain-damaged and helpless. These patterns of progression replace what might ordinarily be considered a plot; each patient's background is sketched and his fate is sealed in the course of the action. The nearest approximation of a main character is Ash, a frustrated teacher with a stomach ulcer who worries himself helping the other patients while undergoing a more gradual decline of his own. His pathetic attempts to educate the helpless cyclist about his British heritage in a closing scene underline a second important irony in the play's title: the equation of the hospital with the failing welfare-state economy of contemporary England.

A third level of theatricality, providing the same kind of bridge between two dramatic levels as the teacher skit in *A Day in the Death of Joe Egg*, exists in the figure of Barnet, a hospital orderly. After his first entrance, in which the lowest man in the hospital, an orderly assigned not to attending the sick but to preparing the dead, has cajoled the ward's patients into good humor, Barnet begins to narrate the story of Staff Nurse Norton—not to the patients but to the theater audience. Barnet, beneath and beyond the hospital's concerns, also delivers a series of macabre monologues that serve to emphasize the difference between conventional representations of hospital life and its grim realities; for example, a comic rundown of his duties serves to mask the disappearance of Rees, one of the most endearing patients, so that his death seems like a successful magic trick. Barnet even provides a running commentary counterpointing the climax of the Nurse Norton melodrama, a spectacular kidney transplant, with the weary, unsuccessful attempts of the hospital staff to resuscitate Foster, another important sympathetic character. At the end of the play, Barnet appears surprisingly in blackface, a device that stresses his purely theatrical identity, and asserts that the audience members are themselves patients of a kind in the national health, not immune to the terrible suffering and humiliation that have befallen those in the hospital ward.

The National Health offers a broader scope on the problems of mercy killing and ethical responsibility explored by *A Day in the Death of Joe Egg*, pointing out that these are not mere personal problems but political issues. Biographical material has been reconstituted in both plays to achieve a layered, communicative structure that allows Nichols's characteristically ironic voice to emerge. The audience is encouraged to use one level of the play's action to see through others, and so the apparently simple situations and language of the plays take on a hidden depth, acquiring an unusual richness in their ability to encourage emotional response. Nichols's next few plays, though sometimes very successful, accomplish less, either because they address a limited range of concerns or because they employ less compelling theatrical techniques.

FORGET-ME-NOT LANE

Forget-Me-Not Lane limits itself almost exclusively to Nichols's troubled memories of his family life. He uses a very flexible theatrical structure, with scenes shifting through three broad time periods, fluidly moving onstage and offstage through a series of hidden doors that constitute the only setting. In *Forget-Me-Not Lane*, this theatrical structure, with its Nichols-like author/narrator providing the usual direct address, serves also to facilitate a more important thesis about the structure of the family. Nichols views the family as a kind of trap, where heredity and the following of role models cause the mistakes of the parents to be repeated by their children, even when such patterns are acknowledged and challenged. The play juxtaposes scenes selected from Nichols's childhood to others from his early married years and his mature years as a parent—the time near his own father's death. Actors double roles, enacting similar events in each time frame to underline the patterns of familial repetition. Nichols deftly orchestrates the shifting scenes, incorporating material from five or more television plays while building slowly to the revelation of the father's death—the son's response to that death. Because the play is so scrupulously atten-

tive to detail, the specific voices and cultural standing of the characters are difficult to translate beyond the time and place of the first British performance. Yet, for those same reasons, Nichols scored one of his largest popular successes in the play's original long-running London production. For critics such as John Russell Taylor, who can fund its themes with a wealth of similar experiences, the play seems to be Nichols's best, summarizing the feelings of an entire generation. From the distance of another culture, however, *Forget-Me-Not Lane* seems extremely eccentric, despite the attraction of its vaudeville elements and the cleverness of its theatrical structure.

NEITHER UP NOR DOWN

Neither Up nor Down, like *The Hooded Terror*, made only a brief appearance onstage. The next popular success for Nichols came with *Chez Nous*, the least ambitious of his major works. The play's sensational subject involves an expert on child-rearing whose fourteen-year-old daughter has a child fathered by his closest friend. The two men and their wives undergo some doubts about the choices they have made in the past, but the play fails to arouse either the deep feelings or the theatrical excitement of Nichols's best work. Though his comic touch makes the play entertaining, particularly during a late visit to the expert by two American protégés, Nichols never introduces a specific political, moral, or personal problem with the scope of the earlier works. Unlike Joe Egg, the daughter never comes onstage, and the promising thematic potential of an itinerant French-speaking vagrant is never really exploited. Like Jean Anouilh, to whom he has been compared, Nichols appears to have employed his considerable theatrical talents in some plays written purely for diversion or profit.

THE FREEWAY AND HARDING'S LUCK

The Freeway is Nichols's only attempt at a *pièce à thèse*. Once again, the amount of theatrical invention has been reduced, the only variety coming from the peculiar combination of comrades who are brought together by the national traffic jam serving as the play's premise. The work's most important aspect seems to be Nichols's new emphasis on narrative invention. Unfortunately, the world he imagines and the story he tells in *The Freeway* seem simplistic in comparison to the richness of plays drawn from biographical sources. The sort of futuristic society, based on the motor car, that Nichols uses to frame the action falls somewhere between fantasy and plausibility, satisfying neither sort of expectation. The various characters, intentionally chosen to represent different strata of British society, like their counterparts in *Forget-Me-Not Lane*, tend to lose their effectiveness when shown in another cultural context. The brief run of *The Freeway* in Jonathan Miller's National Theater production was followed shortly after by *Harding's Luck*, a children's story adaptation about the transformation of a crippled child, which must also be considered a minor work.

PRIVATES ON PARADE

Privates on Parade, on the other hand, marks a new phase in Nichols's development. Here, the theatrical devices of the early plays combine with the techniques of musical comedy to produce one of the playwright's most dynamic works. The material for the play, a portrait of corruption in a Malaysian service entertainment company, comes from Nichols's postwar duty with a similar RAF troupe. As in the first two stage plays, he has transformed the material, breaking it up with a number of different performance techniques, tinkering with theatrical illusion and simultaneous action and manipulating his medium for the most intense emotional effects. Steve, a leading character loosely based on Nichols, provides a bridge into direct address for the other characters when he narrates his letters home. The military also provides a situation in which a wide variety of social classes can plausibly be put together in the same setting; at the same time, the experience of military service cuts across national boundaries, so that the play is readily accessible to non-British audiences. *Privates on Parade* was extremely successful in its London production, which was once again directed by Michael Blakemore, and will probably age well.

The technical advances that Nichols makes in *Privates on Parade* come in two areas. Most obviously, the switch to a musical comedy form allows another level of action to be introduced in the songs, much like the level provided by direct address in the early

plays. Moreover, the freedom of writing lyrics rather than dialogue gives Nichols the chance to comment on the action from an authorial perspective, whether these comments are directed toward characters and actions in the play or toward the broader political questions that Nichols asks about the nature of British colonialism. The use of music clearly marks this new level of writing for the audience, so Nichols is simply able to add it to the kind of complex theatrical structure he had already employed in his first three stage plays.

The second area of technical advance comes in Nichols's decision to use a theater as the location for much of the action. This choice allows Nichols to crosscut from song numbers directly into dramatic scenes that are frequently rehearsals, creating stinging ironic laughter and dazzling suspense by capitalizing on the audience's confusion between the immediate performance in their own theater and performances that may have some place in the dramatic structure of the play. Here, Nichols splits not only the actors but also the theater building and even the normal concept of the theater. As in his earlier extended pun on the hospital's "operating theater" in *The National Health*, in *Privates on Parade* Nichols uses the conventional machinery of the English drag show to expose the brutality of the "theater of war." In this case, the hackneyed devices being exploited and ridiculed are not those of another form, television, but a juxtaposition of wartime bravado with the decadent cross-dress tradition that has been part and parcel of the popular English theater since before the time of William Shakespeare. The military comes off looking much like the kind of theater it sponsors: ridiculously outdated, empty, ineffectual, and above all, embarrassing.

BORN IN THE GARDENS

Compared with *Privates on Parade*, Nichols's next play, *Born in the Gardens*, looks like a retreat. Here, the biographical materials are spread out into a larger, older family than the one so familiar from *Forget-Me-Not Lane* and the television plays. The central character, an elderly widow named Maud, resembles Nichols's mother, but there is no clear biographical parallel for the play's three children. The subject is really Bristol and how life there has changed. Consequently, Nichols chose to direct the first production himself at the Bristol Old Vic, where the slow-moving realistic play was warmly received for its local interest. *Born in the Gardens* reflects interestingly back on the mother-child relationship in *A Day in the Death of Joe Egg* and complements the biographical plays centering on Nichols's father with an outstanding character study of the old woman. Unlike Nichols's major works, however, this play makes no attempt to explain or analyze the events as they are presented. *Born in the Gardens* shows the other side of the range Nichols has acquired, a naturalistic antithesis to the kind of flamboyant play he is most famous for writing.

PASSION PLAY

Nichols followed this interesting but tangential play with one of his finest works. In *Passion Play*, Nichols took a very common, almost banal, topic, marital infidelity, and illuminated it through the clever use of a few theatrical devices. The most striking of these is his decision to introduce, at the point where each partner begins to lie to the other, a second stage figure for the character—one that the spouse cannot see or hear. Each character's double then serves as a kind of passionate alter ego: James spins off a Jim, while Eleanor acquires Nell. These new figures function like conventional whispering temptation figures, arguing in opposition to the consciences of the original characters. This device, quite old, has also been employed by modern writers such as Eugene O'Neill, Bertolt Brecht, and Brian Friel. Nichols uses the split masterfully, overlapping scenes and dialogue in which the characters contradict one another's actions to create his usual blend of comedy, bitterness, and suspense. One might even suggest that Nichols wrote the play only for the sake of the trick's theatrical potential and not out of any interest in the subject or its resolution, for he notes that the play might well end with either Nell or Eleanor leaving the house. *Passion Play* seems to lack any specific biographical parallels; Nichols's lack of commitment to the resolution probably stems from a lack of personal commitment to the material itself.

The other devices that Nichols employs show the lessons he learned from *Privates on Parade*. Rather than writing musical numbers of his own, Nichols chooses to make Eleanor a singer of classical music. This characterization allows Nichols to quote liberally from music associated with Christ's Passion and (as the punning title suggests) to ask some important questions about the relation of Christian moral norms to the challenge of human sexual desire. Similarly, Nichols makes James a restorer of modern paintings, allowing frequent allusions to art history that reinforce the same themes. For a playwright with Nichols's skill in the manipulation of audience response, such a topic provides ideal material: Temptation and passion are as universal as pledges of fidelity, and when treated with the kind of riveting theatricality that Nichols can conjure, the aesthetic response called up becomes unusually intense and fulfilling. *Passion Play*, because of its accessibility and adept use of the medium, has become Nichols's most popular work.

POPPY

Poppy, the last stage work before Nichols announced his "retirement," may be the most accomplished of all of his plays. A musical comedy, *Poppy* draws on a unique set of theatrical resources to create a scathing seriocomic indictment of the imperial British opium wars. In a fairy tale gone wrong, Nichols presents the voyage of Dick Whittington, his merchant partner, his manservant, his mother, and his ward to Asia, where they propose to make their fortunes. A number of things go wrong with this ideal scenario: The fortunes will be made through a combination of evangelism and opium trading; Dick's ward, a schoolmistress who loves him, learns that she is his illegitimate half sister and becomes an opium addict; the efforts of the Chinese rulers to resist exploitation result in civil conflicts and eventually in their defeat by British gunboats. *Poppy* shows a strong commitment by Nichols to demonstrate the havoc wrought by the British empire overseas, inasmuch as the empire was built not on Christian values or on British forthrightness but on greed and deception.

The theatrical potpourri that Nichols uses to make his point is probably his most ambitious mixture ever. With a nod to W. S. Gilbert and Sir Arthur Sullivan's *The Mikado: Or, The Town of Titipu* (pr., pb.1885),

Nichols uses conventional British images of Asia in combination with the form and figures of the holiday pantomime. Unusual turns such as a 1950's-style newsreel report on nineteenth century India are deftly woven into the presentation, while the typical splitting of characters occurs in the cross-dressing of pantomime principals (Dick Whittington is a long-legged girl) and bits such as Queen Victoria's transformations into a statute of herself and a fortune figure. Story integrates with means of representation when Sally, the principal girl, is unable to marry her half brother, who is also played by a woman. The genius of the work comes in the way Nichols uses the traditional machinery of British imperial theater forms to expose the ideology of British imperialism. Tensions within the forms, such as cross-dressed stage figures and chauvinistic choruses, are exploited to reveal the decadence in the culture that created them. All this happens in a colorful spectacle that children might enjoy in the same way that they innocently enjoy a typical innuendo-ridden British pantomime. *Poppy* elevates the theme of innocence-gone-wrong to a national level and employs the materials of the nation's cherished "innocent" performances, holiday entertainments, to make its point.

A PIECE OF MY MIND

Nichols's *A Piece of My Mind*, which marked his return to the stage after a five-year absence, moves his autobiographical method out of his obsessive memories of adolescence and into a concern with the struggles of a mature writer with his literary form, his personal limitations, and his rivals. Like *Forget-Me-Not Lane*, the play uses doubling of parts and shifts through time and place, movements in and out of character. The story, about a man who retires from playwriting to work on an autobiographical novel, closely parallels Nichols's life. Moreover, the rival writers bear resemblance to contemporary British playwrights Charles Wood and Tom Stoppard. The result is a Pirandellian collage of fact and fantasy, truth and fiction, that allows the technical virtuosity of Nichols to shine while underscoring it with a primary theme of failure. In *A Piece of My Mind*, Nichols continues to work with the tools and themes of his best plays, providing a balance between

formalist effect and painful confession that confirms his status as a leading writer of ironic comedy.

A Piece of My Mind embraces Nichols's self-consciousness not only as a writer who uses personal material to write his plays but also as a figure in contemporary culture whose every word is received in the context of his prior achievements. An early scene centers on an article in a reference book, which reports that the play's hero had died of a tumor four years earlier, on April Fools' Day; as the writer in *A Piece of My Mind*, Ted, explains it to his wife, he was suffering from a depression over the opening of his last play, so he pretended to be his own executor and sent in the biosheet announcing his own death. Yet there is nothing solipsistic about the spirit of Nichols's play; the jokes are clean and humorous, the ironic self-perception as cruel and original as in any of his earlier plays. Like the late plays of Anouilh or Stoppard's *The Real Thing* (pr., pb. 1983), Nichols's *A Piece of My Mind* turns the theater in on itself to reveal the fundamental values of the people who make it and try to live with the memory of its vanished performances. The play seethes with quotations, rigged entrances and exits, and inventive bits of writing. Because it never pretends to be more than the shadow of earlier works, it becomes a remarkably vivid shadow.

BLUE MURDER

After a nine-year absence, Nichols returned to playwriting in 1995 with *Blue Murder*, which he also directed through two productions. An absurdist comedy in two acts, the play opens in 1963 at a comfortable suburban home near Shrewsbury. An apparently law-abiding, conventional, well-off middle-class couple host their son Colin, an actor of small expectations and an aspiring playwright, and his new actress girlfriend, Isabel. When a radio report reveals that the next prime minister is defending Secretary of State for War John Profumo against accusations of sexual impropriety, the parents stoutly applaud his decision as the mother relentlessly serves strong drinks and the father voices prejudicial opinions of his class and ogles Isabel's legs. The businessperson father belittles the artistic pursuits of his son, who is constantly jotting down dialogue for a play, and urges the son to work for him as a respectable real estate salesperson.

An uncle, the father's producer brother who reveals the family's cockney past, arrives and surreptitiously slips some money to Isabel.

A working-class producer friend of Isabel arrives unexpectedly and uninvited, discloses her past as a chorus girl of easy virtue and her present as his now-pregnant girl, and insists she return to the city with him. She refuses and faces the rejection of the family, except for Colin. However, she reveals from her personal experience that the uncle is a shameless lecher and the father likes to dress as a maid and entertain men. Protecting the family honor, the mother fatally poisons Isabel's friend, an action that is discovered by Isabel when the father buries the body in the garden. She agrees to stay with the family on the terms that they will keep their secrets hidden. The mother starts to poison Isabel but develops a sexual passion for her and changes her mind. A police officer friend of the father arrives and takes part in the complicity. At the act's end, all gather at the piano to sing a song entitled "Nice People." Decency appears to be fraud, and almost all are shown to be unprincipled and sexually depraved.

The second act, set in a guardsman barracks facing the courtyard of St. James Palace in 1967, introduces a new group of characters (largely guardsmen, petty officials, and women workers)—played by the same actors as in act 1. After a number of continuing farcical concealments and encounters (aided by three doors) involving secretive bisexual love affairs, an unwanted pregnancy, and a leaking of incorrect red-scare information to the press, a playwright and his director arrive seeking approval from the assistant controller to get a play licensed. The play is the one written from the events of the first act. The controller, whose past is as checkered as those of his companions, refuses to approve any line or event deemed improper, which results in the play being destroyed. The playwright acquiesces and the director fumes. The scene shifts to the future in which the writer reworks his script and returns to act 2 to find it is licensed. The play suggests a play-within-a-play format because several characters, events, and issues in the second act closely resemble those of act 1. After the final blackout, the audience hears these lines: "Good au-thors too who once knew better words/ Now only use four-letter words/ Writing prose . . . / Anything Goes." Despite uneven structuring in the second act, the play comically yet firmly comments on the shortcoming of generational mores, class system hypocrisy, and literary developments. Essayist Enoch Brater has observed that Nichols's sophisticated handling of the technical devices of staging "make[s] viewers confront in some small way the shallowness of many of their own endeavors."

OTHER MAJOR WORKS

SCREENPLAYS: *Catch Us If You Can*, 1965 (pb. in U.S. as *Having a Wild Weekend*, 1965); *Georgy Girl*, 1966 (with Margaret Foster; adaptation of her novel); *Joe Egg*, 1971 (adaptation of his stage play *A Day in the Death of Joe Egg*); *The National Health*, 1973 (adaptation of his stage play); *Privates on Parade*, 1983 (adaptation of his stage play); *Changing Places*, 1984 (adaptation of David Lodge's novel).

TELEPLAYS: *A Walk on the Grass*, 1959; *After All*, 1959 (with Bernie Cooper); *Promenade*, 1959; *Ben Spray*, 1961; *The Reception*, 1961; *The Big Boys*, 1961; *The Heart of the County*, 1962; *The Continuity Man*, 1963; *Ben Again*, 1963; *The Hooded Terror*, 1963; *The Brick Umbrella*, 1964; *When the Wind Blows*, 1965; *The Gorge*, 1968; *Majesty*, 1968 (adaptation of F. Scott Fitzgerald's short story); *Winner Takes All*, 1968 (adaptation of Evelyn Waugh's short story); *Daddy Kiss It Better*, 1969; *Hearts and Flowers*, 1970; *The Common*, 1973.

NONFICTION: *Feeling You're Behind: An Autobiography*, 1984; *Aristophanes' Novel Forms: The Political Role of Drama*, 1998; *Diaries, 1969-1977*, 2000.

BIBLIOGRAPHY

Davison, Peter. *Contemporary Drama and the Popular Dramatic Tradition in England*. Totowa, N.J.: Barnes and Noble Books, 1982. Davison surveys the use of popular theater in Nichols's plays up to *Privates on Parade*, arguing for the complexity and value of his artistic achievement. From this essay, it seems clear that Nichols is so unusually adept at manipulating popular materials that his use of sources sometimes goes unnoticed.

Foulkes, Richard. "The Cure Is Removal of Guilt: Faith, Fidelity, and Fertility in the Plays of Peter Nichols." *Modern Drama* 29 (June, 1986): 207-215. Foulkes reviews the marital themes in *A Day in the Death of Joe Egg*, *Chez Nous*, and *Passion Play*, arguing for a common psychological pattern in all three plays' central characters. Contains strong psychological criticism, which does not reduce the author's consciousness to the same simple outline.

Miller, Brian. "Peter Nichols." In *British Television Drama*, edited by George W. Brandt. New York: Cambridge University Press, 1981. The only survey of Nichols's many excellent television plays, well researched, with a modest appraisal of the material. Nichols clearly excelled at television writing, in relation to other writers, and that achievement puts his theatrical skills in a new context, arguing for the diversity of his talents.

Nichols, Peter. "Peter Nichols on His Art, Politics, and Peers: An Interview." Interview by William Demastes. *Journal of Dramatic Theory and Criticism* 3 (Fall, 1988): 101-112. Nichols answers questions about his writing, his politics, and his position in the writing community, issues similar to those that later preoccupy him in *A Piece of My Mind*. Demastes does a thorough job of positioning Nichols in relation to other English dramatists.

Parkin, Andrew. *File on Nichols*. London: Methuen, 1993. Detailed description of Nichols's creative work including biographical information. A useful reference.

Wertheim, Albert. "The Modern British Homecoming Play." *Comparative Drama* 19, no. 2 (1985): 151-165. Considers *Born in the Gardens* in relation to themes in plays by T. S. Eliot, Harold Pinter, and David Storey. The analysis takes for granted Nichols's excellence and demonstrates the traditional quality of even his most personal writings.

Michael L. Quinn,
updated by Christian H. Moe

MARSHA NORMAN

Born: Louisville, Kentucky; September 21, 1947

PRINCIPAL DRAMA

Getting Out, pr. 1977, pb. 1979

Third and Oak, pr. 1978 (includes *The Laundromat*, pb. 1980, and *The Pool Hall*, pb. 1985)

Circus Valentine, pr. 1979, pb. 1998

The Hold-up, pr. 1980, pb. 1987

'night, Mother, pr. 1982, pb. 1983

Traveler in the Dark, pr. 1984, pb. 1988

Sarah and Abraham, pr. 1987, pb. 1998

Four Plays, pb. 1988

The Secret Garden, pr. 1991, pb. 1992 (libretto, music by Lucy Simon; adaptation of Frances Hodgson Burnett's novel)

D. Boone, pr. 1992, pb. 1998 (as *Loving Daniel Boone*)

The Red Shoes, pr. 1993

Trudy Blue, pr., pb. 1995

Collected Plays, pb. 1998

140, pr., pb. 1998 (in *Love's Fire*; based on William Shakespeare's sonnet)

OTHER LITERARY FORMS

Though known primarily as a playwright, Marsha Norman began her career as a journalist, writing a number of highly regarded feature articles and reviews of books, plays, and films for the *Louisville Times* in the mid-1970's. During this same period, she created and edited that newspaper's celebrated children's weekend supplement, "The Jelly Bean

Marsha Norman (© Miriam Berkley)

Journal." She has continued to write reviews as well as articles on playwrights and on women's issues. Her first novel, *The Fortune Teller*, appeared in 1987.

Norman has adapted a number of her works for television and film. Her film version of *'night, Mother* appeared in 1986. Her teleplays include adaptations of *The Laundromat* (1985) and *Getting Out* (1994). This success led to other work for television: *A Cooler Climate* (1999), about an unlikely friendship that develops between a wealthy Maine woman named Paula, just separated from her husband, and her just hired housekeeper Iris, a once-wealthy divorced woman. Especially popular teleplays include *Custody of the Heart* (2000), based on a book by Barbara Delinsky, about a successful woman sued for custody of her children and her much publicized *Audrey Hepburn Story* (2000), a somewhat sensationalized life of the actress.

ACHIEVEMENTS

Marsha Norman's abilities as a playwright were first recognized in 1977 by Jon Jory, director of the Festival of New Plays, Actors Theatre of Louisville. Her first major play, *Getting Out*, was cowinner of the Actors Theatre's playwriting prize. Norman's other awards include the John Gassner New Playwright's Medallion (1979), the George Oppenheimer *Newsday* Playwriting Award (1979), and grants from the National Endowment for the Arts, the Rockefeller Foundation, and the American Academy and Institute of Letters. Her masterwork, *'night, Mother*, won the 1983 Pulitzer Prize in Drama, the prestigious Hull-Warriner Award, the Susan Smith Blackburn Prize, and four Tony Award nominations. Norman also received a Tony Award and a Drama Desk Award for her Broadway musical *The Secret Garden*. She has been playwright-in-residence at the Actors Theatre of Louisville and the Mark Taper Forum in Los Angeles and has been elected to membership in the American Academy of Achievement. She has co-directed the Lila Acheson Wallace American Playwrights Program of the Juilliard School in New York City with Christopher Durang. In 1998 Norman was invited to participate in a theater project of Erindale College, University of Toronto, called *Love's Fire*, eight plays by eight contemporary playwrights each inspired by one of the sonnets of William Shakespeare. Her effort, entitled *140* from the sonnet she chose, concerns betrayal and infidelity.

Norman is known for her ability to write compellingly about the psychic pain of ordinary, often inarticulate, and generally forgotten people. Inevitably, she seizes on the single moment of greatest crisis in the lives of these people, that which allows them to rise to their greatest nobility. Though she is from the South, she makes every effort to create characterizations and settings that rise above regionalism to stand as contemporary and universal.

BIOGRAPHY

Marsha Williams Norman was born on September 21, 1947, in Louisville, Kentucky. She was a solitary child, and she inevitably cites childhood loneliness as having led to writing as a profession. Her mother, a

Fundamentalist Methodist, did not believe that the local children were "good enough," and so Norman spent her childhood reading, practicing piano, and playing with "Bettering," an imaginary friend, in her Audubon Park, Kentucky, home. A high school essay entitled "Why Do Good Men Suffer?" earned first prize in a local contest and was subsequently published in the *Kentucky English Bulletin*.

Norman's earliest works, whimsical reviews and essays published in the 1970's, appeared in local newspapers. Her most widely read pieces appeared in the *Louisville Times* starting in 1976 in "The Jelly Bean Journal," a weekend children's supplement that she created for that newspaper. It was only after Jory asked her to write a serious play that Norman recalled her counseling experiences with disturbed adolescents at Kentucky Central State Hospital (perhaps also the psychological imprisonment of her own childhood) and wrote *Getting Out*. This play was staged successfully by the Actors Theatre in 1977 and enjoyed Los Angeles and New York runs. Her most widely known play, *'night, Mother*, has been translated into twenty-three languages and was produced as a film. *Third and Oak* achieved success in Louisville in its Actors Theatre production; Robert Altman directed the first half of that play, *The Laundromat*, for a Home Box Office production. *Traveler in the Dark* received mixed reviews when presented by the American Repertory Theatre in Boston, but her musical *The Secret Garden* was successful on Broadway. *Sarah and Abraham* premiered at the Actors Theatre in 1987 and was produced at the George Street Playhouse in the fall of 1991. Her later play *D. Boone* premiered in 1992 at the Actors Theatre Humana Festival.

Norman's personal life changed greatly in the late 1970's, a period corresponding to her earliest theatrical success. Her first marriage, to Michael Norman, ended in divorce in 1974, and in November, 1978, she married Dann C. Byck, Jr., a Louisville businessperson with an interest in the theater. After their marriage, Byck increasingly involved himself in theatrical production and support of Norman's work. The couple moved to New York despite Norman's apprehensions that Manhattan life would make her writing

more difficult; as it turned out, Norman's most critically acclaimed works have all been written in New York. Norman continued to serve on the boards of the New York Foundation for the Arts and the Independent Committee for Arts Policy and to carry out her responsibilities as treasurer of the Council of the Dramatists Guild. Yet she remained closely associated with the Actors Theatre of Louisville, where her plays often open.

Her work as a dramatist led Norman to write for television, and two of her teleplays, *It's the Willingness* (1980), for the Public Broadcasting Service series *Visions*, and *In Trouble at Fifteen* (1980), for the National Broadcasting Company series *Skag*, were popularly acclaimed. Indeed, it is probably true that Norman finds television such a congenial medium for her writing because of her gift in portraying the problems of ordinary and forgotten people. It is clear that Norman is a playwright with an unusual gift for writing spare and taut dialogue and that her plays address the concerns of a very broad audience.

ANALYSIS

Marsha Noman has always maintained that it was precisely because she had no models that she came so late to drama. Nevertheless, it is clear from her studies at New York's Center for Understanding Media that she is a serious student of the theater in addition to being one of its most important developing playwrights. Her style is taut and spare, like that of Samuel Beckett, though her settings and characters are realistic. Her plays often have small casts and deal with a single moment of overwhelming importance for the protagonist. The dramatic conflict centers on the recognition of this problem and its resolution. Though this does not seem very different from the pattern of classical drama, Norman's plays focus on some difficulty that relates to the inner life of the protagonist. In consequence, her dramas depend greatly on dialogue rather than stage action, physical movement, or change of scene. They are often the cathartic conversations of ordinary people, given in simple language and without learned allusions but nevertheless profound, because they mirror the unexpressed thoughts of many individuals. Normally inarticulate, often nondescript protagonists find hidden strength and depth of feeling they had never before recognized in themselves, and they face their problems with determination. The solution is often a radical one. Though the outcome may be tragic, the central character is usually personally triumphant.

Norman deals easily with psychological questions, as in *Getting Out*, in which a young woman moves easily between Arlene, her present self, and Arlie, the girl who committed the murder that sent her to prison. In *The Hold-up*, about would-be cowboys at the beginning of the twentieth century in New Mexico, and *Traveler in the Dark*, about a brilliant surgeon unable to cope with the death of his closest coworker, Norman uses dialogue that is witty and eloquent by turns to provide a close psychological scrutiny of characters in pain. Throughout her work, Norman shows an interest in fundamental human relationships as fired in the crucible of both familial and generational conflict. All of her characters, in their own way, are struggling to survive, to find some inner strength to cope with the disabling emotions that their situations inevitably provoke. With similarities in both themes and technique, Norman's work fits easily into the traditional canon of American drama that includes such playwrights as Lillian Hellman, Tennessee Williams, and Arthur Miller, to whom she is often compared.

GETTING OUT

Getting Out deals with the difficulties of Arlene Holsclaw, a newly released parolee who served an eight-year prison term for robbery, kidnapping, and manslaughter. Eight years have greatly changed her, but she must still come to terms with her past as well as face an uncertain future. Her past is first represented by Arlie, her younger and uncontrolled self, that part of her capable of committing the earlier crimes. Played by a second actress, Arlie literally invades Arlene's shabby apartment on the first day of Arlene's new freedom. Arlie is foulmouthed, crude, and defiant in contrast to Arlene's attempt to be quiet, reserved, and self-confident. The alter ego declares that Arlene is not really free, that Arlene remains a prisoner to her younger self, and that this other part of her will surface again.

Though Arlene manages to quell Arlie, she is tormented by three other symbols of her past: a guard Arlene knew in prison who is concerned only with seducing her; her mother, who succeeds in revealing that she is domineering and selfish; and a former pimp who tries to enlist Arlene's help in supporting his addiction. The drama's tension mounts as Arlene, who could be destroyed at any moment, faces each of these temptations. She realizes that "getting out," winning personal freedom, must be accomplished by oneself and that psychological prisons are the most difficult to escape. Norman always mentions in interviews the feelings of isolation and terror she had while writing the play, that *Getting Out* represented her own emotional release.

The play was much acclaimed in its 1977 Actors Theatre production in Louisville; it was voted best new play produced by a regional theater by the American Theatre Critics Association, and it was published in extract in *The Best Plays of 1977-78* (1980), the first non-New York production ever so honored. *Getting Out* was given an Off-Broadway production at Marymount-Manhattan Theatre in the Phoenix Theatre's 1978-1979 season as well as a revival in May, 1979, at the Theatre De Lys, which ran eight months with highly favorable notices.

THIRD AND OAK

Third and Oak comprises a pair of one-act plays that explore psychological terrain similar to that of *Getting Out*. In *The Laundromat*, a widow and a woman trapped in a loveless marriage meet by chance in a local coin-operated laundry and fall into a discussion of the ironic similarity of their lives. Both desperately need love, though neither can find it. As she would often do subsequently, Norman imposes a strict time limit on conversation and action, as long as it takes to finish a week's washing, and the commonplace setting further highlights the banality of her characters' lives. *The Pool Hall*, the second half of *Third and Oak*, takes the form of a parallel conversation between the owner of the hall and the son of a famous pool shark. It similarly deals with personal frustrations and unrealized hopes. *Third and Oak* was the major success of the Actors Theatre's 1978 season, but, more important, it marks a further development of the kinds of characterizations and situations typical in Norman's plays and anticipates the playwright's great achievement *'night, Mother.*

'NIGHT, MOTHER

The simple language and ordinary women presented in *'night, Mother* contrast with the magnitude of the question with which it deals: whether a woman presumably in control of her life can rationally and with dignity end it if she chooses. Jessie Cates is, accordingly, typical of many suicide victims. She has no compelling or overwhelming crisis in her life at the time she chooses to end it. It is simply that she recognizes her life's mediocrity and tedium. Significantly, she blames neither herself nor anyone else for the failure of her marriage or the delinquency of her son. Indeed, she calmly tells her mother, Thelma Cates, what she plans to do, not to be dissuaded but to allow Thelma to understand better why she wants to die and to satisfy her mother's last desires.

Thelma has turned off her television set on the night of her daughter's suicide, no doubt the first time she has changed her usual routine in many evenings. The irony is that it has taken the crisis of Jessie's imminent suicide to force her into frank conversation with her daughter. Apparently, Thelma's life is as unfulfilling as her daughter's, but it is clear Thelma will never take her own life. She seems content with her small house, her sweets, her insipid friendships, and the superficial contacts she has with her son and daughter-in-law. Clearly, Norman has isolated a genuine paradox of the modern world: Crisis or impending catastrophe seems required for simple conversation; communication is otherwise limited to trivialities or sacrificed to television.

Her mother learns more about Jessie in her final ninety-minute conversation with her daughter than she has in a lifetime. The modern world ironically sets a premium on time; Norman emphasizes this with onstage clocks set at real time, 8:15 P.M. at the beginning of the performance, and running to the time of Jessie's suicide just before 10:00 P.M. Jessie makes repeated references to the time, particularly when her conversation with her mother falls into trivialities or becomes repetitive. Jessie's last act is to bequeath her wristwatch to her son. She is deter-

mined to kill herself on this evening, while she is in relative control of her own life. She is, therefore, certain that it is a rational decision, not influenced by her epilepsy or depression concerning her failed marriage or delinquent son.

The play has only two characters: Jessie and Thelma. Their conversation takes place in the small living room of Thelma's house, a room filled with Thelma's possessions: magazines, candy dishes, afghans, quilts, and other examples of Thelma's needlework. The house is cluttered but comfortable, and it is clearly Thelma's: Nothing is clearly identifiable as Jessie's. She does not even own the gun with which she kills herself.

Jessie is in her late thirties or early forties and seems pale and physically unsteady. She has come through a difficult period following her illness and divorce but now seems in complete control. She is systematic and disciplined in her behavior, and the lists she writes, the pencil behind her ear, and the arrangements she makes throughout the play for Thelma's comfort serve to confirm that her decision to take her life, announced to her mother at the play's outset, is both rational and carefully considered.

Thelma is in her late fifties or early sixties and has begun to feel her age. She allows Jessie to do even the simplest tasks for her. Indeed, without realizing it, she has become inordinately dependent on her daughter. The audience, accordingly, comes to realize that the real objections Thelma has to Jessie's suicide involve her concern for herself, not her daughter. By the play's end, it is clear that Jessie, despite her younger age, shows far greater maturity than her mother.

The conversation between Thelma and Jessie that forms this play is a confrontation of life and death. While nearly all the audience obviously will choose life, it is ironic that Thelma clearly loses the argument with her daughter. She is never able to give Jessie a solid reason for continuing a life so obviously unsatisfactory.

Yet it is a tribute to Norman's skill that she allows her audience to reach its own, albeit inevitable, conclusions about Jessie and Thelma. Aside from the plot's requirement that they live somewhere outside town, Thelma's house could be in any section of the country. Though nothing is said about their educational attainments, it is clear that neither woman is intellectually inclined. Jessie has the greater sensitivity and potential, but her inability to realize this potential is the very thing that causes her suicide.

Norman writes all of her plays about largely forgotten people, individuals whose lives seem small, perhaps even mean, but who, faced with some large and overwhelming problem, rise to their own varieties of eloquence. It is for this reason that Norman keeps the dialogue simple in the extreme. There are few extended speeches and little that is philosophical. She does not intend her plays as polemics on the place of suicide in the modern world, and the audience correspondingly views Jessie and Thelma as fully individualized characters. Though this violates a norm of classical tragedy, it intensifies the drama, because the audience, while not admitting the inevitability or irreversibility of Jessie's decision, remains intent on discovering just what provoked it.

OTHER MAJOR WORKS

LONG FICTION: *The Fortune Teller*, 1987.
SCREENPLAY: *Audrey Hepburn*, 1999.
TELEPLAYS: *It's the Willingness*, 1980; *In Trouble at Fifteen*, 1980; *The Laundromat*, 1985; *Getting Out*, 1994; *A Cooler Climate*, 1999; *Custody of the Heart*, 2000.

BIBLIOGRAPHY

Betsko, Kathleen, and Rachel Koenig, eds. *Interviews with Contemporary Women Playwrights*. New York: Beech Tree Books, 1987. The most wide-ranging and useful of the many interviews Norman has granted since winning the Pulitzer Prize in 1983. Topics include Norman's problems with critics, her move to New York, the influence of music on her work, her rules of playwriting, and her thoughts on issues of concern to feminist writers.

Brown, Janet. "*Getting Out/'night, Mother*." In *Taking Center Stage: Feminism in Contemporary U.S. Drama*. Metuchen: The Scarecrow Press, 1991. Deals with Norman's use of women characters, their social class and the moments of crisis that affect the ordinary people of Norman's plays.

Dolan, Jill. *The Feminist Spectator as Critic*. Ann Arbor, Mich.: UMI Research Press, 1988. In an important work, Dolan uses Norman's '*night, Mother* to show how more traditional plays by women, through claims of universality, gain acceptance into a male-dominated canon. Dolan questions the particular precedents set for other contemporary women playwrights by Norman's mainstream success.

Gornik, April. "Interview with Marsha Norman." *Bomb Magazine* 77 (Fall, 2001). The interview focuses on the relationship between the tentative but fortunately inaccurate cancer diagnosis Norman received and its relationship to the crisis-centered themes of her plays.

Hart, Lynda. "Doing Time: Hunger for Power in Marsha Norman's Plays." *Southern Quarterly* 25 (Spring, 1987): 67-79. Beginning with Norman's own comments about her work, Hart traces Norman's complex use of food and hunger imagery to capture the struggle for both nurturing and independence that her characters experience. Such image patterns are crucial to understanding the mother-daughter relationships in Norman's plays.

Keyssar, Helene. *Feminist Theatre: An Introduction to Plays of Contemporary British and American Women*. New York: Grove Press, 1985. In a chapter titled "Success and Its Limits," Keyssar considers Norman along with five other women whose work has gained recognition on the American stage. Special attention is given to '*night, Mother*, which won a Pulitzer Prize.

McDonnell, Lisa J. "Diverse Similitude: Beth Henley and Marsha Norman." *Southern Quarterly* 25 (Spring, 1987): 95-104. In an issue devoted to Southern playwrights, McDonnell examines the work of Henley and Norman, who gained recognition at the same time. Despite their similar gifts for storytelling, gothic humor, use of language, and focus on family, McDonnell finds notable differences in both the styles and worldviews of the two playwrights.

Simon, John. "Theatre Chronicle: Kopit, Norman, and Shepard." *The Hudson Review* 32 (Spring, 1979): 78-88. Simon finds the link between three diverse plays that appeared in the same season— Arthur Kopit's *Wings* (pr. 1978), Sam Shepard's *Buried Child* (pr. 1978), and Norman's *Getting Out*—in the playwrights' powerful visual imagery and exploration of fragmented selves. Simon describes *Getting Out*, with its subtle characterizations and innovative stage techniques, as an "astonishing first play."

Spencer, Jerry S. "Marsha Norman's She-Tragedies." In *Making a Spectacle: Feminist Essays on Contemporary Women's Theatre*, edited by Lynda Hart. Ann Arbor: University of Michigan Press, 1989. This article compares Norman's first three women-centered plays: *Getting Out*, *The Laundromat*, and *'night, Mother*. Despite the characters' differing and sometimes successful coping strategies, they are forced to act within the limited space traditionally offered women in tragedy.

_____. "Norman's *'night, Mother*: Psycho-Drama of Female Identity." *Modern Drama* 30 (September, 1987): 364-375. Attempting to account for differences in male and female reponses to *'night, Mother*, Spencer suggests that Norman's play is as much about issues particular to women as it is a play about suicide or death. Using feminist theory, Spencer closely analyzes the mother-daughter dynamic without suggesting that the play is overtly political.

Wolfe, Irmgard H. "Marsha Norman: A Classified Bibliography." *Studies in American Drama, 1945-Present* 3 (1988): 149-175. A brief general introduction to Norman, followed by an extensive bibliography of critical resources, interviews, and reviews of Norman's work through 1988. Of special interest are reviews of international and regional productions, newspaper articles and essays written by Norman, a list of unpublished screenplays, and several academic articles.

Robert J. Forman,
updated by Jerry S. Spencer

THOMAS NORTON *and* THOMAS SACKVILLE

Thomas Norton
Born: London, England; 1532
Died: Bedfordshire, England; March 10, 1584

Thomas Sackville
Born: Buckhurst, England; 1536
Died: London, England; April 19, 1608

PRINCIPAL DRAMA

Gorboduc, pr. 1561, pb. 1565 (authorized edition pb. 1570; also known as *The Tragedy of Ferrex and Porrex*)

OTHER LITERARY FORMS

Thomas Norton contributed verse to the miscellany of Richard Tottel, *Songs and Sonnets* (1557), one of the most widely read collections of English poetry in the entire Renaissance. In 1561, Norton translated John Calvin's final version of *Institutes of the Christian Religion*, completed only a few years before, and in 1562, he turned twenty-eight psalms into metric versions for the collection of Thomas Sternhold and John Hopkins. Norton also wrote a number of religious pamphlets. As a writer, however, he is remembered almost exclusively for his part in *Gorboduc*.

Thomas Sackville showed considerable early promise as a poet. For the second edition of the famed *A Mirror for Magistrates* (1563), Sackville provided the "Induction" and one of the tragic laments, "Complaint of Henry, Duke of Buckingham." Both poems are in rhyme royal, a stanza of seven lines of iambic pentameter rhyming *ababbcc*.

The "Induction" recounts a Dantesque journey into Hell. As a bitterly cold night falls on a desolate winter countryside, Sackville, pondering the mutability of all living things, muses particularly on the tragic falls of great men in England and wishes that someone would describe their tragedies in order to warn the living to avoid the mistakes of the dead. Suddenly, the pitiful figure of Sorrow, a goddess, appears to lead him into the underworld, where they pass such allegorical figures as Remorse, Misery, Sleep (for whom Sackville composes some of his most beautifully poetic lines), Death, and War before reaching the area where they encounter the ghost of Henry Stafford, duke of Buckingham. The second poem, Buckingham's lament, begins at this point; in it, the duke admits to the crimes he helped Richard III commit on his way to the throne, but he says that he turned against the tyrant and tried to overthrow him. The failure of his enterprise he furiously blames on the common people who deserted him, and he utters terrible curses against one of his own men, Humphrey Banaster, who ultimately betrayed him to Richard. Then, his energy almost spent, Buckingham warns magistrates to learn a lesson from his fall and to rule their subjects wisely and well.

ACHIEVEMENTS

The only achievement of Thomas Norton and Thomas Sackville in drama consists of their collaboration in *Gorboduc*, first performed at one of the Inns of Court, the Inner Temple, on January 6, 1561, where it was enough of a success to gain a second performance, before Queen Elizabeth, on January 18, at Whitehall. The title page of the first printed edition (1565) credits Norton with the first three acts and Sackville with the final two. Although that volume was a piracy, most modern scholars accept the ascription with the reservation that, based on internal evidence, Sackville appears to be the more likely author of the opening scene of act 1 and Norton, the more probable author of the final scene in the play.

The influence of *Gorboduc* is evident from the fact that a second blank-verse tragedy, the *Jocasta* (pr. 1566) of George Gascoigne and Francis Kinwelmershe, appeared at one of the Inns of Court, Gray's Inn, during 1566, the next year after the initial publication of *Gorboduc*. Within the next thirty years, English writers would produce many other tragedies, and a large number of these would contain the unrhymed iambic pentameter first introduced into drama by Norton and Sackville; blank verse would also appear in hundreds of comedies, histories, and other types of plays.

In addition to being a tragedy, *Gorboduc* is also a history play, for the English accepted the story of King Gorboduc, which had been recounted in the twelfth century in Geoffrey of Monmouth's *Historia Regum Britanniae* (1148), as a factual part of their nation's past. Some scholars claim that *Gorboduc* was the first English history play, but that honor surely belongs to John Bale's *King Johan* (pb. 1538), which obviously developed from the medieval morality play tradition. The real significance of *Gorboduc* in the development of the historical drama may be that it was the first English history free from the intrusive abstractions of the morality play.

Norton has no other significant literary achievements, but Sackville does. Sackville has been the recipient of much critical praise for his writing of the "Induction" to the second edition of *A Mirror for Magistrates*, one of the most popular of Elizabethan works. The "Induction" introduces "Complaint of Henry, Duke of Buckingham," which Sackville also penned. Although Buckingham's lament has always been considered inferior to the "Induction," it also contains a number of fine passages, such as that in which Alexander laments the death of Clitus. Praise for Sackville's poems began in his own century, and included compliments from Thomas Campion, Edmund Spenser, and many others. In more recent centuries, the acclaim has continued, culminating in George Saintsbury's famous assertion that Sackville was the author of the best English poetry to appear between the death of Geoffrey Chaucer and the flowering of Spenser.

The full measure of Sackville's achievement and of his promise as a poet may be appreciated if recent theories about the date of composition for the poems are correct. Several scholars have argued for a date as early as 1554 or 1555. If they are correct, then the lavish praise of Saintsbury and others has been given to the work of a poet not yet out of his teens.

BIOGRAPHY

Thomas Norton, born in 1532, was a member of a wealthy London family associated with the Grocer's Company. While still quite young, he entered the household of Lord Somerset, the Protector, proving himself a very intelligent youth and serving that important nobleman well as an amanuensis. Some of Norton's Calvinist ideas were formulated while he served under Somerset. As early as 1552, Norton corresponded with John Calvin.

The lives of Thomas Norton and Thomas Sackville, four years Norton's junior, touched each other several times during their careers. The first such occasion came perhaps in 1555, when they both entered the Inner Temple to study law, of which Norton later made a successful career, serving as counsel for the Stationers' Company and later as solicitor for the Merchant Taylors' Company.

Thomas Sackville (Hulton Archive by Getty Images)

Norton married twice, both times to relatives of Archbishop Thomas Cranmer: first to a daughter, Margery, then to a cousin, Alice. Cranmer was burned by the Catholics in 1556, the year after Norton had married Margery. In the latter part of his life, Norton was virulently anti-Catholic.

Norton and Sackville were associated as members of Elizabeth's first Parliament in 1558. Norton began the main period of his literary career about that time. His translation of Calvin was published in 1561; his collaboration on *Gorboduc* culminated in the performances of 1561-1562; and his verse translations of certain psalms belonged to 1562. He also wrote a few poems in Latin and some in English, as well as a number of polemical attacks against Catholics.

At various times between 1558 and 1580, Norton was a member of Parliament for Berwick and for London. Norton and Sackville both were seated in Elizabeth's second Parliament, convening in January of 1563, which wrote a new petition to request again the same things that the first Parliament had been denied: that for the good of the country Elizabeth should agree to marry and should define the succession to her Crown. Norton was a member of the committee charged with studying the question of succession, and he may even have been its chairman since his was the voice that read the committee report to the second Parliament. Norton also was the probable author of the new petition.

Norton entered Oxford in 1565, receiving a master of arts degree in 1569. In that year, he wrote an attack on the duke of Norfolk because of the proposed marriage of the duke to Mary, Queen of Scots. Norton's religious fervor earned for him a new appointment. He was asked officially to take notes at Norfolk's trial for treason, at which Sackville was one of the men who sat in judgment.

In 1571, the City of London appointed Norton to the newly created position of Remembrancer. His hatred of Catholicism led him to Rome to gather information to be used against English Papists, and in 1581, he officially became the censor of Catholics, carrying out his task with torture and with persecution. Among others, Edmund Campion and Francis Throckmorton evidently suffered from the cruelty of the Puritan zealot who came to be known as "Rackmaster-General." Indeed, Norton's Puritan fanaticism soon led him too far. When he dared to criticize episcopacy, he was removed from office, and when he continued his attacks, he was charged with treason and imprisoned in the Tower of London for a brief time in 1583. When released, his health was broken. He died the next year at the family home, Sharpenhoe, in Bedfordshire.

Thomas Sackville was born in the parish at Buckhurst in Sussex, in 1536, the only son of Sir Richard Sackville, who was a cousin of Anne Boleyn, the mother of Queen Elizabeth. Richard Sackville, who filled important positions at court under Edward VI, Mary, and Elizabeth, sent his heir to Oxford, probably around 1551. In 1555, Sackville married Cicely Baker, daughter of a Privy Councillor. In that same year, he entered the Inner Temple, but he never took a degree as barrister. Even so, the intellectual climate at the Temple must have been pleasing to Sackville. There he began to exchange ideas with Norton, and when the two young authors finished composing a tragedy some years later, they decided to stage the first performance at the law school.

Sackville's political career evidently began in 1558, when he sat as a member of both Mary's last and Elizabeth's first Parliaments. He was seated again in 1563 and by that year had evidently won the notice and the regard of Elizabeth, who requested that he be in attendance on her. Around Christmas of that year, he was in Italy, where he was imprisoned for some two weeks, evidently for speaking too openly of his Protestantism, but his friends secured his release, and he was granted an audience with the Pope. The Vatican may have hoped to use Sackville as a mediator in its relations with Elizabeth, and he seemed willing to sail for England to serve in that capacity, but on his father's urging he stayed on the Continent for some time, and nothing came of his mission.

When his father died on April 21, 1566, Sackville inherited a vast estate. On June 8, 1567, he was knighted and given the title of Baron Buckhurst. From this point to the end of his life, he served his country in many and various capacities, and he served well. In 1571, he was sent to the French court of Charles IX, ostensibly to bear congratulations to the monarch on his wedding to Elizabeth of Austria; in fact, Sackville was also there to further negotiations for a marriage between Elizabeth and the French duke of Anjou, and he was entrusted to carry messages among Elizabeth, Charles IX, and the Queen Mother of France, Catherine de Médicis. In 1572, he was a commissioner at the state trial of the duke of Norfolk, who was charged with treason for his involvement with Mary, Queen of Scots. Years later, in 1586, Sackville was supposedly the officer sent to inform Mary that the sentence of execution had been levied against her. He must have performed his painful task with great kindness, for the doomed woman gave him a gift, a carving of Christ's procession to the Cross.

In 1587, Sackville was sent on the most significant political mission of his career, a mission to smooth out difficulties with the Dutch, whose relationship with England had deteriorated under the earl of Leicester's governorship of the Low Countries. Sackville handled the difficult situation well until forced by Elizabeth to suggest that the Dutch attempt to make peace with Spain. Although disagreeing with Elizabeth on this question, he carried out her orders; predictably, the Dutch objected strenuously, and an irritated Elizabeth returned Leicester to the Netherlands, recalling Sackville in disgrace and banishing him from court. This incident marked the only time in his long career that Sackville incurred the great anger of his royal cousin. His banishment lasted only until the death of Leicester in 1588; Sackville again was the queen's trusted adviser in dealing with the Dutch in 1589, 1596, and 1598.

Honors came rapidly to Sackville after his return to the queen's favor in 1588. In 1589, he became a knight of the Order of the Garter. In 1591, he was made the Lord Chancellor of Oxford University, winning the chancellorship over a potent rival, the youthful earl of Essex, at whose trial for treason, in 1601, Sackville, by then Lord High Treasurer and Lord High Steward of England, sat in judgment and delivered the sentence of death.

When James succeeded Elizabeth as ruler of England in 1603, honors continued for Sackville. He was appointed to the Privy Council and was made Lord High Treasurer for life. On March 13 of the next year, he was made earl of Dorset. Still Chancellor of Oxford, he welcomed James there in August, 1605. He remained active politically for the rest of his life, dying while at the council table in Whitehall on April 19, 1608.

Sackville's funeral services were held in Westminster Abbey, where the sermon was preached by his chaplain, George Abbot, who later became Archbishop. Sackville was buried in the family chapel near the parish church in Withyam. He was survived by Cicely, with whom he had had seven children. In his will, he spoke of her with great love and kindness.

History certainly paints very different pictures of the two authors of *Gorboduc*. Norton became the bitter Calvinist master of a torture chamber, his religious fanaticism finally overpowering his good judgment. Sackville remained a moderate Anglican, respected by all for his humanity and working to the last for king and country.

ANALYSIS

Thomas Norton and Thomas Sackville are two extremely interesting men who wrote an extremely imporant play, *Gorboduc*. The play was the first regular English tragedy, the first English drama of any type to be written in blank verse, and one of the first English history plays. It was written in collaboration by two young, wealthy, well-educated men, trained in law, who had already served as members of Parliament. The authors performed their play before Queen Elizabeth in the troubled early years of her reign. They had no original intention of publishing their play but were forced to do so after a pirated first edition appeared with various corrupt readings. All of these factors lead to highly interesting points of analysis.

GORBODUC

Norton and Sackville wrote *Gorboduc* with one definite purpose in mind: to offer political advice to Elizabeth Tudor, the young relative of Sackville who then sat on the throne of a country sharply divided by political and religious differences. The whole play is an urgent plea for Elizabeth to do everything in her power to keep the nation united.

To dramatize their political statements, the two playwrights made significant changes in the story told by Geoffrey of Monmouth of an ancient British king. In Geoffrey's account, when King Gorboduc grows old, his two sons, Ferrex and Porrex, both desire the Crown. Porrex kills his brother but then is slain by his own mother, Widen, in revenge for Ferrex. Civil war breaks out, and the country is torn apart, eventually being divided into five different kingdoms before it is reunited under one strong leader. The horrors of a divided kingdom and of civil war were already evident in the story, but Norton and Sackville carefully altered other details to make their political arguments clearer and more emphatic, to make their play, in effect, a mirror for one magistrate. The play stresses the necessity of a ruler's heeding wise counsel, distinguishing between flatterers and good advisers, keeping control over the unruly commons, settling all questions of succession to the throne, summoning Parliament at the proper time, and ensuring that the realm will not fall to a foreign ruler.

The political messages begin in the play as early as possible, in the well-known dumb show that precedes act 1. To the music of violins, a group of savages enters with a bundle of sticks, which they try, first individually and then with their combined strength, to break. They fail—until they begin to pull the sticks out one at a time, and then they can snap them easily. The interpretation is clear: Unity is strength; division is weakness. The act that follows contains two scenes. In the first, Queen Videna (Geoffrey's Widen) sorrowfully informs her elder and favorite son that his father plans to divide Ferrex's inheritance and give half of the realm to Porrex. The second scene shows her statement to be true. King Gorboduc, whose mind is already decided on the question, nevertheless asks three of his counselors for their opinions of his plan. The first two, Arostus and Philander, agree to the division of the country, though Philander argues that it should not happen while the king is still living. Only Eubulus, whose name means "good counselor," argues against the dangerous plan, but he is ignored by Gorboduc. After the act has ended, a chorus of four ancient sages of Britain enters to voice their condemnation of the foolish decision of the king.

The tight organizational scheme of the authors is apparent: They begin with a dumb show that clearly relates to the events in the act that follows; then, the chorus comments on the action preceding it and connects that action thematically with the dumb show. The pattern will continue for all five acts, with the exception that there is no chorus after the fifth act.

Before the second act, the music of cornets ushers in a dumb show set in a royal court. A king refuses wine offered him in a glass but accepts liquid offered in a golden goblet. The king falls dead, killed by the poison within the goblet. The dumb show indicates the difference between an honest counselor whose advice is open and plain and a bad counselor who speaks with the poison of flattery.

In act 2, another aspect of the play's structure becomes apparent: Balance and contrast, while present in act 1, are much more obvious in act 2. Again there are two scenes, and in each scene there are three characters, a prince and two advisers, one good and one bad. Ferrex listens to his bad adviser, Hermon, a flattering parasite, and decides to raise an army for defense in case his brother should attack. Dordan, a wise counselor sent by Gorboduc to stay with Ferrex, has spoken against Hermon's counsel, but to no avail. He immediately writes a letter to inform Gorboduc of his son's foolishness.

Scene 2 repeats the pattern of its predecessor. Porrex agrees with Tyndar, another flatterer, who has advised him to invade his brother's realm; they ignore the outspoken opposition of Philander, a good counselor assigned by Gorboduc to stay with Porrex. In dismay, Philander hastens to inform Gorboduc in person of Porrex's invasion plans. The chorus enters to lament that unbridled youth would neglect the good advice of able counselors and listen instead to poisonous words from flattering mouths.

Before act 3, the music shifts from the loud measures of the first two dumb shows to the softer notes of flutes. With this change, another element in the art-istry of the play becomes apparent: The instruments have been selected so that the music will provide as appropriate an accompaniment to the dumb show and as appropriate a prelude to the act that follows as are possible. For example, the sad music of the flutes—which, centuries before Christ, had accompanied the elegiac verse of Greece—accompanies a group of mourners, dressed in black, who march thrice around the stage, indicating the sorrow that will soon come on the realm. In the act that follows, first Dordan's letter and then the personal report of Philander cause Gorboduc great concern, but he still has hope that he can intercede and make peace between his sons. Then, however, the type of character who frequently bears the worst of news in classical drama, the Nuntius or messenger, rushes in to tell of Porrex's invasion of his brother's land and the act of fratricide that has resulted. Gorboduc is left to mourn the death of Ferrex. The chorus then laments the mistakes of Gorboduc and of his children, which have brought black floods of mourning to the land.

The clear connection of the music with the content of the play continues throughout. For act 4, the wild music of hautboys (oboes) introduces the terrifying figures of the Furies, and before act 5 the martial music provided by drums and flutes precedes scenes of warfare. According to his chaplain, Sackville had always been interested in music; undoubtedly, the varied musical effects in the play should be credited to him.

Sackville has always been accepted as the author of act 4, and the formal parallelism that marked Norton's first three acts is no longer present. In the dumb show, each of the frighteningly ugly Furies—Alecto with a snake, Megaera with a whip, and Tisiphone with a firebrand—lashes at a king and queen who have killed their own offspring. This presentation prepares the audience for the slaying of Porrex. The typical Senecan revenge motive appears immediately; Queen Videna, distraught over the news of Ferrex's death, vows to kill her only other child.

In the following scene, Porrex appears before his father, who, although threatening dire punishment, wishes to give his son time to speak in his own defense. Porrex admits that he has killed Ferrex, but adds that he is now full of grief and guilt, so much so that he will not beg for pardon. He does remind his father, however, that the decision to grant Porrex half of the realm was Gorboduc's own and not one planted in the king's mind by Porrex. The young prince then states something not shown in earlier scenes—that Ferrex had planned to have Porrex poisoned, a plot revealed by the servant of Porrex who had been hired to do the deed. Only then did Porrex invade his brother's realm. This account is the one major example of the failure of the two parts of the play to mesh well, giving credence to the contention that composition had shifted to a second hand.

Gorboduc sends Porrex from his sight while he and his advisers determine what action he will take. The king then laments the cruelty of fate that has brought such sorrow to his old age. Arostus, in a speech which recalls Sackville's lines in the "Induction" to *A Mirror for Magistrates*, reminds Gorboduc that all the joys of life are fleeting; in life, only death is a certainty. They are interrupted by a horror-stricken servant, Marcella, who tells them that Videna has stabbed and killed Porrex. The grief of the servant and her affection for Porrex contrast with the cold viciousness and hatred of the woman who killed him. Marcella's anguished speech continues at length and closes the scene.

The chorus emphasizes the idea of Nemesis. A brother has slain a brother; Jove, greatly offended, has sent the Furies to exact vengeance by making Videna kill Porrex. The play's artistry suffers here, for the choric comment meshes imperfectly with the dumb show, in which the Furies were punishing parents who had killed their children. Furthermore, the chorus makes no mention of an uprising by the common people, and this could not have been interpreted from the action of the dumb show itself, though the commentary in the printed edition lists such an uprising as one of the things signified in the dumb show. The fact that the pirated edition of 1565 led Norton and Sackville into print in 1570 may have provided them with the opportunity to insist in print on an interpretation that would not have been understood by anyone who had watched one of the performances several years earlier.

Before act 5, the drums and flutes signal the approach of soldiers, who actually discharge their weapons before the audience. Obviously the show signals war, in this case a civil war that will rage in Britain for half a century.

The play may be charged with a lack of unity because of the handling of the fifth act. Neither Gorboduc nor Videna appears; their deaths are reported in the seventh line. Because Ferrex and Porrex have died earlier, no member of the royal family is left to bring unity into the final act. In act, Eubulus is the only character from the opening portions of the play who appears at the beginning of the final act, though later Arostus will appear. All of the other characters in act 5 are appearing for the first time.

After the murders of Ferrex and Porrex, the common people, horrified by the atrocities within the royal family, have rebelled and slaughtered both Videna and Gorboduc. Eubulus has reason to fear what actions might be committed next by the masses, in whom he has never placed any trust. With the help of some honest lords, Eubulus puts down the rebellion, but trouble immediately flares again when one ambitious nobleman, Fergus, raises an army and tries to seize the throne of a kingdom that as yet has no king clearly and rightfully placed on its throne. As Eubulus prepares to deal with the new danger, he speaks angrily against rulers who do not listen to good advice, and he anachronistically laments that Parliament had not been summoned and that the question of succession to the throne had not been clearly determined. The play has made its essential points over and over again: The land must not be divided, a ruler must listen to the good advice of wise counselors, Parliament should be called, and the succession to the throne should be incontrovertibly settled. Norton and Sackville were saying to Elizabeth what her Parliament of 1558 had already said to her and what her Parliament of 1563 would quickly say to her again.

SENECAN INFLUENCE

Because *Gorboduc* is a tragedy and because the Roman Stoic Seneca is the model for much early Renaissance tragedy as Seneca's tragedies were being translated at the time (Jasper Heywood's translation of *Thyestes* had appeared in 1560—with a preface referring to both Norton and Sackville as poets), it is natural to assume that *Gorboduc* must have been influenced by Seneca. Nevertheless, the extent of the Senecan influence has been the subject of long debate. In 1893, John W. Cunliffe argued that the debt to Seneca was obvious in almost every aspect of the play, but over the next few decades some more moderate voices maintained that the case for Senecan influence was being overstated. The extreme opposite of Cunliffe's position was reached in 1939, when Howard Baker presented his staggering argument that almost everything in *Gorboduc* could be traced to native English medieval dramatic traditions and that influence of Seneca was virtually nonexistent. The truth undoubtedly lies somewhere between the views of Cunliffe and Baker.

The presence of Seneca possibly may be seen in the revenge motive of the play, in the division into five acts with a chorus appearing between the acts to summarize the significance of what has just happened, in the appearance of the Nuntius, in several rhetorical devices, and in the presence of a number of sententious passages. The dumb shows, however, certainly stem from influences other than Seneca, and it should be noted that the play does not observe the classical unities of time, place, and action. In fact, the fifth act is but weakly related to the preceding four, for Gorboduc and his entire family are dead before the fifth act begins and the act seems to exist primarily to provide the advisers and certain lords an opportunity to pronounce the major political theories of the play.

BLANK VERSE

Except for the choruses, *Gorboduc* is written in blank verse. Norton and Sackville often have been criticized for their verse, and certainly it seems inferior when compared with the lines of greater poets writing thirty or forty years later, but when the language of *Gorboduc* is compared with the verse of other plays written in the 1550's and 1560's, it fares very well indeed. Admittedly, in some passages, particularly the long individual speeches, the carefully measured accents make the verse stiff and tedious, but the very first few lines of the opening scene indi-

cate the smooth and successful movement of which the poets were capable.

One of the reasons why the blank verse seems wooden and uninteresting is that it is being made to serve rhetorical purposes. The play abounds with rhetorical devices, and the flow of the verse is often sacrificed for alliteration, antithesis, repetition, and other rhetorical ends. The syntactic balance within individual passages is particularly noticeable. Another factor that causes dissatisfaction with the verse is its lack of metaphor; indeed, there is virtually no imagery in the poetry of the play. Finally, all of the choruses are written in rhyme; the poets generally use a six-line iambic pentameter stanza for the choric passages, but there is a considerable amount of variation.

In the final analysis, *Gorboduc* seems a remarkably successful effort. Norton and Sackville wanted to express certain specific political messages, and the play conveys those clearly and emphatically. The play contains many excellent artistic touches—in organization, in visual effect, and in its music. Only the heaviness of the style has prevented greater appreciation of the play by modern readers, and the style was no barrier to the enjoyment of Renaissance audiences, as is indicated by the compliment paid to it by one of the most discriminating minds of the age, Sir Philip Sidney, who praised it highly in *The Defence of Poesie* (1595).

Strangely, for both Norton and Sackville, *Gorboduc* represented the beginning and the end of their work in drama and, in fact, of their creative literary efforts in general. For Norton, a career in law and his passionate involvement in the religious disputes of the time would occupy the remaining years of his life, and no other of his writings would prove lasting. For Sackville, the peak of accomplishment represented by *Gorboduc* would be followed by more success in 1563, with the publication of the second edition of *A Mirror for Magistrates*, but Sackville's portions of that work had evidently been written some years earlier. After the literary acclaim early in his life, Sackville would enjoy a long and successful career of almost fifty years, but that career was dedicated to the service of the realm rather than the service of the Muses.

OTHER MAJOR WORKS

POETRY (BY SACKVILLE): "Induction," and "Complaint of Henry, Duke of Buckingham," in *A Mirror for Magistrates*, 1563 (second edition).

BIBLIOGRAPHY

Baker, Howard. *Induction to Tragedy: A Study in a Development of Form in "Gorboduc," "The Spanish Tragedy," and "Titus Andronicus."* Baton Rouge: Louisiana State University Press, 1939. This standard work considers the tragic form from two viewpoints: artistry and moral significance. Baker discusses the authorship question of *Gorboduc* and the possible Senecan influence and also considers native English dramatic influences to be very strong. Pays some attention to the historical criticism of the play.

Berlin, Normand. *Thomas Sackville.* New York: Twayne, 1974. Contains discussions of Sackville's life and his work on *A Mirror for Magistrates*, in addition to a substantial chapter on *Gorboduc*, which precedes a plea that Sackville should be more appreciated for his substantial artistic merits. Investigates *Gorboduc* for its political intent, for the mixture of Senecan and native influences, and for the likely division of parts between the co-authors. Useful annotated bibliography.

Graves, Michael A. R. *Thomas Norton: The Parliament Man.* Cambridge, Mass.: Blackwell, 1994. This biography examines the life of Norton, as well as his writings. Bibliography and index.

Walker, Greg. *The Politics of Performance in Early Renaissance Drama.* New York: Cambridge University Press, 1998. Walker examines Norton and Sackville's *Gorboduc*, among other works, in terms of its political implications. Bibliography and index.

Whall, Helen M. *To Instruct and Delight: Didactic Method in Five Tudor Dramas.* New York: Garland, 1988. Finds *Gorboduc* consciously designed for artistic effects, and its authors—unlike John Bale in *King Johan* (pb. 1538)—unsatisfied with simply delivering a powerful message. Shows evidence of their artistic concerns in the elaborate dumb shows, the patterned divisions of the five acts, and their innovative verse. Compares *Gorboduc* frequently with *King Johan*.

Howard L. Ford

O

SEAN O'CASEY
John Casey

Born: Dublin, Ireland; March 30, 1880
Died: Torquay, England; September 18, 1964

<small>PRINCIPAL DRAMA</small>

The Shadow of a Gunman, pr. 1923, pb. 1925
Cathleen Listens In, pr. 1923, pb. 1962
Juno and the Paycock, pr. 1924, pb. 1925
Nannie's Night Out, pr. 1924, pb. 1962 (one act)
Two Plays, pb. 1925 (includes *The Shadow of a Gunman* and *Juno and the Paycock*)
The Plough and the Stars, pr., pb. 1926
The Silver Tassie, pb. 1928, pr. 1929
Within the Gates, pb. 1933, pr. 1934
A Pound on Demand, pb. 1934, pr. 1947 (one act)
The End of the Beginning, pb. 1934, pr. 1937 (one act)
Five Irish Plays, pb. 1935
The Star Turns Red, pr., pb. 1940
Purple Dust, pb. 1940, pr. 1944
Red Roses for Me, pb. 1942, pr. 1943
Oak Leaves and Lavender: Or, A World on Wallpaper, pb. 1946, pr. 1947
Cock-a-Doodle Dandy, pr., pb. 1949
Collected Plays, pb. 1949-1951 (4 volumes; includes *Cock-a-Doodle Dandy, Bedtime Story, Hall of Healing, Time to Go*)
Bedtime Story, pb. 1951, pr. 1952
Hall of Healing, pr. 1951, pr. 1952 (one act)
Time to Go, pb. 1951, pr. 1952 (one act)
The Bishop's Bonfire, pr., pb. 1955
Selected Plays of Sean O'Casey, pb. 1956
Five One-Act Plays, pb. 1958, 1990
The Drums of Father Ned, pr. 1959, pb. 1960
Behind the Green Curtains, pb. 1961, pr. 1962
Figure in the Night, pb. 1961, pr. 1962 (one act)
The Moon Shines on Kylenamoe, pb. 1961, pr. 1962 (one act)
Three More Plays, pb. 1965
The Complete Plays of Sean O'Casey, pb. 1984

<small>OTHER LITERARY FORMS</small>

Along with his drama, Sean O'Casey wrote verse, political tracts, historical sketches, essays, dramatic criticism, short stories, and an extensive six-volume autobiography: *I Knock at the Door* (1939), *Pictures in the Hallway* (1942), *Drums Under the Windows* (1945), *Inishfallen, Fare Thee Well* (1949), *Rose and Crown* (1952), and *Sunset and Evening Star* (1954). The autobiography is also available in a two-volume edition, *Mirror in My House* (1956). Early in his career, O'Casey published two volumes of poetry: *Songs of the Wren* (1918) and *More Wren Songs* (1918). His political pamphlets include *The Story of Thomas Ashe* (1918), *The Sacrifice of Thomas Ashe* (1918), and *The Story of the Irish Citizen Army* (1919). O'Casey's two essay collections are *The Flying Wasp* (1937) and *The Green Crow* (1956). His essays, criticism, short stories, and verse have been collected in several anthologies, including *Windfalls* (1934), *Feathers from the Green Crow: Sean O'Casey, 1905-1925* (1962), *Under a Colored Cap* (1963), and *Blasts and Benedictions* (1967).

<small>ACHIEVEMENTS</small>

Poet, playwright, essayist, and short-story writer Sean O'Casey stands as one of the major figures of the Irish Literary Renaissance. Though he began his career as a playwright late in life, he still managed to complete more than twenty plays, a six-volume autobiography, and numerous short stories and essays before his death in 1964. Along with the works of John

Millington Synge, Lady Augusta Gregory, and William Butler Yeats, his plays sustained the Abbey Theatre during its early years, accounting for its greatest commercial successes, and they are still among the most popular works in the Abbey Theatre's repertory.

During his career, O'Casey moved beyond the confines of dramatic realism to create a new style of expressionism in Anglo-Irish theater. In this regard, he is among the most original and innovative of modern European playwrights. Perhaps only the epic realism of Bertolt Brecht's works rivals the sheer spectacle and vitality of O'Casey's stage. Though his early plays have continued in repertory, these later plays, especially, deserve to be performed more often, despite the demands of their Irish dialect and their variety of song-and-dance material. That they are not reflects the impoverishment of the modern stage, for O'Casey was a master of theatrical entertainment.

BIOGRAPHY

The youngest child in a large Irish Protestant family of modest means, Sean O'Casey was born John Casey in Dublin on March 30, 1880. He was the third child in his family to be named John; two of his siblings with that name had died in infancy. Later, in his twenties, after he had become an Irish nationalist and a member of the Gaelic League, he adopted the Gaelic version of his name, Sean O'Cathasaigh (pronounced O'Casey). O'Casey's father, Michael Casey, who came from a farming family in Limerick, worked as a clerk for the Anglican Irish Church Missions. He went to Dublin as a young man and married Susan Archer, of a respectable auctioneer's family. Michael Casey was a literate man with a good library of English classics, while O'Casey's mother was a woman of great fortitude and devotion to her children, especially her youngest, whom she sheltered because of his physical frailty and a severe eye affliction, which left his vision permanently impaired. Even in the difficult period after her husband's death, she maintained her respectability and encouraged her children to enter professions.

Michael Casey died after a protracted illness on September 6, 1886, when his youngest son was only six. With the loss of his income, the family started a gradual decline into poverty. The Caseys were forced to move to cheaper lodgings in a Dublin dockside neighborhood. There, O'Casey started to associate with working-class Catholic boys who attended the local parochial school. He had been enrolled at St. Mary's National School, where his sister Isabella taught, but when he reached the age of fourteen, his schooling came to an end. His family needed the extra income, so he began to work as a stock boy with a Dublin hardware firm. Though out of school, O'Casey continued his interest in books, and he certainly learned to read before the age of sixteen, contrary to what he later reported to Lady Gregory.

O'Casey became active in the Church of Ireland during this time and was confirmed at the age of seventeen. In his free time, he read William Shakespeare and the Irish playwright Dion Boucicault. He also attended the Mechanics' Theatre with his brother Isaac and even acted in at least one production. His love of drama was strengthened by these early productions, and after the group was later reorganized as the Abbey Theatre, he would see two of his early plays produced there in 1923.

In 1902, O'Casey began work as a laborer on the Great Northern Railway of Ireland, where he was employed for the next ten years. His budding interest in Irish nationalism led him to join the Gaelic League, learn the Irish language, and change his name. Within a short time, he was also a member of the Irish Republican Brotherhood. Through these associations, O'Casey began to shape his identity as Irish nationalist, laborer, and political activist. His interest in writing also emerged as he joined the St. Lawrence O'Toole Club, a local literary society. Above all, he forged the commitment to Irish nationalism that would occupy him for the next twenty years.

O'Casey joined the Irish Transport and General Workers Union in 1909 and was dismissed from his job later that year for refusing to sign a nonstrike pledge during the railway strike. Left unemployed, he turned increasingly to politics while he supported himself as a laborer in the building trade. From his perspective, socialism began to look attractive as an alternative to British economic domination of Ireland. The six-month Dublin labor lockout of 1913 hardened his political views, as he helped organize a relief fund for destitute families. Becoming more militant, he drafted part of the constitution for the Irish Citizen Army, though recuperation from an operation and personal doubts kept him from taking part in the weeklong insurrection of Easter, 1916. Instead, he wrote poems, pamphlets, and broadsides in support of the Irish cause.

His mother and sister died in 1918, leaving O'Casey to board temporarily with the family of his brother Michael. This period marked a low point in O'Casey's fortunes because he was out of work and was forced to accept the charity of others. Yet he was determined to write. In 1921, while living in a small flat, he started work on his three Dublin plays: *The Shadow of a Gunman*, *Juno and the Paycock*, and *The Plough and the Stars*. O'Casey reached the age of forty-three before *The Shadow of a Gunman* was finally produced, in April, 1923, but his career as a playwright had finally begun. *Juno and the Paycock* followed in March, 1924, and *The Plough and the Stars*, two years later.

O'Casey's Dublin play *The Plough and the Stars* presented such an unflattering view of the Easter Week uprising of 1916 that the audience rioted when it opened at the Abbey Theatre in February, 1926. Yeats stood up before the mob and defended the play, but O'Casey was embittered by its hostile reception and decided shortly afterward to leave Ireland for voluntary exile in England.

In 1926, O'Casey won the Hawthornden Prize for *Juno and the Paycock*, and he left for London that spring to accept the award in person. There, he hoped to find greater artistic freedom as a playwright. During his first three years in London, he was introduced to George Bernard Shaw, had his portrait painted by Augustus John, and met the talented and attractive actress Eileen Reynolds (stage name Carey), whom he married on September 23, 1927. They were to enjoy a long and mutually supportive marriage for thirty-seven years, with their three children, Breon, Niall, and Shivaun. Marriage and life in London apparently had a salutary effect on O'Casey's imagination, for he began to work almost immediately after their marriage on the expressionistic play *The Silver Tassie*, which marked a clear departure from his earlier work.

O'Casey had been attracted to socialism as early as 1911, during the Irish railway strike, but the economic hardships of the 1930's and the rise of Fascism drove him further to the left, to the point of tacitly accepting Communism and serving as a member of the advisory board of the London *Daily Worker*. He also became increasingly anticlerical in regard to Ireland, viewing the Catholic prelacy as the oppressor of the Irish people. After World War II, O'Casey spoke out vigorously in favor of the Soviet Union. He opposed the arms race and urged nuclear disarmament.

In 1954, O'Casey moved with his family from London to the resort town of St. Marychurch, Torquay, in Devon. There, in 1956, the family suffered a deep personal loss when the younger son, Niall, died of leukemia. In his mid-seventies when this misfortune occurred, virtually blind and suffering from constant pain, O'Casey still possessed the strength of character to write a moving tribute to his son, "Under a Greenwood Tree He Died," and to continue his play-

Sean O'Casey (Hulton Archive by Getty Images)

writing. Friends remembered him from these last years as a thin, sharp-faced man with a gay spirit and an enchanting Irish brogue, who was usually dressed in a warm turtleneck sweater and one of the brightly colored caps that his daughter had knit for him.

The last decade of O'Casey's life showed an increasing American interest in his work and brought him numerous awards and honors, most of which he declined, including an appointment as Commander of the Order of the British Empire and several honorary doctorates from the Universities of Durham and Exeter and from Trinity College, Dublin. His eightieth birthday was celebrated with much fanfare. After suffering a heart attack, O'Casey died in Torquay on September 18, 1964, at the age of eighty-four.

ANALYSIS

In "O'Casey's Credo," an essay that appeared in *The New York Times* and was written in 1958 for the opening of an American production of *Cock-a-Doodle Dandy*, Sean O'Casey remarked that "the first thing I try to do is to make a play live: live as a part of life, and live in its own right as a work of drama." This concern with the vitality of his plays marked O'Casey's craftsmanship as a playwright throughout his career. "Every character, every life," he continued, "[has] something to say, comic or serious, and to say it well [is] not an easy thing to do." To express this vitality through his characters' actions and dialogue was O'Casey's goal as a dramatist. All of his plays share the blend of comic, serious, and poetic imagination that O'Casey believed should meld in any play worth staging.

O'CASEY'S THREE PERIODS

O'Casey's plays fall into three periods: the early naturalistic tragicomedies, the expressionistic plays of the middle period, and the exuberant, satiric comedies that mark his later work. O'Casey was forty-three years old when his first play, *The Shadow of a Gunman*, was accepted by the Abbey Theatre. Behind him lay four apprentice plays and more than twenty years of hard experience in Dublin as a laborer, nationalist, and political organizer. He might easily have failed to develop his talent but for the encouragement of Lady Augusta Gregory, Yeats, and Lennox Robinson, who read his early scripts and urged him to continue writing. O'Casey was drawn to the theater as a social medium—as the best way for him to express the impact on Dublin's poor of Ireland's struggle for independence.

O'Casey's first play, *The Shadow of a Gunman*, opened at the Abbey Theatre in April, 1923, and ran for only a few performances, but its modest success encouraged O'Casey to submit *Juno and the Paycock* and *The Plough and the Stars* within the next three years. O'Casey had lived through the bitter period when Ireland was torn first by insurrection and later by the bloody struggle between the Irish Republican Army and the notorious Black and Tans. In these plays, his Dublin trilogy, he expresses disillusionment and bitterness about the way in which the Irish struggle for independence degenerated into fratricidal bloodshed. Together, these plays present a chronicle history of the Irish conflict between 1916 and 1921. Naturalistic in style and approach, they are noted, as critics have remarked, for their tragicomic tone, their vivid depictions of Dublin tenement dwellers, and their lively and colorful speech.

The second period of O'Casey's playwriting career began after he left Dublin for London in 1926. Up to this point, he had been an Irish playwright writing for a national theater, but the response to *The Plough and the Stars*, which provoked a riot at the Abbey Theatre when it opened, may have led him to recognize the limitations of conventional dramatic realism. Seeking ways to expand his artistic vision, O'Casey turned to the expressionistic mode in his next play, *The Silver Tassie*. Inspired by a London coal vendor's song, this ambitious play about World War I incorporates songs, chants, ritualistic scenes, allegorized characters, and stylized sets. The play's action alternates between Dublin and the front as O'Casey depicts the cost of war for all the young men who departed as heroes and returned as cripples and invalids.

Like Synge before him, O'Casey opened new possibilities for Irish theater, but unfortunately, the Abbey Theatre was unwilling to accept his stylistic innovations. When O'Casey submitted *The Silver Tassie* to the Abbey Theatre in 1928, Yeats rejected it with a sharply worded reply that initiated a bitter exchange; the two were finally reconciled in 1935. Yeats attacked the play for its alleged introduction of propaganda into the theater, for, despite his own experiments with Japanese Nō theater, he was curiously unreceptive to O'Casey's attempts to move beyond dramatic realism. O'Casey did not aspire to a "pure" art of theater or cherish a dramatic theory, as did Yeats. Instead, he merely intended to expand the range of tragicomedy using the devices of expressionism. He hoped to use the exuberance of music-hall entertainment—its melodrama, boisterous comedy, burlesque, and farce—to animate serious drama, just as Shakespeare had woven comic interludes into even his most somber tragedies.

After the rejection of *The Silver Tassie* by the Abbey Theatre, O'Casey turned to a London producer to stage the play. Henceforth, he was to be a playwright without a permanent theater, often forced to publish his plays before they were staged and to depend on commercial productions of varying quality. Though *The Silver Tassie* enjoyed only a mixed success, O'Casey was committed to expressionism as an artistic direction, and his plays during the next decade show the gradual development of this style.

The 1930's were a period of diversity for O'Casey. Besides writing several one-act plays and the full-length morality play *Within the Gates*, he published drama reviews and short stories and began his six-volume autobiography. In his drama reviews and criticism, O'Casey defended other contemporary, experimental playwrights and called for the use of a wider range of theatrical techniques and for a drama criticism receptive to these innovations. He attacked the British critics' taste for the light drawing-room comedies of Noël Coward and the general lack of variety in the London theater. By this time he had also become a committed left-wing thinker who actively sympathized with Communist causes. His political ideology is evident in two plays of this period, *The Star Turns Red* and *Oak Leaves and Lavender*. Unfortunately, art and politics did not mix well for O'Casey, and these are largely inferior works.

Perhaps O'Casey came to realize the limits of ideological drama, or he may simply have grown tired of the war theme, for in the most successful plays of his middle period, he returned to an Irish setting, combining expressionistic techniques with traditional Irish characters, scenes, songs, and material. Also written during the war years, *Purple Dust* and *Red Roses for Me* show the refinement of expressionistic techniques that O'Casey had introduced in *The Silver Tassie* almost fifteen years earlier. These two plays demonstrate the range and quality of O'Casey's mature lyric imagination as he animates his stage with the song, pageantry, and spectacle of the Elizabethan theater. As he later observed about his plays, "Like [James] Joyce, it is only through an Irish scene that my imagination can weave a way."

The third period of O'Casey's career reflects a further enhancement of his artistic vision through a series of exuberant comic fantasies dramatizing the conflict between the affirmative and repressive forces in Irish culture. Here, he sharpened his critique of the provincialism, clericalism, materialism, and restrictive religious morality that he perceived in modern Irish life. Starting with *Cock-a-Doodle Dandy*, which O'Casey regarded as his favorite, and continuing with *The Bishop's Bonfire*, *The Drums of Father Ned*, and *Behind the Green Curtains*, the plays of this period mark the height of his mature achievement. In these late plays, O'Casey perfected his distinctive blend of broad comedy, farce, song, fantasy, dance, satire, and melodrama. As his favorite dramatists, Shakespeare and Boucicault, had done before him, O'Casey made his plays infinitely richer and more varied than conventional realistic drama. His expressionism became a medium for his lyricism and gaiety of spirit. This determination to broaden the range of contemporary theater perhaps marks O'Casey's most distinctive contribution to the modern stage.

In his long and productive career, O'Casey reanimated the Anglo-Irish theater with a blend of tragicomedy, fantasy, and farce that drew from Elizabethan drama, the music hall, and expressionism to create a vibrant and innovative form of dramatic theater. Though his plays have been criticized for lacking a "pure" dramatic form, his vigorous mixture of theatrical elements has stood in marked contrast to other trends in contemporary theater through its sheer power of entertainment and affirmation. O'Casey had the creative power and vision to transcend the limitations of dramatic theory. His genius was for theatrical vitality rather than pure dramatic art.

THE SHADOW OF A GUNMAN

O'Casey's first play to be accepted by the Abbey Theatre, *The Shadow of a Gunman*, is a two-act tragicomedy set in a Dublin tenement during the May, 1920, struggle between the Irish Republican Army (IRA) and the British Black and Tans. Two hapless young Irishmen, Seumas Shields (a Catholic peddler) and Donal Davoren (a poet manqué) are drawn into the guerrilla warfare when other residents mistake them for IRA fighters and a friend accidentally leaves a bag of terrorist bombs in their rooms. Davoren, the would-be poet, enjoys the hero-worship of his neighbors and the affection of young Minnie Powell, while he writes poor imitations of Percy Bysshe Shelley and pretends to be an insurgent. O'Casey uses the contrast between the self-deceiving appearance and the reality of the two men to debunk romantic myths of Irish heroism and valor. Shields and Davoren are both antiheroes, ordinary men who instinctively shun violence and try to live the semblance of normal lives amid the conflict. This antiheroic theme is the source of both comedy and pathos, for while Shields and Davoren act as cowards, Minnie behaves heroically. In act 2, when British soldiers arrive to search the apartments for snipers or weapons, she volunteers to hide the bag of bombs in her room and is discovered and captured. Sacrificing herself for a sham ideal, she is shot while trying to escape from the British, as Shields and Davoren, who form "the shadow of a gunman," cower in their rooms, terrified of the gunfire.

JUNO AND THE PAYCOCK

Juno and the Paycock is set in 1922 during the period of continued civil war after the Irish Free State had been established. The scene is once again a Dublin tenement, and the play depicts the misfortunes of the Boyle family, impoverished Dubliners temporarily lifted out of their squalor by a spurious legacy, which they quickly squander. This three-act tragicomedy parallels domestic and civil chaos; the Boyles struggle against the disintegration of their family, while outside the provisional Irish Republican Army continues its resistance against the Dublin government. "Captain" Jack Boyle and "Joxer" Daley are among O'Casey's most memorable characters. The Captain struts from apartment to pub, accompanied by the ingratiating Joxer, embellishing on his past adventures, complaining about his hard luck, and deftly avoiding responsibility, while his wife, Juno, struggles both to work and to keep house. As the play progresses, their crippled son, Johnny, becomes an IRA informer, and their daughter, Mary, falls in love with the young lawyer who brings the family news of their supposed inheritance. Despite these misfortunes, the play generates rich humor from the garrulous, irresponsible behavior of the Captain and Joxer, who belong to a long tradition of the stage Irishman and the braggart soldier. Once their inheritance is discovered to be a sham, the family's fortunes swiftly disintegrate, as their furniture is repossessed, Johnny is shot by the IRA, and Mary is left pregnant and deserted by her lover. By the end of the play, bitter and defeated, Juno and Mary mourn Johnny's death, while the Captain and Joxer stagger in, drunk and lugubrious, to lament "the terrible state o' chassis" of the world.

THE PLOUGH AND THE STARS

The title for O'Casey's *The Plough and the Stars* is taken from the original flag of the Irish Citizen Army, with its working-class symbols, but the focus is once again the folly and futility of war. This four-act tragicomedy is set before and during the Easter, 1916, uprising in Dublin and dramatizes the mixed motives of idealism, vanity, and folly that inspired Irish nationalism. The action in the play alternates between a Dublin boardinghouse and the streets and pubs of the city. It dramatizes the trauma of war in separating a young couple, Jack and Nora Clitheroe, recently married. When the call for the uprising takes place, Jack hurries to join his compatriots, while Nora desperately tries to prevent him from leaving and then wanders through the strife-torn city in search of him. After the battle, the city is filled with looters, and O'Casey creates some memorable scenes of rioters fighting over their plunder. The various boarders at the Clitheroes's boardinghouse represent differing attitudes toward the insurrection, from patriotism to scorn. By the end of the play, Dublin is in flames and Jack has died heroically, although Nora, who has lost her baby, cannot be told. Her neighbor, the Unionist Bessie Burgess, is fatally shot by the British while nursing Nora, and the play ends with British soldiers drinking tea in the rooms they have just ransacked.

THE SILVER TASSIE

In style and technique, *The Silver Tassie* marks a clear departure from O'Casey's earlier plays. Though he retains the tragicomic mode, he turns from a realistic to an expressionistic mode to convey the horrors of modern warfare. Symbols and abstractions of war bode large in this play, particularly in act 2, as O'Casey attempts to move his art beyond dramatic realism to a more poetic theater. The protagonist, Harry Heegan, leaves for the front in act 1 after he has won the Silver Tassie, or victory cup, for his Avondale Football Club. He departs as a hero, victorious and in love with Jessie Taite, and returns a crippled, embittered veteran, having lost his youth, vitality, and love. Act 2 invokes the carnage of the front through chant and ritual; an allegorical figure, the Croucher, dominates the action, while Harry is wounded in battle. Act 3 shifts to the army hospital during Harry's recuperation from his injuries, and act 4 brings him back to a dance at the Avondale Football Club. Now a wheelchair invalid, and having lost Jessie to his friend Barney, he drinks the bitter cup of loss and smashes the Silver Tassie on the floor. The dramatic action is quite simple, but O'Casey's expressionistic treatment makes this a powerful and compelling play.

PURPLE DUST

After a period of unsuccessful propaganda plays, O'Casey's next significant play was *Purple Dust*. He called the play a "wayward comedy," though perhaps it is closer in form to a rollicking farce—a humorous confrontation between the English and the Irish national characters reminiscent of Shaw's *John Bull's Other Island* (pr. 1904, pb. 1907). The play is set in the Irish countryside, where two wealthy English dupes, Cyril Poges and Basil Stokes, try to restore a dilapidated Tudor mansion in Clune na Geera. O'Casey's "stage Englishmen" are thwarted by their bungling mismanagement and by the unpredictable Irish weather. By the end of the play, their young Irish mistresses have run off with two Irish workmen and the mansion is about to be destroyed by a flood. Once again, the English are defeated in their attempt to dominate Ireland economically, and, as the title suggests, the pair are left in the ruins of their romantic and extravagant obsession with the "purple dust" of Tudor Ireland.

RED ROSES FOR ME

The most autobiographical of O'Casey's plays, *Red Roses for Me*, presents a romantic, nostalgic evocation of his early manhood in Dublin. The protagonist, Ayamonn Breydon, is a young Protestant railway worker who helps organize a strike in the Dublin yards to win a small wage increase. Ayamonn is in love with a timid Catholic girl, Sheila Moorneen, who, along with Ayamonn's mother, begs him to give up the strike, but Ayamonn is determined that the strike will occur, and he is killed in the labor violence that follows. Before his death, however, he enjoys a moment of ecstatic vision, as, from a bridge across the Liffey, he envisions Dublin transfigured from its drab dullness to a golden radiance. This magnificent scene and the rich language of the play save it from becoming a mere propaganda piece for the cause of Labour.

COCK-A-DOODLE DANDY

O'Casey often remarked that he considered *Cock-a-Doodle Dandy* his best play, although it is by no means the easiest to produce. Reminiscent of the fantastic comedies of Aristophanes, this play features a life-size apocalyptic Cock who comes to banish religious bigotry and puritanism from the small Irish village of Nyadnanave, inciting a series of magical and mysterious events. The village priest and older men are sure the Cock represents some malign spirit, though the young women, especially, are attracted to it. O'Casey himself commented that "the Cock, of course, is the joyful, active spirit of life as it weaves a way through the Irish scene." In three long scenes, the play presents a parable of the Irish spirit in conflict, torn between the powers of affirmation and negation, as the puritanical Father Domineer musters the village forces of superstition, ignorance, and fear to suppress dance and merriment and, ultimately, to banish the most attractive young women from the region. Unfortunately, the enchantment of the Cock does not prevail in this play, although O'Casey implies that the spirit of human joy is irrepressible.

THE BISHOP'S BONFIRE

O'Casey continues his anticlerical theme in *The Bishop's Bonfire*, a satirical farce in which Bishop Bill Mullarky's visit to his hometown is marked by a ritual book-burning of objectionable literature. The forces of piety and respectability are once more in control, as Councillor Reiligan, the richest man in the village, prepares his house to welcome the bishop, while both the upper and lower classes celebrate the homecoming in their own ways. The pompous Reiligan also interferes with his daughters' happiness by preventing them from marrying the men they love because he thinks these men are not respectable enough. Much of the play is farcical or melodramatic, particularly the death scene at the end of the play, in which Fooraun Reiligan is shot by her suitor, Manus Moanroe, when she discovers that he is stealing church funds from her house. Her suicide note absolves him, however, as the sight of burning books welcomes the bishop home.

THE DRUMS OF FATHER NED

O'Casey's continuing satire of Irish morality irritated many of his compatriots, and the controversy surrounding his next play, *The Drums of Father Ned*, seems like a parody of the play itself in a strange instance of life imitating art. Set in the village of Doonavale during the Tostal, or national arts festival, the play depicts the healing of an old feud between two prosperous families, the Binningtons and the McGilligans, when their son and daughter fall in love during play rehearsals. A short "Prerumble," or one-act prelude, reenacts the feud between Alderman Binnington and Councillor McGilligan, enemies since the Irish Civil War, who will talk with each other only about business matters. Through the evocative power of the "drums" of Father Ned, a life-affirming country priest, the families are reconciled, and joy and love of life are restored to the village of Doonavale during the Tostal celebration. Ironically, this seemingly innocuous comedy was scheduled to be performed at the 1958 Dublin Tostal until it was withdrawn at the behest of the archbishop of Dublin, who refused to celebrate Mass at the festival if works by O'Casey, Joyce, or Samuel Beckett were performed. The spirit of negation prevailed, unfortunately, and the festival continued without the works of three principal Irish artists.

OTHER MAJOR WORKS

POETRY: *Songs of the Wren*, 1918; *More Wren Songs*, 1918.

NONFICTION: *The Story of Thomas Ashe*, 1918; *The Sacrifice of Thomas Ashe*, 1918; *The Story of the Irish Citizen Army*, 1919; *The Flying Wasp*, 1937; *I Knock at the Door*, 1939 (autobiography); *Pictures in the Hallway*, 1942 (autobiography); *Drums Under the Windows*, 1945 (autobiography); *Inishfallen, Fare Thee Well*, 1949 (autobiography); *Rose and Crown*, 1952 (autobiography); *Sunset and Evening Star*, 1954 (autobiography); *Mirror in My House*, 1956 (2 volumes; reissue of 6 volumes of autobiography above); *The Green Crow*, 1956; *Under a Colored Cap*, 1963; *Blasts and Benedictions*, 1967; *The Letters of Sean O'Casey*, 1975, 1978 (3 volumes; David Krause, editor).

MISCELLANEOUS: *Windfalls*, 1934 (includes essays, plays, poems, and stories); *Feathers from the Green Crow: Sean O'Casey, 1905-1925*, 1962 (includes essays, plays, poems, and stories); *The Sean O'Casey Reader: Plays, Autobiographies, Opinions*, 1968 (Brooks Atkinson, editor).

BIBLIOGRAPHY

Ayling, Ronald, and Michael J. Durkan. *Sean O'Casey: A Bibliography*. London: Macmillan, 1978. This volume is considered to be the standard bibliographic source on O'Casey's work and the critical reaction to it.

Kearney, Colbert. *The Glamour of Grammar: Orality and Politics and the Emergence of Sean O'Casey*. Westport, Conn.: Greenwood Press, 2000. A study of the Irishness of the literary language of O'Casey, especially his early works.

Krause, David. *Sean O'Casey: The Man and His Work*. 2d ed. New York: Macmillan, 1975. An enlarged edition of an earlier and useful scholarly study. Krause examines O'Casey's life, drama, and experiences in the theatrical world.

Mikhail, E. H. *Sean O'Casey and His Critics: An Annotated Bibliography.* Metuchen, N.J.: Scarecrow Press, 1985. Mikhail's bibliography is the finest later survey of available sources on Ireland's most celebrated playwright.

Mitchell, Jack. *The Essential O'Casey: A Study of the Twelve Major Plays of Sean O'Casey.* New York: International Publishers, 1980. This volume provides a handy summary of O'Casey's most popular works.

O'Connor, Garry. *Sean O'Casey: A Life.* New York: Atheneum, 1988. The best and most readable biography, especially useful on the playwright's rise, through self-education and life as a Dublin laborer, to a major role in the 1916 Easter Rebellion and his Abbey Theatre productions.

Andrew J. Angyal,
updated by Peter C. Holloran

CLIFFORD ODETS

Born: Philadelphia, Pennsylvania; July 18, 1906
Died: Los Angeles, California; August 14, 1963

PRINCIPAL DRAMA

Waiting for Lefty, pr., pb. 1935 (one act)
Till the Day I Die, pr., pb. 1935
Awake and Sing!, pr., pb. 1935
Paradise Lost, pr. 1935, pb. 1936
I Can't Sleep, pr. 1935, pb. 1936
Golden Boy, pr., pb. 1937
Rocket to the Moon, pr. 1938, pb. 1939
Six Plays of Clifford Odets, pb. 1939 (revised as *"Waiting for Lefty" and Other Plays*, 1993)
Night Music, pr., pb. 1940
Clash by Night, pr. 1941, pb. 1942
The Russian People, pr. 1942, pb. 1946 (adaptation of Konstantin Simonov's play *The Russians*)
The Big Knife, pr., pb. 1949
The Country Girl, pr. 1950, pb. 1951
The Flowering Peach, pr., pb. 1954

OTHER LITERARY FORMS

Clifford Odets is also known for his screenplays, which include *The General Died at Dawn* (1936), an adaptation of Charles G. Booth's novel; *Blockade* (1938); *None but the Lonely Heart* (1944), an adaptation of Richard Llewellyn's novel; *Deadline at Dawn* (1946), an adaptation of William Irish's novel; *Humoresque* (1946), an adaptation of Fanny Hurst's story, with Zachary Gold; *The Sweet Smell of Success* (1957), an adaptation, with Ernest Lehman, of Lehman's novel; *The Story on Page One* (1960); and *Wild in the Country* (1961), an adaptation of J. R. Salamanca's novel *The Lost Country*.

ACHIEVEMENTS

In the spring of 1935, Clifford Odets, a young playwright thitherto unknown, had the heady experience of seeing three of his plays produced in New York. Overnight, he was hailed as the rising star of American drama. *Waiting for Lefty*, a timely tour de force dealing specifically with the strike of New York taxicab drivers but more broadly with the stressful socioeconomic situation in which many working people found themselves during the Great Depression, was a pioneering effort in proletarian drama that made its point by presenting six vignettes around a controlling theme and by involving the audience directly in the play's action—it is the audience that gives the strike call in the play's dramatically intense ending. By March, 1935, the play had been brought to Broadway to play as part of a double bill with *Till the Day I Die*, written quickly as an accompaniment to it. By July, 1935, *Waiting for Lefty* had been performed in thirty cities across the United States.

On February 19, 1935, the Group Theatre brought *Awake and Sing!* to Broadway some weeks after *Waiting for Lefty* had first gained its widespread pop-

Clifford Odets (Hulton Archive by Getty Images)

The Depression gave Odets a strong subject, and when it ended, he had difficulty finding subjects about which he could write with the force and conviction of his early work. The Odets who could convincingly argue the case of young lovers unable to marry because of the economic pressures of the Depression was a much less persuasive social protester when, more than a decade later, in *The Big Knife*, he attacked Hollywood's exploitation of Charlie Castle, an actor who had a fourteen-year contract for four million dollars. The social conditions out of which Odets's best artistic achievement grew had largely ceased to exist by 1940, and he was never able to find another theme with which he could identify so fully or in quite the same way as he had with the themes that the Depression provided him. While his last three plays are dramatically sound and compelling, Odets was always forced to work in his own enormous shadow, and his public demanded more of him than he could deliver in his later years.

BIOGRAPHY

Clifford Odets was born in Philadelphia to a twenty-year-old Lithuanian immigrant, Louis J. Odets, and his nineteen-year-old wife, Pearl Geisinger Odets, who had come to the United States from Romania, often called "Austria" by the Geisingers. Odets was the first of three children, and he was closer in many ways to his Aunt Esther and her husband than he was to his sickly, chronically depressed mother and somewhat combative father. "Tante Esther," as he called her, had been just enough older than her sister Pearl when they arrived in the United States that she remembered Yiddish and was able to speak it. Her husband, Israel Rossman, read Yiddish newspapers, and in the Rossman household, the young Odets was exposed to cadences of language that were absent from his parents' home and that he was to use effectively in dialogue throughout his career. Indeed, Odets was more successful than any playwright of his time in capturing the speech cadences and intonations of Jewish Americans.

Odets's father rose quickly to middle-class status. By the early 1920's, Louis Odets was owner of a print shop in the Bronx. As the fortunes of the family im-

ular acclaim, and this warm play of middle-class Jewish family life clearly established its author as a significant and effective playwright.

If ever a dramatist were right for his time, the young Odets was right for the 1930's. A nonconformist with a strong sense of outrage at social injustice, Odets drifted into various acting and radio jobs after he dropped out of high school at age seventeen. During this period, Odets learned a great deal about the struggle to survive and about theater. It was his association with the Group Theatre that gave Odets an identity, a satisfying surrogate family, and the motivation that he had until then been lacking. The Group Theatre, an outgrowth of the Depression, was to become the compelling force in the spirit and structure of Odets's best work, the plays from *Waiting for Lefty* through *Paradise Lost*, excluding only the somewhat inconsequential *Till the Day I Die*. His plays reflected the philosophy of the Group Theatre that there should be no stars; in these early plays, Odets discovered and experimented with the theme of nonfulfillment, which was to be the controlling theme of most of his writing.

proved, however, Odets began to feel spiritually alienated from the bourgeois values of his parents. He was moving gradually into what would be his vocation by affiliating himself with such theatrical groups as the Drawing-Room Players, Harry Kemp's Poets' Theatre, the Mae Desmond Stock Company, and, for a short time in 1929, the Theatre Guild. It was not until 1931, however, that he found his spiritual home in the newly formed Group Theatre. His writing was to be shaped by the philosophy of the Group Theatre, in which, as Harold Clurman wrote in *The Fervent Years*, "there were to be no stars . . . not for the negative purpose of avoiding distinction, but because all distinction . . . was to be embodied in the production as a whole." Odets's plays, reflecting this philosophy, generally contain no starring roles, but rather six or eight substantial roles of essentially equal importance.

With his meteoric rise to fame in 1935, Odets's commitment to the Group Theatre grew, and as the group faced financial difficulties, Odets reluctantly became a Hollywood screenwriter, primarily to earn enough money to keep it from financial collapse. Some argue that Odets compromised his talent by writing for the screen, that he was never again able to write with the force and the conviction that he had demonstrated before "selling out" to Hollywood. Although it is evident that he never again wrote as well as he had in the 1930's, it is overly simplistic to attribute Odets's artistic decline to any single causal factor. The times in which he lived and crucial events in his own life, including his 1937 marriage to and subsequent divorce in 1941 from Austrian film star Luise Rainer, both contributed to Odets's artistic decline in the early 1940's.

Odets's middle range of plays—*Rocket to the Moon*, *Night Music*, and *Clash by Night*—deal largely with questions of love, personal isolation, and nonfulfillment. None reaches the artistic level of the earlier plays. In the seven-year hiatus between *Clash by Night* and the 1949 production of *The Big Knife*, Odets produced three screenplays and an adaptation of Konstantin Simonov's *The Russians*, a propaganda piece. Odets was unable to recapture in his later plays the freshness and the authentic social anger of his early plays.

When he was called before the House Committee on Un-American Activities in 1952, Odets admitted to having been a member of the Communist Party "from toward the end of 1934 to the middle of 1935, covering anywhere from six to eight months." Never a very convinced Party member, Odets favored having a third major political party in the United States but was quickly disenchanted with the rigidity of the Communist Party and dismissed it as a reasonable vehicle for dealing with the social problems that perplexed him.

Odets's last stage play, *The Flowering Peach*, reflects its author's newly found interest in the biblical heritage of the Jewish people. A redaction of the Noah story, *The Flowering Peach* is warm and sensitive, reminiscent in its family orientation of *Awake and Sing!* It is a play of resignation rather than of revolution.

In the last decade of his life, Odets produced little, although in the last year of his life he was working on an ambitious project to write four of the thirteen scripts for *The Richard Boone Show*, a dramatic television series. Odets had completed three of the four scripts he was to write before he succumbed to cancer in Los Angeles on August 14, 1963. The year after Odets's death, the musical version of *Golden Boy*, on which he had been working with William Gibson, reached Broadway.

ANALYSIS

In an interview with Arthur Wagner conducted two years before Clifford Odets's death but not published in *Harper's Magazine* until September of 1966, Odets told Wagner, "The question is really not one of knowing how to write so much as knowing how to connect with yourself so that the writing is, so to speak, born affiliated with yourself." When he was dealing with the pressing social problems of the 1930's, which were times of great national pain that spilled over into the lives of individuals and into the conduct of families, Odets was connecting with himself. He was writing from deep personal conviction intensified by moral outrage at a society that could do no better for its members than to allow the economic and social dissolution that the Depression brought.

WAITING FOR LEFTY

Economic and social determinism is significantly present in all of Odets's major plays, and *Waiting for Lefty* is no exception. Despite its brevity, it makes eloquent statements on a broad range of topics, ranging from family life to anti-Semitism to collective bargaining to the ecological irresponsibility of capitalist producers of poison gas. The overwhelming question posed by the play is whether workers should have control over their own destinies, a question that recurs in Odets's later plays. Although the last curtain leaves no doubt about the answer Odets proposes, it is clear that the social and economic pressure under which his characters are laboring will not magically disappear.

As often happens with social drama, *Waiting for Lefty*, which Brooks Atkinson called "fiercely dramatic in the theater," has become, as Michael Mendelsohn wrote, "as dead as last year's newspaper." This earliest of Odets's plays, an agitprop piece written in great haste to be presented at workers' meetings, was to catapult its author into public recognition and to offer him the opportunity to become a successful Broadway playwright.

Waiting for Lefty was intended to be a play about "the stormbirds of the working class"; the play is more accurately described as being about "declassed members of the middle class," as John Howard Lawson contends. The principals in the play are from various walks of life. They have two things in common: They are taxicab drivers, and they earn their living in this way because the Depression has made it impossible for them to follow other pursuits. The drivers and those close to them are examples of men with thwarted ambitions and broken dreams; external economic forces are determining their lives. They meet to consider whether they should strike, and as the strike is discussed, various drivers tell their stories in the several vignettes of which the play is composed. Mendelsohn rightly perceived that the play succeeds dramatically because of its "interplay between personal lives and collective action." Odets was himself middle-class, his audiences were middle-class, and the play is essentially middle-class, despite Odets's polemics to the contrary. This accounts for the play's initial success with its audiences. A middle-class audience could feel empathy with middle-class protagonists who had been brought to the level of the working class by the Depression.

TILL THE DAY I DIE

Waiting for Lefty, which plays in less than an hour, was too short to be taken to Broadway as an evening's entertainment. The play and its writer were in great demand with all sorts of political groups, and the publicity generated by the play made producers eager to bring it to Broadway, where *Awake and Sing!* had just opened. In order to round out an evening of theater, Odets wrote *Till the Day I Die*, one of the early anti-Nazi plays to appear on Broadway. The play, which focuses on the situation of Communists in Adolf Hitler's Germany, is somewhat trivial, although in it one can recognize the beginning of themes that Odets was to develop later. For example, the protagonist, Ernst Tausig, is brought in for questioning by the storm troopers, who smash his right hand with a rifle butt. This leads eventually to amputation, a particularly difficult outcome for Ernst, who is a violinist. (Similarly, in *Golden Boy*, Joe Bonaparte is a promising violinist, but he destroys his hands by becoming a prize-winning boxer, led into this activity by economic necessity rather than by choice.) Ernst Tausig commits suicide, finally, and if any ray of hope is offered, it is a questionable one: Ernst's mistress, Tilly, is pregnant and presumably will produce a child who will carry on. What this child is likely to become in Hitler's Germany is doubtful. *Till the Day I Die* was dashed off in five days, and the play is less than convincing. As a curtain opener for *Waiting for Lefty*, it served its commercial purposes at the expense of artistic integrity; its value is historical rather than artistic.

AWAKE AND SING!

The backdrop of the Depression pervades *Awake and Sing!* Those who expected another play with the political fervor and intense anger of *Waiting for Lefty* found instead that *Awake and Sing!* was an accurate view of Jewish family life and of the effect of the Depression on three generations of the Berger family, all living under one roof. The play focuses primarily on the two members of the youngest generation, Ralph and Hennie. Both are thwarted because of the economic pressures under which they live. Hennie is trapped in a marriage contrived by her mother, who cannot bear the thought of her daughter mothering an illegitimate child. Her brother, Ralph, the idealist, can proclaim, "We don't want life printed on dollar bills," but his whole existence is so economically determined that he has little control over his life. The grandfather, Jacob, also an idealist, complains, "This is a house? Marx said it—abolish such families." Jacob commits suicide in the end, leaving to Ralph the small legacy that his insurance policy will provide: a slender but unconvincing thread of hope. Bessie Berger, the mother of the household, lives in fear that her family will collapse and her home be taken away: "They threw out a family on Dawson Street today. All the furniture on the sidewalk. A fine old woman with gray hair." Ever concerned with appearances, Bessie proclaims ingenuously, "I like my house to look respectable," and acts to keep it that way no matter what deceptions she must engage in to maintain the appearance. Odets is at his best in *Awake and Sing!* He is close to his blood ties: He knows his characters, and the play exudes authenticity.

PARADISE LOST

Speaking of *Awake and Sing!*, Odets said that his "interest was not in the presentation of an individual's problems, but in those of a whole class." One must bear this statement in mind when approaching *Paradise Lost*, in which the trials visited on the Gordon family are so numerous and so close together in time that they put one in mind of the most melodramatic of soap operas. In this play, which, like *Awake and Sing!*, is Chekhovian in its characterization and structure, Odets deals with an upper-middle-class family caught in the grip of the Depression.

As the threat of economic annihilation closes in on the Gordons, Leo, the father, loses his business, largely through the deception of an unscrupulous partner. One of his sons, Julie, is dying of encephalitis. The other son, Ben, a former Olympic runner, is felled by a policeman's bullets in a chase following a robbery he committed in order to get money for his wife and family. Leo's daughter, Pearl, frustrated in her musical and personal ambitions, becomes a virtual recluse. Ultimately, the family is evicted when Leo's business plunges into bankruptcy.

Odets considered *Paradise Lost* his most profound play. Most of the critics did not agree, with even such perceptive commentators as Joseph Wood Krutch suggesting that the play was a mere burlesque of *Awake and Sing!* Few could see through the melodrama and sentimentality of *Paradise Lost* to what Odets was struggling to communicate. Harold Clurman, writing in his introduction to the published version of the play, contended quite correctly that it is about middle-class people who have the "bewildering perception that everything [they intimately believe] is being denied by the actual conditions of contemporary society." Metaphorically, the play, like *Waiting for Lefty* and *Awake and Sing!*, is about an entire class of people who are being wiped out by the Depression. The Bergers represent the lower range of this class; the Gordons, the upper range. The middle class, upper or lower, is being dragged down by economic conditions over which they have no control. As in most of his plays, Odets wrote in *Paradise Lost* about blocked aspirations. The theme of nonfulfillment controls the play, whose only shred of hope comes in Leo's final lengthy oration, which, in the face of such encompassing despair, is somewhat out of place and unconvincing.

The play, nevertheless, has strong vignettes, the best of which are found in the portrayal of Sam Katz, Leo's dishonest business partner. Sam, sexually impotent, blames his long-suffering wife for their childlessness. Sam's impotence can be taken to represent a general lack of the strength and will that might enable him to live as he desires. His wife-mother, Bertha, endures his taunts and his humiliation, comforting him at the end and calling him "a good boy." In Sam and Bertha, Odets was beginning to develop the characters who emerged more fully developed as Ben and Belle in *Rocket to the Moon* and who reappeared in a somewhat different form in *The Country Girl*. His concern with a weak man in a childless marriage to a woman whose maternal feelings are directed at her spouse pervades these three plays.

GOLDEN BOY

In *Golden Boy*, Joe Bonaparte's artistic nature and his desire to be a concert violinist are at odds with the economic realities of his life. Bonaparte goes into boxing to make money, and in so doing, he ruins his sensitive hands and destroys any possibility that he might ultimately achieve his artistic goal. On a metaphoric level, Odets is suggesting quite cynically a philosophy that Moe Axelrod espoused in *Awake and Sing!*: "One thing to get another." Life kills the dreamer, the artist, in the same way that Odets's father had done everything in his power to make his son practical, to kill the dreamer in him.

Harold Clurman called *Golden Boy* Odets's most subjective play. Odets held the play in some contempt, claiming to have written the play to be a hit in order to keep the Group Theatre together. *Golden Boy*, however, shows commendable control and artistic maturation. If one can overcome the early incongruity of a boxer who is also a sensitive violinist, the rest of the play is plausible and well made. Joe Bonaparte, the "golden boy" of the play's title, falls victim to what Gerald Weales called "the disintegration brought on by success." Joe makes the difficult decision to abandon his musical career in order to pursue a career in championship boxing. Ironically, he wins the championship fight but, in so doing, kills his opponent and forecloses all hope of returning to his music.

Joe grows increasingly alienated from his society as he realizes that he has sold out. His trainer cautions him, "Your heart ain't in fighting . . . your *hate* is." Joe changes in the course of the play from a youth who is sensitive about being cross-eyed to a necessarily hardened figure: Sensitivity, an asset for a musician, is a liability for a boxer. Ultimately, Joe becomes a piece of property (this theme recurs forcefully in *The Big Knife*). Joe gets his Duesenberg, a clear and visible symbol of economic success, but he dies when the car crashes, a conclusion with a dramatic impact not unlike that left on audiences who learn at the end of *Waiting for Lefty* that Lefty has been found shot to death in an alley. Whereas the news of Lefty's death forces the taxicab drivers to rise to action, the news of Joe Bonaparte's death leaves audiences with a dull, pervasive ache for the human condition.

Golden Boy was Odets's first drama to underplay the Yiddish-English dialect of his earlier work. In this departure, one sees a playwright trying to broaden his range, trying to reduce his dependence on his Jewish heritage. *Rocket to the Moon*, *Night Music*, and *Clash by Night* represented a new direction for Odets. The years in which these plays were written were those during which Odets was married to and divorced from Luise Rainer, and the plays themselves are much concerned with questions of love and marriage. *Night Music* is concerned with young love and the effects of economic uncertainty on it, while the other two are concerned with romantic triangles. Odets is tentative in these plays. His personal concerns have shifted from those of an artist struggling to establish himself and to survive during the Depression to those of someone who is concerned primarily with the tensions that two people experience in a love relationship and in marriage.

ROCKET TO THE MOON

Rocket to the Moon is an unfocused drama about the tedious dalliance of a middle-aged dentist with Cleo, his receptionist. Unfortunately, Odets allowed himself to be sidetracked in this play, concentrating more on Ben Stark, the dentist, than on Cleo, the receptionist, who could have been drawn with sufficient psychological complexity to bring some intensity into the drama. The sensitivity with which Odets portrayed Sam and Bertha Katz in *Paradise Lost* was not repeated in *Rocket to the Moon*, although Ben and Belle indisputably resemble Sam and Bertha. This play is at best tawdry and represents an artistic setback for its author. Odets was at this time able neither to distance himself sufficiently from his own problems to practice his profession at its highest level, nor to use his own suffering and confusion to enrich his art. Some of Odets's remarkable ability to sketch characters is, nevertheless, evident in *Rocket to the Moon*. Belle's father, Mr. Prince, is drawn with great skill, and in him one sees a bit of what Odets was beginning to fancy himself to be—someone who had gained material security but who was essentially unloved. When Mr. Prince suggests that Cleo might marry him, she rejects the offer, saying, "Next week I'll buy myself a dog."

NIGHT MUSIC

The theme of *Night Music* is homelessness. Steve Takis, the protagonist, is known as "Suitcase Steve" because he always carries a suitcase with him and constantly moves from place to place. He has been sent East on an incredible errand to pick up two apes for a Hollywood film studio and to accompany them back to the West Coast. One of the apes snatches a gold locket from Fay Tucker, the police become involved, and Steve is arrested and then released, his apes being held as security. He approaches Fay with indignation for the trouble she has caused him, and, predictably, the two fall in love. The play's most sympathetic character, Detective A. L. Rosenberg, helps the couple, but Rosenberg, the symbol of good in a hostile world, is dying of cancer. The play's didacticism overcomes its warmth and its occasional gentle tenderness. The symbols are heavy-handed, and the interesting themes of personal isolation, homelessness, and loneliness, which had been themes of some prominence in all of Odets's earlier plays, here seem completely trivial.

CLASH BY NIGHT

Clash by Night was written as Odets's marriage fell apart and as the Group Theatre was reaching the point of disbanding. Between the time the play opened out of town and the time it opened on Broadway, the Japanese had bombed Pearl Harbor and national attention was on more serious matters than the sordid love triangle around which this play revolves. *Clash by Night* is about Mae Wilenski and her lackluster husband, Jerry. Mae is bored with her life, and before the end of act 1, she is involved in a love affair with Earl Pfeiffer, a boarder in the Wilenski household. The action plays out quite slowly, each act being interlarded with echoes of Odets's social fervor; in a subplot, for example, Joe and Peggy have been engaged for two years and are unable to marry because Joe works only three days a week, a situation rather unconvincing to audiences in a society gearing up for war and recruiting every available able-bodied citizen to work in defense jobs. Ultimately, Jerry is led by jealousy to murder Earl, an interesting outcome in this love triangle involving two men and a woman as opposed to the two women-one man triangle in *Rocket to the Moon*. Whereas Belle takes Ben back, perhaps to nurture him but more likely to torture him for the rest of his days, Jerry must strike out

in a manly way and seek vengeance through killing his rival.

THE BIG KNIFE

A seven-year gap separated *Clash by Night* from Odets's next Broadway production, *The Big Knife*. The play focuses on Hollywood's exploitation of Charlie Castle, an actor who has just been offered a fourteen-year movie contract worth four million dollars. Charlie, however, does not wish to sign. Like Joe Bonaparte in *Golden Boy*, he is in danger of becoming merely a piece of property, and Charlie recoils from allowing the studio to own him. The complication is that Charlie was involved in a fatal hit-and-run accident for which he and the studio have permitted his publicity man, Buddy Bliss, to take the rap. The studio now attempts to force Charlie to sign the contract under threat of revealing the real facts of the accident. In a sense, Odets was back to arguing the worker-management conflict with which he first dealt in *Waiting for Lefty*; the argument against management is somewhat less convincing, however, when management is paying the worker as handsomely as it is here, even though the principle may be similar.

The play sheds some light on the false standards of Hollywood society, presenting interesting scenes that spotlight such realities of Hollywood life as the control that gossip columnists have over actors' lives. Charlie Castle calls free speech "the highest-priced luxury in this country today," and he attacks the superficiality of Hollywood relationships by saying, "I'll bet you don't know why we all wear these beautiful, expensive ties in Hollywood. . . . It's a military tactic—we hope you won't notice our faces." Odets thus gave vent to the resentment that had been growing in him during the decade since he first went to Hollywood as a screenwriter. *The Big Knife* is tightly structured, and its dramatic intensity is at times superb, but its basic premise is difficult to accept, and Charlie Castle's suicide at the end is more melodramatic than artistically valid.

THE COUNTRY GIRL

The Country Girl followed *The Big Knife* in 1950, and in it Odets revived some of the controlling ideas of his earlier plays. The protagonist, Frank Elgin, is an aging actor who has fallen on hard times, largely because of his alcoholism, brought about by the accidental death of his young son, for which he blames himself. Frank's wife, Georgie, is a wife-mother recalling Bertha Katz and Belle Stark. Bernie Dodd, a director, has given Frank one last chance for a comeback. He insists that if Frank begins drinking again, he will dismiss him immediately. Bernie, who first detests Georgie, later is strongly attracted to her, creating a love triangle. This love triangle differs from Odets's previous ones, however, in that Georgie and Bernie are ironically united in their efforts to rehabilitate Frank. The psychological complexity of the play makes it conceptually stronger than *Rocket to the Moon* or *Clash by Night*.

In numerous rewrites, the role of Georgie was drastically changed from that of a nagging wife to that of a firm but understanding and supportive marriage partner. The love relationship that grows between Georgie and Bernie is the timeworn love-hate relationship. Frank remains largely oblivious to it until near the end of the last act. In the end, despite lapses along the way, Frank succeeds in acting his part well and in paving the way for the comeback toward which he has been struggling. The role of Frank provides a challenging vehicle for an actor to play a weak, insecure character, a pathological liar who successfully undergoes a difficult rehabilitation. Still, Frank's triumph at the end, accompanied by Georgie's decision to stay with him, leaves doubts in the minds of the audience. Throughout the play, Georgie's relationship to Frank has been based on her providing strength for a weak husband. If Frank has overcome his weakness, one must seriously question whether the relationship will give Georgie what she needs. If he has not overcome his weakness, then they are back exactly where they began. Odets himself viewed *The Country Girl* as a theater piece and disparaged the play's artistry, although he was pleased with certain technical aspects of it, especially the much-revised ending.

THE FLOWERING PEACH

In his last play, *The Flowering Peach*, Odets returned to his blood sources. The family in the play, reminiscent of the Bergers in *Awake and Sing!*, speaks in the Yiddish-English dialect of Odets's ear-

lier characters. *The Flowering Peach* is a version of the Noah story and largely concerns Noah, to whom God appears in a dream, predicting the Flood; Noah's attempts to build the Ark; and his conflicts with his son, Japheth, who, even when he comes to believe the truth of his father's dream, refuses to enter the Ark as a protest against a cruel God who would destroy the earth. Japheth finds himself on the Ark only because his father knocks him out and has him carried aboard. Once there, the father-son conflict, the conflict between faith and reason, again erupts. Japheth is convinced that the Ark should have a rudder; his father is equally convinced that God will direct the Ark as He intends.

The Flowering Peach is a warm and satisfying play. In it, Odets again explores the family as a unit, and he does so with sensitivity and with a sentimentality that, in this play, is not unbecoming. The dialogue is easy and natural, and tensions are reduced by the inclusion of amusing wisecracks. *The Flowering Peach* was nominated for the Pulitzer Prize, the first time that such recognition had come to an Odets play, but the Pulitzer Prize's advisory board overruled the jurors and gave the prize for the 1954-1955 season to Tennessee Williams for his *Cat on a Hot Tin Roof*. *The Flowering Peach*, a play of great affirmation, has yet to receive the recognition that many believe it deserves.

Odets wrote to Eugene Gross, "Nothing moves me so much as human aspirations blocked, nothing enrages me like waste. I am for use as opposed to abuse." All of his plays, with the possible exception of *The Flowering Peach*, have a deep and controlling concern with the question of blocked aspirations, and this persistent concern with a universal human problem gives Odets's work a lasting value, despite the dated topical themes of many of his plays.

OTHER MAJOR WORKS

SCREENPLAYS: *The General Died at Dawn*, 1936 (adaptation of Charles G. Booth's novel); *Blockade*, 1938; *None but the Lonely Heart*, 1944 (adaptation of Richard Llewellyn's novel); *Deadline at Dawn*, 1946 (adaptation of William Irish's novel); *Humoresque*, 1946 (with Zachary Gold; adaptation of Fannie Hurst's story); *The Sweet Smell of Success*, 1957 (with Ernest Lehman; adaptation of Lehman's novel); *The Story on Page One*, 1960 (directed by Odets); *Wild in the Country*, 1961 (adaptation of J. R. Salamanca's novel *The Lost Country*).

NONFICTION: *The Time Is Ripe: The 1940 Journal of Clifford Odets*, 1988.

BIBLIOGRAPHY

Brenman-Gibson, Margaret. *Clifford Odets: American Playwright; the Years from 1906-1940.* New York: Applause, 2001. This biography of Odets focuses on the earlier part of his career, which many would argue was the better part.

Cantor, Hal. *Clifford Odets: Playwright-Poet.* Lanham, Md.: Scarecrow Press, 2000. Rather than examining Odets from a political or biographical perspective, Cantor concentrates on eleven of his plays, reading closely and identifying common themes. He emphasizes Odets's poetic style and also notes Odets's influence on American theater. Bibliography and index.

Cooperman, Robert. *Clifford Odets: An Annotated Bibliography, 1935-1989.* Westport, Conn.: Meckler, 1990. A useful bibliographic essay evaluates the listed entries, which are divided into primary works (plays, screenplays, teleplays, articles, journals, and diaries), critical studies (on individual plays and politics, and on the Group Theatre), and information on the House Committee on Un-American Activities. Includes a brief chronology and an index.

Demastes, William W. *Clifford Odets: A Research and Production Sourcebook.* New York: Greenwood Press, 1991. The book's main features are summaries of characters and plots, along with overviews of the critical reception of Odets's stage and radio plays. Includes a brief chronology, a biographical essay, a bibliography of Odets's primary works (with unpublished archival sources), an annotated secondary bibliography (1935-1990), a list of major productions, and an index.

Miller, Gabriel. *Clifford Odets.* New York: Continuum, 1989. Critical of the narrow interpretations of Odets as a political playwright of the 1930's, Miller focuses primarily on the published plays, arranged thematically around several "visions": Chekhovian, tragic, romantic, melodramatic, and political. The interest centers on both experimentation with form and the evolution of Odets's "significant thematic and social concerns." Index.

_____, ed. *Critical Essays on Clifford Odets.* Boston: G. K. Hall, 1991. This anthology includes ten reviews of Odets's productions (from *Waiting for Lefty* to *The Flowering Peach*), two 1930's evaluations of Odets, three interviews with Odets dating from the 1950's and 1960's, and a collection of essays, most reprinted from earlier books. The introduction provides an evaluative chronological overview of primary and secondary sources.

R. Baird Shuman,
updated by Elsie Galbreath Haley

ADAM GOTTLOB OEHLENSCHLÄGER

Born: Copenhagen, Denmark; November 14, 1779
Died: Copenhagen, Denmark; January 20, 1850

PRINCIPAL DRAMA

Sanct hansaften-spil, pb. 1803, pr. 1804
(*Midsummer Night's Play*, 1913)

Aladdin, pb. 1805, pr. 1806 (English translation, 1857)

Hakon Jarl hiin rige, pb. 1807, pr. 1808 (*Hakon Jarl*, 1840)

Baldur hiin gode, pb. 1807, pr. 1808

Palnatoke, pr., pb. 1809

Axel og Valborg, pb. 1810, pr. 1811 (*Axel and Valborg*, 1851)
Corregio, pr., pb. 1811 (English translation, 1846)

OTHER LITERARY FORMS

Adam Gottlob Oehlenschläger was an accomplished poet. He wrote very few prose texts but contributed greatly to the genre of the lyric epic poem. In addition, Oehlenschläger is highly acclaimed for his straightforward lyric poetry.

ACHIEVEMENTS

In 1797, one of the most important contemporary Danish journals pronounced the Golden Age of poetry and culture dead, but within five years of this pronouncement some of the giants of intellectual life in Denmark were to make their presence felt. Among them were Bertel Thorvaldsen, whose sculptures in the classic tradition made him famous beyond the national borders, Hans Christian Ørsted, whose contribution to the natural sciences is still recognized today, and Adam Gottlob Oehlenschläger. The celebrated

Adam Gottlob Oehlenschläger (Kongelige Bibliotek)

Danish literary critic Georg Brandes stated in 1886 that Oehlenschläger's *Aladdin* represents the point of departure of more recent Danish literary culture.

Like most other Romantic poets, Oehlenschläger must be seen in his historical context. He grew up in a world that was going through successive political crises. Denmark was to experience its worst trauma in centuries in the English bombing of Copenhagen in 1807, the loss of Norway to Sweden as a result of the Napoleonic Wars, and the state bankruptcy of 1813. Against this political backdrop, the dominant direction of belletristic literature was to turn away from reality to seek solace in aesthetic and religious values. Imagination was the tool with which Romanticism tried to embrace the whole world, to understand its secrets, and to arrive at an explanation for the meaning of life. This aim was not to be achieved by means of scientific striving and research; above all, it was the province of the Romantic poet.

It would be simplistic to say that Oehlenschläger introduced Romanticism into Denmark. The main impetus of his style and subject matter came from the German Romantics, among them mainly the Schlegel brothers, Johann Adolf and Johann Elias, and Novalis. Oehlenschläger, however, did not import the German movement unchanged into his country but subsumed many of its strategies into the particular circumstances of his culture. At times, these circumstances were even limited to his immediate location—Copenhagen and its surrounding area—as is the case in *Midsummer Night's Play*. Oehlenschläger made wide use of a humor, which, although localized and, at times, rather parochial, nevertheless separates him from many of his contemporaries in European Romanticism. His changes introduced a special Danish Romanticism on the belletristic scene.

As a Romantic poet, Oehlenschläger possessed a singular lyric inventiveness, and he made use of the Danish language as few before him had. Evidence for his influence on Danish is to be found in the many quotations from *Aladdin* that have entered the vernacular as proverbs or sayings; these are widely used today without any consciousness of their origin. Oehlenschläger made the Danes aware of the beauty and possibilities of their language.

Oehlenschläger also played a major role in the Danish-German literary relationship. He rewrote *Aladdin* and several other works in German and translated the works of Ludvig Holberg into that language. In addition, he translated the works of the German poet Ludwig Tieck and introduced them to the Danish public.

Linguistically and stylistically, Oehlenschläger created an epoch. Colorful, directly sensual, and plastic imagery reached a new height in his work. He was exposed to many attacks by his fellow authors and poets, but in 1829, the Swedish poet Esaias Tegnér crowned him the "Nordic King of Poetry." In his later years, Oehlenschläger enjoyed a growing appreciation of his role as the creator of Danish national poetry and as a master of the lyric epic poem and Nordic drama. Largely because of his work, romance became a favorite genre in Denmark, as did drama, and following generations tried with varying degrees of success to follow in Oehlenschläger's footsteps.

BIOGRAPHY

Adam Gottlob Oehlenschläger was born in Copenhagen on November 14, 1779, to a Danish mother and a German father. The latter was an organist at first but later became the steward of the palace at Frederiksberg, then the summer residence of the Danish royal family. There can be little doubt that Oehlenschläger's love for nature started in his childhood, a good part of which he spent in the beautiful parks and gardens of the royal palace.

As a young man, he vacillated between law and the theater. During this period, he met and came under the influence of the important Danish intellectuals of his time, whose lives revolved around the natural sciences, art, literature, religion, aesthetics, and the search for "truth." Young Oehlenschläger grew to despise the materialism and the rationalist philistinism (or so his time perceived the spirit of the Enlightenment) that prevailed in his country.

In 1801, Oehlenschläger won second prize in a contest that posed the controversial question of whether it would be useful for Nordic arts if the old Nordic mythology were to be introduced and generally accepted in lieu of the Greek. As might be ex-

pected of a budding Romantic, he answered in the affirmative and thus set the tone for the main subject matter in his literary works. It was the philosopher Henrik Steffens who was crucial in introducing Oehlenschläger to the ideas of Romanticism. Steffens believed that sentiment and nature were vital elements in poetry, and he shared the contemporary Continental (and especially German) preference for imagination and intuition over reason and enlightenment. Oehlenschläger, who at the age of nineteen had read Johann Wolfgang von Goethe's *Die Leiden des jungen Werthers* (1774; *The Sorrows of Young Werther*, 1779), was easily converted to Romanticism.

Oehlenschläger's first collection, *Digte* (1803), broke with the tradition of the eighteenth century and heralded the arrival of a Danish Romanticism. The work was a true testament to the "universal poetry" suggested by Friedrich von Schlegel because it embraced several genres, including lyric poems, a verse drama, and lyric epics. Its publication marked a turning point in Oehlenschläger's literary career. It included the lyric drama *Midsummer Night's Play* and the poem *Guldhornene* (1802; *The Golden Horns*, 1913), which was based on the discovery of two gold drinking horns from Nordic antiquity (they were later stolen from a museum and are believed to have been melted down). Oehlenschläger's imagination turned these relics of antiquity into symbols of true poetry because they were not found by scientists or scholars, but by accident by a "son of nature"—a ploughman—who was selected by the gods.

This theme was further explored in his next collection, *Poetiske skrifter*, which appeared in 1805. It contained, among other works, two lyric cycles and *Vaulundurs saga* (English translation, 1847), but the crucial text was the play *Aladdin*. *Poetiske skrifter* made Oehlenschläger the favorite of the Danish public, and hopes for a Danish national literature were placed on the young poet. The king sponsored an obligatory trip abroad, and from 1805 to 1809, Oehlenschläger journeyed to Germany, France, Italy, and Switzerland, during which time he made the personal acquaintance of Goethe and Friedrich Schleiermacher and renewed his friendship with Steffens.

He matured much during this period and turned toward a bourgeois humanism with a Nordic focus. His literary output was no longer characterized by a lighthearted and witty vein, and he started writing tragedies. It was during his stay in Halle with Steffens that he wrote *Hakon Jarl*, which was published in 1807, together with *Baldur hiin gode* and a dramatic poem entitled *Nordiske digte*.

After his return to Denmark, Oehlenschläger was made professor of aesthetics at the University of Copenhagen. He would never again reach the pinnacle of creativity of his early youth, although he wrote many more lyric poems and epics—of the latter, *Hroars saga* (1817) is worth mentioning. Indeed, Oehlenschläger did not develop as a reflective writer: He blossomed for a short time and then never again. He was thus an example of his own philosophy of literature. On his seventieth birthday, shortly after a Danish victory over Prussia, his countrymen celebrated him as a symbol of Danish national resurrection. He died a few months later in Copenhagen on January 20, 1850.

ANALYSIS

Adam Gottlob Oehlenschläger's choice of subject matter for his plays was very much in line with the philosophy of the time. To him, as well as to other writers of the epoch, the national spirit was to be found in indigenous folklore. This view stimulated enormous research into folk songs and medieval tales, resulting in a rediscovery of the old sagas. Oehlenschläger stated that mythology was the product of a nation's characters and way of thinking. Thus, one must look at his literary production as the point of departure for a new Danish national literary tradition. This fact is one of the prime reasons for his success with audiences.

MIDSUMMER NIGHT'S PLAY

Midsummer Night's Play, a lyric drama, appeared in the collection *Digte* in 1803. This is the only play by Oehlenschläger that is set in contemporary Denmark, and the author uses the local setting as backdrop for a Romantic polemic against the rationalist philosophy of life and its expression in the arts.

The plot line of *Midsummer Night's Play* is very thin and is subordinate to the polemicizing of the proponents of the various viewpoints. Maria has been farmed out and hidden with another family by her mother because she has fallen in love with Ludvig, a man above her in social standing. Ludvig loves Maria also, and they meet surreptitiously at a picnic at the popular Bakken, an amusement park for Copenhageners then and now. Within this framework, Oehlenschläger takes a mildly satiric look at the bourgeoisie and the state of the arts in Denmark. His vehicle is the whole plethora of Pierrots, harlequins, conjurers, minstrels, marionettes, and beggars, together with "art critics" from the general crowd of listeners. The play ends on a happy note when the Goddess of Love takes pity on the unhappy lovers and escorts them to a faraway place where they can live their lives in idyllic harmony.

Midsummer Night's Play is composed of a series of pictures that represents a bourgeois idyll. Oehlenschläger displays a contrapuntal array of figures, images, and ideas that contrast both in form and in content. The bold artists and the philistines, the irreverence of the ideals of the Enlightenment and the sensual representation of the primitive antiquity, the joy at the sight of the full picnic basket and the semireligious reverence of nature—these elements are all present in this youthful, playful drama. Most of the themes are presented in their own style, and lyric and epic episodes interchange freely in Oehlenschläger's first dramatic attempt at universal poetry.

ALADDIN

Aladdin was the main work appearing in Oehlenschläger's collection *Poetiske skrifter*. The source for the play was a 1758 Danish translation from the French of *The Thousand and One Nights*, and the author followed his source very closely, deviating only when dramatic exigency demanded it.

Aladdin is divided into five "actions," rather than the traditional acts. In this way, Oehlenschläger broke with dramatic conventions, immediately establishing the critical stance of Romanticism: nonconformity, challenge, and negation of classicism and rationalism.

Aladdin is the story of a young, handsome idler who wins a princess and a crown. Aladdin meets

Nureddin, who, unknown to him, is a magician and is searching for the Magic Lamp. Nureddin tries to kill Aladdin when the latter has retrieved the Magic Lamp for him but is unsuccessful. The young man returns home to his mother, Morgana, with the aid of the Spirit of the Lamp and proceeds to fall in love with the sultan's daughter, Gulnare, after having spied on her when she was on the way to her bath. He convinces his mother to go to Soliman, the sultan, to ask for the hand of his daughter. Helped by the Spirit of the Lamp, he comes up with the outrageous bridal price that Soliman demands: forty black slaves, each carrying one gold vessel filled with jewels, followed by forty white slaves. In addition, his magic servants build a white marble palace overnight as a wedding gift to Gulnare.

Nureddin, however, has realized that Aladdin is alive and in possession of the Magic Lamp. He appears in the town, disguised, and while Aladdin is away hunting, he acquires the lamp through cunning. When the hunting party returns, there is neither palace nor Gulnare. Consequently, the sultan loses his confidence in his son-in-law and condemns him to death, but the people plead for Aladdin's life, and he goes free on the condition that he return the princess and the palace within forty days.

Aladdin locates and kills Nureddin at the last moment and regains the favor of Soliman. Yet Nureddin's brother, Hindbad, is driven by greed toward possession of the Magic Lamp. He kills a holy woman and, disguised as her, gains entry to the palace, where he is exposed as an impostor and dies in a duel with Aladdin. As Hindbad dies, a messenger tells Aladdin and Gulnare that the old sultan has died, and Aladdin is proclaimed sultan.

Aladdin is essentially an anti-Faustian figure who does not strive for knowledge. In this figure, Oehlenschläger presented his Danish audience with the Romantic paradigm, the "merry son of nature." Many see in the character of Aladdin the forerunner of Joseph von Eichendorff's protagonist in his popular Romantic novella *Aus dem Leben eines Taugenichts* (1826; *Memoirs of a Good-for-Nothing*, 1906, 1955). The evil magician, Nureddin, represents that which the Romantic movement fought with unflagging

energy—the rational, intellectual being who orders, "Nature shall succumb to the power of the intellect." He is first introduced speaking in a meter closely resembling the Alexandrine, very frequently used in the Enlightenment because it is well suited to discursive thought. Oehlenschläger also used obvious formal devices for the characterization of the *dramatis personae*.

HAKON JARL

Hakon Jarl was written at the end of 1805, was published in 1807, and had its premiere on January 30, 1808. The play is a Nordic tragedy focusing on the introduction of Christianity into Scandinavia. Hakon Jarl, the title character, has ruled Norway as earl for some time but longs to be crowned king. His strength and ingenuity are legendary, but in a conversation with the merchant Thorer Klake in Odin's sacred grove, he reveals his fears of Olaf Trygveson, the Christian king of Dublin, and at the same time bemoans his own increasing age and failing strength. During this conversation, Hakon Jarl discovers the strikingly beautiful daughter of the smith and local guildsman, Bergthor. She begs Hakon to let her go and then runs home to her father, who immediately locks her up underneath the house, confirming the audience's suspicion that Hakon is a womanizer. Later, Hakon visits Bergthor's shop to inquire whether the crown is ready for the meeting of the farmers' council where he wants to be crowned. Bergthor replies that the crown is forged according to the measurement of an old, legendary king and that the crown belongs on the head on which it fits. The first real clue to the outcome of the play is found in the revelation that Hakon's head is far too small for the crown.

Meanwhile, Thorer Klake succeeds in tricking the young Dublin king into staying in Norway. Olaf had stopped there on a sentimental visit en route to Russia, and he now declares his love of Norway and Christianity. He believes Thorer's tale about the peasants' dissatisfaction with Hakon and decides to stay to win over the country and its inhabitants to Christianity and himself. Unknown to Thorer, Hakon has in fact given the impetus to a peasants' uprising in Hlade, having sent a group of his bondsmen to take the beautiful Gudrun from her father and her lawfully betrothed. The brave smith and his clan have offered resistance, and the outrage over this attempted misdeed spreads very quickly to other areas; soon an army is raised.

Act 3 of *Hakon Jarl* takes place on the island of Moster, where everything is ready for battle. Hakon is waiting in a coppice for the outcome of his latest cunning attempt to kill King Olaf, but his own kinsmen and warriors are disgusted by his deceit and thwart his plan, and Hakon is forced to flee.

The tragedy depicts the end of the last great heathen warrior and the extent to which he is willing to go in order to please the strict gods of Valhalla. In a pathetic last attempt to appease Odin, Hakon sacrifices his youngest and dearest son, Erling, in the sacred grove. Erling is already showing signs of the change that is to come over the Nordic countries when he shows his fear of the gods' stone images, asking his father who those foul, old men are.

In the final act, the audience and Hakon's sometime lover, Thora, hear word of the last battle, in the style of the old warrior epic and Nordic saga. Hakon has escaped alone on horseback, and Olaf Trygveson and his men are looking for him. Thora, however, allows Hakon to hide in the sepulchral chamber underneath her house. There he spends the last hours of his life with his thrall, Karker, who finally kills him and is executed by King Olaf for this unfaithful deed.

Hakon is indeed a tragic hero in the classic sense. Because of an accident of birth, he lives at a time of great upheaval in the north. He is a true product of his environment and can function only as a warrior and a ruler according to the cruel and dark myths of his time. Olaf Trygveson, on the other hand, is the harbinger of the new light and merciful faith that is changing the face of humanity. Hakon has no alternative but to follow the bidding of his culture and does not understand that the age of the old gods is over.

Oehlenschläger's original intention was to make Olaf Trygveson the main character, but the ancient historical sources made such an impression on him that Hakon's grand, tragic figure became the central one, and his struggle for power and for the values of the old culture became the heart of the tragedy. Oehlenschläger created two allegorical heroes who

are fighting not for themselves but for ideas: the virile Nordic and heathen spirit against a generous, colorful, but weaker southern nature.

BALDUR HIIN GODE

Baldur hiin gode is a tragedy written in iambic hexameter, the traditional epic meter. Here Oehlenschläger turns fully to the Nordic mythology and describes the end of Mithgarth—the realm of the Nordic gods. The god Baldur, representing the principle of Good, has had a dream that he soon shall die. The other gods, who all love Baldur, are horrified at the thought and command all things in the universe that they rule not to harm him. They forget the mistletoe, and Loke, a misfit and only part member of the family of gods, kills Baldur by means of a spear made of mistletoe. Hel, the goddess of the underworld, promises to let Baldur return to life if all things in the world show sorrow. Loke, however, does not weep, and consequently Baldur must remain with Hel.

The characters are types or allegorical figures. Good and evil, and beauty and ugliness, are juxtaposed forcefully in the play. The action is also built on contrasting relationships and historical clashes between ideas, cultures, or personalities. *Baldur hiin gode* portrays the grand passions: happiness and sorrow, love and hate, envy and sacrifice.

Even though the theme is different from that of *Aladdin*, it is interesting to note that the quality of evil, just as in *Aladdin*, has been assigned to the meditating, scheming, more rational figure, Loke. Baldur, on the other hand, is the dreaming, beautiful, naïve character; the audience recognizes the Romantic ideal in his qualities.

OTHER MAJOR WORKS

SHORT FICTION: *Vaulundurs saga*, 1805 (English translation, 1847); *Hroars saga*, 1817; *Oervarodds saga*, 1841.

POETRY: *Guldhornene*, 1802 (*The Golden Horns*, 1913); *Hakon Jarls doed*, 1803; *Langelandsrejsen*, 1805; *Nordiske digte*, 1807; *De tvende Kirkegaarde*, 1807; *Thors reise til Jotunheim*, 1807; *Helge*, 1814; *Hrolf krake*, 1828.

MISCELLANEOUS: *Digte*, 1803; *Poetiske skrifter*, 1805.

BIBLIOGRAPHY

Aage, Jøorgenson. *Idyll and Abyss: Essays on Danish Literature and Theater*. Seattle, Wash.: Mermaid Press, 1992. A chapter in this work is devoted to a discussion of Oehlenschläger, with emphasis on his poetry. Bibliography.

Bernd, Clifford A. *Poetic Realism in Scandinavia and Central Europe, 1820-1895*. Columbia, S.C.: Camden House, 1995. This volume covers poetry in Denmark at the time when Oehlenschläger was writing. Bibliography and index.

Vibeke R. Petersen

YURY OLESHA

Born: Elisavetgrad (now Kirovograd), Ukraine, Russian Empire; March 3, 1899
Died: Moscow, U.S.S.R.; May 10, 1960

PRINCIPAL DRAMA

Zagovor chuvstv, pr., pb. 1929 (*The Conspiracy of Feelings*, 1976)

Tri tolstyaka, pr., pb. 1930 (*The Three Fat Men*, 1983)

Spisok blagodeyaniy, pr., pb. 1931 (*A List of Assets*, 1960; also known as *A List of Blessings*, 1983)

Strogiy yunosha, pr., pb. 1934 (*A Stern Young Man*, 1983)

The Complete Plays, pb. 1983

OTHER LITERARY FORMS

Yury Olesha's main literary contribution was in the field of fiction. The publication of his major work, the novel *Zavist'* (1927; *Envy*, 1936), established him immediately as an important writer. Its theme of the right of individuals to free development of their abilities was contrary to the official line of collectivism, but it was tolerated in the relatively free spirit of the 1920's. As soon as that decade was over, both Olesha and the novel were ostracized for many years. His only works to be published were those in which he tried to accommodate the regime, and publication of even those ceased in the late 1930's. For the rest of his life, he did not publish anything of importance. His memoirs, *Ni dnia bez strochki* (*No Day Without a Line*, 1979), were published posthumously in 1965.

ACHIEVEMENTS

Mainly because of his precarious relationship with the Soviet Union's communist regime, Yury Olesha did not receive any awards. The government tolerated him and his writings until the beginning of Joseph Stalin's reign of terror in the early 1930's. Olesha was very interested in theater and was highly respected by the leading directors such as Konstantin Stanislavsky and Vsevolod Meyerhold, who staged his plays as soon as they were published. Olesha's love for theater also manifested in the rewriting of his novels and stories into plays, with different levels of success. Two of his plays, *The Conspiracy of Feelings* and *A List of Assets*, were considered to be some of the best Russian plays in the late 1920's and the early 1930's.

BIOGRAPHY

The son of a tsarist officer, Yury Karlovich Olesha was born in Elisavetgrad, near Odessa, on March 3, 1899. He grew up in Odessa, where he finished his education. He joined the active literary scene in that city and counted writers Isaak Babel and Valentin Katayev among his friends. He began to write poetry but soon abandoned that genre. He had an ambivalent attitude toward the revolution, which was reflected in almost all his later works. He moved to Moscow in 1920 and continued to write and associate with writers. He wrote some short stories in the mid-1920's but did not publish them right away.

In 1927 he published his first and best novel *Envy*, which was hailed by many critics as one of the best novels in contemporary Soviet literature. Through the views and actions of the protagonist Nikolay Kavalerov, Olesha expresses his own views about the revolution and the role of the intellectuals, which are replete with ambivalence and doubts about the sacrosanctity, and even need, for the drastic revolution carried out by the Bolsheviks. He rewrote *Envy* as a play, *The Conspiracy of Feelings*, which had a successful run at the prestigious Vakhtangov Theater in 1929, as well as at other theaters. This play was followed by *A List of Assets*, staged at Vsevolod Meyerhold's theater in 1931. In this work, Olesha continued to wrestle with his ambivalence about the revolution, attempting to strike a balance between positive and negative developments in the communist state. Because of the views he expressed in these plays and other works, he was viewed with suspicion by the authorities and criticized heavily by the official critics loyal to the system. His literary productivity was reduced to a trickle. Few of his works were reprinted, save for a novel-length fairy tale for children, *Tri tolstyaka* (1928; *The Three Fat Men*, 1964).

With the introduction of Stalin's strict control of every part of life, including literature, Olesha's position became more and more precarious. He found it necessary to publicly explain his position at the first Congress of the Union of Soviet Writers in 1934. He pleaded for understanding of his inability to accept without reservations the official guidelines and averred that the protagonist of *Envy*, Nikolay Kavalerov, as his alter ego, expresses his own ambivalence. The plea fell on deaf ears, and Olesha was condemned to silence and was fortunate not to follow other writers, including his friend Babel, to their death. He was prevented from publishing any new works during his lifetime, although his memoir, *No Day Without a Line*, was published after his death.

ANALYSIS

In his plays, Yury Olesha grappled with the question that was of paramount importance to him, that of the position and role of an individual, especially of an intellectual, in a collectivist society. For this reason he was labeled by many critics as a one-theme writer. Both *The Conspiracy of Feelings* and *The Three Fat Men*, adapted from his longer fiction, as well as his

two original plays, *A List of Assets* and *A Stern Young Man*, are indeed variations on a theme. They constitute his dialogue with his epoch, the Soviet period, during which many other Russian writers also suffered. Olesha's tendency to focus on the problems of the individual in a collectivist society seemed potentially dangerous to the authorities and caused him much trouble and even persecution. It is to his credit that he avoided the pitfalls of monotony; each of his plays stands by itself and adds to the mosaic of the overriding theme. That is why his plays were popular in his time and have lost little of their original charm and significance. In a way, he answered the call of the literary bosses to write about social themes, but he did it in such a way as to ensure his place among the better Russian playwrights.

THE CONSPIRACY OF FEELINGS

The Conspiracy of Feelings generally follows the plot of the novel *Envy*, on which it was based. In the play, Ivan Babichev clings to the old virtues and wages war against the so-called progress brought by the revolution. He attacks his brother Andrey Babichev as the epitome of the new, especially railing against Andrey's reliance on practical things in his efforts to create a cafeteria with the best fast food and sausages for the masses. Ivan, however, does not help his cause by wearing shabby clothes and rampaging through the streets of Moscow, creating the impression that he is a lunatic bum.

Nikolay Kavalerov, a young drifter, vacillates between the two brothers. He is in love with Ivan's daughter, Valya, but he is also grateful to Andrey for picking him drunk out of a gutter and bringing him to his home to start a new life. Interestingly, Kavalerov envies both brothers: Ivan, for his free spirit and his despisal of material things, and Andrey, for his success in what he does. Kavalerov wants to be successful, too, and he is torn between the values represented by the two brothers. However, he is unable either to achieve his goals here and now like Andrey or to live in the past like Ivan. Enraged, Kavalerov decides to kill Andrey, but in the last moment, he changes his mind and kills Ivan, in fact killing his past, according to his own words at the end of the play. This is the only substantial change from the novel.

Because Olesha has publicly admitted that in Kavalerov he portrays himself and because of the Kavalerov's desire and futile attempts to accept the new reality, *The Conspiracy of Feelings* can be viewed as Olesha's catharsis. The writer Olesha wanted to be successful in the here and now, like Kavalerov, but his respect for some indestructible values of the past prevented him from becoming a successful new-style "sausage-maker." In Olesha's view, feelings should prevail over strictly rational concerns, otherwise life would lose all its worth and become a huge sausage factory. Olesha thus expresses a belief that the conspiracy of feelings will triumph in the end.

A LIST OF ASSETS

Olesha's ambivalence about the new system in the Soviet Union is further depicted in his play *A List of Assets*. A successful Moscow theater actress, Yelena Goncharova, makes a dream trip to the cultural center of the world, Paris, to see the hallowed ground trod by her idol Charlie Chaplin and to invoke the Chaplinesque theme of the lonely human being trying to get something out of life. Once there, she is attracted by some aspects of life in the West and repelled by others. She is also brought in touch with Russian émigrés, who try to persuade her to defect from the Soviet Union, which she is reluctant to do. However, during the course of a demonstration, she is killed.

It is revealed that before Goncharova was killed, she had listed in her diary the reasons why she should not defect. She lists both good things and bad things about her home country. In her opinion, the good things prevail, and that is why she refuses to join the émigrés in Paris. In reality, this is the list of pros and cons Olesha himself formulated while wrestling with the dilemma of whether to accept the new system or reject it altogether, a dilemma of which he would later speak while addressing the Congress of the Union of Soviet Writers in 1934. While describing her decision to return to her homeland, Goncharova makes some ingratiating statements about the communist system, perhaps as justification or rationalization of her decision. This is in line with what Olesha did at the writers' congress, to no avail.

THE THREE FAT MEN

Olesha rewrote a short novel, *The Three Fat Men*, into a play with the same title. Ostensibly written as a fairy tale for children, the book, as well as the play, contains issues aimed at adults. The plot of the play follows that of the novel: A revolution in a fairy-tale land results in the triumph of the proletariat, who are ruled by the Three Fat Men, who bear the symbolic names of General, Cardinal, and Miller. To ensure a suitable heir to their regime, the rulers kidnap a small boy named Tutti. The gluttony of these evil dictators demonstrates how they live off the fat of the land. They order Tutti's heart to be replaced by an iron heart so that he can continue their heartless rule, but their order is not carried out. In the course of the play, Tutti undergoes normal human experiences such as feeling love for a young circus dancer, who was also kidnaped by the Three Fat Men and happens to be his sister. A doctor says to Tutti at the end of the play that he has an ordinary heart, a human heart, which cannot be replaced by iron, stone, or ice. Olesha uses the trappings of a modern fairy tale and adventure story, including circus shows and magic, to make the play more attractive for children but also to veil more serious connotations concerning the way of governing and the role of feelings in government.

The Three Fat Men is Olesha's most popular work and the only one approved by the authorities because of its seemingly innocuous contents and of its appeal for children. Once transformed into a play, however, it lost some of the charm meant for juveniles and acquired the seriousness of one of Olesha's basic themes—that a human heart could not, and should not, be forced to betray itself for the sake of rationalistic machinations. This is the message Olesha tried to tell the world.

A STERN YOUNG MAN

In *A Stern Young Man*, Olesha endeavors to depict "the new Soviet man": athletic, good-looking, and loyal to the new society. As he explained in his speech at the 1934 writers' congress, he wanted to portray a young man who would represent the best of his own youth. For Olesha, communism was not only an economic but also a moral system, and he wanted to show that the new socialist attitude to the world was human in the purest sense of the word. However, the qualities of the protagonist, a young communist, fly in the face of the official acceptance, revealing a predilection for dangerous "feelings" such as modesty, truthfulness, generosity, sentimentality, and other "bourgeois aberrations." Thus, Olesha's attempt to present "socialism with a human face" was rejected by the official watchdogs as too idealistic and as "philosophically pessimistic" reveries that were in opposition to the ideals of the revolutionary proletariat.

Olesha wrote a film scenario for the play, and it was made into a motion picture, but it was never shown because of the authorities' objections. His last work to be published during his lifetime, *A Stern Young Man* finally convinced Olesha of the futility of attempting to present an objective artistic assessment of the Soviet socialist society, which he had tried to do in many of his works, notably in *A List of Assets.*

OTHER MAJOR WORKS

LONG FICTION: *Zavist'*, 1927 (*Envy*, 1936); *Tri tolstyaka*, 1928 (*The Three Fat Men*, 1964).

SHORT FICTION: *Lyubov*, 1929; *Vishneyaya kostochka*, 1931; *The Wayward Comrade and the Commissars*, 1960; *Envy and Other Works*, 1967; *Love and Other Stories*, 1967; *The Complete Short Stories and "The Three Fat Men,"* 1979.

POETRY: *Zubilo*, 1924; *Salyut*, 1927.

SCREENPLAYS: *Bolotnye soldaty*, 1938; *Strogiy yunosha*, 1942 (adaptation of his play).

NONFICTION: *Ni dnia bez strochki*, 1965 (memoir; *No Day Without a Line*, 1979).

BIBLIOGRAPHY

Beaujour, Elizabeth K. *The Invisible Land: A Study of the Artistic Imagination of Iurii Olesha*. New York: Columbia University Press, 1970. Although the study emphasizes the interpretation of images in *Envy*, it deals, by implication, with similar phenomena in *The Conspiracy of Feelings* and other plays.

Green, Michael, and Jerome Katsell. "Olesha and the Theater." In *Yury Olesha: The Complete Plays*. Ann Arbor, Mich.: Ardis, 1983. A succinct overview of Olesha's plays and of his career as a writer, paying special attention to how he converted his fiction into plays.

Rudnitsky, Konstantin. *Meyerhold the Director*. Ann Arbor, Mich.: Ardis, 1981. An authoritative study of Meyerhold's work as a director, touching on his dealings with Olesha in staging his plays. Serves as a history of the Russian theater in the first half of the twentieth century, in which Olesha played a brief but important role.

Struve, Gleb. *Russian Literature Under Lenin and Stalin, 1917-1953*. Norman: University of Oklahoma Press, 1971. Extensive discussion of Olesha's contribution to Russian literature and of his struggle with the authorities in his efforts to defend the freedom of expression.

Tucker, Janet G. *Revolution Betrayed: Jurij Olesha's "Envy."* Columbus, Ohio: Slavica, 1996. Examines political and social issues present in *Envy* and *The Conspiracy of Feelings*, focusing on the role of intellectuals and literature in relation to the revolution and ensuing Soviet system.

Vasa D. Mihailovich

EUGENE O'NEILL

Born: New York, New York; October 16, 1888
Died: Boston, Massachusetts; November 27, 1953

PRINCIPAL DRAMA

Bound East for Cardiff, wr. 1913-1914, pr. 1916, pb. 1919

Thirst, and Other One-Act Plays, pb. 1914
Chris Christophersen, wr. 1919, pb. 1982 (revised as *Anna Christie*)
Beyond the Horizon, pr., pb. 1920
The Emperor Jones, pr. 1920, pb. 1921
Anna Christie, pr. 1921, pb. 1923

The Hairy Ape, pr., pb. 1922
All God's Chillun Got Wings, pr., pb. 1924
Complete Works, pb. 1924 (2 volumes)
Desire Under the Elms, pr. 1924, pb. 1925
The Great God Brown, pr., pb. 1926
Lazarus Laughed, pb. 1927, pr. 1928
Strange Interlude, pr., pb. 1928
Mourning Becomes Electra, pr., pb. 1931 (includes
    Homecoming, *The Hunted*, and *The Haunted*)
Nine Plays, pb. 1932
Ah, Wilderness!, pr., pb. 1933
Plays, pb. 1941 (3 volumes), pb. 1955 (revised)
The Iceman Cometh, pr., pb. 1946
A Moon for the Misbegotten, pr. 1947, pb. 1952
Long Day's Journey into Night, pr., pb. 1956
Later Plays, pb. 1967
The Calms of Capricorn, pb. 1981 (with Donald
    Gallup)
The Complete Plays, pb. 1988 (3 volumes)
Ten "Lost" Plays, pb. 1995
Early Plays, pb. 2001

Eugene O'Neill (© The Nobel Foundation)

OTHER LITERARY FORMS

Although primarily known for his plays, Eugene O'Neill also wrote poetry and a large amount of correspondence, collected in several volumes and published posthumously. Among these are *"The Theatre We Worked For": The Letters of Eugene O'Neill to Kenneth MacGowan* (1982), edited by Jackson R. Bryer and Ruth M. Alvarez and containing an introductory essay by Travis Bogard; *"Love and Admiration and Respect": The O'Neill-Commins Correspondence* (1986), edited by Dorothy Commins; and *"As Ever, Gene": The Letters of Eugene O'Neill to George Jean Nathan* (1987), edited by Nancy L. Roberts and Arthur W. Roberts. O'Neill's poems were published in *Poems, 1912-1944* (1979) and were edited by Donald Gallup. His unpublished or unfamiliar writings were published in *The Unknown O'Neill* (1988), edited by Travis Bogard.

ACHIEVEMENTS

Eugene O'Neill has been called, rightly, the father of modern American drama, not only because he was the first major American playwright but also because

of the influence of his work on the development of American theater and on other dramatists. In addition to achieving both popular success and critical acclaim in the United States, O'Neill has achieved an international reputation. Produced throughout the world, his plays are the subject of countless critical books and articles. In many of his plays, O'Neill employed traditional themes such as the quest, while in others he treated subjects that had gone largely unexamined on the American stage, particularly subjects concerning human psychology. Although many of his works are now universally acclaimed, initial critical reaction to the emotional content of some of these plays was mixed. In addition to breaking new ground in theme and subject matter, O'Neill was innovative in his use of technical elements of the theater. He experimented with such devices as masks, "asides," and even the stage itself as vehicles to further themes. Moreover, in an effort to achieve for the drama the broad temporal spectrum of the novel, he experimented with dramatic time, presenting two of his works in trilogies of nine acts each. Although some of O'Neill's dramatic and theatrical experiments were less well received than others, his reputation is now secure; his plays continue to be widely produced throughout the world, both on the stage and on film, because they speak to the human experience that is shared by all.

BIOGRAPHY

Eugene Gladstone O'Neill's parents were James O'Neill, an actor imprisoned by the material success of his role as the Count of Monte Cristo, and Ellen Quinlan O'Neill, a romantic and idealistic woman similarly trapped for much of her life by an addiction to morphine. The complex psychologies of O'Neill's parents and his brother, and the relationships among all the family members, figure significantly as subjects of many of O'Neill's best plays, particularly *Long Day's Journey into Night*. Educated in Catholic schools, O'Neill entered Princeton University in 1906 but left before a year was over. His travels in 1910 and 1911 to South America and England provided background for his early plays of the sea, several of which he wrote during a six-month hospitalization for tuberculosis in 1912. The following year, he participated in George Pierce Baker's Workshop 47 at Harvard University, where he formally studied playwriting. O'Neill was married three times: to Kathleen Jenkins in 1909, to Agnes Boulton in 1918, and to Carlotta Monterey in 1929. He had three children: Eugene, Jr., who was born to the first marriage and who committed suicide in 1950; and Shane and Oona, who were born to the second marriage. O'Neill won four Pulitzer Prizes for his plays: in 1920 for *Beyond the Horizon*, in 1922 for *Anna Christie*, in 1928 for *Strange Interlude*, and in 1957 for *Long Day's Journey into Night*. In 1936, he was awarded the Nobel Prize in Literature. Although ill for the last seventeen years of his life, O'Neill wrote several of his finest plays during that period.

ANALYSIS

Eugene O'Neill has often been criticized for his choice of characters, for their aberrant psychologies,

and for their emotionalism. Certainly he dealt with emotions, but he did so because he believed that emotions were a better guide than thoughts in the search for truth. The struggles of his characters frequently take place, therefore, within themselves, so that there is little real action performed on the stage. Victories, consequently, are in the mind, not quantifiable. The ephemeral nature of such victories has been, for some critics, insufficient.

The popularity of O'Neill's work, however, continues to grow. His plays have been performed throughout the world and transformed into film and opera because they concern truths of human existence. For O'Neill, life *is* a tragedy—but human beings have the resources with which to confront it. The dramatic presentation of that struggle was O'Neill's lifework.

THE EMPEROR JONES

Although O'Neill was fortunate in having several of his earliest plays produced, his first real success was *The Emperor Jones*, produced by the Provincetown Players in 1920. The play was an immense success for the small theater, for O'Neill, and for Charles Gilpin, who performed as America's first black tragic hero in a role later played by Paul Robeson. Devoted to the final hours in the life of Brutus Jones, a former convict who, in the course of two years, comes to be emperor of an island in the West Indies, O'Neill's expressionist play won immediate acclaim, both popular and critical.

The form of the play is particularly interesting, for it is composed essentially of one act with eight scenes. The six interior monologue scenes take place in the forest and in Jones's mind and are peopled by the ghosts and phantoms that plague Jones. These six scenes are enveloped by opening and closing scenes that occur outside the forest and that present real characters. The movement of the play is thus a journey from the civilized world into the primitive world of the forest and of the mind, and a journey for Jones to self-knowledge and to death.

The play's expository opening scene reveals that Jones, who arrived on the island two years earlier as a stowaway and who has come to rule the island, has exploited the natives; has enriched himself by manipulation, thievery, and cruel taxation; and has, as a consequence, become so hated that the natives have withdrawn into the hills to stage a revolution. Jones believes, however, that he is prepared for all possibilities: Should he need to escape suddenly, he has hidden food and has learned the paths of the forest. He has also removed vast amounts of money from the island to a safe place. As he explains, he has learned from white people to steal big, and he proudly asserts that he makes his own good luck by using his brain. Jones has, moreover, created among the islanders a mystique and a mythology for himself; distancing himself completely from the natives, whom he terms "bush niggers" and to whom he feels vastly superior, Jones has propagated the myth that he is magically protected from lead bullets and can be killed only by one of silver. Furthermore, having made for himself a silver bullet that he carries as the sixth in his gun, he has spread the companion tale that he is invulnerable to native assaults because he is the only man big enough to kill himself. Having learned that the natives are rebelling, he congratulates himself on his precautions, boasts about how easy it is to outwit them, and makes his way to the forest through which he must go that night in order to meet the boat that will take him to safety.

When, in the second scene, Jones reaches the edge of the forest, the audience begins to see some of O'Neill's experimental techniques. The edge of the forest, O'Neill tells the audience, is a "wall of darkness dividing the world," a point at which Jones begins to understand the uselessness of his precautions: He cannot find his store of food, and more important, he is not even sure where he is, exactly. When the little Formless Fears appear, amorphous, black, child-size shapes that, with low sounds of laughter, advance writhingly toward him, he is terrified and fires a shot at them. He reveals his thought processes through a continuing monologue, a technique that seems to reflect the influence of August Strindberg on O'Neill. Jones's monologue, which continues throughout the six forest scenes, reveals at this point his fear at having disclosed his location and his determination to make it through the forest. In addition, he begins to have, within his monologue, a dialogue with himself, a dialogue that symbolically suggests a

duality within him, a dissociation between mind and body and between outer bravado and inner fear. The steadily increasing beat of the drum, which had begun with his departure from the palace in the first act, reflects Jones's heightened emotional state and conveys not only the buildup of tension in him but also that in the distant natives.

This first forest scene and the five that follow present a series of vignettes that derive both from Jones's own life and mind and from the racial memory, or collective unconscious. Having first encountered the Formless Fears, he comes next on Jeff, the Pullman porter he killed with a razor in a fight over a crap game and for whose death he went to prison. Both furious and terrified, Jones fires his second bullet into the ghost, who disappears as the drumbeat's tempo once again increases. When, in the fourth scene, Jones reaches a wide road that he does not recognize, his outer appearance is beginning to deteriorate: His glorious uniform is torn and dirty, and he removes his coat and his spurs for comfort. Castigating himself for his belief in ghosts, he reminds himself that he is civilized, not like "dese ign'rent black niggers heah." He is nearly paralyzed with fright, however, when he sees another apparition, a chain gang with a guard who forces Jones to join the prisoners. When the guard beats Jones with his whip, Jones, reenacting his actual break from prison, fires his third bullet into the guard's back.

These first three forest scenes, concerned with aspects of Jones's own life, represent troublesome elements from his individual consciousness. Making him aware of the evil to which he has committed himself, they are important stages in his journey to self-knowledge. Moreover, they indicate, beyond a doubt, the true criminality of his nature. The following scenes, concerned with aspects of his racial memory, present elements that are part of the collective unconscious and thereby reveal some of the cultural forces that have made him what he is.

In the fifth scene, in a clearing in the forest, Jones comes on a dead stump that looks like an auction block. His appearance further deteriorating, his pants torn and ragged, he removes his battered shoes; the outer symbols of his exalted position, and of his difference from the natives, are virtually gone. As he sends an agonized prayer to Jesus, admitting his wrongdoing and acknowledging that as emperor he is getting "mighty low," he is suddenly surrounded by a group of Southern aristocrats of the 1850's who are waiting for a group of slaves to come in. To Jones's utter horror, the auctioneer compels Jones to stand on the auction block; when he is bought, Jones, suddenly coming to life and resisting this treatment, angrily pulls out his gun and fires at both the auctioneer and his purchaser, using his last two lead bullets, as the drum quickens and the scene fades.

The sixth scene goes back to a time preceding the fifth; Jones finds himself in a clearing so overhung by trees that it appears as the hold of a ship. By this time, Jones's clothes have been so torn that he is wearing only a loincloth. Discovering that he is among two rows of blacks who moan desolately as they sway back and forth, Jones finds himself inadvertently joining in their chorus of despair, crying out even more loudly than they. Having used all his lead bullets, he has nothing with which to dispatch them, since he needs his silver bullet for luck, for self-preservation. He is obliged, then, as he was obliged to recommit his crimes, to enter into the racial experience of slavery, to feel the grief and desperation of his ancestors. Unable to disperse this scene, Jones simply walks into the seventh and last of the forest scenes, which takes him to an even earlier time. Coming on an ancient altar by the river, Jones instinctively bows, even as he wonders why he does so. Although he prays for the Christian God's protection, what appears is a witch doctor whose dance and incantations hypnotize Jones and force his participation in an ancient and mysterious ritual. O'Neill's stage directions indicate that Jones is expected at this point to sacrifice himself to the forces of evil, to the forces that have governed his life and that are now represented by a huge crocodile emerging from the river. Urged onward by the witch doctor and unable to stop himself from moving toward the crocodile, Jones, in a last act of desperate defiance, shoots the crocodile with his last bullet— the silver bullet.

The last act at the edge of the forest, an act that serves as an epilogue, is almost anticlimactic, de-scribing how the natives enter the forest to kill the dazed Jones, who has wandered back (full circle) to the spot where he entered. The audience knows, however, that Jones has symbolically killed himself, destroying his evil and his identity with his own silver bullet. It is, moreover, particularly appropriate that the natives shoot Jones with silver bullets, bullets they have made out of melted money.

The journey into the forest has been for Jones a journey to death, but it has also been a journey to understanding. He has come not only to understand the evil of his own life but also to destroy it symbolically by destroying the crocodile with the bullet that affirms his identity. In effect, he is obliged to confront his true nature when the structure he has created for himself collapses. He has also come, however, to understand both his membership in his race and his connection with those natives to whom he felt so superior. By being forced to undergo the primitive experiences of his people, he is able to move from individuation into the group, into an awareness of the experiences common to his race. He is able to return, by means of this backward and inward journey, to his essential self, the self he had denied out of greed and egotism.

O'Neill in this way presents Jones as both a criminal and a victim, as a man whose own character and personality help to create his fate but whose racial and cultural experiences have also shaped him. Part of the play's tragedy, though, is that the knowledge Jones gains is insufficient to save his life. Nevertheless, as the trader, Smithers, concludes at the end of the play, the Emperor Jones "died in the 'eighth o' style, any'ow."

With this play, O'Neill established himself as an important and innovative American playwright. The play is also notable for its lack of autobiographical elements. It is an imaginative creation based on a blend of folktale and psychology that permitted O'Neill to enter the racial memory of another.

DESIRE UNDER THE ELMS

A play differing considerably in kind is *Desire Under the Elms*, first performed by the Provincetown Players in 1924 and perhaps one of O'Neill's most representative works. It reflects a number of the influences that worked significantly on him, including the Bible and classical mythology. It treats several of his favorite subjects, including the tension-ridden family, antimaterialism, and individuals' participation in creating their own fate; and although the play was initially received with considerable skepticism and disapproval (it was banned in both Boston and England), its critical reputation and its popular acceptance have steadily increased with time, and it continues to be produced for appreciative contemporary audiences.

The play is set on a New England farm in the mid-nineteenth century, a thematically important setting. Just as the New England land is rocky, unyielding, and difficult to manage, so is old Ephraim Cabot, who owns the farm, and so is the Puritan ethos that governs the lives of this patriarch and those around him. Accompanying this symbolism of hardness and coldness in the land and in Ephraim is the emotional symbolism associated with the farmhouse: O'Neill's set directions specify that the farmhouse is flanked by "two enormous elms" that "brood oppressively over the house," that "appear to protect and at the same time subdue," and that possess "a sinister maternity in their aspect, a crushing, jealous absorption." Clearly symbolic of Ephraim's dead second wife, and typifying both her physical and mental exhaustion and her unavenged spirit, the elms are also symbolic of the restrictive nature of New England farm life. In signifying that restriction, they are symbolic also of Ephraim, who exercises a jealous and unrelentingly selfish control over everything and everyone within his reach.

When the play opens, Ephraim is away from the farm on a trip, during which he marries Abbie Putnam, a young widow. By means of the marriage, Ephraim can prove his continuing virility and vigor and, he believes, achieve his paramount desire: to perpetuate his power and his hold over the land. His three grown sons, Simeon and Peter, children of Ephraim's first wife, and the sensitive Eben, son of Ephraim's second wife, dislike and distrust their father and recognize that his marriage to Abbie ensures that none of them will satisfy their desire to inherit the farm. One of the French naturalist writers whose

work influenced O'Neill was Émile Zola, and this play seems to be particularly evocative of Zola's *La Terre* (1887; *The Soil*, 1888; also as *Earth*, 1954) in dealing with the human greed for land. This shared desire for land, however, is not the only desire with which the play is concerned. Ephraim, who sees himself as an extension of the Old Testament God, desires to maintain his power forever. Abbie, who marries because of her initial desire for security, comes later to desire love instead, as does Eben, who initially desires revenge on his father for working his mother to death. Although Simeon and Peter also hope for a share in the farm, they are happy to accept Eben's offer to buy them off, realizing that their expectations, because of their father's new marriage, will probably go unrealized.

The play establishes in the first act the many violent tensions existing between father and son. Blaming his father for the death of his mother, Eben also believes his father is cheating him out of the farm. Moreover, although Eben insists that he is like his mother and denies any similarity to his father and although Ephraim likewise considers his son weak and spineless, it is one of the play's ironies that father and son are in fact much alike, as indicated symbolically by the fact that both patronize the same local prostitute. More significant, however, both father and son are governed by strong emotions: Both are quick to anger, stubborn, vengeful, proud, and hard, and both are the victims of seething animal passions that are covered by only a thin veneer of civilization. The psychologically normal conflict between any father and son is thus intensified by their temperamental similarities, and when Abbie, the catalyst, appears as the stepmother who is closer in age to son than to father, the stage is indeed set for a depiction of violent emotions that result in great tragedy.

Because they both desire the farm, Abbie and Eben initially hate and mistrust each other, but their harsh and cruel behavior toward each other is counterpointed by a growing physical desire between them, a reflection, perhaps, of O'Neill's interest in the classical myths of Oedipus and Phaedra. O'Neill's use of a divided set permits the audience to watch this desire growing as they see simultaneously into the bedroom of Eben, as he moves half-unconsciously toward the wall beyond which Abbie stands, and into the bedroom of Ephraim and Abbie, where they continue to hope for the son who will fulfill Ephraim's desire and ensure Abbie's security. As the obvious but unspoken passion between Abbie and Eben mounts and the house grows correspondingly cold, Ephraim is driven to find solace in the barn, among the animals, where it is warm—an opportunity that Abbie uses to seduce Eben in the parlor, where the restless spirit of Eben's mother seems to be concentrated.

This lovemaking between stepmother and son, teetering as it does on the brink of incest, was, as one might expect, an aspect of the play to which censors objected. Abbie is, after all, Eben's stepmother, and she uses her "maternal" relationship to Eben as a means of seduction. At the same time that she vows to kiss him "pure," as if she were his mother, she passionately blurts out that loving him like a mother "hain't enuf," and that "it's got to be that and more." As O'Neill explains in his stage directions, there is in her "a horribly frank mixture of lust and mother love." One further motive for Abbie that O'Neill leaves uncertain is her need to produce a son for Ephraim. It is one of the fine ambiguities of the play that viewers are unable to decide whether Abbie seduces Eben out of greed for the land, out of maternal caring, out of physical lust, or out of genuine love for him. Eben is moved by similarly discordant motives, by both a real desire for Abbie and a desire to avenge his mother by taking his father's woman. He senses his mother's spirit leaving the house and returning to her grave, finally at peace. Eben indicates his understanding of and his satisfaction with the retributive nature of this act the next morning when he offers his hand to his father, remarking to the uncomprehending Ephraim that they are now "quits."

Yet, despite the deliberate calculation with which this love affair begins, Abbie and Eben come in time genuinely to love each other. What was initially, at least in part, a mutually self-serving and opportunistic seduction results in the first warm human relationship the farm has seen. There is, however, no way for the drama to end happily, even though, at the beginning of the third act, all have attained what they at one time desired: Ephraim has a son to prove his virility, Abbie has earned the farm by providing that son, and Eben has avenged his mother. These desires are, to Abbie and Eben, at least, no longer of prime importance, and the party Ephraim gives to celebrate the birth of "his" son serves as an ironic backdrop to the play's tragic climax.

Ephraim, flushed with liquor and pride at producing a son at seventy-six and oblivious to the knowing sneers of the townspeople, in a brutal physical and emotional confrontation with Eben gloats that Abbie wanted a child only to preempt Eben's claim to the farm. Believing that Abbie has seduced him only in order to become pregnant and cheat him, Eben turns violently against her, telling her that he hates her and wishes their son dead. The half-crazed Abbie, hysterically wishing to restore the time when Eben loved her and confusedly identifying the child as the cause of Eben's present hate, smothers the child in its cradle in an appalling inversion of the myth of Medea: Whereas Medea murders her children as an act of revenge against her faithless husband, Abbie murders her child in order to recapture the lost love of Eben. Eben, however, does not respond with love, but with horror and revulsion, and he runs for the sheriff to arrest her. Returning before the sheriff, Eben in a change of heart acknowledges his own guilt and reaffirms his love for Abbie. The play ends with their mutual expression of love as they are taken off by the sheriff, who ironically remarks, with admiration, that "it's a jim-dandy farm."

The play seems, then, to be unmitigatedly naturalistic and pessimistic as the lovers go off to be hanged and as Ephraim is left alone with his farm. Yet O'Neill poses the possibility of a spiritual victory in the play: Although the desire to possess has dominated their lives, Abbie and Eben are freed of that desire at the end—even though their victory is to be short-lived. It is also possible to see a victory over the forces of evil embodied in Puritanism and in the New England patriarchal society, because, even though Eben reacts initially to his father's announcement and to the baby's murder with all the violent self-righteousness one would expect of his father, he comes to transcend this attitude and to acknowledge both his love for Abbie and his own guilt. Although Abbie and Eben have lost everything in the worldly sense, in finding love and faith in each other they do perhaps escape, however briefly and symbolically, from the brooding, confining New England elms.

In this play, O'Neill seems to return to the naturalism that informed his early plays of the sea. His characters are presented as bewildered, struggling beings, blown about like leaves in the gutter, compelled by the external forces of fate, chance, and environment and by the internal workings of their physical nature. It is indeed difficult for these characters to win, but for O'Neill, the salient point is that, in struggling, his characters can transcend their fate.

THE ICEMAN COMETH

The critics, who had difficulty with *Desire Under the Elms* because of its objectionable subject matter, were also troubled by *The Iceman Cometh*, but for different reasons; many considered the latter play unhealthy, pessimistic, and morbid in its depiction of the wasted lives of the habitués of Harry Hope's New York saloon, modeled after those in which O'Neill spent considerable time in 1911 and in 1914-1919. A key theme in the play, and a recurring theme in O'Neill's dramas, is the power and the necessity of illusion to give meaning to life. O'Neill develops this theme through expository conversation and monologues because there is very little onstage action during the two-day period that the play's four acts encompass. Containing both comic and tragic elements, the play, set in 1912, takes place entirely in the back room of Harry Hope's bar, where the regulars gather.

The play opens on a gathering of regulars to await the arrival of Hickey, a hardware salesperson who is the most successful among them and who comes to the bar for periodic drunks, particularly on the occasion of Harry Hope's birthday, when he funds a great drunken party for the regulars. Himself unfaithful to his wife, Hickey maintains a running gag that his apparently saintly wife must, in his absence, be having an affair with the iceman. Hickey and all the other characters live in a world of illusion, a world that ignores today: They all look backward to yesterday, to what they once were or to what their rosy rewriting of

history now tells them they once were, just as they look forward to an equally rosy and improbable tomorrow. The illusion that they all have a future is part of the pipe dream each has, a pipe dream essential to their lives that helps them "keep up the appearances of life." Although these people really have, in Robert Frost's words, "nothing to look backward to with pride" and "nothing to look forward to with hope," they somehow manage to live, to survive in the bleak, drunken world they inhabit, because they possess the illusion that they have a yesterday about which they can feel pride and a tomorrow about which they can hope. That illusion enables them to ignore the dark reality that is their today. Moreover, because they understand one another's illusions and accept them, they can be sympathetic to and tolerant of one another's failings as well as of their own.

Among the characters who frequent the bar are Larry Slade, an elderly anarchist who believes he is uninvolved in life and who claims he wants only to die; Joe Mott, an African American who plans to open a gambling house one day; Piet Wetjoen, a former Boer War commander who believes he can return home; Pat McGloin, who plans to return soon to the police force; Harry Hope, a former Tammany politician who believes he will someday leave his saloon and walk the ward; Willie Oban, previously of Harvard Law School, who plans one day to go to the district attorney and get a law job; Rocky, the night bartender, who, because he works as a bartender, believes that he is not a pimp, even though he "manages" and takes money from two prostitutes; Margie and Pearl, Rocky's two "girls," who make the fine distinction that they are tarts but not whores—because they don't have a pimp; Chuck, the day bartender, who believes he will go on the wagon, marry Cora, and buy a farm in the country; and Cora, who shares Chuck's dream and who also believes that he will forgive her for making her living as a prostitute. Into the circle of regulars comes the eighteen-year-old Don Parritt, whose mother, part of the anarchist movement, is on trial out West for a bombing.

Although many of these regulars stay up all night in the saloon to await Hickey, his arrival is disappointing and strangely troubling: When he appears, he is not the same as before. For one thing, he fails to make his usual joke about his wife and the iceman, and for another, he no longer drinks; he explains that he no longer needs it after he threw away "the damned lying pipe dream" that had made him feel miserable. Moreover, he wants very much to save his friends by persuading them to be honest, to stop lying about themselves, and to stop kidding themselves about their tomorrows. He believes that by giving up their illusions, they can attain peace and contentment, and he systematically embarks on a campaign to make them admit the truth about their pasts and to do immediately what they have always said they will do in the future—even though Hickey knows that they will fail. Hickey insists that if one faces reality and kills one's dreams, then those dreams will not be there to nag or to cause guilt, not haunted by yesterday and not fooling oneself about tomorrow. Then, Hickey believes, his friends will have peace, as he does.

As a result of his campaign, however, the friendly and tolerant atmosphere of the bar wears dangerously thin as the friends, stripped of their protective illusions and their defense mechanisms, become not only sober but also nervous, irritable, and belligerent with one another. Harry's birthday party is a flop, spoiled by fights and bad feeling and finally by Hickey's announcement that his wife is dead. Moreover, the peace that Hickey predicts will come, as an effect of facing reality, does not, even though the characters, with varying degrees of reluctance, attempt to give up their dreams, to leave the bar—actually as well as symbolically—and to face reality. Instead of providing them with peace, the act of facing reality robs them of tolerance for one another and therefore of companionship, of tolerance for themselves and therefore of self-respect, of hope for the future and therefore of happiness. As a result of Hickey's efforts to save them from their illusions, as a result of his forcing them to face their tomorrows and to fail, the habitués of Harry Hope's bar are miserable—quarrelsome, despondent, and hateful toward themselves and one another. Even alcohol loses its kick; it seems to have "no life in it," and they can no longer even pass out.

Hickey is genuinely puzzled by these results because his expectation was that, once they had "killed tomorrow," they would have "licked the game of life." The play's fourth act, which begins by further demonstrating the unpleasantness that has derived from exposure to reality, centers on Hickey's revelation of his new philosophy and how he acted out this philosophy in his marriage, finally murdering his wife. He killed her, he says, to give her peace by ending her pipe dream that he would one day be better, that he would stop drinking and whoring. Continually making vows to her that he was unable to keep, he was then obliged to feel guilty because his wife was continually hurt and disappointed. Juxtaposed to Hickey's story of love and guilt is Parritt's parallel narrative disclosing his betrayal of his mother. The two stories reach a climax when Parritt confesses that he betrayed the movement because he hated his mother as Hickey confesses that after killing his wife he laughed and called her a "damned bitch." Unable to live with what he has admitted, Hickey seizes on the explanation that he must have been insane—insane, that is, to laugh at his wife's death, because everyone surely knows that he has always loved her, and if he laughed at her death, then he must have been insane.

The other characters seize on this explanation as well, because it means they can disregard what he has said before, reestablish their illusions, and thereby once again live with one another and themselves. Don Parritt, however, apparently unable to live with his betrayal of his mother and the reality that his betrayal was motivated by hate, commits suicide by jumping off the fire escape, as, in a sense, does Hickey by calling the police to come for him. He and Parritt, facing the reality about themselves, must destroy themselves because of the pain of that reality. In truth, Hickey hated his wife because she represented his conscience, because although she always forgave him, she also always expected him to try to be better, which he simply did not wish to do. When for one brief moment he admits the truth, that he wanted and was glad to be free of the burden of this conscience, he is unable to live with that truth and he immediately rationalizes that he must have been insane. He thus proves that illusion is, in fact, necessary, in order to accept oneself and in order to live not only with others in the world but also with the reality that death, the iceman, does indeed "cometh."

The play, then, while pessimistic in delineating human weaknesses, seems to hold out the possibility that those weaknesses can be transcended so long as life exists. O'Neill suggests that, in order for life to exist, there must be hope—and hope, very often, is created from illusion. Although Hickey is termed a "nihilist" at one point in the play, he serves, through the dramatic revelation of his own example, to reinforce the necessity, and the positive power, of illusion.

OTHER MAJOR WORKS

POETRY: *Poems, 1912-1944*, 1979 (Donald Gallup, editor).

NONFICTION: *"The Theatre We Worked For": The Letters of Eugene O'Neill to Kenneth MacGowan*, 1982 (Jackson R. Bryer and Ruth M. Alvarez, editors); *"Love and Admiration and Respect": The O'Neill-Commins Correspondence*, 1986 (Dorothy Commins, editor); *"As Ever, Gene": The Letters of Eugene O'Neill to George Jean Nathan*, 1987 (Nancy L. Roberts and Arthur W. Roberts, editors); *Selected Letters of Eugene O'Neill*, 1988 (Travis Bogard and Bryer, editors); *A Wind Is Rising: The Correspondence of Agnes Boulton and Eugene O'Neill*, 2000 (William Davies King, editor).

MISCELLANEOUS: *The Unknown O'Neill: Unpublished or Unfamiliar Writings of Eugene O'Neill*, 1988 (Travis Bogard, editor).

BIBLIOGRAPHY

Bloom, Harold, ed. *Eugene O'Neill*. New York: Chelsea House, 1987. As part of the Modern Critical Views series, this collection includes essays by Lionel Trilling, Doris Falk, Arnold Goldman, Robert Lee, Travis Boyard, Thomas Van Laan, Jean Chathia, C. W. Bigsby, and Michael Manheim, arranged in chronological order by their original publication dates. Bloom describes them as representative of the "best criticism available." The theoretical slant is thematic and philosophical, with detailed characters and plot analyses. Contains a brief bibliography.

Brietzke, Zander. *The Aesthetics of Failure: Dynamic Structure in the Plays of Eugene O'Neill*. Jefferson, N.C.: McFarland, 2001. A controversial but insightful study of O'Neill's literary theory, with particular attention to his "anti-theater" approach to character development and storytelling.

Manheim, Michael, ed. *The Cambridge Companion to Eugene O'Neill*. New York: Cambridge University Press, 1998. A comprehensive reference work that contains a wealth of information on the life and works of O'Neill. Bibliography and index.

Moorton, Richard F., Jr., ed. *Eugene O'Neill's Century*. New York: Greenwood Press, 1991. This collection includes excerpts from more than seventeen plays and collected notes, as well as articles ranging from Spencer Golub's semiotic analysis of *Long Day's Journey into Night* to biographical and psychological analyses by Lowell Swortzell, Jane Torrey, Georgia Nugent, Jeffrey Elliott Sands, and Linda Herr. Some essays focus on how and why O'Neill's extensive stage directions have influenced dramatic practice. Six pages of works cited and thirteen pages of index are useful for scholars.

Ranald, Margaret Loftus. *The Eugene O'Neill Companion*. Westport, Conn.: Greenwood Press, 1984. The author has arranged in alphabetical order a complete compendium of plays, synopses, production histories, characters, personal and professional acquaintances, and critical analysis. Three appendices include a chronology of plays, adaptations, and a critical overview. Twenty-eight pages of notes and thirty-seven index pages make this work an invaluable, encyclopedia resource and guide to further study of O'Neill's work.

Robinson, James A. *Eugene O'Neill and Oriental Thought: A Divided Vision*. Carbondale: Southern Illinois University Press, 1982. Taking a philosophical approach to O'Neill's work, Robinson's 186-page work is a scholarly, detailed analysis of possible connections between O'Neill's plays and Oriental mysticism, particularly Hindu, Buddhist, and Daoist belief systems. The bibliography and index offer more information on philosophy and religions of the East than on O'Neill, but Robinson's analysis of individual plays, such as *The Great God Brown*, *Lazarus Laughed*, *The Iceman Cometh*, and *Long Day's Journey into Night*, sheds new light on the often-stated view of O'Neill's drama as "religious" and "romantic."

Sheaffer, Louis. *O'Neill*. 2 vols. Boston: Little, Brown, 1968-1973. This two-part biography is considered the most complete work on O'Neill's life, and it stands as a model for the genre of literary biography. Including recollections by a variety of O'Neill's colleagues and friends, this work reads smoothly and effectively combines scholarship and human interest. Generally acknowledged as both sympathetic and trustworthy. Notes, index.

Wainscott, Ronald H. *Staging O'Neill: The Experimental Years, 1920-1934*. New Haven, Conn.: Yale University Press, 1988. This highly scholarly yet accessible historical work chronicles the production of O'Neill's plays and the profound influence of his work on American theater practice. Written in a lively style, it is the most detailed work of its kind on O'Neill, although others may have greater scope.

Evelyn S. Newlyn,
updated by Rebecca Bell-Metereau

ISTVÁN ÖRKÉNY

Born: Budapest, Hungary; April 5, 1912
Died: Budapest, Hungary; June 24, 1979

PRINCIPAL DRAMA

Voronyezs, pb. 1948, pr. 1969
Sötét galamb, pr., pb. 1957
Tóték, pr. 1966, pb. 1967 (*The Tóth Family*, 1982)
Macskajáték, pr. 1969, pb. 1970 (*Catsplay*, 1976)
Pisti a vérzivatarban, pb. 1970, pr. 1979 (*Stevie in the Bloodbath*, 1993)
Vérrokonok, pr. 1974, pb. 1975 (*Blood Relations*, 1975)
Kulcskeresők, pr. 1976, pb. 1977
Forgatókönyv, pr. 1979

OTHER LITERARY FORMS

As a writer, István Örkény is not easily categorized. In addition to dramatic works, he produced short stories, novels, and screenplays, several of which are adaptations of earlier works. Örkény's *Sötét galamb* (dark pigeon) is a stage adaptation of his novel *Glória* (1957). *Macskajáték* (1966; catsplay, 1976) and *Tóték* (1964; the Toth family), two of Örkény's most celebrated novels, were first conceived as film scenarios but were left unfinished when the original film projects were abandoned. The unused material was salvaged in the form of novels, which were subsequently adapted for the stage and finally recast as two critically acclaimed films: *Macskajáték* (1974) and *Isten hozta, őrnagy úr!* (1969; welcome, dear major). The difficulty of categorizing Örkény is further demonstrated by his *Egyperces novellák* (1968; *One-minute Stories*, 1994). These writings are sketches imbued with wit and concentrated meaning. As the title of the collection suggests, these stories are highly condensed, bearing a relationship to the conventional-length short story analogous to that of the terse haiku to lyrical poetry.

ACHIEVEMENTS

István Örkény is, more often than not, labeled a writer of the absurd and grotesque. The sardonic and often understated wit that he brought to his writing makes his work unique and readily identifiable. He has been a favorite with many critics and, as far as Hungarian writers go, has enjoyed some commercial success as well. He was practiced and accomplished in several genres: drama, the novel, the short story, and the screenplay. His mature works are historical probes that reach back to retrieve and record the collective psychological plight of a nation—his native Hungary—in its difficult transition from a backward and semifeudal order to a Socialist state characterized by lofty ideals and Stalinist abuses of power alike. The distinctive ambience of Örkény's plays and other writings is in no small part achieved by his terse, pared-down style, in which rhetoric and decorativeness give way to plain diction and simple syntax.

Örkény was twice the winner of the Attila József Prize (in 1953 and 1967), and in 1970, his *The Tóth Family* won the Grand Prize for Black Humor in France. In 1973, he was at long last the recipient of the most coveted award in Hungary, the Kossuth Prize.

BIOGRAPHY

István Örkény was born in Budapest, Hungary, on April 5, 1912. His father, a well-to-do pharmacist, was by Örkény's account a generous man with his money, and through sheer improvidence he eventually lost all four of his Budapest pharmacies. A man of a dying age, he participated in no fewer than twelve duels. Örkény was, on his father's side, of Jewish descent but was reared a Catholic, if not a particularly devout one. He attended the Piarist gymnasium in Budapest, where he studied Latin and Greek. By the time Örkény was graduated in 1930, he was conversant in German, French, and English as well. After an inauspicious two years at the Polytechnic University at Budapest, where he studied chemical engineering, in 1932 Örkény enrolled at the University of Arts and Sciences.

In 1934 he received his diploma, and in the same year he cofounded the short-lived periodical *Keresztmetszet*, of which he would also be main financier. It was in this periodical that Örkény's first writings were to appear, but they did not yet bespeak any great talent. In 1937 he became involved with the liberal-radical periodical *Szép Szó*, where the first version of his short story "Tengertánc" (sea dance) was published. Also in 1937, Örkény married Flóra Gönczi. He spent 1938 in London and much of 1939 in Paris, eking out a living. In 1939, on Hungary's declaration of war, Örkény returned home. That year he reenrolled at the Polytechnic University, earning his degree in 1941.

In 1942 Örkény was recruited into forced labor, was later transported (together with the second Hun-

garian army) to the Soviet front, and had to march on foot all the way from Gomel to the Don. Winter set in, and Örkény and his companions endured the cold in summer clothes. Örkény was eventually wounded and taken prisoner by the Soviets. During his long tenure as a prisoner of war, Örkény wrote three pieces: *Voronyezs*, *Lágerek népe* (1947; people of the camps), and *Emlékezők* (1945; those who remember), a drama and two reportages respectively.

Several years and three prison camps later, Örkény was set free in 1946. One of the first things he would do on his return to Hungary was join the Communist Party. At first Örkény shared the general enthusiasm for the future exhibited by the utopianists and party ideologues, and in the late 1940's and early 1950's he himself contributed to the building of that future with politically unassailable writings. With the publication in 1952 of the short story "Lila tinta" (purple ink), however, dogmatists and ideologues strongly censured Örkény, accusing him, among other things, of immorality.

In 1948, Örkény married Angéla Nagy, with whom he would have two children. From 1951 to 1953, he worked periodically as a dramaturge. In 1956, Örkény's volume of short stories *Ezüstpisztráng* (silver trout) was published, signaling a new period for the writer. In the same year, the Hungarian revolt was suppressed, and Örkény, along with several other writers, would be practically unpublishable until the early 1960's. He was divorced from Angéla Nagy in 1958, but in the same year he became acquainted with Zsuzsa Radnóti, a dramaturge, whom he married in 1965. In that decade, Örkény slowly rejoined Hungarian literary life, creating in succession works both profound and humorous. He died in Budapest on June 24, 1979.

ANALYSIS

The œuvre of István Örkény is characteristically described as absurd and grotesque. The description is accurate, yet the world he depicted is also quite familiar, rendered with realistic details that readers or theatergoers—particularly if they are Hungarian—immediately recognize. At his best, Örkény presented the absurd as he found it in real life and did not go out of his way to manufacture the strange and bizarre. His *ars poetica* argues for clarity and brevity in the service of the truth as he saw it. Rhetorical devices have little or no place in the works of his mature years. His characters are on the whole likable and sympathetic. Yet though they breathe with life, they straddle the border between the realm of flesh-and-blood characters, on one hand, and that of the stereotype and archetype, on the other. The figures that inhabit the world of Örkény are happy to the extent that they are in communication with one another, but as a rule they seem barely to elude one another's reach. Nevertheless, the possibility of establishing and securing bonds between people is affirmed and reaffirmed by Örkény. By the same token, historical forces seem to act as determinants, making the balance that he postulated between man and the controlling environment very delicate and tenuous indeed.

ARTISTIC DEVELOPMENT

Örkény's earliest writings, which at most document the writer's search for a voice of his own, do not offer interesting reading for anyone today but the specialist. In 1941, his first complete volume of short stories was published. *Tengertánc* (1941), named after the 1937 short story, signaled the arrival of a bona fide writer. The combination of realist and surrealist elements so characteristic of his mature years is already in evidence here. The collection is not without distinct left-wing political overtones, another recurring feature in Örkény.

Örkény's next few works were written in prisoner-of-war camps in the Soviet Union. *Voronyezs*, *Lágerek népe*, and *Emlékezők* are clearly the works of a much maturer man than the Örkény who wrote "Tengertánc," one who had since seen and himself suffered the hardships of war and prison. In the late 1940's and early 1950's, Örkény, who had in the meantime joined the Communist Party, produced writings heavily influenced by Socialist Realism. They were overly schematic and heavy-handed treatments of social and political issues that were, however, worthy of being addressed.

By 1956, Örkény had been writing seriously for two decades, yet he still found himself experimenting with subjects, themes, and forms alike. He had not yet found his own voice. In 1956—the year which saw a series of dramatic events in Hungary culminate in the earthshaking anti-Soviet revolt—important changes came for Örkény, too. *Ezüstpisztráng*, which appeared in that year, marked the beginning of Örkény's truly mature period. This volume of short stories struck just the right balance between realism, on one hand, and the grotesque, on the other. It also signaled, according to Örkény, the end of a brief flirtation with colorful and rhetorical language and a return to the laconic and economical style of "Tengertánc."

Örkény's works of this period are all, in one way or another, reflections and commentaries on the peculiar conditions of post-World War II Hungary—indeed of all Eastern Europe—owing in part to, and characterized by, the peculiar "chemical reaction" of a fledgling socialism and a millennium of feudalism. This basically absurd world, fraught with terrible and seemingly irreconcilable contradictions, is starkly rendered by Örkény with language plain and direct. It is not merely the common rhetorical devices such as metaphor that Örkény shunned, it is essentially anything that might call attention to itself and distract the reader from the heart of the matter.

The world of Örkény seems at a glance too infected with humor to be taken seriously. Beneath the armor of wry wit, however, lurks a much darker dimension. Yet even this is a place less sad than it appears. Overcast though it may be, it is penetrated by a ray of hope. Örkény might well be called a realistic optimist. This basic orientation was, Örkény said, formed during his long tenure in the Soviet prison camps. It was there that he experienced how an apparently heterogeneous collection of people, comprising several different nationalities and social classes, can transcend the plane of mere coexistence to cohere into a genuine community. Örkény's conviction that solidarity is the most that one can give to another derives from those years. Even in the contemporary world, where many writers seriously doubt whether real communication is possible, Örkény affirmed that true and lasting bonds can be formed.

As noted above, Örkény's œuvre is extremely varied; he wrote novels, plays, reportages, and novellas without seeming to show preference for one over another. Nevertheless, the last two decades of his career were particularly rich in dramatic works, ones that won critical acclaim abroad no less than at home. When he died in 1979, he left behind him a body of published work neither very big nor very small. The manuscripts of his unfinished and discarded writings could fill several volumes. In reviewing his entire œuvre from beginning to end, particularly the works of his mature years, it is impossible not to notice the common themes, recurring motifs, and characteristic style that forge them into a grand unity.

CATSPLAY

Catsplay was adapted by Örkény for the stage in 1969. Its epigraph reads:

We all want something from each other.
It is only old people whom no one wants anything from.
But when old people want something from each other,
    we laugh.

Catsplay is the story of two elderly sisters—the uncouth Mrs. Orbán and the distinguished Giza—and their relationship. It is set around the late 1950's and early 1960's, when the Iron Curtain, understood in a broad sense, still represented a serious barrier of communication between East and West. The déclassé Mrs. Orban is living in her native country, while Giza has for several years been living in the West, where she occupies an even higher position on the social scale than that which she enjoyed during her childhood years in Hungary.

The differences between them are substantial. Giza is an invalid confined to her wheelchair and is perhaps for that reason more willing than her able-bodied but unshapely sister to see that the sweet flower of youth is gone. It is perhaps their attitude toward aging and death that most distinguishes them from each other. Giza, by all appearances, accepts death as the inevitable and final stage of life; her sister jousts with it like Don Quixote with his windmill. The epigraph, like a musical theme that is varied and developed, appears in many guises and forms. Giza's thoughts on old age recall, and at the same time amend, its message. The only way, she says, that young people can forgive the elderly their old age is if old people themselves show that they accept and are reconciled to their old age.

Though the sisters keep in touch by telephone and by letter, these imperfect means of communication prove insufficient to bridge the cavernous gap between them, caused by two diverse ways of life and thinking. Yet the fact that the sisters persevere, against great odds, to reestablish the bond that has been lost between them is courageous and portends some faint hope.

THE TÓTH FAMILY

The Tóth Family, set during World War II, is the story of a certain visit paid one day by a certain major to a certain family. The family is temporarily without their son, who is away at war. The major who has come as their guest is the boy's commander. Apparently intended as only a short visit, the major's stay begins to look like one of indefinite duration. The family waits in vain to hear from their boy, while in the meantime the major takes over the house, issuing gratuitous and nonsensical commands. His favorite command, repeated with the frequency and force of a recurring nightmare, is that the family assist him in making paper boxes. This they do, with the assistance of a paper cutter that calls to mind the guillotine.

The village in which the story is set serves as a microcosm of the country as a whole, and the major's dictatorial reign over the Tóths suggests the unequal relationship of the Fascists and the common people over whom they rule. As the country in the end deposes the Fascists, so the Tóths, on learning that their son is dead and has been for some time, oust from power the maniacal major, turning the force of the paper cutter against him. The overall effect of *The Tóth Family* is in no small part achieved by the balance Örkény strikes between absurdism and realism. Indeed, the very distinction between the realistic and the absurd becomes blurred. Örkény, here as elsewhere, does not so much invent the absurd as he discovers it in real life.

STEVIE IN THE BLOODBATH

Stevie in the Bloodbath (Pisti in the bloodbath) was finished by Örkény in 1969 but was not actually performed until a decade later, in 1979. Whereas *The Tóth Family* and *Catsplay* are small chamber works, set in a well-defined space and time, *Stevie in the Bloodbath* is a grand production encompassing all

Central-Eastern Europe and the second third of the twentieth century. It is, particularly in comparison to other Örkény plays, highly experimental theater. It is characterized by lengthy discussions, thought fragments, and flights of the imagination. It is an epic of the absurd, the twentieth century counterpart of Imre Madách's *Az ember tragédiája* (wr. 1860, pb. 1862, pr. 1883; *The Tragedy of Man*, 1933). Örkény, not wont in general to instruct or preach, does not assume an omniscient view of history but rather confides in his audience, as a patient might confide in his psychoanalyst, with self-revelatory statements connected only by the thread of free association.

Who or what is the Pisti of the original title? It is not a single character as such but, in Örkény's language, the collective noun for the people or masses. "Pisti" in Hungarian is the diminutive form of the name István (Stephen). Its use therefore might suggest some condescension on the part of the playwright toward his subject, particularly when he uses the emphatic "pistipisti." Yet such is not the case. Örkény, no doubt aware of the tendency in Socialist Realism and even Brechtian drama to idealize the "people," bestowed on the subject of his sympathy a name of endearment rather than risk evoking the familiar image of the people as a race of native geniuses.

Pisti is no less the hero of Örkény's play for his colloquial nickname. Like Christ, he tries to die, for a good cause, a martyr's death. In the twentieth century, however, when the relativity of good and bad has overturned absolute morality, his well-meaning gesture looks absurd. Besides, Pisti can be different things at different times. Now he is a murderer, now a man at the gallows, now a tyrant, now Moses before the burning bush. It is not, however, the interchangeability of slayer and victim that interests Örkény. He merely demonstrates that even the people are only as good or bad, virtuous or wicked, as their historical circumstances will permit.

BLOOD RELATIONS

Blood Relations debuted on March 28, 1974, and a year later appeared in book form. The characters are all railway employees and their wives, all going by the name of Bokor. They have a single passion in common: the railroad. If another subject by chance enters their conversations, it soon becomes apparent that this topic too has, in the minds of the Bokors, some association with the railroad. It would seem, therefore, that the railroad provides for its devotees a very strong bond, and so it does: It is the bonding force of the family, in whose embrace all is one and one is all. The members of the family seem, however, somewhat out of touch with one another, as though they occupy noncontingent planes. Their apparently common obsession is in fact experienced by each person differently and separately. It is as if, when any two of them stand on either side of the tracks or semaphore, they are cut off from each other no less certainly than if they were separated by *Catsplay*'s Iron Curtain.

Örkény would not be Örkény if behind the absurd and bizarre situations of the story there did not lurk a historical examination. One of the Bokors, the most likable of them all, is one day arrested for a crime he never committed, coerced into a phony confession, and eventually "rehabilitated." The reference is to the Stalinist years of Hungary, the late 1940's and early 1950's, during which time such practices were all too common.

KULCSKERESŐK

In *Kulcskeresők* (the key hunters), Örkény probes into the Hungarian collective psyche, in doing so examining an ordinary character with few distinguishing features. At most, the psychoanalysis turns up these facts: Hungarians are a dreaming people whose best successes may well come from their worst failures.

The play is a return to the small-studio format, focusing as it does on a single character. It forms an integral part of Örkény's œuvre, sketching in details omitted from other works. Just as *Stevie in the Bloodbath* studied the relationship between historical forces and the collective consciousness of a people, so *Kulcskeresők* examines the way a national character can shape the individual.

OTHER MAJOR WORKS

LONG FICTION: *Házastársak*, 1951; *Babik*, 1953; *Glória*, 1957; *Macskajáték*, 1966; *Tóték*, 1964; *Rózsakiállítás*, 1977 (*The Flower Show*, 1982).

SHORT FICTION: *Tengertánc*, 1941; *Budai böjt*, 1948; *Hóviharban*, 1954; *Ezüstpisztráng*, 1956; *Jeruzsálem hercegnője*, 1966; *Egyperces novellák*, 1968 (*One-minute Stories*, 1994).

SCREENPLAYS: *Becsület és dicsőség*, 1951; *Babik*, 1953; *Isten hozta, őrnagy úr!*, 1969; *Macskajáték*, 1974.

NONFICTION: *Emlékezők*, 1945; *Amíg idejutottunk*, 1946; *Lágerek népe*, 1947.

BIBLIOGRAPHY

Bales, Ken. "An American Catsplay." *The New Hungarian Quarterly* 19 (Spring, 1978): 198-202. A look at Örkény's *Catsplay*.

Brody, Ervin C. Introduction to *A Mirror to the Cage: Three Contemporary Hungarian Plays*, edited and translated by Clara Györgyey. Fayetteville: University of Arkansas Press, 1993. Introduction contains information about Örkény, in particular, his play *Stevie in the Bloodbath*, a translation of which is included along with translations of works by György Spiró and Mihály Kornis.

Heim, Michael Henry. Introduction to *The Flower Show; The Toth Family*, by István Örkény, translated by Michael Henry Heim and Clara Györgyey. New York: New Directions, 1982. Heim, in his introduction to two works by Örkény, provides valuable insights into the writer.

Riggs, Thomas, ed. *Reference Guide to Short Fiction*. 2d ed. Detroit, Mich.: St. James Press, 1999. Contains information on Örkény's life and works, particularly with reference to his short fiction

Gregory Nehler

JOE ORTON

Born: Leicester, England; January 1, 1933
Died: London, England; August 9, 1967

PRINCIPAL DRAMA

The Ruffian on the Stair, pr. 1964 (radio play), pr. 1966 (staged), pb. 1967 (one act)

Entertaining Mr. Sloane, pr., pb. 1964

The Good and Faithful Servant, wr. 1964, pr. 1967 (staged and televised), pb. 1970 (one act)

Loot, pr. 1965, pb. 1967

The Erpingham Camp, pr. 1966 (televised), pr. 1967 (staged), pb. 1967 (one act)

Funeral Games, pr. 1968 (televised), pr. 1970 (staged), pb. 1970 (as television script; one act)

What the Butler Saw, pr., pb. 1969

The Complete Plays, pb. 1976

OTHER LITERARY FORMS

Joe Orton's novel *Head to Toe* (originally entitled "The Vision of Gombold Proval") was published posthumously in 1971. *Up Against It*, a screenplay written for the Beatles, was published in 1979, although it was never produced. He also collaborated on several novels with Kenneth Halliwell, entitled "The Last Days of Sodom," "Priapus in the Shrubbery," and "The Mechanical Womb"; these were never published.

ACHIEVEMENTS

Joe Orton's meteoric rise as a dramatist during the mid-1960's in Britain was the result of the unique and frequently outrageous tone and style of his plays. Called "the master farceur of his age" by John Lahr and "the Oscar Wilde of Welfare State gentility" by Ronald Bryden, Orton made a radical break with the currently popular naturalistic drama of John Osborne and Arnold Wesker. He was instead influenced by Samuel Beckett and Harold Pinter, although he rapidly moved away from Pinter's "comedy of menace" to experiment with farce and the brittle epigrammatic style of Oscar Wilde. The verbal wit, aggressive sexuality, and black humor of his dramas created a new critical term, "Ortonesque," to describe his own style and that of his imitators. The critical reaction to Orton's drama was and remains mixed; the middle-class audiences that Orton worked so hard to affront frequently reacted with horror and shock to his plays, as did many reviewers. Playwrights as varied as Pinter and Terence Rattigan, however, were impressed by Orton. *Loot* won the best play of 1966 award from the *Evening Standard* and was voted the best play of 1966 by *Plays and Players*. Orton's body of work is small, consisting of four one-act plays and three full-length dramas, but he gained an international reputation before his premature death. At the time of his murder, he had begun work on a play tentatively entitled "Prick Up Your Ears," a farce about King Edward VII's coronation.

BIOGRAPHY

John Kingsley Orton (who later changed his name to Joe Orton to avoid any confusion with playwright John Osborne) was born to William and Elsie Orton in a working-class area of Leicester, England. After failing the eleven-plus examination, he enrolled in Clark's College, a commercial school where one of his teachers described him as "semiliterate." Seeing the theater as a way to escape the drudgery of the menial jobs he was forced to take, Orton joined the Leicester Dramatic Society in 1949 and acted in several small roles in other amateur theatrical groups. In 1950, he was accepted to study at the Royal Academy of Dramatic Art, which he entered in 1951. It was there that he met a fellow student-actor, Kenneth Halliwell, who became Orton's friend, lover, and roommate for the rest of his life.

After receiving his diploma from the Royal Academy of Dramatic Art, Orton worked briefly as an assistant stage manager for the Ipswich Repertory Company and then rejoined Halliwell in London in 1953. They began collaborating on a series of

novels, all of which were turned down for publication. In 1959, Orton, aided by Halliwell, began stealing and defacing books from the Islington and Hampstead libraries. Orton, who would remove the photographs and illustrations from the books and then replace them with his own creations, would also write false blurbs and summaries; after replacing the books on the shelves, he would stand and watch people's reactions to his pranks. In 1962, Orton and Halliwell were arrested and convicted of theft and malicious damage, and both men were sentenced to six months in jail. The jail sentence was a turning point in Orton's life, for it brought him a new sense of detachment from his own writing that had been lacking before this experience. After his release, he began writing plays and no longer collaborated to any great degree with Halliwell.

Orton's sudden fame and fortune during his brief career from 1963 to 1967 put a tremendous strain on his relationship with Halliwell, who, older and better educated than Orton, had considered himself the real creative artist. Deeply resentful of Orton's literary success and sexual promiscuity, Halliwell became more and more deeply depressed and neurotic. On August 9, 1967, a chauffeur who had come to drive Orton to an appointment to discuss his screenplay,

Joe Orton at Wyndham's Theatre in London during a rehearsal of his play, Entertaining Mr. Sloane, *in 1964. (Hulton Archive by Getty Images)*

Up Against It, discovered the bodies of Orton and Halliwell. Halliwell had beaten Orton to death with hammer blows to his head and then committed suicide with sleeping pills. Orton's murder, which was so similar in fashion to many of the events of his plays, made him even more famous in death than in life. The details of Orton's life and career may be found in Lahr's superb critical biography, published in 1978, entitled *Prick Up Your Ears: The Biography of Joe Orton*.

ANALYSIS

Joe Orton's career was launched by the British Broadcasting Corporation's acceptance of his first play, *The Ruffian on the Stair*. By the time the drama was broadcast in 1964, however, Orton had already achieved fame with the successful West End production of *Entertaining Mr. Sloane*. Orton revised *The Ruffian on the Stair* for its stage production in 1966; the revised version is less derivative of Harold Pinter's *The Room* (pr. 1957), although it still shows Orton's early debt to Pinter's techniques.

THE RUFFIAN ON THE STAIR

This one-act play involves three characters: Joyce, a former prostitute; Mike, a thief; and Wilson, the "intruder" who arrives at Joyce and Mike's apartment ostensibly searching for a room to rent. During the course of the play, Wilson reveals that he has had a homosexual relationship with his own brother, whom Mike has recently killed. Wilson's plan is to force Mike to kill him by pretending to sleep with Joyce; in this way, he hopes that Mike will be brought to justice for the murder. Wilson's plan succeeds, and the drama concludes with Mike comforting Joyce, who is weeping not over Wilson's murder but over the death of her goldfish. The play shows Orton, still strongly influenced by Pinter, moving toward the kind of verbal style that would characterize *Entertaining Mr. Sloane*—a style in which characters use media-influenced language to mask their real thoughts and emotions. The emotional sterility of the characters is reflected in the debased, meaningless language of cliché and the popular press, which they use almost exclusively. Although the play suffers from an ending that appears to be arbitrarily forced on the action, *The*

Ruffian on the Stair does show Orton's talent with dialogue and his ability to create a degree of emotional tension among his characters.

ENTERTAINING MR. SLOANE

Orton's first full-length drama was *Entertaining Mr. Sloane*, a three-act play that showed that the playwright had made important advancements beyond *The Ruffian on the Stair*. In much firmer control of his material in this play, Orton perfected his characters' use of media-influenced language and cliché. In addition, he was able to construct a relationship among the characters that made the play's ending believable and inevitable, a problem he had been unable to solve satisfactorily in *The Ruffian on the Stair*.

In *Entertaining Mr. Sloane*, Kath and Ed, Kath's brother, battle for control and possession of Sloane, Kath's young lodger. The double meaning of the play's title becomes clear as the play progresses, for the insidious Sloane is at first wooed and entertained by Kath and Ed and later must provide entertainment in the form of sexual favors for both of them when they become witnesses to his second murder. At the beginning of the play, Sloane takes a room in Kath's house, where she lives with her father, Kemp. Kemp soon recognizes Sloane as the young man who murdered his employer two years earlier. Kath, a middle-aged woman who coyly plays the role of Sloane's "Mamma" while brazenly seducing him at the end of the first act, soon finds herself pregnant by Sloane. Sloane is also being pursued, in a less obvious fashion, by Ed, who gives him a job as his chauffeur. When Kemp threatens to expose Sloane as a murderer, Sloane accidentally kills him and is then at the mercy of Kath and Ed, who both want to possess him exclusively. The brother and sister finally agree to share Sloane, each taking him for six months at a time. Sloane, who at the play's beginning was able to control Kath and Ed completely, is quickly reduced to an object.

Orton insisted that the play should be acted as realistically as possible so that the characters would not degenerate into caricatures or stereotypes. "What I wanted to do in *Sloane*," said Orton, "was to break down all the sexual compartments that people have." Kath and Ed are deadly serious about their designs on the young lodger, and Orton resisted the two male leads being played as effeminate homosexuals, just as he did not wish Kath to be played as a nymphomaniac. Instead, the play is about individual personalities who are constantly maneuvering in their attempts to gain power. Despite the play's realism, however, *Entertaining Mr. Sloane* is, like several of Orton's later dramas, reflexive in the sense that the characters are aware of their own theatricality. Orton also uses the rhetoric of the detective film in the play, just as he would parody the genre of farce in later dramas.

Present throughout the play is Orton's fascination with a debased language that functions to obscure the characters' real thoughts and deeds. John Lahr argues that Orton's dialogue reveals the "sensory overload" of the effects of the media on the individual—what he calls "an eclectic brew of rhythms and idioms which captured and commented on the mutation of language." *Entertaining Mr. Sloane* is the best example of Orton's search for what he described as his "collage" literary style: His characters mix the language of newspaper headlines, scandal sheets, advertising, and cliché in a comical and meaningless speech that nevertheless manages to communicate their obsessions and desires. Pinter's influence is still present in *Entertaining Mr. Sloane*, but Orton's success with the play led him in new directions as a dramatist. His work became increasingly more outrageous and farcical as a result of the self-confidence he gained because of the success of *Entertaining Mr. Sloane*.

THE GOOD AND FAITHFUL SERVANT

Orton's next play, *The Good and Faithful Servant*, was written in 1964 and appeared on television and stage in 1967. It was Orton's first full-scale attack on authority and convention, represented in this case by the company from which the main character, Buchanan, is retiring after fifty years of service. At the time of his retirement, Buchanan is stripped of his uniform and given an electric clock and toaster, neither of which works. Buchanan also encounters Edith Anderson, an elderly maid who is working for the firm and who turns out to have given birth to their illegitimate twins many years ago. The one-act play concerns Buchanan's adjustment to his retirement, his marriage to Edith, and the relationship between his grandson, Ray, and Debbie, who is pregnant with Ray's illegitimate child.

Buchanan's broken-down physical condition is reflective of what his lifelong service to the company has given him. Although he claims to have led "a useful and constructive life," he breaks down coughing at the end of this statement and, in addition to needing glasses and a hearing aid, has also lost an arm in the service of the firm. Buchanan's pitiful reverence for the company is shared by the other employees. Edith is thrilled because she was able to sweep out the canteen one day in the distant past, and Buchanan states that the "high point" of his life came when he appeared in the company's magazine. He also reverentially mentions that he was "almost Staff" and actually opened the door to the chairman of the board on one occasion. Buchanan's death at the end of the play, which occurs after his disillusionment with the party for the elderly, which culminates in his smashing of the toaster and clock with a hammer, is ironically counterpointed by Ray's induction into the corporate life after having been forced by the company's representative, Mrs. Vealfoy, into marrying Debbie. Just as illegitimacy is handed down from generation to generation in the play, so is the grinding and mindless service to a corporation that remains an abstraction to its employees.

Mrs. Vealfoy is the voice both of the corporate mentality and of the social conformity that it uses to manipulate its workers. She advises Ray to "say 'yes' as often as possible. . . . I always do. . . . Always," and she organizes the darkly comic party for the retired workers in scene 16, forcing the dispirited elderly people to sing songs containing the word "happy" while a woman collapses and dies in the background. Mrs. Vealfoy's genial intrusiveness and blind faith in the rightness of the company's policies structure *The Good and Faithful Servant*, which is Orton's most naturalistic assault on the world of authority and convention that he would lampoon in a much more anarchic and farcical style in his later drama.

LOOT

In his novel *Head to Toe*, Orton said that "To be destructive, words had to be irrefutable. . . . Print was less effective than the spoken word because the blast was greater; eyes could ignore, slide past, dangerous verbs or nouns. But if you could lock the enemy into a room somewhere and fire the sentences at them, you would get a sort of seismic disturbance." Not surprisingly, Orton turned from fiction to the theater, where he could attack his audience directly with words, for Orton considered his audience to be his enemy. He chose farce as the most appropriate genre to create a "seismic disturbance," to disturb his audience's conventions and expectations. *Loot* was the first full-length play in which he allowed his taste for anarchic farce a free rein, and if it sometimes too exuberantly celebrates a farcical, outrageous, and topsy-turvy world of madness and corruption, it also shows Orton discovering the proper vehicle for his talent. Farce, observes John Lahr, is an act of "literary aggression," and Orton used farce in order to vent his own anger and to assault a society that he believed to be hypocritical and stultifying. In his farces, he sought what he called in *Head to Toe* a "particularly dangerous collection of words" which could "explode," creating "shock waves [which] were capable of killing centuries afterwards."

In *Loot*, Orton mercilessly lampoons authority, represented most clearly in the play by Detective Truscott. Truscott, who comes to the home of Mr. McLeavy, whose wife has just died, is investigating a theft in which Hal, McLeavy's son, has been involved. McLeavy, the only character in the play with any real respect for authority, is also the only "innocent" character; ironically, it is McLeavy who at the play's conclusion is arrested for a "crime" that Truscott refuses to define.

McLeavy's faith in authority is naïve and pitiful. Early in the play, he says that he likes "to be of assistance to authority" and that public servants can be relied on to behave themselves: "As a good citizen I ignore the stories which bring officialdom into disrepute." All the events of the play work to underscore the irony of McLeavy's blind trust in "officialdom," and his statement in act 2 that "my personal freedom must be sacrificed" so that Truscott can continue with his investigation becomes chillingly significant later in the play. McLeavy's amazement at his own arrest at the conclusion of the play leads to his incredulous comment, "You can't do this. I've always been a law-abiding citizen. The police are for the protection of ordinary people." Truscott's reply, that he does not understand where McLeavy has picked up "such slogans," sums up Orton's view of authority and justice: The conventional law and order of society is merely a mask for corruption, intolerance, and irrationality. As a result, most of the play's references to authority are couched in clichés that render the characters' speeches ludicrous. Fay, the young nurse who has just murdered McLeavy's wife for her money, reacts similarly to McLeavy when she is threatened with arrest: "I'm innocent till I'm proved guilty. This is a free country. The law is impartial." Truscott's response is reminiscent of his reply to McLeavy: "Who's been filling your head with that rubbish?"

As *What the Butler Saw* would later parody farce, *Loot* parodies the detective novel and film. Truscott's comical conclusion that Fay shot her husband at the Hermitage Private Hotel because one of her wedding rings has a roughness associated with "powder burns and salt" shows Orton mocking the detective story's emphasis on rational thinking and deductive reasoning. The world of *Loot* is instead one of madness and illogic in which relationships among people alter rapidly; there is no core of stability or predictability. McLeavy finally asks Truscott, "Is the world mad? Tell me it's not"; his question is answered by Truscott's statement that "I'm not paid to quarrel with accepted facts." *Loot* shows that mysteries cannot be solved, for mysteries only lead to further mystification: Truscott tells the group that "the process by which the police arrive at the solution to a mystery is, in itself, a mystery." In *Loot*, the plot becomes more rather than less complicated as it progresses; the true "criminals" are allowed to go free while the "detective" becomes part of the crime. Fay's final statement in the play, "We must keep up appearances," articulates an important theme: The world is composed of masks, false identities, and lies that exist not to conceal reality but to compensate for its nonexistence. There are only appearances, and the characters who can most effectively manipulate appearance are the most successful. McLeavy's worship of authority reflects his ignorance of appearances. He assumes that those in power are what they claim to be, and he pays the price.

THE ERPINGHAM CAMP

In *The Erpingham Camp*, Orton continues to attack authority and convention and to develop the brilliantly epigrammatic style that culminated in *What the Butler Saw*. Much less naturalistic even than *Loot*, *The Erpingham Camp* is a one-act play composed of eleven short scenes. Its setting is a holiday camp in which chaos and anarchy erupt in what initially appears to be a rigidly organized situation controlled by the proud entrepreneur Erpingham. He is the major symbol of authority in the play and, like Orton's other authority figures, has false notions about the predictability and rational nature of the world. Early in the play, he tells an employee, "We live in a rational world, Riley"; the rest of the drama functions to destroy the validity of this statement.

Problems begin when Riley, who is organizing an evening of entertainment, slaps Eileen, a pregnant woman who is screaming hysterically. Although Riley's action is an attempt to make her stop screaming, a melee ensues and the campers begin, in Erpingham's phrase, to "destroy property," which results in Erpingham refusing to feed them an evening meal. "We've no time for hedonists here. My camp is a pure camp," Erpingham had said earlier, and he tries to punish his "underlings" in an effort to control their behavior. Erpingham, whose usual advice in any situation is to "consult the manual," is unable to understand or deal with the campers' rage and replies to their pleas for food with the statement, "You have no rights. You have certain privileges which can be withdrawn. I am withdrawing them."

Physical and verbal violence breaks out after this incident, with two groups of campers battling for their own "approach" to the situation. Lou and Ted, a right-wing young couple who claim to have met outside the Young Conservatives, call for moderation, remaining "within the law," and adherence to "page twenty of the Civil Defense Booklet." Kenny and Eileen, a working-class couple resentful of Lou and Ted's "advantages," instead want to take the "means of supply" into their own hands and encourage the campers to break into the food stores, screaming,

"Have a bash, I say. Have a bash for the pregnant woman next door!"

The play becomes increasingly anarchic and unrealistic until it concludes with Erpingham falling to his death down a hole in the floor. Attending at the funeral is the Padre, who has just returned from a court appearance in which he has been accused of molesting a young girl and who ironically notes, "As the little foxes gnaw at the roots of the vine, so anarchy weakens the fibers of society." The play ends with one of Orton's most famous epigrams, the Padre's statement that "it's Life that defeats the Christian Church. She's always been well-equipped to deal with Death." Although his themes in this play are similar to the dramas of the past, particularly the attacks on political and clerical authority, convention, and corruption, *The Erpingham Camp* shows Orton's increasing confidence in his ability to write anarchic farce in the epigrammatic style and was an important step in his movement away from naturalistic drama.

WHAT THE BUTLER SAW

Orton's last completed drama, *What the Butler Saw*, was not performed until after his death, and as a result the play did not undergo final rewrites by the playwright. Nevertheless, *What the Butler Saw* is Orton's most accomplished work. The play is a celebration of irrationality that also parodies the farce form by comically exaggerating its structure and characteristics: An absurdist genre is parodically made even more absurd. C. W. E. Bigsby suggests that the "byzantine complexities of the plot of *What the Butler Saw* can be seen as a deliberate attempt to parody the very structure of farce itself," and certainly the play's intricate plot makes summary almost impossible.

Like Orton's earlier work, *What the Butler Saw* attacks authority and tradition. In this drama, Dr. Rance, a government representative who has come to Dr. Prentice's mental clinic to be "given details" about its operations, at first appears to be the voice of conventional authority that wishes to suppress the forces of chaos. Although Rance represents the "Commissioners," however, he is also a spokesperson for unreason, mentioning to Dr. Prentice that he is a representative of "Her Majesty's Government. Your immediate superiors in madness," and opining that "the higher reaches of the Civil Service are recruited entirely from corpses or madmen." In *What the Butler Saw*, Orton's questioning of authority goes beyond that of religious or governmental institutions; here, he tries to destroy the very foundations of logic, reason, and predictability on which his audience's assumptions are based.

One of the most important themes of the play is the very thin line of demarcation between the sane and the insane. The setting is a madhouse in which no actual "insane" patients ever appear; rather, it is the ostensibly sane inhabitants, particularly the psychologists, who are mad. Rance tells the policeman Match that they are in a madhouse where "unusual behavior" is the prerogative of everyone: "We've no privileged class here. It's democratic lunacy we practice." "Democratic lunacy" aptly describes the world of *What the Butler Saw*, in which sanity and insanity are relative conditions that depend entirely on perspective. "The sane appear as strange to the mad as the mad to the sane," Rance tells Dr. Prentice in a statement that echoes the play's epigraph, drawn from Cyril Tourneur's play *The Revenger's Tragedy* (pr. 1606-1607): "Surely we're all mad people, and they/ Whom we think are, are not." Rance tells Mrs. Prentice that her husband's behavior is "so ridiculous one might suspect him of being sane," a Wildean paradox that sums up Orton's view that sanity and insanity are actually mirror images of one another.

In this play, sanity is dependent on a rejection of all evidence of reality; Rance, after denying that the blood on Mrs. Prentice's hand is "real" while admitting that he sees it, says, "I'm a scientist. I state facts, I cannot be expected to provide explanations. Reject any para-normal phenomena. It's the only way to remain sane." Because reality *is* madness, sanity can exist only when reality is denied. In a sense, however, madness is to be preferred to sanity, for Rance tells Geraldine Barclay that the fact that her mind has "given way" will be an invaluable aid in her efforts to "come to terms with twentieth century living." In a world in which irrationality and farcical absurdity rule, the most effective defense is insanity.

Orton's characters also lack any firm sense of their individual identities. Identities and sexes are ex-

changed with dizzying rapidity, with the result that the characters begin to lose their sense of who and what they are. Nicholas Beckett, in an attempt to verify his own existence, tells Rance, "If [my] pain is real I must be real," a statement Rance counters with the observation that "I'd rather not get involved in metaphysical speculation." Rance prefers to construct elaborate and illogical premises on which he bases even more outrageously illogical theories, at one point noting his own "law" that the "relations of apparitions are also apparitions." In *What the Butler Saw*, characters are much like "apparitions" who disappear and reemerge as different people; lacking any core of intrinsic identity, they are capable of endless psychic transformations. This lack of immutable identity, however, is not necessarily a negative characteristic: Like madness, fluidity of identity is a means of survival.

What the Butler Saw posits a universe in which irrationality must rule because all premises are illogical, erroneous, or nonexistent. Rance's comically incorrect "theories" about the reasons for Geraldine Barclay's neuroses and Dr. Prentice's madness are blatant fictions that have, as he is well aware, no relationship to reality. In the play, there is no actual "reality" because there is no truth. Geraldine asserts to Dr. Prentice, "We must tell the truth!" and is answered, "That's a thoroughly defeatist attitude." Rance's repeated admonishments to characters to "face facts" is ironic in this context, and near the end of the play, he admits to Geraldine, who is still trying to discover the "truth" about her situation, "It's much too late to tell the truth," a statement that could have been uttered at the play's beginning.

Indeed, Rance is adept at creating theories that satisfy his imagination much more than any simple truth could. When confronted with an actual "fact," such as Dr. Prentice's attack on Mrs. Prentice, he dismisses it by saying, "Oh, that was a mere physical act with no special psychological significance." Rance, entranced with Freudian symbols and theoretical interpretations, sees the madness around him as culminating in the "final chapters" of his planned documentary novel, which will include "incest, buggery, outrageous women, and strange love-cults catering to depraved appetites. All the fashionable bric-a-brac"—

a list that also describes Orton's dramatic world. Rance's fictive reworking of the "plot" of the drama is similar to the artistic process, and Orton the dramatist creates a character who imaginatively and fictively revels in the madness around him, just as Orton used his own chaotic lifestyle as fodder for his art. His early death ended a career that had, perhaps, only begun to approach its maturity. It is impossible to speculate, given his rapid development as a playwright, in which directions he might have gone.

OTHER MAJOR WORKS
LONG FICTION: *Head to Toe*, 1971; *Between Us Girls*, 1988 (wr. 1957); "*Lord Cucumber*" and "*The Boy Hairdresser*": *Two Novels*, 1999 (*Lord Cucumber*, wr. 1960; *The Boy Hairdresser*, wr. 1954).
NONFICTION: *The Orton Diaries*, 1986, expanded 1996 (John Lahr, editor).
SCREENPLAY: *Up Against It*, 1979.

BIBLIOGRAPHY
Bigsby, C. W. E. *Joe Orton*. London: Methuen, 1982. This brief study contends that Orton developed a style of anarchic farce that was deliberately subversive, not only of the authority figures appearing in his plays but also of language itself and conventionalities of plot and character. Bigsby also relates Orton's work to developments in postmodern literature and contemporary art. Notes, bibliography.
Charney, Maurice. *Joe Orton*. London: Macmillan, 1984. This introductory overview of Orton's œuvre concisely assesses not only all of his plays but also his novel *Head to Toe* and his unproduced screenplay for the Beatles, *Up Against It*. The final chapter offers a useful definition of "the Ortonesque." Photographs, notes, bibliography.
Lahr, John. *Prick Up Your Ears: The Biography of Joe Orton*. 1978. Reprint. Berkeley: University of California Press, 2000. This definitive biography of the playwright, based in part on Orton's diaries, is indispensable to any study of Orton's work. It is not only a readable, detailed study of his life but also an insightful critical appreciation of the plays. The biography was the basis of a feature film of the same name, directed by Stephen Frears and released in 1987. Photographs, notes.
Rusinko, Susan. *Joe Orton*. New York: Twayne, 1995. A basic biography of Orton that covers his life and works. Bibliography and index.
Shepherd, Simon. *Because We're Queers: The Life and Crimes of Kenneth Halliwell and Joe Orton*. Boston: Alyson, 1989. A biography that covers the lives of Orton and his partner Halliwell. Bibliography.
Zarhy-Levo, Yael. *The Theatrical Critic as Cultural Agent: Constructing Pinter, Orton, and Stoppard as Absurdist Playwrights*. New York: Peter Lang, 2001. A look at the connection between absurdism and the theatrical works of Orton, Harold Pinter, and Tom Stoppard. Bibliography and index.

Angela Hague,
updated by William Hutchings

JOHN OSBORNE

Born: London, England; December 12, 1929
Died: Shropshire, England; December 24, 1994

PRINCIPAL DRAMA
Look Back in Anger, pr. 1956, pb. 1957
The Entertainer, pr., pb. 1957 (music by John Addison)
Epitaph for George Dillon, pr., pb. 1958 (with Anthony Creighton)
The World of Paul Slickey, pr., pb. 1959 (music by Christopher Whelen)
Luther, pr., pb. 1961
Plays for England: The Blood of the Bambergs and Under Plain Cover, pr. 1962, pb. 1963

Inadmissible Evidence, pr. 1964, pb. 1965

A Bond Honored, pr., pb. 1966 (adaptation of Lope de Vega's play *La fianza satistecna*)

A Patriot for Me, pr., pb. 1966

The Hotel in Amsterdam, pr., pb. 1968

Time Present, pr., pb. 1968

A Sense of Detachment, pr. 1972, pb. 1973

Hedda Gabler, pr., pb. 1972 (adaptation of Henrik Ibsen's play)

A Place Calling Itself Rome, pb. 1973 (adaptation of William Shakespeare's play *Coriolanus*)

Four Plays, pb. 1973

The Picture of Dorian Gray, pb. 1973, pr. 1975 (adaptation of Oscar Wilde's novel)

West of Suez, pr., pb. 1973

Watch It Come Down, pb. 1975, pr. 1976

Déjàvu, pb. 1991, pr. 1992

Plays, pb. 1993-1998 (3 volumes)

Four Plays, pb. 2000

John Osborne in 1958. (Hulton Archive by Getty Images)

OTHER LITERARY FORMS

John Osborne's considerable output includes, besides his plays, a comparatively unsuccessful musical comedy about a gossip columnist with a dual personality, *The World of Paul Slickey*, and a series of dramatic scripts for television: *A Subject of Scandal and Concern* (1960, originally *A Matter of Scandal and Concern*); *The Right Prospectus* (1970); *Very Like a Whale* (1971); *The Gift of Friendship* (1972); *Ms.: Or, Jill and Jack* (1974, later published as *Jill and Jack*); *The End of Me Old Cigar* (1975); *Try a Little Tenderness* (1978); and *You're Not Watching Me, Mummy* (1980). He adapted several plays and a novel for the stage and wrote the screenplays for several of his own plays. His adaptation of *Tom Jones* (1963) from Henry Fielding's novel earned for him an Academy Award in 1964. He also wrote *A Better Class of Person: An Autobiography, 1929-1956* (1981), and the second volume, titled *Almost a Gentleman: An Autobiography, Volume Two, 1955-1966* (1991), covering his life to 1966.

ACHIEVEMENTS

John Osborne's most generous critics credit him with having transformed the English stage on a single night: May 8, 1956, when *Look Back in Anger* opened at the Royal Court Theatre. He is celebrated as the principal voice among England's Angry Young Men of the 1950's and 1960's, who railed vindictively against Edwardian dinosaurs and the emptyheaded bourgeoisie; it should be noted, however, that his antiheroes rebel against their own frustrations and futility more than they do in the service of any substantial social or political reform. Indeed, they betray their envy of the stability and the "historical legitimacy" of the very generation they condemn. Perhaps Osborne's most profound influence has been his leadership in bringing authenticity into contemporary English theater; a member of what has loosely been defined as the kitchen-sink school, he helped institute a new receptivity to social issues, naturalistic characterization, and the vernacular, thereby revitalizing a theater scene that had been dominated by the verse elevations of T. S. Eliot and Christopher Fry and the commercial conventionality of Terence Rattigan.

In addition to his achievements as a playwright, Osborne was also an accomplished actor, director, and screenwriter. Testimonies to his popular and critical successes include three *Evening Standard* awards (1956, 1965, 1968), two New York Drama Critics Circle Awards (1958, 1965), a Tony (1963), and an Oscar (1964). In the last twenty years of his life, Osborne devoted much of his energy to television plays for the British Broadcasting Corporation. Although some saw this as a confirmation of dwindling artistic resources, Osborne's reputation as a prime mover of the postwar English stage held secure. He created some of the most arresting roles in twentieth century drama, and his career-long indictment of complacency is evident in every "lesson of feeling" he delivered to his audiences.

BIOGRAPHY

John Osborne grew up in Fulham, Ventnor, and Surrey, leading a suburban childhood in somewhat less dire circumstances than one's preconception of Jimmy Porter's alter ego would lead one to expect. In fact, every class subtlety between "upper-lower" and "lower-middle" was represented in his own extended family; Osborne's autobiography traces, with a gusto bordering on the vengeful, the Welsh and Cockney sides of his family, and characterizes, in the spirit of English low comedy, their attempts to sustain outworn Edwardian amenities after having "come down in the world." His father was an advertising copywriter who suffered long spells of illness, and his mother was a barmaid, but the family tree included many connections to the music hall and the theater. (Grandfather Grove, for example, would be revived in the form of Billy Rice in *The Entertainer*.)

Osborne was an only child, rather sickly and bookish. His most vivid memories of adolescence include listening in the air-raid shelter to German bombers and suffering the abuse of bullies at school. Eventually, he went to a boarding school, St. Michael's, and after being expelled for striking back at the headmaster, turned toward journalism as a reporter for a trade journal, *Gas World*. After a failed engagement, he joined a struggling touring company, with which he gained his first experience in acting and playwriting, including an artistic and sexual collaboration with an older actress. The most important result of this picaresque period for the young Osborne was that he realized his ear for speech and developed his ambition to write for the stage. The early 1950's led him into the vital world of provincial repertory—the background for *Epitaph for George Dillon*—and ultimately, to the acceptance of *Look Back in Anger* by George Devine and the English Stage Company. Thus began a prolific career that established Osborne as an influence on the style and subject of contemporary English theater, rivaled only by Harold Pinter. He was married four times, to Pamela Lane (1951-1957), actress Mary Ure (1957-1963), writer Penelope Gilliatt (1963-1968), and actress Jill Bennett, whom he married in 1968. He had one child. Osborne was a member of the Royal Society of Arts, and in 1970, he received an honorary doctorate from the Royal College of Art in London.

In the mid-1970's, after two decades of steady production for the stage, Osborne substantially reduced his playwriting, though he continued to turn out television dramas. Other than occasional adaptations, such as the 1991 televised revision (produced as a stage work in 1975) of Oscar Wilde's *The Picture of Dorian Gray* and an hour-long profile on British television's South Bank Show, Osborne was not highly visible on the theater scene in these later decades of his life. His 1991 play, *Déjàvu*, which opened at the Comedy Theater in London to mixed reviews, was his first major new work to appear on the London stage in more than fifteen years. The 1991 publication of the second volume of Osborne's autobiography, *Almost a Gentleman*, brought his memoirs up to the mid-1960's and kept his name in the news for a short time. He died in 1994 at the age of sixty-five.

ANALYSIS

When the much-heralded John Osborne hero tore into an entire generation yet had no prospect for viable change, he discovered his own nakedness and vulnerability. He was inevitably a man in limbo, caught between nostalgia for the settled order of the past and hope for an idealized future he could not possibly identify. His rage was directed against his own inadequacy, not simply against that of his society. Because it was ineffectual, protesting against the ills of society became primarily a ritual complaint of the self against its own limitations.

Every Osborne play deals with reality's raids on self-esteem. His characters, even those who are most hostile to outworn conventions, are all in search of some private realm where they can operate with distinction. Sadly, that very search, which leads to isolation and denies communication, is as important a contributor to the contemporary malaise as is any governing body or social system. Angry young men and scornful old men, alike, feel disaffiliated and frustrated by the meager roles they occupy, but their greatest failure comes from not making a commitment to anything other than the justification of those feelings. Osborne wrote of a world that is immune to meaningful achievement. The degree to which his characters can move beyond complaint toward some constructive alternative that welcomes other people is the best measure of their heroism.

LOOK BACK IN ANGER

Look Back in Anger is less specifically about rebellion than it is about the inertia that overcomes someone when he feels helpless to rebel. To excuse his own inanition, Jimmy Porter cries that there are no "good, brave causes left"; in fact, he daily rails against dozens of enemies—the bomb, advertisers, the church, politicians, aristocrats, cinema audiences, and others—until one realizes that the problem is that there are *too many* causes worth fighting for, and their sheer magnitude renders Jimmy impotent. His anger, his irreverence, and his castigating wit are all an imposture, an attempt to shield himself from his failure to take meaningful action. While he pricks the illusions and damns the lethargy of those around him, he himself holds fast to the sense that only he suffers, that his anger betokens spiritual superiority over Alison, who irons incessantly and who only desires peace, and over Cliff, who buries his head in the

newspaper and who only desires comfortable seclusion in the Porters' flat. However justifiable his charges against the other characters, Jimmy's anger is less a mark of privilege than it is a standing joke—part of the "Sunday ritual."

Jimmy at times seems almost envious of those he attacks. The man for whom he professes the greatest resentment, Colonel Redfern, is an illusion-ridden, displaced Edwardian whom Jimmy prefers to see as the tyrannical father from whose clutches he saved Alison; nevertheless, the colonel at least had a golden age, whereas Jimmy agitates in a vacuum. Similarly, Helena, Alison's posh actress-friend, inspires in Jimmy equal portions of spite and sexual desire; he not only brings this officious snob down from her pedestal but also makes a place for her in his home after Alison's departure. Even Alison's political brother, Nigel, "the chinless wonder," whose vagueness Jimmy loves to attack, reflects on Jimmy's personal lack of commitment.

The point is that Jimmy cannot afford to see himself as in any way implicated by his own attacks. He resents everyone else's desperate evasion of suffering—he goes so far as to wish that Alison should witness the death of a baby, thereby unwittingly previewing her fate—but he, too, tends to leave the scene at times of crisis, going off to play his horn in the other room, for example, when Alison returns to confront the "traitorous" Helena. At this crucial juncture, Helena decides to opt out of the mess. Rather than risk dirtying her soul, she spouts convenient clichés about doing the decent thing and thus escapes her guilt. Alison's return is itself a compromise made in order to reaffirm the only security she has ever had. To say that Jimmy Porter proves any more willing to handle the pain and difficulty of being alive, however, is to ignore the fact that his has been an exclusive self-interest throughout the play. He is childishly arrogant rather than righteously indignant. So long as some woman is there to iron his clothes, he will not be bothered about his responsibilities to either Alison or Helena. (After all, he reasons, by leaving him, they have betrayed his "love," and so they deserve little more than scorn.) The image that concludes the play—Jimmy and Alison huddled together in a game of bears and squirrels—marks a final repudiation of the complications of adult life. "Let's pretend we're human" is Jimmy's original suggestion at the beginning of *Look Back in Anger*, but the consequences of human thought and feeling are too great; only within the limited arrangement of a "brainless" love game can either of them function at the end of the play.

Look Back in Anger portrays a world that lacks opportunities for meaningful achievement. Jimmy Porter loses his glibness and sarcasm as the "cruel steel traps" of the world close in on him; he trades in his anger for anesthesia. Ironically, even more obsolete than Colonel Redfern's visions of bygone days is Jimmy's own anger; Helena suggests that he really belongs "in the middle of the French Revolution," when glory was available. Jimmy Porter, who embodies the failures of his society, can support no cause other than that of the self in retreat. An impotent reformer and would-be martyr, he is consumed by a burning rage that finds no outlet.

THE ENTERTAINER

Osborne's society is one that seems immune to creativity and inimical to full humanity. In *The Entertainer*, Archie Rice looks back on the past nobility of the music hall (his is now a tawdry striptease joint) and forward to the barren legacy he has to offer his alienated children, and he wonders where all the "real people" have gone. Like Colonel Redfern, he is an anachronism, a personification of degraded values, as exemplified by his adherence to a dead art. He lacks even the satisfaction of the dying Billy Rice, who can at least withdraw into memories of free pudding with a pint of beer and respectable women in elegant dresses. Instead, Archie must console himself as best he can with a pitiful affair, his "little round world of light" onstage, and the conviction that at least he has "had a go at life."

The music hall structure of "turns" on a bill is imitated in the structure of the play itself. In this way, the story of the Rice family becomes an elaborate sketch, including overture, comic patter, heartrending interludes, and skits of love and death. Like the music hall, which has been corrupted by nudity and obscenity, the family unit, once a bastion of British dignity, has fallen on hard times. Phoebe, Archie's wife, in-

dulges her husband's adulteries and failures and seeks shelter in local movie houses (another degraded art form). His son Frank is a conscientious objector who can only manage a "relationship substitute" with his father. His daughter Jean is also estranged from her parents, as she nurses the pain of a failed engagement and teaches an art class to children she loathes. In short, the younger generation is embittered by an inheritance of disappointment and ruined values, and Archie is incapable of communicating with them naturally and openly. He chooses, rather, to relate to them through a contrived performance, as he would to one of his vulgar audiences. In the place of intimacy, there is cajolement and manipulation, so that it becomes impossible for characters to distinguish sincerity from routine, confession from monologue.

"Everybody's all right," croons Archie, and the central tension of *The Entertainer* is that between his efforts to sustain happiness, Britishness, the welfare state, and the state of his private little world, all by sheer theatricality, and the steady deconstruction of those myths. The final blows are the deaths of Billy Rice and young Mick, the one seeming to pass away out of his own irrelevance to the contemporary world, and the other killed in an otherworldly war. The result is shell shock. All that Archie can turn to is a quiet drink and a few awkward old songs in the faded spotlight. Like *Look Back in Anger*, which concludes with a desperate desire for mindless retreat, *The Entertainer* shows the responses to crisis as the familiar patter and the old soft shoe.

LUTHER

Luther was both a departure from and an expansion of familiar themes for Osborne. The move from contemporary middle-class England to sixteenth century Germany makes *Luther* seem an anomalous experiment, but Osborne was once again concerned with the psychology of a sensitive man who prefers to escape the world rather than cope with the burden of mammoth causes that he finds overwhelming. Luther is a direct ancestor of Jimmy Porter: He is frightened by the implications of his own anger. The realization of God's enormous task sends him into an epileptic fit. By embracing a monastic alternative, Luther can rationalize, at least temporarily, his divestment of the trappings and complications of secular life in the protective bosom of the Lord. The Augustinian order is the religious equivalent of the psychological refuges in Osborne's previous plays.

It is not God alone who castigates Luther for his retreat. Luther's father, a practical and rather blasphemous man of the world, argues that his son, who could have been a fine lawyer, has chosen to run away from such a challenge and is now "abusing his youth with fear and humiliation." Luther's response is that his father is narrow-minded and blind to the glory of God, but the indictment still plagues Luther. The other brothers, too, laugh at the intensity of his "over-stimulated conscience"; Brother Weinand says Luther always speaks "as if lightning were just about to strike" behind him. Even Luther's sleep is infested by demons, and his days are soured by constipation and vomiting. Having entered the monastery to find security and certainty, Luther is instead faced with weakness and doubt. Not only does he fail to forge his soul into a human equivalent of sanctuary, but he also finds his worst traits are exaggerated within this restricted arena. As Staupitz will advise him years later, his fanaticism does not guarantee the order's potency, it simply renders it ridiculous. It is paranoia, not faith, that underlies Luther's devotion.

One can appreciate the fact that, despite Luther's ultimate role as world-shaker, he is not a social revolutionary. He consistently sides with the forces of law and order during the Peasants' Revolt. Although he prefers to drink to his own conscience instead of to the pope, he is equally disdainful of the "empty" rampage of revolution, which he deems an affront to what is truly Christian. In short, Luther has never learned the last tool of good works—to hate his own will—and his one-man crusade in the play is not so much against Satan as it is against the devilish fears in his own heart. It is ironic, then, that Luther contributes to the dismantling of the fortress that Cajetan calls a representation of the perfect unity of the world because Luther has never desired anything more than its unassailable safety. As he tries to bargain with God, he insists, "This cause is not mine but yours. For myself, I've no business to be dealing with the great lords of the world. I want to be still, in peace, and alone." *Luther* concludes with the hero crawling into a substitute sanctuary, in the form of marriage to a nun, Katherina von Bora. One is left with a weary man cradling his sleeping son in his arms and praying that God grant both of them sweet dreams. Luther is no different from Osborne's wholly fictional creations in that he is the one who appears to be most afflicted by the fires he has ignited; the fact that Luther is far more successful in having an effect on the world at large than is Jimmy Porter does not free him from the sense that all he has "ever managed to do is convert everything into stench and dying and peril."

INADMISSIBLE EVIDENCE

Inadmissible Evidence resumed Osborne's contention that one can suffer more personal damage from one's own attempts to insulate oneself than from those things—a hostile world, a guilty past, or simply other people—from which one desires insulation. Bill Maitland is an attorney who undergoes a play-long cross-examination about the quality of his own life. Although his detestation of computerized, deculturalized, dehumanized society may in part explain his callousness and conceit, it does not justify his personal inadequacies or his inability to maintain meaningful relationships. The most damaging evidence against him is that, however virulently he argues that the world has discarded him, he appears to be the instrument of his own isolation, and this is what he cannot admit to himself.

The play records Maitland's last hours in a process of collapse. It opens in a "dream-court," in which he conducts an anxious, helpless defense; when he awakens to his real world, he is no longer capable of handling the trials there. Like so many of Osborne's main characters, Maitland turns to rhetoric to defend himself and to convince himself of his own existence. With a lawyer's expertise, he spins convoluted monologues. He proposes to obscure, if he cannot eliminate, the ambiguous "wicked, bawdy and scandalous object" of which he stands accused: a life lived at a distance. Indeed, *Inadmissible Evidence* has the effect of a one-man play, for Maitland is so manipulative and exploitative that other characters in the play are reduced to two-dimensional fact files, existing solely as embodiments of reactions toward Maitland. Their limited existence is a result of his incapacity for engaging in relationships of any real complexity or depth. What he sees as betrayal by his friends and family—one by one they appear in his office or call up to confirm their desertion—is, from another perspective, Maitland's steady disappearance into solipsism. Having treated everyone with the same cynical caution, he grows to feel more and more "like something in a capsule in space, weightless, unable to touch anything or do anything, like a groping baby in a removed, putrefying womb." He is losing the control he once exerted over people both sexually and professionally, and now he cannot stem the tide of their retreat. Eventually, not even taxis notice him, and the newspapers feature the replacement of lawyers by computers that will render them obsolete. Ironically, the sentence for the crime of a practiced detachment is a suffocating anonymity.

Maitland's last clients serve as the most effective witnesses for the "prosecution." The women who complain of the callousness and the adulteries of their men come for legal counsel, but their function in the play is to force Maitland to recognize his own crimes in those of their men. (That all the women are played by one actress seems to insist on their symbolic status; they represent a single indictment.) Maitland can no longer escape into his work, for his work presents further evidence against him. He becomes indistinguishable from his last client, the self-consumed Mr. Maples, who also wants to avoid the ugly issues he has helped to create for himself.

The play ends in plea bargaining. It is no longer possible to keep from being "found out" (his fear in the opening dream sequence), so Maitland considers changing his plea to guilty in order possibly to mitigate the judgment against him. Perhaps he can salvage something by warning his daughter not to make the same mistakes and messes he did. Unfortunately, it may simply be too late to avoid his sentence; after all, can his daughter take to heart the didactic instruction of a man who has shown her nothing but insincerity? *Inadmissible Evidence* leaves one with the image of a man repenting his sins in solitary confinement.

A NEW FOCUS

Osborne never deserted the theme of life's failure to measure up to human desires, and of people's unwitting contribution to that failure by virtue of the self-interest that underlies their complaints. Thus, for example, does Pamela in *Time Present* take up the gauntlet from Jimmy Porter, ridiculing the tawdriness and banality of the 1960's, the drugs, hippies, happenings, and the need to be "cool," with the same fervor that Jimmy railed against the uninspiring prospects of life in the 1950's. Osborne's later approach to this theme, however, was from the point of view of the conservative forces that were the target of the younger heroes of his earlier plays. This approach was not so much the inevitable by-product of an aging playwright's political reassessment as it was a change of focus that intensified his argument. In other words, the materially comfortable Establishment and the stolid aristocracy are as dissatisfied as the disenfranchised younger generation. In *West of Suez*, the first play designating this new focus, the shift from self-righteous anger to anxious unsettledness denotes not only nostalgia for the past and dissatisfaction with the present but also a fear of the future.

WEST OF SUEZ

West of Suez examines yet another cramped refuge: In this case, it is the garden of a villa in the West Indies meant to serve as a retreat from the "cold, uncertain tides and striving pavements. And the marriage of anxieties." What had been intended as a reservation for the vestiges of the old British Empire is instead proof of its degradation. The Suez Canal is closed; the dreams of the empire it once exemplified are choked. The fiction cannot survive unless those who maintain it do so miles away from the reality, "in the West, among the non-descripts of the Bahamas."

Like their literary predecessors, Colonel Redfern and Billy Rice, the nostalgia-ridden members of this "exclusive circle" have been trivialized into comedy. A brigadier is reduced to domestic chores; the aged writer, Wyatt Gillman, gives an interview "like a wounded imperial bull being baited by a member of the lesser breeds"; social gatherings are contaminated by hippies, homosexuals, and tourists. The only defense against this invasion is boorish prejudice, which the traditionalists exhibit throughout the play.

The offspring of their obsolescence, represented by Edward and Frederica, are saddled with a useless legacy, and their marriage encompasses the tension and disappointment of people who must live vicariously on other people's distant memories. Edward immerses himself in pathology because it affords him uncompromised detachment, and Frederica finds her self-possession in a kind of sneering sophistication. Their conversations are nothing more than highly stylized verbal exercises designed to take their minds off the supreme boredom of their lives. In a sense, they aspire to the state of blissful self-importance of Wyatt Gillman, the extreme version of which must be senility. Modern life is not something in which they would choose to involve themselves, but their island home is no escape from vulgarity. Tourists litter the place, cheapening it with their very presence, and the native blacks are charmless and sullen. Finally, there is the anarchist-hippie Jed, something of a reincarnation of Jimmy Porter, who lambastes the befuddled aristocrats with curses and threats of violence. His heavy-handed assault summarizes their ineffectuality, their pathetic irrelevance to the real world, while also demonstrating the ugliness of that world and almost justifying aristocratic stereotypes of the undignified lower classes. The response of Wyatt Gillman to all of this is to ask to go to bed, but there is no hiding from Jed's vicious prophecy. Wyatt is murdered at the end of *West of Suez* by a band of natives. Nothing is sacred anymore, especially not the memory of colonial power and prestige. Wyatt's children, friends, and associates, all of whom have staked claims in a world that no longer exists, stand over his corpse in stupefaction.

DÉJÀVU

In 1992, Osborne returned to the London stage with *Déjàvu*, which brought *Look Back in Anger*'s Jimmy Porter back to life after two and a half decades. In *Déjàvu*, Jimmy, now a middle-aged drunk, still vents his spleen at all those around him. Few critics, though, thought that the new incarnation matched the power of the original.

OTHER MAJOR WORKS

SCREENPLAYS: *Look Back in Anger*, 1959 (with Nigel Kneale; adaptation of his stage play); *The Entertainer*, 1960 (with Kneale; adaptation of his stage play); *Tom Jones*, 1963 (adaptation of Henry Fielding's novel); *Inadmissible Evidence*, 1968 (adaptation of his stage play); *The Charge of the Light Brigade*, 1968 (with Charles Wood).

TELEPLAYS: *A Subject of Scandal and Concern*, 1960 (originally as *A Matter of Scandal and Concern*); *The Right Prospectus*, 1970; *Very Like a Whale*, 1971; *The Gift of Friendship*, 1972; *Ms.: Or, Jill and Jack*, 1974 (later published as *Jill and Jack*); *The End of Me Old Cigar*, 1975; *Try a Little Tenderness*, 1978; *You're Not Watching Me, Mummy*, 1980; *A Better Class of Person*, 1985; *God Rot Tunbridge Wells*, 1985; *The Picture of Dorian Gray*, 1991 (adaptation of Oscar Wilde's novel).

NONFICTION: *A Better Class of Person: An Autobiography, 1929-1956*, 1981; *Almost a Gentleman: An Autobiography, Volume Two: 1955-1966*, 1991; *Damn You, England: Collected Prose*, 1994.

BIBLIOGRAPHY

Banham, Martin. *Osborne*. Edinburgh, Scotland: Oliver and Boyd, 1969. Contains discerning essays on *Look Back in Anger*, *The Entertainer*, and nine other plays, discussed around the thesis statement that "most of Osborne's targets are very clearly observed, defined, and, through his frontal assault, shaken to their foundations." Rich with material for further inquiry, especially when compared with later work. Complemented by a list of first British productions and a select bibliography.

Brien, Alan. "Snot or Not?" Review of *Almost a Gentleman*. *New Statesman Society* 4 (November 15, 1991): 47. In this review of Osborne's second volume of his autobiography, Brien's premise is that an "autobiography is not history. It is a form of entertainment." He finds Osborne's work hostile but valuable. Brien was one of the few defenders of Osborne's aggressively straightforward second volume.

Denison, Patricia D., ed. *John Osborne: A Casebook*. New York: Garland, 1997. Several essays critically examine Osborne's body of work, focusing on his form and technique, the construction of gender, and the relationships between his life and plays.

Ferrar, Harold. *John Osborne*. New York: Columbia University Press, 1973. This booklet on Osborne's first fifteen years of output notes that Jimmy Porter (in *Look Back in Anger*) is a portrait of "the body politic: one either defensively dismisses him or confronts the political implications of his protest and the social etiology of his anguish." Discusses *A Bond Honored*, *The Hotel in Amsterdam*, and other more obscure works. Brief select bibliography.

Gilleman, Luc. *John Osborne: Vituperative Artist*. New York: Routledge, 2002. Provides criticism and analysis of Osborne's life and works. Bibliography and index.

Hayman, Ronald. *John Osborne*. New York: Frederick Ungar, 1972. The World Dramatists series specializes in a factual overview, with play-by-play chapters, copious notes on stage productions, cast lists (here, both of London and New York premieres and productions), and a careful chronol-ogy. The introduction speaks of Osborne's ability to "epitomize something important about England today, not just by expressing moods and stating attitudes but by summing up the condition that the country is in, almost personifying it." Index.

Hinchliffe, Arnold P. *British Theatre, 1950-1970*. Totowa, N.J.: Rowman and Littlefield, 1974. The best book for putting Osborne in the context of the total revolutionary movement in British and European theater, and written when the movement was preparing for the second wave of playwrights. Particularly articulate on European influences, the Theater of the Absurd, and the relation of a national theater to the themes of Osborne and his contemporaries. Select bibliography but no index.

_____. *John Osborne*. Boston: Twayne, 1984. A general introduction to Osborne, with an oddly dated discussion of his most influential works, and not much new. Chronology, index, and bibliography.

Arthur M. Saltzman,
updated by Thomas J. Taylor
and Robert McClenaghan

ALEXANDER OSTROVSKY

Born: Moscow, Russia; April 12, 1823
Died: Shchelykovo, Russia; June 14, 1886

PRINCIPAL DRAMA

Svoi lyudi—sochtemsya, pb. 1850, pr. 1861 (*It's a Family Affair—We'll Settle It Ourselves*, 1917)

Bednaya nevesta, pb. 1852, pr. 1853 (*The Poor Bride*, 1933)

Ne v svoi sani ne sadis, pr., pb. 1853

Bednost ne porok, pr., pb. 1854 (*Poverty Is No Crime*, 1917)

Ne tak zhivi kak khochetsya, pr. 1854, pb. 1855 (*You Can't Live Just as You Please*, 1943)

Dokhodnoe mesto, pb. 1857, pr. 1863

Groza, pr. 1859, pb. 1860 (*The Storm*, 1899)

Vospitannitsa, pb. 1859, pr. 1862 (*A Protégé of the Mistress*, 1917)

Stary drug luchshe novykh dvukh, pr., pb. 1860

Kozma Zakharich Minin, Sukhoruk, pb. 1862, revised pr. 1866

Grech da beda na kogo ne zhivyot, pr., pb. 1863 (*Sin and Sorrow Are Common to All*, 1917)

Voevoda, pr., pb. 1865

Na boykom meste, pr., pb. 1865 (*At the Jolly Spot*, 1925)

Dmitry Samozvanets i Vasily Shuysky, pr., pb. 1867

Na vsyakogo mudresta dovolno prostoty, pr., pb. 1868 (*The Scoundrel*, 1923)

Beshennye dengi, pr., pb. 1870 (*Easy Money*, 1944)

Les, pr., pb. 1871 (*The Forest*, 1926)

Ne vse kotu maslenitsa, pr., pb. 1871 (*A Cat Has Not Always Carnival*, 1929)

Snegurochka, pr., pb. 1873

Volki i ovtsy, pr., pb. 1875 (*Wolves and Sheep*, 1926)

Poslednyaya zhertva, pr. 1877, pb. 1878 (*A Last Sacrifice*, 1928)

Bespridannitsa, pr. 1878, pb. 1879

Nevolnitsy, pr. 1880, pb. 1881 (*Bondwomen*, 1925)

Talanty i poklonniki, pr. 1881, pb. 1882 (*Artists and Admirers*, 1970)

Plays, pb. 1917

Five Plays of Alexander Ostrovsky, pb. 1969

OTHER LITERARY FORMS

Alexander Ostrovsky's only nondramatic writings are the semifictional "Zapiski zamoskvoretskogo zhitelya" (notes of a beyond-the-river resident) and occasional critical articles for various literary journals.

ACHIEVEMENTS

Alexander Ostrovsky was the founder of the modern Russian theater. Though his predecessors Alexander Pushkin and Nikolai Gogol wrote several memorable plays, their primary genres were poetry and prose, respectively, and they did not contribute significantly to the development of drama. Ostrovsky devoted his entire creative life not only to writing plays but also to producing them. In addition, he took a leading part in bringing variety to the stage by breaking the monopoly of the Imperial theaters. His prolific output of forty-seven original plays, supplemented by collaborative efforts and translations, gave Russia its first solid repertoire. In choice of subject matter, he also broke new ground. His plays for the first time presented the rising Russian merchant class to the audience. This social contingent, barely one generation away from humbler country origin, had not been deemed worthy of artistic portrayal previously, and its highly visible presence in many of Ostrovsky's plays aroused immediate interest and controversy. The playwright further used his work to

emphasize the unjust and utterly dependent position of young women without a dowry, the regressive marriage practices of the time, and the abuses perpetrated by Russia's growing merchant class. For illuminating this "realm of darkness," as the prominent critic Nikolay Dobrolyubov called it, and because of his many confrontations with czarist censors, Ostrovsky was considered an important social reformer.

As producer or coproducer of nearly eighty plays, half of them his own, Ostrovsky dominated Russian drama of the nineteenth century. The Maly Theater in Moscow, where most of his plays were performed, came to be known as The Ostrovsky House. The playwright worked hard at creating a more positive image for actors, who were largely treated as vagabonds and prostitutes before he formed guilds for their protection. Two of his plays, *The Forest* and *Artists and Admirers*, depict the high moral qualities of actors.

Ostrovsky's work is difficult to translate because his dramatic language faithfully reproduces the dialects of various social classes and abounds in proverbs and wordplay. As a result, he is not widely staged abroad. His best-known translated piece is *The Storm*. At home, however, he remains the most extensively read and performed playwright. His simple plots and satiric approaches continue to appeal to mass audiences. After the revolution, he was hailed as an exposer of capitalist vices in czarist Russia, which added to his popularity. In the post-Stalin period, as a less restrictive censorship opened the way for more modern and sophisticated drama, Ostrovsky's dominance diminished. His major plays, however, are still regularly performed, especially in the provinces, and new productions draw sizable urban audiences. His place in the development of Russian drama is firmly established.

BIOGRAPHY

Alexander Nikolayevich Ostrovsky was born April 12, 1823, in that part of Moscow in which disreputable lawyers, shopkeepers, and matchmakers plied their trade. He had ample opportunity to chronicle the customs and ethics of such figures, for his father, a government clerk at civil court, performed legal services in the area. His first plays faithfully reproduce the vices observed on "the other side of the river," and most of his later works reflect some phase of the merchant mentality. The elder Ostrovsky eventually achieved the rank of collegiate assessor, which gave him the privileges of petty nobility. After being widowed, he married a baroness with property. These benefits procured a good education for his son. After private tutoring by seminarians, Ostrovsky entered the Moscow Gymnasium in 1835; he was graduated five years later with honors. He then ceded to his father's wishes and enrolled at Moscow University Law School, where he soon slighted the dry legal documents for literature. Forced to repeat his entire second year, he dropped out altogether in the third year. His disappointed father, still insisting on a juridical career for his son, placed Ostrovsky as clerk first in the court of conscience and later, in 1845, in the court of commerce in Moscow. Ostrovsky used these years primarily to gather material for his plays, chronicling the petty intrigues, deceits, and questionable transactions that were brought to light in the courts. He entered the literary world by contributing occasional critical articles to the journal *Moskvityanin* (the Moscovite).

In 1847, Ostrovsky's first work, a comic one-act play, "Kartina semeinogo schastya" (a picture of family happiness), was read to teachers and students of Moscow University in a professor's apartment. The lavish praise of this private audience led to its publication a month later in the liberal newspaper *Moskovsky gorodskoy listok* (Moscow city notes), which presented the piece in the form of a dramatized chronicle from "across the river." When Ostrovsky asked for permission to stage it, the censors refused, dissatisfied with the devastatingly negative portrayal of Moscow merchants. By 1849, the budding author had completed his first full-length play, *It's a Family Affair*, initially entitled "Bankrot" (bankrupt).

Here again, Ostrovsky presented the avaricious lifestyle of tradespeople. The play was first read in various literary circles and was widely discussed. The editor of *Moskvityanin* used his connections to gain printing approval, and the piece appeared in the journal early in 1850. Ostrovsky immediately received critical acclaim and began production preparations. The censors, however, once more denied permission, citing the outrage of merchants and conservatives at being depicted in such unflattering terms. Following a special appeal, Nicholas I himself viewed the work and fully supported his censors. Further discussion in print was prohibited, Ostrovsky was placed under surveillance, and shortly thereafter (1851), he was forced to resign his civil service post. Although this placed him in financial difficulties, he welcomed the chance to devote himself entirely to dramatic work.

His next few pieces were of questionable artistic merit, but in 1852 Ostrovsky recaptured public attention with *The Poor Bride*, which received staging approval after some delay and editing, and met with great success. For a short time, Ostrovsky, eager to get his work past the censors and before the viewing public, adopted a slightly less critical tone toward social vices, supplementing his plots with positive depictions of traditional songs, customs, and behavior. After the death of Nicholas I (1855), however, when the less repressive reign of Alexander II encouraged writers to be more daring, Ostrovsky returned to his earlier critical stance, especially after 1856, when he was no longer under police surveillance. Nevertheless, difficulties with censorship continued to delay productions. *Dokhodnoe mesto* (a profitable position) was briefly allowed staging in the provinces but was later denied all performance, even though Ostrovsky made changes. Similarly, *A Protégé of the Mistress* (also known as *The Ward*) failed to receive approval in 1859 and was staged three years later only after considerable haggling. The still prohibited *It's a Family Affair* saw its first performance in 1861 after the playwright had completely changed the ending to satisfy the government's ethical pretensions. Undaunted by these delays, Ostrovsky continued to turn out plays, producing at least one, often more than one, per year. As progressive voices became louder, access to the public became easier, and Ostrovsky in the end managed to bring all his works to the stage.

In 1862, Ostrovsky went abroad to Germany, Austria, Italy, France, and England. His impressions did not visibly influence his subsequent work, but he widened his range to include other Russian social classes, notably the petty gentry, government clerks, and actors. In 1874, he established the Dramatic Actor Society, and he served as its president until his death. He fought vigorously for social recognition and better remuneration for actors, especially in the provincial theaters, where their standing was low. Ostrovsky's wife, Maria Vasileva, was a leading actress of the Maly Theater, which staged most of his plays. Although Ostrovsky never became rich, his successes permitted him to purchase a country estate in 1867, where he spent many of his summers. In January, 1886, he was appointed artistic director of the Moscow government theaters, finally receiving official recognition after decades of censorial strife with the regime. His health, however, had deteriorated by then, barely permitting him to complete the season. He left for his estate in Kostroma province late in May and died shortly after his arrival, June 14, 1886.

ANALYSIS

Alexander Ostrovsky dominated the nineteenth century Russian stage. He provided audiences with more plays than all previous Russian playwrights combined, and he closely supervised production of his work or directed the staging himself. All his writings satirize the shortcomings of certain social classes, prominent among them the still rather coarse merchant class, which lacked the graces and idealism of the educated elite.

Before Ostrovsky, Russian writers had largely ignored this rising commercial world. Ostrovsky's portrayal of shopkeepers and petty manufacturers is without exception negative. As they appear in his plays, such characters are rapacious, dishonest, and devoid of any measure of goodwill. Still strangers to the city, they band together in ancient clannish patterns. Overwhelmingly preoccupied with enrichment by any means whatsoever, they frequently arrange marriages of offspring, especially daughters, to profit their business ventures. The unchallenged and dictatorially exercised authority of Ostrovsky's patriarchs moves the vulnerable position of women into the foreground of the plays. The office of matchmaker, still powerful among the merchants, is presented as a particularly destructive institution, an unwelcome

vestige of the past. Ostrovsky gradually expanded his subject matter to include hypocritical nobles and bribe-taking lawyers and government clerks, as well as unsympathetic matriarchs and well-meaning but weak-willed, ineffectual idealists.

This exposé of Russia's misfits forced Ostrovsky occasionally to alter a character or theme in order to get his work staged. During the early 1850's, as noted above, Ostrovsky modified his critical approach, producing plays in which tradition assumes a somewhat sentimentally idyllic shading: *Ne v svoi sani ne sadis* (do not sit in another's sleigh), *Poverty Is No Crime*, and *You Can't Live Just as You Please*. Similarly, in the 1860's, Ostrovsky briefly turned his attention to noncontroversial historical subjects. The most notable plays of this group are *Kozma Zakharich Minin, Sukhoruk*; *Voevoda*, made into an unsuccessful opera by Peter Ilich Tchaikovsky; and *Dmitry Samozvanets i Vasily Shuysky*. The bulk of Ostrovsky's work, however, deals with topical, ethical problems. By presenting much of his criticism in comic form, he avoided didactic excesses, never losing sight of the necessity to entertain the public. Twenty-four of his plays carry the comedy label, despite the presence of dramatic conflicts. Another nineteen works are designated as scenes or pictures from life, and this designation best describes Ostrovsky's drama, for most of his plays feature a mixture of dramatic, tragic, and comic elements.

Ostrovsky's mode of presentation is strictly realistic. His plots are transparent, sometimes trivial, and he eschewed overdramatization. Although Ostrovsky's realism often provoked criticism, the playwright insisted on reproducing his characters and conversations in as lifelike a manner as possible so that the audience would at once recognize and judge the topic. Ostrovsky was enough of a craftsperson to avoid a simple copying of reality, but his figures and conflicts do lack psychological complexity, making them less appealing to twentieth century Western audiences. The author's skill in bringing the vernacular to the stage, however, continues to be appreciated by Russian viewers. Ostrovsky's characters express themselves in a style peculiar to their social standing, so that a single drama may contain a blend of shopkeeper and servant lingo, government jargon, the nobility's foreign-laced language, the traditional Church Slavonic of conservatives, and the poetic romanticism of young women, all generously sprinkled with proverbs and sayings. These features, added to the frequent wordplay and mispronunciations of uneducated social climbers, cannot be adequately translated and result in a dearth of foreign publications and stagings. Similarly, non-Russian audiences will miss the connotations of characters' names, such as those of the tyrants in *The Storm*, Dikoy (Barbarian) and Kabanova (Hatchet). With the aid of such naming and other devices such as proverbial titles—for example, *Stary drug luchshe novykh dvukh* (an old friend is better than two new ones) and *Sin and Sorrow Are Common to All*—Ostrovsky imparted a folkloric dimension to his material, evoking a native atmosphere. He even produced a fantastic drama, *Snegurochka* (the snow maiden), set to music by Tchaikovsky and turned into an opera by Nikolai Rimsky-Korsakov. These homespun touches served to make Ostrovsky's revelations of injustice and corruption more palatable.

IT'S A FAMILY AFFAIR

It's a Family Affair, Ostrovsky's first full-length work, demonstrates many of the concerns that preoccupied him throughout his career. In this play, for the first time, Moscow's merchant world appeared on the stage. Dominating the action is a tyrannical patriarch, the rich tradesman Bolshov (Bigman), who decides to enrich himself by cheating his creditors through phony bankruptcy. He temporarily transfers his goods to a trusted clerk, Podkhalyuzin (Sneaky), to whom he also gives his daughter, so that the fortune will remain "in the family." The clerk and daughter, possessed of the same moral failings, refuse to return the money and cause the merchant's imprisonment. The play has no redeeming characters at all; it seeks to show that avarice destroys human relationships at every level. The dishonesty of the daughter and the employee emerges as the inevitable result of the older generation's corruption. This condemnation is embedded in and somewhat tempered by the faithful reproduction of traditional mores and the shopkeeper milieu. Neither comic nor tragic angles are exaggerated, so that the overall image is an accurate one. The censors objected to the ending, which permits the cheating clerk to go unpunished. After eleven years of appeal for staging approval, Ostrovsky had to give in and alter the outcome. In the changed version, Podkhalyuzin is arrested. Since 1881, the play has been performed in its original version to record audiences. Its popularity suffered a decline in the post-World War II decades, but new productions are still periodically mounted in the Soviet Union.

THE POOR BRIDE

In *The Poor Bride*, his second major work, Ostrovsky deals with the exploitation of women. A widowed mother in financial straits automatically assumes, as does everyone else, that her daughter will welcome an arranged marriage to an old drunkard to save the situation. The proud young woman desperately seeks a more companionable mate—at that time, most women were barred from respectable gainful employment—but Ostrovsky's survey of eligibles reveals that the unfortunate Marya has no options. Poor suitors cannot support a dowerless bride. Younger men with positions shop for more substantial wives to secure their future, and rich young men marry within their own class. This leaves only coarse or aged prospects, who do not conceal the fact that they are purchasing youth and comeliness. Matchmakers play a despicable but seemingly indispensable role in the negotiations, and Ostrovsky also adds unwholesome government clerks to his gallery of ethical offenders: Marya's prospective husband is a bribe-taking official, ironically named Benevolensky (Benefactor), who has reached high position and wealth by thoroughly dishonest means. Mindful of censorial objections, the playwright developed the piece in such a way that Marya herself comes to recognize the necessity of the arrangement and enters it with some hope of reforming the erring spouse. This seemingly upbeat conclusion does not alter the basic impression of Marya's desperation and defenselessness. Even as the bride tearfully tells herself that she will be happy and thanks her mother for arranging the union, spectators conclude the play by emphasizing the young woman's pitiful appearance and questionable future.

Although reviewers welcomed discussion of the female topic, they criticized Ostrovsky's casual artistry. The play's theatrical effectiveness suffers because of repetitious dialogue, as each suitor parades before the hapless bride with his story. Marya's reaction to the suitors also exhibits a certain sameness and lacks vitality. In defense of the play, progressive critics, placing content over art, praised the production for bringing a vital social issue before the public in easily understandable form. Nevertheless, before Ostrovsky included the play in a collected edition, he improved it by individualizing some characters and by excising several slow-moving scenes. *The Poor Bride*, like *It's a Family Affair*, is called a comedy, its light touches achieved by imitating official pomposity, middle-class vulgarity, and young people's foolish fancies. The play never achieved the popularity of Ostrovsky's other major pieces, partly because it was banned in the popular playhouses, being limited to infrequent production at the Imperial theaters. The importance of the forced marriage theme, however, had been raised and subsequently found wide, artistically superior expression in Ostrovsky's work. In Soviet times, as female emancipation once more received a high profile, the number of productions increased.

POVERTY IS NO CRIME

Ostrovsky also treated forced marriage in his politically milder comedy *Poverty Is No Crime.* Here again, a positively depicted daughter is ordered by her heartless merchant father to take an aging, lecherous manufacturer to husband, even though she loves a penniless business clerk. The tone and development of this potentially tragic conflict differ markedly from those of previous and later plays. The bumbling, dissolute brother of the family despot saves his niece by exposing the vices of the rich bridegroom. He tricks the egotistic patriarch into permitting the lovers to marry and even regenerates fatherly feelings in him. At the time of this writing, Ostrovsky had fallen briefly under the influence of conservative Slavophils, who urged him not to destroy Russia's cultural heritage through overexposure of social problems. To mollify them, and to gain a reprieve from the censors, he softened his social criticism by including a mer-

chant with a soul in the person of the brother, and numerous songs, rituals, and customs, all presented in a cordial, heartwarming manner. The preponderance of comic elements in the play further mutes its message. Soon, however, during Alexander II's more tolerant reign, the playwright once more concentrated on writing critical exposé.

THE STORM

The Storm, Ostrovsky's most controversial and best-known play, encompasses all his major concerns: merchant greed, patriarchal tyranny, exploitation of young women, the dangers of regressive tradition, religious orthodoxy, budding rebellion, and society-serving idealism. It is atypical of Ostrovsky in that it has a truly disastrous ending and is one of his few pieces designated simply as drama, devoid of the usual satire and comic effusiveness. By transferring the locale to a provincial town, the author stressed that the vices depicted previously in urban settings were deeply ingrained in the Russian psyche. Production restrictions had been liberalized by 1860—the emancipation of serfs was not far away—and permission for staging was given immediately, possibly because casual censorial reading perceived the content to be the love story of a repentant adulteress. *The Storm* is in fact Ostrovsky's most hard-hitting play.

The merchant villains not only terrorize their households but also prohibit all efforts at education and reform in the town. Dikoy represents the greedy miser, whose every waking moment is planned to extort money dishonestly. When confronted by logic, he uses brute force and outmoded irrational arguments to maintain his position. The equally vile matriarch, Kabanikha, defends medieval practices, among them absolute submission by her family. The young men of these respective homes have been mentally emasculated, unable to assert themselves, though they privately recognize the injustice. The feebleness of these latter two figures contributes to the misery and eventual demise of Katerina, Kabanikha's gentle daughter-in-law. Katerina's husband, Tikhon, passively assents to her mistreatment, too fearful of his mother to defend his wife. Katerina's lover, Boris, is similarly weak-willed and sacrifices her to Dikoy's cruel dictates.

The typical Ostrovsky plot line is skillfully supplemented by the carefully developed portrait of Katerina. She is torn between rejecting the strictures of the old and remaining loyal to religious tradition. This agonizing conflict eventually results in her death, and Ostrovsky's depiction of her struggle clearly relates her individual fate to larger issues. Katerina has docilely married Tikhon at the insistence of her mother, only to find that she cannot reconcile her romantic expectations with Kabanikha's cruelty. Driven by her longings to seek relief in an illicit affair, she quickly comes in conflict with deep-seated religious scruples. An approaching thunderstorm symbolizes the upheaval within her. Tradition decrees that lightning is God's punishment for sinners, and Katerina is certain that the flashes are meant for her. Crazed with fear, she confesses, thus submitting to the rage of the vicious mother-in-law. As the latter devises a miserable future for her, Katerina, unable to provoke husband or lover into defensive action, ends her life in the river.

On one level, the play implies that strength of religious tradition has won out over adulterous transgression. A closer inspection, however, reveals other nuances. Although Katerina is unable to live with her sin, she is also unwilling to accept punishment in the form of Kabanikha's savagery. Instead, she commits the cardinal sin of suicide in the hope that a merciful God will overrule earthly ecclesiastical doctrine. This powerful statement is accompanied by downgrading of provincial religious practice. The selfish holy woman, Feklyusha, is counterpointed to the social reformer Kuligin, who gives his labor free to the town, in obvious contrast to the fawning, gossipy pilgrim. Kabanikha's patriarchal rule, meant to preserve traditional family, actually destroys it. Her own daughter rebelliously elopes with a clerk, while her son, in a belated show of courage, accuses her of murder. Ostrovsky thus mirrors the cautious social changes of the era. Young people question and rebel even as traditional patriarchy makes its last malicious stand.

In terms of composition, the play is among Ostrovsky's best. Artful plot development, strong characterization, and forceful if rather heavy-handed symbolism combine to move the action deftly forward. *The Storm* is also one of his most popular pieces at home and abroad. It had close to 3,600 performances before the revolution, and its success continued into Soviet times. Famous directors, among them Vsevolod Meyerhold and Vladimir Ivanovich Nemirovich-Danchenko, have given it innovative productions, and it has been transferred to the screen. Outstanding actresses have vied for the role of Katerina, and productions abroad extended the play's fame. It is likely to remain in the repertoire for many years to come.

THE SCOUNDREL

Although *The Storm* represents the high point of Ostrovsky's career, his literary output continued undiminished for twenty-six more years. Among his best later productions are *The Scoundrel* and *The Forest*. The former is noteworthy for its treatment of lower nobility, to which Ostrovsky now shifted his attention. *The Scoundrel* was possibly inspired by Richard Brinsley Sheridan's *The School for Scandal* (pr. 1777), with which it shares the themes of intrigue, vapid amusements, and social relation rituals. The hero of the title, searching for a comfortable position and a rich wife, ingratiates himself with various important figures and then plays them off against one another for maximum gain. When unmasked, he brazenly reminds them that they need a scoundrel like him to organize their petty schemes. The ending suggests that he will be restored to everyone's favor. The play has been performed abroad, and in the 1920's Sergei Eisenstein revived Soviet interest with an innovative staging featuring experimental sets.

THE FOREST

The Forest has the distinction of being Ostrovsky's most frequently performed drama. It pays homage to the superior moral qualities of actors by contrasting them favorably to a group of scheming, empty-headed landowners. The plot is typical of Ostrovsky: The poor ward of a pretentious rich widow is manipulated into an unwanted marriage but rescued in time by a traveling actor, who facilitates her wedding to her true love, an abused merchant's son. The comedy is understandably a favorite of performers, and this accounts for much of its success. It had more than five thousand performances before 1917, some of them abroad, and continues to be a perennial favorite in the Soviet Union.

BIBLIOGRAPHY

Hoover, Marjorie L. *Alexander Ostrovsky*. Boston: Twayne, 1981. A basic biography of Ostrovsky that covers his life and works. Bibliography and index.

Lyons, Donald. "Chekov and His Forebear." Review of *The Cherry Orchard*, by Anton Chekhov, and *The Forest*, by Alexander Ostrovsky. *Wall Street Journal*, November 5, 1997, p. A20. Lyons compares and contrasts the two Russian plays, which were being performed in New York in 1997.

Rahman, Kate Sealey. *Ostrovsky: Reality and Illusion*. Birmingham, England: University of Birmingham, 1999. A study of Ostrovsky that focuses on his efforts at realism and his idealism. Bibliography and index.

Margot K. Frank

THOMAS OTWAY

Born: Trotton, England; March 3, 1652
Died: London, England; April 14, 1685

PRINCIPAL DRAMA

Alcibiades, pr., pb. 1675
Don Carlos, Prince of Spain, pr., pb. 1676
Titus and Berenice, pr. 1676, pb. 1677 (adaptation of Jean Racine's play *Bérénice*)
The Cheats of Scapin, pr. 1676, pb. 1677 (adaptation of Molière's play *Les Fourberies de Scapin*)
Friendship in Fashion, pr., pb. 1678
The History and Fall of Caius Marius, pr. 1679, pb. 1680
The Orphan: Or, The Unhappy Marriage, pr., pb. 1680
The Soldier's Fortune, pr. 1680, pb. 1681
Venice Preserved: Or, A Plot Discovered, pr., pb. 1682
The Atheist: Or, The Second Part of the Soldier's Fortune, pr. 1683, pb. 1684

OTHER LITERARY FORMS

The writings of Thomas Otway, apart from his plays, are of minor significance. His two most substantial poetic efforts were his first published poem, *The Poet's Complaint of His Muse* (1680), and the posthumously published *Windsor Castle* (1685). The former poem, despite claims made for its autobiographical and political interest, is a disjointed effort that shifts from a seemingly personal apologia to an allegorized presentation of the Popish Plot and the Exclusion Crisis. *Windsor Castle* consists of a mélange of devices, drawn from elegy, topographical poetry, and Restoration advice-to-the-painter poetry, occasioned by the death of Charles II. The rest of Otway's poetry is in typical Restoration modes: dramatic prologues and epilogues, translations (of Ovid and Horace), a commendatory poem (addressed to Thomas Creech on his translation of Lucretius), and a verse epistle (to Richard Duke). Published posthumously were his prose translations from the French, *The History of the Triumvirates*, in 1686, and a group of love letters, supposedly written by Otway to the actress Elizabeth Barry, in 1697.

ACHIEVEMENTS

A proper measure of Thomas Otway's achievement as a dramatist can be taken neither from the current critical reputation of his heroic plays, tragedies, and comedies nor from the success of these works in his own time but, rather, must take into account a popularity and influence that continued through the early nineteenth century. *Don Carlos, Prince of Spain*, *The Orphan*, and *Venice Preserved* were among the most popular of Restoration plays; only by comparison with these plays could Otway's comedies be considered unsuccessful. It is true that his comedies were dropped from the repertory of the London theaters early in the eighteenth century, but this fact reflects a change in taste for which Otway himself might have been partly responsible: It is possible to detect a gradual translation of the affective techniques that characterize Otway's tragedies into the comedies of the late seventeenth and early eighteenth centuries. The frequent revivals of *The Orphan* and *Venice Preserved* suggest these plays' persistent influence and confirm Otway's high standing in English drama. Joseph Addison in *The Spectator* (1711-1712, 1714) anticipated many later comments when he wrote that "Otway has followed Nature in the Language of his Tragedy, and therefore shines in the Passionate Parts, more than any of our English poets." A renewed appreciation of Otway's plays followed from the general revival of critical and scholarly interest in Restoration drama in the 1920's. Most subsequent study has concentrated on *The Orphan* and *Venice Preserved* but, unfortunately, critical interest has rarely led to theatrical production. Harold Pinter, however, has spoken for the dramatic accessibility of *Venice Preserved* to modern audiences, and critics have supplied groundwork for a more extensive treatment of Otway's dramatic production.

BIOGRAPHY

Thomas Otway was born March 3, 1652, in Trotton, Sussex, the son of Humphrey Otway, an Anglican clergyman of distinguished family and of Royalist sympathies, and Elizabeth Otway, of whom little is known. Otway briefly attended Winchester College before entering Oxford University in May, 1669; he left the university in 1671 without taking a degree, perhaps because of the death of his father. Sometime after leaving Oxford, Otway made his way to London, where, at the Duke's Theatre, he was given a role in Aphra Behn's play *The Forced Marriage: Or, The Jealous Bridegroom* (pr. 1670). His performance was a failure; nevertheless, he may for a time have found some marginal employment as an actor. In any event, by 1675, the year in which his first play, *Alcibiades*, was presented at Dorset Garden, he was devoting himself to the financially insecure profession of playwriting. Despite some early theatrical success (notably the extremely popular *Don Carlos, Prince of Spain*), the uncertainty of his fortunes and of patronage by members of the royal court probably led to his decision to join the English forces in Flan-

ders in 1678. Even though Otway received a commission, his military career was brief: The army was recalled from Flanders early in 1679 and disbanded in June. This expedition having improved his fortunes not at all, Otway returned to writing, and thereupon followed his most concentrated period of literary production. The plays *The History and Fall of Caius Marius, The Orphan,* and *The Soldier's Fortune,* and the poem *The Poet's Complaint of His Muse,* were either first produced or first published within the year. He was granted a master of arts degree by St. John's College, Cambridge University, in 1680, and, at about this time, he may have been tutor to one of Charles II's illegitimate children by Nell Gwyn. Nevertheless, Otway seems to have slipped into a state of poverty that the production of his later plays, *Venice Preserved* and *The Atheist,* did little to relieve. Although the circumstances of Otway's death in London on April 14, 1685, became the stuff of legend, they remain uncertain.

ANALYSIS

In his *Lives of the English Poets,* Samuel Johnson says of Thomas Otway's *The Orphan* that "its whole power is upon the affections; for it is not written with much comprehension of thought or elegance of expression. But, if the heart is interested, many other beauties may be wanting, yet not be missed." For one accustomed to Johnson's judicial manner of literary evaluation, his praise of the play rises above the qualifications with which it is voiced. Although Johnson is here addressing himself to only one of Otway's plays, the quality on which he fastens—the ability to elicit an affective response through the representation of the passions—is one that was fitfully apparent even in *Alcibiades* and at least as forcefully realized in *Venice Preserved.* Indeed, in *Venice Preserved,* Johnson discovered a greater virility, if not an elegance, of expression, but this new strength of Otway's imagery and language could not overcome his qualms regarding "the want of morality in the original design, and the despicable scenes of vile comedy with which he has diversified his tragic action." Pathos is the play's sole saving grace; that Otway's "original design" was in fact altered in eighteenth century theatrical productions so that the offensive comic scenes were deleted suggests that Johnson stood very much with his age in his refusal to accept the "thought" that was expressed in *Venice Preserved*. While the pathetic character of Otway's plays remains a matter of critical interest, respect must also be given to those elements of Otway's work that were considered anomalous in the period of Johnson—his seeming immorality, his comic cynicism, and his tragic despair—in order to understand fully the attitudes that informed not only his heroic plays and tragedies but also the comedies (and the comic episodes of *Venice Preserved*), which Johnson dismissed.

The characteristic strengths of Otway's plays seem to depend more on the force of their original conception than on the art with which they are executed. Too often, Otway seems simply unwilling to improve on his first designs. Certainly such a nearly complete lapse of dramatic sense as is seen in the opening exposition of *The Orphan* could have been prevented by even the most cursory reading of François Hédelin, Abbé d'Aubignac's *La Pratique du théâtre* (1657), a contemporary French dramatic treatise. At other times, Otway's original conception, however deficient, seems

Thomas Otway (Hulton Archive by Getty Images)

incapable of being altered without sacrificing its intended effect. To use the example of *The Orphan* again, there appears to be a lack of motivation in Castalio's concealing of his marriage to Monimia from the rest of his family, particularly from his brother, Polydore. That the brothers are rivals in love seems less important than the violation of Castalio's vows of absolute friendship for his brother by his withholding of the truth. Without Polydore's misunderstanding of the situation, however, there could be no tragedy, at least not the kind that Otway intended. Motivation for Castalio's behavior would perhaps be necessary in a tragedy of character, but the focus of the tragedy of *The Orphan*, as in other Otway plays, is not on individual character so much as on the inveterate frailty of human intentions and the circumstances by which human ideals are defeated.

Jessica Munns stresses the analogy between the king/subjects relationship and that between the father and his family, noting the rebellion of fractious sons against cruel fathers in the plays. Munns reads Otway's dramas as subtle subversions of "traditional, monarchical, and non-consent-based power," products of a historical period undergoing profound changes to which the playwright was alert. To explain away the "intense misogyny" of Otway's language, Munns resorts to New Historicist and Marxist arguments that focus on theories of how repressive states manipulate contradictions to achieve containment. She can thus admit that Otway's politics support royal power but nevertheless "go beyond party politics to constitute a critique of the very systems of power and representation the ideology purports and the dramas probably mean to sustain."

Earlier in the Restoration period, the ideals of honor, love, and friendship were given heroic affirmation in the plays of John Dryden and Roger Boyle, earl of Orrery. Even in his later tragedies, so formally different from these heroic plays, Otway typically does not take the position of denying that these ideals are worthy of desire—indeed, the pathos of his plays would be lost if he did—but instead casts doubt on their power to determine actions. The influence of the heroic tradition on Otway persists to the last of his serious plays in the tendency to conceive of dramatic character as representing the radical expression of human possibility, but, instead of being employed to glorify human potential, this mode of characterization is used to indicate human beings' pathetic inability to realize their aspirations. Further, Otway was able to rely on the continued urgency of the heroic play's thematic concerns to direct attention, in a dramatically concise and forceful manner, to his own iconoclasm. The writing of comedy in no way lightened Otway's vision of the human situation, but, because the world represented is closer to the mean of everyday experience, the substance of his comedies may seem trivial in comparison with his heroic plays and tragedies. A comparison of *The Orphan* with *Friendship in Fashion*, however, would also serve to indicate the presence in the comedy of the two thematic motifs, friendship and love, which are the dominant concerns of the later tragedy, and the power of *Friendship in Fashion* to disturb the most commonly held notions of Restoration comedy suggests that Otway approached the conventions of the comedy of manners not with delight but with something close to moral repugnance. Otway, then, looks to a common area of experience in both dramatic modes, exploiting alike the forms and conventions of comic and serious plays.

The high road of the Restoration heroic play is that represented in John Dryden's proselytizing of a dramatic practice based on an epic analogy. His two-part drama produced between 1670 and 1671, *The Conquest of Granada by the Spaniards*, has been considered the apotheosis of his theory of the heroic play, but his earlier play, *Tyrannic Love: Or, The Royal Martyr* (pr. 1669), was more remarkable for its extravagance of language, character, and situation and its accompanying use of theatrical spectacle than for any truly epic qualities. Elkanah Settle's extraordinarily successful 1671 production, *The Empress of Morocco*, and Nathaniel Lee's *The Tragedy of Nero, Emperor of Rome* (pr. 1674, pb. 1675) resemble both of Dryden's plays in the use of rhymed couplets as their basic verse form and in the portrayal of "heroic"

love, but they exploit the theatrical values of *Tyrannic Love* rather than the epic tendencies of *The Conquest of Granada by the Spaniards*. *The Tragedy of Nero, Emperor of Rome* is of particular interest in regard to *Alcibiades*, and not merely because it was Lee's own initial dramatic effort: The choice of classical subject, the fictional elaboration on the facts of history, and the indiscriminate letting of the blood of both protagonists and villains in a manner reminiscent of the Jacobean theater are common to the two plays. Both the plays make use of dramatic sensationalism; *The Empress of Morocco* had previously shown that theatric capital could be made of a blatantly melodramatic approach to the heroic play in which action was forwarded by villainy and lust.

ALCIBIADES

Viewed against the perspective supplied by the repertory of Restoration playhouses, the plot of *Alcibiades* contains no surprises. The plot is built on a single incident drawn from Plutarch—Alcibiades' expulsion from Athens following a night of drunken sacrilege—but the action of the play begins not with the event itself but with its report to the woman to whom he is betrothed, Timandra. This brief scene of exposition concludes with Timandra's rejection of the love of Theramnes, the man who supplanted Alcibiades as Athenian general. The remaining action of the play takes place about the camp of the king of Sparta, where Alcibiades had taken himself on his expulsion from Athens. There, the Spartan king's granting of the title of general to Alcibiades; the secret resentment and desire for revenge of Tissaphernes, the Spartan he replaces; the Spartan queen's sudden, violent passion for Alcibiades; the appearance of Timandra; the victory over the Athenians; and the capture of Theramnes supply more than the necessary means of spasmodically forwarding the action of the play toward its bloody conclusion, in which the only major character left alive is Patroclus, who is the son of Tissaphernes but nevertheless a loyal friend of Alcibiades. Jessica Munns emphasized the depiction of Tissaphernes as "a perverse and vampiric creation who seeks to regain youth through shedding blood . . . ," thereby making him the first exhibit in her gallery of Otway's "dreadful fathers."

Little can be said for the artistic merit of *Alcibiades*. In part, the weakness of its dramatic organization might be simply explained by Otway's failure to amalgamate those materials he had freely and rather too copiously borrowed; nevertheless, *Alcibiades* yet has something of the characteristic tenor of the later plays, and it is possible to find in it an anticipation of the sorts of problems of form and characterization with which Otway, by the very nature of the kind of drama that he was attempting to write, was later forced to confront.

The titular character of *Alcibiades* is a major dramatic liability. The historical character from Plutarch is almost completely lost from sight, and Otway never quite squares his presentation of Alcibiades the martial figure with Alcibiades the sensitive lover. Further, the character of Alcibiades is weakened not merely by the disjunction of his characterization but also by his situation within the plot. Although he is at the center of all the various actions of the play, he is a character more acted on than acting. His military triumph over Athens and Theramnes and the killing of his rival in the act of ravishing Timandra were obviously intended to establish his heroic credibility, but the latter action serves only to precipitate the catastrophe of the play—the murder of the king and of Timandra and the suicide of Alcibiades. It is by the forces of lust, deceit, and revenge that the two lovers, Alcibiades and Timandra, are made vulnerable (although it is not as a necessary consequence that they are doomed). That Timandra's vulnerability seems more emphatic and compelling has much to do with contemporary dramatic and social stereotypes of feminine behavior; from the first scene, however, her articulation of the vulnerability of love places her closer to the realities of the play than is Alcibiades.

The burden of these fears is realized not only in *Alcibiades* but also in later plays by Otway: Loyalty and love cannot survive the way of the world. She and her lover serve as exemplars of this fact. There is, however, a definite irony, one that Otway may not have fully intended, in the situation that forces Alcibiades to suicide: The "heroic" self-absorption that prevents his admitting any real danger to himself, even when Tissaphernes' designs are revealed by Patroclus, also renders him incapable of recognizing the peril to Timandra represented by the queen. The force of his love seems rather too summarily expressed by his suicide. Timandra, on the other hand, has only one role, that of the loved one, and from this role the expression of her fears seems naturally to follow. Moreover, her anticipation of the sad worldly fate of her love for Alcibiades is joined in a corrupt Neoplatonic manner to the belief that their love will find its true reward in an afterlife together. The unusual prominence given to this notion in *Alcibiades*, even as it diminishes its tragic effect, constitutes the most powerful formal demand for the sacrifice of the lovers.

DON CARLOS, PRINCE OF SPAIN

The villainy of Tissaphernes and of Deidama, the queen of Sparta, although in the end self-defeating, is nevertheless efficient in its decimation of the *dramatis personae* of *Alcibiades*, and the characterization of Deidama is a gesture in the direction of the heroic fashion of sensually motivated villainesses. Some traces of this dramatic type remain in the duchess of Eboli in *Don Carlos, Prince of Spain*. Yet even though she aids in the machinations against the prince, it is her husband, Rui-Gomez, who is clearly the central figure in the plot. Reflection on the role of Rui-Gomez suggests some of the changes in dramatic conception that, in the streamlining of the heroic apparatus, made *Don Carlos, Prince of Spain* a markedly better play than *Alcibiades*. The action of *Don Carlos, Prince of Spain*, like that of *Alcibiades*, entails the pursuit of revenge; in the earlier play, however, there exists another major motivating force, the queen's desire for Alcibiades. Although Tissaphernes and the queen are brought together in the murder of the king, the need for some coordination or subordination of their purposes is realized too late in the play. In *Don Carlos, Prince of Spain*, the malevolence of Rui-Gomez, even as it exploits and infects the other characters, is used to concentrate and direct the play's action. Because Rui-Gomez does not attempt anything so crude as assassination, there is no need for him to follow Tissaphernes' almost ludicrous course of failed attempts at murder in order that his revenge might be protracted to the length of the play. Rather, because the revenge of Rui-Gomez is to be effected through the jealousy of King Philip, each stay in his scheme seems only to increase its potential yield, until only the death of his son and wife can satisfy the king's maddened sense of injury.

This concurrent dilation and intensification of the act of revenge resembles the action of William Shakespeare's *Othello, the Moor of Venice* (pr. 1604), as Rui-Gomez resembles Iago. Iago may have also had a part in the conception of Tissaphernes, but the earlier character is so much an epitome of villainy that any particular touches drawn from Shakespeare are lost in generality. The influence of Iago on the characterization of Rui-Gomez is sharply rendered; the effect is to draw the character into a more particular and probable dramatic world than that inhabited by Tissaphernes. J. C. Ghosh overstated the case for *Don Carlos, Prince of Spain* when, in the introduction to his edition of the works of Otway, he said that "the characters are not the bloated abstractions of the heroic play, but real flesh and blood"; yet within the dramatic limits of the heroic form, Otway managed to give his characters touches of life that were absent from *Alcibiades*. The action of *Don Carlos, Prince of Spain*, however, does not approach the dramatic and moral concentration of *Othello*. The focus of the play is not so much on the victim of jealousy, the king, as on those characters who suffer on account of his jealousy—his son, Don Carlos, and his recently married queen. The result would be analogous to an *Othello* more concerned with the fate of Desdemona than with the victimizing of the Moor. As a consequence of the play's design, none of the characters is allowed the intense moral and psychological regard that is given to Othello.

The love of Carlos and the queen, moreover, is represented not as wrong but as unfortunate, and moral evaluation in the play does not depend so much on the nature of particular actions as on their association with the almost schematically opposed guilt and innocence of Rui-Gomez and the queen. Thus, the king, once he is made to realize the treachery of Rui-Gomez's counsel, must be allowed the full weight of the forgiveness by his dying queen and his son, allowing him a share in the pathetic emotions of the play's conclusion. Even the anomalous moral position of Don Juan, whose naturalism is reminiscent of Edmund in Shakespeare's *King Lear* (pr. c. 1605-1606) and near to the contemporary libertinism of John Wilmot, earl of Rochester, is accommodated more by his allegiance to Don Carlos than by his representation as an *honnête homme*. (It must be noticed, however, that the blunt sexuality of his relationship with Eboli, which is not disguised by the preciosity of its expression, serves as a negative counterpoint to the ideal quality of the love of Carlos and the queen.) Don Carlos himself is not so absolute a paragon as the queen. The method in which the vacillation of Carlos's sense of filial duty is made external in his design to defect to the rebels in Flanders adds a hint of moral complexity that aids in forwarding the plot yet, in the end, does not inhibit the pathetic capability of his character. Carlos's plan to go to Flanders ultimately condemns him in the eyes of his father. It is also an indication of his heroic aspirations, but, most important, it is an attempt to escape the emotional agony of his passion for the queen. The catastrophe of the play follows almost the same destructive pattern as does that of *Alcibiades*. That Otway could boast in his preface to *Don Carlos, Prince of Spain* that the play "never fail'd to draw Tears from the Eyes of the Auditors" is a result of his ability to enunciate fully the pity of a love that does not capitulate to the accidents of fate but is destroyed by them.

ADAPTATIONS AND BORROWINGS

In his prefatory discussion of the pathos of *Don Carlos, Prince of Spain*, Otway made reference to Jean Racine's *Bérénice* (pr. 1670; English translation, 1676), and in 1676, his adaptations of this play and of Molière's *Les Fourberies de Scapin* (pr., pb. 1671; *The Cheats of Scapin*, 1701) were combined in a single night's entertainment at the Duke's Theatre. Otway's three acts of *Titus and Berenice*, although faithful to Racine's plot and the tendency of his language, are nevertheless an extremely compressed redaction of the original. While the alternation of emotional states remains, the adaptation's compression short-circuits the sustained dramatic logic of Racine's play, and yet, considering the remarkable efficiency of the heroic couplets of *Don Carlos, Prince of Spain*, Otway's verses seem slack in comparison with Racine's French Alexandrines. Otway's *Titus and Berenice* is similar to the shortened versions of Shakespeare that were produced in the eighteenth century: It supplies the bare bones of the action but little of the quality of the original.

THE HISTORY AND FALL OF CAIUS MARIUS

Otway, in fact, made use of Shakespearean materials in *The History and Fall of Caius Marius*, the first of his plays produced after his return from Flanders. Otway openly admitted his Shakespearean borrowings in the prologue to the play, and, until 1744, *The History and Fall of Caius Marius* replaced Shakespeare's *Romeo and Juliet* (pr. c. 1595-1596) in the repertory of the London theaters. Indeed, what little modern critical interest there has been in *The History and Fall of Caius Marius* has tended to concentrate on its indebtedness to *Romeo and Juliet*, but a refashioning of Shakespeare's love story constitutes only a part of Otway's drama. A more various use of Shakespearean techniques is evident in that portion of the play that represents a historical parallel to current political events in England. Otway's lovers are separated and ultimately destroyed not as a result of the private feuding of their families but because of their fathers' engagement in the political antagonisms of the Marian civil war.

Even though Otway employed Plutarch with more integrity than in *Alcibiades*, his purpose was not simply to dramatize episodes from the life of Caius Marius. Similarly, although his dramatic prologues and epilogues, along with *The Poet's Complaint of His Muse*, proclaim his staunch allegiance to the duke of York, he did not simply allegorize the events of the Exclusion Crisis from a Royalist perspective. Rather, the play uses its historical materials to portray the miseries of civil war, a condition seen by many Royalists as the inevitable consequence of the attempt to exclude the Catholic duke from succession to the English throne. Monarchy could not, without blatant anachronism, be introduced into a treatment of the Marian civil war, but the sort of stabilizing, ordering influence that Royalists credited the monarchy as having on the social economy of England is conspicuously absent from the dramatic world of the play. In

The History and Fall of Caius Marius, political ambition and factional strife are allowed free play in a Hobbesian nightmare of naked self-interest. Caius Marius himself establishes the keynote of the play when he expresses his desire "to be Great, unequall'd, and alone." His ambition functions without regard for the Roman commonwealth or for those human values that are evident in his son's love for Lavinia, the daughter of his political rival. In exposing the hypocrisy of his patriotism, Otway no doubt intended that it should count against those politicians, the first to be called "Whigs," who claimed that their support of Exclusion was in the best interest of the nation, but that *The History and Fall of Caius Marius* was a play of narrow political regard and application is denied by its continued theatrical production in the changed political circumstances of the years following the accession of William and Mary.

In such a dramatic context, for which Shakespeare's history plays, English and Roman, seem a model, the claustrophobic intensity of Shakespeare's treatment of the ill-fated love of Romeo and Juliet was impossible. Instead, Otway used the story as a counter in which the destruction of the love of Marius's son and Metullus's daughter, insofar as it is a symbol of social collapse, serves a wider function than do the similar catastrophes of *Alcibiades* and *Don Carlos, Prince of Spain*. *The History and Fall of Caius Marius* should perhaps be considered a play that marks a transition in Otway's dramatic work. While the use of blank verse in *The History and Fall of Caius Marius* (and of prose in its comic sections) is suggestive of other of Otway's departures from the practice of his heroic plays, the extended focus of the play is nothing like that of the painfully constricted tragedy *The Orphan*, which followed within a year.

FRIENDSHIP IN FASHION

Although Otway's first full-length comedy, *Friendship in Fashion*, is recognizably a product of its dramatic environment, it cannot be made to sit comfortably with William Wycherley's *The Country Wife* (pr., pb. 1675) or Sir George Etherege's *The Man of Mode: Or, Sir Fopling Flutter* (pr., pb. 1676) as a comedy of manners. It is neither a matter of subject—the title of Otway's play accurately describes its social focus, and sex was as much at the forefront of its action as in the two plays of Etherege and Wycherley—nor a matter of dramatic form so much as of emphasis, a different attitude taken to the form as it existed. Otway exploits its satiric potential at the expense of that comic brilliance of surface, which at times has been considered the Restoration comedy of manners's only claim to critical redemption. *Friendship in Fashion*, in fact, has as much (if not more) in common with Wycherley's *The Plain Dealer* (pr. 1676), a play that has been similarly resistant to narrowly prescriptive notions of the comedy of manners, as with his earlier *The Country Wife* (although Otway borrows a character, or at least a name, Mrs. Squeamish, from that play). Yet even *The Plain Dealer*, while pointing in the satiric direction of *Friendship in Fashion*, does not go as far. Both plays are concerned with the betrayal of trust, but Otway does not allow a figure such as Fidelia or the reminiscence of the romantic pattern of Shakespeare's *Twelfth Night* (pr. c. 1600-1602) to obstruct his indictment of love and friendship in its current fashion. The misanthropy of Manly is shown by Wycherley to be in excess of the whole of the play's facts; an unstable but nevertheless a crucial distance is thus established between Manly's perspective and that of the play. There is no such figure as Manly in Otway's play, and there is no ground for ambiguity in its meaning. *Friendship in Fashion* offers the grim sort of entertainment that a Manly might have found in having his views affirmed.

In *Friendship in Fashion*, the cynical, manipulative rake figure was not displaced from the center of the play's action, as he had been in Wycherley's last comedy. Rather, Otway removed the rake both from his position of social power and from his dominant dramatic status. *Friendship in Fashion* seems an almost precise inversion of the dramatic pattern of *The Man of Mode*: The action of the play represents the progressive loss of control of Otway's rake, Goodvile, over his social domain. Goodvile's attempt to combine a rake's career with marriage makes him vulnerable, but it is, significantly, Goodvile's violation of his friendships that is made to seem the effective cause of his cuckoldry, which, in turn, is made palatable by Otway's complete degradation of his

rake. Goodvile not only is morally unattractive but also lacks charm and wit. Indeed, the other major characters of the play are responded to, not on account of their personal characteristics or in terms of their adherence to more or less ideal social or amatory values, but almost purely in respect to their opposition to Goodvile and their frustration of his designs. The play obviously pursues dramatic unity in the compression of its events; there is a coordinate compression, or collapse, of social values.

THE SOLDIER'S FORTUNE

Just as *Friendship in Fashion* depended on the comedy of manners, *The Soldier's Fortune* refined and enlarged the pattern of contemporary farce. The play contains the constitutive figures of sexual farce—the lover, the boorish husband, and the willing wife—and its action depicts the frustration and delay of the sexual engagement of the soldier, Beaugard, with Lady Dunce, but both in characterization and in the tenor of its action, *The Soldier's Fortune* exceeds the limits of farce. The play is heavily weighted with matters that retard a blithe depiction of cuckoldry. Otway is concerned with the subject of unhappy marriage here, as in his other comedies, as something more than grist for the mill of comic invention. The disaffection of Lady Dunce for her husband, Sir Davy, is not represented simply as the pettish response of a willful, sexually frustrated young woman to confinement by an old and unattractive husband, as it would have been in farce. On the contrary, Otway does much to elevate the character of Lady Dunce— she is shown to be clever, discerning, even sensitive—and the fact that her emotional involvement with Beaugard antedated her enforced marriage to Sir Davy extenuates her pursuit of Beaugard and her adultery. In short, her incompatibility with Sir Davy is more than sexual, and her marriage is made to seem a form of injustice.

A sense of injustice is also evident in Beaugard's complaints against his fortune. Forced to leave London (and Lady Dunce) to become a soldier, he is still almost beggared after his departure. The grievances of Beaugard and his military companion Courtine take them into the position of being outsiders on the scene of London, and, from the beginning, *The Sol-*

dier's Fortune is leavened by their acerbic commentary. In this commentary, which distends the dramatic shape of the play, it is tempting to see a reflection of Otway's own experience and attitudes; nevertheless, it is made to serve a dramatic purpose, reinforcing, for example, the apposition of Beaugard and Sir Davy. Beaugard's unrewarded loyalty is in complete contrast with the prosperity of Sir Davy's disaffection with the king. Indeed, the political context in which the play was written exerted a forceful, albeit intermittent, influence. Sir Davy's plan to murder Beaugard and his subsequent disposal of Beaugard's body have a parodic relationship to the Whig version of the events of the Popish Plot, and, fueled by prior allusions to Shakespeare's *Macbeth* (pr. c. 1605-1606), the obsessiveness, the frenzy, and the utter disregard for even the comic conventions of human behavior at the play's conclusion are in apparent similitude to the contemporary state of England.

At the end, when Beaugard has finally obtained sexual possession of Lady Dunce, there is little sense of either delight or permanence in the arrangement. Throughout the play, Sir Jolly Jumble, an impotent, bisexual pimp and voyeur, has served them as a go-between, and his involvement is enough to limit the romantic implications of their relationship. The concurrent courtship and marriage of Courtine and Sylvia that function as an underplot to the main action represent a romantic possibility denied to Beaugard and Lady Dunce, despite the hesitation and even the cynicism that results from the pair's lack of faith in the institution of marriage.

THE ATHEIST

Otway's last play, *The Atheist*, a "second part" of *The Soldier's Fortune*, was probably written for the same reason as was the second of Aphra Behn's *Rover* (pr., pb. 1681) plays: to capitalize on the theatrical success of the original. Beaugard, in the earlier *The Soldier's Fortune*, was the same type of character as the "Rover" Willmore; *The Atheist* was of the same dramatic kind as the *Rover* plays. In the dramatic extravagance of their use of cloaks and daggers and nighttime intrigue, these plays have more in common with the "Spanish" plays of the early years of the Restoration than with the social comedies of the

1670's. Yet the one aspect of *The Atheist* that is an actual sequel to the events of *The Soldier's Fortune*—the treatment of the marriage of Courtine and Sylvia—establishes a thematic link with Otway's earlier comedies. Courtine has reached the nadir of Goodvile's dissatisfaction with marriage, but his attempts to escape its bonds are complete in their lack of success. His situation is contrasted with that of his brother-in-arms, Beaugard, who by the death of an uncle has achieved a fortune totally unencumbered by the demands of marriage. He, it seems, has entered into a rake's paradise of financial and emotional freedom. That Beaugard freely marries a widow who had echoed his consistent objections to marriage suggests, however, that in *The Atheist*, Otway, for once in his comedies, acceded to the satisfaction of a dramatic formula and a romantic pattern. Moreover, both Daredevil, the "atheist" of the title, and Beaugard's father bear a potential for thematic complication that is never realized in the play. Instead, they supply local dramatic interest in the manner of "humours" characters; they are intrinsically entertaining. Otway's increased allowance of the claim of comic entertainment in *The Atheist* may have constituted a recognition that he had exhausted a particular comic vein and may therefore have been an attempt to write a dramatically richer, perhaps a more Shakespearean comedy; it may, on the other hand, have been simply meretricious.

THE ORPHAN

Otway's personal disappointment in the rewards of military service may have been reflected in *The Soldier's Fortune*. In *The Orphan*, produced earlier in the same year, the uncertainty of virtue's reward at court is the reason given by Acasto, himself a disillusioned courtier, for the continued rustication of his twin sons, Castalio and Polydore. Eric Rothstein spoke of the influence that the naturalism of Restoration comedy had on *The Orphan*, while the play's subtitle, *The Unhappy Marriage*, suggests a tragic treatment of one of the topics of *Friendship in Fashion*, and the dramatic prominence of the friendship of the two brothers points to another form of thematic continuity. Although *The Orphan* does not represent a formal assault on heroic ideals as such, its depiction of the corruption of a rural idyll denies that sense of pastoral whose function in the late heroic play, according to Rothstein, was as "a counterpoise to dismal actualities, a psychological possibility of vacationing forever from corrupt courts, the contests of ambition, the dangers of martial glory, the deceitful lures of fortune." Moral corruption in *Friendship in Fashion* seems the common, but local, condition of fashionable life; the tragic power of *The Orphan* results from the unaccommodated recognition of a corruption that, in its adherence to a world so much closer to the pure facts of humankind's nature, is made to seem almost universal.

The central dramatic fact of *The Orphan* is Polydore's taking the place of his brother Castalio on his wedding night with Monimia, their father's ward. Although the act itself is only technically incestuous, it registers the shattering of all the chains of social relationships that have, by various means, been fused into a familial pattern. At the beginning of the play, Acasto's servants mention that Monimia is only his ward and Serina, his only daughter, but in the remainder of *The Orphan*, this distinction is often blurred. Serina's character is remarkable only for its lack of prominence. Indeed, the high point of Serina's dramatic existence begins with her being greeted by Monimia's brother, Chamont, as "another sister." The sudden efflorescence of his love for her and its allowance by Acasto does not, however, divert Chamont from an overwrought and morbid concern for his sister. Moreover, the strangely unmotivated secrecy of Calisto's dealings with Monimia tends to imply that their marriage represents some manner of violation beyond that of the trust of his father and brother. Thus, the celebration in act 2 of his king's birthday by Acasto, divorced from the changes of courtly fortune and content in the security of his newly extended family, achieves a full measure of dramatic irony. Chamont has come from the court, but it is not he who contaminates Acasto's world; corruption is already present in his sons.

Critics have been disturbed (or, more accurately, distracted) by the problem of how Polydore, confined by his father to a country retreat, could have learned the language of a fashionable sexual cynicism. Too strict a conception of dramatic verisimilitude obscures Otway's point: Otway was here using the diction of libertinism, as in the characterization of Don John in *Don Carlos, Prince of Spain*, primarily in order to express a sexual attitude, not a coherent philosophy. It is not, perhaps, an accident of language that "venery" is a word that comprehends Polydore's hunting of the boar as well as his sexual pursuit of Monimia. Polydore's sexual attitude is the efficient cause of the play's tragic dilemma, but not the formal ground of its tragic significance. Otway, both here and in *Venice Preserved*, suggests that the actions determining tragedy are neither matters of simple moral choice nor the products of moral intention. The sensibility evident in Polydore's relationship with his brother, and his regret for his crime, while they offer no protection against, or relief from, the fact of moral pollution, are at the center of the play's pathos. Because the play is uninhibited by sustained and explicit moral judgment, there exists an almost total freedom of response to the emotional dilemmas of the characters. To suggest, however, that pathetic response is the play's only dramatic concern is to ignore the power of the play's moral analysis, a power that resides not in judgment but in recognition.

VENICE PRESERVED

The dramatic progress of *Venice Preserved* is sustained by the series of shifting moral, political, and personal oppositions that confront Jaffeir, the play's central character. While the extensive use of peripeteia as a dramatic device may seem to recall the heroic play, its significance has been radically altered. Peripeteia was employed in Dryden's heroic plays to register the heroic self-consistency of his protagonists in the face of changing fortune; in *Venice Preserved*, it is the impossibility of moral integrity that is the point of the vacillations in the dramatic action, since Jaffeir is implicated in all of them. The initial, domestic antagonism of Jaffeir and his father-in-law, Priuli, is projected, through the agency of Jaffeir's friend Pierre, into his joining in a conspiracy against the entire senatorial order of which Priuli is a member. Priuli had considered Jaffeir's marriage with his daughter, Belvidira, a betrayal of trust; Jaffeir now leaves Belvidira with the conspirators as a pledge of his faithfulness to their cause. Consequently, the first countermovement of the play begins, not as might have been expected, in the initiation of the revolt, but with Jaffeir's learning of the attempted seduction of his wife by Renault, the oldest and the most morally repugnant of the conspirators. On the tide of his emotional reaction, Belvidira is able to lead her husband to the betrayal of the conspiracy. Although the main conspirators have already been apprehended by the time of his betrayal, thus undercutting the public significance of Jaffeir's action, this fact does not diminish his consciousness of guilt. There is no possible resolution of the conflict of love and honor, because these concepts no longer exist as moral ideals capable of being reconciled, as in Dryden's heroic plays. Jaffeir is forced to choose between life with Belvidira or death with his friend Pierre. He chooses death.

Every human relationship, every political act in *Venice Preserved* seems tainted by sexual motivation. Even the friendship of Jaffeir and Pierre is at times represented in imagery that is unequivocally sexual. This pandemic sexuality cooperates in the representation of the action to constrict the moral vision of the play, and, insofar as *Venice Preserved* bears a general political significance, it is that the world of politics reflects this fundamental moral ambiguity. Thus, the so-called Nicky-Nacky scenes must be seen as more than a satiric, political attack (though they are that) on Anthony Cooper, earl of Shaftesbury, perhaps the most important of the Whig leaders during the Exclusion Crisis, or, in dramatic terms, as merely more or less offensive bits of comic relief. Otway's presentation of the perverse sexual relationship of Antonio, himself a senator, with Aquilina, formerly a mistress to Pierre, so precisely echoes and counterpoints the action on the "serious" level of the play that a sense of dramatic equivalence is established that qualifies the audience's understanding of both the senators and the conspirators.

Venice Preserved is the best known of Otway's plays, perhaps because it is the most accessible to modern audiences. In a sense, the public and private dimensions of *The History and Fall of Caius Marius* and *The Orphan* are made to converge in the series of contradictory stances that Jaffeir is forced to adopt. Even though the oppositions that Jaffeir faces are

fully articulated, they are perplexed and problematic. Jaffeir, like Antony in Dryden's *All for Love: Or, The World Well Lost* (pr. 1677), decides on death as the resolution of conflict, but, since his dramatic existence is so much closer to the mean of human experience, his death cannot be considered an act of romantic transcendence. In *Venice Preserved*, even more completely than in *All for Love*, the death of the central character represents a tragic denial of life.

OTHER MAJOR WORKS

POETRY: *The Poet's Complaint of His Muse*, 1680; *Windsor Castle*, 1685.

TRANSLATION: *The History of the Triumvirates*, 1686 (of various works).

MISCELLANEOUS: *Thomas Otway*, 1903; *The Complete Works of Thomas Otway*, 1926 (3 volumes); *The Works of Thomas Otway: Plays, Poems, and Love-Letters*, 1932, 1968 (2 volumes; J. C. Ghosh, editor).

BIBLIOGRAPHY

Armistead, J. M. *Four Restoration Playwrights: A Reference Guide to Thomas Shadwell, Aphra Behn, Nathaniel Lee, and Thomas Otway.* Boston: G. K. Hall & Co., 1984. A superb reference tool, bringing Otway's secondary bibliography through 1981.

Derrick, Samuel. *The Dramatic Censor; Remarks upon the Tragedy of "Venice Preserved."* Los Angeles: William Andrews Clark Memorial Library of University of California, 1985. Reprint of 1752 edition. Derrick was a well-known figure in London literary circles, and this reading is perceptive even if heavily moralistic.

Ham, Roswell Gray. *Otway and Lee: Biography from a Baroque Age.* New Haven, Conn.: Yale University Press, 1931. This volume is an excellent study of two Restoration dramatists whose careers ran parallel on the turbulent London stage. A chapter titled "Shakespeare and Otway" studies Otway's indebtedness to his famous predecessor, and an appreciative chapter, "Venice Preserved," examines that play and the reasons for its success.

Johnson, Samuel. *Lives of the English Poets.* Edited by George Birkbeck Hill. Vol. 1. Oxford, England:

Clarendon Press, 1905. Johnson comments briefly on some of the works and moralizes typically on the life: "Want of morals or of decency did not in those days exclude any man from the company of the wealthy and the gay if he brought with him any powers of entertainment." Hill's notes are excellent.

Munns, Jessica. *Restoration Politics and Drama: The Plays of Thomas Otway, 1675-1683.* Newark: University of Delaware Press, 1995. A major study, drawing on insights from New Historicism, feminist criticism, Lacanian psychology, and other postmodernist approaches. Valuable notes and bibliography.

Noel, Roden. Introduction to *Thomas Otway.* New York: Charles Scribner's Sons, 1903. Collection includes *Don Carlos, Prince of Spain, The Orphan, The Soldier's Fortune,* and *Venice Preserved.* In his introduction, Noel compares Otway to the Greek tragedians and analyzes the four plays he has chosen. An appendix prints six letters supposed to have been written to the actress Elizabeth Barry.

Otway, Thomas. *The Complete Works of Thomas Otway.* Edited by Montague Summers. 3 vols. London: Nonesuch Press, 1926. Reprint. New York: AMS Press, 1967. Summers's long introduction is informative and readable in its gossipy, anecdotal approach. The explanatory notes are brisk, and the source notes are rich with references.

Pollard, Hazel M. Batzer. *From Heroics to Sentimentalism: A Study of Thomas Otway's Tragedies.* Salzburg: Institut für Englische Sprache und Literatur, Universität Salzburg, 1974. Pollard traces the development in Otway's tragedies away from the heroic tragedies of his time toward the mounting psychology of sentimentalism. Among the discussions are "*Caius Marius*: Emancipation from the Heroic" and "*The Orphan*: Domestic Tragedy."

Taylor, Aline Mackenzie. *Next to Shakespeare: Otway's "Venice Preserv'd" and "The Orphan" and Their History on the London Stage.* Durham, N.C.: Duke University Press, 1950. An invaluable account of the stage histories of these two plays, with a list of performances, an excellent bibliography, an essay on Otway's reputation, and an index of actors.

Warner, Kerstin P. *Thomas Otway.* Boston: Twayne, 1982. A fine overview in the format of the Twayne series. A chronology is followed by a biographical sketch and chapters on Otway's political views, Otway's first plays (1675-1678), the playwright's "peak season" (1678-1680), and a chapter titled "After the Playhouses Merged (1682-1683)." A succinct annotated bibliography completes this essential work.

James E. Maloney,
updated by Frank Day

ERIC OVERMYER

Born: Boulder, Colorado; September 25, 1951

PRINCIPAL DRAMA
Native Speech, pr. 1983, pb. 1984
On the Verge: Or, The Geography of Yearning, pr. 1985, pb. 1986
The Double Bass, pr. 1986 (with Harry Newman; adaptation of Patrick Süskind's play *Der Kontrabuss*)
In a Pig's Valise, pr. 1986, pb. 1989 (with August Darnell)
In Perpetuity Throughout the Universe, pr. 1988, pb. 1989
Kafka's Radio, pr. 1990
Don Quixote de la Jolla, pr. 1990, pb. 1993
The Heliotrope Bouquet by Scott Joplin and Louis Chauvin, pr. 1991, pb. 1993
Dark Rapture, pr. 1992, pb. 1993

Eric Overmyer: Collected Plays, pb. 1993
*The Marriage of Figaro/Figaro Gets a
    Divorce*, pr. 1994, pb. 1996 (also known
    as *Figaro/Figaro*; music by Kim D.
    Sherman; adaptation of Pierre-Augustin
    Caron de Beaumarchais's *The Marriage
    of Figaro* and Odon von Horvath's *Figaro
    Gets a Divorce*)
Duke Kahanamoko vs. the Surfnappers,
    pr. 1994
The Dalai Lama Goes Three for Four,
    pr. 1995
Amphitryon, pr. 1995; pb. 1996 (adaptation
    of Henrich von Kleist's play)
Alki, pb. 1997 (adaptation of Henrik Ibsen's
    play *Peer Gynt*)
Don Quixote de Milwaukee, pr. 2000

OTHER LITERARY FORMS

Although Eric Overmyer's reputation rests
primarily on his stage plays, he has also written
for film and television, most notably for such
shows as *St. Elsewhere*, *The Days and Nights
of Molly Dodd*, and the television movie *Rear
Window* (1998), in which he blended the Cornell Woolrich short story with details from ac-
tor-producer Christopher Reeve's book about
life.

ACHIEVEMENTS

Eric Overmyer has received grants and fel-
lowships from the McKnight Foundation, the
National Endowment for the Arts, the New
York Foundation for the Arts, the Rockefeller
Foundation, and Le Compte Du Nouy Foundation. In
1987 he received a grant to write a play for the South
Coast Repertory Theater in Costa Mesa, California.

BIOGRAPHY

Eric Overmyer was born in Boulder, Colorado,
and was raised in Seattle, Washington. He attended
Reed College in Oregon, majoring in theater. After
graduation, he did graduate work at the Asolo Con-
servatory, Florida State University, and at Brooklyn
College and the City College of New York. After

Eric Overmyer in 1987. (AP/Wide World Photos)

serving as the literary manager of Playwrights Horizon from 1982 to 1984, he was associate artist at the
Center Stage in Baltimore. He taught at the Yale
School of Drama, where he was visiting associate
professor of playwriting, 1991-1992, at the Yale Repertory Theatre, where he was associate artist, 1991-
1992, and at the Mark Taper Forum Playwriting
Workshop, where he was a mentor, 1992. He has
lived in New York and New Orleans and worked in
Los Angeles. He married actress Ellen McElduff. He
wrote extensively for television and in 2000 was a

nominee for best writer in a miniseries or movie for his work on *Homicide: The Movie*. In 2000 he also became a coproducer of the American Broadcasting Companies television series *Gideon's Crossing*.

ANALYSIS

Like Mac Wellman and Timberlake Wertenbaker, Eric Overmyer writes "language plays," and his plays are more concerned with language and ideas than they are with action or plot. He has much in common with British playwright Tom Stoppard in that both delight in linguistic virtuosity and cloak their social criticism in puns, metaphors, and language that is stretched, pulled apart, and then reassembled. In his later plays, Overmyer has reduced the amount of wordplay and turned to the world of crime, a world he has successfully written about for television, which may be where his talents will take him.

NATIVE SPEECH

Native Speech, Overmyer's first play, established him as a wordsmith, a writer of language plays, for it includes language that is at once foreign and understandable to audiences, and it is language that is spoken by the natives of a futuristic urban world in which violence and drugs are the norm. Hungry Mother, the protagonist, is a deejay who operates his underground (unlicensed) radio station from a cramped studio "constructed from the detritus of Western Civ" under the city streets. Like the host on Eric Bogosian's *Talk Radio* (pr. 1984, pb. 1988) or Robin Williams's role in *Good Morning, Vietnam* (1987), Hungry Mother is hip and fast talking, but his banter is harder, edgier, and more "on the verge."

The allusion of Hungry Mother, who defines himself as the "argot argonaut" and "the vandal of the vernacular," to William Shakespeare suggests that he, like Macduff, is powerful because both are "not of woman born," but he is reminded that "Mistah Kurtz, Mothah, he dead." The reference to Joseph Conrad's *Heart of Darkness* (1899 serial; 1902) reminds audiences of human mortality and the darkness of the human heart. Hungry Mother not only supplies his listeners with "dope" about drug prices and availability but also with unusual weather reports such as "weather outlook for continued existential dread" and

"intermittent bouts of apocalyptic epiphany." He even touts what he believes are nonexistent musical groups such as Hoover and the Navajos. Unfortunately, what Hungry Mother fabricates becomes real: Hoover and the Navajos visit his studio, provide parodies of contemporary rock groups, and destroy his studio; and his fictitious drug reports are taken seriously by addicts and law officials. Overmyer thereby illustrates the awesome power of the media. According to Hungry Mother, a "fictional fact, a metaphor," "comes back on me."

At play's end, all of Hungry Mother's attempts, through language, to belong to what is essentially a nonwhite culture fail. Some street hoodlums turn on him and beat him; the Mook, a drug-dealing pimp, informs on him to the police; and Janis, who looked to him for assistance, commits suicide. In a long soliloquy, Hungry Mother vacillates between "native language" and formal English, and it is in the latter that he faces the truth about his situation.

ON THE VERGE

In *On the Verge*, his second play, Overmyer continues his verbal acrobatics as he presents three nineteenth century American women traveling through terra incognita, an interior suggestive of a psychic terrain like the unconscious. The three women journey through space and time, 1888 to 1955, as they encounter an abominable snowman, a cannibal who takes on the appearance and speech of his latest repast (a German aviator), and a troll toll taker before they reach Nicky's Havana Paradise, a rock-and-roll haven.

Overmyer uses Alexandra, a malaprop character, to display his wit. She is responsible for confusing "refurbished" with "refreshed," exploring the composition of "imagination" ("image" plus "native"), and supplying the alliterative rhyme "A troll's toll. How droll." As in *Native Speech*, there are numerous allusions, but most of them are anachronistic, such as references to Burma Shave ads, which themselves contain rhymes, "I Like Ike" pins that help the women decipher "Hec-kwhod-ont" ("Heck, who don't?"), and Shakespeare's *The Tempest* (pr. 1611), in which the line, "O brave new world, that has such creatures in it," is given a new twist. The anachronisms include a loofah, a Kodak camera, an eggbeater (regarded as a totem by anthropologist Mary), and a hula hoop. The women "osmose" these items, which, like a time capsule, represent American culture, but Overmyer's selection reflects his criticism of that culture.

Fanny, the most conservative of the trio, is the medium for Overmyer's political commentary. She reads the anachronistic right-wing *National Review*, refuses to wear the trousers that Alexandra recommends, and is married to Republican Grover, who has her declared legally dead while she is absent from her home in Terra Haute, Indiana, a recognizable territory. At the end of the play, she finds romance with Nicky, Alexandra writes rock-and-roll lyrics, and Mary continues her travel into the future.

IN PERPETUITY THROUGHOUT THE UNIVERSE

Like his earlier plays, Overmyer's *In Perpetuity Throughout the Universe* concerns language, in this case, ghostwriting, primarily for anti-Semitic and anti-Asian hate mongers who believe in conspiracy theories. The Montage (the word suggests editing) Agency, Christine Penderecki's employer, is only open at night, the perfect setting for a loose plot involving a white conspiracy to take over the world. Christine and Dennis Wu, a colleague, fall in love and discover the dangerous scheme in Ampersand Qwerty's (the unusual name may be traced to the first six letters in the top row of a computer keyboard) *Yellow Emperor*, "a sort of anti-*Uncle Tom's Cabin*" to be published at an opportune time, one in which a recession has produced paranoia book buyers: "No one ever went broke overestimating the vulgarity of the American public." Qwerty's earlier manuscript was about ZOG, the Zionist Occupational Government. *Yellow Emperor* had been edited by the Jewish Lefkovitz, who has mysteriously disappeared, and there are conspiracy theories to explain his probable demise.

The geography of hate that permeates the play extends to various other conspiracy theories. In fact, the question is asked, "How can you explain the world without a conspiracy theory?" In a litany of ridiculous theories some stand out: "Contraception, a double-bind genocidal plot" and the creation of "an ethnic bomb." The Vatican is also thought to be responsible for Abraham Lincoln's assassination. Christine and Dennis, the "good guys" in the play, have lists of things and people that they despise. When they decide to destroy Qwerty's manuscript, they find that some of their copies are missing and decide that they, too, must be the victims of a conspiracy. Adding to the "conspiratorial" atmosphere of the play is Overmyer's insistence that four of the actors play two or more roles. Having the actor who plays the "good" Dennis also play the "bad" Tai-Tung Tranh adds to the difficulty of determining whom to trust. By the end of the play, even the apparently irrelevant chain-letter scenes are pulled into the conspiracy motif.

DARK RAPTURE

Overmyer's *Dark Rapture* is a theatrical film noir, a kind of dark crime thriller in the tradition of Raymond Chandler, whom Overmyer quoted in *In a Pig's Valise*, and Dashiell Hammett, but the mood is not consistently bleak because Overmyer seemingly cannot resist using his comedic talents. The play concerns the efforts of Ray, a would-be screenwriter (Overmyer's other occupation), to start life over again with the five million dollars he takes from his burning house in California. The money belongs to his wife, Julia, the femme fatale of the play, who is intent on producing films, but she got the money from money-launderers, Vegas and Lexington, who now want the funds back. They enlist the help of Tony and Ron, Armenian hoodlums whose murder of a Turkish American car salesperson serves primarily to demonstrate the ethnic prejudice common in Overmyer's plays. Their efforts to track Ray down take them to Seattle, San Francisco, New Orleans, Santa Barbara (California), and Tampa and finally Key West (Florida), a setting reminiscent of *Key Largo*, a 1948 film noir featuring Humphrey Bogart. Unfortunately, everywhere that Ray goes has "peaked," a word that suggests the decay in American life that Ray professes to like.

Ray cannot hide forever, despite acquiring a new name and a fake passport. Actually, identity is a main theme in the play. Overmyer's practice of having actors play more than one part adds to the identity theme. In addition, some of the characters, including Ray, are not whom they seem to be. For example,

Babcock is actually Jose Marti Chibas Valenzuela, Renee's father, who may have been the second shooter in President John F. Kennedy, Jr.'s assassination, but who finally is revealed as Renee's lover. When the mob finally closes in on Ray, he insists that he is Ray Avila, rather than Ray Gaines; and Julia, who realizes that identifying Ray as her husband might cause her death, helps him deceive the mobsters. Two suitcases in Ray's possession contain not the missing funds, but screenplays, one of which is *Dark Rapture*. Julia is freed to make films, and Ray and his girlfriend Max, who has the two suitcases with the money, are released to spend the money.

Dark Rapture contains several typical Overmyer experiments with language. A Seattle bartender uses "Californicate," and "Ray" is subjected to linguistic stretching: "Ray. El Ray. Ex-Ray. El Ray-o ex." Characters also allude to literary texts, such as when Ray talks, like Huckleberry Finn, about "lighting out for the territory." There are relevant, "cute" sub-themes, one of which concerns screenwriting. Many of the characters in the play create their own scenarios about the past and the future. In fact, Ray's attempt to "reinvent" himself in really an effort to write a new scenario for himself.

OTHER MAJOR WORK

TELEPLAY: *Rear Window,* 1998 (with Larry Gross).

BIBLIOGRAPHY

Andreach, Robert J. *Creating the Self in the Contemporary American Theatre.* Carbondale: Southern Illinois University Press, 1998. Andreach asserts that Overmyer's *Native Speech* is about the collapse of the old world and that *On the Verge* concerns efforts to build a new world. Both plays, which are about language, involve people assimilating images from the unconscious with objects from the real world in order to survive.

_____. "Overmyer's *Amphitryon:* Adapting Kleist for a Contemporary Audience." *Papers on Language and Literature* 36 (2000): 158-176. Andreach discusses several versions of the classical myth about Jupiter, Amphitryon, and Alcmena, and he argues that Overmyer's Surrealistic adaptation modernizes the play at the same time that it contains anachronistic elements, cuts the long speeches, makes the marital relationship of the couple more contemporary and credible, and emphasizes love's irrational power to motivate and affirm life.

DiGaetani, John L. *A Search for a Postmodern Theater: Interviews with Contemporary Playwrights.* New York: Greenwood Press, 1991. In his interview, Overmyer explains that his main concern in writing is language itself; naturalism, he believes, is best served by film and television. Because film is really a director's medium, rather than a writer's, Overmyer prefers writing for the theater, but his writing for film and television provides him with the money to support his playwriting.

Peterson, William. "The Heliotrope Bouquet by Scott Joplin and Louis Chauvin." *Theatre Journal* 44 (1992): 403-404. Peterson describes Overmyer's work as a "memory play in which Joplin's memories clash with Chauvin's." While praising the production's strong visual images, Peterson is not sympathetic with the treatment of Joplin as the Protestant stereotype of a failed black artist.

Wainscott, Ronal, and Kathy Fletcher. Review of *On the Verge: Or, The Geography of Yearning,* by Eric Overmyer. *Theatre Journal* 37 (1985): 357-358. The reviewers discuss the contrast between nineteenth century values and twentieth century ones in the play and comment on the language, which provides another contrast between contemporary slang and Victorian formal, polite discourse.

Thomas L. Erskine

ROCHELLE OWENS

Born: Brooklyn, New York; April 2, 1936

PRINCIPAL DRAMA

Futz, pb. 1961, pr. 1965, revised pb. 1968 (music by Tom O'Horgan)

The String Game, pr. 1965, pb. 1968

Istanboul, pr. 1965, pb. 1968

Homo, pr. 1966, pb. 1968

Beclch, pr. 1966, pb. 1968

Farmer's Almanac, pr. 1968, pb. 1974

Futz and What Came After, pb. 1968 (includes *Beclch*, *Homo*, *The String Game*, and *Istanboul*)

The Queen of Greece, pr. 1969

Kontraption, pb. 1971, pr. 1978 (one act)

The Karl Marx Play, pb. 1971 (one act; in *The Best Short Plays of 1971*, Stanley Richards, editor), revised pr., pb. 1973 (two acts; music by Galt MacDermot)

He Wants Shih!, pb. 1972, pr. 1975 (one act)

The Karl Marx Play and Others, pb. 1974 (includes *Kontraption*, *He Wants Shih!*, *Farmer's Almanac*, *Coconut Folk-singer*, and *O. K. Certaldo*)

Emma Instigated Me, pb. 1976, pr. 1977 (expanded)

Mountain Rites, pb. 1978 (one act)

Chucky's Hunch, pr. 1981, pb. 1982

Who Do You Want, Peire Vidal?, pr. 1982, pb. 1986

Plays by Rochelle Owens, pb. 2000 (includes *Chucky's Hunch*, *Futz*, *Kontraption*, and *Three Front*)

OTHER LITERARY FORMS

Rochelle Owens began writing as a poet and has published several volumes of poetry as well as numerous poems in various journals and small magazines. Her poetry is lyric and metaphysical, depending heavily on juxtapositions that often involve fairly wide leaps between ideas or attitudes. In addition to conventional poetic devices, Owens makes consider-

able use of typographical devices: The spacing between words, phrases, and lines is important both to the sense and to the rhythm of her verse, and she often uses capitalization and punctuation (or the lack of it) in an arresting way, sometimes forming unusual patterns on the page with words or parts of words. These appear to be voice cues, and her voice is, as Toby Olson has written (in a symposium devoted to Owens's work), the controlling element of her poetry. Wit and humor are also essential ingredients, but Owens is by no means a poet of the intellect only; her poetry conveys emotion and sensuality as she probes deeply into her subject, expressing her discoveries energetically if not always with the greatest lucidity.

Owens writes about a variety of subjects, but her chief interests are political and humanistic, combined, for example, in "Purple Worms of Vengeance," a poem that contrasts a fat, gluttonous congressman with a poor Chicano child. In the same volume— *I Am the Babe of Joseph Stalin's Daughter: Poems, 1961-1971* (1972)—are a number of poems about her "Deebler Woman," such as "Deebler Woman's Thoughts on the Nature of the Universe," which is a working woman's meditation on her lot in life and the pleasure she gets from going to see motion pictures: "the movies don't/ really tell it/ honestly/ but I like it." "Radiant Heat," dedicated to her husband, is a moving love lyric about how, through the "radiant heat" of two bodies, true contact is achieved. "Song of the Loving Father of the Stuffed Son" captures the real agony, partly expressed in jokes, felt by an affluent Jewish lawyer whose son is a Cuban-loving Marxist. Owens's Jewishness does not express itself in modish self-hate; she is entirely capable of satiric attacks against Jewish anti-Zionists and others, as in "A Poem for Jewish Collaborators Who Betray Their Ancestral Homeland Israel" or "The Camel Smiles at the Ignorance of the Assimilated Man." Beneath the political, social, or economic concerns, however, is the fundamental human one: "I love my family! I want them to laugh!" cries Karl Marx, even as he recognizes "I am the coming judgment!" ("The Voluminous Agony of Karl Marx"). Owens expands on these themes in one of her most celebrated dramas, *The Karl Marx Play.*

In her later poetry, as in her dramatic work, Owens has continued to experiment with form and content. She sums up her own efforts succinctly and accurately in her note to her poetry collection *Shemuel* (1979): "Imagination is generator of the word as act/event. In *Shemuel* the journey begun in *The Joe Eighty-two Creation Poems* [1974] and *The Joe Chronicles II* [1978] continues to explore through patterns of force the conjunction of the old and the new, the spiritual and the physical."

ACHIEVEMENTS

Throughout her career, Rochelle Owens has received support for her writing from major foundations. In 1965, she received grants from the Rockefeller Office for Advanced Drama Research and the

Rochelle Owens in 1968. (AP/Wide World Photos)

Ford Foundation. The next year she won a Creative Artists Public Service grant, and in 1968, she was awarded a Yale University Drama School fellowship. She received a Guggenheim Fellowship in 1971 and a National Endowment for the Arts grant in 1974, followed by a Rockefeller grant in 1975. Her plays have won Obie Awards in 1968, 1971, and 1982. She also received *The Villager* award for *Chucky's Hunch* in 1982, a New York Drama Critics Circle award in 1983, and a Bellagio fellowship from the Rockefeller Foundation, Italy, in 1993. She served as distinguished writer-in-residence at the University of Southwestern Louisiana in 1997. She has also taught creative writing at the University of Oklahoma and served as writer-in-residence for Brown Univeristy.

Critics have generally shown interest in her plays, which have been reviewed in *The New York Times* as well as *The Village Voice*, often with sympathy and sensitivity, despite their unconventional subject matter and sometimes surrealist manner. Her first successful play, *Futz*, was made into a motion picture by Tom O'Horgan, who directed several of Owens's plays and who also wrote music for them. She is recognized as a major talent among Off-Broadway playwrights, and she is a founding member of the New York Theatre Strategy. Several of her plays were first produced by Café La Mama, either in New York or in Europe, where her work has attracted a considerable amount of critical attention, both favorable and unfavorable. Owens is a member of the Dramatists Guild, of the New Dramatists Committee, of the American Society of Composers, Authors, and Publishers, and of the Authors Guild.

BIOGRAPHY

Rochelle Owens was born Rochelle Bass, daughter of Maxwell and Molly (Adler) Bass. Reared in Brooklyn, Owens was educated in New York City public schools and was graduated from Lafayette High School in 1953. She was married to David Owens in 1956 and divorced in 1959. She began writing poetry early. When George Economou saw "Groshl Monkeys Horses" in a 1960 issue of *Yugen*, he invited her to submit some of her poems to *Trobar*, which he had just begun editing with Robert Kelly.

She sent him a packet of verse, many of the poems appearing in *Trobar* (II), including "Humble humble pinati." Trobar Press also brought out her first book of poems, *Not Be Essence That Cannot Be* (1961), simultaneously with Paul Blackburn's *The Nets*. In 1962, Owens and Economou were married, and many of her books subsequently have been dedicated to her husband, a poet in his own right, who has also appeared in some of her plays (he played the Robed Man, for example, in *Istanboul*).

Although written several years earlier, *Futz* was first produced by the Tyrone Guthrie Workshop in Minneapolis on October 10, 1965, where it played for a single performance. Later revised, it was produced in New York by the Café La Mama Theatre Troupe on March 1, 1967. During this period, several other plays were produced in New York and elsewhere. On February 12, 1965, the Judson Poets Theatre produced *The String Game*, and on September 12, *Istanbul*. Andre Gregory produced *Beclch* at the Theatre of the Living Arts with the Southwark Theatre Company in Philadelphia on December 20, 1966. The controversial production was at least in part responsible for the termination of relations between Gregory and the Theatre of the Living Arts.

By then, Owens's association with Café La Mama had already begun, and *Homo* was taken on tour, to Europe in the summer of 1966, where it played in Stockholm, and later in New York. O'Horgan's production of *Futz* followed early the next year and was made into a film by Commonwealth United in 1969, O'Horgan again directing and Owens contributing additional dialogue for the screenplay. Portions of *The String Game* and *Beclch* were televised by the Columbia Broadcasting System (CBS) and Public Broadcasting Service (PBS). On April 12, 1969, Café La Mama staged two plays: *The Queen of Greece*, a curtain raiser, and *Homo*.

Owens continued writing poetry during this period and began giving readings of her verse throughout the United States, including appearances at universities such as Princeton and Columbia. She has made several recordings, reading both her own verse and some of the primitive and archaic poetry that has obviously influenced her writing.

In the 1970's, several new plays by Owens were produced, most notably *The Karl Marx Play*, which opened at the American Place Theatre in New York on March 16, 1973. For this production, the original one-act version, first published in Stanley Richards's *The Best Short Plays of 1971*, was revised and expanded to a two-act play. The music for the play was composed and directed by Galt MacDermot, with Mel Shapiro in charge of overall direction. The production was honored by the New York Drama Critics Circle. *He Wants Shih!* opened the spring season of Theatre Strategy at the Gate Theater in New York on April 1, 1975, and in 1977, the American Place Theatre performed *Emma Instigated Me* as a work-in-progress, expanded from the original version published in 1976. *Chucky's Hunch*, a play for a single actor, first opened Off-Off-Broadway at the Theater for the New City on March 22, 1981, with Kevin O'Connor. It was revived, again with O'Connor, on February 18, 1982, when it opened at the Harold Clurman Theater in New York. Later in the same year, *Who Do You Want, Peire Vidal?* opened at the Theater for the New City on May 8.

Owens's chief interests remain poetry and drama, and doubtless each nourishes the other. She has written several unpublished works, including the radio play "A Guerre Trois" (1991), and she has written and produced video works, such as "Oklahoma Too" (1987). Although many of her published works in the 1990's were poetry collections, a volume containing four of her plays, *Plays by Rochelle Owens*, was published in 2000. Her reading performances at the Museum of Modern Art, the Guggenheim Museum, and the Whitney Museum are popular with the artistic community of New York.

ANALYSIS

Rochelle Owens first achieved success in the theater in the 1960's. Because she is both a poet and a playwright, her plays contain poetic imagery. In her *Who's Who in America* entry, Owens states that "Creativity, idealism and mental concentration have enabled me to pursue the world of ideas, transforming itself always into art."

FUTZ

Futz was Owens's first play to attract significant critical attention. It is about a gentle farmer, Cy Futz, in love with his sow, Amanda. He lives alone and raises vegetables for himself and his sow, but the people of the community will not leave him alone. Majorie Satz, the town whore, fancies him and finally inveigles him into a three-way sexual encounter with her and his pig, but Cy prefers Amanda.

Cy's amorous devotion to his pig has unfortunate consequences for Oscar Loop, who hears the grunts and groans coming from Cy's barn. The sounds and sight of Cy's lovemaking antagonize Oscar to the point that he murders randy Ann Fox, whom he has brought with him and with whom he is engaging in some amorous activity of his own: He is driven insane by the idea of evil and his need to wipe it out. Oscar is arrested for the murder, and subsequently Sheriff Tom Sluck and Bill Marjoram come to arrest Cy, too. Meanwhile, Majorie has become worse than ever, upsetting the Satz family so much that her brother Ned resolves to take matters into his own hands and vindicate the family's loss of honor.

In jail immediately before his execution, Oscar is visited by his mother, who gives an account of her son's conception and birth. Oscar is obviously mad, thinking that the "spice-seed insects" he gives his mother have miraculous powers. The suggestions of incestuous feelings between them are quite broad, but Mrs. Loop seems interested mostly in her position of respectability and as an object of sorrow in the community.

Neither Oscar's execution nor Cy's murder by Brother Ned has any effect on the sexual mores of the community. Two characters, Buford and Sugford, take Majorie (in a "whorey mood") with them to a field. Majorie suggests that she and her friends kill Cy's pig, offering to do it herself when they demur. They go as Brother Ned prepares to kill Cy because, he says, "You make my brains red!"

Futz thus dramatizes and satirizes some of the worst aspects of humankind's vicious animal nature and counterpoints them to its gentler manifestations. Cy intends no harm to anyone and asks only to be left alone. The members of his community find his besti-ality intolerable but are oblivious to the far more damaging consequences of their own animality toward one another, as in Oscar Loop's treatment of Ann Fox, or in her treatment of him (she leads him on shamelessly, unwittingly preparing the scene for her own murder). The scenes in the field between Majorie and Buford and Sugford are devoid of any of the feelings that Cy has for Amanda; likewise, Mrs. Loop's feelings for her son are a perversion of genuine motherly love. Nothing softens the conclusion of the play: Owens intends that the full force of human brutality should be felt, and it is.

Clive Barnes, in a review that appeared in *The New York Times* in October, 1968, called *Futz* a conventional play about an unconventional subject. The rapid alternation of scenes is hardly novel, and neither is the use of a narrator, who gives stage directions that are dispensable and makes choral comments that are not. The music and dance of the production in New York by O'Horgan doubtless filled out the play, which by itself can hardly take up an evening.

THE STRING GAME

The String Game, Owens's next play, is similarly conventional in structure and in theme as well; only its setting is novel: Greenland. A group of Eskimo are sitting around in a hut playing the string game, guessing at the patterns or pictures that the string makes, usually erotic ones. Father Bontempo, a Maltese priest who is with them, tries to get their minds off sex. He objects to their customs of wife exchange, adult breast-feeding, and other heathenish practices. For their part, the Eskimo cannot understand Bontempo's objections to what they regard as natural behavior.

Cecil, a half-breed (he is half German), also tries to get the Eskimo interested in something else—business. He suggests various schemes, such as a herring factory, the manufacture of clay pipes, and so on, to help them get ahead. Personally very ambitious, he is baffled by the lack of ambition among the others and enlists Father Bontempo's aid in a plan to involve everyone in a shoe-selling business about which he learns from a matchbook cover. At first, the Eskimo resist, seeing nothing creative about this venture as compared with the string game; in any case, they are comfortable enough with their government checks. Under Bontempo's persuasion, however, they acquiesce, though still with misgivings. They recognize only too well how "it's the outer world that wants to change the inner one. The foreign influences." When Bontempo dies, choking on the pasta and sauce with which Cecil had bribed him, the shoe-selling scheme dies with him. The Eskimo throw Cecil out and resume the string game.

ISTANBOUL

The evils of foreign influences are dramatized in *Istanboul* and *Homo* as well. In *Istanboul*, set in fifteenth century Constantinople, the crusaders Godfrigh and Baldwin try to make a commercial deal with Saint Mary of Egypt, while Godfrigh's wife, Alice, and her friend Gertrude compete for the favor of the Byzantine dancer, Leo, also desired by two native women, Mary and Zoe. A robed man watches most of the action of the play in silence. In a religious/sexual frenzy, Saint Mary cuts off Godfrigh's leg, which results in Godfrigh's death and Alice's widowhood. The play ends as Alice lies in bed with Leo, an hour before the Saracens arrive to overthrow Byzantine rule.

HOMO

If effetism, decadence, religious ecstasy and corruption, and the mutual attraction and repulsion of East and West are major themes in *Istanboul*, white European racism and greed are the themes of *Homo*. Bernice is the blonde bitch-goddess worshiped by the horse-man and the Asiatics in the play, while Elizabeth, a fiftyish, fleshy European female, is abused by Asiatic workmen but is also adored by them, especially when she gives them her sugarcoated fingers to suck. Thus, competition is set up between Bernice (the goddess) and Elizabeth (the mother archetype), objects of primal masculine drives. Elizabeth's husband, the Dutch merchant Gelderen, is also abused by Asiatics, officials who allow him to do business at the price of self-abasement. The time shifts between the mid-nineteenth century and the present, and the so-called Asiatics may actually be played (the stage directions tell us) by Mediterranean types, who speak much better English than Gelderen. Owens thus does

not depend on mere verisimilitude to drive home her satiric point about cultural imperialism or to dramatize her themes.

BECLCH

Beclch (pronounced Bek-lek) is one of Owens's most ambitious and difficult plays and her first full-length one. Here she strikingly unveils the violence, lust, sadism, and brutality that she sees at the heart of perverted human nature. Beclch is a power-maddened woman living in Africa, manipulating Yago and others to satisfy her desire to rule supreme among the poor specimens of humankind that surround her. She is unleashed passion personified, finding no reason at all to keep her impulses in check. Succeeding in making her husband, Yago, king through means both cruel and disgusting as well as (to him) extremely painful, she later becomes bored and persuades him to die by self-strangulation, whereupon she becomes queen. She plans to marry her lover Jose, but he recognizes her for what she is, refuses to participate fully in her activities, and eventually runs away, leaving her husbandless and thus ripe for ritual slaughter. Her depravity is best expressed by her words as she faces death: "I hope I drool like an animal."

From all accounts, *Beclch* was a failure, if an interesting one in some respects. Lavishly produced in New York after its original opening in Philadelphia, it was condemned even by usually sympathetic critics, such as Clive Barnes, who found the play badly written or at least badly played and reeking of bad taste. Julius Novick commented on the play's failure finally to shock because it overshot its mark. If excess is its theme, it should not have been allowed to drown in its own excesses.

THE KARL MARX PLAY

Plenitude is also a quality of *The Karl Marx Play*, but here Owens exercises firmer control over her material, even as she allows her innate lyricism full expression. Owens all but abandons traditional concepts of plot in favor of a representation of Karl Marx, the man and the historical figure, surrounded by family, friends, and—in the anachronistic character of Leadbelly (Huddie Ledbetter, 1888-1949), the famed black American blues singer—a nagging and insistent conscience. Like the biblical Job, Marx suffers from boils and must force himself finally to go to the British Museum and write his famous *Das Kapital*. He has reveries about his romantic and aristocratic wife, Jenny von Westphalen, and he thinks of her voluptuous breasts when he should be concocting his theories on economics. Indeed, one of the running jokes in the play is that Marx hates economics and must be driven to write his treatise. His friend and supporter, Friedrich Engels, also emerges as a comical figure. Very *mittel European*, as the stage directions indicate, he speaks with a German accent and, as the heir to his family's manufacturing concern, provides the funds on which Marx and his family live. The language throughout the play is vivid, idiomatic according to character, and often raunchy. Songs are frequent and help to emphasize the essential lyric quality of the drama; in fact, the play opens with Leadbelly singing a kind of hymn. Hymns, however, are by no means the chief kind of song the audience hears.

In keeping with its lyric approach to drama, *The Karl Marx Play* moves back and forth in time easily: One must not look for linear development here. Owens's exuberance is not confusing but refreshing and enlivening, aided by Galt MacDermot's music. *The Karl Marx Play* received many favorable reviews, vindicating Owens's intentions; she says in her author's note:

> The play evolved out of investigations of the circumstances and events, factual and imaginary, of the life of Karl Marx. It is a play with music whose story is told as much by its imagery and tonal "meanings" as it is by its plot. It is a theatrical experiencing of the extreme humanness of Karl Marx, a vision of the man's spirit and fate.

The experiments of Owens's poetry pay off handsomely in this work, which, one critic has said, is as much about the creative process as about Karl Marx. Marxism has never appeared less doctrinaire than it does here, thanks to the humanity that Owens reveals underlying the historical facts.

HE WANTS SHIH!

As restless in dramatic experiments as she is in her verse, Owens has continued to explore the frontiers of her art in other plays, such as *Kontraption* and *He Wants Shih!* The latter was begun as early as 1967 but waited for eight years to be produced. Written partly in a kind of pseudo-Chinese, it is one of Owens's most richly poetic dramas; the Chinese words act as images and enhance through sound and rhythm other aspects of the diction. The play's multiply punning title is ambiguous; in a note, Owens says that *Shih* is pronounced *shur* and means "Law, Command, Poetry." Lan, the young emperor of China and the last of the Manchu Dynasty, strives for complete self-fulfillment to the extent that he is willing to surrender all worldly responsibility in his quest. That quest, Owens says in her author's note, is "toward the supernatural . . . toward an ultimate transformation: the means of entering the Unseen by force, of driving his way into the Power over the world." Instructed by his tutor, a monk named Feng, Lan recognizes the male-female duality within himself and actively courts his half brother, Bok. He also loves the Princess Ling. While China is beset by civil war and foreign invasion, Lan pursues his own goals, longing to answer questions of being and becoming. He is more interested in learning magic tricks and acrobatics than in fighting battles; indeed, he advocates disarmament. According to critic Bonnie Marranca, Lan embodies both the Buddhist thought that informs the play and Neo-Confucian teachings on the infinite number of principles, or laws, that make up the universe. By the final scene, having killed Princess Ling with a golden dart, he transforms himself into both Lan-He and Lan-She, male and female, and carries on a dialogue with himself/herself, dancing and singing as appropriate. Ultimately, however, Lan is a tragic figure: Dethroned and imprisoned, he is murdered by rough Chinese soldiers at the end of the play in an ecstasy of self-abasement and poetry.

KONTRAPTION

Reminiscent of Vladimir and Estragon in Samuel Beckett's *En attendant Godot* (pb. 1952, pr. 1953; *Waiting for Godot*, 1954), Hortten and Abdal—the chief characters in Owens's *Kontraption*—are friends living in an absurdist world in which reality and fantasy freely interchange. Their love-hate relationship oscillates between deep devotion and vigorous attacks. Abdal appears most violent and is punished shortly after he suffocates Mr. Strauss, an Albanian/German laundryman who has asked only to sit down and rest for a while, entertaining them with tales of Gastour, his fantasy ideal of himself as a he-man surrounded by lovely ladies. The master deity of the play's universe, a Chemist, appears and transforms Abdal from "an agreeable bald man" smelling of myrrh and sweet herbs (his own conception of himself) to a square-shaped contraption from the neck down, part mechanical, part animal. Justifying this action, the Chemist says, "I smelled his fear, his longing!" A symbol of technology gone awry, the Chemist boasts that he has now made Abdal into a perfect man, "a blending of nature and graceful art."

Gradually, Abdal recovers from his shocked state and begins dancing and singing. At first, Hortten is impressed with his friend's new form and being, but the alternation of devotion and name-calling in their relationship quickly returns, along with more fantasies and the haunting memory of Mr. Strauss. The fantasies are mostly erotic ones and arouse the passions of the two friends. The Chemist reappears and forbids grief: "We put grief in a mudhole!" he declares. At the end, Abdal dies and ascends to heaven, leaving Hortten in intense despair, imploring his friend to come down to him, promising him food and water and good times again in the summer. "There's nothing up there! In the sky!" he cries, berating himself for not nailing Abdal down while he had the chance.

LATER PLAYS

In her introduction to *The Karl Marx Play and Others*, Owens proclaims that she writes "so that God will not hate you." By portraying our "visceral anguish," as in *Kontraption*, she reveals humanity in its deepest agonies, but she also believes in human joy and its recovery, as in the lighter one-act play *O. K. Certaldo*. "Authentic theatre," she says, "is always oscillating between joyousness and fiendishness." In her later plays, such as *Emma Instigated Me* and *What Do You Want, Peire Vidal?*, she continues to reject theater as entertainment in favor of experimentation. "We are extremists," she says of herself and of

similar playwrights, "and attempt both in our lives and in our art to explore aesthetic possibilities and to become more open to the profound, endless dimensions of creating art." Only in *Chucky's Hunch*, an epistolary drama written for a single actor, does Owens appear to concede anything (but not much) to traditional conceptions of theater. This successful play, with Kevin O'Connor playing Chucky in both New York productions, was quickly followed by the boldly conceived *What Do You Want, Peire Vidal?*, suggesting that Owens has surrendered nothing of her integrity as an innovative dramatist.

OTHER MAJOR WORKS

SHORT FICTION: *The Girl on the Garage Wall*, 1962; *The Obscenities of Reva Cigarnik*, 1963.

POETRY: *Not Be Essence That Cannot Be*, 1961; *Four Young Lady Poets*, 1962 (with others; LeRoi Jones, editor); *I Am the Babe of Joseph Stalin's Daughter: Poems, 1961-1971*, 1972; *Poems from Joe's Garage*, 1973; *The Joe Eighty-two Creation Poems*, 1974; *Poems*, 1974; *The Joe Chronicles II*, 1978; *Shemuel*, 1979; *Constructs*, 1985; *W. C. Fields in French Light*, 1986; *How Much Paint Does the Painting Need*, 1988; *Black Chalk: Discourse on Life and Death*, 1992; *Paysanne, and Selected Earlier Poems, 1961-1990*, 1993; *Rubbed Stones: Poems from 1960-1992*, 1994; *New and Selected Poems, 1961-1996*, 1997; *Luca: Discourse on Life and Death*, 2001.

SCREENPLAY: *Futz*, 1969 (adaptation of her play).

EDITED TEXT: *Spontaneous Combustion: Eight New American Plays*, 1972.

TRANSLATION: *The Passerby*, 1993 (of Liliane Atlan's novel *Les Passants*).

BIBLIOGRAPHY

Cohn, Ruby. *Dialogue in American Drama*. Bloomington: Indiana University Press, 1971. In a longer discussion of major playwrights, Cohn separates Owens as one of the "poets at play." Provides a strong discussion of *Futz*, *Homo*, and *Beclch* ("suggesting beak, belch, cluck, lick—all resonant of animals") and concentrates on how Owens "renders her cruelty mainly through language."

Marranca, Bonnie, and Gautam Dasgupta. *American Playwrights: A Critical Survey*. New York: Drama Book Specialists, 1981. Contains a chapter on Owens, beginning with her poetic output and continuing into a discussion of *Futz*, and an analysis of the "ethnopoetics" and the poetic language inherent in *Beclch*, *Kontraption*, and *The Karl Marx Play*. Most of Owens's plays are set in Africa, Greenland, Europe, and China, but *Futz* and *Emma Instigated Me* have American settings.

Murray, Timothy. "The Play of Letters: Possession and Writing in *Chucky's Hunch*." In *Feminine Focus: The New Women Playwrights*, edited by Enoch Brater. New York: Oxford University Press, 1989. Murray examines in this postmodern linguistic analysis the writing strategies of Owens in her 1981 play: "The primary [strategy] continually positions Chucky's silent and disgusted interlocutors . . . vis-à-vis a crisis of reception posed by his narrative presence." Contains a long essay, divided by sections entitled "Self-Restoration," "Oozing Signs, Early Memories," "Primal Digressions," and "Rebirth or Lack?" Notes.

Novick, Julius. *Beyond Broadway: The Quest for Permanent Theatres*. New York: Hill and Wang, 1968. In a chapter treating André Gregory and the East Coast theaters (Washington to Philadelphia), Owens's play *Beclch* is discussed in Artaudian terms. Owens, says Novick, in her attempt to shock, "generated a feeling of adolescent eagerness that was at odds with the somber impression she was trying to convey." Good discussion of the relation of experimental theater to its audience.

Olauson, Judith. *The American Woman Playwright: A View of Criticism and Characterization*. Troy, N.Y.: Witston, 1981. A feminist reevaluation of traditional literary views of women, divided by decades (Owens is in the 1960-1970 period with Megan Terry, Myrna Lamb, and others), this study sees Owens as "a proponent of the 'underground theatre' movement and insists that modern times require a new artistic response." Owens portrays her two main female characters in *Futz* as predators. No index.

Jay Halio,
updated by Thomas J. Taylor

P

SUZAN-LORI PARKS

Born: Fort Knox, Kentucky; May 10, 1963

OTHER LITERARY FORMS

Though her literary reputation rests primarily on her dramatic writing, Suzan-Lori Parks has also written several screenplays: *Anemone Me*, an independent film released in New York in 1990, *Girl 6*, directed by Spike Lee and released in 1996, and two scripts for Jodie Foster and Danny Glover. Parks has also written several essays that have been published in theater journals.

ACHIEVEMENTS

Suzan-Lori Parks produced her first play, *The Sinner's Place*, in 1984, as a student at Mount Holyoke College. Her second, *Betting on the Dust Commander*, debuted in a Brooklyn garage in 1987, with Parks purchasing five folding chairs to accommodate the audience. From these modest beginnings, Parks has become one of the most celebrated American playwrights of her generation. *Imperceptible Mutabilities in the Third Kingdom*, produced in 1989, earned Parks her first Obie Award for best new American play, and *The New York Times* named her the year's most promising playwright. Parks received her second Obie, for *Venus*, in 1996. Her next play, *In the Blood*, was a Pulitzer Prize finalist in 2000.

Parks has received numerous fellowships and grants, including the Guggenheim Fellowship in 2000 and the MacArthur Foundation Fellowship in 2001. In 2002, Parks became only the fourth African American and the first African American woman to receive the Pulitzer Prize in Drama for her play *Topdog/Underdog*. She has taught at the University of Michigan, Yale University, and New York University. She also served as writer-in-residence at the New School for Social Research (now New School University) in New York from 1991 to 1992. In 2000, Parks became director of the Audrey Skirball Kernis Theatre Projects Writing for Performance program at the California Institute of the Arts.

BIOGRAPHY

Suzan-Lori Parks was born in Fort Knox, Kentucky, in 1963, the daughter of a career army officer. She spent her early childhood in several cities across the United States and lived in Germany, where she attended high school. She began writing short stories as a third grader and continued to focus on prose writing until her undergraduate years at Mount Holyoke College in Massachusetts. There, she met the distinguished author and essayist James Baldwin, who recognized her gift for dialogue and suggested that she explore drama.

Parks wrote her first play, *The Sinner's Place*, in 1984 as a student at Mount Holyoke. Though she earned an honors citation for her work, the college's theater department refused to stage the play. Parks graduated with honors in 1985 and moved to London for a year to study acting. *Betting on the Dust Commander,* her first play to be produced in New York City, debuted in 1987. Two years later, Parks received an Obie Award for *Imperceptible Mutabilities in the Third Kingdom,* and *The New York Times* named Parks the most promising playwright of 1989.

Following the successful production of *The Death of the Last Black Man in the Whole Entire World* at the Brooklyn Arts Council's BACA Downtown Theatre in 1990, Parks produced her next two plays, *Devotees in the Garden of Love* and *The America Play* on smaller stages in Lexington, Kentucky, and Dallas, Texas, respectively. *The America Play* later opened Off-Broadway at the Joseph Papp Public Theatre in New York City in 1994. Parks earned a second Obie Award in 1996, for her play *Venus,* which also debuted at the Joseph Papp Public Theatre. Also in 1996, Parks wrote the screenplay for director Spike Lee's film *Girl 6.*

The productions of *In the Blood,* which was nominated for the Pulitzer Prize in Drama in 2000, and *Fucking A,* both of which draw on elements in Nathaniel Hawthorne's classic novel, *The Scarlet Letter* (1850), continued to earn Parks wide critical acclaim. She received the prestigious Guggenheim Fellowship in 2000 and the MacArthur Fellowship (called the genius grant) in 2001. Parks's growing reputation as a brilliant young playwright reached new heights in 2001 with the production of *Topdog/Underdog.* The play opened on July 22, 2001, at the Joseph Papp Public Theatre in New York City to rave reviews and earned Parks the Pulitzer Prize in Drama in 2002, distinguishing her as the first African American woman and only the fourth African American to win the award. *Topdog/Underdog* opened on Broadway in April of 2002, the first Broadway opening for an African American woman since Ntozake Shange, whose *for colored girls who have considered suicide/ since the rainbow is enuf* opened in 1976.

"I think it's a great moment for all African-American women writers," Parks has explained about becoming the first African American woman to receive the Pulitzer Prize for drama. "And anytime America

Suzan-Lori Parks (AP/Wide World Photos)

recognizes a member of a certain group for excellence—one that has not traditionally been recognized—it's a great moment for American culture." Parks married Paul Oscher, a blues musician, in 2001, and joined the faculty of the California Institute of the Arts in Valencia, California, as the director of the Audrey Skirball Kernis Theatre Projects Writing for Performance program.

ANALYSIS

"I am obsessed with resurrecting," Suzan-Lori Parks explained in a 1996 interview, "with bringing up the dead . . . and hearing their stories as they come into my head." Parks has often described the characters she creates as independent beings, as voices that relate their stories to her. Rather than writing them into existence, Parks allows the characters to speak themselves into being. Drawing on history, myth, and fantasy, she populates her plays with conventional and unconventional characters whose stories excavate the past in order to expose the truths and misconceptions about African American and American history. "Every play I write is about love and distance. And time," she explained in 1994. "And from that we can get things like history." She elaborates further in her essay "Possession," collected in *The America Play and Other Works*. "Through each line of text, I'm rewriting the Time Line—creating history where it is and always was but has not yet been divined."

Language plays a vital role in this creation of history. Using what she calls "rep and rev" (repetition and revision), Parks often employs language as a musical refrain, with characters repeating phrases throughout her plays, the repetition of which adds different shades of meaning. In *Topdog/Underdog*, Booth rehearses his three-card monte street routine, addressing his imaginary audience: "Watch me close watch me close now: who-see-thuh-red-card-who-see-the-red-card?" As the words recur at various points in the play, they take on the quality of a chant, or a chorus that signifies the building tension between the brothers.

The question of identity in Parks's drama, as self-awareness and the identification of an individual within a group, is of central importance. As characters attempt to identify themselves, they must destroy the false identities and histories that have been attributed to them. In *Imperceptible Mutabilities in the Third Kingdom*, the characters Mona, Chona, and Verona, whose names have been changed to Molly, Charlene, and Veronica, meditate on the apparent mutability of their characters. "Once there was uh me named Mona who wondered what she'd be like if no one was watchin," Mona/Molly says. The Foundling Father of Parks's *The America Play*, whose setting is the Great Pit of History, is obsessed by Abraham Lincoln and decides to reenact his assassination in a traveling show. Like the character of Lincoln in *Topdog/Underdog*, who earns his living by reenacting Abraham Lincoln's assassination in a local arcade, the Foundling Father is a captive of history.

IMPERCEPTIBLE MUTABILITIES IN THE THIRD KINGDOM

Rather than separating her first major play into traditional acts, Parks creates four separate stories that provide a nonlinear and sometimes surreal look at aspects of the African American experience in her *Imperceptible Mutabilities in the Third Kingdom.*

"Snails," the first section of the play, looks at a contemporary group of women who possess two names, one they have chosen and another that has been imposed on them. The second section, "Third Kingdom," recreates the tragic Middle Passage, through which enslaved Africans journeyed on their way to America, and the details of which are narrated by characters like Kin-Seer, Us-Seer, and Over-Seer. "Open House," the third section, depicts the life of Aretha Saxon, a black servant/slave in the household of the white Saxon family. Aretha's departure from the family is occasioned by the removal with pliers of all of her teeth. The play's final section, "Greeks," is a modern interpretation of Homer's *Odyssey* (c. 750 B.C.E.; English translation, 1614), with Mr. Seargant Smith in the role of Odysseus. Hoping to earn "his Distinction" in the army, Seargant Smith spends most of his life away from his family, who await his return and the honor he hopes to bring back with him.

The four stories in *Imperceptible Mutabilities in the Third Kingdom* depict characters whose identity and culture are marginalized by others. From the three women in "Snails," whose identities are studied and inevitably altered by the invasive Lutsky, to Miss Faith's extraction of Aretha Saxon's teeth in an act that functions metaphorically as a means of extracting Aretha from the Saxon family history, Parks dramatizes the struggle of African Americans against cultural, historical, and linguistic sabotage. A critical and popular success, *Imperceptible Mutabilities in the Third Kingdom* earned Parks her first Obie Award for best new American play. *The New York Times* also named her 1989's most promising young playwright.

VENUS

Venus received mixed reviews for its portrayal of an African woman whose unconventional physiognomy becomes the basis for her exhibition in a traveling sideshow in Europe. Parks based her play on a historical character, Saartjie Baartman, a South African woman whose body was displayed publicly in London and Paris in the early nineteenth century.

Dubbed the Hottentot Venus, Baartman became a popular spectacle for white audiences who were fascinated and revolted by her appearance. After her death, Baartman's sexual organs and buttocks were preserved and housed in the Musee de l'homme in Paris until the late twentieth century.

As the play opens, Venus is a popular attraction in Mother Showman's traveling show of Nine Human Wonders in London. Because slavery has been outlawed in England, Mother Showman's captivity of Venus sparks a debate about whether such exhibitions constitute slavery. Venus eventually escapes to Paris, where she falls under the influence of the Baron Docteur, who falls in love with Venus but also assures his colleagues that he intends to make her the object of scientific study. A twisted custody battle ensues as Mother Showman and Baron Docteur fight over who has the right to exhibit Venus.

In the character of Venus, Parks explores the objectification of human beings, and particularly African Americans, whose humanity was denied in the nineteenth century (and beyond) on the basis of pseudoscientific theories that reinforced prejudices against physical and cultural difference. Venus, a woman who desires to be treated with love and respect, becomes an oddity in a circus sideshow, reduced to little more in the public consciousness than her "great heathen buttocks."

IN THE BLOOD

A modern interpretation of Nathaniel Hawthorne's novel *The Scarlet Letter*, *In the Blood* depicts a homeless woman's struggle to care for herself and her family. Hester, La Negrita, and her five children, all from different fathers, live under a bridge, making what little money they have from collecting cans. Hester spends much of her time practicing her writing (she knows only the letter *A*). As her health declines, Hester appeals for assistance to a street doctor, her welfare case worker, a former lover and father of her first child, and eventually a local reverend, who is the father of her youngest child.

The actors who portray Hester's five children also double as adult characters. In a series of stage confessions that resemble the chorus of a Greek tragedy, these characters (Amiga Gringa, Chilli, The Doctor,

The Welfare Lady, and Reverend D) explain the ways in which they have taken advantage of Hester, who has been sexually exploited by almost everyone that she knows.

In the Blood is a hopeless tale of a woman undone by poverty and a social system that cannot meet her needs. Individuals in a position to help Hester can think only of how to use her. The word "slut," scrawled on the wall of Hester's makeshift home under the bridge in the play's opening scene, serves a similar purpose as Hawthorne's scarlet letter on Hester Prynne's chest. Both Hesters are defined almost exclusively by what their societies perceive as aberrant sexuality. When every means of salvation is exhausted, Hester is left, in the final scene of the play, with the word "slut," this time on the lips of her oldest child. Hester's murder of her son Jabber at the end of the play functions as an attempt to efface the word, and the identification, both of which have followed her throughout the play. A critical and popular success, *In the Blood* was named a finalist for the 2000 Pulitzer Prize in Drama.

TOPDOG/UNDERDOG

Departing from the unorthodox staging and characterization of her previous plays, Parks presents what appears on the surface to be a traditional tale of sibling rivalry in *Topdog/Underdog*, which opened at the Joseph Papp Public Theatre on July 22, 2001, and opened on Broadway at the Ambassador Theatre in New York less than a year later. However, Parks links the struggle of her two characters, named Lincoln and Booth, to more complex and historical struggles of race, family, and identity.

The two brothers, Lincoln and Booth, share a seedy urban apartment. Lincoln, a former street hustler whose skill at the card game three-card monte is legendary, now works at an arcade where he impersonates Abraham Lincoln for patrons who pay money to reenact his assassination. Booth, who aspires to his brother's greatness at three-card monte, relies on Lincoln's paychecks and whatever he can steal to make ends meet.

As Lincoln and Booth, so named as a joke by their father, try to plan for their future, they confront the realities of the past: their abandonment by their parents and the buried animosities toward each other. In the play's final scene, Booth flies into a rage when Lincoln bests him at three-card monte, thereby winning the family legacy (five hundred dollars rolled in a stocking) left to each son when their parents fled. Lincoln's violent end is foreshadowed by his job at the arcade and by his and Booth's names. How each brother accepts and realizes the roles imposed by family history, circumstance, and the inherent opposition of their names, however, makes the play a deeply compelling one. In 2002, shortly after its debut on Broadway, *Topdog/Underdog* earned Parks the Pulitzer Prize in Drama.

OTHER MAJOR WORKS

SCREENPLAYS: *Anemone Me*, 1990; *Girl 6*, 1996.
RADIO PLAYS: *Pickling,* 1990; *The Third Kingdom,* 1990; *Locomotive,* 1991.

BIBLIOGRAPHY

Frieze, James. "*Imperceptible Mutabilities in the Third Kingdom*: Suzan-Lori Parks and the Shared Struggle to Perceive." *Modern Drama* 41, no. 4 (Winter, 1998): 523. Frieze provides a detailed analysis of Parks's Obie Award-winning play, emphasizing the significance of identity in shaping the actions and thoughts of the play's characters.

Garrett, Shawn-Marie. "The Possession of Suzan-Lori Parks." *American Theatre* 17, no. 8 (October, 2000): 22. This essay provides some background on Parks's beginnings as a playwright and her unconventional approach to the writing process. Garrett provides a good overview of Parks's development as a playwright and the historical, political, and racial forces that inform her work.

Parks, Suzan-Lori. *The America Play and Other Works*. New York: Theatre Communications Group, 1995. This volume combines a sampling of Parks's early plays, including *Betting on the Dust Commander* and *Devotees in the Garden of Love*, with three essays that provide insight on the aims and methods of Parks's writing.

Pochoda, Elizabeth. "I See Thuh Black Card . . . ?" *Nation* 274, no. 20 (May 27, 2002): 36. A review of Parks's *Topdog/Underdog*, following its Broadway debut at the Ambassador Theatre in New York, which touches on the major themes of the Pulitzer Prize-winning play.

Wilmer, S. E. "Restaging the Nation: The Work of Suzan-Lori Parks." *Modern Drama* 43, no. 3 (Fall, 2000): 442. Examines the postmodern elements of Parks's drama and provides analysis of most of her major plays.

Philip Bader

JOHN PATRICK
John Patrick Goggan

Born: Louisville, Kentucky; May 17, 1905
Died: Delray Beach, Florida; November 7, 1995

PRINCIPAL DRAMA

Hell Freezes Over, pr. 1935
The Story of Mary Surratt, wr. 1940, pr., pb. 1947
The Willow and I, pr. 1942, pb. 1943
The Hasty Heart, pr., pb. 1945
The Curious Savage, pr. 1950, pb. 1951
Lo and Behold!, pr. 1951, pb. 1952
The Teahouse of the August Moon, pr. 1953, pb. 1954 (adaptation of Vern Sneider's novel)
Good as Gold, pr. 1957
Everybody Loves Opal, pr. 1961, pb. 1962
Love Is a Time of Day, pr. 1969, pb. 1970
Lovely Ladies, Kind Gentlemen, pr., pb. 1970 (music and lyrics by Stan Freeman and Franklin Underwood)
Opal Is a Diamond, pr. 1971, pb. 1972

Anybody Out There?, pb. 1972

Opal's Husband, pr., pb. 1975

Noah's Animal: A Musical Allegory, pr. 1975, pb. 1976

The Girls of the Garden Club, pr. 1979, pb. 1980

Opal's Million Dollar Duck, pr. 1979, pb. 1980

People, pb. 1980

That's Not My Father!: Three One-Act Plays, pr. 1979, pb. 1980 (included *Raconteur*, *Fettucine*, and *Masquerade*)

That's Not My Mother!: Three One-Act Plays, pr. 1979, pb. 1980 (includes *Seniority*, *Redemption*, and *Optimism*)

The Gay Deceiver, pb. 1988

Sense and Nonsense, pb. 1989

The Doctor Will See You Now: Four One-Act Plays, pb. 1991

OTHER LITERARY FORMS

In addition to his plays, John Patrick was the author of more than thirty screenplays, more than one thousand radio plays for the series *Cecil and Sally* (1929-1933), and a television play, *The Small Miracle* (1972), with Arthur Dales, from the novel by Paul Gallico. It is worth noting that many of Patrick's best-known screenplays are those adapted from novels or plays. *Look Out, Mr. Moto* (1937) and *Mr. Moto Takes a Chance* (1938), written with others, were taken from the detective novels of John P. Marquand. *The President's Lady* (1953), *Three Coins in the Fountain* (1954), *Love Is a Many-Splendored Thing* (1955), *Les Girls* (1957), and *Some Came Running* (1958) were based on novels by Irving Stone, John H. Secondari, Han Suyin, Vera Caspary, and James Jones, respectively. The Philip Barry play *The Philadelphia Story* (pr. 1939) provided the basis for *High Society* (1956), while *The World of Susie Wong* (1960) and *The Teahouse of the August Moon* (1956) were adapted from novels by, respectively, Richard Mason and Vern Sneider, and plays by, respectively, Paul Osborn and John Patrick himself. Patrick is also noted for radio dramatizations of novels, and his adaptations for that medium doubtless contributed to the sure grasp of dramatic structure that distinguished Patrick's stage plays.

ACHIEVEMENTS

John Patrick was one of the most prolific American dramatic writers on record. While his plays range in genre, subject matter, and setting from wartime or postwar experiences in foreign lands to domestic situations and murder mysteries, the majority of them emerge as comedies and evidence both their author's superior craftsmanship and his marked talent for the comic genre.

Patrick's most accomplished and enduring work is *The Teahouse of the August Moon*. One of the greatest critical and popular successes in the history of the American theater, the play garnered in 1954 the Pulitzer Prize in Drama, the New York Drama Critics Circle Award for Best American Play of the Broadway season, the Tony Award, the Donaldson Award, and the Aegis Club Award. Less spectacular in their success yet also notable are *The Hasty Heart*, a serious play set in wartime and popular with audiences and critics in the 1945 Broadway and London seasons, and *The Curious Savage*, a comedy whose regional popularity (it has been a staple of community theater playbills over the years) has far exceeded and outlasted its restrained reception in New York in 1950. All three plays are interlaced with gentle humor and a compassionate view of the human condition, but it is for *The Teahouse of the August Moon* that Patrick will be remembered. A fine craftsman and a productive journeyman playwright in the best sense of the term, Patrick surpassed himself in that play, giving American theater one of its best comedies.

In addition to awards won for *The Teahouse of the August Moon*, Patrick won the Screenwriters Guild Award and the Foreign Correspondents Award for the 1957 musical screenplay *Les Girls*, with Gene Kelly and Cole Porter songs, which was presented as a command performance for Queen Elizabeth II. Patrick also received an honorary doctorate in fine arts from Baldwin Wallace College in Berea, Ohio.

BIOGRAPHY

John Patrick was born John Patrick Goggan on May 17, 1905, in Louisville, Kentucky. Following a rift with his parents, which he did not publicly discuss, Patrick spent a portion of his youth living with relatives and attending boarding schools such as St. Mary's Seminary in La Porte, Texas, and St. Edward's College in Austin, Texas. Later he attended Holy Cross College in New Orleans and was a summer school student at Harvard and Columbia universities. In the early 1930's, Patrick began a career in San Francisco as a scriptwriter for the National Broadcasting Company, where he authored numerous radio scripts and earned a reputation for his radio dramatizations of novels.

In 1935, Patrick's first play, a melodrama titled *Hell Freezes Over*, concerning polar explorers whose dirigible crash-lands in the Antarctic, was produced on Broadway; the production was the directorial debut of Joshua Logan, who went on to gain fame as director of *South Pacific* (1949) and many other Broadway musicals. *Hell Freezes Over* closed after an unfavorable reception, causing critic George Jean Nathan to remark that its playwright should be thrown back to Hollywood. Perhaps taking his cue from Nathan, a talent scout secured for Patrick a Hollywood contract. Returning to California, Patrick developed his craft by writing thirty or more screenplays between 1936 and 1968 for such studios as Metro-Goldwyn-Mayer and Twentieth Century-Fox.

Leaving Hollywood (to which he would often return for screenwriting assignments) in the late 1930's, Patrick established himself in Boston. It was there that he wrote "The Gentle Ghost," a drama about the woman hanged for complicity in Abraham Lincoln's assassination, which appeared on Broadway in 1947 as *The Story of Mary Surratt*. During this period, Patrick also completed *The Willow and I*, a psychological drama about two sisters competing for the love of the same man and destroying him in the process, which opened in New York in 1942. Neither of the two plays was a box office success.

In 1942, Patrick joined the American Field Service, serving overseas as a captain with a British ambulance unit in Egypt, India, Burma, and Syria. He drew on this experience in *The Hasty Heart*, which centers on a dour and terminally ill Scottish sergeant in a British military hospital in Southeast Asia; the play enjoyed both critical and popular success in the 1945 Broadway season. The fruits of his first stage success permitted Patrick to purchase a sixty-five-acre farm in Rockland County, New York, which he appropriately called Hasty Hill. There he lived casually as a gentleman farmer, raised sheep, remained unmarried, and continued to write. In a 1950's interview with Harry Gilroy for *The New York Times Magazine*, he said that strenuous physical activity keeps one aware of life's basic values and that one "can't lead a push-button life and be a writer."

Turning to comedy, Patrick wrote *The Curious Savage*, whose heroine is a wealthy eccentric widow, and *Lo and Behold!*, a comedy-fantasy about a solitude-loving writer who, after stipulating in his will that his house be kept vacant as a sanctuary, returns as a ghost to find it occupied by three incompatible spirits. Both comedies had short runs on Broadway, but the former has enjoyed lasting popularity with community theater audiences. Following these plays,

John Patrick in 1956. (AP/Wide World Photos)

Patrick created his most successful comedy, *The Teahouse of the August Moon*, which won many awards and established his reputation as an American dramatist. Patrick rewrote it as a screenplay and later as a short-lived musical titled *Lovely Ladies, Kind Gentlemen*, with music and lyrics by Stan Freeman and Franklin Underwood.

Patrick is also the author of a number of comedies that, while attaining neither Broadway acclaim nor, in some cases, New York productions, have proved popular with regional theaters. For example, *The Hasty Heart* was successfully performed at the Berkshire Theatre Festival Mainstage in August of 1990; *Opal Is a Diamond*, "as entertainingly silly as the silliest sitcom," was presented by the Arena Players of Baltimore, Maryland, in March of 1991. The Group Repertory Theatre of Los Angeles produced *The Curious Savage*, "this pallid American chestnut," in October of 1991.

ANALYSIS

A versatile, prolific playwright, John Patrick was most successful as a writer of comedy. His comic plays, like the best of his serious ones, are, in the main, marked by cleverly conceived situations, well-drawn characters, effective dialogue, and an overall sense of solid craftsmanship. Patrick's comedies are imbued with charm and humor, wit, a gentle satirizing of misguided conventional attitudes or behavior, and a compassionate view of the human species and its frailties. Implicit is a comic view of the world that sees the need for compromise and mutual understanding, however different from one another people may be.

While Patrick was not ostensibly a "theme" writer, his most effective plays reveal commonalities of theme. In these plays can often be found a sympathetic major character who, by virtue of culture, behavior, or association, is considered an outsider by members of an establishment presumably motivated by conventional and rational standards of judgment, and who meets with misunderstanding or a lack of compassion from that group. In some instances, the outsider's nature makes group acceptance difficult. An encounter occurs between these disparate forces, resulting in a clash from which emerges the realization (on the part of some but seldom all of the characters concerned) of people's need to accept and treat one another with understanding and kindness. Interwoven in such a situational pattern are several interrelated themes: people's need to realize their interdependency with others, however great the differences; the urgency for compassionate understanding and truly rational judgment in human affairs despite pressures to the contrary; and the need to comprehend and value the person who marches to a different drummer. The subsequent examination of three of Patrick's plays will discover, in varying degrees, these characteristic themes and patterns.

THE CURIOUS SAVAGE

The Curious Savage, Patrick's first comedy, tells a fanciful tale about a widow, left millions by her deceased husband, whose adult stepchildren have her committed to a private sanatorium because she insists on endowing a foundation that will enable people to finance their daydreams. The widow, Mrs. Savage, decides in her last years to indulge all the foolish whims she has suppressed in a lifetime of self-denial. In the sanatorium, the gently eccentric but sane Mrs. Savage is greeted by a compassionate staff and by pleasant inmates with such harmless idiosyncracies as fibbing about imagined careers and reading only month-old newspapers (vulnerable men and women who cannot cope with life and require the affectionate understanding that their new arrival can provide). As she comes to know her companions, Mrs. Savage finds them more attractive than her own sane but greedy family. When the latter learn that their stepmother has transformed the family's financial assets into negotiable securities, which she has hidden, they take active steps to find and seize them. After the members of the Savage family have been sent by the wily Mrs. Savage on a wild-goose chase and have been humiliated by performing ridiculous acts in pursuit of the bonds, they angrily threaten to transfer their stepmother to a public mental institution and never release her. Forced to reveal the hiding place of the bonds, Mrs. Savage receives the united help of the institution's kindly staff and fellow inmates in ultimately outwitting her family; she is free to use her money as she will. The institution's doctor, realizing her sanity, tells her she is free to go. After the inmates throw a farewell party in which each demonstrates Mrs. Savage's beneficial influence by acting out the fulfillment of a hopeless dream for something never realized, she reluctantly bids her friends good-bye and departs to the harshness of the world outside. The neglected virtues of kindness and affection have not been entirely lost in a world largely motivated by greed and callousness.

Reminiscent of Jean Giraudoux's *La Folle de Chaillot* (pr., pb. 1945; *The Madwoman of Chaillot*, 1947), the comedy's charmingly irrational characters, and its central figure in particular, are treated with affectionate humor and are solidly supported by a cleverly constructed plot. While the rational "villains," Mrs. Savage's stepchildren, are treated somewhat too stridently, they make excellent foils for the "irrational" characters and contribute effectively to the drama's comic complications. *The Curious Savage* is a minor work in comparison with the two following plays to be discussed, yet it permits a fuller view of the scope of Patrick's work while also reflecting characteristic themes and patterns.

THE HASTY HEART

Patrick's World War II experiences as an ambulance driver with the British Army in Southeast Asia furnished the background for *The Hasty Heart*, a serious comedy with none of the farcical characterizations and action of *The Curious Savage*. Prominent, however, is the figure of the outsider. The action is set in the convalescent ward of a British military hospital behind the Assam-Burma front. A distinctive and convivial company of five convalescent soldiers—an American, an Australian, an Englishman, a New Zealander, and an African Basuto who knows no English—find their tranquillity and good-natured banter disrupted by the arrival of a dour and seemingly healthy Scottish sergeant, Lachlen McLachlen, who is unaware that an operation for a wound has left him with one defective kidney, which will soon fail. A colonel keeps this information from the Scot but imparts it to the five men and to their efficient young nurse, Sister Margaret, asking them to gladden the Scot's last six weeks of life. Their assignment is not an easy one. The young sergeant, whom the men call

Lachie, is friendless, distrustful, and antisocial, hard used by life and hardened by war. Pridefully asserting an uncompromising independence and demand for privacy, Lachie persistently frustrates the men's attempts to befriend him. All of his life, Lachie, who is an orphan, has obstinately repressed the "hasty heart" that accepts and gives fellowship and understanding. Patrick skillfully carries the story this far by the end of the first act. The playwright introduces a group of individualized characters, economically supplies the essential exposition, and establishes the classic dramatic pattern in which a situation of initial equilibrium is thrown out of balance by the incursion of a disturbing force or catalytic agent.

As the action progresses in the final two acts, occurring two weeks after act 1, Lachie's misanthropic sullenness is melted when his wardmates, urged by Sister Margaret to renew their hitherto abortive attempts at friendship, present him on his birthday with a kilt that he has long coveted. This act breaks through the hard crust of suspicion and pride in which the Scot has encased himself. Engulfing himself in a whole new world of fellowship, the taciturn Lachie starts talking nonstop, invites his new mates to pay a peacetime visit to the farm in Scotland in which he has invested, and even shyly proposes marriage to Sister Margaret, who accepts him. At this point, the author introduces a complication leading to the crisis of the play. Lachie learns the truth of his fatal condition, suspects that the friendship extended to him was simply pity in disguise, and rejects his new companions. Ultimately, however, he realizes the value of friendship and again embraces his wardmates' goodwill, resolving to spend his last days with them rather than in Scotland without friends. That act of final acceptance demonstrates Patrick's premise: the importance of a man's acknowledgment of his dependence on others.

Not unlike the typical Molière comedy in which an unreasonable man (be he miser or hypochondriac) is surrounded by reasonable people who eventually pull the former into the circle of society, *The Hasty Heart* displays an outsider at first eschewing the proffered understanding and friendship of a group but eventually coming to trust and value them. There is a warmth and humor to the play, sustained by the good nature and wit of the men, that lends a correctly comic perspective to a serious subject and keeps sentimentality within proper bounds. *The Hasty Heart* demonstrated Patrick's growth as a dramatist, able to deal incisively with plot structure and with the effect of inner states of mind on conduct and character. The drama earned considerable Broadway success in 1945 before it was made into a motion picture.

THE TEAHOUSE OF THE AUGUST MOON

Patrick's award-winning comedy *The Teahouse of the August Moon*, like *The Hasty Heart*, centers on soldiers in a foreign setting. Based on a novel by Vern Sneider, the play is an amusing satire on the efforts of the American Army of Occupation, following World War II, to bring democracy to the people of Okinawa. A young captain, Fisby, with a record of past failure in the military, is assigned to the remote Okinawan village of Tobiki to teach democracy to the natives and make them self-supporting. His commanding officer, a stiff-necked simpleton named Colonel Purdy, demands strict enforcement of Plan B, which calls for the formation of native industry, municipal government, a Ladies League for Democratic Action, and the building of a schoolhouse in the shape of the Pentagon. The young officer, aided by a wily native interpreter named Sakini, attempts to meet his stipulated objectives but at first fails to take into account the traditions and mores of the much-occupied Okinawans, who are experienced in surviving under conquerors. Nor is he prepared to contend with the villagers' ingenuous charm. Within a short time, Fisby finds himself the master of an attractive geisha and, adhering to the democratic principle of the will of the majority, allows the materials sent to him for a schoolhouse to be used to build the teahouse that the male villagers have longed for; he also agrees to the native women's demands for geisha lessons, lipstick, and perfume. Moreover, he encourages the impoverished village to sell its only marketable item, potato brandy, to all the surrounding army and navy officers' clubs—an enterprise astoundingly enriching to the local economy.

Relaxing into village life, Fisby "goes native," as does an army psychiatrist with a yen for organic gardening who has been sent to check up on him. When Fisby's increasingly suspicious commanding officer inopportunely visits the village at the opening of the teahouse, he is outraged at such unorthodox practices and orders the teahouse and the brandy stills to be destroyed. The order is seemingly obeyed, but the resultant mood of despair changes when word arrives from the Pentagon that Congress has received reports that Tobiki is the most progressive village on the island. Colonel Purdy, who has feared demotion, now stands to win unearned credit for Fisby's methods if a soon-to-arrive congressional committee can be impressed. Happily, the teahouse and stills have only been hidden by the villagers and are swiftly reassembled, and Captain Fisby is exonerated for his first success. Although East is East and West is West, both have learned from each other. American capitalist get-up-and-go has brought prosperity to the village, while the kindly people of Tobiki have taught the occupying Americans "the wisdom of gracious acceptance."

Interwoven into the fabric of the drama is the well-made play structure, with its establishment of a problem (the democratization of Tobiki) progressively developed by causally connected and conflict-laden incidents leading to a major crisis (the ordered destruction of the teahouse) and resolution (the exoneration of Captain Fisby's methods and the meeting of East and West). Within three acts and eleven scenes, the carefully constructed linear plot takes the protagonist Fisby through a series of difficult but comedic attempts to achieve his major objective. Even though shifts of locale and parallel scenes (as when Colonel Purdy at General Headquarters is seen talking on the telephone to Fisby in Tobiki) are called for, these are accomplished swiftly and fluently. Crucial in this respect is the conception of Sakini as a frame character who orders locales to be progressively revealed by commanding the raising and lowering of an inner curtain of bamboo panels.

Both characters and scenes are introduced by Sakini, who functions as a character-narrator akin to the Stage Manager in Thornton Wilder's *Our Town* (pr., pb. 1938) or the *waki* figure of the Japanese Nō play. Sakini comments on the action to the audience and connects the scenes while also participating in the action, establishing a friendly rapport between actor and audience and lending a nonrealistic style, borrowed from the Asian theater, to the realistic mode of the episodes. In addition, he establishes the wryly satiric perspective according to which the action and its characters are to be viewed.

The Teahouse of the August Moon was Patrick's masterwork, representing the pinnacle of his achievement as a craftsman of the American theater.

OTHER MAJOR WORKS

SCREENPLAYS: *Educating Father*, 1936 (with Katherine Kavanaugh and Edward T. Lowe); *15 Maiden Lane*, 1936 (with others); *High Tension*, 1936 (with others); *Thirty-six Hours to Live*, 1936 (with Lou Breslow); *Big Town Girl*, 1937 (with others); *Born Reckless*, 1937 (with others); *Dangerously Yours*, 1937 (with Breslow); *The Holy Terror*, 1937 (with Breslow); *Look Out, Mr. Moto*, 1937 (with others); *Midnight Taxi*, 1937 (with Breslow); *One Mile from Heaven*, 1937 (with others); *Sing and Be Happy*, 1937 (with Breslow and Ben Markson); *Time Out for Romance*, 1937 (with others); *Battle of Broadway*, 1938 (with Breslow); *International Settlement*, 1938 (with others); *Mr. Moto Takes a Chance*, 1938 (with others); *Up the River Heaven*, 1938 (with Breslow and Maurine Watkins); *Enchantment*, 1948; *The President's Lady*, 1953 (based on Irving Stone's novel); *Three Coins in the Fountain*, 1954 (based on John H. Secondari's novel); *Love Is a Many-Splendored Thing*, 1955 (based on Han Suyin's novel); *High Society*, 1956 (based on Philip Barry's play *The Philadelphia Story*); *The Teahouse of the August Moon*, 1956 (adaptation of Vern Sneider's novel and Patrick's play); *Les Girls*, 1957 (with Vera Caspary; based on Caspary's novel); *Some Came Running*, 1958 (with Arthur Sheekman; based on James Jones's novel); *The World of Susie Wong*, 1960 (adaptation of Richard Mason's novel and Paul Osborn's play); *The Main Attraction*, 1962; *Gigot*, 1962 (with Jackie Gleason); *The Shoes of the Fisherman*, 1968 (with James Kennaway).

TELEPLAY: *The Small Miracle*, 1972 (with Arthur Dales; adaptation of Paul Gallico's novel).

RADIO PLAYS: *Cecil and Sally*, pr. 1929-1933 (series; 1,100 scripts).

BIBLIOGRAPHY

Atkinson, Brooks. *The Teahouse of the August Moon*. Review of *The Teahouse of the August Moon*, by John Patrick. *The New York Times*, October 16, 1953, p. 32. Patrick's most successful play opened at the Martin Beck Theatre on October 15, 1953, a "light and sagacious comedy . . . ingratiating." "The form is inventive and familiar . . . the point of view is droll," Atkinson states. He praises Patrick as a stylist for the "piece of erotic make-believe in a style as intimate as a fairy story."

_____. "Theatre: *Good as Gold*." Review of *Good as Gold*. *The New York Times*, March 8, 1957, p. 22. "Basing his study of political science on a book by Alfred Toombs, John Patrick says that the number of taxes we pay is foolish," notes Atkinson in this review of *Good as Gold*. Patrick's playwriting, according to Atkinson, indicates "a refreshing lack of reverence for the people who process and implement our society," but "he does not drive straight on through the entire evening in the key of the opening scenes."

Borak, Jeffrey. "Compelling 'Heart' at BTF." *Berkshire Eagle* (Pittsfield, Mass.), August 17, 1990. "This is tough material to play," says Borak of *The Hasty Heart*, adding that "the emotional transitions here are far too abrupt and convenient." Provides a strong discussion of characters, especially Lachlen and Margaret, and gives credit to director Richard Dunlap for giving "unsentimental attention to detail in both the staging and the playing of Patrick's wartime romance."

Watts, Richard, Jr. "A Thoroughly Delightful Comedy." Review of *The Teahouse of the August Moon* by John Patrick. *Post* (New York), October 16, 1953. Watts calls the play "[w]arm, charming . . . a wise, gently satirical and beautifully understanding dramatic fantasy" about East and West. Provides a longer discussion of the play's themes and structure than most reviews offer of this "smiling tribute to the human spirit and the capacity of mankind for mutual understanding."

Christian H. Moe,
updated by Thomas J. Taylor

ROBERT PATRICK
Robert Patrick O'Connor

Born: Kilgore, Texas; September 27, 1937

PRINCIPAL DRAMA

The Haunted Host, pr. 1964, pb. 1972

Lights, Camera, Action, pr. 1967, pb. 1972
(includes *Lights, Camera Obscura*, and
Action)

Still-Love, pr., pb. 1967

Cornered, pr. 1968, pb. 1972

Help, I Am, pr. 1968, pb. 1972

Camera Obscura, pb. 1968

Preggin and Liss, pr. 1968, pb. 1972

Salvation Army, pr. 1968

Fog, pr. 1969, pb. 1971

I Came to New York to Write, pr. 1969, pb. 1972

Joyce Dynel, pr. 1969, pb. 1972

Lily of the Valley of the Dolls, pr. 1969

One Person, pr. 1969, pb. 1972

The Actor and the Invader, pr. 1969 (pr., pb. 1972
as part of *The Arnold Bliss Show*)

The Golden Circle, pb. 1970, pr. 1972

Hymen and Carbuncle, pr. 1970, pb. 1980

La Répétition, pr. 1970 (pr., pb. 1972 as part of
The Arnold Bliss Show)

The Golden Animal, pr. 1970

The Richest Girl in the World Finds Happiness,
pr. 1970, pb. 1972

A Christmas Carol, pr. 1971

The Arnold Bliss Show, pr., pb. 1972 (includes
*Presenting Arnold Bliss, The Actor and the
Invader, La Répétition*, and *Arnold's Big
Break*)

Robert Patrick's Cheep Theatricks!, pb. 1972
(includes *I Came to New York to Write; The
Haunted Host; Joyce Dynel; Cornered; Still-
Love; Lights, Camera, Action; Help, I Am; The
Arnold Bliss Show; One Person; Preggin and
Liss; The Richest Girl in the World Finds
Happiness*)

Play-by-Play: A Spectacle of Ourselves, pr. 1972,
revised, pr., pb. 1975

Judas, pr. 1973, pb. 1979

Simultaneous Transmissions, pr. 1973, pb. 1974
(one act)

Kennedy's Children, pr. 1973, pb. 1975

Cleaning House, pr. 1973, pb. 1978

Ludwig and Wagner, pr. 1974, pb. 1979

My Cup Ranneth Over, pr. 1978, pb. 1979

Mutual Benefit Life, pr. 1978, pb. 1979

One Man, One Woman: Six One Act Plays, pb.
1978 (includes *Mirage, Cleaning House,
Cheesecake, Something Else, Love Lace*, and
Bank Street Breakfast)

T-Shirts, pr. 1978, pb. 1979

Diaghilev and Nijinsky, pb. 1979, pr. 1981

Mercy Drop and Other Plays, pb. 1980 (includes
*Mercy Drop, Ludwig and Wagner, Diaghilev
and Nijinsky, Hymen and Carbuncle*, and *The
Family Bar*)

Michelangelo's Models, pr. 1981, pb. 1993

Blue Is for Boys, pr. 1983

Fairy Tale, pr. 1984

Odd Number, pr. 1984

Sit-Com, pr. 1984

50's 60's 70's 80's, pr. 1984 (includes *Odd
Number, Fog, Fairy Tale*, and *Sit-Com*)

Bread Alone, pr. 1985, pb. 1993

No Trojan Women, pr. 1985

The Trial of Socrates, pr. 1986, pb. 1993

Explanation of a Christmas Wedding,
pr. 1987

Pouf Positive, pr. 1987

*Untold Decades: Seven Comedies of Gay
Romance*, pb. 1988

Hello Bob, pr. 1990

Ruminations, pr. 1991

Harbor, pr. 1992

Raise the Children, pr. 1992

Sugar Cookies, pr. 1993

Interruptions, pr. 1993

Meet Marvin, pr. 1993

November Dodo, pr. 1993

OTHER LITERARY FORMS

Robert Patrick has contributed poetry to several small magazines and has written articles for a number of periodicals, usually with a focus on theater, but he is known primarily for his plays. His only novel, *Temple Slave* (1994), is based on Caffé Cino and is partly a tribute to Joseph Cino and partly a remembrance of the "dreams, work, and hopes" of the founders of Off-Off Broadway.

ACHIEVEMENTS

Robert Patrick has one of the most fertile imaginations in the contemporary American theater, one that is impulsively freewheeling and continually surprising. Because his career has remained considerably Off-Broadway, except for his best-known play, *Kennedy's Children*, he has not had to succumb to conventional Broadway formulas and has been able to give his imagination free rein. His dramatic œuvre is filled with fresh, often startling ideas and striking images, all in the service of dynamic theater, rarely in familiar realistic and naturalistic traditions. Instead, for example, he creates satiric, often surrealistic farces such as *The Arnold Bliss Show*, which mocks the ambitions and struggles of the young actor on his way to fame and fortune, however much he may have to "sell out." Patrick also creates brilliant stage metaphors, as in the brief but effective one-act *Simultaneous Transmissions*, in which United States-Soviet relations (or those of any opposing nations) are represented by two families on opposite sides of the stage. The two sets of parents simultaneously instruct their sons in the proper attitude of distrust, hostility, and aggression regarding the other family, until the play ends with the sons blindly destroying each other's families.

Patrick has also experimented with dramatic form, as in the alternating monologues of *Kennedy's Children*. Occasionally an experiment of his has anticipated a far more famous work of several years later. For example, Patrick's *Still-Love*, like Harold Pinter's *Betrayal* (pr., pb. 1978), traces a love affair backward in time, though somewhat more effectively; even some scenes are broken up so that the audience views the events of one particular encounter in reverse order. In

Robert Patrick in 1975. (AP/Wide World Photos)

this play, Patrick involves the audience intensely, not so much in figuring out what has happened (that is, what they will discover as the play moves backward in time), but rather in looking ahead from the present scene onstage to the earlier scenes that transpire at a later time, to recall the outcome of specific events or snippets of dialogue. Moreover, Patrick's manipulation of stage props and costume changes is masterful (and a stage manager's headache) in getting the audience to think about the story and the characters' relationship.

Patrick likewise preceded Harvey Fierstein in presenting a one-person monologue in which a character not only talks to a number of other people who are present only by implication, but also performs a number of intimate actions. Fierstein's remarkable backroom bar scene in *Torch Song Trilogy* (pb. 1978-1979, pb. 1979), in which Arnold, onstage alone, describes a sexual encounter as he experiences it, may be indebted to Patrick's *One Person*, which Fierstein, whose career also started Off-Broadway, is likely to have seen or at least read before writing his own tremendously successful and unconventional work.

Fierstein is certainly indebted to Patrick for helping to open the theater's closet doors on the subject of homosexuality. In Patrick's plays dealing with gay characters, homosexuality is not really an issue. Mart Crowley's *The Boys in the Band* (pr., pb. 1968) may have introduced the subject to Broadway audiences in a frank way, while *Torch Song Trilogy* progressed to a stronger sense of gay pride and self-assurance when it came to Broadway in 1982, but Patrick, even in 1964, was presenting a gay man in *The Haunted Host* who was completely at ease with his homosexuality and quite unapologetic about it. The story concerns an exorcism, whereby Jay, a blocked playwright haunted by the ghost of his dead lover, proceeds to free himself of the past and resume his own creativity. Jay's homosexuality is simply a given, needing no explanation or defense.

Patrick's other plays dealing with gay people also focus on individuals' particular concerns, such as loneliness, sexual betrayal, or a dissolving (or beginning) love affair. Mere coming-out stories can get repetitious, Patrick believes; finding many other stories that are apropos of gay life, he seeks to present a wide range of them. In an interview in *The Advocate* in October, 1984, he said, "I seem to be expected to write grim, serious plays about gay persecution. That's fine; I've done that and there are others doing it. I am determined to give gay people a rich, dramatic literature, including romances, comedies, musicals."

Among Patrick's honors are the *Show Business* Best Off-Off-Broadway Playwright Award for the 1968-1969 season (for *Fog*, *Joyce Dynel*, and *Salvation Army*), the Glasgow Citizens' Theatre World Play Writing Award in 1973 for *Kennedy's Children*, the Omni One-Act Award, the Rockefeller Foundation grant in 1973, the Creative Artists Public Service grant in 1976, the Janus Award in 1983, and the Bill Whitehead Award for Lifetime Achievement in Gay and Lesbian Literature in 1996. His work has appeared in numerous publications and anthologies, and on television.

BIOGRAPHY

Born in Texas in 1937, Robert Patrick O'Connor, as well as being part Native American, was a product of the Dust Bowl. He and his two older sisters spent their childhood moving around the Southwest with a father who worked as a rigger in the oil fields and a mother who waited on tables. Of greater influence, however, was the popular culture of Patrick's childhood, especially motion pictures, which find their way into many of his plays in references to specific films and stars as well as in familiar story lines and such devices as song-and-dance numbers.

After three years at Eastern New Mexico University and a stint in the United States Air Force, Patrick traveled to New York in 1961. There he wandered by chance into a rehearsal at the Caffé Cino, founded and run by Joseph Cino. He thought that all the repetition common to a rehearsal was part of the real play, and he became entranced with such a new method of theater. He stayed with Caffé Cino until 1968, when Cino committed suicide.

Unlike many playwrights, Patrick came to writing through practical experience in the theater. He spent three years in the Off-Off-Broadway milieu of Caffé Cino, waiting on tables, running errands, and eventually stage managing, before his first play was produced there. In fact, Cino wanted him to stick with stage managing, at which he excelled, rather than take a risk with playwriting. Fortunately, another budding young playwright, Lanford Wilson, persuaded Cino to consider Patrick's work, and *The Haunted Host* was produced in 1964.

Although many of Patrick's contemporaries, including Wilson, Sam Shepard, and David Rabe, are far better known, Patrick has remained loyal to his roots—the grassroots kind of theater in which everyone is involved in all aspects of production. He resigned from his position as artistic director of the Fifth Estate Theatre in Hollywood when Actors' Equity began to propose potentially restrictive measures on Los Angeles' Equity Waiver theaters, threatening the "let's put on a show" feeling that Patrick was familiar with and favored. After all, the company of theater people whose duties are not strictly divided has a long and honorable history: William Shakespeare himself, as a member of the Lord Chamberlain's Company, not only wrote—often with specific actors in mind—but also acted and certainly staged his own work and the plays of others. Patrick may have been alluding to the theater of Elizabethan England when he entitled his 1972 collection of plays

Robert Patrick's Cheep Theatricks! The spelling not only suggests the archaic spelling of Shakespeare's time but also, as is common with Patrick, constitutes a clever pun on the word "tricks," revealing the element of play so important to his concept of theater. Patrick has frequently attached himself to specific theaters, for varying periods of time, in order to work more fully with the plays and the companies. He has been particularly associated with the Old Reliable Theatre Tavern in New York, the Fifth Estate in Hollywood, and La Mama in Hollywood and New York, as well as theaters in other cities.

Patrick is Off-Off-Broadway's most produced playwright but that has not necessarily meant financial success. He has supported himself and his talent with jobs as a dishwasher, an autopsy typist, an accounts receivable correspondent, an astrologer, and a reporter. In 1973, he left New York for Los Angeles, disillusioned with the commercialization and stagnation of Off-Off-Broadway. With *Kennedy's Children*, however, he gained fame and welcomed royalties from the United States and abroad. In fact, that play, his only play to be produced on Broadway, has been translated into sixty languages.

Around 1978, Patrick started spending a considerable amount of time traveling to high schools and colleges, presenting workshops and classes and advocating alternative life views among the student production repertories. He won the International Thespian Society's highest award for "service to theater and to youth" in 1979, an award of which he is very proud. He began curtailing his travels in 1988, because, he said, "I felt I wasn't really making a difference. . . . I would visit, do workshops and they [high schools and colleges] were still having the kids perform *Hello, Dolly!* I decided I was their token liberal, to assuage their guilt."

Patrick voiced his objections in *The New York Times* to *En attendant Godot* (pb. 1952, pr. 1953; *Waiting for Godot*, 1954) and Samuel Beckett, whom he called "a charming writer of lugubrious skits, completely inflated," when Beckett's play was revived on Broadway in 1988. In 1991, two of Patrick's short plays were performed at the Actors Playhouse in New York to good reviews. *The Haunted Host* was revived with Fierstein in the major role; it was followed by *Pouf Positive*, a monologue that Fierstein performed.

ANALYSIS

Robert Patrick's preoccupation as a dramatist with the theme of illusion versus reality may be attributed in part to his experience as a gay man in a society that largely prefers that homosexuality be hidden; in part to a childhood spent riding around Depression and post-Depression Texas as his parents were looking for work, while he turned the dials on a silent Motorola radio and made up programs with his sisters; and in part to other forms of popular culture in which he immersed himself, including paperback books, glossy magazines, and motion pictures. Whatever the source, his plays are filled with illusions— illusions that are frequently deadly but can also be life-giving.

Characters in many of America's greatest plays have dealt with the theme of illusion versus reality— from Tennessee Williams's Amanda Wingfield with her dreams of gentlemen callers, Laura with her glass menagerie, and Blanche DuBois on her streetcar named Desire, to Arthur Miller's starry-eyed salesman Willy Loman with his impossible plans for his sons, to Edward Albee's George and Martha in *Who's Afraid of Virginia Woolf?* with their imaginary son. For some of these characters, the puncturing of illusion brings a tragic end, while for others it allows a hopeful renewal. Patrick's characters respond similarly, but Patrick's concern is rather a further twist on the theme: He generally carries characters not merely into a recognition of illusion but also beyond, into appreciation of the need for illusion. This is not a tragic understanding—that is, that people are crippled because of their reliance on illusion, like Blanche or Mary Tyrone—but rather a tranquil acceptance of the fact that illusion is not merely a crutch for the mentally unbalanced but is present to a degree in every human being's existence. This is one of the central truths of *Kennedy's Children*: The play reveals the many realities present in a single historical era, and not merely one for each of the five characters, but a complex of different realities for each of them.

KENNEDY'S CHILDREN

Kennedy's Children presents the interweaving monologues of five diverse individuals in a bar, each recalling his or her experience of the 1960's from the perspective of the present, February 14, 1974. Each began with hopes and dreams, optimism and vitality, and each has been disillusioned and depleted in some way. Patrick has said that the play is about the loss of heroes, and indeed, it suggests the importance of finding heroism and dreams in oneself rather than in the myths of popular culture.

Carla is probably the most poignant character, building her illusions on the image of Marilyn Monroe. Like two of the other characters, she came to New York in the 1960's as a teenager (one of "Kennedy's children") with dreams of success. Her dreams, she discovers, are shared by millions of others, and her own life becomes a tangle of lofty ideals and harsh realities, all of which she seeks to reconcile through rationalizations. Her illusions come crashing down when she realizes that the symbols of glamour and sex in the 1970's are the artificially perfected body of Raquel Welch and the complete artifice of drag queens. Somehow the surface has become all-important, an illusion overpowering her loftier dreams of inspiring the masses with her own beauty and glamour. Which is the deeper reality, which the frailer illusion? Does Carla kill herself because her brand of glamour has become obsolete, or is it rather that she is unable to reconcile herself to a world of such contradictory realities?

Sparger is an actor, but he never becomes caught up in the illusions of the stage. His approach is that of the cynical realist, well aware of the pretentiousness and insincerity of the underground theater movement (virtually identical with Off-Off-Broadway, quite familiar to Patrick). Yet perhaps Sparger's very cynicism, as he describes the preoccupation with sex and lack of serious artistry motivating the movement, is itself delusion. Was it all merely a mockery? Was there no value in the antiestablishment, nonconformist productions in which he has participated? Theater life is one of Patrick's favorite themes, and he punctures many of the glamorous notions connected with it, showing the venality of the actors and others involved. Yet Patrick clearly believes in its power and its value, as the seriousness of much of his work demonstrates.

In the characters of Rona, the hippie-revolutionary, and Mark, the Vietnam War veteran, Patrick embodies the most serious sides of the 1960's. Each of them has arrived at 1974 quite lost, their high ideals revealed as inadequate for coping with the realities of life. All the movements in which Rona has participated (a bit unrealistically perhaps, but appropriately for effective symbolic representation)—from civil rights to antiwar, from Berkeley's Free Speech movement to rebellion in drugs, dress, and rock music—seem to have culminated in apathy and drug or alcohol dependency for her and her offstage husband, himself a former revolutionary. When she tells him that action and leaders are needed now, he asks ironically, with a sense of despairing futility, "Who do you want me to *kill*? What do you want me to be: Lee Harvey Oswald?"

Mark is one of the saddest casualties of the 1960's, his mind strung out by drugs and the shocks of war. As he reads from his diary of his Vietnam War experiences, he proceeds through the multiple meanings that confront him—and the multiple contradictions (a Robert Patrick hallmark). Humankind should be unified, he believes—but not, he says, in the way that the Communist Vietcong would do this. His friend Chick tells him how important it is not to take sides, in order to save his own hide and not involve himself in another person's war. Yet Mark's mind has become so numbed that when Chick moves to kill a Vietcong about to attack Mark, Mark kills Chick in return, because Chick has taken sides. What is the proper role or belief for a soldier? How do thoughts and feelings and philosophies fit into the midst of war? Which illusion is least delusory, closest to reality—or is that question utterly unanswerable?

It is Wanda who most extensively makes the connection with John F. Kennedy, as she proceeds through her recollections, first of his assassination, then of his impact on her, the era he embodied, his wife, Jackie, and finally the complete oblivion into which he has fallen in the lives and minds of the "subnormal" children with whom she is now working as she pursues her teaching license. Even though she is well aware of the criticisms people have made of both Jack and Jackie, aware of the short memories of people around her, she retains her idealism, her belief in Camelot. She is keeping his memory alive by becoming a teacher. She has not succumbed to disillusionment; she can be aware of reality, but she finds no reason to abandon an illusion that provides a standard by which to live. This is what the other characters have not comprehended.

Kennedy's Children, like many of Patrick's plays, suggests that reality depends on the individual's perceptions of it. Why not, Patrick seems to ask, give the mind positive images, illusions of beauty and love, rather than images that will lead only to despair? Consequently, many of Patrick's plays are comic romps with happy endings, such as *Blue Is for Boys*, in which boy gets boy five times over, with all ten characters happily matched at the end. Patrick is doing nothing more serious in that play than offering the same kind of wish fulfillment represented by traditional romantic comedies dating back to Shakespeare's *As You Like It* (pr. c. 1599-1600) and *Much Ado About Nothing* (pr. c. 1598-1599).

FOG

Yet other plays by Patrick, seemingly more frivolous works, including the outrageous "The Loves of the Artists" trilogy (*Hymen and Carbuncle, Ludwig and Wagner, Diaghilev and Nijinsky*) and the varied *50's 60's 70's 80's* tetralogy, provide keen insights into a wide variety of homosexual relationships. A single short play such as *Fog* (the *60's* segment), for example, can be at once comic and satiric, offering a complex presentation of illusion and reality laced with multiple ironies. In *Fog*, two gay men meet (in a sense) in Central Park during a heavy fog that prevents their seeing each other. The fog allows each to create for the other the reality he prefers for himself: the gorgeous "Stud," in his twenties, presents himself as an unattractive, seventeen-year-old writer whose only attraction is his mind, while the effeminate "Fag" presents himself as an attractive man who belittles the value of looks. Both, it seems, have recently left the same party, the Fag in fact looking for the Stud, as the Stud soon realizes in their conversation, though never letting on,

choosing rather to expound on the party guests' shallow emphasis on beauty. Later, when briefly lighting a match, the Fag discovers the Stud's true identity, but he, in turn, does not let on, and together they proceed into the bushes for a sexual encounter, each thinking the other imagines him to be someone different. The Fag is getting what he wants, but is the Stud? Will he not fault the Fag for his falsehood, or will he simply acknowledge his own as they both proceed to laugh about it, having each indulged in his own deception, created his own image, his own reality? Perhaps the play is simply a shrewd look at the complicated games of contemporary sex and love.

These games and intricate knots of feelings and relationships are explored throughout Patrick's work, in a wide range of homosexual and heterosexual characters. Some plays, such as *Cleaning House*, present characters who can see so many sides of an issue that they cannot decide what they really want. Other plays, such as *T-Shirts* and *My Cup Ranneth Over*, present characters who cover up their hurts with a barrage of gags and one-liners. Sometimes, in fact, elaborate puns and joke sequences come so fast and furiously as to leave the audience behind, and some viewers might find the humor strained. Yet much of Patrick's work has been highly popular with audiences, in the tradition of Neil Simon and Jean Kerr (a writer for whom Patrick has expressed much admiration).

JUDAS

One of Patrick's few wholly serious plays is *Judas*, also one of his most powerful. Like *Kennedy's Children*, *Judas* is a play with many realities—that is, with no single illusion to destroy. Also like *Kennedy's Children*, its topic (Jesus's last days) evokes in audience members their own perspectives and interpretations, the conceptions of reality that they hold when they enter the theater. The story line is familiar, but it is susceptible to numerous retellings in fresh approaches, as in Tim Rice and Andrew Lloyd Webber's rock opera *Jesus Christ Superstar* (1970), Pier Paolo Pasolini's film *The Gospel According to St. Matthew* (1964), or even Patrick's own earlier work *Joyce Dynel*.

Despite its title, the play's focus is actually on Pilate. The ambience of the play is strictly late twentieth century, with Pilate in a business suit and Jesus in work clothes, and the dialogue uses very little direct quotation from the Bible, conveying less the feeling of a biblical epic than of a contemporary political drama.

Patrick presents Pilate as a counterpart to Jesus; Pilate has his own "disciples"—Judas the Jew and Klautus, his Roman assistant—whom he is instructing in proper thought and behavior for government service with Rome. At the end of the play, Pilate, too, is betrayed, not by Judas but, like Jesus, by his own countryman, Klautus, who discovers that his master's highest allegiance is not to Rome after all. Pilate, in fact, comes to believe in Jesus's images of a better world, even if it means denouncing Rome. Pilate is a pragmatist, but he believes above all in truth. Patrick avoids the temptation of having Pilate voice his great question to Jesus from John 18:38—"What is truth?"—for it is amply implicit throughout his discussion with Jesus. What Pilate comes to discover is Jesus's truth—the kingdom of Heaven within—as humanity's highest goal. Though he cannot transcend the sectarianism that would destroy Jesus, Pilate still believes in the inner reality as the path to good. The irony is that Pilate, too, is on his way to destruction, when Klautus discovers that he holds something in higher esteem than Rome itself.

More than any other Patrick work, this is a play of ideas in the tradition of George Bernard Shaw, with a superb theatrical sense as well. In the powerful interrogation scene, for example, which carries reverberations of the great confrontation between Christ and the Grand Inquisitor in Fyodor Dostoevski's *The Brothers Karamazov* (1879-1880), Jesus speaks not at all, while Pilate circles him with extended pleas to save his life by denying himself. Jesus's last words onstage, at the end of this scene—when Pilate, joined by Judas, tries to urge Jesus one last time to use a proto-Machiavellian political lie and deny his role as king of the Jews so that he might live to *become* king of the Jews—are merely those of the Lord's Prayer, through which Jesus restores Judas to his faith in him and inspires Judas to his own act of self-sacrifice.

The true reality, according to *Judas*, *Kennedy's Children*, and many other Patrick plays, is the one within, though others may consider it mere illusion. In a time when many playwrights trade in nihilism and despair, Patrick's message is one of hope.

LATER PLAYS

Although Patrick moved to Los Angeles and found steady work as a ghostwriter, he has continued to produce plays. His last production for the New York stage was *Hello Bob*. The new play, composed of twenty-three monologues, centers on a wide variety of characters, from a male prostitute to a director. These characters all address one character, Robert Patrick, who never appears onstage. Patrick integrated autobiographical details into this play, as he has done with many of his other plays. Patrick had four one-act plays (*Ruminations*, *Evan on Earth*, *Harbor*, and *Raise the Children*) that were staged in New York during the 1990's but overlooked by critics. Other productions, such as *Interruptions* and *Sugar Cookies*, have been produced on the stage of, respectively, a college and a high school.

OTHER MAJOR WORK

LONG FICTION: *Temple Slave*, 1994.

BIBLIOGRAPHY

Evans, Everett. "Revival Proves Sixties Legacy Lives." Review of *Kennedy's Children* by Robert Patrick. *Chronicle* (Houston), February 5, 1992. In this review of a revival of *Kennedy's Children* at the Grassroots Theater Project, Evans finds in the play "interwoven monologues by five characters who exist in the same environment but never speak directly to one another." Evans considers, however, that the play still "asks some valid questions about mixed-up American values."

Evett, Marianne. "Playwright Robert Patrick Champions Artistic Integrity of Off-Off Broadway Theater." *Plain Dealer* (Cleveland), May 19, 1989. A good, long interview article occasioned by Patrick's classroom visits, playwriting workshops, and staged readings in Cleveland. Includes a discussion of *Judas*, which was performed at Case Western Reserve University in 1985. "Write what excites you," Patrick advises his workshop participants. He also expresses his firm belief in theater and states that "it's our only real hope of spreading any idea not already accepted." He also discusses acquired immune deficiency syndrome (AIDS).

Kirkpatrick, Melanie. "Fierstein's Gays." Review of *The Haunted Host* by Robert Patrick. *The Wall Street Journal*, May 7, 1991, p. A16. *The Haunted Host*, a two-person play originally performed in 1964, was staged at the La Mama Experimental Theatre Club (ETC), with raging comic Harvey Fierstein and Jason Workman. It was performed with a new play, *Pouf Positive*, a forty-minute monologue by Fierstein.

Marranca, Bonnie, and Gautam Dasgupta. *American Playwrights: A Critical Survey.* 2 vols. New York: Drama Book Specialists, 1981. Contains a chapter on "playwright-actor-director-general factotum" Patrick, whose presence in the early days of Off-Off-Broadway are chronicled here, more in the analytical than the informational mode. Good recaps of the small, often one-person plays, such as *Cornered, Camera Obscura*, and *Help, I Am. Kennedy's Children*, itself a fragmented play, is Patrick's only full-length play to gain any substantial popularity.

Weeks, Jerome. "An Amusing but Superficial Look at Gay Life." *Morning News* (Dallas), September 10, 1991. Patrick's *Untold Decades* is compared to August Wilson's "ongoing attempt to write a drama for each decade of the black American experience." Two plays from the homosexual cycle, together dubbed "Homosexual Acts," played in Dallas to mixed reviews. The plays illustrate the tendency of homosexuals to work "their way into positions of power; and they use it for their protective advantage," Weeks says.

Scott Giantvalley, updated by Thomas J. Taylor and Andrea E. Miller

---

JOHN HOWARD PAYNE

Born: New York, New York; June 9, 1791
Died: Tunis, North Africa; April 9, 1852

PRINCIPAL DRAMA

Julia: Or, The Wanderer, a Comedy in Five Acts, pr., pb. 1806

Lovers' Vows, pb. 1809, pr. 1811 (adaptation of August von Kotzebue's play *Das Kind der Liebe*)

Trial Without Jury: Or, The Magpie and the Maid, pr. 1815(?), pb. 1940 (adaptation of Louis Charles Caigniez and Jean Marie Théodore Baudouin's play *La Pie voleuse*)

Accusation: Or, The Family of D'Anglade, pr. 1816 (adaptation of Frédéric du Petit-Méré's play *Le Vol: Ou, La Famille d'Anglade*)

Brutus: Or, The Fall of Tarquin, pr., pb. 1818

Thérèse: Or, The Orphan of Geneva, pr., pb. 1821 (adaptation of Victor Ducange's play *Thérèse: Ou, L'Orpheline de Genève*)

Adeline, the Victim of Seduction, pr. 1822

Love in Humble Life, pr. 1822 (one act; based on Eugène Scribe and Henri Dupin's play *Michel et Christine*)

Clari: Or, The Maid of Milan, pr., pb. 1823 (libretto, music by Henry R. Bishop; adaptation of L. J. Milon's play *Clari: Ou, La Promesse de mariage*; also as *Angioletta*)

Charles the Second: Or, The Merry Monarch, pr., pb. 1824 (with Washington Irving; adaptation of Alexandre Duval's *La Jeunesse de Henri V*)

Richelieu, a Domestic Tragedy, pr., pb. 1826 (with Irving; adaptation of Duval's *La Jeunesse du Duc de Richelieu: Ou, Le Lovelace Français*; also as *The French Libertine*)

The Last Duel in Spain, and Other Plays, pb. 1940 (edited by Codman Hislop and W. R. Richardson)

Trial Without Jury and Other Plays, pb. 1940 (edited by Hislop and Richardson)

OTHER LITERARY FORMS

Though John Howard Payne wrote some dramatic criticism and several essays on political subjects, he is chiefly known as a dramatist.

ACHIEVEMENTS

The achievement of John Howard Payne is difficult to gauge. His work is admittedly derivative; much of it consists of close translations and adaptations of other dramas, mostly French. At his best, however, he was a supreme adapter. He worked with astonishing speed, producing more than sixty plays in a career of little more than twenty years. His career, in fact, provides fascinating insight into the lifestyle of the dramaturgical hack of the early nineteenth century.

Theatrical houses of the day hungrily devoured any material, original or adapted, that would fill seats. Plagiarism was a minor concern in an age of uncertain and ill-defined copyright laws, and Payne thus provided a welcome service to theater managers and actors. Though not a creator, he was a literary carpenter, a superlative transmitter of popular drama. His knowledge of the contemporary stage and of what was dramatically effective often resulted not in slavish imitation but in the molding of a truly superior product from existing material, although that material was always suited to the popular taste rather than to the discriminating temper.

Payne's position in the history of the drama can best be understood by comparing him to a scriptwriter; he produced quick-moving melodramatic plays for a general audience that used the theater at that time as general audiences of today use television. Much of his work was entertainment that never had any pretensions to art.

BIOGRAPHY

John Howard Payne's career in the theater began when he submitted some critical reviews to newspapers at the age of twelve. His precocious interest was so intense that he founded his own theatrical newspaper, *Thespian Mirror*, when he was fourteen. Though short-lived—issued only from December 28, 1805, to March 22, 1806—the paper gave Payne a great deal of self-confidence and a few literary contacts. At fifteen he wrote his first play, *Julia*. Though a completely conventional melodrama, the play was a modest success and so impressed his friends that they arranged to send the young playwright to Union College in Schenectady, New York. He was there only two years, however, when his family's bankruptcy forced him to return to New York City and to the pursuit of his overwhelming ambition, acting.

A genial, good-humored, handsome young man, Payne made his debut in 1809, at the age of eighteen. He played a number of roles, from Young Norval (a famous male lead in John Home's popular tragedy, *Douglas*, pr. 1756) to Hamlet. Payne, in fact, was among the first Americans to play Hamlet, and the theatrical season of 1809 was to be the time of his greatest triumph as an actor. His fame as "the American Roscius," a great Roman actor, followed him wherever he played—from Boston, Massachusetts, to Charleston, South Carolina. Whether because the novelty of his boyish good looks soon wore off or because his talent was too undisciplined or because established actors were jealous of his early success, Payne found his career stalling badly. For the rest of his life, in fact, his acting roles were irregular, and he was continually in debt.

John Howard Payne (Hulton Archive by Getty Images)

It was during the time of his success as an actor that Payne wrote his second play, *Lovers' Vows*, an adaptation of August von Kotzebue's *Das Kind der Liebe* (pr. 1790). Payne used an English translation for his own adaptation, and though this work is not particularly noteworthy, it clearly shows Payne's early disposition toward adaptation as a quick and easy way to make money.

Meanwhile, the American theater began to fall on hard times. The public taste, never very sophisticated, was being distracted by the War of 1812 and the resulting instability of the American economy. Still in debt and harboring his great ambition to succeed on the British stage, Payne left New York for Liverpool in January, 1813. His voyage signaled a turning point in his career; he was to remain a part of the European theatrical scene for the next twenty years.

By June, 1813, Payne had played at Drury Lane, one of the two legitimate theatrical companies in England, but there, too, audiences tired of the young actor, so that by the summer of 1814, Payne was penniless and facing an uncertain future. At this point, abreast of the latest dramas of England and France, Payne turned his talent as a speedy adapter of other plays toward earning money between acting engagements, which were becoming less frequent. As he had done in the United States, so he could do in Europe; hence, in August, 1815, he translated a popular French melodrama, *La Pie voleuse* (pr. 1815), and quickly wrote an adaptation, *Trial Without Jury*. He eventually sold it to Covent Garden, the rival house of Drury Lane. There is some doubt as to whether the play was ever performed, but there is no doubt about its effect on Payne's career. The manager of Drury Lane, Douglas Kinnaird, was so impressed with both the speed and the theatrical "rightness" of Payne's adaptation that he offered the twenty-four-year-old American the opportunity to supply Drury Lane with as many adaptations of successful plays as he could turn out. Kinnaird sent Payne to Paris, where, for a brief period, Payne worked as both a translator and an adapter, a virtual literary secret agent, in the service not of the government but of Drury Lane Theatre. Payne, in fact, boasted of a "system" whereby he could provide his employer with a complete adaptation of an original French production within four days.

Kinnaird and Drury Lane, however, treated Payne poorly. He was generally underpaid for his work, derived little or no credit for it, and received few opportunities to act, still his principal ambition. Dissatisfied, he left the employ of Drury Lane and went to work for Covent Garden, for which he labored for two years with the same results.

Payne's ill treatment at the hands of theater managers such as Kinnaird and of actors such as Edmund Kean is a telling commentary on the harsh conditions of the London theater business of that period. Ironically, Payne produced his best work at this time. His *Brutus* is generally acknowledged as his finest play, though Payne himself admitted in his preface to the printed edition that he was indebted to at least seven previous plays on the same subject. Typically, he was paid poorly for it, receiving less than other playwrights customarily got for a curtain raiser. Yet, despite accusations of plagiarism, *Brutus* was to become one of the most famous tragedies in English during the entire nineteenth century. Its popularity in America was such that it held the boards for seventy years, supplying a meaty role for actors such as Edwin Forrest, Edwin Booth, and Kean.

Despite the enormous popularity of *Brutus*, Payne was still struggling against crushing debts, and when at last he despaired of fair treatment from both Drury Lane and Covent Garden, he opened his own theater at Sadler's Wells in 1820. The enterprise was a disaster; Payne's poor business sense and the failure of his own plays to draw audiences plunged him into bankruptcy, and he was arrested for debt.

From debtors' prison, Payne still managed to keep up with the latest plays from the Continent. In three days, he adapted *Thérèse*. Selling the play to Drury Lane, Payne bought his way out of prison and fled to Paris; from there, he continued to sell his adaptations of popular French dramas to the British theaters. One such play was *Clari*. A typical melodrama of little literary value, it is nevertheless a noteworthy play because it contains the song "Home Sweet Home," one of the best-known ballads of the era. Payne wrote only the lyrics; the melody was based on a French or Sicilian air. In the play, it is sung by the heroine, who longs for her rural homestead rather than a life of urban dissipation. Interestingly, Payne had not been "home" for ten years, and it would be yet another decade before he returned.

In Paris, Payne renewed his friendship with Washington Irving. The two had known each other as youths in New York City, and during these later years Irving gave his old friend some financial help as well as literary contacts. For a time, they even shared the same house in Paris, collaborating on a number of plays, among them *Charles the Second*, Payne's best comedy. It clearly shows Irving's hand in the urbane wit and comic verve of such characters as Captain Copp. Like Payne's other works, *Charles the Second* is an adaptation. The plot is drawn essentially from a French comedy, although the characters and situations are made thoroughly British. The play is interesting as an example of Irving's dramatic ability.

Back in London in 1824-1825, Payne courted the newly widowed Mary Wollstonecraft Shelley, but no serious relationship seems to have developed. It is uncertain whether Payne's attentions to her were based on her beauty of mind or her bounty of pocketbook. In any event, her stated preference for Irving (unreciprocated on Irving's part) did nothing to dampen the Payne-Irving friendship.

For the next few years, Payne lived a precarious existence, still adapting dozens of plays and selling them to Drury Lane or Covent Garden. Finally, in 1832, penniless and disappointed, he returned to the United States, where he was surprised to find that he was a famous and respected man of letters. His plays had been popular in America since *Brutus*, and though he had never received royalties from any of them, dozens of his plays were running in American houses through the 1830's. The fame and prestige that he had so long sought in Europe and that had eluded him had now settled on him in the United States. On his arrival, he was treated as the conquering literary man he had wanted to be in England. He was feted in Boston and New York; benefits were given in his honor; and several of his famous plays, including *Brutus* and *Charles the Second*, as well as his "Home Sweet Home," were performed.

Payne's career as a playwright was finished; for the next few years, he busied himself with visionary schemes. The year 1835 saw him in Georgia gathering materials for a projected series of articles on the plight of the Cherokee Indians, but both the material and the magazine for which it was intended died stillborn. While in Georgia, Payne was detained for his abolitionist activities, was called a troublemaker, and was asked to leave the state.

In 1842, still penurious but well known, Payne was appointed American consul at Tunis by President John Tyler. Recalled by the next administration, he again suffered financial difficulties until his appointment to the same post by President Millard Fillmore in 1851. He died, still in debt, in Tunis, the following year. Ironically, the man whose fame throughout the century was yoked to "Home Sweet Home" died in a foreign land, thousands of miles from his home.

ANALYSIS

John Howard Payne wrote in one of his prefaces that it was "almost hopeless to look to the stage of the present days for a permanent literary distinction." A broader view of the drama in England and the United States during most of the nineteenth century suggests that Payne's admission bespoke not only his own limitations but also the relatively undistinguished record of most of the century's dramatists before the arrival of Oscar Wilde and George Bernard Shaw. On balance, one could justly claim that Payne's enormous output in itself provides the scholar with a source sufficient to gauge accurately the dramatic tastes of an age.

TRIAL WITHOUT JURY

Trial Without Jury was one of Payne's first translations, his first play written or adapted in England, and the work that established his position as "supplier" for Drury Lane and, later, for Covent Garden. An adaptation of the French melodrama *La Pie voleuse*, by Louis Charles Caigniez and Jean Marie Théodore Baudouin, the play is a source of controversy among scholars. There is some evidence that Payne's play was never performed, as three other versions of the original exist in English by other adapters, including Thomas Dibdin and Isaac Pocock, both of whom were well-known hacks for Drury Lane.

Aside from such scholarly discussion, however, and the interesting fact that the original version was turned into a libretto for a sparkling opera by Gioacchino Rossini, *La gazza ladra* (pr. 1817), the play is a trivial concoction that relies on a brilliantly theatrical gimmick.

Rosalie is the pretty young heroine, employed as a maid in the household of Mr. Gregory, a rich farmer, and his wife, Nannette. Rosalie is in love with the Gregorys' handsome son, Henry, who is returning from a career in the army. The army is also the career of Everard, Rosalie's father. As the play opens, the Gregorys are preparing a feast to celebrate Henry's return. Rosalie is setting out the silver and plate, assisted by Coody, an honest manservant and country bumpkin. The family's pet magpie sits in an open cage above the table. While Rosalie and Coody are engaged in friendly banter, the magpie swoops down, steals a spoon, and flies away.

Eventually, the loss of the spoon is noted by Nannette, who suspects Rosalie, since other spoons have disappeared over a period of time. Meanwhile, Rosalie's father, facing court-martial for insubordination, visits his daughter for the last time, asking her to sell a silver spoon of his own and to give him the money later, in the woods. Rosalie sells the spoon, but the money is afterward found on her and she is accused of the theft of the Gregorys' silver. A trial ensues; the prosecutor is a villainous magistrate who seeks vengeance on Rosalie because she had spurned his advances.

In the end, Coody spies the magpie stealing again. Following it, he retrieves a cache of plate, silver, and money. He makes all known; Rosalie is acquitted and is pledged to Henry; her father is exonerated; and the justice is relieved of his duties, which are now given to Gregory.

A modern reader might find it difficult to understand how anything could be made of such nonsense, material more suitable to parody and comic opera than to serious drama, but the original play and its adaptations were quite popular in their time. Despite its foolishness, Payne's play proceeds smoothly. Further, Payne anglicizes the tone and feel of the play by a deft reliance on solid English idiom.

BRUTUS

Though it appeared rather early in Payne's career as a playwright, *Brutus* is his finest achievement. First performed in December, 1818, the play held the stage for more than seventy years and became for many the supreme model for romantic historical tragedy. The importance of *Brutus* lies not in the creation of original characters or dramatic material, but rather in Payne's complete mastery of the art of editing, in pruning and selecting scenes and characters from among the welter of dramatic predecessors. *Brutus* brings the skill of a first-rate adapter to the verge of art. Payne's version has survived because he knew what would work dramatically. He combines, for example, the effective language of Hugh Downman's 1779 version with the effective theatricality of Richard Cumberland's contemporaneous treatment, transposing speeches from the middle of a scene to the end, and making the action more concise and logical.

The sheer theatricality of *Brutus* is impressive. The dialogue is crisp and fast-moving. Payne eliminated many of the excesses of orotund phrasing and simplified the plot, removing subplots and scenes of protracted rhetorical passion. Simplicity, in fact, is the play's chief virtue. *Brutus* is remarkably free, for example, of melodramatic absurdity, though melodramatic elements are bound closely to the plot.

Junius Brutus, Rome's leading citizen, has been killed by Tarquin, who now rules as king, together with his queen, the ruthless Tullia. The spirit of Junius is kept alive by his son Lucius, the Brutus of the play, who has survived the Tarquins' onslaught by feigning madness. Throughout his early confrontations with Tullia and her dissolute son, Sextus, Brutus plays the fool, waiting for a propitious moment to rise up and make Rome a republic. Meanwhile, Brutus's own son, Titus, is saddened by what he believes is his father's madness; Titus keeps his own republican sentiments in check because of his love for Tullia's daughter, Tarquinia.

Brutus's propitious moment arrives when Sextus rapes a noble Roman matron, Lucretia. Lucretia kills herself, and the family seeks vengeance. Brutus abandons his pretense of madness, organizes the enemies of the Tarquins, and leads them to victory. Tullia is captured and dies on the tomb of her father (whom she had murdered), and the republic is restored. In the final dramatic scene, Titus, who has joined the Tarquins out of love for Tarquinia, is captured and brought before his father.

Titus faces Brutus without fear, asking only to be allowed to die on his own sword rather than suffer execution as a traitor. Brutus, however, must remain true to his republican principles: Though "a father's bleeding heart forgives," "the sov'reign magistrate of injured Rome" must condemn. As he gives the signal for execution, Brutus declares: "Justice is satisfied and Rome is free."

Brutus's dilemma in the concluding scene might have been dramatically powerful, but its impact is lessened because Payne provides no preparation for the conflict between paternal and national love, no scenes of intimacy between Brutus and his son to prepare for the climactic scene. The play is interesting as an example of sheer theater and controlled rhetoric, but there is in it little real characterization, little emotional charge, and thus little real tragedy.

BIBLIOGRAPHY

Ailes, Milton E. "John Howard Payne: A Strange, Eventful History." *Frank Leslie's Popular Monthly*, December, 1899, 115-130. This short biography of Payne is particularly interesting for its account of the exhumation of Payne's remains from Tunis and their return to the United States, where they were laid to rest at ceremonies attended by then President Chester A. Arthur and his cabinet. Bandmaster John Philip Sousa and the U.S. Marine Band played Payne's "Home Sweet Home." The article clearly shows the esteem in which Payne was held even as late as 1900.

Hanson, Willis T., Jr. *The Early Life of John Howard Payne: With Contemporary Letters Heretofore Unpublished*. 1913. Reprint. New York: B. Blom, 1971. This standard biography of Payne is particularly interesting for the letters that it contains. Bibliography included.

Harrison, Gabriel. *John Howard Payne: Dramatist, Poet, Actor, and Author of "Home Sweet Home"; His Life and Writing*. Rev. ed. New York: B. Blom, 1969. A reprint of the definitive biography published in 1885, detailing Payne's early career as child actor, his life abroad as dramatist, and his final years as editor and consul at Tunis. The study is valuable as a source of original material, such as Payne's letters and excerpts from his voluminous journals. The book also includes Payne's unpublished juvenilia and his critical reviews, and it provides estimates of Payne's character from friends.

Overmeyer, Grace. *America's First Hamlet*. 1957. Reprint. Westport, Conn.: Greenwood Press, 1975. Overmeyer re-creates Payne's career largely through views of him presented by his friends, particularly Washington Irving and Charles Lamb. The study also draws on Payne's diaries, letters, and critical reviews, and it reveals Payne's brilliant, if erratic, personality and his pioneering work in the early American theater.

Edward Fiorelli

GEORGE PEELE

Born: London, England; July 27, 1556 (baptized)
Died: London, England; November 9, 1596(?)

PRINCIPAL DRAMA

The Hunting of Cupid, wr. 1581-1585, pb. 1591 (no longer extant)
The Arraignment of Paris, pr. c. 1584, pb. 1584
The Battle of Alcazar, pr. c. 1589, pb. 1594
Edward I, pr. c. 1590-1591, pb. 1593
The Old Wives' Tale, pr. c. 1591-1594, pb. 1595
David and Bethsabe, pr. c. 1593-1594, pb. 1599
"Mahomet and Hiren the Fair Greek," wr. before 1594 (no longer extant)

OTHER LITERARY FORMS

George Peele's work in other literary forms consists mostly of occasional pieces celebrating public or patriotic events. Somewhat related to his dramatic works are three of the Lord Mayor of London's annual pageants: *The Device of the Pageant Borne Before Woolstone Dixi*, of 1585; the pageant of 1588 (now lost); and *Descensus Astraeae*, of 1591. "A Farewell," a short poem published in 1589, applauds an English naval expedition setting out to destroy the Spanish forces. Longer occasional poems, with their dates of publication, are *An Eclogue Gratulatory* (1589), celebrating the Earl of Essex's safe return from the same ill-fated naval expedition; *Polyhymnia* (1590), written for the Queen's Accession Day, November 17, 1590; *The Honour of the Garter* (1593), marking the Earl of Northumberland's induction into the Knights of the Garter; and *Anglorum Feriae* (printed transcript, c. 1830), written for the Queen's Accession Day, November 17, 1595. Miscellaneous pieces are the short poems "Lines to Watson" (1582) and "The Praise of Chastity" (1593) and the long poem *A Tale of Troy* (1589; revised as *The Tale of Troy*, 1604), a narrative summary.

ACHIEVEMENTS

George Peele's full achievement as a dramatist cannot now be properly assessed because some of his work is missing. Two of his known plays are lost, and possibly others are; in addition, the extent of his collaboration with other playwrights is unknown. Peele was, however, well respected by his fellow writers, and he is one of those from whom a certain "upstart crow," William Shakespeare, was accused of stealing beautiful feathers (by Robert Greene in *Greene's Groatsworth of Wit Bought with a Million of Repentance*, 1592). Along with Greene, John Lyly, and Christopher Marlowe, Peele was one of the so-called University Wits, in whose hands Renaissance English drama was swiftly breaking out of the classical mold. No doubt, Shakespeare did build on their efforts and their risks: The University Wits, with Thomas Kyd, explored the new world of drama, and Shakespeare colonized it. Except for Marlowe, Peele was probably the most original of Shakespeare's predecessors,

though some of Peele's innovations were not taken up by others (for example, biblical drama).

Peele's dramatic talent, unlike Marlowe's, was not for depicting character and conflict but for spectacle, as his writing of pageants tends to confirm. The prevailing mode in his work is narrative, expository, or poetic: Two main influences on Peele were Geoffrey Chaucer and Edmund Spenser, and one of Peele's achievements was to stake out their material for the drama. His plays embody dramatic conflicts, but the conflicts do not generate much tension; thus, his characters sometimes declaim or rant. Balancing the declamation and ranting is some attractive poetry. In addition, if the approximate dating of his plays is roughly correct, Peele improved as a dramatist as he went along, so that his best plays are his latest ones, *The Old Wives' Tale* and *David and Bethsabe*.

BIOGRAPHY

Many of the facts about George Peele's life are unknown or uncertain. What little is known is to some extent eclipsed by a highly unreliable biographical source, *The Merry Conceited Jests of George Peele* (1607), which depicts him as a rascal. Published by an unknown author eleven years after Peele died, the jest book is merely a traditional collection of old pranks and tricks, here ascribed to Peele. Despite the jest book's apparently fictional nature, biographers have been unable to resist its suggestions, especially in combination with Francis Meres's statement (in *Palladis Tamia: Wit's Treasury*, 1598) that Peele died of syphilis: "As Anacreon the poet died by the pot: so George Peele by the pox." Thus, a tradition has grown up that pictures Peele variously as a wastrel, a street person, and a Bohemian who frequented the White Horse Tavern and caroused with fellow writers and University Wits.

The truth is probably more somber, or at least more sober. Peele spent much of his London childhood in the environs of Christ's Hospital, a public home for orphans and indigent old people managed by his father, James Peele, a solid middle-class citizen and author of two works on double-entry bookkeeping. Peele attended school at Christ's Hospital until his midteens, when he entered Christ Church

College of Oxford University. Here he proceeded to earn a bachelor of arts degree in 1577 and a master of arts degree in 1579. He also became involved with drama at Christ Church College, which had a tradition of presenting plays in its large dining hall. Not only did he translate one of Euripides' plays about Iphigenia but also he became expert at stagecraft, as indicated by his later work on London pageants and his return to Oxford in 1583 as a technical director of the Christ Church plays presented during Count Palatine's visit. Possibly he also had another reason for returning to Oxford: In 1580, he had married a sixteen-year-old Oxford heiress, Ann Cooke, and he spent the next four years in court trying, with meager success, to collect the modest inheritance. He and Ann had one daughter, possibly more (Peele's only extant letter refers to "my eldest daughter"); there is inconclusive evidence that Ann died in 1587 and that Peele remarried—taking as his second wife the widow Mary Yates in 1591—and that any other daughters could have been hers.

What is more certain is that Peele's life after Oxford was a constant struggle for money. His fine Oxford education, whose effects can be seen in the historical and mythological content of his plays, fitted him to be a gentleman, but it was a style he had difficulty maintaining. His writing probably did not bring in enough money, and if he married the widow Mary Yates, her small inheritance also came encumbered with lawsuits. Peele's state toward the end of his life is indicated in the poem *The Honour of the Garter*, wherein he describes himself as a poor poet without a patron but with many cares: "I laid me down laden with many cares/ (My bedfellows almost these twenty years)." Peele's only existing letter, dated 1595 and mentioning his "long sickness," is an appeal to Lord Burghley, Lord High Treasurer of England, for patronage; Lord Burghley, however, placed the letter in his file for cranks and crazy people.

ANALYSIS

George Peele was an inveterate experimenter in verse form, types of drama, and subject matter. His five extant plays are extremely diverse: *The Arraignment of Paris* is a mythological pastoral with touches of a court masque; *The Battle of Alcazar* is a historical melodrama with a revenge motif; *Edward I* is a historical chronicle with elements of romantic comedy; *The Old Wives' Tale* is a folklore play; and *David and Bethsabe* is a biblical tragedy. Some of these plays are imitative, combining the influences of other writers, but the last two in particular show Peele breaking new ground. Their diversity is a tribute to Peele's academic background, which gave him the learning to range widely. At the same time, an academic stiffness permeates his work, again less so in the last two plays. The diversity and experimentation that characterize his work suggest that Peele was only completing his apprenticeship and reaching his stride as a dramatist when he died at the age of forty.

Except for *The Old Wives' Tale*, all of Peele's extant plays are concerned with politics, in particular the behavior of rulers. This interest is consistent with Peele's work in other genres, his pageants for the Lord Mayor and his occasional poems celebrating patriotic or court events. Apparently Peele identified closely with the Elizabethan political order, possibly because he saw himself playing an important role in it. To some extent, too, he was on a political bandwagon: Like all the English, he was stirred by the victory over the Spanish Armada in 1588, and the prevailing patriotic fervor accounts for his chauvinism and his anti-Catholic, anti-Spanish sentiments. Like other playwrights of the time, he no doubt was also happy with the stability under Elizabeth I and concerned about the uncertain succession after her death. Therefore, he wrote plays that examined the behavior of rulers and subjects and offered implicit advice to both. Even *The Old Wives' Tale* cannot entirely be exempted here, since its general admonitions about charitable behavior certainly apply to the political context.

THE ARRAIGNMENT OF PARIS

Peele's three earliest extant plays, awkward apprentice efforts for the greater part, all take up the behavior of rulers. Of the three plays, *The Arraignment of Paris* is the least clearly political and also the best written. A veritable anthology of verse forms—fourteeners, heroic couplets, blank verse, and assorted songs—*The Arraignment of Paris*, as befits a pastoral, maintains a leisurely pace and a light touch, except for a brokenhearted nymph and the death of a lovesick shepherd. The tyranny of lovers in the play is paralleled by the tyranny of the gods, as the Trojan shepherd Paris discovers when he has to judge a beauty contest among three goddesses, Juno, Pallas, and Venus. Paris awards the prize, a golden ball, to Venus, and in consequence Juno and Pallas arraign him before a court of the gods for "indifference." The other gods treat the golden ball like the hot potato it is, and they skirt their difficulty by setting Paris free and getting Diana, the virgin goddess, to rejudge the contest. Diana neatly solves the problem by turning to the audience and handing the symbolic prize to Elizabeth I:

> In state Queen Juno's peer, for power in arms,
> And virtues of the mind Minerva's mate:
> As fair and lovely as the queen of love:
> As chaste as Diana in her chaste desires.

Peele's message is clear: The English have a good queen, one not prone to the capricious and irresponsible behavior of mere gods.

THE BATTLE OF ALCAZAR

If Elizabeth I epitomizes the good ruler who "gives laws of justice and of peace," *The Battle of Alcazar* displays a variety of bad rulers. The worst of them is Muly Mahamet, the Moorish usurper of Barbary who slaughters his own uncle and brothers so that his son may succeed him. One uncle, Abdelmelec, survives and, returning to claim his rightful throne, unseats Muly Mahamet. Crying revenge, Muly Mahamet goes to Sebastian, the young king of Portugal, to ask for help, and Sebastian is rash enough to offer it. For the expedition, Sebastian gets an offer of collaboration from Philip, the Spanish king, but at the last moment, the conniving Spanish king reneges. With his modest force, Sebastian goes off to Barbary, there to die on the desert battlefield of Alcazar, along with Abdelmelec, Muly Mahamet, and most of both armies. Significantly, Sebastian is killed by his own soldiers for leading them into disaster. Suffering the same fate at the hands of his Italian mercenaries is the English adventurer Tom Stukley, sidetracked on his way to becoming the Catholic king of Ireland. In case the audience misses the point, each act is preceded by a choruslike "presenter" and a grisly dumb show—for example, "To them enter Death and three Furies, one with blood, one with dead men's heads in dishes, another with dead men's bones." Thus, in *The Battle of Alcazar*, Peele not only shows how blessed the English are in their ruler but also indulges in some typically vehement anti-Catholic propaganda.

EDWARD I

The blank verse of *The Battle of Alcazar* is full of rant, but the language in *Edward I*, mostly a mixture of blank verse and prose, is considerably better. *Edward I* also provides relief from the wars with some pleasant scenes of comedy, romance, and Welsh rebels playing Robin Hood. The inconsistency of mood, however, causes the long play to fall apart, especially the twist into domestic tragedy at the end. There is also inconsistency of character; it is disconcerting to see Queen Elinor, at first benevolent and loving, turn out to be a torturer who suckles a poisonous snake at the breast of the Lord Mayor's wife. Then King Edward, hitherto an ideal exemplar of kingly behavior, poses as a French friar in order to hear Elinor's secret deathbed confession of infidelities with his brother (on her wedding day) and with a friar. One is reminded of Peele's penchant for spectacle when the earth at Charing Green opens up and swallows the evil queen:

> QUEEN: Gape, earth, and swallow me, and let my soul
> Sink down to Hell if I were author of
> That woman's tragedy. Oh, Joan! Help, Joan,
> Thy mother sinks!

Unfortunately, the earth spits her forth again at Potter's Hive, in time for this queen of Spanish origin to decimate her English royal family.

THE OLD WIVES' TALE

For unknown reasons, the first edition of *The Old Wives' Tale* indicated only that the play was "written by G. P." Perhaps the initials G. P. were readily identifiable at the time; in any event, the author was not identified in print as George Peele until 1782, by Isaac Reed in his *Biographia Dramatica*. Reed's identification has not been much disputed because internal evidence of language and style points to Peele as author, as does the play's unrestrained experimentation in content and form.

Indeed, most commentators stress the play's uniqueness among extant Renaissance English drama: its wild mix of folkloric elements. The play is not as original, however, as this mix makes it first appear. The idea of dramatizing folklore could have been suggested by almost any village mumming or old gammer such as the one in the play. It was also only a short step from dramatizing classical mythology to dramatizing native folklore. Here, as in his other plays, Peele made heavy use of sources, except here the sources were likely oral rather than written. In form, too, the play's compact action, suitable for folk material, is reminiscent of medieval drama, while the music and spectacle suggest the sophisticated influence of the court masque. Still, Peele's daring use of folkloric elements opened a rich lode for Shakespeare and other dramatists, helped to bridge the gap between classical and native drama, and helped to legitimate certain "low" material for later romantic comedy.

Some features of the play still seem strikingly new, even modern. One such feature is the dignity accorded the "young master's" retainers, however comically lost, and the old peasant couple, Clunch and Madge, who take the retainers in for the night. In his humble cottage, Clunch the "smith leads a life as merry as a king with Madge his wife." Madge provides the evening's entertainment with her old wives' tale; she is not one of the "rude mechanicals" out of Shakespeare's *A Midsummer Night's Dream*, a play perhaps inspired by *The Old Wives' Tale*. Another notable feature is the association of folklore with the night, with the world of dreams, the irrational, and the supernatural. Here the archetypes flow fast and furiously: the conjurer, the abducted maiden, the quest, the two brothers, the two sisters, the man-bear standing at the crossroads, the grateful dead, the heads in the well, and on and on. Finally, a related feature, familiar to modern audiences from Hollywood's cinematic fade, is the merging of the old lady's spoken narrative into dramatization. As in a modern psychological drama, this convention suggests that the play-within-the-play is taking place in her mind, or at least through her words.

The experimentation in content and form carries over into the play's mix of prose, blank verse, rhymed verse, and songs. As in most Renaissance work, there is a great deal of punning and play with language (including Latin). There is parody of other writers, of Petrarchan conventions, and of the folkloric mode. There is much sexual innuendo, especially in the folklore material.

Some commentators have found only confusion in this mixture of styles, but at least two themes stand out clearly and simply in *The Old Wives' Tale*. First, the old wife tells her tale to entertain her guests. Her purpose suggests that a story—and, by extension, art in general—need be nothing more than pleasant playing, which is a value in itself, a human gesture in a human context, a gift more sustaining than the bread and pudding that the guests refuse. The second theme, related to the first, is suggested by the father of the two sisters, Lampriscus, who pleads with the bear-man Erestus "for charity," "for neighborhood or brotherhood." Erestus gives Lampriscus charity, as he does other characters, in the form of his oracles. Throughout the play-within-the-play, those characters who show charity or "brotherhood" are rewarded, while those who are uncharitable also get their deserts. Even in the framing action, the theme of charity is enforced by Clunch and Madge's hospitality to the lost retainers, by the old wife who shares her food, her fire, and her imagination.

DAVID AND BETHSABE

There is no doubt that *David and Bethsabe*, the only biblical play among extant English Renaissance drama, is Peele's work, but there is evidence that the text is corrupt (for example, in one startling textual fragment, Absalom bounces forth, alive and well, after he has just writhed through one of those sensational and prolonged Elizabethan deaths). It is thus uncertain whether one should criticize Peele or a corrupt text for occasional instances of awkward or obscure imagery and action. Such imagery may be a result of Peele's striving for a biblical richness, which he sometimes achieves (with the help of his source) but which he sometimes inflates into purple passages or bombast. Any awkward action may be attributable to Peele's condensation of time and action here, as in

The Old Wives' Tale. Despite the play's tendency toward long speeches, events move rapidly, covering the David-Bethsabe affair, the incest of Amnon and Thamar, and the rebellion of Absalom. During this time, Salomon is born to David and Bethsabe, grows to a youth, and begins spouting his traditional wisdom. The rambling plot is held together by an Aeschylean curse wherein the evils visited on David's children are presumably caused by the sins of the father, in particular his affair with Bethsabe. With his many wives and concubines and his close relationship to God, David may have reminded contemporary audiences of Henry VIII, Elizabeth I's father.

Aside from the sometimes rich blank verse, the sordid action, and the plot's biblical basis, the play's main attraction is the conjunction of theology, politics, and character, though modern audiences might find the theme offensive. David is depicted as an Asian tyrant whose greatness is measured by his self-indulgence; hence, it is natural in the play to see outward events as an extension of his ego. He forces himself on Bethsabe, sends her soldier-husband Urias into the front lines to die, appears at the siege of Rabbah in time to take credit for the victory, and orders all the town's inhabitants slaughtered. Then, for his sins, punishment is visited on his children: Amnon forces himself on Thamar, Absalom kills Amnon, and Absalom is killed in a rebellion against David. Modern audiences might view Absalom as a force for reform, but they would be wrong. Absalom's vanity makes him an unworthy successor to David; instead, the wise Salomon, son of David and Bethsabe, is the next chosen one. In rebelling against David, proud Absalom has also tried to usurp the authority of God, whose prerogative it is to punish chosen ones. The proper role of subjects is illustrated by the submissive Bethsabe and the sycophantic Urias. In all of English Renaissance drama, one could hardly find a more enthusiastic endorsement of the divine right of kings.

David and Bethsabe, like much of Peele's work, shows that the playwright was more than a budding sycophant himself. A member of the London middle class who worked his way up from a Christ's Hospital scholar to an Oxford gentleman to a University Wit and would-be court hanger-on, Peele identified with the greatness of the ruling class in his writing. When he was not offering outright flattery to the queen and members of the nobility, he was usually giving implicit advice on the proper behavior of rulers and subjects. He apparently felt that, as a writer, a volunteer poet laureate, he played an important part in the ruling order. It is therefore ironic that the Lord High Treasurer of England scorned his dying plea for patronage; it is also ironic that Peele should be best remembered for *The Old Wives' Tale*, a play that dignifies humble people.

OTHER MAJOR WORKS

POETRY: *An Eclogue Gratulatory*, 1589; *A Tale of Troy*, 1589 (revised as *The Tale of Troy*, 1604); *Polyhymnia*, 1590; *The Honour of the Garter*, 1593; *Anglorum Feriae*, c. 1830 (wr. c. 1595).

MISCELLANEOUS: *The Life and Works of George Peele*, 1952-1970 (3 volumes; Charles Tyler Prouty et al., editors).

BIBLIOGRAPHY

Braunmuller, A. R. *George Peele*. Boston: Twayne, 1983. An attempt to rebuild Peele's reputation by noting how thoroughly he studied the folk motifs used in *The Old Wives' Tale* and how frequently he rearranged historical facts for *The Battle of Alcazar* and *Edward I* to relate those plays to current political concerns. Asserts that Peele is a careful artist worthy of reexamination as one learns more about Elizabethan art and thought.

Clemen, Wolfgang. *English Tragedy Before Shakespeare: The Development of Dramatic Speech.* Translated by T. S. Dorsch. London: Methuen, 1961. Peele's five extant plays are analyzed in turn. Clemen concludes that Peele had considerable gifts for poetic expression and could create effective dramatic moments, but he lacked a talent for consistency in characterization or plot structure. Emphasis on Peele's language and the set speeches in his plays.

Dreher, G. K. *Samples from the Love of King David and Fair Bethsabe.* Chicago: Adams Press, 1980. This unusual brief volume relates passages from the play *David and Bethsabe* to their biblical sources, followed by commentary on these passages.

Horne, David H. *The Life and Minor Works of George Peele*. 1952. Reprint. Westport, Conn.: Greenwood Press, 1978. A lengthy study of Peele's life and family backgrounds, with some historical and critical information about the plays. Contains illustrations and references from public records concerning the Peele family. Informative and readable.

Hunter, G. K. *Lyly and Peele*. London: Longmans, Green, 1968. This thin volume, although containing only some ten pages on Peele, provides comments on every play. Peele is seen as highly patriotic, using Christopher Marlowe's style and Marlowe's flamboyant actor, Edward Alleyn, to express his views. Comments on Peele's stylistic decorum and his varying use of language to suit the audience and/or subject matter. Hunter states that Peele could reach members of the audience because he knew and shared their assumptions.

Harold Branam,
updated by Howard L. Ford

BENITO PÉREZ GALDÓS

Born: Las Palmas, Canary Islands; May 10, 1843
Died: Madrid, Spain; January 4, 1920

PRINCIPAL DRAMA

El hombre fuerte, wr. 1864-1868, pb. 1902
Un joven de provecho, wr. 1867, pb. 1935
Realidad, pr., pb. 1892 (adaptation of his novel)
La loca de la casa, pr., pb. 1893
Gerona, pr. 1893, pb. 1908 (adaptation of his novel)
La de San Quintín, pr., pb. 1894 (*The Duchess of San Quintín*, 1917)
Los condenados, pr. 1894, pb. 1895
Voluntad, pr. 1895, pb. 1896
Doña Perfecta, pr., pb. 1896 (adaptation of his novel)
La fiera, pr. 1896, pb. 1897
Electra, pr., pb. 1901 (English translation, 1911)
Alma y vida, pr., pb. 1902
Mariucha, pr., pb. 1903
El abuelo, pr., pb. 1904 (adaptation of his novel; *The Grandfather*, 1910)
Bárbara, pr., pb. 1905
Amor y ciencia, pr., pb. 1905
Pedro Minio, pr. 1908, pb. 1909
Zaragoza, pr., pb. 1908 (music by Arturo Lapuerto; adaptation of his novel)
Casandra, pr., pb. 1910 (adaptation of his novel)
Celia en los infiernos, pr., pb. 1913
Alceste, pr., pb. 1914
Sor Simona, pr., pb. 1915
El tacaño Salomón, pr., pb. 1916
Santa Juana de Castilla, pr., pb. 1918
Antón Caballero, pr. 1921, pb. 1922 (completed by Serafín and Joaquín Álvarez Quintero)

OTHER LITERARY FORMS

Benito Pérez Galdós is known primarily for his novels. Between 1873 and 1912, he wrote forty-six historical novels, called *Episodios nacionales*. In addition, he produced thirty-two other novels, the first of which, *La sombra* (1871; *The Shadow*, 1980), may have been written as early as 1865. A journalist by profession, Pérez Galdos wrote many articles, as well as prologues to his own works and those of his contemporaries.

ACHIEVEMENTS

Benito Pérez Galdós wrote some two dozen plays. Critics are divided with regard to their merit, although there is an increasing appreciation of the works he wrote for the stage. Contemporaries of Pérez Galdós criticized the novelistic traits they saw in his dramas. In 1893, Leopoldo Alas, known by his pseudonym Clarín, wrote that Pérez Galdós had only managed to put on the stage, with a few changes, *ideas novelescas*. Other critics agreed that Pérez Galdós's theater suffered from an overabundance of detail, which encumbered the plot and failed to advance the action. They complained of excessive dialogue and of the author's inability to achieve dramatic intensity. In short, many of the same qualities that Pérez Galdós's admirers praised in his books, his detractors criticized in his plays. Indeed, one obstacle to the appreciation of Pérez Galdós's dramas may be that so many of them are theatrical adaptations of novels. Audiences familiar with the richly woven fabric of the author's fiction may have felt dissatisfied with his dramas, for which the plot had necessarily to be compressed and from which powerful scenes sometimes had to be omitted because of staging difficulties. For example, the suicide pact between Don Pío and the Count of Albrit is absent from the stage version of the novel *El abuelo* (1897), possibly because it is set on a steep cliff. Nevertheless, not all critics were dissatisfied with Pérez Galdós's theater, and after his death, a reevaluation began. In 1929, H. Chonon Berkowitz affirmed, "From a purely literary standpoint, his dramas share the merits of his novels; in so far as genius expresses itself in substance and not in form, Galdós the dramatist will stand the test of time as well as Galdós the novelist."

From a commercial point of view, about half of Pérez Galdós's dramas were successful. Critic Federico Carlos Sainz de Robles qualifies four of them as "glorious successes"; these are *Realidad*, *The Duchess of San Quintín*, *Electra*, and *The Grandfather*. Those Sainz de Robles calls "great successes" are *La loca de la casa*, *Doña Perfecta*, *Pedro Minio*, *Celia en los infiernos*, and *Sor Simona*. Other "successes" are *Mariucha*, *El tacaño Salomón*, and *Santa Juana de Castilla*. The rest of Pérez Galdós's dramas were not particularly well received. Modern critics judge *Electra* and *The Grandfather* to be among Pérez Galdós's best plays.

Pérez Galdós's drama is considered transitional: It bridged the gap between the melodramatic, sensation-

Benito Pérez Galdós (Library of Congress)

alist theater of José Echegaray y Eizaguirre, who dominated the Spanish stage during the late nineteenth century, and the more realistic, satirical, problem-oriented schools of the early twentieth century. Like Echegaray and his followers, Pérez Galdós emphasized social questions, but he differed from them in his disregard for passion and rhetoric, and in his preference for conversational language. While the writers of Echegaray's school tended to write in verse (although they eventually abandoned this practice), Pérez Galdós always wrote in prose.

Although Pérez Galdós's theatrical achievements were largely overlooked during his lifetime, today critics recognize that Pérez Galdós was instrumental in freeing Spanish drama from the conventions of Romanticism and in reintroducing the social realism that had characterized theater in Spain since the early sixteenth century and that would become fundamental to the works of twentieth century playwrights such as Antonio Buero Vallejo and Alfonso Sastre. With Pérez Galdós, Spanish theater regained the popular bent that had always been one of its most salient characteristics.

BIOGRAPHY

Considering the immense amount of critical attention that Benito Pérez Galdós's writing has attracted, it is surprising that so little is known about his life. Pérez Galdós was a man of the written word, not of the spoken word. His reticence is legendary. Modest and reserved, Pérez Galdós spoke little about himself and left few memoirs. In a group he was an attentive listener, not an avid participant. He appears to have confided little to his friends because they have been able to provide biographers with a minimum of significant information. His writing is not a reliable source of biographical material, either, since he sought to maintain a distance between himself and the characters and situations he depicted.

Pérez Galdós was born in the Canary Islands, a fact that is often cited to explain his fascination with life on the peninsula. H. Chonon Berkowitz, a major Pérez Galdós scholar, writes that if the author had been born on the mainland, he might not have become such a meticulous observer of Spanish traits.

Pérez Galdós's father was a military officer. His mother, the daughter of a former secretary of the Inquisition in the Canary Islands, was a devout Christian. Pérez Galdós was educated in an English school until he was thirteen and later traveled in England. He had a good knowledge of English literature, and critics have often pointed out similarities between Pérez Galdós's novels and those of nineteenth century English writers, especially Charles Dickens. Pérez Galdós received his *bachillerato*, or secondary school degree, from the Colegio de San Agustín, where he excelled in literature. He also studied music and painting, interests that are reflected in his writing. His own illustrations appear in several volumes of his *Episodios nacionales*, and he painted many of the watercolors in his summer home in Santander.

Pérez Galdós's interest in theater dates from his secondary school days. In the 1840's, a dramatic society had been formed in Las Palmas. The group had both artistic and social functions, and the most prominent families in the area participated. By 1844, a cultural center with a small theater and areas for literary and other activities had been constructed. When he was still a student at the Colegio de San Agustín,

Pérez Galdós wrote his first article for a student newspaper. Given the importance that theater occupied in the province, it is not surprising that this was a review of a performance by a zarzuela and opera group.

After he left Las Palmas, Pérez Galdós studied law in Madrid, although he felt little enthusiasm for the profession. He did finish the course, but seems to have spent most of his time acquainting himself with the capital, attending the theater, and participating in literary discussions at the cafés. Although he had already written for newspapers in Las Palmas, his career actually began in Madrid, in 1865, with the publication of a series of articles on the arts that appeared in *La nación*. Journalism was not Pérez Galdós's primary interest, however, even though he continued to write articles as a source of income. He had his heart set on becoming a dramatist, and in 1865 he wrote "La expulsión de los moriscos," a Romantic drama in verse (which eventually was lost). Neither this work nor Pérez Galdós's second Romantic play, *El hombre fuerte*, was ever produced.

For many years it was thought that Pérez Galdós turned to writing novels in 1868, after a recent trip to Paris. The author himself affirms that in the French capital he became fascinated with Honoré de Balzac and decided to attempt his first novel, which was completed during a second visit to France that same year. In his *Memorias* (1930), Pérez Galdós writes that in the period between these two trips to Paris, he became disillusioned with his attempts to write good theater: "I pulled my plays and dramas out of a drawer and found them turned to dust; what I mean is, they seemed ridiculous to me, they seemed worthy of being burned." Critic Rodolfo Cardona has shown, however, that Pérez Galdós had actually read at least fifteen of Balzac's novels before going to France and that his first novel was not *The Golden Fountain Café*, the work completed in Paris in 1868, as previously thought, but *La sombra*, probably written in 1865. Pérez Galdós's decision to abandon the theater and to write novels had nothing to do with his trip to France or his discovery of Balzac, argues Cardona, but rather with an inner struggle between his Romantic tendencies, manifested in his plays, and his desire to observe and accurately describe his world, manifested in his novels. According to Cardona, Pérez Galdós was profoundly influenced by Johann Wolfgang von Goethe's *Wilhelm Meister* novels, which constitute a repudiation of the Romantic concept of life. Pérez Galdós, torn between Romanticism and realism, opted for the latter and, as a result, began to cultivate the realistic novel.

One of the most important events in Pérez Galdós's life occurred immediately after his second trip to France. In 1868, on his way back to Spain, Pérez Galdós passed through Barcelona, where he witnessed the Revolution of September. The event appears to have affected him deeply, sparking a reflection on national problems that was enriched in later years by his contacts with important political and literary figures.

In 1869, Pérez Galdós joined the staff of *Las cortes*. He also contributed to *Revista de España* and later became editor of *El debate*. Through his work as a journalist, Pérez Galdós met many prominent statesmen and artists, but in 1873—now author of three novels—he broke off relationships with his friends and entered into a period of isolation and intense creative activity. During this year, he wrote the first four of his forty-six historical novels, known as *Episodios nacionales*. In 1874, he wrote five, and the following year he wrote three. In 1876, he produced not only three historical novels but also one contemporary novel, *Doña Perfecta* (1876; English translation, 1880). Thereafter, Pérez Galdós continued to keep up this pace until 1879, when he finished the second series of *Episodios nacionales*. During the following years, he wrote contemporary novels, until, in 1898, he began the third series of *Episodios nacionales*.

In spite of his amazing prolificacy, Pérez Galdós found time to travel. In 1883 he went to London—the first of many trips to England—where he visited the locations immortalized by Dickens in his novels. He also traveled to other European countries and throughout Spain. Never having married, he was free to jaunt about as he wished. Often he went third-class, stopping at rural inns, where he came into contact with all kinds of people. With his keen eye and

unobtrusive manner, he gleaned a wealth of detail that would enrich his novels.

Roughly twenty-five years after his first modest attempts at writing drama, Pérez Galdós turned once again to the theater. During the interim, he had not lost interest in drama entirely. The element of dialogue in his novels had increased in importance, while the narrative element had decreased, until the author finally developed a new form called the *novela dialogada*. An example is the novel *Realidad* (*Reality*, 1992), published in 1889.

Pérez Galdós's reasons for returning to the theater are not completely clear, but in 1912 he stated in an interview that the dramatic genre had been his first love and had always attracted him. By the time he wrote the play *Realidad* in 1892, he was a well-known novelist. Rodolfo Cardona points out that in late nineteenth century Spain, the novel was flourishing, but the drama was languishing. He suggests that Pérez Galdós wished to regenerate the Spanish theater, imbuing it with a sense of realism and immediacy. According to Cardona, Pérez Galdós was motivated by a personal need and a sense of social mission; he wanted to indoctrinate his audiences in the truth at the same time that he hoped to revitalize a moribund genre. Whatever the impetus for Pérez Galdós's return to drama, however, his new plays were entirely different from his early attempts. Rather than Romantic fantasies, the works of this later period are realistic and anticonventional.

Realidad was immediately followed by seven other plays. Then, between *La fiera* (1896) and *Electra* (1901), Pérez Galdós temporarily abandoned the theater and concentrated on the historical novel. Berkowitz has suggested that in this period, during which Spain was involved in the Spanish-American War and the writers of the Generation of 1898 were engaging in intense analysis of the national psyche, Pérez Galdós did not feel free to comment on contemporary events. At any rate, when Pérez Galdós did return to the stage, it was to produce a flow of plays nearly uninterrupted until his death.

Pérez Galdós was elected to the Royal Spanish Academy in 1889, and he took his seat in 1897. He was recommended for a Nobel Prize in Literature (which he did not receive). It has been suggested that the Nobel Prize committee feared giving offense to a Catholic country by conferring a distinction on a rabid anti-Catholic. Pérez Galdós also became active in politics, and in 1907 he was elected deputy of the republican party in Madrid.

Toward the end of his life, Pérez Galdós began to lose his sight. He went completely blind in 1912, yet continued his literary activities until his death, dictating his works to others. His persistence was caused by economic necessity, for, in spite of being the most widely read writer of his generation, he was impoverished during his old age, the victim of poor management and unscrupulous business partners. He died on January 4, 1920.

ANALYSIS

Benito Pérez Galdós sought to develop his own dramatic technique and thus deliberately divorced himself from prevailing conventions. He recognized that his tendencies toward psychological analysis, slow exposition, long scenes, and occasional use of obscure symbolism ran against current tastes but argued for an open-minded approach to theater. Pérez Galdós believed that dramatic art was in a constant state of evolution and should never be fixed by canons.

Like his novels, Pérez Galdós's plays depict Spanish reality in great detail, although toward the end of his career his theater tended to become less local and more universal. In many works, he analyzed the national state of mind and those aspects of Hispanic society that he viewed as stifling or degenerating—among these, political and moral corruption, the obsession with family honor and lineage, decadent aristocracy, social climbing, and the adherence to a social hierarchy that made the use of connections and interpersonal protection inevitable.

Pérez Galdós was fascinated with the complexities of human behavior, and much of his drama reveals considerable psychological understanding. Although his characters usually represent a particular idea and in this sense are philosophical abstractions, they are often vivid and convincing. The array of characters Pérez Galdós created for the theater is nearly as wide as that which he created for his novels. His gallery of creations is a cross section of nineteenth century Spain. It includes people from all walks of life: sophisticated, cosmopolitan types, provincial figures, rural folks. Aristocrats, professionals, government workers, petty officials, clerks, peasants, Gypsies, servants, beggars, and bums all appear in this microcosm of Spanish society. There are religious men and women and degenerates, idealists and opportunists, dreamers and visionaries, fanatics and moderates. There are Spaniards and foreigners. Pérez Galdós's characters are of every occupation, every background, every age, and a variety of origins.

THE GRANDFATHER

One type that appears frequently in both Pérez Galdós's novels and his plays is the impoverished aristocrat who retains a keen sense of social superiority. In *The Grandfather*, one of Pérez Galdós's most successful dramas from both the commercial and the literary standpoint, the aging Count of Albrit, Don Rodrigo de Arista-Potestad, returns from an unsuccessful venture in Peru to his family lands in the north of Spain. Now penniless, the count must accept hospitality from Venancio and his wife, Gregoria, former tenant-farmers on the Albrit estate who are currently the owners of the manor, known as La Pardina. Don Rodrigo's son has died, and his daughter-in-law, Lucrecia, Countess of Laín, is a foreigner and a libertine who has engaged in several affairs. Her daughters, Dolly and Nell, live at La Pardina with Venancio and Gregoria.

The play's plot and philosophical message revolve around the paternity of Don Rodrigo's two grandchildren, Dolly and Nell. When the count learns that one of the girls is not the daughter of his deceased son and therefore not a legitimate Albrit, he is torn with anguish. Proud, arrogant, and obsessed with his bygone glory, he seeks desperately to verify which granddaughter is genuine and which is fraudulent, but Don Rodrigo is nearly blind and cannot distinguish between them. In any event, the physical evidence is inconclusive, and both girls seem to love the count equally. Furthermore, both are independent and rebellious. There seems to be no unmistakable sign of the superiority of either one. Don Rodrigo's sightlessness symbolizes his doubt or inability to "see" the truth.

The only clue is that Dolly (the illegitimate granddaughter) is a talented painter; her mother's lover was an artist. Don Rodrigo, however, sees Dolly's gift only as an indication of her greater sensitivity. Throughout most of the play, he grapples with evidence—all of it circumstantial—and finally reaches the conclusion that Dolly is his legitimate heir, for he sees in her the pride, loyalty, and hauteur he associates with the aristocracy.

Like Pérez Galdós's finest novelistic creations, the Count of Albrit is a complex character who is both pathetic and irritating, lovable and abominable. An irascible old man who insists on having his own way, he demands submissiveness from all who surround him. Given his circumstances, his pretentiousness is as offensive as it is absurd. Although Pérez Galdós is known as a realist, his characters are often distortions in which one or two features are exaggerated. Indignant when he is not served the finest coffee and infuriated that his servant is taken away, Don Rodrigo borders on the caricaturesque. The shabby old man does elicit sympathy, however, for he has been deeply afflicted by the death of his son and suffers greatly from his present disgrace. Furthermore, the anguish that his uncertainty causes him is genuine. The count truly loves Dolly and Nell, and the knowledge that one of them is not of his blood torments him. The image of Don Rodrigo, known as the Lion of Albrit, struggling to hold on to his dignity amid the vestiges of his shattered world, is deeply moving.

In his prologue to *Los condenados*, Pérez Galdós wrote: "The goal of every dramatic work is to interest and move the audience, snaring its attention, exciting an interest in the issue and creating an attachment to the characters, so that a perfect fusion is achieved between real life, contained in the public's mind, and the imaginary world that the actors create on the stage." Typically, each of Pérez Galdós's plays revolves around one central issue—philosophical, social, political, or moral—that was of concern to his audience and which he elucidated through the creation of interesting, psychologically complex characters. This fusion of the abstract and the tangible is beautifully achieved in all the author's best works.

In *The Grandfather*, the central problem is lineage. Which of the girls, Nell or Dolly, has inherited her grandfather's nobility? The count becomes convinced that Dolly is an authentic descendant of the Arista-Potestad line when she flies into fury at the suggestion that her grandfather be forced to leave the family estate. In his eyes, Dolly displays the fierceness and sense of honor that define her as a true aristocrat, while Nell, who is willing to let her grandfather be taken away, lacks these qualities. After reassessing Nell's behavior, he concludes that she is somewhat frivolous and vulgar. When it turns out that Dolly is the spurious granddaughter, Don Rodrigo is forced to admit that love, not the superficial bonds of name and lineage, is the essence of a relationship; it is Dolly, not Nell, who not only defends him but sacrifices everything to stay with him. The work ends somewhat melodramatically, as the grandfather rejects those values to which he had always adhered: "I see now that the thoughts, calculations, and resolutions of human beings are worth nothing. All of that is rust that crumbles and falls. . . . What is inside is what remains. . . . The soul does not oxidize. . . . My child . . . love . . . the eternal truth." Once he has rejected the old order and accepted a new, healthier outlook, the count achieves a sense of liberation. The naturalists of the late nineteenth century—Emilia Pardo Bazán and Leopoldo Alas, for example—had stressed the role of heredity in the development of the individual. Pérez Galdós does not deny the role of heredity (Dolly has inherited her father's artistic talent), but he does stress that emotional ties are far more meaningful than blood ties.

MEMORABLE CHARACTERS

Pérez Galdós produced an impressive number of strong female characters. In addition to Dolly, Isidora of *Voluntad* and Victoria of *La loca de la casa* are admirable for their determination and energy. Yet not all the women who populate Pérez Galdós's plays are positive characters. Perfecta (*Doña Perfecta*), Augusta (*Realidad*), and Bárbara (*Bárbara*) are examples of women whose egotism and mistaken values cause heartbreak or disaster.

As in Pérez Galdós's novels, the name of a character is often the key to his or her personality. For example, in *The Grandfather*, Arista (Don Rodrigo's paternal surname) means "bristle," and Potestad (his maternal surname) means "power." Thus, he is a bristling, irritatingly rigid aristocrat. Lucrecia's name is an ironic reference to the Roman heroine who prided herself on her virtue. Don Pío Coronado (pious, tonsured cleric), the sisters' tutor, is virtuous to the point of foolishness, for he allows everyone to abuse him; the name of Don Salvador Ángulo (savior, angel), who is a doctor, is an allusion to the saving power of science; the name of the mayor, Don José Monedero (counterfeiter), suggests the corruption of politicians. Similarly, in *Celia en los infiernos*, Don Infinito's name suggests the fantasy world in which he lives; in *La loca de la casa*, Victoria's name suggests her "victory"; in *Doña Perfecta*, Perfecta's name is an ironic allusion to her self-righteousness—she believes herself to be perfect but is actually a domineering, destructive woman.

The strength of Pérez Galdós's drama lies not only in his creation of memorable characters but also in his depiction of social tensions. In *The Grandfather*, the characters of inferior lineage take pains to show the count courtesy—at least, at first—but their adherence to etiquette becomes increasingly transparent. Venancio, Gregoria, and Senén (a former servant of Lucrecia) smolder with resentment at the count's pretentiousness. A sense of repressed hostility charges the atmosphere. When, at last, the animosity surfaces and explodes, the count is forced to come to terms with his circumstances.

Pérez Galdós's characters are never mere mouthpieces for the author's own convictions. Although Pérez Galdós was sympathetic to the lower classes and critical of the aristocracy, he created small-minded, antagonistic peasants such as Venancio and Gregoria, and opportunistic, social-climbing servants such as Senén. None of his aristocrats is truly hateful, and some are actually attractive. In spite of his own anticlerical leanings, Pérez Galdós presents a progressive priest in *Mariucha*.

Pérez Galdós was far too subtle an artist to produce characters or situations that are clear-cut. He under-stood the fundamental ambiguity of all human reality. He conveys a degree of sympathy for almost all of his characters, even those who embrace mistaken ideals. The conventional villain is nearly absent from his theater. Pérez Galdós shows that every reality is multi-faceted, and it is precisely this perspectivism that prevents his works from becoming mere thesis plays.

A METICULOUS TALENT

Pérez Galdós was meticulous in his attention to detail. He took great pains to be accurate in his depiction of characters and their surroundings in both his contemporary and his historical dramas. He investigated his subjects thoroughly, often traveling to different parts of Spain and even to other countries in order to create accurate settings. He went to Paris in order to research the staging of the *pastorela* in *Alma y vida*. In *La fiera*, *Alma y vida*, *Bárbara*, *Alceste*, and *Santa Juana de Castilla*, Pérez Galdós displayed the same care for historical authenticity as he did in the *Episodios nacionales*.

Pérez Galdós was equally careful in his re-creation of language. His characters speak a lively, conversational Spanish imbued with the savor of their class and surroundings. In like manner, his historical plays reproduce language that is appropriate to the period he depicts.

BENEVOLENCE AS A THEME

Pérez Galdós worked with a wide variety of themes, although the need for benevolence and humanitarianism is a constant in a large part of his work. In several of his plays, he examines different aspects of tyranny. In *La fiera*, for example, he explores the kind that is practiced in the name of an ideal. In *El tacaño Salomón*, he deals with the problems of avarice and charity. In *Electra* and *Doña Perfecta*, he condemns religious fanatics and empty, ritualistic Catholicism. Several dramas treat moral deviations or sexual infractions. In most cases, Pérez Galdós displays tolerance, even indulgence toward characters who stray from the accepted code of behavior, especially when their repentance is sincere. In the case of characters who are deliberately cruel, however, he is less flexible. Although there is playfulness and irony in many of Pérez Galdós's plays, *Pedro Minio* is his only real comedy.

OTHER MAJOR WORKS

LONG FICTION: *La fontana de oro*, 1868 (*The Golden Fountain Café*, 1989); *El audaz*, 1871; *La sombra*, 1871 (*The Shadow*, 1980); *Episodios nacionales*, 1873-1912 (forty-six historical novellas written in five series, many of which were also published separately and are included in this list); *La corte de Carlos IV*, 1873 (*The Court of Charles IV: A Romance of the Escorial*, 1888); *Trafalgar*, 1873 (English translation, 1884); *Gerona*, 1874; *Zaragoza*, 1874 (*Saragossa: A Story of Spanish Valor*, 1899); *La batalla de los Arapiles*, 1875 (*The Battle of Salamanca: A Tale of the Napoleonic War*, 1895); *Doña Perfecta*, 1876 (English translation, 1880); *Gloria*, 1876-1877 (English translation, 1879); *La familia de León Roch*, 1878 (*The Family of León Roch*, 1888; also as *León Roch: A Romance*, 1888); *Marianela*, 1878 (English translation, 1883); *La desheredada*, 1881 (*The Disinherited Lady*, 1957); *El amigo Manso*, 1882 (*Our Friend Manso*, 1987); *El doctor Centeno*, 1883; *La de Bringas*, 1884 (*The Spendthrifts*, 1951; also as *That Bringas Woman*, 1996); *Tormento*, 1884 (*Torment*, 1952); *Lo prohibido*, 1884-1885; *Fortunata y Jacinta*, 1886-1887 (*Fortunata and Jacinta: Two Stories of Married Women*, 1973); *Miau*, 1888 (English translation, 1963); *La incógnita*, 1889 (*The Unknown*, 1991); *Realidad*, 1889 (*Reality*, 1992); *Torquemada en la hoguera*, 1889 (*Torquemada in the Flames*, 1956; also as *Torquemada at the Stake*, 1986); *Ángel Guerra*, 1890-1891 (English translation, 1990); *La loca de la casa*, 1892; *Tristana*, 1892 (English translation, 1961); *Torquemada en la cruz*, 1893 (*Torquemada's Cross*, 1973; also as *Torquemada on the Cross*, 1986); *Torquemada en el purgatorio*, 1894 (*Torquemada in Purgatory*, 1986); *Halma*, 1895; *Nazarín*, 1895 (English translation, 1993); *Torquemada y San Pedro*, 1895 (*Torquemada and Saint Peter*, 1986); *El abuelo*, 1897; *Misericordia*, 1897 (*Compassion*, 1962); *Casandra*, 1905; *Prim*, 1906 (English translation, 1944); *El caballero encantado*, 1909; *La razón de la sinrazón*, 1915; *Torquemada*, 1986 (collection contains *Torquemada at the Stake*, *Torquemada on the Cross*, *Torquemada in Purgatory*, and *Torquemada and Saint Peter*).

NONFICTION: *Discursos académicos*, 1897; *Memoranda*, 1906; *Arte y crítica*, 1923; *Fisonomías sociales*, 1923; *Nuestro teatro*, 1923; *Política española*, 1923; *Cronicón*, 1924; *Toledo*, 1924; *Viajes y fantasías*, 1928; *Memorias*, 1930; *Cronica de Madrid*, 1933; *Cartas a Mesonero Romanos*, 1943; *Crónica de la Quincena*, 1948; *Madrid*, 1956.

BIBLIOGRAPHY

Condé, Lisa P. *Women in the Theatre of Galdós: From "Realidad" (1892) to "Voluntad" (1895).* Lewiston, N.Y.: Edwin Mellen, 1990. A look at the portrayal of women in the plays of Pérez Galdós. Bibliography and index.

Labanyi, Jo, ed. *Galdós*. New York: Longman, 1993. A critical analysis of the works of Pérez Galdós. Bibliography and index.

McGovern, Timothy Michael. *Dickens in Galdós*. New York: Peter Lang, 2000. McGovern compares and contrasts the works of Pérez Galdós and Charles Dickens. Bibliography and index.

Percival, Anthony. *Galdós and His Critics*. Buffalo, N.Y.: University of Toronto Press, 1985. An analysis and interpretation of the works of Pérez Galdós, with emphasis on critical reaction to his work. Bibliography and index.

Ribbans, Geoffrey. *Reality Plan or Fancy? Some Reflections on Galdós's Concept of Realism.* Liverpool, England: Liverpool University Press, 1986. Ribbans examines the works of Pérez Galdós, paying particular attention to the use of realism. Bibliography.

Urey, Diane F. *Galdós and the Irony of Language*. New York: Cambridge University Press, 1982. A study that focuses on the use of irony in its examination of the works of Pérez Galdós.

Willem, Linda M., ed. *A Sesquicentennial Tribute to Galdós, 1843-1993.* Newark, Del.: Juan de la Cuesta, 1993. A group of essays on various aspects of Pérez Galdós's life and works. Bibliography.

Barbara Mujica

CARYL PHILLIPS

Born: St. Kitts, West Indies; March 13, 1958

PRINCIPAL DRAMA

Strange Fruit, pr. 1980, pb. 1981
Where There Is Darkness, pr., pb. 1982
The Shelter, pr. 1983, pb. 1984
The Wasted Years, pr. 1984, pb. 1985 (radio play)

OTHER LITERARY FORMS

Caryl Phillips's early work in drama brought him immediate acclaim as a young writer worthy of attention. Although his first three plays, produced in the 1980's in London, were praised by reviewers, he is better known for his six novels and his three collections of essays. He has also written for film, radio, and television, both drama and documentaries. His literary criticism, particularly of writers on multicultural and ethnic subjects, and his commentary on social issues have appeared in a number of academic and popular journals. He also writes about sports and music. Phillips has served on several editorial boards and is the editor of the Faber and Faber Caribbean Series. His papers are collected at the Bienecke Rare Book and Manuscript Library at Yale University.

ACHIEVEMENTS

Caryl Phillips won his first playwriting award in 1984 from the British Broadcasting Company for his radio play *The Wasted Years*. In that year he also received the Arts Council of Great Britain Bursary in Drama, as well as a British Council Fiftieth Anniversary Fellowship. However, he is better known for his six novels, whose themes are an outgrowth of those in the three plays. His first novel, *The Final Passage* (1985), won the Malcolm X Prize for Literature in 1987. His 1987 collection of travel essays, *The European Tribe*, won the Martin Luther King Memorial Prize for Literature. In 1992 he was awarded a Guggenheim Fellowship and was named by the London Sunday Times as Young Writer of the Year. His novel *Crossing the River* (1993) was a finalist for the Booker Prize in 1993. In 1994 he received the Lannan Literary Award and the James Tait Black Memorial Prize. In the same year he was awarded a Rockefeller Foundation residency. He holds an honorary Master of Arts degree from Amherst College and an honorary doctorate from Leeds Metropolitan University.

BIOGRAPHY

Caryl Phillips was born on March 13, 1958, in St. Kitts, then a Caribbean colony of Great Britain. Shortly after his birth, the family, which later included four more children, migrated to England, establishing a home in Leeds, Yorkshire. Both parents stressed the importance of a good education; however, they were divorced when Phillips was eight years old. As a child Phillips lived with his mother, who worked in an office and attended night school to earn a teaching degree. As a teenager he lived with his father, a social worker who had a strong, positive influence in his life. An immigrant and a black child in a school in which most students were working-class whites, young Phillips was painfully aware of being an outsider. He was a good student, however, and was encouraged by his teachers to further his education. He was accepted at Queens College of Oxford University.

At Oxford, Phillips was a well-rounded student, an accomplished athlete and head of the drama society. Nevertheless, he was deeply troubled by an ugly racial incident that undermined his confidence. His initial goal was to become a film director, but he became immersed in the theater and directed six plays in just more than a year, ranging from the works of William Shakespeare and Henrik Ibsen to those of Tennessee Williams. After his second year at Oxford, he went to the United States where he experienced firsthand the racial problems of American blacks. His traditional British education had included no writing by black authors. In the United States, the discovery of *Invisible Man* by Ralph Ellison (1952) and *Native Son* (1940) by Richard Wright was a revelation that convinced him to become a writer.

He returned to Oxford to complete his bachelor of arts degree in 1979 with honors in English language and literature. Shortly after his graduation, he achieved recognition as a playwright. With the royalties from his first play, he visited St. Kitts with his mother, observing that despite the island's new independence, the paternalism of the colonial culture still persisted. He recognized that his identification with different cultures and his sense of displacement and confusion could give him a unique viewpoint as a writer. He began a lifetime of travel in Europe, Asia, and Africa, using his experience as an outsider to report on the worldwide consequences of slavery and colonialism. After a series of appointments as visiting professor in several countries, including India, Ghana, and Poland, Phillips was named writer-in-residence at Amherst College in Massachusetts in 1992. In 1998 he was appointed Henry R. Luce Professor of migration and social order at Barnard College in New York City. In addition to teaching, Phillips writes prolifically in the field of literary criticism and social commentary and regularly participates in conferences. He is widely recognized as a public intellectual.

Phillips divides his time among his three homes in England, St. Kitts, and United States, a choice emblematic of his diverse geographic identity. His sense of displacement, so evident in his early plays, has evolved into a complex self-definition that defies racial or ethnic identification. He believes that in the contemporary world of refugees, migrants, and people whose lives are disrupted by social disorder, everyone will be metaphorically homeless. When his lawyer asked about his final wishes, Phillips responded: "I want my ashes to be scattered in the middle of the Atlantic Ocean at a point equidistant between Britain, Africa, and North America."

ANALYSIS

Caryl Phillips's body of work is marked by his experience as an immigrant from the former British colony of St. Kitts to the Yorkshire city of Leeds where he spent his childhood and was educated. His most significant dramatic works are the three plays written and performed in the early 1980's, which have their origins in his firsthand knowledge of the painful cultural displacement that causes family conflict and breakdown among immigrants. His first two plays, he says, are based on his emotional identification with his characters, not on his own experience. In both plays, a central motif is the bitter disillusionment of West Indian immigrants with the paternalistic British society that marginalizes them. Their psychological security is undermined by the historical forces of colonialism and their own self-delusion. These two plays were traditional in form and, Phillips says, easy to write because of his youth and inexperience.

In writing the third play, *The Shelter*, however, Phillips suffered a period of intense difficulty. His solution to the problems of his material was to experiment with form, locating each of the two acts in a different historical time, requiring the audience to complete the connection. In this play, he confronted what he views as the ultimate taboo: the sexual relationship between a black man and a white woman that evokes hatred and fear in white people. Phillips wanted to force his audience to identify with the lives of Britain's immigrants, whose stories had been ignored in England and continental Europe, and to acknowledge the racial prejudice that underlies both English and European society.

Phillips has continued to use this fracturing of historical time in his work, most notably in his novel *Cambridge* (1991, 1992), evoking mixed responses from literary critics. He has continued to explore the themes of his early plays in his fiction. He believes strongly in his responsibility as an artist to correct the myths of history and to reveal the truth. He echoes the words of Langston Hughes in defining the dilemma of the black writer: "The Negro artist works against an undertow of sharp criticism and misunderstanding from his own group and unintentional bribes from the whites."

Phillips believes that critics have judged his work in terms of writing by white authors, rather than respecting his perspective as a black man. While acknowledging the horrors of the history of racial persecution, he describes a more subtle danger that white people do not understand. This is best expressed by the black male slave in *The Shelter* who says to the white woman: "I have much to fear in any man's presence but it is not the chains that I dread, it is the manner of thought that flashes between a man's clapping eyes on me and the opening of his mouth. It is not his touch but the hesitation before his touch."

Phillips has said that he enjoys writing in several genres, suiting the format to his subject matter. His close friendship with James Baldwin, his mentor, resulted in several interviews and a television documentary. He also admires the work of Jean Rhys, Toni Morrison, and Caribbean writers who share his heritage. He cites Derek Walcott as a writer who has a unique insight into the history of the islands, the heritage of Africa, and the colonialism of Great Britain and Europe.

STRANGE FRUIT

The title of his first play was no doubt drawn from Phillips's familiarity with Billie Holiday's song about lynching. The central character, Vivienne Marshall, is a single mother who has emigrated from the Caribbean to Britain with her sons Alvin and Errol. The mother has kept secret from her sons the tragic story of their alcoholic father's life and death. Alvin's crisis occurs when he goes to the Caribbean for his grandfather's funeral. Alvin's alienation in Britain has drawn him into an emotional identification with Africa. However, during his visit to the Caribbean he is badly treated by his West Indian relatives and rejects his African heritage, causing a painful break with his brother. Minor characters include Vernice, Vivienne's West Indian friend, and Errol's girlfriend Shelley. The play offers no resolution to the fracturing of family relationships that results from racial prejudice toward immigrants. Phillips sees this breakdown as the tragic legacy of slavery and colonialism.

WHERE THERE IS DARKNESS

The protagonist in the play is Albert Williams, a West Indian native who, after living in Britain for many years, reviews the meaning of his life at a farewell party before his return to the Caribbean island of his birth. The drama is a journey of self-discovery, told in a series of flashbacks of events in his life in both the Caribbean and in Britain. Albert owes his financial success to his deception of his first wife Lynn, the white woman he impregnated so that her father would pay their passage to Britain where they hoped for a better life. Albert, a social worker whose friends are white, recognizes the wrong he has done

in achieving his personal ambition. His son Remi, in an ironic payback, tells his father he is leaving his university to marry his pregnant black girlfriend. This play, performed in London where Phillips had developed strong ties to the black community, reveals his sense of urgency in bringing public awareness to the tormented lives of Britain's immigrants from its former West Indian colonies.

THE SHELTER

This play introduces a continuing theme in Phillips's work: the troubled sexual relationship between black men and white women. Here he begins the experiment with juxtaposition of historical time and place that is one of the hallmarks of his work. Act 1 takes place in the late eighteenth century with two unnamed characters: Him, a slave; and Her, a white woman. They are the only survivors from a shipwreck and have landed on a deserted island. Some critics find the formal eighteenth century speech patterns awkward. However, the dialogue suggests the deep irony that although the two are equals in their predicament, she does not recognize that it is his skills that will ensure their survival. She refuses to acknowledge his humanity, insisting on her superiority as a white woman. Fully aware of her blind racism but increasingly confident of his own humanity, he will take responsibility for saving her life.

Act 2 takes place in a London pub in the 1950's. Louis, a black man, and Irene, a white woman, meet and relive their troubled relationship. Louis speaks in poetic images, expressing his despair and his need to go "home" to the Caribbean; he cannot live with the hatred of the white community that despises a black man's relationship with a white woman. Irene, who is pregnant with his child, will not accompany him and will bear the child and raise it by herself. The play ends without resolution; it is understood that the next generation will inherit the consequences of the terrible history of slavery and racism.

OTHER MAJOR WORKS

LONG FICTION: *The Final Passage*, 1985; *A State of Independence*, 1986; *Higher Ground*, 1989; *Cambridge*, 1991, 1992; *Crossing the River*, 1993; *The Nature of Blood*, 1997.

SCREENPLAY: *The Mystic Masseur*, 2001 (adaptation of V. S. Naipul's novel).

TELEPLAYS: *Welcome to Birmingham*, 1983; *The Hope and the Glory*, 1984; *The Record*, 1984; *Lost in Music*, 1985; *Playing Away*, 1987; *The Final Passage*, 1996.

RADIO PLAYS: *Crossing the River*, 1985; *The Prince of Africa*, 1987; *Writing Fiction*, 1991.

NONFICTION: *The European Tribe*, 1987; *The Atlantic Sound*, 2000; *A New World Order: Selected Essays*, 2001.

EDITED TEXTS: *Extravagant Strangers: A Literature of Belonging*, 1997; *The Right Set: The Faber Book of Tennis*, 1999.

BIBLIOGRAPHY

Davison, Carol Margaret. "Crisscrossing the River: An Interview with Caryl Phillips." *Ariel* 35, no. 4 (October, 1994): 91-99. This interview follows the publication of *Crossing the River*. Phillips traces the origin of the novel to his play *The Shelter* and gives critical insights into black-white power relationships under colonial regimes, a continuing theme in his work.

Ledent, Bénédicte. *Caryl Phillips*. New York: Manchester University Press, 2002. An examination of the literary works of Phillips. Bibliography and index.

Marjorie Podolsky

ARTHUR WING PINERO

Born: London, England; May 24, 1855
Died: London, England; November 23, 1934

PRINCIPAL DRAMA

£200 a Year, pr. 1877

Two Can Play at That Game, pr. 1877

La Comète: Or, Two Hearts, pr. 1878

Daisy's Escape, pr. 1879

Bygones, pr. 1880

Hester's Mystery, pr. 1880, pb. 1893

The Money Spinner, pr. 1880, pb. 1900

Imprudence, pr. 1881

The Squire, pr., pb. 1881

Girls and Boys, pr. 1882

Lords and Commons, pr. 1883

The Rector, pr. 1883

The Rocket, pr. 1883, pb. 1905

Low Water, pr. 1884, pb. 1905

The Ironmaster, pr. 1884 (adaptation of George Ohnet's play *Le Maître de forges*)

In Chancery, pr. 1884, pb. 1905

The Magistrate, pr. 1885, pb. 1892

Mayfair, pr. 1885 (adaptation of Victorien Sardou's play *Maison neuve*)

The Hobby Horse, pr. 1886, pb. 1892

The School Mistress, pr. 1886, pb. 1894

Dandy Dick, pr. 1887, pb. 1893

Sweet Lavender, pr. 1888, pb. 1893

The Weaker Sex, pr. 1888, pb. 1894

The Profligate, pr. 1889, pb. 1892

The Cabinet Minister, pr. 1890, pb. 1891

The Plays of Arthur W. Pinero, pb. 1891-1915 (25 volumes)

Lady Bountiful, pr. 1891, pb. 1892

The Times, pr., pb. 1891

The Amazons, pr. 1893, pb. 1905

The Second Mrs. Tanqueray, pr. 1893, pb. 1895

The Benefit of the Doubt, pr. 1895, pb. 1896

The Notorious Mrs. Ebbsmith, pr., pb. 1895

The Princess and the Butterfly: Or, The Fantastics, pr. 1897, pb. 1898

The Beauty Stone, pr., pb. 1898 (libretto, with J. Comyns Carr; music by Sir Arthur Sullivan)

Trelawny of the "Wells," pr., pb. 1898

The Gay Lord Quex, pr. 1899, pb. 1900

Iris, pr. 1901, pb. 1902

Letty, pr. 1903, pb. 1904

A Wife Without a Smile, pr. 1904, pb. 1905

His House in Order, pr., pb. 1906

The Thunderbolt, pr. 1908, pb. 1909

Mid-Channel, pr. 1909, pb. 1910

Preserving Mr. Panmure, pr. 1911, pb. 1912

The "Mind the Paint" Girl, pr. 1912, pb. 1913

The Widow of Wasdale Head, pr. 1912, pb. 1924

Playgoers, pr., pb. 1913

The Big Drum, pr., pb. 1915

Mr. Livermore's Dream, pb. 1916, pr. 1917

Social Plays, pb. 1917-1922 (4 volumes)

The Freaks: An Idyll of Suburbia, pr. 1918, pb. 1922

Monica's Blue Boy, pb. 1918 (ballet-pantomime; music by Frederick Cowen)

Quick Work, pr. 1919

A Seat in the Park, pr., pb. 1922

The Enchanted Cottage, pr., pb. 1922

A Private Room, pr., pb. 1928

Dr. Harmer's Holiday, pr. 1930, pb. 1931

A Cold June, pb. 1931, pr. 1932

Three Plays, pb. 1985

"Trelawny of the 'Wells'" and Other Plays, pb. 1995

OTHER LITERARY FORMS

Unlike his great contemporary George Bernard Shaw, Arthur Wing Pinero wrote very little other than plays. His nondramatic works consist of less than a dozen essays and the collected letters. The essays contain comments on theatrical technique, appreciations and criticisms of his fellow playwrights, retrospective accounts of the late nineteenth century London stage, and vignettes of his own life in the theater. The letters constitute a more substantial document; written in a style that varies from the businesslike to the witty and urbane, they provide invaluable glimpses of London theatrical life during the several decades in which Pinero was a dominant figure in British drama.

ACHIEVEMENTS

During his extraordinarily productive career, Arthur Wing Pinero wrote more than fifty plays, nearly all of which were produced and most of which were popular successes. Although his reputation is no longer what it once was, during the last two decades of the nineteenth century and the first decade of the twentieth, he was one of Britain's most acclaimed playwrights. His prolific output was the financial mainstay of many a London theater, and his plays brought him both great wealth and international fame. The foremost performers of his day acted the roles he created, often achieving triumphs that they could never again equal. Nothing in the career of Edward Terry, for example, could match his popularity as Dick Phenyl, the amiable drunkard of *Sweet Lavender*.

Pinero achieved success in a variety of dramatic forms. He wrote a series of farces for the Court Theatre that brought that institution from the brink of financial collapse to immediate prosperity. The first of these, *The Magistrate*, set a London record by running for more than three hundred consecutive performances. The play is still occasionally revived, a retitled version having been produced in London as recently as 1983. His sentimental comedies were also immensely popular, especially *Sweet Lavender*, which outdid even *The Magistrate* with an unprecedented first run of 684 performances. More historically important were Pinero's problem plays, which demonstrated that drama with a serious social purpose could succeed on the nineteenth century British stage. Such plays as *The Profligate*, *The Second Mrs. Tanqueray*, and *The Notorious Mrs. Ebbsmith* lack the intellectual subtlety and dramatic power of the works of Shaw, but they did help to prepare the way for Shaw. Although Pinero never challenged his audience's social assumptions as directly as Shaw did, he showed that British playgoers were willing to think as well as to be entertained.

Another of Pinero's accomplishments was his successful advocacy, along with Henry Arthur Jones, of dramatic realism. An admirer from his youth of Thomas William Robertson's cup-and-saucer drama, Pinero wrote in a colloquial rather than a declamatory style and avoided extreme melodramatic flourishes. Like Robertson, he drew his characters and plots from ordinary life, especially the life of the upper-middle class. He made meticulous use of place references and of speech mannerisms to establish dramatic verisimilitude, and because of its greater naturalness for the performance of social drama, he preferred the three-walled-box stage to all other arrangements. As director of his own plays, he insisted that his actors avoid artificiality in the delivery of their lines, a practice that helped rid the theater of its last vestiges of bombast. Pinero's determination that his plays not be distorted during their preparation for performance induced him, in fact, to exert complete directorial control over the final product, and the key place of the director in modern theater owes much to Pinero's thoroughness.

The extreme care with which Pinero created his realistic effects did not preclude the occurrence in his plays of sentimental and sensational moments reminiscent of melodrama. Indeed, sentiment and surprise are vital elements in most, if not all, of Pinero's works, but these elements develop with a logical inevitability from character portrayal and plot construction rather than springing up, as they so often do in melodrama, with inappropriate suddenness. Unfortunately, the plot construction necessary to bring about some of the effects at which Pinero aimed is not as realistic as other aspects of his writing, and his plots often seem contrived. In imitation of Eugène Scribe, Victorien Sardou, and Alexandre Dumas, *fils*, Pinero was a writer of well-made plays, plays that Shaw compared to "cats'-cradles, clockwork mice, mechanical rabbits, and the like." Such plays relied heavily on compressed exposition through convenient exchanges of letters and unlikely conversations between characters. Their well-made plots contained obtrusive foreshadowings of later events, especially of the startling, but carefully prepared-for, plot reversal. They then moved to their inevitable denouement, in which every plot complication was resolved and every uncertainty clarified.

Although Pinero's fusion of realism, sentiment, and plot contrivance may sound like an unpromising amalgam, the craftsmanship with which he drew these elements together suited the taste of his audiences well enough to make him the most popular playwright in the English-speaking world for more than two decades and to earn for him, in 1909, a knighthood—the second to be granted to a play-wright for his contributions to the theater; no one but W. S. Gilbert had been so honored previously. Moreover, the conventions of popular theater that Pinero helped shape are not drastically different from the conventions that exist today. It would take very little rewriting to transform *The Magistrate* into the most up-to-date of situation comedies, and it would take only slightly more effort to make *Sweet Lavender* a believable contemporary screen romance. For his considerable contributions to popular theater, then, and for his pioneering efforts in serious social drama, Pinero is worthy of more attention than he has, in the past, received.

BIOGRAPHY

Sir Arthur Wing Pinero was born into an upper-middle-class family in London, England, on May 24, 1855. He was the youngest child and only son of Lucy Daines Pinero and John Daniel Pinero, a couple described by Pinero's biographer, Wilbur Dunkel, as "liberal-minded." Pinero's maternal ancestors were of long-established English stock. His paternal forebears, whose name was originally Pinheiro, were Portuguese Jewish immigrants who had arrived in England in the early eighteenth century.

Pinero's parents were frequent theatergoers, and one of his earliest memories was of attending a Grecian Theatre pantomime with his parents and his sisters, Frances and Mary. Very early, too, he discovered the wonders of Sadler's Wells, where, for a mere eighteen pence, he could indulge his growing fascination with plays and actors. His parents never objected to this fascination, but it was always understood that Arthur, like his father and his grandfather, would become a lawyer.

Because of family financial difficulties, Pinero was removed from school and began his legal apprenticeship at age ten. He worked in his father's law office, without great enthusiasm, until his father's retirement in 1870 and then found employment as a library clerk. He soon left that job to accept a position in a solicitor's office, but he felt no more interest in the law while working for his new employer in Lincoln's Inn Fields than he had felt while working for his father in Great James Street.

Meanwhile, Pinero's fascination with the theater continued to increase: He discovered Thomas William Robertson's dramas at the Prince of Wales's Theatre and became absorbed in the new theatrical realism. He learned much that would later be of great use to him from Marie Wilton's purposely understated productions of Robertson's plays, and he began to haunt the street outside the David Garrick Club in hopes of catching an occasional glimpse of the performers he so much admired. He wrote plays that no theater manager would produce, took elocution lessons that intensified his interest in the actor's art, and decided finally to seek a theatrical career of his own.

In 1874, soon after the death of his father, Pinero became an extra with the Edinburgh Theatre Royal. A year later, he moved on to Liverpool, where Wilkie Collins saw him and secured for him a part in his newest play, *Miss Gwilt*, which opened at the Globe Theatre, London, in April of 1876. Henry Irving liked Pinero's unpretentious style of acting and offered him the role of Claudius in a Lyceum Theatre tour of William Shakespeare's *Hamlet, Prince of Denmark* (pr. c. 1600-1601). Pinero accepted the part and spent most of the next five years performing in various Lyceum Theatre productions.

Pinero also succeeded for the first time in having one of his own plays produced. In October of 1877, *£200 a Year* was performed as a curtain raiser at the Globe Theatre, which borrowed him back from the Lyceum for the evening to play the male lead. During the next three years, five more of his plays were produced, with varying degrees of success, followed at last by his first undeniable hit, *The Money Spinner*, which opened in Manchester during November of 1880 and moved to London the following January. His next several plays also turned a profit, and he retired from acting in 1882 to dedicate himself fully to the creation of new works for the stage.

Pinero's work habits were almost compulsive in their regularity, and even after marrying Myra Holme, a widowed actress, in 1883, he refused to deviate from his accustomed writing schedule. Between teatime and breakfast, he wrote and slept, a routine that he maintained with stubborn perseverance and that helped him turn out an amazing number of plays.

Many of these early efforts were farces, farce being the first dramatic form of which Pinero was an acknowledged master. *The Rocket* and *In Chancery*, which premiered in December of 1883 and December of 1884 respectively, brought Pinero considerable success, but it was with the opening of *The Magistrate*, the first of the Court farces, on March 21, 1885, that his reputation soared. During the next several years, he supplied the Court Theatre with four more farces, *The School Mistress*, *Dandy Dick*, *The Cabinet Minister*, and *The Amazons*, all of which were resoundingly popular.

In this same period, Pinero was also writing sentimental comedies and had begun to experiment with the problem play. *Sweet Lavender* commenced its record first run on March 21, 1888, and the more modestly successful but equally sentimental *Lady Bountiful* opened on March 7, 1891. The first of the significant problem plays, *The Profligate*, premiered in the spring of 1889 and caused a considerable critical stir. The play was hailed for its daring treatment of a serious social theme, and hope was expressed that further plays of the same sort, from Pinero or from others, might soon appear.

This hope was realized on May 27, 1893, with the premiere of *The Second Mrs. Tanqueray*, Pinero's most acclaimed play. Pinero had dedicated a year of his life to putting the play together and another several months to getting it staged. Despite Pinero's prodigious reputation, none of the London theater managers was at first willing to touch it. Finally, with some reluctance, George Alexander accepted it for production at the St. James's Theatre and cast an unknown actress, Mrs. Patrick Campbell, in the title role of Paula Tanqueray. In a part that was later to provide triumphs for Sarah Bernhardt, Eleonora Duse, and Ethel Barrymore, Mrs. Campbell was brilliant, and the play was an unqualified critical and popular success. It was compared favorably to Dumas's *Camille* (pr. 1852) and was declared to be superior to every English drama since the time of Richard Brinsley Sheridan.

For the next fifteen years, Pinero was at the top of his profession. Theaters clamored for his work, his plays were performed throughout the world, and nearly everything he wrote gained an enthusiastic reception. There were occasional failures, such as *The Princess and the Butterfly* and the ill-advised Sir Arthur Sullivan collaboration, *The Beauty Stone*, but the successes far outnumbered the infrequent lapses. When Pinero's knighthood was announced in 1909, there were few to cavil. After all, his two most recent plays, *His House in Order* (which earned for him an astounding £50,000) and *The Thunderbolt*, were among his very best works, and the immediately following *Mid-Channel* was equally fine.

Preserving Mr. Panmure, however, was not so fine, and *The "Mind the Paint" Girl* was booed. The materials Pinero was shaping were not so very different from those he had used in the past, but he had begun to lose his craftsman's touch, and his audience's interests had begun to shift in ways he could not understand. He was becoming old-fashioned, and try as he might, he could never regain the knack for creating successful plays.

The last twenty-five years of Pinero's life were marked by a gradual decline. He wrote fewer and fewer plays, and they received less and less attention. He remained financially prosperous, but he was no longer the theatrical lion that he had once been. The death of his wife in 1919 reduced his creative energies still more, and when he died in London on November 23, 1934, it had been many years since he had experienced a theatrical triumph.

ANALYSIS

Because of its earnest self-importance and prudish restrictiveness, Victorian England was as ripe for comic deflation as the Rome of Plautus, and few of his contemporaries were as skillful as Arthur Wing Pinero at producing subversive, farcical laughter. In the typical Pinero farce, the young and uninhibited gain the upper hand over their proper, authoritarian elders with dazzling ease. In the course of the play, the well established and the vain, the powerful and the pompous are teased and tormented until nothing remains of their cherished propriety but a sheepish grin. All of this is accomplished without rancor, however, and even the figures of fun are treated with warmhearted sympathy.

THE MAGISTRATE

In *The Magistrate*, the primary victims of comic deflation are the mock-heroically named Aeneas Posket, a stuffy but charitable police magistrate who fills his household with those convicted in his court, and his deceiving second wife, Agatha. The instigator of their discomfiture is Agatha's delightfully irresponsible son, Cis Farringdon. The unlikely premise on which the plot depends is that, out of vanity and a desire to catch a second husband, Agatha has subtracted five years from her own age and five years from that of her son, thereby convincing both Aeneas and Cis that she is thirty-one and that Cis is fourteen. As she explains to her sister Charlotte in one of Pinero's contrived expository dialogues, "If I am only thirty-one now, my boy couldn't have been born nineteen years ago, and if he could, he oughtn't to have been, because, on my own showing, I wasn't married till four years later." Because she lives in a society that has taught her that no man is likely to propose to a middle-aged woman and that no respectable woman has a child out of wedlock, Agatha has set a trap both for herself and for her unsuspecting husband.

The trap is sprung by Cis, who, despite believing himself to be fourteen, cannot help acting nineteen. He flirts with his sixteen-year-old music teacher, gambles quite skillfully, and lures his dignified stepfather, at a key moment, into a night of carousing. The carousing is made possible through Pinero's use of another of his favorite plot contrivances, the fortuitous arrival of important letters. One of these letters announces an upcoming visit by Colonel Lukyn, a friend of Agatha's first husband, who will be sure to expose Agatha's deceit unless she intercepts him. A second letter informs Agatha of the sickness of a friend, Lady Adelaide Jenkins, which gives Agatha the excuse she needs to leave the house in quest of Colonel Lukyn. A third contains an overdue bill for charges incurred by Cis and his friends at the Hotel des Princes, a bill that Cis decides to manipulate his stepfather into paying. The fourth, whose significance in Pinero's jigsaw puzzle plot becomes clear only later in the play, declares the intention of Charlotte's straitlaced, sententious fiancé, Captain Horace Vale, to break off their engagement because of the impulsive Charlotte's flirtation with another man.

What the characters are unaware of is that all of them are headed for the same place, the Hotel des Princes, where the intricately prepared comic reversal awaits them. Cis is there to get his bill paid for him and to have a good time; Aeneas is there to see his wondrous new fourteen-year-old son in his unlikely natural habitat; Colonel Lukyn is there to visit old haunts; Captain Vale is there because he knows Colonel Lukyn; Agatha is there to plead for Lukyn's silence; and Charlotte is there because Agatha is.

Pinero milks the scenes that follow for all of their humorous possibilities, and in the process, he puts his dignified characters through absurd torments. The proper Captain Vale, for example, is asked to step onto a rickety balcony during a torrential rainstorm when Agatha and Charlotte request a private meeting with the colonel. He later creeps back into the room, soaked to the skin and wearing a bedraggled, oversized hat, mistakenly handed to him by Lukyn, and hides behind a curtain. In the meantime, the colonel has peppered his speech with so many babbling asides about his poor friend on the balcony that Agatha suspects him of suffering the aftereffects of sunstroke. Nevertheless, she does win his pledge to keep her secret, and the three sit down to dinner, while the grumbling, half-starved captain acts as a disembodied waiter from behind the curtain.

After an absurd discovery scene in which Vale, visible to the audience, converses from his hiding place with the principals, Pinero begins the true humbling of his characters. As Vale and Charlotte attempt a reconciliation and as the infuriated Agatha realizes for the first time that the voices from the next room are those of her husband and her son—both of whom, like Agatha herself, have lied about their plans for the evening—the hotel is raided for serving food and drink after hours. Aeneas, the ostensible upholder of the laws, and Cis escape by leaping through a window and falling through a roof, while the magistrate's wife and her three companions are dragged off to jail.

After several hours of running from the authorities, Aeneas again becomes a figure of authority himself and prepares, as best he can, to judge the wrongdoings of others. What a shock it is, however,

when he finds that the first case before him involves his wife's friend, Colonel Lukyn, and three of Lukyn's comrades. In a face-to-face interview with the colonel before the trial begins, Aeneas refuses to give special treatment to any of the four, not even the two ladies, and he exclaims, in righteous indignation, "I am listening, sir, to the guiding voice of Mrs. Posket—that newly-made wife still blushing from the embarrassment of her second marriage, and that voice says, 'Strike for the sanctity of hearth and home, for the credit of the wives of England—no mercy!'" The result is that he hears the four malefactors plead guilty to exactly the crime he himself has committed and sentences them to seven days in jail, at the very moment that his wife, who has lied about her identity, pulls back her veil.

In a play of this sort, in which self-righteousness and rigid social conventions are held up to ridicule, the appropriate conclusion is a liberating relaxation of the rules, and Pinero chooses just such a conclusion for *The Magistrate*. Mr. Bullamy, Aeneas's fellow magistrate, finds a way of skirting the letter of the law and secures the prisoners' release. The warring parties, much chastened by their experiences, are reconciled, and every concealed truth is revealed. Pinero even makes use of that most ancient symbol of reconciliation, a marriage, to bring the play to an end. Aeneas agrees to bless the upcoming union of the music teacher and Cis, who was fourteen yesterday but is nineteen today, especially if the two will accept his gift of a thousand pounds and take themselves off to Canada.

SWEET LAVENDER

Pinero's most successful sentimental comedy, *Sweet Lavender*, also makes use of ego deflation to bring its characters to their senses, but here laughter is less important than pathos for winning the audience's approval of the playwright's resolution of his plot. The play centers on one of the themes dealt with in *The Magistrate*, the sometimes rocky progress of love, but *Sweet Lavender* manages to explore much more dangerous ground without giving the impression of considering controversial materials. Essentially, the play asks whether one should follow the dictates of one's heart or the expectations of society when choosing a spouse; the emphatic, and unabashedly maudlin, answer is that, if it is sensitive to innocence and virtue, the heart is the better guide.

The exposition is again handled through convenient conversations, but this time with less artificiality than in *The Magistrate*. From these conversations, the audience learns that Clement Hale, a law student and the adopted son of wealthy banker Geoffrey Wedderburn, is sharing rooms with Dick Phenyl, a drunken but kindly barrister, and that Clement loves Lavender Rolt, the young daughter of housekeeper Ruth Rolt. He has not yet told Lavender of his love, and Dick Phenyl is convinced that such a declaration would destroy Clement's future. The simple, poverty-stricken young lady is an unworthy match for Clement, he argues, and Mr. Wedderburn expects Clement to marry his niece, Minnie Gilfillian. Dick himself is very familiar with poverty and failure and would hate to see his young friend ruin his own expectations.

From Lavender's first entrance, however, Pinero makes it clear that she and Clement are destined for each other and that whatever snobbishness interferes with their union is unjust and must be overcome. Barriers of rank and wealth are of no consequence when two people are as well matched as Clement and Lavender, and the audience is in perfect sympathy with the two lovers when Clement, early in the play, proposes marriage and Lavender accepts him. Their decision to marry is so obviously right that the Wedderburns and anyone who sides with them must be convinced of their error in resisting such a perfect union.

Dick Phenyl is the first to be won over. An impractical romantic himself, and for that very reason an admirable character, he quickly succumbs to the sentiment of the situation and acts as the lovers' ally. Minnie becomes a collaborator with equal ease; her love for Clement is more nearly sisterly affection than passion, and besides, she herself is too busy flouting social conventions by playing the coquette with an upstart American to worry about a lost match with Clement.

Mr. Wedderburn and his sister, Mrs. Gilfillian, are more stubborn in their interference, and it is only af-

ter both have been humbled that the marriage can occur. In one of his most extreme reversal scenes, Pinero has Wedderburn deliver an ultimatum to Clement to abandon Lavender or be cut off without a cent at the very moment when his own ruin is about to be announced. Barely has Clement reaffirmed his loyalty to Lavender and Wedderburn cursed him as a penniless fool when Dick Phenyl carries in a telegram that tells of the collapse of Mr. Wedderburn's bank. At the same instant, Ruth Rolt appears at the door, and Wedderburn stares at her in shock. He has just been using himself as an example of a man who escaped the consequences of an improvident love affair by leaving the woman he loved; that woman was Ruth.

In fact, the young lady whom Wedderburn has branded as unworthy of his stepson is Wedderburn's own daughter, and the poverty for which he despised her becomes, temporarily, his own. Mrs. Gilfillian, who performs the housekeeping tasks once taken care of by the Rolts, is also drawn down, by necessity, to the level of those whom she has scorned. Both learn respect for their erstwhile inferiors and drop all objection to Clement's marriage to Lavender. Mrs. Rolt, who had taken Lavender away out of fear that her daughter would either enter an incestuous marriage or have to be told the closely guarded secret of her illegitimacy, also relents when she discovers that Clement is an adopted son and that Mr. Wedderburn, who still loves her, will never reveal the truth. Finally, Dick Phenyl crowns the play's triumphant ending when he announces that he has it in his power to restore Mr. Wedderburn's bank to solvency. He knew of the bank's collapse because he had been informed of his unexpected inheritance of the estate of his Uncle George, all of whose money had been placed in Mr. Wedderburn's bank. By withdrawing his claim to the money, he can put the bank back on its feet. With this announcement, the play comes to its ecstatic conclusion.

Despite the play's popular success, Pinero was well aware that *Sweet Lavender* is artistically flawed. It slips perilously close to pure melodrama, and its fairy-tale ending is outrageously contrived. Shakespearean comedy contains elements as unlikely as those found here, but as many commentators have pointed out, such plays as *The Winter's Tale* (pr. c.1610-1611) and *As You Like It* (pr. c.1599-1600) make no claims to verisimilitude, whereas *Sweet Lavender* purports to be realistic. The incompatibility that exists between its real and its contrived elements hurts the play's artistic integrity.

Nevertheless, *Sweet Lavender* does contain elements of serious drama, however flawed it may be. In its contrast of happy and unhappy couples, it attempts to make a statement about male sexual irresponsibility and about the double standard that allows such irresponsibility to flourish. The victimizing male is forced to see the consequences of his insensitivity to the abandoned female, and he feels appropriately ashamed. A more idealistic male is then permitted to right the wrongs of the past by treating the virginal female with proper love and respect.

THE PROFLIGATE

Such a neatly symmetrical combination of parts, however, is not often reflective of the complexities and compromises of real life. Of much deeper human interest is the use Pinero makes of the same four character types in his fascinating, but again flawed, problem play, *The Profligate*. Here, innocence is married to experience, and the virginal female to the victimizing male, while the idealistic male and the abandoned female move into and out of their lives, sometimes in troublesome ways.

Hugh Murray, a thirty-year-old solicitor, is self-lessly in love with Leslie Brundenell, a naïve but charming schoolgirl. Unfortunately for Hugh, "a pale, thoughtful, resolute-looking man," Leslie has fallen in love with the gallant and worldly Dunstan Renshaw, the sort of man that Hugh himself admits to be more often successful with the ladies than men of his own kind. Leslie and Dunstan are to be married, and Hugh has agreed to be best man at their wedding, but he has second thoughts about his participation in the ceremony when Dunstan's friend Lord Dangars drops by to pick up his latest divorce decree. After all, how could the friend of such a libertine as Dangars, a friend whose past is probably as shameful as Dangars's own, behave honorably toward the innocent Miss Brundenell? Hugh will not actively inter-

fere with the young couple's union, but he will also not help it take place.

Almost as soon as the wedding party departs, Janet Preece appears, a woman in search of her seducer. He had called himself Lawrence Kenward when he had known her in the country, but Janet is well aware that that name was as false as the man himself. She wants Hugh Murray to help her find him, and when he guesses the man's identity, he agrees.

If the audience is unfamiliar enough with Pinero's use of foreshadowing not to have discovered that Lawrence Kenward is Dunstan Renshaw, Murray makes that fact explicit during a later conversation with Renshaw. Leslie and Dunstan have been living together blissfully in an Italian villa for several weeks when Murray arrives to warn Renshaw of his danger. He has compromised his professional ethics for a month by concealing what he knows from Janet Preece, but the secret will soon be out, and for Leslie's sake, Dunstan had best be prepared.

Unfortunately, when the secret does come out, Dunstan is not the least prepared, and the results are disastrous. In a series of coincidences as unlikely as the events which bring the characters in *The Magistrate* together at the Hotel des Princes, Janet, Leslie, Dunstan, and Lord Dangars suddenly find themselves in a distressing confrontation at the Italian villa. Janet has been stranded at the villa by her former employer and has confessed her sordid past to the kindly Leslie, who has nursed her through a serious illness. Soon thereafter, Dunstan returns from a visit with Lord Dangars. Dangars has accompanied Dunstan to the villa, since Dangars's latest fiancée, who is Leslie's closest friend and the daughter of Janet's former employer, is staying there. When Janet sees the two approaching, she shouts, "It's the man—the man!" and Leslie's imagination does the rest. In order to protect her affianced friend, she prepares for Lord Dangars's unmasking and unmasks her own husband instead. Despite Dunstan's pleas for mercy, Leslie leaves him, and Dunstan commits suicide.

This summary of events seems to support the frequently enunciated interpretation of the play as an attack on the double standard, which makes its point by punishing the erring male as severely as the more conventional moral tale punishes the erring female. According to this view, then, men ought to guard their honor as diligently as women do, for who knows what the eventual consequences of sin may be? Such an interpretation undervalues the play's complexity.

First, Dunstan is not destroyed by his sin but by the moral rigidity of his wife. Dunstan has been cruel in his abandoning of Janet Preece, and it was his lust that led him astray, but he has changed since that premarital adventure and has become worthy of Leslie's love. Because of her own upbringing as an overprotected Victorian young lady, however, Leslie cannot see this and classes Dunstan with the play's one true profligate, Lord Dangars. So serious is this inability to discriminate, in fact, that, in the moment of her greatest distress over the discovery of Dunstan's past, Leslie loses the power to protect her close friend from the truly dangerous male, and Dangars escorts his reluctant fiancée from the stage. Furthermore, human sexuality is not as one-sided as Leslie assumes, and in a startling confession toward the end of the play, Janet admits to having been the sexual aggressor in her affair with Dunstan, a confession that Leslie dismisses without considering its implications. She does finally forgive Dunstan, however, and in the final scene of the play, she exhibits a sadder but deeper humanity than she possessed at the play's beginning. Unfortunately, the man to whom she speaks her forgiveness has already taken his life.

THE SECOND MRS. TANQUERAY

The dialogue in *The Profligate* is too wooden and a number of the scenes too sensational for the play to be a fully successful work of art. In *The Second Mrs. Tanqueray*, Pinero largely solved such aesthetic problems to produce what is generally regarded as his masterpiece. The play again concerns Victorian sexual mores, and it again centers on the confrontation between innocence and experience, with innocence once more learning the lesson of tolerance and humanity too late.

In the play's opening act, which contains some of Pinero's most skillfully handled exposition and foreshadowing, Aubrey Tanqueray is bidding a tentative farewell to the friends of his single life, to whom he announces that tomorrow he will be married for the second time. The first Mrs. Tanqueray had been "one of your cold sort . . . all marble arms and black velvet." She had had no lack of Victorian respectability, but sexually, "She *was* an iceberg! As for kissing, the mere contact would have given him chapped lips." The second Mrs. Tanqueray will be different; just how different is implied by Aubrey's uncertainty that his friends will continue to socialize with him after the marriage has occurred. It is also implied by the discomfort with which he listens to the account given by his best friend, Cayley Drummle, of Sir George Orreyed's marriage to a woman of low repute. The best people will cut him dead, Cayley asserts. The man should have known better.

At the end of the act, when the men have left, the audience is introduced directly to the future Paula Tanqueray and indirectly to her pure and innocent opposite, Aubrey's daughter Ellean. Paula, who has been the mistress of many men, has arrived at an outrageously late hour to deliver a letter to Aubrey containing an account of her various sexual escapades. She wants Aubrey to enter married life with no illusions about his wife's past, but Aubrey assures her that he has no doubts about the wisdom of marrying her and gallantly burns the letter. She begs him to be sure, very sure, of what he feels; reminds him of the suicide of one of her close friends; and leaves him for the evening. He then opens a letter from his daughter, who has treated him with the same bloodless coldness as her mother had done before her, and discovers that Ellean has suddenly decided to leave the convent in which she has been educated in order to come home to her father. The potential difficulties of his decision are immediately obvious. How can such a creature of the spirit as Ellean and such a creature of the flesh as Paula be brought under the same roof without tragic results? How, in the age of Victoria, can the soul and the body be reconciled?

The confrontation between the two women develops gradually and occurs, ironically enough, after they appear to have made peace. During the first days of their acquaintance, Paula is constantly attempting to win Ellean's friendship and is constantly being treated with a maddening, dutiful politeness. Paula's self-respect is totally dependent on being accepted and understood by Aubrey's virginal daughter, a fact of which Aubrey himself is partially aware, and when that acceptance and understanding are not forthcoming, Paula lashes out at those around her. As Aubrey had feared, he and Paula have not been received into polite society, and their ostracism has intensified Paula's contradictory feelings of shame and anger. She wants very much to be an untainted woman, and despite the power of her personality, a power that sometimes suggests a Phaedra or a Hedda Gabler, she has a deep need for approval. If Ellean, the embodiment of the purity she herself had once possessed, can love her, all will be well.

For that to occur, however, each woman needs to learn something about the other's attitude toward human relationships. That reeducation takes place for Ellean when she accompanies Aubrey's friend, Mrs. Cortelyon, on a trip to Paris, a trip that Paula mistakenly assumes is intended to separate her forever from her stepdaughter. Paula's own reeducation occurs when, in retaliation for the carrying off of Ellean and in direct defiance of her husband's wishes, she invites the Orreyeds to visit. Lady Orreyed had been a close friend during their days as mistresses to the wealthy, and Paula has frequently expressed a desire to see her again.

What she sees, however, is a vulgar gold digger who has married a stupid drunkard and who seems well on her way to bankrupting him. The married Paula Tanqueray is no more like Lady Orreyed than the married Dunstan Renshaw is like Lord Dangars, but after watching Lady Orreyed in action, Paula can hardly fail to see why anyone whose situation even superficially resembles Lady Orreyed's might have difficulty winning her way into the hearts of the respectable and the well-to-do. Sexual prudery is part of the problem, but not the whole problem.

The more drastic transformation has taken place in Ellean. This cold, spiritual young lady has experienced a sexual awakening, and the drives that have determined so much of Paula's life are suddenly comprehensible to her. While in Paris, she has fallen in love. The young man is reputed to have had a wild youth, but he has since performed an act of heroism

in India, and no one is more dashing and handsome. She now understands and accepts Paula, or seems to, and she kisses her in acknowledgment of their shared womanhood. At last, Paula is happy.

Then the catastrophe occurs. Ellean's sweetheart was once Paula's sweetheart, and out of a false sense of duty, Paula informs Aubrey. Aubrey forbids Ellean to see him again. Ellean guesses the reason, and her love for Paula becomes hatred. In response, Paula surrenders to the sense of worthlessness that society has tried for so long to force on her and kills herself. Ellean hears "the fall" of this fallen woman's body and runs to tell her father, crying out as she does so, "But I know—I helped to kill her. If I had only been merciful!"

The Second Mrs. Tanqueray exhibits Pinero's talents at their best, but it also suggests why Pinero is not praised today as enthusiastically as he once was. His craftsmanship is there for all to see, no matter in which literary epoch they live, but his serious social statements come through in their full power only when one is familiar with their Victorian context. His pronouncements lack the ring of lasting truth of the words of a Shakespeare or a Shaw, whatever he might have taught his Victorian (and later his Edwardian) audiences. Nevertheless, he helped to prepare the way for modern English social drama, and he perfected many of the techniques of modern popular drama, accomplishments that assure his place in British dramatic history.

OTHER MAJOR WORK

NONFICTION: *The Collected Letters of Sir Arthur Pinero*, 1974 (J. P. Wearing, editor).

BIBLIOGRAPHY

Beerbohm, Max. *Around Theatres*. London: Rupert Hart-Davies, 1953. A collection of theater pieces by one of England's most brilliant and perceptive writers and cartoonists. Contains reviews of four Pinero plays, *The School Mistress*, *Iris*, *Letty*, and *The Notorious Mrs. Ebbsmith*, valuable precisely because Beerbohm wrote them after he succeeded George Bernard Shaw as drama critic for the *Saturday Review*.

Dawick, John. *Pinero: A Theatrical Life*. Niwot: University Press of Colorado, 1993. Dawick provides a look at Pinero's long history with the theater. Contains bibliography and index.

Griffin, Penny. *Arthur Wing Pinero and Henry Arthur Jones*. New York: St. Martin's Press, 1991. Griffin examines English drama in the late nineteenth and early twentieth centuries, focusing on a comparison of the works of Pinero and Henry Arthur Jones. Bibliography and index.

Lazenby, Walter. *Arthur Wing Pinero*. New York: Twayne, 1972. A basic look at the life and works of Pinero. Bibliography.

Shaw, G. B. *Dramatic Opinions and Essays*. 2 vols. New York: Brentano's, 1907. These reviews, published when Shaw was still a drama critic, remain the most perceptive ever written about Pinero. Despite Pinero's extraordinary popularity, Shaw exposed the conventionality of the playwright's ideas and his inability to come to grips with the situations he had created.

Smith, Leslie. *Modern British Farce: A Selective Study of British Farce from Pinero to the Present Day*. Totowa, N.J.: Barnes and Nobles, 1989. Smith examines British farce, with emphasis on Pinero and his legacy. Bibliography and index.

Robert H. O'Connor,
updated by Mildred C. Kuner

ROBERT PINGET

Born: Geneva, Switzerland; July 19, 1919
Died: Tours, France; August 26, 1997

PRINCIPAL DRAMA

Lettre morte, pr., pb. 1959 (*Dead Letter*, 1963)

La Manivelle, pr., pb. 1960 (radio play; *The Old Tune*, 1960)

Architruc, pr., pb. 1961 (English translation, 1967)

Ici ou ailleurs, pr., pb. 1961 (*Clope*, 1963)

L'Hypothèse, pr., pb. 1961 (*The Hypothesis*, 1967)

Plays, pb. 1963, revised pb. 1967

Autour de Mortin, pb. 1965 (radio play; *About Mortin*, 1967)

Identité, pr., pb. 1971

Abel et Bela, pr., pb. 1971 (*Abel and Bela*, 1987)

Paralchimie, pr., pb. 1973

Lubie, pr. 1981, pb. 1986 (radio play)

Un Testament bizarre et autres pieces, pb. 1986 (*A Bizarre Will and Other Plays*, 1989; includes *Un Testament bizarre* [*A Bizarre Will*], *Mortin pas mort* [*Mortin Not Dead*], *Dictée* [*Dictation*], *Sophisme et sadisme* [*Sophism and Sadism*], *Le Chrysanthème* [*The Chrysanthemum*], and *Lubie*. [English translation])

OTHER LITERARY FORMS

Robert Pinget began his literary career with the 1951 publication of *Entre Fantoine et Agapa* (1951; *Between Fantoine and Agapa*, 1982), a collection of short stories. Later he wrote more than a dozen experimental, highly innovative novels. Among these are *Mahu: Ou, Le Matériau* (1952; *Mahu: Or, The Material*, 1966), *Baga* (1958; English translation, 1967), *Le Fiston* (1959; *No Answer*, 1961; also as *Mr. Levert*), *Clope au dossier* (1961), *L'Inquisitoire* (1962; *The Inquisitory*, 1966), *Quelqu'un* (1965; *Someone*, 1984), *Le Libéra* (1968; *The Libera Me Domine*, 1972), *Passacaille* (1969; *Recurrent Melody*, 1975; also as *Passacaglia*, 1978), *Cette Voix* (1975; *That Voice*, 1982), *Le Harnais* (1984), and *Du Nerf* (1990; *Be Brave*, 1995).

ACHIEVEMENTS

In his fiction, and in the plays that derive from it, Robert Pinget created and peopled the mapless region of Fantoine and Agapa. This is a world not of being but of becoming, constantly changing from work to work and even within particular books. As Pinget described his fictional universe in a lecture at Williams

College on April 21, 1970, his characters and setting "exist not as defined but as in the process of definition." This "continual metamorphosis"—Pinget's term—mirrors the uncertainty and instability of the late twentieth century.

For many readers and viewers, Pinget's techniques rendered his works inaccessible. Although his works have been translated into eleven languages, he enjoyed less recognition than such fellow experimenters as Samuel Beckett and Eugène Ionesco. Still, critical response was warm. *The Inquisitory* won the Prix des Critiques (1963), and two years later, *Someone* received the Prix Femina. The Ford Foundation awarded him a grant in 1960, and the French government recognized his achievements with a subsidized sabbatical (1975-1976).

BIOGRAPHY

Robert Pinget was born in Geneva, Switzerland, on July 19, 1919. After receiving a law degree from the University of Geneva and practicing briefly (1944-1946), he turned to painting. A one-man showing of his works was fairly successful, but he grew dissatisfied with this career as well. He taught design and French in England; then, in 1951, after settling in Paris, he completed a manuscript collection of stories, *Between Fantoine and Agapa*, which was published by a provincial press at the author's expense.

Having at last found his vocation, he began to write extensively, publishing his first novel, *Mahu*, in 1952. This book won for him the admiration of another avant-garde writer, Alain Robbe-Grillet, who reviewed the work favorably. Pinget's second novel gained for him another significant admirer; he submitted the manuscript to the prestigious publishing house Gallimard, whose reader, Albert Camus, was much impressed. Subsequently, Pinget continued producing a series of novels that received critical acclaim.

Pinget's dramatic career began in 1959 when he translated Beckett's *All That Fall* (pr., pb. 1957) as *Tout ceux qui tombent*. Beckett soon reciprocated by translating *La Manivelle* into *The Old Tune*, broadcast by the British Broadcasting Corporation (BBC) on August 23, 1960. Pinget's first original play, *Dead*

Letter, followed shortly afterward, and in the spring of 1960 it shared the stage with Beckett's *Krapp's Last Tape* (pr., pb. 1958). Although Pinget claimed to prefer the novel, he used his plays to explore more fully the themes, characters, and situations that he presented in his fiction. He died of a stroke in Tours, France, in 1997.

ANALYSIS

Although Martin Esslin includes Robert Pinget among the playwrights examined in *The Theatre of the Absurd* (1961), Pinget himself claimed that he more accurately belongs to the "theater of the ear." In a 1962 interview he replied to the question "What am I trying to do?" by stating that he sought "to translate into the language of today the problems of today." Elsewhere, he talked of his efforts to capture the proper tone that will reify his characters. "Only the manner of speaking interests me," he observed in a lecture in Philadelphia (May 7, 1964).

Consequently, there is little action on the stage. Instead, all the emotion and energy are concentrated into highly evocative, often poetic language, which is itself one of the chief concerns of these works. How can people communicate? Can people communicate? While rejecting the antiliterary bias of many contemporary playwrights, Pinget shared their interest in the pitfalls that seem hidden within words.

For Pinget, language was the only means to recapture the past, know the present, establish a personality, and bond with others. Yet because this language is so elusive, characters often are isolated from their own history and identity, divided from relatives and associates. An existential anxiety pervades Pinget's writing, as each person fails to understand himself or make himself understood to others. Clope's groping for his past in the darkness at the beginning of the second act of *Clope* represents the universal plight of mankind. At the same time, Pinget found much humor and even occasional glimmers of hope in this struggle for sense in what may be a meaningless world.

In 1968, frustrated by the inability of language to retain or convey meaning, Pinget vowed to stop writing. The fascination with the quest for the magical "two or three key words," however, drove him back to his desk to explore the central dilemma of the age. In *Le Mythe de Sisyphe* (1942; *The Myth of Sisyphus*, 1955), Albert Camus observed that in the modern world man has become "an exile because he is deprived of memories of a lost homeland as much as he lacks the hope of a promised land to come." At the end of *Clope*, Pierrot and Clope embark on an actual quest for that land, in which Madame Flan also believes. More often in Pinget's works, the search is verbal. Always, though, the conclusion, whether more or less promising, remains open-ended, the answer still unfound, and Pinget's characters seem condemned, like Sisyphus, to continue the never-ending search for meaning and fulfillment in a world that may not contain either.

DEAD LETTER

Like the dramas to follow, Pinget's first play, *Dead Letter*, derived from a novel, in this case *No Answer*. In the first act, set in a bar, Edward Levert talks about his son, who has left him, as a waiter listens to this story that he has heard many times before. The second act resembles the first, except that the setting is a post office. Levert again speaks of his son, while a clerk, who is the bartender in another guise, halfheartedly listens. This repetition highlights the futility of Levert's quest, indicating that it will be repeated in various settings but never achieve a successful resolution.

Pinget further emphasized the hopelessness of the situation by introducing a play-within-a-play. Toward the end of the first act, Fred and Lili enter the bar and perform part of a piece they have just finished, *The Prodigal Son*. In this conventional play, the father's letters succeed in winning back his son, but Pinget implies that such happy endings occur only in artificially contrived dramas. In the real world that his work represents, such happy resolutions are unlikely if not impossible.

The father's failure to reach his son with his letters represents language's inability to connect people, for the son never responds. The bartender/clerk, despite his irritation with Levert and his oft-told tale, tries to be comforting, but his words, too, become in effect dead letters. At the end of the first act he can offer only the cliché, "Oh, you know how it is." The second act concludes even less satisfactorily, as he tells Levert, "Letters don't matter. What matters is. . . . What matters is. . . . What matters."

The play raises questions about identity as well as about language. The bartender metamorphoses into a postal clerk, and he may be Levert's missing son, too. In the first act his title is *garçon*, meaning either waiter or boy. The bartender's father, like Levert, owns a villa on the Mediterranean, and the bartender, like Levert's son, never writes letters to his father. Physically, too, there seems to be some similarity; at least Levert tells the man, "You're like my son."

Other incidents raise further questions about who is who. Fred and Lili's fellow actors have names like theirs—Bed and Quiqui—and in the bar, Fred and Lili assume their colleagues' roles. In the second act, the clerk and Levert watch the funeral of a girl whose history mirrors that of the clerk's sister. The clerk tells Levert of a man who used to come in looking for a letter from Heaven; that man may have been Levert.

As Levert observes, "We never know anyone." He does not know the history of the bartender, he cannot even be sure who the bartender is. In an attempt to learn more about him, he asks the man to strip himself, and he offers to undress also, but the bartender tells him that the mystery of existence lies deeper than the skin. The quest for truth must therefore proceed in a bewildering universe that holds out little hope for success.

THE OLD TUNE

The Old Tune raises a number of the same issues as *Dead Letter*, letting the audience eavesdrop on Pommard and Toupin, two old men trying to review their youth. Because this is a piece for radio, the audience would rely on the voices to distinguish the characters, but the two sound alike. Both have cracked voices, both stop for breath even in the middle of a word or sentence, both whistle their sibilants. Moreover, Pommard seems to know Toupin's past better than Toupin, and the reverse is also true. Hence, their attempt to reestablish a friendship through their conversation leads instead to quarrels. Also, at times they seem not to be paying attention or are unable to hear each other because of the roar of the traffic. The resulting confusion is both humorous and sad. One cannot help laughing as the "happy memories" repeatedly prove false, yet one also realizes that these characters are doomed to fail in their effort to rekindle a former alliance. Symbolic of this failure is their attempt to smoke a cigarette. Neither has a match, nor will any passerby provide one. The cigarettes thus remain unlit, unsmoked, just as their old friendship remains unrevived and cold.

CLOPE

Clope once more traces this search for union. Clope and Madame Flan live in a railway station kiosk, where she sells newspapers and he tells fortunes with a Tarot deck. While their trades are therefore similar—telling others what is happening in their world—their personalities differ. Madame Flan is the idealist, dreaming of an escape to China or Clysterea. Clope, on the other hand, is the cynic. He tells Madame Flan that a trip to China—or anywhere—would be pointless; he does not believe that life will change for her or anyone else. Hence, he gives everyone the same reading of the cards, and when they return the next week, he repeats that reading yet again.

Devoid of illusions and hope, Clope persuades a would-be traveler, Pierrot, to abandon his intention of seeking a better life elsewhere. Instead, Pierrot builds a second kiosk at the train station and becomes a surrogate son to Clope. As in *Dead Letter*, though, this son finally goes away, but he does leave hope behind. Clope resolves to pursue him and so embarks on another of Pinget's quests. As the play ends, each character clings to an expectation: Pierrot thinks that he will find a better life somewhere else, Clope wants to find Pierrot to reestablish their former relationship, and Madame Flan, clutching Clope's old grammar book, longs for her colleague to return.

IDENTITÉ

In a poetic sequence opening the second act of *Clope*, Clope searches for something in his past that will allow him to make sense of his life. This search for self-understanding, already evident in *Dead Letter*, serves as the central issue of the aptly named *Identité*. The protagonist, Mortin, had already appeared in *The Hypothesis* and the radio drama based on it, *About Mortin*, in which he vainly attempted to determine why a manuscript, perhaps his own, had

been tossed into a well. As *Identité* opens, Mortin, apparently a writer, sits before a stack of papers and urges his physician to leave so that he, Mortin, can get on with his work.

Quickly, however, confusion sets in, for the doctor is not onstage as Mortin makes his request. Two scenes later, at the urging of the maid, Naomi, Mortin reverses his position, but again the doctor does not hear a word of what is being said to him. To add to the confusion, Naomi afterward tells Mortin to send the doctor away, and the doctor threatens to leave the other characters. Just as one is uncertain as to who wants whom to do what, so one cannot tell who is interfering with whose work—assuming that anyone has work to do. Naomi claims that Mortin prevents her from doing her job, Mortin blames the doctor, and the doctor blames Mortin. As Naomi and the doctor say, "One is never sure of anything."

This lack of certainty results from and is reflected in the slippage of language. When, for example, Mortin speaks of *l'analyse* (analysis), Naomi hears Anne-Lise and begins a conversation about that woman, sidetracking their discussion about the doctor. Also indicative of the treachery of words is the frequent discussion of an anticipated duck dinner, but in the end Naomi produces only an empty plate. Words have lost their significance; they do not represent real objects, and at times they lose all coherence, as when the doctor and Naomi speak at once, telling two stories by uttering selected phrases from each. The result is gibberish. In the final scene, the audience remains with noise followed by silence, both of which are as meaningful—or meaningless—as the dialogue that has filled the preceding two acts.

ABEL AND BELA

As an artist, Pinget frequently explored the creative process. *The Inquisitory* is on one level an examination of how to write a novel, and Mortin in both *The Hypothesis* and *Identité* attempts to produce a coherent manuscript. *Abel and Bela* translates this problem to the stage, as the two title characters discuss a projected play. Initially, they consider a traditional, elegant piece set before World War II and filled with upper-class characters circulating in opulent settings. The first act soon degenerates into an orgy, though, and the projected second and third acts merely repeat the first, indicating that in the contemporary world, one no longer can compose a conventional or traditional work for the theater because life has become too chaotic. *Dead Letter*, rather than *The Prodigal Son*, should serve as the playwright's model.

Abel and Bela therefore propose a psychological examination of their own lives, but they fail again because they realize how dull their existence has been. Because reality lacks the stuff of drama, and since the old forms no longer serve, they next turn to Surrealism, imagining a play about the lives they have not led. Even this idea does not work, though, for their plot becomes too bizarre. Bela imagines himself a nun, Abel a swan. As with *Clope*, the ending does leave room for hope nevertheless, for as Pinget's piece ends, the audience sees the beginning of Abel and Bela's first suggested play.

Like all of Pinget's other works for the stage, *Abel and Bela* explores questions of identity and language. The very names of the two characters are virtually identical, as are their accounts of their past. Moreover, Pinget acted in this piece, so he was both writer and a character trying to write. Because the similarities between Abel and Bela are linguistic, however, they can create new lives by saying other words. "Everything is a question of vocabulary," Abel insists; if they tell other stories about themselves, they can give themselves different, fantastic histories.

In fact, language may change itself and its users. "One word changes and all the rest follow," Abel insists. When Abel begins to speak of the playwright's freedom and uses the word "liberty," Bela immediately adds "fraternity," one word drawing forth the other. Like Lewis Carroll, Pinget here posed the question every communicator, certainly every writer, must face: Do people control words or do words control people? *Abel and Bela* implies that the latter is closer to the truth.

PARALCHIMIE

This transforming quality of language provides the title for *Paralchimie*, a word itself exhibiting linguistic shifts. It can mean "by alchemy" (*par alchimie*), "word chemistry" (*parole chimie*), or, by extension, "word alchemy." For Mortin, who appears

yet again, words are the philosopher's stone that can transform the dross of his life into gold. Despite the abundance of words, though, all the efforts of the first act produce only sleep and silence.

In the second act, Naomi and the doctor return from *Identité* to continue their shaggy dog stories. Mortin joins them in constructing a fable about a shepherd, but its meaning never becomes clear, nor can they complete their tale. The play concludes with a thunderstorm that leaves Mortin blind and speechless. The quest for the magical "two or three key words" has ended in sound and fury that signify nothing.

OTHER MAJOR WORKS

LONG FICTION: *Mahu: Ou, Le Matériau*, 1952 (*Mahu: Or, The Material*, 1966); *Le Renard et la boussole*, 1953; *Graal flibuste*, 1956; *Baga*, 1958 (English translation, 1967); *Le Fiston*, 1959 (*No Answer*, 1961; also known as *Mr. Levert*); *Clope au dossier*, 1961; *L'Inquisitoire*, 1962 (*The Inquisitory*, 1966); *Quelqu'un*, 1965 (*Someone*, 1984); *Le Libéra*, 1968 (*The Libera Me Domine*, 1972); *Passacaille*, 1969 (*Recurrent Melody*, 1975; also known as *Passacaglia*, 1978); *Fable*, 1971 (English translation, 1980); *Cette voix*, 1975 (*That Voice*, 1982); *L'Apocryphe*, 1980 (*The Apocrypha*, 1980); *Monsieur Songe*, 1982 (English translation, 1989); *Le Harnais*, 1984; *Charrue*, 1985; *L'Ennemi*, 1987 (*The Enemy*, 1991); *Du Nerf*, 1990 (*Be Brave*, 1995); *Théo: Ou, Le Temps neuf*, 1991 (*Theo: Or, The New Era*, 1995); *Taches d'encre*, 1997 (*Traces of Ink*, 2000).

SHORT FICTION: *Entre Fantoine et Agapa*, 1951 (*Between Fantoine and Agapa*, 1982).

NONFICTION: *Robert Pinget à la lettre*, 1993.

BIBLIOGRAPHY

Chambers, Ross. *The World Around Mortin: A Reading of Robert Pinget's Autour de Mortin*. North Ryde, Australia: Macquarie University, School of Modern Languages, 1973. Offers a close reading and interpretation of Pinget's radio play, *Autour de Mortin*.

Esslin, Martin. *The Theatre of the Absurd*. 1961. 3d ed. New York: Penguin Books, 1991. Examines an important movement in twentieth century drama, one with which Pinget has been associated. Some specific discussion of Pinget included. Bibliography and index.

Henkels, Robert M., Jr. *Robert Pinget: The Novel as Quest*. Tuscaloosa: University of Alabama Press, 1979. Examines the overriding theme of search and journey in Pinget's works.

The Review of Contemporary Fiction. 3, no. 2 (Summer, 1983). An issue devoted to analysis of Jack Kerouac and Robert Pinget.

Rosmarin, Leonard A. *Robert Pinget*. New York: Twayne, 1995. Provides criticism and interpretation of Pinget's life and works. Bibliography and index.

Joseph Rosenblum

HAROLD PINTER

Born: London, England; October 10, 1930

PRINCIPAL DRAMA

The Room, pr. 1957, pb. 1960 (one act)
The Birthday Party, pr. 1958, pb. 1959
The Dumb Waiter, pr. 1959 (in German), pr., pb. 1960 (in English; one act)
The Caretaker, pr., pb. 1960
The Collection, pr. 1961, pb. 1963
"A Slight Ache" and Other Plays, pb. 1961
The Lover, pr., pb. 1963 (one act)
The Homecoming, pr., pb. 1965
Tea Party, pb. 1965, pr. 1965 (televised), pr. 1968 (staged)
The Basement, pb. 1967, pr. 1967 (televised), pr. 1968 (staged)
Landscape, pb. 1968, pr. 1968 (radio play), pr. 1969 (staged; one act)
Silence, pr., pb. 1969 (one act)
Old Times, pr., pb. 1971
No Man's Land, pr., pb. 1975
Plays, pb. 1975-1981, revised pb. 1991-1998 (4 volumes)
Betrayal, pr., pb. 1978
The Hothouse, pr., pb. 1980 (wr. 1958)
Family Voices, pr., pb. 1981
Other Places: Three Plays, pr., pb. 1982 (includes *Family Voices*, *Victoria Station*, and *A Kind of Alaska*; revised in 1984, includes *One for the Road* and deletes *Family Voices*)

Mountain Language, pr., pb. 1988
The New World Order, pr. 1991
Party Time, pr., pb. 1991
Moonlight, pr., pb. 1993
Ashes to Ashes, pb. 1996
The Dwarfs and Nine Revue Sketches, pb. 1999
Celebration, pr., pb. 2000
Remembrance of Things Past, pr., pb. 2000 (with Di Trevis; adaptation of Marcel Proust's novel)
Press Conference, pr., pb. 2002 (sketch)

OTHER LITERARY FORMS

In addition to his works for the stage, Harold Pinter has published poetry and a few short stories in magazines. Early in his writing career, he contributed poems to *Poetry London* under the pseudonym Harold Pinta. He has written a number of radio plays as well as screenplays adapted from his own works and those of other writers. In 1972, Pinter was approached by Joseph Losey, who had directed the films made from Pinter's screenplays *The Servant* (1963), *Accident* (1967), and *The Go-Between* (1971), with the idea of adapting Marcel Proust's *À la recherche du temps perdu* (1913-1927; *Remembrance of Things Past*, 1922-1931, 1981) for the screen. The task of turning Proust's monumental seven-volume novel into a workable screenplay was daunting, and although the screenplay was published in 1977, the film was never made. However, Pinter has written that the time devoted to the Proust project was the best working year of his life. Three collections of Pinter's screenplays were published in 2000, and a collection of his prose and poetry *Various Voices: Prose, Poetry, Politics, 1948-1998* was published in 1998.

ACHIEVEMENTS

Harold Pinter has won many awards, including the *Evening Standard* Award (1960, for *The Caretaker*), the Italia Prize (1963, for the television version of *The Lover*), the British Film Academy Award (1965, for *The Pumpkin Eater*), and the Common Wealth Award (1981). He has a long list of honorary degrees, and he was elected an Honorary Fellow in the Modern Language Association in 1970.

Harold Pinter (R. Jones)

BIOGRAPHY

Harold Pinter was born October 10, 1930, in England, the son of a hardworking Jewish tailor whose business eventually failed. Pinter grew up in a run-down working-class area, full of railroad yards and bad-smelling factories. When World War II broke out in 1939, Pinter, like most London children, was evacuated to the countryside to be safe from the German bombing. Living in the countryside or by the sea was not, for Pinter, as idyllic as it might have been: "I was quite a morose little boy." He returned to London before the end of the war and remembers seeing V-2 rockets flying overhead and his backyard in flames. After the war ended, the violence did not cease; anti-Semitism was strong in his neighborhood, and Jews were frequently threatened. Perhaps these early brushes with war and violence decided him; when he was eighteen and eligible for National Service, he declared himself a conscientious objector. He was afraid he would be jailed, but in fact, he was merely fined. In grammar school, he was a sprinter and set a record for the hundred-yard dash. He was also an actor in school plays, playing Macbeth and Romeo, and he received a grant in 1948 to study acting at the Royal Academy of Dramatic Art. He did not stay long, however, and spent the next year tramping the streets. He published a few poems in literary magazines (he was only nineteen when the first were published) and got an acting job with a Shakespearean company touring Ireland; other acting jobs followed. He met the actress Vivien Merchant and married her in 1956; she was to perform in a number of his plays. They were divorced in 1980, and in November of that year Pinter married Lady Antonia Fraser, a highly regarded writer of historical biographies and one of England's great beauties. The match of the famous, working-class playwright and the beautiful, aristocratic biographer was the object of much attention in London literary circles and in the popular press. Pinter has one son, Daniel, from his first marriage.

In 1957, a friend of Pinter who was studying directing at Bristol University told him he needed a play, and Pinter wrote *The Room* for him in four afternoons. The play was performed and was favorably reviewed by Harold Hobson in the *Sunday Times*. Pinter seemed to have found himself. Immediately after writing *The Room*, he wrote *The Birthday Party* and *The Dumb Waiter*. The plays were performed, and though Harold Hobson continued to champion him, many drama critics gave the plays scathing reviews. *The Birthday Party* closed after a week. In the following years, though Pinter's plays continued to be attacked, they also continued to be revived and performed, and his work began to receive considerable critical attention. After his play *The Caretaker* became his first commercial success, Pinter emerged as a productive and versatile writer for stage and screen, as well as a political activist and spokesperson for the arts in general.

In 1989, he came to the United States to direct his play *Mountain Language*. Directing his own and others' work and acting in such touring shows as *Old Times* (with Liv Ullmann, in 1986), he has become very well respected in the theater community. His film work includes, in addition to adaptations of his plays, *The Handmaid's Tale* (1990; adapted from Margaret Atwood's novel), *The Heat of the Day* (1990; based on Elizabeth Bowen's novel), and original works such as *Reunion* (1989).

Politically and culturally, Pinter protested the imprisonment of writers through his activities with the International Association of Poets, Playwrights, Editors, Essayists, and Novelists (PEN Club), donated proceeds to Václav Havel, protested against the Margaret Thatcher government in Great Britain and U.S. involvement in Central and South America, founded the Arts for Nicaragua Fund, delivered a speech by Salman Rushdie while the writer was in hiding, and raised funds for famine relief in Ethiopia. In 1990, he organized a celebration in honor of Samuel Beckett at the National Theatre. Since the early 1990's, Pinter has been less active as a playwright.

ANALYSIS

Harold Pinter is sometimes associated with the generation of British playwrights who emerged in the 1950's and are known as the Angry Young Men. His first plays, with their dingy, working-class settings and surface naturalism, seemed to link Pinter with this group, but only the surface of his plays is naturalistic; most of a Pinter play takes place beneath the surface. His closest affinities are with a more centrally important movement, the Theater of the Absurd. As a young man, before he started writing plays, the works of Franz Kafka and Samuel Beckett made a great impression on Pinter. Like Kafka, Pinter portrays the absurdity of human existence with a loving attention to detail that creates the deceptive naturalism of his surfaces. It is particularly with the meticulously rendered, tape-recorder-accurate language

of his characters that Pinter pulls the naturalistic and absurdist strands of his drama all together. The language of his characters, bumbling, repetitive, circular, is actually more realistic—more like actual human speech—than the precise and rhetorically patterned dialogue found in what is considered to be "realistic" drama. Yet that actual language of human beings, when isolated on the stage, underlines the absurdity of human aspirations and becomes both wonderfully comic and pathetic as it marks the stages of human beings' inability to communicate what is most important to them. Pinter, however, is more than an accurate recorder of speech; he is also a poet. The language of his characters, for all of their inarticulateness, is finally profoundly communicative of the human condition. What makes Pinter one of the most important modern British dramatists is his consummate skill as a dramatist; the fact that in language and pattern he is a poet, especially a poet of contemporary language, both its spoken expression and its expressive silences; and his existential insight into human beings' place in the universe, which connects him with the most profound writers and thinkers of his time.

THE ROOM

Pinter's first play, *The Room*, contained a number of features that were to become his hallmarks. The play is set in a single small room, the characters warm and secure within but threatened by cold and death from without. *The Room* is overtly symbolic, more so than Pinter's later work, but the setting and characters are, for the most part, realistic. Rose sits in the cheap flat making endless cups of tea, wrapping a muffler around her man before she lets him go out into the cold; her husband, Bert, drives a van. Under the naturalistic veneer, however, the play has a murky, almost expressionistic atmosphere. The room is Rose's living space on earth. If she stays within, she is warm and safe. Outside, it is so cold it is "murder," she says. She opens the door, and there, waiting to come in, is the new generation, a young couple named Mr. and Mrs. Sands (the sands of time? Mr. Sands's name is Tod, which in German means "death"). They are looking for an apartment and have heard that Rose's apartment is empty. "This room is occupied," she insists, obviously upset at this premonition of her departure. A man has been staying in the basement. She imagines it to be wet and cold there, a place where no one would stand much of a chance. The man wants to see her. Again the door opens, to reveal a terrifying intruder from the outside. He comes in. He is a black man—the color of death—and he is blind, tapping in with his stick, blind as death is when claiming its victims from the ranks of the good or the bad. "Your father wants you to come home," he tells her. Rose's husband comes in at this moment, shrieks "Lice!" and immediately attacks the man, tipping him out of his chair and kicking him in the head until he is motionless. On the naturalistic level of the play, the action seems motivated by racist hatred, perhaps, but at the symbolic level, Bert seems to have recognized death and instinctively engages it in battle, as later Pinter characters kick out violently against their fate. It is, however, to no avail: Rose has been struck blind, already infected by her approaching death.

While this summary stresses the symbolic dimension of the play, it is Pinter's genius to achieve such symbolic resonance at the same time that he maintains an eerily naturalistic surface—although less so in this first play than in later plays. Critics have objected to the heavy-handedness, the overt symbolism, of the blind black man, and characters with similar roles in later plays are more subtly drawn.

THE BIRTHDAY PARTY

The Birthday Party was Pinter's first full-length play; in effect, it is a much fuller and more skillful working out of the elements already present in *The Room*. The scene once more is restricted to a single room, the dining room of a seedy seaside guesthouse. Meg, the landlady, and Petey, her husband, who has a menial job outside the hotel, resemble Rose and her husband of *The Room*. Meg is especially like Rose in her suffocating motherliness. In this play, however, she is no longer the main character. That role has been taken by Stanley, the only boarder of the house, who has been there for a year. He is pinned to the house, afraid to go out, feeling that intruders from outside are menacing bringers of death. Although he is in his late thirties, he is being kept by Meg as a spoiled little boy. He sleeps late in the morning, and when he comes down to breakfast, he complains querulously about everything she fixes for him. He is unshaven and unwashed, still wearing his pajamas. What is enacted symbolically by his refusing to leave the house is his fear of going out and engaging life, his fear that an acceptance of life—meaning going outside, having a job, having normal sexual relations with a woman his age—would also mean accepting his eventual death. He is refusing to live in an absurd world that exacts so high a price for life. It is an untenable position, and his refusal to live as an adult human being has left him a wrinkled and aging child. Further, it does him no good to remain in the house: If he does not go out into the world, the world will come in to him. In fact, he hears that two men have come to town and that they are going to stay at the guesthouse. He knows at once that they have come for him and is thrown into a panic. In the meantime, Meg decides that it is his birthday and gives him a present. The unintentionally chilling reminder of his aging is cut across by the present itself, a child's toy drum, which Stan begins beating frenziedly as the first act ends.

The symbolic action, though more complex, resembles that of *The Room*: What is new is the much finer texture of the realistic surface of the play. The relationship between Stan and his surrogate mother, Meg, beautifully handled, is both comic and sad—comic because it is ridiculous for this nearly middle-aged man to be mothered so excessively and to behave so much like a spoiled child; sad because one believes in both Meg and Stan as human beings. Both comedy and pathos, realism and symbolic undercurrents, grow out of the fully developed language of the dialogue. Its richness, its circumlocution—all elements that have come to be called "Pinteresque"—are evident even in this early play.

It is obvious that the two men who come, Goldberg and McCann, have indeed come for Stan. There is no concealment between them and Stan. He is rude to them and tries to order them out. They make it equally clear to him that he is not to leave the premises. McCann is gloomy and taciturn; Goldberg, the senior partner, is glib and falsely jovial. His language is a wonderfully comic—and sinister—blend of politicians' clichés, shallow philosophy, and gangster argot. There is a brilliant scene when they first confront Stan, cross-examining him with a dizzying landslide of insane questions ("Why did you kill your wife?... Why did you never get married?... Why do you pick your nose?") that finally leaves him screaming, and he kicks Goldberg in the stomach, just as the husband in *The Room* kicks the blind black man. It is too late, however, for they have already taken his glasses, and he has had his first taste of the blindness of death.

Meg comes in, and they stop scuffling, the two henchmen putting on a show of joviality. They begin to have a birthday party for Stan. Lulu, a pretty but rather vulgar young woman, is invited. Lulu in the past has frequently invited Stan to go outside walking with her, but he has refused. She and Goldberg hit it off together, and she ends up in his lap kissing him as everyone at the party drinks heavily. They begin a drunken game of blindman's buff—"If you're touched, then you're blind"—and the recurring image of blindness serves as a foretaste of death. McCann, wearing the blindfold, comes over and touches Stan, so that it is Stan's turn to be "blind." To make sure, McCann breaks Stan's glasses. The drunken Stan stumbles over to Meg and suddenly begins strangling her. They rush over to stop him, and suddenly the power goes out. In the darkness, Stan rushes around, avoiding them, giggling. The terrified Lulu faints, and when someone briefly turns on a flashlight, the audience sees that Stan has Lulu spread-eagled on the table and is on top of her. With his mortality approaching him anyway, Stan, buoyed up by drink, makes a desperate effort to get out of the house, out of his entrapment in sterile childhood. He struggles to strangle the mother who is suffocating him and to have a sexual relationship with an appropriate female—a taste of the life he has denied himself in order to escape paying the debt, death. It is too late. In the morning, a nearly catatonic Stan is brought downstairs by the two henchmen. He has been washed and shaved and dressed in a suit, as if for burial. A black limousine waits outside the door. Petey, Meg's husband, makes a halfhearted attempt to save Stan from the henchmen, but to still his protests, they need only

invite him to come along. One is reminded of the medieval morality play *Everyman*. When Death is carrying off Everyman, Everyman's friends and family promise to be true to him and help him in any way, but the moment they are invited to come with him, they find some excuse to stay behind.

The play in some ways points one back to other possible intentions in *The Room*. Perhaps Rose, like Stan, has denied life. Afraid to go out in the cold, she does not escape having the cold come in after her. What she has lost is the pleasure she might have had in actively engaging life. Her husband, for example, comes home after a cold, wintry day out driving his van and talks with almost sexual relish about the pleasure he has had in masterfully controlling his van through all the dangers of his route.

THE DUMB WAITER

The Dumb Waiter has much in common with *The Room* and *The Birthday Party*. Again, the setting is a single room in which the characters sit, nervously waiting for an ominous presence from the outside. The two characters are a pair of assassins, sent from place to place, job to job, to kill people. They are, then, rather like McCann and Goldberg of *The Birthday Party*. What is interesting is that the cast of *The Birthday Party* has been collapsed into only these two, for they are not only the killers who come from outside, they are also the victims who wait nervously inside. While they wait in an anonymous room for their final directions on their new job, a job in which everything begins to go wrong, they pass the time by talking. The conversation ranges from reports of what one character is reading in the paper to discussions of how to prepare their tea, but in this oblique fashion it begins circling around to much more pressing speculations on the nature of their lives, questions with which these semiliterate thugs are poorly equipped to deal. The dialogue is quite comical at first, the verbal sparring between the two Cockneys handled with Pinter's customary assurance, but the play is also witty in a more intellectual, allusive manner.

In the opening scene, a number of direct allusions are made to Beckett's play, *En attendant Godot* (pb. 1952, pr. 1953; *Waiting for Godot*, 1954). There is, for example, a great deal of comic business made over putting on and taking off shoes and shaking things out of them, and at one point a character walks to the apron, looks over the audience, and says, "I wouldn't like to live in this dump." Ben and Gus (like Didi and Gogo) are waiting, with varying amounts of patience and impatience, for the arrival of a mysterious presence to reveal the meaning of things to them—the person who makes all the arrangements and sends them out on their jobs. Also Beckettian is the way an entire life is described in the most minimal terms: "I mean, you come into a place when it's still dark, you come into a room you've never seen before, you sleep all day, you do your job, and then you go away in the night." The many parallels are intentional: *The Dumb Waiter* is Pinter's urban, Cockney version of *Waiting for Godot*. In *Waiting for Godot*, there was at least a tree; here, there is only a squalid room, with no windows, in the basement of an old restaurant. The two characters do not have any intellectual or poetic aspirations, as do the two characters representing humankind in Beckett's play. In Beckett's play, Godot's name suggests at least a remnant of belief in a benevolent, loving God—if only by parody. *The Dumb Waiter* lacks even such a remnant. The name of Gus and Ben's boss, Wilson, is deliberately lacking in any allegorical resonance. Further, Wilson is depicted as being increasingly arbitrary in his treatment of them, even though they have been faithful and pride themselves on their reliability. If God exists in this contemporary world, he is God as a fascist.

Early in the play, mysteriously, an envelope slides under the outside door. It contains twelve matches. Is a benevolent power giving them fire, the great civilizing agent, to help them stave off chaos? They use the matches to light a fire under their kettle, but a moment later, the gas fails, and they have no tea. It is not benevolence, but the power of chance, which rules their absurd world, as soon becomes manifest. There is a dumbwaiter in the room. A tray comes down to them from upstairs. They open the dumbwaiter and take it out. There is a message, ordering an elaborate meal. They do not know what to do, and a moment later the tray goes back upstairs. They are quite worried. When it comes down again, ordering an even

more elaborate meal, they desperately fill it with everything they have—biscuits, tea, potato chips. A message comes down telling them that it is not good enough.

Earlier in the play, Ben had read to Gus items from the newspaper, accounts of bizarre accidents and killings, and they had been astounded that such things could go on. The popular press represented their access—from their safe room—to the absurd goings-on in the arbitrary world outside. They try to go back to remarking on the news items now, but they are no longer really interested in the news from outside, because now the absurd has invaded their safe room. They have passed all of their tests, they have been reliable and faithful on the job—yet absurdity is still with them. Their good behavior has not, after all, been able to save them. Ben, the senior partner, falls back on what has been successful for him before: He follows instructions more and more rigidly, becoming increasingly punctilious over the least detail of formal instructions. Gus, who from the beginning has shown himself to be more sensitive, reacts in a quite different way. He begins questioning the absurdity; he begins, to Ben's horror, to question authority.

Gus's first questions have to do with his job. He does not have the luxury of being a guiltless victim, such as the two tramps in *Waiting for Godot*. He lives in his modern society by being a part of its violence. Others die that he may live and hold his place in the world. This has already been bothering him, and when he finds out that on top of his burden of guilt, he will not even be treated fairly by authority, he begins to rebel; he criticizes Ben, his superior, and even shouts angrily up the dumbwaiter shaft. He wanders off stage left to get a glass of water. Then Ben is notified by the authority that the person he is to kill is coming in the door at stage right (to the audience's left). He shouts for Gus, his partner, to come help him.

The door at stage right flies open. Ben levels his revolver. It is Gus, thrust in, his coat and tie and revolver stripped from him, to stand there, stooped and awkward; he slowly looks up to meet Ben's eyes. The play ends there, but it is clear that Ben, who, faced with absurdity, reacts by following orders all the more unquestioningly, will shoot his partner. He will be the ostensible winner, the survivor, although in an absurd world, what can really be won? He will in the end be nothing. When Gus spoke earlier about coming in at night, doing a job, and leaving at night—a realistic statement but also a metaphor of a human being's life—he went on to say that he wanted a window, a bit of a view, before he left. His perceptions of absurdity and guilt, a first step toward moral choice, constitute his bit of a view, his wresting of some meaning out of life.

THE CARETAKER

The Caretaker, generally considered to be Pinter's greatest play, is in many ways an even more complex permutation of the elements that were developed in his first few plays. Though *The Caretaker* is much more realistic on the surface than the earlier plays and has much less overt violence, it retains its tie with absurdist theater in the fact that it readily lends itself to allegorical interpretation. The setting, again, is a single room, and once more, it is made clear that at least a degree of security exists within the room, and that outside, in the endlessly rainy weather, there is little chance for survival. Davies, the old tramp, is the man struggling to stay in the room, but he is ultimately thrown out to his destruction. The two young men, the brothers Aston and Mick, though in much more subtle and complex ways, occupy the role of the killers. It is they who throw Davies out.

The setting is a run-down room in an old house, with a leaky roof and piles of miscellaneous junk stacked everywhere. As the scene opens, Mick, the younger brother, is scrutinizing the room. He hears a door slam and voices offstage, and he quietly exits. Aston, the older brother, enters. He has brought Davies, the old tramp, along. It is revealed that Aston had found him in a fight, had saved him from a bad beating, and is now taking him into his house and giving him a place to sleep. Davies is the worst kind of garrulous old man, puffed up with self-importance, constantly justifying himself, and running down everyone else, especially blacks and aliens. Aston seems kindly, ingenuous, almost a bit simple. Davies, who is wearing old sandals, says he needs shoes. Aston immediately rummages through his things and

brings out a solid pair of shoes to give him. Davies regards them very critically and rejects them as too narrow, throwing them aside.

In a nice bit of theatercraft on Pinter's part, the audience initially tends to see the play from the kindly Aston's point of view and wonders why he has taken in this tiresome and ungrateful old bum. Very shortly, however, as Aston begins to act more strangely and as his brother Mick shows his own erratic and unpredictable behavior, the audience slowly realizes that it is seeing the play from Davies' point of view—that Davies, disagreeable as he is, is Everyman.

Davies, who is shabby and bad-smelling, continues truculently to insist on his personal worth. He evidently does this no matter what the cost. He lost his job, which he sorely needed, and got in the fight, which might have killed him, because he was asked to carry out a bucket of slops when he had been hired to sweep up. He also values himself for not being a black or an alien and therefore, he believes, having a higher place in the scheme of things. He is rude and choosy when Aston offers him gifts. Obviously, however, these are all pathetic attempts by a man with nothing to preserve but a certain dignity. When Aston goes out the next morning, Davies is incredulous that Aston lets him remain behind, actually trusting him in the room alone. In other words, Davies knows that his position is low, but he desperately wants to keep it above the very bottom. It is all he has left.

Aston, though apparently kindly, is very strange. He goes out every day and buys more worthless junk to pile up in the room. He is constantly tinkering with electric appliances, though obviously without a clue as to how to fix them. He plans eventually to fix up the room but obviously, from day to day, is accomplishing nothing. When he leaves, Mick comes in. If Aston is slow in everything he does, Mick is dazzlingly quick. He deluges Davies with torrents of language, holds Davies completely in his power, and torments him with words—threats alternating with attractive-sounding offers. It is his house, it turns out, in which Aston merely lives. Both Mick and Aston, at different times, offer Davies the job of being caretaker of the house. The offer is tempting. Davies keeps saying he needs shoes so he can get down to

Sidcup and pick up his papers and get his life sorted out. Yet as he refuses offers of shoes, it becomes clear that he does not want to go; he wants to remain in this room, which, for all of its shortcomings, is at least out of the rain. One night, in a long monologue, the usually taciturn Aston tells Davies about the time he was committed to an asylum and given shock treatment. Davies, who knows that he is himself near the bottom, only marginally above the blacks, now decides that, being sane, he is also above Aston. Although Aston has befriended him and put him up, and Mick has only offered him extravagant promises, Davies decides he will be Mick's man and perhaps work to ease out Aston.

Aston has been waking Davies up in the middle of the night, complaining that his muttering and groaning make it impossible to sleep. Davies is fed up with this treatment, and the next time Aston wakes him up, Davies explodes and tells him that he is crazy and should go back to the asylum, and that he, Davies, and Mick will start running things—perhaps Aston had better leave. It is a typical outburst from Davies, overstepping himself, but he relies on Mick—though Mick has been erratic and unpredictable in the past— to back him up. At this point, Aston tells Davies that he had better look for a place somewhere else, and Davies is forced to leave. Davies comes back the next day to the room when only Mick is there, but Mick turns on him savagely, and Davies realizes he has been had. Aston comes in, and Mick exits. All Davies' truculence is gone, and he begs Aston to take him back, but Aston ignores him, and it is clear that Davies must depart.

The play is moving enough only on its surface, by turns comic, ominous, perhaps even approaching the tragic. It does not remain at the surface, however, but pushes toward allegorical interpretation. There are many possible readings of the play, none of which necessarily excludes the others. Martin Esslin, in *The Peopled Wound: The Work of Harold Pinter* (1970), sees the play as an Oedipal confrontation: The father lords it over the sons while he has the power, but when he gets too old to defend himself, their covert antagonism against him comes to the surface, and they destroy him, throwing out the old generation so that the new generation has room in which to live. An even older archetype, however, might fit the play more closely. A kindly God puts together a world for man and invites him to come live in it. Man, rather than being grateful, as he ought, becomes puffed up with self-importance and lets a tempting Satan (Mick) convince him that he, humankind, is the equal of God; as a result, he is thrown out of his paradise. Pinter has updated his allegory. It is a rather trashy and rundown paradise, a Cockney paradise in a London slum. Obviously, the temptation and fall, the ejection from paradise, is a pattern that can be read into many stories. There is evidence in the text, however, that Pinter intended this particular reading. Aston is referred to in terms that would suggest such an interpretation. "There was someone walking about on the roof the other night," Davies says. "It must have been him." Aston, of course, is the giver of all necessary things—a roof, money, bread. When Davies wakes in the morning, he is startled to find that Aston is sitting smiling at him. Davies, characteristically, immediately begins complaining that Aston's gifts are not enough. Aston gives him bread but no knife with which to cut it (reminiscent of Wilson, in *The Dumb Waiter*, sending the two men matches to light the stove but providing no gas for the stove); gives him shoes with unmatching shoelaces; and does not give him a clock.

Aston's curious life history suggests an identification with Christ. He tells Davies that he used to talk to everyone, and he thought they listened, and that it was all right. He used to have hallucinations, in which he would see everything very clearly. When he had something to say, he would tell the others, but some lie got spread about him, and they took him away, and gave him shock treatment (the Crucifixion?), after which he was no longer able to work or get his thoughts together. After his long confessional monologue to Davies, Aston seldom speaks to him again, and Davies feels deserted. In suggestive words, Davies says: "Christ! That bastard, he ain't even listening to me!" By this time, Davies has also deserted Aston. He listens to Mick, forgetting Mick's previous bad treatment of him and forgetting Aston's many kindnesses to him.

It is a hopeless situation for Davies, because Aston does indeed seem feckless and unstable; Mick seems to own the world now, and in a world of increasing absurdity, Davies has to make his decision, has to struggle for survival and some sort of existential sense of personal value. In the final scene before Davies' expulsion, Mick and Aston meet briefly and smile faintly, and there is almost, for the moment, the hint of collusion between them, as if God and the Devil worked in concert to destroy humankind, as if, working together, they were indeed the two hit men sent out to annihilate humankind after human beings' brief sojourn in an absurd world.

The Caretaker carries to full maturity the themes and techniques that Pinter first adumbrated in *The Room* and developed over his next few plays. With its characters, its allegory, and its brilliant language and stagecraft, it is a quintessentially Pinteresque play, the perfection of all he was feeling his way toward as a playwright. Thereafter, he had to change direction if he were going to avoid merely imitating himself. He felt increasingly that he "couldn't any longer stay in the room with this bunch of people who opened doors and came in and went out." He changed his milieu, writing plays with middle-class characters, leaving behind the Cockney language of the first plays but demonstrating that he had just as accurate an ear for the absurdities and banalities of middle-class speech and could hear just as clearly what was trying to be said under the affectations of its language.

THE HOMECOMING

The Homecoming, perhaps the most Kafkaesque of Pinter's plays, firmly established his dramatic idiom as unique. In the play, a professor who has been teaching in the United States returns to his London home so that his wife might meet his father and his brothers. He is greeted with oblique suggestions of enmity and sexual overtures toward his wife. In the end, the detached professor (like so many of Kafka's passive protagonists) acquiesces when his wife announces her decision to move in with the father and the two brothers.

LATER PLAYS

With plays such as *Landscape* and *Silence*, Pinter began working with more lyrical language. In *One*

for the Road, Mountain Language, and The New World Order, Pinter began writing overtly political works that reflected his growing activism as a self-styled "citizen of the world." In each new direction he has taken, he has continued to show that the essence of Pinter is not one or another easily imitated mannerism, but rather his poetic brilliance with language, his flawless stagecraft, and his insights into the human condition.

In February, 2002, nine of Pinter's sketches, none longer than ten minutes, were performed at the Lyttleton Theatre. Seven dated from around 1959, but "Tess" was two years old, and "Press Conference" was new. "Tess" is a slight work featuring a smiling lady from a comically disreputable upper-crust family. In "Press Conference," Pinter himself (battling cancer and chemotherapy) played the lead, a Minister of Culture who was recently head of the secret police. This sketch reveals the same skepticism of, even hostility toward, supposedly democratic governments as reflected in *One for the Road* and *Ashes to Ashes*. During the press conference, the urbane Minister blandly announces what his response will be to those people who resist the free market. Their women will be raped, and their children will be killed or abducted. Dissent will not be tolerated. The journalists greet the Minister's program with chuckles and applause. In the latter part of his career, Pinter appears to draw little distinction between governments of the capitalistic West and brutal dictatorships elsewhere in the world.

OTHER MAJOR WORKS

LONG FICTION: *The Dwarfs*, 1990.

POETRY: *Poems*, 1968 (Alan Clodd, editor); *I Know the Place*, 1979; *Ten Early Poems*, 1992.

SCREENPLAYS: *The Servant*, 1963; *The Guest*, 1964; *The Pumpkin Eater*, 1964; *The Quiller Memorandum*, 1966 (adaptation of Adam Hall's novel); *Accident*, 1967; *The Birthday Party*, 1968 (adaptation of his play); *The Go-between*, 1971; *The Homecoming*, 1971 (adaptation of his play); *The Last Tycoon*, 1976 (adaptation of F. Scott Fitzgerald's novel); *Proust: A Screenplay*, 1977; *The French Lieutenant's Woman*, 1981 (adaptation of John Fowles's novel); *Betrayal*,

1983 (adaptation of his play); *Turtle Diary*, 1985; *Reunion*, 1989; *The Handmaid's Tale*, 1990 (adaptation of Margaret Atwood's novel); *The Heat of the Day*, 1990 (adaptation of Elizabeth Bowen's novel); *The Comfort of Strangers*, 1991; *Party Time*, 1991 (adaptation of his play); *The Remains of the Day*, 1991 (adaptation of Kazuo Ishiguro's novel); *The Trial*, 1992 (adaptation of Franz Kafka's novel); *Collected Screenplays*, 2000 (3 volumes).

NONFICTION: *Pinter at Sixty*, 1993; *Conversations with Pinter*, 1996.

EDITED TEXT: *One Hundred Poems by One Hundred Poets*, 1991 (with Geoffrey Godbert and Anthony Astbury).

MISCELLANEOUS: *Various Voices: Prose, Poetry, Politics, 1948-1998*, 1998.

BIBLIOGRAPHY

Billington, Michael. *The Life and Work of Harold Pinter*. New York: Faber and Faber, 2001. This 432-page update of a 1997 study covers the life of Pinter and provides critical analysis of his major works.

Burkman, Katherine H. *The Dramatic World of Harold Pinter: Its Basis in Ritual*. Columbus: Ohio State University Press, 1971. A fairly early study dealing with mythic structures in the stylized staging of Pinter's work, especially *The Birthday Party* (viewed as an agon) and *The Caretaker*, "a poignant portrayal of man's self-destructive nature, his seeming compulsion to live his life in the image of the cruel ritual of the priesthood of Nemi." Bibliography and index.

Dukore, Bernard F. *Harold Pinter*. 2d ed. London: Macmillan, 1988. An updating of Dukore's earlier 1982 work, this study serves as a condensation of the essential critical vision: the sense of menace, the acknowledgment of the absurd, struggles with realism, the nature of power, and the place of memory. Notes Pinter's "minimalist theorizing." Bibliography; index of proper names and play titles.

Gale, Steven H. *Butter's Going Up: A Critical Analysis of Harold Pinter's Work*. Durham, N.C.: Duke University Press, 1977. After a brief biographical chapter, Gale examines "the comedies of menace," a group of Pinter's plays that "collectively . . . defines the themes and establishes the techniques which will be basic in all of his works." Following chapters analyze the metaphor of "the room" and sum up Pinter's writing patterns over a long and varied career. Contains lists of first performances, casts and directors, productions directed by Pinter, and several other valuable appendices. Strong chronology, annotated bibliography (including select reviews), and index.

Gordon, Lois, ed. *Harold Pinter: A Casebook*. New York: Garland, 1990. Honoring Pinter on his sixtieth birthday, this collection of insightful essays is a good source for later plays and revisionist criticism on earlier plays. Best is Gordon's "observation," full of contemporary information, of Pinter's 1989 visit to the United States, where the playwright came to stage *Mountain Language*, among other projects. Appendix of photographs from Pauline Flanagan's collection, select bibliography, and valuable index to all articles.

Gussow, Mel. *Conversations with Pinter*. New York: Grove/Atlantic, 1996. The playwright discusses his technique and aesthetic.

Merritt, Susan Hollis. *Pinter in Play: Critical Strategies and the Plays of Harold Pinter*. Durham, N.C.: Duke University Press, 1990. Centering her discussion on "criticism as strategy" and comparing criticism to "playing" in Pinter's work, Merritt puts a postmodern twist to her study. Divided into "Perspectives on Pinter's Critical Evolution," "Some Strategies of Pinter Critics," and "Social Relations of Critical and Cultural Change," this work is a major statement, sophisticated and astute. Supplemented by a list of works cited and an index.

Morrison, Kristin. *Canters and Chronicles: The Use of Narrative in the Plays of Samuel Beckett and Harold Pinter*. Chicago: University of Chicago Press, 1996. Compares narrative movement and, especially, Pinter's absurdist approach to dialogue with that of his early idol.

Quigley, Austin E. *The Pinter Problem*. Princeton, N.J.: Princeton University Press, 1975. This early study of Pinter's "problems of identity, illusion, menace, and verification" is the first to examine the contradiction between the concrete and the abstract approaches to understanding Pinter's work, up to *Landscape*. Bibliography and index of proper names only.

Thompson, David T. *Pinter: The Player's Playwright*. New York: Schocken Books, 1985. Taking a performance approach, and starting from Pinter's own acting career, this short but information-packed work helps get the plays off the page and onto the stage. Subtleties of movement and dialogue, and Pinter's concentration on "the positioning of characters" in the stage picture, are well discussed, with theatrical examples throughout. Claims more attention should be paid to stage directions. Includes a list of plays acted by Pinter in the 1950's and a good index.

Norman Lavers, updated by Thomas J. Taylor
and Patrick Adcock

LUIGI PIRANDELLO

Born: Girgenti (now Agrigento), Sicily, Italy; June 28, 1867
Died: Rome, Italy; December 10, 1936

PRINCIPAL DRAMA

La morsa, pb. as *L'epilogo*, 1898, pr. 1910 (*The Vise*, 1928)

Scamandro, pb. 1909, pr. 1928

Lumìe di Sicilia, pr. 1910, pb. 1911 (*Sicilian Limes*, 1921)

Il dovere del medico, pb. 1912, pr. 1913 (*The Doctor's Duty*, 1928)

Se non così . . ., pr. 1915, pb. 1916

All'uscita, pr. 1916, pb. 1922 (*At the Gate*, 1928)

Liolà, pr. 1916, pb. 1917 (English translation, 1952)

Pensaci, Giacomino!, pr. 1916, pb. 1917

Il berretto a sonagli, pr. 1917, pb. 1920 (*Cap and Bells*, 1957)

Così è (se vi pare), pr. 1917, pb. 1918 (*Right You Are [If You Think So]*, 1922)

La giara, pr. 1917, pb. 1925 (*The Jar*, 1928)

Il piacere dell'onestà, pr. 1917, pb. 1918 (*The Pleasure of Honesty*, 1923)

Il giuoco delle parti, pr. 1918, pb. 1919 (*The Rules of the Game*, 1959)

Ma non è una cosa seria, pr. 1918, pb. 1919

La patente, pb. 1918, pr. 1919 (*The License*, 1964)

L'innesto, pr. 1919, pb. 1921

L'uomo, la bestia, e la virtù, pr., pb. 1919 (*Man, Beast, and Virtue*, 1989)

Come prima, meglio di prima, pr. 1920, pb. 1921

La Signora Morli, una e due, pr. 1920, pb. 1922

Tutto per bene, pr., pb. 1920 (*All for the Best*, 1960)

Sei personaggi in cerca d'autore, pr., pb. 1921 (*Six Characters in Search of an Author*, 1922)

Enrico IV, pr., pb. 1922 (*Henry IV*, 1923)

L'imbecille, pr. 1922, pb. 1926 (*The Imbecile*, 1928)

Vestire gli ignudi, pr. 1922, pb. 1923 (*Naked*, 1924)

L'altro figlio, pr. 1923, pb. 1925 (*The House with the Column*, 1928)

L'uomo dal fiore in bocca, pr. 1923, pb. 1926 (*The Man with the Flower in His Mouth*, 1928)

La vita che ti diedi, pr. 1923, pb. 1924 (*The Life I Gave You*, 1959)

Ciascuno a suo modo, pr., pb. 1924 (*Each in His Own Way*, 1923)

Sagra del Signore della nave, pb. 1924, pr. 1925 (*Our Lord of the Ship*, 1928)

Diana e la Tuda, Swiss pr. 1926, pr., pb. 1927 (*Diana and Tudo*, 1950)

L'amica della mogli, pr., pb. 1927 (*The Wives' Friend*, 1949)

Bellavita, pr. 1927, pb. 1928 (English translation, 1964)

La nuova colonia, pr., pb. 1928 (*The New Colony*, 1958)

Lazzaro, pr., pb. 1929 (*Lazarus*, 1952)

O di uno o di nessuno, pr., pb. 1929

Sogno (ma forse no), pb. 1929, pr. 1936 (*I'm Dreaming, But Am I?*, 1964)

Come tu mi vuoi, pr., pb. 1930 (*As You Desire Me*, 1931)

Questa sera si recita a soggetto, pr., pb. 1930 (*Tonight We Improvise*, 1932)

I giganti della montagna, act 1 pb. 1931, act 2 pb. 1934, act 3 pr. 1937 (*The Mountain Giants*, 1958)

Trovarsi, pr., pb. 1932 (*To Find Oneself*, 1943)

Quando si è qualcuno, pr. 1933 (*When Someone Is Somebody*, 1958)

La favola del figlio cambiato, pr., pb. 1934

Non si sa come, pr. 1934, pb. 1935 (*No One Knows How*, 1960)

Naked Masks: Five Plays, pb. 1952

OTHER LITERARY FORMS

Luigi Pirandello wrote seven novels, more than three hundred short stories, a number of critical essays, and six volumes of poetry. The standard edition of his works, *Opere* (1966), published by Mondadori in Milan, consists of six volumes, including *Novelle per un anno* (1956-1957); *Tutti i romanzi* (1957); *Maschere nude* (1958); and *Saggi, poesie, scritti vari* (1960).

ACHIEVEMENTS

Italy's most acclaimed modern writer, Luigi Pirandello is known in the United States primarily for three or four of his forty-four plays, written between 1917 and 1924 and collected by Eric Bentley in *Naked Masks* (1952). Of these plays, *Six Characters in Search of an Author* has earned for Pirandello a reputation as a major figure in the development of modern drama. Assessing the impact of that play's 1923 production in Paris, Georges Neveux remarked that "the entire theatre of an era came out of the womb of that play." Another critic affirmed Pirandello's seminal importance by referring to his plays as the symbolic beginning of a new form of drama, for which the phrase "after Pirandello" has become a critical shorthand.

Critics who have tired of plays that explore the theme of reality and illusion have complained that Pirandello is more philosopher than playwright, but his plays endure as theatrically surprising and provocative contributions to the modern stage. Himself influenced by Luigi Chiarelli and the *teatro del grottesco*, Pirandello in turn has influenced virtually every playwright of reputation writing since the 1920's, including Jean-Paul Sartre, Albert Camus, Samuel Beckett, Eugène Ionesco, Eugene O'Neill, Harold Pinter, Edward Albee, Thornton Wilder, Jack Gelber, Jean Anouilh, Jean Giraudoux, and Jean Genet. With Beckett, Pirandello stands as the most influential playwright of this century.

Luigi Pirandello (© The Nobel Foundation)

BIOGRAPHY

Luigi Pirandello was born on June 28, 1867, at Villa del Caos in Girgenti (now Agrigento), Sicily, and moved to Palermo with his family when he was fourteen. Son of an owner of sulfur mines, Pirandello entered into an arranged marriage in 1894 with Maria Antonietta Portulano, the daughter of one of his father's business associates. Their first son, Stefano (named after Pirandello's father), was born a year later; Lietta, a daughter, was born in 1897, and Fausto, a son, in 1899. In 1903, when his father's mines were flooded and Pirandello's assets were lost, his wife suffered a shock that progressed into paranoia, finally necessitating her confinement in a nursing home (where she remained for forty years). Until 1919, however, when he consented to the transfer, Pirandello cared for his wife at home, an experience that undoubtedly stimulated the writer's preoccupation with the distinctions between sanity and madness.

Pirandello was a well-educated man, who studied at the universities of Palermo, Rome, and Bonn. In 1891, he completed a dissertation on his native Sicilian dialect, receiving the Doctor of Philosophy degree from Bonn. In 1898, he accepted a position as a professor of Italian at a normal school, Istituto Superiore di Magistero Femminile, in Rome. Ten years later, he was given that institution's chair in Italian language.

Pirandello published his first poems as early as 1883; he wrote his first play, "Gli uccelli dell'alto" (birds that fly), in 1886; his first novel, *L'esclusa* (*The Outcast*, 1925) in 1901; and he published his first collection of short stories, *Amori senza amore* (loves without love), in 1894. Until the early 1920's, Pirandello's work was known primarily in Italy. He gained international recognition, however, with performances of *Six Characters in Search of an Author* in Rome, London, New York City, Paris, Vienna, and Berlin between 1921 and 1924. Also active as the first director of the Teatro d'arte di Roma, Pirandello toured Europe, North America, and South America between 1924 and 1928. Pirandello's frequent travel was followed by residences in Paris and Berlin and by a period of intense creativity. Two years before his death of pneumonia in Rome on December 10, 1936, Pirandello was awarded the Nobel Prize in Literature.

ANALYSIS

In *Each in His Own Way*, Luigi Pirandello playfully has one of his characters ask another to justify his incessant "harping on this illusion and reality string." So persistent is Pirandello's dramatic examination of the multiplicity of personality, the nature of truth, and the interplay between life and art that the term "Pirandellian" has become synonymous with the complexities that result from any attempt to define the fluid line between what is illusory and what is real. In his inquiry into the nature of truth, Pirandello constructs and demolishes layers of illusion, probing the multiple perceptions and identities of his characters to reveal yet conceal the "naked mask." In his fascination with his own power as artist-creator, he dramatizes the dialectic between the fluid, spontaneous, sprawling nature of life and the fixed, predictable, and contained nature of art.

The typical Pirandellian character—Signora Ponza in *Right You Are (If You Think So)*, for example, or Leone in *The Rules of the Game*—presents himself through both "mask" and "face," a dichotomy that is more generally reflected in the playwright's treatment of theater as both illusory and real. For Pirandello, character creation involves a less-than-subtle but endlessly clever interplay among the psychological, the social, and the theatrical, which consistently reiterates the playwright's preoccupation with the multiple facets of reality and illusion.

The relationship between reality and illusion provided Pirandello with a seemingly inexhaustible fund of dramatic material. In part this is a tribute to his creative imagination, but it also suggests that this theme is not merely one among others, one that—as some critics have charged—has been worn out through overuse. Rather, the very nature of theater ensures that this theme will be forever fresh in the hands of a playwright who, like Pirandello, has the audacity to make it new.

RIGHT YOU ARE (IF YOU THINK SO)

Right You Are (If You Think So), also known as *It Is So! (If You Think So)*, is at once a traditional melodrama and a clever investigation into the nature of truth. The dramatic question propelling the play's action involves the identity of Signora Ponza, the woman whom Signor Ponza claims is his second wife and Signora Frola claims is her daughter. A group of curious members of the community into which the trio has recently moved is determined to discover the truth and, in a series of revelations, is led to believe first Signor Ponza and then Signora Frola. In order for either to be believed, however, the other must be thought to be mentally unstable. Signor Ponza's story is that Signora Frola was the mother of his first wife, who died, but for her sake he has continued the pretense that his present wife is her daughter. Signora Frola's story is that the woman is indeed her daughter and that during the daughter's illness, which necessitated her stay at a nursing home, Signor Ponza went mad. Believing that his wife had died, he refused to accept her as his wife on her return, marrying her a second time as though she were another woman. The two claims are logically irreconcilable: Signora Ponza cannot be both Ponza's second wife and Signora Frola's daughter.

The neatly constructed plot unfolds gradually as each new piece of information is revealed. Instead of adding to what has already been established, however, each new bit of information invalidates what was previously believed, leaving the town gossips, as well as the audience, suspicious and unsure. The promise of relief by forthcoming official records from the trio's previous residence is short-lived, for an earthquake has destroyed all evidence. Encouraged by Laudisi, who is amused by the others' insistence on one truth when he knows there may be several, the townspeople confront the veiled Signora Ponza herself, who reveals that she is both Signor Ponza's second wife and Signora Frola's daughter. The reply satisfies no one but Laudisi, but it is, as Signora Ponza understands, the only solution that compassion will allow.

In his monograph on *Modernism in Modern Drama* (1966), Joseph Wood Krutch speaks of Pirandello as making the most crucial denial of all: the denial of the existence of a continuous, identifiable self. The play, however, is less a modern skeptic's dramatization of the dissolution of self than it is a forceful suggestion that truth is not an external, objective fact but an internal, psychological reality. In demonstrating dramatically that Signora Ponza is both women, de-

pending on what her perceiver chooses her to be, *Right You Are (If You Think So)* sets the stage for Pirandello's subsequent, more complex inquiries into the nature of reality and illusion.

SIX CHARACTERS IN SEARCH OF AN AUTHOR

The first of a trilogy of stage plays that includes *Each in His Own Way* and *Tonight We Improvise*, *Six Characters in Search of an Author* is a spectacularly theatrical play that leaves its audience as confused as the Stage Manager and Actors whom a family of Characters interrupts, hoping that they will dramatize its story. Those Characters—the Father, his estranged wife, his son, and three stepchildren—claim to have been created by an author who, having given them life, has abandoned them. Driven by the need for self-actualization, the Father insists on enacting—or living—the family's story onstage, which the Characters do in increasingly provocative episodes that culminate in the drowning of one child and the suicide of another.

Some years earlier, when the couple had only one child, the Father recognized the attraction his wife had for an employee, so he sent the two of them off to live in a common-law relationship that resulted in three children. A number of years later, the Father visits Madame Pace's brothel, where the Stepdaughter has been forced, by poverty, to work, and he then becomes her client. The Father insists that the Mother's interruption of the encounter and the discovery of the young woman's identity prevented a consummation, but the Stepdaughter's bitterness hints otherwise.

The family's intensely emotional story constitutes the dramatic center of the play, but the play's greatest interest rests in the interplay among the dimensions of reality and fiction it presents. Although the Characters insist that they are living, not reenacting, their story, the Stage Manager believes otherwise. His attempt to cast the Actors as the Characters, however, results in a patently false performance, lending curious authenticity to the presumably fictive Characters. For the Characters, the script, though unfinished, is their destiny, compelling them to define themselves through what their author has created and constantly to live their story and their suffering.

As drama, *Six Characters in Search of an Author* is exceptionally self-conscious, dramatizing not only the relationship between reality and illusion in a philosophical sense but also the process of character creation. The play boldly presents character in the making, from the author's conception through the independent, seemingly autonomous transformations that each character undergoes before achieving full realization. When the Actors play the Characters, it becomes evident that their interpretation of character does not coincide with that of the author, thus making the actor a participant in the creation as well. Still, the Father, who feels confident that he knows his own essential nature, argues that the fictive character's life is fixed and identifiable, unlike the human life, which changes daily.

In his preface to the play, Pirandello speaks of how the Characters surfaced in his imagination one day, but how, finding no special meaning in them, he decided to abandon them. The Characters, though, remained, virtually demanding that they live and making Pirandello realize it was no longer in his power to deny them life. Thereafter, they chose their own time to reappear in his imagination, each time enticing him to give them a story, until Pirandello found himself obsessed with them. It was then that he had the idea of dramatizing this peculiar, but artistically typical, situation itself, to present the autonomy of these dramatic characters. The result, he remarks, was a combination of "tragic and comic, fantastic and realistic" that finally suggested the conflict between an ever-changing life and a fixed, immutable form.

Pirandello's manipulative powers are at their best in this play, which ends with the Actors, as well as the audience, questioning whether the deaths of the children are real, and hence a onetime occurrence, or fictive, and hence performable night after night. The unsettling ending is a fitting climax to the ongoing dialectic between reality and illusion and life and art that the Characters' invasion of the Actors' stage has caused.

HENRY IV

A play as provocative dramatically and philosophically as *Six Characters in Search of an Author*, *Henry IV* introduces an unnamed protagonist who, some twenty years earlier, suffered a fall during a masquerade party. Dressed as Henry IV at the time, he has since lived his life as though he were the eleventh century German king, with a host of retainers who support the pretense. The protagonist repeatedly replays one particular incident in the life of the historical king, Henry's penitent journey to Canossa, where he knelt before Pope Gregory VII. At the masquerade, the woman whom the protagonist loved, Donna Matilda, was dressed as Matilda of Canossa, and she has remained that figure in the mind of the madman.

Early in the play, Donna Matilda, along with four others—Carlo Di Nolli, the protagonist's nephew; Frida, Donna Matilda's daughter and Carlo's fiancée; Belcredi, the rival for Donna Matilda's affection; and Dionysius Genoni, a physician—visit the throne room, intending to administer a treatment that they hope will restore the protagonist's memory. Through dressing the young woman as her mother in masquerade twenty years earlier, then presenting her along with the older woman, who has aged, they hope to telescope time and shock the protagonist into sanity. The group does not know, however, that the protagonist recovered his memory after twelve years and has for the past eight years only pretended to be Henry IV.

The plan proceeds and backfires. When the protagonist sees the young woman looking exactly as her mother did twenty years earlier, he loses his sense of certainty in his sanity; thinking the younger woman to be Donna Matilda, he becomes obsessed with her, as he had been years before with her mother. As with the earlier play, the ending leaves the visitors and the audience questioning whether the final event occurs in the realm of reality or illusion, whether Henry IV is sane or insane when, in an act of revenge, he slays Belcredi. Either way, the protagonist must now remain in an "eternal masquerade," permanently fixed in the identity of Henry IV. The love triangle is central to *Henry IV*, just as the family's story was to *Six Characters in Search of an Author*, but as with the earlier drama, the play's contribution to dramatic innovation rests in the philosophical and artistic questions that it raises.

Henry IV is perhaps the richest of Pirandello's plays in its treatment of the complexity of identity, for each of its characters possesses at least two distinct selves. In the case of Donna Matilda, the character moves among several identities as the action shifts from the distant past to the recent past to the present. Which of these several selves she is at any given moment depends on the director of the play-within-the-play, Henry IV. If the protagonist is playing the penitent, Donna Matilda must assume the role within that scenario. So also might Donna Matilda be the young woman of twenty years earlier, whom the masquerading protagonist loved, or the middle-aged woman of the present, depending on the protagonist's perception of her. The protagonist is well aware of his manipulative powers and of the superiority that his position grants him. When the protagonist pretends to be mad, he is fully conscious that his role is an illusion, but he sustains the role to amuse and protect himself. Even when he is actually mad, though, he is curiously superior to the others, for then he is so totally committed to his one, fixed identity as Henry IV that for him no distinction exists between the mask and the face.

Henry IV's madness and sanity also serve to suggest the division between life and art that so fascinated Pirandello. As the playwright remarks in his 1908 essay, *L'umorismo* (revised 1920; partial translation *On Humor*, 1966; complete translation, 1974), we are constantly trying to stop the continuous flow of life and to fix it in determinate forms. In *Henry IV*, the protagonist, unlike the others in the play, succeeds through his self-created fiction, which, in its immunity to time, belies his own graying hair. Yet in his success, the protagonist has sacrificed the spontaneity that only the "continuous flow" of which Pirandello speaks can offer. The ongoing dialectic between motion and form that characterizes life is exemplified in the play's final moments, when Frida steps out of the picture frame where she posed as the youthful Donna Matilda and the protagonist embraces her, in a ground swell of emotion that has been suppressed for twenty years. Within moments, however, the protagonist loses the possibility of embracing the pure life that Frida symbolizes, for in slaying

Belcredi, he must reclaim and perpetuate his fictive role.

EACH IN HIS OWN WAY

Though less often performed in the United States than the three plays discussed above, *Each in His Own Way* exemplifies the theatrical innovation on which Pirandello's fame rests. In this play, the audience itself is involved in the action, informing the already complex dialectic between the fictive and the real with yet another dimension. The play being performed is presumably based on the recent scandal involving Amelia Moreno, an actress who betrayed her sculptor fiancé, Giacomo La Vela, by running off with Baron Nuti, leading the distraught sculptor to suicide. Onstage, two men attempt to blame the dramatic counterparts of the three involved in the love triangle. As with *Right You Are (If You Think So)*, the audience vacillates between believing first one person and then another, but here the playwright has added reversals that leave the audience uncertain as to whether the young woman, Amelia Moreno, is to be blamed. At the moment when she has been vindicated, she appears to take full responsibility and to apologize. The first-act curtain falls in a seeming intermission, but before the audience can parade out into the lobby, the "intermission" begins to take form onstage, which is now set as a theater with audience members and critics discussing the Pirandello play. In a wonderful invasion of this already unusual performance, a woman who is apparently Amelia Moreno rushes onstage to protest this intrusion of her privacy.

Act 2 begins with Amelia and the man for whom she left her artist fiancé arguing, embracing, then going off together as the guilty pair. Again, the curtain falls and is raised on the intermission set, and Amelia Moreno rushes onstage to protest. This time, however, the audience witnesses a presumably real-life scene among the characters on whom the drama is based. In a clever reversal, Pirandello has set up a situation in which life imitates art rather than the other way around. The annoyed actors refuse to perform the third act, and the play ends, presumably incomplete but having perfectly achieved Pirandello's goal.

OTHER MAJOR WORKS

LONG FICTION: *L'esclusa*, 1901 (*The Outcast*, 1925); *Il turno*, 1902 (*The Merry-Go-Round of Love*, 1964); *Il fu Mattia Pascal*, 1904 (*The Late Mattia Pascal*, 1923); *Suo marito*, 1911 (*Her Husband*, 2000); *I vecchi e i giovani*, 1913 (*The Old and the Young*, 1928); *Si gira . . .*, 1916 (*Shoot! The Notebooks of Serafino Gubbio, Cinematograph Operator*, 1926); *Uno, nessuno, centomila*, 1925 (*One, None and a Hundred Thousand*, 1933); *Tutti i romanzi*, 1941 (collected novels).

SHORT FICTION: *Amori senza amore*, 1894; *Beffe della morte e della vita*, 1902-1903 (2 volumes); *Quando'ero matto . . .*, 1902; *Bianche e nere*, 1904; *Erma bifronte*, 1906; *La vita nuda*, 1910; *Terzetti*, 1912; *Le due maschere*, 1914; *Erba del nostro orto*, 1915; *La trappola*, 1915; *E domani, lunedì*, 1917; *Un cavallo nella luna*, 1918; *Berecche e la guerra*, 1919; *Il carnevale dei morti*, 1919; *A Horse in the Moon and Twelve Short Stories*, 1932; *Better Think Twice About It! and Twelve Other Stories*, 1933; *The Naked Truth and Eleven Other Stories*, 1934; *Four Tales*, 1939; *The Medals and Other Stories*, 1939; *Short Stories*, 1959; *The Merry-Go-Round of Love and Selected Stories*, 1964; *Selected Stories*, 1964; *Short Stories*, 1964.

POETRY: *Mal giocondo*, 1889; *Pasqua di Gea*, 1891; *Pier Gudrò*, 1894; *Elegie renane*, 1895; *Elegie romane*, 1896 (translation of Johann von Goethe's *Römische Elegien*); *Scamandro*, 1909 (dramatic poem); *Fuori de chiave*, 1912; *Saggi*, 1939.

NONFICTION: *Arte e scienze*, 1908; *L'umorismo*, 1908, revised 1920 (partial translation *On Humor*, 1966; complete translation, 1974); *Saggi*, 1939.

MISCELLANEOUS: *Opere*, 1966.

BIBLIOGRAPHY

Alessio, A., D. Pietropaolo, and G. Sanguinetti-Katz, eds. Ottawa, Ont.: Canadian Society for Italian Studies, 1992. A selection from the proceedings of the International Conference on Pirandello and the Modern Theatre, held in Toronto in November, 1990. Bibliography.

Bassanese, Fiora A. *Understanding Luigi Pirandello*. Columbia: University of South Carolina Press, 1997. In her scholarly examination of Pirandello's works, Bassanese looks at the question of reality and illusion, focusing on *Right You Are (If You Think So)* and *Henry IV*. Bibliography and index.

Biasin, Gian-Paolo, and Manuela Gieri, eds. *Luigi Pirandello: Contemporary Perspectives*. Buffalo: University of Toronto Press, 1999. This collection of essays provide modern perspectives on the work of Pirandello, including his quest for truth, his use of theater-within-the-theater, and use of characters and actors on the stage.

Dashwood, Julie, ed. *Luigi Pirandello: The Theater of Paradox*. Lewiston, N.Y.: Edwin Mellen Press, 1996. This volume examines the works of Pirandello, particularly his creation of paradoxical scenes in his drama. Bibliography and index.

O'Grady, Deidre. *Piave, Boito, Pirandello: From Romantic Realism to Modernism*. Lewiston, N.Y.: Edwin Mellen Press, 2000. O'Grady traces the development of Italian literature, from romantic realism to modernism, examining the works of Pirandello, Arrigo Boito, and Francesco Maria Piave, among others. Bibliography and index.

Parilla, Catherine Arturi. *A Theory for Reading Dramatic Texts: Selected Plays by Pirandello and García Lorca*. New York: P. Lang, 1995. Parilla contrasts and compares Pirandello and Federico García Lorca, focusing on Pirandello's *Six Characters in Search of an Author* and *Henry IV* and García Lorca's *Yerma* (pr. 1934; English translation, 1941) and *La casa de Bernarda Alba* (wr. 1936, pr., pb. 1945; *The House of Bernarda Alba*, 1947).

Stella, M. John. *Self and Self-compromise in the Narratives of Pirandello and Moravia*. New York: P. Lang, 2000. Stella examines the concept of self in literature, comparing and contrasting the works of Pirandello and Alberto Moravia.

June Schlueter

GUILBERT DE PIXÉRÉCOURT

Born: Nancy, France; January 22, 1773
Died: Nancy, France; July 27, 1844

PRINCIPAL DRAMA

Sélico: Ou, Les Nègres généreux, pr. 1793
Claudine: Ou, L'Anglais vertueux, pr. 1793
Marat-Mauger: Ou, Le Jacobin en mission, pr. 1794
Les Petits Auvergnates, pr. 1797, pb. 1799
Victor: Ou, L'Enfant de la forêt, pr. 1798, pb. 1803 (based on François-Guillaume Ducray-Duminil's novel)
Cœlina: Ou, L'Enfant du mystère, pr. 1800, pb. 1803 (*The Tale of Mystery*, 1802)
L'Homme à trois visages: Ou, Le Proscrit, pr., pb. 1801 (*The Venetian Outlaw*, 1805)
La Femme à deux maris, pr., pb. 1802 (*A Wife with Two Husbands*, 1803)
Robinson Crusoë, pr., pb. 1805 (music by Alexandre Piccini and Gérardin Lacour)
Marguerite d'Anjou, pr., pb. 1810 (music by Lacour)
Le Chien de Montargis: Ou, La Forêt de Bondy, pr., pb. 1814 (*The Forest of Bondy: Or, The Dog of Montargis*, 1815)
Cristophe Colomb: Ou, La Découverte de nouveau monde, pr., pb. 1815
Le Belvéder: Ou, La Vallée de l'Etna, pr., pb. 1818
Valentine: Ou, La Séduction, pr. 1821, pb. 1822 (*Adeline: Or, the Victim of Seduction*, 1822)
Théâtre choisi, pb. 1841-1843 (4 volumes)

OTHER LITERARY FORMS

Guilbert de Pixérécourt is known only for his plays.

ACHIEVEMENTS

Guilbert de Pixérécourt is known as the father of melodrama. In his hands, melodrama became a colorful dramatic instrument that included the components of tragedy, comedy, pantomine, comic opera, fantasy, and vaudeville. In his *Théâtre choisi* (selected plays),

he lists among his 120 plays 63 dramas and melodramas, 9 comedies, 21 comic operas and lyric dramas, 8 fantasies and pantomimes, and 17 vaudevilles. In the large enterprise of adapting the popular genre to please his contemporary audience, Pixérécourt at times collaborated with other writers and with musical composers, such as Nicolas Brazier and Victor Ducange.

Literary historians have advanced several theories on the evolution of melodrama and Pixérécourt's role in it. Although scholarly arguments represent a diversity of opinions, there tends to be agreement that melodrama is an extension of the dramatic tradition of both the neoclassical and the bourgeois theater that preceded it. Although traditional neoclassical drama was intended for a more erudite audience, the melodrama addressed itself to a less well educated public. Consequently, the genre disregarded many of the codes and rules governing conventional theater in favor of a more colorful, realistic, and emotional representation. Jules Marsan, a well-known literary critic of the period, points out that the melodrama constituted a predictable step in the evolution of eighteenth century theater because of the increasing demands of a larger and more popular audience. Classical masterpieces by such famous playwrights as Pierre Corneille, Jean Racine, Molière, and their imitators no longer expressed the mood of the times. The modern spectator preferred an entertaining and rapidly moving social drama to detailed analysis, and the prose of everyday speech to poetry. In addition, as its name indicates, melodrama was interspersed with song and instrumental music.

Having chosen the genre as his preferred vehicle of expression, Pixérécourt dedicated his creative talent to its development. Known as the "Corneille of the boulevards," he supervised the many details—music, scenery, costumes—in the production of his plays and carefully directed rehearsals. "Enfin j'ai régné pendant trente ans comme un roi absolu" (in a word, for thirty years I reigned supreme), he commented on his long-lived ascendancy in the boulevard theaters. Beyond Paris as well, Pixérécourt's melo-dramas were celebrated. Many were staged for enthusiastic provincial audiences, and some were translated and performed in other countries, including England, Germany, Italy, Portugal, Holland, and Russia.

BIOGRAPHY

In many ways, the emotional situations of René-Charles Guilbert de Pixérécourt's melodramas reflect the upheavals and perils that he experienced first-hand. From his early youth until the end of his life, he was subject to dramatic events. Pixérécourt was born on January 22, 1773, into a noble provincial family, which included several distinguished members. His grandfather had served as adviser to Charles of Lorraine, and his uncle, for whom he was named, was a doctor of theology who had served as chaplain to King Stanislas of Poland. The family had received the title of nobility at the beginning of the eighteenth century. Although little is known about his mother, his father is characterized by Edmond Estève as having "une âme de féodal" (the soul of a feudal lord). Nicolas Charles Georges Guilbert, a former army officer, fully intended to rear his son in the strict manner of the *ancien régime*. Consequently, the young Pixérécourt's upbringing was severe. "Ma première jeunesse a été arrosée de larmes" (my earliest youth was sprinkled with tears), the playwright reminisced in his declining years. He also observed that his sadness and need of affection in his childhood underlay the sentimental perspective of his plays.

Although the young Pixérécourt was interested in art and literature, he received neither encouragement nor recognition until he was in secondary school, where he won books as prizes for his academic excellence. The year 1785 was important because the book awards marked the beginning of a lifelong pleasure of book collecting and a step toward the definition of his career goals. During his school years, Pixérécourt also demonstrated a talent for drawing, which would help him to earn a living later in Paris and would attract his interest in the scenic design of his plays. He did not, however, pursue a career in the arts immediately but chose law as his future profession. Unfortu-

nately, it was impossible for him to realize his plans, for at the conclusion of his studies, the Revolution erupted, and his family's financial condition changed dramatically. Although Pixérécourt was horrified by revolutionary terror and abuses, he decided not to emigrate as other young men of aristocratic families were doing. Nevertheless, his father insisted on enrolling him in a royalist army in Coblentz. No doubt remembering the harsh military exercises of his childhood, Pixérécourt was repelled by army life and yearned to escape. He requested a month's leave and, disguised as a beggar, returned to France. He was able to reach Nancy without incident but in continuing on to Paris encountered numerous obstacles. Having no money and in danger of being arrested as a defector, he was saved only through the intervention of a friend who took him in.

As it was impossible to look for work, Pixérécourt spent his time reading Edward Young and Jean-Pierre Claris de Florian, whose influence proved decisive in his choice of a career. In fact, he was so impressed with Florian that he prepared an edition of the playwright and novelist's unpublished works. Energized from his reading and experiences, Pixérécourt began writing immediately and within a short time had composed a drama in four acts, *Sélico: Ou, Les Nègres généreux* (Selico: or, the noble Negroes), which he sold outright to the director of the Théâtre Molière. Even though unforeseen circumstances prevented the play from reaching the stage at that time, the author, encouraged by the sale of his first work, enthusiastically composed another, *Claudine: Ou, L'Anglais vertueux* (Claudine: or, the virtuous Englishman), a one-act comedy that was accepted at the Théâtre Favart.

Just as the young artist was becoming deeply involved in his work and felt success within his reach, he was again interrupted. This time, the French government required all Frenchmen between the ages of eighteen and twenty-five to register for conscription. Therefore, the young artist returned to Nancy, where he entered the eleventh cavalry division. While in military service, he encountered an unusually cruel government official, about whom he wrote a one-act play, *Marat-Mauger*. The production was halted by the revolutionary committee at the moment of its opening at the Théâtre de Nancy. Pixérécourt escaped arrest and somehow maneuvered a medical discharge from the army. Back in Paris, he continued to live precariously and in constant danger. Yet, in spite of reversals, an influential friend, Lazare Carnot, came to his aid, obtaining for him an appointment as clerk in the war office. It was only through the constant intervention of Carnot that Pixérécourt, who was under threat of being recognized as a former rebel emigrant, could continue to earn his living and not fall into Maximilien Robespierre's hands. Yet even with the security of having suitable employment, he yearned to return to the theater. Accordingly, in 1795, he left his post in the war office in order to write, and, in addition, he married Marie Jeanne Françoise Quinette de la Hogue. In his memoirs, he speaks of the financial difficulties of his first years of marriage, when he was attempting to support a wife and child and, at the same time, to establish himself in the theatrical world. At this point, he returned to his talent of drawing to help meet his financial obligations.

Professional success came in 1797, with his one-act comedy *Les Petits Auvergnates* (the little Auvergnates). Seventy-three showings in Paris and thirty-nine in the provinces gave Pixérécourt the means to dedicate himself to his first love, the theater. During the following thirty years, he became the recognized master of melodrama, delighting large audiences both in Paris and in provincial cities. His works held universal appeal, as was proved by numerous translations. Though 120 plays represent an impressive body of work, they do not comprise the sum of his literary activity. The playwright did not confine his energetic talent to composition; he also became an administrator in Parisian theaters: the Opéra-Comique and the Gaîté. In 1835, a fire at the latter theater nearly ruined Pixérécourt financially and brought his brilliant career to an abrupt end. Consequently, he was forced to sell his beloved country home at Fontenay-sous-Bois and the library he had cherished. This catastrophe, exacerbated by declining health, forced him to leave the theater. Although Pixérécourt withdrew from active life, he spent his final years preparing a valuable edition of his selected plays. He returned to his birthplace, where he died in 1844.

ANALYSIS

In his memoirs, Guilbert de Pixérécourt speaks of his inspiration and his artistic intentions: "C'est avec des idées religieuses et providentielles; c'est avec des sentiments moraux que je me suis lancé dans la carrière épineuse du théâtre" (I launched out into the thorny career of theater with religious and providential ideas and with moral sentiment). Pixérécourt accomplished what he set out to do; a high moral purpose uplifts all of his works. In the struggle between good and evil that dominates the plots of the melodramas, good always triumphs, and in its victory the virtues of generosity, charity, and love are constantly rewarded while the vices of avarice, egotism, and hatred are scorned.

With this moral basis in mind, Pixérécourt invented a dramatic system that would achieve his ethical objectives while pleasing the audience by encouraging participation and evoking both laughter and tears. Rejecting the neoclassical preference for artificial, formal language—which, he said, made the peasant sound like the prince—Pixérécourt was nevertheless fundamentally conservative in his dramaturgy. He was not eager to overturn all vestiges of theatrical tradition, such as the three unities that had governed classical drama; instead, he adapted these elements according to the requirements of each plot in an attempt to render the play convincing and well organized. Pixérécourt not only insisted on careful preparation and high standards in artistic composition but also required professionalism in his actors and recommended constant interaction among author, director, producer, stage manager, and actors. He believed that the playwright should be present at all rehearsals.

THE TALE OF MYSTERY

Pixérécourt achieved his objectives in his first melodrama. *The Tale of Mystery*, enthusiastically received more than three hundred times in Paris and more than one thousand times in the provinces and translated into several foreign languages as well, serves as an excellent and in many ways typical example of Pixérécourt's melodrama. Although he did not invent the genre of melodrama, he was praised by one critic as having begun a renaissance in the theater with this play.

The principal appeal of the play resides in its successfully communicated message and colorful and musical staging. Indeed, Pixérécourt rarely invented new material; instead, he borrowed his protagonists and situations from history, contemporary life, or popular novels. In the case of *The Tale of Mystery*, he took his theme from a novel written in 1798 by François-Guillaume Ducray-Duminil. Notwithstanding the thematic borrowing, which because of name recognition heightened interest in the play, *The Tale of Mystery* is not a subservient imitation. Pixérécourt transformed the story into a lively performance filled with music, dance, colorful scenery, pantomime, and rapid dialogue. The author embodies the polarized concepts of good and evil in his protagonists; virtuous qualities are exemplified in the innocent Coelina, whose parents are dead and who is threatened with the loss of her inheritance to her uncle, the evil Truguelin, who is conspiring for his niece to marry his son Marcan. Coelina is surrounded by her cousin Stephany, who loves her; Tiennette, her confidante and housekeeper to her uncle, with whom she lives; and a devoted mute beggar, Francisque, who is eventually revealed as her real father. Truguelin is assisted in his ambitions by an obedient servant.

The spectators, knowing the outcome in advance, can applaud the virtuous throughout the play and await the final happy union of Coelina and Stephany with pleasant anticipation. Nevertheless, the expectation of a triumphant conclusion does not exclude suspense. Pixérécourt holds the spectator in a state of uncertainty as the villain Truguelin's sinister plans constantly threaten the lives and happiness of the innocent. Interest is further heightened by staccato dialogues in single alternate lines that underscore moments of conflict and fear. In contrast to the rapid colloquy that casts the antagonist against the heroine and her supporters, longer and majestically placed grandiloquent statements on virtue serve to strengthen the moral communication of the play. Moreover, the delineation of good and evil is reinforced by a tremolo from the orchestra announcing the entrance of virtuous and malevolent characters and thus preparing the audience for the following scene.

The movement of the play is smooth, transitions are artfully prepared, and expository remarks are woven into the design of the plot in a natural manner. The overall structure of the melodrama, typified in *The Tale of Mystery*, supports the play's basic message. Each act performs a distinct function. The first presents a happy, innocent situation and introduces the problem that will jeopardize the happiness of the main characters. The second act shows the maneuvers of the antagonist and the extent to which he will go to accomplish his desires. Finally, the third act witnesses the struggle between good and evil and the eventual triumph of virtue. The success of *The Tale of Mystery* must be attributed in large part to its clear organization, audience participation, and gratifying surprise *coup de théâtre* in the final denouement. No doubt the audience gave a standing ovation on learning through the discovery of her birth certificate that Coelina was the daughter of Francisque, whom they had come to love during the course of the play.

In fact, the role of Francisque is an important unifying element in the play. While interpreting his gestures and sensitive facial expressions, the spectator becomes curious and intently follows the revelations that lead to his identification. The contrast between the lively musical and conversational background and Francisque's silence renders the mute's every movement telling and intriguing. Developing the role of a nonspeaking character proved successful, and Pixérécourt used the device in other melodramas as well, including *The Forest of Bondy* and *Christophe Colomb*. *The Tale of Mystery* constitutes a powerful beginning to Pixérécourt's melodrama and to the development of the art of pantomime. The play makes a vital statement on the significance of gesture in literary expression. Audiences were particularly appreciative of this visual communication, which complemented and at times even surpassed the symbolic richness of the dialogue.

ROBINSON CRUSOË

In keeping with his objective to impart a moral message within a colorful and entertaining framework, Pixérécourt concentrated on immersing the audience in a changing environment from act to act and from play to play. Always conscientious in creating an authentic physical setting, the playwright specialized in generating the atmosphere of the locale and historical time in which the action occurs. To this end, local color included not only visible elements such as scenery, costumes, and properties but also audible features such as music and song. *Robinson Crusoë* stands out as a model work that transports the audience into another world. The success of the three-act melodrama, with its 366 showings in Paris and 386 in the provinces, confirmed the popular approval of Pixérécourt's plays. Enthusiastic boulevard theatergoers were willing to wait in line for hours before curtain time at the Porte Saint-Martin.

Assuredly, the success of *Robinson Crusoë* must be attributed to its popular subject and the playwright's imaginative approach. The hero was known and appreciated from Daniel Defoe's novel of 1719. Yet, having borrowed the protagonist, his faithful servant Vendredi (Friday), and his parrot, Pixérécourt proceeded to apply both creativity and research that culminated in an innovative work. To the small core of original characters, the playwright added a host of others, so that there would be an ample range of relationships with their accompanying emotions necessary to the genre.

In the melodrama, the heretofore deserted island is filled with Caribbean natives, including Friday's father, Iglou, and a ship of mutineers led by Atkins, an English petty officer, who abandon their captain, Don Diégo. As the first act unfolds, it is discovered that Don Diégo is Crusoë's devoted brother-in-law who had set out with Crusoë's wife, Emma, and son Isidor to find the sailor who was shipwrecked sixteen years earlier. These innocent victims are seconded by a faithful and humorous sailor from Provence and an elderly housekeeper, who, along with Friday, intervene constantly on behalf of their mistress and master. The ensuing conflict for possession of the boat favors alternately Crusoë's small group, then the mutineers. When nearly all hope is lost, Iglou mobilizes his Caribbean tribe, and, disguising them as a forest, turns defeat into a stunning victory for the virtuous friends of his son. The scene of the moving forest, reminiscent of William Shakespeare's *Macbeth* (pr. 1606), constitutes a colorful and amusing *coup de théâtre*. At the conclusion of the play, there is jubilant celebration with singing, dancing, and smoking of the peace pipe before the departure of Crusoë, his family, and his friends.

Although the hero rejoices on returning to his family and civilization, referring to the island as "témoin de mes longues souffrances" (witness of my long suffering), he states at the end of the play that he hopes to return one day. It is possible that this statement represented as well the feelings of the spectators, for they had been absorbed in a beautiful and exotic atmosphere that had been carefully constructed. Scene after scene of natural splendor, colorful native traditions, costumes, and music produced an exciting theatrical event and constitute the genuine innovation of the play.

The structure of the melodrama follows a well-established pattern with each act performing a function. A state of innocence and impending gloom prevails in the first act, followed by full-blown conflict and multiple reversals in the second and a final reversal in the third. Virtue and happiness are restored at the conclusion; evil is literally brought to its knees as the mutineers beg for pardon. In his characters, too, the playwright continues to depict virtues and faults in a simplified fashion; Peter Brooks well describes Pixérécourt's characters as "pure forms." Always faithful to their essential definition, they do not undergo development in the course of the action; instead, their strength lies in the clarity with which they present conflicting values.

It was through such larger-than-life creations that Pixérécourt chose to bring morality to his audience without incurring the risks inherent in dealing with specific events and people of his times. His early and unsuccessful attempt, in *Marat-Mauger*, to dramatize a political event persuaded him of the advantage of concentrating on a universal message. *The Tale of Mystery* and *Robinson Crusoë* are important because they illustrate in both form and content the qualities that made Pixérécourt's theater so popular and influential, as well as the limitations which have determined his place in literary history.

BIBLIOGRAPHY

Brooks, Peter. "The Aesthetics of Astonishment." *The Georgia Review* 30 (Fall, 1976): 615-639. This article looks at the lively performance style that marked the melodramas of Pixérécourt.

_____. "The Text of Muteness." *New Literary History* 5, no. 3 (Spring, 1974): 549-564. This essay looks at the contrast between the muteness of the character Francisque and the music and conversation that characterize Pixérécourt's melodramas.

Marcoux, J. Paul. *Guilbert de Pixérécourt: French Melodrama in the Early Nineteenth Century.* New York: P. Lang, 1992. Marcoux examines Pixérécourt's life and work and the French popular theater. He focuses on *The Forest of Bondy: Or, The Dog of Montargis* and *The Tale of Mystery.*

Ann R. Hill

JAMES ROBINSON PLANCHÉ

Born: London, England; February 27, 1796
Died: London, England; May 30, 1880

PRINCIPAL DRAMA

Amoroso, King of Little Britain, pr., pb. 1818 (music by Tom Cooke)

The Vampire: Or, The Bride of the Isles, pr., pb. 1820 (adaptation of a French melodrama)

Kenilworth Castle: Or, The Days of Queen Bess, pr. 1821

The Pirate, pr., pb. 1822

Cortez: Or, The Conquest of Mexico, pr., pb. 1823 (libretto; music by William Reeve)

Der Freischütz: Or, The Black Huntsman of Bohemia, pr. 1824, pb. 1825 (music by B. Livius; based on J. F. Kind's opera)

Success: Or, A Hit If You Like It, pr. 1825, pb. 1879

Oberon: Or, The Elf-King's Oath, pr., pb. 1826 (libretto; music by Carl Maria von Weber)

Charles XII: Or, The Siege of Stralsund, pr. 1828, pb. 1830

The Mason of Buda, pr., pb. 1828 (libretto; music by George Rodwell)

Der Vampyr, pr. 1829 (libretto; music by Heinrich Marschner; adaptation of his play)

Olympic Revels: Or, Prometheus and Pandora, pr. 1831, pb. 1834 (with Charles Dance)

Olympic Devils: Or, Orpheus and Eurydice, pr. 1831, pb. 1836 (with Dance)

The Paphian Bower: Or, Venus and Adonis, pr. 1832, pb. 1879 (with Dance)

The Deep, Deep Sea: Or, Perseus and Andromeda, pr., pb. 1833 (with Dance)

Secret Service, pr., pb. 1834

The Two Figaros, pr. 1836, pb. 1837

The Child of the Wreck, pr. 1837, pb. 1859 (music by Cooke)

Caractacus, pr. 1837 (adaptation of Francis Beaumont and John Fletcher's play *Bonduca*; music by Michael Balfe)

Puss in Boots, pr., pb. 1837 (with Dance)

The Drama's Levee: Or, A Peep at the Past, pr. 1838, pb. 1879

Blue Beard, pr., pb. 1839 (with Dance)

The Garrick Fever, pr. 1839, pb. 1855

Beauty and the Beast, pr., pb. 1841

The White Cat, pr., pb. 1842 (music by J. H. Tully)

The Drama at Home: Or, An Evening with Puff, pr., pb. 1844

Queen Mary's Bower, pr. 1846, pb. 1847

The Jacobite, pr. 1847, pb. 1852

The Island of Jewels, pr. 1849, pb. 1850

A Day of Reckoning, pr. 1850, pb. 1852

My Lord and My Lady: Or, It Might Have Been Worse, pb. 1852, pr. 1861

Mr. Buckstone's Ascent of Mount Parnassus, pr. 1853, pb. 1879

The Camp at the Olympic, pr. 1853, pb. 1854

Mr. Buckstone's Voyage Round the Globe (in Leicester Square), pr. 1854, pb. 1879

The Knights of the Round Table, pr. 1854

The New Haymarket Spring Meeting, pr. 1855, pb. 1879

Orpheus in the Haymarket, pr. 1865, pb. 1879 (music by Jacques Offenbach)

King Christmas, pr. 1871, pb. 1879 (masque, one act)

Babil and Bijou, pr. 1872 (with Dion Boucicault)

The Extravaganzas of Planché, pb. 1879 (5 volumes)

Plays, pb. 1985 (Donald Roy, editor)

OTHER LITERARY FORMS

James Robinson Planché's literary versatility extended well beyond the theater. He was an inveterate traveler, recounting one of his many Continental journeys in his *Descent of the Danube from Ratisbon to Vienna* (1828). He was also an antiquarian and a historian, and his *History of British Costume* (1834) and *A Cyclopaedia of Costume: Or, Dictionary of Dress* (1876-1879) became standard reference works for theatrical costumers. Furthermore, Planché's two-volume history, *The Conqueror and His Companions* (1874), was considered "definitive" in his own day. Always adept at languages, Planché also translated, edited, or adapted works by French, Spanish, Italian, and German authors, including, in 1853, a translation of E. T. A. Hoffmann's *Nussknacker und Mausekönig* and, in 1855 and 1858, translations of the seventeenth century fairy tales of the Countess d'Aulnoy.

When Planché was asked to write about his extraordinarily long and successful theatrical career, the result was his informative and witty *Recollections and Reflections* (1872), which offers invaluable insights into nineteenth century theatrical practices. Planché was concerned, however, not only with the theater's past but also with its future. Shortly before his death, he published a pamphlet, *Suggestions for Establishing an English Art Theatre* (1879). The proposed theater was to produce plays of merit without regard for commercial considerations. Five volumes of Planché's extravaganzas were also published in 1879. His songs and poems appeared posthumously in 1881.

James Robinson Planché (Courtesy of the New York Public Library)

ACHIEVEMENTS

By his own count, James Robinson Planché wrote seventy-two original plays, ten of those in collaboration with Charles Dance. He adapted or translated an additional 104 plays. Thus, Planché's pen produced some 176 stage entertainments, embracing such diverse genres as historical drama, melodrama, comedy, farce, burlesque, extravaganza, opera libretto, and revue.

Planché's achievements were not limited to playwriting. His antiquarian interests, especially his passion for the history of British costume, led him in 1823 to persuade Charles Kemble, then manager of Covent Garden Theatre, to stage William Shakespeare's *King John* (pr., c. 1596-1597) with historically correct costuming instead of the contemporary dress that had been customary. Kemble's production was an unprecedented success. Similarly, in 1831, Planché persuaded Madame Vestris (Lucia Elizabeth Bartolozzi), chief actress and manager of the Olympic Theatre, to stage his burlesque *Olympic Revels* with authentic costuming. Again, Planché's innovation was remarkably successful.

Planché was also adept at stagecraft, especially set design and scene painting. For his production of *The Vampire*, he invented the "vampire trap," which enabled an actor to come and go through seemingly solid scenery. Indeed, when Madame Vestris became manager of the Lyceum Theatre in 1847, Planché wrote for that theater and supervised its scenery.

Shortly before his death, Planché published his *Suggestions for Establishing an English Art Theatre*, a theater "not wholly controlled by the predominant taste of the public." Although he did not live to see his project realized, Planché was responsible for two other important reforms. In 1828, an unauthorized performance of Planché's popular historical drama, *Charles XII*, led him to seek legal protection. Five years later, in 1833, Parliament, as a result of the efforts of Planché's friend Edward Bulwer-Lytton, passed the Dramatic Authors Act, providing fines for appropriating a play without the consent of its author. Similarly, in 1829 Planché sued George Rodwell, who was about to publish the lyrics to Planché's operetta *The Mason of Buda* without payment to the author. Planché won his suit and thereby broke the custom of publishers paying royalties to the composer of the music for an operetta but nothing to the writer of the lyrics, which were considered of little value. Thus, Planché's reforms and innovations touched almost every aspect of nineteenth century theater, much of whose history can be discerned from his works alone.

Biography

James Robinson Planché, son of Jacques Planché, a watchmaker, and Catherine Emily Planché (his father's cousin), was born in London on February 27, 1796. In his youth, Planché studied geometry and perspective—arts he later applied to his stagecraft. His apprenticeship to a bookseller also enabled him to read widely.

Planché began his theatrical career as an amateur actor at several private theaters. At twenty-two, he wrote his first play, *Amoroso, King of Little Britain*, which was staged successfully at Drury Lane on April 21, 1818. From that date until 1872, one or

more new entertainments by Planché appeared on the London stage nearly every year.

Planché's diverse talents led to his supervising the music at Vauxhall Gardens during the 1826-1827 season. In 1830, he managed the Adelphi Theatre, and in 1831, he began his long association with Madame Vestris, first at the Olympic Theatre and later at the Lyceum. Planché not only wrote for her theaters but also designed and decorated their sets. In addition, he wrote and staged entertainments for many other theaters, including the Haymarket.

Although Planché's first love was the theater, his second was antiquarianism. He was elected to the Society of Antiquaries in 1829 and also helped found the British Archaeological Association in 1843. From 1866 to 1871, he held the post of Somerset Herald. Indeed, Planché's expertise eventually led to his being permitted to arrange chronologically the collection of armor in the Tower of London.

In 1821, Planché married Elizabeth St. George, who was also a dramatist. The couple had two daughters, Katherine Frances and Matilda Anne. Planché died on May 30, 1880.

Analysis

In his *Recollections and Reflections*, James Robinson Planché categorized contemporary English drama as "mere amusement." Although critical of this situation, Planché both capitalized on and contributed to it. Indeed, he was the master of nearly every popular dramatic form of his day, including the melodrama.

The melodrama had been popular in England since the end of the eighteenth century. The term literally means "musical drama," and therefore songs and sometimes dances were often an integral part of the entertainment. Songs were also necessary to circumvent the theatrical licensing regulations of Planché's day, which placed many restrictions on the kinds of dramatic fare the minor London theaters were able to offer. Although the nineteenth century enjoyed several specific varieties of melodrama (such as the nautical or the gothic), exotic settings, excessive emotions, and extravagant dialogue characterized the genre as a whole.

Despite Planché's criticism of popular dramatic forms, the majority of his own works were written to satisfy commercial dictates. Indeed, his instincts for what would work on the stage of his era were remarkably acute (a talent also shared by his most direct dramatic descendant, W. S. Gilbert). Although content with the personal profitability of the popular theater, Planché was never content with the status quo. He attempted to change the English stage by experimenting with new dramatic forms and theatrical techniques; by presenting satiric, sentimental, or sensational plays with an underlying serious point; and by proposing the establishment of an "English Art Theatre" to revive "the masterpieces of the last three centuries" in a theater in which commercialism would be subordinated to the highest production standards. The result of Planché's creative efforts was 176 dramatic entertainments and perhaps the most successful career of any nineteenth century playwright.

THE VAMPIRE

One of Planché's early melodramas was *The Vampire*, which Planché adapted from a French melodrama, *Le Vampire*, at the invitation of Samuel James Arnold, then proprietor of the Lyceum Theatre. Indeed, it was Arnold who refused to allow Planché to change the play's setting from Scotland, "where the [vampire] superstition never existed," to somewhere in Eastern Europe.

This "Romantic Melo-Drama," as Planché called his play, consists of two acts and an "Introductory Vision"—the latter set in the moonlit interior of "the Basaltic Caverns of Staffa." Lady Margaret, soon to be wed to the Earl of Marsden (the vampire), is sleeping fitfully. Unda, the Spirit of the Flood, and Ariel, the Spirit of the Air, recount the vampire legend and try to warn Margaret of danger by raising a vision of the vampire, who emerges from a nearby tomb, springs at Margaret, and then "sinks again, shuddering." Planché's invention of the so-called vampire trap enabled T. P. Cooke, as the vampire, to repeat his spectacular exit at the end of the play.

The action of *The Vampire* is confined to Lady Margaret's wedding day. Neither she nor her family is aware that her fiancé Ruthven is a vampire who must wed a virgin bride and drink her blood before the moon sets or forever vanish into nothingness. Although Ruthven loves Margaret and tries to forestall their wedding by eloping with a servant girl, his plans are thwarted, and he presses for an immediate ceremony. Margaret's father at first consents, but later he reflects on two miraculous reappearances of Ruthven, each after Ruthven has supposedly been killed, and concludes that Ruthven himself must be the legendary vampire. Margaret's father tries to prevent the wedding, but Ruthven discredits his warnings as the ravings of a madman. To Ruthven's distress, however, Margaret promises to humor her father and to heed his plea not to marry until after the moon has set. As the moon sets, the desperate Ruthven draws a dagger and attempts to seize his bride but is disarmed by Margaret's father and his servants. With a peal of thunder overhead, the lost Ruthven falls to the ground and vanishes forever.

Although Planché often condemned the public's preference for a theater of "mere amusement," he succeeded more often than any other of his contemporaries in catering to that preference. Planché himself attested that *The Vampire* became one of the most popular plays of its day. Its curious Scottish vampire-villain, its suspenseful though contrivance-ridden plot, its Gothic setting, and its spectacular vampire trap precisely suited public tastes. In 1829, Planché converted his melodrama into a libretto for the German opera *Der Vampyr*, changing its location to Hungary and substituting a "Wallachian Boyard" for the play's "Scotch chieftain." Planché also designed costumes that were, in his own words, "novel as well as correct." Taken together, these two "vampire" works testify to Planché's talents as playwright, translator, set and costume designer, librettist, and theatrical entrepreneur.

CHARLES XII

One of Planché's most successful ventures into what he termed "historical drama" was *Charles XII*. The play's title character, the Swedish King Charles XII (1682-1718), was renowned for his obsession with war. Not having been content to rule his own country, he had attacked Denmark, Saxony, and Poland before being defeated by the Russians at Poltava in 1709. As Samuel Johnson later observed, "the name at which the World grew pale" would henceforth be used only "to point a Moral, or adorn a Tale"—in this case, Planché's drama.

Planché's *Charles XII* avoids the moral ambiguities of the king's military escapades, using war only as a background menace that sometimes threatens to intrude into the play's comedy. Instead, the focus is on Charles's incognito visit to an inn kept by a Mr. Firmann, who is really one Major Vanberg, unjustly convicted of treason and under Charles's own death sentence. Charles is both charming and charmed, especially by the innkeeper's daughter Ulrica, who in turn is in love with Gustavus, one of Charles's officers. Charles has come to the town in search of Adam Brock, the play's liveliest and most popular character. Brock, something of a good-humored philosopher, had earlier lent money to the king, who now comes to repay him and cancel the debt. Brock's daughter Eudiga is in love with a Colonel Reichal, and when the king uses that name for his alias, Brock assumes he has come to propose to his daughter. The ensuing comic confusions are finally straightened out when Charles reveals his identity. Potentially tragic complications soon follow. Triptolymus Muddlewerk, a clerk and a busybody, reveals Vanberg's identity. Brock, who had earlier refused the king's debt repayment, claims Vanberg's life instead and later clears Vanberg's name as well, leaving Charles still indebted to him. Eudiga and Ulrica are united with their fiancés, and Charles returns to his war.

Unlike the sensationalism of *The Vampire*, characterization is the strength of *Charles XII*. Charles, momentarily removed from his primary obsession, exhibits all the charm, wit, and repartee of the cultivated eighteenth century gentleman. Likewise, Adam Brock maintains his composure and especially his good humor whether he is dealing with the machinations of Muddlewerk, kneeling before his newly discovered king, or saving Vanberg's life. Eudiga and Ulrica resemble the spirited heroines of eighteenth century comedy, while the meddling Muddlewerk is straight out of the humors tradition. Nevertheless, *Charles XII* also anticipates George Bernard Shaw's *The Man of Destiny* (pr. 1897). Planché's Charles is no more "historical" than is Shaw's Napoleon. Both playwrights

depict the softer side of a military hero: Shaw to deflate the pretensions of authority, Planché to show what happens when the softer values predominate, even if only for a moment. Charles's tragedy is that he cannot sustain those values beyond the moment. Unlike Adam Brock, he cannot synthesize honor and courage with a peaceable disposition—a misfortune in a private man, a disaster in a public one.

OLYMPIC REVELS

In addition to his forays into historical drama and melodrama, Planché also experimented with burlesque, a form that treats a lofty subject in a lowly manner. The first of Planché's classical burlesques, *Olympic Revels*, which opened at the Olympic Theatre on January 3, 1831, became, in Planché's words, "the first of a series which enjoyed the favour of the public for upwards of thirty years." *Olympic Revels* retells the myth of Olympic characters in doggerel verse, often laced with puns. Jupiter is angry with Prometheus for "making creatures out of clay beneath us" and especially for heating their passions with "pilfered coals" from Jupiter's "kitchen range." Jupiter proposes to punish Prometheus by giving him the gift of a woman, Pandora, newly forged by Vulcan himself. With Pandora comes a mysterious casket and Jupiter's injunction not to open it. A jealous Juno also gives her the gift of curiosity. Pandora soon opens the box, from which immediately issue "fiends of every description." Jupiter punishes Pandora by turning her into "an ugly old maid" while Prometheus is condemned "to die of a liver complaint." Both are reprieved, however, when Hope arises out of Pandora's box to pardon them and provide the conventional happy ending. The play concludes with an appeal to the audience to "fill with patrons all Pandora's boxes."

Olympic Revels derives its title both from its classical subject and from the name of the Olympic Theatre where it was performed. Indeed, Madame Vestris, manager of the Olympic, chose Planché's play to open her new theater. Before the play began, she delivered an address to her audience, promising them joy, mirth, song, whim, fancy, humor, wit, music, and vaudeville from France. *Olympic Revels* itself comes close to fulfilling most of those promises. In the tradition of eighteenth century ballad opera, the action was interrupted by songs whose original lyrics were set to popular tunes. Planché, however, departed from the convention of presenting burlesques using outlandish costumes. Instead, he insisted on classically correct costumes, dressing Prometheus, he says, in a "Phrygian cap, tunic, and trousers" instead of "in a red jacket and nankeens, with a pinafore all besmeared with lollipop."

Planché, in his *Recollections and Reflections*, confesses that the idea for his *Olympic Revels* came from *The Sun Poker*, by George Colman the younger. Planché had originally written his burlesque several years earlier but had been unable to produce it. He then suggested to Dance, with whom he had previously collaborated, that they revise the piece and present it to Madame Vestris. Its overwhelming success inspired Planché's similar treatment of the Orpheus and Eurydice myth a year later in *Olympic Devils*, which was nearly as well received as its predecessor.

THE ISLAND OF JEWELS

Planché's fascination with fairy tales led him not only to translate but also to dramatize many of them, including one of his most popular, *The Island of Jewels*, which opened December 26, 1849, at the Lyceum Theatre. Laidronetta, daughter of the King and Queen of Pharitale, has been made ugly by a spell cast by the wicked fairy Margotine, who was accidentally overlooked and thus not invited to Laidronetta's christening. While lamenting that her ugliness prevents anyone from loving her, Laidronetta is interrupted by a large, green serpent—himself a victim of Margotine's spells—who declares his love for Laidronetta and then disappears when she faints. Later, she and her servant are shipwrecked on the Island of Jewels—a fabulously wealthy land governed by the mysterious King Emerald. The king, carried about in a covered sedan chair, offers his hand and his kingdom to Laidronetta if she will marry him sight unseen. She at first agrees, but, prompted by her beautiful and envious sister, she peeks at her intended bridegroom, who is none other than the green serpent. Margotine reappears to threaten both of them, but her power is finally broken by the intervention of

the good fairy Benevolentia and by Laidronetta's unselfish choice to give happiness to the serpent at the cost of having to remain forever ugly. The serpent is transformed into King Emerald, who immediately weds Laidronetta, while Margotine is condemned to live tormented by her "own bad spirits." The fairy extravaganza concludes with the maxim "If mortals would by happy here below,/ The surest way is making others so!"

Planché's play is a tour de force of pun and parody. For example, the King of Pharitale, distraught over his daughter's supposed loss of a kingdom, begins to recite King Lear's "Blow winds and crack your cheeks" when the rains come and the thought strikes him that he is "a king more rained upon than reigning." A moment later, the king shouts: "I tax not you, ye elements, you pay/ No duty under schedules D or A." Nevertheless, under the foolery there lies a nugget of truth, for *The Island of Jewels* underscores the folly of judging by appearances, both individually and as a country. The irony, though, is that the play itself was finally to be judged chiefly by appearances, for its costumes and scenery were so elaborate that they overshadowed everything else. "It was not," Planché himself complains, "the precise tissue of absurdity I had calculated for effect." Indeed, "calculated absurdity"—the satirist's ability to create a controlled chaos that looks beyond the appearances of order—accounts for much of Planché's theatrical success.

MR. BUCKSTONE'S ASCENT OF MOUNT PARNASSUS

Planché was to use this talent to its fullest in his dramatic revues—a form whose freedom allowed him to satirize the popular entertainments of his day, usually those running at competing theaters. *Mr. Buckstone's Ascent of Mount Parnassus*, for example, pokes fun at specific genres such as the Italian opera, at specific plays such as Dion Boucicault's *The Corsican Brothers* (pr. 1848), and at specific theaters such as Drury Lane and the Lyceum. It even satirizes the contemporary craze for dramatic adaptations of Harriet Beecher Stowe's *Uncle Tom's Cabin* (1852), which were appearing at many of the London playhouses.

Planché's protagonist is Mr. John Buckstone, "Sole Lessee and Manager" of the Haymarket Theatre, who acted the part himself. As the play opens, Mr. Buckstone is contemplating a pile of manuscripts, attempting to choose the most profitable entertainment for his theater. As he is reading "Arsenic: a Tragedy in fifteen acts,/ and forty tableaux, founded upon facts," the Spirits of Fashion and Fortune appear and suggest that Mr. Buckstone emulate Mr. Albert Smith's *The Spirit of Mount Blanc*—a combination travelogue and display of scene painting currently appearing at the Egyptian Hall. Mr. Buckstone eventually returns to this suggestion but not before he has heard an aria from an Italian opera, has talked with the spirits of Drury Lane and the Lyceum, and has considered scenes from *The Corsican Brothers* and George L. Aiken's *Uncle Tom's Cabin* (pr. 1852).

Observing that Fortune has its ups and downs, Mr. Buckstone determines that he will go "up or down something wonderful" and selects Mount Parnassus, home of the classical Muses, because "nobody lately has gone high up there." With the aid of his scene painter, Mr. Buckstone presents a series of views beginning with Mount Parnassus, followed by the Greek villages of Crisso and Delphi and concluding with the summit of Parnassus on which Phoebus Apollo is enthroned. Throughout these proceedings, the Muses appear and comment on contemporary corruptions of their arts. Euterpe, for example, laments that her "ancient concerts" have been displaced by the "discords and sharps" of "rival operas." Urania bemoans the star system, which emphasized individual actors at the expense of the ensemble, and Mr. Buckstone himself calls it "the ruin of the stage." Nevertheless, he vows to continue his climb until he can learn from Apollo in person "those fine arts [which] may the drama raise." His final plea is for his audience's "assent" to assure his "ascent."

Planché was an admirer of the eighteenth century dramatic satirists, and *Mr. Buckstone's Ascent of Mount Parnassus* is the descendant of such pieces as Henry Fielding's *The Author's Farce* (pr. 1730), in which emblematic representations of the "pleasures of the town" contest for the honor of being declared the Goddess of Nonsense's most devoted servant. Indeed, both Fielding and Planché capitalized on the dramatic revue's episodic plot structure, which conveniently permits the presentation of diverse topical material and the easy removal of or substitution for some or all of that material whenever it needs to be updated. More important, however, the dramatic revue constitutes a form of criticism in and of itself because it uses the conventions of its own medium to challenge those same conventions and sometimes to change them.

OTHER MAJOR WORKS

NONFICTION: *Descent of the Danube from Ratisbon to Vienna*, 1828; *History of British Costume*, 1834; *Recollections and Reflections*, 1872; *The Conqueror and His Companions*, 1874 (2 volumes); *A Cyclopaedia of Costume: Or, Dictionary of Dress*, 1876-1879; *Suggestions for Establishing an English Art Theatre*, 1879.

TRANSLATIONS: *King Nutcracker*, 1853 (of E. T. A. Hoffmann's *Nussknacker und Mausekönig*); *Fairy Tales*, 1855 (of the Countess d'Aulnoy's fairy tales); *Four-and-Twenty Fairy Tales*, 1858 (of d'Aulnoy's fairy tales).

MISCELLANEOUS: *Songs and Poems from 1819 to 1879*, 1881.

BIBLIOGRAPHY

Booth, Michael, et al. *The Revels History of Drama in English, 1750-1880*. Vol. 6. London: Methuen, 1976. Richly illustrated with portraits of important theatrical personalities and drawings of the innovative stagecraft of the early nineteenth century, this readable survey considers Planché among the most important playwrights between 1810 and 1850. Contains a thorough bibliography of primary sources on the Georgian and Victorian theaters.

Emeljanow, Victor. "Dramatic Forms and Their Theatrical Context." In *Victorian Popular Dramatists*. Boston: Twayne, 1987. Planché is one of many dramatists on whose work Emeljanow comments as he investigates the paradox of Victorian theater: Its audiences grew and its technical expertise increased even as the literary quality of the drama declined—not only in Great Britain but also throughout the English-speaking countries worldwide.

Jenkins, Anthony. "Breaking Through the Darkness." In *The Making of Victorian Drama*. Cambridge, England: Cambridge University Press, 1991. This important study touches briefly on Planché but offers an enlightening, introductory account of the rise of realistic, spectacular stage production of the sort at which Planché excelled. Jenkins details the crucial role of the Olympic Theatre in breaking the patent theater monopoly under the direction of Planché's sometime coentrepreneur, Madame Vestris (Lucia Elizabeth Bartolozzi).

Nicoll, Allardyce. *A History of English Drama, 1660-1900.* 6 vols. Cambridge, England: Cambridge University Press, 1959-1962. Planché is frequently mentioned in Nicoll's account of "illegitimate drama," by which is meant melodrama, farce, burlesque, burletta, and extravaganzas. Nicoll has little sympathy for Planché or any other writer who experimented outside conventional comedy and tragedy, but he provides an exhaustive list of Planché's prolific output between 1818 and 1850.

White, Eric Walter. *A History of English Opera.* London: Faber and Faber, 1983. An expanded version of White's earlier *The Rise of English Opera* (1951). Aimed at a general audience, *A History of English Opera* is a readable and sympathetic account of an art form that Nicoll derides as "illegitimate drama." Although this volume traces opera from the early 1660's through the 1980's, it devotes generous attention to Planché and other Victorian practitioners, mainly through anecdotes about personalities and performances rather than the analysis of texts.

Valerie C. Rudolph,
updated by Robert M. Otten

PLAUTUS

Born: Sarsina, Umbria (now in Italy); c. 254 B.C.E.
Died: Rome; 184 B.C.E.

PRINCIPAL DRAMA

External evidence suggests the following order for the plays of Plautus. It is possible, however, to give exact dates to only two of his plays.

Asinaria (*The Comedy of Asses*, 1774)
Mercator (*The Merchant*, 1767)
Miles gloriosus (*The Braggart Warrior*, 1767)
Cistellaria (*The Casket*, 1774)
Stichus, 200 B.C.E. (English translation, 1774)
Aulularia (*The Pot of Gold*, 1767)
Curculio (English translation, 1774)
Mostellaria (*The Haunted House*, 1774)
Poenulus (*The Carthaginian*, 1774)
Pseudolus, 191 B.C.E. (English translation, 1774)
Epidicus (English translation, 1694)
Bacchides (*The Two Bacchides*, 1774)
Rudens (*The Rope*, 1694)
Captivi (*The Captives*, 1767)
Trinummus (*The Three-penny Day*, 1767)
Truculentus (English translation, 1774)
Amphitruo (*Amphitryon*, 1694)
Menaechmi (*The Twin Menaechmi*, 1595)
Persa (*The Girl from Persia*, 1774)
Casina (English translation, 1774)
The Comedies, pb. 1769-1774 (5 volumes)
Works, pb. 1928-1938 (5 volumes)
Plautus: The Comedies, pb. 1995 (4 volumes)

OTHER LITERARY FORMS

Plautus is remembered only for his plays.

ACHIEVEMENTS

Writing in the second century C.E., Aulus Gellius recorded that 130 plays of Plautus were in circulation, of which twenty-one were agreed on by all as genuine plays of Plautus, at least according to Marcus Terentius Varro, the most respected scholar of the first century B.C.E. It is this set of twenty-one that survives, though the twenty-first, the *Vidularia* (*The Tale of a Travelling Bag*), is only four pages of fragments. In addition to the twenty complete plays, fragmentary lines from thirty-two plays ascribed to Plautus survive in the form of quotations in other writers' works.

Partly through merit and partly through fortune, Plautus stands as the fountainhead of comic drama. A central fact is that each play of Plautus is rendered from a Greek original; twice the prologue identifies which play of which Greek author Plautus is adapting or rendering. None of the Greek originals survives. In fact, until Menander's *Dyskolos* (317 B.C.E.; *The Bad-Tempered Man*, 1921; also known as *The Grouch*) surfaced in a papyrus codex in the twentieth century, no Greek New Comedy survived at all. The work of Plautus—with the six similar plays of his countryman Terence—therefore represents an entire ancient genre and an unmatched source for modern drama. The contemporary critical wisdom is that the course of drama went from Euripidean tragicomedy to Greek New Comedy to Plautus to modern drama.

Old Comedy refers to Aristophanes, whose plots are mythic and fantastic; the humor is bisexual and flatulent and ad hominem. For New Comedy, perhaps "boy meets girl" is the most succinct description. This is Plautus's œuvre in the main: His plots involve mortals, not gods, and though the humor may still be "indecent," it is human rather than ad hominem. Plautus's contemporary Gnaeus Naevius demonstrated that Rome was no market for Old Comedy: Assaying its ad hominem humor, he was jailed for calumny. Old Comedy is represented in Plautus by *Amphitryon*, a mythic burlesque.

What Roman stylists appreciated about Plautus was savor. Aulus Gellius uses a verb of tasting to define what is "Plautine." A line could "taste" like Plautus. This taste was a salty, direct simplicity, peppered with wordplay. Plautine Latin style has even been recognized, among scholars of Saint Jerome, as an influential factor in the Latin Vulgate. Saint Jerome's versions are marked by a boisterous energy and a breadth of both meters and subject matter.

On the larger scale of dramatic structure, the firmest evidence for Plautus's originality lies in the prologue of Terence's *Andria* (166 B.C.E.; English translation, 1598). From it, readers learn that Menander's *Andria* and *Perinthie* "differed more in speech and style than in plot," and that Terence took what he liked from the latter into his version of the former. When this was objected to as contamination of the original, Terence offered the precedent of Plautus in his defense. That Plautus was known to have mixed two plays into one strongly suggests that he was eclectically building, rather than simply translating, plays. Such weaving has been recognized in *The Braggart Warrior* and in *The Carthaginian*.

Plautus's material has been a gold mine for William Shakespeare, Molière, Henry Fielding, and others who have done unto Plautus as he did unto his Greek sources. Plautus, or Plautine material, still "plays," as the success of *The Boys from Syracuse* (1938) and *A Funny Thing Happened on the Way to the Forum* (1962) attests. *The Boys from Syracuse*, a musical by Richard Rodgers and Lorenz Hart, follows Plautus's *The Twin Menaechmi* much more closely than did Shakespeare's *The Comedy of Errors* (pr. c. 1592-1594). *A Funny Thing Happened on the Way to the Forum* weaves together many Plautine plots, scenes, and ideas, principally from *Casina*, *The Haunted House*, *The Braggart Warrior*, and *Pseudolus*. The character names "Miles Gloriosus" and "Pseudolus" in fact pay homage to these last two sources.

Mapping the scope of Plautus's originality vis-à-vis his sources is an abiding scholarly quest. Though this will not be settled, it can be comprehended. Reading or viewing one of the two musicals named above helps, given familiarity with Plautus as a starting point, to understand the adaptive process. Some adaptive concept of Plautus's originality is necessary: Axiomatically, pure translation of past drama produced for another culture would not play. It must be adapted to its own audience or that audience would walk away from it—which in fact happened the first two times Terence tried to present his *Hecyra* (165 B.C.E.; *The Mother-in-Law*, 1598). There is no record of an audience walking away from Plautus.

BIOGRAPHY

The life of Titus Maccius Plautus is known from three ancient notices, two chance remarks in the works of Cicero, and a paragraph in Gellius's *Noctes Atticae* (c. 180 C.E.; *Attic Nights*, 1927). While contending that old age is pleasant if intellectually productive, Cicero observes "how pleased . . . Plautus must have been with the *Truculentus*, with the *Pseudolus*!" The passage shows how flimsy a construction the life of Plautus must be: The original production notice, the *didascalia*, has survived for the *Pseudolus*. This provides the firm date 191 B.C.E. From Cicero, one can infer that Plautus was old in 191 B.C.E. The traditional date for his birth, 254 B.C.E., is owing to nothing more and arbitrarily defines "old" as the age of sixty-three.

Several details of Plautus's life come to light in Gellius's *Attic Nights*:

> Varro and others relate that he wrote the *Saturio* and the *Addictus*, and a third one which I can't remember, while working in a bakery turning a pushmill. The money he had saved working as a stage carpenter he had lost in business, and he came back to Rome looking for a living.

Supposing that Varro was correct, Plautus first made a living as a stage carpenter. In that period, he would have been working on the Latin plays of a Greek slave named Livius Andronicus. This raises a point of contrast with the mainstream of Latin literature: Plautus was not an independently wealthy man writing in the leisure time that wealth afforded but a professional. As such, his market consisted of four Roman officials, called aediles, whose purview included organization and supervision of the public games, which were public holidays with public entertainments. Around the year 240 B.C.E., one aedile saw an intellectual and satisfyingly economical way of fulfilling his duties: Drama would not, like some other entertainments, cost the lives of perhaps half the trained personnel each performance. Livius Andronicus, the slave of Marcus Livius Salinator, was engaged to produce a Latinized script of a Greek play. Drama in Rome thus was established on a large scale. Building sets for these early hybrids was Plautus's apprenticeship. After the failure of his business enterprise, Plautus's ticket out of drudgery was the realization that he could sell plays to the aediles as competently as Andronicus, who may, in fact, have bought Plautus's freedom—Plautus did end up a freedman. After three sales, Plautus was free, if Varro is right.

The remaining relevant passage in Cicero names the consuls for the year Plautus died, giving a certain date, 184 B.C.E., for his death.

ANALYSIS

New Comedy is characterized by a program filled with certain stock roles. First, there is the *adulescens*, or youth. He is fickle, he is incompetent, he is in love; his father is rich and away on business. The *adulescens'* modern acme is P. G. Wodehouse's Bertie Wooster. The *senex*, or old man, is befuddled, doddering, philandering, and irascible. He strikes terror in the heart of his son, the *adulescens*, and lives in terror of his wife, the *matrona*. The *scortum*, or courtesan, sometimes has a house of her own, and it is next door. Or she is owned by the *leno*, always a practical businessman. The money that the youth must pay to the *leno* comes from the *danista*, the moneylender, who will demand payment. The driving force is the essential character, *servus callidus*, the clever slave. He extemporizes intermediary solutions, finds ways for the youths, dupes the old men, and runs a gauntlet between them, for satisfying the young master means a whipping at the hands of the old one. The braggart soldier, *miles gloriosus*, rival for the hand of the maiden, is no match for him, even with an army. *Virgo*, the maiden, was kidnapped in early childhood but has kept with her always the tokens of her last day of freedom. These serve as the sufficient proofs of her identity: She is recognized as the freeborn daughter of a good family. This is the recognition scene, *recognitio*, which is New Comedy's counterpart to the *deus ex machina* of tragedy in that it solves the insoluble and brings the play to its end. Where it is used, it makes the slave girl eligible to marry the *adulescens*.

Of the plays described below, the relative uniqueness of *Amphitryon*, a holdover from an earlier age of drama; *Casina*, with melded *adulescens-senex* and vicarious father-son rivalry; and *The Twin Menaechmi*, a comedy of mistaken identity, argues against the sameness of all Roman comedy, or at least of all Plautine comedy. Of these plays, *The Haunted House* most closely follows the type, with most of the stock characters appearing in their stock situations. A sustained metaphor from musical composition best answers the question of the perceived sameness, the question of Plautus's originality with regard to his Greek sources, and the matter of Plautus's place in the art of drama. When one thinks of Plautus's originality, one should think of Johannes Brahms composing the *Academic Festival Overture*. He incorporated student songs into it, with the song "Gaudeamus Igitur" for climax. The audience knows that the song is old; that someone else wrote the melody; that the selection, orchestration, and the overture itself are Brahms. The matter of perceived sameness and the position of Plautus in the history of drama are both picked up in the inevitable question which the dilettante has ready for the contemporary composer, "You know what that reminds me of?" There are only eight notes in the scale. Plautus's stock characters, *senex*, *matrona*, *adulescens*, *virgo*, *scortum*, *danista*, and *miles gloriosus*, are taken from life and resound all its centers and epicenters: family, love, power, money, and biological urges.

AMPHITRYON

Though the above must serve as the *dramatis personae* and prologue for the twenty surviving plays, it would be misleading if from it one were to expect a sameness about them. *Amphitryon*, in fact, is not a New Comedy. Mercury, speaking the introduction, first calls it tragedy (the audience scowls), then comedy, then mixes them to call it tragicomedy. The title character of *Amphitryon* suggests divine ribaldry and mortal tragedy: He is the father of Heracles, or rather, the cuckolded husband whom Jupiter displaced for a night to sire the future hero and god. Its burlesque of myth and its adultery of a married woman make it unique in Roman comedy. It fulfills Mercury's promise and is a sampling of the breadth in Plautus, who does not always write a simple variation of the boy-meets-girl story.

THE CAPTIVES

There is a thrill of the newness of the whole art in Plautus. *The Captives* is a very human comedy with the triumph in the end, not of lust, but of family, in the loyalty of slave to master and the reuniting of father and son. The prologue warns—or boasts—of the difference from the expected: "It is not the same as the others: no indecent, unrepeatable lines, no pimps, no whores, not even a braggart soldier."

CASINA

Alone of the plays, *Casina* has a prologue that stems from a much later Roman production in a time that looks on Plautus as ancient, is nostalgic about him, and speaks of *Casina* as a perennial favorite. This comedy will show, then, what noble Romans on a holiday appreciated. *Casina* opens with two slaves, Olympio and Chalinus, challenging each other over the hand of Casina, a foundling reared in the house as a slave, who is now sixteen years old. Cleustrata, the lady of the house, knows that her husband, Lysidamus, wants Olympio, the overseer of his farm, to wed Casina, so he can, with Olympio winking, slake his "love," as he calls it, for Casina. Part of the comedy is that the old man is in the role of the *adulescens* and is as unable as the inexperienced youth to discern between lust and love. Cleustrata would have the slave Chalinus, armor-bearer to her son, marry Casina. It is understood that Cleustrata's son would then cuckold the groom. Father and son are thus vicarious rivals for the same woman. Lysidamus settles the issue by lot. His choice, Olympio, wins. Lysidamus next arranges an overnight detour for the wedding party on the route to the farm: The neighbor and his entire family are to spend the night in Lysidamus's house, to leave the house next door vacant for Lysidamus's seigneurial wedding night with Casina. The slave Chalinus overhears this detour plot and relates it to Cleustrata.

A novelty here is a nonstock character, the clever matron: Cleustrata arranges a series of contretemps to vex and foil her errant husband. The series begins with neighborly altercations and culminates in the dressing and veiling of vengeful Chalinus as the bride. This results in bruises, puns, and bawdy jokes as the two intending husbands first conduct the "bride" away and then report their ardor-cooling experiences as each man attempts to be first with "Casina." Their reports are the climax of the play.

The resolution is that the husband, foiled, is forgiven by the *matrona*. Casina, the object of all desiring, never appears. Nor in fact does the son, Euthynicus: A closing speaker, in two lines before the request for applause, says that Casina will be acknowledged as the neighbor's daughter and will marry the master's son. Here Plautus has not even bothered to dramatize the *recognitio*; in asking the audience to pretend that he did, he practically boasts of not bothering with the typical fare. The play is Plautus at his salty and language-twisting best.

The untranslatability of puns makes them, by definition, a measure of Plautine originality and individual contribution. He crowds them thickly. In *Casina*, as Olympio and Lysidamus conduct the "bride," Lysidamus exclaims in pain, "She almost spread me out with her elbow!" Response: "Therefore she wants to go to bed." "Cubito" means "with an elbow," and "cubitum" is a supine form meaning "to go to bed."

THE TWIN MENAECHMI

Shakespeare's favorite play by Plautus, if imitation is the sincerest form of flattery, is *The Twin Menaechmi*. Before the action begins, twin sons, Menaechmus and Sosicles, were born to a Sicilian merchant. During a business trip to Italy, this merchant and his son Menaechmus became separated at the public games. The lost Menaechmus was adopted by a man from Epidamnus. The grieving father died of a broken heart, leaving a grandfather to rear Sosicles, whom he renamed Menaechmus after the lost twin. As the play opens, the renamed Menaechmus, grown to maturity, has searched the world for the lost Menaechmus and is disembarking at the home of Epidamnus. The Epidamnian twin, heir to his stepfather's estate, is an established householder and henpecked husband. His heart belongs to the girl next door, a professional woman named Erotium. Her lines of greeting are laden with M's. It is not simply that Erotium is greeting Menaechmus: Plautus typically crams a courtesan's greeting lines with M's: "Mmmmmmm." It is part of his art.

The local Menaechmus appropriates his wife's best dress and gives it to Erotium. This dress becomes an Ariadne's thread that winds through the labyrinth of the play, an audience guide to the action. At each turning, the wrong Menaechmus possesses it, whether it is a ticket to a good time or a lightning rod to attract trouble. Finally, the twin Menaechmi are onstage together, and the clever slave who proves to them that they are brothers wins his freedom.

THE HAUNTED HOUSE

The Twin Menaechmi is a jewel, complete and artistic in its balanced neatness. If such quality were everywhere maintained, it would be insufficiently appreciated, and some Plautine jewels lack such complete settings. *The Haunted House*, at least two scenes of which are reworked in *A Funny Thing Happened on the Way to the Forum*, has a scene deserving of comic immortality, but it nevertheless limps. Tranio, the clever slave, is left in charge of the master's son while the master is absent on a long trip. A slave in charge of a young adult free citizen? The situation is an impossible one, comic in itself. Unhindered by Tranio, the *adulescens* has embarked on a nonstop party, has fallen in love with a slave girl, borrowed money from a *danista*, and bought the slave girl from her pimp. He gives her freedom. Amid his revelry, lovemaking, and the dunning administered by the *danista*, the breathless news comes from the harbor: His father is back.

Tranio keeps the *senex* away for the moment by convincing him that his house is haunted. Tranio explains the moneylender's inopportune dun by adding that because the haunt has made their house uninhabitable, his son had to go into debt to buy another one. One lie requires another, leading one scholar most aptly to call *The Haunted House* a house of cards, as the metaphor suggests onlookers just waiting to see which additional pasteboard will make the whole structure collapse.

Tranio claims to have bought the neighbor's house, and he must now lie to the *senex* next door: His master wants to inspect the house, to model his own remodeling after it. The tour of the house is the heart of the comedy. Once inside, Tranio takes the two old men—and the audience—in with their own bamboozling. He asks them to admire the painting of the two old donkeys being led around by the crow. Where? The two old men do not see any such painting, but the audience sees the play, and there is, clear as life, such a picture before them. Tranio, when the inevitable occurs, takes refuge at an altar. After much worthwhile comic repartee, there comes along a young man bringing the end of the play with him: As he had just slept off a drunk when the news came, the partiers selected him to face the returning father, suggesting that the others are in no condition to speak to anyone. He entreats the angry *senex* by stages first to forgive his son and then his rascal slave.

BIBLIOGRAPHY

McCarthy, Kathleen. *Slaves, Masters, and the Art of Authority in Plautine Comedy.* Princeton, N.J.: Princeton University Press, 2000. A look at the relation of slaves to their masters, with emphasis on the work of Plautus. Bibliography and index.

Moore, Timothy. *The Theater of Plautus: Playing to the Audience.* Austin: University of Texas Press, 1998. A study of Plautus that focuses on his endeavors to adapt works to suit his audience's taste and culture. Bibliography and indexes.

Riehle, Wolfgang. *Shakespeare, Plautus, and the Humanist Tradition.* Rochester, N.Y.: D. S. Brewer, 1990. A comparison of William Shakespeare and Plautus, examining Plautus's influence on Shakespeare. Bibliography and index.

Slater, Niall W. *Plautus in Performance: The Theater of the Mind.* Amsterdam: Harwood Academic, 2000. This study focuses on the production of the plays of Plautus. Bibliography and index.

Sutton, Dana Ferrin. *Ancient Comedy: The War of the Generations.* New York: Twayne, 1993. An examination of early comedy that looks at Plautus, Aristophanes, Menander, and Terence.

Thomas N. Winter

BERNARD POMERANCE

Born: Brooklyn, New York; 1940

PRINCIPAL DRAMA

High in Vietnam Hot Damn, pr., 1971, pb. 1972
Hospital, pr., 1971, pb. 1972
Thanksgiving Before Detroit, pr., 1971, pb. 1972
Foco Novo, pr., 1972
Someone Else Is Still Someone, pr., 1974
A Man's a Man, pr. 1975
The Elephant Man, pr. 1977, pb. 1979
Quantrill in Lawrence, pr. 1980, pb. 1981
Melons, pr. 1985, pb. 2001
The Collected Plays of Bernard Pomerance, pb. 2001 (includes *Superhighway*, *Quantrill in Lawrence*, *Melons*, and *Hands of Light*)

OTHER LITERARY FORMS

Bernard Pomerance's main contribution to literature consists of his many plays, but he also wrote *We Need to Dream All This Again: An Account of Crazy Horse, Custer, and the Battle for the Black Hills* (1987), a book-length narrative poem that recreated the events surrounding the Battle of the Little Big Horn in 1876. Pomerance has also contributed poetry to *Harper's Magazine*.

ACHIEVEMENTS

Bernard Pomerance has been awarded the Antoinette Perry (Tony) Award, the New York Drama Critics Circle Award, the Drama Desk Award, and the Obie Award, all in 1979, and all for *The Elephant Man*, which ran for more than two years at the Booth Theatre in New York City.

BIOGRAPHY

Bernard Pomerance was born in Brooklyn in 1940. He received an A.B. from the University of Chicago in 1962, and in the early 1970's, he left the United States for London. His early ambition was to be a novelist, but he found that his greatest talent lay

in playwriting. He became involved in the fringe theater groups that flourished in London in the 1970's,
and together with director Roland Rees, he founded
the Foco Novo Theatre Group, which produced all of
his early plays, including *High in Vietnam Hot Damn*
and *Someone Else Is Still Someone*. In 1977 he wrote
The Elephant Man, which was a critical and commercial success. It had an extended run at London's
Hampstead Theater before arriving at the Theatre at
St. Peter's Church in New York in January, 1979, and
then on Broadway at the Booth Theater in April,
1979.

Pomerance, an elusive figure who rarely gives
interviews, quickly returned to England after *The
Elephant Man* opened in New York City. He has
remained productive, writing *Quantrill in Lawrence*
and *Melons*. Both plays produced mixed reviews, and
neither approached anywhere near the success of *The
Elephant Man*.

ANALYSIS

Bernard Pomerance occupies an unusual position
in contemporary drama. He is an American, often
writing plays set in the United States, but he lives in
London. Although he has written more than ten plays
over a period of more than thirty years, he has had
only one unqualified dramatic success, on both sides
of the Atlantic, with *The Elephant Man*, a play set in
nineteenth century London. Pomerance's early plays
express a political orientation toward the left, but *The
Elephant Man* has psychological rather than political
implications. Since his play based on the historical
figure, Pomerance's best work has been inspired by
American historical settings, and his plays have
probed some dark issues in the American past, such
as atrocities committed on the fringes of the Civil
War and the exploitation of Native Americans by a
white society that deprived them of their rights in the
name of progress.

THE ELEPHANT MAN

The Elephant Man was based on the true story of
Joseph Merrick, who suffered from a disease that
produced gross physical deformities. The disease is
now known as neurofibromatosis, a genetic disorder.
Merrick's head was enormous, with bony protrusions

and spongy growths of skin. The circumference of his
skull was equal to that of his waist. His nose and upper lip had a trunk-like appearance, which in profile
gave the impression of an elephant's head. His feet
and legs were covered by thick, pendulous skin.
Many people were terrified when they first saw him.

Merrick was exhibited at a London freak show before it was closed by police, after which he was exhibited in Belgium. In 1886, Frederick Treves, a
young surgeon from the London Hospital, rescued
Merrick and took him to the London. There it was
discovered that underneath his deformities, Merrick
was an intelligent, gentle, religious human being.
When word got out of his plight, sufficient donations
were received to allow Merrick to stay at the London
Hospital for the rest of his life. There he read widely
and received visits from people high in British society. He died in 1890 when he fell asleep and was suf-
focated by the weight of his head pressing on his
windpipe.

In the play, Merrick's deformity is suggested only
by the distorted physical postures that the actor playing the part takes up, unlike the film *The Elephant
Man* (which was not based on the play), in which
makeup was used to present his appearance realistically. Pomerance preferred to use slide projections to
show photographs of the real Merrick.

The play is not a tribute to the goodness of Treves
and the hospital. It implies that Merrick is still being
exhibited, if in a more subtle way. The point is emphasized when Ross, the man who did exhibit Merrick,
tries to persuade Merrick to charge his visitors fees,
with Ross to receive 10 percent. Merrick refuses.

The play also explores the concept of what is normal, but rather than putting Merrick under examination, it turns the spotlight on Treves and his visitors.
Treves declares his desire to make Merrick "normal,"
as far as is possible. He tries to train him to adopt socially acceptable responses to his condition, such as
cultivating good manners and accepting that the hospital rules are for his benefit. When one of Merrick's
visitors, the actress Mrs. Kendal, satisfies Merrick's
curiosity about what a naked woman looks like by
partially undressing for him, Treves is so scandalized
that he banishes the offending woman. Merrick, tak-

ing a dig at Treves's complacency, asks whose standards were offended. A few scenes later, the roles of the two men are explicitly reversed. Treves, who despite his high status suffers from self-doubt, dreams that he, rather than Merrick, is on exhibit. He also dreams that Merrick is lecturing about him, just as Treves had earlier lectured about Merrick. In the dream, Merrick describes Treves as being in a state of "benevolent enlightenment, what we believe to be a kind of self-mesmerized state." He is self-satisfied and unable to change; his charity is merely a guise for the assertion of authority, but he cannot tell the difference. He is sexually repressed and unable to feel what others feel, a situation that he declares to be prevalent in society as a whole.

This point had been dramatized earlier in the play. No one is able to meet Merrick on his own terms and genuinely empathize with the reality of his condition. All his high-born visitors present him with gifts, but they are of use only to the giver, not the recipient: brushes and combs, for example, when Merrick is almost bald, and a walking stick for a man who does not take walks. They naïvely convince themselves that he is really like them. Mrs. Kendal thinks him artistic; for the bishop, Merrick is devout; for Gomm the administrator, he is practical. They all make him in their own image, as Treves eventually realizes: "I conclude that we have polished him like a mirror, and shout hallelujah when he reflects us to the inch."

It could be argued that Merrick, despite his physical affliction, is the most healthy person in the play. This is suggested not only by his behavior but also by a recurring visual metaphor: Merrick builds a model of a church with his one good hand. Terribly damaged though he is physically, his mind aspires to the spiritual and compensates for his infirmity; a deformed man, he can still create something of beauty, "An imitation of grace flying up and up from the mud."

QUANTRILL IN LAWRENCE

Pomerance turned again to a historical source for his one-act play *Quantrill in Lawrence*, which is set in Lawrence, Kansas, in 1863, during the Civil War. At that time, many bloody border skirmishes were taking place between Kansans loyal to the Union and proslavery forces in Missouri. William Clarke Quantrill was a confederate fighter who was responsible for a raid on Lawrence that resulted in the city being burned. However, Pomerance adheres only very loosely to the historical facts. He is more concerned with creating in the character of Quantrill a strange, mercurial figure and setting up a conflict between Quantrill and the fictional mayor of Lawrence, John Cane.

Quantrill is despised and feared by the Union men. Major Blood, a Union cavalry officer, tells of the lewd practices, fueled by alcohol and opiates, that the raiders, who are camped in the woods outside Lawrence, supposedly indulge in at night. The dangerous situation is compounded by the fact that some of the girls in Lawrence sneak out at night and befriend the rebels. The girls are soon captured and imprisoned in a disgusting converted stable. Blood is seized by Quantrill's men and blinded, and Cane too is captured and humiliated by Quantrill. Past massacres by the Unionists are recalled, and the picture is one of atrocities by both sides, which have set up a cycle of violence and revenge that seems to have no end. Quantrill himself seems to represent an avenging force of nature as much as a real human being, as is shown when, in the midst of a killing spree during his final raid on the town, his hands turn to roses, dripping red.

This lurid image provides a clue to the mythological element in the play, which owes much to *Bakchai* (405 B.C.E.; *The Bacchae*, 1781), a play by the ancient Greek dramatist Euripides. *The Bacchae* revolves around a conflict between Dionysus, the god of wine, revelry and ecstasy, and Pentheus, the king of Thebes, who, like Cane in Pomerance's play, is a puritanical, law-and-order man. In *Quantrill in Lawrence*, Quantrill embodies many of the qualities associated with Dionysus. He is in tune with the natural impulses of life and has a habit of speaking in lyrical tones about nature. In *The Bacchae*, Dionysus outwits Pentheus, tricking him into embracing the very things he despises and getting him to dress in women's clothes. In Pomerance's play, Cane meets exactly the same fate after Quantrill gives him opiates that drive him almost crazy and persuades him to don women's attire.

There are other parallels between the two plays: The mysterious destruction of the stable in which the girls are held is similar to the supernatural destruction of Pentheus's jail in Thebes by Dionysus. The implication is that the relentless buildup of violence has awakened an elemental force in nature that can now only bring chaos.

The play also has a number of Shakespearean echoes. Like King Lear, Cane goes mad and through suffering learns pity. Near the end of the play he says he will devote himself to working for the common good. Blood, who wanders around blinded, resembles Gloucester in William Shakespeare's *King Lear* (pr. c. 1605-1606), who meets the same fate. There is also an echo of Shakespeare's *Macbeth* (pr. 1606) in the prophecy that Quantrill cannot die until the sun rises in the west. In *Macbeth*, the witches prophesy that Macbeth will not be conquered until Birnam wood moves to Dunsinane—like the sun rising in the west, a seeming impossibility. However, the forecast comes true in *Quantrill in Lawrence* when the torches of five hundred of Quantrill's men bearing down on Lawrence from the west are so bright they look like the sun rising.

MELONS

Pomerance was inspired to write *Melons* by reading the memoirs of Geronimo and accounts of injustices inflicted on the Pueblos of New Mexico by U.S. authorities. The play is set in a melon patch in New Mexico in the fall of 1906. Thematically, it revolves around the conflict between the old Indian ways of living, with their ancient ceremonies and beliefs, and the imposition of foreign ways by the European American settlers. Issues at the center of the conflict are Christianity, the education of Indian children in U.S. government schools, and most important for the plot, the concept of land as something that can be parceled up and bought and sold, as opposed to a gift from the creator, held in common by the community.

The principal character is Caracol, a notorious old Apache warrior, now in his seventies, living anonymously and peacefully on Hopaho Pueblo land. The U.S. authorities believe he has been dead for years. However, a former U.S. Cavalry officer, Mike Stolsky, who is vice president for Tribal Affairs for Hopaho

Oil, knows who Caracol is, although he wishes him no harm. Stolsky is involved in the central action of the play, which revolves around an attempt by the oil company to drill on the Pueblo land for oil deposits. Caracol orders the two visiting oil men, the hot-tempered, hostile Hartman and the more reasonable Fleming, off the land. Carlos Montezuma, an assimilated Indian who was raised by whites in the north and is now a journalist on issues affecting Indians, tries to persuade Caracol to use the law to enforce Indian rights. He claims to know that the whites gained leases on the land by deception and that Caracol can fight them with their own weapons. However, Caracol, inspired by an Indian prophesy about a coming savior and believing it to be himself, kills Hartman and Fleming in a gruesome fashion and then decapitates them. Stolsky kills him and is killed in his turn by a U.S. Marshal, who also happens to be Stolsky's estranged brother. The irony is that it turns out that there are no usable oil deposits for the Hopaho Oil on the Pueblo land, so the deaths are unnecessary, only serving to reveal a clash of cultures that no one knows how to resolve.

OTHER MAJOR WORK

POETRY: *We Need to Dream All This Again: An Account of Crazy Horse, Custer, and the Battle for the Black Hills*, 1987 (prose poem).

BIBLIOGRAPHY

Bayles, Martha. "Deformation of Character." *Harper's Magazine* 262 (May, 1981): 66-68. Discusses the differences between the play and the film, *The Elephant Man*. Bayles prefers the film. Unlike most reviewers, Bayles objects to the fact that in the play, Merrick's physical deformity is not represented onstage. She also takes a negative view of the play's implication that the hospital is little better than the freak show from which Merrick was rescued.

Graham, Peter W., and Fritz H. Oehlschaeger. *Articulating the Elephant Man: Joseph Merrick and His Interpreters*. Baltimore, Md.: Johns Hopkins University Press, 1992. Includes a wealth of information about Joseph Merrick. Also has chapters on

Pomerance's play, plays by other dramatists that are based on the same story, and David Lynch's 1979 film *The Elephant Man*.

Kroll, Jack. "The Playing's the Thing." *Newsweek* 95 (June 16, 1980): 83. A review of *Quantrill in Lawrence*, a play that does not meet with Kroll's approval. He regards it as shallow and written in "pseudo-poetry," while Quantrill himself is "a kind of Confederate Charlie Manson."

Larson, Janet Karsten. "Poetry of Religion on Broadway: *The Elephant Man*." *Christian Century* 97, no. 1 (January 2-9, 1980): 14-18. Argues that *The Elephant Man* has religious implications, emphasizing the need for faith in the face of a malignant nature and superficial culture. Merrick is a symbol of transcendence on the stage.

Lawson, Steve. "Beauty of the Beast: The Elephant Man." *Horizon* 22, no. 6 (June, 1979): 16-24. Highly positive review of *The Elephant Man*, which places it in the context of many plays of the 1970's, including Peter Shaffer's *Equus*, that focus on disease, debilitation, or mental disturbance. In Lawson's opinion, Pomerance's play is the best of them all.

Montagu, Ashley. *The Elephant Man: A Study in Human Dignity*. 3d ed. Acadian House, 1995. The book that inspired the play. Montagu discusses the mystery of how Merrick was transformed from a frightened, inarticulate creature into a gentle and inspiring human being.

Bryan Aubrey

FRANÇOIS PONSARD

Born: Vienne, France; June 1, 1814
Died: Paris, France; July 7, 1867

PRINCIPAL DRAMA

Lucrèce, pr., pb. 1843
Agnès de Méranie, pr., pb. 1846
Charlotte Corday, pr., pb. 1850
Horace et Lydie, pr., pb. 1850 (*Horace and Lydia*, 1855)
Ulysse, pr., pb. 1852
L'Honneur et l'argent, pr., pb. 1853
La Bourse, pr., pb. 1856
Ce qui plaît aux femmes, pr. 1860
Le Lion amoureux, pr., pb. 1866
Galilée, pr., pb. 1867

OTHER LITERARY FORMS

François Ponsard abandoned a career as a lawyer to devote himself almost exclusively to writing for the theater. For a short while, he edited several ephemeral magazines having to do with his literary philosophy as well as the theater in general, and in 1858, he published a short poem entitled *Homère-Ulysse*, which was composed as a framework for a translation into French of the fifth song of Homer's *Odyssey* (c. 750 B.C.E.; English translation, 1614).

ACHIEVEMENTS

During his lifetime, François Ponsard was admitted into the ranks of the best-known literary lights. The public welcomed many of his plays with great enthusiasm, and the literary critics of France published many articles about his drama, whether to praise or to condemn him. Today, if his name is remembered at all, it is probably in relation to the literary coincidence that occurred in 1843: the failure, in March, of *Les Burgraves*, Victor Hugo's long, complex Romantic play, and the success, a few weeks later, of Ponsard's neoclassical drama, *Lucrèce*. For this one reason alone, Ponsard has been credited with having struck the *coup de grâce* at Romanticism in France. In his capacity as "the new Molière" and the leader of the "school of good sense" (*l'école de bon sens*), to which Émile Augier and Alexandre Dumas, *fils*, also belonged, he espoused commonsense, bourgeois values in the theater.

BIOGRAPHY

Ironically, it was not the theater that first attracted François Ponsard to literature. It was George Gordon, Lord Byron, whose *Manfred* (1817) he translated into French in 1837, some twenty-three years after he was born in Vienne, a small town just south of Lyons and northwest of Grenoble. As a young man, he studied law and eventually became a lawyer, but when he first saw Rachel on the stage at Lyons in the classical tragedies of Pierre Corneille and Jean Racine, he knew the theater was where his heart lay.

Toward the end of the year 1842, the reading committee of the Théâtre de l'Odéon accepted *Lucrèce*, a tragedy by an unknown author, for presentation on the stage. Until that time, Ponsard's name had not been heard beyond the confines of his native town of Vienne, where the young lawyer had already achieved a modest literary renown for several articles in the local journal *Revue de Vienne*, including poems, a "proverb," and a short assessment of the classical versus the Romantic theater. In writing *Lucrèce*, Ponsard was motivated by a desire to move from the *drame romantique* back to the "pure" classical style of the seventeenth century.

The various Parisian literary journals of the time were seemingly unrestrained in their interest in the upcoming play, proclaiming its author "a new Racine" possessing a brilliance accorded by God to the rarest of authors. The evening of the premiere of *Lucrèce*, Parisian society arrived in droves, expecting, on one hand, the revelation of a new Corneille or Racine and a return to the strict classical formula that had been superseded by Romanticism, and, on the other hand, an even greater and more resounding defeat of the Romantic theater than the drubbing it had received with the failure of *Les Burgraves*.

Few were disappointed. The author saw his play greeted with thunderous applause and repeated kudos from critics willing to pardon him the many Romantic elements and undeniable weaknesses in the play. Yet, while many would have placed Ponsard immediately in the same pantheon as that inhabited by Molière, Corneille, and Racine, others were less impressed. Victor Hugo, understandably, found *Lucrèce* unoriginal; the great novelist Honoré de Balzac noted in a letter to his future wife that *Lucrèce* was not only mediocre at best but also childish, sophomoric, and boring. Alfred de Vigny, the great poet and dramatist, pointed out that while Ponsard was attempting with his tragedy to revive the classical theater and destroy the Romantic, its success was a result, precisely, of the Romantic elements therein, along with inspiration from William Shakespeare's *Coriolanus* (pr. c. 1607-1608) and *Julius Caesar* (pr. c. 1599-1600). The poet and critic Charles Baudelaire also characterized Ponsard as far more Romantic in his play than was suspected at large.

In any case, following on the heels of the premiere, all the best salons of Paris opened their doors to Ponsard, the "messiah" of the French theater, who had trouble finding time to answer the many invitations he received, including one from the monarch himself, Louis-Philippe. Two important consequences of his monumental early success are worth noting: First, he did make some important contacts (Alphonse de Lamartine, for one) in the world of literature, politics, and society, receiving a sinecure as librarian of the Senate. Second, he was introduced into the milieu of the upper bourgeoisie, to whose values and norms he would adapt his works.

In 1845, the Académie Française awarded *Lucrèce* its prize for best tragedy. It was time for Ponsard to present a new play to the public, lest it be decided that his initial success was only a fluke. Therefore, after much deliberation and many false starts, his second play, *Agnès de Méranie*, finally opened, on December 22, 1846. Though the public, whose appetite had been whetted by *Lucrèce*, crowded into the theater with much anticipation, they were not to witness a dramatic event of earthshaking proportions. Polite, reserved applause signaled the end of Ponsard's second play, which was not very warmly received in the press, either. The reaction of public and critics alike was a grave disappointment to Ponsard, who had slaved over the composition of *Agnès de Méranie* far more than he had over *Lucrèce*, hoping to make it as true to the former classical tradition as possible.

Ponsard's third play, *Charlotte Corday*, which premiered in 1850, managed to recoup some of the reputation he had lost with the tepid reception of his second play. Even some of the Romantics who had excoriated *Lucrèce* were able to find good things to say about his latest dramatic venture. Both Alfred de Musset and Gérard de Nerval, eminent Romantic poets and dramatists, praised the play, the latter noting that his hands were still red from applauding. Perhaps the greatest compliment came from Ponsard's former arch-enemy, Victor Hugo, who in a letter to Ponsard congratulated him on the strength and verve of the play, as well as on its humanity and style. Yet the reputation that he did partially save came from the critics almost uniquely, for the public disliked the "revolutionary" air of the drama during this agitated period in the unstable Second Republic.

Mention should be made of the importance of the great and famous French actress Rachel, in Ponsard's career. It was, in fact, in part because of this much-respected interpreter of Corneille and Racine that *Lucrèce*, in which she starred, became a hit. Because of the failure of *Agnès de Méranie*, in which Rachel also played the lead role, she chose not to accept the title role in *Charlotte Corday*, a decision she regretted. Then, a few months after this play's run, Ponsard presented a short comedy based on an ode by Horace and written for Rachel; *Horace et Lydie* would be his first play on which both public and critics agreed, and it remains his third most popular play in terms of numbers of times staged.

In 1852, a disastrous love affair and the censoring of his plays by the government left Ponsard despondent almost to the point of suicide and caused him to cease writing for the stage for some time. In the same year, the government of Louis-Napoleon (soon to be Napoleon III, emperor of his self-proclaimed Second Empire) prohibited Ponsard's extant writings. He resigned his chair as librarian of the Senate and for several years experienced financial hardship. Nevertheless, the success of *La Dame aux camélias* (1852), by Alexandre Dumas, *fils*, suggested to Ponsard a new direction: He would combine the grand tradition of classical comedy with the more recent comedy of manners, which had been popular in the eighteenth

century. With *L'Honneur et l'argent* (honor and money), Ponsard succeeded in melding the two styles, and with this play's critical and public acclaim, he would be acknowledged, not the "master of the comedy of manners"—that title best suited Dumas, *fils*, or Ponsard's associate and disciple, Émile Augier—but "the new Molière." In 1855, Ponsard was also accorded the ultimate honor of France: election to the Académie Française. In what was reported by Charles-Augustin Sainte-Beuve, the literary critic and author, as a moving speech, Ponsard paid tribute to Victor Hugo and other great Romantics who had inspired him and his work, on his reception into the Academy.

Ponsard followed *L'Honneur et l'argent* in 1856 with *La Bourse* (the stock exchange), a play dealing with a common phenomenon of the Second Empire, stock speculation. The excitement of opening night was magnified by the presence of the emperor, Napoleon III, and many highly placed dignitaries. The critics and public alike praised the play, though the latter less than the former. In the next seven years, Ponsard was subject to various setbacks, both amorous and financial, which also left him sick and despondent, until 1863, when he began composing what would be his last successful play. At the premiere of *Le Lion amoureux* (the amorous lion), the audience was filled with anticipation—an atmosphere not unlike that which had greeted the appearance of *Lucrèce*, for the excesses of realism in the theater were beginning to make the public desirous of returning to a more "chaste" theatrical art. The premiere was an enormous success; everyone approved: The author, the theater management, the public, the critics, and even the emperor and his cohorts were once again present at an opening of a Ponsard play. The Comédie-Française, where it was staged, had not seen such success for many years.

Ponsard, now extremely ill, decided to attempt to add one more point to his crown. In great haste, he composed a three-act play, *Galilée*, which debuted at the beginning of 1867. Its success was undoubtedly attributable to the public sympathy felt for its dying author (indeed, even the emperor had softened, lifting the interdiction that had been placed on his plays in 1852 and granting him a small stipend), as well as to the esteem that he had finally found among the majority of French literary critics. When he died a few months later, his passing was widely mourned.

ANALYSIS

It is claimed that François Ponsard acted only as a renovator of the classical theater and that, in such a role, he failed. In fact, he set about to be an innovator, for although he did reinvigorate the seventeenth century style of tragedy, he actually sought to combine elements of classicism with those of Romanticism. To that extent, he can be considered somewhat successful.

Ponsard was a dramatist who, though he never had a firm grasp on the technical aspects of dramaturgy, did, on occasion, reach sublime points in his dramas. Although the consensus of critics appears to be that he was a mediocre playwright, he did create a theater of ideas that formed a transition between the Romantic theater and the Naturalist and Symbolist theaters to come soon after him. Together with the fact that two or three of his plays do provide good drama, this element should afford Ponsard a somewhat higher place in the rankings of playwrights than that which he has occupied in the past.

LUCRÈCE

His play *Lucrèce* retells the ancient story, recounted by Livy, of Lucretia, wife of Tarquinius Collatinus (Tarquin Collatin), who is related to Tarquinius Superbus (Tarquin le Superbe). The latter's son, Sextus, is impassioned by Lucretia and rapes her, whereupon she, to prove her virtue, stabs herself to death in front of her husband and father. Immediately, Junius Brutus rattles the death dagger still dripping with blood, rouses the people to revolt, and proclaims the fall of the Tarquins.

CHARLOTTE CORDAY

Throughout his literary career, Ponsard would choose his themes and settings from a wide variety of historical and contemporaneous tableaus. *Agnès de Méranie*, for example, had for its setting an event and characters from the Middle Ages, which was, ironically, the favored period of the Romantics. *Charlotte Corday*, considered by many his best play, amplifies the story of the slaying of the revolutionary Jean-Paul Marat in his bathtub by the exiled Girondin, Charlotte Corday during the time of the Terror, in 1793. With fervor and conviction reminiscent of Joan of Arc, Charlotte views herself as the person chosen by God (she arrives at this notion through her own interpretation of the Bible) to infiltrate the revolutionaries and assassinate Marat, who has sworn to rid France of the Girondins (among others). There are some powerful moments in the play, which run the gamut from the impassioned oath of commitment taken by Charlotte to the chilling description of Marat as a man without heart or conscience.

SUBJECTS AND STRUCTURE

With *Horace et Lydie*, Ponsard returned briefly to antiquity for inspiration, as he did with the slight *Ulysse*, but by 1853, he had changed direction, choosing a contemporary motif for his highly rated play *L'Honneur et l'argent*, which he followed three years later with the theme of excessive speculation as a vice and ruination in *La Bourse*. In his last great play, *Le Lion amoureux*, Ponsard returned once again to the late eighteenth century for events and characters in the period of the Directoire. Ponsard's last play, *Galilée*, though very weak, represents a subject he had wanted to explore all his life: the Man from Galilee.

As for the structure of his plays, it does not follow the exigencies of the classical theater. Ponsard ignores the unities for the most part, and his sense of action is perhaps the weakest point of his dramaturgy altogether. There is a profusion of events leading to a lack of focus in the action, and the characters tend to express their many ideas rather than execute them—in short, they tend to "preach" onstage. The characters move about almost like puppets and seem to be there only to deliver the author's message. Ponsard divides his plays into short and long acts and scenes willy-nilly, an aspect that produces an unbalanced play at best.

Ponsard is more adept at creating a sense of tragedy in his principal characters, where called for. For *Lucrèce*, the tragedy is innate, the conflict born within her, and in *Agnès de Méranie*, the audience sees the tragic aspect develop with the conflicting actions between Church and State. As mentioned, Charlotte Corday also conjures a sort of nobility of character that leads to the tragic. Yet for the most part, Ponsard's sense of the tragic is not sustained in each character; rather, episodes provide glimpses of impending tragedy in lieu of building momentum. His attempts at creating comic action are even less successful than his attempts at tragic action.

The three principal areas that interested Ponsard are morality, politics, and religion. The theatergoer, on leaving the theater where a play by Ponsard has been staged, has the feeling that morality and virtue are always rewarded or, conversely, evil is always punished. The author is not necessarily subtle about his message, for at the ends of his plays, he frequently delivers it unequivocally through the mouth of the protagonist. In the various plays, greatness of character, victory over prejudice, and faithfulness are rewarded, while political crimes (such as that in *Charlotte Corday*), weakness of character (in *La Bourse*), weakness vis-à-vis the seducer, and blind submission to authority are all punished. In the area of politics, Ponsard, who had once briefly attempted to become a politician, was forthright in his opinions.

A liberal Republican (that is, on the Left), he was often in trouble with the somewhat repressive government of Louis-Napoleon (the future Napoleon III), as he was with the Church. At heart a Voltairian, Ponsard was anticlerical to some extent, having an abiding faith in humankind.

OTHER MAJOR WORKS

POETRY: *Homère-Ulysse*, 1858.

MISCELLANEOUS: *Œuvres complètes*, 1865-1876 (3 volumes).

BIBLIOGRAPHY

Carlson, Marvin. *The French Stage in the Nineteenth Century.* Metuchen, N.J.: Scarecrow Press, 1972. An overall look at French drama in the nineteenth century that provides background information helpful in understanding Ponsard.

Howarth, W. D. *Sublime and Grotesque: A Study of French Romantic Drama.* London: Harrap, 1975. A basic look at French drama in the nineteenth century, when Ponsard was active.

Christopher R. McRae

HENRIK PONTOPPIDAN

Born: Fredericia, Denmark; July 24, 1857
Died: Charlottenlund, Denmark; August 21, 1943

PRINCIPAL DRAMA

De vilde fugle, pb. 1902, pr. 1932 (adaptation of his novel *Højsang*)

Asgaardsrejen, pb. 1906, pr. 1907

Thora van Deken, pr. 1914 (with Hjalmar Bergstrøm; adaptation of his novel *Lille Rødhætte*)

OTHER LITERARY FORMS

Henrik Pontoppidan's reputation rests almost exclusively on his novels and short stories. His three voluminous novel cycles, published between 1891 and 1916, are considered masterpieces of Scandinavian prose. They not only sketch broad and satirical pictures of the political and intellectual developments of contemporary Denmark but also portray and analyze characters in conflict with society as well as with their own passions. In all three works, the focus is on a protagonist who becomes increasingly disillusioned, leading to isolation and death. In his later years, Pontoppidan wrote four autobiographical volumes, *Drengeaar* (1933), *Hamskifte* (1936), *Arv og Gæld* (1938), and *Familjeliv* (1940), which rank among the most accomplished biographical writing in Danish literature. In these volumes as well as in his other works, which are characterized by irony and harsh judgments of contemporary societal trends, Pontoppidan emerges as a stern moralist, constantly emphasizing the individual's own responsibility in shaping his or her life.

ACHIEVEMENTS

Henrik Pontoppidan, independent of any literary school or clique, was one of the most respected writers of his time. He ranks among the most prominent writers in any presentation of Danish or Scandinavian literature. In 1917, he shared the Nobel Prize in Literature with another Danish writer, Karl Gjellerup; it was awarded to him primarily for his three novel cycles. In 1929, he received an honorary doctorate from the University of Lund, Sweden, and in 1933, he was made an honorary citizen of Randers, the town in which he grew up.

BIOGRAPHY

Henrik Pontoppidan was born on July 24, 1857, in the Jutland, Denmark, town of Fredericia. His parents were Dines Pontoppidan, a Lutheran clergyman, and Birgitte Christine Marie, née Oxenböll. In 1865, his father became a minister in Randers, where Pontoppidan spent his childhood. He graduated from high school in 1873 and moved to Copenhagen, where he began studying engineering. In 1876, he traveled to the Swiss Alps, and the following year, he completed the first part of his course work at the Polytechnic Institute. In 1879, the same year that his father died, he decided to pursue a career as a writer and gave up further studies.

After having spent the summer of 1880 in military service, Pontoppidan worked as a science teacher until 1882 at two folk high schools north of Copenhagen that were run by his brother, Morten. In 1881, he made his debut with a short story, "Et Endeligt" (an end), which he submitted to the journal *Ude og Hjemme*, and a collection of short stories, *Stækkede Vinger* (clipped wings), introducing a major theme in his writings: the futile battle against the influence on human life of heredity and environment. The honorarium for the book made it possible for Pontoppidan at the end of the same year to marry Mette Marie Hansen, a farmer's daughter from the area. During his marriage, Pontoppidan traveled extensively in Denmark and abroad and wrote a series of shorter works. Some are based partly on his nega-

Henrik Pontoppidan (© The Nobel Foundation)

tive experiences of the folk high school as being hypocritical and pseudo-religious as shown in *Sandinge Menighed: En Fortælling* (1883; Sandinge parish); others expose with crass realism the misery of the rural population as well as the general corruption of the clergy, as in *Fra Hytterne: Nye Landsbybilleder* (1887; from the cottages). From 1887 to 1889 Pontoppidan worked as a journalist for the influential liberal Danish newspaper *Politiken*, writing informal and light sketches under the heading *Enetaler* (soliloquies) and drama reviews, and from 1889 to 1991 for *Kjøbenhavns Börstidende*, writing various articles, mostly under the pseudonym of "Urbanus" (city dweller). Pontoppidan and his wife began living separately in 1887, and in 1892, they were divorced. The same year, he married Antoinette Caroline Elise, née Kofoed, who belonged to the well-established Copenhagen bourgeoisie. After journeys to Germany and Italy, Pontoppidan settled in the provincial town of Fredensborg north of Copenhagen. After 1910, he lived permanently in Copenhagen.

Pontoppidan's works until the late 1880's, when he came under the influence of the romantic and Symbolist renaissance in Danish literature, clearly belong to the school of critical and radical naturalism. However, the short novel *Ung Elskov: Idyl* (1885; young love) already signaled a change through its attack on the naturalist concept of free love, and in *Krøniker* (1890; tales), a collection of partly ironic tales, some of which are based on local folk legends, Pontoppidan chose a new lyrical and metaphoric style. Characteristic of the neoromantic trend is Pontoppidan's contrasting of the rural and the urban as well as nature and culture. This contrast dominates the narrative in the love story *Spøgelser: En Historie* (1888; ghosts) and is further elaborated in the two stories of the volume *Natur: To smaa Romaner* (1890; nature). The theme becomes fully developed in the books of the trilogy *Det forgættede* (1891, 1892, 1895) and is later taken up in the poetic novel *Højsang: Skildring fra Alfarvej* (1896; song of songs), rewritten in dramatic form as *De vilde fugle* (the wild birds) in 1902.

Partly as a result of his new marriage, Pontoppidan changed the setting of his writings from a rural to an urban milieu, although he continued to employ autobiographical features. After the youthful, first phase of his authorship, Pontoppidan created a series of shorter novels that analyze the tension between realism and poetic imagination and portray people who strive beyond themselves and therefore must pay a tragic price. This theme is fully developed in Pontoppidan's second epic cycle, his masterpiece *Lykke-Per* (1898-1904; lucky Per).

As a prelude to his third major prose work, Pontoppidan wrote a series of shorter novels, among them *Lille Rødhætte: Et portræt* (1900; Little Red Riding Hood), which in 1914 was dramatized together with Hjalmar Bergstrøm as *Thora van Deken*,

and *Den kongelige gæst* (1908; *The Royal Guest*, 1977). These novels, like several of the previous works, analyze the tension between the establishment of marriage and the reign of uninhibited passion, a theme that is also taken up in the two plays *De vilde fugle* and *Asgaardsrejen*, which is closely related to the artist's novel *Nattevagt* (1894; night watch). Although Pontoppidan had usually included a social component in earlier works, he began to increasingly focus on the psychological implications of human isolation and the ensuing fear, themes that in the five-volume novel *De dødes rige* (1912, 1913, 1914, 1915, 1916; the realm of the dead) take on an existential dimension, concluding with a deeply pessimistic realization of the nothingness of life.

Pontoppidan's smoldering disappointment with the Danish political system blazes up in his last novel, *Mands Himmerig* (1927; man's heaven), in which he denounces the spirit of compromise and greediness that ruled Denmark immediately before the outbreak of World War I. The protagonist's battle to unveil the rampant hypocrisy and materialism turns out to be in vain, and like most of Pontoppidan's heroes, he ends his life in tragic defeat.

Pontoppidan is a writer who consistently aims at painting as precise a picture of his time as possible, of its intellectual and political movements and its people. He succeeds in doing this both on an individual level through in-depth, psychological analyses of his characters' attitudes toward values such as honesty and commitment and as a judge of the entire nation's moral decline. Pontoppidan's indignation increased with the years and also became reflected in his style, which he constantly reworked to achieve objectivity and lucidity, moving his prose close to that of the laconic Icelandic sagas. Nevertheless, under the calm surface, Pontoppidan, the vehement fighter for truth and existential commitment, remained a subtle, concerned, and ironic portrayer of individuals who at all times are ruled by vanity and weakness. He never stopped searching for meaning in life, a search that made him transgress the border into the metaphysical realms of the soul. This rather universal perspective of human behavior raises his authorship to a timeless level.

ANALYSIS

Henrik Pontoppidan's earliest work as a writer was a play, *Hjemve* (homesickness), in which he depicted his love for a young girl he had met during his stay in Switzerland in 1876. He submitted it to the Royal Theater in Copenhagen, but the play was rejected and he burnt the manuscript a few years later. During his years as a journalist, he frequently wrote about the world of the stage, producing ten articles from 1889 to 1891 and six in 1897. In these articles, Pontoppidan time and again rejects the aloof world of Romantic drama in favor of the realistic concept one finds, for example, in the works of William Shakespeare. During a visit to Berlin, he sent reviews of two performances of plays by Henrik Ibsen back to his newspaper in Copenhagen, one of which contained a rather negative critique of *Hedda Gabler* (1890; English translation, 1891), a play that later would serve as a source of inspiration for his own drama *De vilde fugle*.

Although Pontoppidan is highly regarded as a prose writer, he never became successful as a playwright. His strengths as a writer were the short story, whether ironic or poetic and evocative, and the large, epic novel, like those that make up his three cycles. Two of his three plays are adaptations of his prose works, and all three dramas lack dramatic tension as well as an eye for stage effects. Pontoppidan's only long-lasting theatrical success was the dramatization by fellow writer Svend Leopold of the novel *The Royal Guest*. It was turned into a one-act comedy and set to music by Hakon Börresen. It premiered on the Royal Theater of Copenhagen in 1919 and has been performed several times since.

DE VILDE FUGLE

The play is an adaptation of the novel *Højsang* and shares to a great extent its plot and characters. The common theme is a glorification of passionate love—a major theme in Pontoppidan's works—as it develops on the stormy Jutland west coast between Mrs. Lindemark, who is withering away in a tedious marriage to a noble and wealthy but wooden gentleman farmer and is desperately longing for a passionate, erotic adventure, and the local inspector of the dunes, Lieutenant von Hacke, an apparent Don Juan

character, but lacking the latter's grandeur. A third important role is played by a philosophizing character named Glob. If Pontoppidan had been a more skilled playwright, he could have used these people to create a dramatic play about the eternal love triangle. However, the potential conflict fizzles out when the lieutenant at one point thinks that Glob is the man Mrs. Lindemark is truly in love with and, in a melodramatic scene, drops dead at her feet. Before the curtain falls, Mrs. Lindemark becomes reconciled with her husband.

Pontoppidan vacillates between glorifying and ridiculing the couple but is unable to create that balance that might have made the plot credible. His female protagonist is nothing but a semipedestrian gadabout, and the lieutenant turns out to be rather seedy and mendacious, completely lacking even the slightest degree of sex appeal. Although Ibsen successfully based his drama *Hedda Gabler*, Pontoppidan's inspiration for *De vilde fugle*, on a somewhat similar constellation, Pontoppidan's work fails in part because he did not create three-dimensional characters. The playwright even takes the drama out of his play by not having the lieutenant shoot himself out of jealousy, as he did in the novel—his only noble act—resulting in Mrs. Lindemark's becoming insane. The play was never performed on stage but in 1932 was broadcast as a radio drama by Denmark's State Radio.

ASGAARDSREJEN

This three-act play, in which Pontoppidan challenged contemporary Danish political life, was submitted to the Royal Theater of Copenhagen in 1906 when it was published but was rejected. It premiered at Folketeatret the following year but without any success. In 1991, an adaptation by Svend Metling entitled *Ragna* was performed. The title of the play refers to the wild ride of the Old Norse gods through the air, which would terrify but also bring salvation. In this play, which takes place after Denmark has gained political freedom, two comrades-in-arms, Nordby and his brother-in-law, Otto Kall, have chosen different goals to pursue. Nordby has become a self-effacing principal of a school in the provinces, quietly trying to promote a spirit of humanity. Kall, on the other hand, has not given up his former fighting spirit, claiming that the battle for freedom never ceases. Between them Pontoppidan has positioned Nordby's daughter, Ragna. After various attempts at rebellion, she leaves home and decides to make a living in Copenhagen as a journalist (and as such she resurfaces in the 1927 novel *Mands Himmerig*). Thus, Ragna resembles her uncle much more than her father, and when the former is about to die, she realizes that she must carry on his fight for freedom and justice. However, in spite of the dramatic contrast between two worldviews, Pontoppidan does not succeed in transforming epic material into a viable play. The two male protagonists represent ideas but do not become living figures on the stage; only Ragna is a somewhat credible character.

THORA VAN DEKEN

Together with the playwright Hjalmar Bergstrøm, Pontoppidan, using his novel *Lille Rødhætte* as the point of departure, wrote a play in four acts, which premiered at the Dagmar Theater in Copenhagen in 1914 and was used as a film script in 1920 but has remained unpublished. The play centers on a woman, Thora van Deken, who was raised in poverty because her father squandered his wife's fortune. As a young adult, she marries a wealthy landowner in order to find financial security. After eighteen years of marriage, the landowner decides to divorce her to marry a much younger woman. However, before this happens, he dies, and Thora discovers that in his will he has turned his estate into a foundation. She hides the document, but her seventeen-year-old daughter betrays her to her fiancée, who alerts the authorities. When Thora realizes that she has been betrayed by her own daughter, she confesses, is sentenced, and dies shortly afterward in prison. This play about the power of the past over humans recalls Ibsen's drama *Gengangere* (1881; *Ghosts*, 1885) but, as is the case with Pontoppidan's other plays, it lacks Ibsen's dramatic force and credible and lively characters.

OTHER MAJOR WORKS

LONG FICTION: *Sandinge menighed: En Fortælling*, 1883; *Ung Elskov: Idyl*, 1885; *Mimoser: Et Familjeliv*, 1886 (*The Apothecary's Daughters*,

1890); *Isbjørnen*, 1887; *Spøgelser: En Historie*, 1888; *Natur: To smaa Romaner*, 1890; *Muld: Et Tidsbillede*, 1891 (*Emmanuel: Or, Children of the Soil*, 1892); *Det forjættede Land: Et Tidsbillede*, 1892 (*The Promised Land*, 1896); *Minder*, 1893; *Nattevagt*, 1894; *Den gamle Adam: Skildring fra Alfarvej*, 1894; *Dommens dag: Et Tidsbillede*, 1895 (with *Muld* and *Det forjættede Land* forms the three-novel cycle *Det Forgættede*); *Højsang: Skildring fra Alfarvej*, 1896; *Lykke-Per*, 1898-1904 (8 volumes); *Lille Rødhætte: Et portræt*, 1900; *Det ideale Hjem*, 1900; *Borgmester Hoeck og Hustru*, 1905 (*Burgomaster Hoeck and His Wife*, 1999); *Det store Spøgelse*, 1907; *Hans Kvast og Melusine*, 1907; *Den kongelige gæst*, 1908 (*The Royal Guest*, 1977); *Torben og Jytte*, 1912; *Storeholt*, 1913; *Toldere og Syndere*, 1914; *Enslevs Død*, 1915; *Favsinghold*, 1916 (previous 5 novels collectively known as *De dødes rige*); *Et Kærlinghedseventyr*, 1918; *Mands Himmerig*, 1927.

SHORT FICTION: *Stækkede vinger*, 1881; *Landsbybilleder*, 1883; *Fra Hytterne: Nye Landsbybilleder*, 1887; *Folkelivsskildringer*, 1888-1890 (2 volumes); *Skyer: Skildringer fra Provisoriernes Dage*, 1890; *Krøniker*, 1890; *Kirkeskuden*, 1897.

NONFICTION: *Reisebilder aus Dänemark*, 1890; *Kirken og dens mænd*, 1914; *En Vinterrejse*, 1920; *Drengeaar*, 1933; *Hamskifte*, 1936; *Arv og Gæld*, 1938; *Familjeliv*, 1940; *Enetaler*, 1993 (originally published in *Politiken*, in 1897).

BIBLIOGRAPHY

Ingwersen, Niels. "The Modern Breakthrough." In *A History of Danish Literature*, edited by Sven H. Rossel. Lincoln: University of Nebraska Press, 1992. This excellent chapter on Danish realism and naturalism offers a brief but precise introduction to Pontoppidan, stressing his pessimistic worldview, but his plays are not mentioned.

Marker, Frederick J., and Lise-Lone Marker. *A History of Scandinavian Theatre*. Cambridge, England: Cambridge University Press, 1996. This richly illustrated overview of Scandinavian drama from the Middle Ages to 1990 gives special emphasis to Henrik Ibsen and August Strindberg but does not discuss Pontoppidan.

Mitchell, Phillip Marshall. *Henrik Pontoppidan*. Boston: Twayne, 1979. A full-length monograph and an excellent introduction to the writings of Pontoppidan; not much detail, however, is given to the plays. The volume contains a selected bibliography of primary and secondary sources.

Rossel, Sven H. "Henrik Pontoppidan: 1917." In *The Nobel Prize Winners: Literature*, vol. 1. Englewood Cliffs, N.J.: Salem Press, 1987. An introduction to Pontoppidan's writings with special reference to the Nobel Prize he was awarded in 1917.

Sven H. Rossel

J. B. PRIESTLEY

Born: Bradford, England; September 13, 1894
Died: Stratford-upon-Avon, England; August 14, 1984

PRINCIPAL DRAMA

The Good Companions, pr. 1931, pb. 1935 (adaptation of his novel, with Edward Knoblock)
Dangerous Corner, pr., pb. 1932
The Roundabout, pr. 1932, pb. 1933
Laburnum Grove, pr. 1933, pb. 1934
Eden End, pr., pb. 1934
Cornelius, pr., pb. 1935
Duet in Floodlight, pr., pb. 1935
Bees on the Boat Deck, pr., pb. 1936
Spring Tide, pr., pb. 1936 (with George Billam)
People at Sea, pr., pb. 1937
Time and the Conways, pr., pb. 1937
I Have Been Here Before, pr., pb. 1937
Music at Night, pr. 1938, pb. 1947
Mystery at Greenfingers, pr., pb. 1938
When We Are Married, pr., pb. 1938
Johnson over Jordan, pr., pb. 1939
The Long Mirror, pr., pb. 1940
Goodnight, Children, pr., pb. 1942
They Came to a City, pr. 1943, pb. 1944
Desert Highway, pr., pb. 1944
The Golden Fleece, pr. 1944, pb. 1948
How Are They at Home?, pr., pb. 1944
An Inspector Calls, pr. 1946, pb. 1947
Ever Since Paradise, pr. 1946, pb. 1950
The Linden Tree, pr. 1947, pb. 1948

The Rose and Crown, pb. 1947 (one act)
The High Toby, pb. 1948 (for puppet theater)
Home Is Tomorrow, pr. 1948, pb. 1949
The Plays of J. B. Priestley, pb. 1948-1950 (3 volumes)
Summer Day's Dream, pr. 1949, pb. 1950
Bright Shadow, pr., pb. 1950
Seven Plays of J. B. Priestley, pb. 1950
Dragon's Mouth, pr., pb. 1952 (with Jacquetta Hawkes)
Treasure on Pelican, pr. 1952, pb. 1953
Mother's Day, pb. 1953 (one act)
Private Rooms, pb. 1953 (one act)
Try It Again, pb. 1953 (one act)
A Glass of Bitter, pb. 1954 (one act)
The White Countess, pr. 1954 (with Hawkes)
The Scandalous Affair of Mr. Kettle and Mrs. Moon, pr., pb. 1955
These Our Actors, pr. 1956
The Glass Cage, pr. 1957, pb. 1958
The Pavilion of Masks, pr. 1963
A Severed Head, pr. 1963, pb. 1964 (with Iris Murdoch; adaptation of Murdoch's novel)
An Inspector Calls and Other Plays, pb. 2001

OTHER LITERARY FORMS

J. B. Priestley's plays may be his most lasting contribution to literature, yet as a consummate man of letters, he mastered many genres in a canon consisting of nearly two hundred works. Beginning his writing career as critic and essayist on subjects ranging from William Shakespeare to Thomas Love Peacock, from the art of conversation to political theory, Priestley became a household name in 1929 with the extraordinarily popular success of *The Good Companions*, a picaresque novel about a concert party, which, translated into many languages, was an international best-seller. In all, he wrote more than thirty novels, eighteen books of essays and autobiography, numerous works of social commentary and history, accounts of his travels, philosophical conjectures on the nature of time, even morale-boosting propaganda during World War II, as well as an occasional screenplay and an opera libretto. Poetry was the only genre he neglected, after publishing, at his own expense, a single slim volume of verse in 1918, *The Chapman of Rhymes*. He was a popular professional writer, vitally concerned with every aspect of human life, and no subject escaped his scrutiny. As a result, the gruff, pipe-smoking Yorkshireman held a unique position in English letters as a highly respected sage who was also a man of the people.

For more than half a century, he remained loyal to a single publishing house, William Heinemann, which brought out nearly all of his massive output in various genres. Heinemann published single editions of most of his plays as well as thematically linked collections of two, three, and four plays. Heinemann's major collection of his drama, consisting of twenty-one of his plays, both comedies and dramas, was published as *The Plays of J. B. Priestley* in three volumes from 1948 to 1950.

ACHIEVEMENTS

J. B. Priestley's achievements as a dramatist outshine his work as a novelist. If he was a mainstream figure, albeit a minor one, in a vastly rich period of the English novel, in drama, he was the single serious English writer of the first half of the twentieth century, bridging the gap between George Bernard Shaw and John Osborne. Only Sean O'Casey, an Irishman like Shaw, had a reputation as dramatist greater than Priestley's in the same period. The plays of John Galsworthy were quickly dated, while much of the work of Sir James Barrie, aside from the 1904 production of the immortal *Peter Pan*, was too cloying to survive its own generation. The plays of W. Somerset

Maugham and Noël Coward may have been more successful with contemporary audiences, but they remain monuments to triviality rather than attempts to illuminate the plight of twentieth century humankind.

Priestley's focus was England and the Englishman, not the aristocrats and idle wastrels who people Maugham's and Coward's elegant drawing rooms but the middle classes, the workers—the backbone of the country, England's defenders and its hope for a workable future. Priestley was an optimist who believed that human beings working in and for the community can overcome any obstacle. A socialist, he firmly believed throughout a long career that the golden world in which he grew up before World War I could be reestablished once people rid themselves of sloth and greed and willingly accept responsibility for others. His view, which may seem overly romantic to modern readers, was fueled by a belief in a quasi-

J. B. Priestley (Library of Congress)

scientific theory of the coexistence of all time, popularized by J. W. Dunne in *An Experiment with Time* (1927), and was tempered by a clear-sightedness concerning his compatriots' failings, which may have caused a decline in his popularity at home after World War II at the same time that his plays were embraced in the communist world. Priestly was offered a knighthood and a life peerage but insisted on remaining a man of the people and refused them. In 1973, however, he received the conferment of the Freedom of the City of Bradford. In 1977, he accepted membership in the Order of Merit, a prestigious honor limited to twenty-four living Britons, privately expressing the opinion that it had come too late to bring him satisfaction for very long. Nevertheless, Priestley lived to enjoy the honor for seven years.

After attempting comedies of manners in such works as *The Roundabout* and *Duet in Floodlight* but rejecting the mode as a shallow one, Priestley revealed that the influences on his drama were more Continental than native. Specifically, he attempted to demonstrate, like dramatist Henrik Ibsen, that the present is the inevitable result of the deeds and actions of one's past. The present, in turn, inevitably colors the future. Here, too, the reader can detect the effect of theorizing about time as a fourth dimension in which human beings live. The single most important influence on Priestley's drama, however, was the dramatist Anton Chekhov. Like Chekhov's dramas, Priestley's best plays capture and sustain an elegiac atmosphere in which imperfect individuals lose their way but also touch others and their families with love. Again like Chekhov, the dramatist could love his characters despite their failings, but unlike Chekhov, Priestley did not always successfully universalize his situations. Whereas *Vishnyovy sad* (pr., pb. 1904; *The Cherry Orchard*, 1908) becomes a metaphor reaching beyond Russia to evoke a world, *Eden End* remains a view of provincial England. As a result, Priestley never touched American audiences as he did his own people. Nevertheless, in such plays as *Eden End*, *Cornelius*, and *The Linden Tree*, Priestley evoked a sense of loss more subtly than any dramatist since Chekhov.

Exploring the family circle in such early plays as *Laburnum Grove* and *Eden End*, Priestley eventually widened his focus to the nation as family in *They Came to a City* and *How Are They at Home?* and inevitably to the world as family in *Home Is Tomorrow* and *Summer Day's Dream*. The unifying thread through these works is the Jungian concept of the unity of all human beings, a concept most clearly expressed in such innovative plays as *Johnson over Jordan* and *Music at Night*, works that enabled Priestley to handle time and place in the fluid manner of the expressionists. Priestley, however, denied that his work was expressionistic; he preferred to believe instead that his theory of coexisting time, in which persons are at all times beyond mere chronological time, proved that expressionist "distortion" does not take place in his work.

Priestley's experimental dramas, again influenced by Continental writers, as well as his insistence on thrusting the common person to the very center of the stage in his realistic plays, were important blows in freeing the English theater from a stultifying conservatism. Never losing sight of the fact that a dramatist must be able to entertain his audience, Priestley found the way to make audiences think as well, to face hard truths about themselves, and to confront these truths with love rather than with anger. Although the Angry Young Men who came after him mistakenly thought him to be, as Osborne has stated, an Edwardian relic, Priestley's plays are in fact precursors of their own. Their concerns were his before them, but his voice was gentler and, unlike theirs, forgiving.

BIOGRAPHY

Bradford, once the wool-merchandizing center of Northern England, provided the perfect atmosphere for a budding writer. A commercial hub on a more human scale than sprawling London, the city nurtured the arts. There were two theaters, two music halls, a concert hall visited by the world's most renowned musicians, play-reading societies, arts clubs, a good library, and a local paper that accepted contributions from young writers. Nearby were the Yorkshire dales, providing solace from the city's bustle. John Boynton Priestley, encouraged by his Socialist schoolmaster father and his kindly stepmother, took advantage of all that his native city had to offer. He lived a culturally rich childhood balanced by long weekend walks on the moors. The environment of his home, where his father led discussions on the arts, education, and politics, stimulated him as well. To Richard Pendlebury, his English master, Priestley attributed his awakening interest in literature and his early desire to be a writer.

Priestley furtively wrote poetry and short stories in his notebooks during the days he spent as a junior clerk in a wool firm. Unable to concentrate on commerce, he began placing his pieces in popular London weekly magazines. In 1913, he became a regular contributor to *The Bradford Pioneer*, a Labour weekly, with a cultural column he called "Round the Hearth."

World War I interrupted a tranquil, idyllic, if directionless, existence, and, in 1914, Priestley enlisted in the duke of Wellington's West Riding Regiment. Shipped to France, he was wounded near Souchez and returned to England. In 1917, after his recuperation, he received a commission as lieutenant. Back in France, Priestley, along with several members of his Devon Regiment, was gassed. In his writing, he hardly mentioned the wartime horrors that he witnessed and suffered, yet World War I remains the key to an understanding of his work. Priestley never shed his sense of waste and loss. The war spelled an end to a simpler life, which, in retrospect, always seemed to him a better life. The world he was brought up to inhabit no longer existed, and Priestley's own boyish innocence died with it. Much of his work was a romantic attempt to recapture the vitalizing spirit of an earlier time, of a world in harmony.

After three unsatisfying years at Cambridge, from 1919 to 1922, where he studied literature, history, and political science, Priestley abandoned plans for a teaching career and moved to London to try his luck as a freelance writer. At the time, he and his wife, Pat Tempest, whom he married in 1919, were expecting their first child. Aided by J. C. Squire, who ran *The London Mercury*, he established himself as essayist and critic. In 1925, after a long illness, his first wife died. A year later, he married Mary (Holland) Wyndham Lewis. As a result of the two marriages,

Priestley had five children: four daughters and a son.

The almost immediate worldwide success of *The Good Companions* in 1929 made it possible for Priestley to live the life he had chosen, that of a professional writer. He began to travel widely at home and abroad to find new subjects to explore and entered the world of the commercial theater, which had seemed, until his success, too much of a risk for a family man. Beginning a new phase of his career in 1931 with the adaptation (in collaboration with Edward Knoblock) of *The Good Companions*, the novel that had won for him fame and a newfound security, Priestley achieved theatrical success on his own a year later with a well-crafted melodrama, *Dangerous Corner*, which was soon produced around the world. Shortly afterward, he formed a company for the production of his own work. In addition to writing various types of plays, Priestley occasionally directed them as well, and even acted in one, *When We Are Married*, while a leading actor was indisposed. For a time Priestley thought of himself as primarily a dramatist, but in later life, he left the theater to concentrate again on novels and essays.

Priestley became one of his nation's most beloved figures during World War II, rivaling Sir Winston Churchill in popularity, with the weekly broadcasts of his "Postscripts" for the British Broadcasting Company. These began in 1940 after Dunkirk and ended the next year when the Germans launched their blitz on London. The talks stirred a nation and comforted those who, like Priestley, hoped that a better world would be the outcome of this devastating war.

In 1952, Priestley divorced his second wife and a year later married Jacquetta Hawkes, the distinguished anthropologist with whom he occasionally collaborated. The two lived in a gracious Georgian home, Kissing Tree House, in Alveston, just outside Stratford-upon-Avon. After a short illness in 1984, he died in his home one month before his ninetieth birthday.

ANALYSIS

Much of J. B. Priestley's drama explores the oneness of all human beings. That notion leads the dramatist to view individuals as members of a charmed or magic circle. The circle is continually broken, but Priestley, the essential optimist, believed that the circle can and must be mended as people accept responsibility for their fellow human beings. The family, then, with its temporary victories, its too frequently dashed dreams, its individuals pulling the circle out of shape only to have it reshaped by the family's wiser members, becomes the microcosm of the world. That world, however, is continually buffeted by time. Priestley therefore viewed the family through a multiple time perspective. He was conscious of time past, time present, even future time. Occasionally he enabled an especially perceptive character to understand his place in flowing time, but he always led his audience to an awareness that all time is one. Even in an early commercial success such as the melodramatic *Dangerous Corner*, Priestley implied that a family shattered by the sordid past deeds of one of its members can find life anew. It need not be bound by the past, and a new awareness in the present may even reshape a past. The return to the beginning and a second chance for the characters of *Dangerous Corner*, though perhaps a mere theatrical gimmick in this early play, foreshadows Priestley's more thoughtful view of the Family of Man in time in *Eden End*, *Time and the Conways*, *Johnson over Jordan*, and *An Inspector Calls*.

EDEN END

Time provides *Eden End* its richest dimension. Eschewing the gimmickry of *Dangerous Corner*'s celebrated time twist, Priestley made extraordinary use of dramatic irony in *Eden End*, a realistic family drama set in 1912. Not only are his characters about to lose their innocence but also an entire world is about to be plunged into the horrors of a war from which it can never recover. As characters speak of a better time to come, the audience is fully aware of darkening shadows on the horizon. Time itself evokes *Eden End*'s autumnal atmosphere, making the play a threnody for a glorious but doomed world, which must inevitably give way to a material, technological advancement, spelling the end of the safe and sane values of love and loyalty and the quiet pleasures of a life lived in the service of others. As the Kirby family inevitably breaks apart, Eden comes to an end.

The widower Dr. Kirby, a general practitioner who has always longed for something more from his career, is suffering from a heart condition that will soon kill him. He has with him in Eden End, in Northern England, his younger daughter, Lilian, who serves as his housekeeper, and crotchety old Sarah, who was nurse to his three children and has been retained beyond her years of usefulness. Expected to arrive is Wilfred, the youngest of the children, home on leave from the British West Africa Company. However, an unexpected arrival, Stella, Lilian's older sister and the family prodigal, disrupts a stable family situation. Stella had left the limited horizons of Eden End to pursue an unsuccessful career as an actress. Aware now that the only happy period in her life was her youth in Eden End, she learns before the play ends that one's youth cannot be recaptured; to expect miracles is a pointless pastime. Eden End can no longer be for her the haven she has imagined, and she must return to the actress's life of tiring railway journeys, uncomfortable lodgings, and dusty dressing rooms. Before her departure, which signals a return to normalcy for the others, she attempts to rekindle the love of Geoffrey Farant, who runs a nearby estate. Lilian, however, herself interested in Geoffrey, retaliates by bringing Charlie Appleby, another second-rate actor and Stella's estranged husband, to Eden End to confront her. On learning that Stella is married, Geoffrey plans to relocate in New Zealand, inadvertently dashing the hopes of Lilian, who has for many years been quietly contemplating a home of her own with the man she loves. Reconciled, Stella and Charlie make a seemingly futile attempt to renew their life together, while Wilfred, frustrated by an aborted relationship with a local barmaid, takes his disappointment back with him to Nigeria, where he will wait patiently for his next unfulfilling leave.

Knowing that his own death is approaching, Dr. Kirby ironically comforts himself with the mistaken notion of a bright future that he believes life holds in store for his children and for the baby he has just delivered. If no dreams come true, if life holds only the promise of hardship and heartbreak in Eden End, it is left to Charlie Appleby to proclaim the reward that life offers to all. That he is inebriated at the time does not diminish the truth of his observation that life is full of wonder. Pain is part of life's wonder, and humankind is the richer for experiencing it, especially in those moments in which the experience is shared with others. Dr. Kirby is not the failure he believes himself to be, but a good man who has shared the life of family and community.

In a brief critical study, *Anton Chekhov* (1970), Priestley makes clear his admiration and affection for the plays of the Russian master, and in *Eden End* he demonstrates that he has been an apt pupil. Priestly's method is Chekhov's own as he sustains a mood dependent on depth of characterization and wealth of detail. Stella incorporates the qualities of Madame Ranevskaya of *The Cherry Orchard*, Nina of *Chayka* (pr. 1896, rev. pr. 1898; *The Seagull*, 1909), and Elena of *Dyadya Vanya* (pb. 1897; *Uncle Vanya*, 1914) as she tries to win the man loved by her more practical sister Lilian, who recalls *Uncle Vanya*'s Sonia and Varya of *The Cherry Orchard*. Lilian even has a brief exchange with Geoffrey Farant in which, like Varya and Lopakhin, they avoid any discussion of their personal relationship by talking about the weather instead. Wilfred is as much the idle dreamer as Gaev, and Dr. Kirby recalls a number of Chekhov's sad and wise doctors. Like old Firs, Sarah emphasizes a bewildering, rapidly changing world. She still thinks of her charges as children and fails to come to terms with the technology of motorcars and phonographs. When the others go off to the station at the play's end, Sarah, like Firs, is left behind and ignores the ringing telephone that replaces Chekhov's breaking string.

Despite the similarities, however, *Eden End* is no mere imitation of Chekhov. The play exquisitely evokes the life of provincial England in the second decade of the twentieth century, and English audiences, deeply moved by it, responded enthusiastically. The minute details of English life in another era, however, may finally work against the play's achieving universality, and it has not found favor abroad. Acknowledging that Chekhov has influenced many English dramatists, Priestley himself suggested that he and others were better for that influence. *Eden End* ranks among the finest plays of the Chekhovian mode.

TIME AND THE CONWAYS

Priestley, who called himself "a Time haunted man," inevitably turned again to time as the controlling factor in human life in *Time and the Conways*, a play highly influenced by the theories of Dunne. In *An Experiment with Time*, Dunne, the designer of Great Britain's first military aircraft, attempts to explain the experience of precognition, that sense of déjà vu in which human beings, through the distortion of dream, receive foreknowledge of future events displaced in time. Dunne's quasi-scientific theory provides for a series of observers within every person existing in a series of times. To a person's ordinary self, Observer One, the fourth dimension appears as time. The self within dreams, however, is Observer Two, to whom the fifth dimension appears as time. Unlike the three-dimensional outlook of Observer One, Observer Two has a four-dimensional outlook that enables him or her to receive images from the coexisting times of past and future. Part of the appeal of Dunne's so-called theory of Serialism is its provision for immortality: Observer One dies in time one but lives on within Observer Two in time two, and so on to "infinite regression." *Time and the Conways* is Priestley's rendering of abstruse theory into poignantly effective literature. Revisiting the world of his own past, he infuses it with an awareness of the effects of time on all human beings, a sense of waste and loss tempered with a note of hope and an intimation of immortality.

The play begins in 1919 in the Conway home, in a prosperous suburb of a manufacturing town, where a party is under way to celebrate Kay's twenty-first birthday. An aspiring novelist, Kay is joined by her widowed mother, five brothers and sisters, friends, and neighbors. With the war ended, all of them look forward to a bright future. Madge is eager to be part of a new Socialist order; Robin, home from the Royal Air Force, expects to make his fortune in car sales; Hazel, the family beauty, awaits her Prince Charming, while Carol, the youngest, is bursting with an overflowing sense of life. Alan, a clerk in the Rate Office and the only member of the family with no great hopes or plans, is the most contented of the lot as he savors what seems to the others to be merely a humdrum existence. Once their game of charades is over and the costumes are put away, everyone goes into the next room to hear Mrs. Conway's rendering of Robert Schumann's "Der Nussbaum." Kay, however, returns to the sitting room. She cannot let go of this moment of blissful happiness, the happiest moment any of the young Conways will ever experience. Sitting on a window seat, her head bathed in moonlight, Kay, with the special sensitivity of the artist, is about to be granted a vision of her family's future as the curtain falls on the first act.

The action of act 2 seems to be continuous as the rising curtain reveals Kay in the same position. When Alan enters and turns on the lights, however, it is obvious that several years have passed. It is again Kay's birthday, but the year is 1937, the year in which the play was written, and Kay is now forty. Act 2, as Priestley explained it, is Kay's precognition or glimpse of the future. In terms of Dunne's Serialism, her Observer Two sees what will happen to her Observer One.

Mrs. Conway, as impractical as Madame Ranevskaya, has called her children together to discuss her financial difficulties but has attempted to turn the homecoming into a party. Her children, however, are not in a party mood this time. Kay, no celebrated novelist, merely a hack journalist, is involved in an unhappy affair with a married man. Madge is an embittered schoolmistress, and Robin is unable to hold on to a job. He has frittered away much of the family funds and has deserted his wife and children. Hazel, too, has changed. Married to a wealthy mill owner who resents the family for snubbing him years before when he had first come to town, she is terrified of her husband. Conspicuously absent from the family group is Carol. On the threshold of life in the first act, she has been dead for sixteen years in the second.

The air is full of insult, accusation, and recrimination. Once the others have gone their separate ways, a miserable Kay tells her brother Alan that life seems pointless to her now as she remembers the happiness of their younger days. At forty, she is constantly aware of every tick of the clock, of that great devil in the universe called time. Alan, still the one stable ele-

ment in the family, manages to soothe her. She is again alone at the window as the act ends.

Act 3 continues the action of act 1. Mrs. Conway can be heard singing as Kay is again discovered at the window. It is again 1919 and her twenty-first birthday. The events of act 2 have not yet taken place; life has not yet exacted its toll. Kay, however, has an awareness the others do not share. For her and for the audience, act 3 has a terrible poignancy as the carefree Conways unwittingly plant the seeds of their future unhappiness and destroy one another in ignorance and innocence. The doomed Carol tells the rest how full her life will be. She will act, paint, travel, but the point of it all, she explains with Priestley's acquiescence, is to live. Moved, Kay begins to cry and asks Alan for comforting words. As the play ends, Alan replies that one day he will have something to tell her that may comfort her.

What Kay needs to hear, what Alan will tell her in eighteen years, he has already told her at the end of Kay's precognitive vision that is act 2—that all human beings are at any moment only a cross-section of their real selves. At the end of their lives, they are all of themselves in all of their times and may find themselves in yet another time that is another kind of dream. If the ideas are Dunne's, Priestley transcends theory in a profoundly moving play that affords insight into a person's plight in a bewildering age and offers an audience something to cling to in the midst of the pain of life. Pseudoscientific explanations are beside the point.

The play is no bag of tricks, as some critics have complained, with a third act where the second ought to be. Performed chronologically, the three acts would not have the meaningful impact that Priestley's dramatic irony unleashes. In *Time and the Conways*, Priestley revealed himself as innovator, liberating the stage from the limiting convention of realism, paving the way for such later works as Harold Pinter's 1971 production of *Old Times* and his 1975 production of *No Man's Land*, in which past and present coexist on the stage.

JOHNSON OVER JORDAN

The enthusiastic acceptance and understanding of *Time and the Conways* convinced Priestley that audiences were ready for more daring experimentation, that he could challenge himself and them with the form and content of untried materials. In *Johnson over Jordan*, which he called "a biographical morality play," Priestley made maximal use of all the resources the theater offered in a drama stressing the timelessness that was one of his favorite themes. The play calls for intricate musical effects requiring a full orchestra, even ballet sequences, as characters are taken outside time and presented four-dimensionally.

Influenced by the Tibetan Book of the Dead, Priestley was especially struck by an account of the Bardo, a dreamlike state after death, filled with hallucinatory visions. *Johnson over Jordan* is an attempt to simplify the complex Bardo into a Westernized version in which Robert Johnson, an English Everyman, moves back and forth in time examining the quality of the life he has just departed.

The manager of a small business firm, Johnson cannot let go of his material concerns even after death. He wanders through a distorted landscape of documents, ledgers, and tax forms, a nightmare world with which he cannot cope. Like the officer in August Strindberg's *A Dream Play*, he becomes a schoolboy again, confused by life's contradictions, reminded of his petty deeds and thoughtless actions. Eventually he takes refuge, like Ibsen's Peer Gynt in the land of the trolls, in the Jungle Hot Spot. Here, he confronts his animal self as he mingles with men and women in grotesque, piglike masks. A mysterious figure, who, like Peer's Button Moulder, reappears throughout his spiritual journey, directs him on to the Inn at the End of the World. All who have illuminated Johnson's mind and touched his heart, members of his immediate family and characters from beloved books, reappear to him through a window at the inn. He recognizes his wife, like Peer's Solveig, as Eternal Woman. His love for her, stronger than material desires, is a lasting one that makes him finally aware of life's wonders and its prosaic joys. At last Johnson, acknowledging himself a less than perfect being, is granted entry into an unknown universe.

Despite a now legendary performance by Sir Ralph Richardson, effective music by Benjamin Britten, and inventive choreography by Antony Tudor,

Johnson over Jordan failed to find its audience. To some extent Priestley attributed that failure to the critics who dwelled on the work's expressionistic style, frightening away its potential audience. Priestley's own view of the expressionistic theater is that it is peopled entirely by symbolic figures and flattened characters. In the case of *Johnson over Jordan*, he believed, the realistic portrayal of the protagonist, despite the distorted trappings of his environment, made a mockery of the dreaded label. His own explanation of what he was attempting, however—to make use of objective form to present material that was deeply subjective—suggests that the work in fact derives from the expressionist tradition. Like those of expressionist drama, the characters, apart from Johnson himself, are types. All, Johnson among them, speak a heightened language, and the play, in its exploration of a dreamworld devoid of time and space, deals abstractly with a basic expressionist theme—the worth of human beings. The play's very theatricality is the measure of its achievement. Without becoming a commercial success, *Johnson over Jordan* was a landmark occasion in a London theater long resistant to dynamic change. It encouraged others to press on with efforts to expand the limits of a too confining stage.

AN INSPECTOR CALLS

Priestley's work for the theater during World War II expressed his lifelong theme of commitment to community. Plays such as *Desert Highway* and *How Are They at Home?* appear to have been written more from a sense of duty than from a spark of creativity, but one play of the war years stands apart from the rest. Written during the last winter of the war, *An Inspector Calls* was first performed by two Soviet theater companies in Moscow at a time when no London theater was available for its production. When it was produced at home in 1946, in a weighty production full of realistic detail, it was dismissed with indifference. Priestley believed that acclaim with which Russian audiences had greeted it resulted from a more sympathetic symbolic production. There were no walls to the set, only an illuminated acting area. The symbolic setting made the audience aware that the play concerned more than its immediate and continuous action, was in fact concerned with the history of a generation that had just come through a worldwide conflagration. Sharing with *Dangerous Corner* the form of a conventional melodrama, *An Inspector Calls* is a committed social drama that focuses on one man's family while insisting inevitably on the Family of Man.

On an evening in 1912 in an industrial city in the North Midlands, the Birlings are celebrating their daughter Sheila's engagement to Gerald Croft. The coming wedding will signal the merger of Birling and Company and Crofts Limited. Dashing the festive mood of the occasion is the visit of an Inspector Goole, new to the district, to announce the death that evening of a young woman, Eva Smith, who swallowed a disinfectant and died in agony in the infirmary. One by one the Birlings are shown a photograph of the girl, and each recognizes her. By the time Goole departs, everyone is implicated in the girl's death. Birling had fired her for her part in a strike at his factory, and Sheila had had her discharged from a dress shop for impertinence. Croft, who knew her as Daisy Renton, had made her his mistress for a time, but she had later become pregnant by Birling's son Eric. When she had asked for assistance from a charity organization, she had been denied by the interviewing committee, chaired by Mrs. Birling. Frustrated at every turn, she had committed suicide.

The Birling children are shaken by Goole's statement that the world is full of Eva Smiths, and that everyone is responsible for his or her own destiny. The elder Birlings and Croft, on the other hand, are more concerned with their reputations and with covering up the scandal than they are convinced of their guilt and responsibility. It even occurs to them that they may have been shown different photos, that Eva Smith and Daisy Renton may not have been the same girl. Checking with the police a few minutes later, they are overjoyed to learn that there is no Inspector Goole on the force and that no girl has died in the infirmary. Believing that they have been the victims of an elaborate hoax, they prepare to carry on as before, much to the dismay of Sheila and Eric. Suddenly the phone rings, and Birling reports his telephone con-

versation to the others. The police have just informed him that a girl has died on the way to the infirmary after swallowing disinfectant. An inspector is on his way to ask some questions. The curtain abruptly falls on five stunned characters.

In one of Priestley's tautest and best-crafted works, what seems to be a realistic drama suddenly moves outside time. No particular time theory is under illustration here. Instead, time reinforces the notion that human beings must take responsibility for their actions and their consequences. In the present, individuals prepare their future. Even Inspector Goole is taken outside time. Is he police officer or imposter? Perhaps he is the very embodiment of the Birlings' collective guilt, which has been called forth by their need to account for their actions.

Like *Eden End*, *An Inspector Calls* is set in 1912, enabling the dramatist to make astonishing use of dramatic irony. The Birlings' world, like the Kirbys', is about to disintegrate. The Kirbys were victims of their own innocence, but the Birlings, no innocents, have caused the demise of their comfortable world through a lack of compassion, a disregard for those members of their community less fortunate than themselves. Priestley added a further dimension to the play, which he wrote as World War II was ending, by setting it on the eve of World War I. When will humankind benefit, he was asking, from the lessons of the past?

LATER PLAYS

Priestley's wartime despair eventually gave way to a cautious optimism, despite the uncertainties of the future, in such later plays as *Summer Day's Dream* and *The Linden Tree*. After collaborating with Iris Murdoch on a successful adaptation of her novel *A Severed Head* in 1963, he abandoned the theater.

OTHER MAJOR WORKS

LONG FICTION: *Adam in Moonshine*, 1927; *Benighted*, 1927; *Farthing Hall*, 1929 (with Hugh Walpole); *The Good Companions*, 1929; *Angel Pavement*, 1930; *Faraway*, 1932; *I'll Tell You Everything*, 1933 (with George Bullett); *Wonder Hero*, 1933; *They Walk in the City: The Lovers in the Stone Forest*, 1936; *The Doomsday Men: An Adventure*, 1938; *Let the People Sing*, 1939; *Blackout in Gretley: A Story of—and for—Wartime*, 1942; *Daylight on Saturday: A Novel About an Aircraft Factory*, 1943; *Three Men in New Suits*, 1945; *Bright Day*, 1946; *Jenny Villiers: A Story of the Theatre*, 1947; *Festival at Farbridge*, 1951 (published in the United States as *Festival*); *Low Notes on a High Level: A Frolic*, 1954; *The Magicians*, 1954; *Saturn over the Water: An Account of His Adventures in London, South America, and Australia by Tim Bedford, Painter, Edited with Some Preliminary and Concluding Remarks by Henry Sulgrave and Here Presented to the Reading Public*, 1961; *The Thirty-first of June: A Tale of True Love, Enterprise, and Progress in the Arthurian and Ad-Atomic Ages*, 1961; *The Shape of Sleep: A Topical Tale*, 1962; *Sir Michael and Sir George: A Tale of COMSA and DISCUS and the New Elizabethans*, 1964 (also known as *Sir Michael and Sir George: A Comedy of New Elizabethans*); *Lost Empires: Being Richard Herncastle's Account of His Life on the Variety Stage from November, 1913, to August, 1914, Together with a Prologue and Epilogue*, 1965; *Salt Is Leaving*, 1966; *It's an Old Country*, 1967; *The Image Men: "Out of Town" and "London End,"* 1968; *The Carfitt Crisis*, 1975; *Found, Lost, Found: Or, The English Way of Life*, 1976; *My Three Favorite Novels*, 1978.

SHORT FICTION: *The Town Major of Miraucourt*, 1930; *Going Up: Stories and Sketches*, 1950; *The Other Place and Other Stories of the Same Sort*, 1953; *The Carfitt Crisis and Two Other Stories*, 1975.

POETRY: *The Chapman of Rhymes*, 1918.

SCREENPLAY: *Last Holiday*, 1950.

NONFICTION: *Brief Diversions: Being Tales, Travesties, and Epigrams*, 1922; *Papers from Lilliput*, 1922; *I for One*, 1923; *Figures in Modern Literature*, 1924; *Fools and Philosophers: A Gallery of Comic Figures from English Literature*, 1925 (published in the United States as *The English Comic Characters*); *George Meredith*, 1926; *Talking: An Essay*, 1926; *The English Novel*, 1927, 1935, 1974; *Open House: A Book of Essays*, 1927; *Thomas Love Peacock*, 1927; *Too Many People and Other Reflections*, 1928; *Apes and Angels: A Book of Essays*, 1928; *The Balconinny and Other Essays*, 1929 (published in the United States as *The Balconinny*, 1931); *English Humour*, 1929, 1976; *The Lost Generation: An Armistice Day Article*, 1932; *Self-Selected Essays*, 1932; *Albert Goes Through*, 1933; *English Journey: Being a Rambling but Truthful Account of What One Man Saw and Heard and Felt and Thought During a Journey Through England During the Autumn of the Year 1933*, 1934; *Four-in-Hand*, 1934; *Midnight on the Desert: A Chapter of Autobiography*, 1937 (published in the United States as *Midnight on the Desert: Being an Excursion into Autobiography During a Winter in America, 1935-1936*, 1937); *Rain upon Godshill: A Further Chapter of Autobiography*, 1939; *Britain Speaks*, 1940; *Postscripts*, 1940 (radio talks); *Out of the People*, 1941; *Britain at War*, 1942; *British Women Go to War*, 1943; *The Man-Power Story*, 1943; *Here Are Your Answers*, 1944; *The New Citizen*, 1944; *Letter to a Returning Serviceman*, 1945; *Russian Journey*, 1946; *The Secret Dream: An Essay on Britain, America, and Russia*, 1946; *The Arts Under Socialism: Being a Lecture Given to the Fabian Society, with a Postscript on What Government Should Do for the Arts Here and Now*, 1947; *Theatre Outlook*, 1947; *Delight*, 1949; *Journey Down a Rainbow*, 1955 (with Jacquetta Hawkes); *All About Ourselves and Other Essays*, 1956; *The Writer in a Changing Society*, 1956; *The Art of the Dramatist: A Lecture Together with Appendices and Discursive Notes*, 1957; *The Bodley Head Leacock*, 1957; *Thoughts in the Wilderness*, 1957; *Topside: Or, The Future of England, a Dialogue*, 1958; *The Story of Theatre*, 1959; *Literature and Western Man*, 1960; *William Hazlitt*, 1960; *Charles Dickens: A Pictorial Biography*, 1962; *Margin Released: A Writer's Reminiscences and Reflections*, 1962; *The English Comic Characters*, 1963; *Man and Time*, 1964; *The Moments and Other Pieces*, 1966; *All England Listened: J. B. Priestley's Wartime Broadcasts*, 1968; *Essays of Five Decades*, 1968 (Susan Cooper, editor); *Trumpets over the Sea: Being a Rambling and Egotistical Account of the London Symphony Orchestra's Engagement at Daytona Beach, Florida, in July-August, 1967*, 1968; *The Prince of Pleasure and His Regency, 1811-1820*, 1969; *Anton Chekhov*, 1970; *The*

Edwardians, 1970; *Over the Long High Wall: Some Reflections and Speculations on Life, Death, and Time*, 1972; *Victoria's Heyday*, 1972; *The English*, 1973; *Outcries and Asides*, 1974; *A Visit to New Zealand, Particular Pleasures: Being a Personal Record of Some Varied Arts and Many Different Artists*, 1974; *The Happy Dream: An Essay*, 1976; *Instead of the Trees*, 1977 (autobiography).

CHILDREN'S LITERATURE: *Snoggle*, 1972.

EDITED TEXTS: *Essayist Past and Present: A Selection of English Essays*, 1925; *Tom Moore's Diary: A Selection*, 1925; *The Book of Bodley Head Verse*, 1926; *The Female Spectator: Selections from Mrs. Eliza Heywood's Periodical, 1744-1746*, 1929; *Our Nation's Heritage*, 1939; *Scenes of London Life, from "Sketches by Boz" by Charles Dickens*, 1947; *The Best of Leacock*, 1957; *Four English Novels*, 1960; *Four English Biographies*, 1961; *Adventures in English Literature*, 1963; *An Everyman Anthology*, 1966.

BIBLIOGRAPHY

Atkins, John. *J. B. Priestley: The Last of the Sages.* New York: Riverrun Press, 1981. Atkin's attempt to illustrate Priestley's development as essayist, critic, novelist, dramatist, autobiographer, social commentator, historian, and travel writer in a "leap-frogging method" leads inevitably to overlapping and repetition. The 309-page book is most useful on the political, social, and economic background of the late 1920's and 1930's, the period of Priestley's most significant contributions to literature.

Brome, Vincent. *J. B. Priestley.* London: Hamish Hamilton, 1988. Brome offers an affectionate but candid portrait of the writer in public and private life. Brome rightly argues that the prolific writer has been denied his proper niche by overly harsh critics who do not deal fairly with those who write for a wide, general audience. Brome points to the popularization of Carl Jung's theories as an important aspect of Priestley's work.

Cook, Judith. *Priestley.* London: Bloomsbury, 1997. Cook provides a biography of Priestley, examining both his prose and dramatic works. Includes bibliography and index.

DeVitis, A. A., and Albert E. Kalson. *J. B. Priestley.* Boston: Twayne, 1980. After a biographical chapter that includes a discussion of Priestley's time theories, the 257-page book divides into two sections, the first half dealing with Priestley as novelist, the latter half dealing with Priestley as dramatist. All Priestley's works in the two genres are discussed, the more significant ones in some detail. Includes a chronology of the important events in the writer's life and a useful bibliography.

Gray, Dulcie. *J. B. Priestley.* Stroud, England: Sutton, 2000. This volume in the Sutton Pocket Biographies series provides a concise look at Priestley's life and many works. Includes bibliography.

Klein, Holger. *J. B. Priestley's Plays.* New York: St. Martin's Press, 1988. Klein states that his goal is "to further an understanding" of Priestley's "dramatic objectives and methods," but his seeming inability to differentiate between Priestley the serious dramatist and Priestley the occasional hack working to order occasionally invalidates his findings in the confusing first section of the book that deals with dramatic structure. Klein's study is more useful in its latter half in its discussion of Priestley's ideas concerning contemporary issues, pointing especially to *The Linden Tree* as the dramatist's condemnation of Great Britain's post-World War II malaise.

Albert E. Kalson

JAMES PURDY

Born: Near Fremont, Ohio; July 14, 1923

PRINCIPAL DRAMA

Mr. Cough Syrup and the Phantom Sex, pb. 1960
Children Is All, pb. 1961 (stories and plays)
Cracks, pb. 1962, pr. 1963
Wedding Finger, pb. 1974
Clearing in the Forest, pr. 1978, pb. 1980
True, pr. 1978, pb. 1979
A Day After the Fair, pb. 1979
Now, pr. 1979, pb. 1980
Two Plays, pb. 1979 (includes *A Day After the Fair* and *True*)
What Is It, Zach?, pr. 1979, pb. 1980
Proud Flesh: Four Short Plays, pb. 1980
Strong, pb. 1980
The Berry-Picker, pb. 1981, pr. 1984
Scrap of Paper, pb. 1981
In the Night of Time, pb. 1992
Ruthanna Elder, pb. 1992
Enduring Zeal, pb. 1992
In the Night of Time and Four Other Plays, pb. 1992
The Paradise Circus, pb. 1992
The Rivalry of Dolls, pr., pb. 1992

OTHER LITERARY FORMS

Although he has written poems and plays throughout his career, James Purdy's reputation rests primarily on his work as a novelist and writer of short stories. His first two novels, *Malcolm* (1959) and *The Nephew* (1960), caused the most critical stir. In fact, *Malcolm* was adapted for the stage in 1966 by American dramatist Edward Albee. In the 1960's, Purdy was touted as one of the United States' most promising writers, especially because of his experimentation with the conventions of the fiction genre.

By the end of that decade, however, the critical response to Purdy's work had become increasingly fractured. Purdy himself claims that his public unhappiness with the literary establishment was the reason for this mixed response; others point to his con-

troversial themes and grotesque characters and plots. Although Purdy has continued to have his ardent admirers, frequently his works have been disparaged and ignored.

ACHIEVEMENTS

Some commentators have asserted that James Purdy's work has found greatest acceptance in Europe, especially in England and the Netherlands. In reality, his native America has not failed to recognize his creative output. He was the recipient of many grants, including a National Institute of Arts and Letters grant in 1958, Guggenheim Fellowships in 1958 and 1962, and a Ford Foundation grant in 1961. Purdy was also nominated for a PEN-Faulkner Award in 1985, and he won the Morten Dauwen Zabel Fiction Award from the Academy of Arts and Letters in 1993.

BIOGRAPHY

Born in Ohio on July 14, 1923, James Purdy has consistently avoided personal publicity, arguing that his work is his biography. As a result of this decision, the details of his personal life are often sketchy. One of three sons born to William and Vera (Covick) Purdy, who divorced when he was only a small child, Purdy spent his teenaged years in Chicago. He attended both the University of Chicago and the University of Puebla in Mexico.

Purdy spent a number of years abroad, particularly as an interpreter in Latin America, Spain, and France. In addition to his linguistic work, he tried teaching, first as a faculty member at Lawrence University in Wisconsin from 1949 to 1953, then as a lecturer for the United States Information Agency in Europe in 1982, and finally as an instructor of fiction writing at New York University in the 1980's.

Still, most of Purdy's life has been devoted to his writing. At the beginning of his career, he could not attract the attention of editors and publishers, and he had his first two books privately published. Purdy sent copies of these two books to writers that he admired, and one in particular, the English poet Dame Edith Sitwell, helped him acquire a European publisher, a development that led eventually to an American publishing contract.

From that moment, his output has been prolific. In fact, over the years, Purdy has published more than fifty volumes of fiction, poetry, and drama. Although his works have not garnered him a popular audience, he has continued to hone his craft. Purdy lives and works in Brooklyn Heights, New York.

ANALYSIS

James Purdy has consistently experimented with the dramatic medium since the beginning of his writing career. Some of his short plays exist only on the printed page; others have been produced onstage, mostly in New York theaters Off-Broadway.

Critical examination of Purdy's one-act dramas in the late twentieth century can be credited largely to the revival of interest in this genre, thanks in part to theater companies such as the Ensemble Studio Theater of New York. For example, Purdy's one-act play *Clearing in the Forest* had its world premier at the Ensemble Studio Theater in 1978, the first year of the company's later celebrated annual marathon productions of short plays.

Purdy's short dramatic pieces can be said to be the theatrical equivalents of his short stories. Over the years, a number of these works have been published along with the short fiction in mixed collections. Because both his short plays and short stories rely heavily on vivid characterization and the use of dialogue, there is often a blurring of genres. In 1963, for example, the short play *Cracks* and five stories from the collection *Children Is All* were adapted for the stage, packaged under the title *Color of Darkness: An Evening in the World of James Purdy*, and performed at the Writer's Stage in New York.

The characters in Purdy's plays, like those in his fiction pieces, grapple with issues of self-identity. Their attempts to define themselves are complicated by the simultaneous desire for independence and the yearning to belong. Sometimes the latter longing is confined to the level of personal relationships, especially that of parent and child. At other times, Purdy

pits the individual against society as a whole, in a setting informed either by the middle-class values of small town life or the often-bewildering lifestyle options afforded by residency in a big city.

Although recounted in the generally spare language of everyday speech, the hopes and dreams of Purdy's characters are complicated and charged by a strong undercurrent of sexual tension and pent-up violence. These two factors Purdy attributes largely to an essential flaw in modern American society, which he feels is "based on money and competition" and "terrified of love."

CHILDREN IS ALL

This early play is representative of one of Purdy's major thematic preoccupations—the child's essential need for and often betrayal by his parents. In ironic contrast to its title, *Children Is All* focuses on one woman's inability to live up to the demands of motherhood.

After a fifteen-year absence, Edna's son Billy sends his mother a hastily scribbled postcard indicating his intention to return home. Imprisoned for em-

James Purdy (Fabian Bachrach)

bezzlement, a crime for which he may have been framed, Billy desperately needs Edna's acceptance. For her part, however, she cannot reconcile herself to her son's homecoming, fearing that he will resent her for not having supported him at his trial and never having visited him in prison. Furthermore, Edna fears that she will not be able to recognize her thirty-three-year-old son when he does return.

True to her own premonition, Edna fails to acknowledge Billy when he arrives, fatally wounded while escaping from prison. As her son dies, his bloody head in her lap, Edna mechanically comforts "the stranger" while lost in personal reverie. Their posture, seated mother and dying child, is reminiscent of the Pieta, the classic image of the Virgin Mary mourning for the dead Christ, but Purdy's unflattering portrait of Edna Cartwright serves to distance the character from the reader, and there is an absence of pity for her fate.

A DAY AFTER THE FAIR

Another play with archetypal aspects is *A Day After the Fair*, which features the stock character of the clown who laughs on the outside while he is crying on the inside. In this case, there is a pair of clown brothers. Neil, the younger brother, is the object of all of the other characters' projected desire, both psychological and physical. Arnold, the older brother, is his possessive protector. Oswin, a professional assassin, is willing to kill for Neil; Oswin's wife Elga is willing to accept her own death in a botched abortion rather than impede her husband's greater passion for Neil. Even the evil Clown Master feels compelled to banish both Arnold and Neil from the circus because he cannot abide his not being able to possess them both.

This tangled web of sexual obsession and barely repressed violence is indicative of so much of Purdy's work, especially in connection with his depictions of the relationships between men. In this regard, critics have been quick to note Purdy's groundbreaking use of homosexual subject matter as early as the 1950's. For his own part, however, Purdy has resisted being labeled as a gay writer; for him the troubled male relationships in his works are one of many symptoms of the general inability of individuals in contemporary American society to reach out to others in significant, reciprocal, and life-enhancing ways.

One of the reasons that people have problems in relating to others is what Purdy sees as the basic treachery of language. For many of Purdy's characters, their words betray them. In *A Day After the Fair*, for example, both Arnold and the Clown Master have their tongues posthumously cut out, the former by Neil and the latter by Oswin, because they are perceived as liars.

PROUD FLESH

In *Proud Flesh*, perhaps Purdy's most important collection of short plays, are four works that bring together some of his abiding character configurations and thematic concerns, including the often unbearable tension brought about by the simultaneous struggle for autonomy and acceptance.

Strong, a play that attracted the early attention of American dramatist Tennessee Williams, focuses on one of Purdy's characteristically dysfunctional families: a dutiful and self-sacrificing son named Dana, a rebellious and self-destructive son named Corey, and a mother unwilling, like Edna Cartwright in *Children Is All*, to face unpleasant realities. In the face of Corey's continuing trouble with the law, Dana presumes to take on the role of their absent father by adopting a stern, censorious stance while their mother persists in trying to mitigate the seriousness of Corey's personal problems by saying that the "poor little fellow is confused." The tension resulting from their contradictory responses takes its emotional toll on Corey, and when he cannot escape his family and their acceptance of the suburban values of 1950's America, he kills himself.

A similarly violent ending awaits the two characters in the short play *Clearing in the Forest*. Gil and Burk are a pair of male lovers who are facing the dissolution of their relationship because of the younger Gil's decision to marry Louise, a woman whose unseen presence permeates the farmhouse both men have shared for two years.

As the story's title indicates, both Gil and Burk have reached a point in their partnership when their complicated feelings for one another are stripped bare and fully exposed for their own scrutiny and judgment. During the course of this mutual examination, Burk extols the storminess of their partnership while young Gil confesses that he cannot "stand a life of all storms and flashes of lightning." He yearns, in part, for the sanctuary of marriage, symbolized by the forest, and he fears the emotional and physical tension inherent in his homosexual relationship with Burk.

In the end, Gil stabs and kills himself, an act that gay critics point to as evidence of Purdy's inability to entertain the possibility that love between two men can be viable and that some commentators see as just another example of the author's abiding insistence that love cannot endure in a world whose values do not support its flourishing.

IN THE NIGHT OF TIME AND FOUR OTHER PLAYS

The five plays featured in the 1992 collection *In the Night of Time and Four Other Plays* call attention to one of Purdy's persistent compositional tendencies. He is prone to revisiting earlier works and translating them from one genre to another. The play *Ruthanna Elder*, for instance, first appeared as a five-page short story in the 1987 collection *The Candles of Your Eyes*.

In the short story, an elderly physician recalls the tragic tale of a young woman whose innocent beauty serves as a catalyst in the death of two men. Ruthanna visits the doctor out of her concern that she may have been impregnated during a single, passionate encounter with a fifteen-year-old male relative. Although her fears prove groundless, Jess, to whom she has been betrothed for years, intuits her changed status, elicits a confession from the young seducer, subsequently kills the boy, and then commits suicide.

The play version retains the essential threads of the short story but increases the role of the boy, now given the name of Judd. Like so many of Purdy's physical and spiritual orphans, Judd is looking for any shelter in the storm. In part, he loves Ruthanna as a sister; in part, he looks to Jess as his brother and father. In either case, Judd's need to belong leads to tragedy as he seeks a moment of intimacy with Ruthanna and then readily confesses his indiscretion to Jess, for whom he professes worship. In essence, therefore, the play retains the story's basic love trian-

gle but magnifies the roles of all three characters, particularly that of Judd.

OTHER MAJOR WORKS

LONG FICTION: *Malcolm*, 1959; *The Nephew*, 1960; *Cabot Wright Begins*, 1964; *Eustace Chisholm and the Works*, 1967; *Jeremy's Version*, 1970; *I Am Elijah Thrush*, 1972; *The House of the Solitary Maggot*, 1974; *In a Shallow Grave*, 1976; *Narrow Rooms*, 1978; *Mourners Below*, 1981; *On Glory's Course*, 1984; *In the Hollow of His Hand*, 1986; *Garments the Living Wear*, 1989; *Out with the Stars*, 1992; *Gertrude of Stony Island Avenue*, 1997.

SHORT FICTION: *Don't Call Me by My Right Name and Other Stories*, 1956; *Sixty-three: Dream Palace*, 1956; *Color of Darkness: Eleven Stories and a Novella*, 1957 (contains *Don't Call Me by My Right Name and Other Stories* and *Sixty-three: Dream Palace*); *The Candles of Your Eyes*, 1985; *The Candles of Your Eyes, and Thirteen Other Stories*, 1987; *Sixty-three: Dream Palace: Selected Stories, 1956-1987*, 1991.

POETRY: *The Running Sun*, 1971; *Sunshine Is an Only Child*, 1973; *She Came Out of the Mists of Morning*, 1975; *Lessons and Complaints*, 1978; *The Brooklyn Branding Parlors*, 1986.

MISCELLANEOUS: *An Oyster Is a Wealthy Beast*, 1967 (story and poems); *Mr. Evening: A Story and Nine Poems*, 1968; *On the Rebound: A Story and Nine Poems*, 1970; *A Day After the Fair: A Collection of Plays and Stories*, 1977.

BIBLIOGRAPHY

Adams, Stephen D. *James Purdy*. New York: Barnes & Noble, 1976. Concentrating primarily on eight early novels, Adams places Purdy in the great tradition of American symbolic writers such as Nathaniel Hawthorne and Herman Melville. This volume includes analysis of two early plays, *Children Is All* and *Cracks*.

Canning, Richard. *Gay Fiction Speaks: Conversations with Gay Novelists*. New York: Columbia University Press, 2000. The extensive interview contained in this twelve-author volume focuses primarily on Purdy's identity as a gay novelist, but it does include some material on his plays. In particular, Purdy acknowledges his interest in and debt owed to the Jacobean theater of the early seventeenth century in England, especially those plays by John Webster and Thomas Middleton that fixate on the existence of evil as a major force in human destiny.

Chupack, Henry. *James Purdy.* Boston: Twayne, 1975. This is the most comprehensive treatment of Purdy's work to date. Although Chupack focuses on the author's early fiction, there is some reference to Purdy's plays and to his fiction adapted for the stage by others.

Guy-Bray, Stephen. *The Gay and Lesbian Literary Heritage.* Edited by Claude J. Summers. New York: Henry Holt, 1995. In this short article, Guy-Bray tries to identify some of Purdy's most pervasive themes, including the betrayal of love, the use of violence to resolve inner conflict, and the malevolence of fate.

Tanner, Tony. *City of Words.* New York: Harper & Row, 1971. One of Purdy's earliest critical supporters, Tanner devotes the fourth chapter of this volume to an overview of the author's themes, particularly the quest for identity, and the author's frequent creative commentaries on the art of writing.

Weales, Gerald. *The Jumping-Off Place: American Drama in the 1960's.* New York: Macmillan, 1969. A scholar of Anglo American theatre, Weales attempts to place Purdy's early plays in the context of dramatic trends during the decade of the 1960's. Special attention is paid to Purdy's *Cracks* and *Children Is All* and to Edward Albee's stage adaptation of Purdy's novel *Malcolm.*

S. Thomas Mack

ALEXANDER PUSHKIN

Born: Moscow, Russia; June 6, 1799
Died: St. Petersburg, Russia; February 10, 1837

Principal drama

Boris Godunov, wr. 1824-1825, pb. 1831, pr. 1870 (English translation, 1918)

Skupoy rytsar, wr. 1830, pr., pb. 1852 (*The Covetous Knight*, 1925)

Kamyenny gost, wr. 1830, pb. 1839, pr. 1847 (*The Stone Guest*, 1936)

Motsart i Salyeri, pr., pb. 1832 (*Mozart and Salieri*, 1920)

Pir vo vryemya chumy, pb. 1833, pr. 1899 (*The Feast in Time of the Plague*, 1925)

Stseny iz rytsarskikh vryemen, wr. 1835, pr., pb. 1937

Rusalka, pb. 1837, pr. 1838 (*The Water Nymph*, 1924)

Little Tragedies, pb. 1946 (includes *The Covetous Knight, The Stone Guest, Mozart and Salieri,* and *The Feast in Time of the Plague*)

Other literary forms

In addition to his masterful short dramas and more famous long play, *Boris Godunov,* Alexander Pushkin was the author of numerous short lyrics that have achieved critical acclaim as well as wide popularity. He was the author of a novel in verse, *Evgeny Onegin* (1825-1832, 1833; *Eugene Onegin,* 1881), and several long poems including *Ruslan i Lyudmila* (1820; English translation, 1936), *Kavkazskiy plennik* (1822; *The Prisoner of the Caucasus,* 1895), *Gavriiliada* (1822; *Gabriel: A Poem,* 1926), *Graf Nulin* (1827; *Count Nulin,* 1972), *Poltava* (1829; English translation, 1936), *Domik v Kolomne* (1833; *The Little House at Kolomna,* 1977), and *Medniy vsadnik* (1841; *The Bronze Horseman,* 1936). Pushkin also wrote a number of prose works later in life; his *Povesti Belkina* (1831; *The Tales of Belkin,* 1947) includes five beautifully wrought short stories, and his *Kapitanskaya dochka* (1836; *The Captain's Daughter,* 1946) is a masterful treatment of the Pugachev Rebellion of the eighteenth century.

ACHIEVEMENTS

Alexander Pushkin has always been regarded as the greatest Russian poet. He began writing when still a student and matured as a poet while a young man in St. Petersburg. His verse is distinguished for its clarity and simplicity, yet Pushkin was a complex thinker whose insights into the human psyche, great ethical and moral issues, and political questions of the day were sophisticated and profound. His famous novel in verse, *Eugene Onegin*, is an unparalleled depiction of the society of early nineteenth century Russia, while his greatest longer poem, *The Bronze Horseman*, demonstrates a penetrating understanding of the relationship between the private citizen and the state.

In addition to being a poet of genius, Pushkin was a great prose writer. Written in the 1830's, at a time when Russian literature was beginning to be dominated by prose rather than poetry, *The Tales of Belkin* are short story gems that demonstrate exciting twists of plot and were conceived as literary polemics as well as belles lettres. The hero of his longer story, *Pikovaya dama* (1834; *The Queen of Spades*, 1896), can be considered a precedent for the tortured protagonists of Fyodor Dostoevski.

One of Pushkin's most significant contributions to Russian literature was that his works could be regarded as models for the writers who came after him. In addition to providing a prototype for Dostoevski's hero-villains, Pushkin wrote in a clear, straightforward prose style that had an enormous impact on such nineteenth and twentieth century writers as Ivan Turgenev, Anton Chekhov, and Ivan Bunin. Pushkin's worth as an exemplar is a measure of his greatness.

BIOGRAPHY

Alexander Sergeyevich Pushkin was born in Moscow, Russia, on June 6, 1799. His mother, Nadezhda Osipovna, née Hannibal, was a descendant of the Abyssinian (Ethiopian) godson of Peter the Great. Sergei Lvovich Pushkin, his father, was the son of an old noble family; his ancestor Afanasy Pushkin makes an appearance in *Boris Godunov*. Although close to his older sister, Pushkin never developed a warm relationship with his parents. French was the language of the household, and the family belonged

Alexander Pushkin (Library of Congress)

to a society of aristocrats who lived beyond their means and engaged in an endless round of social activities, including theatricals and contact with the poets of the day. Pushkin is said to have done his first writing in French.

When Pushkin was twelve, his parents sent him to the newly opened lycée at Tsarskoe Selo. It was there that he received his six years of formal education, doing his best work in Russian and French literature. The friendships he formed at the lycée, especially with his fellow poet, Baron Anton Delvig, were the closest of his entire life. He was graduated in 1817 and entered into an undemanding position in the Ministry of Foreign Affairs office in St. Petersburg. Pushkin immediately plunged into a life of the theater and ballet, drinking and women, spending his less frenetic hours on discussions of subversive liberal ideas with his friends. His liberal sympathies found their way into his verse, and he was sent to the Caucasus, to a new job with the Board of Protection of Foreign Colonists in South Russia, to keep him out of trouble. Although Pushkin's southern exile probably prevented him from taking part in the Decembrist

Uprising of 1825, he was suspected of complicity in the Decembrist Movement and arrested. The emperor Nicholas I, who promised to serve as his personal protector (and later, personal censor), pardoned him in 1826.

Pushkin married the frivolous society beauty Natalia Nikolayevna Goncharova in 1831. He was unable to share his intellectual and literary interests with her and was anxious about her flirtations, especially at court. Natalia caught the eye of the emperor, and so that she could spend more time in his presence, the emperor made Pushkin a gentleman of the bedchamber, an insulting offer that the poet deeply resented. Natalia extended her flirtations to Baron Georges d'Anthès, a Frenchman in Russian service who was the adopted son of the Dutch diplomat Baron Louis Beveriwaert van Heeckeren. When d'Anthès's attentions to Natalia became insultingly obvious, Pushkin challenged him to a duel. Pushkin was gravely wounded, and perished in agony on February 10, 1837. Nicholas himself, who found the poet an inconvenience, was no doubt implicated in the affair.

ANALYSIS

Alexander Pushkin's dramas represent an interesting point of development in his career as a writer, for they were written during a period of flux after some of his finest lyrics and longer poems and before his later prose works. They contain many of the elements, such as the development of characters and their interaction, that are central to prose writing. They were conceived and written, however, in verse, not prose, and the characters must be coordinated and portrayed within this formal scheme. Pushkin's dramatic works, and particularly the *Little Tragedies*, combine successfully the formal strictures of poetry with the in-depth character analysis that proved to be so influential in later Russian literature.

BORIS GODUNOV

Although not one of Pushkin's greatest works, *Boris Godunov* is an interesting and important play. Pushkin conceived of it primarily as an example to later writers, demonstrating greater concern with the literary form itself than with the subject matter. The

play was based on a Shakespearean model. Like his illustrious predecessor, Pushkin was casual about observing the three unities of time, place, and action. He wrote his play, like William Shakespeare's dramas, in blank verse, occasionally introduced prose dialogues, and had frequent scene changes.

Boris Godunov is a chronicle play that centers on the reign of Czar Boris Godunov, prime minister and power behind the throne during the reign of his brother-in-law, Fyodor. Boris was chosen for the throne after the death of Fyodor in an election that his enemies decried as false. He was also assumed to have had Fyodor's younger brother Dimitry, the only surviving member of the Ryurik Dynasty, murdered in 1591. Although this charge has since been repudiated, it was accepted at the time when Nikolai Karamzin published his great history of Russia, *Istoriya gosudarstya rossiyskogo*, Pushkin's source, in 1816-1829. Although the reign of Boris began on a good note, he eventually ran into problems accentuated by the great famine of 1601-1603. Once his popularity had waned, he was easy prey for pretenders to the throne. It is on this note that the play begins.

Boris Godunov opens with a conspiratorial conversation between two boyars, followed by a scene in the Kremlin in which the boyars reaffirm Boris's right to rule. The action shifts almost immediately to the Chudov Monastery and the monk Grigori Otrepev, the future False Dimitry and Pretender to the throne. Hearing of the murder of the child Dimitry, who would have been his contemporary, Grigori decides on a scheme to escape the deadening routine of the monastery. He will claim that Dimitry has survived after all and is none other than himself. Donning secular attire, he flees from the monastery. He is intercepted at the Lithuanian border but escapes into Lithuania (at that time united with Poland). With the assistance of the Poles and the aid of disgruntled boyars who are indifferent to his true identity (including Pushkin's forebear, Afanasy Pushkin), he eventually ascends the Russian throne.

In Cracow, Grigori meets and falls in love with the beautiful Marina Mniszek, the only person to whom he reveals his true identity. Marina's partiality for him is linked to her own political ambition, not to affection. Her scornful rebuff of his attentions prompts him to be proud in turn with her, a move that earns her respect and opens her eyes to the possibility that he will indeed be able to attain his goal. Anxious to subdue a potentially threatening neighbor, the kingdom of Poland-Lithuania lends military support to the claims of the Pretender and invades Russia. Boris assumes that he will not need foreign help to overcome this threat and makes the fatal mistake of rejecting the aid of the Swedish king.

The Pretender harnesses the discontent of local military forces, and Ukraine rises in revolt. With the death of Boris (from a heart attack), the boyars are free to act; Prince V. V. Golitsyn has Boris's wife and son murdered. The triumphant Pretender enters Moscow, and the play concludes with the boyar Mosal'skij exhorting the populace to hail the Czar Dimitry Ivanovich, a command that is met with silence. Pushkin had in fact intended for the people to respond; this is one instance in which the censor's meddling produced a more desirable ending.

Because Pushkin believed that Boris was responsible for the murder of Dimitry, the play depicts the rise of the Pretender as retribution for Boris's crime. One of Pushkin's great strokes of characterization is to have Boris die with a clear conscience, having accepted the punishment due to him. Nevertheless, his guilt is visited on his own son, who is killed at the end of the play.

Pushkin's dialogic style is stiffer and his metrical structure less adequate in *Boris Godunov* than in the four plays collected in English as *Little Tragedies*. His major characters are less interesting and complex. *Boris Godunov* attained greater stature as Petrovich Mussorgsky's opera than it enjoyed as a play. Although not Pushkin's greatest drama, it prepared the way for the later tragedies.

According to the critic D. S. Mirsky, Pushkin's *Little Tragedies* are "dramatic investigations" of character and situation, a designation that Pushkin himself had applied to them. Written in blank verse, they can be considered closet dramas rather than stage plays. Their brevity enabled Pushkin to focus on a single climactic situation illuminating the major characters.

THE COVETOUS KNIGHT

The Covetous Knight is purported to be a scene from a play of the same name by the Englishman Chenstone. Perhaps Pushkin confused his name with that of the writer William Shenstone, author of *The Schoolmistress* (1742) but not of this play. Like the other *Little Tragedies*, *The Covetous Knight* has a fairly simple plot. The poor knight, Albert, is unable to pay for a new helmet and is embarrassed to appear in a shirt of mail when the other knights are wearing satin and velvet. His problems would be alleviated if his avaricious father, the baron, a miserly knight with large quantities of gold, would bestow some on his son. Albert's servant Ivan has attempted to borrow money from the Jewish moneylender Solomon but has not succeeded. Solomon suddenly appears, reluctant to lend money but with a plan to help Albert obtain a large sum. Acquainted with an apothecary, Solomon confides to Albert that a few tasteless, colorless drops of poison in the baron's wine will make the son a rich man. Albert is disgusted and chases Solomon away.

As the second scene opens, the baron is in his vault ready to drop yet a few more gold coins into the sixth of his treasure chests. He contemplates the power that his money represents. Not only can he control the arts and "free genius," but virtue itself would submit to him and "bloody villainy" would obey him. He gloats over the suffering he has caused, the crimes he has forced others to commit. When the moment comes to unlock the chest, he is seized with fear. As he inserts the key into the lock, a strange feeling grips him, and he feels like a murderer plunging a knife into a victim's body. This is a foreshadowing of his own death.

Albert visits the baron's castle with his friend the duke, who has promised Albert that he will attempt to wrest some money from the covetous father. The baron slanders his son, claiming that Albert had wanted to kill him or had at least longed for his death. When Albert, who has been concealed, comes rushing into the room to cry that his father's statements are lies, the duke banishes him from his presence. Thereupon the baron does in fact die, calling for his keys while choking. The cause of his death is not explained in the play; it would seem to have been a consequence of his own greed. Perhaps Albert has, in fact, poisoned him.

MOZART AND SALIERI

The shortest of the *Little Tragedies* is *Mozart and Salieri*, based on a legend that Salieri poisoned Mozart. As the play opens, Salieri is delivering a monologue, recounting the single-mindedness with which he devoted himself to his art. Yet now, having tasted success, he has come to be consumed by envy for his friend Mozart. Salieri is especially tormented by Mozart's lack of earnest diligence, and by his love of silliness and practical jokes.

Mozart enters, accompanied by a blind fiddler who plays for them something "from Mozart," and Salieri is stunned to see his rival willingly desecrate his art. Mozart has brought a new piece for Salieri to hear. He asks Salieri to imagine that he, Mozart, is with a beautiful woman or a friend, "perhaps with thee," and then has a sudden vision of darkness or the grave. Then he plays. It is a brilliant prefiguring of the actual outcome of the plot. Salieri responds ardently, saying, "Thou, Mozart, art a god, and thyself knowest it not;/ I know, I." In this he expresses the essence of their relationship, for Mozart seemingly toys with his divine gift, one that Salieri recognizes but does not share. Salieri invites Mozart to dine with him, and Mozart leaves to make arrangements.

On Mozart's departure, Salieri delivers his second long monologue. He is determined to get rid of Mozart, who has eclipsed his fellow composers and is so great a genius that he could never leave any musical heirs. Salieri brings out a vial that he always carries against the day when he might wish to commit suicide, having decided instead to use it to poison Mozart.

The two meet, and Mozart is uncharacteristically solemn. When pressed, he reveals that he had been thinking about his *Requiem Mass*. Salieri expresses surprise at Mozart's choice of so solemn a piece, whereupon the latter tells him a strange story. A stranger dressed in black commissioned Mozart to write a requiem mass and then vanished. Mozart finished the piece, but the man never returned to claim it, and Mozart is reluctant to part with his work. Then

Mozart reveals that he feels the constant presence of the man in black and senses him sitting at the table with them. The man is death, and the *Requiem Mass* for Mozart's funeral.

Pushkin's inclusion of this episode serves not only to foreshadow the ending of the play, but also to reveal the differences between the two protagonists. Salieri knows that Mozart is sufficiently gifted to have had a presentiment of his own fate. He suggests that they uncork a bottle of champagne (the better to poison his rival) or read *The Marriage of Figaro* (1786), an obvious attempt to flatter and distract his enemy. The brilliant Mozart is blind to the fact that his "friend" loathes him, is consumed by jealousy, and might possibly be tempted to kill him. Mozart alludes to Salieri's inability to get along with his fellow musicians, mentioning that Beaumarchais had been Salieri's friend. He innocently asks if Beaumarchais had really poisoned someone and receives a casual reply from Salieri. Salieri then pours the poison into Mozart's glass and suggests that he drink. Mozart utters an ironic speech: "To thy/ Health, friend, to the sincere tie/ Uniting Mozart and Salieri,/ Two sons of harmony." He drinks to the health of his murderer—who, by his lack of sincerity, precisely because of the absence of any tie joining them, has killed him. Salieri has inserted the ultimate disharmony into Mozart's life. Mozart then plays part of his *Requiem Mass*, and Salieri weeps with pain and pleasure, distressed at the tragedy but simultaneously relieved. Calling them both "priests of beauty," Mozart says that he feels unwell and goes home to die. Pushkin's drama inspired Peter Shaffer's play *Amadeus* (pr. 1979), which in turn served as the basis for the Academy Award-winning film of the same title (1984).

THE STONE GUEST

The Stone Guest, often considered the greatest play of *Little Tragedies*, draws on the Don Juan legend. Don Juan has been exiled from Madrid for having killed the commander of the municipal garrison. He goes to the monument for the slain man and encounters Doña Anna, his widow. Concealing his true identity, he attracts her attention and excites her interest. They arrange to meet at her home. He says that he desires only death at her feet, an ironic reference to his later fate. On her departure, he invites the statute to come, too. When it nods in agreement, he is horrified.

Don Juan arrives at Doña Anna's, tells her who he really is, and swears (with seeming sincerity) that he loves her. Thereupon the statue itself appears and tells Don Juan to give it his hand. He perishes as the statue crushes him. Just as *The Covetous Knight* is about the dehumanizing effect of avariciousness, and *Mozart and Salieri* is concerned with the deadly power of envy, so in *The Stone Guest* does one encounter the fatal consequences of extreme emotion.

THE FEAST IN TIME OF THE PLAGUE

The Feast in Time of the Plague is Pushkin's translation of one scene of the play *The City of the Plague* (1816), by the Scottish writer John Wilson; the translation is generally accurate. The two songs of the scene are, however, original. The plot is simple. A group of young men and women are having a feast during a plague. The principal characters consist of a speaker, the singer Mary, Luisa, a young man, and a priest. As the scene begins, the young man speaks movingly of Jackson, so recently one of their number and a merry addition to their company. He is a victim of the plague, and his armchair has been left empty in tribute.

Mary's is the first song; unlike the blank verse of the dialogue, it is written in trochaic tetrameter. Mary sings of the sorrow brought by the plague, focusing on the death of her alter ego, Jenny: "I beg thee, do not come near,/ To the body of the Jenny;/ Do not touch the dead lips,/ Go far from her." She remembers how her parents had loved to hear her sing, how innocent her voice had been before the plague. The young man wants free, dynamic song that will distract them from their sorrow. Thereupon the speaker himself sings in celebration of the plague, remarking on the intoxication of its breath. His blank verse song is strongly reminiscent of the songs of Shakespeare.

An old priest appears and reproaches them for being ungodly madmen, celebrating a "godless feast." "Is it thou," he reminds the speaker, "who three weeks ago, on thy knees/ Sobbing, embraced the body of thy mother." The speaker leaves the feast and is sunk in deep pensiveness as the rest continue. Like

Mozart and Salieri, *The Feast in Time of the Plague* contains the suggestion that those who are endowed with the creative impulse are jealously persecuted by the less gifted. Indeed, all four of the *Little Tragedies* can be seen as a defense of art and freedom, whether threatened by the tyranny of official control or by the envy of the untalented.

THE WATER NYMPH

Pushkin's remaining dramatic works, *The Water Nymph* and *Stseny iz rytsarskikh vryemen* (scenes from knightly times), remained unfinished and were published as fragments. The first concerns the seduction of a miller's daughter by a prince. When he deserts her to marry someone more fitting his station, she casts herself into the Dnieper. She becomes a water nymph, and years later, the child-nymph with whom she had been pregnant lures the father to a doom not specified by the end of the scene. Although the play is in blank verse, it closely resembles Nikolai Gogol's later prose tales and, like them, is based in part on Ukrainian folk legend. It differs from the *Little Tragedies* and from *Stseny iz rytsarskikh vryemen* as well in having a native setting rather than a Western European one.

STSENY IZ RYTSARSKIKH VRYEMEN

Stseny iz rytsarskikh vryemen is a blank verse playlet similar to *The Covetous Knight*. Not only is the setting in medieval Western Europe, but also the main characters are similar. After the knight, Albert, has accidently killed his groom, Jacob, with a heavy slap of his gauntleted hand, Francis agrees to take Jacob's place. From having been Albert's friend and equal (although he is impoverished), Francis becomes an inferior and a servant. This difference is stressed by Albert's use of the familiar form of the pronoun "you" with Francis, while the latter must respond with the formal, respectful form of the pronoun.

Albert's beautiful sister, Clothilda, ridicules Francis's love for her, and Francis's smoldering resentment explodes when Albert expects him to be a butler as well as a groom. He leaves in fury. He returns home to find his father dead. With no other recourse, Francis turns highwayman with other disenchanteds and ambushes Albert and Rothenfeld. Francis is captured and brought to Rothenfeld's castle. He sings a beautiful song (in iambic tetrameter) about a poor knight, and Clothilda begs that, as a reward, he be spared the noose. Rothenfeld agrees but casts Francis into the dungeon for life.

Both *Stseny iz rytsarskikh vryemen* and *The Covetous Knight* strongly prefigure the works of Dostoevski. Both have proud heroes who are disinherited aristocrats, men who might be willing to plot crimes for material gain but, more important, for vengeance. The proud man is the victim of an inferior, unjust society, a character echoed later in Raskolnikov, from Dostoevski's *Prestupleniye i nakazaniye* (1866; *Crime and Punishment*, 1866) and Stavrogin from *Besy* (1871-1872; *The Possessed*, 1913).

OTHER MAJOR WORKS

LONG FICTION: *Evgeny Onegin*, 1825-1832, 1833 (*Eugene Onegin*, 1881); *Arap Petra velikogo*, 1828-1841 (*Peter the Great's Negro*, 1896); *Kirdzhali*, 1834 (English translation, 1896); *Kapitanskaya dochka*, 1836 (*The Captain's Daughter*, 1846); *Dubrovsky*, 1841 (English translation, 1892); *Yegipetskiye nochi*, 1841 (*Egyptian Nights*, 1896); *Istoriya sela Goryukhina*, 1857 (*History of the Village of Goryukhino*, 1966).

SHORT FICTION: *Povesti Belkina*, 1831 (*Russian Romance*, 1875; better known as *The Tales of Belkin*, 1947); *Pikovaya dama*, 1834 (*The Queen of Spades*, 1858).

POETRY: *Ruslan i Lyudmila*, 1820 (*Ruslan and Liudmila*, 1936); *Gavriiliada*, 1822 (*Gabriel: A Poem*, 1926); *Kavkazskiy plennik*, 1822 (*The Prisoner of the Caucasus*, 1895); *Bratya razboyniki*, 1824; *Bakhchisaraiskiy fontan*, 1827 (*The Fountain of Bakhchisarai*, 1849); *Graf Nulin*, 1827 (*Count Nulin*, 1972); *Tsygany*, 1827 (*The Gypsies*, 1957); *Poltava*, 1829 (English translation, 1936); *Domik v Kolomne*, 1833 (*The Little House at Kolomna*, 1977); *Skazka o mertvoy tsarevne*, 1833 (*The Tale of the Dead Princess*, 1924); *Skazka o rybake ir rybke*, 1833 (*The Tale of the Fisherman and the Fish*, 1926); *Skazka o tsare Saltane*, 1833 (*The Tale of Tsar Saltan*, 1950); *Skazka o zolotom petushke*, 1834 (*The Tale of the Golden Cockerel*, 1918); *Medniy vsadnik*, 1837 (*The Bronze Horseman*, 1899); *Collected Narrative and Lyrical Poetry*, 1984; *Epigrams and Satirical Verse*, 1984.

NONFICTION: *Istoriya Pugacheva*, 1834 (*The Pugachev Rebellion*, 1966); *Puteshestviye v Arzrum*, 1836 (*A Journey to Arzrum*, 1974); *Dnevnik, 1833-1835*, 1923; *Pisma*, 1926-1935 (3 volumes); *The Letters of Alexander Pushkin*, 1963 (3 volumes); *Pisma poslednikh let 1834-1837*, 1969.

MISCELLANEOUS: *The Captain's Daughter and Other Tales*, 1933; *The Works of Alexander Pushkin*, 1936; *The Poems, Prose, and Plays of Pushkin*, 1936; *Polnoye sobraniye sochineniy*, 1937-1959 (17 volumes); *The Complete Prose Tales of Alexander Pushkin*, 1966; *Pushkin Threefold*, 1972; *A. S. Pushkin bez tsenzury*, 1972; *Polnoye sobraniye sochineniy*, 1977-1979 (10 volumes); *Alexander Pushkin: Complete Prose Fiction*, 1983.

BIBLIOGRAPHY

Feinstein, Elaine. *Pushkin: A Biography.* Hopewell, New Jersey, 1999. Drawing on recently discovered documents, Feinstein explores the life of one of nineteenth century Russia's greatest writers.

Ryfa, Juras T., ed. *Collected Essays in Honor of the Bicentennial of Alexander Pushkin's Birth.* Lewiston, New York: Edwin Mellen Press, 2000. A selection of scholarly essays devoted to various works by Pushkin and his influence on his literary descendants.

Tertz, Abram. *Strolls with Pushkin.* New Haven, Conn.: Yale University Press, 1994. A free-flowing and sometimes irreverent analysis that critically contests the major works, artistic habits, and persisting cultural legacy of the prominent Russian poet and novelist.

Janet G. Tucker

Q

PHILIPPE QUINAULT

Born: Paris, France; June, 1635
Died: Paris, France; November 26, 1688

PRINCIPAL DRAMA

Les Rivales, pr. 1653
L'Amant indiscret, pb. 1654 (*The Indiscreet Lover*, 1976)
La Comédie sans comédie, pb. 1655
Amalasonte, pb. 1657
Stratonice, pb. 1660
Astrate, pb. c. 1664-1665 (English translation, 1968)
La Mère coquette, pr., pb. 1665
Pausanias, pr. 1668, pb. 1669
Bellérophon, pr., pb. 1671
Psyché, pr. 1671 (libretto, with others)
Cadmus et Hermione, pb. 1673 (libretto)
Alceste, pr., pb. 1674 (libretto; English translation, 1977)
Thésée, pr., pb. 1675 (libretto)
Proserpine, pr., pb. 1680 (libretto)
Roland, pr., pb. 1685 (libretto)
Armide, pr., pb. 1686 (libretto; English translation, 1906)

OTHER LITERARY FORMS

Philippe Quinault is remembered only for his plays and librettos.

ACHIEVEMENTS

During his lengthy literary career, from 1653 to 1686, Philippe Quinault made significant contributions to both drama and opera. His career can be divided into two separate periods. Between 1653 and 1671, he wrote sixteen plays for important Parisian theatrical troupes. Like his eminent contemporary Pierre Corneille, Quinault was a skillful playwright in many dramatic genres. His sixteen plays include seven tragicomedies, five tragedies, three comedies, and *La Comédie sans comédie* (the comedy without comedy), which contains four separate plays-within-a-play. Quinault's masterpieces are *La Comédie sans comédie* and his tragedy *Astrate*. His major dramatic achievements are his well-constructed plots and his elegant and profound treatments of the theme of love. Unfortunately, many critics since the seventeenth century have misinterpreted Quinault's plays. In his *Satires* (1666) and *Dialogue des héros de roman* (c. 1665), the influential critic Nicolas Boileau-Despréaux described Quinault as a playwright incapable of portraying any passion stronger than sentimental love. Many critics have blindly accepted Boileau's simplistic judgment and thus have failed to understand the complex treatment of love in Quinault's plays.

In the early 1670's, Quinault began a new career. On January 17, 1671, there was a lavish court performance of *Psyché*, a play that included musical intermezzos. Corneille, Quinault, Molière, and the composer Jean-Baptiste Lully collaborated on *Psyché*. Quinault wrote the words for three of the intermezzos, which Lully set to music. This performance of *Psyché* was very well received. After this success, Quinault began writing opera librettos for Lully. Lully and Quinault in fact created French opera and had an enormous influence on French opera composers and librettists for more than a century, producing eleven operas between 1673 and 1686.

BIOGRAPHY

Philippe Quinault was baptized in the Parisian church of Saint Eustache on June 5, 1635. Although the date of his birth is unknown, French children then were normally bapitzed within a few days after birth.

Quinault's father was a baker. At the age of ten or eleven, Quinault became a servant to the French playwright Tristan L'Hermite; it appears that Tristan was responsible for the education which Quinault received. In the early 1650's, Quinault began the study of law, and by 1655, he was a lawyer. Quinault was only eighteen years old when a prominent Parisian theater company performed his first play, *Les Rivales*. Between 1653 and 1671, sixteen plays by Quinault were performed in Paris. In 1670, Quinault was elected to the Académie Française.

After the performance in early 1671 of *Bellérophon*, Quinault began a new career. Between 1673 and 1686, he wrote eleven opera librettos for Lully. Their first opera, *Cadmus et Hermione*, was so well received at the royal court that Lully did not want to lose such a valuable librettist. He agreed to pay Quinault four thousand pounds for each libretto. In addition to this substantial sum, Quinault also received an annual pension of two thousand pounds from King Louis XIV. Louis XIV granted such pensions to artists, musicians, and playwrights who had contributed significantly to the cultural life of his

Philippe Quinault (Hulton Archive by Getty Images)

court. When Quinault died in Paris on November 26, 1688, he was a wealthy man. He had also enjoyed a normal family life. On April 29, 1660, Quinault married a young widow, Louise Goujon. They had six children: five daughters, and one son who died in infancy. Two daughters married, while the other three entered religious life. Quinault's widow died on May 5, 1710.

ANALYSIS

Philippe Quinault made significant contributions to the history of French theater and opera. His contemporaries recognized both the brilliance of Lully's music and the high literary quality of Quinault's librettos. Later commentators, including Voltaire, Jean-Jacques Rousseau, and Denis Diderot, who disliked Lully's music, still expressed great admiration for Quinault's librettos. During his eighteen-year career as a stage playwright, Quinault demonstrated his artistry in three separate dramatic genres: tragicomedy, comedy, and tragedy. Though the theme of love dominates Quinault's sixteen plays and eleven operas, Quinault did portray love in several different modes. Since the seventeenth century, Quinault has been famous for his descriptions of altruistic and sentimental lovers, but he also described love in a comic vein and as a destructive passion. Quinault was a gifted playwright and librettist whose works merit the serious attention of theater historians.

Although Quinault wrote twenty-seven full-length works, his masterpieces are clearly the plays *La Comédie sans comédie* and *Astrate* and his libretto *Alceste*. Fortunately, modern editions exist for these three masterpieces.

LA COMÉDIE SANS COMÉDIE

La Comédie sans comédie is a fascinating series of four one-act plays-within-a-play. Quinault wrote *La Comédie sans comédie* for the Parisian Theater of the Marais, and members of this troupe are themselves the major characters in this play, whose unifying theme is theatrical illusion. In the opening act, the characters explain that the main obstacle to their happiness is a middle-class merchant named La Fleur, himself a member of their troupe. La Fleur disdains actors and actresses and does not want his son and daughter, also members of this troupe, to marry people engaged in such a disreputable profession. The other members of the troupe conclude that it is in their own self-interest to convince La Fleur of the excellence of their profession. For the edification of La Fleur and other spectators in the Theater of the Marais, they perform four one-act plays.

Each play-within-a-play illustrates a different contemporary dramatic genre. Act 2 is a pastoral play, act 3 is a farce, act 4 is a tragedy, and act 5 is a tragicomedy that utilizes elaborate stage machinery. Each dramatic genre would normally require three or five acts for a complete play, but the twenty-year-old Quinault was already such a skillful playwright that in each one-act play, he expressed the essential elements of a specific dramatic genre. Both the pastoral play and the farce are very witty. His pastoral play is in fact an elegant parody of traditional pastoral comedies. While act 2 stresses the artificiality of pastoral drama, act 3, the farce entitled "The Glass Doctor," deals with a very strange type of madness. The doctor is convinced that he is made of glass; if others touch him, he may break into pieces. This disturbed doctor also speaks French in a ludicrous and highly Latinate style.

The literary source of acts 4 and 5 is the epic *Gerusalemme conquistata* (1593; *Jerusalem Conquered*, 1907), written by the Italian poet Torquato Tasso (1544-1595). Act 4 describes the fatal love between the Christian prince Tancrède and the pagan warrior Clorinde. Despite their religious differences, the crusader and the infidel love each other deeply. During a battle, however, Clorinde's helmet and armor hide her true identity from Tancrède, who kills her. After her death on the stage, Tancrède pronounces a moving monologue and then commits suicide. The costume worn by the actress playing Clorinde hid her identity and sex and thus created a theatrical illusion. This one-act tragedy also establishes a close link between love and violence.

Act 5 further develops the intimate connection among love, violence, and fate. The main characters in this tragicomedy with machines, set on the enchanted island of Armide, are the pagan magician Armide and the Christian knight Renaud. During the Crusades, Renaud killed many enemies, including several of Armide's cousins, yet after having seen a portrait of Armide, Renaud fell madly in love with her. When he reaches her enchanted island, Armide plans to kill him. The god of Love, however, intervenes and shoots an arrow into her heart. All ends well for the two lovers in this tragicomedy, which illustrates the adage *omnia vincit amor* ("love conquers all"). Quinault makes good use of extensive stage machinery—Armide and the god of Love are frequently suspended in the air—and using such elaborate devices was an essential element in the eleven operas on which he collaborated with Lully. *La Comédie sans comédie* illustrates the fluency and the range of a young playwright who would later write very successful comedies, tragicomedies, tragedies, and opera librettos.

ASTRATE

Astrate is Quinault's masterpiece. Like the one-act tragedy "Tancrède" in *La Comédie sans comédie*, *Astrate* describes a beautiful love that is nevertheless doomed to failure. Like many heroes and heroines in the tragedies of Jean Racine (1639-1699), the two major characters in *Astrate*, the lovers Astrate and Queen Elise, understand lucidly the inexorability of fate and their personal responsibility for setting in motion fate's destructive mechanism.

Long before the action of this tragedy began, Elise's father has overthrown and imprisoned King Adraste. One of King Adraste's young sons was saved from capture by a loyal but unknown subject. After having ascended to the throne herself, Elise ordered the execution of the imprisoned King Adraste in order to ensure the eventual transfer of power to her beloved subject Astrate. She thus committed murder for the sake of love. Despite Astrate's low social status, she prefers him to the politically influential General Agénor, whom her father had designated as her future husband. She realizes that her refusal to marry Agénor may well provoke a military uprising in her kingdom, but she willingly accepts this danger.

The last three acts of *Astrate* are dramatically very successful. Following the second act, Elise transfers to Agénor the royal ring, which symbolizes both her troth and royal power. As she fully expects, Agénor quickly abuses this new power, which gives Queen Elise a convenient excuse to have Agénor arrested. At the very moment when Agénor orders his guards to arrest Astrate, Géraste, the captain of the Queen's guards, enters, arrests Agénor, and transfers the royal ring to Astrate. Elise thus humiliates the haughty Agénor and demonstrates publicly her true love for Astrate.

At the beginning of act 4, however, Astrate learns that there is an insurmountable obstacle to his marriage with Elise. The courtier Sichée has reared Astrate as his own son. Astrate now discovers that he is the son of King Adraste and thus the legitimate heir to the throne. Thanks to the efforts of Sichée, other loyal subjects will soon overthrow the murderous tyrant Elise and place Adraste's sole surviving son on the throne. Sichée argues that justice requires Astrate to sacrifice love for honor. Sichée cannot believe that his "son" could marry a regicide. Whatever he chooses, Astrate will never attain happiness.

When Astrate reveals his true identity to Elise, she is shocked but answers him in a calm and philosophical manner. She now recognizes the close link between fate and personal responsibility. Both she and Astrate realize that it is her fate to die, thus reestablishing moral order in the kingdom. When for the sake of love she freely chose to have King Adraste executed, she grossly violated the moral law and set in motion the destructive and irreversible mechanism of fate.

Act 5 further illustrates the destructive potential of a criminal passion. In order to avoid an ignominious death at the hands of the rebels, Elise must commit suicide. Astrate is unable to accept her death, and he loses all desire to live. At the end of this tragedy, Elise is dead onstage and Astrate has either died of a broken heart or gone mad; the ending is ambiguous. Elise's heinous "crime of love" thus produces three victims: Adraste, herself, and Astrate.

ALCESTE

After *Astrate*, Quinault wrote three more stage plays: one comedy, *La Mère Coquette*, and two tragedies, *Pausanias* and *Bellérophon*. After eighteen years as a successful and prolific playwright, Quinault became the opera librettist for Lully. Although

Quinault and Lully collaborated on eleven operas between 1673 and 1686, *Alceste* is generally considered to be their finest opera.

Alceste exemplifies a creative use of the classical tradition in a new dramatic form. The literary source of this opera is Euripides' powerful tragedy *Alkēstis* (438 B.C.E.; *Alcestis*, 1781). Euripides describes the immense sacrifice made by Alcestis, who, after the death of her husband, Admetus, takes his place in Hades so that he may live again. Quinault's opera contains a fascinating blend of both comic and tragic elements. Quinault totally transformed Euripides' serious tragedy by introducing several comic subplots. In the fourth act of his libretto, Quinault even portrays the crossing of the river Styx, and Charon, the ferryman in the underworld, in a very lighthearted manner. Quinault and Lully strove to furnish elegant and aesthetically pleasing entertainment for Louis XIV and his court. As the chief French patron of the arts during his reign, Louis XIV rewarded handsomely playwrights and composers who had contributed to court performances of plays and operas.

Alceste was first performed on January 12, 1674, in the Parisian theater of the Palais Royal. Six months later, a lavish performance of *Alceste* took place on the Marble Courtyard at the Palace of Versailles before the royal family. *Alceste* became Louis XIV's favorite opera. The five acts of *Alceste* are preceded by a formal overture and an allegorical prologue in praise of Louis XIV's recent military victories. Each of Quinault and Lully's eleven operas begins with an overture and a prologue.

During the first act, preparations are being made to celebrate the forthcoming marriage of Alceste and Admète. In order to complicate the simple plot of Euripides' tragedy, Quinault added several sets of comic and serious lovers. Both the sentimental Alcide and the violent Lycomède still hope to dissuade their beloved Alceste from marrying Admète. Lycomède kidnaps Alceste and imprisons her on his island. While trying to liberate Alceste, Admète is mortally wounded. In addition to these lovers, Quinault created three comic lovers: the fickle Céphise, whom both Straton (Lycomède's confidant) and Lychas (Alcide's confidant) love. One of the highlights of act 1 is a duet between Straton and Céphise. Straton sings the virtues of perfect fidelity in love, while Céphise praises inconstancy. This duet is an elegant parody of a conventional love duet.

Unlike Euripides, Quinault does not limit his work to the magnanimity of his title character. In his opera, Alceste, Admète, and even Alcide all strive to surpass one another with extraordinary acts of generosity. In act 3, Admète discovers to his horror that Alceste has taken his place in Hades. He then expresses both his love for Alceste and his despair in a beautiful recitative: *"Sans Alceste, sans ses appas,/ Croyez-vous que je puisse vivre!"* ("Without Alceste, without her charms,/ Do you believe that I can live!"). Life without Alceste has no meaning for him. Alcide then promises to descend into Hades to bring Alceste back alive, if Admète will yield Alceste to him. Although he loves Alceste, Admète sacrifices his own happiness so that she may live again. For his part, Alcide willingly risks his life for the sake of love.

The fourth act demonstrates the incredible power of love. Charon, the ferryman of the river Styx, opens this act with his recitative: *"Il faut passer tôt ou tard/ Il faut passer dans ma barque"* ("Sooner or later everyone must pass into my boat"). This beautiful set piece has become the most famous recitative in the eleven operas of Quinault and Lully. Alcide's passion is so pure that the eternal laws governing the universe are changed in his favor. Charon must transport him, a living person, across the Styx; Pluto and Proserpina, god and goddess of Hades, allow the dead Alceste to live again and to return to her homeland. As Pluto and Proserpina both agree, love must be stronger than death.

Once back in Greece, Alcide quickly realizes that Admète and Alceste will never be happy if they are separated. Alcide then makes a supreme gesture of magnanimity by yielding Alceste to Admète. Quinault and Lully end their opera in a very lighthearted manner. Straton and Céphise sing witty recitatives on the pleasures of love.

BIBLIOGRAPHY

Connon, Derek, and George Evans, eds. *Essays on French Comic Drama from the 1640s to the 1780s.* New York: Peter Lang, 2000. Provides information on French drama in the seventeenth and eighteenth centuries, when Quinault was active. Bibliography and index.

Norman, Buford. "Ancients and Moderns, Tragedy and Opera: The Quarrel over *Alceste.*" In *French Musical Thought, 1600-1800,* edited by Georgia Cowart. Ann Arbor: University of Michigan Research Press, 1989. An examination of Quinault's *Alceste.*

Norman, Buford, and Michele Vialet. "A Woman's Fate in the Balance: The Persephone Myth in Quinault and Lully's *Proserpine.*" In *Images of Persephone: Feminist Reaching in Western Literature,* edited by Elizabeth T. Hayes. Gainesville: University Press of Florida, 1994. A look at the Persephone myth in Quinault's work.

Smith, Patrick J. *The Tenth Muse: A Historical Study of the Opera Libretto.* New York: Alfred A. Knopf, 1970. This study of librettos touches on Quinault's contribution.

Trott, David, and Nicole Boursier, eds. *The Age of Theater in France.* Edmonton, Alberta, Canada: Academic Printing and Publishing, 1988. This group of papers examines the state of drama in France in the seventeenth and eighteenth centuries, when Quinault was writing.

Edmund J. Campion

R

DAVID RABE

Born: Dubuque, Iowa; March 10, 1940

PRINCIPAL DRAMA

Sticks and Bones, pr. 1969, pb. 1972

The Basic Training of Pavlo Hummel, pr. 1971, pb. 1973

The Orphan, pr. 1973, pb. 1975

In the Boom Boom Room, pr. 1974, pb. 1975 (originally as *Boom Boom Room*, pr. 1973)

The Burning, pr. 1974

Streamers, pr. 1976, pb. 1977

Goose and Tomtom, pr. 1982, pb. 1986

Hurlyburly, pr. 1984, pb. 1985

Those the River Keeps, pr. 1991, pb. 1994

The Vietnam Plays, pb. 1993

A Question of Mercy, pr. 1997, pb. 1998

The Dog Problem, pr. 2000

OTHER LITERARY FORMS

David Rabe is known primarily for his plays and screenplays. He is also the author of two novels, neither of which has been received as favorably as his dramatic works. *Recital of the Dog* (1993), the story of a painter terrorized by a dog, is told with Rabe's characteristic humor and violence. Rabe has also written the novelization of a Sean Penn film, *The Crossing Guard* (1995).

ACHIEVEMENTS

While the aesthetic effectiveness of David Rabe's dramas remains a matter for discussion and debate, it is an easier task to place his work within the context of his contemporaries and their concerns. Modern drama asserts, among other fundamental precepts, that the notion of heroism is outdated and that the principle of the individual's alienation from the community provides the normative social standard. In his plays of disorder, violence, and lack of choice—in his "war" plays, in other words—Rabe conforms to the prevailing tradition as he addresses both psychological and political issues.

Like Eugene O'Neill, Tennessee Williams, and Arthur Miller, Rabe works on both the symbolic, or nonrealistic, and the naturalistic, or realistic, levels. Like Edward Albee, he uses surrealist or absurdist elements as he explores the implications of the failure of human contact, the enervation of American social values, the interplay between past and present, and the overwhelming finality of death. His misfits, like those of Lanford Wilson, endure a course of failure that he ordains for them, and Rabe attempts, as does Arthur Kopit, to chart their psychological landscapes as they struggle with the perennial question of identity. As Sam Shepard reveals the distorted, destructive fabric of family relationships and the commercialized corruption of American society, so does Rabe attempt to account for the same bewildering phenomena.

Although Rabe's characters exist too firmly in an abstracted, topical dimension, his ritualistic evocation of their alienated conditions functions, in an inverse manner, to call attention to their need for genuine human interaction. If he is not as successful as many of his contemporaries in sustaining dialogue with his audience, if the impact of his works is not as likely to endure, Rabe still asks significant questions in his plays.

Rabe has been the recipient of many awards. *The Basic Training of Pavlo Hummel* received the Obie Award, the Drama Desk Award, and the award of the *Variety* Critics Poll. The Outer Circle Critics Award and the New York Drama Critics Circle citation went to *Sticks and Bones*. Rabe received the National Institute of Arts and Letters Award in 1974 and a second award from the prestigious New York Drama Critics Circle in 1976 for *Streamers*. He was nominated for the Antoinette Perry (Tony) Award for best play in 1974 for *In the Boom Boom Room* and in 1985 for *Hurlyburly*; he won the Tony Award for best play in 1971-1972 for *Sticks and Bones*.

BIOGRAPHY

David Rabe was born on March 10, 1940, in Dubuque, Iowa, where he attended Roman Catholic parochial schools. He began to write short stories and plays while an undergraduate at Loras College, a Catholic institution in Dubuque, from which he was graduated in 1962 with a B.A. in English. He was drafted into the army in 1965 and served with a hospital support unit at Long Binh, South Vietnam. Although he did not go into actual combat himself, he observed many casualties. After his discharge in early 1967, he resumed his interrupted graduate studies at Villanova University and earned a master's degree in 1968. While at Villanova, he wrote the draft scripts of *The Basic Training of Pavlo Hummel* and *Sticks and Bones*, inspired by his experiences of Vietnam and then of the United States as encountered by a returned Vietnam veteran. Under the auspices of Joseph Papp's New York Shakespeare Festival, *The Basic Training of Pavlo Hummel* opened in New York at the Public Theatre on May 20, 1971, with *Sticks and Bones* following, also at the Public Theatre, on November 7 of the same year. With these productions, Rabe was saluted by many critics as a most promising young dramatist.

Rabe's third play, *The Orphan*, a puzzling retelling of the dramas of Aeschylus that made repeated allusions to Vietnam, was roundly criticized. With his fourth play, *In the Boom Boom Room* (originally produced in 1973 as *Boom Boom Room* and later revised and retitled), Rabe turned his focus away from

the Vietnam experience to depict the life of a young go-go dancer, but the play received a lukewarm response. In 1976, though, Rabe returned to the Vietnam War as the setting for *Streamers*, which again brought him wide praise.

Rabe's long professional relationship with Joseph Papp and the Public Theatre in New York was jeopardized in 1982, when a production of *Goose and Tomtom* was put into rehearsal at the Public Theatre but was disavowed by Rabe because of aesthetic differences in interpretation. "I despaired of it," said Rabe, when Papp misinterpreted the relationship between the two title characters.

Despite the critical and commercial success of *Hurlyburly* on Broadway in 1984, it did not receive any major awards (although Judith Ivey won a Tony

David Rabe in 1972. (AP/Wide World Photos)

Award for her performance in the play). Rabe was dissatisfied with Mike Nichols's direction of the production and reworked the play for a later production (1989) under his own direction.

After six years of silence, except for screenplay work such as *Casualties of War* (1989), Rabe's play *Those the River Keeps* was produced in 1991. It tells the story of Phil, a popular character from *Hurlyburly*, before the action of *Hurlyburly* begins. Although audiences continued to respond to Phil, the prequel did not receive the praise of *Hurlyburly*.

In 1997, Rabe adapted an essay by physician-writer Richard Selzer into a new play, *A Question of Mercy*. It tells the story of a physician whose patient, dying of AIDS, asks the doctor to help him commit suicide. For many critics, *A Question of Mercy* was a triumph, Rabe's most powerful play in decades. It was followed in 2000 by *The Dog Problem*, a comedy about the Italian Mafia, adapted from his own early fifteen-minute play.

During the 1990's, Rabe continued to work on screenplays, including the adaptation of John Grisham's *The Firm*, and also wrote two novels, *Recital of the Dog* (1993) and *The Crossing Guard*, a novelization of a Sean Penn screenplay. *In the Boom Boom Room* was revived in New York in 2002, to generally favorable reviews, demonstrating Rabe's ability to craft works that transcend their original time period.

Rabe has been married since 1979 to actress Jill Clayburgh, who starred in the 1982 *I'm Dancing As Fast As I Can*, a Rabe screenplay.

ANALYSIS

Many of David Rabe's strongest works are closely linked thematically to the late 1960's and early 1970's in America. He expresses this turbulent era of the debilitating war in Vietnam, racial strife in the streets, the horrific murders by Charles Manson's clan, the puzzling generation gap, and the confusing sexual revolution as a dramatic world of violent confrontation. For the individual living in this setting, its most salient features are racial and sexual turmoil, family disintegration, social isolation, and personal inarticulateness. Whether the scene is an army barracks room, a middle-class American home, the an-

cient Greece of Aeschylus's *Oresteia* (458 B.C.E.; English translation, 1777), or a slimy bar in Philadelphia, Rabe's characters live on a metaphoric battlefield. His plays, then, are war plays, and his protagonists lose their separate struggles with dispiriting inevitability. The chaos of their lives is figured, institutionalized, and sometimes justified by ritualistic activities that are symbolic of their alienation and lack of choice rather than of the communal experience and support that ritual ordinarily celebrates.

THE VIETNAM PLAYS

Rabe's intense, critical reflections on the interrelatedness of war, sex, racism, the family, past, and present as they define the contemporary American battlefield are frequently provocative. His dramatic world of streamers is, however, all of a piece. Lacking complexity and nuance, it only sporadically achieves, beyond the transitory moment, the sustained dialogue between dramatist and playgoer or reader that is the essence of great art.

The title of *Streamers* suggests the bleak vision of Rabe's work: A "streamer" is a parachute which unexpectedly fails to open, a fragile ribbon of silk that simply trails the unlucky jumper as he plummets toward his death. As he leaps out of the secure womb of the airplane, he is born, after a few seconds, into a brief life characterized by the terror of circumstance, the rule of irrationality, and the absence of alternatives to the destruction awaiting him. There is no possibility of introspection or insight and no reality except for the unambiguous fact of personal annihilation. Like the parachutist, the main characters in Rabe's plays are hurriedly discovering death.

Although *The Basic Training of Pavlo Hummel*, *Sticks and Bones*, and *Streamers*, with their episodes of ritualistic violence, are often referred to as Rabe's "Vietnam trilogy," only the first includes actual combat, and that only briefly. Rabe uses the war in Vietnam as a generalized background for his presentation of the violence endemic to American life. In response to critics who proposed the "antiwar" label as an appropriate description of his work, Rabe asserted that he expected to achieve no political effect but simply sought to identify and diagnose the informing cultural and social phenomena around him.

THE BASIC TRAINING OF PAVLO HUMMEL

In *The Basic Training of Pavlo Hummel*, the time-honored ritual of army basic training generates the controlling metaphor: the four-beat cadence of a basic training company's marching and singing, the formal dance of bayonet practice, the impending trainee proficiency test. Into this arena, the classic loser Pavlo enters, leaving his dreary existence behind and seeking the clear confirmation of physical courage and sexual virility he expects military heroism to afford him. The two-act play opens with Pavlo's ironic, nonheroic death in a Saigon whorehouse, following an argument with an army sergeant over a prostitute. The play then flashes back to portray the stages of Pavlo's journey to this grim end. The drill sergeant's tower, a constant reminder of army ritual, commands the stage.

Unfortunately for Pavlo, his pathetic expectations of army life clash with everything the audience sees about the army and the war. His enthusiasm for a career as an army "lifer" and his desire to excel in the community that is superficially symbolized by army ritual actually exclude him from his fellow draftees and from a realistic perspective on the war itself. As a foil to almost everyone else in the play, Pavlo is most clearly exemplified by his consistent naïveté and stupid fervor. For example, he persistently volunteers for menial duties and eagerly performs supplemental physical training. He takes solitary bayonet and port arms practice when he should be in formation and anxiously studies the conduct manual for the upcoming proficiency test.

In act 2, Pavlo enjoys the sexual experience that eluded him on his leave, despite his snappy dress uniform. The sergeant drills the men on one side of the stage as Pavlo makes four-beat love to Yen on the other. Reluctantly serving as a medic in a field hospital, Pavlo refuses to comprehend the vivid example of a soldier blown into a living stump. Only after he is actually wounded in combat does Pavlo recognize the vicious truth of the infantryman's plight on the field. Whereas he formerly associated acts of violence in the barracks or on the battlefield with an affirmation of manhood, Pavlo simply wants to go home after he is wounded for the third time. Rewarded, instead, with a Purple Heart, he retreats to the whorehouse for a dalliance with Yen and the assignation with the grenade that finally kills him.

From start to finish, Pavlo Hummel is doomed—as trainee, medic, or combat infantryman. Army ritual overtly offers community, song, and some humor as both a mask and an excuse for the violence that awaits Pavlo. Life for the enlisted man in Vietnam, however, actually means every man for himself. The interweaving of past and present, the use of simultaneous action, and the play's Surrealist and absurdist elements demonstrate Pavlo's self-centered confusion and his failure to develop. In some respects, he is so one-dimensional that it is difficult to maintain sympathy for him.

STICKS AND BONES

Like *The Basic Training of Pavlo Hummel*, *Sticks and Bones* begins with the ending, the ritualistic suicide of the protagonist David, a blinded Vietnam veteran. Shockingly, his father, mother, and younger brother encourage and assist him in this act. As Pavlo's army "family" rebuffs him, so do Ozzie, Harriet, and Ricky reject David. Unlike Pavlo, however, David denies his family, too; they mutually repel one another. In his naming of the characters, Rabe parodies the popular situation comedy *The Adventures of Ozzie and Harriet*: This middle-class American family is the antithesis of the television Nelsons.

The ritual matter of *Sticks and Bones* arises from what Rabe considers the symbols of modern American culture: racism and television. Both destroy communication and, thus, indicate the mutual alienation of David and his family. Television offers a desirable fantasy life redolent of money and materialism. Related to sexual fear and insecurity, racism answers the need to feel superior to some group. From the instant when David is virtually delivered home, he and his family are strangers to one another. Ozzie even considers checking his son's dental records to verify his identity.

Although he is physically blind, David's moral vision has been expanded by his experiences in Vietnam and also by his sense of guilt over the Vietnamese girl, Zung, whom he loved but, typically, deserted. A symbol of continuity between his past and present, the wraithlike Zung appears intermittently throughout the play and, until the climax, is "seen" by David only. She embodies the immediate motivation for the mission he assumes in his parents' home, as their moral blindness is exemplified by virulent racial and sexual prejudice. Their contempt for the Vietnamese recalls that of the soldiers in *The Basic Training of Pavlo Hummel* in its perverted preoccupation with sex. Neither Ozzie nor Harriet can tolerate the notion that David might have engendered children with yellow faces and, worse, that he might have brought them home. Both in the field and at home, Rabe charges, the Vietnamese are despised by the Americans, who profess to help them.

David's abrasive presence and his withering accusations cause his parents' superficial veneer of middle-class respectability to blister and peel away. Ozzie is deeply troubled that his combat experience has been confined to his safe childhood, when he regularly beat up "Ole Fat Kramer." During World War II, his army service consisted of truck maintenance. Operating as a catalytic agent, then, David releases his father's suppressed capacity for violence. Zung becomes visible to Ozzie, who, refusing to "see" her, nevertheless strangles her. Ricky suggests that David should cut his wrists, and Harriet provides pans and towels so that the blood will not stain the carpet. With this ritualistic self-sacrifice, David is exorcised from the mainstream of the middle-class consciousness and can pose no further challenge to the self-deluded but triumphant American way of life.

In this grotesque family portrait, Rabe demonstrates that domestic violence is as terrible as the military violence in Vietnam. Through language and action, he indicates the irreconcilable division within the family and charges that racism was a basic cause of the war in Vietnam. The polarization of the family, concurrently, is a source of the play's most disabling flaw. The dramatist would have his audience simplistically concede that a blinded Vietnam veteran, by definition, possesses greater moral stature than his family, that he is entitled, because of his combat experiences, to instruct them in moral concerns. David's sufferings, however, have not enhanced his capacity for understanding and compassion, the requi-

sites for the moral stature he assumes, but have only refined his ability to hate. Like Ozzie, Harriet, and Rick, David remains a cipher despite the truth of much of his indictment of American life.

Additionally, the names of the characters finally detract from Rabe's message as well because their names isolate them from the audience. The television Nelson clan, in all its saccharine perfection, is so one-dimensional a target that the playwright's generalizations about middle-class America become increasingly difficult to accept. Nevertheless, taken in conjunction with *The Basic Training of Pavlo Hummel*, *Sticks and Bones* presents a disturbing portrayal of the divisive features of American military and domestic experience in the late 1960's.

THE ORPHAN

The Orphan is Rabe's most intellectually complex play, but it is marred by thematic diffuseness. Instead of using modern war as the background, the playwright employs Aeschylus's *Oresteia*, with its informing theme of violence within the family, as a framework for his consideration of the related phenomena of Vietnam and My Lai, governmental apathy, commercial obsession, and the Manson murders. As in *Sticks and Bones*, the source of all corruption resides in the family. Touchstones of modern American culture are sex, drugs, business, and killing. The rigid progression of cause to effect enslaves men, and past becomes present as men and women seem literally born to kill.

Murder is so common that it achieves the status of ritual, its rites observable in governmental policy statements, the entrails of birds, current scientific explanations, and hallucinatory drug rampages—all the same and all unavoidable. As a part of this ritual, language itself becomes automatic and thus debased: It helps to isolate people from one another by preserving the gaping distinctions between them. As such, it, too, is a blunt instrument of destruction.

Act 1 concerns the sacrifice of Iphegenia over the impassioned opposition of Clytemnestra 1 and the resultant murder of Agamemnon by Clytemnestra 2 and Aegisthus; act 2 entails Orestes' revenge on his mother and her lover. From the tub in which Agamemnon is slaughtered, Orestes is born in act 2, blood-soaked and wrapped in the placenta-like net in which his father died: Life's violent course is ordained from the moment of birth. In this same tub, the bound Clytemnestras—their simultaneous presence indicative of the identity between past and present—will be killed by Orestes. The womb, then, greatly resembles a grave.

Orestes' revenge against Aegisthus reiterates both the Manson murders and the My Lai massacre; depravity and murder are nearly sanctified by their regularity in this world. Tainted by violence, Orestes is left literally suspended between the uncaring gods of heaven and the waiting Furies on earth, abandoned and deluded.

Although *The Orphan* makes provocative statements about modern American society, it founders on its diffusion of images and on its categorical statement that the United States is a murderous wasteland. If Orestes' revenge is justifiable according to the myth, then the Manson murders and My Lai cannot be explained according to the same criterion. The audience withdraws because, to an even greater extent than in *The Basic Training of Pavlo Hummel* and *Sticks and Bones*, the characters are totally manipulated in the service of the prevailing doctrine. Without alternative or ambiguity, they and *The Orphan* become morally artificial and intellectually confused. The spurting gore undercuts its own effect.

IN THE BOOM BOOM ROOM

With *In the Boom Boom Room*, the scene shifts to a deteriorating, neon-lit section of Philadelphia in the mid-1960's. Once more, sex, violence, racism, self-deception, and inarticulateness are the interrelated themes. Although Vietnam is not a factor in this play, the characters live in an urban jungle in which the strong defeat and brutalize the weak. Chrissy, an aspiring go-go dancer who wants to become good enough to succeed in New York, is doomed in her struggle for individuality because she is a vulnerable woman in a man's world. Ironically, the lives of the various men in Chrissy's sphere are as rigidly circumscribed and hopeless as hers.

Chrissy is Rabe's only female protagonist, but she has much in common with her male counterparts. Past and present intermingle to show that she is vic-

timized by everyone she knows: her parents, her boyfriends, her lover, her homosexual neighbor, and the bisexual dance captain at the Boom Boom Room. Like Rabe's other protagonists, she has little self-awareness.

With their associations of physical and mental imprisonment, spiritual isolation, and sexual exhibitionism, the go-go cages provide the continuous backdrop for the action. The controlling metaphor—and the ritual—grows out of the animalistic, solitary go-go dance itself. To be able to perform the Monkey and the Jerk fluidly and sensually will enable Chrissy to transfer to the elite realm of the go-go world, but the names of these dances symbolize the degradation that is her actual present and her future lot. Everyone wants something from her, most often sex, but no one loves her, starting with the mother who nearly aborted her.

A thief and a drunk like her father, Chrissy's brutal, emotionally impotent lover, Al, destroys her professional hopes and, concomitantly, her ability to order her life. In an argument suffused with the sexism and racism also fundamental to *The Basic Training of Pavlo Hummel* and *Sticks and Bones*, Al beats Chrissy bloody. In the final scene of the play, she has come to New York, but as a masked topless dancer. She is completely anonymous, alone, and dehumanized.

In the Boom Boom Room is like *The Orphan* in its consistent despair about the human condition, but it lacks the intellectual gamesmanship that is the major interest of *The Orphan*. Rabe's reflections on violence in modern America as seen through an Oresteian glass invite the audience—or more effectively, perhaps, the reader—to become sufficiently engaged by his philosophical comparisons between ancient and contemporary, mythical and mundane to treat them skeptically. The action of *In the Boom Boom Room*, however, adheres to a static, linear structure in which Chrissy does not develop as a personality but in which the quality of her life inexorably deteriorates. Although it is finally difficult to sympathize with Pavlo and David, one can discern a measure of conflict and vitality in their lives. Chrissy never has a chance.

STREAMERS

Rabe returns to the thematic background of the American experience in Vietnam in *Streamers*, his most persuasive play because it is his most straightforward. It concentrates exclusively on the interactions of four young army enlisted men, each of whom exemplifies a different facet of American society. Foregoing the flashbacks and the special effects of his earlier plays, Rabe here achieves sustained focus: The four characters form a desperate Family of Man in the barracks room.

Their clashing ideas about war, sex, and racism transform this barracks crucible into a battlefield on which violence is as certain, and as deadly, as the violence that awaits them in Vietnam. Their metaphorical parachutes have failed to open, and the matter of the play chronicles their fall to earth, streamers floating uselessly above them. Two older sergeants, Cokes and Rooney, one suffering from leukemia and the other an alcoholic, represent the general way that the four recruits are destined to go. As the exhausted members of the previous generation of cannon fodder, they introduce the song, set to the tune of Stephen Foster's "Beautiful Dreamer," which provides the ritualistic foundation of the play: "Beautiful streamer,/ Open for me,/ The sky is above me,/ But no canopy."

Like the parachutist and like Rabe's other characters, Roger, Billy, Richie, and Carlyle have no control over their lives. For them, there is no escape from the barracks except through violence. If they survive the battlefield in the barracks, then the elephant traps in Vietnam loom before them. Isolated from the external world, they find no philosophical, racial, or sexual comradeship within the army either.

For example, Cokes and Rooney are embittered career men whose prolonged experiences of combat in World War II cause them simultaneously to envy and despise the two-year recruits. Blacks, represented by Roger and Carlyle, and whites, represented by Billy and Richie, live together warily, with ready recourse to a switchblade or an epithet. The homosexual Richie belongs to the army's least visible, most defensive, minority. Rabe clearly establishes these categories within the army of the Vietnam era, but he succeeds in transcending them to an extent that he does not achieve in *The Basic Training of Pavlo Hummel* and *Sticks and Bones*: The army in *Streamers* is a credible microcosm of American society at large.

Roger and Billy, black and white, exemplify the conventional middle-class stance. They ambitiously want to leave this holding company and get into the real army, yet it is understandably difficult for them to absorb the fierce prospect of Vietnam into their lives. Carlyle is a ghetto black terrified of the deadly fate that the army obviously, and casually, reserves for him, and Richie is a spoiled white in the process of adjusting to his homosexuality. They constitute a counterpoint to Roger and Billy, and their personal relationship inspires the crisis. Carlyle is the patented Rabean grenade who shatters the delicate equilibrium achieved by the other three; in this sense, his function resembles that of Pavlo and David in earlier Rabe plays. Alienated by his race, education, and social status, Carlyle loathes American society in general and the war in particular.

The two outcasts, Carlyle and Richie, deserted by their fathers and by conventional society, connect in a sexual relationship born as much from lonely despair as from physical craving. Roger can accept this situation, while Billy, on the other hand, is enraged by this desecration of his barracks "house." His aggressive cries of outrage abruptly end as Carlyle repeatedly stabs him in the stomach in a fatal parody of the sexual act. The drunken Rooney literally stumbles into the fight's aftermath and inadvertently becomes Carlyle's next victim. As in many of Rabe's plays, mindless violence prevails.

Richie and Roger, white and black, homosexual and heterosexual, have survived the barracks, but Vietnam, with its myriad opportunities for the unanticipated situations that produce streamers, awaits. If they survive Vietnam, there is always, as *Sticks and Bones* reveals, the home front.

There are no simple explanations for the characters' motivations and actions in *Streamers*, and thus Rabe surpasses his previous work. He blends the themes of war, sex, racism, family, and resultant chaos without relying upon a schematic, predictable plot, exhibited at its least effective in *In the Boom Boom Room.*

Although *Streamers* is a sounder play, structurally, than Rabe's prior dramas, it partakes of a full measure of their informing cynicism and despair. In all of his plays through *Streamers*, the dramatist establishes some expression of ritual as a reflection of disorder. People live in a world so irrational that there is virtually no order to subvert. This ethos contributes much to the spectacular, bloody stageworthiness of the plays and is, further, a direct function of their topicality. Their effectiveness depends crucially on an audience's experience of American political, social, and cultural history in the second half of the 1960's and the early 1970's.

This topicality is the source of both the strength and the weakness of Rabe's plays. For those who lived through the Vietnam era, the plays have a visceral, emotional impact that compensates, to some degree, for the stylization of the characters, their lack of alternatives, and their failure to develop. At the same time, however, like Rabe's characters, the plays become victims of this topical concentration. With the exception of *Streamers*, they cannot transcend their particular time and place.

HURLYBURLY

Rabe's *Hurlyburly* appeared in New York in 1984 to general critical acclaim. This play marks both a continuation from and a break with his artistic past. The battlefield moves from Vietnam to the vicious jungle of Hollywood, but the prevailing violence and the fragmentation of the characters' lives preclude the need for even a gesture toward the sort of ironic ritual that pervades his earlier plays.

The bungalow shared by Eddie and Mickey, two casting directors, provides a drug-inspired arena for the testing conflicts that are acted out between the male characters and, even more hideously, for their brutal expressions of fear and hatred for the various women who pliantly stumble into their lives. The world of *Hurlyburly* lacks moral focus of any sort. As Rabe stated in an interview in *The New York Times* that accompanied the play's opening, the contemporary scene offers "philosophies that aren't philosophies, answers that aren't answers, one pharmaceuti-

cal solution after another." Repellently dazzling as the play's language is, it reiterates the playwright's recurring theme: the willed failure to communicate, to care.

THOSE THE RIVER KEEPS

Those the River Keeps focuses on the character Phil, a former convict who had also appeared as a struggling actor in *Hurlyburly.* In *Those the River Keeps*, Phil is confronted by an acquaintance from his criminal past who attempts to lure him back to a life of crime. Rabe once described the play as an "invitation/seduction" and remarked cryptically, "It's literal in one way, and in another way it's not."

The title, according to Rabe, refers to forces from one's past that are strong enough to keep pulling, no matter how one tries to pull away. Although the theme—that human attempts to move forward are ultimately doomed—is rather bleak, the play is darkly humorous, as characters express their frustration with life by wittily insulting each other.

A QUESTION OF MERCY

A Question of Mercy marked Rabe's triumphant return to critical and popular acclaim after more than a decade of lukewarm reception. Unlike many of Rabe's most significant plays, *A Question of Mercy* is informed less by the perils of a particular location (Vietnam or California) than by the struggles within one human heart. This difference is due in part to the fact that Rabe wrote the play as an adaptation of a nonfiction article by another writer, the physician Richard Selzer. However, the play is unmistakably Rabe's, sharing with the earlier work a theme of the hopelessness of human endeavor, and a focus on contemporary concerns, in this case the issues of AIDS (acquired immunodeficiency syndrome) and assisted suicide.

When Anthony, the young man at the center of the play, realizes he is dying of AIDS, he turns to his lover Thomas for help in ending his life painlessly. Together Thomas and Anthony turn to a retired doctor, Robert Chapman, to assist Anthony in committing suicide. As the group works through a plan to end Anthony's life, their good intentions go wrong, and the plan and the bonds begin to unravel. The play follows the conflicts of the three main characters:

Thomas, torn between his desire to help Anthony and his fear of legal trouble; the doctor, torn between his longing for meaningful contact with his patients and the realization that what Anthony needs from him is not a cure, but help dying; and Anthony himself, who is unconvincing in his declarations that he is ready to die.

In the end, the question of the merits of assisted suicide is unresolved; this is not a diatribe. Rabe is more interested in the characters' struggles than in what ultimately happens to Anthony, who swings back and forth from dying to living to dying again in the last act. The focus in the end is on the survivors who, like Rabe's other significant characters, are left isolated and unfulfilled.

THE DOG PROBLEM

Like *Those the River Keeps*, *The Dog Problem* draws on jokes about organized crime on the East Coast, but in *The Dog Problem* the gangsters are merely clowns. This parody of gangster stories revolves around a couple, Ray and Teresa, who share a sexual encounter with their dog Ed. When Teresa's brother learns of the affair, he contacts a friend in the mob to avenge the family honor. The critics dealt harshly with the play, finding the jokes weak and the violence needlessly cruel.

OTHER MAJOR WORKS

LONG FICTION: *Recital of the Dog*, 1993; *The Crossing Guard*, 1995 (adaptation of Sean Penn's screenplay).

SCREENPLAYS: *I'm Dancing as Fast as I Can*, 1982 (adaptation of Barbara Gordon's novel); *Streamers*, 1983 (adaptation of his play); *Casualties of War*, 1989; *The Firm*, 1993 (with Robert Towne and Davis Rayfiel; adaptation of John Grisham's novel); *Hurlyburly*, 1998 (adaptation of his play).

BIBLIOGRAPHY

Bigsby, C. W. E. *Beyond Broadway*. Vol. 3 in *A Critical Introduction to Twentieth-Century American Drama*. Cambridge, England: Cambridge University Press, 1985. The introduction to part 5, "The Theatre of Commitment," includes a long discussion of Rabe's work. Bigsby is respectful of the power and importance of Rabe's work through *Streamers*. He says that Rabe's Vietnam plays are less "about war than about loneliness and self-betrayal; less an account of political perfidy than of the failure of private morality."

Cohn, Ruby. *New American Dramatists, 1960-1990*. 2d ed. New York: St. Martin's Press, 1991. Cohn once called this chapter "Narrower Straits" but renamed it "Roaming Around" to point at an orientation away from Broadway conventions in the plays of Rabe, Ronald Ribman, John Guare, and David Henry Hwang. Notes the revision of the early version of *In the Boom Boom Room* in 1986 but is silent regarding the hiatus from *Hurlyburly* to 1990.

Cole, Susan Letzler. *Playwrights in Rehearsal: The Seduction of Company*. New York: Routledge, 2001. Cole participated in rehearsals of plays by eight contemporary playwrights, to discover the writer's role in bringing a script to the stage. The chapter on Rabe follows the creative process in developing *A Question of Mercy*.

Demastes, William W., and Michael Vanden Heuvel. "The Hurlyburly Lies of the Causalist Mind: Chaos and the Realism of Rabe and Shepard." In *Realism and the American Dramatic Tradition*, William W. Demastes, ed. Tuscaloosa: University of Alabama Press, 1996. Examines realism and its relationship to chaos in plays by Rabe and by Sam Shepard.

Herman, William. *Understanding Contemporary American Drama*. Columbia: University of South Carolina Press, 1987. Places *Hurlyburly* in the Shakespearean context of despair as an aftereffect of war. Discusses some individual works at length but calls others "a small body of less assured and less coherent drama," including Rabe's favorite, *Goose and Tomtom*. Good bibliography of primary and secondary sources.

Kolin, Philip C. *David Rabe: A Stage History and a Primary and Secondary Bibliography*. New York: Garland, 1988. The first source for factual information and continuing study of the playwright, including a chronology of productions. The secondary bibliography is valuable for pursuing criticism on individual plays and reviews of first productions.

McDonough, Carla J. *Staging Masculinity: Male Identity in Contemporary American Drama*. Jefferson, N.C.: McFarland, 1997. McDonough examines typical male characters by eight contemporary male playwrights, including Rabe. She finds that in Rabe's work, masculinity itself is a problematic issue for his troubled characters.

Savran, David. *In Their Own Words: Contemporary American Playwrights*. New York: Theatre Communications Group, 1988. Rabe is interviewed here in 1986 after the success and anguish of *Hurlyburly*. The brief biographical notes include discussions of his writing habits, his relations with directors, and his problems with Mike Nichols's direction of *Hurlyburly*.

Zinman, Toby Silverman. "What's Wrong with This Picture? David Rabe's Comic-Strip Plays." In *Modern Dramatists: A Casebook of Major British, Irish, and American Playwrights*, Kimball King, ed. New York: Routledge, 2001. This essay, which compares the bold characterization in Rabe's plays to that in comic strips, appeared in the earlier volume *David Rabe: A Casebook*. Its inclusion here makes it easier for readers to see Rabe's work in the context of work by other writers from the latter third of the twentieth century.

Zinman, Toby Silverman, ed. *David Rabe: A Casebook*. New York: Garland, 1991. Contains nineteen articles, including an interview. Separate chapters provide Rabe's comments on Vietnam, *Streamers*, *Sticks and Bones*, and *Goose and Tomtom*.

Janet S. Hertzbach,
updated by Thomas J. Taylor, Robert McClenaghan,
and Cynthia A. Bily

JEAN RACINE

Born: La Ferté-Milon, France; December, 1639
Died: Paris, France; April 21, 1699

PRINCIPAL DRAMA

La Thébaïde: Ou, Les Frères ennemis, pr., pb. 1664 (*The Theban Brothers*, 1723)

Alexandre le Grand, pr. 1665, pb. 1666 (*Alexander the Great*, 1714)

Andromaque, pr. 1667, pb. 1668 (*Andromache*, 1674)

Les Plaideurs, pr. 1668, pb. 1669 (*The Litigants*, 1715)

Britannicus, pr. 1669, pb. 1670 (English translation, 1714)

Bérénice, pr. 1670, pb. 1671 (English translation, 1676)

Bajazet, pr., pb. 1672 (English translation, 1717)

Mithridate, pr., pb. 1673 (*Mithridates*, 1926)

Iphigénie, pr. 1674, pb. 1675 (*Iphigenia in Aulis*, 1700)

Phèdre, pr., pb. 1677 (*Phaedra*, 1701)

Idylle sur la paix, pb. 1685 (libretto, with Jean-Baptiste Lully)

Esther, pr., pb. 1689 (English translation, 1715)

Athalie, pr., pb. 1691 (*Athaliah*, 1722)

The Dramatic Works of Jean Racine, pb. 1889

The Best Plays of Racine, pb. 1936

Five Plays, pb. 1960

The Complete Plays, pb. 1967

OTHER LITERARY FORMS

Jean Racine's reputation rests on a relatively limited dramatic œuvre. Nevertheless, Racine published a number of other works during his literary career. Among these are several odes celebrating Louis XIV in the early 1660's; a polemical letter attacking his

Jansenist mentors in 1666; a collection of religious poems, *Cantiques spirituels* (1694); and an unfinished defense of the Jansenists, *Abrégé de l'histoire de Port-Royal* (1742, 1767). To accompany his plays, Racine also wrote critical prefaces in which he vigorously defended himself against his detractors.

ACHIEVEMENTS

Racinian tragedy is the supreme expression of French seventeenth century classical literature, a period called *le grand siècle* (the grand century), a golden age of French art, literature, and architecture. This cultural efflorescence centered on the Sun King, Louis XIV, whom the ambitious Jean Racine assiduously courted. For the playwright, the famous rules of French drama were not fetters that hampered the full realization of his genius but rather intrinsic elements of what only can be called the Racinian "tone." Racine offers, as he states in the preface to *Britannicus*,

Jean Racine (Library of Congress)

"A simple action, charged with little subject matter, necessary in an action which must occur in a single day, and which, moving forward by degrees, is sustained only by the interests, the sentiments, and the passions of the characters." The simplicity, violence, and elegance of Racine's style create a tone of "majestic sadness" (an expression of Racine) concerning the human condition. His noble and grandiose protagonists confront their tragic destiny with lucidity and humanity. The result is a fusion of psychological realism and a restrained grandeur that is the soul of classical art.

Like all great artists, Racine has enjoyed periods of adulation alternating with periods of scorn and derision. In his own century, he rapidly eclipsed Pierre Corneille's renown with apparently simple plays in which pathos and emotion replaced Corneillian intellectuality and complexity. It is significant that the great codifier of French classicism, Nicolas Boileau, defined tragedy according to the Racinian model in his *L'Art poétique* (1674). The struggle between disciples of Corneille and Racine continued in the eighteenth century, but most commentators looked on Racinian tragedy as a model of perfection. Its adherence to the rules of reason and nature, according to the Age of Voltaire, made it the quintessence of the French spirit. With the rise of Romanticism in the nineteenth century, a polemical criticism developed that declared that the slavish imitation of the Racinian model had impeded the evolution of French theater in the eighteenth century. This reaction saw Racine as too cramped by convention and courtly etiquette to permit a true depiction of human emotions. Later in the century, however, a new nationalistic fervor elevated Racine to the status of a national idol, the epitome of *le grand siècle*. In numerous and varied studies, the twentieth century, for the most part, rescued Racine from the purely historical approach of the preceding century. Most recent studies adopt a sociological, theological, or psychoanalytical premise that serves to elucidate Racine's life and work. Thus, Racine's plays emerge as an expression of Jansenist theology, a firm rejection of the baroque style, or as a genuine reflection of Racine's psyche. Other studies have focused on the recurrent elements and structural patterns that are then used to define Racine's work.

BIOGRAPHY

Born in December, 1639, to a bourgeois family of La Ferté-Milon (about forty miles northeast of Paris), Jean Racine was left an orphan at the age of four and was adopted by his paternal grandmother. In 1649, his penurious grandmother sought refuge at the celebrated center of Jansenism, Port-Royal, where Racine received an excellent education in Latin as well as Greek. Jansenism, which upheld the doctrine of predestination and insisted on the helplessness of humankind without divine grace, can be described as a kind of Calvinistic Catholicism. Denying free will and practicing a very rigorous code of morality, the Jansenists reproved the more relaxed tenets of the dominant and rival Jesuits. Although many critics have focused on a Jansenist orientation in the plays, it is uncertain whether Racine was a Jansenist during his literary career or indeed whether his teachers actually inculcated their theology in their pupils.

After four years at Port-Royal, Racine spent two years at the Collège de Beauvais, then three more at Port-Royal, and finally completed his education in Paris at the Collège d'Harcourt. Racine's austere and scholarly masters (called *solitaires*, the solitary persons) introduced the young Racine to the Bible and ancient literature. In an age in which education was based on Latin, Racine was fortunate to acquire a thorough knowledge of Greek. He read in the original ancient Greek tragedy, notably Sophocles and Euripides, and most critics point to the Hellenistic simplicity and the mysterious force of destiny so characteristic of Racine's plays. In Paris, the ambitious Racine wrote poetry and cultivated many literary acquaintances. His first published piece, an ode in honor of Louis XIV's marriage, appeared in 1660, and earned for Racine a small royal gratification. Racine's first play, "L'Amasie," now lost, was rejected; a second attempt at the theater, "Théagène et Chariclée," remained unfinished. Torn between worldly ambition and the lingering influence of Port-Royal, which con-

demned a literary career as frivolous and sinful, Racine spent an unhappy year in southern France, at Uzès, where he had hoped to gain an ecclesiastic sinecure. His decision to return to Paris in 1663 was rewarded by some literary success; the publication of several poems put Racine on a list of royal pensioners.

Although Racine's first two dramatic ventures did not reach the stage, they brought him into closer contact with Molière, who, as director of an important theatrical troupe—the Théâtre du Marais—was to premiere Racine's first two performed dramas, *The Theban Brothers*, a success, though a mediocre one, and *Alexander the Great*, an instant popular success. After several performances, Racine, apparently feeling that Molière's troupe was misinterpreting *Alexander the Great*, gave the play to the rival, more prestigious troupe of the Hôtel de Bourgogne without informing Molière, an act of ingratitude characteristic of Racine's overwhelming desire to arrive as a dramatist. This ambition also explains his break with his Jansenist mentors at Port-Royal. Realizing that the Jansenists, deeply suspect as dissenters by the government, would never help him in his literary career, Racine took great care to dissociate himself from the *solitaires* in two sarcastic letters (one of which was published) attacking Port-Royal, which had condemned a writer as a "public poisoner."

In 1667, Racine was secretly married to Thérèse Du Parc, a famous actress whom he had lured away from Molière's troupe. In the same year, *Andromache* premiered, with Du Parc in the leading role. The popular and critical acclaim of what is considered Racine's first masterpiece helped him to replace the aging Pierre Corneille as supreme French tragedian. Racine's triumph occasioned a series of personal and critical attacks from the partisans of Corneille, initiating a prolonged and bitter polemic. After his only comedy *The Litigants*, Racine responded to his detractors with *Britannicus*, called by some a Corneillian tragedy because of its Roman subject and political emphasis. In the play's preface, Racine virulently attacked his adversary. Racine's next play, *Bérénice*, was performed in direct competition with Corneille's *Tite et Bérénice* (1670), over which Racine's version won a clear victory. Elected to the French Academy in 1673 and finding himself in possession of a growing fortune and elevated social standing, Racine continued to present a string of hits when in 1677 he produced *Phaedra*, which, because of a rival play on the same subject, appeared at first to be a failure. The superiority of the Racine play asserted itself, however, and *Phaedra* became a huge success.

At the age of thirty-seven, at the height of his renown, Racine retired from the theater, a retirement he thought definitive at the time. Much speculation has centered on this withdrawal. Historians emphasize a reconciliation with Port-Royal or simply a reasoned career move: Just married to Catherine de Romanet (with whom he had seven children), and appointed with Nicolas Boileau to the lucrative position of the king's historiographer, Racine, ever the shrewd courtier, may simply have decided that higher social elevation and greater security would come if he abandoned the theater. At any rate, Racine led the life of a courtier, a permanent resident at Versailles, in constant contact with Louis XIV, while remaining the best-known and most popular playwright in France.

In 1689, Racine made a modest return to the stage, composing, at the request of the king's morganatic wife, Mme de Maintenon, *Esther*, a biblical drama to be performed by the young ladies at the school at Saint-Cyr. In 1691, he composed another sacred drama, *Athaliah*, also for Saint-Cyr. Written and performed for an extremely limited audience of courtiers, Racine's last two plays are nevertheless judged masterpieces by most critics. Racine developed closer ties to Jansenism in his last years, composing the unfinished "Abrégé de l'histoire de Port-Royal"; he died in April, 1699, and was buried at the feet of a former master at Port-Royal. A destitute orphan at his origins, Racine died "fabulously rich." Biographers see contradictory images of the man: a calculating, cruel arriviste and courtier in opposition to the pious family man of the later years.

ANALYSIS

The outer form of Racinian tragedy differs little from that of his predecessors. His five-act plays are written in regular twelve-syllable Alexandrine verse;

Jean Racine adheres to the three unities of time, place, and action, to the concept of *bienséance*, which prohibited vulgarity of language and overt violence on the stage, and to the required "unity of tone," a sustained elegance and dignity proper to tragedy. The concept of *gloire*, which informs the work of Corneille, however, is modified in Racine. An exulted self-esteem and worldly fame arising from the exercise of total freedom, *gloire* in Racine loses its compelling force. Whereas in Corneille, the hero achieves self-realization through the domination of his or her love, the hero in Racine accepts fully this passion and the destiny that it entails. The dependent, yet far from weak, lover in Racine knows and acknowledges that he or she cannot exist without the beloved. This "demolition of the hero" reveals a new psychological realism that spurns the illusory ambition of complete self-mastery and independence. From a social and historical viewpoint, this new perspective bears witness to the decline of the ancient aristocratic ideals after the subjugation of the nobility during the absolutist regime of Louis XIV.

ANDROMACHE

Although famous after the resounding success of *Alexander the Great* in 1665, Racine created in his next play, *Andromache*, what is unanimously called his first true masterpiece. This play presented something new to contemporary audiences: love as an overwhelming, ultimately destructive passion in both men and women, who, under its sway, are bereft of honor, pride, resolve, and self-control. This play proved beyond doubt that Corneillian heroism was *passé*, and Racine was generally hailed as the great man's successor despite vehement criticisms leveled at the play by Corneille's supporters.

Evoking the epic grandeur of Vergil's *Aeneid* (c. 29-19 B.C.E.; English translation, 1553), *Andromache*, set at the court of Pyrrhus in Epirus, opens with Oreste sent by the vengeful and fearful Greeks to demand Hector's son, Astyanax, who has been held captive by Pyrrhus since the Fall of Troy one year earlier. Because of his passionate love for the captive Andromache, Pyrrhus refuses to deliver the boy to the Greeks. He intends to use Astyanax as blackmail: He will turn him over to the Greeks if Andromache does not marry him. Oreste, ostensibly on a diplomatic mission, has other motives for visiting Epirus: He loves Hermione, Pyrrhus's betrothed, whom Pyrrhus has neglected because of his passion for Andromache. Oreste hopes that his mission will fail so that he will be able to persuade Hermione to renounce the unfaithful Pyrrhus and return with him to Greece. Pyrrhus's blackmail means that the entire situation revolves on Andromache's decision: If she accepts his offer, he will reject Hermione, thus making her available to Oreste; if she refuses, Pyrrhus will accept Hermione, Andromache will lose Astyanax—the last vestige of her dead husband Hector—and Oreste will lose all hope of winning Hermione.

While Andromache ponders this momentous decision, Pyrrhus, angered by her hesitations, has a change of heart. He will fulfill his official duty by marrying Hermione and delivering Astyanax to the Greeks. Thinking that he must now yield Hermione to Pyrrhus, Oreste is disconsolate when he learns of this. Andromache is in despair; Hermione, who is apparently triumphant, exults. The depth of Pyrrhus's passion, however, forces him to weaken. In a fateful interview with Andromache, he again falls under her spell, allowing her more time to choose between marrying him or losing her son. Andromache's long-awaited decision emerges at the beginning of act 4: To save her son, she will marry Pyrrhus, then commit suicide. Neglected once again, Hermione, in a jealous rage, demands that Oreste murder the double-dealing Pyrrhus. In act 5, scene 3, the deed is done; Oreste, believing that this act has earned for him possession of Hermione, is astounded when she bitterly blames him for the murder of her beloved Pyrrhus. He goes mad after learning that Hermione has killed herself over the body of Pyrrhus. Of the four principal characters, Andromache, the Trojan captive, alone survives, indeed triumphs, at the play's close, for she has assured the survival of her son, and, as widow of Pyrrhus, assumes control over Epirus.

The outward simplicity of the play's plot structure belies the complex psychology at work. Because the action of the play is psychological, time and space play no role: Racine has made use of the unities to create a taut work that concentrates on the emotional

crisis provoked by Oreste's arrival. Once this occurs, the dominant emotions of the individuals affected inexorably lead to the final catastrophe. Aside from the Greeks' demand, revealed in act 1, scene 1, no external event influences the emotional interplay among the four protagonists. The three Greek characters are at the mercy of their passions: Pyrrhus, son of the great Achilles, is a horribly tormented king who, almost despite himself, is ready to sacrifice all for Andromache. Oreste, son of Agamemnon, whose incipient madness is suggested in the opening scene, actually hopes that his diplomatic mission will fail so that he might win Hermione. Hermione, daughter of the beautiful and celebrated Helen, is overwhelmed by Pyrrhus's rejection of her. She, like Oreste and Pyrrhus, can rule neither her heart nor her mind.

Illumined by the grandeur that was Troy, Andromache, however, does not belong to the psychological universe of the Greek characters. Her fidelity to her destroyed city and above all to her dead husband, Hector, both incarnate in the person of Astyanax (who never appears onstage, thereby reinforcing his value as symbol), is the keystone of her complex character. Her dilemma—to marry Pyrrhus or to see her son die—entails in each case treason against Troy. Her solution, which, she says, the spirit of Hector has ordered, constitutes a heroic self-sacrifice in the name of a higher value. The irony of her triumph—a captive who imposes her will on the others—reflects the more general theme of revenge in the play. Troy, in the person of Andromache, avenges itself on its Greek enemies. Repeated allusions to the destruction of Troy and to its hero Hector reinforce this interpretation. The means of revenge is the insurmountable power of passion. Pyrrhus, a cruel warrior who played a major role in Troy's final destruction, now suffers the intolerable pangs of unrequited love as well as remorse for his murderous barbarism at Troy. The seemingly conventional image of love's flame is rejuvenated by Racine to evoke Troy's revenge on Pyrrhus; he is *"Brûlé de plus de feux que je n'en allumai"* ("Burned by more fires than I lit"). Just as he had burned Troy in a passion of hatred, he himself now "burns" in a passion of love that Andromache's eyes have kindled within him. Racine's mastery of imagery and vocabulary is also apparent in what one critic calls the "poetics of the glance": The eyes of the lover can only imperfectly "grasp" the beloved, yet the latter's eyes maintain an inescapable power over he who loves.

The situation in which one character has absolute physical control over another, yet loves passionately and without recompense the same character, exists in many of Racine's plays. The main structure of Racinian tragedy appears to be based on a relationship of force and authority. As a consequence, a trial of strength lies at the foundation of his theater. Although the characters in *Andromache*—and in this they are characteristically Racinian—appear to be carried away with their emotions, they arrive at essential decisions lucidly: Pyrrhus, in wishing to marry a Trojan captive, knows very well that he is disowning his country and repudiating his past deeds as well as those of his father Achilles. Like Oreste, he accepts fully his passion and its tragic consequences. His acquiescence to blind destiny constitutes his self-realization. Unlike the autonomous, strong-willed heroes of Corneille, Racinian heroes enjoy no genuine freedom.

THE LITIGANTS

The Litigants, Racine's only comedy, is an anomaly in his rather unified tragic œuvre, and for this reason it has been relatively neglected by scholars. A scathing satire of the French legal system, the play exhibits, by its parodies, puns, and acrobatic versification, Racine's mastery of language and poetry.

BRITANNICUS

The huge success of *Andromache* prompted the partisans of Corneille to charge that Racine was merely a poet of love and tenderness and that he would never master the more significant historical and political subjects of Corneille's drama. To answer these criticisms, Racine presented *Britannicus*, a political play of jealousy and ambition set in Nero's Rome. At first a failure, *Britannicus* later established itself; it ranks third, after *Phaedra* and *Andromache*, in the number of performances at the Comédie-Française.

As in *Andromache*, the plot is rather simple. Intending to continue her own rule, Agrippine, mother of Néron, has put her own son on the throne in place of Britannicus, its rightful heir. Néron, however, does not prove to be the obedient and docile son: At the opening of the action, he has just abducted the young princess Junie, whom Agrippine had intended for Britannicus, and with whom Néron, finding himself in a loveless political marriage, has fallen in love. Junie loves Britannicus, which Néron will not tolerate: In a famous scene (act 2, scene 6), the hidden Néron watches as Junie, under his command, must reject the stunned Britannicus. At a critical moment in his infamous career, Néron oscillates between two antithetical political conceptions: Burrhus counsels a policy based on morality, respect of law, and trust in the basic virtue of the people, whereas the Machiavellian Narcisse maintains that Néron must subdue the capricious mob and all those who oppose him. Warned by Narcisse, Néron discovers that Junie, aided by Agrippine, has been able to inform Britannicus of the real reason for her rejection. In this key scene (act 3, scene 8), Néron has the defiant Britannicus arrested on the spot while Agrippine and Junie are put under house arrest. In act 4, Narcisse finally prevails over Burrhus: Néron makes the momentous decision to murder his rival and to marry Junie. In act 5, during a feast of reconciliation, Britannicus is poisoned. Junie flees to the Vestal Virgins: Agrippine curses Néron, who lapses into a despair verging on madness. The play thus closes just as Néron is beginning his murderous career. Racine in his preface describes the play as the depiction of a *monstre naissant*, a nascent monster. The political conflict among Néron, Agrippine, and Britannicus ends with Néron's victory: He now has the absolute power required for a reign of tyranny and terror.

Like other Racinian heroes, Néron is predestined, determined by heredity to sadistic cruelty and madness. External circumstances converge to force him to reveal this fatality to all. In the course of the play, Néron's behavior is unpredictable—which undoubtedly creates great suspense—yet the logic of his actions becomes clear after the entire plot unfolds: Néron unmasks himself, revealing the true character that had been hidden during his three years of rule before the opening of the play. The image of the glance, so important in *Andromache*, also emerges in *Britannicus*: Néron seeks to seize and possess another by means of his eyes (act 2, scene 6, for example); his constant avoidance of Agrippine's formidable presence, his desire to escape her glance and its influence, stress the power of the eyes. Despite his efforts to escape his mother's tutelage, Néron never succeeds in gaining control over others or events: His adviser Narcisse is killed by a mob, and Junie escapes.

Inasmuch as Néron is probably the play's most dynamic, interesting character, critics have questioned its title. Britannicus is a courageous, noble, yet extremely naïve and imprudent young man whose political ineptitude makes his murder inevitable. Yet in his preface, Racine insisted on the innocence of Britannicus. A sympathetic character who, through political machinations cannot inherit his rightful place, arouses the compassion and pity of the audience: hence the title of the play.

With the longest role in the play, Agrippine presents an intelligent, proud, unscrupulous, and hugely ambitious woman, a typically formidable Racinian heroine. Her fall is inextricably tied to the death of Britannicus, and, as such, it forms a major subject of the play. She is the outsider, rejected by the young lovers as well as her newly independent son. Just as Pyrrhus in *Andromache* is torn between Hermione and Andromache, Néron is torn between Agrippine and Junie. In both cases the male character loves, and is rejected by, the gentler woman; each is trying to escape from a domineering, violent woman, a possessive fiancé in one play, a possessive mother in the other. The basic structure of an all-powerful protagonist (Néron) who loves a weaker character (Junie), who in turn has other emotional loyalties, also obtains in this play.

BÉRÉNICE

Racine's success continued in the 1670's. His next play, *Bérénice*, is remarkable for its extreme simplicity. In his preface, the author expresses his thoughts on simplicity of action: "There are some who think that this simplicity [of *Bérénice*] is evidence of little inventiveness. They don't believe that, on the contrary, all inventiveness lies in making something from nothing." Written, apparently, as a challenge to Corneille's *Tite et Bérénice* (pr. 1670), this play contains only three main characters and their confidants, whose roles are minor. Set in ancient Rome, the action is intimate: The new emperor Tite, whose father Vespasien has recently died, has loved the queen of Palestine, Bérénice, for five years. Although he wishes to marry her, the Senate opposes the marriage of a head of state with a foreign queen. After much pain and hesitation, Tite sacrifices Bérénice and his love to the reason of state. Thus a strangely Corneillian denouement, in which duty triumphs over passion, closes this most Racinian of Racine's dramas; it is in effect a play of personal sacrifice, quite different in this respect from Racine's other works.

BAJAZET

After creating a play in which nothing happens, Racine in *Bajazet*, his next work, presented the violent, even sadistic world of the Turkish court in the 1630's. *Bajazet* was Racine's first play published without a polemical, apologetic preface, suggesting, perhaps, that his self-confidence was increasing. Full of suspense, court intrigues, and bloody passions, *Bajazet*, like *Andromache* and *Britannicus*, depicts a character (Roxane) whose power of life or death over another character (Bajazet) is mocked by the enslaving power of love. Roxane swings violently between love and hatred—allied emotions in the complex of Racinian passion—depending on whether she believes that Bajazet returns her love or not and finally has him killed. Despite her cruelty and deceit, Roxane remains a pathetic figure: All of her power cannot erase the fact that her happiness is utterly dependent on Bajazet. Although set in an exotic locale, *Bajazet*, like Racine's other plays, is a psychological study revealing the eternal truth of the human heart.

MITHRIDATES

A huge success from its first performance, *Mithridates*, Racine's only serious play with what could be called a happy ending, enjoyed the acclaim of the court, the city, and even of the Corneille clique. Set in Rome, the work depicts the cagey, longtime foe of the Romans, Mithridates, at the end of his life. The relatively involved plot and large number of dramatic surprises or *coups de théâtre*, the heroic apotheosis of

Mithridates, whose generosity wins over others who had feared and despised him, and generally strong characters who put duty before sentiment, mark this play among all Racine's works as the most strongly influenced by Corneille.

IPHIGENIA IN AULIS

Racine's next play, *Iphigenia in Aulis*, once again demonstrated his supremacy on the French stage. Returning to Greek myth for his subject matter, Racine imitated Euripides' *Iphigeneia ē en Aulidi* (405 B.C.E.; *Iphigenia in Aulis*, 1782). It was necessary, however, to adapt the ancient story to the tastes of the seventeenth century French audience. To accomplish this, Racine invented the character of Eriphile, who, because of an ambiguity in the oracle that apparently demands the sacrifice of Iphigenia before the Greek fleet can depart for Troy, is substituted for her and dies on the altar, thus allowing the Greeks to continue their voyage. By substituting a more *vraisemblance*—or verisimilar—denouement for the miraculous ending of Euripides, Racine satisfied the demand for *bienséance* (propriety or decorum), for the treacherous and ungrateful Eriphile is much less sympathetic than the virtuous Iphigenia. The enormous suspense generated just before the audience learns that Iphigenia is saved attests Racine's skill in plot construction. Alternately savage and lyric, *Iphigenia in Aulis* has been called Racine's most Homeric play.

PHAEDRA

Racine's greatest masterpiece, easily his most celebrated play, *Phaedra*, was presented in January, 1677, at the same time as a competing "Phaedra." Jacques Pradon had composed a rival *Phèdre et Hippolyte* (competing authors often wrote in direct competition), which was at first more successful. After several months, however, Racine's *Phaedra* surpassed Pradon's in popular acclaim. That the play was the inaugural performance of the Comédie-Française in 1680 confirmed its appeal. As in *Iphigenia in Aulis*, in *Phaedra*, the mythic element dominates; humanity is in eternal opposition to the seemingly perfidious gods. At the opening of the play, Thésée, king of Troezen, has been absent for six months. His son Hippolyte, apparently concerned about his father, wishes to leave Troezen in search of Thésée. In fact, other reasons motivate Hippolyte's departure: his love for Aricie, whom Thésée has forbidden him to marry because of her link to the rebellious Pallantides, and his desire to flee the overt hatred of his stepmother Phaedra. After Hippolyte's revelation that he loves Aricie, a dying Phaedra takes the stage and confesses to her confidante Oenone that she loves Hippolyte and that her enmity toward him has been a means of avoiding an unwilling declaration of her love. A peripeteia closes the first act: News (Aricie calls it "incredible") arrives that Thésée is dead. This external event effects profound changes in the internal situation: Hippolyte is now free to woo Aricie, and Phaedra can now pursue Hippolyte without fear of incest and adultery.

On the urging of Oenone, Phaedra determines to speak privately to Hippolyte on a political pretext relating to the rights of succession. In perhaps the most famous scene in French classical theater (act 2, scene 5), Phaedra, carried away by her passion, declares her love. While Hippolyte stands dumbfounded, Phaedra seizes his sword, thinking to kill herself but does not. In act 3, the humiliated, rejected Phaedra oscillates between love and hatred for Hippolyte. In her confused state, against the advice of Oenone, she decides to use political blackmail to gain Hippolyte's love. Devastating news then arrives: Thésée is alive. The desperate and helpless Phaedra, fearful that Hippolyte will tell his father of her incestuous love, is persuaded by Oenone that she must accuse Hippolyte of attempting to seduce her before he can reveal the truth. Putting herself in the hands of Oenone, Phaedra greets Thésée coldly, refusing to accept his sincere affection. Stunned and suspicious, Thésée demands an explanation from Hippolyte, who has naïvely vowed never to reveal Phaedra's shame to his father.

This oath puts Hippolyte in an untenable position, for he has no effective means of defending himself against Oenone's lies. The violent, vengeful, and quick-tempered Thésée is convinced by Hippolyte's sword, left in the hands of Phaedra after act 2, scene 5, and by his son's diffident behavior. In a stormy interview, Thésée asks Neptune to wreak vengeance on his son; in an attempt at self-defense, Hippolyte confesses his real love for Aricie, which Thésée judges a cowardly ruse. Phaedra, who now realizes that Hippolyte is in mortal danger, resolves to reveal the truth to Thésée. Her regret and pity, however, change to furious hatred and jealousy when Thésée tells her that Hippolyte told him that he loves Aricie. This news makes her continue to hide the truth. Although Thésée begins to guess that Hippolyte was not lying, inexorable destiny is played out in act 5. Hippolyte kills a sea monster sent by Neptune, but then Neptune himself causes the horses of Hippolyte's chariot to stampede, killing the innocent young hero. Overwhelmed by the enormity of her crime, Phaedra poisons herself. Right before she dies, Phaedra finally tells the truth; the desolate Thésée determines to protect the bereft Aricie.

A malevolent destiny hovers over the action of *Phaedra*. A descendant of the Sun, daughter of Minos and Pasiphaé, Phaedra bears the curse of Venus. Her mother's indomitable passion for the White Bull of Crete, the issue of this passion, the Minotaur and its Labyrinth, the doomed love of Phaedra's sister Ariadne for Thésée—all figure prominently in the play and serve as background to the fateful, "monstrous" passion of Phaedra for Hippolyte. The gods in *Phaedra*, if one wishes to consider them such (they have been interpreted as symbols for humanity's unbridled passions), emerge as incomprehensible powers with no moral purpose. Phaedra, who wishes to die throughout the play, knows that escape from her anguish is impossible, for her own father Minos sits as judge at the gates of Hades. Racine presents a universe in which the innocent are punished for uncommitted crimes, in which people are forced by the gods to commit crimes for which they will suffer eternal torment. Such a universe seems absurd; it is truly a tragic vision of the human condition.

True to the Aristotelian concept of the tragic hero, Racine emphasized in his preface that Phaedra is "neither totally guilty nor totally innocent." Victim of an unrelenting divine vengeance, Phaedra condemns herself for a passion to which she has never yielded. She feels herself responsible for a love over which she has absolutely no control. Phaedra aspires to good, but the gods force her to submit to evil. Both Phaedra and Hippolyte view their respective passions

as a *mal*, a kind of sickness that destroys sovereign reason and thus transforms he who loves. Racinian passion is inimical to self-control and equilibrium, a monster that destroys independence and harmony.

Critics have frequently declared that *Phaedra* summarizes all Racine's drama. The universality of the play, its unremitting depiction of human nature aspiring to virtue but condemned to vice, has undoubtedly contributed to its status as Racine's crowning achievement. The play poses the fundamental problem of liberty. Predetermined, whether by the gods, heredity, or other forces, humanity is unable to escape the monsters that pursue it. Nevertheless, humankind never ceases to assume responsibility and thus affirms an illusory freedom. Phaedra's awareness of her crime and its shame constitutes, perhaps, a kind of individual liberty and tragic grandeur.

Key words and images converge in the play to reinforce the major themes and conflict. Poison plays a central role as symbol for the fatal passion that courses through the veins of Phaedra. A complex network of images relating to light and darkness also pervades the work. Unable to face her formidable ancestor the Sun, Phaedra retreats from the accusing light of purity and innocence like a furtive nocturnal creature; Phaedra's desire for darkness evokes not only her shame but also her wish to discover in death eternal darkness. Hippolyte and Aricie, however, share an innocence and purity that revel in the light: "Every day rose clear and serene for them," whereas Phaedra says of herself: "I hid from the day, I fled from the light." *Phaedra* is also a play of monsters: The fruit of Pasiphaé's passion, the Minotaur, was destroyed by the heroic monster-killer Thésée, whom Hippolyte wishes to emulate. Hippolyte kills the sea monster sent by Neptune, yet dies a victim of Phaedra, whose love, like that of her mother for the White Bull, is against nature, monstrous.

ESTHER AND ATHALIAH

After *Phaedra*, twelve years passed before Racine's next play. Whatever the true reasons for his long silence, it is clear that he became reconciled with his Jansenist masters at Port-Royal. Racine's second wife, whom he married in 1677, the year of *Phaedra*, never read her husband's tragedies; their seven children received a most austere Jansenist up-bringing. Racine's last two plays, *Esther* and *Athaliah*, attest the piety of his later years; overtly didactic, both derive from the Old Testament. Although some scholars have hesitated to view these religious plays as integral components of Racine's œuvre, all agree that both obviously bear the imprint of Racine; many consider *Athaliah* one of his best plays.

OTHER MAJOR WORKS

POETRY: *Cantiques spirituels*, 1694.

NONFICTION: *Abrégé de l'histoire de Port-Royal*, 1742 (first part), 1767 (full text).

BIBLIOGRAPHY

Barthes, Roland. *On Racine*. 1983. Reprint. Berkeley: University of California Press, 1992. A French scholar discusses Racine's tragedies. Bibliography and index.

Caldicott, Edric, and Derval Conroy, eds. *Racine: The Power and the Pleasure*. Dublin, Ireland: University College Dublin Press, 2001. This study examines the concepts of power and pleasure in Racine's dramas.

Goodkin, Richard E. *Birth Marks: The Tragedy of Primogeniture in Pierre Corneille, Thomas Corneille, and Jean Racine*. Philadelphia: University of Pennsylvania Press, 2000. Goodkin examines the works of Racine and the two Corneilles, placing special emphasis on their treatments of primogeniture.

Hawcroft, Michael. *Word as Action: Racine, Rhetoric, and Theatrical Language*. New York: Oxford University Press, 1992. Hawcroft examines Racine's use of language in his dramatic works. Bibliography and indexes.

Parish, Richard. *Racine: The Limits of Tragedy*. Seattle, Wash.: Papers on French Seventeenth Century Literature, 1993. An examination of the tragedies written by Racine. Bibliography.

Phillips, Henry. *Racine: Language and Theatre*. Durham, England: University of Durham, 1994. A look at the language of Racine and how he used it in his dramas. Bibliography.

Tobin, Ronald W. *Jean Racine Revisited*. New York: Twayne, 1999. A basic biography of Racine that covers his life and works. Bibliography and index.

Robert T. Corum, Jr.

FERDINAND RAIMUND
Jakob Raimann

Born: Vienna, Austria; June 1, 1790
Died: Potenstein, Austria; September 5, 1836

PRINCIPAL DRAMA

Der Barometermacher auf der Zauberinsel, pr. 1823, pb. 1837 (*The Barometer-Maker on the Magic Island*, 1996)

Der Diamant des Geisterkönigs, pr. 1824, pb. 1837 (*The Diamond of the Spirit King*, 1996)

Das Mädchen aus der Feenwelt: Oder, Der Bauer als Millionär, pr. 1826, pb. 1837 (*The Maid from Fairyland: Or, The Peasant as Millionaire*, 1962)

Moisasurs Zauberfluch, pr. 1827, pb. 1837

Die gefesselte Phantasie, pr. 1828, pb. 1837

Der Alpenkönig und der Menschenfeind, pr. 1828, pb. 1837 (*Mountain King and Misanthrope*, 1962)

Die unheilbringende Krone: Oder, König ohne Reich, Held ohne Mut, Schönheit ohne Jugend, pr. 1829, pb. 1837

Der Verschwender, pr. 1834, pb. 1837 (*The Spendthrift*, 1949)

OTHER LITERARY FORMS

Ferdinand Raimund is known only for his plays. There exist a few poems from his hand, notably an

Ferdinand Raimund (Hulton Archive by Getty Images)

ode to Friedrich Schiller and a poem "An die Dunkelheit" (to darkness). His letters have been collected, and later editors have compiled separate editions of the most famous couplets (songs) from his plays.

ACHIEVEMENTS

Ferdinand Raimund has been called "the first great humoristic dramatist of the Germans in the nineteenth century." He freed the Viennese Popular Theater from coarseness and bawdiness and elevated it to the level of literary acceptability. This Popular Theater, which had its roots in the Baroque and its first significant representative in the famous J. A. Stranitzky at the beginning of the eighteenth century, achieved its fulfillment with the plays of Ferdinand Raimund between 1823 and 1834, and reached its

conclusion with Raimund's sardonic rival Johann Nestroy, who died in 1862. Both Raimund and Nestroy were actors initially, and both began writing plays because they were dissatisfied with the comedies in which they acted. Although the younger Nestroy embraced the new age of heightened realism, which ridiculed idealism and the dreamy fairyland of a waning Romantic age, Raimund clung to this idealism and made the dreamworld an integral and often overwhelming part of his plays. Raimund's comedies are marked by a sensitivity that sometimes descends to sentimentality; Nestroy was incapable of either, and his plays were frequently criticized because of his return to the somewhat bawdier robustness of a former era.

Raimund, the idealist, also attempted to free the Popular Theater from another tradition inherited from the Italian *commedia dell'arte*, that of excessive improvisation, which related the plays all too closely to the affairs of the day. Raimund thus was searching for eternal truth and beauty beyond the moment; he sometimes overshot his goal with too much pathos. Nestroy, on the other hand, returned the Viennese *posse* (comic play) to the realm of improvisation, abandoning the carefully constructed play in favor of the incidental comical situation or word.

Measured against the volume of more than eighty plays that Nestroy wrote during his lifetime, Raimund's achievement seems rather small. In little more than ten years, he wrote all of his eight finished plays and perhaps worked on but abandoned a ninth one; its title is said to have been "Eine Nacht auf dem Himalaja" (a night in the Himalayas). He did not labor on his plays for long periods of time; most of them were written within a span of two to three months. Raimund's extreme sensitivity, his rather fragile and hypochondriac nature, seem to have required rather lengthy periods of rest and reflection, when he also devoted himself entirely to his acting again. Doubt of his own ability apparently forced him to withhold a finished play from the stage for as much as a year and a half, as was the case with *Die gefesselte Phantasie* (phantasy in chains), which had been finished in the fall of 1826, but did not reach the stage until January of 1828.

Such self-doubt can perhaps be attributed to Raimund's lack of formal education. The author compensated for this perceived lack through high aspirations and ideals, through many allusions to names and themes of classical antiquity, and through his often lofty language. His veneration of Friedrich Schiller in the poem "To Schiller's Posthumous Fame" ("Who wrote, as you did, for the German nation?") must be seen in this light, as Schiller also succeeded in the face of adversity. Throughout his life, Raimund seemed intent on overcoming obstacles, whether real or imagined. He failed his first audition as an actor, because he could not produce the rolled *r* sound required for the German-speaking stage. Relentlessly, he practiced until he could make the required sound. He wrote his first play because the playwright Karl Meisl, to whom he had given the material, was too slow and incompetent. He lamented that the playwrights of his age proved to be "more and more miserable, they practice their craft only to make money, not to receive laurels."

Once he had found his own dramatic style in *The Maid from Fairyland*, Raimund strove to improve on it by treating more elevated themes, for example, the tale of Orpheus mixed with the fable of Alcestia in *Die gefesselte Phantasie*. He failed but had success with critics and audience alike in *Mountain King and Misanthrope*. He tried to break away a second time with *Die unheilbringende Krone* (the fateful crown) and failed even more dismally. His earnest attempt at being a comic actor and playwright led Constant von Wurzbach to observe that "for other comedians comedy is comical, for him it was serious." Comedy for Raimund was supposed to be more than mere entertainment; it was to teach a lesson, as well as have high moral standards.

Raimund's life and art were full of such contradictions. This comic actor with the serious disposition, a playwright in spite of himself, was filled with a desire for public renown and an ardent longing for the solitude of nature. He praised the institution of marriage in one of his plays while he was forced to live with his beloved Toni Wagner in a common-law relationship for most of his life. He was the foremost representative of the lower-class Viennese folk play, yet he favored elevated themes, classical allusions, and lofty language. In his plays, real and imaginary worlds were always set against one another, and his main characters, like the playwright himself, seemed to want to escape the ambience of Vienna simply to be able to long for it. Viennese charm permeated his plays. His upper-class characters spoke High-German, but the servants, whose essence he captured masterfully, used the Viennese dialect. His language, Hugo von Hofmannsthal observed, was a "mixture of higher and lower elements, half grandiose style, half the language of the Viennese Hanswurst" (a character similar to the English Punch). The use of the couplet—the typical Viennese song—was another of his trademarks.

The Viennese baroque tradition of grandiosity was evident not only in his characters but also in the stage settings which he required. The machinery necessary for the production of Raimund's works was simply overwhelming. Spectacular alpine landscapes, enchanted forests, and ornate palaces abounded. Magical open scene changes dazzled the eyes of the spectators. It should be noted how often the word *Zauber* (magic) appears in the titles of his plays. Visitors from abroad flocked to Vienna to see these performances. Lord Stanhope, who saw Raimund in *Mountain King and Misanthrope*, was so impressed that he supposedly translated the story into English and gave it to the playwright John Baldwin Buckstone to fashion a theatrical adaptation. Buckstone's *King of the Alps and Misanthrope* played to full houses at the Adelphi Theatre in London for three months in the spring of 1831. Acting editions were published in that year and again in 1852. Buckstone's translation, however, hinted at the limitation that Raimund would encounter outside Vienna: The English version omitted several of the supernatural scenes involving the King of the Alps because they were considered unappealing to English audiences. A melodramatic subplot was substituted instead. Not many other foreign-language productions or adaptations of Raimund's plays have been attempted. The German stage of St. Louis apparently gave some thirty-four performances of *The Spendthrift* in the original language between 1842 and 1911. The German theater in San Francisco is also recorded as having performed the play several times in the 1860's. *The Spendthrift* appeared again in English translation in New York in 1949. Aside from these few exceptions, Raimund's plays have been confined to the Austrian and German stages, and on the latter, they are considered a typically Viennese phenomenon.

BIOGRAPHY

Ferdinand Raimund's father, Jakob Raimann (for whom Raimund was named at birth), was a turner with little means to provide his son with a good education. Raimund was sent to the school of St. Anna in Vienna, where he acquired not only rudimentary skills but also learned drawing, the violin, and some French. He became an orphan when he was fifteen, and his older sister was put in charge of his upbringing. Unable to provide for the boy, she apprenticed him to a confectioner. This confectioner supplied cake and candy to Josephstädter Theater for sale during intermissions, and Raimund became a so-called *Nummero* (vendor) at the theater. He had to attend performances almost daily, and he quickly grew to love the stage.

After three years, Raimund quit his apprenticeship virtually overnight, attaching a note to some nuts he was to prepare that read, "*Diese vierzig Nuss sind meine letzte Buss*" ("These forty nuts are my last penance"). He went to the town of Meidling near the castle of Schönbrunn, where a traveling theater company performed at the time. Its director, Kralitschek, let the young boy try out but found him so unsuitable because of his unassuming looks and the inability to pronounce the German stage-*r* that he sent him away immediately. Undaunted, Raimund continued on to Pressburg, where he was given a second chance. Again he failed, but this time at least during his first performance. He wandered farther away from Vienna and deeper into the Hungarian provinces to the town of Steinamanger, where he finally got his first con-

tract, which forced him to play all kinds of parts, including even the "Pierot in the pantomime" (Wurzbach). After this theater disbanded, Raimund found a new engagement with the director Kunz, and played under dismal conditions for four consecutive years on the stages of Raab and Oedenburg. Villains and comical old men were his most frequent roles. In this period, Raimund wrote a few coarse prologues in verse.

Finally, in 1814, Raimund returned to Vienna, which had been his ambition all along. He received a contract at the Josephstädter Theater and had moderate success in a comedy by August von Kotzebue and as Karl Moor in Schiller's *Die Räuber* (pb. 1781; *The Robbers*, 1792). He was given both serious and comic roles and had a chance to improve his acting from mere imitation of the greats of the Viennese stage to his own individualized style. His pathos in the serious roles was much exaggerated. According to reports of the time, the critic Eduard von Bauernfeld called his Karl Moor "simply disgusting." Nevertheless, it must have taken a long time to quell Raimund's ambition to become a tragedian at the much renowned Burgtheater. The same critic Bauernfeld quotes a later tongue-in-cheek confession by Raimund, "I was born a tragedian, and I lack nothing for it, except the figure and the voice."

In 1815, Raimund had his first major success as the jealous musician Adam Kratzerl in the comedy *Die Musikanten am hohen Markt* (1815; the musicians at high market) by Josef Alois Gleich. Five continuations had to be written to satisfy audiences. In the same year, he was invited to give a first guest-performance at the Leopoldstädter Theater, which he knew well from his cake-selling days, and in 1817, he transferred there altogether. His opening role at the Leopoldstädter Theater was again in a play by Gleich, who also assumed importance for him on a more private level: In 1820, Raimund reluctantly married Gleich's daughter Luise on a second try, after failing to show up on the original wedding date. The marriage was dissolved in 1822, and a child from it died in infancy. Altogether, his relationships with women seem to have been more stormy than felicitous. Bauernfeld claims that Raimund, during his days at the theater in Raab, was so shaken by the unfaithful-ness of a beloved girl that he threw himself into the river, where he was barely saved from drowning. In 1818, his insane jealousy even led to an entry in the Vienna police blotter. He persuaded his young fellow-actress Therese Grünthal to move in with him, but she left him after a week because of his "irascible, coarse character." Raimund was insulted, chased after her, and caught her with a new beau in the foyer of the theater. When she refused to return to him, he re-viled and threatened her and finally beat her up on the steps toward the box seats. The police intervened, and Raimund went to prison for three days.

Instead of jumping into the river as in former times, Raimund jumped at his next best opportunity and married Luise Gleich, but not before he had met Toni Wagner, the daughter of a prominent Viennese restaurant owner who had rudely rebuffed this unsta-ble suitor of his daughter. During his marriage, Raimund began to pursue Toni again, and after his di-vorce, she became his constant companion until his death (a second marriage was not possible under Austrian law). Toni seems to have had a somewhat calming effect on him, because for the next decade, Raimund was able to devote himself to his stage ca-reer, and he began writing his plays in 1823. Starting in 1824, however, the hypochondria that had plagued him in earlier years took on more serious and omi-nous forms, and he had to withdraw from the stage for some time. He did not reappear until the fall of 1825.

From then on, Raimund's plays appeared with regularity until the end of the decade, when his con-tract with the Leopoldstädter Theater ran out. He chose not to renew it. Instead, he accepted invitations for guest performances within Vienna and went on tour to Munich, Hamburg, Frankfurt, Stuttgart, and Berlin during the next two years. He was successful everywhere, mostly appearing in his own plays. In the meantime, he had bought a villa in the country outside Vienna and withdrew to it with increasing frequency, appearing only occasionally in the city for guest performances between 1832 and 1834. In 1834, his last and perhaps greatest play, *The Spendthrift*, was completed, and Raimund gave forty-five perfor-

mances in it at the Josephstädter Theater. In 1835 and 1836, he went on tour again. It is perhaps symbolic that Raimund's last stage appearance was in Ham-burg—as far away as he had ever ventured from Vi-enna—on May 11, 1836.

Raimund returned to his villa at Gutenstein for the summer months, and on August 25 was bitten by his own dog, whom he immediately presumed to be ra-bid. After some hesitation, he attempted to reach Vi-enna for medical help. As if his life and his theater had come together for a grand finale, a severe thun-derstorm prevented him from traveling on. He was forced to spend the night at the inn in Potenstein. Toni accompanied him. Outside, thunder and light-ning raged; inside, his soul was racked with fear of painful death. During the night, he asked Toni to get him a glass of water. While she was absent, he shot himself in the mouth with the small handgun that he always carried. He wrestled with death for another five days and died on September 5, 1836.

ANALYSIS

Ferdinand Raimund entered the theater as an ac-tor, and he became a playwright almost unintention-ally. His plays must be seen as an attempt to synthe-size the Viennese Popular Theater with the classical German drama of the eighteenth and the beginning of the nineteenth century. John Michalski (*Ferdinand Raimund*, 1968) observes that Raimund

> obtained his effects by means of a picturesque, some-times melancholy idiom, which combines the delight-fully musical Viennese dialect with standard High German. Allegorical figures and characters from the Viennese milieu speak and act in a manner that sug-gests no division between the worlds of reality and imagination. The action . . . is frequently treated from the vantage point of a naïve, almost child-like human being.

It has been suggested that Raimund's suicide in 1836 was not only brought on by his hypochondria, but that it was also prompted by a change in theatrical taste, which threatened to take him out of the lime-light very soon. Ever since the success of *Der böse Geist Lumpazivagabundus* (the evil spirit Lumpazivagabundus) in 1833, the star of Johann Nestroy had risen brighter and brighter on the theatrical skies of Vienna. Raimund's ability—and willingness—to adapt, to accommodate changing tastes, was in question. Raimund was disturbed by what he saw happening on the stage, and when he went to see Nestroy's play, he was horrified. The title alone had offended him with its suggestions of low life, drunkenness, and slovenliness. In a letter to Toni Wagner, Raimund observed that Viennese audiences had been led astray by charlatans. Honest talent was being subverted through "the cabals of these theatrical bushrangers." He ended by stating that "my physical and moral life is inseparable from my honor."

Raimund's plays were the product of a political age of innocence; his success as an actor and a playwright fell into a time when the final defeat of Napoleon Bonaparte and the Congress of Vienna had brought peace to the troubled city. Prince Metternich attempted to maintain peace and prosperity by means of espionage, censorship, and the repression of liberal ideas, and the populace sought distraction in the theater. Here one could catch concealed allusions to the real political conditions interwoven with fantastic fairy tales or harmless farces. Nevertheless, the moral of most plays was that, however exciting other places around the world might be, Vienna was still the most delightful abode.

THE BAROMETER-MAKER ON THE MAGIC ISLAND

This is exactly the sentiment expressed in Raimund's first play, *The Barometer-Maker on the Magic Island*. Raimund's authorship was disputed at first, forcing him to state publicly that he had indeed written the play. The music was composed by Wenzel Müller, with whom Raimund collaborated on several of his later plays, notably *Mountain King and Misanthrope*. Raimund played the lead of Bartholomäus Quecksilber in the premier performance at the Leopoldstädter Theater on December 18, 1823.

The Barometer-Maker on the Magic Island depicts the conflict between the Viennese wit and trickster Bartholomäus Quecksilber and the cunning princess Zoraide of the enchanted isle. Bartholomäus has obtained three magical gifts from the fairy Rosalinde,

who must dispense them once every one hundred years. One by one, Zoraide succeeds in stealing these gifts from him, but she is forced to return them in the end when Bartholomäus appears at her court with figs that produce enormous noses on everyone who eats them, and for which only he holds the antidote. The fig magic was nothing new; it had appeared in a number of baroque court operas and also was a well-known motif in fairy tales. Zoraide's father, King Tutu, seems to be a soul mate of Georg Büchner's famous King Peter in his *Leonce und Lena* (wr. 1836, pb. 1850; *Leonce and Lena*, 1927), and critics did not fail to notice his resemblance to the ruling Austrian emperor, Francis I. In all events, the play contained little to distinguish it from the usual comedy fare of the time.

THE DIAMOND OF THE SPIRIT KING

In his second play, *The Diamond of the Spirit King*, Raimund succeeded in the creation of a servant role (Florian) that hinted at the author's superior talent in drawing believable characters for the stage. He played Florian in the opening performance at the Leopoldstädter Theater on December 17, 1824. The music was written by the theater's resident composer, Josef Drechsler. Florian's counterpart, the servant maid Mariandel, was portrayed by Therese Krones, one of the leading actresses of the period. Both of these servants deviated from the norm because they were not only cunning but also faithful servants of their master. Again, the plot is simple in its synthesis of the real and the imaginary world. Master Eduard, the son of a deceased magician, has inherited six valuable magic statues from his father and must obtain the seventh, the most valuable, from the Fairy King Longimanus. This seventh statue has been fashioned from a rose-colored diamond. Longimanus is willing to part with it if Eduard in turn can find him a girl who has never lied in her life. She is finally found: She is the English girl Amine, on the Island of Truth, who is just about to be cast out to sea because she does not pay lip service to its king, Veritatius. The Island of Truth and its king resemble some venerable traditions in Metternich's Austria that could not bear too much scrutiny. In the end, Eduard has recognized that love is more important than wealth, and he is willing to give up the statue for his beloved Amine. The play ends with the double betrothal of Eduard and Amine and of their servants Florian and Mariandel. In the character of Eduard, Raimund seems to have summed up his philosophy of life when he has him declare that "true virtuousness is not a matter of outward form, it lives innermost in the heart."

THE MAID FROM FAIRYLAND

On November 10, 1826, Raimund appeared as Fortunatus Wurzel in the premiere of his third play, *The Maid from Fairyland*. The title role was suited to his talent, especially as he was able to show off his versatility in changing from a middle-aged man to an old man, from pride to remorse, from millionaire to ashman. Two songs from the play became popular folk songs virtually overnight: "Brüderlein fein" (my fine little brother) and Wurzel's famous "Aschenlied" (ash song). The plot concerns the fairy Lacrimosa and her baby girl from a marriage with a mortal man. According to her mother's wish, this "Girl from the Land of the Fairies" should marry the Prince of the Fairies. The Queen of the Fairies, outraged by this presumption, has deprived Lacrimosa of all her magic powers and has also decreed that Lottchen must marry a virtuous mortal before she turns eighteen. The peasant Fortunatus Wurzel, her guardian, is instructed to marry her off as required. Lottchen, educated in the virtues of honesty and simplicity, has been promised to the fisherman Karl Schilf. Meanwhile, the allegorical figure of Envy has showered Wurzel with an immense fortune and thereby corrupted him, and he vows to find a wealthy husband for his ward. Lacrimosa's cousin, the magician Ajaxerle, who has been sent by the desperate mother to change Wurzel's mind, is told by the haughty Wurzel that he would have to turn old and weak before he would permit Lottchen's marriage to Karl. In the scene that follows immediately—and which some critics consider the best the age has to offer—the allegorical figure of youth leaves Wurzel, singing "Brüderlein fein . . . ," and Old Age arrives. Lottchen and Karl can marry, Lacrimosa has regained her powers, and Wurzel has recognized that wealth has only corrupted him. He returns to his peasant state and

will be happy without wealth from now on. *The Maid from Fairyland* was a great success. Raimund had finally perfected his formula of synthesizing the real and the imaginary world, and he had created, in Fortunatus Wurzel, a character who had no equal in the Popular Theater at that time.

The two plays that followed, *Moisasurs Zauberfluch* (Moisasur's magic curse) and *Die gefesselte Phantasie*, were much less successful. The happy balance between the two worlds that Raimund had struck in *The Maid from Fairyland* became unbalanced in favor of the imaginary one, and the real world was shortchanged. The fusing of the two spheres was also imperfect, leaving the reader to wonder about the compelling necessity of their connection. *Die gefesselte Phantasie* has been considered "the fragment of an autobiography" in which Raimund set out to prove that he, a man without education, could write plays in the Shakespearean vein. The plays had some redeeming qualities, however, and one critic of the time remarked that he considered the avaricious peasant Gluthahn in *Moisasurs Zauberfluch* among Raimund's greatest accomplishments.

MOUNTAIN KING AND MISANTHROPE

A rich and misanthropic peasant was the focal character of Raimund's next play, *Mountain King and Misanthrope*. Raimund himself, with his distrust for his environment and his friends, was the model for Rappelkopf, whom he portrayed at the opening performance at the Leopoldstädter Theater on October 27, 1828. Herr von Rappelkopf has gone into seclusion from the world and from other human beings, whom he hates and mistrusts. His fourth and current wife has to endure his moods and unjustified suspicions, which have apparently killed the three wives before her. Rappelkopf's only daughter, Malchen, must keep her love for the young painter August Dorn hidden from her father, who would not approve of such a worthless suitor. Rappelkopf's paranoia, which extends to everything and everyone, makes him also suspect his servant Habakuk, who happens to enter the room on a kitchen errand with a knife in his hand. Rappelkopf surmises that his wife has sent the servant to assassinate him. After breaking all the furniture, he runs from the house out into the forest, where he encounters the family of the poor charcoal-burner Christian Glüwurm. He, his wife, their four children, and a grandmother live in a dilapidated hut that appeals to Rappelkopf because of its solitude. He buys it from them for a good price and rudely drives them from their abode. At this hut high up in the mountains, he encounters the King of the Alps, Astralagus, who tells him that he has only himself to blame for his misanthropy. To prove it, Astralagus transforms himself into Rappelkopf and Rappelkopf into his own brother-in-law, so that Rappelkopf may observe his behavior toward his family as an outsider. Once Rappelkopf recognizes that his suspicions are unfounded, he puts an end to Astralagus's torture of his family in his own guise. A reformed misanthrope, he gives his blessing to his daughter's marriage and holds his wife and servant in high esteem. Peace and tranquillity have finally entered his house.

The play exceeded all Raimund's previous successes to that point. Franz Grillparzer called the scene in the charcoal-burner's hut a portrayal "unsurpassed in all of Dutch genre-painting." A literary debate ensued immediately as to Raimund's sources. Was he indebted to Molière, to William Shakespeare's *Timon of Athens* (pr. c. 1607-1608), or to Schiller's fragment "Der Menschenfeind" (the misanthrope)? In the end, it was Raimund's own shaping of the material that produced one of his two greatest plays. Raimund had again found the perfect expression for his formula of fusing together the worlds of fantasy and reality.

DIE UNHEILBRINGENDE KRONE

This great success was followed by Raimund's greatest failure, *Die unheilbringende Krone*. The author even failed initially in his attempt to title the play, having to change "Crown" to "Magic Crown" in order to avoid a seeming allusion to the Austrian Imperial Crown. The plot was confusing and dull, fraught with too many characters and subplots. The audience objected to Raimund's departure from a simple comical story line, which it had come to expect in his work. Instead, Raimund had indulged in his passion to create a theater that was to measure up

to Shakespeare's historical tragedies or perhaps Johann Wolfgang von Goethe's *Faust: Eine Tragödie* (pb. 1808, pb. 1833; *The Tragedy of Faust*, 1823, 1828). The critics found the play marred by bombast and false pathos. In his disappointment, Raimund did not produce another play for four years.

THE SPENDTHRIFT

After this self-imposed silence, Raimund created his last and perhaps greatest play of all, *The Spendthrift*, which again reduced the emphasis on fantasy elements and pathos in favor of a plot placed squarely in the center of Raimund's beloved Vienna. In more ways than one, Raimund's career seemed to have come full circle, because the author had again written a servant role for himself, as in his early plays. *The Spendthrift* opened at the Josephstädter Theater on February 20, 1834, with Raimund in the role of the servant Valentin. For the first time, Raimund divided his play into three acts rather than the customary two. In the first act, the audience hears about the wealthy nobleman Julius von Flottwell through his servants and his secretary Wolf. Flottwell is careless with his money, indulging his every whim and leaving all decisions to Wolf. Wolf, the incarnation of evil, interviews two competing architects who are bidding for a contract to build Flottwell's new castle, and the secretary intends to give the contract to the one who will pay him the higher bribe. Into this web of corruption enters the honest servant Valentin, with his dependent, the chambermaid Rosa. Both of them are happy to be in the service of such a kind and generous master, but they despise the shallow and coarse friends whose company Flottwell keeps. Eventually, Flottwell himself and his companions appear, ready to engage in their favorite pastime, hunting. Toward the end of the act, it becomes evident that Flottwell not only associates with mortals but also has a protective spirit, Cheristane, who had provided Flottwell's father with all his wealth because she felt a deep fondness for young Flottwell. Now, however, she recognizes that wealth is an impediment to Flottwell's maturity. She dispatches her assistant, Azur, disguised as a beggar, to give Flottwell a taste of things to come unless he reforms his reckless life, but Flottwell does not recognize the impending doom.

In the second act, which takes place three years later, Flottwell is wooing Amalia, the daughter of President Klugheim, who refuses to give his daughter's hand to such a spendthrift. Meanwhile, Valentin and Rosa are dismissed from the household by Wolf on a trumped-up charge of theft. In reality, Rosa has incurred Wolf's ire by refusing his advances. At the end of the act, Flottwell has fled with Amalia to England; he squanders much of his fortune there and eventually loses his wife Amalia and a child on a voyage to South America.

In the third act, twenty years later, Flottwell returns home a beggar, while his secretary is now the ailing master of the castle. Valentin, now a carpenter, has married Rosa, and they have several children. In one of Raimund's most famous songs, the so-called "Hobellied" ("Carpenter's Song"), Valentin expresses his philosophy that all people will end up in the same condition eventually. He has remained loyal to Flottwell, who had always been kind to him and had given him many a ducat in good times. Together with Valentin and his family, Flottwell can spend the remainder of his life in modest comfort on the income from the gifts he had once carelessly bestowed on Azur.

With *The Spendthrift*, Raimund created the classical play of the Viennese Popular Theater, unsurpassed to this day. The realms of the real and the imaginary world appear side by side, as if this were the most normal state of affairs, but their juxtaposition no longer serves to hint at a doddering Austrian emperor or the empire's despicable lip service to truth—or, more gravely, at the paranoia that had pervaded everything during that age of political repression. Rather, Raimund returned to his contention, from *The Maid from Fairyland*, that wealth corrupts. It is moderation which Flottwell must learn; he has lived too "flott" (sumptuously) in every sense of the word.

Raimund's praise of moderation may also be interpreted as showing his affinity with the Biedermeier movement, which represented a withdrawal from the political and public scene to the privacy of home and hearth. Raimund had proved, however, that he was sensitive to the problems of his age, and perhaps his last play should be seen rather as a warning against the consequences of an unchecked materialism, which was on the rise with the advent of the Industrial Revolution.

BIBLIOGRAPHY

Harding, Laurence V. *The Dramatic Art of Ferdinand Raimund and Johann Nestroy*. The Hague, Netherlands: Mouton, 1974. Harding compares and contrasts the works of Raimund and Nestroy. Bibliography and index.

James, Dorothy. *Raimund and Vienna: A Critical Study of Raimund's Plays in Their Viennese Setting*. Cambridge, England: Cambridge University Press, 1970. A study of Raimund's dramatic works and their setting in Vienna. Bibliography.

Kimbell, Edmund. Introduction to *The Barometer-maker on the Magic Island and The Diamond of the Spirit King*, by Ferdinand Raimund. New York: Peter Lang, 1996. In his introduction to his translation of two of Raimund's plays, Kimbell provides critical analysis and useful insights. Bibliography.

Michalski, John. *Ferdinand Raimund*. New York: Twayne, 1968. A basic biography of Raimund that covers his life and works. Bibliography and index.

Yates, W. E., and John R. P. McKenzie, eds. *Viennese Popular Theatre: A Symposium*. Exeter, England: University of Exeter, 1985. This group of essays on the Viennese popular theater examines Raimund as well as Johann Nestroy and the theater of Austria. Bibliography.

Klaus D. Hanson

TERENCE RATTIGAN

Born: London, England; June 10, 1911
Died: Bermuda; November 30, 1977

PRINCIPAL DRAMA

First Episode, pr. 1933
French Without Tears, pr. 1936, pb. 1937
Flare Path, pr., pb. 1942
While the Sun Shines, pr. 1943, pb. 1944
Love in Idleness, pr. 1944, pb. 1945 (also as *O
    Mistress Mine*, pr., pb. 1946)
The Winslow Boy, pr., pb. 1946
*Playbill: "The Browning Version" and
    "Harlequinade,"* pr. 1948, pb. 1949 (2 one-acts)
Adventure Story, pr. 1949, pb. 1950
The Deep Blue Sea, pr., pb. 1952
The Collected Plays of Terence Rattigan, pb. 1953-
    1978 (4 volumes; Hamish Hamilton, editor)
The Sleeping Prince, pr. 1953, pb. 1954
*Separate Tables: "Table by the Window" and
    "Table Number Seven,"* pr. 1954, pb. 1955 (two
    playlets; commonly known as *Separate Tables*)
Ross, pr., pb. 1960
Man and Boy, pr., pb. 1963
A Bequest to the Nation, pr., pb. 1970 (adaptation
    of Rattigan's teleplay *Nelson*, pr. 1964)
*In Praise of Love: "Before Dawn" and "After
    Lydia,"* pb. 1973, pr. 1974 (as *In Praise
    of Love*)
Cause Célèbre, pr. 1977, pb. 1978 (adaptation of
    his radio play)
Plays, pb. 1981-1985 (2 volumes)

OTHER LITERARY FORMS

Terence Rattigan wrote many screenplays, including a number of adaptations of his own plays. For
the film of *The Browning Version*, he won the 1951
Cannes Film Festival Award for best screenplay. In
1958, the screenplay of *Separate Tables*, adapted
from Rattigan's play in collaboration with John Gay,
was nominated for an Academy Award. The triumvi-
rate of Rattigan, cowriter/producer Anatole de Grunwald, and director Anthony Asquith created a number

of films, including *Quiet Wedding* (1941, based on
Esther McCracken's play), *English Without Tears*
(1944, based on *French Without Tears*; also as *Her
Man Gilbey*), *The Way to the Stars* (1945; also as
Johnny in the Clouds, 1946), *While the Sun Shines*
(1946, adapted from Rattigan's play), and *The Winslow Boy* (1948, adapted from Rattigan's play). These
films were significant contributions to Great Britain's
postwar film renaissance. *The Sound Barrier* (1952;
also as *Breaking the Sound Barrier*), from Rattigan's
screenplay, is considered by some aficionados the
finest film ever made about aviation. His best-known
films are probably *Separate Tables* (for which David
Niven won an Academy Award as Best Actor), *The
Prince and the Showgirl* (1957, starring Marilyn
Monroe and Sir Laurence Olivier in the adaptation of
Rattigan's stage comedy *The Sleeping Prince*), and
The VIPs (1963, with an all-star cast headed by Elizabeth Taylor and Richard Burton).

Of Rattigan's seven original television scripts and
one radio script, *The Final Test* (1951) was released
as a film in 1954; *Nelson—A Portrait in Miniature*
(1964) was adapted as the play *A Bequest to the Nation* in 1970, with the film version appearing in 1973
under that title; and the radio script *Cause Célèbre*
(1975) was adapted for the stage.

Rattigan also wrote numerous theoretical essays.
Most important to his career were "Concerning the
Play of Ideas" and "The Play of Ideas," both published in 1950 in *The New Statesman and Nation*, and
the prefaces he wrote for the first three volumes of
The Collected Plays, published by Hamish Hamilton.
In *The New Statesman and Nation*, Rattigan defended
story and character—as opposed to intellectual debate and propagandizing—as the timeless values of
drama. He was rebutted, wholly or partly, by James
Bridie, Benn Levy, Peter Ustinov, Sean O'Casey,
Christopher Fry, and George Bernard Shaw. In his
second and third prefaces, Rattigan invented a
prototypical theatergoer, Aunt Edna, intended as a
humorous salute to the good common sense of audiences throughout the ages but attacked as evidence of

his own pandering to lowbrow sensibilities. His theoretical essays are too gentlemanly in tone to persuade with the sheer moral fervor of Shaw's, yet Rattigan was as sincere in his convictions and as true to his own values. His championship of the craft of playwriting and of the judgment of the dedicated theatergoer, his exploration in his first preface of the significance of dramatic implication, his musings in American newspaper articles on why plays suffer a "sea change" when produced in foreign countries, and his concept of the "farce of character" (in a 1947 *Strand* magazine article) are all valuable contributions to the literature of dramatic theory.

ACHIEVEMENTS

The first author ever to have had two plays (*French Without Tears* and *While the Sun Shines*) run for more than one thousand performances each on London's West End, Terence Rattigan was one of the most commercially successful playwrights in theater history. With striking versatility, he achieved his goal of moving audiences to laughter or tears in romantic comedy, comedy of manners, farce, fantasy, history plays, courtroom drama, and dramas about troubled middle-class characters. He also attracted many of the finest acting and directing talents of his period. Roles in Rattigan plays made stars of such young actors as Rex Harrison, Paul Scofield, and Kenneth More, and enhanced the careers of such luminaries as Peggy Ashcroft, Sir Laurence Olivier, Sir Alec Guinness, Margaret Sullivan, Margaret Leighton, and Alfred Lunt and Lynn Fontanne (a couple who had enjoyed the longest run of their stage careers in the American version of *Love in Idleness*).

Rattigan's success, however, was often held against him by critics, who did not bother to look beyond the polished surfaces of his plays. Failing to grasp the depth of psychological insight and the serious themes that usually characterized even his light comedies, most critics rated him as a good boulevard playwright at best. During the 1950's and the 1960's, the heyday of the Angry Young Men and the Theater

Terence Rattigan in 1971. (AP/Wide World Photos)

of the Absurd, Rattigan's work was derided as representing the establishment culture that younger playwrights and critics sought to demolish. London revivals of five of his plays between 1970 and 1977, the year of Rattigan's death, led to a greater appreciation of his worth. With the widely hailed National Theatre's production of *Playbill* in 1980 and the Roundabout Theatre Company's acclaimed New York revivals of *The Winslow Boy* in 1980 and *The Browning Version* in 1982, Rattigan began to be recognized as an artist of high stature.

BIOGRAPHY

Terence Mervyn Rattigan was born in Kensington, London, on June 10, 1911, to William Frank Rattigan and Vera Houston Rattigan, ten days before the coronation of George V. His father, a career diplomat, was a minor functionary in the coronation and his mother missed the ceremony because of her confinement. Forty-two years later, when Rattigan wrote his sophisticated fantasy *The Sleeping Prince* as a *pièce d'occasion* for Elizabeth II's coronation, he said that he used George V's coronation for the background of the play as a present to his mother for having missed the real thing.

Both of Rattigan's parents came from distinguished families of Irish lawyers, a heritage that fascinated Rattigan and showed itself not only in the characters of the lawyers in *The Winslow Boy* and *Cause Célèbre* but also in such scenes as the hotel residents' "trial" of Major Pollock in *Table Number Seven*. Rattigan's father, who failed in his own career and was pensioned off in 1922, hoped that Rattigan would find a career in the diplomatic service.

From early boyhood, however, when his parents first took him to the theater, Rattigan was determined to be a playwright. He hoarded his allowance and sneaked off to the theater, began writing plays at eleven, and read plays avidly while on scholarship at Harrow from 1925 to 1930. At Oxford on a history scholarship, he acted, wrote criticism for the *Cherwell*, and collaborated with fellow student Philip Heimann on a play about Oxonian high jinks and their sad consequences entitled *First Episode*, which enjoyed respectful reviews and a brief run on the West End in the 1933-1934 season. On the strength of this success, he persuaded his father to give him a modest allowance to enable him to write for two years, at the end of which he either would be a successful playwright or would bow to his parents' wishes for his career.

Rattigan's Oxford years were far from wasted; his reading of history helped inspire his studies of Alexander the Great (*Adventure Story*, 1949), T. E. Lawrence (*Ross*), and Lord Nelson (*A Bequest to the Nation*), and summers spent taking language courses in Germany and France prompted *French Without Tears*, whose spectacular success enabled Rattigan to win his career gamble with his father. From then until the last decade of his life, even though he suffered his

share of flops and personal sorrows, Rattigan was depicted in the press as fortune's favorite, an image enlarged by his exceptional good looks and elegant lifestyle.

Virtually all of Rattigan's work was influenced directly or indirectly by his personal experience. Several of his wartime plays and film scripts, for example, grew out of his service as a Royal Air Force flight lieutenant. *In Praise of Love* was dually inspired by his friendship with Rex Harrison and Harrison's wife, Kay Kendall, when she was dying of leukemia and by a false diagnosis of leukemia in Rattigan himself in 1962. Examples of more pervasive influences are his parents' unhappy marriage, his attempts to love and be loyal to both his mother and his father, and his own homosexuality. Rattigan's comedies and dramas often feature compassionate portraits of mismatched couples, bewildered youths in contention with their elders, and individuals tortured by sexual repression, deviation, or frustration. Rattigan's protagonists generally meet their problems with the dignity and courage that he brought to his own life, particularly during his two-year battle with bone cancer. After a self-imposed seven-year exile to write film scripts during the period of his greatest vilification by younger critics and colleagues, Rattigan lived to see himself welcomed back into the British theater community with his knighthood in 1971, the beginning of his artistic renaissance through revivals of his earlier plays, and the positive reception of a new work, *Cause Célèbre*, only months before his death.

ANALYSIS

In a 1962 *Theatre Arts* interview, Terence Rattigan told John Simon that playwrights were born Ibsenites or Chekhovians and that he was the former longing to be the latter. In fact, he blended the influences of both. Like Henrik Ibsen in his problem plays, Rattigan reshaped the Scribean well-made play to his own ends, imbuing it with psychological complexity and moral passion. Unlike Ibsen, he seldom allowed his characters to debate ideas and issues, taking instead a firm stand against ideological drama. Like Anton Chekhov, Rattigan focused on the personal problems of predominantly middle-class characters who are left with no neat solutions; his comedies end with a respite instead of a celebration; his dramas, with a delicate balance of losses and gains. Rattigan's characters are, like Chekhov's, bound in a rich tapestry: Their fates are to varying degrees interrelated, but their essential aloneness is poignantly conveyed. Unlike Ibsen or Chekhov, Rattigan was not a radical innovator, and as yet there is no evidence of his direct influence on successors. Each of Rattigan's plays displays innovative touches, however, and the body of his work reveals an artist with a distinct personal vision that he expressed in both the content and the form of his plays.

Rattigan's attacks on doctrinaire drama and his dismissal by most critics as an ideologically empty playwright are ironic, for his work is deeply ideological. His pervading theme is a passionate defense of the most oppressed minority throughout history: the individual. In a 1982 *Contemporary Review* retrospective, a writer recalled Rattigan's saying: "People should care about people, and I've some doubts that the ideologists do. They may care about the starving millions, but they're not worried too much about those millions' particular concerns." Rattigan was.

All but three of his plays are set in the twentieth century, most in the period from the 1930's to the 1960's. Rattigan captured the bewilderment of people living in a world without a firm moral and social structure to give them a sense of place and security. Theirs is a stark existence in which confusion and loneliness predominate, compounded by stale ideas and conventions. The philosophical idea Rattigan implicitly condemned throughout his work was the mind-body dichotomy, or the belief that human beings' physical and spiritual natures are irreconcilable, that one can be satisfied only at the expense of the other, and that spiritual love is superior to physical love. The social conventions Rattigan most abhorred were the prohibition against expressing emotion and the ostracism of individuals for deviating from various norms. His plays show that the individual's best resources are self-reliance and self-respect, understanding and compassion for others, and the healing bonds of kindness and friendship.

Rattigan's characters are influenced by outside factors, but all have a range of choice in their values and actions. His plots delineate the cause-and-effect relationship between the nature of the values that individuals pursue, evade, or betray and their psychological and existential well-being. The form of a Rattigan play is determined by and inseparable from its content. In a *Daily Telegraph* tribute after the playwright's death, William Douglas-Home likened the beauty of Rattigan's structures to those of classical architecture and the symphony. The *Contemporary Review* writer stated that Rattigan's plays have "'good bones'—a prime requisite for aging well." The sinews of his plays are his extraordinarily rich dialogue—naturalistic but so precisely stylized that a few simple words can, as Harold Hobson frequently pointed out, convey a world of meaning. Rattigan's personal signature on the form and content of his work may be seen by surveying one play from each of the five decades of his playwriting career.

FRENCH WITHOUT TEARS

Even when one recalls that Rattigan had been writing plays diligently from the age of eleven, the artistic wholeness of *French Without Tears*, his first produced solo effort, seems remarkable. In varying degrees, the characteristics of his body of work are all present in this early work.

The innovative element of this romantic comedy is Rattigan's reversal of the cliché of a femme fatale who turns friends into enemies. At a small language program in France, several young Englishmen try to learn French while one student's alluring sister, Diana, tries to distract them. She entraps Kit, much to the distress of the French tutor's daughter, Jacqueline, and then entices a newly arrived, more mature naval commander. Alan, a diplomat's son yearning to be a novelist (an autobiographical touch), feigns indifference to Diana, cheers Kit, and ridicules the Commander. In a scene reminiscent of the Elyot-Victor clash in Noël Coward's *Private Lives* (pr. 1930), Kit and the Commander fight until they discover that Diana has used the same "line" on them. They unite in friendship, accompanied by Alan, and confront Diana with her perfidy. She confounds them all by declaring that she really loves Alan. Kit turns to Jacqueline, and Diana chases Alan as he, taking the Commander's advice, bolts to London to tell his father that he is taking up writing instead of diplomacy. Although structured on the Chekhovian model of short scenes between groups of characters, building up a central situation through accumulation of detail, the plot has the vitality of a mixed-doubles grudge match in tennis, with changes of partners topped by one player taking off after the referee.

The play examines the relationship of love and sex at a depth unusual in light comedy. Alan and Kit are caught in the mind-body dichotomy, desiring an attractive girl with little character and feeling only friendship for the plainer but more worthy Jacqueline. At the end, she and Kit decide timidly to see if love and friendship, sex and liking, can mix. For all of his sophisticated airs, Alan is a little English gentleman who can sail only calm waters. He feels comfortable in friendship with Jacqueline but panics over Diana, afraid of sex and of having his emotions aroused.

Friendship is a bond bridging social and economic gaps and changing people's lives throughout Rattigan's work. When they stop fighting with the Commander, Kit and Alan discover that he is not the stodgy figure they mocked but a sensitive and sensible man. This revelation is also an instance of Rattigan showing characters as individuals, not types. He accomplishes this with Diana in a sequence in which she admits to Jacqueline that she cannot give up the chase because she knows that men can only love but never like her.

Rattigan's use of dramatic implication is illustrated by a short scene in which Alan describes the plot of his rejected novel to Kit and the Commander. His story not only mirrors the conflict between his listeners and its resolution but also foreshadows the war clouds gathering around the students—a point reinforced by other touches in the play. Historically, the comedy is a sunny look at the youth of a generation soon to fight World War II. Rattigan's biographers, Michael Darlow and Gillian Hodson, cite *French Without Tears* as the best comedy of the 1930's and the representative British play of that decade.

PLAYBILL

In spite of the success of his war drama *Flare Path*, his comedy of manners and romance *Love in Idleness*, and his courtroom-like drama set entirely in a drawing room, *The Winslow Boy*, Rattigan had difficulty finding a producer for *Playbill*. Most managements thought bills of one-acts commercial folly. T. C. Worsley noted in a *London Magazine* essay that Rattigan's defense of the artistic integrity of the one-act form and his reintroduction of it to the West End after the war proved boons to his successors.

Though *The Browning Version* and *Harlequinade* are often produced separately, their coupling in *Playbill* represents an artistic design. The overall structure is psychological, encompassing studies of vastly different personalities—the severely repressed and the flamboyantly theatrical. They are embodied in plots ingeniously similar enough—in each play, errors from the past press on the protagonists—to highlight the contrast between psychologies.

The Browning Version, which won the Ellen Terry Award for best play of 1948, probes a psychological state that Rattigan had used as a leitmotif of characterization in his earlier plays. As Kay Nolte Smith pointed out in a 1971 *Objectivist* essay, the drama's theme is the tragedy of emotional repression. This is Rattigan's most original theme, and a difficult one to dramatize. His genius lay in making the causes and effects of repression intelligible and dramatic in a classically severe plot, without the use of soliloquy, of a narrator or *raisonneur* figure to offer explanations, or even of the word "repression."

The setting is the living room of a schoolmaster's apartment at a British boy's school. Andrew Crocker-Harris, once a brilliant and idealistic Greek master but now a dessicated pedant, is retiring early because of ill health. Visits by his young successor, the Headmaster, a pupil, and a colleague, and constant taunts by his sexually and socially frustrated wife, recall Crocker-Harris to his hopes and failures as a teacher and as a husband. Two gestures of kindness—the pupil's parting gift of Robert Browning's version of Aeschylus's *Agamemnōn* (458 B.C.E.; *Agamemnon*, 1777) and the colleague's offer of friendship—help Crocker-Harris to overcome what he calls his state of being a spiritual corpse, to break with his wife and to assert himself to the Headmaster. The play's penultimate line, when Crocker-Harris claims from the Headmaster his right to speak last at a school ceremony, "I am of opinion that occasionally an anti-climax can be surprisingly effective," is a characteristic Rattigan understatement, conveying his protagonist's recovery of self-respect in a simple phrase. Reviewing a 1976 London revival in the *Sunday Times*, Harold Hobson called *The Browning Version* "a masterpiece if ever there was one, the best one-act in the language."

Crocker-Harris was inspired partly by Rattigan's Greek master at Harrow. The famed acting team playing an aging Romeo and Juliet, whose dress rehearsal is interrupted by unwelcome visitors in *Harlequinade*, bore resemblances to Alfred Lunt and Lynn Fontanne, with whom Rattigan had worked so closely on *Love in Idleness*. The focus is on the Romeo, a quintessential actor-manager oblivious of events outside the theater, who embodies Rattigan's theory that farce may be based on character. The comedy has been compared favorably with George Villiers's *The Rehearsal* (pr. 1671, pb. 1672), Richard Brinsley Sheridan's *The Critic: Or, A Tragedy Rehearsed* (pr. 1779), and Arthur Wing Pinero's *Trelawny of the "Wells"* (pr., pb. 1898) as a classic play about theater life.

THE DEEP BLUE SEA

Though usually cited as one of Rattigan's finest works, *The Deep Blue Sea* has yet to be fully appreciated. Eleven years before the women's movement began with the publication of Betty Friedan's *The Feminine Mystique* (1963), Rattigan produced a prescient drama about the effects of a woman's "raised consciousness."

The play is structured like a thriller, beginning with a landlady's discovery of Hester Collyer, unconscious from a suicide attempt, in a run-down London boardinghouse. Hester no longer feels worthy or desirous of living; gradually, the action reveals why. Daughter of a clergyman, wife of a judge honored with knighthood, she has fallen passionately in love with a feckless younger man and run off with him. A war pilot who has never found an equivalent challenge in civilian life, Freddie Page loves Hester in his

way but is incapable of returning her ardor sexually or emotionally, and determines to leave rather than ruin Hester's life further. Hester's loving husband, Sir William, views her attachment as an ignoble but pardonable sex obsession and wants her to return to being his companionable wife.

Hester's sexual awakening with Freddie has released her need for more intense relationships than either man can offer. She feels deep shame at the pain she has caused, terror at the prospect of losing Freddie, and anger at the religious and societal view—pressed by her background, Sir William, and a young neighbor—that spiritual love is superior to physical. Another neighbor, a former doctor who lost his license and bears his disgrace with dignity, is able from his perspective as a social outcast to help Hester view herself as a worthy individual. In the end, after saying goodbye to her husband and lover, Hester takes her first step toward independence by lighting the gas heater she may still decide to use to escape life. *The Deep Blue Sea* was ahead of its time not only in Rattigan's sympathetic portrait of a woman who must virtually start life again almost at middle age, but also in his equally compassionate portrayals of men who are bewildered, wounded, and threatened by women's changing needs.

THE ADVENTURE STORY AND ROSS

Rattigan applied principles of craftsmanship from the well-made play to the epic form with impressive results. Although his portraits of Alexander the Great in *Adventure Story* and T. E. Lawrence in *Ross* are marred by earnest but ultimately unconvincing attempts to explain each man's motivations, Rattigan captures the personal charisma of both figures and the sweep of their lives through world history with narrative mastery.

Like *Adventure Story*, *Ross* traces the psychological destruction of a brilliant military leader. The first three scenes dramatize Lawrence's attempt to find peace after World War I as a Royal Air Force aircraftman enlisted under the pseudonym of Ross. Recognized and awaiting expulsion, he drifts into a malarial dream that becomes a bridge to scenes depicting the wartime exploits that made him famous but sickened him spiritually. He is torn by exulting in his triumphs while wading through carnage to achieve them and then destroyed psychologically by being awakened to his homosexual and masochistic tendencies in his (offstage) beating and rape by Turkish soldiers. Lawrence had trusted in the supremacy of his will and cannot face the realization that behind his will are not strength and integrity but inclinations that shame him. In the end, he decides to seek sanctuary in the service again under another assumed name.

In terms of Rattigan's attempt to integrate an expansive narrative structure with a comprehensive character study, *Ross* is his most complex and ambitious play. There is a density in its texture because of the sheer weight of material it encompasses. Rattigan had to explain the British, Arab, and Turkish positions during the World War I Middle Eastern conflict while simultaneously exploring the inner conflicts of a character who is both a man of action and a deeply repressed, tormented intellectual. Without narration, Rattigan was able to organize his mass of material in theatrical terms, judiciously balancing humor, suspense, and pathos.

IN PRAISE OF LOVE

The last third of *In Praise of Love*, Rattigan's penultimate play, contains some of his finest writing. About an Eastern European war refugee dying of leukemia, her apparently callous British husband, their sensitive son, and an old family friend, the work is structured as a psychological suspense story. Two-thirds of the play are devoted to creating a negative picture of the husband as a childish, boorish, selfish man. The wife confides her illness to the friend because she fears boring her husband, as she thinks she once bored him with her refugee tales, and tries to reconcile the contentious husband and son, both of whom she adores. In a *coup de théâtre*, the husband is forced to tell the friend that he has known of his wife's illness all along and is determined to keep it from her lest she relive her wartime anticipation of death at any moment. His callousness, once a habit, is now a mask he dons to foster the illusion that all is normal. He finds the mask torturous to wear because he has realized how much he loves his wife yet cannot tell her. He remarks that the English people's worst vice is their refusal to admit to their emotions.

Rattigan's condemnation of emotional repression is explicit in *In Praise of Love*, but particularly noteworthy in the play is the most daring use he ever made of implication. Rattigan's dramas are all dotted with comic dialogue and business that further his goals without undercutting the seriousness of his subjects. With *In Praise of Love*, he used comic dialogue and action throughout to build a picture of a household under almost unbearable emotional pressure, a household in which characters use banter to mask their own feelings and to try to spare the feelings of others. The contrast between the characters' veneer and the depth of their love and grief is profoundly poignant.

On Rattigan's death in 1977, the *Guardian*'s Michael Billington, representative of a post-Angry-Young-Man generation of theater critics, maintained that Rattigan was misunderstood as an exemplar of the cool and gentlemanly school of English playwriting: "The real truth is that his plays are a remorseless attack on English emotional inhibition, and a moving plea for affection and kindness and understanding in the everyday business of life. . . . Few dramatists [in the twentieth] century have written with more understanding about the human heart." Giving evidence that this revaluation is not confined to British critics, Susan Rusinko concludes in her 1983 study of Rattigan for Twayne's English Authors series: "Polished without being slick, natural without untidiness, Rattigan's art has given firm shape to the mid-twentieth century mainstream of English life, chronicling the sweeping changes in the moods and attitudes of the time, as [did] Chekhov for his time."

OTHER MAJOR WORKS

SCREENPLAYS: *Quiet Wedding*, 1941 (based on Esther McCracken's play); *English Without Tears*, 1944 (with Anatole de Grunwald; also known as *Her Man Gilbey*); *The Way to the Stars*, 1945 (with de Grunwald; also known as *Johnny in the Clouds*); *While the Sun Shines*, 1946; *The Winslow Boy*, 1948 (with de Grunwald); *Bond Street*, 1948; *Brighton Rock*, 1948 (later as *Young Scarface*; with Graham Greene; based on Greene's novel); *The Browning Version*, 1951; *The Sound Barrier*, 1952 (also known as *Breaking the*

Sound Barrier); *The Final Test*, 1954; *The Prince and the Showgirl*, 1957 (adaptation of *The Sleeping Prince*); *Separate Tables*, 1958 (with John Gay; adaptation of Rattigan's play); *The VIPs*, 1963; *The Yellow Rolls-Royce*, 1965; *A Bequest to the Nation*, 1973.

TELEPLAYS: *The Final Test*, 1951; *Heart to Heart*, 1964; *Nelson—A Portrait in Miniature*, 1964.

RADIO PLAY: *Cause Célèbre*, 1975.

BIBLIOGRAPHY

Darlow, Michael, and Gillian Hodson. *Terence Rattigan: The Man and His Work*. London: Quartet Books, 1979. A 360-page critical biography, thoroughly researched, using archives from the British Broadcasting Corporation. In this eminently readable narrative of Rattigan, his plays, and their times—all three led inexorably to one another—the authors write with authority and with permission from Rattigan to reveal much of what he had been unable to write about directly in his own plays. Includes photographs, a bibliography, a list of British and American opening dates and casts, and an index.

O'Connor, Sean. *Straight Acting: Popular Gay Drama from Wilde to Rattigan*. Washington, D.C.: Cassell, 1998. A look at homosexuality and literature that traces gay writers from Oscar Wilde and W. Somerset Maugham to more modern writers such as Noël Coward and Terence Rattigan. Bibliography and index.

Rusinko, Susan. *Terence Rattigan*. Boston: Twayne, 1983. A chronological summary-analysis of the complete stage, film, and television plays, analyzing Rattigan's major plays, from his early sunny comedies to his later dramas about dysfunctional families in a dysfunctional society. Photograph, chronology, bibliography, index.

Wansell, Geoffrey. *Terence Rattigan*. New York: St. Martin's Press, 1997. A biography of the British dramatist that covers his works for the stage as well as those for television and the movie theater. Bibliography and index.

Young, B. A. *The Rattigan Version: The Theatre of Character*. New York: Atheneum, 1988. A personal memoir by an author who knew Rattigan. Leisurely in pace and impressionistic in style, it raises some questions, as in the descriptions of Rattigan's manner of throwing "his dialogue down on the page, caring only for its gist rather than its style." Includes index, cast lists, and photographs that tell their own story.

Holly Hill,
updated by Susan Rusinko

JAMES REANEY

Born: South Easthope, Ontario, Canada;
September 1, 1926

PRINCIPAL DRAMA

Night-Blooming Cereus, wr. 1952, pr. 1959 (radio play), pr. 1960 (staged), pb. 1962 (libretto; with John Beckwith)

The Sun and the Moon, wr. 1959, pb. 1962, pr. 1965

The Killdeer, pr. 1960, pb. 1962, revised pr. 1970, pb. 1972

One-Man Masque, pr. 1960, pb. 1962

The Easter Egg, pr. 1962, pb. 1972

Names and Nicknames, pr. 1963, pb. 1969

Let's Make a Carol, pr. 1964, pb. 1965 (music by Beckwith)

Apple Butter, pr. 1965, pb. 1973 (puppet play)

The Shivaree, wr. 1965, pb. 1978, pr. 1982 (libretto; music by Beckwith)

Listen to the Wind, pr. 1966, pb. 1972

Ignoramus, pr. 1966, pb. 1973

Colours in the Dark, pr. 1967, pb. 1969

Three Desks, pr. 1967, pb. 1972

Geography Match, pr. 1967, pb. 1973

The Donnellys: Part I, Sticks and Stones, wr. 1968-1972, pr. 1973, pb. 1975

The Donnellys: Part II, St. Nicholas Hotel, Wm Donnelly, Prop., wr. 1968-1973, pr. 1974, pb. 1976

The Donnellys: Part III, Handcuffs, wr. 1968-1974, pr. 1975, pb. 1977

Masks of Childhood, pb. 1972 (includes *The Easter Egg*, *Three Desks*, and *The Killdeer*)

All the Bees and All the Keys, pr. 1973, pb. 1976 (music by Beckwith)

Baldoon, pr., pb. 1976 (with C. H. "Marty" Gervais)

The Dismissal, wr. 1976-1977, pr. 1977, pb. 1978

Wacousta!, pr. 1978, pb. 1979

King Whistle, pr. 1979

Antler River, pr. 1980

Gyroscope, pr. 1981, pb. 1983

The Canadian Brothers, pr. 1983, pb. 1984

The Donnellys, pb. 1983 (includes the Donnelly trilogy)

Crazy to Kill, pr., pb. 1988 (libretto; music by Beckwith)

Lewis Carroll's "Alice Through the Looking Glass," pr., pb. 1994 (adaptation of Carroll's novel)

OTHER LITERARY FORMS

Since the late 1940's, when James Reaney first distinguished himself as one of Canada's most provocative writers, he has amassed an impressive list of publications in all areas of creative and scholarly writing. In addition to more than twenty-five plays produced on stage, radio, and television, Reaney has written four volumes of award-winning poetry (*The Red Heart*, 1949; *A Suit of Nettles*, 1958; *Twelve Letters to a Small Town*, 1962; *The Dance of Death at London, Ontario*, 1963). His individual pieces, published in a wide variety of literary magazines and academic journals, have been collected into three separate volumes by editor Germaine Warkentin (*Poems*, 1972; *Selected Shorter Poems*, 1975; *Selected Longer Poems*, 1976). With composer John Beckwith, Rea-

ney developed skills as a librettist, setting his poetry to Beckwith's music for radio broadcast in the late 1950's and early 1960's.

Like his drama, much of Reaney's poetry concerns the power of language as a redemptive catalyst in a corrupt and evil world. Geographically set in his native region of southwestern Ontario, his poetry is essentially lyric pastoral with characters, situations, and the landscape transformed by the imagery and such diverse poetic structures as eclogues, dialogue, and prosaic narrative. Reaney's poetry is a testament to his fascination with the musical patterns of rhyme and rhythm, demonstrating the author's talent for iambic pentameter, doggerel, rhyming couplets, blank verse, and lyric stanzas.

Reaney's short stories, written between 1946 and 1955, are also set in small-town Ontario. Young women with disturbing and unresolved emotional conflicts dominate the action of these stories. Beneath the calm, romantic façade of domesticity, Reaney's heroines hide a passionate intensity, which is revealed in the often surprising climaxes to the stories. Two juvenile novels and a journal of the cross-country tour of the Donnelly trilogy fill out his creative dossier. As a highly respected professor of literature, Reaney has published works on a variety of scholarly and literary topics in numerous academic publications.

ACHIEVEMENTS

A distinguished poet, playwright, and scholar, James Reaney has won three Governor General's Awards for poetry and drama, as well as a Chalmer's Award for drama. His first major dramatic work, *The Killdeer*, collected five of the top awards at the Dominion Drama Festival in 1960 for Reaney, Pamela Terry (director), the designer, and two performers. The numerous awards and accolades garnered during his career are but one measure of Reaney's impact on modern Canadian literature. The success of *The Killdeer* thrust Reaney into the limelight of a small, elite group of contemporary Canadian writers who had a marked effect on the growth of professional theater (and dramatic literature) in Canada.

Reaney has been involved in theatrical production since his high school days, and the sheer number of plays that he has written and had produced (more than twenty-five) is an enormous achievement in a country whose theatrical traditions began to reach maturity more than twenty years after he began writing drama. One of his early goals was to provide Canadians with a portrait of their own unique experiences. As he said in a 1977 interview with *University of Western Ontario News*, "We need new plays, and Ontario is a very fascinating place."

Besides the significant contribution that Reaney has made to Canadian literature, he has also been influential in his role as teacher. Through his children's literature, his courses in creative writing, and his Listeners' Workshops, Reaney has led a new generation of young Canadians to an appreciation of poetry, drama, and their own unique history.

BIOGRAPHY

James Crerar Reaney, born in 1926 on a small farm in Fundamentalist southwestern Ontario (about ninety miles from the major cultural center of Toronto), grew up in a family and a community that was predominantly Irish and Scottish. The family broke with the conventional teachings of their congregation, Gospel Hall, and conducted prayer meetings at home. As Reaney grew older, he was sent to attend an Interdenominational Sunday school and later a combination Presbyterian and Congregational Sunday school, where the evangelical nature of the teachings had a dramatic effect on his imagination. The gothic tones and melodrama of the church teachings are clearly evident in his early plays *The Killdeer*, *The Sun and the Moon*, and *Listen to the Wind*.

By the time Reaney was graduated from high school, he was an accomplished musician and linguist. On a scholarship, he moved to Toronto to study Greek and Latin at the country's most distinguished college, the University of Toronto. It was during his study of classical languages that Reaney began his exploration of the alphabet and his fascination with the creative possibilities of a flexible language. He began to experiment with word lists as a way of developing an inventory of life, imagination, and experience; these word lists grew into volumes of highly acclaimed poetry. The underlying concept of the

word catalogs is an iconography of the imagination—a concept that came to fruition with the founding of an unusual literary journal, *Alphabet*, published from 1960 to 1971. Reaney's experimentation with language as an integral part of dramatic structure is demonstrated in his 1967 play *Colours in the Dark* but shows itself in its most mature form in the Donnelly trilogy, written between 1968 and 1974. The trilogy brought Reaney national acclaim as one of Canada's foremost playwrights.

By 1947, Reaney had already achieved national notoriety as a provocative young talent with the publication of his short story "The Box Social" in the July 19, 1947, issue of *New Liberty Magazine*. This macabre story, which tells of a young man whose girlfriend presents him with a stillborn fetus during a church social, set the tone for much of his early writing. Reaney's world is an unsettling mixture of good and evil where pastoral romance, rural realism, and strong strains of melodrama are held together by the common thread of childhood experience, simultaneously innocent and corrupt.

While completing his M.A. at the University of Toronto in 1949, Reaney published his first volume of poetry, *The Red Heart*, which won the Governor General's Award, the most prestigious literary prize in Canada (comparable to the Pulitzer Prize). It was also during this time that the young writer came under the influence of Northrop Frye, the internationally acclaimed scholar and literary critic whose pioneering study of William Blake, *Fearful Symmetry* (1947), was to revolutionize modern literary analysis. Although Reaney was not yet a student of Frye, he was very much a part of the literary elite at the university who were preoccupied with discussion and analysis of Frye's important work. *Fearful Symmetry* provided Reaney with an archetypal vision of the Bible that became the impetus for much of the imagery and metaphor in both his poetry and drama. As Ross Woodman says in his excellent introduction to *James Reaney* (1971), Frye's work transformed "in a comprehensive and systematic way Reaney's earlier evangelical world into a literary one."

With his M.A. completed and the Governor General's Award in hand, Reaney accepted a position at the University of Manitoba in Winnipeg (the gateway to the Canadian West) to teach English and creative writing. The years in Winnipeg (until 1956) were difficult for Reaney, who felt isolated from the creative activity of southern Ontario, but it was also a time when he forged important friendships with people such as stage director John Hirsch (who later founded the Manitoba Theatre Centre, one of Canada's leading performing arts facilities) and playwright Tom Hendry. Both men, along with Keith Turnbull of the NDWT (Ne'er-Do-Well-Thespians) Company, would have an important influence on Reaney's development as a dramatist.

It was also during this period that Reaney began writing librettos for composer John Beckwith, whom he had met as an undergraduate at the University of Toronto. Their first coproduction, *Night-Blooming Cereus*, was also Reaney's initial attempt at dramatic writing and was produced on radio by the Canadian Broadcasting Corporation (CBC) in 1959 and staged in 1960.

Each summer during the Winnipeg years, Reaney returned to Stratford to write and to take part in an important cultural event in his hometown. Internationally famous actor/director/producer Tyrone Guthrie had come to Stratford (from London, England) to found the Stratford Shakespeare Festival. The festival began in a large marquee in the early 1950's and had grown by the late 1960's to encompass the Festival Theatre (a Shakespearean thrust stage), the Avon Theatre (a proscenium arch theater), and the Third Stage (a flexible, experimental space). Reaney's participation in the formative years of the Stratford experiment solidified his desire to write for the stage. His first attempt at a full-length play, "The Rules of Joy" (later rewritten and retitled *The Sun and the Moon*), was conceived with the Festival Theatre stage in mind, but it was not until 1967 that the festival commissioned Reaney to write a major work for the Stratford stage. *Colours in the Dark*, which was performed at the Avon Theatre in 1967, was not only a watershed piece in Reaney's evolution as a dramatist but also a celebration of the nation itself—written to commemorate Canada's one hundredth birthday.

At home in Stratford for Christmas of 1951, Reaney married Colleen Thibaudeau, an accomplished poet of Irish and Acadian French background whom he had met during his years at the University of Toronto. Both had been members of a small literary group at the university, and Reaney respected both her accomplishments and her advice on his writing. Thibaudeau, whose poetic style was very different from his, had a substantial impact on the tone and quality of Reaney's writing. The often negative view of marriage and family life presented in his early works changed and mellowed after their marriage and the birth of their first son, James Stewart, in 1953. The Reaneys had another son, John Andrew, in 1954, and a daughter, Susan Alice, in 1959. While Reaney was in rehearsal with one of his most romantic plays, *Listen to the Wind*, John Andrew died at the age of eleven. The published version of *Listen to the Wind* is dedicated to Reaney's son.

In 1956, Reaney took a two-year sabbatical from the University of Manitoba and returned to the University of Toronto in 1956 to write his doctoral thesis, "The Influence of Spenser on Yeats." He enrolled in Northrop Frye's course on literary symbolism and finally came under the direct influence of the great scholar when Frye became Reaney's thesis supervisor. His studies with Frye brought together the many facets of literature and myth that Reaney had been exploring for decades. His love of nursery rhymes, fairy tales, and all other literary paraphernalia of childhood began to take on a new meaning: Childhood fantasy, evangelism, and the magic of pastoral romance merged with marionettes, children's games, and his growing understanding of the many possibilities of stage business. Reaney, who had bicycled more than one hundred miles to see the opening of Walt Disney's *Fantasia* (1940), was on the brink of creating his own very personal vocabulary for poetry and drama.

With his doctorate completed, Reaney returned to Winnipeg and to the business of teaching and writing. In 1958, his second volume of poetry, *A Suit of Nettles*, was greeted with critical enthusiasm and, in 1959, a second Governor General's Award. In Winnipeg, Reaney began work on his first major play, *The Killdeer*, the story of an emotionally retarded young man and the young lovers who help him reach both maturity and reality. Reaney had difficulty restraining the narrative to fit the dramatic structure. He sent the play to Toronto to his friend Pamela Terry (who was later to marry composer Beckwith), and with her assistance the play was rewritten and finally produced, with Terry as director, in 1960. This first version of *The Killdeer* won five awards at the Dominion Drama Festival, and in 1962, the play and Reaney's radio poem, *Twelve Letters to a Small Town*, won for him a third Governor General's Award.

The year of *The Killdeer* was a new beginning. Reaney began dedicating more and more time to his dramatic writing. He returned from Winnipeg and accepted a professorship at the University of Western Ontario, in London, Ontario. The year 1960 also saw the first volume of *Alphabet: A Semiannual Devoted to the Iconography of the Imagination* and the flourishing of his scholarly writings in such esteemed academic and literary journals as *Tamarack Review*, *Canadian Literature*, *Canadian Forum*, and the *University of Toronto Quarterly*.

Reaney understood that it was essential to develop actors, directors, and creative support-staff simultaneously with the evolution of his writing style — artists whose diverse approaches to theater would enhance his writing. To this end, he established the Listeners' Workshops, which began at the Alphacentre in London, Ontario, in 1967. The workshops were a joint project of many in the artistic community who believed that performers need to relearn how to play and to be inventive in the way children are as they engage in make-believe. Children and adults, amateurs and professionals all participated in the Saturday morning sessions, directed by Reaney, which explored sound, music, movement, poetry, play, myth, and magic in an effort to develop a vibrant ensemble theater. The freedom of imagination that evolved in the workshops redefined for Reaney the meaning of ensemble playing. From the workshops grew a core of fiercely loyal, creative people who ultimately formed the nucleus of the NDWT Company, the troupe with which Reaney worked on the Donnelly trilogy.

Reaney continued to write both poetry and plays. In the mid-1960's, he was particularly influenced by

a performance of the Beijing opera, where mime, movement, and masks replaced traditional properties and stage sets. Fascinated by the circus-like nature of the production, Reaney assimilated the experience and began work on his major opus, the Donnelly trilogy, which was to take nearly ten years to complete. The story of an outcast Irish family in rural Ontario at the turn of the century, the Donnelly plays brought to fruition the various threads of poetry, music, drama, dance, documentary, mime, circus, and magic that appear in embryonic form in the early plays. In 1974, *The Donnellys: Part II, St. Nicholas Hotel, Wm Donnelly, Prop.*, the second of the three Donnelly plays, won the Chalmers Award for Drama, the prize for outstanding stage writing in Canada.

The success of the trilogy was unlike anything that had happened before in Canadian theater. Over a period of three years, each of the three plays was a huge box-office and critical success when it was first presented in Toronto. Even more remarkable was the reception of the trilogy tour across eight of the ten provinces — proving that Canadian audiences were as interested in poetry, drama, and local history as was the author. In 1975, Reaney and the NDWT Company took the three plays from coast to coast, ending the tour in Toronto, where all three plays were presented again. Audiences in Toronto had the opportunity to see the entire trilogy performed in one day (each play is more than three and a half hours long) with a break for lunch and dinner. This once-in-a-lifetime opportunity sold out. The experience of the tour has been recorded in Reaney's book *Fourteen Barrels from Sea to Sea* (1977). With the tour complete, Reaney was awarded the Order of Canada in 1975. In the wake of this success, Reaney turned increasingly to dramas focused on the history and culture of southwestern Ontario, but such plays as *Wacousta!* and *The Canadian Brothers* met with mixed receptions.

ANALYSIS

James Reaney has said "William Blake's poetry is the kind of ideal I have in which there's painting and dance and rhythm and poetry and sound, a whole world on various levels. . . . I'm not interested in writing a play that's two dimensional. It's got to have references to your whole psyche." Reaney had fulfilled his vision of multidimensional drama in his masterpiece, the Donnelly trilogy, by the time he made this statement in 1976. In retrospect, one can see that it is a vision equally applicable to his earliest attempts at stage drama.

THE KILLDEER

The original three-act version of *The Killdeer*, produced by the University College Alumnae Association in Toronto in 1960, brought Reaney national acclaim as a playwright. This work is an excellent model for investigating the Reaney universe of themes, symbols, characters, and techniques common throughout his drama. A study of *The Killdeer* has this to recommend it as well: The play was rewritten in a more economical two-act version in 1968 at a time when Reaney began mulling the task of turning the legend of the Black Donnellys into a major stage presentation, a project that took nearly ten years of writing and research to complete.

Both versions of *The Killdeer* share elements of romance, mystery, and melodrama. In the original three-act version, the structure of the play hints strongly of a "well-made play" formula, with a third-act trial scene in which a *deus ex machina* figure delivers previously unknown evidence that resolves the plot complications.

The story concerns two families who are inextricably bound through generations of greed, lust, love, and murder. At the center of attention are two innocents—a young boy, Eli, who raises angora rabbits, and a girl, Rebecca, who delivers farm eggs to the townsfolk. Rebecca and Eli are about to marry. They are the offspring of two half sisters and share a common history of horror. Eli's mother, Madam Fay, is responsible for the death of Rebecca's mother and brothers, and her own husband, who was Eli's father, and she is also responsible for the mental breakdown of Rebecca's father. Both youngsters have grown up essentially as orphans (a favorite Reaney character-type). Rebecca's hope is that their marriage will be "love's solution to the puzzle of hatred." As she says, "Eli and I will untie the evil knot."

Unbeknownst to Rebecca, she and Eli are trapped in separate but intersecting worlds of malevolence and horror that threaten to destroy the beneficent, regenerative power they represent. A hired man named Clifford, who has reared Eli, plots to destroy them both. Rebecca's other dilemma is that she is in love with Harry Gardner, a young bank clerk whose life is dominated by his overpowering mother, just as Rebecca's life is dominated by her sense of duty. What is common to all is that they cannot follow their true instincts; circumstances that are the legacy of the previous generation force each character into a loveless, death-in-life existence that leads irrevocably to violent death.

As in all Reaney plays, the strong narrative line of *The Killdeer* implies that his primary concern is to resolve the mystery and to allow virtue to triumph, but a close examination of his works reveals another purpose. Reaney is interested in exploring the subtext, the subconscious realm of imagination and instinct. He probes inside the human and social psyche, looking beneath the surface of settings that are often romantic, pastoral, and idyllic. There, he finds greed, lust, hatred, malice, and fear, but also love.

Appropriately, the first characters that one meets in *The Killdeer* are Mrs. Gardner and Madam Fay—two mothers, starkly contrasting types. Reaney is both fascinated and repelled by the power of motherhood. Typical of most of Reaney's married women, Mrs. Gardner and Madam Fay are widows who stand alone against the world. They are strong personalities, powerful obstacles in the way of their children's happiness and development into adulthood.

Mrs. Gardner is a typical small-town, churchgoing woman whose veneer of good manners conceals her narrow-mindedness, her ambition, and her fascination with things sinful and evil. She has dominated her son into a state of compliance and despair. Madam Fay, at the other end of the spectrum, is the local bad girl, talking tough, feeling nothing but contempt for the holier-than-thou townsfolk. She has knowledge of the real world and therefore no use for its false pretenses to civility and manners. She wears her sordid past as if it were a badge of honor.

Madam Fay is an interestingly drawn character (of a type that recurs throughout Reaney's works): She appears to have no sense of right and wrong, no guilt.

She is in no way the conventional "whore with a heart of gold." She admits responsibility for the deaths of her half sister, two nephews, and husband. She reveals that she abandoned her own son and cares nothing for him. She laughs at her part in the mental breakdown of her illicit lover. Yet despite her confessions, the viewer is intrigued rather than repulsed by her character, wanting to know the motivation behind such action; thus, the author creates the curiosity that moves the play along to its dramatic conclusion.

In addition to the dominating hypocrite (Mrs. Gardner) and the demoniac yet honest primitive (Madam Fay), the play presents other character-types that recur throughout Reaney's works. Rebecca is exactly what one would expect of the heroine of a melodrama and much more—she is candid, untainted, naïve, loving, calm, brave, loyal, and bright. Most important, she is an orphan, and like the other orphans of Reaney's world (including Madam Fay), she is independent, intelligent, and self-sufficient. Like Polly in *The Easter Egg* and Susan Kingbird in *The Sun and the Moon* (two other young heroines), when confronted with the necessity to sacrifice her own needs for the betterment of those around her, Rebecca is willing to make the sacrifice—made with no hint of martyrdom or melodrama, as one might expect. Reaney seems to be saying that such women are necessary to absolve the play world of the sins of the other characters. To ensure ultimate justice, none of his heroines has to live long with her sacrifice: Justice is restored by the end of the play.

Two more significant figures are introduced before the canvas is complete. Eli, the unwilling bridegroom, and his mentor-tormentor, Clifford, one of Reaney's finest villains, appear next. Eli is half man, half child, emotionally stunted by the traumatic experiences of his past and mesmerized by Clifford's evil. Clifford has forced Eli into the marriage as a way of getting possession of Rebecca and her land. Eli is the ultimate battered and abused child. His real tragedy is that he is intelligent and perceptive enough to understand Clifford's machinations, but he does not have the power to stop him.

Eli's powerlessness is important. He is as trapped by his history as Harry Gardner is by his mother's conditioning. Eli and others like him (Kenneth in *The Easter Egg*, Andrew Kingbird in *The Sun and the Moon*, and Rogue in *Listen to the Wind*) are all trapped in a limbo between adolescence and manhood. Such characters need to be freed by the power of love, the power of language, the power of knowledge. In contrast to these brutalized and immature male characters, Reaney presents female characters who, despite common histories of childhood neglect and abuse, have grown to be mature and self-reliant. Repeatedly in Reaney's plays, the maturation of male characters is facilitated by the strength of female characters.

In 1968, Reaney rewrote *The Killdeer*, telescoping the action and characters into two acts and making considerable changes in the plot line. Technically, the second version is more adventurous: Flashbacks, choruses, significant properties, and clarified symbols dominate the stage directions. The revision demonstrates that Reaney had gained considerable confidence in the interim between the two versions, teaching himself to simplify the poetry, the plot, and the stage business. He allows his characters to be more explicit, adding a sense of urgency and eliminating much of the melodramatic formula of the first version. What feels confessional in the first version becomes exciting, forthright dialogue in the second version. By looking at the two versions in combination, one can see much of the landscape of what has come to be known as Reaneyland. Both his thematic concerns and his fascination with developing a new, exciting vocabulary of stagecraft are manifest here, as are his striking character-types.

The revision of *The Killdeer* was an important step toward achieving an unencumbered drama. As Reaney's stagecraft began to match his poetic skills and his visionary gift, as in such works as *Colours in the Dark, Listen to the Wind*, and the Donnelly trilogy, he began to experiment more and more with structure, language, and imagery, following his conviction that drama should be a process of dreaming.

LISTEN TO THE WIND

Listen to the Wind, which premiered in 1966, before the revision of *The Killdeer*, is one of Reaney's most popular and successful plays. It was this work that brought him together with Keith Turnbull, the director who has made a significant contribution to Reaney's career. *Listen to the Wind* is symbolic, romantic, and melodramatic. It depends on a play-within-a-play device that allows two separate yet similar worlds to intersect. Significantly, it developed out of the Listeners' Workshops, where the ability to "pretend" was the most important talent necessary for the participants, both actors and audience.

The play is set in rural southwestern Ontario in the 1930's. A young boy, Owen, is confined to bed by a serious and mysterious illness. At the same time, he is burdened by the knowledge that his parents' marriage has come to an end. Thus, his malaise is both physical and spiritual. He is visited, for the summer, by three female cousins who want to cure both his body and his soul. The children decide to produce a play, *The Saga of Caresfoot Court*, in the hope that the adults not only will be entertained but also will get involved and therefore resolve their problems. Owen's life parallels the life of the saga's heroine, Angela: Both are surrounded by a terrifying world of indifference, neglect, and violence; both are innocent and naïve, overwhelmed by the evil around them.

The Caresfoot Court play focuses on Angela's corruption in a debased world; her life attests the dictum that the sins of the parents are visited on the children. Owen tries to avoid Angela's fate by writing alternative endings for the play—a happy and a tragic conclusion. Thus, he attempts to determine events in the real world (his parents' divorce) by controlling the internal fantasy, wherein everything, including parental reconciliation, is possible.

Particularly noteworthy is the manner in which the play proper and the play-within-a-play interact, illuminating each other. As Jay Macpherson observed in a 1966 article in *Canadian Forum*, "They do so through numerous cross-references in image and situation, and through the revelation of the capacities of the characters of the outer story by the roles they play in the inner one. . . . While the outer story is slight, gentle, and touching, the inner one consists of a series of explosive confrontations."

The device of using a play-within-a-play also allows Reaney to present both sides of the story at once—a technique that he used again in a more radical form in the medicine show of the Donnelly plays. This device juxtaposes Owen's reality to the deeply sentimental world of the inner play and becomes Owen's way of "listening to the wind." The play was a giant leap forward in the development of Reaney's craftsmanship. One sees here the beginning of a theater that relies on minimal directions, few properties, and a large cast, and one that requires the audience to be an active participant in the creative process. It is a dramatic world in which past and present are no longer clearly delineated.

COLOURS IN THE DARK

To re-create Victorian England, in the play-within-a-play of *Listen to the Wind* Reaney employed a brilliant theatrical device borrowed from ancient Greece, the chorus—in this play, composed of children—which can create anything possible within the scope of the audience's imagination by chanting, singing, stomping, clapping, miming, dancing, and generally acting out, or making believe. This device led Reaney to a turning point in his career: *Colours in the Dark*, a landmark play, produced at the Stratford Festival in 1967. Reaney himself described the work as "a play box"; it is a collage of images, colors, objects (toys), songs, dances, myths, symbols, and sounds, culminating in the "existence poem" that is the central image of the play and the focus of its structure.

Colours in the Dark demands much of an audience. There is overlapping dialogue, and the same actors play several different parts. Multiscreen images are projected behind the action as the plot unravels in a linear and historically chronological fashion. To hold the many scenes together, the playwright uses scene codes—codes that are held up on banners labeling them by color and a related word. White is Sunday, but it is also a flower, a type of music, and a symbol of innocence and goodness. Color, word, and symbol are signposts to the action of each scene.

Colours in the Dark is Reaney's testament to the power of language. It proposes that there are many nontraditional ways of interpreting the world. The story begins with a game in which a child is blindfolded so that he will have to develop other senses to guide him through the matrix of life. Without the use of his eyes, he must depend on touch, smell, sound, and imagination—leading the audience to the experience of synesthetic knowledge, whereby sensory perception creates a new vocabulary of equivalents, breaking down boundaries between word, symbol, and image. What *Colours in the Dark* achieves is a recapitulation of the history of civilization in the life of a single individual. It is a kaleidoscope that proves "our ancestors are we, our descendants are us, and so on like a sea."

THE DONNELLY TRILOGY

Reaney's masterpiece, the Donnelly trilogy, was a logical next step. In it one sees much that has developed directly from *Colours in the Dark*: catalogs of names, the use of local color, important chorus sections, the juxtaposition of the real and absurd worlds, and much more. The trilogy is truly the fulfillment of Reaney's artistic vision. In it, with help from Keith Turnbull and a talented, loyal crew of actors and technicians, he was able to synthesize poetry, dance, music, and movement to create a powerfully unified theater experience.

All three plays, *The Donnellys: Part I, Sticks and Stones, The Donnellys: Part II, St. Nicholas Hotel, Wm Donnelly, Prop.,* and *The Donnellys: Part III, Handcuffs,* are consistent in their style of presentation, although each has separate symbols: sticks and stones, wheels and tops, grains and seeds. Reaney deliberately uses familiar props, stage furnishings, and styles in all three plays. The best description of this technique comes from critic Urjo Kareda in his review in *The Toronto Star* on November 26, 1973:

> The eleven performers, always present, using beautiful props which are always on view, work through choric chanting, songs, children's games, soliloquies, plays-within-plays, indirect narration, mime, and even marionettes to express Reaney's collage of history. The play has an exceptionally simple and evocative range of symbols and imagery; like the props, they are chosen from a common experience. The seven sons are represented by seven white shirts hanging on a line; horizontal country roads are seen as vertical ladders; the lieutenant-governor and his lady are dolls; a greedy

fat woman is her "darling little laundry stove"; the Donnellys themselves are the solid stones, while their enemies are the dry, crackling sticks.

In the Donnelly trilogy, Reaney achieved the dream first hinted at in *The Killdeer*: He found a way to make his universal themes pertinent to the real history of the people in his community. The poetic language of the three plays reverberates with musical structures of duet, trio, and quartet. The structure is interwoven with symbol, myth, and significant props. Most important, Reaney's vision has grown to accommodate documented, historical truth. What results is a smooth, rich mixture of language, action, structure, and stagecraft—a theater in which everything can be something.

OTHER MAJOR WORKS

SHORT FICTION: "Clay Hole," 1946; "The Elevator," 1946; "The Book in the Tree," 1947; "Mr. Whur: A Metamorphosis," 1947; "The Box Social," 1947; "Afternoon Moon," 1948; "The Young Necrophiles," 1948; "The Bully," 1952; "Dear Metronome," 1952; "To the Secret City: From a Winnipeg Sketch Book," 1954; "Winnipeg Sketches," 1955; *The Box Social and Other Stories,* 1996.

POETRY: *The Red Heart,* 1949; *A Suit of Nettles,* 1958; *Twelve Letters to a Small Town,* 1962; *The Dance of Death at London, Ontario,* 1963; *Poems,* 1972 (Germaine Warkentin, editor); *Selected Shorter Poems,* 1975 (Warkentin, editor); *Selected Longer Poems,* 1976 (Warkentin, editor); *Imprecations: The Art of Swearing,* 1984; *Performance: Poems,* 1990.

TELEPLAY: *An Evening Without James Reaney,* 1960.

RADIO PLAYS: *The Great Lakes Suite,* 1950; *Message to Winnipeg,* 1959; *Poet and City—Winnipeg,* 1960; *The Journals and Letters of William Blake,* 1961; *Wednesday's Child,* 1962; *Canada Dot—Canada Dash,* 1965-1967 (in 3 parts).

NONFICTION: "The Influence of Spenser on Yeats," 1958 (Ph.D. thesis); "The Canadian Imagination," 1959 (in *Poetry*); "Isabella Valancy Crawford," 1959; *Alphabet: A Semiannual Devoted to the Iconography of the Imagination,* 1960-1971 (20 volumes); "The Canadian Poets' Predicament," 1962 (in *Masks of Poetry*); "An Evening with Babble and Doodle," 1962; "Ten Miles High on a Song," 1966 (in *The Globe and Mail* newspaper); *Ten Years at Play*, 1969; *Fourteen Barrels from Sea to Sea*, 1977; "Some Critics Are Music Teachers," 1982 (in *Centre and Labyrinth: Essays in Honour of Northrop Frye*); "Digesting the Bible," 1982 (in *Saturday Night Magazine*).

CHILDREN'S LITERATURE: *The Boy with an R in His Hand*, 1965; *Take the Big Picture*, 1986.

BIBLIOGRAPHY

Grandy, Karen. "Playing with Time: James Reaney's *The Donnellys* as Spatial Form Drama." *Modern Drama* 38, no. 4 (Winter, 1995): 462. Explores some of Reaney's unique techniques for dealing with time—both linear history and a circle of myth.

Lee, Alvin. "A Turn to the Stage: Reaney's Dramatic Verse." In *Dramatists in Canada: Selected Essays*, edited by William H. New. Vancouver: University of British Columbia Press, 1972. Offers "a description of the major writings . . . in an attempt to show something of his [Reaney's] development as a verse dramatist." Deals with *The Red Heart*, *A Suit of Nettles* (briefly), and the chamber opera *Night-Blooming Cereus*. Long discussion of *The Killdeer* and *The Easter Egg*.

Parker, Gerald. *How to Play: The Theatre of James Reaney*. Toronto: ECW Press, 1991. Three long chapters explore the importance to Reaney of Canada and Ontario, the symbolic and visual elements in his theater, and his linguistic versatility. Bibliography and index.

_____. "The Key Word . . . Is 'Listen': James Reaney's 'Sonic Environment.'" *Mosaic* 14 (Fall, 1981): 1-14. This article on the Donnelly trilogy is a model of Reaney's use of "the sonic environment through various forms of instrumentation and vocal gesture." Examines a large part of Reaney's dramatic work, praising "the preoccupation with the theatrical values of sound" and Reaney's appreciation of filmic and operatic techniques. Notes provide a bibliography for further inquiry.

Reaney, James. *Masks of Childhood*. Toronto: New Press, 1972. An afterword, by editor Brian Parker, accompanies this edition of three plays, *The Easter Egg*, *Three Desks*, and *The Killdeer*. Parker sees "the interplay of man and child" as the central idea in Reaney's work. A brief but informative analysis of the three plays is followed by a chronology of plays and works for radio.

Tait, Michael. "Everything Is Something: James Reaney's *Colours in the Dark*." In *Dramatists in Canada: Selected Essays*, edited by William H. New. Vancouver: University of British Columbia Press, 1972. Tait concentrates on *Colours in the Dark*, produced at the Stratford Festival in 1967, and finds much of merit in his "attempt to define some of Reaney's strengths as a dramatist, and more particularly, those qualities of *Colours* that set it apart from earlier, less successful stage pieces." He finds Reaney's play "*sui generis*, a luminous structure . . . lyric in subjective intensity of mood; dramatic in the articulation of large conflicts; epic in its breadth of statement."

_____. "The Limits of Innocence: James Reaney's Theatre." In *Dramatists in Canada: Selected Essays*, edited by William H. New. Vancouver: University of British Columbia Press, 1972. An alternative, more critical view than Alvin Lee's essay (above) in the same collection. Tait claims that "a pattern of striking imagery, in the absence of plausible characterization and coherent action, is not enough to hold any play together." After more of the same criticism, he concludes: "No one else has his capacity to write for the stage at once so badly and so well."

Eleanor R. Goldhar,
updated by Thomas J. Taylor

JEAN-FRANÇOIS REGNARD

Born: Paris, France; February 8, 1655
Died: Dourdan, France; September 4, 1709

PRINCIPAL DRAMA

Le Divorce, pr., pb. 1688
La Descente d'Arlequin aux Enfers, pr., pb. 1689
L'Homme à bonnes fortunes, pr. 1690, pb. 1694
La Critique de "L'Homme à bonnes fortunes," pr. 1690, pb. 1700
Les Filles errantes, pr. 1690, pb. 1700
La Coquette, pr. 1691, pb. 1700
Les Chinois, pr. 1691, pb. 1700
La Baquette de Vulcain, pr. 1693, pb. 1694
La Naissance d'Amadis, pr. 1694, pb. 1697
Attendez-moi sous l'orme, pr., pb. 1694
La Sérénade, pr., pb. 1694 (*The Serenade*, 1777)
La Foire de Saint-Germain, pr. 1695, pb. 1696 (*The St. Germain Fair*, 1718)
Les Momies d'Égypte, pr. 1696, pb. 1700
Le Bal: Ou, Le Bourgeois de Falaise, pr., pb. 1696
Le Joueur, pr. 1696, pb. 1697
Le Distrait, pr. 1697, pb. 1698
Le Carnaval de Venise, pr., pb. 1699 (ballet scenario)
Démocrite, pr., pb. 1700
Le Retour imprévu, pr., pb. 1700 (*The Unexpected Return*, 1715)
Les Folies amoureuses, pr., pb. 1704
Les Ménechmes, pr. 1705, pb. 1706
Le Légataire universel, pr., pb. 1708 (*The Universal Legatee*, 1796)
La Critique du "Légataire universel," pr., pb. 1708
Sapor, pb. 1731
Les Vendages, pb. 1731

OTHER LITERARY FORMS

Jean-François Regnard wrote a romantic novel, *La Provençale* (1731), satires and occasional verses, *Epîtres* (1731), and accounts of travels, *Voyage de Flandre et de Hollande* (*A Journey Through Flanders, Holland, etc.*, 1801) and *Voyage de Laponie* (*Journey to Lapland, etc.*, 1808), both published posthumously in 1731.

ACHIEVEMENTS

Literary history has been unkind to Jean-François Regnard. It was his misfortune to begin writing his comedies shortly after Molière's death. By then, the classical conception of comedy in France meant comedy as conceived by Molière. Therefore, in the last decades of the seventeenth century, the chief preoccupation of French playwrights was almost exclusively with character studies. Plot became subordinated to the study of contemporary manners, and authors concentrated more on character portrayals. Hence, while most writers of comedies after Molière were striving to imitate him in painting contemporary manners and in creating living characters, Regnard concentrated all of his efforts in creating amusing, witty plays that filled audiences with delightful merriment. He considered the ability to amuse, to induce laughter, as the *sine qua non* of comedy. For this reason, many critics have rendered unfavorable judgments on his dramatic output, particularly in the area of characterization. Conceding that Regnard's comedies are very funny, these critics claim that his characters are pale creatures in comparison with Molière's and that his plays are bereft of penetrating psychology and moral instruction. Unfortunately, the preoccupation of an era of French scholarship centering on human motivation and human foibles produced a negative attitude toward comedy that is based on robust laughter, and too many critics of the French theater have shared this cultural attitude.

When Regnard's comedies are studies without any preconceived notions, they may be appreciated from various points of view. To begin with, his plays are very theatrical. Indeed, much of his strength as a dramatist lies in the area of dramaturgy, that repository of devices and methods that are the very heart of the playwright's craft. His skill in creating movement without impeding the progress of the plot, his gift for dramatic irony and contrast, his ability to give variety and freshness to the treatment of common theatrical devices, the ingenious manner in which he works out the intrigues—in brief, his talent to manipulate adroitly the strictly dramatic aspects of his art is one of his principal appeals.

In conjunction with these high dramatic qualities, Regnard's comedies can be appreciated from the standpoint of verbal technique. He was naturally gifted with a talent for choosing the right words in a comic situation, and his plays exude an atmosphere of the sheer delight that comes from playing with words. He is an acknowledged master of the language. Even his detractors have agreed that his style of writing is admirable for the purpose of lighthearted comedy—easy, vivacious, humorous, picturesque, graceful—more akin to the style of Marivaux (1688-1763) than to that of Molière. Indeed, although Regnard was born and lived most of his life in the seventeenth century, by style and temperament he belongs to the eighteenth. Regnard was able to exploit fully his two major assets as a comic playwright: a prodigious abundance of comic verbal inventiveness combined with an uncommon aptitude for happy versification. The so-called comedy of words as an effective medium of comic expression achieved its highest level in his plays. Regnard showed much cleverness in writing sparkling dialogue imbued with an effervescent quality and humorous wit. Perhaps this style of writing was a reaction against the sobriety of court life under the strictures of Madame de Maintenon as well as a distraction from the disastrous period through which the country was passing. In any event, Regnard's unbridled merriment was well received by his contemporaries.

One of Regnard's greatest contributions to French classical comedy was to bring about a renewal of verse as the primary means of expression. Toward the end of the seventeenth century, most writers of comedies had discarded verse in favor of prose in their plays. Regnard's decision to write his major comedies in verse was a significant reversal of this trend, and his success as a playwright ensured a revival of verse comedy during the first half of the eighteenth century. It is true that he was not a faultless versifier. His critics have often noted that his style is somewhat careless, and

that it abounds in poetic license and improper rhymes. Nevertheless, he handled the Alexandrine and the shorter verse measures with great skill. His poetic expertise can best be seen in the subtle interplay of the rhythmic and harmonic resources of the Alexandrine, in evocative combinations of sounds, and in his use of *vers libres* (a loose sort of verse) which accounts for much of the graceful, chatty style of his comedies.

Regnard's seven principal verse plays have retained a remarkable vitality, attested by the fact that they have received more than four thousand performances by the prestigious Comédie-Française down through the centuries. Moreover, five of these plays are still performed in the twenty-first century, a claim that can be made about the plays of no other seventeenth century writer of comedies except Molière.

BIOGRAPHY

Jean-François Regnard was born into a prosperous Parisian family of merchants. He was the only son in

Jean-François Regnard (Hulton Archive by Getty Images)

a family of five children. When he was only two years old, his father died, and he was reared by his mother and four elder sisters. He seems to have been very close to his mother, a shrewd businesswoman in whose hands the family business flourished. Regnard received a good education without, however, applying himself seriously to his studies. At the age of fifteen, he went to work for his brother-in-law, who sold jewelry and all types of dress goods. His brother-in-law's business firm was also involved in exporting, and this gave the young Regnard the opportunity to travel extensively to many exotic places such as Turkey.

On coming of age, Regnard found himself independently wealthy and this newly inherited fortune allowed him to indulge further his passion for travel. He set forth for Italy in 1673 and proceeded to Constantinople (now Istanbul), where he spent nearly two years. On his way home, he again passed through Italy, and at Venice is said to have been lucky enough to win at the gaming table a sum that enabled him to pay all the expenses of his journey and bring home, in addition, the sum of ten thousand crowns. After a brief interval in France, he undertook a second trip to Italy in 1678, where he met another young Frenchman, Aucousteaux de Fercourt, who shared his penchant for traveling. The new friends went to Bologna, where Regnard made the acquaintance of a charming young woman, Elvire de Prade. A strong attachment developed between the two. Unfortunately, she was already married. Regnard and Fercourt continued their journey, but on their return to France, they happened to embark on the same vessel with M. and Mme de Prade. During the voyage, they were attacked by Algerian pirates who specialized in the slave trade. They were caught and spent some months in captivity. Regnard and his friend were soon ransomed, and they were also able to secure the freedom of the lovely Mme de Prade, leaving her husband for the time being still a prisoner in Algiers. This episode, with its story of shipwreck, corsairs, and a romantic love affair with a pretty captive lady, formed the basis of Regnard's novel, *La Provençale*.

Regnard set out again on another long journey in 1681. With Fercourt and another companion, he visited the Netherlands, Denmark, Sweden, Lapland, Poland, Hungary, Austria, and Germany, finally reaching Paris in 1682. He left a written account of these journeys in his *Journey to Lapland, etc.* Shortly after his return to Paris, he bought a position as treasurer in the Bureau des Finances in Paris. He spent the rest of his life at his house on the Rue Richelieu or at his château near Dourdan, in Normandy, where he entertained his friends lavishly.

It was shortly after he established himself in Paris that Regnard's desire to write became more pronounced. He turned to playwriting initially as a lark. Regnard and certain friends used to put together comic scripts for the Italian troupe in Paris. They did this mainly as an amusing hobby, without any remuneration. As his skills developed, however, Regnard began to write plays for the reputable Hôtel de Bourgogne. He wrote at least a dozen plays for this theater house, some on his own, some with Charles Rivière Dufresny. These plays are never performed today and have only a historical interest to specialists in the theater of the period. His association with the well-established Théâtre-Français (later known as the Comédie-Française) began in 1694, when he wrote two amusing little prose comedies in one act, entitled *Attendez-moi sous l'orme* and *The Serenade*. The former concerns a valet who takes revenge on his master for not paying his wages by frustrating his marriage with a peasant girl, while the latter is about an old miser and his projected marriage with the lady to whom his son is secretly betrothed. Both plays were well received by the public.

In his next seven plays, Regnard abandoned the kind of farcical low comedy with which his name had been associated in order to embrace high comedy, a neoclassical type of comedy written in verse and consisting of five acts in which the time required for the action to unfold rarely exceeded a day. These are the plays on which his fame as a dramatist rests. The success of these seven verse plays was such that they made Regnard the leading playwright in France at the turn of the eighteenth century. He was praised by the literati of his day, and aspiring young authors paid him tribute. Although Regnard enjoyed much fame during his lifetime, he never married. He died suddenly at his château on September 4, 1709.

ANALYSIS

Jean-François Regnard's fame as a dramatist rests on his mature plays—the seven major comedies that he wrote for the Comédie-Française. Of the seven plays, four still remain in the repertory of this famous theater company. They are, in order of production, *Le Joueur* (1696), *Les Folies amoureuses* (1704), *Les Ménechmes* (1705), and *The Universal Legatee* (1708). After nearly three centuries, Regnard's seven verse plays still retain their original liveliness as well as their infectious humor. An overview of these comedies shows the influence of the Italian *commedia dell'arte*, particularly in the use of stock characters (such as clever valets, old misers, and foolish lovers) and comic leitmotifs (such as mistaken identities, disguises, quid pro quos, and so on). The ultimate goal in all the plays is marriage. In terms of plot structure, the action is primarily built on the removal of numerous obstacles confronting the protagonists. In this period, it was common practice for playwrights to borrow ideas, lines, and sometimes entire scenes from a predecessor or a contemporary, presenting them as one's own work. Regnard was no different from other dramatists of the time in this respect, but the changes that he wrought on his source material reveal his distinctive gifts. Regnard also displayed ingenuity in his handling of verbal comic devices: The vivacity of his language has seldom been equaled in French comedy.

LE JOUEUR

Some critics consider the first of Regnard's major comedies, *Le Joueur*, to be his masterpiece. As the title indicates, the play concerns a chronic gambler, Valère, who is torn between his love of gambling and his love for his mistress, Angélique. Regnard took the subject of gambling from a play by Florent Carton Dancourt, *La Désolation des joueuses* (1687). *Le Joueur* resembles in many ways the *Le Chevalier joueur* (1697), which was acted two months later and written by his former collaborator, Dufresny. Each playwright accused the other of plagiarizing his work, and scholarly research has never been able to prove satisfactorily who borrowed what from whom, but Regnard's play is unquestionably superior to his rival's. The major character, Valère, returns home one evening penniless after a gambling bout and immedi-

ately inquires what efforts his valet has made to get him more money. His valet informs him that his fiancé, Angélique, weary of his gambling habit, is ready to break off the engagement and marry his uncle, Dorante, instead. She finally gives in to Valère's protestations, and as a sign of their reconciliation gives him her portrait. He immediately pawns it and does not redeem it when he has the chance. Valère loses everything in another game and seeks consolation from his fiancé, but he is unable to produce the missing portrait when requested to do so. He accuses his servant of having misplaced it. His uncle, who is also his rival, has come into possession of the portrait and now shows it to Angélique. The latter reproaches Valère and expresses her intention to marry the uncle. A dejected Valère departs despairingly, still hoping that someday gambling will change his fortune.

The play is more a comedy of manners than of character (gambling as a mania plagued France at the end of the seventeenth century). The manners of gamblers are depicted, various card games are described, and a number of gaming expressions are used. The structure of the play itself reflects the fluctuations of a gambler's fortunes, as the action shifts back and forth—loss of money, remorse, love, a gift, winning, and eventually losing both girl and money. The scenes are skillfully arranged. Regnard develops to the full the play's amusing aspects. His dry humor is shown in several scenes, notably in act 1, scene 2 and act 4, scene 13. He parodies a tragic tirade when he has the servant describe his master's melodramatic speeches in scene 2 of act 4; a pseudomarquis makes an absurd entrance in scene 4 of act 2, and in act 4, this boastful marquis evokes laughter by poking fun at the new class of *parvenus*. Regnard maintains a lighthearted tone throughout his play, which is a prime example of good theater and good entertainment.

LE DISTRAIT

Regnard's next comedy, *Le Distrait*, was first performed on December 2, 1697. The play is based on one of Jean de La Bruyère's "characters," Ménalque, an absentminded type. The play is not a satire of contemporary manners but rather a caricature, a comic portrait. Léandre is in love with Clarice, but in order to inherit money from his wealthy uncle, he has signed a contract to marry Isabelle. The latter is loved by a chevalier, the brother of Clarice. He and Clarice have an uncle, Valère, who wishes for them to marry according to their wishes. In his absentmindedness, Léandre forgets that a marriage contract has been signed. This infuriates his rich uncle, who disinherits him shortly before dying. Isabelle's mother now refuses to let her daughter marry Léandre. Valère, by offering to make the chevalier his heir, wins her consent to the proposed marriage between her daughter and the chevalier. Valère also promises a considerable sum to Clarice, removing the financial obstacle to her marriage to Léandre. She consents to the marriage and is ready to reconcile herself to the fact of Léandre's distractions and absentmindedness. The chief merit of the plot is to accentuate the peculiar trait of the protagonist, Léandre, in amusing scenes, as when, for example, he does not notice that his stocking is down, asks for gloves when he already has them on, takes someone else's carriage, throws away his watch, writes a letter to one lady and sends it to another, forgets an important communication, and even forgets that his marriage contract has been signed. Still, when the plot depends on a series of incidents, however amusing, the action is bound to languish. In terms of plot structure, then, *Le Distrait* is perhaps the least successful of Regnard's major plays. This fact notwithstanding, the language in the play remains vintage Regnard. There are many witty, graceful phrases, and the overall tone is that of light banter. Irony and parody abound, especially in the Léandre-chevalier exchange in act 4, scene 6. The author indulges his love of wordplay by interspersing Latin jargon, military idioms, musical expressions, and legal phrases rather conspicuously throughout his rhyme scenes. The play had a very short run when it was first produced (only four performances), but was successfully restaged in 1731 and continued in the repertory of the Comédie-Française well into the twentieth century.

DÉMOCRITE

Regnard's third full-length comedy, *Démocrite*, was markedly different from the two that preceded it. He intended it to be a more serious play. The action takes place in Greece, and the plot contains run-of-the-mill Romanesque elements not found in his previous plays. It had its premiere on January 12, 1700. Regnard was initially disappointed with the public's response, but he persuaded the actors and the theater management to keep the play running. He was soon vindicated when it was performed seventeen times in succession. The plot is a variation of the familiar theme of a royal princess identified by means of a valuable bracelet. Criséis, the adopted daughter of the peasant, Thaler, is the pupil of the misanthropic philosopher Démocrite. One day, Agélas and Agénor, king and prince of Greece, meet by chance Criséis, Thaler, Démocrite, and the latter's disciple, Strabon. The king falls in love with the girl and invites them all to court. When he proposes marriage, his betrothed, Isabelle, protests. Because of the bracelet and the recollections of Thaler and Cléanthis, who was involved in the substitution of the young girl at birth, Criséis is identified as the long-lost daughter of the King of Athens. According to a previous pact, she must now marry Agélas. Isabelle will marry Prince Agénor instead. Strabon and Cléanthis, who are attracted to each other, also decide to live together. As the play ends, Démocrite is left alone to pine over the loss of Criséis, whom he had secretly loved all along. He returns to his desert cave to ponder over the vicissitudes of life and to laugh at the follies of others. Although Démocrite gives his name to the comedy, his role is not well-developed. He has little in common with the historical Greek philosopher, Democritus. Like Alceste in Molière's play, he is in love, but he is a reluctant lover who makes excuses for his passion and human weakness. The play is still a comedy of manners, in spite of the Romanesque elements. The Athenian court is a parody of the court of Versailles. Regnard uses the character of Démocrite to depict the shallowness and hypocrisy of court society, particularly in act two, scene 5. Indeed, the artificiality of court life in act 2 contrasts with the simple, idealistic, rustic life encountered in act 1. This dichotomy of lifestyles is very pronounced in the play, yet Regnard never lets one forget that one is seeing or reading a comedy. Thaler's use of peasant dialect throughout the play not only lends amusement but also adds a touch of realism. The most successful comic element occurs in the scenes with Strabon and Cléanthis. Their scenes are filled with the rapid-fire dialogue and comical stichomythia of which Regnard was a master. These scenes have often been detached and produced separately as comic skits. *Démocrite* remained in favor with the public for a long time. Its greatest success, however, occurred in the eighteenth century, when it received nearly four hundred performances. It was performed more than fifty times in the twentieth century.

THE UNEXPECTED RETURN

The Unexpected Return is based on the *Mostellaria* (date unknown; *The Haunted House*, 1774) of Plautus. The same subject had been treated by Pierre de Larivey in his comedy *Les Esprits* (1579). A profligate son, Clitandre, sells his miserly father's possessions during his absence in order to support his expensive tastes. The father, Géronte, returns unexpectedly from Spain while his son is lavishly entertaining his friends and his mistress, Lucile. The plot turns on the ruses employed to keep the father out of the way. The nimble-minded servant, Merlin, comes up with all kinds of stratagems and ideas to delay Géronte from entering his own home. He announces that the house is presently haunted, the cause of the trouble being in the cellar. The astonished Géronte is greatly disturbed on hearing this, confessing to Merlin that he has twenty thousand francs hidden in the cellar. Merlin hurries to tell the maid, Lisette, who later emerges from the alleged haunted house with a treasure bag in her hand. A drunken marquis wanders in and informs Géronte of his son's duplicity. Clitandre avows everything and promises to change his ways and to see that his father gets his treasure back if he will allow him to marry Lucile. The play ends when Géronte agrees to the marriage in order to recover his treasure. Regnard follows rather loosely his Latin model. He adds most of the early scenes and some of the later scenes crucial for the denouement (for example, the money left in the house by its owner is not found in *The Haunted House*). Although the plot is far-fetched, the play is important in another respect; it shows Regnard's increasing reliance on intrigue to produce comic effects. Increasingly, his

plays were characterized by the use of conventions and devices usually associated with this genre, such as stock characters, trickeries, disguises, surprises, and numerous imbroglios. The dialogue is lively and full of gaiety. There are some hilarious scenes, especially the one with the double accusation of madness and the last two scenes with the drunken marquis. Despite its amusing qualities, the comedy is no longer performed. It remained in the repertory until 1836, enjoying a total of 265 performances.

LES FOLIES AMOUREUSES

Regnard's next comedy, *Les Folies amoureuses* (January 15, 1704), is one of his most frolicking plays. The plot is the familiar one of the elderly guardian who wishes to marry his young ward. The theme had been treated by Molière in *L'École des femmes* (pr. 1662, pb. 1663; *The School for Wives*, 1732). In Regnard's play, however, it is the heroine, Agathe, who instigates her own escape from her jealous guardian by pretending to be mad. Unlike Molière's play, *Les Folies amoureuses* makes no pretense at moral instruction. It is mainly farcical, full of action and vivacity from beginning to end. When the action starts, Agathe is a virtual prisoner of Albert, an old fool, in an isolated château. Albert, who is vain and suspicious, entertains thoughts of marrying her. A handsome young man, Eraste, and his valet, Crispin, happen to stroll by one day and unexpectedly come face to face with Agathe and her guardian. The old man quickly ushers away his ward, but not before the latter has had an opportunity to apprise her would-be suitor of her misfortune. Eraste pretends to approve of Albert's marriage plans in order to win his confidence while he tries to arrange an elopement with Agathe. At this point, Agathe's maid, Lisette, runs out to announce her mistress has taken leave of her senses. In three bogus "mad" scenes, Agathe manages to make Eraste understand her plan of action for her escape. In the first of these scenes, she appears as a swashbuckling braggadocio, then as a scatterbrained old woman, and finally as an army officer. The dull-witted Albert is convinced that she has become insane. He enlists the aid of Crispin, who has claimed to have a vast knowledge of herbs and medicines. As a result of the medicine administered by "doctor" Crispin, Agathe and Eraste are able to escape at a moment when Albert is preoccupied. Crispin and Lisette soon join them, and the play ends in a double marriage.

Even if the plot is predictable, the madcap antics of the young heroine give the play a special flavor. The scenes of lunacy are full of verbal fun and comedy of gesture. For example, in the second scene—the mad musician scene in which Agathe impersonates a giddy old woman—she babbles about a certain "duo" while shaking Albert's hand vigorously and allowing Eraste to kiss the other. Pretending to rehearse a concert, she simultaneously gives a sheet of music to Albert and a love letter to Eraste. Toward the end of the scene, she has managed to revenge herself on Albert by beating time on his head with the baton, all the while communicating successfully with her lover in a musical code filled with puns and double meanings. The play is tailor-made for a good actress who can exploit its comical possibilities; it provokes as much mirth today as it did when it was first performed.

LES MÉNECHMES

Les Ménechmes (December 4, 1705), although based on the *Menaechmi* (date unknown; *The Twin Menaechmi*, 1595) of Plautus, is very different from its Roman model, rewritten by Regnard from beginning to end. It is a well-constructed play, the most classical of Regnard's works. The plot is based on the familiar theme of identical twins who are the cause of all sorts of complications arising from mistaken identity (as in William Shakespeare's *The Comedy of Errors*, pr. c. 1592-1594). When the play opens, neither twin is aware of the existence of the other. Though exactly alike in appearance, they present a complete contrast in temperament and manners—a contrast that occasions many misunderstandings and some hilarious quid pro quo scenes. One of the twins, an outspoken, clumsy provincial, comes to Paris to claim an inheritance, which is conditional on his marrying a lady named Isabelle. The other twin is a suave, debonair chevalier who happens to be in love with the same Isabelle. His servant, Valentin, comes across the other twin's luggage through an accidental substitution. Examination of its contents reveals the inheri-

tance information and the recommendation that Ménechme wed Isabelle. The chevalier puts on mourning attire and sets out to collect his brother's inheritance. As the play progresses, the twins are mistaken for each other a total of eight times, and Valentin only adds to the confusion by attempting to serve both brothers. In due time, the chevalier puts an end to these confusing escapades by explaining everything. He shares with his brother part of the inheritance and claims Isabelle for himself.

On the whole, *Les Ménechmes* found favor with the critics, who admired its sustained vivacity, the brilliance of its verse, and, above all, Regnard's skill in weaving an intricate plot. Indeed, he plays up the sense of rapid movement in this comedy. The incidents of mistaken identity—with their boisterous humor—are utilized expertly, and the spectators are hurried on to another amusing situation before the previous situation has had time to pall on them. Regnard succeeds marvelously in keeping a rather complicated plot moving smoothly without too much confusion in the minds of his audience. For example, he adroitly begins with a relatively mild confusion, that between Ménechme and Araminte, which introduces the spectator or reader to the dominant theme of confusion. The next mistake in identity, however, has more serious repercussions. From then on, the plot thickens, and the characters are plunged into a morass of confusion until the brothers can no longer be kept apart. Even though the incidents are the result of chance, the spectator's or reader's pleasure is increased by the fact that the groundwork has been carefully laid through a dexterous combination and succession of events.

THE UNIVERSAL LEGATEE

The last play to be performed during Regnard's lifetime, *The Universal Legatee* (January 9, 1708), is generally considered to be his best comedy. Unquestionably the most original of his plays, it concerns the impersonation of a man in a comatose state, the forging of a will that is supposed to be that of the incapacitated man, and the care taken by the impersonator to advance his own interests. The entire play hinges on a twofold problem: Will Eraste be recognized as his uncle's only heir, and will he marry the enchanting

Isabelle? As the comedy begins, the wealthy Géronte announces to his nephew, Eraste, that he desires an heir and intends to marry Isabelle. Unknown to him, Eraste is in love with the lady. His nephew dissuades him from the project, but another obstacle to his prospective inheritance soon emerges: Géronte decides to divide his estate three ways, between Eraste, another nephew, and a niece whom he has never seen. The cunning valet, Crispin, solves the matter by giving comical impersonations of the two coheirs. He and his master are confronted anew with another problem: Géronte has had one of his frequent blackout spells shortly after agreeing that Eraste should be his sole heir. With a notary coming to write the will, Crispin, disguised as Géronte in a darkened room, dictates the will, which includes a large legacy for himself and the maid, Lisette, along with the main bequest to Eraste. Shortly thereafter, Géronte awakes from his *léthargie*. Everyone now tries to convince him that he is the author of this improbable will. Even the duped notary persuades old Géronte that the document was dictated by him. When Géronte claims that he does not recall doing so, the conspirators remind him of his recurring blackouts. Eraste can now wed Isabelle, and Crispin will live a life of leisure.

Such an amoral subject was not well-received by certain righteous individuals who failed to see any merriment in cheating an old man out of his money. Yet, the characters in the play are not real people. The world of the play is a fantasy world of laughter—the supposed end of all comedy—and *The Universal Legatee* is extremely funny in spite of the shameful behavior of the conspirators. Regnard's handling of the plot is particularly masterful. The basic situation remains confused, and the principals are repeatedly thrown off balance by the appearance of some unforeseen event or character. Regnard manipulates turns and counterturns while keeping the plot moving forward with a comic impetus. Just when the situation seems to be under control, he introduces a new twist in the plot. Whether a plot construction of this kind is good dramaturgy may be a question of taste, but its effectiveness as an amusing complicating factor cannot be denied. Finally, Regnard's verse is more polished here than in any of his comedies. *The Universal*

Legatee has enjoyed more than one thousand performances at the Comédie-Française alone, making it the most popular of his works.

There is no doubt that Regnard's comedies are essentially comedies of intrigue rather than of character. The primary source for most of them was the imbroglio play of Italian inspiration. Like the Italians, he knew how to build a play and keep it moving. He was not interested in probing deeply into human psychology; his characters remain stereotypes rather than flesh and blood individuals. Nevertheless, his plays are far from being dull, and his superb command of the French language has kept his best work fresh for centuries. If entertainment is the ultimate aim of comedy, Regnard belongs among the foremost playwrights in the genre.

OTHER MAJOR WORKS

LONG FICTION: *La Provençale*, 1731.

NONFICTION: *Epîtres*, 1731; *Voyage de Flandre et de Hollande*, 1731 (*A Journey Through Flanders, Holland, etc.*, 1801); *Voyage de Laponie*, 1731 (*Journey to Lapland, etc.*, 1808).

BIBLIOGRAPHY

Connon, Derek, and George Evans, eds. *Essays on French Comic Drama from the 1640s to the 1780s.* New York: Peter Lang, 2000. This collection of essays focusing on French drama from the mid-seventeenth century to the late eighteenth century looks at comedy during the period in which Regnard was active. Bibliography and index.

Harrison, Helen L. *Pistoles/Paroles: Money and Language in Seventeenth Century French Comedy.* Charlottesville, Va.: Rockwood Press, 1996. This study of French comedy in the seventeenth century centers on the prevalent writers such as Molière, Pierre Corneille, Monsieur Scarron, and Thomas Corneille. However, it presents a broad discussion of comedy and the topics of money and social class in literature. Bibliography and index.

Orwen, Gifford P. *Jean-François Regnard.* Boston: Twayne, 1982. A basic biography that covers the life and works of Regnard. Bibliography and index.

Yeh, J. "Heir Today, Gone Tomorrow." Review of *The Universal Legatee*, by Jean-François Regnard. *The Village Voice*, April 24, 2001, p. 119. Yeh reviews a performance of Regnard's *The Universal* *Legatee* (translated here as *A Will of His Own*) by the Pearl Theater Company in New York City.

Raymond LePage

YASMINA REZA

Born: Paris, France; May 1, 1959

PRINCIPAL DRAMA

Conversations apres un enterrement, pr., pb. 1987 (*Conversations After a Burial*, 2000)

La Traversee de l'hiver, pr., pb. 1989 (*Winter Crossing*, 2000)

"Art," pr., pb. 1994 (English translation, 1996)

L'Homme du hasard, pr. 1995, pb. 1998 (*The Unexpected Man*, 1998)

Trois Versions de la vie, pr., pb. 2000 (*Life × 3*, 2000)

OTHER LITERARY FORMS

In addition to stage plays, Yasmina Reza translated (from Steven Berkoff's English version) of Franz Kafka's *Die Verwandlung* (1915; *The Metamorphosis*, 1936) into French for Roman Polanski in 1988 and has written screenplays, a novel, and a memoir. Published in France in 1997, her memoir *Hammerklavier* (English translation, 2000) is part interior monologue and part sketchbook for short-story ideas. Its slim narrative moves randomly through a sequence of fleeting autobiographical vignettes, as Reza draws on memories of friends and her family— especially her dead father—to focus on themes of memory and time (passing and lost). Two years later came her novel, *Une désolation* (1999), about an old man's failed existence. It was translated into ten languages, establishing her international appeal. Reza's screenplay for *Le Pique-nique de Lulu Kreutz* was filmed by Didier Martiny in 2000, starring Philippe Noiret and Stephane Audran. It tells the story of a world-famous violinist, who, weary of his profession and celebrity, falls in love with a fellow violinist who, however, prefers her scientist-husband.

ACHIEVEMENTS

Yasmina Reza has won more awards than any of her contemporary French playwrights. Her remarkable string of awards began with her first play, *Conversations After a Burial*, which won France's prestigious Molière Award for Best Author. In 1988, her French translation of Kafka, *La Metamorphose*, earned for her the Molière translation prize. Two years later, *Winter Crossing* won a Molière for best fringe production. Her play *Art* brought her three Molières for Best Play, Production, and Author in 1994; the 1996 *Evening Standard* Theatre Award and 1997 Olivier Award in England, after Christopher Hampton had translated the play; and a Tony award the next season on Broadway. Other international awards for the piece include Teater Heute Best Play, 1996/97; Drama Critics Circle Award, 1998; Fany Award, 1998; Ace Award Best Dramatic Comedy, 1998; and the Premio Max de la SGAE in 1999. *Art* has been produced in more than twenty languages and has been a hit in more than forty countries. Reza won the distinction of being the first French playwright since Jean Anouilh to have a hit in the West End of London. In November, 2000, *Life × 3* opened simultaneously in Vienna, Athens, London, and Paris.

BIOGRAPHY

Yasmina Reza was born in Paris on May 1, 1959, to Jewish parents. Her mother was the daughter of a Hungarian violinist from Budapest, and her father hailed from a family of Sephardic Jews from Russia.

He was born in 1918, in the middle of the Russian Revolution, when the family (whose original name had been Gedaliah) fled first to Persia where they changed their surname to Reza and pretended to have become Muslims when, in fact, they observed Judaism at home. Their next move was to Paris when Reza's father was five. He became an engineer who ended up in the shirt business. Partly because of these genealogical roots, Reza writes plays and fiction that are informed by nostalgia, rupture, and a sense of loss, even though her wealthy family vacationed in Switzerland.

Both parents had musical taste and aptitude. Her father was an impassioned amateur pianist—just as Yasmina is—and her mother played the violin. Yasmina mentions music in several of her writings, and for her, music is heaven. As she explains, it touches us profoundly and speaks to us in a way that words cannot. She points to Ludwig von Beethoven's sonatas and Johann Sebastian Bach's suites as possessing an absolute integrity and brave expressiveness. What she particularly likes about music is its pauses and silences, for she finds in their mysteries possibilities of dramatic human truth. When she gave up sociology after earning a license in it, she acquired a diploma in theater studies at Nanterre after failing her drama school entrance examinations. She performed in classics by Molière and Marivaux and in new French plays. She revealed her acting talent in a Sacha Guitry play (*Le veilleur de nuit*) in 1985. Indeed, her passion for music and her experience as an actress have helped her find a way of deploying si-

Yasmina Reza, left, accepting the 1998 Tony Award for Best Play for Art, *with the play's producers, Joan Cullman, center, and actor, Sean Connery.*
(AP/Wide World Photos)

lence most effectively in her plays. Words, for her, become parentheses of silences.

Reza turned to playwriting so that she could continue to explore human character and truth after her acting career had reached a peak. "I see the problems for actresses of my age," she remarked in an interview. "After you are thirty, you are finished, while as a writer I am considered very young." Moreover, she likes stories that have a plot and are lively and sensual. Her acting background helped her discover how things could be left unsaid or half-said and yet felt on stage by the performer's sheer skill. She continued to act but writing pulled her like a strong magnet. Acting was not intellectual enough for her, and she did not want to be a slave to any director. Her father was so filled with pride when her first play was produced in 1987 that he accosted the former prime minister, Raymond Barre, outside the Brasserie Lipp to tell him the good news. When her father died, Reza felt she had lost not only a friend and accomplice but also someone who had "the folly and humor of a Jew of his time, that ability to laugh at the world and weep three minutes later."

Her playwriting showed talent from the outset, though no single piece brought her as much acclaim as did *Art*, which grew out of an autobiographical incident. Her friend Serge Goldszal, a dermatologist, had spent 200,000 francs on the purchase of a plain white canvas. When he showed it to her, she burst out laughing and then felt greatly embarrassed. However, Goldszal joined in her laughter, which was a relief to her. She pondered the significance of this incident: If he had not laughed with her in complicity, their friendship might have been seriously harmed. This is how the idea of *Art* came to her, and she made the issue of male friendship the main theme, using the painting as a comic and dramatic hook. Micheline Connery, wife of actor Sean, wanted to buy the film rights for her husband, but Reza turned her down because she felt that a writer had no power or influence over film. So Micheline Connery agreed to an English stage version, with her husband serving as producer. Noted playwright Christopher Hampton did the translation, and the English production was headed by Albert Finney and Tom Courtney. Reza be-

came a major figure in international theater when *Art* went on to become a commercial and critical hit everywhere it played. However, all of her plays attract famous actors: Michael Gambon, Eileen Atkins, Alan Bates, Alan Alda, and Victor Garber are but some of the performers who have acted in English-language versions of her plays.

A very private person who does not divulge much about her personal life, Reza is married to filmmaker Didier Montiny, and they have two children, a daughter, Alta, and a son, Nathan. Reza has maintained her acting career on stage, on television, and in film while she continues to write.

ANALYSIS

Although Parisian critics once compared Yasmina Reza's plays to works by Arthur Schnitzler, Anton Chekhov, Harold Pinter, and Nathalie Sarraute, they are not modish or derivative either in form or content. Most of them use autobiographical material as they focus on facets of real life, from family relationships to male friendships, disillusionment, love, and betrayal. Compact in length and shape, they are unspectacular on the surface and linger in silences and inarticulate feelings to reveal what often lies beneath the ripples of daily existence. Some critics have labeled her plays "middlebrow entertainments," which is not a term of endearment to the French intellectual elite.

Reza's serious side is attracted to the ways in which people are abandoned in life, daily, by someone or something. The playwright has remarked: "I think that moving through life means being abandoned and abandoning. I have a lot of sympathy for those who are alone. I understand them. I feel very alone although I am not the slightest bit alone." However, she balances this seriousness by a wry wit that helps keep serious subjects light enough for broad appeal. This is not to say that her plays are merely funny even when their wit flashes forth. Rather, it is to say that their wry comedy indicates an intelligence that is alert to the foibles and follies of the human condition.

CONVERSATIONS AFTER A BURIAL

Set on a family property in the Loiret region, this intimate drama opens in flashback on a November noon with a man pouring earth onto his father's coffin. However, death is not the true subject; it is the shadow within which mourning isolates six characters. The three men and three women in the story seem to be enjoying the last moments of a summer holiday, but the play proceeds to expose family conflicts and regrets, as well as the savagery and comedy of love and its betrayals. Although all six characters are essential to the unfolding drama, the focal ones are Edith and her two brothers, Alex and Nathan. Alex's former mistress, Elise, whom he has not seen for three years shows up unexpectedly at the funeral. Her motive is simple respect for bourgeois convention, but her appearance provokes unsettling moments. Nathan who, unlike his brother, has loving memories of his deceased father, has sex with Elise over his father's grave, and Edith confronts him about this, turning hysterically abusive toward Elise, who becomes distraught. In the process, Nathan reveals a dark secret about their father, who, he suggests, might have had an affair with his chiropodist. However, the issue is left ambiguously unclear, just as is the case with the intimacy of all the characters, though the ending is not very effective in dramatic terms.

THE UNEXPECTED MAN

Maintaining an intimate tone (as in her first play), Reza sets this comedy-drama in a train compartment in which two strangers sit across from each other on the way from Paris to Frankfurt. The play unfolds as a series of internal monologues until very late when the characters finally address each other. The man is a senior novelist with highly polished shoes, aristocratic fingernails, and an elegance that is countered by his rage and vitriolic energy. He is, in fact, Paul Parsky, a novelist who muses on his vocation, latest book, friends, daughter and her lover, the workings of his own digestive system, and his faithful but droning secretary. It is clear from his mordant, satirical remarks that he is a bitter cynic who has no love or intimacy in his life. Even sex is bitter to him, and his lip seems to curl with every thought. He is a disappointment to himself as a writer and feels that he has not lived up to his own potential. He wonders if there is a single person who understands his latest book, *The Unexpected Man*.

Reza's irony is clever, for the woman (Martha), who muses on her own life, loves, and friendships, is depressed herself, especially as she is traveling with nothing to read but the very book he has just published. The novelist, of course, is unaware of this fact—as he is of anything that revolves in her mind, just as she is of his own musings. She is that single person who seems to understand his work, and an audience is led to see how she is attracted to the novelist because of his literary achievement. Her inner monologues are a way of talking to him secretly in her own mind.

The irony is underscored by mature comedy, as the man begins to speculate just who the woman might be and what her destination and its motive might be. For her part, she feels that she is being secretly watched by him, though when she decides to converse with him silently, he is somewhere else—really in his own mental ambit.

The entire play proceeds in this elliptical manner, developing unexpected connections through human intersubjectivity. However, despite its fundamentally abstract or cerebral nature, the material is surprisingly affecting, perhaps because it deals with loneliness and the difficulties of making deep and lasting connections to people.

Finally, the man speculates how this encounter with the woman who is reading his novel would make a good short story, and he is suddenly touched by the indelicacy of the situation when Martha and he begin to converse. As he denigrates his own worldview and work, she defends him and his writing. She impulsively declares her love for him, but he just laughs. This little ending underlines yet another irony in the play's title, for he is truly an unexpected man in her life and has strangely impelled her to forget her disappointment for a brief moment. What makes him further unexpected as a person is the very nature of his reaction to her spontaneous declaration of love.

ART

On the surface a satire against pretentious trends in modern art and the politics of aesthetic taste, *Art* is really about tests of male friendship. Reza uses an entirely white oil painting as her dramatic and comic hook. Serge, a Parisian dermatologist and aspiring art collector, has spent 200,000 francs on a large, untitled white canvas with diagonal white stripes by the famous Antrios, two of whose paintings are in the collection of Centre Pompidou. However, when Marc, an aeronautical engineer, scoffingly dismisses his friend's acquisition as "a piece of shit," Serge is offended. Their mutual friend, Yvan, attempts to be diplomatic, but he has his own agonizingly comic problems stemming from his forthcoming marriage to his boss's niece, and he quickly gets caught in the middle of the violent altercation that develops between Serge and Marc.

Reza's comedy makes two significant points: One is about what Reza has called the "terrorism of modernity," which amounts to the fascism of dictating what people are required to like, and the other is about strains on friendship. By standing by his painting, Serge can lose his best friend, while Marc can stay his friend only by accepting the painting as legitimate. To show that friendship is more important than modish art, Serge hands Marc a blue felt-tip pen (borrowed from Yvan who has gone into the stationery business), and Marc, after a dramatic pause, defaces the painting and then draws a skier gliding downhill. Marc ends the play with a soliloquy that restores tranquillity.

OTHER MAJOR WORKS

LONG FICTION: *Une désolation*, 1999.

SCREENPLAY: *Le Pique-nique de Lulu Kreutz*, 2000.

NONFICTION: *Hammerklavier*, 1997 (English translation, 2000).

TRANSLATION: *La Metamorphose*, 1988 (of Franz Kafka's novella).

BIBLIOGRAPHY

Blume, Mary. "Yasmina Reza and the Anatomy of a Play." *International Herald Tribune*, 1998. A good introduction to the genesis of *Art*, with significant comments from Reza on her father and craft.

Danto, Arthur C. "Art, from France to the U.S." *The Nation*, June 29, 1998, p. 28. Reveals the significance of *Art* as a commentary on the politics of art and its worth. Danto's thesis is that *Art* is an allegory of the search to define what art is and what it is worth.

Hill, Diane. "Yasmina Reza: Master of *Art*." *France Today* (1998). A discussion of *Art* and how it has transformed Reza into an international phenomenon. Also discusses her other plays and memoir to show her artistic development.

Hohenadel, Kristin. "Going Beyond Laughs: Yasmina Reza Hopes Her Successful Play *Art* Can Deliver Insights As Well As Humor to Her Audiences." *Los Angeles Times*, January 17, 1999, p. 66. Hohenadel interviews Reza before the opening of *Art* at the James A. Doolittle Theatre in Hollywood, California, in 1999, discussing the audience reaction to the play and her attitude toward writing.

Keith Garebian

RONALD RIBMAN

Born: New York, New York; May 28, 1932

PRINCIPAL DRAMA

Harry, Noon and Night, pr. 1965, pb. 1967

The Journey of the Fifth Horse, pr. 1966, pb. 1967 (based in part on Ivan Turgenev's short story "The Diary of a Superfluous Man")

The Ceremony of Innocence, pr. 1967, pb. 1968

Passing Through from Exotic Places, pr. 1969, pb. 1970 (includes three one-acts, *The Son Who Hunted Tigers in Jakarta*, *Sunstroke*, and *The Burial of Esposito*)

Fingernails Blue as Flowers, pr. 1971, pb. 1973

A Break in the Skin, pr. 1972

The Poison Tree, pr. 1973, pb. 1977

Cold Storage, pr. 1977, pb. 1978

Five Plays, pb. 1978 (includes *Harry, Noon and Night*, *The Journey of the Fifth Horse*, *The Ceremony of Innocence*, *The Poison Tree*, and *Cold Storage*)

Buck, pr., pb. 1983

The Cannibal Masque, pr. 1987

A Serpent's Egg, pr. 1987

Sweet Table at the Richelieu, pr., pb. 1987

The Rug Merchants of Chaos, pr. 1991, pb. 1992

The Rug Merchants of Chaos and Other Plays, pb. 1992

The Dream of the Red Spider, pr. 1993

OTHER LITERARY FORMS

Ronald Ribman has worked extensively as a screenwriter, both for film and for television. Among those scripts that have been produced are *The Final War of Olly Winter*, an original television play produced by the Columbia Broadcasting System (CBS) in 1967; *The Angel Levine*, a screenplay written with William Gunn and based on a story by Bernard Malamud, produced by United Artists in 1970; and *Seize the Day*, a teleplay based on the novel by Saul Bellow, produced by the Public Broadcasting Service (PBS) in 1987. Three of Ribman's stage plays have also been adapted for television: *The Journey of the Fifth Horse* for NET in 1966 and for the Canadian Broadcasting Company in 1969, *The Ceremony of Innocence* for NET in 1972 and for Granada Television in London in 1974, and *Cold Storage* for the Entertainment Channel in 1983.

ACHIEVEMENTS

Since the beginning of his career in the late 1960's, Ronald Ribman has been recognized by a relatively small number of discriminating critics, and by foundations dedicated to improving the literary merit of the American theater, as one of the most significant voices of the stage, one that rings out with poetry in the face of the prosaic norm that values language itself: Ribman's language emphasizes the beauty and fluidity of words. Though *The Journey of the Fifth Horse* was savaged by the mainstream critics, it re-

ceived the Obie Award for the best Off-Broadway play of the 1965-1966 season. *The Final War of Olly Winter* was nominated for five Emmy Awards; *The Poison Tree* won the Straw Hat Award for Best New Play in 1973, and *Cold Storage* won the Hull-Warriner Award of the Dramatists Guild in 1977. *The Rug Merchants of Chaos* was the winner of an award from the Kennedy Center Fund for New American Plays. Ribman received Rockefeller grants in 1966 and 1968, and in 1975 the Rockefeller Foundation awarded him a fellowship "in recognition of his sustained contribution to American theatre." In 1976, Ribman was awarded the Creative Artists Public Service grant, and in 1984, he received the Playwrights USA award for *Buck*. He has also been awarded a Guggenheim Foundation grant in 1970 and National Endowment for the Arts fellowships in 1973 and 1986-1987.

BIOGRAPHY

Ronald Burt Ribman was born in New York City on May 28, 1932, the son of Samuel M. Ribman, a lawyer, and Rosa Lerner Ribman. As a teenager he took an aptitude test that indicated that he should be a writer, but it made no sense to him; at that time he despised all forms of literature. His earliest career choice was science. "I was the worst chemistry major in the history of Brooklyn College," he has said. "Things bubbled strangely and blew up in my retorts." He abandoned science, and for his sophomore year, he transferred to the University of Pittsburgh, where in 1954 he received his bachelor's degree in business administration.

Soon after graduation he was drafted. To while away the long hours off duty while he was stationed in Germany, he began to write: long letters at first, and then poetry. "I wrote a lot of terrible poems which they broadcast over the Armed Forces Network, which led to all kinds of suspicions about me—whether I was the right kind of gung-ho military material the Army was looking for."

On his discharge, he started working at one of his father's business concerns, a coal brokerage in Pennsylvania. He continued to write—short stories as well as poetry—and decided to apply to the graduate school at the University of Pittsburgh to study the very subject he had once despised above all others, English literature. He supported his application with copies of his recent writing and was accepted. (His writing was returned with a critical comment: "Mr. Ribman has a penchant for the bizarre, which a few writing courses that stress concrete imagery will take out of him.") After earning his M.Litt. in 1958, he was accepted for doctoral work at the Universities of Edinburgh and Minnesota. "Faced with a choice, I of course picked the wrong one." After "one freezing quarter" in Minnesota, he returned to "Pitt," where he earned his Ph.D., with a dissertation on John Keats, in 1962. He then entered the academic world as an assistant professor of English at Otterbein College in Westerville, Ohio. This career lasted only one year. He resigned to devote himself full-time to writing, which he has done ever since.

In New York, Ribman collaborated with his father on an article about the poor treatment indigent defendants were getting in the federal court system; the piece appeared in *Harper's*. He was thus a published writer, but he had not yet discovered his form. That discovery came while he was watching an amateur production of Edward Albee's *The Sandbox* (pr., pb. 1960) in Johnstown, Pennsylvania. It hit him rather suddenly: "I'm a playwright. That's what I am. I recognize myself now."

Ribman wrote a one-act play called "Day of the Games" and sent it to the American Place Theatre in New York. The artistic director, Wynn Handman, came across it while slogging through a stack of manuscripts one Saturday morning in 1963, and it leaped out at him. "It was the language: fantastic, actable language, rich, evocative, poetic." He immediately telephoned Ribman and asked him to write a companion piece that would fill up an evening of theater.

The "companion piece" turned out to be a full-length play, *Harry, Noon and Night*, which was staged as the second major production in the American Place Theatre's first season, with two then-unknown actors in the leads, Joel Grey and Dustin Hoffman. Another Off-Broadway production followed immediately, with Robert Blake in the cast. In 1966, the American Place Theatre produced Ribman's second full-length play, *The Journey of the Fifth Horse*, with Hoffman as Zoditch and Michael Tolan as Chulkaturin.

The following year, Ribman married Alice Rosen, a nurse; the couple had two children, James and Elana.

A number of critics—among them Robert Brustein, Martin Gottfried, and Gerald Weales—immediately identified Ribman as one of the few playwrights who represented the future of American playwriting and a rejection of the relatively mindless fare that was becoming the staple of Broadway. Mainstream critics have never embraced him, though, and only two of his plays have been produced on Broadway: *The Poison Tree* in 1976 and *Cold Storage* in 1977. Many of his subsequent plays have been produced by Handman at the American Place Theatre and by Brustein at the Yale Repertory Theatre in New Haven, Connecticut, and the American Repertory Theatre in Cambridge, Massachusetts.

Ribman has refused to create his plays according to any notion of what an audience might want to see. "The thing for me that has always been the most difficult," he has said,

is to be faithful to my own creative instincts, to what I want to do. There are powerful market forces out there that push you into more conservative directions because more conservative directions are what pay. To be true to yourself means that if you are going to find your authentic, individual voice you may at first be pushed aside because it doesn't sound like anyone else, and if it doesn't sound like anyone else they don't know what to do with it. It's been said that we are all born originals, but most of us die as copies. That's what an artist must avoid.

ANALYSIS

Ronald Ribman is a virtuoso of style. The shape of his imagination is protean, its colors those of a chameleon. He has the ability to project himself, from play to play, into different locales, times, levels of reality and fantasy, and to sound, against all odds, persuasive, consistent, compelling.

Each of his plays adopts a different approach to

the question of how reality is to be refracted through the playwright's prism before being presented to the audience. He can write snappy, amusing dialogue, and he can adopt the tone of a parable: simple, lapidary, but suggestive. He can hew very close to realism, but at other times he approaches surrealism, jumping back and forth in time, presenting different levels of fantasy and reality simultaneously, with a poet's eye and ear journeying deep into the thickets of the imaginary to create new worlds—worlds that resemble our own but differ in time, locale, and in their idiosyncratic approaches to reality.

As a result of this virtuosity, it is difficult to identify Ribman with any one particular style. "Some writers," he has said,

> are very fortunate in that they find the vein, the seam in their mind that they can mine right at the beginning and they just keep hacking away at it. I keep finding it and I keep losing it and keep picking it up somewhere else. People have told me, "None of your plays looks like the one that went before. They all look very different from each other." That's because I'm mining different areas.

Nevertheless, there are certain themes and patterns that have recurred from play to play throughout his career, preoccupations and threads of consistency that tie together all the disparate forms of his protean shape. One of these is an interest in the process of victimization, in which, frequently, the victim and the victimizer reverse roles; both are revealed as no more than clowns, and the conflict itself as nothing more than an absurd game.

Often the characters and the plots are created with a bizarre, dreamlike logic, a grotesque, nightmarish quality. Sometimes the fevered imagination of one character seems to create the rest of the cast, as distorted reflections of his fears or preoccupations; they speak and act as if they had never felt the inhibitions of civilization, as if they were capable of keeping nothing inside, as if every unspeakable thought had to emerge immediately—as if, in fact, they had no insides, as if their insides were all on the surface. Grotesque images and incidents appear, too, that are distorted images of what is disturbing the protagonist.

Characters often speak past one another, rather than to one another. They misunderstand one another, and so make it easy for the audience to misunderstand them. In fact, as Ribman himself has often insisted, the plays are ambiguous; there are no single meanings, and each will and should be understood in a number of different ways. Their exact natures are as difficult to seize as Proteus. Ribman's poetry, then, is not simply a matter of rich, supple language; it is also a matter of poetic ambiguity, of ineffability.

One other recurring concern of Ribman is his preoccupation with the persistence of the past in the present—a recognition that all people carry a heavy baggage of seeds, each of which began sprouting at a different time in the past and never stopped shooting out tendrils: a bag of memories that can never simply be dumped. The figure that embodies this preoccupation, in play after play, is a character who seldom appears onstage: the lost one, the dear one who has disappeared, never to be recovered. He has often been swept away in a horrifying instant, a moment that can never be forgotten, that will always live in the present but can never be reversed.

HARRY, NOON AND NIGHT

Harry, Noon and Night, the first of Ribman's plays to be produced, is set in Munich in 1955, during the American occupation. Each of the three scenes of this black comedy is essentially a confrontation between two people. In the first, Harry, posing as an impossibly inept journalist, is interviewing a thick-witted soldier in a bar while both of them fondle a local prostitute. The interview is a wild, improvisatory put-on; the soldier submits to all of Harry's addled questions because Harry promises to give him money for the girl when it is over, but the audience never learns Harry's reason for going through this charade.

In the second scene, the audience meets Immanuel, Harry's insectlike roommate (and bedmate), in their chaotic, filthy apartment; he is conducting a similar put-on of Harry's brother Archer, a gung-ho Air Force gunner during the war, now a can-do Ohio businessman. Harry is an artist who has abandoned the sugary, commercial pictorial realism he learned at home in favor of an ugly, inchoate expressionism that he has never succeeded in selling; Archer has come to fetch him home. Immanuel conducts a masterful put-on of Archer, posing alternately, and successfully, as a student of philosophy, a raging queen, and a vendor of religious relics, and befuddling him with fish scales, dry-cleaning fluid, talcum powder, and an overflowing toilet. In the last scene, Harry returns to the apartment to pack his bags to meet Archer at the train station but causes such an uproar—he ties Immanuel up in the bedding and assaults the neighbors—that he is arrested and misses the train.

The plot is as chaotic as Harry's life and art, but through it, by indirection, the audience begins to see relationships and histories; it is never made clear exactly what Harry's problem is, or what his youth with Archer was like, but subtly a picture emerges. The one image that emerges most clearly is that of Moko the failure clown, whom Archer had brought Harry to see at the circus; Archer had found him hilarious, but Harry had seen only his pain.

THE JOURNEY OF THE FIFTH HORSE

One of the clowns in *The Journey of the Fifth Horse* is Chulkaturin, an impoverished landowner in czarist Russia, whose story is adapted from Ivan Turgenev's short story "Dnevnik lishnyago cheloveka" ("The Diary of a Superfluous Man"). Dying at the age of twenty-eight, Chulkaturin confides to his diary that he has never really lived, never succeeded in love, or indeed in making any impression at all on other people. Ribman creates another clown as counterpoint to Chulkaturin: Zoditch, the lowly first reader in a publishing house, whose task it is to evaluate the manuscript of Chulkaturin's diary. As he reads the diary in his miserable rooming house, Chulkaturin's story comes to life, and Zoditch peoples it with analogous characters from his own loveless, pointless existence. In the end, Zoditch, dripping with scorn for Chulkaturin—especially for those qualities that resemble his own—rejects the manuscript and consigns him to oblivion.

Throughout the play, scenes from Chulkaturin's diary alternate with scenes from Zoditch's life and fantasies. This interweaving of plots and levels of reality is quite ingenious, but the technical ingenuity only enhances the pain and ludicrousness of the two

protagonists. It is a bittersweet play, its laughter tinged with death. One of its most remarkable aspects is the way Ribman, through his mastery of language, convincingly creates two separate levels of nineteenth century Russian society.

THE CEREMONY OF INNOCENCE

His leap of imagination is even greater in *The Ceremony of Innocence*. This play was written, in a sense, as a response to the war in Vietnam, but the story that Ribman tells is a fanciful revision of the history of Ethelred the Unready, king of England in the eleventh century. Ribman creates a sense of war as an entity unto itself, with its own momentum and a tenacious hold on the minds and spirits of the people. Ethelred (who is generally seen by historians in a harsher light) is depicted as standing alone for peace, for common prosperity and the spread of literacy, and for justice; appalled at the prejudice and treachery of his court—even his son and his mother—toward the Danes, he simply refuses, as a matter of principle, to take the field at the head of his troops in defense of England.

Ribman begins his play with Ethelred's refusal to meet with the earls of Sussex and Kent and the bishop of London, who have come to his retreat on the Isle of Wight to importune him to do battle. His refusal seems bullheaded, a bit deranged, and positively untenable—especially in that the subject matter inevitably calls to mind William Shakespeare's histories, in which the welfare of the English throne is assumed to be the greatest good. The playwright then leaps backward a full year to reveal the underpinnings of Ethelred's convictions; then he works forward to the last scene, which is set a few hours after the first; and by the end of the play Ribman has managed to justify, both ethically and emotionally, the king's refusal to lead his country into war even in defense of its borders. Ribman's achievement is all the more remarkable in that he creates a persuasive language for his characters, a diction that mixes some of the direct, prosaic idiom of modern American speech with Elizabethan locutions—a factitious language that, in less skillful hands, might have come across as clumsy or downright silly, but which Ribman wields into an eloquent sort of poetry.

THE POISON TREE

The linguistic audacity of *The Poison Tree* is very different but no less perilous and no less successful; Ribman sets the play in a prison, for the most part among African American prisoners, and writes for them a number of varieties of black dialect. (A few years earlier, in 1967, another white writer, William Styron, had been excoriated for using black dialect—and, indeed, for daring to imagine the workings of a black man's mind—in *The Confessions of Nat Turner*, 1967.) The racism of the white prisoners and guards is a palpable, oppressive force throughout the play, but it is only one of a number of oppressions wearing away at the souls of prisoners and guards alike.

The play begins with the murder of a white guard by a black prisoner. The victim, his neck snapped, falls into the arms of another guard, Di Santis. He becomes obsessed with the senseless loss of his comrade, and, through direct violence and covert manipulation, he wreaks a terrible vengeance on the innocent as well as on the guilty. In the end, though, the tables are turned again, and the victimizer becomes the victim.

COLD STORAGE

In *Cold Storage*, Ribman's most successful play commercially, the language is very close to his own natural speech: that of modern New York. In technique, it is his most realistic, straightforward play. It dares, though, to forge snappy comedy from a situation of inevitable catastrophe; set on the roof garden of a hospital, it presents the relationship between two patients: an old man who is dying and a prosperous middle-aged designer who may have cancer.

BUCK

Buck, also set in modern New York, is somewhat more complex stylistically. It concerns a television director who is hired to make sleazy exploitation tapes for a cable channel but gets so involved in trying to create a true picture of the realities he is restaging that the scenes he films take on a life of their own.

SWEET TABLE AT THE RICHELIEU

Sweet Table at the Richelieu is set in a mysterious, elegant spa in an unspecified (though probably Germanic) corner of Europe. It consists of nothing but an after-dinner conversation among the guests; the guests, however, are a most curious, nightmarish assemblage of Eurotrash, and the discussion is brutal, feral, flaying—more direct, probing, and yet poetical than any real-life chitchat could ever be. Among the guests are a widowed baroness avid to enforce the prerogatives of her rank despite the humiliations of a more democratic age; a half-man, half-beast clairvoyant; an American author of best-selling pulp novels and her lover, a Moroccan given to violent fantasies; and a French Lothario who constantly humiliates his wife, who is always hanging on his neck. The presiding figure is Dr. Atmos, a cheerful but treacherous unlicensed physician who attracts guests to the Richelieu with promises of eternal youth.

The central character, Jeanine Cendrars, is a Pennsylvania woman who speaks very little. Early in the play, the audience learns that her marriage is in trouble, and toward the end Dr. Atmos, who dabbles in psychology as well as in rejuvenation, reveals to all that she is haunted by the loss of a child who was swept from her side on a boat by a wave during a moment of inattention. Although the other characters are intent on obliterating their pasts, Jeanine clings tenaciously to the image of her lost child, keeping him alive in her mind. In fact, the entire play can be seen as an emanation of her mind, and all the other characters as dream-figures brought to palpable form as combatants in her struggle with a tragic past that remains ever present.

The Cannibal Masque and *A Serpent's Egg* are one-act plays that were conceived to form a trilogy with *Sweet Table at the Richelieu*. Each of the three plays has for its central image people eating: In *Sweet Table at the Richelieu*, a cornucopia of sweets from a groaning board; in *The Cannibal Masque*, a fat pork dinner in the midst of a famine in Bavaria in 1923; and in *A Serpent's Egg* (set some thirty years later), a skimpy picnic on a German mountainside under the greedy eye of a rapacious landowner. Although the longer play deals with excess through luxuriant verbiage, the one-acts are spare and parabolic, like little allegories of inhuman victimization, but each with a sudden shift of fortunes.

Though there are similarities with *Sweet Table at the Richelieu*, the other plays in the trilogy are very different in form and feel. Indeed, one of the most curious aspects of Ribman's playwriting career is its diversity, the breadth of imagination that puts him into so many different times, places, idioms, and styles. "I think of Keats," he has said, "who likened a career to the sun which gradually rises, reaches its zenith, and gradually sets. A playwright produces a body of work—he doesn't just produce one or two plays—because what he's doing is mining his life, and a life encompasses more than one or two plays."

THE RUG MERCHANTS OF CHAOS

Ribman's oft used themes are present in *The Rug Merchants of Chaos*. The play is a comedy about a couple who are engaged in questionable business endeavors over the years. Although constantly on the edge of catastrophe, they manage to avoid a downfall through sheer chance.

OTHER MAJOR WORKS

SCREENPLAY: *The Angel Levine*, 1970 (with William Gunn; based on a story by Bernard Malamud).

TELEPLAYS: *The Final War of Olly Winter*, 1967; *The Most Beautiful Fish*, 1969; *Seize the Day*, 1987 (based on Saul Bellow's novel); *The Sunset Gang*, 1991.

BIBLIOGRAPHY

Brustein, Robert. "Journey and Arrival of a Playwright." In *The Third Theater*. New York: Alfred A. Knopf, 1969. In this discussion of *The Journey of the Fifth Horse*, Brustein, who was the drama critic for *The New Republic*, highlights the flexibility of Ribman's language, which can move from evocative tenderness to stinging rebuke. He also praises the way the dramatist suggests the hidden affinities of his two central characters, men who, at first glance, seem worlds apart.

Gottfried, Martin. *Opening Nights: Theater Criticism of the Sixties*. New York: G. P. Putnam's Sons, 1969. Theater critic Gottfried reviews *The Journey of the Fifth Horse* and compares it favorably to a contemporary British drama. Gottfried gives Ribman high marks for his fluid use of structure and his compassion for those tormented by loneliness.

_____. *A Theater Divided: The Postwar American Stage*. Boston: Little, Brown, 1967. In this work, Gottfried argues that the American theater after World War II was divided between left (liberal) and right (conservative) wings, each contesting the shape of drama in the United States. Ironically enough, though, the critic notes that Ribman's works were rejected by both camps. Even if, as Gottfried states, *Harry, Noon and Night* was "the best new American play produced anywhere in New York that year," it divided the critics because it proved unassimilable to fashionable viewpoints.

Lamont, Rosette C. "Murderous Enactments: The Media's Presence in the Drama." *Modern Drama* 28 (1985): 148-161. This essay analyzes how plays by Ribman and Janusz Glowacki present the mass media as violator of people's selfhood and sense of community. In Ribman's play *Buck*, "the true villains are the media and society; the circulation of money, as well as need and avarice, generates violence." In such an outlook, according to Lamont, one sees a reversal of the optimistic picture of technology that appeared in earlier generations of modern dramatists, as in the work of the Surrealists.

Weales, Gerald. *The Jumping-Off Place: American Drama in the 1960's*. New York: Macmillan, 1969. Comparing Ribman's three earliest plays, Weales finds the greatest strength to be in the first two. Although they are idiosyncratic, they are full of surprises, feeling, and black comedy. In the first, *Harry, Noon and Night*, Ribman is able to "transform a potentially conventional character and situation into a statement about human beings that transcends the specific."

Jonathan Marks, updated by James Feast and Andrea E. Miller

ELMER RICE
Elmer Leopold Reizenstein

Born: New York, New York; September 28, 1892
Died: Southampton, England; May 8, 1967

PRINCIPAL DRAMA

On Trial, pr. 1914, pb. 1919
The Passing of Chow-Chow, pr. 1915, pb. 1925
   (one act)
The Iron Cross, wr. 1915, pr. 1917, pb. 1965
The House in Blind Alley, wr. 1916,
   pb. 1932
Wake Up, Jonathan, pr. 1921, pb. 1928 (with
   Hatcher Hughes)
The Adding Machine, pr., pb. 1923
The Subway, wr. 1923, pr., pb. 1929
Street Scene, pr., pb. 1929
See Naples and Die, pr. 1929, pb. 1930
The Left Bank, pr., pb. 1931
Counsellor-at-Law, pr., pb. 1931
The Black Sheep, pr. 1932, pb. 1938
We, the People, pr., pb. 1933
Judgment Day, pr., pb. 1934
Between Two Worlds, pr. 1934, pb. 1935
Not for Children, pr., pb. 1935, revised pr.,
   pb. 1951
American Landscape, pr. 1938,
   pb. 1939
Two on an Island, pr., pb. 1940
Flight to the West, pr. 1940, pb. 1941
A New Life, pr. 1943, pb. 1944
Dream Girl, pr. 1945, pb. 1946
Street Scene, pr. 1947, pb. 1948 (libretto;
   adaptation of his play; music by Kurt Weill,
   lyrics by Langston Hughes)
Seven Plays, pb. 1950
The Grand Tour, pr. 1951, pb. 1952
Love Among the Ruins, wr. 1951, pr.,
   pb. 1963
The Winner, pr., pb. 1954
Cue for Passion, pr. 1958, pb. 1959
Three Plays, pb. 1965
Court of Last Resort, pb. 1985

OTHER LITERARY FORMS

Elmer Rice was a versatile and prolific writer. He was not only a serious dramatist, with more than thirty published plays to his credit at the time of his death, but also a novelist of some skill. In 1930, he published *A Voyage to Purilia*, a satire on Hollywood based on his experiences there during his stint as a writer for Samuel Goldwyn shortly after World War I. In the novel, Rice satirizes the shortcomings and triteness of the movie industry. That the book was accepted for serialization in *The New Yorker* attests Rice's skill as a stylist and craftsperson. Rice's second novel, *Imperial City* (1937), was written during his four-year retirement from the theater. The work examines the variegated pattern of New York City life and offers a panoramic view of that fascinating metropolis. Rice was praised for the completeness of his depiction. In his third and final novel, *The Show Must Go On* (1949), Rice drew on his experiences in the theater world. The book received some acclaim, both in the United States and in England, and has been translated into several foreign languages.

Rice is not remembered for his success as a screenwriter. He did, however, work in Hollywood after World War I and again in the 1930's, and still later in the 1940's. In the 1930's, Rice was hired by Universal to serve as scenarist for the film version of his own play *Counsellor-at-Law*. In the late 1940's, Rice agreed to do a screenplay based on *Earth and High Heaven* (1944), a novel by a Canadian writer, Gwethalyn Graham. The screenplay was completed, but the film was never made.

Rice also published a wide-ranging book on the theater, entitled *The Living Theatre* (1959). In it, he distinguishes the theater from the drama and covers other areas such as the status of the theater in Japan, England, and the Soviet Union, the beginnings of the theater in the United States and its growth, the Federal Theatre Project, commercialism in the arts, and censorship. In 1963, Rice published his autobiography, *Minority Report*, which is fascinating reading for any student of modern American drama.

ACHIEVEMENTS

Ever an innovator, ever seeking to improve the quality of the American theater, Elmer Rice began his Broadway career with a play, *On Trial*, that used the flashback technique for the first time on an American stage. The use of the technique created a production problem, the solution to which required yet another innovation. In order to shift scenes rapidly from various interior settings to a permanent courtroom setting, as required by the play, a two-platform stage had to be developed. In due course this was accomplished, and the device, called a jackknife stage, was introduced for the first time to the American theatergoing public. This development was a boon to playwrights, to whom it offered greater freedom and flexibility in choosing settings.

Rice was responsible for a number of other innovations. In *A New Life*, he was the first American playwright to present a birth scene in full view of the audience, shattering a long-observed taboo and leading the way for other American dramatists. In *The Winner*, Rice again broke with tradition: For the role of the judge who presides over a hearing involving a contested will, Rice chose an African American actor, Frederick O'Neal. This was a departure from the accepted practice of casting black people only in subordinate, menial, or other stereotypical parts. For casting a black person in an unconventional role, and thus opening up the American theater to racial equality, Rice was presented with the Canada Lee Foundation Award.

The most prestigious award Rice received as a playwright was the Pulitzer Prize. This was accorded him for his precedent-shattering play *Street Scene*. It was such a departure from the standard stage fare of the time that some thought it was not a play at all. There were simply too many characters, too many stories to be followed, Rice was told; the play would not be able to hold the attention of the audience. Nevertheless, when Rice persisted in his "folly," and finally found a producer, the play turned out to be his greatest hit—commercially as well as critically. It ran

for 601 performances and was later produced in Europe, South America, Australia, New Zealand, the Near East, the Far East, and South Africa. Again it shows Rice's penchant for innovation: He introduced to the stage a dramatist's version of the collective novel.

Rice's disenchantment with the rampant commercialism of the American theater, its cliché-ridden plots, and its appeal to the puerile instincts of theatergoers caused him to become involved with organizations that were attempting to improve the quality of American theater fare. To that end, he contributed both financial support and advice to the Group Theatre, the Theatre Union, and the Theatre Alliance; he helped in the organization of the latter. On the whole, the purpose of these groups was to produce plays of social significance, to increase and make more important the contribution of those creative individuals—playwrights, directors, actors, and others—involved in putting on plays, and generally to improve the quality of American drama.

To the same end, Rice and four other successful and highly regarded American dramatists—Maxwell Anderson, S. N. Behrman, Sidney Howard, and Robert E. Sherwood—founded the Playwrights' Producing Company in 1938. Its purpose was to extirpate the purely commercial influences of producers and theater owners by having the playwrights themselves furnish the money for producing plays. In this way, dramas of high quality—plays that might not otherwise be produced because of financial considerations—could be staged. The Playwrights' Producing Company was a successful enterprise that survived for more than twenty years.

With the advent of the Depression, Rice became concerned with the price of theater admission tickets, which were no longer affordable to a large segment of the public. This problem compounded another one: the unemployment of many theater workers, unemployment that threatened to become permanent as the Depression spread and deepened. Rice's response to this crisis was to call for some sort of government sponsorship. His leadership here resulted in the formation of the Federal Theatre Project, the genesis of which was his letter to Harry Hopkins in 1935. The

Federal Theatre priced tickets at a dollar or less, and sometimes gave them away. The effect was to build up a theater audience for the future and to provide employment for vast numbers of professional theater workers. Thus, Rice was in some measure responsible for keeping the American theater going during a critical period in its history.

BIOGRAPHY

Elmer Rice was born Elmer Leopold Reizenstein, in an apartment on Ninetieth Street in New York City, in 1892. It was a name he kept until the first production of his play, written in collaboration with Hatcher Hughes, *Wake Up, Jonathan*, in 1921. On opening night, the program listed the playwright for the first time under his newly assumed pen name, Elmer L. Rice.

Rice attended public schools in New York but had to drop out after his sophomore year in high school because his parents could no longer afford to support him. Jobs were hard to get, but Rice finally secured employment as a filing clerk in a law office. Though he did not really wish to become a lawyer, he decided that it was the only career open to him and enrolled in the New York Law School. There he found that classes bored him, and he began bringing reading materials to class to relieve the tedium. The classes were two hours long, and Rice discovered that he could read a play in that length of time. Thus, plays became his preferred reading material. In this way, he developed and nurtured his interest in the drama.

In 1913, Rice took and passed the bar examination, but he soon became appalled by legal ethics and decided that the practice of law was not for him. At this point, he had already written three plays: "A Defection from Grace," "The Seventh Commandment," and *The Passing of Chow-Chow*. The first two, written in collaboration with Frank Harris, a fellow law clerk, have never been published or produced; the third, a solo effort, was entered in a one-act-play contest sponsored by Co-

lumbia University in 1915 and won the aspiring playwright a silver cup. With his apprenticeship over, Rice was ready for Broadway.

Rice's first professionally produced play, *On Trial*, opened in New York on August 19, 1914. It was a blockbuster. The play ran for 365 performances, then went on the road to play in numerous cities throughout the United States. Later, it was performed in Europe, in South Africa, in South America, in Central America, and in the Far East. Eventually, it was made into a film.

During the remainder of the 1920's, Rice demonstrated his versatility and revealed his penchant for using drama to expose the major social and economic diseases of his day. For example, in *The Iron Cross*, written in 1915 but not performed until 1917, Rice, a pacifist, excoriated the glorification of war. He also

Elmer Rice (Hulton Archive by Getty Images)

attacked in this work the puritanical element in American society and the distorted view of sex that it has produced.

In *The House in Blind Alley*, Rice considered some of the evils of the American economic system; in particular, he inveighed against the inclusion of children in the workforce. The play was written in 1916 but has never been produced.

In the 1920's, Rice was at his best; it was during this period that his two greatest plays were produced. *The Adding Machine* and *Street Scene* are at least minor classics of the American theater. Although Rice continued to produce work at a prolific rate during this period, most of the plays he completed were collaborations, one-acts, or adaptations; the lone exceptions were *See Naples and Die* and *The Subway*, both produced in 1929.

During the 1930's, Rice was unable to maintain the high standard that he had set with his two masterpieces, *The Adding Machine* and *Street Scene*. His best drama of this period is undoubtedly *Counsellor-at-Law*, but that play, good as it is, hardly approaches the artistic merit of the two earlier ones. It was during the Depression years, however, that Rice was most effective as a social critic. In such plays as *The Black Sheep* and *The Left Bank*, Rice deplored the status of the creative artist in American society. In *We, the People* and in *American Landscape*, he lamented the plight of the American worker during this economically chaotic period. In *Judgment Day* and in *Between Two Worlds*, he attacked totalitarianism.

In the war years, Rice continued to write prolifically: Between 1940 and 1945, he had four plays produced. *Two on an Island*, a comedy, depicts the struggles of an aspiring young playwright and an embryonic actress to achieve success on Broadway. *Flight to the West* is another attack on fascism. Rice's next play, *A New Life*, also expressed his desire that freedom and liberty flourish. Instead of the Nazis, however, it is dictatorial grandparents who are the recipients of the playwright's wrath. Rice concluded the period as he began it, with a comedy. *Dream Girl*, Rice's greatest commercial success since *Counsellor-at-Law*, is reminiscent of James Thurber's short story "The Secret Life of Walter Mitty."

Rice's first dramatic production of the postwar years, unless one counts his writing of the libretto for the musical version of his 1929 hit *Street Scene* and a revised version of his 1935 drama *Not for Children*, was *The Grand Tour*. One must not assume, however, that his energies were diminished. In addition to the libretto, he had written a novel, *The Show Must Go On*, and had taken two trips abroad, one of which provided him with the setting for a later play. Moreover, he hurled himself into several controversies involving censorship, or attempted censorship, of a number of movies. Finally, in the early 1950's, he was to be found defending the civil liberties threatened by the excesses of the House Committee on Un-American Activities and by McCarthyism.

The Grand Tour, principally a love story, also treats extensively materialism as a negative factor in American life. It is not one of Rice's better dramas. *The Grand Tour* was followed three years later by *The Winner*. Like its predecessor, it is not one of the playwright's serious plays, though it does point out the hypocrisy that is to be found everywhere in American society. The fragility of American marital relationships, another Rice staple, also receives its share of attention. One might add that the play revealed that Rice's low opinion of lawyers, first indicated when he gave up the practice of law, had not changed for the better. *Cue for Passion* reached the stage in 1958. It is William Shakespeare's *Hamlet, Prince of Denmark* (pr. c. 1600-1601), converted to modern times and reeking with twentieth century psychology.

The playwright's last play to reach the stage, though only in a college production with Rice employed in an advisory capacity, was *Love Among the Ruins*, written twelve years earlier. In it, Rice deals with the death of love in the postwar world.

Among Rice's accomplishments between 1945 and his death in 1967 is *The Living Theatre*, a book of essays that reveals Rice's views on world theater, and much about his principles and practices as a dramatist. Also, his autobiography, *Minority Report*, not only offers many insights into Rice the man and Rice the playwright but also serves as a history of the American theater between 1914 and 1963.

ANALYSIS

Elmer Rice is unquestionably a major American playwright. His durability—his first play was produced in 1914, his last in 1963—and the sheer scope of his output ensure his stature in the history of American drama. Like many writers who came to maturity in the 1920's and the 1930's, he combined a dedication to art and craftsmanship with a commitment to social reform. In his autobiography, Rice mentions his particular attraction to works of literature that unmask the evils of society. This predilection serves to explain his preference for such dramatists as Henrik Ibsen, George Bernard Shaw, and August Strindberg. Of this group, it was Shaw with whom Rice most felt an affinity. Like Shaw, Rice believed that it was the playwright's duty to improve society by exposing its false values and hypocrisies. In this pursuit, virtually all of his attention was focused on America and Americans. Even when Rice's plays are set abroad, it is principally the weaknesses of Americans and of American society that he lays bare. Though he employed a variety of dramatic forms and though his work covers a wide range of subject matter, his œuvre is consistent in at least one respect: All of his dramas reveal his perennial engagement with improving the quality of American life by uncovering its many imperfections.

THE ADDING MACHINE

The Adding Machine, Rice's first masterwork, represented a departure from the realism of his earlier plays. In it, he adapted to the American stage the devices of German expressionism. Indeed, *The Adding Machine* is quite possibly the best full-length expressionistic play by an American dramatist. The play had its genesis in Rice's visit to the Ford Motor Company plant in Detroit, quickly followed by his tour of the Chicago stockyards. These firsthand observations of industrialization left Rice appalled. He watched in some horror the robotlike actions of workers who were obliged to perform their monotonous tasks while hovering over a relentless conveyer belt. Some time later, after a period of germination, Rice wrote, in the remarkable time of seventeen days, the play based on his observation of the effect of the machine age on humankind.

Expressionism, a technique for making inner experience concrete, is exemplified in the play in a number of ways: in the externalization of thought processes; in the treatment of the characters, who are numbered instead of named to indicate their dehumanization and loss of individuality; and in the rows of numbers that decorate the wallpaper, signifying the ascendance of a quantified society.

Although *The Adding Machine* represented a departure in both form and technique from Rice's previous work, he remained the social critic he had always been. Among the targets of the play are hypocrisy, the depersonalization of the modern business world, bigotry, the impersonality of the law, and Puritanism.

The hypocrisy that permeates American life is demonstrated by Rice through his depiction of his protagonist, Zero, and Zero's wife. Zero, who has taken delight in watching a prostitute who neglects to pull the shade across her window even when she is not dressed, finally reports her to the police. Although he deplores her lack of modesty and her extravagant use of makeup, he later regrets that he had not taken advantage of his wife's absence to pay the prostitute a visit.

For her part, Mrs. Zero claims that she prefers movies that portray highly moral, wholesome love stories, but in the dialogue that follows, one discerns that Mrs. Zero's real predilection is for love stories that incorporate risqué scenes—scenes that may be cut before the movies reach the neighborhood theaters where she can see them.

To Rice, the business world is a competitive one where human beings and human values get short shrift. In such a world, there is little room for personal considerations. This depersonalization of relationships is shown both in Zero's boss's failure to know Zero's name—even though he has been his employee for twenty-five years—and his lack of concern for the consequences that await a man fired at an advanced age with no warning.

Racial bigotry, a frequent subject in Rice's drama, and sexism also receive attention in *The Adding Machine*. Early in the play, the Zeros host a party. Those who attend all dress alike, have the same tastes, share the same views and prejudices. If business conditions are bad, it is because of foreign agitators; women's suffrage is ridiculous; a woman's place is in the home; women have no business meddling in politics.

Rice's disenchantment with the legal profession, expressed when he refused to practice law shortly after receiving his degree and passing the bar examination, is revealed again here. Rice believed that the spirit of the law, not the letter, should be paramount. He believed that in practice, however, the reverse is true. Therefore, Rice finds the courts to be impersonal, even indifferent to those whose fates they determine—an attitude embodied by the judge in the courtroom scene, who is nothing but an impassive automaton. Similarly, Rice's belief that justice does not always prevail and that court cases are frequently won by trickery, theatrics, and obscuration is exemplified by Zero's lawyer's insistence that the blood on the murder weapon is red ink, even though Zero fully admits to his guilt and wishes to be punished. Later, Zero complains about court procedure that requires yes or no answers. Some questions necessitate more complex answers if justice is to be served.

The deleterious effects of Puritanism on the American psyche are revealed by Zero and Shrdlu, whom Zero (who has been executed for murder) meets in the afterlife. Shrdlu is also a murderer: He has killed his mother, and his conscience demands that he suffer the torture of the damned in hell for his unspeakable crime. What has happened to justice, to morality, that he should be permitted to spend eternity in the Elysian Fields? Schooled in a puritanical tradition, he cannot accept forgiveness and a happier fate, and he insists on eternal punishment.

Zero, imbued, like Shrdlu, with the Puritan morality of his earthly existence, cannot understand a heaven that admits murderers. Moreover, he is shaken by his discovery that he is living in the midst of drunkards, thieves, vagabonds, and adulterers. Unable to reconcile this knowledge with his own ingrained ideas about what is respectable, Zero is consigned to return to Earth to begin life anew in another identity.

Though *The Adding Machine* was neither a critical nor a commercial success when it first appeared in 1923, it is now highly esteemed and often per-

formed; Rice himself compiled a list showing that between 1958 and 1963, *The Adding Machine* had a total of ninety-two productions. Today, more than a half century after its first performance, with machines encroaching at an ever-increasing rate on territory previously held by human beings, the play remains relevant.

STREET SCENE

In *Street Scene*, Rice's second major work, the playwright returned to realism with a vengeance. To convey the sounds associated with the New York City setting of his play—automobile horns, squealing brakes, steamboat whistles—Rice recorded them, then put the records on two record players started a minute apart during the performance so as to duplicate the overlapping effect of heavy traffic and other assorted noises of the busy metropolis. Not satisfied with the unrealistic sound of footsteps moving across a wooden stage that purported to be a city street, Rice had a thin layer of cement placed on the boards. Finally, and on a different level, Rice increased the play's authenticity by drawing his characters from a rich diversity of national and ethnic backgrounds.

In this play, Rice seeks to reveal the lives and problems of various families living in an apartment house in a lower-middle-class neighborhood in New York. His realistic depiction of character and circumstance, however, does not prevent him from mounting the soapbox to decry the inadequacies of America's social and economic system.

To begin with the latter, Rice focuses on organized charity, which is a concomitant of the capitalistic system, since under capitalism there will always be those who are unable to support themselves and who have no other source of aid. In the 1920's, accepting charity was considered demeaning, and those who had to depend on it—often through no fault of their own—were considered inferior. Rice, with his strong socialistic bent, sought to point out the unfairness of such an attitude and to invoke sympathy for its victims.

Therefore, in *Street Scene*, the playwright's depiction of charity's representative, Miss Simpson, is highly critical. He begins by describing her as an unattractive spinster and then heightens the unfavorable impression by having her upbraid the small, timid, bewildered Mrs. Hildebrand for spending charity money to take her two children to the movies. That these two children cling to their mother in fear of the austere Miss Simpson only increases the audience's sympathy for the Hildebrands and one's dislike for Miss Simpson and the charity she represents.

There are other flaws in the American economic system, Rice would have us know. His spokesman here is Abraham Kaplan, who is appalled by the eviction of the Hildebrands by their landlord. The institution of private property, which places those without property at the mercy of the property-owning classes, is the real culprit, Kaplan contends.

Then, broadening the scope of his diatribe, he laments the status of the worker, whom he calls a wage slave, at the mercy of the all-powerful leaders of industry. Although these sentiments sound Marxist, one must not assume that Rice was a communist. He was merely pointing out the need for social reform.

Racial bigotry, a ubiquitous element in American society, and one that Rice abhorred, is also treated in *Street Scene*; the play's mixture of Italian, Swedish, Irish, and Jewish characters provides Rice with an excellent opportunity for comment. At the same time, Rice, ever cognizant of the plight of women in American society, provides a sympathetic portrait of Mrs. Maurrant, one of the casualties of the virulent gossip of the bigoted Joneses. Though she is engaged in an adulterous relationship with Steve Sankey, the neighborhood collector for the milk company, Mrs. Maurrant is portrayed as a victim rather than a victimizer. Rice shows her to be a compassionate, loving woman joined in an unhappy marriage to a man who cannot satisfy her emotional needs and who treats her as though she were his personal property rather than as a human being.

OTHER MAJOR WORKS

LONG FICTION: *A Voyage to Purilia*, 1930; *Imperial City*, 1937; *The Show Must Go On*, 1949.

NONFICTION: *The Living Theatre*, 1959; *Minority Report*, 1963.

BIBLIOGRAPHY

Durham, Frank. *Elmer Rice*. New York: Twayne, 1970. Durham's book progresses chronologically through Rice's work, first in farce, then in realist melodrama, through expressionism and naturalism, propaganda plays, and finally through the period of psychological and symbolic drama. Durham writes of Rice's ethical qualities and his ability to turn types into real characters with his "vivid, life-giving touch." Offers detailed analyses of all Rice's work, as well as nineteen pages of notes, bibliography, and index.

Hogan, Robert. *The Independence of Elmer Rice*. Carbondale: Southern Illinois University Press, 1965. Hogan offers a comparative analysis, discussing Rice's connection to Honoré de Balzac, Émile Zola, Marcel Proust, William Faulkner, Clifford Odets, Tennessee Williams, Eugene O'Neill, and others. His appreciation for Rice is evident with the statement that Rice "is rivalled in our theatre only by O'Neill." Hogan adds that "as a master of every kind of plot structure he probably stands alone." Hogan provides extensive analysis of major and lesser known works, as well as fourteen pages of notes, bibliography, and index.

Palmieri, Anthony F. R. *Elmer Rice: A Playwright's Vision of America*. Rutherford, N.J.: Fairleigh Dickinson University Press, 1980. Palmieri argues that "Rice's greatest strength is related to his chief failing." His reformer's impulse leads at times to didactic or propagandistic writing. Palmieri details how Rice struggled against censorship and strove to make the theater an agent of social change, being one of the first to attack such evils as child labor and Nazism. Contains bibliography and index.

Vanden Heuvel, Michael. *Elmer Rice: A Research and Production Sourcebook*. Newport, Conn.: Greenwood Press, 1996. This study looks at the plays of Rice, paying particular attention to how they were staged and produced. Bibliography and indexes.

Anthony F. R. Palmieri,
updated by Rebecca Bell-Metereau

LYNN RIGGS

Born: Near Claremore, Indian Territory (now
    Oklahoma); August 31, 1899
Died: New York, New York; June 30, 1954

PRINCIPAL DRAMA

Knives from Syria, pr. 1925, pb. 1927 (one act)
Big Lake, pr., pb. 1927
Rancor, pr. 1927
A Lantern to See By, pb. 1928, pr. 1930
Sump'n Like Wings, pb. 1928, pr. 1939
Roadside, pr., pb. 1930
Green Grow the Lilacs, pr., pb. 1931
Russet Mantle, pr., pb. 1936
The Cherokee Night, pr., pb. 1936
A World Elsewhere, pb. 1939
The Year of Pilar, wr. 1940, pb. 1947
The Cream in the Well, pr., pb. 1941
Dark Encounter, pb. 1947
Four Plays, pb. 1947
Laughter from a Cloud, pr. 1947
Hang on to Love, pb. 1948
Borned in Texas, pr. 1950 (revision of *Roadside*)
Toward the Western Sky, pr., pb. 1951 (music by
    Nathan Kroll)

OTHER LITERARY FORMS

In addition to writing more than twenty plays, Lynn
Riggs was the author of many poems, which appeared
in such periodicals as *Poetry: A Magazine of Verse*
(edited by Harriet Monroe), *The Smart Set* (edited by
H. L. Mencken), and *The Nation*. A number of these
poems were collected and published in a volume entitled *The Iron Dish* (1930). Riggs also authored screenplays in Hollywood for Metro-Goldwyn-Mayer, including *Laughing Boy* (1933), *Delay in the Sun*
(1935), *Garden of Allah* (1936), and, perhaps most
notably, *The Plainsman* (1936), on which he collaborated with Waldemar Young and Harold Lamb.

ACHIEVEMENTS

Lynn Riggs achieved early recognition from such
notable theatrical authorities as Barrett H. Clark and

Arthur Hopkins, both of whom championed his work,
although most later critics labeled him a minor regionalist. When Clark was speaking of Riggs's first
full-length production for the commercial stage, *Big
Lake*, he called Riggs "one of the few native dramatists who can take the material of our everyday life
and mould it into forms of stirring beauty." Speaking
of *Green Grow the Lilacs*, Hopkins said that "Riggs
caught our fading glory and left it for posterity." It
was this play and the comic *Russet Mantle* that were
Riggs's greatest commercial successes for the stage
during his lifetime, although he continued to write for
the theater until 1951. His chief posthumous claim
to fame has been as the author of *Green Grow the Lilacs*, which provided the basic text for the epoch-
making Richard Rodgers and Oscar Hammerstein
musical *Oklahoma!* (1943). As tastes change, however, so do literary reputations, and it may be that, as
interest in regional and ethnic literature and in plays
about women increases, Riggs's work will come to be
more highly regarded.

As noted by critic Richard Watts, Jr., Riggs's
plays are "invariably rich and lyric folk [dramas,
with] true feeling for atmosphere and period." "He
wrote of people he had known," said his colleague Joseph Benton, "entwining their foibles, weaknesses
and strengths, their garrulous chatterings and grassroots wisdoms throughout his plays." Of Cherokee
extraction, growing up the son of a farmer in Oklahoma in its earliest days as a state, Riggs wrote of
the disappointed expectations and compromised human values that resulted among simple farm people
from their conflicts with the changing values of
American society. Perhaps his outstanding characteristics as an American playwright are his unwillingness to write cheap or empty plays, his facility
with strong situations, his ability to write powerful
two-person scenes, his appreciation for the genuine
folk music of his region, and his gift for expressing the lyricism half-consciously felt and beautifully revealed in the lives of humble and ordinary
people.

BIOGRAPHY

When Lynn Riggs was born in 1899, Claremore was still part of the Indian Territory that was later incorporated into the state of Oklahoma. Son of an Indian farmer, he enjoyed the simple amusements and "play parties" of his neighbors as well as their unselfconscious folk traditions. He did various odd jobs in his youth, first as an itinerant farmhand and cowpuncher and then as a singer at the local movie house. Later, he traveled around the country, working as a proofreader on a newspaper in San Francisco, as a clerk in the book section of Macy's department store in New York City, and as a newspaper reporter in Tulsa. At the age of twenty-one, Riggs enrolled in the University of Oklahoma as a music major, later changing his major to English so that he could qualify for a readership position. He continued to hold the position of second tenor in the solo quartet organized by the university, which toured in a professional summer Chautauqua and minstrel show. He had two farces, *Cuckoo* and *Honeymoon*, produced at school while he was still an undergraduate.

Riggs's dramatic successes at the university and his early one-act *Knives from Syria*, with its Ali Hakim-like peddler character, all showed originality and humor, and he was encouraged to continue playwriting. The production of the full-length *Big Lake* by the American Laboratory Theatre attracted some critical attention and won for Riggs a Guggenheim Fellowship. In 1928, Riggs resided in France, where he wrote *Green Grow the Lilacs* and much of *Roadside*, which was produced by Arthur Hopkins and starred Ralph Bellamy as Texas. At this point, Riggs was considered one of America's most promising playwrights, but critics qualified their praise. By 1936, when *Russet Mantle* succeeded as a comedy, although it had been conceived as a serious work, reviewers were generalizing about Riggs's failure to master the needs of the theater in terms of probability of plotting and characterization. They seemed to believe that Riggs's promise had somehow missed fire. During this period, Riggs was working with some success as a screenwriter.

Riggs was inducted into the United States Army in 1942, serving in the Army Air Corps, and his plays of the 1940's reflect his concern with the international chaos that rocked that era. His last work produced on Broadway was the 1950 *Borned in Texas*, a revision of the 1930 *Roadside*; in 1951, he wrote a "music play" on commission from Western Reserve University to celebrate the school's 125th anniversary. He was working on his first novel when he died of stomach cancer at the age of fifty-four. Riggs was survived by a sister and several brothers; there is no evidence that he ever married. A memorial for him was erected in the town of Claremore, Oklahoma, in 1958, and the library at Rogers University in Claremore has a collection of materials both by and about him.

ANALYSIS

Lynn Riggs is known almost exclusively as a regional dramatist in the tradition of Susan Glaspell and Paul Green, but his work is more varied in both content and style than this label would suggest. For example, it is accurate to call Riggs an ethnic regionalist, but only if one includes the Cherokees in *The Cherokee Night*, the Hispanics in *The Year of Pilar*, *A World Elsewhere*, and *Laughter from a Cloud*, the farmers and ranchers of *Green Grow the Lilacs*, and braggart frontiersmen in *Roadside* as ethnic groups associated with Riggs. A favorite theme deals with the attempts, in Arthur Hopkins's words, to show "beauty in rebellion . . . now successful self-assertion, now frustration—usually girlhood or womanhood fighting for the right to self, for adventure, for love." This theme finds expression not only in the lightly sketched romance between Curly and Laurey in the well-known *Green Grow the Lilacs*, but also in almost all Riggs's other plays, which include tragedies, comedies, and two naturalistic studies of uneducated, lower-class women.

Stylistically, Laurey's dream ballet in *Oklahoma!* is a natural extension of elements already present in *Green Grow the Lilacs*, where Riggs successfully portrays Jeeter's perverse and lurid lust while remaining almost within a naturalistic framework. The authentic folk songs in this, as well as several other of his plays, typify his desire to extend the stage's bounds beyond realism. Thus, most of his plays are infused with a poetic diction that goes far beyond naturalistic speech, as in *Roadside*, or deal with highly melodramatic situations that reflect deep, unconscious drives, as in *The Cream in the Well*, or move overtly beyond naturalism in setting, language, situation, or onstage use of supernatural elements, as does *The Cherokee Night*.

Riggs's plays demonstrate various kinds and strands of excellence, mixed with a number of structural problems. His poetic gift surfaces whenever the beauty of the natural world is invoked. This sensitivity to natural beauty, for example, resulted in the charming opening stage directions for *Green Grow the Lilacs*, which were translated into the lyrics of the title song in *Oklahoma!* In a number of his plays, Riggs uses songs and poetic diction in situations of heightened emotion. The same desire for lyricism finds expression in the effective use of scenic elements, such as the mountains in *Laughter from a Cloud*. In the play that Riggs himself considered his best, *The Cherokee Night*, a Cherokee burial ground looms in the background of each scene, dominating the stage action in an effective symbolic statement.

The Cherokee Night, however, also illustrates Riggs's weaknesses as a playwright. The play has strong moments and a significant, fresh theme, but the characters are present more to illustrate the theme than to exist on their own, while the structure (the play's seven scenes are not in chronological order) lacks clarity. Another play that illustrates Riggs's weaknesses as well as his strengths is *The Cream in the Well*, a story of incest based on the premise that an intelligent, sensitive woman may yet be a despoiler of all those around her because of the secret desires that poison her and her brother's life. Aware that individual scenes showed real power, reviewers nevertheless asked why this melodramatic, contrived plot had been chosen. The theme of incest is a powerful element in *A Lantern to See By* as well and lurks in the background of *Sump'n Like Wings*. It is doubtful that Riggs chose the theme in order to write a successful play. Rather, this was a serious playwright who was wrestling with a theme that engaged him.

The Riggs protagonist searching for love is more often female than male, an emancipated woman, struggling to make some sort of active life for herself in which she will not be dependent on the superior strength or initiative of a man. It seems as though those plays end happily in which both the man and his "women" agree on a common set of values—either mutually accepting the division into traditional, sharply defined masculine and feminine roles or both being willing to adjust to the newer emancipation of women—while those plays end unhappily in which some external condition or some restlessness within the characters forces an irresolvable confrontation over traditional values. It should not be assumed that Riggs was trying to assert the superiority of traditional values. He understood that the forces causing change were irresistible, and he was trying to chart what happened as people tried to accommodate such changes.

Riggs was one of thirty-three playwrights who responded to a questionnaire from W. David Sievers, who was researching his book *Freud on Broadway* (1955). Riggs said that he had read some of Sigmund Freud's work, that he felt his plays were "doing the same thing" as analysts did, and that "he had sought for dramatic devices to dramatize the workings of the unconscious." The need of Riggs's characters to express their libidinous impulses—a need that seemed overstrained to some reviewers and critics—is insistent throughout his plays. In *Dark Encounter*, for example, the heroine, Gail Atwood, seems to have fallen in love with three different men (although engaged to marry Ancil Bingham, she becomes involved sexually with Teek and Karl on day one and day two of the play, respectively), while Riggs portrays her throughout as a sensitive and sympathetic character. Similarly, in *Russet Mantle*, Kay spends night one with one man and night two with another without losing Riggs's sympathy.

The first group of plays written by Riggs, dating from the 1925 *Knives from Syria* through the 1931 *Green Grow the Lilacs*, are studies of young people struggling to find themselves within the context of the kind of harsh farm environment made familiar by Eugene O'Neill in *Desire Under the Elms* (pr. 1924), which the early, tragic *A Lantern to See By* resembles.

A LANTERN TO SEE BY

In *A Lantern to See By*, John Harmon, the father of six living sons, treats his wife as a child breeder and servant. Only the youngest boy, Jodie, seems to have any sensitivity to his mother's situation. When Jodie tries to protect her, the father almost deliberately misinterprets his motives and beats him with an iron bar. In act 2, the mother dies after her eleventh childbirth, and a neighbor's daughter, Annie Marble, comes to do the mother's work for the family. Jodie sees a potential for both mothering and loving in Annie. He falls in love with her, whereas she is willing to make use of his infatuation. She tells him that to win her he must take her away to the big city—Muskogee—which she had admired on a visit to a friend. Jodie leaves to take a job so that he can earn enough money to start his own life with Annie. Meanwhile, act 2 ends with Annie accepting John Harmon's advances. Act 3 opens a month later on the evening of a play party at the Harmons'. Annie is asking for her salary of eight dollars a month, plus the unspecified amount promised for her "extra services" to her employer. Harmon puts off the payment, rightly fearing that she will leave as soon as she gets the money. Then Jodie arrives, angry because his employer, his father's friend, had said he would pay Jodie's wages only to John Harmon. Learning of the situation between his father and Annie, Jodie becomes even angrier, and he kills his father off stage with an iron bar. The play ends as the neighbors speculate over Jodie's fate and the audience learns that Annie's goal was to reach a friend in Muskogee, a prostitute, and join her in her chosen occupation.

This naturalistic tragedy of lower-class farm life, with its theme of father and son fighting first over the mother and then her replacement, was clearly indebted to O'Neill's farm play. Taken on its own, Riggs's play is an effective drama. The father is a driven man, though without the religious ecstasy of O'Neill's Ephraim Cabot, and his crude energy provides an effective contrast of Jodie's poetic sensitivity. Less complex and melodramatic than *Desire Under the Elms*, it is more squalid, as is its companion piece, *Sump'n Like Wings*.

SUMP'N LIKE WINGS

In *Sump'n Like Wings*, the protagonist is a young girl, Willie, whose mother has tried to keep her "good" not by moral persuasion but by locking her up, for example, when she goes swimming with some boys. Finally, Willie rebels and runs off with a ne'er-do-well. Riggs makes no attempt to glamorize Willie or her environment. She gets into the kinds of trouble endemic to such situations (a baby that dies, a husband who simply takes off, never to be seen again). Though a kindly uncle offers help, Willie declares that she must learn to stand on her own. She refuses his offer of a refuge and ends the play alone, trying to put a lock on her door so that strange men will not be able to enter her room whenever they choose.

The audience is intended to see Willie's determination to earn her own way as a victory; she is trying to grow up and become responsible for herself without giving up her right to express her own sexuality. This theme is developed in parallel through an extended conversation in act 1 between Willie and Elvie Rapp, an odd young vagabond whose bold sexuality has gotten her into trouble but who is sympathetically presented by Riggs. Writing in 1936, drama historian Arthur Hobson Quinn deplored Riggs's choice of a protagonist such as Willie, saying that she "escapes from the deadly hotel life not into anything worthwhile, but only into the world of her own desires, which are entirely selfish." Because Willie's is a "narrow soul," this play, like its heroine, is a "little one." From a more modern perspective, the play can be seen, rather, as an early attempt to deal with the theme of overt female sexuality—a theme that is still likely to raise the hackles of some male critics.

GREEN GROW THE LILACS

The issue of healthy versus neurotic sexuality again underlies the seemingly simple *Green Grow the Lilacs*. The attraction of Curly and Laurey for each other, like the attraction of Texas and Hannie in *Roadside* (which seems to be a more broadly drawn caricature of some of the same themes that are found in *Green Grow the Lilacs*), is set in a context in which people pair off as a part of the fecund natural world. As the opening stage directions say, "men, cattle in a meadow, blades of the young corn, streams" give off "a visible golden emanation." Curly is associated with the outdoors and nature, both by his rhapsodic appreciation of its beauty in several long speeches that serve no other dramatic function and by his job as a cowboy. Laurey, too, is part of nature. When Curly tells her he loves her, it is by describing how he saw her while she was growing up: first, "a little tyke" "pickin' blackberries"; next, riding "a little gray filly of Blue Starr's"; then, the year before, when she had been "out a-pickin' flowers" and "had a whole armful of Sweet Williams and wild roses and morning glories." In contrast, Jeeter, the hired hand on Aunt Eller's and Laurey's farm, lives "in a dark hole bent over a table a-fingerin' a pack of cards 's greasy 's a ole tin spoon." Laurey has made the mistake of being kind to Jeeter when he was ill, and his feelings of inferiority, his fascination with sadistic tales of sexual obsession, murder, and revenge, lead to his sexual advances on and threats to Laurey.

Laurey is afraid not to go to the play party with Jeeter, imagining that he might burn down her home in revenge, but when he goes too far at the play party, seizing and threatening her, she sends him off, relying on Curly. They soon agree to marry, but their wedding night is marred by the locals, who set on them to tease them in a "shivoree" (defined by Riggs as a bawdy, community-wide marriage celebration). Then Jeeter emerges from the crowd, setting fire to the haystack holding the young couple. He and Curly fight, and Jeeter is accidentally impaled on his own knife. Curly is arrested but breaks out of jail before the hearing that will determine his fate. In the play's last scene, he visits his bride, who assures him, "I'll put up with everything now. You don't need to worry about me no more." There is an implied happy ending, but there is not the onstage trial and freeing of Curly that occurs in *Oklahoma!*

There are other differences between the play and the adaptation. Riggs used traditional folk songs, whereas Rodgers and Hammerstein wrote the many famous songs, including "People Will Say We're in Love," "The Surrey with the Fringe on Top," and "Oh, What a Beautiful Morning," which enrich the musical. In Riggs's play, Ado Annie has no steady beaux. She comes to visit Laurey with the peddler, who is unnamed, but her significant role in the musical, as well as her fiancé, Will, do not exist in the play. Jeeter, Curly, and Aunt Eller are the play's chief figures. Laurey starts out as somewhat of a spoiled child who is taught by Aunt Eller that she's "got to look at all the good on one side and all the bad on the other, and say: 'Well, all right, then!' to both of 'em."

In his introduction to the play, Riggs explained his intention to use "the simplest of stories." His play could have been subtitled "An Old Song," he wrote. He wanted to illustrate his characters' "quaintness, their sadness, their robustness, their simplicity, their hearty or bawdy humors, their sentimentalities, their melodrama, their touching sweetness." His success cannot be measured by the fate of the play. Although it was produced by the prestigious Theatre Guild with Franchot Tone as Curly, Helen Westley as Aunt Eller, June Walker as Laurey, and Lee Strasberg as the peddler, it ran for only sixty-four performances. In the musical version, however, it ran for more than five years and was one of the American theater's truly great events.

RUSSET MANTLE

Russet Mantle, first produced in 1936, was Riggs's biggest hit. Ironically, although he intended it as a serious study of love versus convention and the materialistic values of American society, the minor character provided as comic relief came to dominate the play. It was produced as a comedy and thus provided an effective balance between Riggs's interests and Broadway standards. In the play, Kay Rowley and her mother visit Kay's retired aunt and uncle living in New Mexico. Kay spends her first night there in bed with a cowboy whom she has met that day. Kay's scandalized aunt and uncle try to discipline her, while Kay's mother, Effie, who is the comic creation largely responsible for the play's success, wants to know none of the details so that she will not have to be upset. The audience learns that the aunt did not marry the poor boy she loved in her youth but settled for financial security with her present husband. Their marriage, then, is an empty one, and their scandalized reaction to Kay's sexual aggressiveness may mask their own dissatisfaction. A young poet named John comes to the farm seeking a job and is hired. He sees through Kay's pose of pseudosophistication, and the two have a love affair. When Kay's pregnancy is discovered, she refuses to name the father, but John is delighted to acknowledge the child. Their hosts now threaten to throw them out into the harsh Depression world, which has been evoked by John's job search and Kay's talk of "Riot squads, strikebreakers, nausea gas, bayonets and starvation! And voices crying out, for what? A little bread, a little sun, a little peace and delight." For their part, the young people are ready to go out into the world together, having affirmed the primacy of true love over convention. In the last line of the play, however, the aunt suggests that she and her husband talk things over before ejecting the young couple, implying that they may find a way to help their niece, even though they disapprove of her behavior.

Critics particularly enjoyed Effie Rowley, and the play enjoyed a good run of more than one hundred performances. Riggs's other 1936 effort, *The Cherokee Night*, a serious statement, fared very poorly with reviewers when performed by the Federal Theatre Project, yet this unique play deserves discussion.

THE CHEROKEE NIGHT

Each of the seven scenes of *The Cherokee Night* is separately titled and constructed so that it can be performed independently of the others. Yet the point of the play, that the Cherokees have become weak, materialistic, and immoral as a result of abandoning their cultural heritage and mixing through intermarriage with the whites, is made most effectively by implication through seeing the entire play and realizing the relationship between the various scenes. The play's structure may well owe some elements to O'Neill's *The Emperor Jones* (pr. 1920), in which supernatural elements and racial memory are similarly implied, and effective use is also made of a drumbeat, but *The Emperor Jones* proceeds in a straight chronology (backward through time) in its supernatural scenes and prepares the audience for the supernaturalism by establishing Jones's superstition and by introducing the transitional symbol of the silver bullet. *The Cherokee Night* lacks that clarity of structure. The chronological order is confusing as the scenes take place, severally, in 1915, 1927, 1931, 1906,

1913, 1919, and 1895. Brooks Atkinson claimed that the play was "pushing into real poetic tragedy," that this "story of a world that has lost its heritage . . . is the universal complaint." At the same time, like other reviewers, Atkinson complained of the play's incoherence, and there was, no doubt, much confusion among audiences because of the demands the play made on their attention. Whether audiences today would be equally bewildered, when flashbacks and flash-forwards have become commonplace in films, is an open question.

In the play's first scene, "Sixty-seven Arrowheads," a desultory picnic of bickering, young, half-breed Cherokees is interrupted by the entrance of the Cherokee Jim Talbert. He tells them that he has been digging for arrowheads, the relics of the once proud nation whose burial ground they have chosen for their picnic site. He wants them to remember their heritage, but they drive him, and it, off and out of their minds as the mound begins to glow in the gathering darkness. In the subsequent scenes, with the symbol of the burial ground always present, the picnickers are seen at various points in their lives. One becomes a prostitute, another becomes rich by denying her heritage entirely, another becomes a murderer. A fourth becomes a parasite, wasting his time in aimless joyriding, living off a land grant given to an Osage woman instead of earning his own. Two scenes (4 and 5) imply the supernatural. In the last scene, a full-blooded Cherokee, Gray Wolf, says to the dying criminal, "You though—like my boy. He's dead. He was half white, like you. They killed him, had to kill him! Not *enough* Indian. The mixture."

OTHER MAJOR WORKS
    POETRY: *The Iron Dish*, 1930.
    SCREENPLAYS: *Laughing Boy*, 1933; *Delay in the Sun*, 1935; *Garden of Allah*, 1936; *The Plainsman*, 1936 (with Waldemar Young and Harold Lamb).

BIBLIOGRAPHY
Braunlich, Phyllis. *Haunted by Home: The Life and Letters of Lynn Riggs*. Norman: University of Oklahoma Press, 1988. In this important biography and critical analysis of Riggs's works, Braunlich

discusses the universal themes in Riggs's plays, which are all set in the early days of the Oklahoma territory. His plays deal with the worst human frailties. Attention is given to *Green Grow the Lilacs*, on which was based the book for the Richard Rodgers and Oscar Hammerstein musical *Oklahoma!* (1943). Illustrations, complete listing of Riggs's works, extensive bibliography, and index.

Brenton, Joseph. "Some Personal Reminiscences About Lynn Riggs." *Chronicles of Oklahoma* 34 (Autumn, 1956): 296-301. A warm remembrance of Riggs by Brenton, who knew him from his earliest college days in Oklahoma to his death in New York. Brenton places some of Riggs's major decisions and accomplishments into biographical context.

Downer, Alan S. *Fifty Years of American Drama.* Chicago: Henry Regnery, 1951. In the chapter entitled "Folk Drama," Downer suggests that *Green Grow the Lilacs*, and more important, *Roadside*, epitomize the American folk drama. The plays are distinguished above other Western melodramas by their poetry of speech, warm humanity, and characters. Index.

Erhard, Thomas. *Lynn Riggs: Southwest Playwright.* Austin, Tex.: Steck-Vaughn, 1970. This forty-four-page monograph provides an excellent biography and critical introduction to Riggs's plays. Erhard comments on the playwright's use of the territorial Oklahoma dialect and settings to tell universal stories of human drama.

Sper, Felix. *From Native Roots: A Panorama of Our Regional Drama.* Caldwell, Idaho: The Caxton Printers, 1948. Sper briefly describes the conflicts and plots of nine Riggs plays. He concludes that Riggs's use of violence, fury, incest, and murder seem to give the plays an air beyond reality. Bibliography and index.

Vera Jiji,
updated by Gerald S. Argetsinger

THOMAS WILLIAM ROBERTSON

Born: Newark-on-Trent, England; January 9, 1829
Died: London, England; February 3, 1871

PRINCIPAL DRAMA

A Night's Adventure: Or, Highways and Byways, pr., pb. 1851 (adaptation of Edward Bulwer-Lytton's novel *Paul Clifford*)

David Garrick, wr. c. 1857, pr. 1864, pb. 1870(?) (adaptation of Mélesville's play *Sullivan*)

The Cantab, pr., pb. 1861 (one act)

Constance, pr. 1865 (libretto; music by Frederick Clay)

Society, pr. 1865, pb. 1866

Ours, pr. 1866, pb. 1890

Caste, pr. 1867, pb. 1878

Play, pr. 1868, pb. 1890

School, pr. 1869, pb. 1874

Home, pr. 1869, pb. 1879 (adaptation of Émile Augier's play *L'Aventurière*)

Dreams, pr. 1869, pb. 1875? (originally as *My Lady Clara*, pr. 1869)

M.P., pr. 1870, pb. 1890

Not at All Jealous, pr. 1871, pb. 1872

War, pr. 1871, pb. 1891

A Row in the House, pr., pb. 1883

The Principal Dramatic Works of Thomas William Robertson, pb. 1889, 1977 (2 volumes)

OTHER LITERARY FORMS

Thomas William Robertson was a prolific writer of periodical articles and stories before he achieved success as a playwright. However, none of this work is of lasting interest, and none of it advances theories of dramaturgy. Robertson produced one novel of interest, *David Garrick* (1865). Four of his prose works are easily accessible to modern readers. "The Poor Rate Unfolds a Tale," in *Rates and Taxes and How They Were Collected*, edited by Thomas Mood and published in 1866, anticipates the play *Caste* in many important ways, including similar characters, motifs, and themes. "After Dinner," in *The Savage Club Papers* of 1867, is a spoof on marriage customs that gently suggests that neither cold calculation nor lusty romance guarantees a happy marriage. "Exceptional Experiences," in *The Savage Club Papers* of 1868, is a modestly witty essay aimed at exploding a variety of social myths: the brutality of miners, the rapacity of innkeepers, the jolliness of sailors, and the snobbishness of successful men toward their former acquaintances. Robertson's restiveness about the unfairness of stereotyping is characteristic of his plays as well. His introduction to *Artemus Ward's Panorama* (1869) is essentially an effusion memorializing his friend, the American humorist Charles Farrar Browne.

ACHIEVEMENTS

The front matter of *The Principal Dramatic Works of Thomas William Robertson* lists forty-seven plays, all but fourteen of them published. Of the total, *The Principal Dramatic Works of Thomas William Robertson* reproduces sixteen. Except for the plays *David Garrick*, a highly successful potboiler adapted from Mélesville's *Sullivan*, and *Dreams* (retitled version of *My Lady Clara*), a somewhat less successful one, Thomas William Robertson's reputation rests on the six plays produced at the Prince of Wales's Theatre: *Society*, *Ours*, *Caste*, *Play*, *School*, and *M.P.* These plays form the body of a dramatic revolution whose reality is universally recognized but whose extent has not been finally set. Robertson teamed with sympathetic managers, Sir Squire and Marie Wilton Bancroft, to achieve a new sort of production. It featured ensemble acting, which emphasized the totality of the dramatic situation and eschewed the then dominant star system. This was combined with a realistic treatment of theme and staging within a cameo theater setting. Less clear than the fact of Robertson's signal success is the extent to which he should be given credit for achieving a breakthrough from melodrama to realistic serious drama a decade and a half before Henrik Ibsen; also a

Thomas William Robertson (Hulton Archive by Getty Images)

matter of critical debate is his contribution to the Little Theater movement that began to sweep Europe and eventually the United States.

As early as 1875, an anonymous critic for the magazine *Temple Bar* gave Robertson credit for revitalizing British drama and exerting a continuing influence after his death. This critic asserted that Robertson's success was in part a result of his novel treatment of social conflicts in a manner drawn from life; Robertson's skills as a stage manager, the critic said, were also crucial to his success. This early evaluation of Robertson's career anticipated the boundaries of much subsequent criticism.

George Bernard Shaw took two occasions to refer to Robertson's work in passing. In the first, he used a recently revived production of *Caste* as a club with which to hammer Arthur Wing Pinero's *The Second Mrs. Tanqueray* (pr. 1893), observing that a comparison of Pinero's characters, in the matter of realism, to those of *Caste* would be as absurd as a comparison of

Caste's realism with that of Ibsen's *Et dukkehjem* (pr., pb. 1879; *A Doll's House*, 1880). In a hardly less restrained mood, Shaw declared in another essay, "Mr. John Hare," that young people seeing *Caste* for the first time in 1884 could form no clear idea of the extent of its impact on their fathers, who had spent a lifetime watching dramas whose staging was so far removed from natural representation that a production of Giuseppe Verdi's opera *La Traviata* might be considered "photographically realistic" in comparison.

Shaw's most extensive consideration of Robertson's achievement came in "Robertson Redivivus." He described *Caste* as an epoch-making play, newly revived. While he conceded that the epoch and the play were both "very little," he suggested that few critics encountered more than two plays of such importance in a lifetime. Shaw pointed out, as have most subsequent critics, that Robertson's new, realistic characters were, in fact, the old stage types very thinly "humanized": the stage swell, the Dickensian caricature of a rogue, the sentimental hero and heroine, and the conventional haughty mother. Still, Shaw noted, even the swell and the haughty mother were indeed humanized, compared with their counterparts on the stage in the 1860's. He held that Robertson gave sympathetic qualities to characters previously treated as "beyond redemption."

Less kind than Shaw, W. Wilding Jones wrote in "Robertson as a Dramatist," published in 1897, that Robertson's plays owed their success to the strength of their actors, to Robertson's good sense in keeping the plays short enough not to try the audience's patience, to bright dialogue and concise structure, and to the novelty of seeing a play of "home manufacture" on a stage dominated by French adaptations.

Cecil Ferard Armstrong's "Thomas William Robertson," published in 1913, was probably the first serious and extensive critical approach to Robertson's life and plays. Armstrong, too, argued that *Caste* began two revolutions, but not the revolutions identified by his predecessors. The first he defined as the innovation of highly professional London companies, which, being sent on tour, doomed the old-fashioned provincial stock companies. The second he defined as

the establishment of international dramatic copyright laws, triggered by a fuss over a pirated edition appearing before the New York production of *Caste*. Armstrong refused to acclaim Robertson as a writer who understood the society he undertook to reform, but in compensation, he declared that in the process of keeping "his garden [plays] very neat, and tidy, and pretty," he "uprooted a host of noxious weeds."

In contrast, during the centennial year of Robertson's birth, 1929, Harrison Dale declared, in an article in *Contemporary Review*, that the history of modern drama begins with Robertson. His work, Dale said, was a "miracle of freshness" beyond the experience of contemporary audiences. For Dale, Robertson's strongest point as a playwright was his ability to see "light as well as shadow." Dale came close to ascribing an overarching philosophy to Robertson in asserting that Robertson both "knew vice" and "believed in the existence of virtue."

In the same year, Frank A. Rahill opened his assessment of Robertson's work on a much less sympathetic centenary note. In the *Theatre Arts Monthly*, he argued that Robertson's "modern social comedy" was an isolated incident, confined to a single theater, and that, failing to take root, its influence had all but disappeared within a decade. He characterized Robertson's point of view as "pure, unadulterated Victorian cant." After suggesting that Charles Matthew anticipated Robertson's innovations in understated acting, that Dion Boucicault actually preceded Robertson in attention to stage business techniques, and that Charles Fechter took precedence in introducing improved set construction and manipulation, Rahill rather surprisingly declared that the production of Robertson's play *Society* signaled the birth of realism and that modern British theater "dates as legitimately from Robertson's plays as from Ibsen's."

Modern scholar Maynard Savin, whose critical biography *Thomas William Robertson: His Plays and Stagecraft* appeared in 1950, argued that previous criticism had reduced Robertson to a mere link between the "theatrical claptrap" of the early nineteenth century and the dramatic revival of its last two decades. Savin was willing to accept the reduction of Robertson's role from that of a revolutionary to that of a transitional figure but argued for the genuine contribution he believed Robertson's leadership had made. Far from seeing Robertson as an imitator of Eugène Scribe's "well-made play," he saw him as one who mastered the form and then struggled to escape its restrictions. While accepting the proposition that other attempts at realism preceded Robertson's, Savin argued that Robertson succeeded in synthesizing the contributions of playwright, director, actor, and stage designer to achieve "a theatre united in aim." The elements working against Robertson were, according to Savin, a monopoly of management, commercialization of playwriting, censorship (a problem against which Shaw fulminated but which he did not raise in estimating Robertson's problems), and what he termed "the decadent resurgence of the poetic tradition."

In a minor vein, Savin took note of Robertson's skill in having two conversations going forward on the stage simultaneously. The technique allows for dramatic contrasts and a great deal of character-highlighting. Although Savin did not say so, this technique also allows an unusual opportunity to intensify dramatic irony, by means of which the audience is put into possession of knowledge denied to the characters. Savin also discussed Robertson's constant use of the tableau and double tableaux. In the former, the action is held suspended at a point of heightened dramatic interest for a moment before the curtain is dropped. If the audience reaction warrants, the curtain is raised again to reveal that the characters have taken the next logical step suggested by the action. The trick was common enough in the nineteenth century theater and may be viewed either as one of the outworn conventions to which Robertson clung or as a clever, popular, and theatrically effective technique, not unlike the cinematic practice of freezing the action in intense situations, especially at the end of a film.

Still, Savin was under no illusion about the limitations of Robertson's realism. He remarked that a combination of very superficial realism and the conventions of the melodrama "cheated" Robertson's audiences into believing that they had seen a mirror "held up to nature." Among these conventions, Savin

identified the following: The nature of woman was held to be either frail or self-sacrificing, with love being regarded as holy and secret; the English class system was represented as both natural and desirable (Robertson distrusted, even rejected, political power for ordinary people; upward mobility, he held, could be permitted safely only to the morally virtuous); militarism was glorified, and soldiers were invariably splendid fellows—notions that permeate most of even his best plays. Robertson's obsession with these unexamined conventions, Savin argued, smothered his "creative energy" and revealed him as merely a rebel-against theatrical conventions, not against the more deadly Victorian conventions. Even so, Savin insisted that Robertson's efforts cleared the way for the emergence of the problem play and of the evolution of realism into naturalism.

Allardyce Nicoll, whose judgments can rarely be safely ignored, observed, in *Late Nineteenth Century Drama, 1850-1900* (1962), that several men have been credited with the introduction of stage managing in the modern sense of directing, including Robertson and Bancroft, W. S. Gilbert, and Boucicault. He also noted that Gilbert gave full credit to Robertson in his *Green-Room Recollections* (1896). Nicoll ultimately attached great importance to Robertson's collaboration with Lady Bancroft, which, he concluded, elevated plays from "merely virtuoso entertainments" to "artistic unities," with realism of action coordinated with realism in staging. Nicoll also praised Robertson's comparatively natural dialogue, a virtue he felt is often hidden from modern readers by the elements of sentimentalizing and moralizing that Robertson retained. To the charge that Robertson continued to make use of the older character types, Nicoll responded that Robertson's reintroduction to the theater of individually conceived characters was a great contribution to the revival of good drama. Less acceptable is Nicoll's notion that Robertson introduced genuinely serious themes into his plays and attempted a balanced view of his entire society, a task of which Robertson was not capable either philosophically or intellectually. Still, Nicoll's placement of Robertson, not first in merit among playwrights of the past but "first in time among the dramatic writers of the present," is a stand to be reckoned with.

Errol Durbach, in his 1972 article "Remembering Tom Robertson (1829-1871)," observed that Robertson combined "emotional impulses" with opposing "social" ones, which was a major contribution to the English comedy of domestic realism. Certainly the technique continued to be used by John Osborne, Tom Stoppard, and many others. Durbach concluded that Robertson's plays tend to support the status quo and suggested that the popularity of Arthur Wing Pinero's *Trelawny of the "Wells"* (pr. 1898) established the myth of Robertson as a revolutionary. Durbach then concluded rather oddly that Robertson brought drama to "a point from which significant European drama might develop."

The penultimate estimate may well belong to Hans Otto Thieme, who argued, in *Das englishe Drama im 18 und 19 Jahrhundert: Interpretationen* (1976), that without doubt, Robertson's new drama swept aside old conventions and, with its realism and its focus on central themes, aided the movement from society drama to the problem play and social drama, despite the necessity for Robertson to master the art of feigned reality.

A critical consensus of sorts emerges. It seems that Robertson was an innovator who was willing to use whatever means were necessary to achieve an intellectually honest drama during a time that could boast of little integrity in that art. His plays show that he was willing to refurbish old techniques and character-types to achieve his end: an intellectually significant play, highly entertaining, produced in a setting that imitated reality by actors who were willing to subordinate their roles to the overall needs of the play. That he was not always clear about these goals, that he produced potboilers along with significant drama throughout the glory years, is demonstrated well enough by the plays themselves. Even so, considering that, except for the aid of the Bancrofts and the support of a few friends, he struggled alone for most of his career, it is rather astonishing that in a period of almost universal decadence, he produced even a half dozen plays that were hailed by contemporary audiences as marvels and remain readable today. That he was the best of his theatrically none-

too-impressive time is clear; that he was the first considerable writer of modern drama in Britain is at least arguable.

BIOGRAPHY

Biographical materials for Thomas William Robertson's life necessarily begin with the "Memoir" to *The Principal Dramatic Works of Thomas William Robertson* by his son, T. W. Robertson, and with the two Bancroft memoirs of 1889 and 1909. Additional material is to be found in *Dame Madge Kendal, by Herself* (1933), by Robertson's sister, a famous actress.

Robertson's life was bound up in the theater from beginning to end. For several generations, his family had been actors and managers in the old theater circuits in the north of England. As a young child, he appeared in bit parts before being sent off, under the care of his actress-poet great-aunt, Fanny Maria Robertson, to attend such undistinguished schools as Henry Young's Spalding Academy in 1836 and Moore's School at Whittlesea in 1841. He seems to have been a normal, fun-loving child, inclined to be frail of health.

At the age of fourteen or fifteen, Robertson rejoined the family acting company based in Lincoln. There he gained practical experience in all aspects of the theater business except playwriting itself. During all of this activity, Robertson found time to continue studying under the supervision of his father, who was a cultured literary man. The regimen included mastering French, a skill that later would prove useful in translating and adapting French plays for the English stage, a process that contributed much to Robertson's understanding of the playwright's business.

In 1848, the family business was in a bad way, and Robertson went to London to seek his fortune. As things went badly, Robertson involved himself in an escapade that haunted him the rest of his life. He simply dropped out of sight for six weeks, to the distress of his family, spending the time miserably in Utrecht, the Netherlands, as a sort of assistant teacher. The mutual antipathy he felt for a fellow assistant teacher eventually surfaced in the character of Krux in the play *School*.

In 1851, Robertson met H. J. Byron, who became a lifelong friend. Together they produced a dramatic fiasco that attracted a single spectator who ultimately demanded his money back. The pair also made an abortive attempt to enlist in the Horse Guards. Meanwhile, Robertson freelanced articles, adapted plays for a publisher, Thomas Hailes Lacy, and saw the production of an early play, *A Night's Adventure*, at the Olympia. In 1854, he found steady work as a prompter at the Lyceum Theatre.

By 1855, Robertson was back with the family troupe, which proceeded to get itself stranded in Paris when their production of William Shakespeare's *Macbeth* (pr. 1606) folded. Later that year, he met an actress, Elizabeth Burton, at the Queen's Theatre (later called the Prince of Wales's), inelegantly known to members of the trade as "the Dust Hole." They were married on August 27, 1856. A son, Thomas William Shafto Robertson, was born December 2, 1857, and a daughter, Betty, died in infancy in 1858.

An acting tour of Ireland followed the marriage, after which Robertson plunged once more into the bohemian life of the backwaters of literary London, acting occasionally and seeing some minor plays and farces produced. He became a member of two clubs, the Savage Club in 1861 and, later, the Arundel. His cronies there included other literary figures, among them the younger Tom Hood and W. S. Gilbert. The bohemian life of the Savage figured realistically in the play *Society*.

On February 14, 1861, Robertson achieved success with his farce *The Cantab* at the Strand Theatre and became drama critic for *The Illustrated Times* at about the same time. In 1863, he wrote a novel, *David Garrick*. In 1864, he produced the play *David Garrick*, an adaptation of a French play, Mélesville's *Sullivan*. The "drunken scene" was reckoned a *coup de théâtre* by Robertson's contemporaries. The play's production in April at the Haymarket was Robertson's first considerable dramatic success.

On May 8, 1865, *Society* opened in Liverpool. In the late summer, on August 14, Robertson's first wife died. She had been loving and supportive, and her loss was a terrible blow. Meanwhile, Byron, who had arranged the Liverpool engagement of *Society*, found

London managers unreceptive to the play. John Baldwin Buckstone, a crusty actor-manager, pronounced it "rubbish." After much maneuvering, Byron succeeded in interesting the Bancrofts, the actor-managers of the small, newly refitted and renamed Prince of Wales's Theatre on Tottingham Court Road, and *Society* opened there November 11, 1865.

From this point onward, Robertson's life of Bohemian penury was over. The play was an immediate success with its first London run of 150 nights. Robertson, for the first time, had theater owners who agreed entirely with his notions of acting, setting, and stage management. Triumph followed triumph with productions of *Ours*, *Caste*, *Play*, *School*, and *M.P.*, all at the Prince of Wales's Theatre. In 1867, Robertson had four other plays running in London, and in the glory year of 1869, he had six plays on the London stage and one each in Liverpool and Manchester.

In the midst of this triumph, Robertson married again, this time to a charming German woman, Rosetta Feist, in Frankfurt, Germany, on October 17, 1867. Never an especially well man, though generally described as robust, Robertson's health declined with the onset of success. His last years were marked by increasingly painful bouts of lung disease, heroic efforts to continue to write and direct, and a nagging sense that, in spite of his obvious success, his work was middling and would not survive.

Robertson died on February 3, 1871, and was buried six days later in Abney Park Cemetery, attended by, among others of note, Tom Hood, Dion Boucicault, and Squire Bancroft.

ANALYSIS

Savin was unquestionably right in dubbing many of Thomas William Robertson's plays "potboilers." Robertson spent much of his life as a literary hack, turning a pound the best way he could, when he could. He continued to grind out inferior work even during the period of his greatest success, 1865 and after. Two late plays, produced in 1871 and 1883 respectively, are cases in point: *Not at All Jealous* (Court Theatre) and *A Row in the House* (Toole's Theatre). The first is simply a running farce centered on jealousy and mistaken identity, puns and concealment. The other is equally mechanical, being a farce in which an uncle sorts out the confusion created among three couples by jealousy. In it, Robertson uses his famous double-dialogue technique but fails to achieve freshness.

Robertson was a playwright who knew his craft completely, who had luck in his friends and wives, who was fortunate enough to find managers who would give his ideas scope, and who adapted more than he innovated in preparing the English stage for its modern renaissance.

DAVID GARRICK

David Garrick is theatrically better than and shares many characteristics with Robertson's best work. Savin observed that Robertson worked in this play as an adapter rather than as a mere translator and was encouraged by the play's success to trust his own originality. The play is essentially a dramatization of an old chestnut: the man who pretends drunkenness to shock the prudish. To that business, however, Robertson attached a theme that became his trademark, the vulgar snobbery of the newly rich mercantile class, which allowed itself to sneer at "mere" actors, as well as a situation, the tender love between two sensitive persons, which also became a recurring feature of his plays. While the tradition of the well-made play is present in some force, that of the farce is not. In the end, the class conflict between the snobbery of the city and that of the theater is reconciled, and the reconciliation is confirmed by a marriage between two superior people.

DREAMS

The last of the better potboilers, and perhaps Robertson's most underestimated drama, is *Dreams*, which was staged under the title *My Lady Clara* in Liverpool before coming to London as *Dreams* at the Gaiety Theatre on March 27, 1869. That Robertson thought highly of *Dreams* is suggested in a headnote of the published acting version, which indicated that it should be played as a comedy, not as a melodrama. The relative seriousness of two of its themes supports his view. The first and lesser theme turns on the difficulties a young man encounters in trying to establish himself as a composer of music in England, a difficulty parallel to that encountered by Robertson in es-

tablishing himself as a writer. The second is an extended examination of the merits and demerits of a social system based on caste. The conclusion, as usual, is that caste is a good thing that should be challenged only by superior merit. Although Savin dismissed the play as "a rusty excrescence scraped up from the bottom of the pot," that estimation is extreme at best. A melodramatic interpretation, exaggerating the more sensational features of the play, would certainly be possible, and some such consideration must have led to Robertson's caveat at the beginning of the script. It is also possible, however, that a troupe, playing as an ensemble and employing Robertson's by then established understated method of acting, could achieve something delicate, if not entirely fragile.

Even Robertson's best plays, four of which will be considered here, are far from perfect. In some ways, they could be said not to merit attention from modern readers who have available not only the superb dramas of the past but also those of the present, the best of which make even Ibsen's work seem quaint, timid, and old-fashioned. Be this as it may, Robertson's plays are still very readable. If this is so, the odds are that, in skillful hands, they are still good theater and even have some claim to treating serious themes seriously. That they can be treated thematically without much need for plot summary is another clue to their continuing value.

SOCIETY

Society, Robertson's first play in London's Prince of Wales's Theatre, followed a year after the success of *David Garrick*. The play examines the place of wealth in the marriages of the upper-middle classes, the repulsiveness of the newly moneyed social climber, and the plight of the impoverished gentry. The play was celebrated for the novelty of its low-key love scenes set in a realistically staged park (leaves actually fell), for its accurate portrayal of the lives of journalists, and for the "Owl's Roost" scenes, set in a club modeled after the Savage Club, in which the journalists and other bohemians enjoy themselves.

In regard to dynastic marriage, an old aunt advises her niece to marry for money and thereby restore the honor of the family. She argues that sentiment is the province of servant girls who romance police officers, a pastime beneath a lady. In her view, a commonplace person with an uncommonplace purse is better than the reverse. Later, this theme is picked up in the "Owl's Roost" when the rejected lover quotes from Alfred, Lord Tennyson's "Locksley Hall": "Thou are mated to a clown." Later in the play, the heroine rejects a marriage of convenience in a speech worthy of Ibsen or Shaw. She will not prostitute herself to a man she despises for the privilege of dressing herself at his expense and controlling his household, leading a life "that is a daily lie." Neither will she share the poverty of a man who does not treat her as an equal and has doubted her. All is sorted out in the end, and after the misunderstandings are cleared away, the deserving young lovers are rewarded with each other. As one might expect, in the final outcome, the impoverished young man turns out to be wealthy after all.

OURS

After opening in Liverpool, *Ours* began a 250-night run at London's Prince of Wales's Theatre on November 26, 1866. Jingoistic to the hilt, the play not only reflects Robertson's often noticed penchant for things military but also demonstrates his instinct for what will appeal to his audience—in this case, a sentimental feeling for the local regiment (hence the title) and a probably genuine patriotic feeling that is also clearly sentimental. The list of characters includes many stock figures from the old melodrama: a comic sergeant, a bouncing girl, an eccentric noblewoman, and a noble foreigner.

The plot is simple enough. Several English women, incredibly, follow their lovers and husbands to the Crimea and manage a reunion in a hut just behind the lines. Two realistic bits of business drew strong admiration: Snow blows in each time the outer door is opened, and Mary makes a roly-poly pudding onstage, converting military equipment into kitchen utensils in the process. Even more impressive is the departure of the regiment at the close of act 2. The movements of the troops offstage, complete with shouted orders, band music, and the sound of marching feet, all with modulations of volume indicating their changes of position, form the background against which the actors onstage react to the departure.

In addition to the theme of patriotism, the nature of love and marriage and its appropriateness at various social levels is explored. The sergeant must leave family behind, wife and children alike. For him, this is merely an inconvenience, because the gentry will see them through. Mary's problem is more serious; she is an impoverished gentlewoman who prefers her relative independence as a paid companion, a demeaning enough position, to marrying simply for the sake of escape. At one point, Mary argues, in a burst of sarcasm, that society makes it a duty for a woman to marry in order to subjugate a man. Blanche, who is not impoverished, is likewise under pressure to marry a prince because he is a good match in spite of the difference in their ages. In the sorting out, everyone either stabilizes a threatened marriage, withdraws from an inappropriate courtship, or is matched with a suitable partner. Even Mary finds a husband she can respect.

SCHOOL

School is not genuinely autobiographical, although the character of the evil teacher, Krux, was drawn from Robertson's unhappy Utrecht experience. The benevolent Dr. Sutcliffe and his foolish, jealous wife run an institution for young ladies that cannot much resemble the penurious Dutch one. *School* is also not entirely original; Robertson drew freely on Roderick Benedix's German play *Aschenbrödel* (1868) and used the Cinderella motif as a charming framing device.

The plot turns on the adventures of Bella, a sort of pupil-teacher who is unjustly turned out because of the obsessive jealousy of Mrs. Sutcliffe and the talebearing of Krux. To everyone's horror, she disappears for six weeks just at the point when her long-lost grandfather shows up to claim her. Right on cue, Bella reappears with her "prince" as a Cinderella bride. Comic justice is satisfied with the thrashing, offstage, of the villainous Krux, while romantic justice is fulfilled at the curtain with the splendid Lord Beaufoy fitting a glass slipper on the foot of the virtuous Bella.

School depends on big scenes for its impact. They begin with Bella's reading the Cinderella story aloud to the assembled girls. Another centers on the school examination, with its nonsensical questions followed by Krux's tyrannizing over the girls after the guests leave the stage. Perhaps as whimsical a scene as any in Robertson's work is the scene in which Lord Beaufoy insists on carrying the milk jug for Bella, an act far beneath his station and accountable only by eccentricity or love. That Robertson substitutes strong scenes for careful plotting is clear and surely identifies the play as more nearly fantasy than realism. This is not surprising, since, for Robertson, plot meant the marshaling of events with an eye to surprise and intensifying effect, rather than action growing logically out of situation and character. In this, he more closely resembles Oscar Wilde than he does Ibsen or Shaw.

CASTE

Caste, which opened at the Prince of Wales's Theatre on April 6, 1867, is a triumph of theatrical craftsmanship. In spite of its reputation as a thematic play, a forerunner of realism and a British anticipation of Ibsen, it is nothing of the sort. It is, however, exactly what Robertson's development as writer-manager suggests he meant it to be—a basically sentimental play, expertly cast and produced, to which his audience could respond with appreciation and applause. All the old situations are there, as well as all the old stereotyped characters. For stereotypes, there are the aristocratic, snobbish mother-in-law, the Marquise de St. Maur; her love-smitten and wholesome son, George D'Alroy; the military swell, Captain Hawtree; the nearly saintly, certainly virtuous woman and wife, Esther Eccles; and the madcap girl, Esther's sister, Polly. There is also the Dickensian eccentric, Sam Gerridge, the pipe fitter who is courting Polly, and the roaring, drunken father, who is a lamb before the gentry and who harks back to Shakespeare's Sir Toby Belch and forward to Shaw's Alfred Doolittle. For situations, there is the aristocrat's love affair and secret marriage to a lower-class woman who has suffered in order to support her drunken, sometimes brutal, and always unappreciative father, and who will suffer to support her supposedly orphaned boy.

There is also a cradle scene in which the villain, in this case the unprincipled Eccles, steals a jewel from the baby, a variation of the thieving Gypsy routine. Finally, there is the stock motif of the soldier, suppos-edly lost in battle, who miraculously turns up again when things are darkest to save the day. That Robertson was able to present such threadbare situations so freshly that his jaded audiences mistook them for something new and significant is itself remarkable. Thus, the enthusiasm and feistiness of Sam Gerridge was taken for the sturdy independence of the respectable working class; the socialistic jargon of Eccles seemed to be in its proper place, in the mouth of a drunken shirker; and the nobility and virtue of George and Esther was seen not only as a triumph of youth over old age, a long-standing comic motif, but also as a daring challenge to the caste system under which many of the audience—the wealthy middle classes who hoped to rise—writhed. In retrospect, the whole show is given away. George is not, after all, a very great aristocrat, although his mama is. Captain Hawtree, if not quite a cad, is at best a social climber who does not quite belong. When his own suit for the hand of a titled lady is rejected for that of a potential marquis, he quite understands. In the denouement, all the couples are sorted into their proper social levels, except Esther, whose virtues place her above caste. While the revelation that Robertson's social revolution was hardly more than a dramatic ploy cannot be said to destroy the play, it does bring the play into focus. With its pathos, its wit, its occasions of boisterous comedy, and its web of tensions and cross-tensions, all realistically mounted and understated in presentation in an intimate theater, *Caste* confirms that Robertson had orchestrated the techniques that would pave the way for the influx of genuine realism a decade later.

OTHER MAJOR WORK

LONG FICTION: *David Garrick*, 1865.

BIBLIOGRAPHY

Armstrong, Cecil Ferard. *Shakespeare to Shaw: Studies in the Life's Work of Six Dramatists of the English Stage*. Freeport, N.Y.: Books for Libraries Press, 1968. The early significance of Robertson is established as he is assessed with William Shakespeare, William Congreve, Richard Brinsley Sheridan, Arthur Wing Pinero, and George Bernard Shaw as the best of English playwrights. A brief literary biography shows the development of the writer in conjunction with the major events of his life.

Barrett, Daniel. *T. W. Robertson and the Prince of Wales's Theatre*. American University Studies Series 26: Theatre Arts Vol. 23. New York: Peter Lang, 1995. Barrett examines Robertson's plays within their theatrical, political, and social contexts. He notes the influence on future dramatists of Robertson's writing style, efforts regarding copyright and compensation, and his work directing plays. Bibliography and index.

Dale, Harrison. "Tom Robertson: A Centenary Criticism." *Contemporary Review* 135 (April, 1929): 356-361. Dale reassesses Robertson's accomplishments on the occasion of his centennial. Even though the work is faulty by modern standards, it marked a turning point in English comedy. Robertson's "cup-and-saucer" drama, with its realistic, domestic interior that now draws sneers, drew applause and acclaim from his contemporary audience.

Durbach, Errol. "Remembering Tom Robertson (1829-1871)." *Educational Theatre Journal* 24 (October, 1972): 284-288. A retrospective of Robertson's contributions to the theater on the occasion of the centennial of his death. His contemporaries praised his drama for its freshness, nature, and humanity. Although Robertson is almost forgotten, he was revolutionary in his day and provided a point from which significant European drama could develop.

Nicoll, Allardyce. *British Drama*. 6th ed. London: Harrap, 1978. Nicoll describes how Robertson created a new "cup-and-saucer" drama, inviting people to bring their "fireside concerns" to the playhouse and look on reality. Robertson was successful in bringing life back into the theater. He was influential in showing how to write characters who speak in natural tones and in showing how to write about themes.

Pemberton, T. Edgar. *The Life and Writings of T. W. Robertson*. London: Richard Bentley and Son, 1893. The standard biography of Robertson, tracing his life and literary development. Robertson's son provided pertinent family information to Pemberton, who offers no literary criticism of the plays. Instead, he invites his audience to judge the works for themselves, as they were still standards on the London stage. Index.

Tydeman, William, ed. Introduction to *Plays by Tom Robertson*. New York: Cambridge University Press, 1982. Tydeman demonstrates why Robertson's plays were so acclaimed in their day and claims that the plays have since been vastly underrated. He draws attention to the features in the best of those genteel, optimistic comedies that enable them to endure for modern audiences. Illustrations, chronology, and bibliography.

B. G. Knepper,
updated by Gerald S. Argetsinger

LENNOX ROBINSON

Born: Douglas, Ireland; October 4, 1886
Died: Dublin, Ireland; October 14, 1958

PRINCIPAL DRAMA

The Clancy Name, pr. 1908, pb. 1909 (one act)
The Cross Roads, pr., pb. 1909
The Lesson of His Life, pr. 1909
Harvest, pr. 1910, pb. 1911
Patriots, pr., pb. 1912
The Dreamers, pr., pb. 1915
The White-Headed Boy, pr. 1916, pb. 1921
The Lost Leader, pr., pb. 1918
Crabbed Youth and Age, pr. 1922, pb. 1924
The Round Table, pr. 1922, pb. 1924
Never the Time and the Place, pr., pb. 1924 (one act)

Portrait, pr. 1925, pb. 1926

The White Blackbird, pr. 1925, pb. 1926

The Big House: Four Scenes in Its Life, pr. 1926,
    pb. 1928

The Far-off Hills, pr. 1928, pb. 1931

Plays, pb. 1928

Give a Dog, pb. 1928, pr. 1929

Ever the Twain, pr. 1929, pb. 1930

The Critic, pr. 1931 (modernization of Richard
    Brinsley Sheridan's play)

All's Over Then?, pr. 1932, pb. 1935

Drama at Inish, pr., pb. 1933 (also known as *Is Life
    Worth Living?*)

Church Street, pr. 1934, pb. 1935 (one act)

When Lovely Woman, pr. 1936

Killycreggs in Twilight, pr. 1937, pb. 1939

Bird's Nest, pr. 1938, pb. 1939

Let Well Alone, pr. 1940 (radio play), pr. 1941
    (staged), pb. 1941

Roly Poly, pr. 1940 (adaptation of Guy de
    Maupassant's story "Boule de suif")

Forget Me Not, pr. 1941

The Lucky Finger, pr. 1948, pb. 1949

The Demon Lover, pr. 1954

Selected Plays, pb. 1982

OTHER LITERARY FORMS

Lennox Robinson's nondramatic writings are of interest only because of the insights they provide into his development as a nationalist and man of the theater. Central in this regard are two volumes of autobiography, *Three Homes* (1938) and *Curtain Up* (1942), and *A Young Man from the South* (1917), published as a novel but little more than a fictionalized autobiography. In the last of these, Willie Powell, the hero, is a Protestant Anglo-Irishman from southwest Cork, a physically weak fellow who has become a successful dramatist (writing plays that are like Robinson's). As a result of a confrontation between nationalists and unionists, Powell reappraises his commitment to nationalist extremism and decides to seek more reasonable outlets for his patriotism. The book is a lucid portrait of the social, intellectual, and political milieu of Ireland in the decade leading up to the Easter Rebellion, but it is not much of a novel. From

the same period and of interest for similar reasons is the 1918 collection of political sketches, *Dark Days*. These pieces give Robinson's reactions to Ireland's troubles and show how his growing nationalism was tempered by doubts about the extremist methods of the Sinn Féiners. The attitudes and problems that Robinson dramatized in *The Big House* in 1926 emerged for the first time in such earlier nondramatic works as *A Young Man from the South* and *Dark Days*.

ACHIEVEMENTS

Lennox Robinson's relationship with Dublin's Abbey Theatre spanned half a century, beginning in 1908 when his first play, *The Clancy Name*, was presented there. During this period, he was one of the theater's most prolific dramatists; its manager for a time; a producer, director, and board member; and author of an officially commissioned Abbey history. The most prominent of the Irish playwrights known as the Cork Realists, Robinson helped chart the course of the theater during the period that included World War I and the height of Ireland's political turbulence, leading the transformation of the literary theater of the Abbey's founders into a realistic one.

In addition to his work for the Abbey, Robinson also acted in productions of the Dublin Drama League, of which he was a founder; edited collections of Irish poetry; wrote drama criticism and other articles for newspapers; and turned out a novel, two volumes of autobiography, short stories, and two biographies. A frequent judge at amateur drama festivals throughout Ireland, he also lectured in the United States, China, and on the Continent. Both at home and abroad, he was widely recognized for several decades not only as one of Ireland's leading playwrights and theatrical figures but also as an important all-around man of letters.

Robinson's most enduring achievement is his dramatic œuvre, thirty plays written between 1908 and 1954. Among these, the conventional comedies and realistic dramas were his most popular works. *The White-Headed Boy*, his first full-length comedy, was an immediate Abbey success and gained for him an international reputation. His second most successful play, *The Far-off Hills*, also a comedy, focuses on provincial life and satirizes foibles of the Irish character. His most notable serious work is *The Big House*, which dramatizes the tragedy of Anglo-Irish Protestants in a Catholic country during the tumultuous period following World War I. This play and others of its type have echoes of Henrik Ibsen, a major influence on Robinson as on most of his Abbey contemporaries. Robinson also ventured into political drama: *Patriots*, *The Dreamers*, and *The Lost Leader* all reflect William Butler Yeats's political views. Though Robinson's major contributions to the Irish drama were as a realist, he shows the influence of Eugene O'Neill in the expressionistic *Ever the Twain*, and in *Church Street*, he employs techniques and themes of Luigi Pirandello. In addition, while Abbey manager, he introduced Dublin audiences to plays by such non-Irish dramatists as Gerhart Hauptmann, August Strindberg, and Rabindranath Tagore.

Although Robinson possessed some of Yeats's romantic idealism, he followed more closely in the footsteps of such realists in the Irish Literary Renaissance as Padraic Colum, John Millington Synge, and Lady Augusta Gregory. His contemporaries so admired his early plays that they also wrote morbidly realistic peasant dramas. T. C. Murray's *Birthright* (pr. 1910) is one such, and A. P. Wilson, Robinson's successor as Abbey manager, said that 95 percent of the manuscripts he received were of this type. Perhaps second only to Lady Gregory as the most prolific twentieth century Irish dramatist, Robinson was much more versatile than his sometime mentor and, during his long career, provided the Abbey and other Dublin stages with comic and serious plays that remain penetrating studies not only of his compatriots but also of the human condition. Although not a dramatist of the first rank, Robinson indeed may be, as a biographer has characterized him, "a modern Goldsmith."

BIOGRAPHY

Esmé Stuart Lennox Robinson was born on October 4, 1886, in Douglas, southeast of Cork, to Andrew Craig and Emily Jones Robinson, Anglo-Irish Protestants. He was the youngest of seven children.

His father, who had been a stockbroker, was ordained a minister of the Church of Ireland in 1892 at the age of fifty and given a parish in Kinsale, County Cork, where the family lived until he was transferred in 1900 to Ballymoney in West Cork. In the same year, young Robinson, who had been tutored at home, began attending Bandon Grammar School for Protestants, but this formal education ended in a year because of his ill health, and his father again became his tutor. Robinson long after wrote of how, during this period, he devoted himself "to music, to rough shooting, and fishing, to reading, to a little boyish writing." He recalled, too, how he and a cousin started *Contributions*, a monthly magazine that ran for three years: "At first many relatives and friends contributed; later they fell away, and my cousin and I had to write it all ourselves under a bewildering variety of *noms-de-plume*." During this period in his late teens, Robinson also became friendly with a Catholic family connected to the nationalist Daniel O'Connell and began to stray from his family's unionist sentiments.

The landmark event in Robinson's progress toward identification with the cause of Irish nationalism and the theater as vocation occurred in August, 1907, when he saw a performance at the Cork Opera House of Yeats's *Cathleen ni Houlihan* (pr., pb. 1902) and *The Hour Glass* (pr. 1903) and Lady Gregory's *The Jackdaw* (pr. 1907) and *The Rising of the Moon* (pb. 1904). He wrote years later: "Certain natural emotions and stirrings . . . were crystallized for ever by *Cathleen ni Houlihan*. . . . Those two hours in the pit of the Opera House in Cork made me an Irish dramatist."

The first product of his new vocation was *The Clancy Name*, a one-act play based on a story by his sister; it was produced at the Abbey on October 8, 1908, "a play as harsh as the stones of West Cork, as realistic as the midden in front of an Irish farm house," according to Robinson (who reacted to criticism of the harshness by rewriting the tragic melodrama for the next Abbey season). His second work, *The Cross Roads*, opened on April 1, 1909; a full-length problem play with overtones of Ibsen, it was well received by the Abbey's audiences mainly because the actors—Sara Allgood, Maire O'Neill, and Arthur Sinclair—obscured its defects (which Robinson unsuccessfully attempted to correct for a 1910 production).

Recognizing Robinson's talent, Yeats and Lady Gregory made him the Abbey's producer and manager late in 1909, and to prepare him for the responsibilities, they sent him to London early the next year to see plays, observe rehearsals, and get to know such luminaries as George Bernard Shaw and Harley Granville-Barker. As manager, Robinson was an arbitrator of disputes among actors and promoter of the Abbey; he also directed plays, including some of his own; and he led the troupe on its 1911 and 1913 American tours. On returning from the latter tour, he resigned his post, mainly because of conflicts with Lady Gregory that stemmed from Abbey financial matters, but also because he wanted more time to write. The next year, he joined the Carnegie United Kingdom Trust as an organizer and developer of libraries, a position he held until 1919, while continuing to write plays, a novel, short stories, and newspaper and magazine articles. During this period, his nationalism emerged in political sketches published as *Dark Days* as well as in the novel *A Young Man from the South* and in *The Lost Leader*, a play dealing with Charles S. Parnell (and which also reveals Robinson's growing interest in spiritualism and psychic phenomena). In 1919, he returned to the Abbey as manager and presided over the theater for four years at a time of financial stress (which led the government in 1924 to recognize the Abbey as the official national theater of Ireland and to grant it a subsidy) and artistic advances (with playwrights Brinsley MacNamara, George Shiels, and Sean O'Casey being introduced to its audiences).

When Robinson again was free of Abbey administrative responsibilities, he was able to devote more time to the Dublin Drama League, and after marrying Dorothy Travers Smith (an Abbey scene designer) in 1931, he began to make lecture tours of the United States and to teach and direct on American campuses. His last trip to the United States was in 1947-1948. On his return, Trinity College, Dublin, awarded him an honorary doctor of literature degree. Though his health was failing, he continued to direct and write plays (his last, *The Demon Lover*, a reworking of a 1914 manuscript, was produced in 1954), to judge amateur theatricals, to write a weekly newspaper column, and to represent Ireland at gatherings in China and Norway. He died on October 14, 1958, and is buried in St. Patrick's Cathedral, Dublin.

ANALYSIS

Lennox Robinson's real strength was in his comedies, with their brilliant technique, sharp observation, and deft touch. In *The White-Headed Boy* and *The Far-off Hills*, he created his masterworks. Although he never attained the stature of a first-rank dramatist, Robinson's contribution to the Irish national theater was crucial, for he did much to create a climate favorable to the development of indigenous talent.

THE WHITE-HEADED BOY

The White-Headed Boy, Robinson's masterpiece, was first presented at the Abbey on December 13, 1916. A gentle satire of his compatriots with a plot and characters that are wholly complementary, it may have autobiographical origins because Robinson's own frail health as a youth caused his mother to be overprotective and to treat him (like Denis in the play, a youngest son) as her pet, or "whiteheaded boy." He previously had used the theme in his first play, *The Clancy Name*, in which a doting mother orchestrates a marriage for her only son and then shields him—and the family name as well—after he accidentally kills a man.

Though Robinson later lamented that everyone had overlooked his political intent in *The White-Headed Boy*, his humorous asides to the reader and stage directions in Irish idiom demonstrate that laughter, not allegory, was his primary goal. The action begins with the Geoghegans—a widowed mother, two sons, three daughters, and a visiting aunt—awaiting the return of Denis, the third and youngest son, from Dublin, where he has been studying medicine and has twice failed his examination. All expect a triumphant homecoming this time, however, and Mrs. Geoghegan looks forward to Denis's becoming a Dublin doctor, not "one of your common dispensaries, hat in hand to every guardian in the country." However, while family members sacrificed so the mother's favorite could get an education, Denis wasted his allowance on horse races and neglected his work. When a telegram comes for him ("Hard luck. Geoghegan's Hope also ran. Sorry, Flanagan"), brother George, the family breadwinner, correctly interprets it as reporting that Denis has failed a third time, and all except Mrs. Geoghegan agree that they no longer will subsidize the prodigal.

When Denis returns, he at first appears to be vain and irresponsible; told of this third examination failure, he reacts indifferently: "Isn't that a beastly nuisance? I'm not surprised; I guessed I hadn't got it." He had not wanted to be a doctor after all but had allowed himself to be led by his mother's misguided expectations for him and hope of enhanced reputation for the family. When brother George offers him passage to Canada as a final familial gesture, Denis retorts:

I never asked to be sent to College; I never asked to have all this money spent on me. I'd have been content to live here with the rest of you—Yes, I'm different now, but whose fault is that? It's not mine. Who was it made me out to be so clever; who insisted on making a doctor of me, or sending me to Trinity? It was all of you.

He shows more spunk and good sense when George also offers to pay passage to Canada for Delia Duffy, Denis's fiancé: "Thank you for nothing. I'm asking no money from you, and I've no intention of asking Delia to come out and rough it in Canada. She wasn't brought up to that sort of thing." Jilting Delia, however, arouses the wrath of her father, who threatens to sue for breach of contract. This prospect and its possible consequences frighten the family into frenetic attempts to forestall public shame, and Duffy reaps a harvest as George, Mrs. Geoghegan, and Aunt Ellen offer him payoffs, and Aunt Ellen (who years earlier had rejected him) agrees to become his wife. Ironically, though all had intended to rid themselves of the burden of Denis, they remain in his thrall.

Delia and Denis, meanwhile, confound the schemers by marrying. Further, instead of emigrating to Canada, Denis gets a job in Ballycolman as a laborer on a work crew. Duffy and the Geoghegans are shocked. George says, "Think what everyone will say of you, and what sort of name will they put on us to say we drove you out on the road!" Again, reputation is a prime consideration, and they offer Denis the payoffs previously tendered to Duffy, but Denis wants independence: "I only want to be able to do what I like with my own life—to be free." He agrees, nevertheless, to go to Kilmurray and manage a cooperative shop, the latest enterprise of rich Aunt Ellen, and he accepts the family's money, the prospect of Aunt Ellen's estate, and Delia's promise to look after everything: "An easy life, no responsibility, money in your pocket, something to grumble at—What more do you want?"

Robinson said that *The White-Headed Boy* "is political from beginning to end, though I don't suppose six people have recognised the fact." It is easy to miss, for the play moves briskly through a series of comical situations, with the second-act wooing scene between Aunt Ellen and old Duffy a comic classic. It is Duffy who expresses the political theme. He is "one of the solidest men in Ballycolman, Chairman of the District Council, Chairman of the Race committee, and a member of every Committee and every League in the village," and he mocks Denis's desire for independence: "Free? . . . Bedad, isn't he like old Ireland asking for freedom, and we're like the fools of Englishmen offering him every bloody thing except the one thing? . . . Do Denis, do like a darling boy, go out to Kilmurray and manage the shop."

Denis (like Ireland) desires the freedom to chart his own course, but the family (like England) assumes that financial support will suffice. "Will I never be free from you?" Denis asks, but he acquiesces in almost the same breath. Futile though his assertion of self-determination may seem, at least he marries. The prospects for his brothers and sisters, however, are bleaker, their dreams of marriage and careers still mere illusions at the final curtain. Robinson's satiric portrayal of ineffectual Irishmen trapped by their environment and sense of inadequacy is softened by his whimsical handling of their conflicts and problems, and given the tense political situation in Dublin in 1916, perhaps it is just as well that almost everyone missed the subtle allegory and serious intent of *The White-Headed Boy.*

THE FAR-OFF HILLS

There are no such hidden purposes in *The Far-off Hills,* which opened at the Abbey on October 22, 1928, and was Robinson's first three-act comedy of Irish life since *The White-Headed Boy* in 1916. A lighthearted portrayal of the marriage game, it has its roots in the same provincial background as that of the earlier plays but ends on a more optimistic note, for all the characters (except the fickle servant Ellen) realize their ambitions. Though its spirit, characters, and milieu are Irish, the central motif of woman as matchmaker may come from Searfín Álvarez Quintero and Joaquín Álvarez Quintero, four of whose plays were translated by Helen and Harley Granville-Barker and published in 1927.

In this second most successful of Robinson's plays, the Clancy family, like the Geoghegans of *The White-Headed Boy,* is overseen by a woman, in this instance the eldest daughter, Marian, who puts off becoming a nun because of her widowered father's blindness. Severe in demeanor, she is a strict disciplinarian who reins in her exuberant younger sisters but fails to gain similar control over Patrick Clancy's drinking, smoking, and socializing with cronies. The girls Ducky and Pet, however, plot to get their father married so Marian will be free to enter the convent and they will be rid of her stern control. Susie Tynan, an eligible old flame of Clancy, is available and willing, so the girls' plan succeeds, but Marian then decides to postpone going to the convent until the girls are older, primarily because she has begun to have doubts about a religious vocation. When Pierce Hegarty, Susie Tynan's nephew, calls her a pretty girl, for example, "she drifts to a mirror and does something to her hair," and later, when Harold Mahony, another young man, loses his wife, Marian invites him to propose to her, but the gloomy pessimist turns her down. Ambitious and personable Pierce is a better man, however, and, encouraged by Pet and Ducky, he eventually prevails. Patrick Clancy delivers the valedictory: "This little room is as full of happiness as an egg is full of meat. Marian dear, Pierce . . . good luck, God bless you both."

The blind father is married to a woman who will tolerate his drinking, smoking, and cronies; Marian, no longer a tyrant, is soon to be wed; and the younger girls have freed themselves from unwanted control. Everyone, in other words, discovers that though far-off hills beckon, those closer to home may be just as verdant. The message of this play, then, is more optimistic than that which most Irish plays deliver, and though some have remarked about a padded plot, the seemingly irrelevant farcical interludes contribute significantly to the play's pervasive blitheness of spirit as well as providing opportunities for character development.

Though in his plays he ranged far and wide in subject matter and form, Robinson regularly returned to what he called "this strange Irish thing, the commanding force in my life." He wrote in the manner of O'Neill and Pirandello, and he adapted Richard Brinsley Sheridan and Guy de Maupassant, but he was at his best in plays that have, as one critic put it, "their inspiration in the warp and woof of Irish life."

THE BIG HOUSE

Robinson's third most successful play deals with the "Irish thing" in a serious manner. *The Big House* opened at the Abbey on September 6, 1926. Robinson focuses on a favorite Anglo-Irish literary theme, the decay and destruction of the Big Houses, aristocratic country homes of Protestant families whose forebears had come from England as long ago as the seventeenth century but were still regarded—and saw themselves—as different from their Irish Catholic neighbors. The decline of the Big Houses and the departure of many Anglo-Irish families were inevitable when the conflict between the Irish and the English reached its peak following World War I, and a number of the estates were destroyed by nationalists as reprisals for actions of the government, but as early as 1912, Synge had written: "If a playwright chose to go through the Irish country houses he would find material, it is very likely, for many gloomy plays that would turn on the decaying of these old families." In his 1931 biography of Bryan Cooper, an Anglo-Irish landlord, Robinson recalls his reaction to a decaying Big House:

Perhaps . . . in that Georgian house or sham Gothic castle there remained an old father and mother and a couple of aged daughters. The house was too large for their needs or too large for their purse and what reason was there for clinging to it? Meanwhile the old house was too full of memories of past greatness, too full of memories of boys who had shot rabbits in the long summer evenings.

A decade later, he wrote in his autobiography of the same experience: "I fell into a reverie and spoke no word until we reached home. A play of mine was born then." *The Big House* is a lament on the passing of an old order that Robinson admired, and at the same time it rallies the young Anglo-Irish to a dynamic commitment to Protestantism and their country.

The play is set at Ballydonal House, County Cork, ancestral home of the Alcocks, atypical Anglo-Irish landlords in that they have not lapsed into penury or decadence (unlike the O'Neills, with whom they are contrasted). Mr. Alcock has devoted himself to public service for years but continues to remain apart from his Catholic neighbors, though without Mrs. Alcock's overt sense of alienation.

The first scene takes place in 1918 on Armistice Day, with the Alcocks celebrating the end of a war in which two of their sons served. Reginald, the elder, died, but they await the return of Ulick, the younger. With them is their daughter Kate and a visiting English officer, Montgomery Despard, who served with Reginald and met Kate in London, where he fell in love with her. Despard, who sees the atypicality of Ballydonal House—"It doesn't seem to be so awfully Irish . . . the way it's run, and—everything"—asks Kate to marry him and come to London, but she is unwilling. She is committed to Ballydonal House and dreams of running it with Ulick after the war: "Reggie wouldn't have cared if he had dragged Ballydonal down. But Ulick and I do care—tremendously. We're going to hold our heads above water, hold Ballydonal above water, proudly and decently." So strong is Ulick's tie to the estate, she says, that "I see him sometimes when he's not here at all," the most recent vision having occurred three evenings before: "That was just when the armistice had begun to seem inevitable. He was dreaming it all over you

see, he was dreaming he was home." The vision was a prescient one, for a telegram arrives with news that Ulick was killed three days earlier.

The next scene takes place in 1921 during the terror wrought by the Republicans and the Black and Tans. The O'Neills, burned out, have left for England (where Irish refugees, Mrs. Alcock supposes, "will soon become as *distingué* as the Russians"), and Mrs. Alcock wants to join them ("I know that we're living in a community of criminal lunatics and that the sooner we get out of it the better"), but Mr. Alcock intends to stay until he is "put out . . . burned out . . . or starved out." To avenge an ambush the night before, the Black and Tans have shot Maggie Leahy, who had been Kate's childhood nurse. Kate, who has been working to overcome the alienation between the Anglo-Irish and the Irish Catholics, returns from Maggie's wake to report that despite her efforts ("I threw a bridge across the gulf and ran across it"), she remained an outsider, "different, away from them. . . . Yes, there was religion to make me feel outside but lots of other things too; education, I suppose, and tradition and—and everything that makes me me and them them." Though she always has felt this separation, she "thought it could be broken down." Alcock tells her that she never will be like the neighbors: "It will be always 'them' and 'us.'" Later, while alone, Kate is surprised by a drunk Despard, now a member of the Auxiliary Police, whose men are searching for nationalists. He proposes to her, but she again rejects him, and the scene ends with a solitary Despard firing his revolver at the voice of Ulick he thinks he hears, as if the protective spirit of Ballydonal has begun to haunt him, too.

Two years later, the Alcocks, almost destitute, have closed off most of the house. Kate, who had taken a job in London, returns, unable to stay away from "country-houses going up in flames, senators being kidnapped and all kinds of thrilling goings-on." Her report of the financial and social successes of the O'Neills in London contrasts vividly with the Alcocks' stoic endurance and Kate's rejection of the "sentimental play-acting" of London life and her decision to return, to "criticize and dislike Irish people—some of them—and be either a Free Stater or a

Republican." The family reunion is interrupted when three Republicans come to blow up Ballydonal House in retaliation for the execution of a young Republican by the Free State government, ironically the very fellow whose life Mr. Alcock had been trying to save.

The next morning, the family gathers in the aftermath of the destruction to retrieve some possessions. Mr. and Mrs. Alcock will go to England after all. Mrs. Alcock is happy to return home after more than two decades in a foreign country; he is relieved that the turmoil will be part of his past, though he still cannot understand the aspirations that have fostered it. Kate, however, will try to shape a new life amid the ruins, renouncing her "poor attempt to pretend" that she was not different from her compatriots and quoting Yeats: "We must glory in our difference, be as proud of it as they are of theirs." Her intentions notwithstanding, she remains tied to the past, for a vision of Ulick appears at the end of the play, smiling with apparent satisfaction at his sister's heroic resolve. Sean O'Casey's *Juno and the Paycock* (pr. 1924) and *The Plough and the Stars* (pr. 1926, seven months before the *The Big House*) dramatize the political upheavals from the perspective of Dubliners. Robinson's play provides a realistic portrait of a different aspect of the era: the tragedy of an Ascendancy family.

OTHER MAJOR WORKS

LONG FICTION: *A Young Man from the South*, 1917.

SHORT FICTION: *Eight Short Stories*, 1919.

NONFICTION: *Dark Days*, 1918; *Bryan Cooper*, 1931; *Three Homes*, 1938; *Curtain Up*, 1942; *Towards an Appreciation of the Theatre*, 1945; *Pictures in a Theatre: A Conversation Piece*, 1946; *Palette and Plough*, 1948; *Ireland's Abbey Theatre*, 1951.

BIBLIOGRAPHY

Dorman, Sean. *Limelight over the Liffey*. Fowey, Cornwall, England: Raffeen Press, 1983. These essays, first serialized under the title "My Uncle Lennox," describe Robinson's life and the theater in Ireland. Index.

Hogan, Robert. *The Abbey: Ireland's National Theatre, 1904-1978*. New York: Columbia University Press, 1979. This history of the Abbey Theatre by one of its former directors contains an account of Robinson's two significant connections with that institution. Describes Robinson's years as a director and examines his work as a playwright. Includes a complete listing of Abbey Theatre productions.

Hunt, Hugh. *The Abbey: Ireland's National Theatre, 1904-1978*. New York: Columbia University Press, 1979. This history of the Abbey Theatre by one of its former directors contains an account of Robinson's two significant connections with that institution. Describes Robinson's years as a director and examines his work as a playwright. Includes a complete listing of Abbey Theatre productions.

Journal of Irish Literature 9 (January, 1980). This special Lennox Robinson issue contains hitherto fugitive and unpublished materials. Perhaps the most important item is the controversial short story "The Madonna of Slieve Dun." In addition to another short story, a full-length play entitled *The Red Sock*, written pseudonymously by Robinson, is published here for the first time. Also contains an article on Robinson's relationship with William Butler Yeats.

O'Neill, Michael J. *Lennox Robinson*. Boston: Twayne, 1964. This study provides a thematic approach to Robinson's wide-ranging and productive career, including his nondramatic writings. The biographical material is related to the development of the playwright's themes and techniques. Contains a detailed chronology that functions both as a bibliography and as a calendar of productions of Robinson's plays.

Gerald H. Strauss,
updated by George O'Brien